$32.00

Computers and Their Applications

Third Edition

Computers and Their Applications

Third Edition

Charles S. Parker
The College of Santa Fe, Santa Fe, New Mexico

The Dryden Press
Harcourt Brace Jovanovich College Publishers
Fort Worth Philadelphia San Diego New York
Orlando Austin San Antonio Toronto
Montreal London Sydney Tokyo

Editor in Chief	Robert A. Pawlik
Acquisitions Editor	Richard Bonacci
Developmental Editor	Michele Tomiak
Project Editor	Jennifer Johnson
Production Manager	Alison Howell

To Mom and Dad

Printed in the United States of America

Computers and Their Applications, Third Edition
Library of Congress Catalog Number: 92-072127
ISBN: 0-03-096821-6

Computers and Their Applications with Productivity Software Tools, Third Edition
Library of Congress Catalog Number: 92-082774
ISBN: 0-03-096883-6

3 4 5 6 7 8 9 0 1 2 048 9 8 7 6 5 4 3 2 1

The Dryden Press
Harcourt Brace Jovanovich

The Dryden Press Series in Information Systems

Arthur Andersen & Co.,
Boynton and Shank
Foundations of Business Systems: Projects and Cases

Arthur Andersen & Co., Flaatten, McCubbrey, O'Riordan, and Burgess
Foundations of Business Systems,
Second Edition

Anderson
Structured Programming Using Turbo Pascal: A Brief Introduction,
Second Edition

Bradley
Introduction to Data Base Management in Business,
Second Edition

Brown and McKeown
Structured Programming with Microsoft BASIC

Carney
Advanced Structured BASIC for the IBM PC

Coburn
Beginning Structured COBOL

Coburn
Advanced Structured COBOL

Dean and Effinger
Common-Sense BASIC: Structured Programming with Microsoft QuickBASIC

Electronic Learning Facilitators, Inc.
The DOS Book

Electronic Learning Facilitators, Inc.
The Lotus 1-2-3 Book

Electronic Learning Facilitators, Inc.
Stepping Through Excel 4.0 for Windows

Electronic Learning Facilitators, Inc.
Stepping Through Harvard Graphics for Windows

Electronic Learning Facilitators, Inc.
Stepping Through Windows 3.1

Electronic Learning Facilitators, Inc.
Stepping Through Word for Windows

Electronic Learning Facilitators, Inc.
Working Smarter with DOS 5.0

Electronic Learning Facilitators, Inc.
Working with WordPerfect 5.0

Electronic Learning Facilitators, Inc.
Working with WordPerfect 5.1

Ellis and Lodi
Structured Programming Using True BASIC

Federico
WordPerfect 5.1 Primer

Goldstein Software, Inc.
Joe Spreadsheet, Macintosh Version

Goldstein Software, Inc.
Joe Spreadsheet, Statistical

Harrington
Making Database Management Work

Harrington
Microsoft Works: A Window to Computing

Harrington
Relational Database Management for Microcomputers: Design and Implementation

Laudon and Laudon
Business Information Systems: A Problem-Solving Approach,
Second Edition

Laudon, Laudon, and Weill
The Integrated Solution

Lawlor
Computer Information Systems,
Second Edition

Lawlor
Introducing BASIC: A Structured Approach

Liebowitz
The Dynamics of Decision Support Systems and Expert Systems

McKeown
Living with Computers,
Fourth Edition

McKeown
Living with Computers with BASIC
Fourth Edition

McKeown
Working with Computers

McKeown
Working with Computers with Software Tutorials

McKeown and Leitch
Managing with Computers

Martin and Burstein
Computer Systems Fundamentals

Martin and Parker
Mastering Today's Software with DOS, WordPerfect 5.0/5.1, Lotus 1-2-3, dBASE III PLUS (for dBASE IV)

Martin and Parker
Mastering Today's Software with DOS, WordPerfect 5.0/5.1, Lotus 1-2-3, dBASE III PLUS (or dBASE IV) and BASIC

Mason
Using IBM Microcomputers in Business: Decision Making with Lotus 1-2-3 and dBASE III PLUS (or dBASE IV)

Parker
A Beginner's Guide to BASIC

Parker
Computers and Their Applications,
Third Edition

Parker
Computers and Their Applications with Productivity Software Tools,
Third Edition

Parker
Microcomputers: Concepts and Applications

Parker
Productivity Software Guide,
Fourth Edition

Parker
Understanding Computers and Information Processing: Today and Tomorrow
Fourth Edition

Parker
Understanding Computers and Information Processing: Today and Tomorrow with BASIC
Fourth Edition

Robertson and Robertson
Microcomputer Applications and Programming: A Complete Computer Course with DOS, WordPerfect 5.1, Lotus 1-2-3, dBASE III PLUS (or dBASE IV), and BASIC

Robertson and Robertson
Using Microcomputer Applications
(A Series of Computer Lab Manuals)

Roche
Telecommunications and Business Strategy

Swafford and Haff
dBASE III PLUS

Preface

We are living at a time when the key to success in virtually every profession or career depends on the skillful use of information. Whether one is a teacher, lawyer, doctor, politician, manager, or corporate president, the main ingredient in the work involved is information—knowing how to get it, how to use it, where to keep it, and how to disseminate it to others.

At the root of all of these information-based work activities are computers and the applications that are supported by them. Currently there are millions of computer systems in the world, and collectively, they are capable of being used in thousands of different ways. Some of the applications that computer systems can now handle—such as making movies and creating art, or "speaking," "seeing," and "listening"—were thought impossible not too long ago. Few professions remain untouched by computers today or will remain so in tomorrow's world. No matter who you are or what you do for a living, it is highly likely that computers somehow affect the way you work.

The importance of computers in virtually every profession brings us to the purpose of this book. *Computers and Their Applications,* third edition, has been written with the end user of computers in mind. This nontechnical, introductory text explains in straightforward terms the importance of learning about computers, the types of computer systems and their components, the principles by which computer systems work, practical applications of computers and related technologies. The goal of the text is both to provide knowledge of computer basics and to impart a perspective for using this knowledge effectively in the workplace.

The textbook is available in two versions—one with an appendix on productivity software tools and one without. The textbook is but one component of a complete and flexible instructional package—one that can easily be adapted to virtually any teaching format. Supplementing the textbook is a comprehensive set of student and teacher support materials.

The Textbook

Computers and Their Applications, third edition, is designed for students taking a first course in computers and information processing. The text meets the requirements proposed for the first course in computing by both the Data Processing Management Association (DPMA) and the Association for Computing Machinery (ACM). Although it provides a comprehensive introduction to the world of computers, the text is not overly technical. Coverage is given to both commercial and personal applications of computers and large and small computer systems.

Key Features

Like previous editions, the third edition of *Computers and Their Applications* is current and comprehensive. It offers a flexible teaching organization and a readable and engaging presentation. Learning tools in each chapter help students master important concepts. Tomorrow boxes and Feature boxes provide insight on current issues of interest. The eight thematic "Windows," each of which highlights a major aspect of information processing, bring the world of computers to life. A glossary at the end of the book gives concise definitions of important terms. The appendix on productivity software tools, for those who adopt the version of the text that contains it, provides a comprehensive, hands-on introduction to WordPerfect, 1-2-3, and dBASE in a style students will find easy to use.

Currency. Perhaps more than textbooks in any other field, computer texts must reflect current technologies, trends, and classroom needs. The state-of-the-art content of this book and its support package reflect these considerations. Before the third edition was started, reviews were commissioned and meetings were held to identify key areas of change for the text and support package. Also, throughout the writing and production stages, enhancements and new developments were continually being made to ensure that the final product would be as state-of-the-art as possible throughout its life. A glance at the Windows, Tomorrow boxes, Feature boxes, User Solution boxes, and chapter outlines should illustrate why this text has been and will continue to remain among the most current in the marketplace.

Comprehensiveness and Depth. In planning for the third edition of this book, the publisher conducted an extensive research study to determine the selection of topics, degree of depth, and other features that instructors of introductory information processing courses most want to see in their texts. As the manuscript evolved, instructors at a variety of institutions around the country were asked for their comments. The resulting textbook accommodates a wide range of teaching preferences. It not only covers traditional topics thoroughly but also includes the facts every student should know about today's "hot" topics, such as telecommunications, microcomputers, database processing, desktop publishing packages, decision support and expert systems, fourth-generation-language products, user and programmer productivity tools, office automation, computer graphics, and nontraditional approaches to systems development.

Flexible Organization. A textbook locked into a rigid organization, no matter how thorough, will inevitably find its uses limited. To appeal to a wide audience, this book is designed to be flexible. Its 13 chapters are grouped into five modules: Introduction (Chapters 1–2), Hardware (Chapters 3–5), Support Systems (Chapters 6–7), Productivity Software (Chapters 8–10), and Information Systems (Chapters 11–13). Every effort was made to have each chapter as self-contained as possible, making it easy for one to skip chapters or learn them in a sequence other than the one in the book. And each chapter is organized into well-defined sections, so you can assign parts of a chapter if the whole provides more depth than you need.

Readability. We remember more about a subject if it is presented in a straightforward way and made interesting and exciting. This book is written in a conversational, down-to-earth style—one designed to be accurate without being intimidating. Concepts are explained clearly and simply, without use of overly technical terminology. Where technical points are presented, they are made understandable with realistic examples from everyday life.

Chapter Learning Tools. Each chapter contains a number of learning tools to help students master the materials.

1. **Outline** An outline of the headings in the chapter shows the major topics to be covered.
2. **Learning Objectives** A list of learning objectives is provided to serve as a guide while students read the chapter.
3. **Overview** Each chapter starts with an overview that puts the subject matter of the chapter in perspective and lets students know what they will be reading about.
4. **Boldfaced Key Terms and Marginal Glossary** Important terms appear in boldface type as they are introduced in the chapter. These terms are also defined in the margin of the page on which they appear and in the end-of-text glossary.
5. **Tomorrow Boxes** These special elements, one in each chapter, provide students with a look at possible future developments in the world of computers and serve as a focus for class discussion.
6. **Feature Boxes** Each chapter contains one or more Feature boxes designed to stimulate interest and discussion about today's uses of information processing technology.
7. **User Solution Boxes** New to this edition, User Solution boxes describe how real-world organizations are using technology to solve business-related problems. Each chapter contains at least one of these features.
8. **Photographs and Diagrams** Instructive, full-color photographs and diagrams appear throughout the book to help illustrate important concepts. The use of color in the diagrams is a functional part of the book.
9. **Summary and Key Terms** This is a concise, section-by-section summary of the main points in the chapter. Every boldfaced key term in the chapter also appears in boldface type in the summary. Students will find the summary a valuable tool for study and review.

10. **Review Exercises** Every chapter ends with a set of fill-in, matching, discussion, and critical thinking questions.

Windows. The book contains eight spectacular photoessays. Each of these "Windows" on the world of computers is organized around a major text theme and vividly illustrates state-of-the-art uses of computer technology.

End-of-Text Glossary. The glossary at the end of the book defines over 450 important computer terms mentioned in the text, including all boldfaced key terms. Each glossary item has a page reference indicating where it is boldfaced or where it first appears in the text.

Appendix A: Numbering Systems. At the end of the book is an appendix that covers numbering systems. Contained in it are explanations of the binary, decimal, and hexadecimal numbering systems, as well as rules both for converting numbers from one system into another and for doing simple arithmetic.

Productivity Software Tools. The version of this book that contains an appendix on productivity software tools provides a comprehensive introduction to DOS, WordPerfect, 1-2-3, and dBASE. More than a list of rules and procedures, it is an engaging, easy-to-read tutorial that encourages students to begin creating applications immediately. Systematic application development techniques and the honing of problem-solving skills are also an integral part of the presentation. A separately bound *Instructor's Manual and Test Bank* is available free to adopters of the version of *Computers and Their Applications* that has the productivity software tools supplement.

Changes from the Second Edition

Although the second edition of this text was highly successful, the pace of technological advances has necessitated a number of key changes. Among the noteworthy differences between the second and third editions of *Computers and Their Applications* are the following:

1. A large number of business and problem-solving examples have been added to the text, giving the text a much more applications-oriented flavor. Some of these examples are highlighted in User Solution boxes throughout each chapter. Each of these boxes shows how a real-world organization is using state-of-the-art technology to creatively solve business problems.
2. The text contains a marginal glossary; that is, boldfaced key terms are defined in the margins of the pages on which they appear.
3. A large number of line illustrations and virtually all of the photos are new, reflecting the most recent advances in technology and applications.

4. The chapter on microcomputer systems has been completely revised. Gone are the sections on hardware, which mostly repeated materials covered in earlier chapters of the book, and in their place are end-user-development issues such as acquiring and maintaining a microcomputer system, backup, and troubleshooting and repairs.
5. Coverage on networks, the Apple Macintosh, desktop publishing, expert systems, computer-aided software engineering (CASE) tools, social issues dealing with computers, and graphical user interfaces has been expanded considerably.
6. The Summary and Key Terms section at the end of each chapter has been reorganized by section headings, making it easier to follow.
7. The chapter on applications software development has been moved to an information-systems module, where it appears right after coverage of systems development. The end-user-development (microcomputers) chapter has been resequenced as the last chapter in this module.
8. The chapters on telecommunications and systems software have been consolidated into a support-systems module.

Student and Teacher Support Materials

Computers and Their Applications is available with a complete package of support materials for instructors and students: Included in the package are an *Instructor's Manual* with transparency masters, *Transparency Acetates*, a *Test Bank* in hard-copy and computerized form, videotapes from Dryden's Information Processing Video Library, and a variety of productivity software manuals and supporting documentation to meet lab needs.

Instructor's Manual

In the *Instuctor's Manual* I draw on my own teaching experience to provide instructors with practical suggestions for enhancing classroom presentation. The *Instructor's Manual* contains suggestions for adapting this textbook to various course schedules, including one-quarter, two-quarter, one-semester, two-semester, and night courses. For each of the 13 chapters of the text, the *Instructor's Manual* provides

1. A list of **Learning Objectives**.
2. A **Summary,** oriented to the instructor, with teaching suggestions.
3. A list of the **Key Terms** in the chapter and their definitions.
4. A **Teaching Outline** that gives a detailed breakdown of the chapter, with all major headings and subheadings, as well as points to cover under each. References to the Transparency Acetates and Transparency Masters are keyed in to this outline.

5. **Teaching Tips,** with recommended topics for class discussion, important points to cover on the transparency acetates, and mention of additional instructor resources.
6. **Notes for Windows and Boxes,** which include both capsule summaries of these materials and points to raise in class.
7. **Lecture Anecdotes** providing additional stories, news items, and information specific to chapter content to liven up lectures.
8. **Transparency Scripts** for each transparency acetate and transparency master in the instructional package.
9. **Answers to Discussion Questions** that appear at the end of the chapter.
10. **Additional Discussion Questions,** for in-class discussion or testing, and their answers.
11. **Answers to Critical Thinking Questions** that appear at the end of the chapter.
12. **Transparency Masters** covering the chapter objectives and other key topics for classroom discussion.

Transparency Acetates

A set of approximately 100 *Transparency Acetates* for use with an overhead projector is available to help explain key points. Included among the acetates are outlines for every chapter, figures derived from selected text diagrams, and new pieces of art. The Teaching Outlines in the *Instructor's Manual* indicate when to show each of the acetates (as well as the Transparency Masters), and the Transparency Scripts in the *Instructor's Manual* list points to make about each.

Test Bank

The *Test Bank*—covering all 13 chapters of the text and the numbering-systems appendix—contains over 2,300 test items in various formats, including true/false, multiple-choice, matching, fill-in, and short-answer questions. Answers are provided for all but the short-answer questions. The *Test Bank* is available in both hard-copy and computerized forms. The electronic versions—available for use with IBM and Macintosh microcomputers—allow instructors to preview, edit, or delete questions as well as to add their own questions, print scrambled forms of tests, and print answer keys.

A key indicating the chapter section from which each question was taken is also provided as part of the *Test Bank*. Keys are included with each question, except for the matching questions. Also provided is a ten-question, ready-to-copy-and-distribute multiple-choice quiz for every chapter, which tests students on a representative sample of important topics.

Videotapes

Videotapes from Dryden's Information Processing Video Library will be available to adopters of *Computers and Their Applications*, Third Edition. Videos focus on applications and cutting-edge technology involving computers, and illustrate concepts such as hardware, software, and systems; database management; graphics; and telecommunications. Adopters will have immediate access to professional-quality videotapes that explore such landmarks of technology as the electrical digital computer, the laser, and communications satellites; information theory; and the role of computers at Florida's Sea World theme park.

Acknowledgments

I could never have completed a project of this scope alone. I owe a special word of thanks to the many people who reviewed the text—those whose extensive suggestions on the first two editions helped define the third, those whose comments on drafts of the third helped mold it into its final form, and those who reviewed the instructional package.

James Ambroise, Jr., *Southern University, Louisiana;* Virginia T. Anderson, *University of North Dakota;* Linda Armbruster, *Rancho Santiago College;* Gary E. Baker, *Marshalltown Community College;* Phillip Barnhart, *Mt. San Antonio College;* Richard Batt, *Saint Louis Community College at Meremec;* Jerry Booher, *Scottsdale Community College;* James Bradley, *University of Calgary;* Curtis Bring, *Moorhead State University;* Cath Brotherton, *Riverside Community College;* James Buxton, *Tidewater Community College, Virginia;* Dick Callahan, *Mississippi State University;* Gena Casas, *Florida Community College, Jacksonville;* Thomas L. Case, *Georgia Southerm University;* John E. Castek, *University of Wisconsin–La Crosse;* Carl Clavadetscher, *California State Polytechnic University;* Vernon Clodfelter, *Rowan Technical College, North Carolina;* Laura Cooper, *College of the Mainland, Texas;* Marvin Daugherty, *Indiana Vocational Technical College;* Donald L. Davis, *University of Mississippi;* Robert H. Dependahl, Jr., *Santa Barbara City College, California;* John DiElsi, *Mercy College, New York;* Mark Dishaw, *Boston University;* Eugene Dolan, *University of the District of Columbia;* Hyun B. Eom, *Middle Tennessee State University;* Hilda Federico, *Jacksonville University;* Michael Feiler, *Merritt College;* J. Patrick Fenton, *West Valley Community College, California;* William C. Fink, *Lewis and Clark Community College, Illinois;* Gene Garza, *University of Montevallo;* Kay H. Gray, *Jacksonville State University;* David W. Green, *Nashville State Technical Institute, Tennessee;* George P. Grill, *University of North Carolina, Greensboro;* Rosemary C. Gross, *Creighton University;* Dennis Guster, *Saint Louis Community College at Meremec;* Donald Hall, *Manatee Community College;* Susan Hansen, *University of Nebraska;* L. D. Harber, *Volunteer State Community College, Tennessee;* Hank Hartman, *Iowa State University;* Richard Hatch, *San Diego State University;* Mary Lou Hawkins, *Del Mar College;* William Hightower, *Elon College, North Carolina;* Sharon A. Hill, *Prince George's Community College, Maryland;* Stanley P. Honacki, *Moraine Valley Community College;* L. Wayne Horn, *Pensacola Junior College;* J. William Howorth, *Seneca College, Ontario, Canada;* Peter L. Irwin, *Richland College, Texas;* Elizabeth Swoope Johnston, *Louisiana State University;* Richard Kerns, *East Carolina*

University, North Carolina; Glenn Kersnick, *Sinclair Community College, Ohio;* Gordon C. Kimbell, *Everett Community College, Washington;* James G. Kriz, *Cuyahoga Community College, Ohio;* Joan Krone, *Ohio State University;* Shelly Langman, *Bellevue Community College;* Liang Chee Wee, *University of Arizona;* Alden Lorents, *Northern Arizona University;* James McMahon, *Community College of Rhode Island;* Wayne Madison, *Clemson University, South Carolina;* LaVonne Manning, *University of the District of Columbia;* Richard Manthei, *Joliet Junior College;* Gary Marks, *Austin Community College, Texas;* Ed Martin, *Kingsborough Community College;* Don B. Medley, *California State Polytechnic University;* Mary Meredith, *University of Southwestern Louisiana;* Marilyn Meyer, *Fresno City College;* Marilyn Moore, *Purdue University;* Donavan J. Nielsen, *Golden West College;* George Novotny, *Ferris State University;* Bob Palank, *Florissant Community College;* James Payne, *Kellogg Community College;* Robert Ralph, *Fayetteville Technical Institute, North Carolina;* Laura Rao, *Central Missouri State University;* Alfred C. St. Onge, *Springfield Technical Community College, Massachusetts;* Larry Schwartzman, *Trident Technical College;* John J. Shuler, *San Antonio College, Texas;* Susan Silvera, *Los Angeles Trade-Technical College;* Harold Smith, *Brigham Young University;* Sandra Stalker, *North Shore Community College;* Michael L. Stratford, *Charles County Community College, Maryland;* Sandra Swanson, *Lewis and Clark Community College, Illinois;* Jane M. Thompson, *Solano Community College;* Sue Traynor, *Clarion University of Pennsylvania;* James R. Walters, *Pikes Peak Community College;* Joyce V. Walton, *Seneca College, Ontario, Canada;* Joseph Waters, *Santa Rosa Junior College, California;* Charles M. Williams, *Georgia State University;* James D. Woolever, *Cerritos College;* A. James Wynne, *Virginia Commonwealth University.*

I am indebted to scores of people at dozens of organizations for the photographs they provided for this text. I would especially like to thank Jessie O. Kempter at IBM, Nancy Winters of Adobe, Peter Heyne of Compaq, Bruce Fox of Evans and Sutherland, Carol Parcels of Hewlett-Packard, Christy Gersich of Microsoft, Doug Morgan of Silicon Graphics, and Helen Kendrick of Software Publishing for the particularly outstanding contributions they made. Also, I extend heart-felt thanks to Jeff Glickman and Lew Witz at The College of Santa Fe (CSF) for the help they provided in preparing the computer programs that are contained in this text. Additionally, I deeply appreciate the continuing help and support on this textbook from my departmental colleagues and good friends at CSF, Dan Breheny and Pat Donahoe.

At The Dryden Press, a special word of thanks to my publisher, Bob Pawlik, to my acquisitions editor, Richard Bonacci, and to my developmental editor, Michele Tomiak, for the suggestions they made that produced a better manuscript. Also, I would like to thank Bill Barnett, Lisa Rittby, DeVilla Williams, Karen Hill, Alan Wendt, Patti Arneson, Cate Rzasa, Jane Perkins, Doris Milligan, Barb Bahnsen, and the many others who worked hard on behalf of the book.

Charles S. Parker

Brief Contents

Windows

Contents

Today computers ensure a high-quality paint job on your new Corvette. Tomorrow the car dealer may invite you to step up to a computer screen and create a unique color for the new car you're ordering.

Module A Introduction

We are living in an age of computers. Businesses, government agencies, and other organizations use computers and related technologies to handle tedious paperwork, provide better service to customers, and assist managers in making better decisions. As the benefits to using computers continue to mount, and as the costs of computing resources continue to decrease relative to the price of everything else, computer technology will become even more widespread in our society. It is therefore essential to know something about it.

The chapters in this module introduce you to computers and some of their uses. Chapters 1 and 2 orient you to what computer systems are, how they work, and how they're used. These chapters also present some key terminology that you will see repeatedly throughout the text.

What could a longshoreman possibly want with a computer? As you will learn in this chapter, computers are becoming useful tools at virtually every level of the organization—from the executive suite to workers in the field.

1 Introduction to the World of Computers

Outline

Overview

Computers in the 1990s Workplace

What's a Computer and What Does It Do?

- Computer Systems
- Data and Programs
- A Look at Computer Storage
- Hardware and Software
- Users and the Experts

Computer Systems to Fit Every Need and Pocketbook

- Microcomputers
- Minicomputers
- Mainframes
- Supercomputers

Using Computers: Some Examples

Computers and Society

Computers in Action

Learning Objectives

After completing this chapter, you will be able to:

1. Understand why it's especially important to learn about computers today.
2. Identify some of the major components in a computing environment and their relationships to one another.
3. Describe several applications in business and other areas of society in which computers play an important role.
4. Define several terms that are useful to know when reading about or discussing computers.
5. Appreciate the social impact of computers.

Overview

Unless you plan to spend your life living off the land in the upper reaches of the Yukon, computers and other forms of high technology will probably have an important impact on your life.

Computer systems keep track of our bank accounts and credit card purchases. They, along with sophisticated communications systems, are the cornerstones of the airlines' massive reservations systems. Computers perform the millions upon millions of computations needed to send astronauts into outer space and bring them back safely. Computers also direct production in our factories and provide executives with the up-to-date information they need to make decisions. Computers are embedded in watches, microwave ovens, television sets, phones, fax machines, automobiles, and probably even the stationary workout bike at your local spa. The applications are almost endless. Fifty short years ago, computers were part of an obscure technology of interest to only a handful of scientists. Today they are part of almost everyone's daily life.

Computers are very much like cars in that you don't need to know everything about them to use them effectively. You can learn to drive a car without knowing about internal combustion engines, and you can learn to use a computer without knowing about technical details such as logic circuits. Still, with both cars and computers, a little knowledge can give you a big advantage. Knowing something about cars can help you make wise purchases and save money on repairs. Likewise, knowing something about computers can help you use them for maximum benefit.

This book is about computers—what they are, how they work, and what they do. It is intended to give you the knowledge you need to use them effectively today and, through the Tomorrow boxes, give you a look into the future. Other boxed features throughout the text provide additional insights into the dynamic world of computers.

This book is not designed to make you a computer expert. It's a beginner's guide. If you're considering a career as a computer professional in business, this book will give you a comprehensive introduction to the field. If you're not, it will give you the basic knowledge you need to understand and use computers in school and on the job.

In this chapter, we'll first take a look at how computers are reshaping the workplace in the 1990s. From there, we turn to what computers are and how they work. Then we'll look at the various sizes in which computers come. Finally, we'll examine several examples of computer systems in action. Window 1, which follows Chapter 1, gives you a glimpse of the myriad applications of computers in today's world.

Computers in the 1990s Workplace

Prior to 1980, it was not critical for an ordinary person to know how to use a computer in his or her job. Computers were expensive, and few people had access to them. Furthermore, the use of computers generally required a lot of technical knowledge. Worse yet, most business computers were equipped to do little but carry out high-volume paperwork processing, such as issuing bills and keeping track of customer-account and inventory balances. Not only were most ordinary working people afraid of computers, but also there were few good reasons for getting familiar with them.

Then, suddenly, things began to change. Microcomputers—small, inexpensive computers that you will read about later in this chapter—were created. Consequently, today there are thousands of times more computers and hundreds of times more people involved with computers than just a decade or so ago. This has resulted in a flood of high-quality, high-technology products in the marketplace.

The usefulness of computers is due to more than their low price, their availability, and their high quality. Computers abound in today's workplace largely because we are living in an era when most jobs heavily depend on the collection, use, creation, and dissemination of information. Whether you become a teacher, lawyer, doctor, professional athlete, executive, or blue-collar worker (see Tomorrow box), your performance will largely depend on information and your use of it. Because computer systems can process facts at dizzying speeds, their availability may be equivalent to having an army of clerks at your disposal.

Following are several examples of computers being used in the workplace to enhance personal productivity (see also Figure 1-1):

- Virtually everyone who needs to type in a job uses a computer system or electronic typewriter to do word processing. *Word processing*—which enables keystrokes to be stored and edited electronically—produces documents such as letters and books faster and better than an ordinary typewriter.
- Managers and professionals at all levels of the business world use computing products called electronic *spreadsheets*—which in essence are powerful calculators—to perform analytical tasks in minutes that once took hours or days to do by hand. Not only can these people assemble information faster than they did before, they also can do tasks that once were impossible to perform manually. By being able to study "all the angles" of strategies or propositions, these individuals often find that they make better decisions.
- Executives are relying increasingly on *database management systems*—tools that provide instant access to local or remote banks of information—to learn about business conditions. Many of these systems are so easy to use that even the most computer-shy executives are being won over to their use, knowing that failure to keep up will give competitors an edge. Worker groups such as lawyers, doctors, and stockbrokers, who need to search through mounds of data to draw conclusions, have also found that database technology has improved their performance.
- Many companies have given thousands of *laptop computers*—computers the size of a notebook—to their field sales forces. These devices often give salespeople an advantage when dealing with clients, be-

Tomorrow

Technology Changes and Tomorrow's Workforce

Will Lower-Level Workers Be Able to Keep Pace?

Until the middle of this century, the principal on-the-job skill that a factory operator had to master was how to manually work a machine. The operator was often responsible for such matters as deciding how fast to run the machine, deciding when to replace certain parts, knowing when something could affect product quality, and deciding when to call other personnel for help. Operating a machine was largely a craft, and experience was valued more highly than a high-school diploma.

As machine automation in the factory became prevalent, jobs changed. Machines were devised throughout the 1940s, 1950s, 1960s, and 1970s that could duplicate certain manual operations at the push of a button. Such machines could also sound an alarm if something strange was happening, making it possible for them to be unattended for long periods of time. The most noticeable effect of these factory improvements was a reduction in the number of workers needed to produce the same volume of output.

The surge in computer technology in the past decade has changed the operation of factory machines even further. Take the newspaper business, for example. Operators of printing presses are, to a large extent today, computer operators. They need to be able to request and read computer outputs and to set up and run the presses through computer instructions. What's more, they also must know how to generate troubleshooting reports and operations memos, sometimes by computer. Many factory jobs in other industries have changed similarly.

The increase in requirements for computer and general literacy (reading and writing) skills at the factory comes at an especially bad time. Dropout rates in high schools are particularly high, and the cost of going to college is rising at an alarming rate. Also, more people are expected to retire from the workforce than to enter it in the next few decades, and the population as a whole is shifting from heavily industrialized cities. The bottom line is that there will be fewer qualified people to operate the sophisticated equipment that requires a wide array of new skills.

The factory floor. Technology is making greater literacy demands on the blue-collar worker.

To meet the demands that technology will continue to bring to the factory, many companies expect to take a more active role in education. In many cases, this means looking for motivated, trainable employees and setting up on-site programs to give these employees the general computing and literacy skills needed to perform their jobs. Some companies are also borrowing from the Japanese team approach to work by training workers to acquire a multitude of skills. This way, as people leave or as assembly lines need to be quickly refitted to produce new products, workers can easily adjust to new roles.

Companies that are investing in the blue-collar worker are reaping some impressive dividends. Workers who are given special treatment are likely to be more motivated and not so likely to look for another employer.

Figure 1-1 Two important ways in which computers are shaping the 1990s workplace.
(a) Laptop-sized computers enable computer work to be performed outside the office. (b) Modern communications systems make it possible for computerized business information to be transmitted around the world within seconds.

(a) (b)

cause the salesperson can analyze a client proposal on the spot, while the client is in a receptive mood. The laptop can also be used to access remote data—possibly supplying information that will help close the sale. And, at the end of a day, the laptop can be used to quickly prepare sales reports to send to headquarters (see User Solution 1-1).

- At all levels of business, computers are helping workers put *presentation materials* together by creating stunning charts and slides to help sell a live audience and by enhancing written materials. Researchers have found that people who use computers in this manner often are considered by others to be more "professional."
- In fields such as design and publishing, computers have completely revolutionized the way people work. Products such as cars, packages, buildings, shoes, and fabrics are all widely computer designed today. The rise of powerful *desktop publishing systems*—computer systems that fit on a desktop and enable ordinary people to produce work that looks as if it came from a professional printing press—has altered the structure of the entire publishing industry.
- Many businesses are now using some form of modern *communications system* to get faster and better information. For instance, facsimile (fax) machines are today widely used to transmit documents between sites almost instantaneously. This allows people to complete within a few hours a task that could stretch out over days or even weeks with just a physical delivery system at hand. Also, electronic mailbox and messaging systems enable people to work in groups more easily, even though they may be at different locations.

These applications only scratch the surface in demonstrating how computers are affecting the workplace in the 1990s. As you read further in

User Solution 1-1

Using Computers for Personal Productivity

Telenet salesman Bobby Rogers takes full advantage of his laptop computer to increase his personal productivity when on the road. At night in his hotel, he uses his computer's built-in communications feature to access Telenet's sales management system. This enables him to review sales data, update revenue forecasts, and send reports directly from his computer to his clients' premises. Also, using a spreadsheet, he can check hand-cranked formulas to make sure figures are correct. He once discovered $7,000 worth of errors in contracts that he was able to correct before passing the contracts to a customer.

this text, you will learn about dozens of others. A categorization of the way computers benefit organizations is described in Feature 1-1.

What's a Computer and What Does It Do?

Input.
What is supplied to a computer process.

Processing.
The conversion of input to output.

Output.
The results of a computer process.

Storage.
An area that holds materials going to or coming from the computer.

Input device.
A machine used to supply materials going to the computer.

Output device.
A machine used to accept materials coming from the computer.

Support equipment.
The machines that work with the computer.

Four words sum up the operation of a computer system: **input, processing, output,** and **storage.** To see what these words mean, let's look at something you probably have in your own home—a stereo system.

A simple stereo system often consists of a turntable and/or compact disk (CD) player, an amplifier, and a pair of speakers. To use the system, you place a record (or CD) on the turntable (or CD player) and turn the system on. The turntable or CD player converts the patterns in the grooves or tracks into sounds and transmits them to the amplifier as electronic signals. The amplifier takes the signals, strengthens them, and transmits them to the speakers. The result is music. In computer terms, the turntable or CD player sends signals as *input* to the amplifier. The amplifier *processes* the signals and sends them to the speakers, which produce a musical *output.* The turntable and CD player are **input devices,** the amplifier is a *processing unit,* and the speakers are **output devices.** The amplifier is the heart of the system, whereas the turntable, CD player, and speakers are examples of **support equipment.**

Most stereo systems have a variety of other support equipment. An antenna, for example, is another kind of input device. Headphones are another type of output device. A tape recorder is both an input and output device—you can use it to send signals to the amplifier or to receive signals from it. The tapes, records, and compact disks in your collection

Feature 1-1

How Computers Benefit Organizations

By Enabling People to Work More Efficiently or Effectively

Virtually every benefit for a business boils down to making people do their jobs either more efficiently or more effectively. Computers are popular because they further these objectives.

Efficiency. Efficiency relates to how well a given job is done. Because computers can do work faster than humans and with fewer errors, many organizations acquire computers for the efficiency they provide. Also, because human labor is expensive, replacing humans with computers often results in less money spent in the long run. In most cases, greater efficiency means doing work faster, more accurately, or cheaper.

Until the last decade, organizations acquired computers mostly because of their efficiency at doing specific types of work. Some examples of such work are issuing payroll checks, keeping track of customer purchases and payments, replacing certain types of workers (such as bank tellers or assembly-line workers) with machines, managing reservations and cancellations, balancing the company books, and the like.

Effectiveness. Whereas efficiency relates to doing something the right way, effectiveness relates to doing the right thing. Efficient uses for the computer generally affect the costs of an organization (i.e., the money going out), whereas effective uses have an impact on the revenues (i.e., the money coming in). Some examples follow:

- **Better Service** Computers are increasingly used to provide better service to clients. For instance, the automatic teller machines (ATMs) used at banks and the telebrokerage services that work with 800-area-code phone numbers and touch-tone phones enable people to withdraw money or place stock orders (and get stock quotes) 24 hours a day. In fact, people have now come to expect the level of service that computer technology provides.
- **Product Creation and Improvement** One classic example of the use of computers to create a product is Merrill Lynch's Cash Management Account (CMA). CMA is a financial package that combines a credit card, checking account, money-market fund, and brokerage service. The product, which could have been created only through advanced information processing technology, was a huge success and left competitors to play catch up.

Quality control. Computers spot dangerous trends before they become problems.

- **Spotting Opportunities and Potential Problems** Computers are often used today to detect subtle changes in markets or products, enabling companies to react more quickly to events. For instance, because virtually all of the major auto companies, including Ferrari (see photo), have sophisticated quality-control procedures for their parts and cars, they can spot dangerous trends well before they turn into major problems. Many of the quality-control checks involve sophisticated statistical algorithms that would be infeasible to calculate by hand.
- **Selling Computer Services** Because large companies often spend a great deal on computer resources, many have seized the opportunity to leverage these large investments by selling computer services on the side. John Deere, the farm equipment company, is one case in point. It acquired such a strong skill base when building its own systems that other companies asked it if it would sell some of its expertise. Thus, Deere Tech Services was formed.

Input/output (I/O) media. Objects used to store computer-processed materials.

Machine-readable. Any form in which data are represented so that they can be read by a machine.

are, in computer terms, **input/output (I/O) media.** They *store* music in a **machine-readable** form—a form that the associated input device (tape recorder, CD player, or record turntable) can recognize (that is, "read") and convert into signals for the amplifier to process.

Computer Systems

Computer system. A collection of elements that includes the computer as well as all the components that contribute to making it a useful tool.

All the elements in a stereo system have their counterparts in a computer system. A **computer system** consists of the computer itself, all the support equipment, and the machine-readable instructions and facts it processes, as well as operating manuals, procedures, and the people who use the system. In other words, all the components that contribute to making the computer a useful tool can be said to be parts of a computer system.

Computer. The piece of hardware, also known as the **central processing unit (CPU),** that interprets and executes program instructions and communicates with support devices.

At the heart of any computer system is the **computer** itself, or **central processing unit (CPU).** The CPU is the equivalent of the stereo amplifier. Like its counterpart, the CPU can't do anything useful without support equipment for input and output and I/O media for storage. Computer input and output devices include, to name just a few, keyboards, display devices, disk units, tape units, and printers. I/O media include disks, tapes, and paper. We will discuss these and many other items in Chapters 2, 4, and 5.

A computer system, of course, is not a stereo system, and a computer is much more versatile than a stereo amplifier. For example, a computer system can perform an enormous variety of processing tasks and a stereo system only a few. Also, a computer can support a much greater variety of input and output devices than can a stereo amplifier.

What gives a computer its flexibility? The answer, in a word, is *memory.* A computer has access to a memory, or "workspace," that allows it to retain whatever inputs it receives and the results it produces from these inputs. An ordinary home stereo amplifier has no such memory; what's playing on the turntable, tape recorder, or compact disk player passes directly through the amplifier to the speakers. Because computers can hold materials in such a workspace, they can be directed by *programs* to rearrange or recombine those materials in an amazing variety of ways before sending them along as output.

Data and Programs

Data. A collection of raw, unorganized facts.

Program. A set of instructions that causes the computer system to perform specific actions.

The material that a computer receives as input is of two kinds: data and programs. **Data** are essentially raw, unorganized facts (such as any event or proposition, whether true or not). **Programs** are instructions that tell the computer how to process those facts to produce the results that you, the computer system user, want. Returning to our example of a computer-driven music system, we could say that the tunes inputted to the system by the turntable, tape deck, or compact disk player are data (facts) and the instructions that tell the music system the order in which to play those tunes are a program. Now let's discuss these important terms in a little more detail.

Data. Almost any kind of fact can become computer data—facts about a company's employees, facts about airline flight schedules, or facts about baseball batting averages. Even picture images and sounds can become data. When we input data into a computer system, we usually aren't interested in getting them back just as we entered them. We want the system to process the data and give us new, useful *information.* **Information,** in the language of computers, refers to data that have been processed into a *meaningful* form.

Information.
Data that have been processed into a meaningful form.

We might want to know, for example, how many employees earn over $15,000, how many seats are available on Flight 495 from Los Angeles to San Francisco, or what Rickey Henderson's batting average was during last year's regular baseball season. The difference between data and information lies in the word "meaningful." Rickey Henderson's batting average may be meaningful to you because it will enable you to make a prediction about an upcoming game or merely because it will make watching the game more interesting. To a friend who doesn't follow baseball, however, Rickey Henderson's batting average may be meaningless—just ordinary data, not information. Thus, information is a *relative* term; information is something that has meaning for a specific person in a specific situation. Like beauty, the difference between data and information is strictly in the eye of the beholder.

Of course, you don't necessarily need a computer system to get information from a set of facts. For example, anyone can go through an employee file and make a list of people earning a certain salary. But to do so would take a lot of time, especially for a company with thousands of employees. In contrast, with their electronically fast speeds, computers can do such jobs almost instantly. Computer processing of data into information is called by a variety of terms, one of which is **information processing.**

Information processing.
Computer operations that transform data into meaningful information.

Information processing has become an especially important activity in recent years because most jobs depend heavily on the wise use of information. What use would a company president be without information about key trends in the world, consumer tastes, industry happenings, hot opportunities, or last quarter's performance? Or a store manager without information about which products are selling well and where to position them on the shelves (see User Solution 1-2)? Increasingly, such information is becoming available in electronic form, and the computer is providing those who know how to use it with a competitive edge. Many companies, in fact, recognize that information is one of their most important assets.

Programs. Like many other machines, the amplifier in your home stereo system is a *special-purpose* device. It is designed to support only a few specific tasks—play a record, make a recording on tape, play music into speakers or headphones, and so forth. These functions are built into its circuitry. To put it another way, it is "hardwired" to perform a very limited number of specific tasks.

Most computers, in contrast, are *general-purpose* devices. They must perform an enormous variety of tasks—for instance, preparing letters to clients, analyzing sales figures, and creating slide presentations, to name

User Solution 1-2

Using Information to Position Products

Serving more than 4,800 retail food stores in 36 states, Fleming is the largest wholesale food distributor in North America. It buys products in volume from thousands of food-processing companies and companies selling perishables and, in turn, supplies retail food stores (the places we shop) with a one-stop solution to stocking their shelves. Fleming also sells food stores a computerized shelf-management program, shown here, that allows stores to effectively allocate shelf space. The program enables each store to more accurately match its product offerings to both its sales and changing customer tastes.

just a few. Because most computers must be flexible, they can't be hardwired to do all the tasks they may be required to do. Instead, they rely on program instructions for guidance. As each program is read into the computer system, it is provided data by the user to process. The program then directs the circuits in the computer to open and close in the manner needed to do whatever task needs doing with these data.

Programming language. A set of rules used to write computer programs.

Programs cannot be written in ordinary English. They must be written in a **programming language**—a code the computer system can read and translate into the electronic pulses that make it work. Programming languages come in many varieties. In the early days of computers, they consisted of strings of numbers that only experts could comprehend. Over the years, they have become easier for ordinary mortals to understand and use. Some "languages" of today, in fact, do not bear much resemblance to languages of only a decade or so ago. Instead of learning and then typing in complicated commands, users only need to point to instructions on the display screen.

Programming languages are not universal; any given computer system will understand some languages but not others. Most computer systems, however, are capable of understanding several different languages. We will discuss programs and programming languages in detail in Module E.

A Look at Computer Storage

So far we've seen that if you want to get something done on a computer system, you must supply it with both facts (data) and instructions (a program) specifying how to process those facts. For example, if you want the

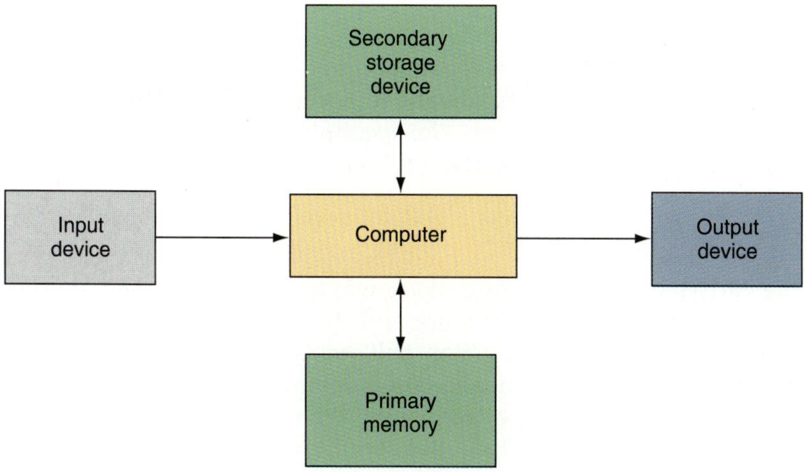

Figure 1-2
Input, processing, output, and storage.
Often, the computer fetches most of the programs and data it needs from secondary storage, from instructions given to it by a user at an input device. While it is working on specific programs and data, the computer uses primary memory as a "scratchpad" area. When finished, results are transferred from primary memory to an output device.

system to write payroll checks, you must supply such data as employees' names, social security numbers, and salaries. The program instructions must "tell" the system how to compute taxes, how to take deductions, where and how to print the checks, and so forth. Also, the computer relies on a memory (storage) to remember all these details as it is doing the work.

Actually, computer systems contain two types of storage. A **primary memory** (sometimes called **memory, main memory,** or **internal memory**), which is often contained in the unit that houses the computer, holds the data and programs that the computer is currently processing. When data are "captured" in the computer's primary memory or "workspace," they can be rearranged or recombined by the instructions in the program.

Primary memory. Also known as **memory, main memory,** and **internal memory,** this section of the computer system temporarily holds data and program instructions awaiting processing, intermediate results, and processed output.

Data and programs the computer doesn't need for the job at hand are stored in **secondary (external) storage.** In large computer systems, secondary storage is usually located in a device separate from the computer itself. In smaller computer systems, secondary storage is usually implemented by a device that is fitted into the unit containing the computer. Whatever the case, this piece of equipment is called a *secondary storage device.* It enables us to conveniently save large quantities of data and programs in machine-readable form so that we need not rekey them into the system every time we use them. Some secondary storage devices are capable of storing thousands of programs and billions of pieces of data.

Secondary storage. Storage on media such as disk and tape that supplements primary memory. Also called **external storage.**

When the CPU needs a certain program and set of data, it requests them from the secondary storage device—much as you might request a particular song from a jukebox—and reads them into its primary memory for processing. Unlike the turntable, however, which puts the original record in play, the CPU puts only a copy of the original program or data into primary memory for use. It is often useful to think of secondary storage as a large "library" of programs and data resources on full-time call to the CPU.

Figure 1-2 illustrates the relationships among input, processing, output, primary memory, and secondary storage.

Hardware and Software

Hardware.
Physical equipment in a computing environment, such as the computer and its support devices.

Software.
Computer programs.

In the world of computers, it is common to distinguish between hardware and software. The word **hardware** refers to the actual machinery that makes up a computer system—for example, the CPU, I/O devices, and storage devices. The word **software** refers to computer programs.

Users and the Experts

In the early days of computing, there was a clear distinction between the people who made computers work and those who used the results computers produced. This distinction still exists, but as computers become more available and easier to use, it is breaking down.

End user.
A person who needs in his or her job the results computers produce.

End users, or *users,* are the people who need the output computer systems produce. They include the accountant who needs a report on a client's taxes, the secretary who is word processing a letter, the engineer who needs to know whether a bridge will be structurally sound, the shop-floor supervisor who needs to know whether the day's quotas were met, and the company president who needs a report on the firm's profitability over the last ten years.

Programmer.
A person whose job is to write, maintain, and test computer programs.

Programmers, on the other hand, are the people who write the programs that produce such outputs. Programming is their primary job responsibility. Thus, although end users may do modest amounts of programming as part of their jobs, the distinction between an ordinary end user and a professional programmer is based on what the person has actually been hired to do.

There are many other types of computer professionals whom organizations employ. For instance, *systems analysts* are hired to build large computer systems within a company. *Computer operations personnel,* in contrast, are people responsible for the day-to-day operation of large computer systems.

Computer Systems to Fit Every Need and Pocketbook

A great variety of computer systems are available commercially to serve computer users' needs. Here we'll consider one important way in which computers differ from one another: size.

Computers are generally classified in one of four size categories: small, or microcomputers; medium-sized, or minicomputers; large, or mainframe computers; and super-large, or supercomputers. In practice, the distinction among these different sizes is not always clear-cut. Large minicomputers, for example, often are bigger than small mainframes.

In general, the larger the computer, the greater its processing power. For example, big computers can process data at faster speeds than small computers. Big computers can also accommodate larger and more powerful support devices. Naturally, the larger the computer and its support

Figure 1-3 Four microcomputer systems.
(a) Compaq Deskpro 486/33L desktop computer. (b) IBM PS/2, Model P75 486 portable computer. (c) Macintosh Portable laptop computer. (d) Texas Instruments Spell-Checker handheld computer.

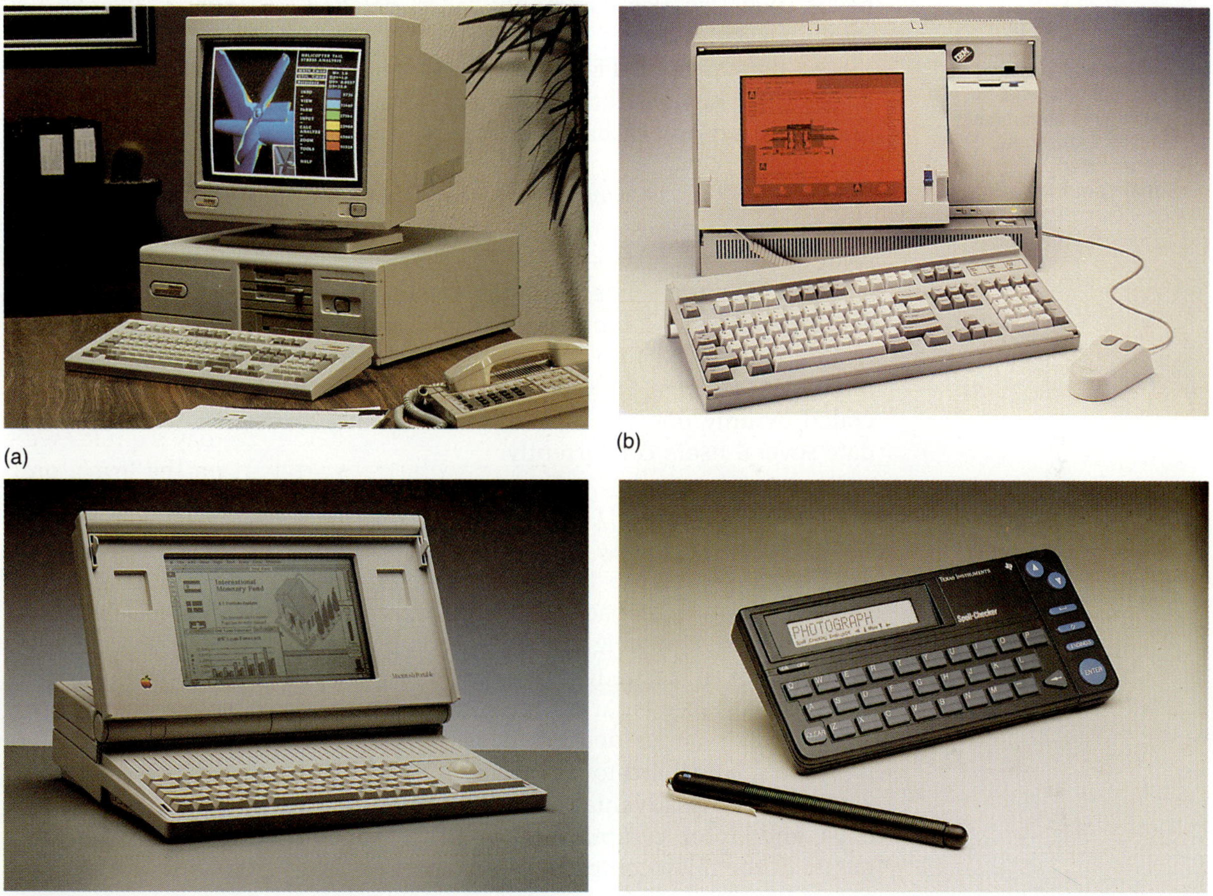

(a) (b) (c) (d)

equipment, the greater the price. A computer system can cost anywhere from a couple of hundred dollars to many millions.

Microcomputers

A technological breakthrough in the early 1970s made it possible to produce an entire CPU on a single silicon chip smaller than a dime. These "computers-on-a-chip," or *microprocessors,* could be mass produced at very low cost. Microprocessors were quickly integrated into all types of products, making possible powerful hand-held calculators, digital watches, a variety of electronic toys, and sophisticated controls for household appliances such as microwave ovens and automatic coffee makers. Microprocessors also made it possible to build inexpensive computer systems, such as those in Figure 1-3, small enough to fit on a desktop or even in a shirt pocket. These small computer systems have informally come to be called **microcomputers** (or *micros*). Because they are inexpensive and small enough for one person to use at home or work for personal needs, they are also commonly called **personal computers** *(PCs)* or *personal computer systems.*

Microcomputer system. The smallest and least expensive type of computer system. Also known as **microcomputer** (*micro*), **personal computer** (*PC*), or *personal computer system.*

As illustrated in Figure 1-3, most **microcomputer systems** currently available for business and home use can be classified as desktop, portable (including laptop), or hand-held units.

Desktop Units. *Desktop computers* are those found most often in schools, homes, and businesses. These are the computer systems that have become household names—IBM PC; IBM PS/1 and PS/2; Apple II, IIe, IIc, and the Macintosh line; Compaq Deskpro 286, 386 and 486 (see Figure 1-3a); the NeXT Computer System; Commodore Amiga; and so forth. Desktop units fall into one of two categories: single-user systems and multiuser systems. *Single-user systems,* as their name implies, can be operated by only one user at a time, while *multiuser systems* can accommodate several users concurrently.

Portable and Laptop Units. *Portable computers* are designed for users who would like to use the same microcomputer at several sites. These computers (see Figure 1-3b) are characterized by being lightweight (1 to 18 pounds) and compact (able to fit into a briefcase). Technically speaking, the most lightweight portable computers—which can be used on a person's lap, if desired—are called *laptop computers* or, sometimes, *notebook computers* (see Figure 1-3c). Although many portables are just as powerful as their larger desktop cousins, they tend to be more expensive, have small and hard-to-read screens, and have a dense arrangement of keys. These disadvantages notwithstanding, portability is "in" these days, and laptop computers currently are one of the fastest-growing segments of the microcomputer industry.

Hand-Held Units. *Hand-held computers*—or *palmtop computers*—look and behave a lot like standard pocket calculators. You can generally hold the entire computer system in your hand while operating it. Today, most hand-held computers are relegated to specialized tasks—keeping track of golf or bowling scores, translating words into foreign languages, checking the spelling of words (see Figure 1-3d), and providing synonyms and antonyms for words.

Micros are widely used in both small and large businesses. Small businesses use them to keep track of merchandise, prepare correspondence, bill customers, and do routine accounting. Large businesses use them as productivity tools for secretaries and as analysis tools for decision makers, to name just two important applications. Also, laptops are popular with salespeople making presentations at client sites and with managers who need a computer as they travel about. Microcomputers are increasingly being networked into large communications systems, where they are used as data-entry devices or as general-purpose workstations.

Figure 1-4
Minicomputers.
Minicomputers are particularly useful in environments in which several people need to share a common system and, as shown here, in environments such as factories or warehouses, where they are dedicated to managing production and inventory operations.

Minicomputers

Minicomputers, or *minis,* generally are regarded as medium-sized computers (see Figure 1-4). Most of them fall between microcomputers and mainframes in their processing power. The very smallest minicomputers, however, are virtually indistinguishable from the largest microcomputers, and the largest (sometimes called *superminis*) closely resemble small mainframes. Minicomputers usually are far more expensive than microcomputers and are unaffordable for most individuals.

Minicomputer.
An intermediate-sized and medium-priced type of computer.

Any of several factors might lead an organization to choose a minicomputer over a micro or mainframe. A small or medium-sized company may simply find microcomputer systems too slow to handle its current volume of processing. Or a company may need a computer system that can do several jobs at once and interact with multiple users at the same time. Many microcomputer systems lack sufficient power for such applications. Mainframes, of course, have these capabilities, but they are much larger and more expensive than minis.

Mainframes

The **mainframe** (see Figure 1-5) is the standard for almost all large organizations. It often operates 24 hours a day, serving hundreds of users on display devices during regular business hours and processing large jobs such as payroll and billing late at night. Many large organizations need several mainframes to complete their computing workloads. Typically these organizations own or lease a variety of computer types—say, mainframes, minis, and micros—to meet all their processing needs.

Mainframe.
A large, transaction-processing-oriented computer.

Most mainframes are employed to handle high-volume processing of business transactions and routine paperwork. For most businesses, this

Figure 1-5
IBM mainframe.
IBM's 3090 series and newly released ES/9000 series set the standard for today's mainframes. IBM accounts for close to 75 percent of all mainframes sold.

includes tasks such as keeping track of customer purchases and payments, sending out bills and reminder notices, paying employees, and maintaining detailed tax records. These operations were some of the earliest applications of computers in business and have been the responsibility of mainframes from day one.

Supercomputers

Supercomputer. The fastest and most expensive type of computer.

Some organizations, such as large scientific and research laboratories, have extraordinary information processing needs. Applications such as sending astronauts into outer space and weather forecasting, for example, require extreme degrees of accuracy and a wealth of computations. High-quality animation, which produces the special effects you see in computer-generated movies and commercials, also demands enormous amounts of high-speed computation. To meet such needs, a few vendors offer very large, sophisticated machines called **supercomputers** (see Figure 1-6). These machines are very expensive, often costing several millions of dollars.

Using Computers: Some Examples

Now that we've briefly seen how a computer system works, let's "walk through" a few applications within a typical organization to put many of the concepts you've just read about into sharper focus.

Large System. Paradise Beach Resort is a large hotel on the Florida coast. It uses a *mainframe* computer system to keep track of such things as guest reservations, bills, and employees. Without the mainframe, the hotel would never be able to accommodate the number of guests it han-

Figure 1-6
Cray X-MP supercomputer. Supercomputers are faster than conventional computers because they pack circuits much more tightly. Cray produces more than half of the supercomputers sold worldwide.

dles with its current staff, nor would it be able to provide the high level of service its guests expect.

In the precomputer days, operations were far less efficient. For instance, it was quite common for bills to be incorrect, misplaced, or mismanaged. Frequently, if a reservation was improperly recorded, the guest was detained in the lobby. In fact, often two desk clerks would be in the process of booking different guests for the same room—an embarrassing mishap for the hotel and one that sometimes resulted in lost business.

Today, with a computer keeping track of guests, these types of problems occur very infrequently. The mainframe also handles various other types of accounting tasks—paying employees and preparing comprehensive reports for management and taxing agencies, for instance. It does these tasks much more quickly and accurately than was possible in the precomputer days. Some of the information that management now routinely receives was impossible to obtain before the computer arrived.

The hotel's mainframe is run by a staff of just four people. A *director* of computing oversees all planning in computer-related areas. A *systems analyst* decides which new software and hardware must be bought and which programs must be custom written to meet the evolving needs of the hotel. A resident *programmer* attends to the latter need, coding programs from specific guidelines provided by the systems analyst. An *operations person* ensures that the mainframe runs smoothly on a daily basis and troubleshoots potential technical problems when the computer system malfunctions.

Figure 1-7 The catering manager's microcomputer system.
The system unit contains the microprocessor, primary memory, and secondary storage devices—two diskette drives and a hard-disk drive.

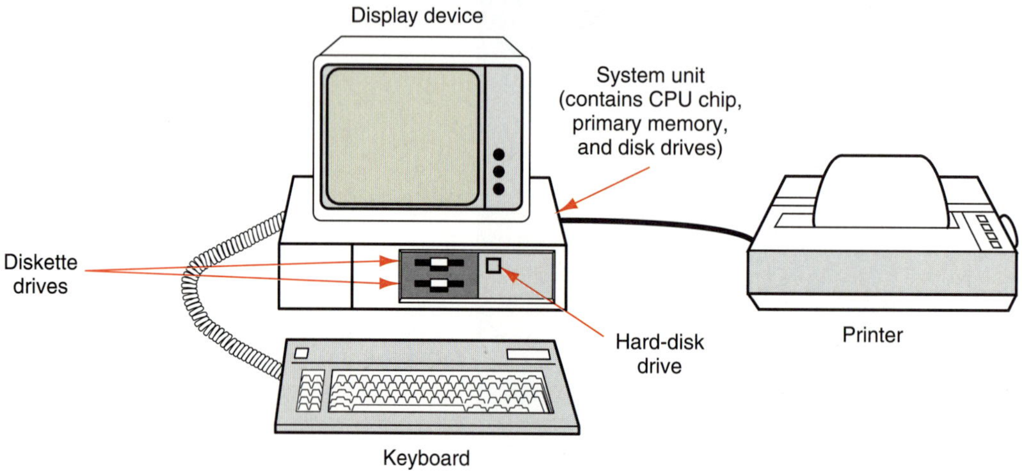

User 1. Lydia Maxwell is the catering manager at Paradise Beach Resort. She has no need for the mainframe but finds a desktop *microcomputer system* a useful tool in her work. The hardware in Lydia's microcomputer system consists of four pieces of equipment: a keyboard, a display device, a printer, and a system unit (see Figure 1-7). Within the *system unit* are the CPU chip or microprocessor, primary memory, and secondary storage devices—two diskette drives and a hard-disk drive—as well as a lot of circuitry that we'll talk about later in the book.

The *keyboard,* which resembles that of an ordinary typewriter, enables Lydia to direct the microcomputer system to do what she wants. Everything she inputs at the keyboard and the computer system's responses to these inputs are shown on the *display device,* which resembles a television screen. When Lydia wants something printed out, she directs the computer system to send the output to her *printer.*

The *diskette unit* on Lydia's microcomputer system consists of two *drives.* On the drives, Lydia can mount *diskettes,* or *floppy disks*—small platters capable of storing, say, 100 or more pages of data or programs. Often users such as Lydia keep their *data* and *programs* on separate diskettes. The diskettes must be properly inserted into the computer system's disk drives if the system is to access the programs and data on them. Diskettes make it convenient to transport data to and from the computer system in machine-readable form.

The *hard-disk unit* on Lydia's system, on the other hand, has almost 100 times the capacity of a single diskette and permits much quicker accessing of both programs and data. Three years ago, Lydia acquired the hard-disk unit for her system because her collection of programs and data

Figure 1-8 Meal-planning data stored on disk.
Each set of data consists of several filled-in "forms." Several hundred such forms can be stored on a single diskette and several thousand on hard disk.

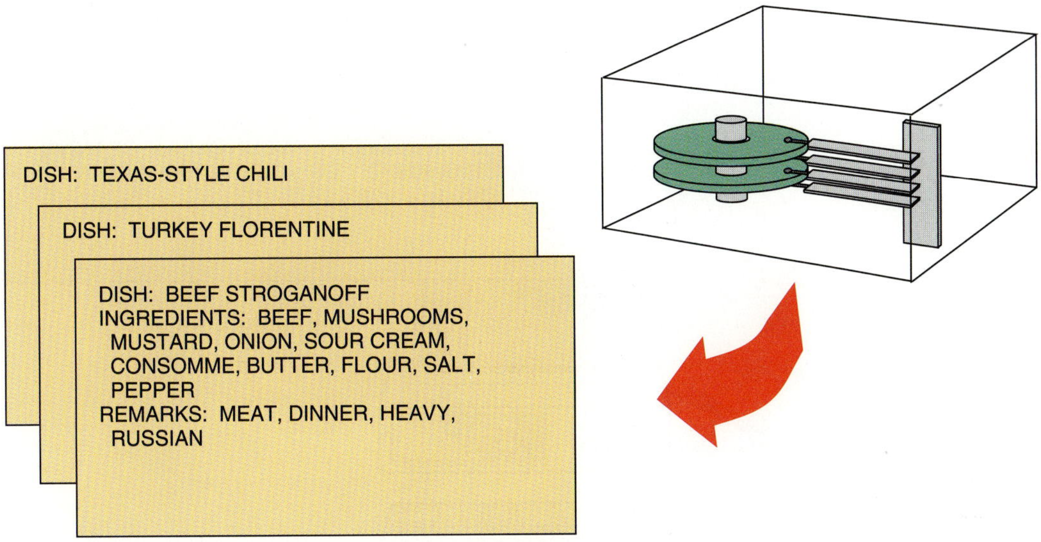

was expanding rapidly and she was getting tired of mounting and dismounting diskettes every time she wanted to use a particular program or set of data.

Once a program and its data are loaded into primary memory from any of the disk devices, the computer is transformed into a powerful calculating tool. One application for which Lydia finds her computer system useful is meal planning. Here she uses it to search through descriptions of food dishes to find ones that will fit a particular client's needs. On her hard disk are stored thousands of filled-in "forms," one form for each food dish Lydia can offer to guests (see Figure 1-8). Each form contains three separate types, or *fields,* of data—the name of the dish, its ingredients, and a few remarks.

Therefore, if Lydia is helping a client plan a Saturday night banquet over the phone, and the client wants a beef dish with mushrooms, Lydia can summon a program stored on her hard disk called a *database management system* to search for all forms on her entrées disk file in which "ingredients" contains "beef" and "mushrooms" and "remarks" contains "dinner." Then she can have the names of these dishes directed to her display screen.

Of course, Lydia can rely on her memory, but having the computer system make the search for her often turns up good alternatives that didn't cross her mind. Also, she can save a lot of phone time by having her computer system do the searching in the background while she attends to other matters with the client. Lydia's database manager lets her add new forms to the file when she wants them, delete forms, and mod-

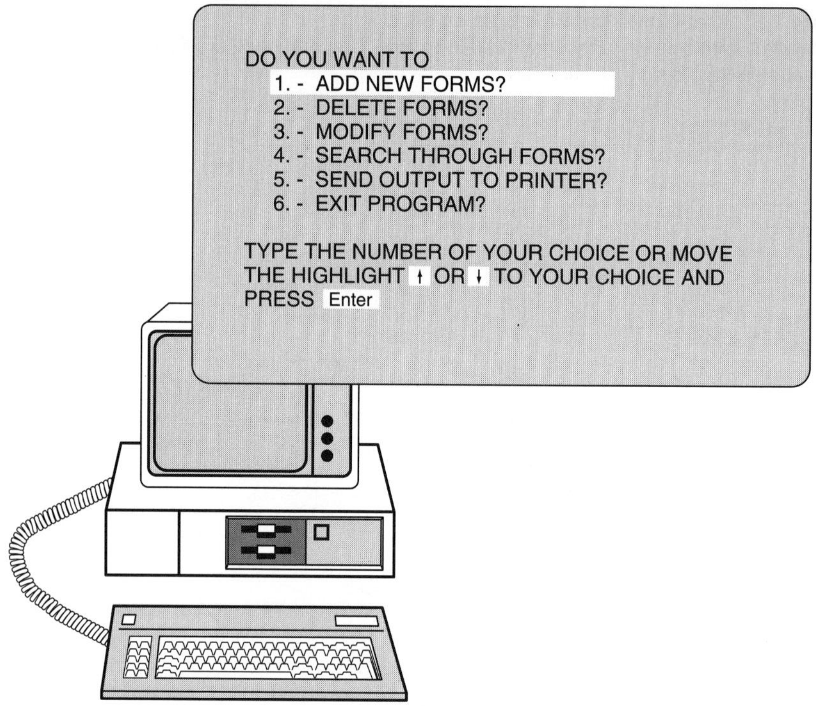

Figure 1-9
A computer menu.
Menus beckon a user to choose a specific course of action. Using them effectively requires neither typing skills nor an extensive knowledge of computers.

ify forms. She does this with a *menu* of processing alternatives (not to be confused with a food menu) that the database manager sends to her display screen, asking her what she wants to do (see Figure 1-9).

User 2. Don Kawashima is the convention manager at Paradise Beach Resort and also a very heavy computer user. His job responsibilities are many. He promotes the hotel to convention groups, arranges for groups to reserve hotel facilities, and performs a variety of other tasks. There's a lot of paperwork involved—sending letters back and forth, booking facilities, establishing budgets, filing reports, and so on. Also, Don finds that success in his job involves lots of little things that aren't in his job description, such as preparing an immediate thank-you letter to an important client when the secretary is swamped with other tasks.

To assist him in his work, Don has a microcomputer system on his desk (see Figure 1-10). Don's system is more sophisticated than Lydia's because he often needs to interact with the hotel's mainframe and frequently must prepare correspondence to clients.

For instance, Don's system has a *communications interface,* which enables him to interact with the hotel's mainframe. It gives him the option of using his own computer or the mainframe to do his work. For secondary storage, his system, like Lydia's, has both diskette units and a hard-disk unit. Of course, since Don can tap into the mainframe, he can also use the secondary storage on that system, which may be 100 or so times greater than that of his own.

Figure 1-10 The convention manager's microcomputer system.
The system depicted here is more sophisticated than the one shown in Figure 1-7, demonstrating how microcomputer systems can be configured to virtually any specific set of needs.

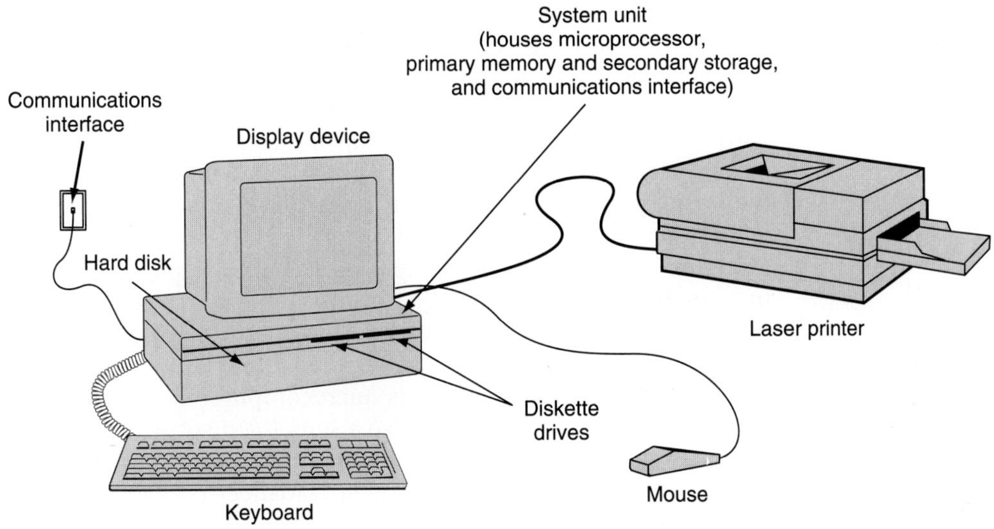

Don also has a *laser printer,* which enables him to prepare crisp-looking correspondence and newsletters to his clients, and a *mouse,* which he uses to select commands or menu choices from the screen. As he moves the mouse along a desktop, an onscreen arrow, called a *pointer,* moves correspondingly. When he "clicks" a button on the mouse, the selection (usually in the form of a graphic symbol, or *icon*) to which the arrow currently points is invoked (see Figure 1-11). Although the mouse cannot directly be used for such things as typing letters or keying in numbers, it is very helpful for making screen selections—especially for a person such as Don, who considers himself a relatively poor typist.

Don interacts with the hotel's mainframe daily to get reservations information necessary for his job. If an important client phones to request a particular set of dates for a conference, Don must be able to get to up-to-date reservations data stored on the mainframe while talking to the client. Or, if an angry client complains about a bill, Don must quickly retrieve billing data from the mainframe to sort out the problem. Don performs these types of tasks with a database management system stored on the mainframe. This system is much more sophisticated than the one Lydia uses because it must handle bigger tasks.

One reason for Don's success at his job is his skill at getting to key information quickly when dealing with clients, thereby allowing him to give them first-class service. Hotel management realizes fully that a $50,000 booking can easily be won or lost on service to clients, so they are more than happy that Don is hooked up to the mainframe with his own system.

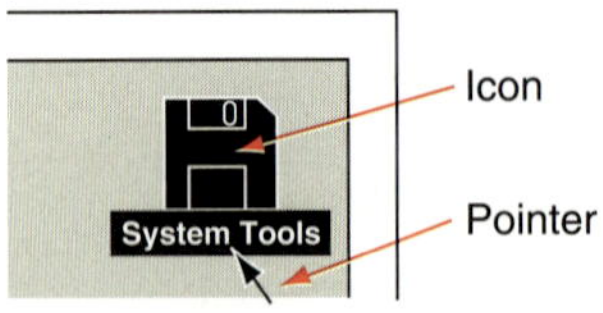

Figure 1-11
Pointing with a mouse. When the user "clicks" a button on the mouse, the selection to which the arrow is currently pointing is invoked. Here the "System Tools" selection—which will provide a set of computer system options—is chosen.

Don also does a lot of computing work that doesn't involve communicating with the mainframe. For instance, when a letter must be quickly prepared and sent to a client to confirm a booking date or to thank the client for his or her patronage, Don uses a *word processing* software package and a form letter (called a "boilerplate"), both of which are stored on his hard disk. To prepare the client letter, he first summons the word processor by selecting an appropriate menu choice or icon on the screen with his mouse. Next, also via the mouse, he may select a file-folder-shaped icon corresponding to the boilerplate letter. In doing this, he asks the word processor to find the boilerplate letter in storage. When the letter is retrieved and displayed onscreen, Don uses the keyboard to type in certain parts of the letter to make it appear personalized. When he finishes typing, he will use the mouse to select an icon that will store a copy of the letter on his hard disk and then to choose another icon that will output the letter on his printer.

Don also frequently uses his microcomputer system to prepare budgets, a task that requires him to use a *spreadsheet* software package. He may summon this package with a special icon similar to the one he uses to summon the word processor. The spreadsheet package also has a facility that enables Don to manage the enormous number of budgets he prepares. And, of course, he can send completed budgets to his printer when he requires them in printed form.

Computer systems, such as those used by Lydia and Don, are making a profound impact in today's workplace. Not only do such systems improve the types of information people need to do their jobs, but also they are fundamentally changing the way work is done.

Computers and Society

The examples we've just presented should give you some idea of why computer systems have become such an important part of modern life. Their ability to sort through massive amounts of data and quickly produce useful information for almost any kind of user—from payroll clerk to president—makes them indispensable in a society like ours. Without computers, neither the catering manager nor the convention manager in our example could possibly provide the level of service they now extend to clients. The government would be unable to tabulate all the data it collects for the census every ten years. Banks would be overwhelmed by the job of tracking all the transactions they must process. The efficient airline and telephone service we are used to would be impossible (see User Solution 1-3). Moon exploration and the space shuttle would still be science fiction fantasies. The list is virtually endless.

But along with the benefits computers bring to society have come some troubling problems, ranging from health to personal security and privacy to ethics. The catering manager in our example, for instance, spends many hours in front of a display screen. Do the radiation and glare emanating from the screen impair her health? Banks keep data on

User Solution 1-3

Providing Better Service at a Lower Cost

At London's Heathrow Airport, British Airways self-service ticketing machines—which work like the automatic teller machines (ATMs) that banks use for 24-hour cash withdrawals—enable shuttle passengers to buy a ticket and check in within 40 seconds. The machines save on clerical labor and provide better service to customers. To handle their information processing, which includes ticketing, British Airways maintains 16 mainframes that collectively store over a trillion characters of data.

customers' accounts on external storage devices. Can they prevent clever "computer criminals" from using their computer systems to steal from those accounts? The Internal Revenue Service has confidential information about every American taxpayer. Can it protect that information from unauthorized use? Because commercial software exists in electronic form, it can be easily copied. What restrictions should be placed on who can copy and use this software?

These are serious issues, but we can only mention them briefly in this chapter. Feature 1-2 covers the growing concern over computer crime and ethical abuses in the technology area.

Computers in Action

Where would you expect to find computers? In our discussion so far, we've seen some of the amazing variety of ways in which computers have become part of our lives. As you read through this book, you should get a good idea of what computer systems can and cannot do and where they

Feature 1-2

Computer Crime and Ethics

Two Major Concerns for the 1990s

We are living in an age when an unprecedented number of people have access to computer resources. A major concern as the 21st century approaches is the potential for abuse of those resources, through both criminal acts and ethically questionable behavior.

Computer Crime

Computer crime is loosely defined as the use of computers to commit unauthorized acts.

Computer crime has many forms. Some cases involve the use of a computer for theft of money or equipment. Others concern the copying of programs or data to the owner's detriment. Still other cases involve manipulation of data such as grades for personal advantage. The cost of computer crime is estimated at billions of dollars annually.

As in many fields, a specialized jargon has evolved in the area of computer crime. Following is a sampling.

Data Diddling. *Data diddling* involves altering key production data on the computer system in some unauthorized way. Data diddlers often are found changing grades in university files, falsifying input records on bank transactions, and the like.

The Trojan Horse. The *Trojan horse* is a procedure for adding concealed instructions to a computer program so that it will still work but will also perform unauthorized duties. For example, a bank worker can subtly alter a program that contains thousands of lines of code by adding a small "patch" that instructs the program not to withdraw money from a certain account.

Salami Shaving. *Salami shaving* involves altering programs so that many small dollar amounts—say, a few cents' worth of interest payments—are shaved from a large number of selected transactions or accounts and deposited in another account. The victims generally are unaware that their funds have been tapped, because the amount taken from each individual is trivial.

Superzapping. *Superzapping* is a technique made possible by a special program that bypasses all system controls when the computer "crashes" and cannot be restarted with normal procedures. This program, in effect, is a "master key" that can provide access to any part of the system.

Trapdoors. *Trapdoors* are diagnostic tools, used in the development of systems programs, that enable programmers to gain access to various parts of the computer system. Before the programs are marketed, these tools are supposed to be removed. Occasionally, however, some are overlooked, enabling unauthorized peeking.

Logic Bombs and Computer Viruses. *Logic bombs* are programs or short code segments designed to be executed at random or at specific times to perform unauthorized acts. In one case, a programmer inserted into a system a logic bomb that would destroy the company's entire personnel file if his name was removed from it. Sometimes the term *computer virus* is used to describe a logic bomb in which piece of unauthorized code is transmitted from program to program during a copy operation and destroys data or crashes the computer system as soon as it is unwittingly executed.

Scavenging. As its name implies, *scavenging* involves searching through trash cans, offices, and the like for information that will permit unauthorized access to a computer system. Students, for example, will sometimes look through discarded listings at the mainframe computer site for ID numbers that will access others' accounts.

Data Leakage. In *data leakage,* confidential data are coded in ways so that they can be removed from an organization's premises undetected. For example, sensitive data can be transformed through a coding process into useless nonsense. Then, after they leave the premises unnoticed, they are decoded.

Wiretapping. There are many documented cases of people who have *wiretapped* computer systems to obtain information illegally. Some transmission facilities, such as satellites, are highly susceptible; others, such as fiber optic cable, are difficult to penetrate.

Software Piracy. *Software piracy,* the unauthorized copying or use of a computer program, is often a crime. A person who makes an unauthorized copy of a program can be guilty of breaking copyright laws. It is definitely a crime to copy a program and then attempt to sell it for profit. Using an unauthorized copy that was made by someone else may constitute a crime as well.

Hacking. *Hacking* is a computer term referring to the activities of people who "get their kicks" out of using computers or terminals to crack the security of some computer system. Many people engage in hacking purely for the challenge of cracking codes; others do it to steal computer time or to peek at confidential information.

Counterfeiting. Microcomputer-based color-copier technology is so sophisticated today that it has opened the door to a brand new type of computer crime—counterfeiting. The U.S. Secret Service, for instance, recently arrested a person who made over $1 million worth of photocopied money and traveler's checks.

Ethics

Ethics refers to standards of moral conduct. For example, telling the truth is a matter of ethics. An unethical act isn't always illegal, but sometimes it is. For example, purposely lying to a friend is unethical but normally is lawful, but perjuring oneself as a courtroom witness is a crime.

Today, with regard to computers, one of the most important concerns in the ethics area is the use of someone else's property in an unauthorized way. Let's look at two examples.

- People tend to casually use computer resources in ways that, although not criminal, are ethically questionable. For instance, some people regularly use a software package they don't own for personal purposes, claiming they are doing so just to "get the feel of it." Although most vendors encourage limited experimentation with their products, they frown on someone who hasn't bought the package but owns and uses it regularly.
- A student may casually eavesdrop, on a university mainframe system, on data not intended for his or her use. This may entail neither a prosecutable crime nor a major security threat, but that make the act no less ethically reprehensible.

Some questions that you should ask yourself when considering an action that might be ethically questionable are provided in the accompanying figure.

An Ethics Checklist

Answering "yes" to any of these questions may be a tip-off of an unethical act.

- ☐ Will you benefit in any way from the action you are considering taking?
- ☐ Are you not disclosing certain facts to others because you are afraid they will disapprove?
- ☐ Are you purposely coloring facts to portray a situation as being better or worse than it actually is?
- ☐ If the same action that you are considering was instead done to you, would you feel badly?
- ☐ Could anyone possibly object to the action as being unfair?
- ☐ Will anyone be harmed by the action?
- ☐ Do you find yourself rationalizing your behavior?
- ☐ Could the action ultimately result in a destructive practice or socially undesirable trend?

do and do not belong. Window 1 presents an extensive picture essay of computers in action in just a few of the many settings in which you are likely to encounter them.

Summary and Key Terms

Computers appear almost everywhere in today's world. They're embedded in consumer products, used to run businesses, and employed to direct production in our factories, to name just a few applications.

Computers in the 1990s Workplace. Computers abound in today's workplace largely because we are living in an era when most jobs heavily depend on the collection, use, creation, and dissemination of information.

What's a Computer and What Does It Do? Four words summarize the operation of a **computer system: input, processing, output,** and **storage.**

The processing function is performed by the **computer** itself, which is sometimes called the **central processing unit,** or **CPU.**

The input and output functions are performed by **support equipment,** such as **input devices** and **output devices.** Just as your stereo amplifier would be useless if it had no speakers, headphones, tape deck, or turntable to supplement it, the computer would be helpless without this support equipment.

On some of the support equipment are mounted **input/output (I/O) media.** Many of these media *store* materials in **machine-readable** form, which the computer system can recognize and process.

The material that a computer receives as input is of two kinds: data and programs. **Data** are facts the computer has at its disposal; **programs** are instructions that explain to the computer what to do with these facts. Programs must be written in a **programming language** that the computer can understand.

Data that have been processed into a useful form are called **information.** The processing of data into information on computers is called **information processing.**

Computer systems have two types of memory, or storage. **Primary memory** (sometimes called **memory, main memory,** or **internal memory**) is often built into the unit housing the computer itself; it holds the programs and data that the system is currently processing. **Secondary (external) storage** holds other programs and data. In many systems, secondary storage is located in a separate hardware device.

In the world of computers, it is common to distinguish between hardware and software. **Hardware** refers to the actual machinery that makes up the computer system, such as the CPU, input and output devices, and secondary storage devices. **Software** refers to computer programs.

End users are the people who need the output that computer systems produce. In a computing environment, there are many types of experts who help users meet their computing needs; for example, **programmers** are responsible for writing programs.

Computer Systems to Fit Every Need and Pocketbook. Small computers are often called **microcomputers (microcomputer systems)** or **personal computers** *(personal computer systems)*, medium-sized computers **minicomputers**, and large computers **mainframes.** The very largest computers, which are used for applications that demand the most in terms of speed in memory, are called **supercomputers.** Although categorizing computers by size can be helpful, in practice it is sometimes difficult to classify computers that fall on the borders of these categories.

Using Computers: Some Examples. The hotel industry is but one example of an environment where computers—from mainframes to microcomputers—serve a variety of uses.

Computers and Society. Although computer systems have become an indispensable part of modern life, their growing use has created troubling problems, ranging from health to personal security and privacy to ethics.

Computers in Action. As you read through this book, you should get a good idea of what computer systems can and cannot do and where they do and do not belong. Window 1 presents an extensive picture essay of computers in action in just a few of the many settings in which you are likely to encounter them.

Review Exercises

Fill-in Questions

1. Four words sum up the operation of a computer system: input, output, ________, and storage.
2. When programs and data are being processed, they are stored in ________ memory.
3. Processed data that are in a useful form are called ________.
4. Another name for computer programs is ________.
5. When programs and data are not being processed but need to be "at the fingertips" of the computer, they are stored in ________ storage.
6. A term used for the equipment in a computing environment is ________.
7. A series of instructions that direct a computer system is known as a(n) ________.
8. The hardware, software, data, procedures, and personnel needed to process data successfully are called a(n) ________.

Matching Questions

Match each term with the description that fits best.

a. minicomputer	d. supercomputer
b. input device	e. hardware
c. mainframe	f. microcomputer

_____ 1. The equipment that makes up a computer system.

_____ 2. Another name for personal computer.

_____ 3. A medium-sized computer.

_____ 4. A large computer used to process business transactions in high volume.

_____ 5. Any piece of equipment that supplies programs and data to a computer.

_____ 6. The most powerful type of computer.

Discussion Questions

1. Name several ways in which computers are used in today's workplace.
2. Provide some examples of input devices, output devices, processing devices, and input/output media that are found in the average household and are not necessarily computer related.
3. What is the difference between a computer and a computer system?
4. Name as many computer support devices as you can. What is the purpose of each?
5. What are the major differences between primary memory and secondary storage?
6. What is the difference between programs and data?
7. Define and give some examples of end users of a computer system.
8. Identify some social problems created by the existence of computer systems.

Critical Thinking Questions

1. Should everyone getting a degree from a college or university today be required to take an introductory computer course? Defend your response.
2. The section on the workplace of the 1990s provides several examples describing how computers are changing the way ordinary people work. Can you think of any additional examples not mentioned in this section?
3. The term "computer literacy"—knowing something about computers—is widely used today. In your opinion, what types of things about computers should people such as yourself be literate about?

Window 1

Computers in Our World

A Visual Portfolio of the Widespread Use of Computers

Computers rapidly have become an important force in almost every segment of our society. This first "window to the world of computers" presents a small sample of the many tasks to which computers may be applied. Included are examples from the fields of business, education, and government.

1. One of the most impressive technological feats today is computer art and animation. As the art of computerized movie making advances, it will become harder than ever to tell the difference between fantasy and reality.

2

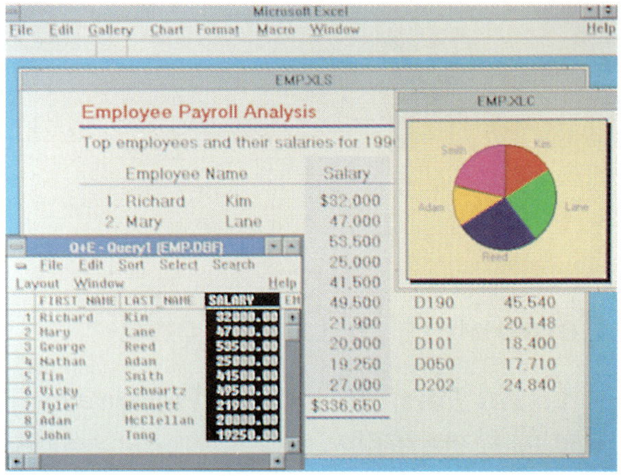

3

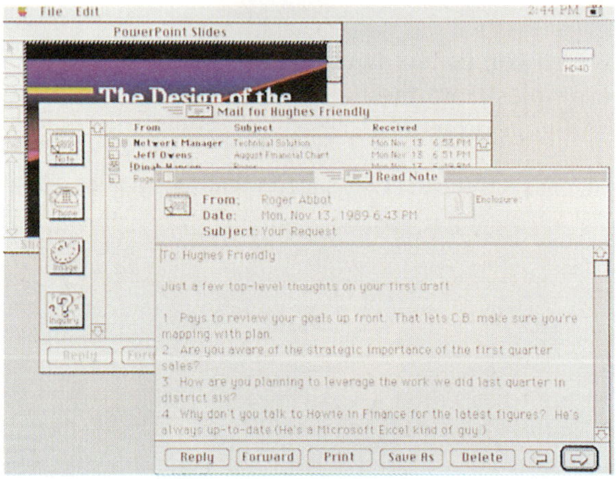

4

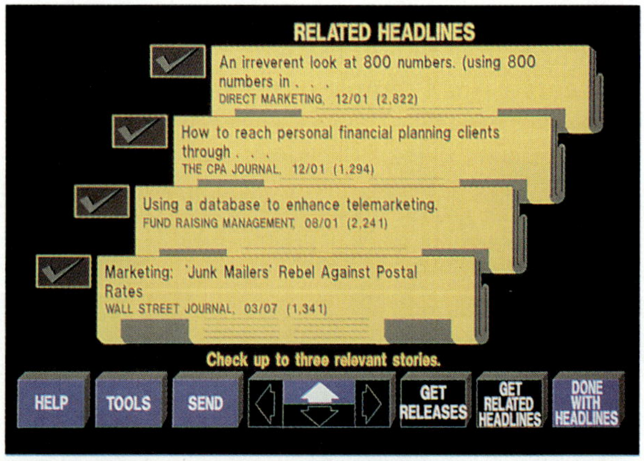

5

6

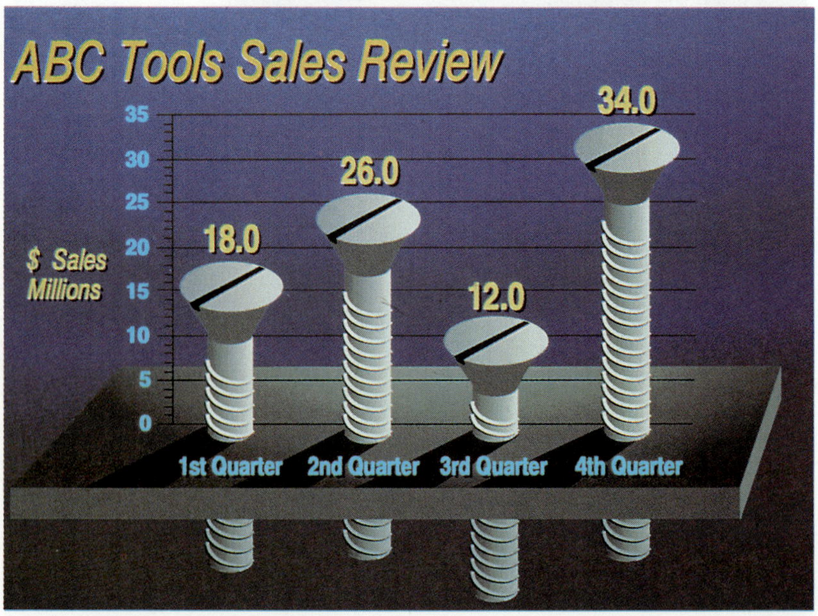

2–6. Many workers use desktop computers to increase their personal productivity. Some favorite applications are spreadsheets (3), electronic mail (4), information retrieval (5), and slides for presentations (6).

7. By using computers, banks need fewer tellers, keep more accurate customer accounts, and provide faster and better service.

8. Computers are widely used today in retailing to record sales and to apprise management quickly of product activity.

9. Many firms have equipped their salesforces with laptops, enabling them to provide clients on-the-spot analysis of buying alternatives and to file sales reports easily and rapidly with headquarters.

10. Manufacturing firms often have sophisticated computer systems that monitor key areas of operation.

11. Fabric designs can be generated by computer much more quickly than by hand. If the customer doesn't like the colors or the pattern, new alternatives can be generated in seconds.

12. Today the design of many buildings—such as this soccer stadium—is done on computer. It is easy to make changes quickly, and the computer keeps track of the completeness of the design specifications and automatically tests the structure for safety.

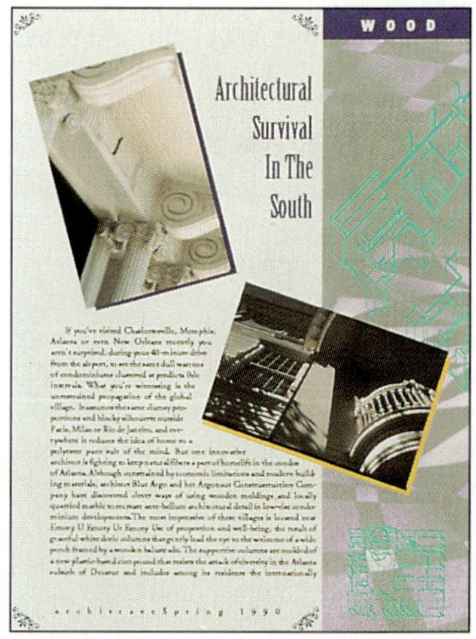
WOOD

Architectural Survival In The South

13. Desktop publishing systems—which produce professional-looking output and cost less than $10,000—have created new publishing opportunities and have enabled virtually anyone to enter the publishing business.

14. It's getting more commonplace to see desktop computers on the counters or in the back rooms of small businesses. These computers accurately keep track of transactions and do bookkeeping and tax work as well.

16

15

15,16. Artists of all types are becoming increasingly skilled at using computers. The art shown here was done with illustration software on ordinary microcomputer systems.

17

18

17,18. Computers are commonly used today in producing animated television logos and commercials.

19. One of the earliest uses of computers, and still one of the most popular, is in research, an area in which calculations can be complex and time-consuming and can require high degrees of accuracy.

20. Few libraries can function effectively today without a computer system to speedily and accurately complete the check-out and check-in process and to keep track of collections and overdue materials.

21. In education, computers are widely used to teach a variety of subjects—including, of course, computers.

22. Multimedia computer applications enable text data to be combined onscreen both with moving and still pictures and with sound. Note at the lower right of the screen the "buttons" that enable you to go forward or reverse through the video clip in the upper right.

23. In the 1940s, the military began using computers to produce ballistics tables automatically. Today, leading-edge defense technology is illustrated by this Patriot missile and its computerized guidance system.

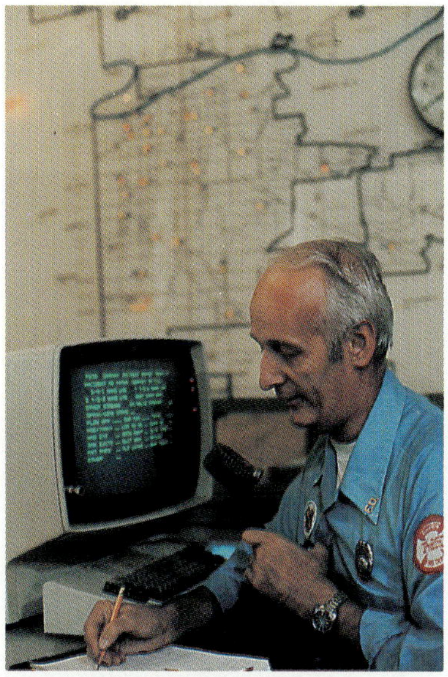

24. In law enforcement, vast computer networks keep track of crime data and make it easier to apprehend criminals.

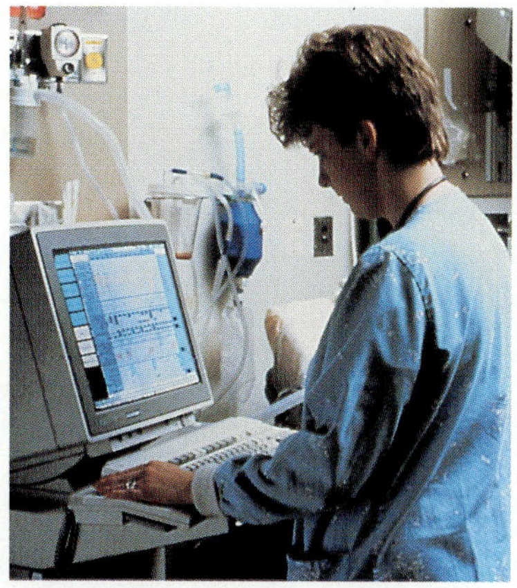

25. Computers are important in medicine as tools for diagnosing and monitoring patients and as control devices when administering treatment.

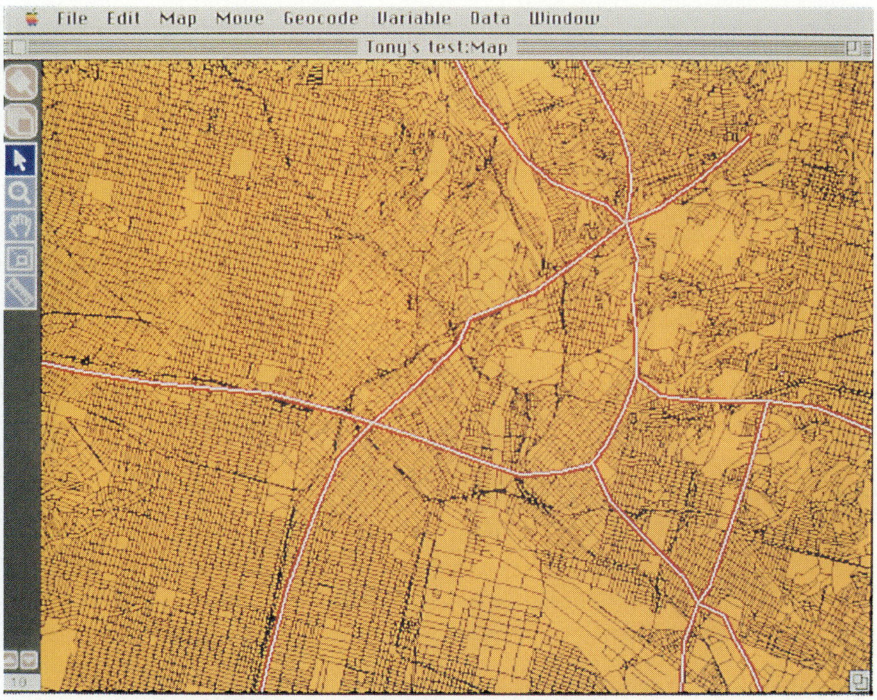

26. Increasingly, maps are being stored in computers, making it possible for police and firefighters to arrive quickly at destinations and for marketers to track selling activity throughout geographical areas.

How are computers used to provide onscreen realistic-looking road conditions in driver's training instruction? It is through realtime processing, covered in this chapter, which enables the computer to make updates immediately upon each operator input.

2 Computer Systems and Information Processing

Outline

Learning Objectives

After completing this chapter, you will be able to:

1. Identify several major classes of input, output, processing, and storage hardware.
2. Explain how data are organized in a computing environment.
3. Distinguish between applications and systems software.
4. Describe some of the ways in which computer systems process data into useful information.
5. Define several more key terms that are useful to know when reading about or discussing computers.

Overview

As you learned in Chapter 1, input, processing, and output, together with storage, are the major components of any computer system. In this chapter, you will see how they work together in more detail.

First, we'll take a look at computer system hardware. We'll cover some basic hardware concepts and discuss some of the most important kinds of input, output, and storage equipment. Then we'll see how this equipment can be linked, first in a small computer system and then in a large one. This section will prepare you for the detailed discussion of hardware in Module B.

From there, we'll take up the subject of data, specifically how data must be organized for processing on a computer system. Study the terms introduced in this section carefully, because you will encounter them frequently throughout the rest of the book.

Then we'll go on to a discussion of program software to introduce you to a subject we cover extensively in Module D.

Following this, we'll discuss information processing on computer systems. We'll examine representative examples of some of the most common types of processing to see how hardware, data, software, procedures, and users interact to do useful work.

Finally, to integrate many of the chapter materials, we'll look at how the hardware, software, data, and information-processing procedures you read about in earlier sections combine with people to form a sophisticated computer system. Although most types of organizations are relatively bullish about integrating computers into their operations to reap the benefits they bring, not all users are quite as enthusiastic, as Feature 2-1 describes.

Computer Hardware

Computer.
A device that can perform arithmetic, make comparisons, and store and retrieve facts. Also called the *central processing unit* (*CPU*).

System unit.
The hardware unit that houses the computer and its storage, as well as a number of other devices.

Support equipment.
The machines that work with the computer.

All computer systems consist of some combination of computers and support equipment. The main **computer,** often called the *central processing unit,* or *CPU,* is the heart of the system; it controls the actual processing of data and programs. Closely tied to the CPU is its *primary memory,* which is almost always housed in the same hardware device, called the **system unit.** Many people, in fact, refer to the system unit as the computer, but strictly speaking it is merely the "box" that contains the computer. **Support equipment** consists of all the machines that make it possible to get data and programs into the CPU, retrieve processed information, and store data and programs for ready access to the CPU.

Support Equipment

There are a number of ways to classify support equipment for computer systems. One of the most basic is by function: Is the device predominantly for input, output, or storage? Another is by medium: Does it use

Feature 2-1

What Do Lawyers and Baseball Managers Have in Common?

A Relatively Low Commitment to Computers

Although many professions have been quick to embrace computers and the advantages they bring, two that are relatively slow in getting off the mark are lawyers and baseball managers.

Why? Consider lawyers. Some say that most lawyers think in terms of delegating authority and feel that keyboarding and compiling data are what secretaries and administrative assistants should do. Besides, legal data aren't as number intensive as business data. Baseball managers, in comparison, are often from the "old school" of thinking—that is, the school of hard knocks, where training in computers and sophisticated statistical analysis is not in the core curriculum. Some also argue that technology makes baseball too mechanical and that intuition about people is more important than anything a computer can spit out.

Nonetheless, both lawyers and baseball managers have been dragged squarely into the computer arena by the need to keep competitive. Even though they may not be pushing the keyboard keys themselves, people in both professions are finding it increasingly necessary to know something about how they can use computing technology for competitive advantage.

Lawyers. Today, the text of court cases, statutes, and many other important legal data are in both electronic and conventional paper form. However, computers can do something that books can't do; they allow the user to search at electronically fast speeds through court records to compile information. The principal software tools for law offices are Lexis and Westlaw, both of which provide access to thousands of legal records. Many lawyers know how to use these packages, and most of those who don't are at least aware of what they contain so that they can direct their assistants.

Another computer application widely used in law firms is office accounting packages. These software products—which are available for doctors and dentists as well—are geared to record-keeping tasks, such as collecting fees from clients, processing payroll, keeping tax records, and generally managing office operations.

Because many law firms have branches in several cities, electronic mail systems are rapidly making solid inroads into law offices. These packages enable lawyers to send memos to colleagues in other offices, to transfer legal briefs, and to coordinate projects that people in several offices are working on simultaneously.

Of course, no law office today is complete without some type of document processing system, which enables contracts to be electronically stored and easily revised by word processing.

Baseball Managers. For a sport that relies so heavily on performance statistics, baseball has taken a surprisingly long time to realize the full potential of computers. Yet things are changing.

Many teams are now starting to use laptops to keep track of data during a game. In the old days, all that was recorded was what the player did at the plate. Now data are gathered on individual pitches. Teams want to know whether a pitch was, say, a slider or a curve and how fast it was. They also want to know whether the batter swung, made contact, or "took" (did nothing with) the pitch. It's also important to know, when a hit or contact out is made, where the ball went, how the fielders shifted, and who were on the bases and how far they advanced.

It may sound as if all of these data produce an information overload, but, to the contrary, they yield some interesting facts. For instance, if a certain batter "takes" the first pitch 90 percent of the time, the opposing pitcher probably should be advised to throw a strike on the first pitch to get ahead of the batter. The computer can also determine whether a specific batter is likely to swing at the first pitch in a scoring situation. And it's vital information if the computer says that a pitcher's performance is degraded after throwing 70 or more pitches. As any baseball fan knows, millions of dollars and a set of championship rings can ride on just one pitch or on stealing a single base.

Computers are being used by some teams to develop "total performance" statistics on players. These statistics weigh such factors as a player's batting average, slugging percentage, on-base percentage, number of stolen bases, speed, defensive skills, and so on. Each of these factors can be weighted to favor certain strengths over others. So, for instance, if a team needed a long-ball hitter with speed, it could weight those characteristics more heavily than others and then input the stats of five promising prospects into the computer to see which player appeared to be worth the most to the team. This information allows teams to look at player trades more objectively.

Computers, although not yet sophisticated enough to replace managers, can certainly help them uncover interesting information that is overlooked by the naked eye.

Figure 2-1
Input devices.
The keyboard (center) is the most widely used input device for entering instructions and data into a computer system. The mouse (bottom) is useful for rapidly moving the cursor around the display screen and for pointing to onscreen selections.

tapes or disks? A third is by relation to the CPU: Is it peripheral or auxiliary? Online or offline? Let's consider each of these in turn.

Input, Output, or Storage?

Input device.
A machine used to supply materials going to the computer.

Output device.
A machine used to accept materials coming from the computer.

Secondary storage device.
A machine, such as a tape or disk unit, that supplements primary memory.

Input devices are machines that convert data and programs into a form that the CPU can understand and process. **Output devices** are machines that convert processed data into a form that users can understand. **Secondary storage devices** are machines that make frequently used data and programs readily available to the CPU. These functions often overlap in a single machine. Some machines, for example, work as both input and output devices, and all secondary storage devices also function as both input and output devices. Now let's discuss some of the most common kinds of support equipment in terms of these three functions.

Computer *keyboards* (see Figure 2-1) are input devices that closely resemble typewriter keyboards. They are used to type in programs and data and to interactively issue instructions to the computer system. As Figure 2-1 shows, people are increasingly using a pointing device called a *mouse* to supplement computer keyboard operations.

Display devices (see Figure 2-2) appear in almost all computer systems. Many of these devices use a televisionlike picture unit called a cathode ray tube, or CRT. Display devices are used for output. The operator enters commands to the computer system through a keyboard or mouse; then both the input the operator enters and the output the CPU produces appear on the screen. A *display terminal* is a display device and a keyboard that are packaged together and used as a communications workstation to

Figure 2-2
Display device.
Display devices show both the input users type at the keyboard and the resulting output the computer produces.

a large computer. The local display devices commonly found with microcomputers are generally referred to as *monitors*.

Printers also produce output (see Figure 2-3). Printers come in a variety of different sizes and capabilities. The printers found in microcomputer systems might cost only a few hundred dollars, print very limited graphics, and output only a page or two a minute. Printers used with larger computers, on the other hand, may cost several hundred thousand dollars or more, print crisp text and sophisticated graphics (possibly even in color), and output several hundred pages per minute.

Secondary storage devices hold frequently used data and programs for ready access to the CPU. They also function as both input and output devices; that is, they contain stored data and programs that are sent to the CPU as input, and the CPU transmits new data and programs to them as output. The most common types of secondary storage devices are *magnetic disk units* and *magnetic tape units* (see Figure 2-4).

- *Disk units* store data and programs on magnetized platters called disks. *Hard-disk units,* which work with fast-spinning, rigid disks, are designed to make relatively large volumes of material immediately available to the CPU. *Diskette units,* which work with small, plastic disks coated with a magnetizable material, are slower than hard-disk units and have much less data-carrying capacity. However, they are far cheaper. Hard-disk units play an important role in both large and small computer systems, whereas diskette units generally are associated with smaller systems.

Figure 2-3 Printers.
(a) A microcomputer-oriented printer. (b) A printer targeted to minicomputers and mainframes.

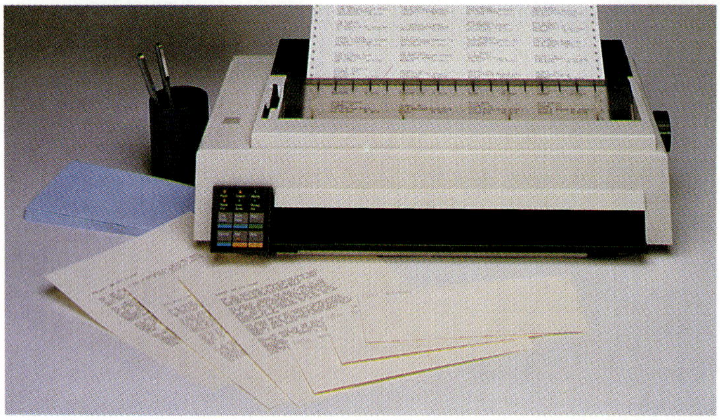

(a)

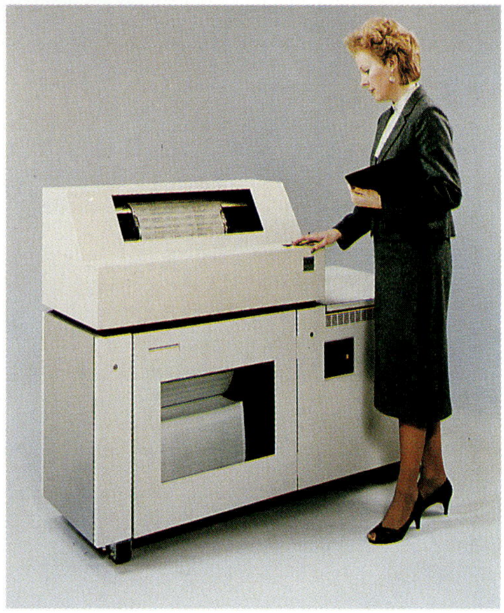

(b)

Figure 2-4
Secondary storage.
Disk units, in the foreground of this large computer system, store the programs and data that an organization must get to most quickly.

(a) (b)

Figure 2-5
Disks and tapes.
(a) Hard disks. (b) Magnetic tape cartridge (left background), detachable-reel tape (right background), and diskettes (foreground).

- *Tape units* are designed to use tapes—either those in detachable-reel form or those packaged in cartridges. Traditionally, the tape units on large computers have used detachable tape reels. Many of the newer tape units use tape cartridges—tapes that are enclosed in a plastic case. Cartridge tape units are also the most common type of tape unit found on smaller computer systems.

Input/Output Media

Input and output devices are, respectively, machines for getting data and programs into a computer and machines for getting the results out in a usable form. Often, however, data and programs are not permanently stored in a particular device. Instead they are recorded on **input/output (I/O) media** in a form the associated device can read and transmit to the CPU. In other words, just as the tape deck on your home stereo system works with tape cassettes, input/output devices work with specific input/output media. Four of the most common input/output media in use today are *hard magnetic disks, diskettes, detachable-reel magnetic tapes,* and *magnetic tape cartridges.* These are illustrated in Figure 2-5 and will be discussed in detail in Chapter 4.

Input/output (I/O) media. Objects used to store computer-processed materials.

Peripheral and Auxiliary; Online and Offline

Support equipment is either peripheral or auxiliary and online or offline.

Peripheral equipment consists of devices that are designed principally to be "plugged into" some computer as they do work. All of the devices we have discussed so far—keyboards, display devices, printers, and secondary storage devices—fall into the peripheral equipment category.

Peripheral equipment. The input devices, output devices, and secondary storage devices in a computer system.

Figure 2-6 Auxiliary devices.
(a) Electronic notepad for collecting supermarket data. (b) Document processor for sorting checks, forms, bills, and other types of documents.

(a) (b)

Auxiliary equipment.
Equipment designed to work in a standalone mode, independent of the main CPU.

Auxiliary equipment principally consists of devices that work away from a general-purpose computer system in what is called the *standalone mode.* A wide variety of auxiliary devices are available, each of which is designed for a specialized task. The electronic notepad shown in Figure 2-6a is used to collect field data onto diskette. Later (such as at the end of the day), these data can be sent over the phone lines to the main computer system for immediate processing and analysis. The document processor in Figure 2-6b can be used to sort documents such as checks, bills, and tax forms so that they can be routed elsewhere for further processing. As these documents are sorted, the machine-readable data on them are collected and later transferred to the main computer.

Online.
Refers to any device ready to communicate with the CPU.

Offline.
Refers to any device not ready to communicate with the CPU.

Any device that is ready to communicate with the computer is said to be **online.** User Solution 2-1, for example, describes how Pier 1 Imports keeps member stores online to a headquarters mainframe so as to have the freshest sales information possible and better control over store pricing. If a device isn't online, it's **offline.** So, for instance, if a microcomputer in the Pier 1 system were to become disconnected in some way from the mainframe, it would be offline to the mainframe.

Organizing Data for Computer Systems

Data, as we said before, are essentially facts. But you can't just randomly input a collection of facts into a computer system and expect to get results. Data to be processed in a computer system must be organized in a systematic way. A common procedure is to organize data into fields, records, files, and databases. Each of these words has a precise meaning in a computing environment, and you should use them with care.

User Solution 2-1

Online Processing for Fresher Information and Better Control

Because the products that Pier 1 Imports sells come from exotic locations, it may take months of bargaining and string-pulling to get certain stock to the stores. To have greater control over sales and inventories, Pier 1 is installing a system that will enable its more than 570 stores and distribution centers to hook up online, by means of PCs, to an IBM mainframe at headquarters. The mainframe keeps track of current store sales, forecasts product demand, alerts distribution centers when to send more stock to stores, and tells buyers when to replenish inventory. When a clerk punches in the code of an item being sold, the remote mainframe even supplies the price.

A **field** is a collection of characters (such as a single digit, letter of the alphabet, or special symbol like a decimal point) that represents a single type of data. A **record** is a collection of related fields. A **file** is a collection of related records. Files, records, and fields normally are stored on an input/output medium such as a disk or a tape. Your school, for example, probably has a *file,* perhaps stored on disk, of all students currently enrolled (see Figure 2-7). The file likely contains a *record* for each student. Each record has several *fields* containing various types of data about each student: ID number; name; street, city, and state of residence; major subject area; and the like.

Field.
A collection of related characters.

Record.
A collection of related fields.

File.
A collection of related records.

The concept of a **database** is a bit more complicated to explain at this point, but you can safely consider it a collection of data that contains the contents of several files. For example, a student database may contain the contents of a student address file (such as the one in Figure 2-7), a student grade file (containing courses completed and grades earned by each student), and a student medical file (containing data that might help in medical emergencies), as illustrated in Figure 2-8. In other words, most of the information about students would be found in the student database. We'll discuss the concept of a database more formally in Chapter 10.

Database.
An integrated collection of data that contains the contents of several files.

In most large computer systems, many data files are kept on disk storage for rapid access. These files often contain operational data. For example, most businesses (such as your local department store) have files storing data such as the following:

- Key customer data, such as names, addresses, and credit standings (called a *customer master file*). A **master file** is a file containing relatively permanent data.

Master file.
A file containing relatively permanent data, such as customer names and addresses.

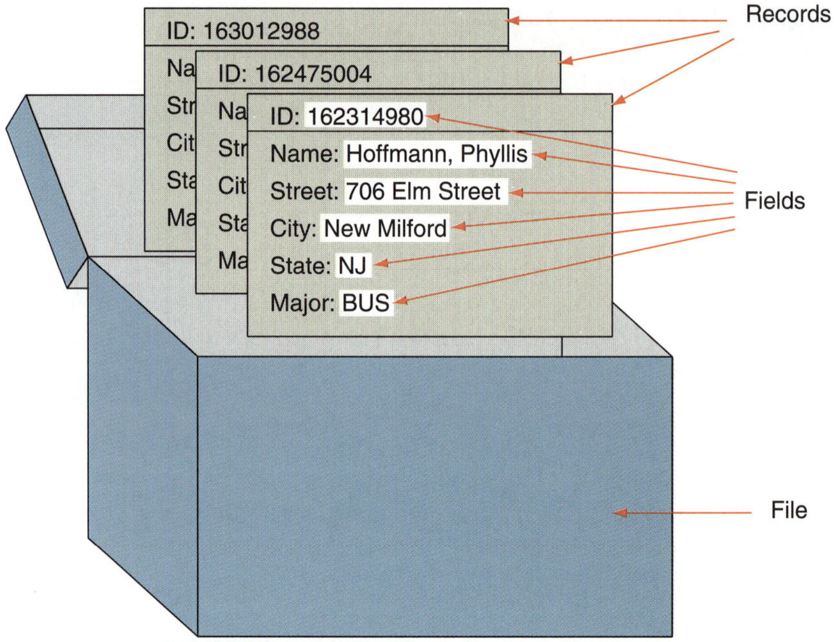

Figure 2-7
Differences between a file, record, and field.
The file shown contains name and address data on students enrolled at a college. If there were 2,000 active students at the college, this file would contain 2,000 records. Each record in the file has six data fields—student's number, name, street, city, state, and major.

Transaction file.
A file of occurrences, such as customer payments and purchases, that have taken place over a period of time.

- Daily customer transactions, such as purchases and payments (called a *customer transaction file*). A **transaction file** is a file containing data that are used to update or modify data in a master file.

As mentioned previously, data from related files often are stored in databases. For example, data that normally would appear in the customer transaction file and customer master file might be collectively stored in a customer database.

Whatever the medium on which they are stored, entities such as files and databases always have names. The computer system uses these

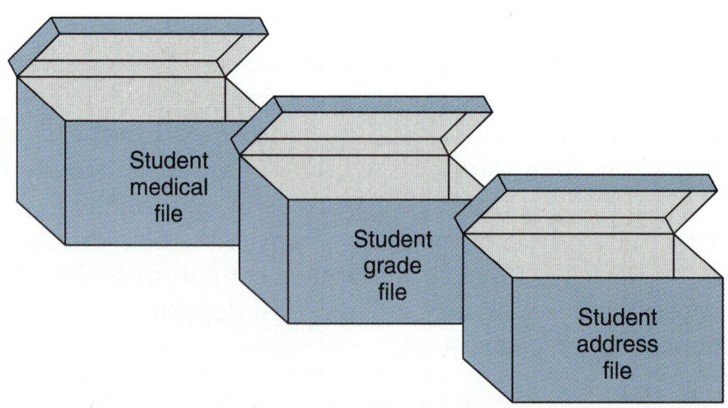

Figure 2-8
A student database.
Databases, such as the one shown here, enable data that might otherwise exist in several separate files to be easily interrelated. Database technology has made it possible for users to ask the computer system complex questions—questions that require data to be drawn from multiple sources within the database.

names to identify the files or databases when it needs to access them. For example, "CUSTOMER-MASTER-DATA" may be the name of a customer master file.

A Brief Introduction to Software

As mentioned earlier, the word *software* refers to computer programs. Programs direct the computer system to do specific tasks, just as your thoughts direct your body to speak or move in certain ways. There are two classes of software: applications software and systems software.

Applications Software. **Applications software** is written by people to perform tasks such as computing the interest on or balance in bank accounts, preparing bills, creating documents, preparing and analyzing budgets, managing files and databases, playing games, scheduling airline flights, or diagnosing hospital patients' illnesses. In other words, applications software makes possible the types of "computer work" end users have in mind when they acquire a computer system. You can buy applications software prewritten or write it yourself. If you write it yourself, you must be familiar with a specific programming language.

Applications software. Programs that do the type of work that people acquire a computer system to do.

Productivity software, which we will discuss in detail in Module D, is the class of easy-to-learn, easy-to-use applications software designed to make workers more productive at their jobs. Some important types of productivity software are described in Figure 2-9. Many organizations cre-

Package Type	Description
Word processor	Turns the computer system into a powerful typewriting tool
Spreadsheet	Turns the computer system into a sophisticated electronic calculator and analysis tool
Presentation graphics	Turns the computer into a tool that can be used to prepare overheads, slides, and presentation materials for meetings
File manager and database management system	Turn the computer system into an electronic research assistant, capable of searching through mounds of data to prepare reports or answer queries for information
Communications software	Enables users to call up remote computers for such things as financial information, marketing information, and news
Desktop publishing	Turns the computer system into a tool that can produce documents that look as if they were produced at a professional print shop
Desk accessory	Provides the electronic equivalent of tools commonly found on an office desktop—calendars, address files, and calculators, for instance
CASE (computer-assisted software engineering)	Automates and integrates many of the tasks performed by computer professionals, thus enabling them to develop systems and software far more effectively
Expert system	Enables workers to tap into expert knowledge to support their work

Figure 2-9
Types of productivity software.
Productivity software packages are designed to make both ordinary users and computer professionals more productive at their jobs.

User Solution 2-2

Productivity Software for On-Site Store Planning

Jack in the Box has decided to go all out in helping its store managers solve problems, by placing personal computers in most of its outlets and planning to have them in all outlets in the future. With the pool of available labor in the 16-to-24-year-old age bracket shrinking, the PCs make optimal use of current help. Based on estimated sales, the PC uses customized software that tells the store owner how many laborers to have for each shift, how much of each type of food to prepare, and how to eliminate waste. By knowing the amount of food that is on hand, being delivered, and thrown out, the computer can tell if the store owner is ordering or preparing too much.

ate their own customized productivity software to deal with the specialized problems of their business, as User Solution 2-2 illustrates.

Systems software. Computer programs, such as the operating system, that do background tasks for users and programmers.

Systems Software. Systems software consists of "background" programs that enable applications software to run smoothly on a given set of hardware devices. One of the most important pieces of systems software is the *operating system,* a set of control programs that supervise the computer system's work. Viewed another way, the operating system enables applications software to interface with a specific set of hardware. Many recent Hollywood movies have portrayed the role of the operating system in an overly exaggerated manner—for example, as a demon master-control program that tries to take over the world. Fortunately, operating systems don't control people; rather, people control operating systems. We'll address operating systems and other types of systems software in more depth in Chapter 7.

Information Processing

Computer systems process data into information. When we talk about information processing, however, what kinds of processing do we have in mind?

The number of ways in which a full-fledged computer system can turn data into useful information is truly staggering and defies a simple, systematic enumeration at this early stage in the book. So rather than trying to look at all of them, let's focus on just a few commonly encountered information-processing tasks. This will help you appreciate the types of work you will likely need a computer system to do.

Some common information processing tasks are

- Selection
- Summarizing
- Issuance
- Sorting
- Information retrieval
- Updating

We will discuss each of these in turn and illustrate each with an example. All of our examples will use the personnel file in Figure 2-10. This file is housed in a secondary storage device, such as the hard-disk unit shown in the figure. We've used a small, five-record file here to simplify the examples (in reality, many personnel files contain thousands of such records). Also, each record shown contains only five fields. The sixth column, "Other Data," indicates that we could have added many more fields had we wanted to.

Each of the information-processing operations we'll describe should be located in a program somewhere in secondary storage. For example, if we want to sort our data file, we will need a program that will enable us to sort data records.

In each of our examples, output can be directed to one or more output devices in the system—the display device, the printer, or secondary storage. Again, to make things straightforward, we've shown output directed to only one device in each of the six example applications in Figure 2-10.

Selection. **Selection** involves going through a set of data and picking out only those items that meet certain criteria. Figure 2-10a illustrates a selection problem and shows how a computer system could handle it. The problem illustrated here is selecting the names of all employees in department A and printing out those names. Naturally, if we wished, we could have directed the names to the display screen instead (and saved paper, too). Selection criteria can be either simple or complex. For example, we could have asked the computer system to extract and display the names of all department A employees who were hired either last year or before 1990.

Selection.
The process of going through a set of data and picking out only those data elements that meet certain criteria.

Summarizing. **Summarizing** involves reducing a mass of data to a manageable form. This could require making a tally of items, determining sums for items in a particular class, and so forth. For example, in Figure 2-10b we have had the computer system output to the printer the number of people in each department and in the personnel file. Still another possible summarizing application would be to have the computer system output the number of people hired in each of several years, such as 1990, 1991, 1992, and so on. Software packages such as spreadsheets, file managers, and database management systems have strong facilities for summarizing data.

Summarizing.
The process of reducing a mass of data to a manageable form.

Issuance. Computer systems are also widely used to input records, perform a series of calculations on each record, and prepare a document for each record based on these computations. This process is sometimes

Figure 2-10 Information processing.
Depicted are six fundamental ways in which computers are capable of processing data into useful information.

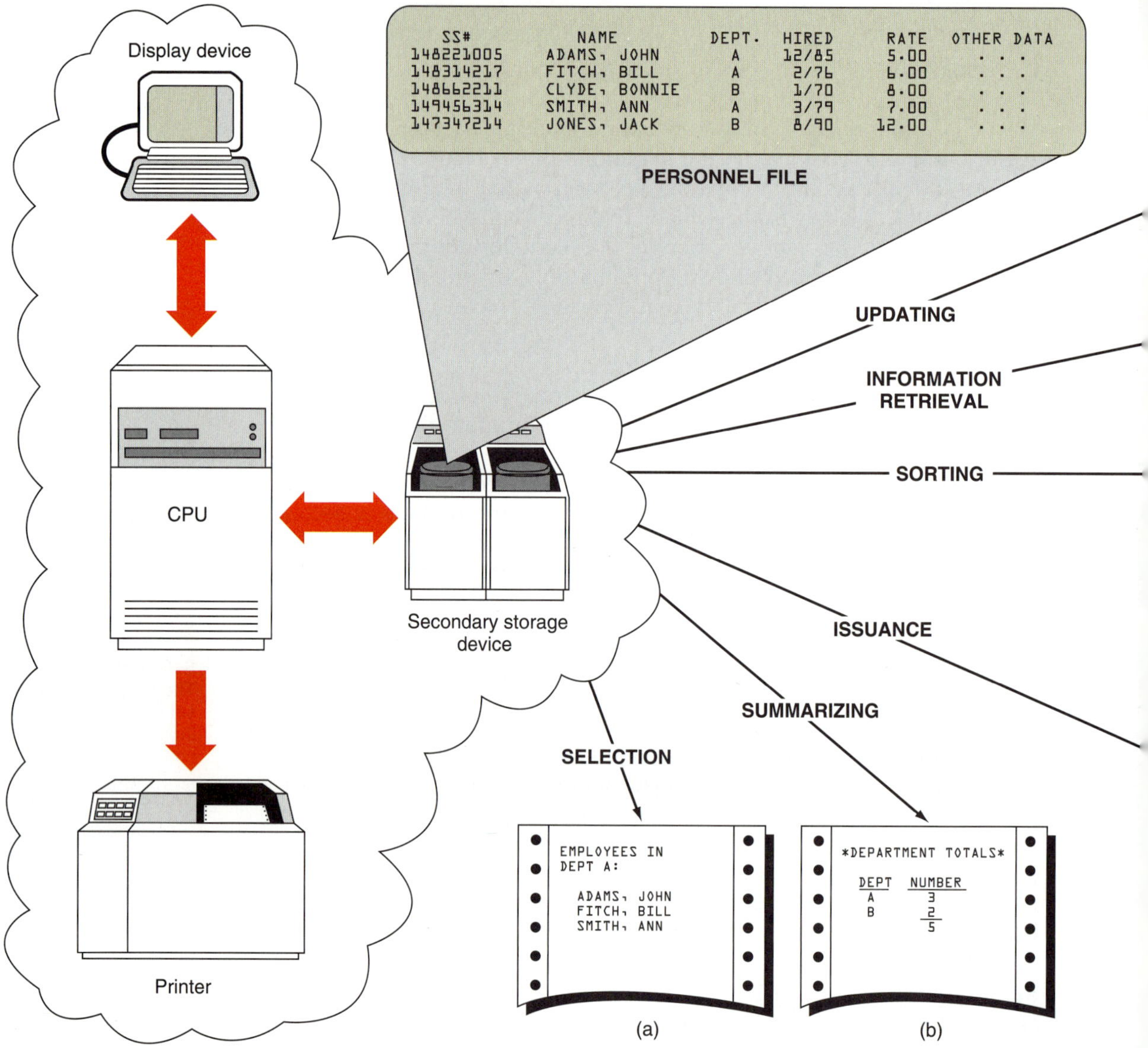

Issuance.
The use of computers to produce transaction-oriented documents such as paychecks, bills, and customer reminder notices.

called **issuance,** since the end result is the issuing of documents. In billing operations, for example, the computer system reads a record of payments and purchases for each customer, computes the amount due, and prepares a bill. Payroll processing, illustrated in Figure 2-10c, is another example.

Checks such as those shown in Figure 2-10c cannot be generated from the personnel file alone. After all, how is the computer system to know how much to pay each employee? Therefore, to produce paychecks, the

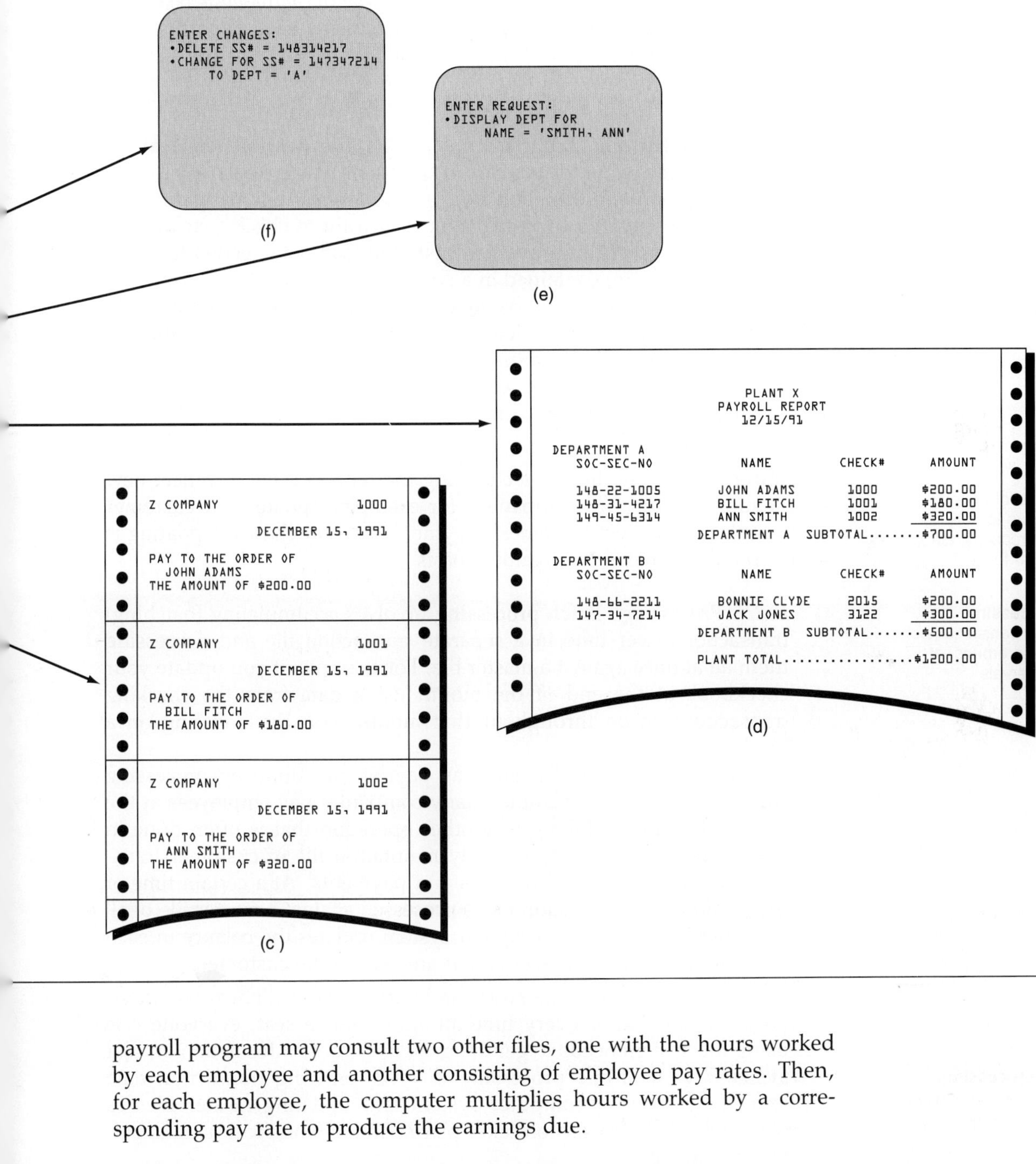

payroll program may consult two other files, one with the hours worked by each employee and another consisting of employee pay rates. Then, for each employee, the computer multiplies hours worked by a corresponding pay rate to produce the earnings due.

Sorting. **Sorting** involves arranging data in a specific order—a list of names in alphabetical order, for example, or a list of numbers in ascending or descending order. Figure 2-10d shows a computer report in which

Sorting.
The process of arranging data in a specified order.

data from the personnel file are sorted first by department and then by name within each department.

The report in Figure 2-10d is also an example of *control-break reporting.* As illustrated, the computer breaks after processing each department to print a subtotal and breaks again at the end of the report to print a final total.

Information retrieval.
Online inquiry to computer files or databases.

Information Retrieval. Programs created for **information retrieval,** or *query,* enable users to enter a series of questions at the keyboard for the purpose of extracting information from a database or from many different data files. For example, a bank manager may want to check a customer's credit rating. The checking, savings, trust, and loan data needed to determine credit ratings are contained in a customer database. An information-retrieval program that responds to the manager's request for a credit check could extract all the needed information from the database and calculate the customer's credit rating automatically. Figure 2-10e illustrates a query to the personnel file, in which the operator is trying to determine the department in which Ann Smith works.

Updating.
The process of bringing something up to date by making corrections, adding new data, and so forth.

Updating. **Updating** involves changing the data in a file to reflect new information. Credit card companies, for example, update their customer files regularly to reflect customers' payments and purchases. Updating is done on either a batch or a realtime basis.

Batch processing.
Processing transactions or other data in groups, at periodic intervals.

- *Batch Processing.* **Batch processing** involves accumulating (batching) transactions over time in a separate transaction file and processing them all at once against a master file. For example, if you update your checkbook at the end of the month using data from the checking transactions made throughout that month, you are updating on a batch basis.

  Many issuance tasks, such as payroll, are done by processing work in a batch. For example, many companies pay employees at the end of the month. Billing is another operation that is often done in the batch mode. A company may maintain a file of customer transactions, which include purchases and payments. At a certain time of the month, this transaction file is processed against a master file of all customer balances. The computer system updates the balance in each account and issues statements that are sent to the customers.

Realtime processing.
Updating data immediately in a master file as transactions take place.

- *Realtime Processing.* The airline industry updates flight reservations on a realtime basis. Every time an agent sells a seat, everyone else using the system needs to get the most up-to-date information on seat availability. **Realtime processing** involves entering transaction data immediately into a computer system and updating master files as each individual transaction takes place. All realtime processing is performed online.

  Another example of realtime processing occurs in banking. Tellers with terminals can update an account as soon as a customer makes a withdrawal. If the customer makes a withdrawal at an automatic teller machine, the machine updates the account immediately. The ability to check and update accounts on the spot protects the bank from overwithdrawals. Deposits, however, usually are not recorded in a customer's balance until the end of the day, when all deposits made by all customers that day are processed together. In other words, deposits typically are processed in the batch mode.

Figure 2-10f illustrates updating of the personnel file to show that Bill Fitch has left the company and Jack Jones has moved to department A. If changes such as these are immediately reflected in the computer system, realtime processing is in effect; if they are done at the end of a day or week, batch processing is taking place. The Tomorrow box features virtual reality, perhaps the ultimate in realtime processing.

Getting It All Together: Combining Elements into a Complete Computer System

Now that you understand a few concepts about hardware, software, and data, it's time to learn how these elements interact with people and procedures to form a complete computer-based information processing system. Along the way, you'll be introduced to a few new concepts, ones that you will read about in detail later in the text.

The example that follows describes the sales information system in a hypothetical firm called The Casual Look (see Figure 2-11). The Casual Look is a national chain of 316 retail stores throughout the United States and Canada that sells casual and recreational clothing.

Input. Each store owner has a microcomputer system, containing a hard disk, that is used to record sales. When a customer makes a purchase, data such as the current date and the identification number, quantity, and price of each item bought are electronically recorded. Many of these data are entered by keyboard and, when the item being sold has a bar-coded tag, by a handheld scanner (see Figure 2-12). The scanner reads the bar code into the computer system, where the product and its current price are identified. According to a strictly followed procedure at each store, every sale is recorded by computer.

All of the purchase data a store gathers are automatically stored on its local computer's hard disk. Every evening, Casual Look's mainframe system in Dallas calls each store computer and automatically has that day's sales data transferred (or "uploaded") over the phone lines from the store's hard disk to a hard disk on the mainframe system. (In Chapter 6, you'll learn in more detail exactly how this can be done.)

Processing. The raw data coming into Dallas from 316 sites are coordinated automatically by the mainframe system and processed in various ways.

Tomorrow

Virtual Reality

Hanging Out in Cyberspace

You're lazing away on a warm beach in Mexico when the sun begins to nudge toward the horizon. The hills to your left take on an orange glow, gulls are diving for fish, and each harmless cloud in the sky looks three-dimensional and painted with its own special color. "If only this could go on for another hour," you think. It does . . . and not because it's actually happening. You've used your computer system to create a virtual reality.

Virtual reality refers to the use of computers to create special, customized environments that seem, to the computer operator, as if they were real. Although we are still far from the virtual reality that science fiction writers tell us about, there are many who believe that computer technology will someday make it possible to create such illusions. To some extent, pioneering virtual-reality applications are arriving in the marketplace today.

In architecture, for instance, it is now possible to take "tours" of buildings whose foundations are yet to be poured. How? A computer model of the building is made in three dimensions. Once the building is mathematically specified, what a person can see if standing at a specific point in the building, looking in a specific direction, can be mathematically determined. Thus, a tour can be developed by predefining a trail of points and telling the computer how quickly to show a certain view from each point. But this scratches only the surface of what the computer can do today in such an application.

Let's say the client taking the tour wants to look at the top floor first and see the lounge before the offices. The tour can be taken in real time, which enables the client to move as he or she so chooses, deciding which facilities to view before others, how much time to spend at each facility, and what to see there. Lighting routines are available that show how natural light falls in the building on a sunny day and how artificial light changes a room. Does the client hate the look and size of the lounge? No problem. With a remodeling package, it can be reshaped, repainted, relighted, refurnished, and ready for reinspection—in just a few minutes.

What the computer still can't do at this point is create a room in which the client can physically walk around. That may just be a matter of time, though. All the computer will have to do is direct laser beams of light into the air in a certain way to block out what's really there and to create the illusion of something else. Child's play, say the believers.

Virtual reality and indoor golf. Now you can play the greatest holes at the world's greatest courses at your local athletic club.

Anyway, expect virtual reality applications to hit it big in the future—especially in the entertainment industry, where illusion is the principal product.

A start in this direction has been made in golf with a product that combines computer technology with video equipment (see photo). On the screen are projected holes at some of the most famous golf courses in the world. When the ball is struck, the computer calculates from the golfer's swing the speed, angle, and spin at which the ball is hit. Then it calculates the distance of the shot and, on the screen seconds later, you see your ball drop in the appropriate place on the fairway or green—or, if you can't golf worth a scratch, in the rough or sand trap.

Figure 2-11 The Casual Look's sales information system.
Each store has a microcomputer system that sends daily sales data to the mainframe at headquarters and receives daily performance reports from it. Sales executives at headquarters can access reports and other relevant sales information through their desktop workstations.

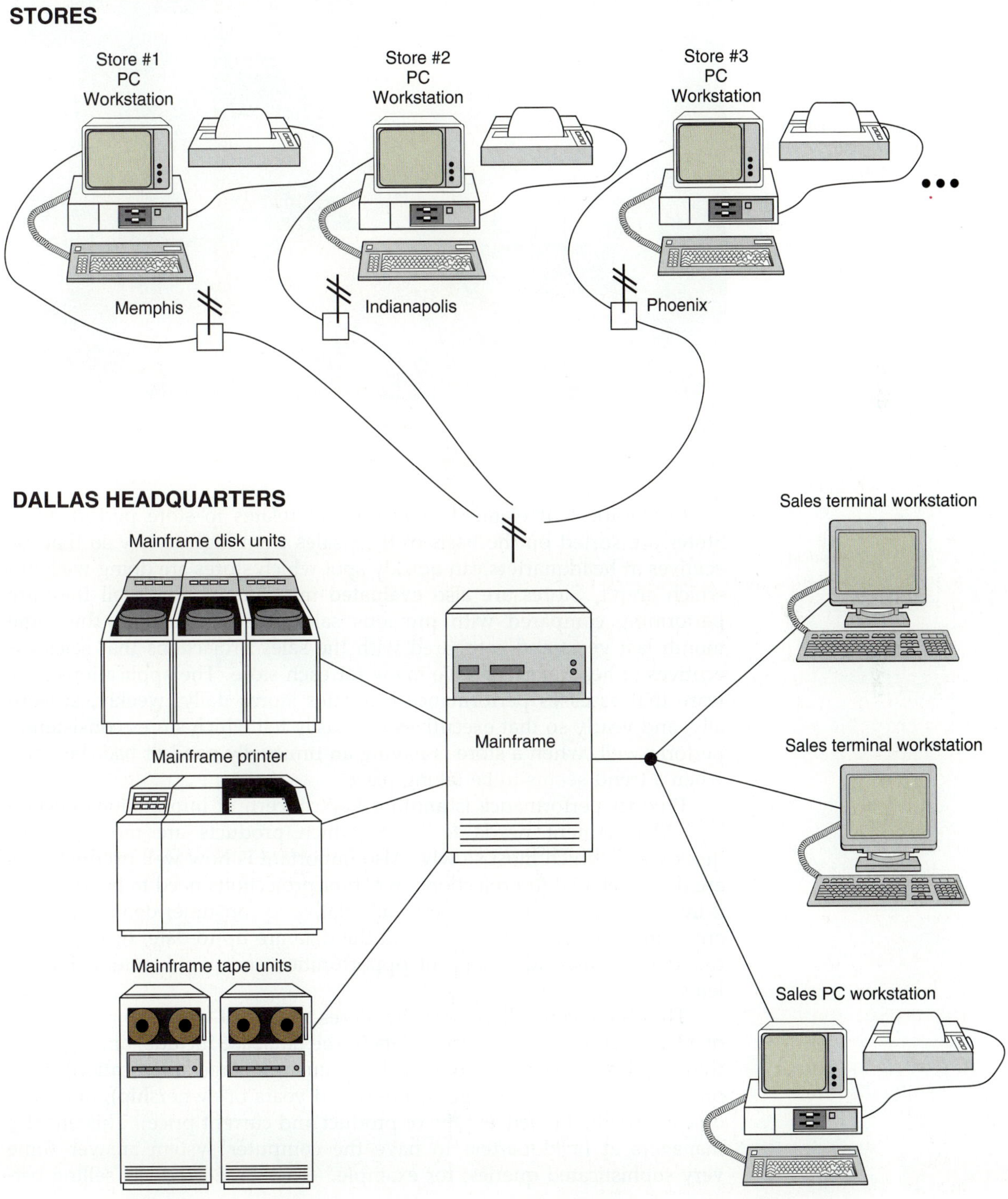

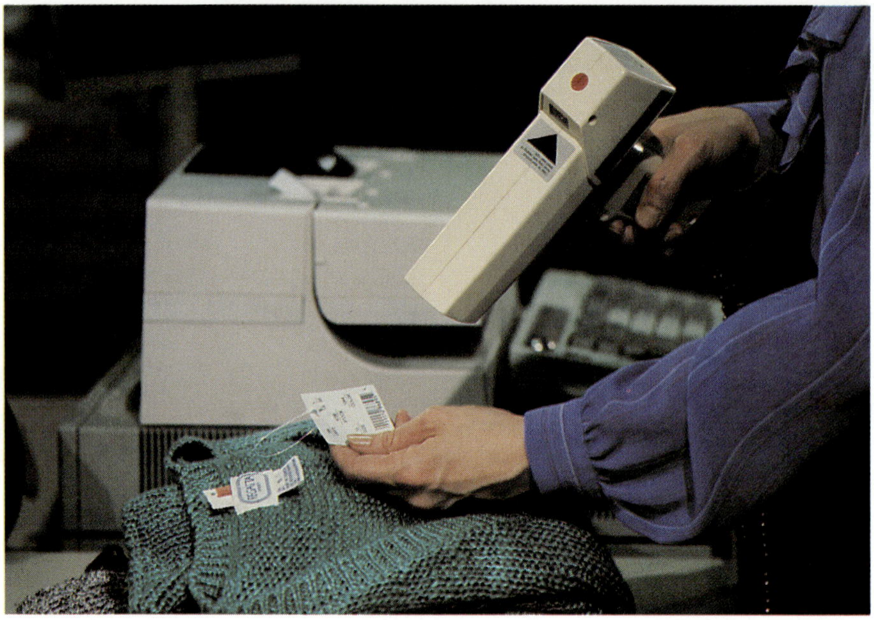

Figure 2-12
Recording transactions.
When the label attached to each purchased item is read with a hand scanner connected to the computer system, valuable sales data are collected quickly and virtually without error. These data can be used to prepare customer receipts and are sent daily to headquarters for rapid management analysis.

One important element in processing relates to store performance. Stores are sorted on the basis of their sales from high to low so that executives at headquarters can quickly spot which stores are doing well and which aren't. Stores are also evaluated in terms of how well they are performing compared with previous sales periods (such as the same month last year) and compared with the sales projections that sales executives at headquarters have made for each store. The applications software that assesses performance evaluates stores daily, weekly, seasonally, and yearly so that executives can easily tell which stores consistently perform well, when a store is having an unusually good or bad day, and when a trend seems to be taking place.

Product performance is another key concern of information processing. Management needs to know which products are moving most quickly and which most slowly. Also important is how well product lines are doing relative to projections, whether projections need to be updated, if inventory is too large or too small relative to consumer demand, and if any trends are evident. Because all the data are up-to-date, headquarters can quickly take advantage of opportunities and avoid potential problems.

The sales data collected at the stores represent only one component of a large sales database. Other data in the database include, among other things, facts on each building (such as square footage and location), facts on each owner (such as age, gender, and years of ownership), and facts on each product (such as type of product and current price). This enables managers at headquarters to have the computer system answer some very sophisticated queries; for example, "Are some products selling better than others in specific areas of the country?" "Are years of ownership related in any way to sales?" "How sensitive are sales of each product to price changes?" Five years ago, when the data used to answer these questions were in separate files that couldn't be interrelated and the Dallas mainframe couldn't communicate daily with each of the stores, it took two or three weeks of intensive research to get answers. Most of the time, managers didn't bother.

Output. Computer output occurs at several levels in this sales information system.

At headquarters, sales executives are most concerned with how the stores and product lines are performing on the whole and in relation to competitive products. Every evening, computer data reflecting the day's activity are summarized into graphs and reports that sales executives can summon on display screens as soon as they arrive for work in the morning. Executives can also electronically browse through any other facts in the sales database to answer questions that go beyond the information available in the graphs and reports (see Figure 2-13).

An electronic mail system enables sales executives and store owners to communicate. If, for instance, an executive has important news to announce to store owners, it is typed as a memo and routed, in seconds, to the hard disks of individual store computers. At each store, a small icon shows up on the display screen, indicating a message has been sent. Store owners can also send memos to headquarters on the electronic mail system.

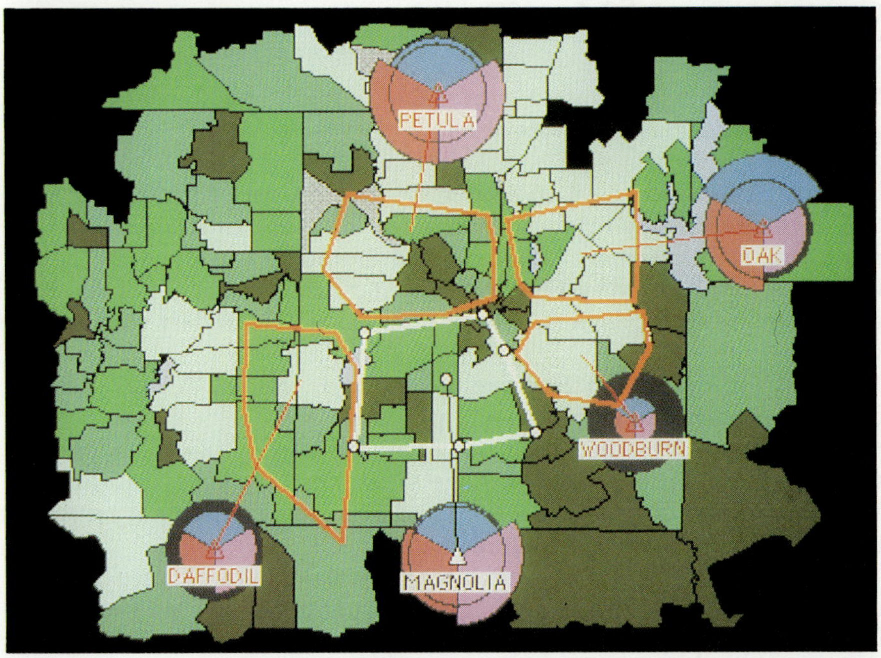

Figure 2-13 Sales information system. Computer systems are increasingly offering executives and managers better types of information to help run their organizations. For instance, the computer can display the geographic penetration of store sites and, using population and other important data, calculate the expected dollar potential of any market area.

At the store level, details of each purchase are output in the form of a receipt given the customer and in the form of a transaction entry that is written to the hard disk.

Sales reports are sent daily to individual store managers. These reports are automatically routed by headquarters through the electronic mail system and are available to each store owner when stores open for business. These reports show owners how well their store has performed relative to expectations, show goods that will be delivered during the next few weeks, make suggestions for purchasing, and provide interesting news items about other stores in the chain and about trends in the industry. The reports are intended to be both informational and motivational, and store owners are free to make their own decisions. Store owners do not have access to the full sales database at headquarters, however.

Storage. There are two types of electronic storage used in Casual Look's sales information system: disk and tape.

Both locally and at headquarters, sales data are stored and processed on hard disk. Today, magnetic disk is the most popular means of online secondary storage because it is relatively fast, capacious, and inexpensive. Hard disk, however, is not so capacious that it doesn't get filled over time. Rather than add more hard-disk capacity online, many organizations, including Casual Look, store hard-disk data they no longer need on tape and then store these tapes offline. For instance, because few managers are interested in looking at raw, detailed sales data from two or three years past, such data are put on tape.

Summary and Key Terms

Chapter 2 explains how input, processing, output, and storage work together to produce useful information.

Computer Hardware. All computer systems consist of some combination of **computers,** their primary memories, and **support equipment.** The computer and its primary memory often are housed in the same hardware device, called the **system unit.** The most common types of support equipment are **input devices, output devices,** and **secondary storage devices.**

Input and output devices include keyboards, display devices such as display terminals and monitors, and printers.

Secondary storage devices include hard-disk units, diskette units, detachable-reel tape units, and cartridge tape units. These devices use, respectively, hard disks, diskettes, detachable tape reels, and cartridge tapes as their **input/output (I/O) media.**

Support equipment that is designed principally to be plugged into the computer in order to function is considered **peripheral equipment;** if not, it's **auxiliary equipment.** Equipment may be either **online** or **offline** to the CPU at any point in time.

Organizing Data for Computer Systems. Data are commonly organized into fields, records, files, and databases. A **field** is a collection of individual characters, such as digits and letters of the alphabet. A **record** is a collection of related fields. A **file** is a collection of related records. As transaction data are generated, they are stored as records in a **transaction file;** a **master file** contains more permanent types of data. A **database** contains the contents of several files.

A Brief Introduction to Software. Software falls into one of two categories: applications software and systems software. **Applications software** is the "computer work" most end users have in mind when they buy a computer system. **Systems software** consists of support programs that keep the applications software running smoothly on a given set of hardware devices.

Information Processing. Six common information processing tasks are selection, summarizing, issuance, sorting, information retrieval, and updating. **Selection** involves extracting from files only those fields or records that meet certain criteria. **Summarizing** consists of reducing a mass of data to a manageable form. **Issuance** involves inputting records, performing a series of calculations on each record, and preparing a document for each record based on the computations. **Sorting** means arranging data in some specified sequence, such as alphabetical order or numeric order. Summarizing, sorting, and issuance often are combined to do *control-break reporting.* **Information retrieval,** or *query,* enables users to extract information from data files. **Updating,** which involves changing data in a file to reflect new information, can be done on a periodic or immediate basis. These types of updating are called **batch processing** and **realtime processing,** respectively.

Getting It All Together: Combining Elements into a Complete Computer System. The case study featuring The Casual Look shows how the hardware, software, data, and informaiton-processing procedures you read about in earlier sections combine with people to form a sophisticated computer system.

Review Exercises

Fill-in Questions

1. To be read by a computer system, data must be recorded in machine-readable form on some type of ______________ .
2. Devices that always work in a standalone mode are referred to as ______________ equipment.
3. Any device that is set up to communicate with the CPU is said to be ______________ .
4. ______________ software is written by users or programmers to perform tasks such as computing the interest or balance in bank accounts.

5. ____________ software consists of "background" programs that enable other programs to run smoothly on a computer system.
6. A(n) ____________ is a collection of characters that represents a single type of data.
7. ____________ processing refers to collecting transactions until the end of the day or week and processing them all at once.
8. The method of updating that the airline industry uses for passenger reservations is called ____________ processing.

Matching Questions

Match each term with the description that fits best.

a. information retrieval
b. issuance
c. batch processing
d. realtime processing
e. control-break reporting
f. sorting

____ 1. A company prepares a reminder notice for a customer whose payment deadline has passed.

____ 2. A company produces an employee phone book with names in alphabetical order.

____ 3. A bank records all deposits made to customer accounts at the end of each day.

____ 4. A report shows information on the sales of a single product, with three subtotals and a grand total.

____ 5. A librarian keys in the title of a book on a display terminal to see whether it has been checked out.

____ 6. Jane Williams withdraws $100 from her checking account, and that amount is immediately subtracted from her account balance.

Discussion Questions

1. Name some common types of computer support equipment, and state whether each is used for input, output, storage, or some combination of these functions.
2. Name some common types of secondary storage devices and the I/O media each uses.
3. Create a small file of data. Can you identify the records and fields?
4. What is the difference between applications software and systems software?
5. What is the difference between a master file and a transaction file?
6. Identify and define the types of information processing discussed in this chapter. Can you think of any other examples of information processing?

Critical Thinking Questions

1. Identify several uses for computers in a videocassette rental store.
2. You have joined a small computer club on your campus. The club has about 20 members. At a recent meeting, you agreed to conduct a sur-

vey to find out how members feel about tours that the club may make of local businesses next semester. You've designed a two-page questionnaire that consists of seven to eight questions. Answers to most of the questions will be in the form of ideas or opinions that will likely run about two or three sentences. The thought has crossed your mind that the computer might be of some help in tabulating the results of the questionnaire. Will it?

3. In the Casual Look example, it is mentioned that store owners do not have unlimited access to mainframe data. Do you think this is a mistake?
4. Virtual reality, covered in the Tomorrow box, is expected to help eliminate unnecessary animal experimentation in medical research. How do you see virtual reality techniques assisting in this area?

Today poll takers can use notebook computers to record public opinion door to door. Given the rate at which computers are shrinking in size, tomorrow's portable computer may be as small as a watch.

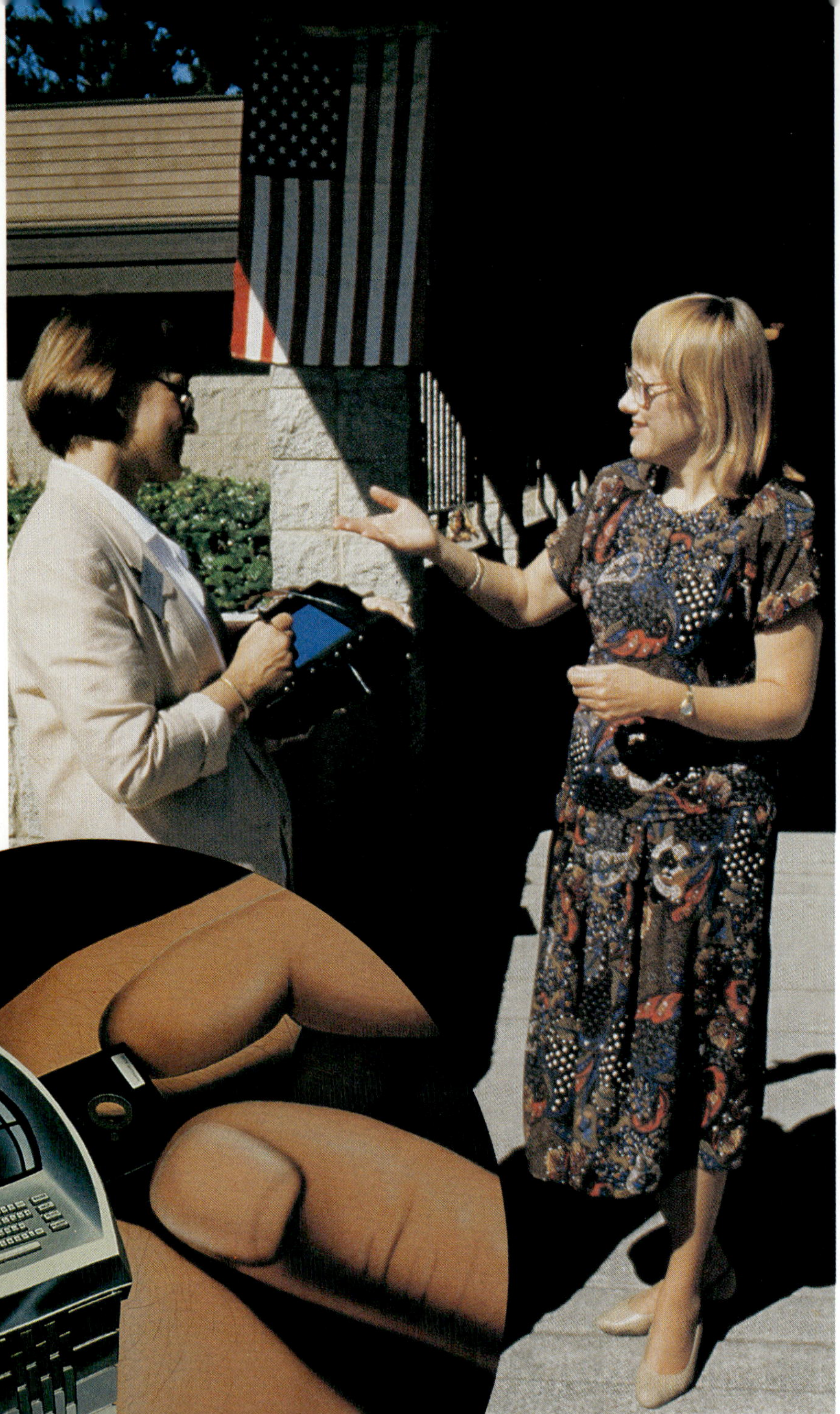

Module B Hardware

When most people think of computers or computer systems today, hardware most readily comes to mind. Hardware comprises the exciting pieces of equipment delivered in crates or boxes when you buy a computer system. As you'll learn in this module, a rich variety of computer hardware is available in today's marketplace. But as you'll see later in this book, hardware needs a guiding force—namely, software—to be of any use. Hardware without software is like a human without the ability to reason and manipulate thoughts.

The hardware discussed in this module is divided into three areas. Chapter 3 describes the role of the CPU—the computer itself. Chapter 4 discusses the class of hardware that provides an indispensable library of resources for the CPU—secondary storage devices. Chapter 5 delves into input and output equipment.

How fast are computers? The computer chip blown up in this photo transmits data at a rate of 3 billion "bits" (a term you will learn about in this chapter) per second. That's roughly equivalent to transmitting 40 encyclopedia volumes every second.

3 The Central Processing Unit and Primary Memory

Outline

Overview
How the CPU Works
- The CPU and Its Primary Memory
- Registers
- Machine Cycles

Data and Program Representation
- ASCII and EBCDIC
- Machine Language

The System Unit
- CPU Chip
- Specialized Processor Chips
- RAM
- ROM
- Add-in Boards
- Ports
- I/O Bus

Making Computers Speedier

Learning Objectives

After completing this chapter, you will be able to:

1. Describe how the CPU and its primary memory process instructions and data.
2. Identify several binary-based codes used in a computing environment.
3. Explain the function of the various pieces of hardware commonly found under the cover of the system unit.
4. Name several strategies for making computers speedier.

Overview

So far we've considered the system unit, which houses the CPU and its primary memory, to be a mysterious "black box." In this chapter, we'll demystify that notion by flipping the lid off the box and closely examining the functions of the parts inside. In doing so, we'll try to get a feel for how the CPU, primary memory, and other devices commonly found in the system unit work together.

To start, we'll examine how a CPU is organized and how it interacts with primary memory to carry out processing tasks. Next, we'll discuss how data and programs must be represented in the computer system. Here we'll talk about the codes developed for translating back and forth from symbols the CPU can understand to symbols people find meaningful. These topics lead us into a discussion of how the CPU and its primary memory are packaged with other computing and memory devices inside the system unit. Finally, we look at strategies used to speed up the work of the CPU.

Since the first, room-sized electronic computers were sold to businesses almost 50 years ago, computers have been getting cheaper, faster, smaller, and able to support more storage. If the cost of other things had decreased as fast as that of computers has, you'd be able to pay for both an around-the-world trip and a Rolls Royce with a $5 bill . . . and receive change! Someday, in the not-too-distant future, computers the size of a pinhead will be commercially available (see Tomorrow box).

How the CPU Works

Every CPU is basically a collection of electronic circuits. Electronic impulses enter the CPU from an input device. Within the CPU, these impulses are sent under program control through circuits to create a series of new impulses. Eventually a set of impulses leaves the CPU, headed for an output device. What happens in those circuits? To begin to understand this process, we need to know first how the CPU is organized—what its parts are—and then how electronic impulses move from one part to another to process data.

The CPU and Its Primary Memory

The CPU works closely with its primary memory to carry out processing inside the system unit. This relationship is described in the next sections and illustrated in Figure 3-1.

Arithmetic/logic unit (ALU). The part of the computer that contains the circuitry to perform arithmetic and logical operations.

The CPU. The CPU has two principal sections: an arithmetic/logic unit and a control unit.

The **arithmetic/logic unit (ALU)** is the section of the CPU that performs arithmetic and logical operations on data. In other words, it is the

Tomorrow

Here Come the Micromachines

Complete with Computers Smaller than a Pinhead

In 1966 a movie was made called *Fantastic Voyage*. It was about a medical team that was reduced to microscopic size and injected into a human body. The film, rich in special effects, was perceived in its day as highly imaginative, if not farfetched. Even Leonard Maltin liked it.

Today, roughly a quarter of a century later, a real-life sort of Fantastic Voyage II is taking place. *Micromachines*—smart machines that are smaller than a pinhead or snowflake—are being successfully developed in laboratories. One type of micromachine (see top part of figure) has rotating, chisel-like blades and is equipped with an onboard computer and memory—making it capable of both cleaning surfaces and processing information as a regular computer system does. When injected into a human body by the thousands, such devices may someday be capable of scrubbing away life-threatening plaque, the substance that builds up over years in the arteries and causes heart attacks and strokes.

The potential for micromachines in the field of medicine is enormous. Imagine tiny devices that could someday navigate through the bloodstream of AIDS or cancer patients and be capable of identifying and straining out infected cells (see bottom part of figure). Or microminiaturized devices that, once injected into the bloodstream, monitor the glucose levels of diabetics and automatically release insulin when levels become too high.

Medicine is not the only field expected to benefit from micromachines.

For instance, imagine a house paint containing millions of micromachine particles. When you want to change the look of a room you just expose the micromachines to a special sound or light ray that causes microtanks on the machines to release a new color. Because the micromachines can, at least theoretically, be accurately programmed to yield any color out of a range of alternatives, today's problem of getting new paint to match old may be tomorrow's nonproblem.

Want an ecology application or two? Micromachines may someday be capable of being released into polluted wells to collect toxic chemicals. And, perhaps, environmental disasters like the nuclear holocaust at Chernobyl could be held in check if airborne micromachines became available to do some cleaning up.

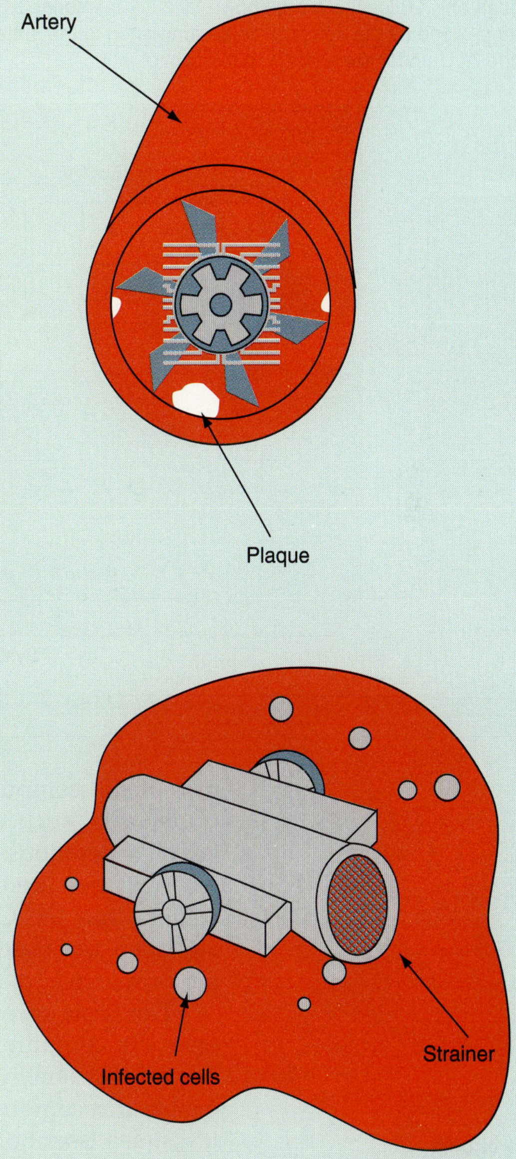

Micromachines. Atomic-level, computer-age cures for whatever ails you.

Figure 3-1 The CPU and its primary memory.
Primary memory temporarily stores the program on which the computer is currently working, as well as input data, intermediate computations, and output. Each location in the memory has an address, and often a single address can store a single character. Although only 20 locations are shown, primary memories typically contain from a few thousand addresses to several billion. All "figuring" done by the computer is accomplished in the arithmetic/logic unit (ALU). Data are transferred between primary memory and the ALU under supervision of the control unit.

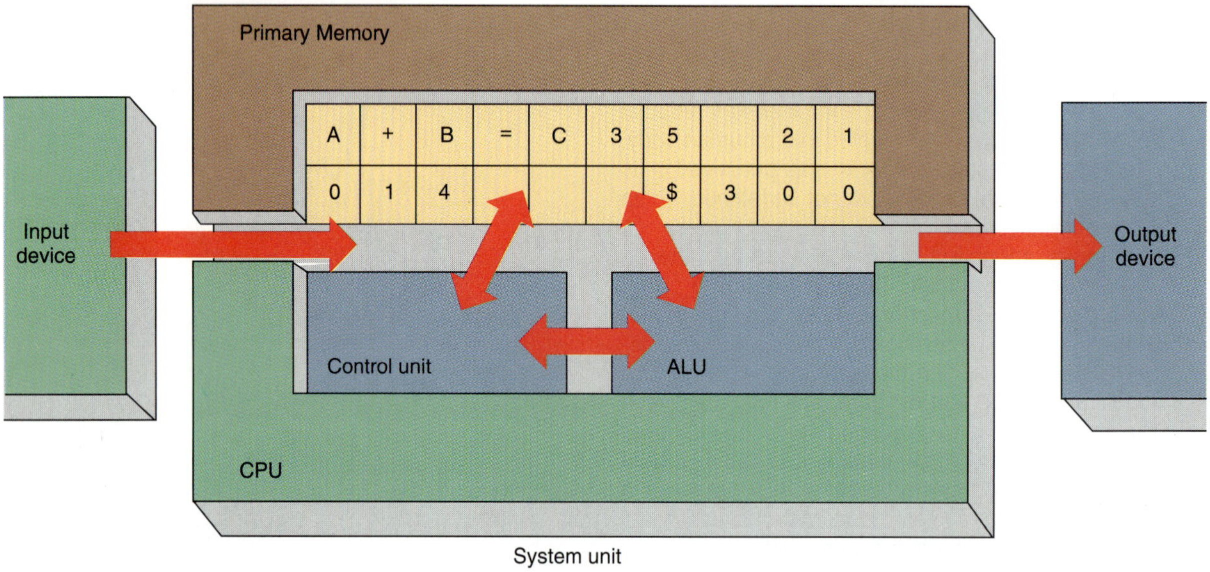

Control unit. The part of the CPU that coordinates the operation of the computer.

Primary memory. The section of the computer system that holds data and program instructions awaiting processing, intermediate results, and processed output. Also called **memory, main memory,** and **internal memory.**

part of the computer that does the computing. *Arithmetic* operations include tasks such as addition, subtraction, multiplication, and division. *Logical* operations involve comparing two items of data to determine whether they are equal and, if not, which is larger. As we'll see, all data coming into the CPU, including nonnumeric data such as letters of the alphabet, are coded in digital (numeric) form. As a result, the ALU can perform logical operations on letters and words as well as on numbers.

The basic arithmetic and logical operations just described are the only ones the computer can perform. That might not seem very impressive. But when combined in various ways at great speeds, these operations enable the computer to perform immensely complex and data-intensive tasks (see User Solution 3-1).

The **control unit** is the section of the CPU that directs the flow of electronic traffic between primary memory and the ALU and between the CPU and input and output devices. In other words, it is the mechanism that coordinates or manages the computer's operation.

Primary Memory. **Primary memory**—also called **main memory, internal memory,** or just **memory** for short—holds the following:

- The programs and data that have been passed to the computer for processing

User Solution 3-1

Number Crunching to Measure Service

How does a large, successful overnight packager use computers to provide better service? At Federal Express, which handles more than 1.5 million packages each day, computers crunch out daily important customer-service statistics and provide them to top management. Each day, executives are provided such information as how many of yesterday's packages were on time or late, how many packages were damaged, and how many billing corrections were made. Each key piece of information is weighted—for example, losing a package is counted ten times as much as a package arriving a little bit late—to arrive at a single quantifiable measure that shows if service is getting better or worse. FedEx's information system must be doing something right; in 1990 the company won the Malcolm Baldridge National Quality award and FedEx's president, Fred Smith, has credited technology for the honor.

- Intermediate processing results
- Output that is ready to be transmitted to secondary storage or to an output device

Once programs, data, intermediate results, and output are stored in primary memory, the CPU must be able to find them again. Thus, each location in primary memory has an *address*. In many computer systems, a table is automatically set up and maintained that provides the address where the first character of each stored program or data block can be found. Whenever a block of data, an instruction, a program, or the result of a calculation is stored in memory, it is assigned an address so that the CPU can locate it again when it is needed.

The size of primary memory varies among computer systems. The smallest computers can accommodate a memory of only a few thousand characters and the largest a few billion. Because primary memory is relatively expensive, it is usually limited in size and used only temporarily. Once the computer has finished processing one program and set of data, another program and data set are written over them in the storage space they occupy. Thus, the contents of each storage location are constantly changing. The address of each location, however, never changes. This process can be compared with what happens to the mailboxes in a post office: The number on each box remains the same, but the contents change as patrons remove their mail and new mail arrives.

Registers

Register.
A high-speed staging area within the computer that temporarily stores data during processing.

To enhance the computer's performance, the control unit and ALU contain special storage locations that act as high-speed staging areas. These areas are called **registers.** Since registers are actually a part of the CPU, their contents can be handled much more rapidly than can those of primary memory. Program instructions and data are normally loaded (that is, staged) into the registers from primary memory just before processing. These devices play a crucial role in making computer speeds extremely fast.

There are several types of registers, including the following:

Instruction register.
The register that holds the part of the instruction indicating what the computer is to do next.

Address register.
A register containing the memory location of data to be used.

Storage register.
A register that, prior to processing, temporarily stores data that have been retrieved from primary memory.

Accumulator.
A register that stores the result of an arithmetic or logical operation.

- *Instruction Register and Address Register.* Before each instruction in a program is processed, the control unit breaks it into two parts. The part that indicates what the ALU is to do next (for example, add, multiply, compare) is placed in the **instruction register.** The part that gives the address of the data to be used in the operation is placed in the **address register.**
- *Storage Register.* The **storage register** temporarily stores data that have been retrieved from primary memory prior to processing.
- *Accumulator.* The **accumulator** temporarily stores the results of ongoing arithmetic and logic operations.

The instruction and address registers are often located in the control unit, whereas the storage register and accumulator are frequently found in the ALU.

Machine Cycles

Microcode.
Instructions that are built into the CPU to control the operation of its circuitry.

System clock.
The timing mechanism within the computer system that governs the transmission of instructions and data through the circuitry.

Machine cycle.
The series of operations involved in the execution of a single machine-level instruction.

I-cycle.
The part of the machine cycle in which the control unit fetches an instruction from main memory and prepares it for subsequent processing.

E-cycle.
The part of the machine cycle in which data are located, an instruction is executed, and results are stored.

Now that we've described the CPU, primary memory, and registers, let's see how these elements work together to process an instruction.

Every instruction that you issue to the computer, whether it is in the form of a command that you type in or an icon that you point to with a mouse, is broken down by your computer system into several smaller machine-level instructions called **microcode.** Each piece of microcode corresponds directly to a set of the computer's circuits.

The computer system has a built-in **system clock** that synchronizes its operations, just as a metronome can synchronize work for an orchestra. During each clock tick, a single piece of microcode can be executed, a single piece of data can be moved from one part of the computer system to another, and so on. Microcode instructions are coded in *machine language,* which will be covered later in the chapter.

The processing of a single, machine-level instruction is called a **machine cycle.** A machine cycle has two parts: an *instruction* cycle (I-cycle) and an *execution* cycle (E-cycle). During the **I-cycle,** the control unit fetches a program instruction from primary memory and prepares for subsequent processing. During the **E-cycle,** the data are located and the instruction is executed. Let's see how this works in a little more detail, using simple addition as an example.

I-cycle

1. The control unit fetches from primary memory the next instruction to be executed.
2. The control unit decodes the instruction.
3. The control unit puts the part of the instruction that shows what to do into the instruction register.
4. The control unit puts the part of the instruction that shows where the associated data are located into the address register.

E-cycle

5. Using the information in the address register, the control unit retrieves data from primary memory and places them into the storage register.
6. Using the information in the instruction register, the control unit commands the ALU to perform the required operation.
7. The ALU performs the specified operation, adding together the values found in the storage register and in the accumulator.
8. The result of the operation is placed back into the accumulator, destroying the value that was there previously.

Figure 3-2 depicts how the machine cycle works.

All this may seem like an extremely tedious process, especially when a computer must go through thousands, millions, or even billions of machine cycles to process a single program fully. But computers are *very* fast. In the slowest of them, cycle times are measured in **milliseconds** (thousandths of a second). In others, they are measured in **microseconds** (millionths of a second). In the fastest computers, they are measured in **nanoseconds** (billionths of a second) or in **picoseconds** (trillionths of a second).

Millisecond.
One thousandth of a second.

Microsecond.
One millionth of a second.

Nanosecond.
One billionth of a second.

Picosecond.
One trillionth of a second.

Data and Program Representation

The electronic components of most computer systems work in two states. For example, a circuit is either open or closed; a magnetic spot is either present or absent; and so on. This two-state, or **binary,** nature of electronics is illustrated in Figure 3-3. It is convenient to think of these binary states as the *O-state* and the *1-state.* Computer people refer to such zeros and ones as **bits,** which is a contraction of the words *BInary digiTS.* Being primarily electronic, computers do all their processing and communicating by representing programs and data in bit form. Binary, then, is the symbol set that forms the computer's "native tongue."

Binary.
The number system with two possible states.

Bit.
A binary digit, such as 0 or 1.

People, of course, don't speak binary. You're not likely to go up to a friend and say,

"0100100001001001"

Figure 3-2
The machine cycle.
Each statement that you code in languages such as BASIC or Pascal actually requires several machine instructions, or cycles.

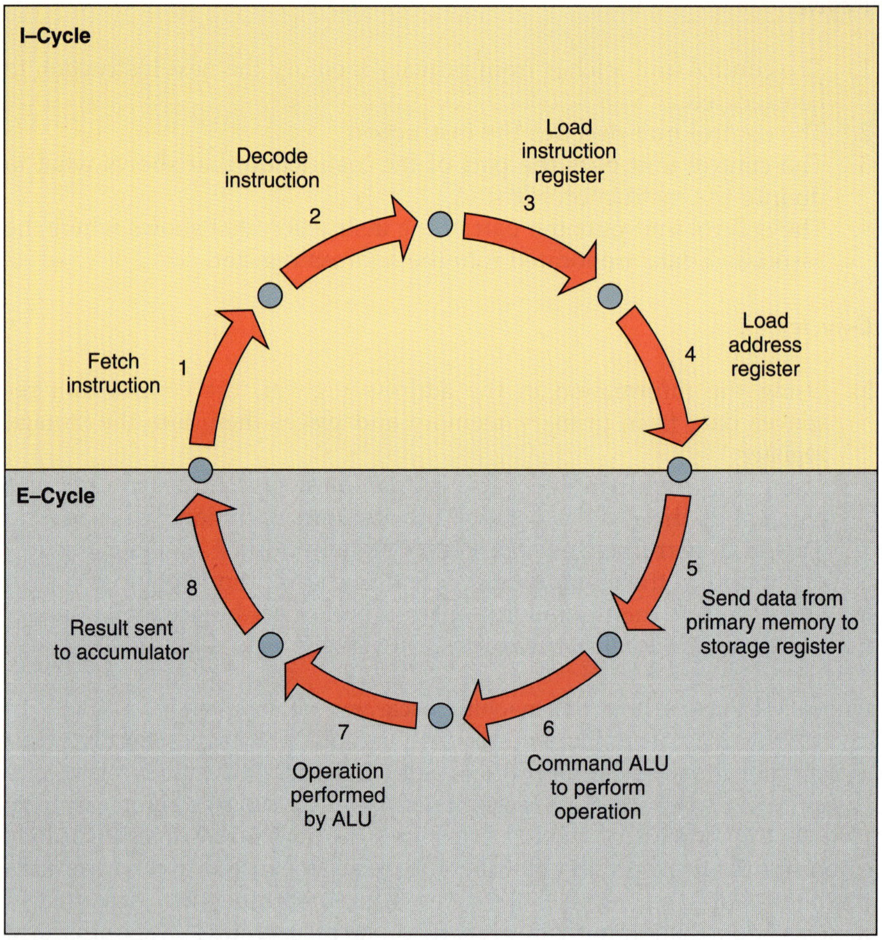

which in one binary-based coding system translates as "HI." People communicate with one another in *natural languages,* such as English, Chinese, and Spanish. In our part of the world, we speak mostly English. Also, we write with a 26-character alphabet, and we use a number system with 10 rather than just 2 digits. Computers, however, understand only 0 and 1. So in order for us to interact with a computer, our messages to it must be translated into binary form and its messages to us must be translated from binary into a natural language.

The programming languages most people use to interact with computer systems consist of a wide variety of natural-language symbols. When we type a message such as

```
DISPLAY NAMES
```

at a keyboard, the computer system must translate all the natural-language symbols in the message into 0s and 1s. After processing is finished,

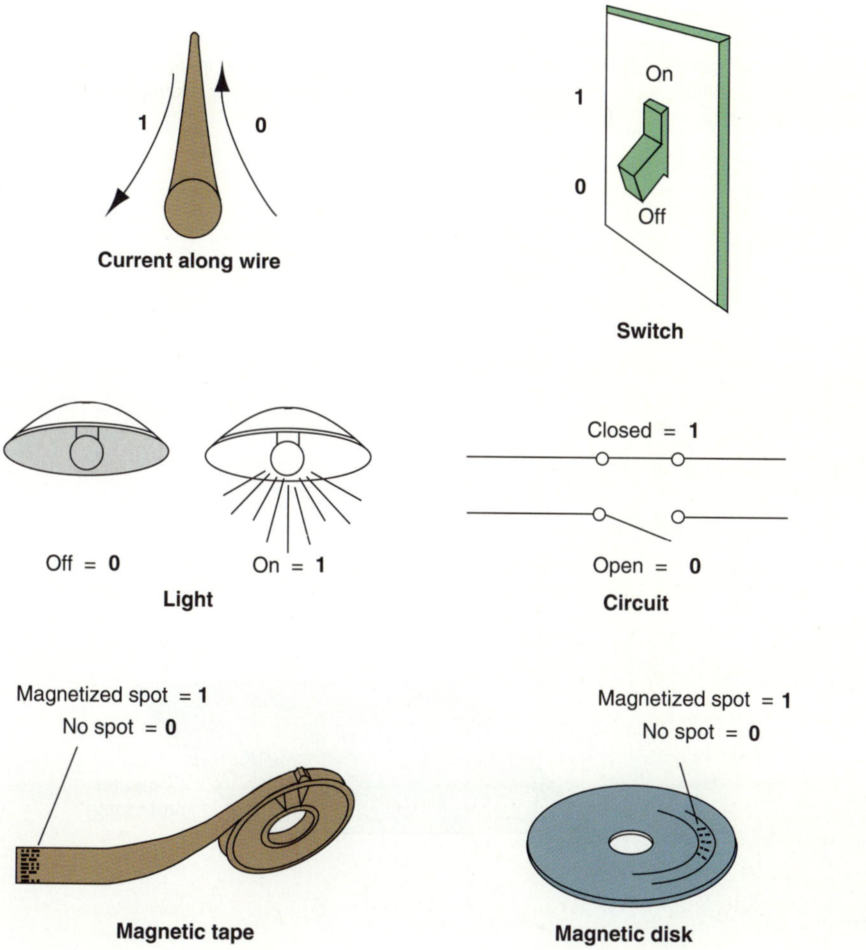

Figure 3-3
The binary nature of electronics.
Circuits are either open or closed, a current runs one way or the opposite way, a charge is either present or absent, and so forth. The two possible states of an electronic component are referred to as *bits* and are represented by computer systems as 0s and 1s.

the computer system must translate the 0s and 1s it has used to represent the program's results into natural language. This conversion process is illustrated in Figure 3-4. (If, incidentally, a mouse rather than a keyboard is being used for input, the conversion process remains unchanged. That is, any selections made by the user are automatically translated into 0s and 1s by the computer system.)

Computer systems use a variety of binary-based codes to represent programs and data. For example, when data and programs are being sent to or from the CPU (steps 2 and 4 in Figure 3-4), a fixed-length, binary-based code such as ASCII or EBCDIC is often used to represent each character transmitted. We will cover these two codes shortly.

Once data and programs are inside the CPU (step 3 of Figure 3-4), other types of binary-based codes typically handle them. For example, when a program is about to be executed, it is represented by a binary code known as machine language. Data, in contrast, may be represented by several different binary-based codes when being manipulated by the

Figure 3-4 Conversion to and from binary-based form.
(1) The user types in a message in natural-language symbols. (2) The computer system translates the message into binary-based form (this conversion often takes place in the input device). (3) The CPU does all the required processing in binary-based form. (4) The computer system translates the output back into natural-language symbols (this conversion usually takes place in the output device). (5) The user is able to read the output.

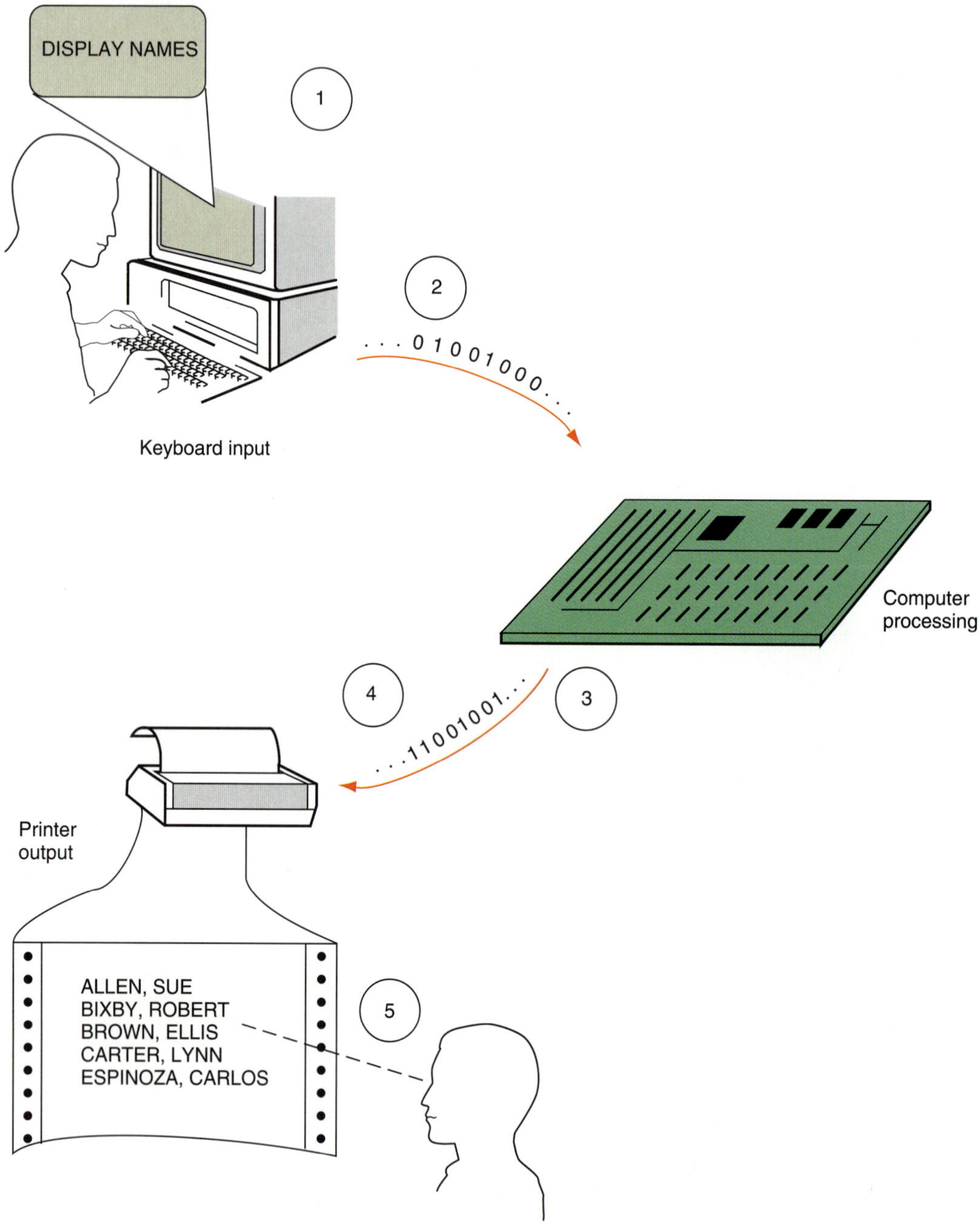

Figure 3-5 ASCII and EBCDIC.
These two common fixed-length codes represent characters as unique strings of bits.

Character	Standard ASCII-8 Bit Representation	EBCDIC Bit Representation	Character	Standard ASCII-8 Bit Representation	EBCDIC Bit Representation
0	00110000	11110000	I	01001001	11001001
1	00110001	11110001	J	01001010	11010001
2	00110010	11110010	K	01001011	11010010
3	00110011	11110011	L	01001100	11010011
4	00110100	11110100	M	01001101	11010100
5	00110101	11110101	N	01001110	11010101
6	00110110	11110110	O	01001111	11010110
7	00110111	11110111	P	01010000	11010111
8	00111000	11111000	Q	01010001	11011000
9	00111001	11111001	R	01010010	11011001
A	01000001	11000001	S	01010011	11100010
B	01000010	11000010	T	01010100	11100011
C	01000011	11000011	U	01010101	11100100
D	01000100	11000100	V	01010110	11100101
E	01000101	11000101	W	01010111	11100110
F	01000110	11000110	X	01011000	11100111
G	01000111	11000111	Y	01011001	11101000
H	01001000	11001000	Z	01011010	11101001

computer. One such code, which everyone learning how computers store numbers should know, is *true binary representation.* This code, as well as some fundamentals of number systems, is covered in Appendix A.

ASCII and EBCDIC

As mentioned earlier, when data or programs are being sent between the computer and its support equipment, a *fixed-length,* binary-based code is commonly used. With a fixed-length code, the machines that are in communication can easily tell where one character ends and another begins. Such codes can be used to represent digits, alphabet characters, and other symbols.

Among the most popular of these codes are **ASCII** (American Standard Code for Information Interchange) and **EBCDIC** (Extended Binary-Coded Decimal Interchange Code). ASCII, developed largely through the efforts of the American National Standards Institute, is used on virtually all microcomputers. It is also widely adopted as the standard for data communications systems. EBCDIC, developed by IBM, is used primarily on IBM mainframes.

ASCII.
A fixed-length, binary-based code widely used to represent data for processing and communications.

EBCDIC.
A fixed-length, binary-based code widely used to represent data on IBM mainframes.

Both ASCII and EBCDIC represent each printable character as a unique combination of a fixed number of bits (see Figure 3-5). EBCDIC uses 8 bits to represent a character. A group of 8 bits has 256 (2^8) different combinations; therefore, EBCDIC can represent up to 256 characters. This is more than enough to account for the 26 uppercase and 26 lowercase characters, the 10 decimal digits, and several special characters.

User Solution 3-2

Extra Bytes Make Research Easier

Only a decade or so ago, many PCs had only 64 kilobytes of RAM and, if they had hard disks at all, they handled only 180-kilobyte diskettes. Fortunately for brokerage firm Dean Witter Reynolds's Equity Research Group, times have changed. The group recently was able to consolidate all of its electronic equity research information on a single Compaq Systempro PC that has 20 megabytes of RAM and 1.7 gigabytes of disk capacity. This single, powerful microcomputer serves as an information hub for thousands of brokers and clients around the world, transmitting electronic copies of research reports to those who need them.

ASCII originally was designed as a 7-bit code that could represent 128 (2^7) characters. Several 8-bit versions of ASCII (called ASCII-8 codes) have also been developed because computers are designed to handle data in chunks of 8 bits. Many computer systems can accept data in either coding system—ASCII or EBCDIC—and perform the conversion to their native code. The 8 (7) bits used to represent a character in ASCII or EBCDIC are collectively referred to as a *byte*.

Byte.
A configuration of seven or eight bits used to represent a single character of data.

Kilobyte (K-byte or **KB).**
Approximately 1,000 (1,024, to be exact) bytes.

Megabyte (M-byte or **MB).**
Approximately 1 million bytes.

Gigabyte (G-byte or **GB).**
Approximately 1 billion bytes.

Terabyte (T-byte or **TB).**
Approximately 1 trillion bytes.

A **byte** represents a single character of data. For this reason, many computer manufacturers use the byte measure to define their machines' storage capacity. As you may have noticed, computer advertisements are filled with references to kilobytes, megabytes, gigabytes, and terabytes. One **kilobyte** (**K-byte** or **KB**) is equal to a little over 1,000 bytes (1,024, to be precise), one **megabyte** (**M-byte** or **MB**) equals about 1 million bytes, one **gigabyte** (**G-byte** or **GB**) equals about 1 billion bytes, and one **terabyte** (**T-byte** or **TB**) equals about 1 trillion bytes. So, for example, when you read about a computer system with a 640 K-byte system unit and a 40 M-byte hard-disk storage unit, it means that the system's primary memory (RAM) can store about 640,000 characters of data and the disk unit an additional 40 million. As User Solution 3-2 shows, microcomputer storage capacities are now comparable with those of mainframes of just a few years ago, thereby enabling departments within companies to create and manage their own powerful computer applications.

The conversion from natural-language words and numbers to their ASCII (or EBCDIC) equivalents and back again usually takes place on an input/output device. For example, when a user types in a message such as

```
RUN
```

at a keyboard, an encoder chip inside the keyboard usually translates it into ASCII and sends it as a series of bytes to the CPU. The output that the CPU sends back to the display or to some other output device is also in ASCII, which the output device—with the aid of another encoder chip—translates into understandable words and numbers. Therefore, if the CPU sent the ASCII message

0100100001001001

to your display device, the word "HI" would appear on your screen.

Computers usually handle data in byte multiples. For instance, a 16-bit computer is built to process data in chunks of two bytes; a (faster) 32-bit computer processes data in chunks of four bytes. These byte multiples are commonly called *words*. We'll look at words in more detail later in the chapter.

The Parity Bit. Suppose you are at a keyboard and press the *B* key. If the keyboard encoder supports ASCII coding, it will transmit the byte "01000010" to the CPU. Sometimes, however, something happens during transmission and the CPU receives a garbled message. Interference on the line, for example, might cause the sixth bit to change from 0 to 1 so that the CPU receives the message "01000110." Unless the CPU had some way of knowing that a mistake was made, it would wrongly interpret this byte as the letter *F*.

To enable the CPU to detect such transmission errors, EBCDIC and ASCII have an additional bit position. This bit, called the **parity bit,** is automatically set to either 0 or 1 to make all the bits in a byte add up to either an even or an odd number. Computer systems support either an even or an odd parity. In *odd-parity* systems, the parity bit makes all the 1-bits in a byte add up to an odd number. In *even-parity* systems, it makes them add up to an even number. Figure 3-6 shows how the parity bit works for the ASCII representation of the word "HELLO" on an even-parity system.

Parity bit.
An extra bit added to the byte representation of a character to ensure that there is always either an odd or an even number of 1-bits transmitted with every character.

The parity bit is automatically generated by the keyboard's processor. Thus, if you typed the *B* character on an even-parity system, "010000100" would be sent up the line to the CPU. If the message were garbled so that the even-parity computer received "010001100" (an odd number of 1-bits), the CPU would sense the error immediately.

The parity check is not foolproof. For example, if two bits are incorrectly transmitted in a byte, they will self-cancel. A two-bit error, however, will rarely occur.

Machine Language

Before any program instruction can be executed by your computer, it must be converted into a binary-based code known as **machine language.** An example of a typical machine-language instruction appears below:

Machine language.
A binary-based programming language that the computer can execute directly.

01011000011100000000000100000010

Figure 3-6
The parity bit.
If the system used supports even parity, as shown here, the 1-bits in every byte must always add up to an even number. The parity bit is set to either 0 or 1 in each byte to force an even number of 1-bits in the byte.

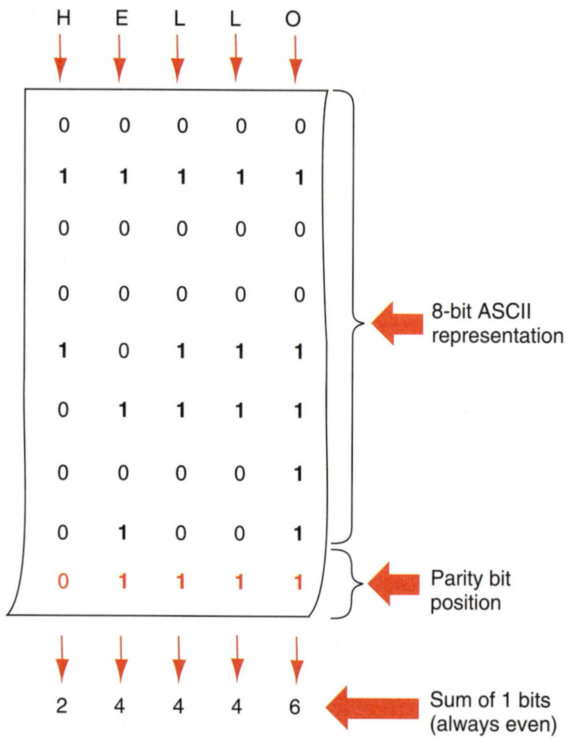

A machine-language instruction may look like a meaningless string of 0s and 1s, but it actually consists of groups of bits that represent specific storage locations and operations. The instruction shown here for an IBM mainframe, for instance, transfers data between two specific memory locations.

In the earliest computers, including even the first microcomputers, all programs were written in machine language. Today, although it is still possible to write in machine language, hardly anybody does. Instead, most people rely on *language translators,* special systems programs that convert instructions automatically into machine language. The translation is so transparent that most users aren't even aware that it is taking place.

Each computer has its own machine language. A code used on an IBM PS/2 computer will be totally foreign to an Apple Macintosh. Incidentally, this is why, when you buy a program package such as a word processor or spreadsheet, you must get the version intended for your specific type of computer system. You don't want the program package translating all of your commands to Macintosh machine language if you have an IBM PS/2 computer that understands only PS/2 machine language.

The System Unit

Now that we've talked conceptually about how the CPU and primary memory work, let's consider how they're realized in hardware and how they relate to other devices inside a system unit of, say, a typical microcomputer.

Almost all computers sold today use a modular hardware approach; for example, related circuitry is etched onto memory or processor chips, the chips are mounted onto carrier packages that are plugged into boards, and the boards are fitted into slots inside the system unit.

The **system unit** often consists of at least one CPU chip, specialized processor chips, memory (RAM and ROM) chips, boards on which these and other chips are mounted, ports that provide connections for external devices, a power supply, and internal circuitry to hook everything together (see Figure 3-7). Here we'll be discussing these devices. System units also often have built-in diskette and hard-disk units and sometimes even a tape drive. Disks and tapes will be covered in detail in Chapter 4.

System unit.
The hardware unit that houses the computer and its primary memory, as well as a number of other devices.

CPU Chip

Every microcomputer system unit contains a specific microprocessor chip as its CPU. This chip is put into a carrier package, as shown in Figure 3-8, and the carrier package is mounted onto a special board—called the **system board**—that fits inside the system unit (see Figure 3-9). This board is located on the floor of the system unit shown in Figure 3-7.

System board.
A board that contains the computer.

Most microcomputer systems made today use CPU chips that are manufactured by either Intel or Motorola. The Intel line of chips—such as the 8086, 8088, 80286, 80386, and 80486—is used on the microcomputer systems made by IBM, Compaq, and companies that make "IBM-compatible" microcomputer systems. The Motorola line of chips—including the 68000, 68020, 68030, and 68040—is used on the Apple Macintosh line of computers and the NeXT Computer System. Figure 3-10 lists the names of some popular system units and the CPUs that run them. Intel chips are commonly referred to by their last three digits—for example, a '386 computer means an Intel 80386 chip is in use.

The type of CPU chip in a computer's system unit greatly affects what you can do with the computer system. Software is written to work on a specific chip, and a program that works on one chip may not function on another unless modified. For instance, software is not very portable between Intel and Motorola chips, as these chips employ a somewhat dissimilar design philosophy. Also, a program designed for an Intel 80386 chip will probably not work on the earlier 80286 chip, which is less capable. And, even though a program designed for an 80286 chip may work on an 80386 chip, some of the 80386's power will be wasted.

CPU chips differ in many respects, one of the most important of which is word size. A computer **word** is a group of bits or bytes that may be manipulated and stored as a unit. It is a critical concept, because the internal circuitry of virtually every computer system is designed around

Word.
A group of bits or characters that are treated by the computer system as a unit.

Figure 3-7 The inside of a system unit.
With the cover of the system unit removed, you can see the parts inside. Generally, the system board is located on the floor. Most system units also contain a fan to keep the parts from overheating.

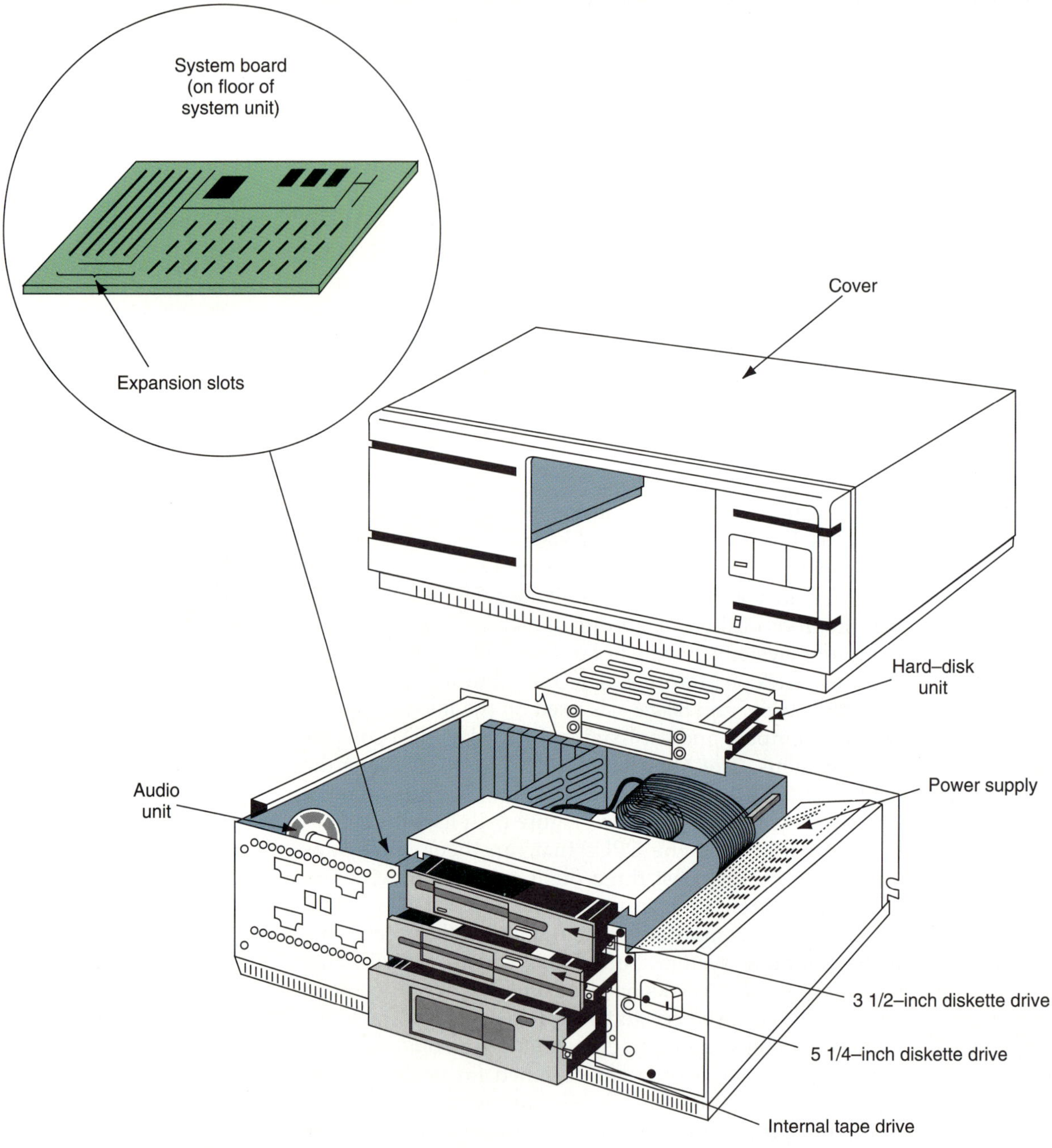

Figure 3-8
Microcomputer in a carrier package.
Shown is the Intel 80486, or '486, microprocessor, which packs over a million circuits into a fingernail-sized area.

Figure 3-9
System board.
The system board contains the CPU chip, RAM, ROM, and circuitry for a number of other functions.

a certain word size. The Apple Macintosh II and IBM PS/2 Model 80 computers, for example, use the Motorola 68030 and Intel 80386 chips, respectively. Both the 68030 and 80386 chips have a 32-bit-word internal architecture, which means that data are transferred within each CPU chip itself in 32-bit chunks. Both chips also have a 32-bit-word I/O bus, mean-

Figure 3-10 Some widely used system units and their CPUs.
Virtually all of the leading microcomputer systems use a CPU chip made by either Intel or Motorola.

Vendor	Product	Type	CPU
Apple Computer, Inc.	Macintosh, Macintosh 512KB Enhanced, Macintosh Plus, Macintosh SE	Desktop	Motorola 68000
	Macintosh Powerbook series	Portable	(Varies)
	Macintosh II	Desktop	Motorola 68020
	Macintosh IIx, IIcx, IIcxi, IIci; IIfx, IIsi; Macintosh Classic II	Desktop	Motorola 68030
	Macintosh Quadra series	Desktop	Motorola 68040
Compaq Computer Corp.	Deskpro 286	Desktop	Intel 80286
	Deskpro 386	Desktop	Intel 80386
	Deskpro 386s	Desktop	Intel 80386SX
	Deskpro 486	Desktop	Intel 80486
	Systempro	Desktop	Intel 80486
	Portable	Portable	Intel 8088
	Portable II, Portable III	Portable	Intel 80286
	LTE 386s	Portable	Intel 80386SX
Dell Computer Corporation	System 325P	Desktop	Intel 80386
	System 316SX, System 320LX	Desktop	Intel 80386SX
	System 316LT, System NX20	Portable	Intel 80386SX
	System 425E, System 486D/33	Desktop	Intel 80486
	System 486D/25, System 486P/20	Desktop	Intel 80486SX
Everex Computer Systems	386	Desktop	Intel 80386
	386is	Desktop	Intel 80386SX
	486	Desktop	Intel 80486
Gateway 2000	2000-386	Desktop	Intel 80386
	2000-386SX	Desktop	Intel 80386SX
	2000-486	Desktop	Intel 80486
IBM Corp.	PC, PC/XT	Desktop	Intel 8088
	PC AT, PS/1	Desktop	Intel 80286
	PS/2 Model 25, PS/2 Model 30	Desktop	Intel 8086
	PS/2 Model 50, PS/2 Model 60	Desktop	Intel 80286
	PS/2 Model 70, PS/2 Model 80	Desktop	Intel 80386
	PS/2 Model 55SX, PS/2 Model 65SX	Desktop	Intel 80386SX
	PS/2 Model 95	Desktop	Intel 80486
	PS/2 Model P70	Portable	Intel 80386
	PS/2 Model P75, PS/2 Model P90	Portable	Intel 80486
	N51SX, CL57SX, L40SX	Portable	Intel 80386SX
Tandy Corp./Radio Shack	Tandy 3000HL	Desktop	Intel 80286
	Tandy 4000, 4000LX, 5000MC	Desktop	Intel 80386
	Tandy 4000SX	Desktop	Intel 80386SX
	Tandy 4825	Desktop	Intel 80486
	Tandy 4833	Desktop	Intel 80486SX
Zeos International, Ltd.	286 Notebook	Portable	Intel 80286
	386	Desktop	Intel 80386
	386SX	Desktop	Intel 80386SX
	486	Desktop	Intel 80486
	486SX	Desktop	Intel 80486SX

ing that there is a 32-bit-wide data path from each CPU to external devices. Often, the greater the word size, the faster the computer system (see Feature 3-1).

Specialized Processor Chips

Working alongside the CPU chip in many system units are *specialized processor chips,* such as numeric coprocessors and graphic coprocessors. The role of these "slave chips" is to perform specialized tasks for the CPU, thereby enhancing overall system performance. For instance, a *numeric (math) coprocessor* chip helps the CPU perform arithmetic; a *graphic coprocessor* chip helps the CPU with the computationally intensive chore of creating complex screen displays. It is not unusual to boost the speed of a computer system several times over by using specialized chips such as these.

RAM

RAM (for **random access memory**), also known as *primary memory* or *main memory,* is used to store the programs and data on which the computer is currently working. Like the microprocessor, the RAM of a microcomputer system consists of circuits etched onto silicon-backed chips. These chips are mounted onto carrier packages, just as the CPU is, and the packages are plugged into the system board. Most desktop microcomputer systems in use today have enough RAM to store 256 thousand to 4 billion bytes of data. Many computer systems allow memory expansion (within limits) directly on the system board or through an add-in board (which we will discuss shortly) when RAM is insufficient. RAM is *volatile,* meaning that the contents of memory are lost when the computer is shut off.

Random access memory (RAM).
Primary memory.

ROM

ROM, which stands for **read-only memory,** consists of nonerasable hardware modules that contain programs. Like RAM, these software-in-hardware modules are mounted into carrier packages that, in turn, are plugged into one or more boards inside the system unit. You can neither write over these ROM programs (that's why they're called read-only) nor destroy their contents when you shut off the computer's power (that is, they're nonvolatile). A program stored in ROM can be fetched more quickly by the CPU than if it were stored on disk, where it would have to be loaded into main memory before the computer could work on it. Key pieces of systems software are often stored in ROM.

Read-only memory (ROM).
A software-in-hardware module that can be read but not written on.

ROM is an example of **firmware,** software-in-hardware modules that are available in several other forms. For instance, *programmable read-only memory (PROM)* is identical to ROM except that the module is blank and the buyer writes the program. Special equipment is needed to write a program onto a PROM module, and once the program is on, it can't be

Firmware.
Software instructions that are written onto a hardware module.

Feature 3-1

But How Fast Will It Do a Payroll?

Factors Affecting System Performance

When comparing the performance of two computer systems, it's easy to get lost in the dense forest of confusing-sounding terms. Getting your mips crossed with your flops perhaps.

How effective a computer system will be depends on a number of factors. Each of these factors interacts in different ways in different situations; consequently, it is difficult to predict computer system performance. The most important determinants of system performance usually include the type of work being done, the speed of the computer in use, the size of the data paths in the system, the amount and type of storage available (and the way it is managed), and the software in use.

Work Being Done. Some computer systems, like some people, are good at doing certain types of jobs and poor at doing others. For instance, one computer system may perform calculations quickly but be relatively slow when handling input and output operations. Another system may be great for text processing but just awful for computer graphics. Probably the most important question to answer when buying a computer system is how the system under consideration will handle the particular types of work it will be expected to do. Usually the only ways to answer this question satisfactorily are to personally try the system out on a particular job and to read unbiased product reviews (found in computer journals) written by people who have used or tested the system.

Assessing system performance. The best way to evaluate a system is to try it out.

Speed of Computer. All computers are designed to run at certain speeds. Among mainframes, speeds are often rated in *mips,* or *millions of instructions per second,* whereas for supercomputers, speeds are calibrated in *flops* (*floating point operations per second*). The more mips or flops, as you might guess, the faster the system. Microcom-

erased. *Erasable programmable read-only memory (EPROM),* on the other hand, is like PROM except that its contents can be erased and a new program written. Firmware is usually supplied when a computer system is purchased, but it can also be bought separately.

Add-in Boards

Add-in board. A board that may be inserted into the computer's system unit to perform one or more functions.

Many microcomputer system vendors enable you to customize your system by choosing your own **add-in boards**. These boards are cardlike pieces of hardware that contain the circuitry for performing one or more specific functions. They plug into *expansion slots* within the computer's system unit (refer back to Figure 3-7), thereby enabling you to either interface with specific types of peripheral devices or add new capabilities. For example, if you want a certain model of display unit attached to your computer, you may need a special *display adapter board* that contains the proper software routine for establishing the connection. Similarly, you puters, by contrast, are rated in *megahertz* (*MHz*), or *millions of "clock ticks"* (*cycles*) *per second.* Each microprocessor has a system clock that coordinates the computer system's operation, just as a metronome coordinates work for an orchestra. During each clock tick, a single piece of a machine-language instruction may be executed and a single piece of a machine-language instruction may travel along any circuit. The original IBM PC has a clock speed of 4.77 MHz; today's top-of-the-line microprocessors are rated at 33 MHz or more.

Size of Data Paths. A computer system includes a set of wires, or paths, along which data pass. The wider the path, the more data that can be passed along it during a single tick of the system clock. On the IBM PC, for instance, there is a 16-bit-wide path on the CPU chip (so the ALU and control unit can pass data between them in 16-bit chunks), but there is only an 8-bit bus. On newer chips, the paths both *on* the CPU chip and *to* or *from* it are 32 bits wide, allowing more data to be transferred in a given time interval. An analogy can be made here with the human circulatory system, which contains many arteries through which blood flows. The wider the arteries, the more blood that can be transferred to body cells during a single heart beat. Also, just as a single narrowed artery can cause the entire body to have problems, a critical data path in the computer system that is too narrow can cause the entire system to bottleneck—regardless of the speed of the CPU or size of the other data paths.

Storage. The amount and type of storage in use, and the way it is being managed, are often critical to computer system performance. For instance, if a system has a large amount of RAM, applications can be transferred from disk to RAM, where they can be performed more quickly by the computer. As you will learn in the next chapter, not all storage devices are equally fast. A hard disk, for instance, will work much faster than a floppy disk. The way in which storage is managed can also be extremely important, and storage management methods can differ substantially from one system to another. This will be discussed more thoroughly in Chapter 4.

Software in Use. The quality of a software product depends on the skills of the programmers and the uses they intend for it. While one programmer may find a clever, speedy way to do work, another doing the same task might find an alternative, slower method. Consequently, the program's performance may depend largely on who wrote it. Also, some software products are upgraded in only modest ways to run on the newer computer chips. Thus, even though you have a fast, 32-bit computer, if the software you are using still handles data in 8-bit chunks, there may not be much you can do to improve performance.

can get your computer system to communicate with facsimile (fax) machines by getting a *fax board*.

Many types of add-in boards currently are available in the marketplace. Most of these boards provide either a basic function that is unavailable with the system unit or a "value-added" capability that enhances an existing function. With new machines and new capabilities being announced regularly, the number of types of add-in boards is increasing rapidly. Figure 3-11 lists several types of these boards and the functions they perform.

System units that allow you to customize with add-in boards are said to possess an *open architecture. Closed-architecture* machines generally are faster and easier to deal with, but they lack the flexibility you get from being able to configure a wide variety of devices to your computer. Virtually all of the leading computers made today, whether microcomputers, minicomputers, mainframes, or supercomputers, are open-architecture devices.

Figure 3-11
Add-in boards for microcomputer systems.
Add-in boards can provide a microcomputer system with either brand new capabilities or enhancements to existing features.

Board Type	Purpose
Cache card	Provides the microcomputer system with logic to improve disk performance
Concurrent-processor board	Contains a CPU that can be run concurrently with the CPU on the system board
Coprocessor board	Uses specialized processor chips that speed up overall processing in the microcomputer system
Disk controller card	Enables a certain type of disk unit to interface with the microcomputer system
Display adapter board	Enables a certain type of display device to interface with the microcomputer system
Emulator board	Allows the microcomputer system to function as a communications terminal to a large computer system
Fax board	Provides facsimile capabilities for the microcomputer system
Graphics adapter board	Enables the computer system to conform to a particular graphics standard
Memory expansion board	Allows additional RAM to be put into the microcomputer system
Modem board	Provides communications circuitry on a board
Multifunction board	Provides several independent functions on a single board
Upgrade board*	Contains a CPU that can be used in lieu of the CPU on the system board

*Also known as an accelerator board or a turbo board.

Ports

Port.
An outlet on the computer's system unit through which a peripheral device may communicate.

Most system units contain built-in sockets that enable you to plug in external hardware devices. These sockets, which often are found on the exterior of the system unit, are known as **ports.** Printers, for instance, generally hook up to microcomputers through either *parallel* ports or *serial* ports. IBM microcomputers and similar devices typically connect printers with parallel ports, whereas Apple computers connect printers with serial ports. Most computers also use serial ports to permit connection to remote devices over phone lines. The technical differences between serial and parallel transmission will be explained in Chapter 6.

When an I/O device needs to be plugged into the system unit and there is not a built-in port for it, you normally must buy a special add-in board that has a port on it. When you install the board, the port will extend through a hole in the system-unit cover so that you can plug the I/O device into it.

There is a practical limit to the number of peripheral devices a CPU can handle. Generally, each new device interfaced through an add-in board or port adds to the burden the CPU must manage, thereby possibly degrading system performance.

I/O Bus

Bus.
A set of wires that acts as a data highway between the CPU and other devices.

The CPU connects to RAM, ROM, boards, and ports through circuitry called an I/O (for input/output) **bus,** as shown in Figure 3-12. The bus links the CPU to every hardware device in the system, enabling data to be exchanged and processed.

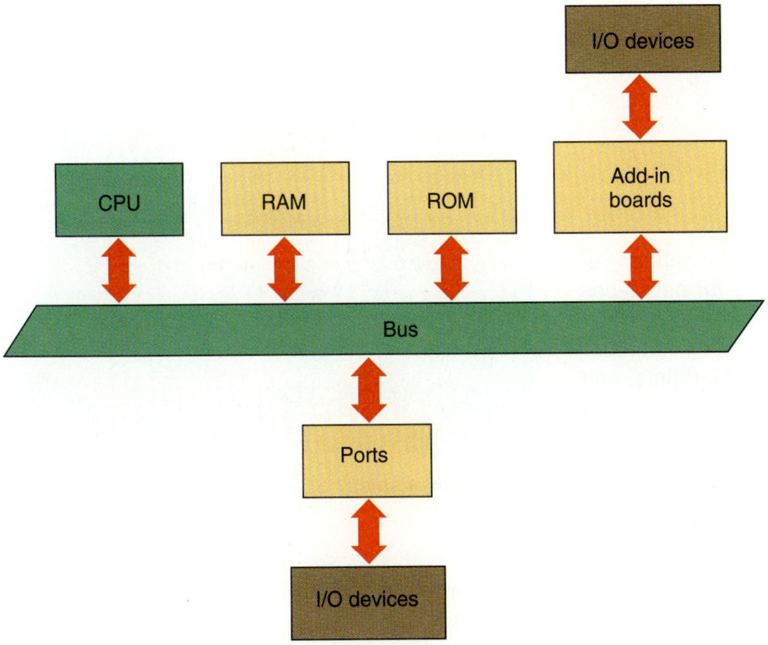

Figure 3-12
How devices are linked.
A set of wires or circuits called a *bus* allows the CPU to communicate with RAM, with ROM, and with peripheral devices connected through either boards or ports.

Today, there are a number of bus standards in existence. The three state-of-the-art standards are IBM's *Micro Channel Architecture* (used on the high end of the IBM PS/2 line of computers), Apple's *NuBus* (used on the most recent Macintoshes), and the *EISA*, or Enhanced Industry Standard Architecture (used on computers made by Compaq and several other vendors). Each of these standards enables you to configure your computer system with several CPUs, including the native CPU and alternate CPUs on add-in boards. Thus, the native CPU can be working on a spreadsheet application while a CPU on an add-in board is performing a background database search. Such an arrangement will, of course, make the work go much faster than it would if the native CPU alone had to do everything.

Making Computers Speedier

Over the years, a number of strategies have been used to make computers faster. Four of these are moving circuits closer together, finding new materials with which to make computers, developing reduced instruction set computers (RISC), and using parallel processing.

Moving Circuits Closer Together. As complex as computers seem sometimes, there is one intuitive natural law that all must follow: the shorter the length of the circuit paths, the shorter the time it takes to move programs and data along them. During the last several decades,

Feature 3-2

The Coming Chip Technologies

What Will Be the Next Major Challenger to Silicon?

Since the beginning of modern computing, researchers have constantly searched for new types of circuit technologies to hold data and to manipulate them faster. The earliest computers used hardware such as vacuum tubes, magnetic drums, and core planes as their principal circuit components. In the 1970s, when it was possible to etch circuitry into an area the size of the head of a pin, another major medium evolved: silicon-backed chips. Silicon became popular because it is an unusually pure substance and will not interfere with the metal circuitry etched onto its surface.

Today, although it is possible to place more than a million microminiaturized circuit elements onto a silicon chip, that may not be enough. So researchers are pressing forward with other approaches. Five of the leading challengers to silicon are the following:

Gallium Arsenide. Probably the most promising new computer chip technology involves gallium arsenide (GaAs). GaAs chips are superior to those made of silicon because:

- They move electronic impulses around up to ten times faster.
- They enable optical transmission, something silicon can't do.
- They can operate at much higher temperatures and emit less heat, enabling circuits to be packed closer together.

How small is small? Silicon-backed chip compared to a pencil.

Gallium arsenide products are already moving into the marketplace. Some of the more critical components of large computers now consist of GaAs chips, and GaAs is rapidly taking hold in areas such as high-speed communications.

But gallium arsenide has some drawbacks. GaAs chips are still often several times more expensive than those made of silicon. And because

computer manufacturers have been able to pack circuitry ever closer together. Today, it is now possible to fit more than a million circuits on a single fingernail-sized chip.

Unfortunately, when the circuits are in use, they generate heat. And, when circuits are placed too close together, they melt. To circumvent this problem, researchers have used such strategies as immersing circuits in helium "baths" to cool them. Helium baths are found in some supercomputers.

New Materials. Most CPU chips today consist of metallic circuitry that is etched onto a silicon backing. Silicon-backed chips have been popular since the 1970s, when manufacturing techniques to microminiaturize circuitry became widely available.

Today, because limits are quickly being reached on the number of circuits that can be packed onto a chip without heat damage, several other alternatives are getting considerable attention. Among these are gal-

the newer technology is still in its infancy, GaAs designers can currently squeeze only tens of thousands of circuits onto a single chip.

Superconductors. One of the problems with conventional circuitry is that it heats up. When circuits get hot, their electrical resistance increases, impeding the flow of message-bearing electrons. If circuits are placed too close together, they can melt. Superconductive materials are those that can transfer electrons without the worry of electrical resistance or heat buildup.

Every year new materials are being discovered that more closely approach the ideal of superconductivity. While most of the superconductors of today must be cooled in order to lose resistance and avoid a meltdown, the search continues for materials that are superconductive at room temperature. If and when naturally superconductive materials emerge from the laboratories and are successfully implemented in products, they may result in circuitry that's 100 times faster than today's silicon-backed chips.

Optical Processing. Optical processing uses light waves to do the work of the silicon-backed chip's electrons. Optical chips currently available in the marketplace can move data around about ten times faster than silicon-backed chips. Theoretically, an optical processor would be capable of speeds hundreds of times faster than silicon—if data could be gotten into and out of it fast enough. Optical chips are today surfacing in such applications as collision-avoidance systems for cars, artificial vision systems for robots, and sensors for image processing.

Biotechnology. Biotechnology offers yet another compelling alternative to today's silicon chip. Scientists have shown that tiny molecules can be grown and shaped to act as circuits. With such a technology, electrons are passed from molecule to molecule. Some scientists believe that if such a technology is ever perfected, it could possibly result in circuits 500 times smaller than those on today's silicon chips.

Tubes on a Chip. Just when everyone thought that it was dead and buried, vacuum electronics—popular in the 1940s and 1950s—is making a comeback. Scientists are now talking about the very real possibility of putting up to ten billion microscopic tubes on a five-inch wafer. Why vacuum tubes? Electrons can travel much faster when placed in a vacuum. Unlike their predecessors, which needed heat to work, these new tubes work by an entirely different set of principles. Some researchers believe that tubes on a chip are capable of packing 1,000 times the power of today's silicon chips.

lium arsenide chips, superconductors, optical processing, biotechnology, and vacuum electronics (see Feature 3-2).

Reduced Instruction Set Computers (RISC). To process data effectively, computers must be equipped with a variety of instructions, called the computer's *instruction set*. Each instruction in the set corresponds to a microcode instruction.

Studies have shown that computers are actually faster if they are given only a fraction of the instructions with which computers have traditionally been provided. (The old adage "too many cooks spoil the broth" applies in the world of computers, too.) The instructions that the computer doesn't need just get in the way of efficient and speedy processing.

In the mid-1970s, CPUs with limited instruction sets became available. These machines have aptly been named **reduced instruction set computers (RISC).** In certain test studies, RISC-based computers have

Reduced instruction set computing (RISC). A term referring to a computer system that gets by with fewer instructions than conventional computer systems.

been shown to work ten times faster than conventional computers with larger instructions sets. Today, RISC devices are rapidly becoming the standard in engineering applications environments and in communications systems. The downside to RISC-based computers is that conventional software needs to be modified to work on them.

Parallel Processing. Despite the astounding evolution of computer systems over the past 50 years, most are still driven by a single CPU. A single CPU can perform instructions only in serial, or one step at a time, whether working exclusively on one program or juggling several concurrently.

In the race to develop ever-faster computer systems for tomorrow, scientists are experimenting with ways to have two or more CPUs and memories perform tasks in parallel. For example, instead of relying on one processor to solve a lengthy calculation, a computer system using **parallel processing** assigns portions of the problem to several CPUs operating simultaneously. But just as it is difficult to coordinate two or more workers who are dedicated to completing a single job, so too is it difficult to integrate the parallel efforts of several processors working together at superhuman speeds. Nonetheless, many industry insiders see parallel processing as an unstoppable future reality. As it becomes harder and harder to make computers themselves faster—by, say, packing circuits closer together—parallel processing will become an increasingly important strategy for reducing the time it takes to do work.

Parallel processing. Refers to computing in which two or more CPUs share work and process pieces of this work simultaneously.

Today several approaches to parallel-processing computer systems are observable in the marketplace. One popular approach is represented by the Cray-2, a supercomputer that carries a price tag of several million dollars. The Cray, like most other supercomputers, employs a common parallel design philosophy—namely, hooking up a small number of expensive, state-of-the-art CPUs. The Cray-2 uses four such processors, which carry out both parallel and serial processing.

Since not everybody can afford a supercomputer, other parallel processing approaches have evolved. Another common tack is to design parallel machines with thousands of relatively inexpensive, off-the-shelf microprocessors. Although devices built this way are less versatile than supercomputers, together they can pack a respectable amount of power at a fraction of the cost.

Summary and Key Terms

In Chapter 3 we flip the lid off of a typical system unit and examine the function of the parts inside.

How the CPU Works. The CPU has two major sections. The **arithmetic/logic unit (ALU)** performs arithmetic and logical operations on data. The **control unit** directs the flow of electronic traffic between primary memory and the ALU and, also, between the CPU and input and output devices.

Both of these units work closely with primary memory to carry out processing tasks inside the system unit.

Primary memory—also called **main memory, internal memory,** or just **memory**—holds the programs and data that have been passed to the computer, the results of intermediate processing, and output that is ready to be transmitted to secondary storage or an output device.

Registers are high-speed staging areas within the CPU that hold program instructions and data immediately before they are processed. The part of a program instruction that indicates what the ALU is to do next is placed in the **instruction register;** the part showing the address of the data to be used in the operation is placed in the **address register.** Before data are processed, they are taken from primary memory and placed in the **storage register.** The **accumulator** is a register that temporarily stores the results of ongoing operations.

The processing of a single, machine-level instruction is called a **machine cycle**. Each such instruction is broken down further into subinstructions called **microcode,** and each piece of microcode corresponds directly to a set of the computer's circuits. The computer system has a built-in **system clock** that synchronizes the processing of microcode.

A machine cycle has two parts: an **I-cycle** (instruction cycle), in which the control unit fetches and examines an instruction, and an **E-cycle** (execution cycle), in which the instruction is actually executed by the ALU under control unit supervision. A computer may need to go through thousands, millions, or even billions of machine cycles to fully process a single program. Computer cycle times generally are measured in **milliseconds** (thousandths of a second), **microseconds** (millionths of a second), **nanoseconds** (billionths of a second), or **picoseconds** (trillionths of a second).

Data and Program Representation. The electronic components of digital computers work in a two-state, or **binary,** fashion. It is convenient to think of these binary states as the 0-state and the 1-state. Computer people refer to such 0s and 1s as **bits.**

The computer uses several binary-based codes to process data. Two popular codes are **ASCII** and **EBCDIC.** These fixed-length codes can represent any single character of data—a digit, alphabet character, or special symbol—as a string of seven or eight bits. This string of bits is called a **byte.** ASCII and EBCDIC allow for an additional bit position, called a **parity bit,** to enable computer systems to check for transmission errors.

The storage capacity of computers often is expressed in **kilobytes** (**K-bytes** or **KB**), or thousands of bytes; **megabytes** (**M-bytes** or **MB**), or millions of bytes; **gigabytes** (**G-bytes** or **GB**), or billions of bytes; and **terabytes** (**T-bytes** or **TB**), or trillions of bytes.

Machine language is the binary-based code used to represent programs. A program must be translated into machine language before the computer can execute it.

The System Unit. Almost all computer systems sold today use a modular hardware approach; that is, related circuitry is etched onto *processor chips* or *memory chips,* the chips are mounted onto carrier packages that are later fitted into boards, and the boards are positioned into slots inside the **system unit.**

Every microcomputer system unit contains a specific microprocessor chip as its CPU. This chip is put into a carrier package that is mounted onto a special board, called the **system board,** that fits inside the system unit. CPU chips differ in many respects; one difference is word size. A computer **word** is a group of bits or bytes that can be manipulated as a unit. Often the larger the word size, the more powerful the processor.

Working alongside the CPU chip in many system units are specialized processor chips, such as *numeric coprocessors* and *graphic coprocessors.*

The primary memory chips on microcomputer systems are commonly referred to as **RAM**, for **random access memory.** Memory chips that contain nonerasable programs are referred to as **ROM,** for **read-only memory.** ROM is an example of **firmware.** There are several other types of firmware, including PROM (programmable read-only memory) and EPROM (erasable programmable read-only memory).

Many system units contain a limited number of internal expansion slots, into which **add-in boards** can be mounted by the user. These boards can be used to customize a computer system by supplying more memory, adding facsimile-machine (fax) capability, and so on. Also, many system units have external I/O **ports** into which peripheral devices may be plugged.

The CPU connects to RAM, ROM, and peripherals (interfaced by add-in boards and ports) through circuitry called an I/O **bus**. Some widely used bus architectures include *Micro Channel Architecture,* used on the high end of the IBM PS/2 line of computers; *NuBus,* used on the recent Apple Macintosh line of computers; and *EISA,* used extensively on Compaq computers and those of many other vendors.

Making Computers Speedier. Over the years, a number of strategies have been used to make computers faster. Four of these are moving circuits closer together, finding new materials with which to make computers, developing **reduced instruction set computers (RISC),** and using **parallel processing.**

Review Exercises

Fill-in Questions

1. The register that temporarily stores the results of ongoing arithmetic and logic operations is called the ______________.
2. A millisecond is one ______________ of a second.
3. One trillion bytes are referred to as a(n) ______________.
4. ROM is an acronym for ______________.
5. System units that allow you to customize with add-in boards are said to possess a(n) ______________ architecture.
6. RISC is an acronym for ______________.
7. The operation of two or more computers working together is known as ______________ processing.

Matching Questions

Match each term with the description that fits best.

a. ALU
b. binary
c. bit
d. EBCDIC
e. ASCII
f. word
g. EPROM
h. parity bit

____ 1. The base-2 numbering system.
____ 2. The fixed-length code most associated with IBM mainframes.
____ 3. A type of firmware that is erasable.
____ 4. A fixed-length code developed by the American National Standards Institute.
____ 5. Used to check for transmission errors.
____ 6. The section of the CPU in which computations are performed.
____ 7. A group of bits or bytes that may be manipulated and stored as a unit.
____ 8. A binary digit.

Discussion Questions

1. Describe the various sections of the CPU and their roles.
2. Explain how a program instruction is executed.
3. Why is the binary system used to represent data and programs?
4. What is the purpose of the parity bit, and how does it work?
5. What are the differences between a bit, a byte, a kilobyte, a megabyte, and a word?
6. How does RAM differ from ROM?
7. What devices are located under the cover of the system unit? What functions do these devices perform?
8. What is the principle advantage of a reduced instruction set computer (RISC)?

Critical Thinking Questions

1. The chapter mentions the continuing quest for faster computers. What difference could it make to have mainframe computing power on the desk of ordinary end users or computers that are, say, hundreds or thousands of times faster than those we have today?
2. The earliest computers were decimal rather than binary machines. In other words, they broke down each piece of data into ten states instead of just two. Why, would you guess, were decimal computers slower than binary computers?
3. Comment on this statement: "Computers are now so easy to work with that it's no longer necessary for the average user to know any of the technical details about how they work." In making your comments, be sure to state how much technical knowledge you think the average business student should have about computers.

Have you ever wondered how the airlines and shipping companies keep close track of the millions of pounds of cargo they handle each day? It's by storing shipment data on high-speed magnetic disks, a technology you will learn about by reading this chapter.

4 Secondary Storage

Outline

Learning Objectives

After completing this chapter, you will be able to:

1. Name several general properties of secondary storage systems.
2. Identify a number of disk storage systems as well as describe how they work and where they are particularly useful.
3. Describe the roles of other secondary storage media and equipment.
4. Explain several types of data access and organization strategies and identify situations in which each is appropriate.

Overview

In Chapter 3, we discussed the role of primary (internal) memory. Primary memory is designed to provide immediate access to stored items. It is here that programs, data, intermediate results, and output are temporarily stored. However, as soon as a program has been executed, new data and programs are written over the existing ones. Thus, if data, programs, and processing results are to be preserved for repeated use, additional storage capacity must be made available. Secondary (external) storage serves this purpose. Although slower than primary memory, secondary storage is less expensive and consequently provides far greater storage capacity for each dollar spent.

We will begin this chapter with a discussion of certain common characteristics of secondary storage systems. One of the most important is data access—the way in which data are retrieved from secondary storage. Then we'll cover the two most important kinds of secondary storage systems in use today: those that use magnetic disk and those that use magnetic tape. Next we'll look at some other secondary storage systems, such as those that use optical disk or magnetic bubbles. Finally, we'll cover data organization—methods of storing data on a medium for efficient access.

Properties of Secondary Storage Systems

In this section, we'll look at several important properties and characteristics of secondary storage systems. We will consider in turn (1) the two physical parts of a secondary storage system, (2) the nonvolatility property of secondary storage, (3) the removability of media from the secondary storage unit, and (4) sequential versus direct access.

Physical Parts. Any secondary storage system involves two physical parts: a *peripheral device* and an *input/output medium.* A disk unit and a tape unit are examples of peripheral devices; magnetic disk platters and magnetic tape cartridges are types of media. Data and programs are written onto and read from some type of medium. The medium must be situated on a peripheral device for the CPU to process its contents.

Read/write head.
A magnetic station on a disk access mechanism or tape unit that reads or writes data.

In most secondary storage systems, media must pass by a **read/write head** in the peripheral device to be read from or written to. For instance, when you play or record to a music tape on your home stereo system, the tape passes by a head on the tape recorder, which will either play or record music. Magnetic tapes on computer systems work by an identical principle. Magnetic disks also use read/write heads that perform similar types of reading and writing tasks.

Nonvolatile storage.
Storage that retains its contents when the power is shut off.

Nonvolatility Property. Secondary storage media are **nonvolatile.** This means that when the power on the peripheral device is shut off, the data stored on the medium remain there. This is in contrast to most types of primary memory, which are **volatile.** With volatile storage, the data on the medium disappear once the power is shut off.

Volatile storage. Storage that loses its contents when the power is shut off.

Removable versus Nonremovable Media. In many secondary storage systems, although the peripheral device is online to the computer, the associated medium must be loaded into the device before the computer can read from it or write to it. These are called *removable-media* secondary storage systems. Diskettes, many types of hard disks, magnetic tape cartridges, and magnetic tape reels are examples of removable media used on such systems. Other secondary storage systems, such as those that use Winchester disks (discussed later in this chapter), are *fixed-media* secondary storage systems. In Winchester disk systems, the disk is encased in a sealed unit within the peripheral device, and it cannot be conveniently removed.

Removability of media provides virtually unlimited storage capacity, because the medium can be replaced when it is full. Removability also facilitates backup (covered extensively in Chapter 13). *Backup* occurs when a duplicate set of data or programs are written onto a disk or tape and are stored offline, for use if the originals are lost or destroyed. *Security* is also enhanced by removability, because programs or data do not have to stay on the disk unit. Finally, removability makes it possible to assign a specific application to a specific medium—say, assigning all customer accounts to one disk and all vendor accounts to another. Fixed media, in contrast, generally offer the advantages of higher speed, greater storage capacity, and better reliability.

Sequential versus Direct Access. When the computer system is instructed to use data or programs residing in secondary storage, it first must be able to find the materials. The process of retrieving data and programs in storage is called *access.*

There are two basic access methods: sequential and direct. With **sequential access,** the records in a file can be retrieved only in the same sequence in which they are physically stored. With **direct access,** also called **random access,** records can be retrieved in any sequence.

Sequential access. Fetching records in storage in the same sequence in which they are physically ordered.

Direct access. Reading or writing data in storage so that the access time involved is relatively independent of the location of the data. Also known as **random access.**

The distinction between sequential and direct access can be seen on a typical home stereo system. Suppose you have both a cassette tape and a phonograph record of the same music. You want to hear the fifth song on side one of the record and this song is also the fifth selection on the tape. With the tape, you must pass sequentially through the first four songs to hear the fifth one. With the phonograph record, however, you can place the needle directly on the fifth song and listen to it immediately.

The phonograph record is also an effective sequential-access device. If you want to listen to the entire first side of the album, you simply place the needle at the beginning of the record and play the tunes in sequence. Thus, the phonograph record is really both a sequential- and direct-access medium because you can play a series of songs sequentially or pick individual ones in random order.

Now let's apply this distinction to computer systems. Machine-readable magnetic tape has the sequential properties of music tape, and magnetic disk has both the sequential and direct properties of the phonograph record.

Some information processing applications are essentially sequential in nature, while others are direct. For example, the preparation of mailing labels is often a sequential operation. If you want to send Christmas cards to all employees in a company, you can process the computerized employee file sequentially—that is, from the beginning of the list to the end. As names and addresses are extracted from the file, they are printed on the mailing labels. Obtaining the latest inventory information about products, on the other hand, often involves direct processing, because requests are made to the inventory file in random order. For example, suppose a salesperson wants to find out how many units of item number 6402 are on hand. A minute later, a customer calls to get the price of item number 36. Then a question comes up regarding deliveries of item number 988. In this case, you move back and forth randomly through the records to obtain information from this file.

Magnetic Disk

Magnetic disk.
A secondary storage medium consisting of platters made of rigid metal (hard disk) or flexible plastic (diskette).

Today **magnetic disks** are undoubtedly the most widely used secondary storage medium for information processing. Because they allow direct access to data, disks permit much faster retrieval of information than do tapes, and at a reasonable cost as well. Without disk storage, many of the computer applications we see around us would not be possible. Banking with automatic teller machines and making airline reservations are just two of the many activities that depend on the rapid access to data that magnetic disks provide (see also Feature 4-1).

Hard disk.
A rigid platter coated with a magnetizable substance.

Two common types of magnetic disks are hard disks and diskettes. **Hard disks** are round, rigid platters. Because of their large storage capacities and fast data-retrieval capabilities, hard disks are by far the preferred medium on minicomputer and mainframe systems. A growing number of microcomputer users are also finding hard disks indispensable in their work. There are many types of hard-disk systems in use today; the most common are those that use either a removable-pack or sealed-pack design.

Diskette.
A small, removable disk made of a tough, flexible plastic and coated with a magnetizable substance.

The advantages of hard disks notwithstanding, inexpensive **diskettes,** which are packaged in small plastic cases, are still widely used—because of their low cost and removability—on many microcomputer systems today. Diskettes also are used occasionally with minicomputers and mainframes as a medium for transferring small amounts of data from one system to another and for small amounts of backup. Although most users of diskettes store their own programs and data on them, diskettes are also used as instructional and promotional tools (see Feature 4-2).

In this section, we'll discuss disk systems for large computers first. Since mainframes were commercially available before any other type of

Feature 4-1

Electronic Markets

A Story of Disk Technology and How Business Competition Evolved around It

Disk technology, which makes possible the random accessing of records, is one of the principal forces behind today's electronic marketplaces. An electronic marketplace is a computerized transaction processing system that offers online ordering of goods and services. Because transactions are entered into the system in a random fashion, only storage systems that can randomly process records—such as magnetic disk—are suitable.

Airlines reservations systems were the first major electronic marketplaces. At first only plane tickets were sold through these systems; today, hotel reservations and car rentals are handled as well. There are many other electronic markets. Computer database services such as Prodigy and CompuServe are also electronic markets—ones in which information is the principal product sold.

Some companies that built computer systems originally tried to keep the electronic markets in which they operated all to themselves. Consider the airlines, for instance. Only a few companies in the airlines industry are large enough to build and support a reservations system. Those that were wanted to list only their own flights. When this became impractical, they wanted to list their own flights first in a preferential manner. The smaller airlines called foul, claiming this to be an anticompetitive practice, and the government had to intercede to straighten the matter out.

Some years ago in the health-care industry, a company named American Hospital Supply (AHS) built a computer system to sell health-care products to clinics, hospitals, and pharmacies. This company gave away computer terminals to its big customers to make it easy for them to order supplies electronically over the phone lines. The system became very popular, and other suppliers of health-care

Electronic markets for health care. Ordering convenience makes a big difference in sales.

products found themselves "locked out." After all, even though a customer might want one desktop computer terminal to make ordering convenient, it would be impractical to have three or four terminals and to learn three or four different systems.

Times changed for AHS, however. Customers became particular and wanted to order products from competitors, too. AHS had to decide whether it could survive by locking out the rest of the market. Today AHS's computer system (now operated by Baxter Healthcare) makes available not only the firm's own products but those of competitors as well.

computer, many of the principles guiding their disk systems influenced disk systems on other types of computers. Next we'll turn to smaller computers, focusing primarily on diskettes and hard-disk systems and, secondarily, on hard cards and cartridge disks. Finally, we'll look at some methods for optimizing disk processing.

Feature 4-2

Sales Diskettes

Giving New Meaning to the Old Soft Sell

If you are tired of high-powered salespeople, now there's a less pressured and even "fun" shopping alternative. It's called the sales diskette.

Sales diskettes are diskette-based programs designed by manufacturers to provide interesting and useful information about products. So that you won't get bored, many of them have built-in games and exciting graphics. Perhaps the most attractive feature is the price; many of them are giveaways, and the rest typically cost less than a couple of hamburgers and fries at a fast-food restaurant.

Let's look at a few examples. To help prospective buyers assess their computer needs, Apple has a sales-diskette game that works like TV's "Wheel of Fortune" show. The Coca-Cola Company has recently released a diskette-based game that provides information about Coke along with exciting graphics, animation, and sound. And MCI, the telecommunications company, has an enticing diskette that helps business managers develop cost-effective telecommunications strategies.

One of the most ambitious computer-based information packages has been undertaken by Ford Motor Company. For $6.95 you get a two-diskette package that shows off the Ford lineup of approximately 100 cars, provides animation showing moving engine and brake parts, and has an interactive driving simulation game that is reminiscent of Microsoft's popular Flight Simulator game. In addition, a built-in spreadsheet program enables you to compute the best package of car options, and it will even figure out monthly payments for you. BMW has a similar diskette product called Desktop Showroom (see photo).

Will sales diskettes become a trend? With the buying public becoming more computer literate and less patient—and with products becoming more complex—it may be easier to place information on a diskette and have the customer peruse it at his or her convenience. The customer avoids a high-pressure sales pitch, and the selling takes place in the comfort of his or her own home. Also, the diskette has an advantage over printed brochures; because the diskette is interactive, it can contain a help feature to handle common customer concerns. An added bonus to the seller is that the more fun the diskette is, the more the customer focuses on the product.

BMW test drive. Simulated situations test your reactions and driving skills.

The potential for sales diskettes is exciting. Imagine that it's the year 2000 and a sales diskette arrives from your favorite mail-order catalog company. You pop it into your computer system, in which a three-dimensional, full-bodied image of yourself is stored. When you select an item of clothing from the electronic catalog, your digital body is dressed onscreen so that you can see how you look. You can also have the catalog default to your stored measurements, so it will automatically pick the right size. Want to see how you look in blue instead of black? Hit a few keys and presto. When you've finished choosing your ensemble, hit another few keys and the system will total your catalog order for you. You can, if you wish, place an order without ever interacting with another human being.

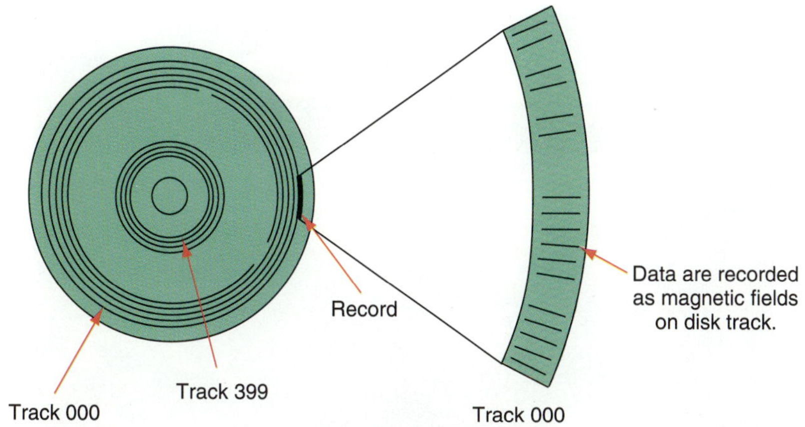

Figure 4-1
Surface of a disk.
Unlike a phonograph record, which bears a single spiral groove, a disk is composed of concentric tracks. The number of tracks per surface varies among manufacturers. The hard disk shown here has 400 tracks. Diskettes commonly have only 40 or 80 tracks.

Disk Systems for Large Computers

The disks used by large computers—mainframes, superminis, and supercomputers—are commonly 14-inch-diameter aluminum platters that are coated on both sides with a magnetizable substance such as ferrous oxide. Records are stored in concentric rings, or **tracks** (see Figure 4-1). Characters are represented by binary bits, which appear as magnetic fields on the tracks. Each track may consist of several records.

Track.
A path on an input/output medium on which data are recorded.

On most disk systems that serve large computers, each track is designed to carry the same total amount of data, even though the tracks near the outer edge are much longer than those nearer the center and move past the read/write heads faster. This design constraint keeps the data transfer rate constant throughout the system, independent of the location of the track being accessed. The number of tracks per disk varies among manufacturers, but it is typically several hundred. Data are read or written by a read/write head, which moves above or below the spinning disk to access the disk tracks.

Disks on disk systems designed for large computers often are assembled into groups of six, eight, ten, twelve, or some other number, depending on the manufacturer, and mounted on a shaft that spins all the disks at the same rate of speed. The disks are spaced far enough apart to permit the read/write heads to move in and out between the disks. Such an assembly is called a **disk pack.** Depending on the disk system in use, packs may be removable or nonremovable.

Disk pack.
A group of tiered hard disks that are mounted on a shaft and treated as a unit.

Figure 4-2 shows a removable disk pack. The pack is encased in a plastic shell, similar to a cake cover, to protect the recording surfaces from foreign objects. On removable-pack systems, the top and bottom surfaces of the pack aren't used, because they are the ones most exposed to dust. Nonremovable-pack disk systems use hermetically sealed packs and are much less vulnerable to exposure to foreign matter.

Disk unit.
A direct-access secondary storage device that uses magnetic or optical disk as the principal medium.

Disk packs function on a device called a **disk unit.** Figure 4-3 shows a removable-pack disk unit, onto which packs are manually mounted by operators. These units are plugged into the computer, enabling it to ac-

Figure 4-2
A disk pack.
A disk pack such as the removable one depicted here must be mounted in a disk unit like the one in Figure 4-3 in order for data on any of the disk surfaces to be processed.

Figure 4-3 A removable-pack disk system.
Disks are assembled into disk packs, which are mounted in the disk unit for processing.

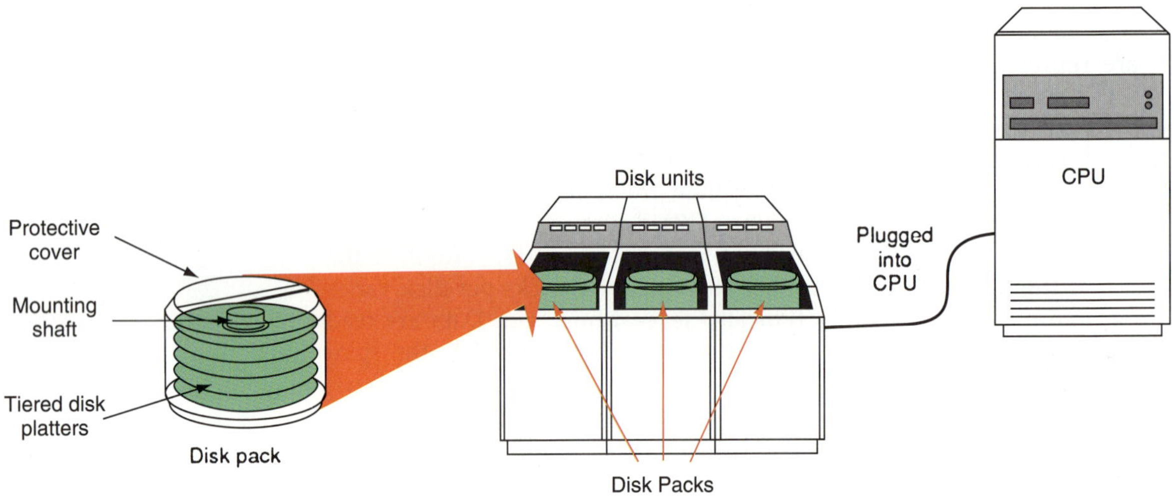

cess any of the data recorded on the disks. A disk pack bears the same relation to a disk unit as a row of phonograph records does to a jukebox. Figure 4-3 also illustrates the relationship between a disk pack and disk unit.

Access mechanism.
A mechanical device in the disk pack or disk unit that positions the read/write heads on the proper tracks.

Reading and Writing Data. Most disk systems have at least one read/write head for each recording surface. These heads are mounted on a device called an **access mechanism.** Figure 4-4 shows how access is accomplished with a *movable access mechanism.* The rotating shaft spins at high speeds (3,600 revolutions per minute is common), and the mecha-

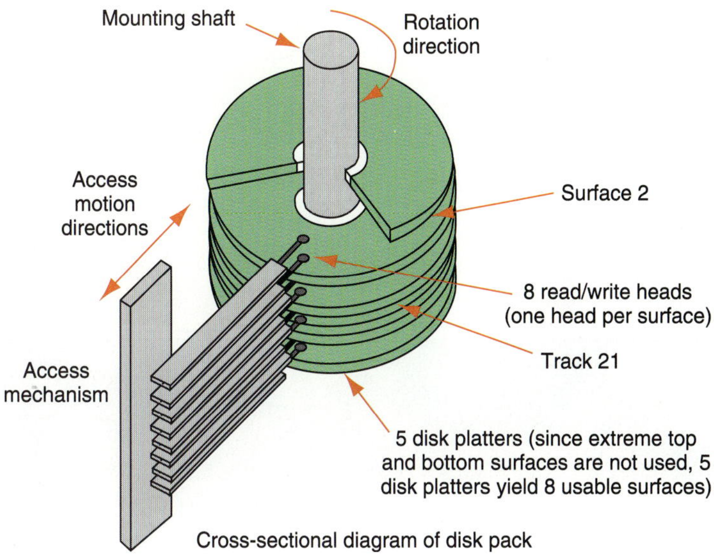

Figure 4-4
A movable access mechanism.
Each read/write head is assigned to a particular disk surface. As the mounting shaft spins the disks, the comblike access mechanism moves the heads in or out between the disks to read or write data on the tracks. On most systems, all the heads move together. Thus, if you need to retrieve data from track 21 on surface 2, all the read/write heads must move together to track 21. At that point, the head assigned to surface 2 will read the data. Only one head may be actively reading or writing at any given time.

nism moves the heads in and out *together* between the disk surfaces to access the required data. Movable devices are by far the most popular type of access mechanism.

A head never touches the surface of a disk at any time, even during reading and writing. Head and disk are very close, however. The IBM 3350 disk heads, for example, glide 17 millionths of an inch above the recording surfaces. A human hair or even a smoke particle (about 2,500 and 100 millionths of an inch, respectively), if present on a surface, will damage the disks and heads—an event known as a *head crash.* As Figure 4-5 shows, the results are like placing a pebble on your favorite phonograph album while playing it.

Disk Cylinders. In disk systems that use disk packs, an important principle for understanding disk storage and access strategies is the concept of **disk cylinders.** Again consider the disk system in Figure 4-4. In the disk pack shown, there are 8 possible recording surfaces with 400 tracks per surface. One might envision the disk pack as being composed of 400 imaginary concentric cylinders, each consisting of 8 tracks, as illustrated in Figure 4-6. Outer cylinders fit over the inner ones like sleeves. Each cylinder is equivalent to a track position to which the heads on the access mechanism can move. With a movable access mechanism, all the read/write heads are positioned on the same cylinder when data are read from or written to one of the tracks on that cylinder.

Disk cylinder.
All tracks on a disk pack that are accessible with a single movement of the access mechanism.

Disk Access Time. In a removable-pack disk system with a movable access mechanism, three events must occur in order to access data.

First, the read/write head must move to the cylinder on which the data are stored. Suppose, for example, that the read/write head is on cyl-

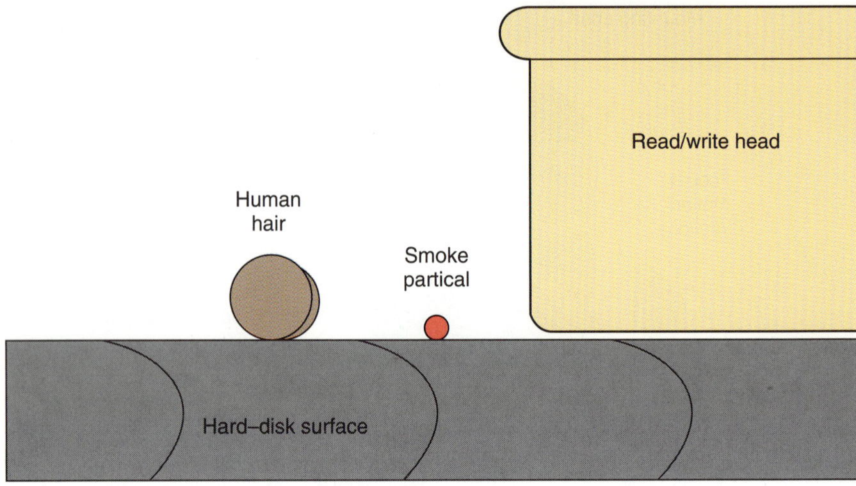

Figure 4-5
The space between a disk and a read/write head compared with a smoke particle and a human hair. A human hair or even a smoke particle, if present on a fast-spinning hard-disk surface, can damage both the surface and the read/write head.

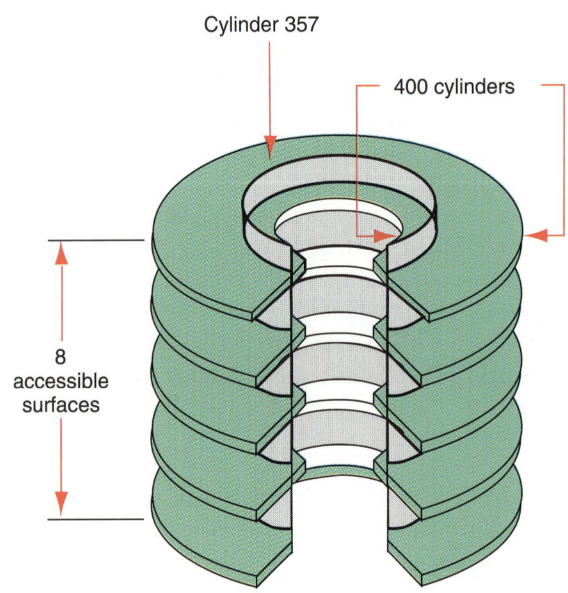

Figure 4-6
The cylinder concept. To envision a particular cylinder, think of pushing an actual cylinder such as a tin can downward through the same track in each disk in the pack. In this example, cylinder 357 is made up of track 357 on surfaces 1 through 8.

inder 5 and we wish to retrieve data from cylinder 36. For us to do this, the mechanism must move inward to cylinder 36. The time required for this task is referred to as *seek time.*

Second, when a read or write order is issued, the heads usually are not aligned over the position on the track on which the desired data are stored. So some delay occurs while the mounting shaft rotates the disks into the proper position. (The disks are always spinning whether or not reading or writing is taking place.) The time needed for completing this alignment is called *rotational delay.*

Tomorrow

Disk Arrays

How a Gang of Small Disks Can Team Up to Outperform a Larger Disk

It's a new and radical idea but one that some experts say may signal an important trend for disk technology in the near future. It's called the *disk array,* and it consists of a set of several small disks that work together as a unit.

Preliminary findings have shown that disk arrays made up of 5¼-inch hard disks can outperform a single 14-inch disk of the same capacity. Performance increases of several orders of magnitude have been observed in five critical areas: cutting access times, increasing reliability, reducing power consumption, slicing the cost of storing each byte, and reducing the physical size of storage hardware.

Several reasons account for the initial success of disk arrays. First, small disks theoretically can spin faster than larger ones. The larger a disk gets, the greater the potential for wobble at the outer edge of the disk, which causes reading and writing problems. (The more the wobble, the farther away from the disk surface the read/write heads must be positioned to prevent a head crash.) Second, data retrieved from a single disk is read from a track serially, one character after another. When several disks work together, they can be hooked up so that data are drawn off simultaneously—that is, in parallel—speeding up processing considerably (see figure).

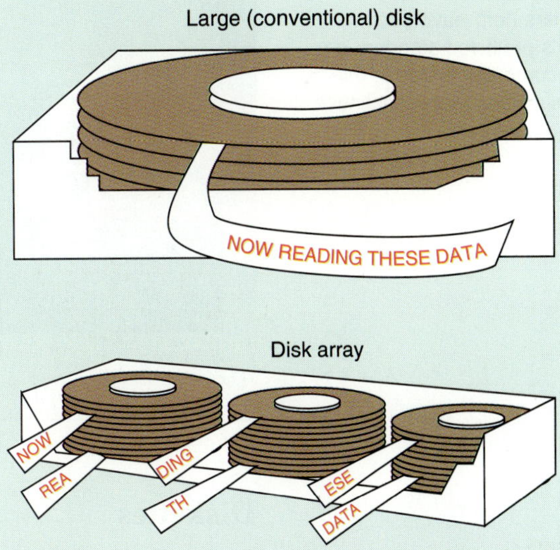

Disk arrays. By reading and writing track data in parallel rather than serially, access times can be sharply reduced.

A switch to disk arrays is likely to cause the greatest upheaval in the mainframe disk marketplace. Currently, about $12 billion is spent annually on mainframe disk products.

Third, once the read/write head is positioned over the correct data, the data must be read from disk and transferred to the computer (or transferred from the computer and written onto disk). This last step is known as *data movement time.* The sum of these three components is known as **disk access time.**

Disk access time. The time taken to locate and read (or position and write) data on a disk device.

To minimize disk access time on a system such as the one depicted in Figure 4-4, related data should be stored on the same cylinder. This strategy sharply reduces seek time. The use of disk arrays—covered in the Tomorrow box—is a new disk access strategy that may signal a new trend in disk technology.

Addressing. Every disk system is *addressable.* This means that each data record or program may be stored and later accessed at a unique *disk address,* which can be automatically determined by the computer system. Procedures for locating records on disk are discussed in the section entitled "Data Organization."

Figure 4-7
Diskettes.
Despite the fact that 3½-inch diskettes (left) have become today's preferred standard on microcomputer systems, 5¼-inch diskettes (right) continue to enjoy wide use.

Diskettes

Diskettes, or *floppy disks,* are small, round platters encased in a plastic jacket. The platters are made of a tough Mylar plastic coated with a magnetizable substance. As with hard disks, each side of the diskette contains concentric tracks, which are encoded with 0- and 1-bits when data and programs are written to them (refer back to Figure 4-1). The jacket is lined with a soft material that wipes the disk clean as it spins.

Unlike their counterparts in hard-disk systems, read/write heads touch a diskette's surface. Also, while hard disks often spin continuously even when not in use, a diskette spins only when a read or write command is issued to its drive. Both of these facts, as well as their removability and flexible surface, account for the diskette's relatively slow rate of speed (400 to 600 rpm) and lengthy access time.

Types of Diskettes. There are dozens of types of diskettes commercially available. If one were to cite a single property that most distinguishes one of these products from another, however, that property would probably be *size.*

Diskettes are widely available in two sizes (diameters)—3½ inches and 5¼ inches—as shown in Figure 4-7. Historically, the 5¼-inch diskettes came along first, then their 3½-inch counterparts. The 5¼-inch diskettes are encased in flexible, plastic-coated cardboard jackets, whereas the 3½-inch diskettes are contained in rugged plastic cases that can fit into a shirt pocket. Strange as it may seem, 3½-inch diskettes can store more data than 5¼-inch ones.

Despite their small size, diskettes can store a respectable amount of data. Common capacities are 360 kilobytes and 1.2 megabytes for 5¼-inch diskettes, and 720 kilobytes and 1.44 megabytes for 3½-inch diskettes. A 360-kilobyte diskette can store over 100 typewritten pages of information; thus, 1.44-megabyte diskettes can store up to 400 pages. The 1.2- and 1.44-megabyte diskettes are often called *high-density* diskettes; the 360-

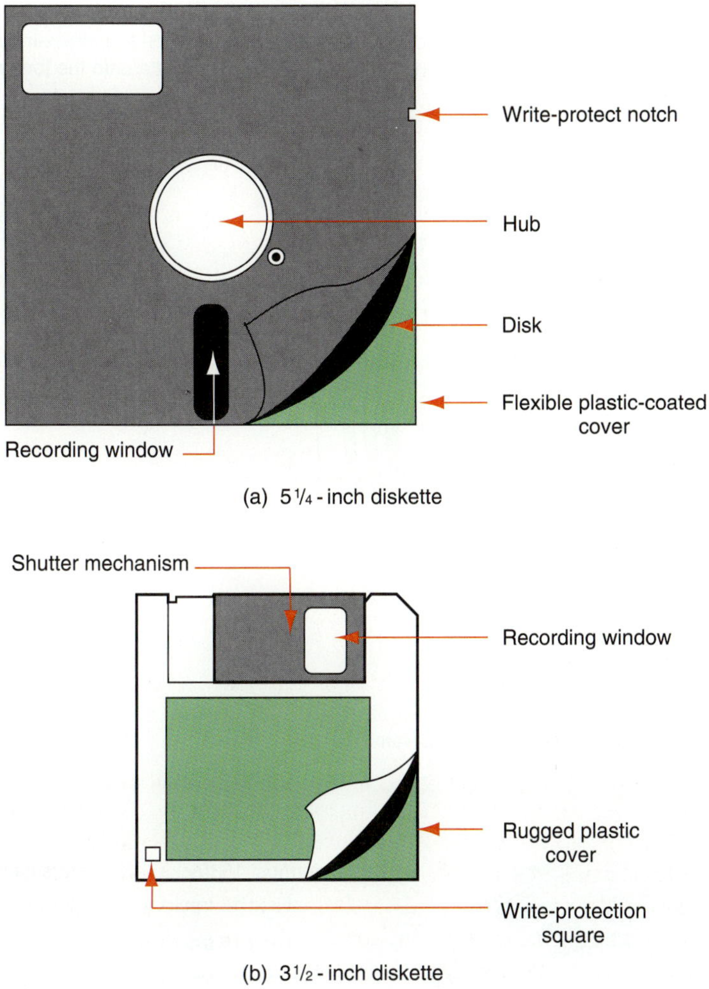

Figure 4-8
5¼-inch and 3½-inch diskettes compared.
(a) In a 5¼-inch diskette, the recording window is always open, meaning that the disk surface is constantly exposed. (b) In a 3½-inch diskette, the recording window exposes the disk surface only when the shutter mechanism is slid to the left, which happens during reading and writing operations. In addition to offering this improved design feature, having a more rugged cover, and being more compact, 3½-inch diskettes can store more data than can 5¼-inch diskettes.

and 720-kilobyte diskettes, *double-density* or *low-density*. (Density refers to how tightly bits of data are packed on the diskette.)

To protect data, diskettes also contain a write-protect notch or square (see Figure 4-8). This prevents the user from accidentally writing on the disk. Covering the notch on 5¼-inch diskettes makes it impossible to write on the surface. The convention on 3½-inch diskettes is the opposite: Exposing the notch or square makes writing impossible.

Sectoring on Diskettes. Computer systems differ in the number of **sectors** into which they divide, or format, a disk. Sectors divide a diskette into addressable, pie-shaped pieces. For example, diskettes formatted with IBM and similar computer systems commonly are formatted into 8, 9, 15, or 18 sectors, depending on the type of diskette and operating system used. Typically there are 512 bytes per sector (see Figure 4-9a). On the Apple Macintosh line of computers, which uses 3½-inch diskettes, the

Sector.
An addressable pie-shaped area on a disk.

Figure 4-9 Formatting (sectoring) a diskette.
(a) IBM microcomputers and similar machines use the same number of sectors on every track with both 3½- and 5¼-inch diskettes. (b) The Apple Macintosh line of computers uses a variable sectoring scheme, packing more data onto the longer, outer tracks.

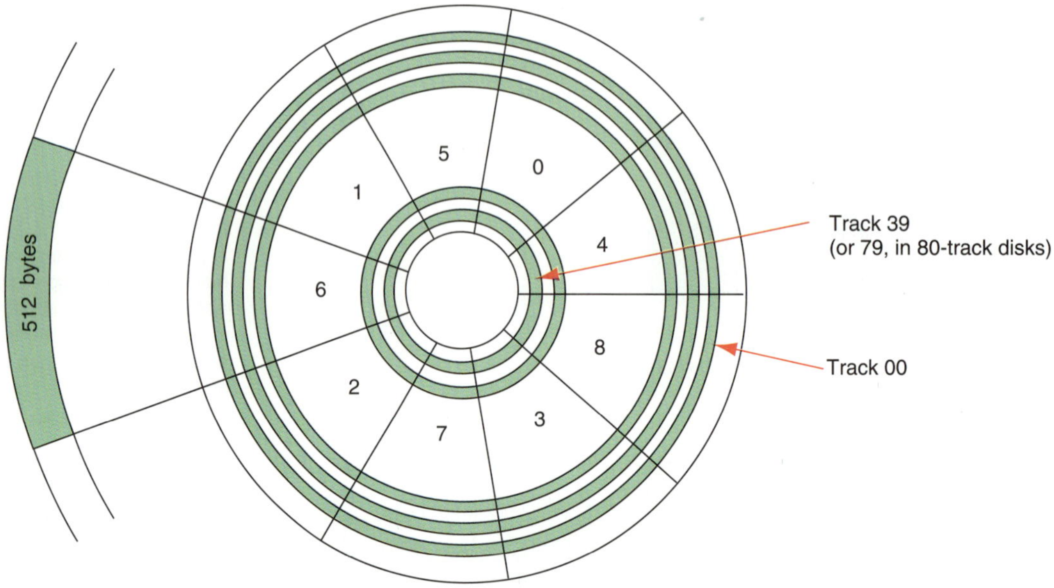

(a) Formatting 5¼-inch diskettes on IBM PC–family microcomputers and similar machines

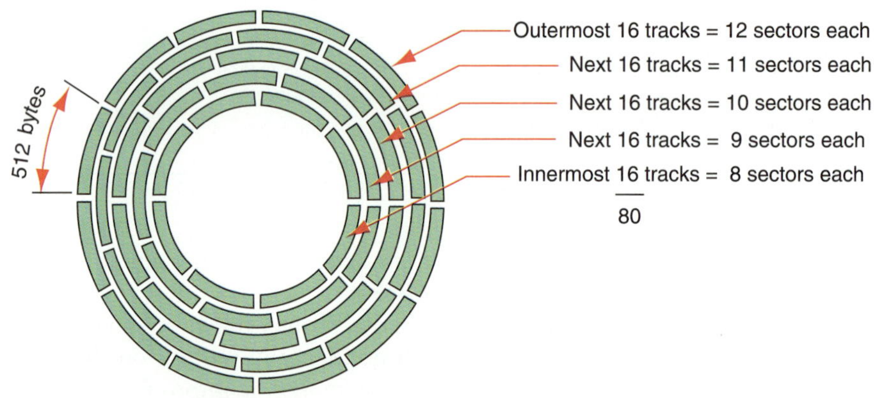

(b) Formatting 3½-inch diskettes on the Apple Macintosh line

number of sectors varies on a single disk. The outermost 16 tracks have 12 sectors each, the next 16 tracks have 11 sectors, the next 16 have 10 sectors, and so forth (see Figure 4-9b).

Formatting a diskette organizes it into addressable storage locations, as Figure 4-9 illustrates. For instance, let's assume that the diskette in Figure 4-9a has 40 tracks, as do most disks used with the IBM PC, and

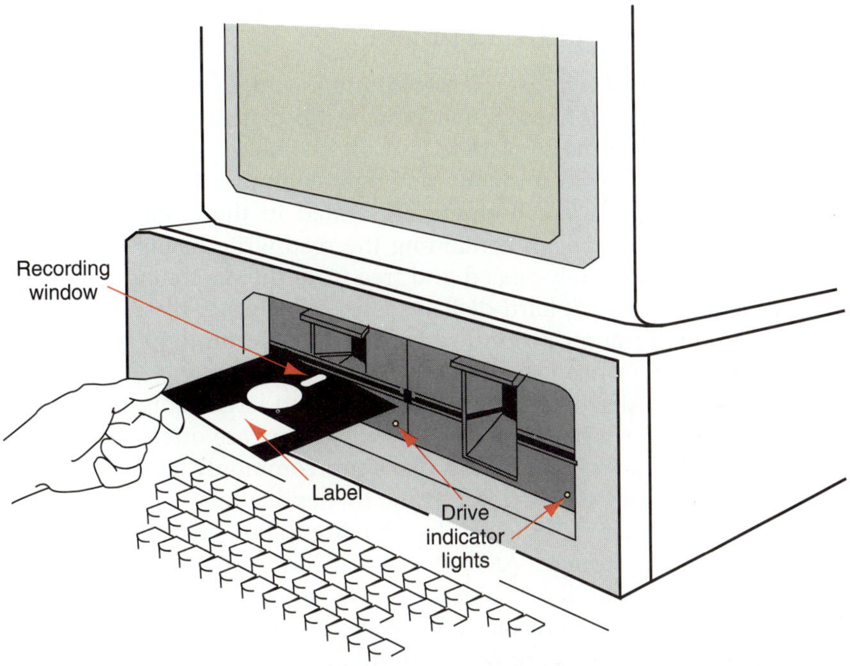

Figure 4-10
Inserting a diskette into a drive.
Diskettes correctly fit into the drive only one way—usually with the label up and the recording window toward the drive door, as shown.

that the computer system divides the diskette into 9 sectors, as shown. Formatting the diskette causes it to be divided into nine pie-shaped sectors, 0 through 8. Because the diskette has 40 tracks, this results in $9 \times 40 = 360$ addressable storage locations per side. On many microcomputer systems, a FORMAT command is used to *format* the diskette, and a diskette is not usable for storage unless it has been formatted.

A **file directory** on the diskette, which the computer system automatically maintains, keeps track of the contents of each location. This directory shows the name of each diskette file, its size, and the sector in which it begins.

File directory.
A listing on an input/output medium that provides such data as name, length, and starting address for each file on the medium.

Using Diskettes. To use a diskette, the operator inserts it into a device called a *diskette drive* (see Figure 4-10). When using 5¼-inch diskette drives, the operator must manually shut the drive door before the diskette can be accessed. Drives for 3½-inch diskettes do not contain a door as such; instead, the operator just inserts the diskette into the appropriate slot. In both cases, there is only one correct way to insert the diskette into the drive.

While the diskette is rotating, the read/write heads access tracks through the recording window. While the indicator light for a drive is on, meaning that the read/write heads are accessing the diskette in the drive, you must not try to remove the diskette.

Caring for Diskettes. Diskettes may look like unsophisticated pieces of plastic, but they are extremely sensitive items and must be cared for accordingly. Care of diskettes is covered in detail in Chapter 13.

Hard Disks for Small Computers

Small computers—such as microcomputers and low-end minicomputers—often employ nonremovable Winchester disks. *Winchester disk* systems consist of rigid metal platters that are tiered on a mounting shaft in the same way as disks accompanying larger computers, discussed earlier. However, these disks are hermetically sealed in the storage unit along with the access mechanism containing the read/write heads. Because the storage unit is completely sealed and free from the air contamination that plagues removable-pack hard-disk systems, Winchester disks need not go through an air filtration procedure before they are brought online. Also, they result in fewer head crashes if maintained properly.

Winchester disks are used on both small and large computer systems. On larger computer systems—where Winchesters are often referred to as *fixed disks* or *sealed-pack disks*—the disks are commonly 14 or 8 inches in diameter. Companies that don't want to handle removable packs find these systems attractive, but they face having to buy additional disk units if they need more storage. Also, they must have room in their data centers for the additional disk cabinets.

Although many microcomputer systems still use diskettes heavily, Winchester disk systems are now a standard feature on virtually all computer systems sold for business purposes. In the microcomputing world, Winchesters are commonly referred to as *hard disks.* They are especially appropriate when an organization needs greater amounts of online storage and faster access to programs and data than diskettes can provide. If you have a 40-megabyte Winchester unit, you have the storage equivalent of about 100 double-sided/double-density 5¼-inch diskettes online the minute you turn on the power. Also, you don't have to constantly shuffle diskettes in and out of disk drives.

Hard-disk units for microcomputers are most commonly found in capacities of roughly 20, 40, 60, and 80 megabytes. Devices that store 100 megabytes or more are now also available. For desktop micros, hard disks are most widely available in 3½-inch diameters. The IBM PS/2 Model 70 386 computer, for instance, is available with either a 60 MB or 120 MB 3½-inch hard disk, whereas the IBM PS/2 Model 95 XP 486 computer comes with either an 80 MB, 160 MB, or 320 MB 3½-inch drive.

Hard-disk units on microcomputer systems can be internal or external. An *internal* hard-disk system is fitted into your computer's system unit in the space normally occupied by one of the diskette drives (see Figure 4-11). An *external* system is a detached hardware unit that has its own power supply. Many external systems also have a built-in bay for a tape cartridge, which can be used to back up important programs and data. On larger computer systems, hard-disk units are always external.

Sectoring. Hard-disk systems, like those that accompany the IBM PC AT, PS/2, and similar computers, use a sectoring scheme similar to that for diskettes to store data. On the internal hard disks available with some PS/2 models, for instance, tracks are broken into 17 sectors. On each of the 4 recordable surfaces, there is a total of 732 tracks. In the language of hard disks, the tracks on these surfaces trace out 732 cylinders.

Figure 4-11
Internal hard disks.
Hard-disk systems for desktop microcomputers most commonly use 3½-inch disks. Capacities often range from 20 megabytes to a few hundred megabytes.

Subdirectories. Because hard disks have large storage capacities, files commonly are organized hierarchically into *subdirectories.* As Figure 4-12 shows, at the top of the hierarchy is a "master" directory called the root directory. The *root directory,* among other things, contains a list of subdirectories on the hard disk. You can store all of your operating system programs in one subdirectory, word-processed documents in another subdirectory, and so forth. Moreover, you can further divide these subdirectories. As shown in Figure 4-12, you can organize your word processing subdirectory by putting letters and school papers into two lower subdirectories. If you so wish, you can add several additional levels of subdirectories.

Later, when you want to access a file in any subdirectory, you must specify the *path* through the subdirectories to get to the file; for example,

```
C:\WORD\LETTER\MARY
```

Here the hard disk is the C drive and WORD and LETTER are the names of the two subdirectories on the path to a subdirectory of letters named MARY. On most microcomputer systems, the *A* and *B* drive designations are reserved for floppy drives.

Partitioning. *Partitioning* a hard disk enables you to divide a hard disk into separate disk drives, such as *D, E, F,* and so forth. You can change the number and size of the partitions at any time, although doing so will destroy any data in the partitions. Thus, you have to download any affected data onto diskettes or tape first and then load the data back onto the repartitioned hard disk.

Figure 4-12 Organizing files into subdirectories.
Shown here is a root directory and three levels of subdirectories. The subdirectory MARY, for instance, would contain all letters (files) written to Mary.

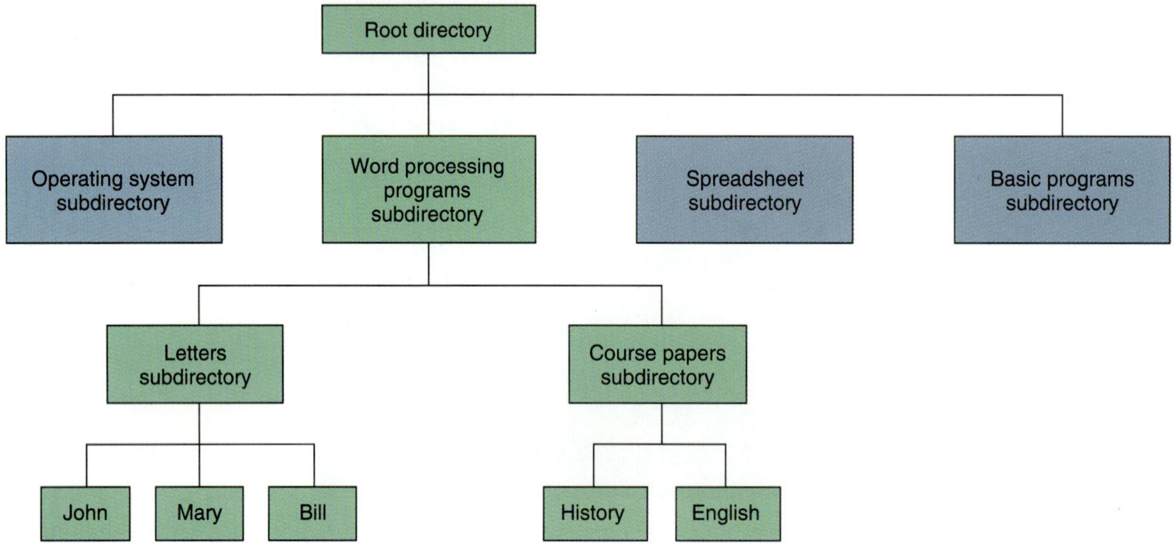

Partitioning a hard disk enables you to use different operating systems on it—say, PC-DOS, OS/2, and UNIX. Each operating system has its own method of formatting and managing disk space. By assigning each operating system to a different partition, you avoid the problem of having an operating system deal with a partition that works in a manner foreign to it.

Disk Standards. When buying a hard disk for a microcomputer system, it is easy to become confused when vendors throw around such acronyms as MFM, RLL, ESDI, and SCSI. These acronyms generally refer to the density with which data can be packed onto the disk, the speed of the disk, and the way the disk interfaces to the board (sometimes called the *disk controller*) that runs it.

The oldest standards are *MFM* (modified frequency modulation) and *RLL* (run length limited). These standards use 17 and 26 sectors per track, respectively, and are commonly found on disks with a capacity of 40 or fewer megabytes. *ESDI* (enhanced small device interface) is widely used today by IBM and IBM-compatible '386 computers with a hard-disk capacity of 60 or more megabytes. It uses 34 sectors per track, packing data more tightly than both the MFM and RLL formats. It is also faster. Unfortunately, like MFM and RLL, an ESDI interface allows users access to only two disk drives at one time.

Some industry experts predict that *SCSI* (small computer system interface) will become the main hard-disk standard by the late 1990s. SCSI (pronounced "scuzzy") allows 26 or 36 sectors per track and faster access

Figure 4-13
A hard card.
Hard cards, such as Plus Development's Hardcard, the original hard-disk-on-a-card product, are popular with users who are looking for a compact alternative to the conventional hard disk.

speeds than ESDI. It is now the prevailing standard for Apple Macintosh computers and allows connection of up to seven devices—disks and other hardware—on one board. SCSI, like ESDI, is widely used on disks with a capacity of 60 or more megabytes.

Other Types of Magnetic Disks

Although Winchester disks dominate the hard-disk scene for small computers, there are alternatives. Two of these are the hard card and the cartridge disk.

Hard Cards. An increasingly popular alternative to the Winchester disk in the microcomputer hard-disk marketplace is the hard card (see Figure 4-13). **Hard cards** are hard disks that are configured onto an add-in board. As with any other board, the hard card fits into a slot in the computer's system unit. The card contains both the disk and the interface circuitry necessary for dealing with the CPU. Although relatively expensive, this type of hard-disk alternative is ideal for people who need hard-disk speed and capacity in a limited space.

Hard card.
A hard disk that has been configured onto an add-in board.

Cartridge Disk. Cartridge disk devices are commonly found on microcomputer and minicomputer systems. **Cartridge disk** devices used on microcomputer systems are external hardware units that accept small, removable high-capacity disk cartridges (see Figure 4-14). The high-capacity disk is packaged into a square case (i.e., the cartridge) to protect the

Cartridge disk.
A magnetic disk in which a single disk platter is contained in a sealed plastic case.

Figure 4-14
Microcomputer cartridge disk.
Cartridge disk provides a storage alternative with the capacity and performance of a conventional hard disk and the removability of a diskette.

disk's contents. The operator inserts a cartridge into a cartridge drive in a manner similar to inserting a diskette into a diskette drive. Cartridge disks are commonly 3½ inches in diameter and have a capacity of about 10 to 90 megabytes. Their biggest pluses are large storage capacity and, because of their removability, backup and security. The biggest drawback is cost—the disk unit can cost $2,000 to $3,000 and the cartridges about $100 apiece.

Cartridge disks also exist for minicomputers. The "removable pack," or disk cartridge, usually consists of a single 14-inch platter encased in an opaque plastic shell (see Figure 4-15). Because cartridge disks have only one platter, they have less data-carrying capacity than do multiplatter packs.

RAM Disk and Cache Disk

RAM disk and cache disk are two strategies for creatively using RAM to compensate for the access-speed differences between primary memory and secondary storage. Both methods overcome the slow speeds involved with fetching instructions or data from disk, and both can be implemented inexpensively under certain conditions. On many computer systems sold today, RAM disk and cache disk are built-in features.

RAM disk.
A disk management system in which a portion of RAM is set up to function as a disk.

RAM Disk. **RAM disk,** sometimes referred to as *electronic disk, E-disk,* or *disk emulation,* is a storage alternative in which the computer's operating system is "tricked" into thinking it is dealing with secondary storage when in fact it is dealing with primary memory.

When computer systems process programs or data files, typically only a limited number of program instructions or data records are in primary memory at any given time. When more instructions or data are needed, the operating system must fetch them from disk. However, if your system has enough RAM to store the entire program or data file, you can use an emulation package to load it into RAM and point the system to this part of RAM every time it would go to the disk to fetch additional program commands or data. Thus, the emulation software essentially tricks the system into thinking it's dealing with the disk drive when it actually is dealing with RAM. Such a technique can boost the speed of applications processing considerably.

Figure 4-15
Minicomputer cartridge disk. Most cartridge disks for minis consist of a single hard-disk platter in a plastic casing.

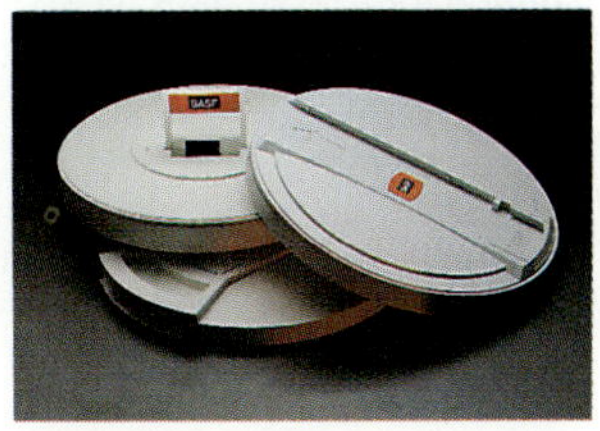

RAM disk is implemented in a number of ways. For instance, a vendor selling such a product might offer it as a "plain vanilla" software routine, available through coded instructions on a multifunction board or through a disk-based program. The routine enables you to "tell" your computer system how many bytes of primary memory you want to set aside as RAM disk. This inexpensive approach to RAM disk is commonly used on microcomputer systems.

Another vendor selling a RAM-disk product might offer it as a dedicated add-in board with a built-in, RAM-like static memory that can be established as RAM disk. Although this second approach is more expensive than the first, it affords the luxury of not using up primary memory and can provide access speeds 50 to 200 times faster than that of rotating disks.

Cache Disk. **Cache disk** refers to a strategy whereby, during any disk access, program or data contents in neighboring disk areas are also fetched and transported to RAM. For instance, if only a single data record needs to be read, a cache-disk feature may read the entire track on which the record is located. The theory behind cache disk is that neighboring program commands and data will likely have to be read later anyway, so one can save disk accesses by bringing those commands or data into RAM early so that they can be accessed more quickly. Thus, caching saves time as well as wear and tear on the disk unit. In portable computers, it can also extend battery life.

Cache disk. A disk management scheme whereby more data than are necessary are read from disk during each time-consuming disk fetch and are stored in RAM to minimize the number of fetches.

Cache disk, like RAM disk, can be implemented in several ways. One method is through an add-in board called a cache card, which contains a semiconductor memory. Some of these memories are five to ten times faster than conventional RAM while costing a fraction of the price of registers. Another method is through a disk controller (the board that manages a hard-disk or diskette unit) that contains a cache-disk feature. Still another possibility is through a software routine (say, as part of an operating system) that will set up a portion of RAM into a cache area. Whichever option one chooses, the cache-disk feature will intercept and process every disk-access command that the operating system issues.

Magnetic Tape

Magnetic tape.
A plastic tape with a magnetic surface for storing data as a series of magnetic spots.

Detachable-reel tape.
Magnetic tape that is wound onto a single reel, which in turn is mounted onto a tape unit with an empty take-up reel.

Cartridge tape.
Magnetic tape in which the supply and take-up reels are contained in a small plastic case.

For years, **magnetic tape** has been one of the most prominent secondary storage alternatives. Although less popular than disk, it is still widely used on all sizes of computer systems. The tapes often are stored either on detachable reels or in cartridges.

Detachable-reel tapes are commonly ½-inch wide and are made of plastic Mylar coated with a magnetizable substance. A standard reel diameter is 10½ inches, although smaller "minireels" are also quite common. A typical 2,400-foot reel can pack data at densities as high as 6,250 bytes per inch. When such a tape is read, it can transfer more data in one second than many secretaries could type in a month—and error free.

Cartridge tapes are housed in a small plastic casing. On microcomputer systems, cartridges are commonly used to back up the contents of a hard disk. These tapes can have huge capacities and work very fast. A ¼-inch tape up to 1,000 feet long can hold 10, 20, 40, or 60 or more megabytes of data and copy the contents of a disk in a matter of minutes. Recently cartridges using *helical-scan* recording methods, which store data at an angle to the edge of the tape rather than perpendicular to it, have permitted storage capacities in the 2 GB range. Cartridge tapes designed specifically for disk backup are sometimes referred to as *streaming tapes.*

The IBM 3480 tape storage system, which is used with the IBM 3090 series of mainframe computers, also uses cartridge tapes. These tapes have twice the number of tracks as traditional detachable-reel tapes and a storage capacity of 200 megabytes. In contrast to streaming tapes, which are intended solely for backup, the IBM 3480 cartridges are designed for general use, including both regular input/output processing operations and backup.

The discussion that follows in this section is based principally on the nine-track, detachable-reel tapes that have been used with mainframes and minicomputers for years. These tape systems are still the most prevalent in the marketplace. Nonetheless, many of the principles described here apply to cartridge tapes as well. Figure 4-16 shows a tape cartridge compared with a conventional, detachable-reel tape.

Processing Tapes

Tape unit.
A secondary storage device on which magnetic tapes are mounted for processing.

A tape must be mounted onto an online **tape unit** (see Figure 4-17) to be processed. Detachable-reel tape units are about the size of a common household refrigerator. The *supply reel* on the unit contains the tape that is to be read from or written to by the computer system. The *take-up reel* collects the tape as it unwinds from the supply reel. As it is processed, the tape passes by a read/write head, which reads data from the tape or records data on it. On many devices, the tape is allowed to droop in a vacuum chamber so that it will not break if the two reels move at different speeds. After processing, the tape is rewound onto the supply reel and removed from the unit. The take-up reel never leaves the unit. On cartridge tape units, the handling of supply and takeup reels is eliminated.

Figure 4-16
Magnetic tape.
Shown here are two tape cartridges and, underneath, a conventional tape reel.

Storing Data on Tape

Figure 4-18 shows how data are stored on nine-track magnetic tape. Data may be coded using the eight-bit byte of either EBCDIC or ASCII-8, depending on the equipment used. Magnetized spots of iron oxide represent 1s; nonmagnetized spots represent 0s. The tape contains a track for

Figure 4-17 Magnetic tape units.
Magnetic tape is often used for backup and for many types of batch processing. (a) In conventional detachable-reel systems, any reels of programs or data to be run must be selected manually from the tape library (background) and mounted on the tape unit, as illustrated here. (b) In cartridge systems, several cartridges can be loaded into hoppers for automatic processing.

(a)

(b)

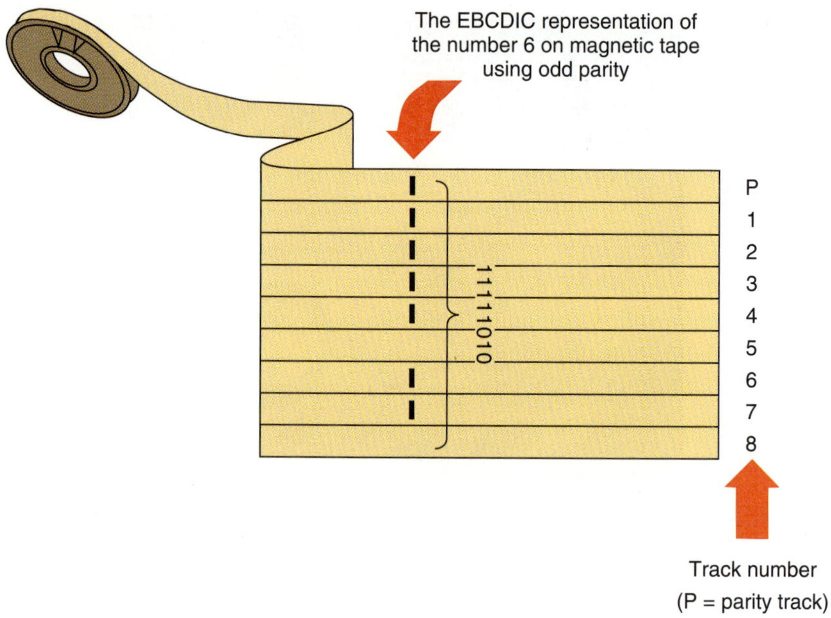

Figure 4-18
Storing data on nine-track magnetic tape.
Shown here is the number 6 represented in EBCDIC (11110110, or 111110110 with the odd-parity track). In the shaded cross-section of the tape, the magnetized spot representing the 1-bit is shown by a vertical mark in the appropriate track. The 0-bit is characterized by the absence of a mark.

each bit of information in a character, plus an additional parity track to allow the computer system to check for transmission errors. The tape unit reads across the nine tracks to identify the character represented in each column. Recall from Chapter 3 that in odd-parity machines, all 1-bits add up to an odd number and in even-parity machines to an even number. An incorrect sum indicates an error. The parity bit is included with the byte representation of each character when it is placed onto tape.

Key field.
A field used to identify a record.

A magnetic tape is basically a long, narrow strip. Thus, when the records in a data file are stored on it, they must be alongside one another in sequence. The sequence often is determined by a **key field,** such as customer ID number, which can be ordered numerically. Every record's key field generally has a different value.

If you want to read a particular record from a tape, you can't go directly to it. Instead, you must pass through all the records that precede it. In a sense, this is similar to the fast forwarding you do on a music tape when the tune you want to hear is in the middle of it. Retrieving records in the order in which they are stored is called *sequential access,* and organizing data in sequence by a key field is called *sequential organization.* We will talk more about data access and organization later in the chapter.

Protecting Tapes

Tape reels are equipped with safety features that prevent operators from accidentally destroying the contents of the tape. One such device is the *file-protection ring* (see Figure 4-19). When tapes are stored offline, these rings are not mounted on the reel. To write onto any part of the tape, thereby destroying any data already stored there, the operator must insert this ring into the center of the reel. The tapes can be read, however, whether or not the ring is present.

Another device designed to protect tapes is the *internal header label.* This label appears at the beginning of the tape and identifies it. The identifying information in the label is usually generated automatically by the computer system or data-entry device. Thus, if you commanded the computer system to process tape AP-601 and the operator accidentally mounted tape AR-601 instead, no processing would occur. Also, the operator would receive a warning message.

Figure 4-19
A magnetic tape with a plastic file-protection ring. When the ring is off the reel, you can read from the tape but you can't write onto it. When the ring is on, you can both read from and write onto the tape.

Other Secondary Storage Alternatives

Magnetic tape and disk systems are by far the most common form of secondary storage. However, a number of other alternatives are possible. In this section, we will discuss the mass storage unit, optical disk storage, and magnetic bubble storage.

Mass Storage Unit

Disk storage units can make large amounts of data available online, but they have limitations. In many systems, disk packs must be manually loaded onto the disk unit, which takes time. Disk systems with nonremovable packs avoid this problem but are limited in the amount of data they can store. For most applications, these drawbacks are not serious. But because the capacity of the largest disk units is only a few billion characters, organizations that must keep massive amounts of data online to the computer have found **mass storage units** extremely useful. A device such as the IBM 3850 mass storage unit can store 472 billion bytes of data, the equivalent of almost 50,000 reels of magnetic tape.

Mass storage unit. A storage device capable of storing billions of bytes of data online.

The IBM 3850 consists of 9,440 cylindrical data cells, each capable of storing 50 million bytes of data. Each cell contains a spool of 770 feet of 3-inch magnetic tape. The cells reside in a honeycomb-shaped rack, as Figure 4-20 shows. When the data in a cell must be retrieved, a mechanical arm pulls the correct cell from its container. Next, the tape is unwound, the data are transferred to disk, and processing is performed. All this takes place automatically, without the aid of human operators.

With mass storage, the user sacrifices speed to gain storage capacity. Retrieval of the data cell and transfer of the data to disk may take as long as 15 seconds. Compared with the fraction of a second that elapses during access to disk, 15 seconds is a long time. Therefore, mass storage is feasible only for applications that require enormous online storage and do not need extremely high speed.

Optical Disk Storage

An emerging technology that many expect will have a profound impact on mass storage strategies in the 1990s is the **optical disk.** With this technology, laser beams write and read data at incredible densities, thousands

Optical disk. A disk read by laser beams rather than by magnetic means.

Figure 4-20
Mass storage unit.
The honeycombed device shown in the photo stores small, cylindrical cartridges containing magnetic tape. The device shown here, the IBM 3850, has enough memory capacity to store a 100-character record for every person in the world or, alternatively, as many words as exist in 27 million pages of a typical daily newspaper.

Figure 4-21 Optical disk units and their optical disks.
(a) Optical disk units targeted to ordinary microcomputer users often accept only a single disk at a time. (b) Optical jukeboxes targeted to commercial users often chain several disk units together. Each disk unit accepts a cartridge (magazine) of several disks. The jukebox shown here has online access of up to 42 optical disks.

(a)

(b)

of times finer than the density of a typical magnetic disk. Data—which can consist of text, graphics, voice, or video images—are placed onto optical disks with high-intensity laser beams that burn tiny holes into the disks' surface. Then a lower-intensity laser beam reads the data inscribed.

Today 3½-inch optical disks can store almost 1 gigabyte of data. Roughly translated, that's close to 1 million pages of text or, alternatively, the contents of approximately 2,500 diskettes. So-called *optical jukeboxes,* which offer online access to scores of optical disks, also have become available. These devices can store 300 or more billion bytes of data (see Figure 4-21).

Figure 4-22
Interactive learning through optical disks.
(a) Compton's *Multimedia Encyclopedia* is a single optical disk containing all 26 volumes of Compton's *Encyclopædia Britannica* and more—in all, about 9 million words, 15,000 pictures, 45 minutes of animated sequences, and an hour of audio. (b) Nursing application at University of Cincinnati Medical Center provides students with an interactive birthing experience that's as close to real life as possible.

(a)

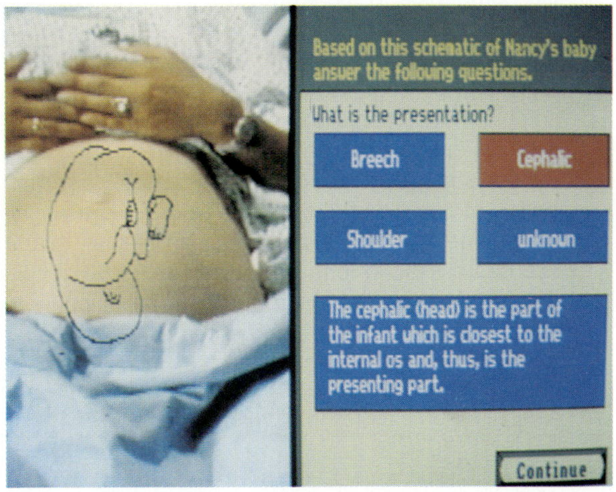

(b)

Optical disk systems have started to become widely used on microcomputer systems, which did not have mass storage available to them until recently. Most optical disk units are of the *CD-ROM* (Compact Disk/ Read-Only Memory) type; that is, you buy a prerecorded disk and "play" (read) it on the optical disk unit attached to your computer. You cannot write new data to the disk in any way. CD-ROM optical disk units are now available for microcomputers for less than $1,000.

There are also systems available that will let you write once to the disk; once written, the data cannot be erased. These are called *WORM* (Write Once, Read Many) disk systems. Since optical disks have very large storage capacities, most users can write to the disk for a year or more before using it up. Optical disk systems that allow you to erase unwanted data—called *fully erasable systems*—have also recently become available.

Uses of optical disk technology abound in today's marketplace. Interactive learning is one major applications area (see Figure 4-22). Helping children in school, for instance, is Compton's *Multimedia Encyclopedia* (Figure 4-22a), a learning product that fits onto a single optical disk 8,784,000 words, 15,000 pictures (many in full color), 45 animated sequences, and

User Solution 4-1

Processing Invoices with Optical Disks

North American Van Lines is one of the first trucking companies in the world to move to an optical-disk-based document system. The system, which costs slightly over a million dollars, is designed to store and process the 4,000 to 7,500 invoices and shipping documents that must be handled daily. The system can manage up to 64 twelve-inch optical disks at one time—collectively about 3.5 million pages of complex data, or over 300 five-drawer filing cabinets worth. (A page with a complex image such as a filled-in form on it can require 50 to 500 times the number of bytes as a page of conventional text data, so the storage capacity of this system is much more impressive than it may initially sound.) North American's system is expected to result in lower operating costs, faster document processing, and, since staff at corporate headquarters can electronically retrieve an important document while a customer is on the phone, better service.

about an hour of audio (featuring music and speeches by John F. Kennedy and Martin Luther King). And, at University of Cincinnati Medical Center, nursing students learn about proper birthing techniques by participating in an instructive video disk segment (Figure 4-22b). If students get confused, they can request help such as a graphic overlay showing the correct position of the fetus. Optical disks are also widely used in document-processing environments, as illustrated in User Solution 4-1.

Despite the excitement over optical disks, hard magnetic disks still have two important advantages. First, hard disks are much faster; 10 to 15 times faster is not unusual. Second, there's a great deal of software written for hard disks that will have to be modified to work on optical disks.

Magnetic Bubble Storage

Magnetic bubble storage. Storage that uses magnetic bubbles to indicate the 0- and 1-bit states.

Magnetic bubble storage is a storage technology in which thousands of magnetized bubbles, each a fraction of the diameter of a human hair, are arranged on a thin film of magnetic material. The presence of a bubble in a location represents a 1-bit and its absence a 0-bit. Bubble storage often is packaged in chip form.

Today magnetic bubbles are popular components in several niche markets. They are used as memory units in terminals, desktop computers, robots, and communications devices.

Data Organization

When a computer system is instructed to use data or programs residing in secondary storage, it first must be able to find the materials. The process of retrieving data and programs in storage is called **data access.** Arranging data for efficient retrieval is called **data organization.**

Data access. Fetching data from a device either sequentially or directly.

Data organization. The process of setting up a data file so that it may subsequently be accessed in some desired way.

As we have seen, a major difference between, say, tape and disk is that data on tape can be *accessed* only sequentially, whereas data on disk can be retrieved both sequentially and in a direct (random) fashion. With sequential access, the records in a file can be retrieved only in the same sequence in which they are physically stored. With direct, or random, access, the time needed to fetch a record is relatively independent of its location in secondary storage.

The need for certain data access methods necessarily dictates the choice of ways to *organize* data files. Let's consider a practical example. Most book libraries are organized with card indexes ordered by title, author, and subject, so you can retrieve books directly. To locate a particular book, you simply look under the book's title in the index, find its call number, and go directly to the appropriate shelf.

However, suppose there were no card indexes and books were organized alphabetically by title on shelves from the first shelf to the last (say, the 758th shelf). With this sequential organization of books, it would take you much longer to retrieve the title you wanted—although you would get a lot of exercise. As you can see, sequential organization does not permit straightforward access to a specific book.

Data organization on computers works in a similar fashion. First, you decide on the type of access you need—direct, sequential, or both. Then you organize the data in a way that will minimize the time needed to retrieve them with the access method selected.

There are many ways to organize data. Here we will describe three—sequential, indexed-sequential, and direct organization.

Sequential Organization. In a file having a **sequential organization,** records follow one another in a predetermined sequence. Sequentially organized files generally are ordered by a key field or fields, such as ID number. Thus, if a four-digit ID number is the key field being used to order the file, the record belonging to, say, ID number 0612 will be stored after number 0611 but before number 0613 (see Figure 4-23).

Sequential organization. Arranging data on a physical medium either ascendingly or descendingly by some key field.

Now that you have an idea of what sequential organization is, let's see how it is used in information processing. Many companies update customer balances and prepare bills at the end of the month. Such an operation is known as a *sequential update.* Two data files are used. The *master file* normally contains the customer's ID number, the amount owed at the beginning of the month, and additional information about the customer. This file is sorted by the key field, customer ID number, and records are arranged in ascending sequence—from the lowest ID number to the highest. The *transaction file* contains all the transactions made during the month by old customers, who appear in the master file, and by new

Figure 4-23 Sequential organization of records on tape.

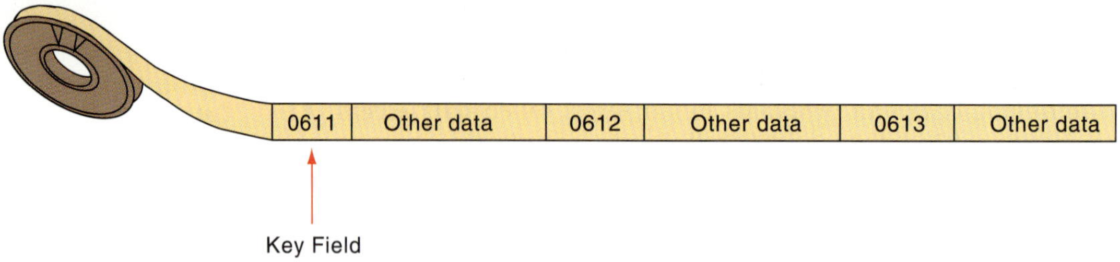

customers, who do not. Transactions might include purchases and payments. Like the master file, the transaction file is ordered in ascending sequence by customer ID number.

In a sequential update, the two files are processed together in the manner shown in Figure 4-24. The sequential-update program reads a record from each file. If the key fields match, the operation specified in the transaction file is performed. Note that in Figure 4-24, the key fields of the first records in each file match. Thus, record 101 is updated to the updated customer master file. For example, if the transaction file shows that customer 101 bought a toaster, data on this purchase are added to the master file. Next, both files are "rolled forward" to the next records. Here the program observes that customer 102 is not in the master file, since the next master file record after 101 is 103. Therefore, this must be a new customer, and the program will create a new record for customer 102 in the updated master file. At this point, only the transaction file will be rolled forward, to customer 103. The program now observes that this record matches the one to which it is currently pointing in the master file. However, the transaction file indicates that 103 is a new customer. Hence, there appears to be an inconsistency, since the master file contains only old customers. The program makes no entry in the updated master file but sends information about this transaction to the error report.

The processing continues in this manner until both files are exhausted. The processing is sequential because the computer processes the records in both files in the order in which they physically appear.

Indexed-sequential organization.
A method of organizing data on a direct-access medium so that they can be accessed directly (through an index) or sequentially.

Indexed-Sequential Organization. **Indexed-sequential organization** is a way of organizing data for both sequential and direct access. This type of organization requires disk, since tapes can't provide direct access. Records are ordered on the disk by key field. Also, several indexes are created to locate these records later. These indexes work similarly to those in a phone book. For example, if the top of a phone book page reads "Alexander—Ashton," you'll know to look for the phone number of Amazon Sewer Service on that page. When implemented on a computer, as Figure 4-25 shows, such indexes permit rapid access to records.

Many computer systems have systems programs that help programmers set up indexes and indexed-sequential-organized files painlessly. As

Figure 4-24 A sequential update of a master file.
Each customer record in the original master file might contain the customer's ID number (the key field), name, address, amount owed, and credit limit. For simplicity, only the key field is shown in the illustration. The transaction file contains a record of each customer transaction. Each record in this file might contain the customer's ID number (the key field), the amount of the purchase or payment, and the type of transaction involved (update, add, or delete). Only the key field and type of transaction are shown in the illustration. As both files are processed together, an updated master file is produced, as well as a printed listing of records that couldn't be processed because of some discrepancy.

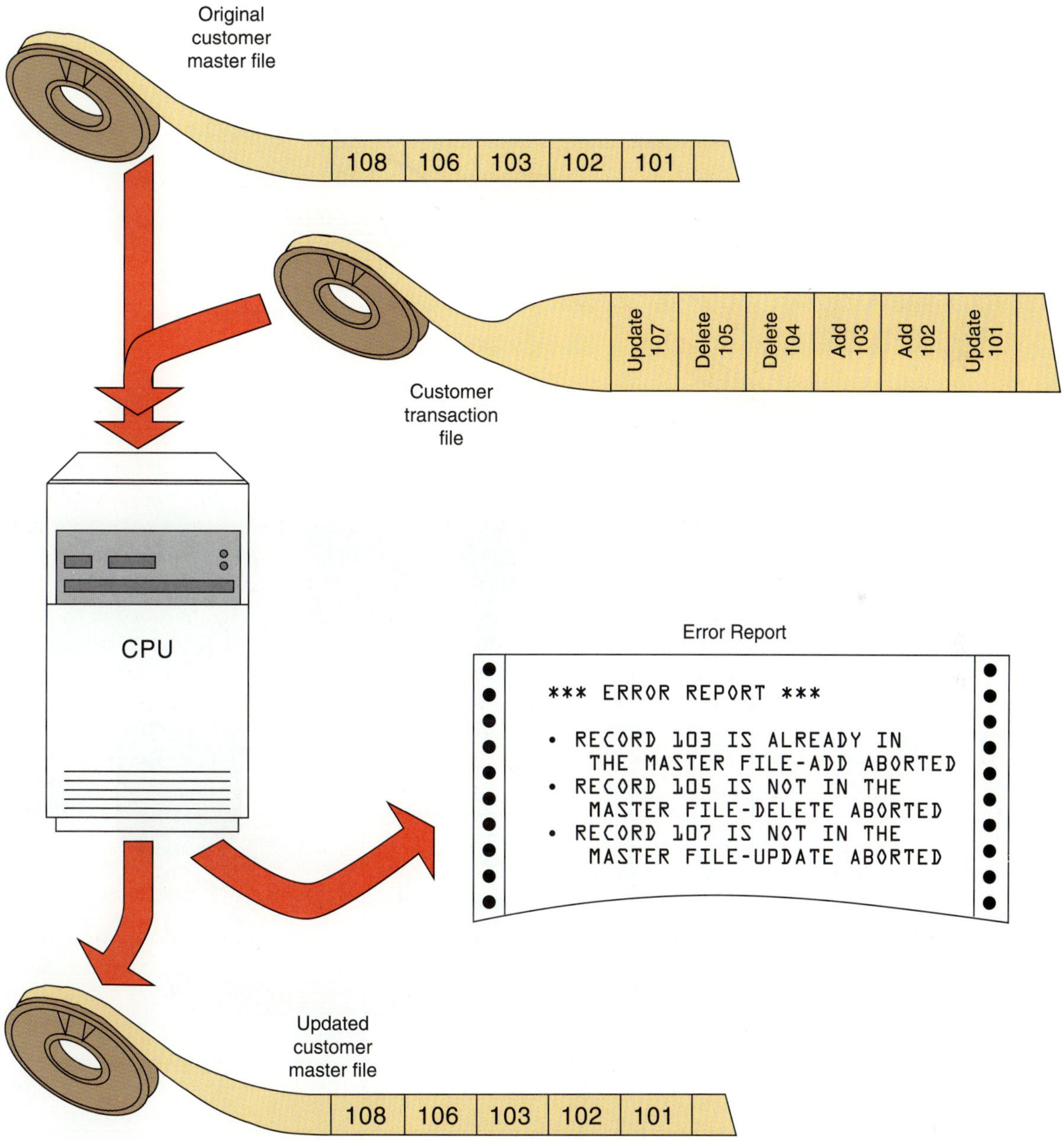

Figure 4-25 Indexed-sequential organization.
Records are ordered on disk by key, and all record addresses are entered in an index. To process a request to find a record—say, record 200—the computer system first searches a cylinder index and then a track index for the record's address. In the cylinder index, it learns that the record is on cylinder 009. The computer system then consults the track index for cylinder 009, where it observes that the record is on track 2 of that cylinder. The access mechanism then proceeds to this track to locate the record.

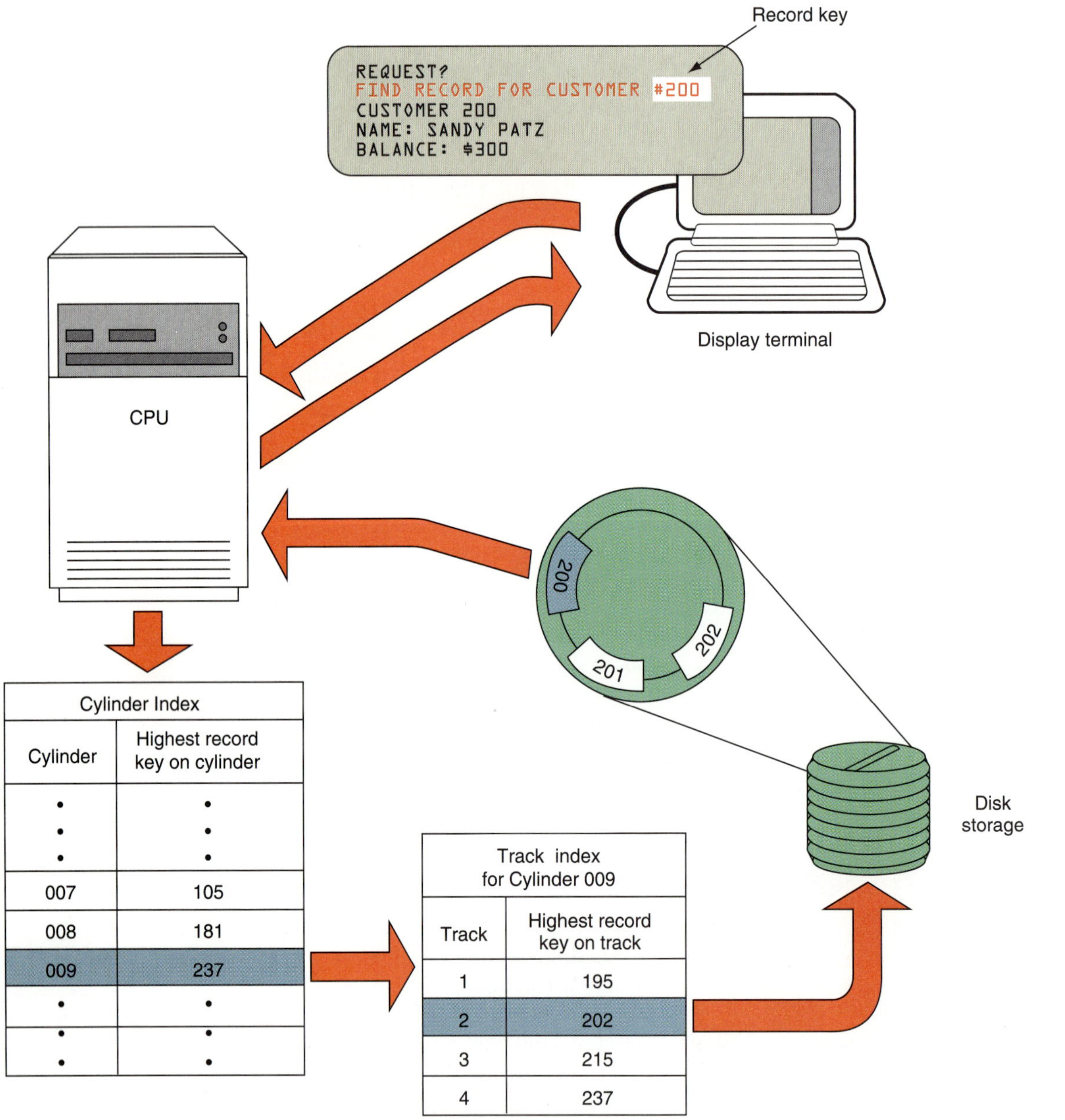

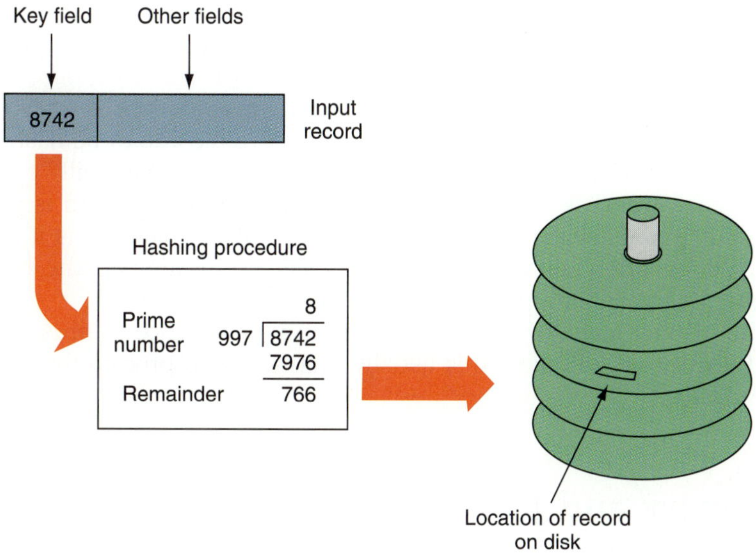

Figure 4-26
Hashing illustrated.
The CPU follows a hashing procedure to assign a record to a disk address. In this case, the hashing procedure involves dividing the key field by the prime number closest to 1,000—997. The remainder corresponds to an actual disk address.

records are added to or deleted from a file, the systems software automatically adds them to or deletes them from the disk and updates the index. Because the records remain organized sequentially on the disk, the file can be processed sequentially at any time.

Direct Organization. Although indexed files are suitable for many applications, the process of finding disk addresses through index searches can be time consuming. Direct-organization schemes have been developed to provide faster direct access.

Direct organization eliminates the need for an index by translating the record's key field directly into a disk address. This is done with the use of mathematical formulas called *hashing algorithms.* Several hashing procedures have been developed. One of the simplest involves dividing the key field by the prime number closest to, but not greater than, the number of records to be stored. A prime number can be divided evenly by itself and 1 but not by any other number. The remainder of the division by the prime number (not the quotient) becomes the address of the relative location in which the record will be stored.

Direct organization.
A method of organizing data on a device so they can be accessed directly (randomly).

Let's consider an example. Suppose that a company has 1,000 employees and therefore 1,000 active employee numbers. Also suppose that all employee identification numbers (the key field) are four digits long. Therefore, the possible range of ID numbers is from 0000 to 9999.

Assume that this company wants to place the record of employee number 8742 onto disk. The hashing procedure will be as follows. The prime number closest to 1,000, the number of records to be stored, is 997. Figure 4-26 shows that the hashed disk address computes to 766. After the record has been placed at an address corresponding to this number, the computer can retrieve it as needed by applying the hashing procedure to the key field of the record again. Calculation of an address in this manner usually consumes much less time than would a search through one or more indexes.

Hashing procedures are difficult to develop and pose certain problems. For example, it is possible for two or more records to be hashed to the same relative disk location. This, of course, means they will "collide" at their common disk address. When this happens, one record is placed in the computed location and assigned a "pointer" that chains it to the other, which often goes in the closest-available location to the hashed address. Good hashing procedures result in few collisions.

The disadvantage of direct organization is that, since records are not stored sequentially by key, it is usually impractical to process the records sequentially.

Summary and Key Terms

Secondary storage technologies make it economically feasible to keep large quantities of programs and data online to the CPU. The most common types of secondary storage media are magnetic disk and magnetic tape.

Properties of Secondary Storage Systems. Any secondary storage system involves two physical parts: a peripheral device and an input/output medium. In most systems, media must pass by a **read/write head** in the peripheral device to be read from or written to.

Secondary storage media are **nonvolatile**—that is, when the power to the peripheral device is shut off, the data stored on the medium remain intact. This contrasts with most types of primary memory, which are **volatile.** Also, media on secondary storage devices can be either *removable,* meaning they must be mounted onto the peripheral device every time they are used, or *fixed,* meaning they are permanently mounted, or nonremovable.

Two basic access methods are used on secondary storage systems: sequential and direct. With **sequential access,** the records in a file can be retrieved only in the same sequence in which they are physically stored. With **direct,** or **random, access,** records can be retrieved in any sequence.

Magnetic Disk. Magnetic disk is most commonly available in the form of hard disks and diskettes. **Hard disks** are rigid platters. **Diskettes,** or *floppy disks,* in contrast, are flexible platters.

The disks used with large computers frequently are 14 inches in diameter. Data are represented in byte form on the concentric **tracks** of each disk surface. Often the same amount of data is stored on each track of a disk to keep the data-transfer rate constant throughout the disk system.

In the disk systems serving larger computers, several platters are usually assembled into a **disk pack.** The disk pack, in turn, is mounted either permanently or temporarily on a **disk unit,** which makes the data on the disks online to the computer. In most systems, a read/write head is assigned to each recordable disk surface. The heads are mounted onto an **access mechanism,** which can move them in and out among the concentric tracks to fetch data. All tracks in the same position on the tiered platters of a disk pack form a **disk cylinder.**

Three events determine the time needed to read from or write to most disks. *Seek time* is the time required for the access mechanism to reach a particular track. The time needed for the disk to spin to a specific area of a track is known as *rotational delay.* Once located, data must be transferred to or from the disk, a process known as *data movement time.* The sum of these three time components is called **disk access time.**

Diskettes are commonly used with microcomputers and small minicomputers. Diskettes are available in a number of sizes (diameters) and densities. **Sectors** divide a diskette into addressable, pie-shaped pieces. The disk's **file directory,** which the computer system maintains automatically, keeps track of the contents at each disk address. A diskette drive works only when the appropriate type of diskette is inserted into it correctly.

Sealed hard-disk units called *Winchester disks,* for many years popular on large computers, are now commonly found on microcomputer systems. Winchesters, which most microcomputer users informally refer to as *hard disks,* are faster and have greater data-carrying capacity than diskettes. **Hard cards** and **cartridge disk** devices are two other hard-disk alternatives for microcomputer systems.

Two strategies for reducing the number of time-consuming disk accesses are RAM disk and cache disk. **RAM disk** is a storage strategy whereby the computer's operating system is "tricked" into thinking it is dealing with secondary storage when in fact it is dealing with primary memory. **Cache disk** refers to a strategy whereby during any disk access, program or data contents in neighboring disk areas are also fetched and transported to RAM.

Magnetic Tape. **Magnetic tape** commonly consists of ½-inch-wide plastic Mylar coated with a magnetizable substance and wound on a 10½-inch-diameter reel. Each character of data is represented in byte form across the tracks in the tape. Many **detachable-reel tapes** contain nine tracks—eight corresponding to the eight bits in a byte and an additional parity track to check for transmission errors. **Cartridge tapes,** in which both supply and take-up reels are enclosed in a plastic case, are also widely available.

To be processed by the CPU, the tape must be mounted on a hardware device called a **tape unit.** The drives on the tape unit spin the tape past a read/write head, which either reads from or writes to the tape. Often records are systematically organized on a tape by means of a **key field,** such as customer ID numbers.

Other Secondary Storage Alternatives. Several devices other than disk and tape may be used for secondary storage. The **mass storage unit** is particularly suitable for storing enormous quantities of data online. Although slower than magnetic disk, mass storage is more cost effective when the CPU must have large quantities of data readily accessible. **Optical disks,** which work with laser read/write devices, are a relatively recent secondary storage technology. Most optical disk systems available today are *CD-ROM, WORM,* or *fully erasable* systems. **Magnetic bubble storage** is used in devices such as terminals, desktop computers, robots, and communications devices.

Data Organization. The process of retrieving data and programs in storage is called **data access.** Systematically arranging data for efficient retrieval is called **data organization.**

There are three major methods of storing files in secondary storage: sequential, indexed-sequential, and direct organization. With **sequential organization,** records are arranged with respect to a key field. With **indexed-sequential organization,** records are arranged sequentially by key field on the disk to facilitate sequential access. In addition, one or more indexes are available to permit direct access to the records. **Direct organization** facilitates even faster direct access to data. It uses a process called *hashing* to transform the key field of each record into a disk address.

Review Exercises

Fill-in Questions

1. A storage medium is ____________ if it loses its contents when the power is shut off.
2. A tiered assembly of disk platters enclosed in a protective cover is known as a(n) ____________ .
3. For rapid access, related data often are stored on the same ________, a collection of disk tracks that are in the same relative position on different disk surfaces of a pack.
4. A hard disk on an add-in board is called a(n) ____________ .
5. SCSI is an acronym for ____________ .
6. Each character of data on magnetic tape is represented in byte form across parallel ____________ of the tape.
7. In order to write data onto a tape, a(n) ____________ must be mounted in the center of the tape.
8. A(n) ____________ is a secondary storage device capable of storing almost 500 billion bytes of data online and using tapes stored in a honeycomb-shaped rack.

Matching Questions

Match each term with the description that fits best.

a. diskette
b. cache disk
c. removable-pack disk unit
d. hard disk
e. mass storage unit
f. RAM disk

____ 1. Used when one needs a lot of fast, random access to run a business on a microcomputer system.

____ 2. A storage alternative, often under one or two megabytes in capacity, that is available in double-density or high-density format.

____ 3. A common storage alternative for minicomputers and mainframes.

____ 4. Used to "trick" the operating system into thinking it is dealing with secondary storage when it is really dealing with primary memory.

____ 5. Used by organizations needing extremely large amounts of data online.

____ 6. Used to fetch more data from disk on each access than the amount of data needed immediately.

Discussion Questions

1. What is the difference between volatile and nonvolatile storage?
2. Describe the advantages and disadvantages of removable media.
3. Identify several types of magnetic disk, and for each type describe a situation in which it may be useful.
4. Provide examples of sequential access and direct access to data.
5. What physical differences exist among diskettes?
6. What advantages do 3½-inch disks have over 5¼-inch disks?
7. What potential do optical disks offer?
8. Name several standards for hard disks and explain in what way these standards differ.
9. Explain how data are stored on magnetic tape.
10. How does indexed-sequential organization work?

Critical Thinking Questions

1. Does the user of a microcomputer with a hard-disk drive really need diskette drives, too?
2. Some people believe that magnetic tape will completely disappear early in the 21st century. What argument(s) do you think support this contention? Do you think that there are any types of applications for which magnetic tape will continue to hold a strong competitive edge?
3. In comparing computers to humans, many observers have pointed out the similarities of computer primary memory to human memory and of the CPU chip to the human mind. Extending this analogy further, what would computer secondary storage resemble?

What roles do specialized support devices serve? Many, as you will learn in this chapter. There are, by far, more different types of input and output devices than any other type of computer-related equipment. This giant Sony JumboTron monitor, beaming over New York's Times Square, is one of the largest hardware devices in the world.

5

Input and Output Equipment

Outline

Overview

Input and Output

Keyboards

Display Devices

- Text versus Graphics
- Monochrome and Color Display Devices
- CRT and Flat-Panel Display Devices

Printers

- Impact Printing
- Nonimpact Printing
- Printers for Microcomputers
- Printers for Large Computers

Source Data Automation

- Optical Character Recognition (OCR)
- Image Scanners
- Magnetic Ink Character Recognition (MICR)
- Digitizers
- Voice-Input Devices
- Handwriting Recognition Devices
- Smart Cards

Special-Purpose Output Equipment

- Computer Output Microfilm (COM)
- Plotters
- Voice-Output Devices
- Film Recorders

Learning Objectives

After completing this chapter, you will be able to:

1. Identify several types of input and output devices and explain their functions.
2. Describe some of the differences that exist among keyboards, among display devices, and among printers.
3. Explain what source data automation means and discuss several ways to accomplish it.
4. Discuss several types of special-purpose output equipment.
5. Appreciate the large variety of input and output equipment available in the marketplace.

Overview

In Chapter 4, we covered secondary storage devices. Although most of those devices perform both input and output operations for the computer, storage is their main role. In this chapter, we turn to equipment designed primarily for input of programs and data into the computer, for output, or for both. Many of these devices possess a limited amount of storage capacity as well.

We'll begin the chapter with a look at keyboards, which most users turn to for entering commands, programs, or data into the computer system.

Following that, we'll explore display devices. These hardware units are ideal for applications that require considerable interaction between the operator and the computer. We'll also highlight some of the qualities that distinguish one display device from another.

Next, we will turn to printers. Printers place the results of computer processing onto paper, sometimes at incredible speeds.

From there, we'll cover hardware designed for source data automation. This equipment provides fast, relatively error-free input for certain kinds of applications.

Finally, we'll describe some special-purpose output equipment. Included among these devices are machines that can record output onto microfilm, machines that can speak, plotters, and film recorders.

Keep in mind that the hardware described in this chapter is only a small sample of the kinds of input/output equipment available today. There are, in fact, thousands of products in the marketplace, and these can be put together in so many ways that it is possible to create a computer system to fit almost any conceivable need (refer to Tomorrow box).

Input and Output

Input device.
A machine used to supply programs and data to the computer.

Output device.
A machine used to output computer-processed results.

Input and output equipment allows people and computers to communicate. **Input devices** convert data and programs that humans can understand into a form the computer can comprehend. These devices translate the letters, numbers, and other natural-language symbols that humans conventionally use in reading and writing into the configurations of 0- and 1-bits that the computer uses to process data. **Output devices,** on the other hand, convert the strings of bits the computer uses back into natural-language form to make them understandable to humans. These devices produce output for screen display, output onto paper or film, and so forth.

The equipment we are about to discuss can be classified in a number of ways. Some of it is *peripheral equipment.* This includes input or output devices that are normally under the computer's direct control. Display devices and printers are examples. Other input or output equipment, such as many electronic cash registers and computer output microfilm

Tomorrow

Interactive Television

High-Tech Thrills for the Couch Potato

It's the Giants versus the 49ers. Joe Montana is fading back for a pass. The camera cuts to Jerry Rice running the sideline. He's open for a second, but the pass is high and out of bounds. Interesting. But what was the Giant's defensive star, Lawrence Taylor, doing? You run the play back on your remote control, watching it at an angle that keys in on the defensive linebackers. When you finish and get back into real time, there's a commercial coming up. So you hit another button on your remote control that keeps you posted on what's happening in other games.

Does this sound too good to be true? Actually, it *is* true. *Interactive television,* as it's called, is a service that's now being tested in selected cities. Advocates in the industry say that interactive television may be in more than a third of American and Canadian homes by the year 2000.

Interactive TV. Watching television no longer has to be passive.

What makes interactive television possible is the increased information-carrying capacity of the communications channels going into homes. Satellites and new types of optical cable can bring in hundreds, and someday thousands, of stations. In addition to that are new, sophisticated capabilities for interleaving information. Thus, a "program" going to the home can now consist of several layers. One layer is the main program itself. Other layers, which you can summon by remote control, bring in features such as other camera angles, background sports analysis, action in other games, and profiles of players.

Interactive sports viewing is only the beginning. Would you like to watch a game show and become a contestant yourself, in your own living room? Consider a program such as "The Price Is Right." As contestants are playing on television, there is a special track for you to guess prices by pressing buttons on your remote control. If you beat all the other viewers, you can win a special prize. Maybe the first generation of prizes will be cheap watches, but as interactive television hits its stride, look for millions of viewers to be involved in lottery-style games worth millions of dollars.

Perhaps you are interested in watching the news, but you're tired of hearing about violent crime. Interactive television can respond to that need, too. It will provide menus from which to choose the news topics you would like to watch. If you want to change to another topic, just activate the menu system again and make another choice. An aerobics class would work in the same way—you can choose the level of aerobic intensity at which you're interested in working. And, when watching music videos, you can choose which ones you want to see, in whatever order you want.

Of course, the advertisers are not going to be idle on the sidelines with Joe Montana's errant pass while all of this is happening. Because interactive television also has a memory, marketing information about what you like to watch can be automatically analyzed to target specific commercial messages to you. Oh well, there's always a catch to every good thing.

(COM) devices, are *auxiliary equipment.* These devices normally work independently of the main CPU. Some auxiliary devices prepare input data for later mounting onto a peripheral device. Others convert output produced on a peripheral device into a form more useful to humans.

This equipment, of course, can also be discussed in terms of its input or output functions. Display terminals, for example, are capable of both input and output. Keyboards and optical character recognition devices are designed primarily for input. Printers, monitors, and most computer microfilm devices specialize in output. Most input and output devices contain limited storage capacity as well.

Hard copy.
A permanent form of usable output—for example, output on paper or film.

Soft copy.
A nonpermanent form of usable output—for example, display output.

Output devices produce results in either hard copy or soft copy form. The term **hard copy** generally refers to output that has been recorded onto a medium such as paper or microfilm—in other words, output that is in a permanent and highly portable form. Printed reports and program listings are among the most common examples. The term **soft copy** generally refers to display output—output that is temporary and of limited portability.

Keyboards

Keyboard.
An input device composed of numerous typewriterlike keys, arranged in a configuration similar to that of a typewriter.

For most people, a computer system would be useless without a **keyboard**, which often is the main vehicle for input. Keyboards vary tremendously in number of keys, key arrangement, types of special keys, and touch. Figure 5-1 shows the Enhanced Keyboard developed for the IBM PS/2 line of computers and describes the purpose of several of these keys. Potential buyers should carefully evaluate keyboards, considering several factors.

First, the keyboards on most computer systems have several special keys that involve specific software routines. A Delete key, for example, deletes characters from the screen, and an Insert key enables characters to be added onto the screen. Also, there are several *function keys* (see the top of Figure 5-1). These keys are often labeled F1, F2, F3, and so on and are located in a cluster on the left-hand side or at the top of the keyboard. When depressed by the operator, these keys initiate a command or even an entire computer program. Generally speaking, each software package you work with will define the function keys differently. For example, depressing the F2 key may enable you to block-indent text with your word processor but edit cells with your spreadsheet package (see also User Solution 5-1). Most keyboards also have a *numeric keypad* (see rightmost part of Figure 5-1), which is activated by the NumLock key and makes it easy to enter numbers quickly. The number of special keys, as well as their capabilities and placement, varies widely among manufacturers.

Second, not all keyboards have the same key arrangement as that on a standard typewriter. For example, the QWERTY keyboard uses the conventional typewriter format, whereas the newer and more sensibly designed Dvorak keyboard uses another arrangement, placing the five vowels under the fingertips of the left hand and the five most-used consonants under the fingertips of the right. One interesting story has it that the QWERTY keyboard, which became a standard a century or so ago, was actually created to slow down typists, so that they wouldn't get their fingers stuck in the keyboard. Despite the QWERTY keyboard's

Figure 5-1 Keyboard.
This 102-key Enhanced Keyboard is sold with many IBM PS/2 computers. For operator convenience, this keyboard features two Ctrl, Alt, Insert, and Delete keys, as well as an extra set of arrow keys.

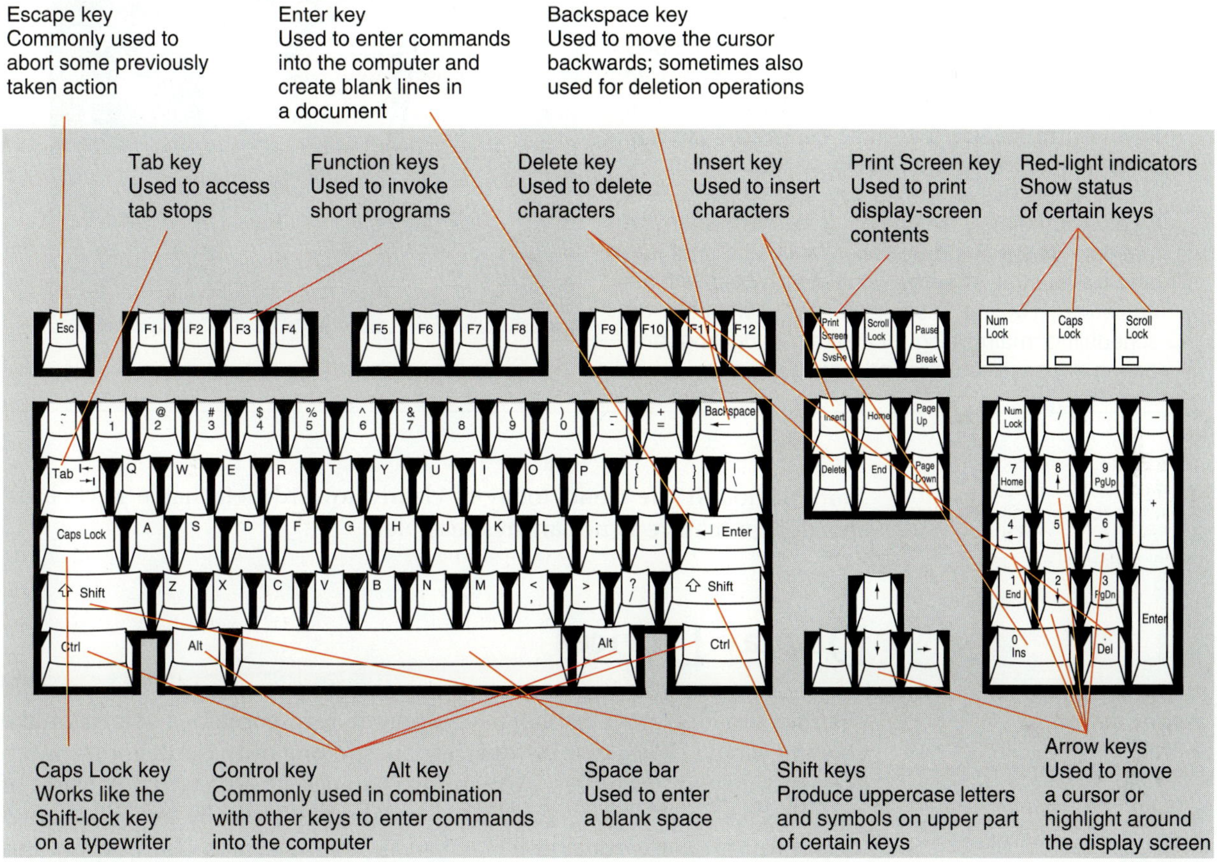

somewhat awkward design, most typists have been trained on it and wouldn't think about switching.

Third, keyboards differ with respect to touch. Some are sculpted to match the contours of the fingertips, for instance, whereas others have either flat, calculator-style keys or a flat membrane panel with touch-sensitive keys. Also, manufacturers space keys differently, so keys that feel just right to one person may seem too far apart to another. Key spacing can be a real problem for word processing users who need a laptop computer, because the keyboards on these units are designed to be as compact as possible. Still another difference regarding touch is that some keyboards make a faint clicking sound each time you depress a key, while others are completely silent.

Finally, many keyboards are detached hardware units that you can place wherever convenient. Others are built into the display or system

User Solution 5-1

Using Function Keys for Fast Access

Sportscaster Frank Herzog, whose play-by-play coverage brings Washington Redskins games to millions of radio listeners, has adapted the function keys on his keyboard to meet his special applications needs. When the Redskins block a punt, for instance, he hits a special key and types in "last time." Immediately the computer tells him when the last time was that the Redskins blocked a punt and who it was against, so he won't miss a beat with his audience. Herzog also uses his computer for scheduling, maintaining a calendar, budgeting, preparing expense reports, and writing memos.

unit. Although the trend today is clearly toward detachable keyboards, this design feature is not always feasible.

Display Devices

Display device.
A peripheral device that contains a viewing screen.

Monitor.
A display device without a keyboard.

Display terminal.
A communications workstation that consists of a display device and a keyboard.

Display devices are peripheral equipment that contain a televisionlike viewing screen. Most display devices fall into one of two categories: monitors and display terminals. A **monitor** is an *output* device that consists of only the viewing screen. A **display terminal** is typically an *input/output* "communications workstation" that includes the screen (for output) and an attached keyboard (for input).

In practice, one commonly finds monitors plugged into and sitting on top of the system units of microcomputers. The keyboard is usually a separate input device that also connects to the system unit. Although the monitor is strictly an output device, the user can also see keyboard input on the display because the computer routes it to the monitor as output. Display terminals, on the other hand, are generally hooked up to either mainframes, minicomputers, or supercomputers in communications networks. After all, communication is the primary function of these display devices. The keyboard unit is cabled directly to the display unit, which in turn is hooked up to the computer.

Cursor.
A highlighting symbol that appears on a display screen to indicate the position where the next character typed in will appear.

As each key on the keyboard is depressed, the corresponding character representation of the key appears on the display screen at the cursor position. The **cursor** is a highlighted position on the screen indicating where the next character to be typed in will be placed. Alternatively, the cursor may point to the option the operator can select next. To have even greater flexibility in manipulating the screen cursor, many people supplement keyboard operations with a mouse, light pen, or other such cursor-movement device. These devices are examples of *digitizers,* which we'll discuss at length later in the chapter.

Display devices are handy when the user requires only small amounts of output and has to see what is being sent as input to the computer system. A student word processing a paper for a class, an airline clerk making inquiries to a flight information database, a stockbroker analyzing a security, and a bank teller checking the status of a customer account would each employ a display device. However, the display is useful only up to a point. If, for example, the student writing the paper wanted to take a copy of it home, he or she would have to direct the output to a printer.

Many features differentiate the hundreds of display devices currently in the market (see Figure 5-2). A discussion of some of the more noteworthy features follows.

Text versus Graphics

Many of the display devices sold today are capable of providing both text and graphics output. *Text* output consists of only letters, digits, and special characters. Two examples are program listings and letters to friends. *Graphics* output includes complex picture images, such as maps and drawings.

Resolution. A key characteristic of any display device is *resolution,* or sharpness of the screen image. On many displays, images are formed by lighting up tiny dots on the screen. On such devices, resolution is measured by the density of these dots, or **pixels** (a contraction of the phrase *picture elements*). The more pixels per square inch of screen, the higher the resolution (i.e., the clearer the picture). A display resolution of, say, 640 by 480 means that the screen consists of 640 columns by 480 rows of dots—that is, 640 × 480 = 307,200 pixels.

Pixel.
A single dot on a display screen that is used to compose images.

Text characters are formed on the screen in a dot-matrix configuration, as shown in Figure 5-3. Generally, several specific matrix sizes—say, 5 by 7 (= 35 pixels) or 7 by 12 (= 84 pixels)—are available for users to display text. For instance, a user may be able to display 25 rows of 65-character lines for one application and 50 rows of 132-character lines for another. The more pixels used to form characters and the more pixels packed per square inch of screen, the higher the text resolution.

Pixels are electronically maintained and manipulated at lightning-fast speeds. For instance, the pixels on a typical desktop display screen are *refreshed*—that is, recharged with a built-in electron gun so they will remain bright—at a rate of about 30 or more times each second. The computers onboard Tomahawk missiles used in the Persian Gulf war compared electronic terrain pictures they took while in motion with pictures stored in their databases at a rate of a billion pixel pairs per second.

Bit Mapping. The earliest display devices were strictly *character addressable;* that is, only text could be output. Every character sent to the screen was the same size and was fitted into a specific block of pixels in a pre-

Figure 5-2 A variety of display devices.
(a, top left) Monochrome, CRT-type display terminal. (b, top right) Color, CRT-type monitor. (c, bottom left) Monochrome, flat-panel display terminal. (d, bottom right) Grey-scale monitor.

(a)

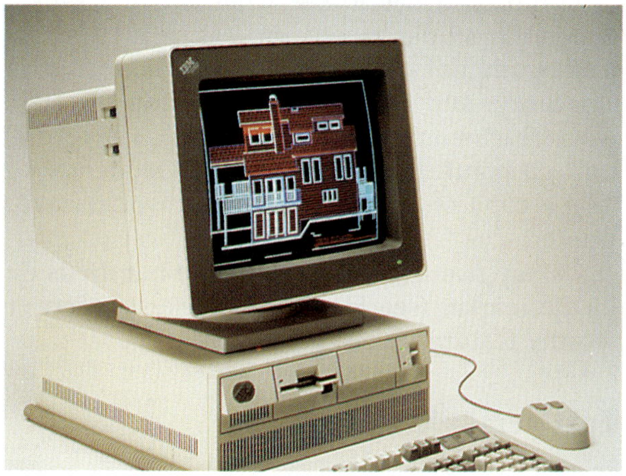

(b)

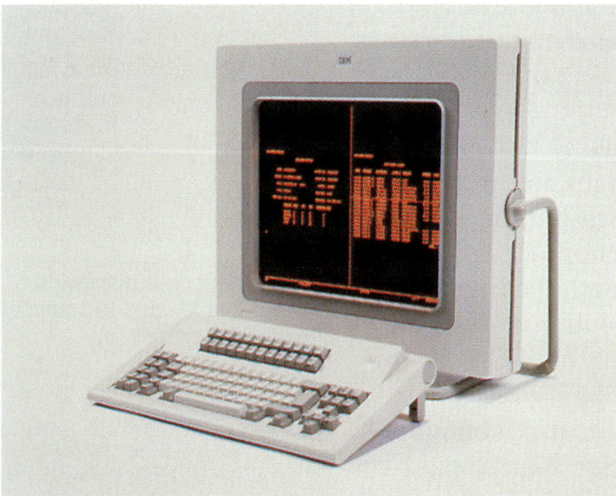

(c)

(d)

designated grid. As demand for graphics devices grew, manufacturers developed techniques to make displays multipurpose—that is, capable of both graphics and standard text output.

Bit mapping.
A graphical output technique in which each of the dots in the output image may be individually operator controlled.

Display devices that produce graphics output often use a technique called **bit mapping.** With bit-mapped graphics, each pixel on the screen (rather than simply a block of pixels) can be individually controlled by the operator. This enables the operator to create virtually any type of image on the screen.

The largest markets for graphics display devices today are in the engineering, science, and art fields. Powerful devices called *technical workstations,* or "diskless PCs," are used for mapping, circuit design, mechanical

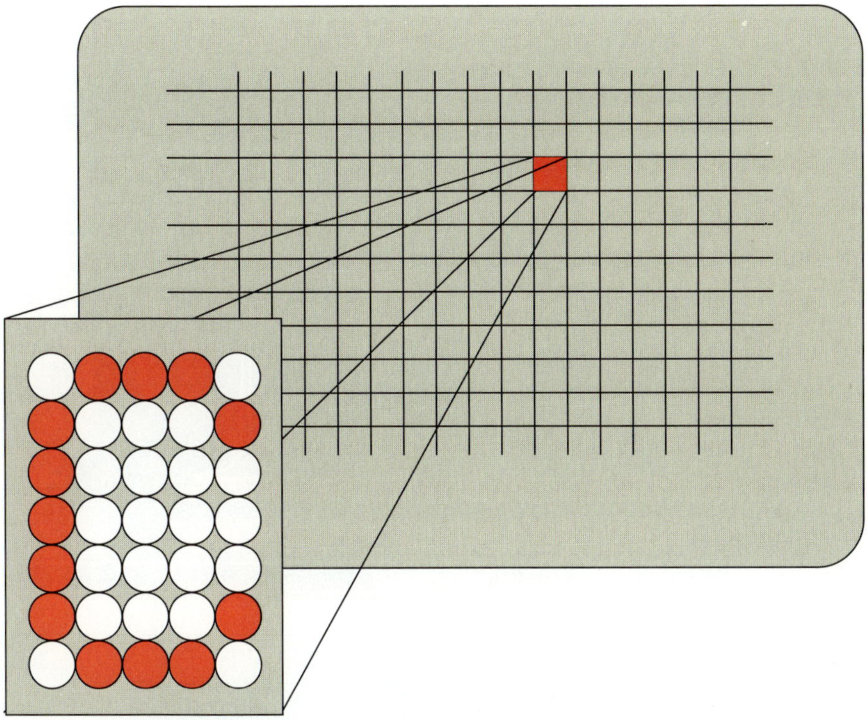

Figure 5-3
A C character as formed by a 5-by-7 dot matrix of pixels. When the screen is set up for a given type (mode) of text display—as it would be when you are using your word processor under normal conditions—it is mapped out with a specific grid of cells. For instance, a mode specifying 25 lines of 80 characters each would provide a grid of 2,000 cells. Each cell will accept only one character, and each character will be composed from the same-sized matrix of dots.

design, drafting, art, advertising, and other graphics-intensive tasks. Such applications collectively fall under the heading of *computer-aided design (CAD).* We will discuss CAD in greater detail in Chapter 11.

Another large market for computer graphics is in the business sector. Managers can easily become overwhelmed as they try to make decisions from piles of raw data. A possible solution lies in the old adage "One picture is worth a thousand words." Using a graphics image, a decision maker can more easily spot problems, opportunities, and trends. Many business applications of computer graphics fall into the general category of *presentation graphics,* which we'll cover in Chapter 9 and Window 5. With presentation graphics, computer images are used to increase the effectiveness of managerial and sales presentations (Figure 5-4).

Recently, computer graphics techniques have brought many businesses squarely into the age of *electronic document handling,* a practice in which digital images of paper documents and photographs are electronically maintained by organizations and processed by workers at their display workstations (see Figure 5-5). The paper documents and photographs are initially read into the computer system with an image scanner, a device we'll discuss later in the chapter. Once in digital form, the images are stored on a high-capacity optical disk system. Workers having access to the system can summon documents to their workstations, where they can cull, sort, summarize, or repackage the information to their heart's content. Workers may also be authorized to annotate certain

Figure 5-4
Computer-generated presentation graphics.
Presentation graphics images are useful for making dramatic and easily understood points in meetings, and they make the presenter look more professional as well. Presentation graphics can be shown to an audience through a variety of media, including a monitor screen, printer or plotter hard copy, and slides or overhead transparencies.

Figure 5-5
Electronic document handling.
Graphics terminals, optical disk storage, and superfast processors have made it possible to maintain digital images of photos and paper documents and to access them at electronic speeds.

documents with comments or approvals and send them to other workers who are hooked into the system.

Graphics Standards. A number of standards for display devices are currently in effect. In the IBM microcomputing world, these standards include Hercules monochrome, Monochrome Display Adapter (MDA),

Color Graphics Adapter (CGA), Multi-Color Graphics Array (MCGA), Enhanced Graphics Adapter (EGA), and Video Graphics Array (VGA). Such standards specify "modes" in which the display device can run. For example, the most current and most powerful of these standards—VGA—can run in 17 different modes. One mode, for instance, divides the screen into a matrix of 320 by 200 pixels and allows 256 colors to be displayed simultaneously; another divides the screen into a matrix of 720 by 400 pixels and permits monochrome display only. The Apple Macintosh line has a similar set of graphics standards.

In response to the large number of standards and modes now available for display, many monitor manufacturers in the microcomputing marketplace have developed *multiscan (multisync) monitors.* These monitors can work under a wide variety of graphics standards. Thus, for instance, such a monitor might be able to support software designed to work under either CGA, EGA, or VGA. Also available are a number of monitors that, in combination with special graphics adapter boards, produce super-high-resolution images—images that go beyond those available with VGA—for an IBM PS/2, a Macintosh II, or virtually any other 32-bit computer.

Monochrome and Color Display Devices

Most display devices in use today are classifiable as monochrome or color. *Grey-scale displays,* which provide output similar to that on a black-and-white TV screen (see Figure 5-2d), have also recently become available for specialized applications.

Monochrome. *Monochrome displays* output images using a single foreground color (see Figure 5-2a). Many of the earliest monochrome devices were of the black-and-white variety, providing white text on a black background. Through a technique known as *reverse video* (reversing the color of the pixels), black text on a white background is also possible. Over the years, a number of studies have shown that people become less fatigued when working with amber or green on a black background. Although such studies have produced conflicting results, many of the display devices now available in the marketplace are of the amber or green type.

Color. Most *color displays* (see Figure 5-2b) are of the *red-green-blue (RGB)* type. That is, all colors available on the screen are formed by intermixing light beams of only these three colors. Depending on such factors as the sophistication of the display unit itself and the amount of RAM available with the computer, users may be able to display from 8 to 16,000,000 colors. Business users who require presentation graphics output often need only a few colors, but people such as artists and product designers need many more. Display devices that meet the latter set of needs often cost several thousand dollars. Nonetheless, users who have only eight or so colors available can create the illusion of many more colors by painting alternate pixels different colors. For example, painting alternate pixels yellow and green produces a lime color.

User Solution 5-2

Flat-Panel Displays Create New Shopping Product

How do you attract customers into a supermarket and get—at the right time—the right type of shopping information to them? VideOcart of Chicago thinks it has the answer. Weatherproof, flat-panel displays that fit onto standard shopping carts (see photo) are programmed to receive product data from sensors and transmitters located strategically throughout the store. When the cart enters a particular aisle, the screen displays ads for nearby products and prompts shoppers to press buttons for electronic coupons and for such information as sale items and recipes. And no need to worry about long lines at the checkout stations; there, the screen can provide you with news, weather, sports trivia, and movie reviews.

Monochrome display devices have advantages over color ones because they are cheaper, generally provide better resolution for text display (an important consideration if the display will be used extensively for word processing), and emit less radiation. But if you need more than a single color, only a color monitor will suffice.

CRT and Flat-Panel Display Devices

Cathode-ray tube (CRT). A display device that contains a long-necked display tube similar to that used in television sets.

Traditionally, most display devices have used a large picture-tube element similar to the one inside a standard TV set. This type of display device (see Figure 5-2b) is commonly called a **CRT (cathode-ray tube).** CRT technology is relatively mature. Over the years, CRTs have become very inexpensive and capable of providing excellent color output. These features notwithstanding, CRTs are bulky, fragile, and consume a great deal of power.

Flat-panel display. A slim-profile display device.

Recently monitors and display terminals that use charged chemicals or gases sandwiched between panes of glass have become popular alternatives to CRTs. These slim-profile devices are called **flat-panel displays.** Although they can be relatively expensive and have only recently become commercially viable for color output, flat-panel displays are compact, are lightweight, and require little power. Because of these features, they are commonly found on laptop and notebook computers and in portable handwriting recognition devices. Also, as described in User Solution 5-2, flat-panel displays are today helping to create new technology products that virtually nobody imagined a decade or so ago.

Figure 5-2c features a flat-panel display that uses a *liquid crystal display (LCD)* technology. LCDs are by far the most common type of flat-panel display devices in use. Among the major advantages of LCD technology over CRTs are low cost, low power consumption, and compactness. However, LCDs provide less contrast, produce more glare, and have poorer screen resolution than CRTs. To overcome the contrast problem, many LCDs are back-lit.

Two other flat-panel technologies in use are *gas plasma* displays and *electroluminescent (EL)* displays. Although devices that use these technologies are more costly and less common than LCD devices, they offer better screen resolution and contrast as well as greater color potential.

Printers

Display devices have two major limitations as output devices: (1) only a small amount of data can be shown on the screen at one time, and (2) output, being in soft copy form, is not very portable. To obtain output in portable form, you must either take notes or use a device that captures output onto paper or film.

Printer.
A device that places computer output onto paper.

Printers overcome these limitations by producing hard copy—a permanent record of output. Hard copy is created when digital electronic signals from the computer are converted into printed material in a natural language that people can easily read and understand. A great deal of output can be placed onto computer printouts, although hard copy can become difficult to handle and store as it accumulates. In fact, many executives now complain that they are literally drowning in a sea of computer-generated paperwork.

Impact printing.
The formation of characters by causing a metal hammer to strike a ribbon into paper or paper into a ribbon.

Solid-font mechanism.
A printing element that produces solid characters.

Printers differ in a number of important respects. One involves the printing technology used—namely, whether it is *impact* or *nonimpact*. Another concerns speed of operation. *Low-speed printers* are capable of outputting only one character at a time, whereas *high-speed printers* can output either a full line or a full page at a time.

Impact Printing

Impact printing is the method used by conventional typewriters. In some types of impact printing, a metal "hammer" embossed with a character strikes a print ribbon, which presses the character's image onto paper. In other types, the hammer strikes the paper and presses it into the ribbon. Characters created through impact printing can be formed by either a solid-font or dot-matrix printing mechanism.

Solid-Font Mechanisms. A **solid-font mechanism** produces fully formed characters similar to those on conventional typewriters.

A popular device for producing fully formed characters on low-speed printers is the daisywheel print element, shown in Figure 5-6. *Daisywheel printers* operate at very slow speeds—often in the neighborhood of 30 to 80 characters per second—but their output quality is very high. Thus, daisywheel printers are sometimes called *letter-quality* printers, because

Figure 5-6
Daisywheel print element.
Daisywheel printers result in superb output quality, but their lack of speed, text-only orientation, and noise level have caused them to lose out to inexpensive laser printers in many applications environments.

they are often used to produce attractive correspondence to be sent outside the user's organization. *Print-thimble printers,* popularized by NEC, are another example of low-speed, solid-font, letter-quality printers. A print thimble looks like a daisywheel with its spokes bent upward in the shape of a sewing thimble.

Many high-speed printers also employ a solid-font mechanism to produce fully formed characters. In band printers, for example, all characters are mounted on a *print band* that revolves rapidly past the print positions, as Figure 5-7 shows.

Impact dot-matrix mechanism.
A print head that forms dot-matrix characters through impact printing.

Dot-Matrix Mechanisms. Most low-speed printers in use today employ a print head that's an impact dot-matrix mechanism. Typically, an **impact dot-matrix mechanism** constructs printed characters by repeatedly activating one or more vertical rows of pins, as illustrated in Figure 5-8. Impact dot-matrix printers are usually much faster than solid-font printers; a speed of 100 to 200 characters per second is common. Top-of-the-line impact dot-matrix printers are currently rated at about 700 characters per second.

The quality of output on impact dot-matrix devices is often lower than that on solid-font devices. Nonetheless, many relatively inexpensive impact dot-matrix printers are capable of printing very respectable-looking output. These printers use techniques such as packing as many pins as possible on the print head, overstriking by making multiple passes on a line, and blending overstrike dots into previous dots by shifting the paper

Figure 5-7
A print band.
Band printing is one of the most widely used kinds of high-speed printing. As the band revolves, one or more hammers strike it to form images on paper.

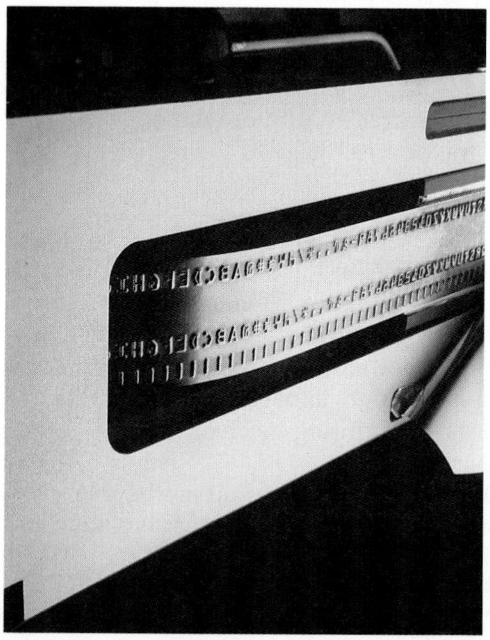

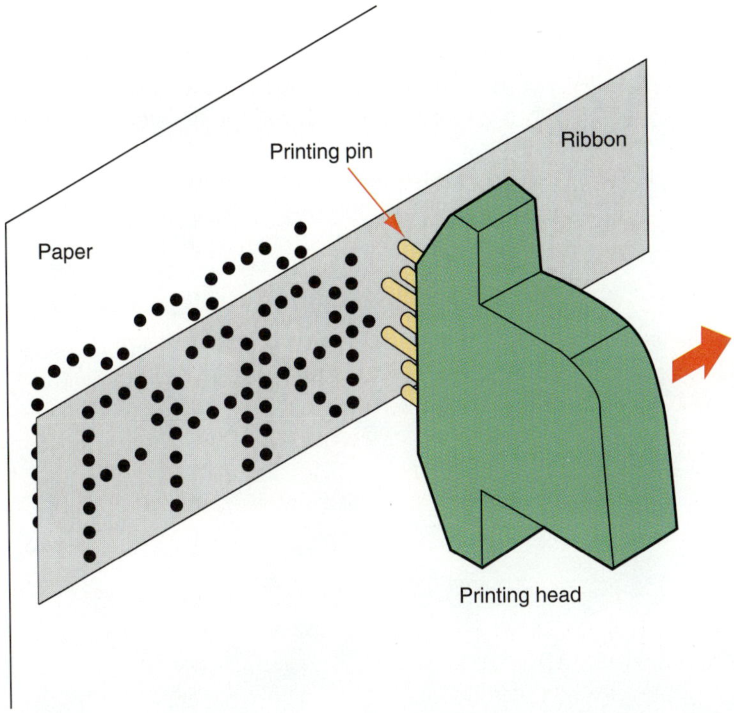

Figure 5-8
Impact dot-matrix printing.
This character-formation technique is similar to the one used to light up electronic scoreboards at sports stadiums. The printing mechanism contains a vertical line of pins that form the characters on the paper. Depending on the character to be represented, different pins in the mechanism are activated. The characters shown are formed from a 5-by-7 dot matrix. The more dots in the matrix, naturally, the higher the quality of the printed character.

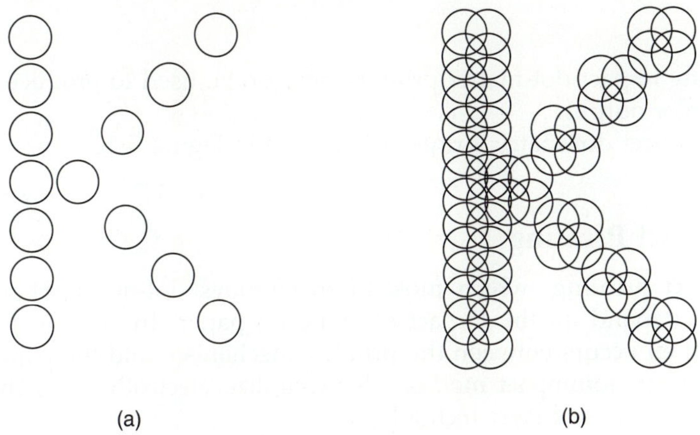

Figure 5-9
Overstriking on a dot-matrix printer.
(a) Single striking.
(b) Overstriking with multiple passes produces denser characters.

very slightly (see Figure 5-9). Top-of-the-line impact dot-matrix printers have 24 pins on their print heads, configured in two 12-pin rows. Generally, these printers can create characters that are virtually indistinguishable from those produced by solid-font printers. In the world of impact dot-matrix printing, low-quality output is often referred to as *draft-quality* printing and presentation-quality output as *near-letter-quality (NLQ)* print-

Figure 5-10
Impact dot-matrix printer. Often costing only a few hundred dollars, impact dot-matrix printers are widely used in microcomputer systems.

ing. Many impact dot-matrix printers can also be used to produce graphical or color output.

An impact dot-matrix printer is featured in Figure 5-10.

Nonimpact Printing

Nonimpact printing. The formation of characters on a surface by means of heat, lasers, photography, or ink jets.

Nonimpact printing, which most often employs dot-matrix characters, does not depend on the impact of metal on paper. In fact, no physical contact at all occurs between the printing mechanism and the paper. The most popular nonimpact methods today utilize electrothermal, thermal-transfer, ink-jet, and laser technologies.

In *electrothermal printing,* characters are burned onto a special paper by heated rods on a print head. Electrothermal printers are available at a very low cost, but they have the disadvantages of poor output quality, requiring special paper (which some people find unpleasant to touch), and being unable to produce color output. Electrothermal printing is the technology most used by fax machines, which are covered in Chapter 6.

Thermal-transfer printers, which represent a relatively new technology, thermally transfer ink from a wax-based ribbon onto plain paper. These printers can produce output that rivals a daisywheel's and, because they use a dot-matrix print head, can support high-quality graphics as well

Figure 5-11
Thermal-transfer printer.
Thermal-transfer printers are ideal for users who need high-quality color output as well as crisp-looking text.

Figure 5-12
Ink-jet printer.
While ink-jet technology is found on various sizes of printers, perhaps it is today most popular for creating the miniature printers used with laptop computers.

(see Figure 5-11). In addition, thermal-transfer printers can produce overhead transparencies for use at meetings.

Ink-jet printers spray small dots of electrically charged ink onto a page to form images (see Figure 5-12). Some models can hold several color

Figure 5-13
Laser printer.
Laser printers are most useful when users need high-resolution, black-and-white text or graphics—and want output quickly.

cartridges simultaneously, so they are excellent for producing color output. Many ink-jet printers are flexible enough to be used as plotters, an output device we'll discuss later in the chapter, and as transparency-making machines.

Laser printers form images by charging thousands of dots on a platen with a very-high-intensity laser beam. Then, as with photocopiers, toner is affixed to the charged positions and, when paper is pressed against the platen, an image is formed. Laser printers quickly produce high-resolution text and graphics (see Figure 5-13), but they are usually more expensive than other types of printers.

Impact versus Nonimpact Printers. There are many important practical differences between impact and nonimpact printers. For one, because nonimpact printers contain fewer moving parts, they generally are much faster and subject to fewer breakdowns. In addition, because they don't use hammers, nonimpact printers are quiet. But unless you require very high speeds or high-quality color, these printers are often an expensive alternative. Figure 5-14 highlights some other differences between the most common types of impact and nonimpact printers.

Printers for Microcomputers

A rich assortment of printers is available today for microcomputers. Most of these printers are of the low-speed variety and output a single character at a time. By far the most common low-speed printers are of the impact dot-matrix type. Daisywheel, print-thimble, thermal-transfer, and ink-jet printers are also used with microcomputers.

Figure 5-14 Comparison of printing technologies.

	Device					
Criterion	**Impact Dot Matrix**	**Daisywheel and Print Thimble**	**Ink Jet**	**Electrothermal**	**Thermal Transfer**	**Laser**
Type	Impact	Impact	Nonimpact	Nonimpact	Nonimpact	Nonimpact
Speed	Fast	Slow	Medium to very fast	Medium to fast	Medium to fast	Very fast
Print quality	Fair to very good	Excellent	Good to excellent	Fair to very good	Excellent	Excellent
Cost	Low	Medium	Medium to high	Low	Medium to high	High
Graphics capabilities	Fair	Very limited	Fair to excellent	Good	Good to excellent	Excellent
Color	Fair	Very limited	Excellent	Not available	Excellent	Very limited

Low-speed printers typically operate in the range of 30 to several hundred characters per second. The slower units print in a single direction, like a conventional typewriter. The faster ones print in two directions (i.e., *bidirectionally*) to save a time-consuming carriage return. Usually the latter devices are also *logic-seeking* in that they are always "peeking" at the next line to decide how to print it the fastest way. Many low-speed printers can output subscripts, superscripts, color, graphic material, or multilingual and scientific text.

Many low-speed printers offer adjustable character widths, enabling the operator to change the number of characters per line or lines per inch. On dot-matrix units, the operator can make these adjustments by setting a switch or through the use of software. With solid-font devices, however, the operator must usually change the printing element by hand.

Changing *fonts*, or typefaces, is also usually easily achievable. On dot-matrix printers, fonts are usually changed by switching font cartridges, which contain character descriptions. On solid-font printers, fonts are changed by replacing the printing element.

Perhaps the greatest potential for high-speed printing on microcomputer systems exists with laser printing. Only since the mid-1980s have relatively inexpensive laser devices—costing about $1,000 and printing about four to eight pages per minute—become available for microcomputers. Many of these print at a resolution of 300 dots per inch (dpi), meaning that every square inch of the output image is broken down into a 300-by-300 matrix of dots. That's 90,000 dots packed into every inch! Such devices have become especially popular in business in the last few years, because they can produce letter-quality output that rivals that of solid-font printers, can quickly create presentation graphics for reports and meetings, and permit performance of certain publishing functions on a desktop. Laser printing is a special case of page printing, which we shall cover shortly.

Printers for Large Computers

Most printing on large computer systems is accomplished with high-speed printers. Whereas low-speed printers top out at speeds of several hundred *characters per second*, the slowest high-speed printers operate at

Figure 5-15
A line printer.
Line printers are targeted to larger computers—most notably minicomputers and mainframes—and produce output at speeds ranging from 300 to 3,000 lines per minute (lpm).

several hundred *lines per minute* (roughly twice the speed of the fastest low-speed printer). In many commercial settings that use both kinds of printers, you will often find the high-speed printers operating at speeds of from 10 to 30 times higher than the low-speed printers.

High-speed printers fall into two major categories: line printers and page printers.

Line printer.
A high-speed printer that produces output a line at a time.

Line Printers. **Line printers** (see Figure 5-15) are so called because they print whole lines at a time rather than just characters. Most line printers use impact printing technologies. For instance, many line printers use the solid-font, impact chain mechanism, which IBM introduced in 1959 on its 1403 printer. This device has proved to be the most popular printer of all time and is still used today. Band printers, which use a character-embossed print band instead of a chain, are currently the most popular type of line printer. Other forms of line printers use mechanical devices such as print trains, drums, wheels, and belts. Impact line printing typically occurs at speeds ranging from 300 to 3,000 lines per minute.

Page printer.
A high-speed printer that delivers output one page at a time.

Page Printers. As the term suggests, **page printers** (see Figure 5-16) can produce a page of output at a time. These devices, which can print up to a few hundred pages of output per minute, all employ nonimpact technology. Many of them utilize an electrophotographic process similar to that used by the copying machines found in many offices. The printing commonly occurs on 8-by-11-inch paper, which is cheaper than the larger, sprocket-fed paper line printers typically use. The smaller-size paper is cheaper to file and mail as well. Some page printers can print in color or on both sides of the page.

Figure 5-16
A page printer.
Operating at peak capacity over a weekend, some page printers produce well over a million pages of output.

A useful feature of page printers is their ability to store digital images of forms and letterheads. In fact, users of such systems often can design their own forms and letterheads if they have art or illustration software. Thus, page printers offer considerable savings over line printers, which require changing of paper and printing elements when output dictates a new form or format.

Page printers generally cost considerably more than line printers. Line printers range from $3,000 to $100,000, whereas page printers for large computers may cost between $100,000 and $300,000. In general, an organization that produces over a million lines of output per month should investigate the feasibility of acquiring one of these machines.

Source Data Automation

Often data must be translated from handwritten form into machine-readable form so that they can be processed, a procedure that sometimes consumes thousands of hours of duplicated effort and that can result in many mistakes and delays. Data must be hand-entered on documents or forms, keyed into machine-readable form on a data preparation device, verified, and read into the computer. Usually, several people will be involved in this process, complicating matters further.

Source data automation. The process of making data available in machine-readable form at the time they are collected.

Source data automation eliminates much of this duplicated effort, delay, extra handling, and potential for error by making data available in machine-readable form at the time they are collected. Because ready-to-process transaction data are collected by the people who know most about them, source data automation is rapidly becoming the dominant form of data entry today.

Source data automation has been applied to a number of tasks. For example, many orders taken over the phone today are entered directly into display terminals. Or, a microchip designer draws some circuits on a special pad, and the drawings are immediately digitized and displayed on screen. Source data automation has also been used to speed up check-out lines and inventory at supermarkets, quality control operations in factories, and processing of checks by banks.

In the next few pages, we will discuss several technologies that can be used to achieve source data automation: optical character recognition (OCR), magnetic ink character recognition (MICR), digitizing, image scanning, voice input, handwriting recognition, and smart cards.

Optical Character Recognition (OCR)

Optical character recognition (OCR).
The use of light reflectivity to identify marks, characters, or codes.

Optical character recognition (OCR) refers to a wide range of optical-scanning procedures and equipment designed for machine recognition of marks, characters, and codes. These symbols are transformed into digital form for storage in the computer. Most symbols designed for OCR can be read by humans as well as by machines. Optical recognition of hand-printed characters is also technically possible but is still in its infancy. OCR equipment is among the most varied and highly specialized in the information processing industry. A scanner that can read one type of document may be totally unable to read another.

Optical Marks. One of the oldest applications of OCR is the processing of tests and questionnaires completed on special forms using *optical marks*. Take the case of grading a test in which the student darkens the bubbles on the answer sheet to indicate the answers to multiple-choice questions. An optical document reader scans the answer sheets offline. This machine passes a light beam across the spaces corresponding to the set of possible responses to each question. The light is reflected where a response is penciled in, and the machine tallies that choice.

Optical Characters. *Optical characters* are characters specially designed to be identifiable by humans as well as by some type of OCR reader. Optical characters conform to a certain font, such as that shown in Figure 5-17. The optical reader reflects light off the characters and converts them into digital patterns for recognition. The reader can identify a character only if it is familiar with the font used.

In the early days of optical character reading, fonts differed widely among OCR manufacturers. As the years passed, however, a few fonts became industry standards. Today many machines are designed to read several fonts even when these fonts are mixed in a single document.

Point-of-sale (POS) system.
A computer system, commonly found in department stores and supermarkets, that uses electronic cash register terminals to process sales transactions.

Probably the best-known use of optical characters is in **point-of-sale (POS) systems,** which are employed widely in retail stores. POS systems allow a store to record a purchase at the time and place it occurs. A sale is often automatically recorded from machine-readable information on a

ABCDEFGHIJKLMN
OPQRSTUVWXYZ
1234567890

Figure 5-17
A selection of characters from an optical character set.

price tag attached to the product. The information on the tag is input to a special cash register. Today many cash registers are equipped with local, direct-access memories containing descriptions of stocked items, so they can print what each item is along with its price on the customer receipt (see Figure 5-18).

Another common application of optical characters is in billing operations, such as the processing of insurance and utility bills.

Optical Codes. The most widely used type of *optical code* is the **bar code,** and the most familiar bar code is the *universal product code (UPC)* commonly found on packaged goods in supermarkets (see Figure 5-19). Because they enable immediate recording of purchases, bar codes also fall into the category of POS systems.

Bar code.
A machine-readable code consisting of sets of bars of varying widths.

Image scanner.
A device that can "read" into memory a hard-copy image such as a text page, photograph, map, or drawing.

Bar codes such as the UPC often consist of several vertical bars of varying widths. Information in the code describes the product and identifies the manufacturer. Bar codes can be read either by passing a wand or gun containing a scanner over the coded label or by sending the item past a fixed scanning station (see Figure 5-20). Using the data from the code, the terminal/cash register can identify the item, look up its latest price, and print the information on a receipt such as the one in Figure 5-18. The UPC has been in use since 1973, and currently more than 80 percent of the products sold in supermarkets carry it.

Figure 5-18
An informative cash register receipt made possible by a local memory.

```
      YURI'S FOODMART

04/02/91 11:09 2 201 48
KETCHUP                .89*
RAISIN BRAN           1.09*
   2.34 LB @ 39/LB
PEACHES                .91*
QT NONFAT MILK         .79*
DOZ LARGE EGGS         .98*
  SUBTOTAL            4.66
    TAX                .27
  TOTAL               4.93
  CASH TEND           5.00
    CHANGE DUE         .07
```

Image Scanners

Image scanners, such as the one in Figure 5-21, are used to digitize images of photographs, drawings, and documents into computer memory. Many image scanners sold for PCs scan at a resolution of 300 dpi. As you might expect, the more dots the computer uses to store the image, the better the resolution will be when the image is finally output. Typeset-quality imaging, available through professional print shops, generally starts at a resolution of about 1,000 dpi.

Many image scanners are "dumb," meaning that they can't recognize any of the text they read. "Intelligent" image scanners, on the other

Figure 5-19
A UPC code used on supermarket goods.
The digit to the left of the bars denotes the product category, while the two numbers below identify the manufacturer and product.

0 48001 26568

hand, are accompanied by optical character recognition (OCR) software, which enables them to recognize as well as read characters. Thus, a person with an OCR-capable image scanner can later edit any text on a standard word processor once it is read in. Although such software packages allow only a limited number of fonts to be read, many of them contain routines that enable scanners to learn new fonts.

Magnetic Ink Character Recognition (MICR)

Magnetic ink character recognition (MICR).
A technology that involves the processing of checks inscribed with special characters set in a special magnetic ink.

Magnetic ink character recognition (MICR) is a technology confined almost exclusively to the banking industry, where it is used for processing checks in high volume. Figure 5-22 illustrates a check that has been encoded with MICR characters. The standard font adopted by the industry contains only 14 characters—the ten decimal digits (0 through 9) and four special symbols.

The characters are written on the check with a special magnetic ink. As with OCR readers, a machine called a MICR reader/sorter senses the identity of a MICR-encoded character on the check by recognizing its shape. But in contrast to OCR, the characters must be magnetized in order to be sensed by the reading device; no optical recognition is used. With MICR, checks can be quickly sorted, processed, and routed to the proper banks.

Figure 5-20 Bar code applications.
Bar codes are useful in environments in which products need to be quickly and accurately identified. (a) A scanning gun is frequently used to read bar-coded labels in retail stores. (b) A scanning station is the usual type of device that reads bar codes in supermarkets.

(a) (b)

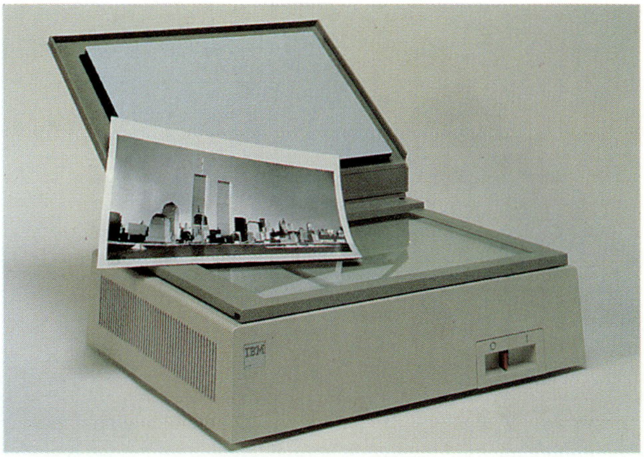

Figure 5-21
An image scanner.
Image scanners are used to digitize images of photographs, drawings, and documents into computer memory. Some scanners are also equipped with software than enables them to recognize text.

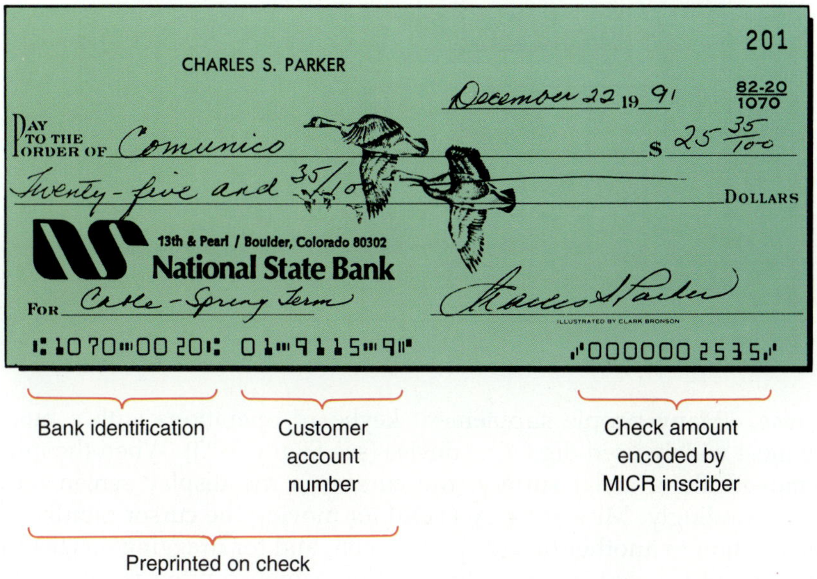

Figure 5-22
Check encoded with MICR characters.
The MICR characters are contained on the bottom line of the check. The characters at the bottom left of the check are preprinted and contain identifying information, including the customer's account number. The characters at the bottom right show the amount of the check and are imprinted by an operator after the check has been cashed.

Digitizers

A **digitizer** is a device that converts a measurement into a digital value. By being moved along a surface or, alternatively, staying stationary and having another device move along them, digitizers determine position, distance, or speed and move the cursor on the display screen accordingly. Digitizers aid source data automation because they directly collect data on events in machine-readable form. Six common types of digitizers are the mouse, light pen, joystick, trackball, crosshair cursor, and digitizing tablet.

Digitizer.
An input device that converts a measurement into a digital value.

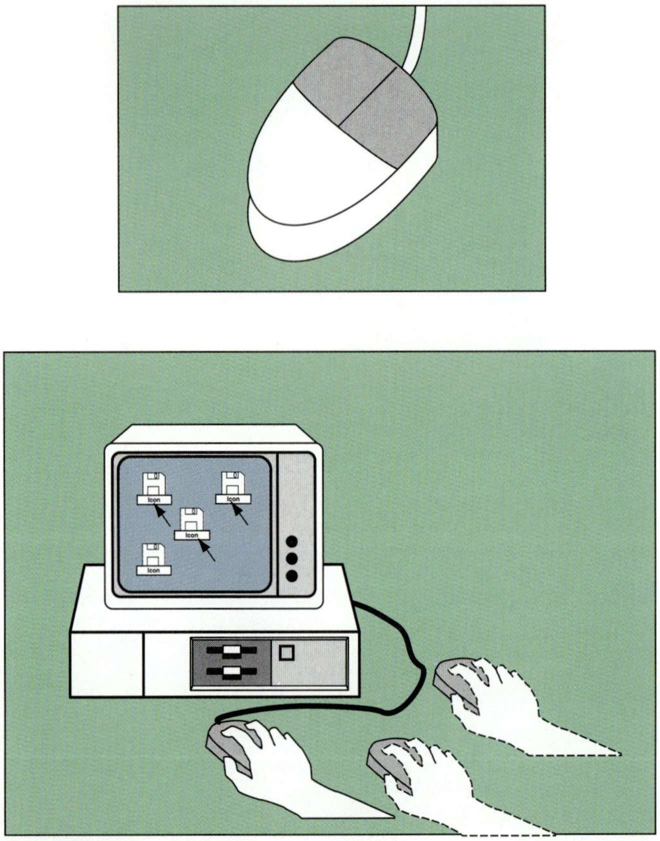

Figure 5-23
Mouse input.
When the mouse is moved along a flat surface, the cursor on the display screen moves correspondingly.

Mouse.
A device used to rapidly move a cursor around a display screen.

Icon.
A graphical image on a display screen that invokes a particular program action when activated by the operator.

Mouse. Many people supplement keyboard operations with a **mouse,** the most widely used digitizing device (see Figure 5-23). When the mouse is moved along a flat surface, the cursor on the display screen moves correspondingly. Mice are very useful for moving the cursor rapidly from one location to another on a display screen, and for dragging images from one part of the screen to another. Using a mouse often is much faster than pressing combinations of cursor-movement keys on keyboard. Mice are especially handy when pointing to **icons** on the screen—small geometric symbols that represent commands or program options. When you use the mouse, say, to move to an icon on the display screen, you select or activate that icon by clicking a button on the mouse once or twice.

Light pen.
An electrical device, resembling an ordinary pen, used to enter input.

Touch-screen device.
A display device that can be activated by touching a finger to the screen.

Light Pen. A **light pen,** such as the one in Figure 5-24a, contains a light-sensitive cell in its tip. When the tip of the pen is placed close to the screen, the display device can identify its position. Some pens are even equipped with a remote-control press-button feature so that when the button is clicked, the computer system flips forward or backward to successive page-length images on the display screen. Display devices that are designed to allow a finger rather than a light pen to activate the screen are commonly called **touch-screen devices** (see Figure 5-24b).

Figure 5-24 Digitizers.
The wide variety of digitizing devices on the market today powerfully illustrates the large number of ways it is possible for ordinary users to input data at their desk tops. (a) Light pen. (b) Touch screen. (c) Joystick. (d) Trackball. (e) Digitizing tablet with crosshair cursor. (f) UnMouse, a miniature, finger-activated digitizing tablet.

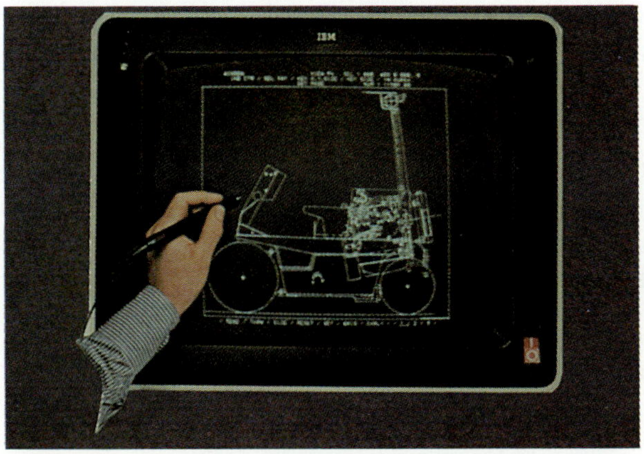

(a)

(b)

(c)

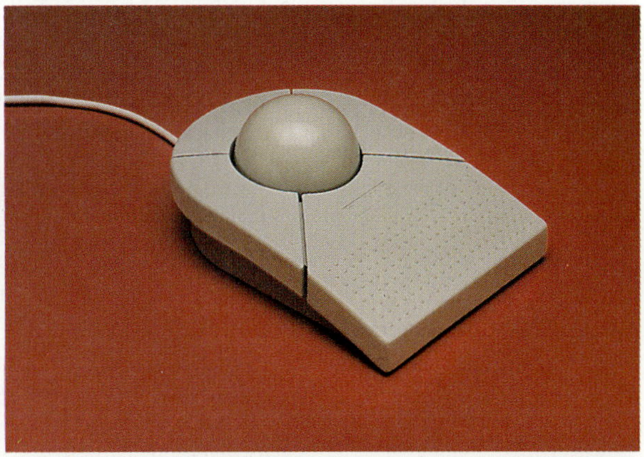

(d)

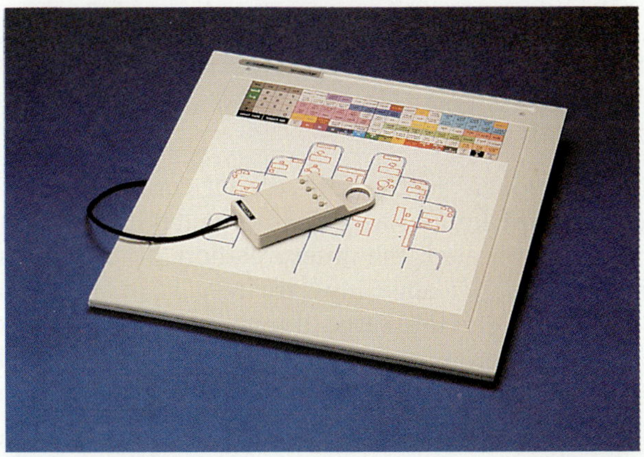

(e)

(f)

Joystick.
An input device that resembles a car's stick shift.

Joystick. A **joystick** (see Figure 5-24c), which looks like a car's stick shift, is often used for computer games and for computer-aided design (CAD) work. With many joysticks, the speed at which they move and the distance they travel determine the speed and distance traveled by the screen cursor. Today, some electronic games are using gloves with built-in sensors in place of joysticks, enabling the computer to directly detect hand movements.

Trackball.
A cursor-movement device that consists of a sphere resting on rollers, with only the top of the sphere exposed outside its case.

Trackball. A **trackball** (see Figure 5-24d) consists of a sphere in a case that rests on rollers, with only the top of the sphere exposed. The screen cursor travels in whatever direction the operator spins the sphere. A mouse is merely a trackball turned upside down.

Crosshair cursor.
A digitizing device that is often moved over hard-copy images of maps and drawings to enter them.

Crosshair Cursor. A **crosshair cursor** (Figure 5-24e) can be moved over hard-copy images of maps, survey photos, and even large drawings. The image is digitized into the computer system's memory as the cursor passes over it. Using a keypad on the cursor, the operator can enter supplementary information into the memory. With maps, for example, features such as rivers, roads, and buildings may be scanned with the crosshair and any identifying labels keyed in from the pad. Once the maps are in digital form, the operator can call them up for display on the screen and modify them.

Digitizing tablet.
A digitizer that consists of a flat board and a device that traces over the board, storing the traced pattern in computer memory.

Digitizing Tablet. A **digitizing tablet** usually employs either a crosshair cursor or a penlike stylus. The operator uses one or the other of these devices to trace over the flat tablet (Figure 5-24e). You can think of the tablet as a matrix of thousands of tiny dots. Each dot has a machine address. When you trace a line on the tablet, the stylus or cursor passes over some of the dots, causing their status in computer memory to change from a 0-state to a 1-state. When the drawing is complete, it is stored in digital form as a large matrix of 0s and 1s and may be recalled at any time. Recently available are also miniature, finger-activated digitizing tablets that compete directly against the mouse (see Figure 5-24f).

Voice-Input Devices

Voice-input device.
A device capable of recognizing the human voice.

Machines that can convert spoken words into digital form for computer storage and processing are known as **voice-input devices.** If you stop to think about how complicated the interpretation of a spoken word can be for humans, you can realize how tricky it is to design a voice-input device to do essentially the same thing. Two people may pronounce the same word differently because of accents, personal styles of speech, and the unique quality of each person's voice. Even the same person can pronounce words differently at various times. Moreover, in listening to others, we not only ignore irrelevant background noises but decode sentence fragments.

User Solution 5-3

Voice Input for Easier Report Preparation

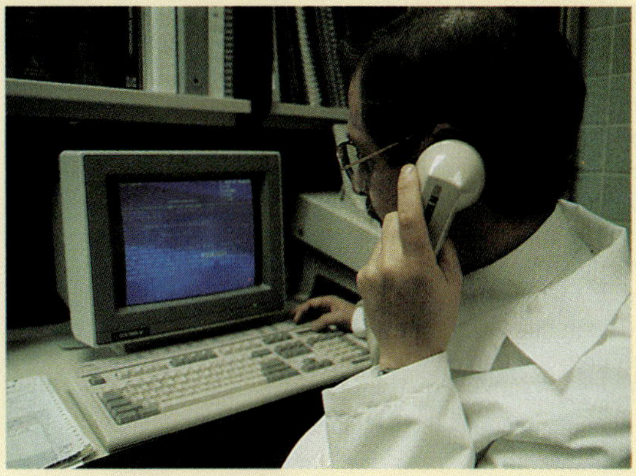

At Mercy Hospital in Springfield, Massachusetts, voice input is the solution of choice to enable emergency-room physicians to prepare patient reports more rapidly. Each day, physicians in the emergency room see 30 to 50 patients and must compile a report on each case. Using a Kurzweil AI voice recognition system, physicians can create and print an average report in about two minutes. The system recognizes both words and "trigger phrases"—single words or phrases that generate entire report segments. The system saves time and produces reports that are more complete and more polished. The latter benefit has provided the unexpected result of cutting down on malpractice suits.

Equipment designers have tried to overcome these obstacles in a number of ways. Some voice-input devices are designed to be "trained" by users, who repeat words until the machines know their voices. These devices can also screen out background noise. Unfortunately, most voice-input devices can recognize only a limited number of isolated words and not whole sentences composed of continuous speech. Thus, the complexity of the messages to which they can respond is quite limited.

Still, the possible applications of this technology are exciting. Imagine yourself speaking into a microphone while a printer automatically types your words. Such a system is, in fact, commercially available today; however, the number of words the computer can "understand" is extremely limited, typically under 1,000. Experts say that voice-actuated word processing will require recognition of at least 10,000 words.

The use of a voice-input system to help doctors prepare reports at a Massachusetts hospital is the subject of User Solution 5-3.

Handwriting Recognition Devices

Handwriting recognition devices generally consist of a flat-screen display tablet and a penlike stylus (see Figure 5-25). Theoretically, as users write words and numbers on the tablet, they are machine recognized. Practically speaking, however, handwriting recognition devices are still in the pioneering stage, and virtually all systems commercially available today can recognize only hand-printed characters. That computer systems have difficulty recognizing characters should not strike you as surprising. After all, if humans have difficulty reading each others' handwriting, how can computers be programmed to fare much better?

Handwriting recognition device.
A device that can read handwritten characters as input.

Figure 5-25
Handwriting recognition.
To reduce paperwork in processing routine police reports, the city of San Jose, California, is experimenting with handwriting recognition equipment. With nearly 1,000 officers collectively filing 100,000 reports a year, the time savings is expected to be enormous. The recognition equipment works best when handwritten characters are written onto the pad with the attached stylus.

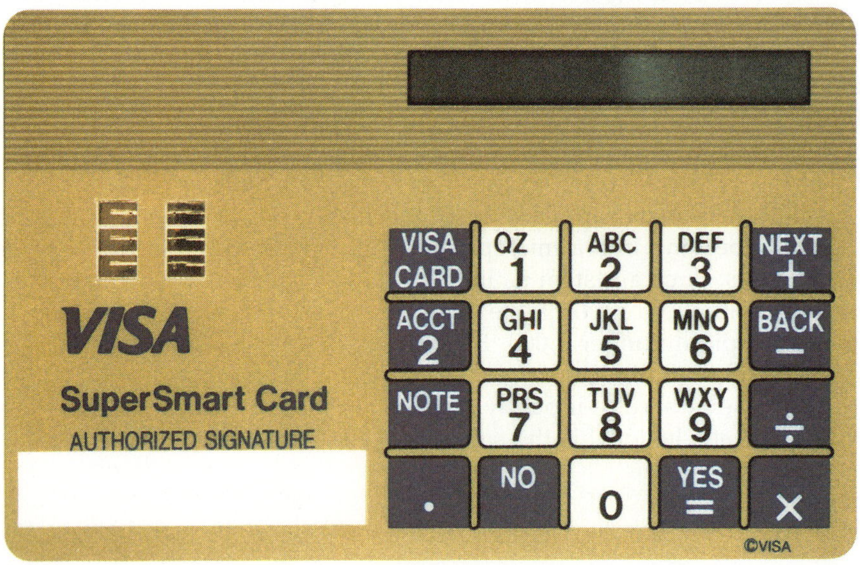

Figure 5-26
Smart card.
The VISA SuperSmart Card shown here contains a keyboard and tiny display to complement its CPU and memory. © *Visa International Service Association. All Rights Reserved. Reproduced with the permission of Visa International Service Association.*

Smart Cards

Smart card.
A credit-card-sized plastic card with storage and a microprocessor.

Smart cards are credit-card-sized pieces of plastic that contain, at a minimum, a microprocessor chip and a memory (see Figure 5-26). The memory capacity may be as small as a few thousand characters or as large as a few million.

Smart cards, which were pioneered in France and are still in the pilot stage in many places, are most often used to make electronic purchases or to transfer funds between accounts—say, between the cardholder's account and the account at a bank or credit card company.

The uses for smart cards abound. In the health care industry, such cards could be used to store a patient's identity and address, insurance data, next of kin, allergies, and a brief medical history. If the card carrier were disabled in an accident, the card could immediately be put into use to assist with treatment. A university issuing such cards could use them to allow students access to grade or financial data. Smart cards also could be useful for making phone calls; a cardholder would have an electronic record of all phone calls made—useful for tax and billing purposes—right on the card. In security applications, such a card could carry a digitized version of a fingerprint or voice and thereby serve as an electronic passkey, allowing an authorized user into restricted areas or access to a sensitive computer network.

In some areas, smart cards are now being tried out at toll booths. The card is mounted in a specific place on the front window of the booth and scanned electronically by a transmitter as the cardholder cruises by. Then the cardholder's account is debited for the toll.

Special-Purpose Output Equipment

In this section, we will consider output devices that are appropriate for specialized uses. The technologies we will describe are computer output microfilm (COM), plotters, voice-output devices, and film recorders.

Computer Output Microfilm (COM)

Computer output microfilm (COM) is a way of placing computer output on microfilm media, typically either a *microfilm reel* or *microfiche card*. Microfilming can result in tremendous savings in paper costs, storage space, the mailing of document images, and handling. For example, a 4-by-6-inch microfiche card can contain the equivalent of 270 printed pages. COM is particularly useful for organizations that must keep massive files of information that do not need to be updated. It's also useful for organizations that need to manipulate large amounts of data but find fast methods of online access too costly.

Computer output microfilm (COM).
A term that refers to reducing computer output to microscopic form and putting it on photosensitive film.

The process of producing microfilm or microfiche output generally takes place offline on a special COM unit. This device displays an image of each page on a screen and produces microfilmed photographs from these images. To read the microfilm or microfiche that COM produces, people either select the reels or cards by hand and mount them onto the appropriate reading device or use an auxiliary retrieval system driven by a minicomputer that automatically locates and mounts the desired frames. Reading usually takes place offline.

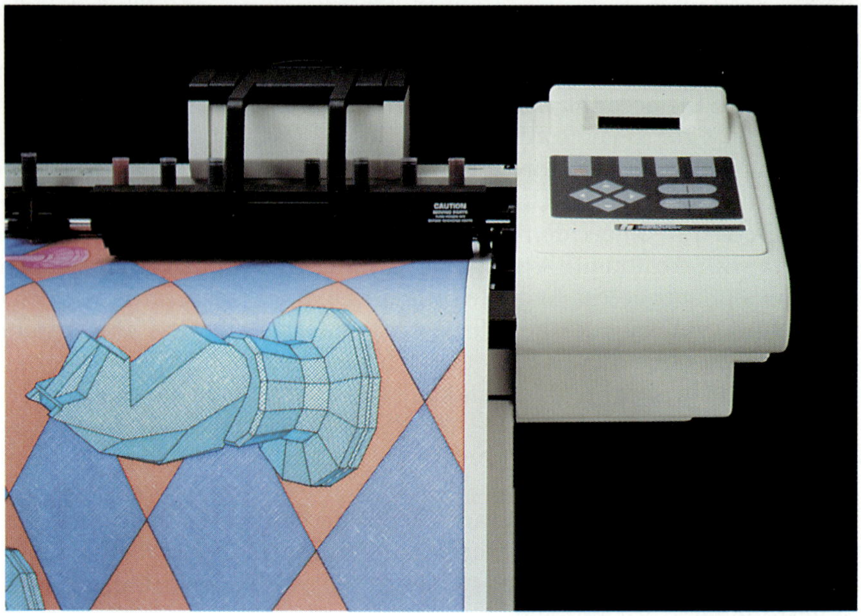

Figure 5-27
A pen plotter.
Pen plotters, such as the drum plotter shown here, can produce very high-quality output but do it at low speeds.

Plotters

Plotter.
An output device used for drawing graphs and diagrams.

A **plotter** is an output device that is primarily used to produce charts, drawings, maps, three-dimensional illustrations, and other forms of hard copy. The two most common types of plotters are pen plotters and electrostatic plotters.

A *pen plotter* (see Figure 5-27) is an output device that employs pens, which create images by moving across the paper surface. Watching these machines draw is an experience and always attracts interest among people who are seeing them for the first time. The plotter looks like a mechanical artist working in fast motion. As the machine switches colors and begins new patterns, the audience is hard put to guess what the plotter will do next. Many pen plotters can accept either standard fiber-tipped pens or, if the highest possible output quality is desired, high-precision, technical drafting pens.

Electrostatic plotters are also very popular for graphics output. These devices work with a toner bed similar to that of a copying machine, but instead of light they use a matrix of tiny wires to charge the paper with electricity. When the charged paper passes over the toner, the toner adheres to it and produces an image. Electrostatic plotters are relatively fast, but their output quality is lower than that of pen plotters. Nonetheless, the output quality of electrostatic devices is improving, and many industry experts expect them to eventually replace the slower, mechanically intensive pen plotters.

Whether they employ pens or electrostatic printing, plotters are of either the flatbed or drum type. A *flatbed plotter* resembles a flat drafting board. By contrast, *drum plotters,* such as the one in Figure 5-27, draw on paper that is rolled onto a drumlike mechanism.

Voice-Output Devices

For a number of years, computers have been able to communicate with users, after a fashion, by "speaking" to them. How often have you dialed a phone number only to hear, "We're sorry, the number you are trying to reach, 774–0202, is no longer in service," or "The time is 6:15 . . . the downtown temperature is 75 degrees"? **Voice-output devices,** the machines responsible for such messages, convert digital data in storage into spoken messages. These messages may be constructed as needed from a file of prerecorded words, or they may be synthesized using other techniques.

Voice-output device.
A device that enables the computer system to produce spoken output.

Computerized voice output is also used extensively at airline terminals to broadcast information about flight departures and arrivals, in the securities business to quote the prices of stocks and bonds, and in the supermarket industry to announce descriptions and prices of items as they are scanned. Voice output has great potential in any company with employees who do little else all day but, say, give out balances and status reports.

Currently one of the main shortcomings of this technology is that the number of potential messages is limited if the system must create them extemporaneously. Most voice-output devices have a vocabulary on the order of a few hundred words and a limited ability to combine words dynamically to form intelligible sentences. As a result, these devices are most useful when short messages are required—a telephone number, a bank balance, a price, and so on (see Feature 5-1).

Film Recorders

Film recorders are cameralike devices that capture high-resolution, computer-generated images directly onto 35mm slides, transparencies, and other film media. Just a few years ago, film recorders served only large computers, with which they were used for applications such as art, medical imaging, and scientific CAD work. Today they are increasingly being used with PCs for applications such as spicing up corporate business meetings or client presentations with slide shows. Some experts predict that such computer-generated slides will soon account for a large percentage of all business slides made. Because film recorders, like cameras, are "dumb" and need not recognize an image in order to record it, they can easily transfer onto film virtually any image that can be captured on a display screen. Most of the images in Window 2 were produced on film recorders, which by far provide the highest resolution of any of the output devices discussed in this chapter.

Film recorder.
A cameralike device that captures computer output onto film.

Feature 5-1

The Telephone as a Computer Terminal

Voice I/O Begins to Take Off

You're impatiently waiting beside a phone booth while the guy inside is hitting key after key on the touch-tone phone. Finally, he is finished. What a waste; it looks as if he never got through to anyone or even had a chance to open his mouth.

"Hard to get any business done during the lunch hour," you say, trying to make some small talk.

"On the contrary, I just bought 500 shares of Oracle, sold 200 shares of Peripherals Unlimited, and got quotes on three other stocks."

What we've just described is an example of *telebrokering.* It is now possible in some areas to buy and sell stocks and to get stock quotes over a touch-tone phone without ever talking to a human operator. The ordinary phone essentially becomes a computer terminal. Telebrokering can be done at any time of the day or night. Although not every type of brokerage interaction can be handled by such a system, some analysts in the industry say that around 20 percent of business transactions are routine enough to be accommodated.

When you use telebrokering, you are engaged in a dialogue with a brokerage house's computer. Let's say that you want to buy some Microsoft stock. You identify the stock by its unique symbol (MSFT), hit "B" for buy, and punch in the number of shares. The computer prompts you separately for each individual input. As you respond to each prompt, the computer uses a voice chip to echo back what you are entering, and it asks you to verify that the information is correct. If it isn't, you can cancel what you've just typed in and re-input the data. With the echo feature, there's no doubt about what took place when you've finished. Before an order is executed, the computer repeats all of the information it has and asks you for a final verification. If the computer can execute the deal, you will know that before you hang up the phone.

The brokerage business is not the only application for which an ordinary phone is the principal input device. At some universities, including Ohio State and Brigham Young (to name just two) you can now register for classes over a touch-tone phone. Almost 90 percent of the students at Ohio State, for instance, sign up for classes by phone. In the field of marketing research, data are often collected by a computer instead of by a human interviewer. And in the travel business, it is becoming increasingly common for people to call up a computer that will supply them with specific weather or travel information as well as updates on conditions at the ski slopes or shore.

Telebrokering. Doing deals without talking to anybody.

In the transportation business, several companies now have phone numbers that are connected to vast global networks. As goods are transferred from one vehicle or ship to another, they pass through a station where bar-coded tags are automatically read by radio signals that identify the cargo. This cargo information is then uploaded to a computer that you can call at any time of the day or night to find out the location of your shipment.

Of course, the compelling advantage to telephones is that most homes have phones, and you can also find them in business offices, airports, restaurants, malls—virtually everywhere that people tend to congregate. In the future, as this technology becomes more commonplace, phones may have built-in display devices and printers. Then you won't have to wait for a computerized voice to tell you what to do, and you'll be able to get a receipt for any transaction on the spot.

Summary and Key Terms

A wide variety of input and output devices is available in today's marketplace.

Input and Output. Input and output devices enable people and computers to communicate. **Input devices** convert data and programs into a form that the CPU will understand. **Output devices** convert computer-processed information into a form that people will comprehend.

Output devices produce results in either hard copy or soft copy form. The term **hard copy** generally refers to output that has been recorded into a *permanent* form onto a medium such as paper or microfilm. The term **soft copy,** in contrast, generally refers to display output, which is *temporary.*

Keyboards. For most people, a computer system would be useless without a **keyboard,** which is often the main vehicle for input. Keyboards vary tremendously in terms of such factors as number of keys, key arrangement, types of special keys, and touch. On most computer keyboards, there are several *function keys*—labeled F1, F2, and so on—that can be used to activate single commands or entire computer programs. There is usually also a *numeric keypad* that allows numbers to be keyed in faster.

Display Devices. **Display devices** are peripheral devices that contain a televisionlike viewing screen. Most display devices fall into one of two categories: monitors and display terminals. A **monitor** is an output device that consists of only the viewing screen. A **display terminal** is an input/output communications workstation that consists of a screen for output and a keyboard for input. As each key on the keyboard is depressed, the corresponding character representation of the key appears on the display screen at the **cursor** position.

A key characteristic of any display device is *resolution,* or the sharpness of the screen image. On many display devices, resolution is measured by the number of dots, or **pixels,** on the screen. With **bit mapping,** the operator can control each pixel on the screen.

One common way to classify display devices is according to whether they are monochrome or color. *Monochrome* display devices output using a single foreground color, whereas *color* display devices often are capable of outputting in eight or more colors.

Most display devices on the market today use a large picture-tube element similar to those found inside standard TV sets. These devices are called **CRTs (cathode-ray tubes).** Recently, slim-profile devices called **flat-panel displays** have also become available.

Printers. Unlike display devices, **printers** produce hard-copy output. *Low-speed printers* output one character at a time. Because of their relatively low cost, they are popular units for small computer systems. *High-*

speed printers, which can output either a line or a page at a time, are popular for larger computer systems.

All printers use either an impact or a nonimpact printing technology. In **impact printing,** a hammer strikes the paper or ribbon to form characters. A **solid-font mechanism** is an impact device that produces fully formed characters like those a typewriter creates. Most low-speed printers in use today employ a print head that's an **impact dot-matrix mechanism,** which constructs printed characters out of a series of closely packed dots. **Nonimpact printing,** which outputs dot-matrix characters, uses a variety of techniques to form printed images. The most popular nonimpact printing methods today use *electrothermal, thermal-transfer, ink-jet,* and *laser* technologies.

The printers most commonly available for microcomputer systems are low-speed devices that use either daisywheel, print-thimble, impact dot-matrix, thermal-transfer, or ink-jet technologies. Although impact-dot matrix printers are still the most widely used, relatively high-speed laser printers have become especially popular in business in the last few years. Laser printers produce letter-quality output that rivals that of solid-font printers, quickly generate presentation graphics for reports and meetings, and enable certain publishing functions to be performed on a desktop.

Most of the printing done on large computer systems is accomplished by high-speed printers. High-speed printers fall into one of two major categories: **line printers,** which produce a line of output at a time, and **page printers,** which produce a page of output at a time.

Source Data Automation. **Source data automation** refers to technologies for collecting data in machine-readable form at their point of origin. Among these technologies are optical character recognition (OCR), magnetic ink character recognition (MICR), digitizing, image scanning, voice input, handwriting recognition, and smart cards.

Optical character recognition (OCR) refers to a wide range of optical-scanning procedures and equipment designed for machine recognition of marks, characters, and codes. *Optical marks* are most frequently used in test-taking situations in which students darken bubbles on special forms to show responses. Probably the best-known use of *optical characters* is in the **point-of-sale (POS) systems** widely used at checkout stations in stores. In many of these systems, the characters on the price tag are coded in a special font readable by both machines and humans. Some POS systems use *optical codes,* such as **bar codes.** The most widely used bar code is the *universal product code (UPC),* which appears on the labels of most packaged supermarket goods.

An **image scanner** is used to input images such as photographs, drawings, and documents into computer storage. In the case of text documents, some image scanners are accompanied by software that enables the scanners to recognize the inputted characters.

Magnetic ink character recognition (MICR) is a technology confined almost exclusively to the banking industry. MICR characters, preprinted on bank checks, enable the checks to be rapidly sorted, processed, and routed to the proper banks.

A **digitizer** is an input device that converts a measurement into a digital value. One of the most widely used digitizers is the **mouse,** which, when rolled along a flat surface, moves the screen cursor accordingly. Mice are especially handy when pointing to **icons** on the screen. Some other widely used digitizing devices are the **light pen, joystick, trackball, crosshair cursor,** and **digitizing tablet.** Display devices that are designed to allow a finger rather than a light pen to activate the screen are commonly called **touch-screen devices.**

Voice-input devices enable computer systems to recognize the spoken word. Voice-input technologies have tremendous work-saving potential but have been slow to mature because of their relative complexity.

Handwriting recognition devices generally consist of a flat-screen display tablet and a penlike stylus. Practically speaking, handwriting recognition devices are still in the pioneering stage, and virtually all systems commercially available today can recognize only hand-printed characters.

Smart cards are credit-card-sized pieces of plastic that contain a microprocessor chip and a memory.

Special-Purpose Output Equipment. A number of special-purpose output devices exist for a variety of information processing applications. Among these are computer output microfilm (COM) equipment, plotters, voice-output devices, and film recorders.

Computer output microfilm (COM) is a way of placing computer output on microfilm media such as microfilm reels or microfiche cards. COM can result in tremendous savings in paper costs, storage space, and handling.

A **plotter** is an output device that is used primarily to produce graphic output such as charts, maps, and engineering drawings. The two most common types of plotters are *pen plotters,* which use drawing pens to create images, and *electrostatic plotters,* which create images through electrostatic charges. Whether they employ pens or electrostatic charges, plotters are of either the flatbed or the drum type. A *flatbed plotter* uses a drawing surface that resembles a drafting table. A *drum plotter* draws on a cylindrically backed surface.

Voice-output devices enable computer systems to compose intelligible spoken messages from digitally stored words and phrases.

Film recorders are cameralike devices that are used to capture computer-generated images directly onto 35mm slides, transparencies, and other film media. Virtually any image that can be captured on a display screen can be output onto film.

Review Exercises

Fill-in Questions

1. The term ____________ generally refers to output that has been recorded onto a medium such as paper or film.
2. Resolution on a display screen is measured by the number of dots, or ____________.

3. A highlighted position on a display screen indicating where the next character the operator types in will be placed is called a(n) ______________.
4. A display device that outputs images in a single foreground color is known as a(n) ______________ display.
5. High-quality dot-matrix printing is sometimes called ______________ (NLQ) printing.
6. A(n) ______________ printer heats ink from a wax-based ribbon onto paper.
7. A(n) ______________ printer sprays small droplets of electrically charged ink onto paper to form images.
8. Two types of pen plotters are ______________ and ______________ plotters.
9. A display device in which all screen pixels can be controlled by the operator is called ______________.
10. A(n) ______________ is a cameralike device used to capture computer-generated images directly onto 35mm slides.

Matching Questions

Match each term with the description that fits best.

a. crosshair cursor	e. MICR
b. OCR	f. COM
c. POS	g. plotter
d. UPC	h. mouse

_____ 1. Used almost exclusively by the banking industry.

_____ 2. Refers to microfilmed output.

_____ 3. A type of output device used to produce graphical images on paper with pens.

_____ 4. Refers to a collection of different technologies used for optical recognition of marks, characters, and codes.

_____ 5. A code that is prominent on the packaging of most supermarket goods.

_____ 6. A device that would be useful for digitizing a map into computer storage.

_____ 7. A device used to move the cursor rapidly around the display screen.

_____ 8. Refers to the use of electronic cash registers, optical scanning devices, and so forth in retail establishments.

Discussion Questions

1. List several types of input and output devices. State whether each device is used for input, output, or both.
2. Identify several ways in which display devices differ.
3. Name some hardware devices that are used in conjunction with display devices for entering data into the computer system.

4. In what major respects do printers differ?
5. What is source data automation, and why is it significant?
6. How does MICR differ from OCR?
7. What are the limitations of voice-input and voice-output devices?
8. What major advantages does COM offer?

Critical Thinking Questions

1. A page of typed text that is created and saved with a word processor takes up a different amount of storage than a copy of that same page read by a scanner. Why do you think this is so? Which would take up more space?
2. Some people predicted years ago that there would never be a significant market for color CRTs among office workers. This prediction proved dead wrong. What do you think motivated this prediction and why would you guess it proved wrong?
3. The president of J.C. Penney has stated that the leading retailers in the future will be those who make the best use of information processing technologies. Do you agree with this point of view? Explain why or why not.

Window 2

The Electronic Canvas

A Peek at the Leading Edge in Computer Output

Probably nothing exemplifies the rapid advances made in computer output over the last few years better than the field of computer art. As you examine the images on the next few pages, keep in mind that only since about 1980 has the computer emerged as a viable tool for artistic expression. All of the early computer artists were scientists with a keen knowledge of both computers and mathematical modeling, and they worked on large, general-purpose computers. As the potential and demand for computer-generated art in business-related fields such as advertising, publishing, and movie production evolved, specialized hardware and software for noncomputer professionals began to emerge. The field of computer art is still in the pioneering stage, and one can only guess what the leading edge of computer output will look like ten years from now.

1. A moose created on a Genigraphics art system. The computer can be used as a tool that enables art to be created from scratch—or read into storage with an image scanner—and treated with special effects.

2

3

4

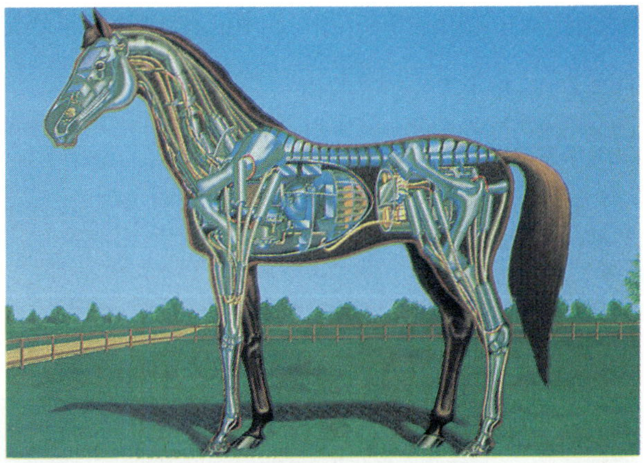

2–9. Computer artists often electronically create highly imaginative, somewhat surreal images that bear only a passing resemblance to reality.

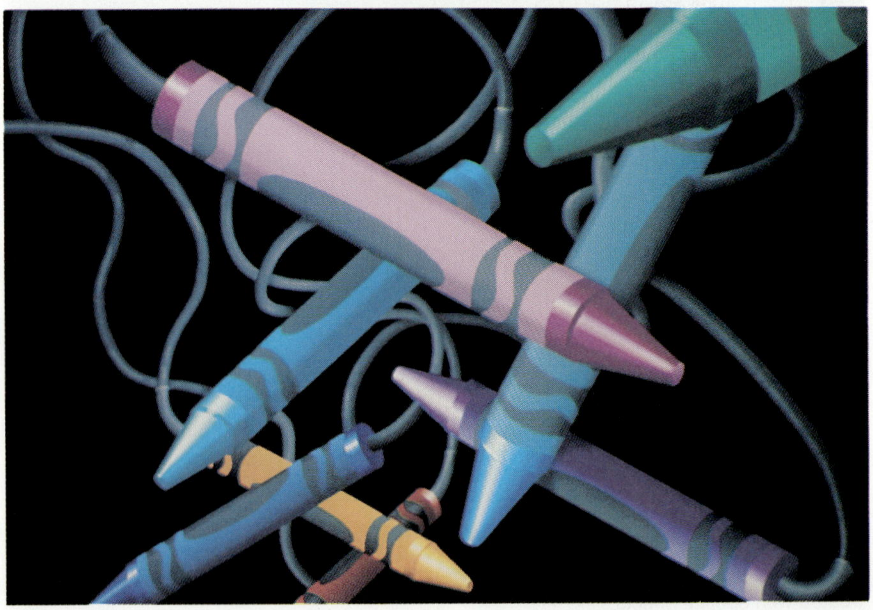

5

6

7

8

9

10

11

12

13

14

15

16

10–16. Many art packages have painting tools that enable artists to imitate traditional art forms, creating images that look as if they were produced with pastels or watercolors, were sketched, or were done with oils.

17

17, 18. Computers are often used to produce natural- and unnatural-looking representations of nature.

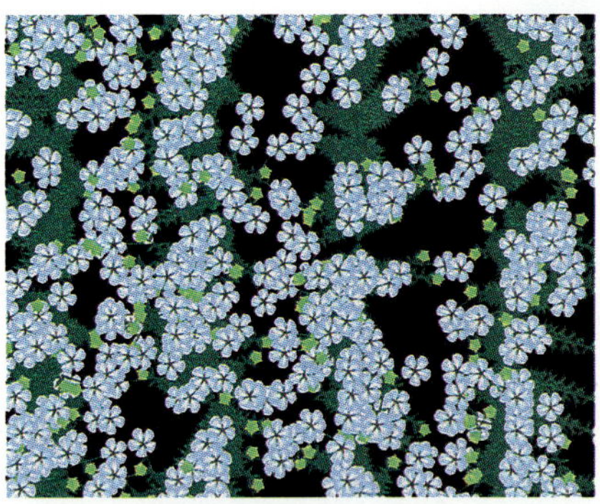

18

19, 20. Computer art usually forms the basis for computer animation, such as the stills shown here from a computer-created film.

19

20

21–24. Computers are often used in the creation of commercial art such as cards, posters, and advertisements.

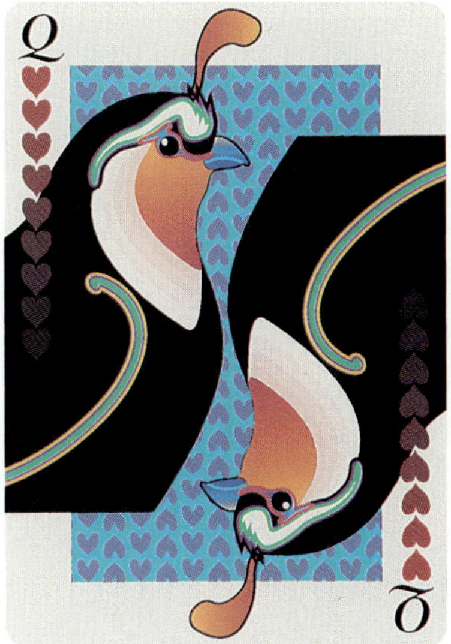

21

22

23

24

Today communications technologies are paving a global data highway, in which information on international events is instantly available to corporations. Tomorrow the global data highway will theoretically enable individuals sitting in their homes to access customized, electronic information anywhere throughout the world.

Module C Support Systems

In this module we examine two areas that play support roles in a computer system—telecommunications and systems software.

Telecommunications, covered in Chapter 6, refers to applications that involve data traveling over distances, as well as the hardware and software that enable this to be done. For instance, special hardware devices send data over ordinary phone lines, and software is required to ensure that the receiving devices understand exactly what the sending devices are communicating. Because companies need up-to-date information to operate successfully in today's highly competitive world, telecommunications is a top priority on managers' agendas.

Systems software, the topic of Chapter 7, refers to the background programs that enable applications software to run on hardware devices. Systems software allows you to start up your computer system, summon applications programs so that you can work on them, recover lost files, reorganize disk storage, and translate applications software into the machine language native to your computer. Everybody who uses a computer system must in some way interact with systems software.

Why are more companies than ever establishing their own worldwide communications centers, such as the one shown here for General Motors? As the world moves to a global economy, corporate survival depends on reacting instantaneously to events both at home and abroad. About half of GM's total information processing costs are communications related, underscoring the importance of telecommunications today.

6 Telecommunications

Outline

Overview

Telecommunications Applications

Communications Media

- Types of Media
- Media Speed
- Media Mode
- Media Signal
- Parallel versus Serial Transmission
- Asynchronous versus Synchronous Transmission

Wide Area Networks and Local Networks

- Wide Area Networks
- Local Networks

Network Topologies

Communications among Devices

- Protocols
- Hardware for Managing Communications Traffic

Learning Objectives

After completing this chapter, you will be able to:

1. Describe several uses of telecommunications technology.
2. Identify the hardware and software components of a telecommunications system.
3. Describe various types of communications media and explain how messages can be sent over them.
4. Identify some types of communications services and network facilities that organizations may acquire.
5. Explain the conventions that devices use to communicate with one another.
6. Describe some of the strategies used to manage networks.

Overview

Telecommunications. A term that refers to transmitting data over a distance.

Telecommunications, or *telecom,* refers to communication over a distance—over phone lines, via privately owned cable, or by satellite, for instance. Today, telecommunications technologies are integrated in a variety of ways into many organizations' routine operations. Through telecommunications, for example, a marketing manager at company headquarters can instantly receive information on inventories from a warehouse at another location and then transmit that information to a division office across the country or even across the globe. Or a purchasing agent on the 25th floor of an office building can use a personal computer workstation to call up the status of a purchase order stored on the mainframe system located in the building's basement. Later, the agent can use the same workstation to dial up a computer owned by a supplier, 1,000 miles away, and get a list of prices. User Solution 6-1, on Wal-Mart, provides a good example of how companies are increasingly relying on telecommunications to keep competitive.

In this chapter, we'll look first at several business applications of telecommunications. Then we'll consider how data are sent over distances. We'll begin by describing the media that carry data, such as phone lines and microwaves, as well as the types of signals that encode the data. Next, we'll discuss the various ways in which people or organizations can get the resources they need to transmit data. Finally, we'll examine several issues concerning the management of telecommunications traffic.

Telecommunications Applications

Today a wide variety of important business applications involve telecommunications. Here we'll briefly discuss several.

Distributed Transaction Processing. At one time, transaction processing operations such as accounts receivable and order entry were totally centralized. As communications systems made it possible to *distribute* workloads to multiple sites, many organizations modified their systems accordingly. The airlines' passenger reservation system is one noteworthy example; thousands of agents located across the globe use display terminals or microcomputer workstations to tap into computerized databases located elsewhere that contain flight, hotel, and rental-car information. While a computer in, say, Chicago is processing a Cerritos, California, agent's request for flight information, that same agent may be processing a ticket for another client locally. Credit-card systems, such as the one for VISA shown in Figure 6-1, are also good examples of distributed transaction processing. Once a store clerk inserts your credit card into a verification terminal, computers hundreds or thousands of miles away approve or deny the purchase.

Virtually every large organization today has several types of distributed transaction processing systems in place. For instance, chain stores

User Solution 6-1

Keeping Competitive with Communications Technology

Large retailers like Wal-Mart depend heavily on sophisticated computer and communications systems. Wal-Mart was the first retailer to have its own private satellite network. Its 1,500-plus stores each has an IBM Series/1 minicomputer that hooks into the network, as well as numerous hand-held terminals, electronic registers, and PCs. Through the register-fed data, Wal-Mart can tell when a product is moving slowly or quickly and can rapidly adjust floor space. Also, product-movement data enables management to forecast inventory needs more accurately and to communicate those needs at once to suppliers. About 1,800 of Wal-Mart's 5,000 suppliers use EDI (Electonic Data Interchange) links to it, which enables them to exchange purchase orders and invoices electronically with Wal-Mart's computers.

often collect and process data locally, then transmit these data to a headquarters site for timely analysis. Mail-order firms frequently process orders at one site and then transmit transaction data to a warehouse site to initiate packing and delivery. The applications are virtually endless.

Strategic Alliances. Recently, many companies have gone a step further with their distributed transaction processing systems by creating *interorganizational systems (IOSs),* in which their computers are strategically linked to the computers of key customers and/or suppliers. For instance, many of the major automakers use their own computer systems to constantly monitor their suppliers' computer systems to ensure that proper inventory levels for critical parts are kept. They also may use the IOSs to shop electronically for the best prices.

Another widely used type of interorganizational information system used now by many companies is **electronic data interchange (EDI).** EDI enables standard business documents such as purchase orders and invoices to be exchanged from one company's computer system to the computer system of another company (see Figure 6-2). The company doing the purchasing often is able to electronically track its order's progress on the seller's computer system.

Electronic data interchange (EDI). A computer procedure that enables standard business documents—such as purchase orders and invoices—to be exchanged electronically between companies.

Companies that wish to exchange transaction documents through EDI must have compatible systems for this. If they don't, they can take advantage of EDI by contacting an intermediary firm that has the hardware

Figure 6-1 Distributed processing: trailing a VISA transaction.
(a) In Chicago, a VISA card is used to pay for a $1,295 computer. (b) The transaction data travel by satellite or by ground to a processing center in New Jersey. (c) Because the transaction tops $50, it is routed to a computer in Atlanta for closer scrutiny. (d) The computer in Atlanta sends the transaction to California for processing. (e) The California computer finds that the card was issued by a Portland bank and checks that bank's computer system to see if the transaction request should be approved or denied. The answer retraces the same path back to the store. The total elapsed time of the transaction is 15 seconds.

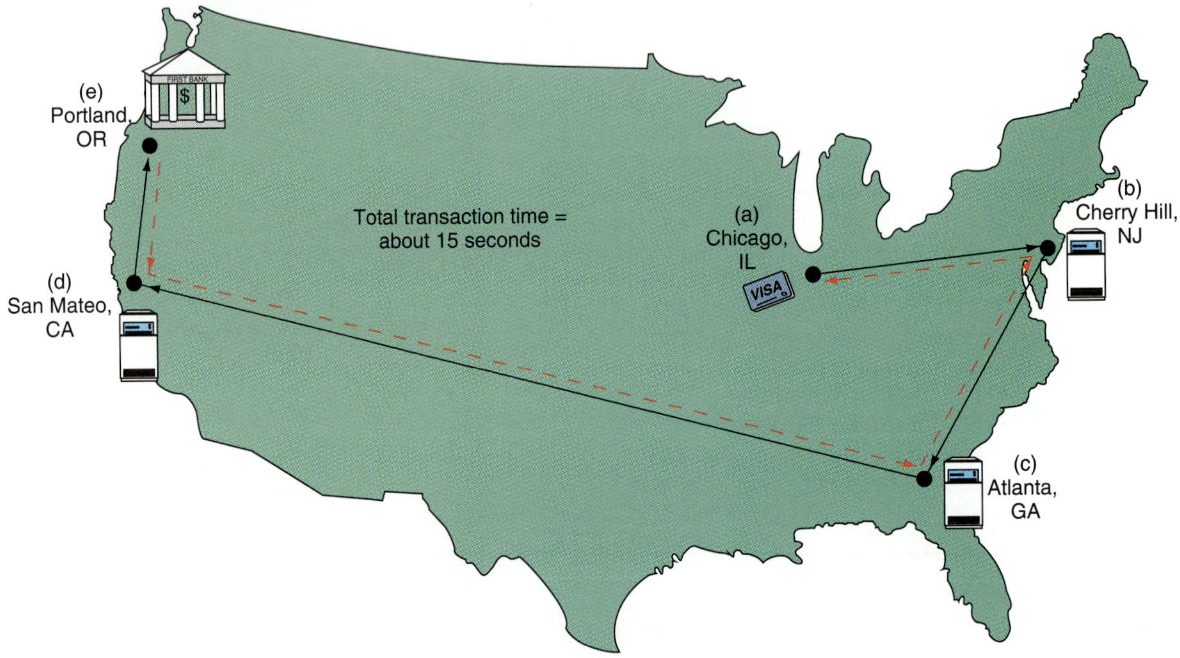

and software to take EDI transmissions from one company and recode them in a form that can be sent to the other company. Many large companies today order a sizable percentage of their supplies and raw materials through computer-to-computer order processing, and many that don't are moving in this direction.

Electronic mailbox.
A storage area used to hold messages, memos, and other documents sent to a person.

Voice mail.
An electronic mail system in which spoken phone messages are digitally recorded and stored in an electronic mailbox.

Electronic Mailboxes and Voice Mail. **Electronic mailboxes** are the computer-age equivalents of traditional mailboxes. They consist of files on hard disk, belonging to specific individuals or accounts, authorized to receive electronic messages. In one common application, a manager types a memo and electronically routes it to the electronic mailboxes of selected company employees (see Figure 6-3).

Voice mail, which involves voice data, is a telecommunications technology that takes electronic mailboxes one step further. In a voice-mail system, the sender's spoken messages are digitized by voice tone and stored in bit form on an answering device at the receiver's location. When the receiver presses a "listen" key, the digitized message is reconverted to voice data.

Figure 6-2 Electronic data interchange.
Electronic data interchange enables companies to electronically exchange documents such as purchase orders (POs) and bills.

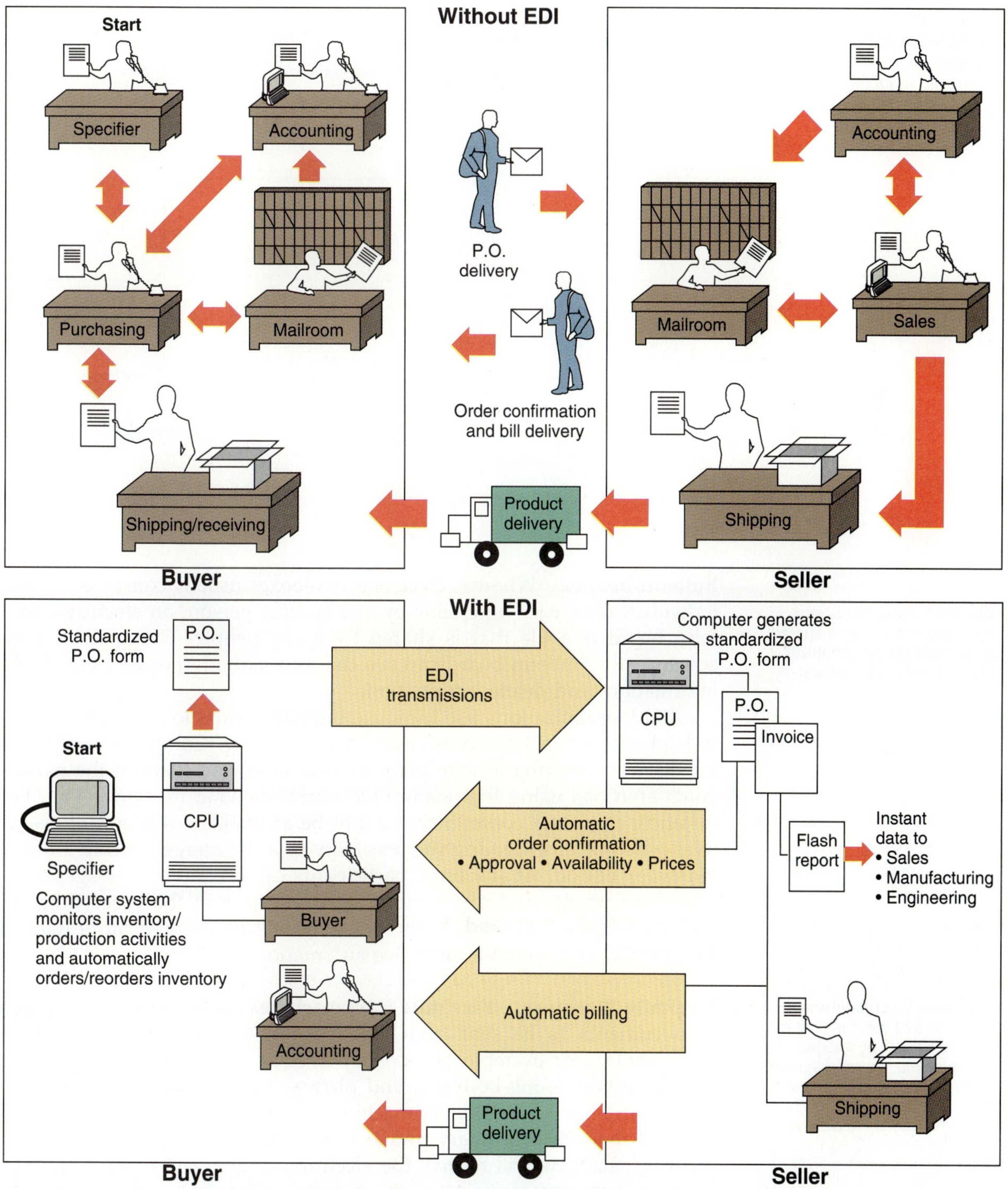

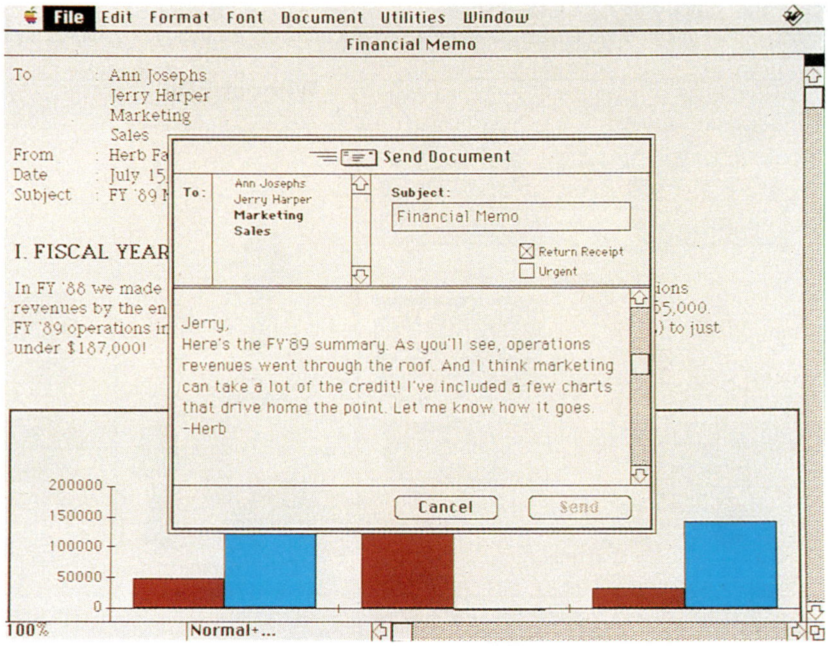

Figure 6-3
Electronic mailboxes.
With software packages such as Microsoft Mail, users can collect electronic documents together, attach a memo to them, and route them to the electronic mailboxes of selected individuals.

Electronic bulletin board. A computer file that is shared by several people, enabling them to post or broadcast messages.

Bulletin Boards. Whereas electronic mailboxes usually consist of several individual files, each accessible by one specific person, an **electronic bulletin board** is a file that is shared by many people. Each person with access to the bulletin board can see the information "posted" on it, add information, and delete information.

Many organizations use in-house bulletin boards to carry out a high-tech phenomenon known as *computer conferencing*. Computer conferencing allows a meeting to take place by computer—even when the participants aren't all using their computer workstations at the same time. For instance, computer conferencing might be available to a group of executives who are investigating the feasibility of a big merger during a hectic two-week period. At any time, participants can broadcast messages to all other participants and can retrieve all or any part of the proceedings of the "conference." Computer conferencing will be covered more fully in Chapter 12, in the section on office automation (OA).

Facsimile (fax) machine. A device that can transmit or receive hard-copy images of text, pictures, maps, diagrams, and the like over the phone lines.

Facsimile Machines. **Facsimile (fax) machines** enable hard-copy images of documents to be sent from one location to another over ordinary phone lines. For example, a secretary in Kansas City may place a short document containing both text and pictures into a fax machine, such as the one in Figure 6-4. The fax machine will digitize the page images and transmit them over ordinary phone lines to New York. In New York another fax machine will receive the electronic page images and reproduce them in hard-copy form. All of this may take place in less than a minute. Also, microcomputer systems can be equipped with *fax boards* that enable them to communicate with fax machines.

Figure 6-4 Fax transmission.
A three-page memo can be sent from Kansas City to New York in less than a minute. In Kansas City, pages are placed in an input hopper in the back of the fax machine. As they are read, they exit out the front. The images are sent over the phone lines in electronic form, and when they reach New York, they are converted into natural-language form—identical to the originals—and output on continuous-roll fax paper.

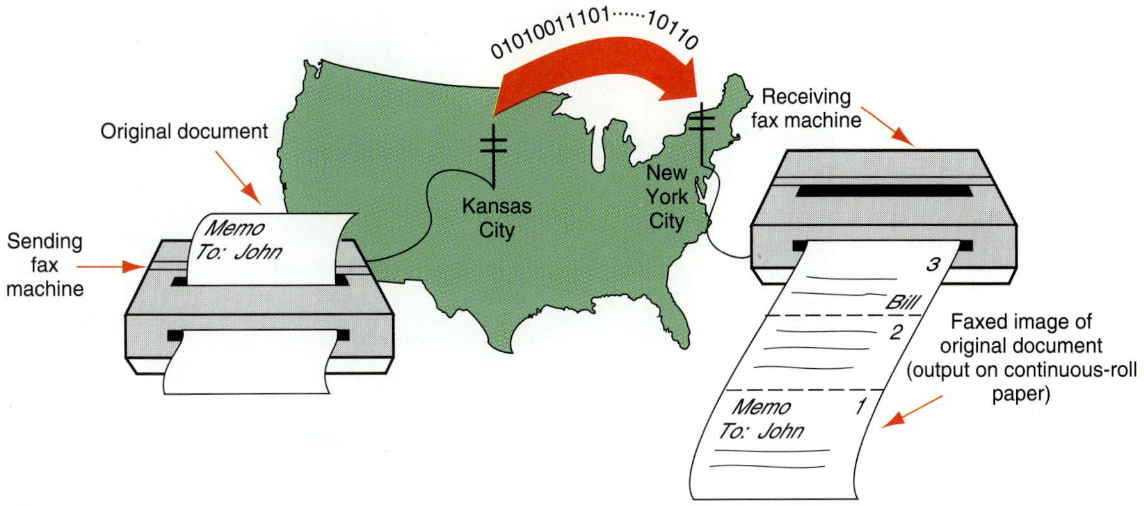

Facsimile machines have been in use for a long time. If you're an old-movie buff, you may remember the 1948 film *Call Northside 777*, in which a young Jimmy Stewart proves that a key trial witness has lied by summoning from across the country a timely fax image contradicting her testimony. It has only been since the recent development of both the microprocessor and improved manufacturing techniques, however, that inexpensive faxing—and the ensuing boom in personal fax machines—has occurred.

Information Retrieval. The assortment of information you can get over the phone lines today is, in a word, amazing. Over 5,000 public databases are currently available for online *information retrieval.* Among these are services for recreational users, shoppers, businesses, researchers, travelers, and other microcomputer users with specialized information needs.

Businesspeople can summon a variety of corporate financial reports, such as those available from Moody's, Standard & Poor's, and Dun & Bradstreet. Also available is a never-ending stream of information from news wires such as those of Dow Jones and Reuters.

For researchers and others who read a lot, virtually every major general-interest or trade magazine, newspaper, and journal published worldwide is now online. Also, many regional newspapers in dozens of U.S. cities are available in electronic versions that can be "delivered" to your monitor screen. There are even clipping services that will scan publications for you and save articles in an electronic mailbox on subjects you designate.

Figure 6-5
Prodigy.
The PRODIGY® service is an easy-to-use information retrieval service that's targeted to the needs of the average person. It contains consumer-oriented shopping, banking, brokerage, financial, travel, news and weather, and educational information. It also provides transaction processing (buying stocks, airline tickets, consumer goods, etc.), electronic mail services, and games.

(a) Weather information

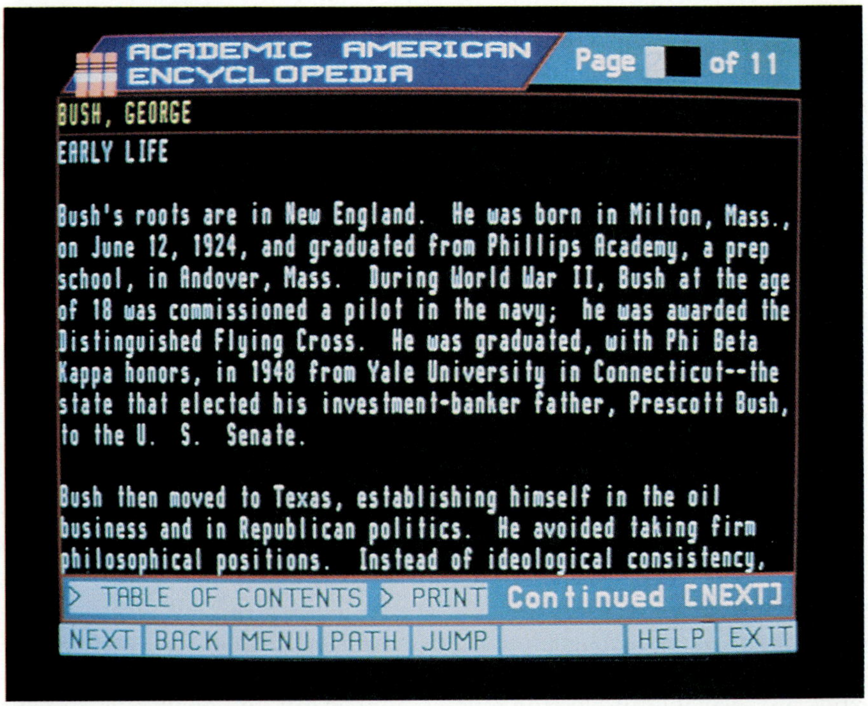

(b) Educational information

Figure 6-6
Cellular phones.
Before heading home after a Chicago Cubs baseball game, a cellular phone user calls a Chicago-area database to find out about the traffic situation on local expressways. On the way home, the user can also access such services as weather and sports information and stock-market reports.

Professionals such as lawyers and doctors also have databases targeted to their specialized needs. Mead Corporation, one of the largest electronic publishers, has been extremely successful with Lexis, a legal database. For the medical professional, there's Medis.

Most people get their online information through a particular services company, which works similarly to a pay-television network. When you subscribe to the services company, you gain access to the variety of participating databases to which it, in turn, subscribes. Prodigy and CompuServe, for instance, are targeted to information useful to the average person and they include news and weather, personal investing and money management, travel, and shopping (see Figure 6-5). Many services companies have a one-time fee and, perhaps, an hourly hookup charge. They may also impose special charges for some types of services.

Cellular Phones. **Cellular phones** are mobile phones that do not need to be hooked up to a phone outlet in order to work. They can put two people into contact with each other anywhere, even if they are in motion (see Figure 6-6).

Cellular phone.
A mobile phone that uses special stations called cells to communicate with the regular phone system.

Currently those who most benefit from the cellular phone boom are people who need to be in constant contact with the office or clients but must be on the move as well, such as a busy executive, salesperson, or real estate agent. Such a user might, for instance, take a cellular phone out of a briefcase and use it while waiting in line, sitting at a traffic light, or taxiing down a runway. People who work outdoors, such as farmers and ranchers, who may need to be in contact with others but can't afford the time it takes to get to a regular phone, are also reaping the benefits of cellular phone technology. You can even hook up a laptop computer

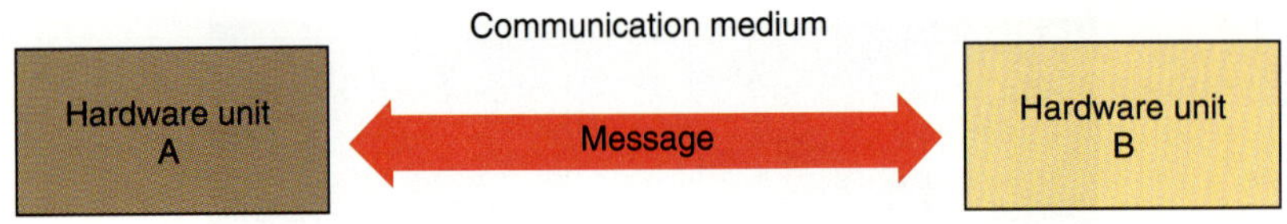

Figure 6-7
A simple telecommunications system.
As complicated as telecommunications systems may seem, they reduce simply to one device being able to communicate effectively with another.

with a cellular phone and gain access to huge databases of information while you are far from an office or a regular phone.

Cellular phones operate by keeping in contact with transmitter stations called *cell stations,* or *cells.* These stations, which resemble tall metal telephone poles, are strategically placed throughout a calling area. Cells perform two essential functions: (1) They provide an interface with the regular public phone network, and (2) they enable a moving vehicle with a phone to receive uninterrupted transmitting power by passing signals off to contiguous cells located in the zone into which the vehicle is moving.

Communications Media

Communications medium. The intervening substance, such as a telephone wire or cable, that connects two physically distant hardware devices.

Figure 6-7 shows a simple telecommunications system. Two hardware units that are distant from each other transfer messages over some type of **communications medium.** The hardware units may be a terminal and a computer, two computers, or some other combination of two devices. The medium may be privately operated, or it may use public phone lines, microwave, or some other alternative. When a message is transmitted, one of the hardware units is designated as the *sender* and the other as the *receiver.* There are several ways to send the message over the medium, as this section will demonstrate.

Types of Media

Communications media fall into one of two classes: physical lines and microwaves.

Physical Lines. Three types of physical lines are used in telecommunications systems today: twisted-pair wires, coaxial cable, and fiber optic cable.

Twisted-pair wires. A communications medium consisting of pairs of wires twisted together and bound into a cable.

Twisted-pair wires, in which strands of wire are twisted in twos, is the communications technology that has been in use the longest. The telephone system, which carries most of the data transmitted in this country and abroad, still consists heavily of twisted-pair wires. In some cases, several thousand pairs may be placed into single cables, which might connect switching stations within a city. In contrast, only a few pairs are needed to connect a home phone to the closest telephone pole. Twisted-pair wires can be manufactured and installed at a very low cost,

Figure 6-8
Fiber optic cable.
Fiber optic cable is commonly used in cities today to connect major communications arteries. A fiber optic cable the width of a pencil may contain as many as 144 optical fibers, each capable of carrying more than 1,000 telephone conversations simultaneously.

but when used over long distances, they are appropriate only for relatively unsophisticated applications such as text and voice transmission.

Coaxial cable, the medium pioneered by the cable television industry, was developed primarily to provide high-speed, interference-free video transmission. Coaxial cable is now also widely used in other types of communication systems. And it is employed extensively by the phone companies, typically as a replacement for twisted-pair wires in large "trunk" lines.

Coaxial cable.
A transmission line developed for transmitting text and video data at high speeds.

One of the most promising developments in cable technology is fiber optics. An innovation whose potential is just beginning to be realized, **fiber optic cable** (see Figure 6-8) consists of as many as hundreds of clear glass fiber strands, each approximately the thickness of a human hair. Transmission is made possible by the transformation of data into light beams, which are sent through the cable by a laser device at speeds on the order of billions of bits per second. Each hairlike fiber has the capacity to carry a few television stations or a few thousand two-way voice conversations.

Fiber optic cable.
A cable composed of hundreds of hair-thin, transparent fibers along which data are passed from lasers as light waves.

The principal advantages of fiber optics over wire media include speed, size, weight, resistance to tapping, and longevity. The speed differences between wire and fiber optic cable can be enormous; in the six seconds it takes to transmit a page of Webster's *Unabridged Dictionary* over wire, the entire 2,000-plus pages of the work can be transmitted over a single fiber strand. Fiber optic cable is especially suitable in situations involving heavy point-to-point transmission between two stations.

Microwaves. **Microwaves** are high-frequency radio signals. Text, graphics, voice, and video data can all be converted to microwave impulses.

Microwave.
An electromagnetic wave in the high-frequency range.

Figure 6-9
Terrestrial microwave station.
Stations normally are placed on mountaintops and tall buildings when they must transmit with other terrestrial stations.

Microwave transmission stations need not be within sight of each other; however, they should have a relatively unobstructed path along which to communicate. When one microwave station receives a message from another, it amplifies it and passes it on. Because of mountains and the curvature of the earth, microwave stations often are placed on tall buildings and mountaintops to ensure an obstacle-free transmission path.

Microwave signals can be sent in two ways: via terrestrial stations or by way of satellite. Both technologies can transmit data in large quantities and at much higher speeds than can twisted-pair wires.

Terrestrial microwave station.
A ground station that receives microwave signals, amplifies them, and passes them on.

Terrestrial microwave stations, illustrated in Figure 6-9, must be no more than 25 to 30 miles apart to communicate with each other directly. This limitation arises because the moisture at the earth's surface causes interference, which impedes communication between stations. As you can imagine, it is quite impractical to build all the repeater stations needed to connect distant locations.

Communications satellite.
An earth-orbiting device that relays communications signals over long distances.

Communications satellites were developed to reduce the cost of long-distance transmission via terrestrial repeater stations as well as to provide a cheaper and better overseas communications medium than underseas cable. Communications satellites, such as the one shown in Figure 6-10, are placed into *geosynchronous orbit* about 22,300 miles above the earth. "Geosynchronous" means that, because they travel at the same speed as the earth's rotation, they appear to remain stationary over a given spot.

Both communications satellites and terrestrial microwave stations are most appropriate for transmitting large amounts of data one way at a time. Thus, they are ideal for applications such as television and radio broadcasting. Because of the long transmission distances involved, they are often not feasible for rapid-response, interactive communications.

Figure 6-10 Communications satellites.
Satellites move in correspondence to the earth's rotation, so they appear stationary to an observer on earth. Because each satellite can communicate effectively over slightly less than half the circumference of the earth, it takes a minimum of three satellites to provide worldwide service.

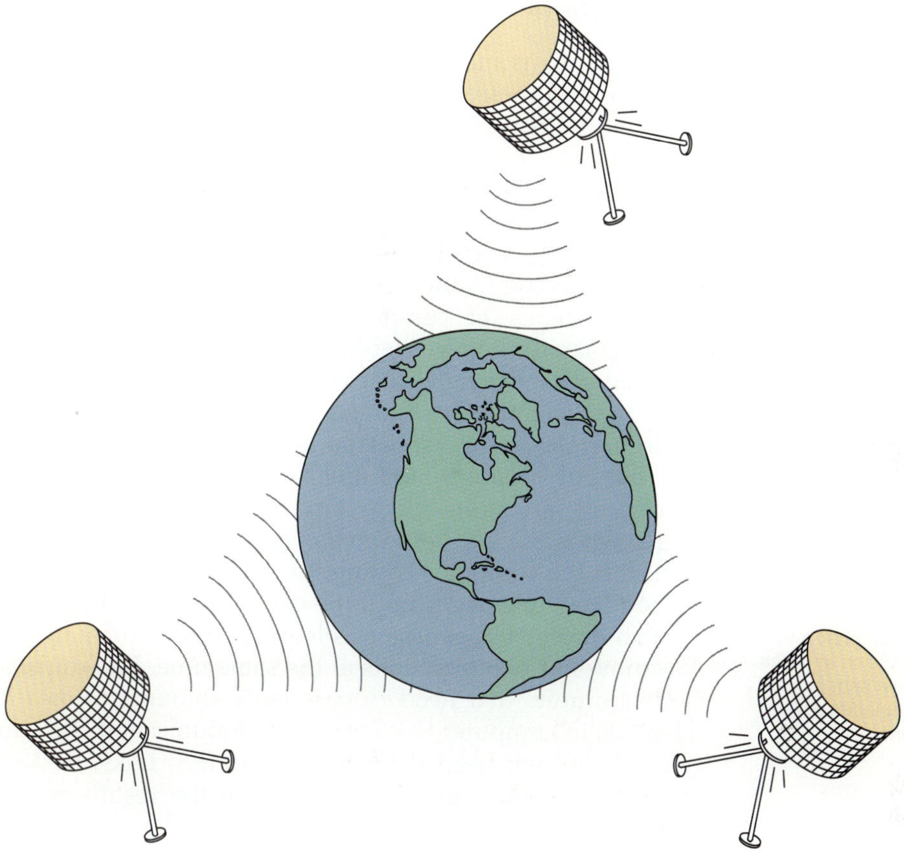

Media Speed

The capacity of a communications medium, generally measured in terms of the number of bits that can be transmitted per second (**bits per second,** or **bps**), partly determines the uses to which the medium can be put. Media can be grouped by speed into three grades, or bandwidths. The speed of transmission is proportional to the width of the frequency band.

Bits per second (bps). A measure of the speed of a communications device.

Narrowband transmission refers to a medium with a data-carrying capacity in the range of 45 to 150 bps. These rates are suitable only for very-low-speed operations, such as telegraph and teletype communication.

Narrowband transmission. Low-speed transmission, characterized by telegraph transmission.

Voice-grade transmission (300 to 9,600 bps) represents a medium level of speed. This kind of transmission is so called because spoken messages can be transmitted in this speed range. On regular telephone lines, the most common voice-grade lines, speeds in the area of 2,400 bps are common for transmitting data.

Voice-grade transmission. Medium-speed transmission characterized by the rates of speed available over ordinary telephone lines.

Wideband transmission. High-speed transmission characterized by the rates of speed available over coaxial cable, fiber optic cable, and microwave.

Wideband transmission rates (19,200 to 500,000 or more bps) are possible only with coaxial and fiber optic cable and with microwave media.

Media Mode

Communications media also can be classified in terms of whether or not they can send messages in two directions. In the terminology of communications, transmission mode is said to be simplex, half-duplex, or full-duplex.

Simplex transmission. Any type of transmission in which a message can be sent along a path in only a single prespecified direction.

In **simplex transmission,** data can be transmitted only in a single, prespecified direction. An example from everyday life is a doorbell—the signal can go only from the button to the chime. Another example is television broadcasting. Although simplex lines are cheap, they are uncommon for many types of computer-based telecommunications applications, which generally involve two-way communication. Even devices that are designed primarily to receive information, such as printers, communicate an acknowledgment back to the sender device.

Half-duplex transmission. Any type of transmission in which messages may be sent in two directions—but only one way at a time—along a communications path.

In **half-duplex transmission,** messages can be carried in either direction, but only one way at a time. The press-to-talk radio phones used in police cars employ this mode of transmission; only one person can talk at a time. Often the line between a display terminal and its host CPU is half-duplex. If the computer is transmitting to the terminal, the operator cannot send new messages until the computer is finished.

Full-duplex transmission. A type of transmission in which messages may be sent in two directions simultaneously along a communications path.

Full-duplex transmission is like traffic on a busy two-way street: The flow moves in two directions at the same time. Full-duplexing is ideal for hardware units that need to pass large amounts of data between themselves, as in computer-to-computer communication. Full-duplex channels generally are not needed for terminal-to-host links, because the terminal operator's response usually depends on the results sent back from the computer.

Media Signal

Signals sent along a medium can be analog or digital.

Analog transmission. The transmission of data as continuous wave patterns.

Digital transmission. The transmission of data as discrete impulses.

The phone system, established many years ago to handle voice traffic, carries signals in an **analog** fashion—that is, by a *continuous* wave over a certain frequency range. The continuous wave reflects the myriad variations in the pitch of the human voice. Unfortunately, most business computing equipment is **digital;** it is built to handle data coded into two *discrete* states—that is, as 0- and 1-bits. This difference between analog and digital states is illustrated in Figure 6-11.

Modem. A communications device that enables computers and their support devices to communicate over ordinary telephone lines.

Modems. Because digital impulses can't be sent over analog phone lines, some means of translating each kind of signal into the other had to be developed. Conversion of signals from digital to continuous-wave form is called *modulation,* and translation from continuous waves back to digital impulses is termed *demodulation.* A single device called a **modem** (coined from the words *MOdulation* and *DEModulation*) takes care of both operations. As Figure 6-12 shows, when a workstation sends a remote CPU a message that must be carried over an analog line, a modem is needed at both the sending end (to convert from digital to analog) and the receiving end (to convert from analog to digital).

Modems are available on add-in boards, which can be inserted into an expansion slot within the computer's system unit, and as standalone hardware devices (see Figure 6-13), which are physically detached from the system unit. Cellular modems, which do not require wires, are also now becoming available and are expected to play an increasing role in the laptop computer market. Common bps rates on modems targeted to microcomputer users are 300, 1,200, 2,400, 4,800, and 9,600 bps. Often modems capable of higher speeds have independent circuitry that enables them to function at the lower rates as well.

Figure 6-11
Analog and digital transmission.

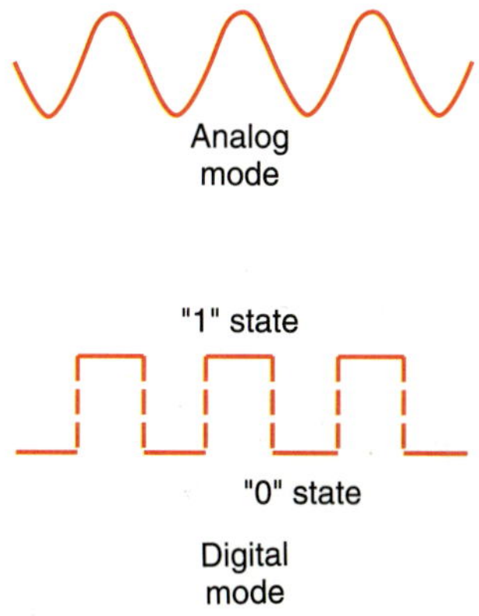

Digital Lines. Although physical lines traditionally have been analog, *digital lines* are also available. These lines can transmit data considerably faster and more accurately than their analog counterparts. Also, with digital lines, several types of data (say, text, voice, and video) can be sent along the same circuit. And, of course, no modem is necessary. The public phone network is still far from being all digital, but urban areas are rapidly moving in that direction.

During the last several years integrated, all-digital communications networks, called *integrated services digital networks (ISDNs)*, have started to appear throughout the world. These networks are designed to carry several different types of data—text, graphics, voice, and video, for instance—at greater speeds than those realizable with conventional, analog networks. ISDN will someday make it possible for you to instantaneously send data from your microcomputer workstation screen to someone else's as you talk to them on the phone. It will also make the long-awaited "picture phone," which lets people see each other as they are engaged in a phone conversation, a reality.

Figure 6-12 How modems work.
An operator at a display workstation types in data that are encoded digitally and sent to modem A. Modem A converts the data to analog form and sends them over the phone lines to modem B. Modem B reconverts the data to digital form and delivers them to the CPU. When the CPU transmits back to the workstation, these steps are reversed.

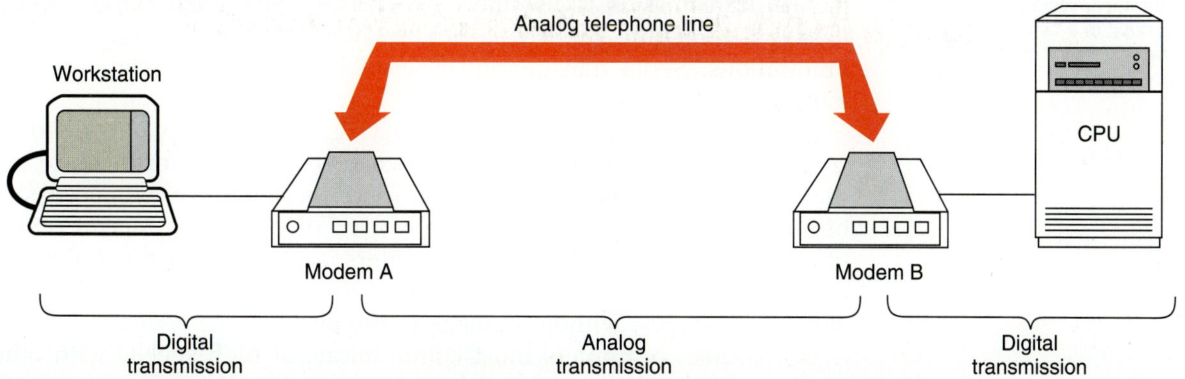

Figure 6-13 Modems.
(a) An external modem is detached from the system unit.
(b) A board (internal) modem fits in an expansion slot within the system unit.

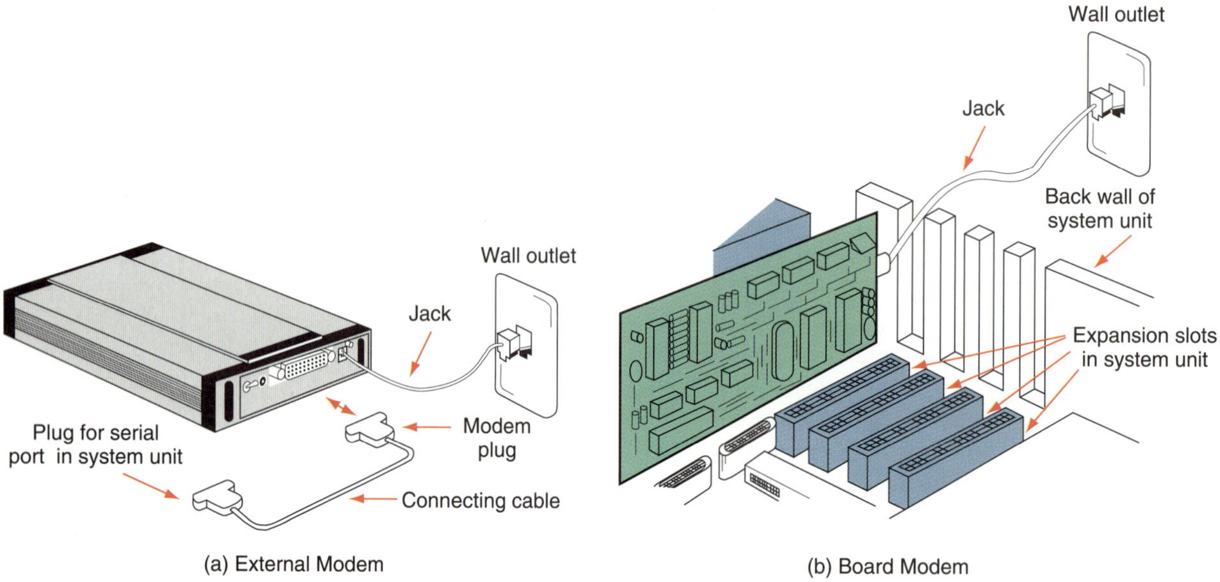

Parallel versus Serial Transmission

Parallel transmission. Data transmission in which each bit in a byte has its own path and all of the bits in a byte are transmitted simultaneously.

Serial transmission. Data transmission in which every bit in a byte must travel down the same path in succession.

Transmission devices differ in the number of channels, or tracks, that they use to transmit data. The bits used to represent characters may be transmitted in parallel or in serial. If, for example, all the 8-bits needed to convey the letter *A* are sent out at once in eight separate channels, **parallel transmission** is being used. On the other hand, if the bits representing *A* are sent out one at a time over a single channel, **serial transmission** is occurring. Figure 6-14 illustrates the difference between the two.

As Figure 6-14 suggests, parallel transmission is much faster than serial transmission. However, because it requires many more channels, parallel transmission is also more expensive. Thus, parallel transmission usually is limited to short distances, such as computer-to-computer communications. Serial transmission is used to connect workstations to remote computer systems.

A common serial interface, the RS-232C, was developed to standardize remote computer-to-terminal connections. Modems, for instance, use this particular interface on many computer systems. An enhanced form of this interface, the RS-422, is widely used on the Apple Macintosh line of computers to connect modems, printers, and electronic musical instruments. These ports will also accept most RS-232C devices, which operate at higher voltages, without damage to the ports.

Of course, computers must communicate at high speeds with other nearby peripherals, such as disk and tape units. Since the distance in-

Figure 6-14 Serial and parallel transmission.
In serial transmission, all of the bits of a byte follow one another over a single path. In parallel transmission, the bits of a byte are split into nine channels (for each of the eight bits and a parity bit) and transmitted. Parallel transmission is faster but more expensive per foot of cable used. Shown in the figure is transmission of the ASCII representation of the letter *A*.

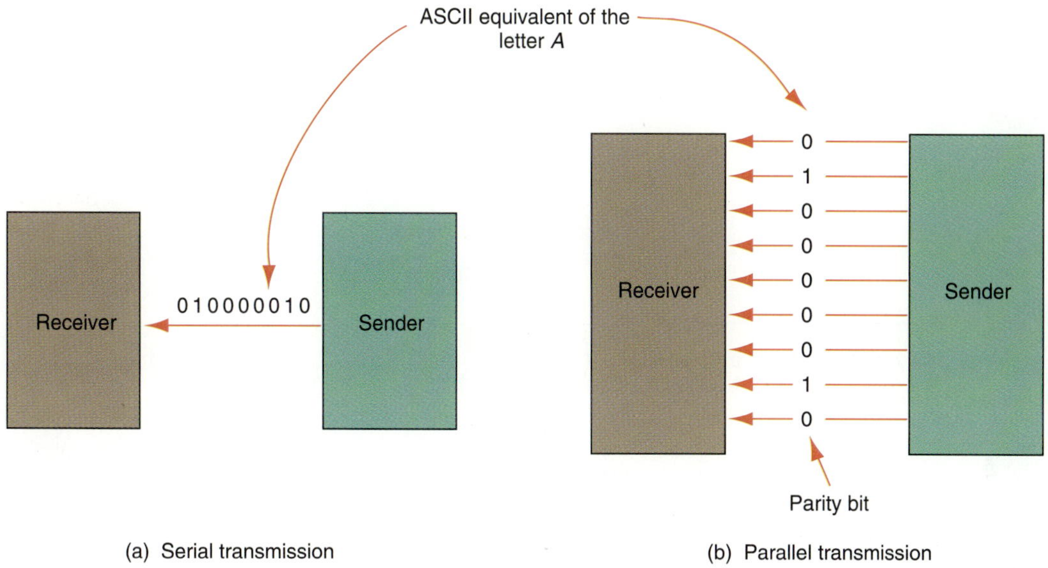

volved is short, parallel transmission is feasible for this purpose. In many IBM microcomputer systems, nearby printers are connected in parallel to the computer's system unit with a popular standard known as the *Centronics* interface.

Asynchronous versus Synchronous Transmission

Serial transmission can be further classified in terms of whether it's asynchronous or synchronous.

In **asynchronous transmission,** one character at a time is transmitted over a line. When the operator strikes a key on the terminal, the character's byte representation is sent up the line to the computer; striking a second key sends a second character; and so forth. But because even the fastest typist can generate only a very small amount of data relative to what the line can accept, a lot of idle time occurs on the line. Furthermore, each character sent must be packaged with a "start bit" and "stop bit," resulting in substantial transmission overhead.

Asynchronous transmission. The transmission of data over a line one character at a time.

Synchronous transmission corrects for this deficiency by dispatching data in blocks of characters rather than one at a time. Each block can consist of thousands of characters. Because no idle time occurs between transmission of individual characters in the block and less transmission overhead is required, the utilization of the line is much more efficient. Synchronous transmission is made possible by a *buffer* in the terminal—a

Synchronous transmission. The transmission of data over a line a block of characters at a time.

Figure 6-15 Asynchronous and synchronous transmission.
In asynchronous transmission, each byte is sent up the line as soon as it is generated. In synchronous transmission, bytes are collected in a buffer and sent in blocks.

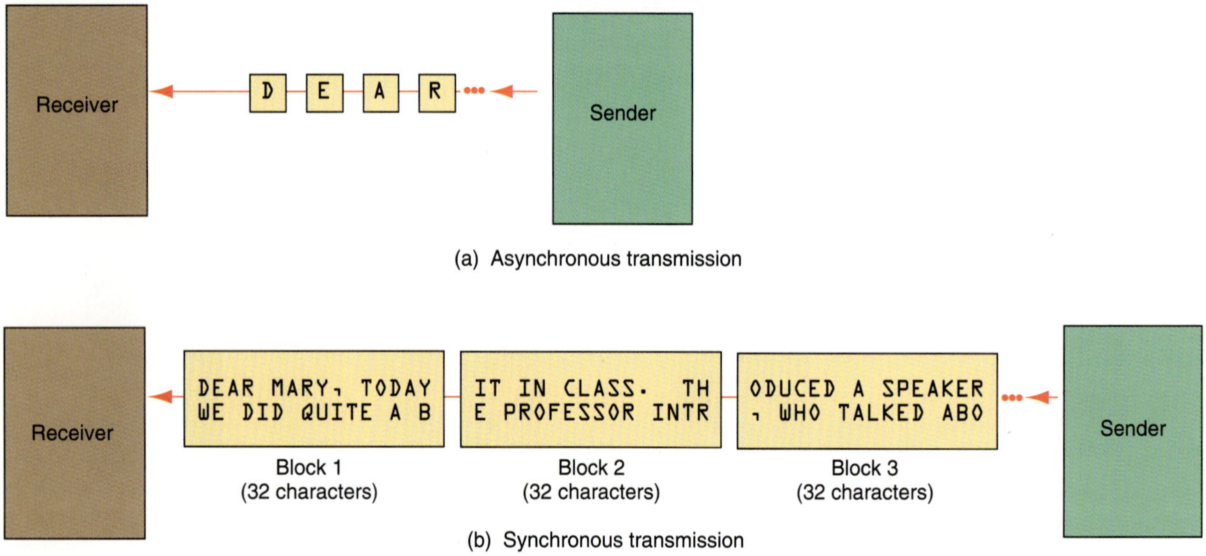

storage area large enough to hold a block of characters. As soon as the buffer is filled, all the characters in it are sent up the line to the computer.

Figure 6-15 illustrates the differences between asynchronous and synchronous transmission. Synchronous transmission is commonly used for data speeds greater than 2,400 bps.

Wide Area Networks and Local Networks

An organization generally has two choices for transmitting data: using a wide area network or using a local network.

Wide Area Networks

Wide area network (WAN).
A network that covers a wide geographic area.

Public-access network.
A network—such as the phone system—that is designed to be used by the general public.

Common carrier.
A government-regulated private organization that provides communications services to the public.

Wide area networks (WANs) are communications networks that encompass a relatively wide geographic area. Three common types of wide area networks are public-access networks, value-added networks, and private wide area networks.

Public-Access Networks. **Public-access networks** are those maintained by phone companies, or common carriers. **Common carriers** are companies licensed by the government to provide wide area communications services to the general public. Although there are dozens of phone companies in the United States alone, virtually all are interconnected so that they appear to be a single, seamless network.

Among the most familiar common carriers are the Bell-system phone companies and firms such as US Sprint, MCI, and AT&T Communications. The Bell-system companies provide in-state and nearby-state communications services, and the other firms serve a wider area. Among the less familiar common carriers are the *specialized carrier companies,* such as those that provide satellite transmission facilities.

Value-Added Networks (VANs). **Value-added network (VAN)** vendors are firms that use the facilities of a common carrier to offer the general subscribing public additional services using those facilities. These services include information processing, information retrieval, electronic mail, and the like. Organizations that use the services are billed by both the common carrier (if toll charges are involved) and the VAN company.

Value-added network (VAN). Use of the phone network by a firm other than the phone company to offer communications-related services over the network.

One of the most popular types of VAN service is information retrieval, which we discussed earlier. Examples of firms that offer such services are Prodigy, CompuServe, Dow Jones News/Retrieval, and The Source. Once users make phone contact with the VAN company, the firm's software systems generally provide easy-to-use menus of available options. After users make a request from their keyboards, the selected services become available over the phone lines for use at the users' remote workstations. Feature 6-1, "Communications Software," explores the use of modem software to call up a VAN service.

In the United States, phone companies were for years blocked by law from offering information processing and related services over phone lines. That is, regional phone companies such as those that serve your area could not become VANs (ironically, by using the phone lines they lay themselves). In recent years, however—especially with the onslaught of competition from foreign organizations—there has been within the federal government a strong deregulation movement regarding communications. Many of the phone companies want to enter the cable TV business; if the courts back recent government rulings, that could result in lower cable TV rates and better cable TV service.

One controversial type of VAN is the company with the 900-prefix phone number. Today, these firms are often collectively more famous for public abuses than for the useful services they actually do offer. While some companies may wrongfully charge teenagers hundreds of dollars for interacting with an alluring voice at the other end of the line, a number of other, reputable 900-line companies offer the public such useful information as technical support on computer products, legal and tax advice, and news. Considering the appetite of people for instant information, 900 lines seem to be an unstoppable business trend. The issue of what types of regulatory controls you think government should place on operators of 900 lines is the subject of a Critical Thinking question at the end of the chapter.

Private Wide Area Networks. Because many organizations today have such massive communications requirements, a number of them have set up their own exclusive **private wide area networks.** These networks are created by building certain facilities, leasing capacity on existing satellites,

Private wide area network. A wide area network that is built by an organization for its own use.

Feature 6-1
Communications Software

The Programs That Power Modems

Modems, like computers, are hardware devices that use software to work. The programs used with modems are commonly referred to in the microcomputing world as *communications software.*

When you buy a modem, you often get communications software bundled in with it. If not, or if you prefer to buy your own software separately, you usually can acquire it from an independent vendor. There is a variety of well-tested products from which to choose, including Smartcom, Crosstalk, PC-Dial, Blast, and PC Talk. The prices of such products typically range from about $25 to $200.

Although products in the communications-software marketplace differ in terms of features, most of them let you do the following:

- Access information services such as CompuServe, The Source, Prodigy, and Dow Jones News/Retrieval Service.
- Connect to electronic mail services.
- Connect to computer bulletin boards.
- Exchange disk files with other microcomputers.
- Turn your microcomputer system into a terminal that can access a mainframe or minicomputer.

In addition, some packages will automatically place and answer calls for you, interface with voice machines, provide security for your files, and simplify a number of routine, phone-related tasks (such as accessing phone directories and keying in passwords to an information service or bulletin board). The accompanying figure shows some of the typical information you must supply when interacting with communications software.

When you summon the software from your operating system, one of the first tasks you need to do is type in the phone number you want the software to dial or, alternatively, declare the name associated with the database service, bulletin board, or party you would like to call. In the figure, a phone number is supplied by the user. Most communications packages allow you to establish files that store frequently used phone numbers and communications settings. So, for instance, if you regularly call CompuServe, you can create a file with its phone number, your passwords, and other pertinent calling data. Then, upon supplying the filename associated with CompuServe and declaring "Y" to the auto sign-on prompt, your call will be put through automatically. If you declare "Y" to the auto redial prompt, the modem will keep redialing the phone number at periodic intervals if it gets a busy signal.

Transmission parameters, such as the type of parity and duplexing involved, communications speed, code used, and number of stop bits, ensure that your modem sends data in the form the receiver expects. Generally, when you subscribe to a communications service, you are told what settings for these parameters are acceptable. Virtually all communications software packages allow you to edit any parameter files you create, in the event settings later need to be changed.

and generally stitching together a variety of cost-effective land- and air-based communications media dedicated to delivering a certain level of performance to the organization.

One such network has been built by Sears, the large Chicago-based retailer. The Sears network hooks up more than 50,000 hardware devices nationwide and supports the communications needs of the Sears merchandising group and Sears' member organizations—AllState (insurance), Coldwell Banker (real estate), and Dean Witter (brokerage services). The network is hosted by an IBM mainframe in Chicago and handles both management information requests and transactions from the millions of users of the Sears Discover card. Sears has also set up a separate organization to sell excess capacity in the network as well as to

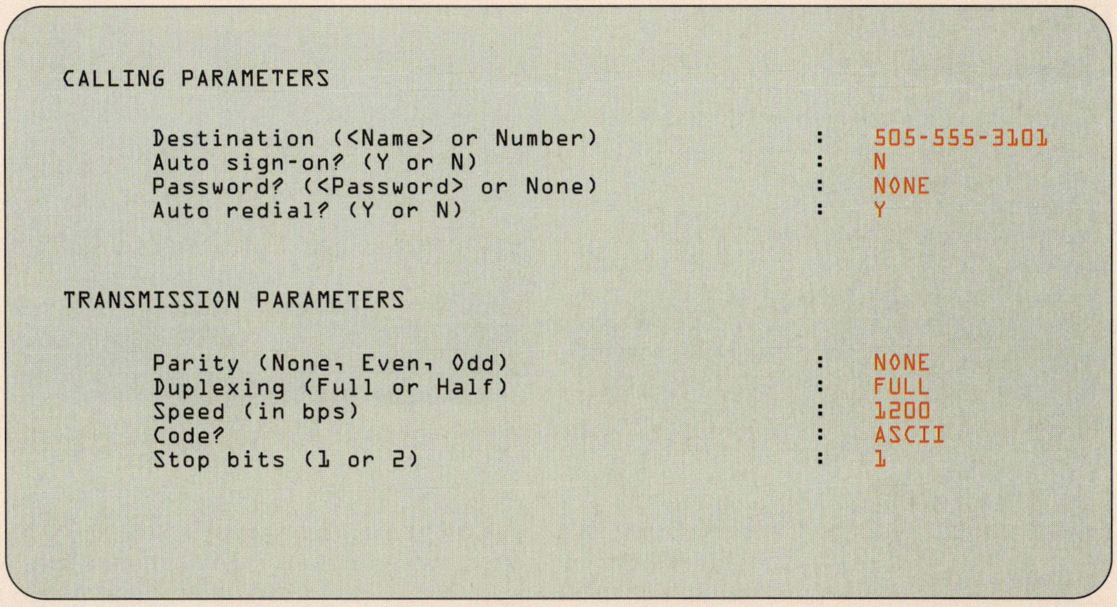

Modem programs. Most communications software costs under $100.

The screen shown in the figure is but one of many a communications package may use. As soon as you dial up a communications service or an electronic bulletin board, the software of these companies controls your computer system. Each of them has its own set of menu screens and retrieval procedures to follow.

Communications software can also turn your microcomputer into a type of answering machine. If you want your computer to receive incoming, electronically encoded messages while you are away from it, you must leave your computer on with the communications software set to a "receive calls" mode. As calls come into the system, they are answered by your modem, which establishes a connection with the remote device. The modem sets up a path so that the remote device can send data over the phone lines onto your system's hard disk.

sell the communications expertise it has acquired in building the network. American President Companies is another organization with a large private network—one that enables its customers to track the status of their orders across the globe (see User Solution 6-2).

Local Networks

Although wide area networks certainly are useful, many firms need communications facilities that connect local resources—say, computers and terminals located on the same college campus or several microcomputer workstations located in the same office. These types of networks are known as **local networks.**

Local network.
A privately run communications network of several machines located within a mile or so of one another.

User Solution 6-2

Realtime Management of Cargo and Fleet

Oakland-based American President Companies is a Pacific Basin shipping company with its own fleet of trains, trucks, and seagoing vessels. Data-entry equipment, database technology, and a sophisticated network created from both physical lines and microwave combine to keep close track of both cargo and transit equipment. Using a touch-tone phone, import/export customers can determine the whereabouts of a particular shipment, 24 hours a day, from a computerized voice-response system.

Local networks often are acquired from communications media vendors—firms that sell or lease media for private rather than public use. These media may consist of dedicated point-to-point lines, shared lines, switched lines that are unavailable for public use, or perhaps networks composed of a combination of these lines. Three common types of local networks are host-independent local area networks (LANs), private branch exchanges (PBXs), and hierarchical local networks.

Local Area Networks (LANs). For many years, most networks consisted of a remote, central *host computer*—such as a mainframe—that controlled a large number of display terminals. With the arrival of inexpensive microcomputers, which could do their own local processing, local area networks (LANs) became possible.

Local area network (LAN). A local network without a host computer that usually consists entirely of microcomputer workstations and shared peripherals.

Server. A computer that manages shared devices, such as laser printers or high-capacity hard disks, on a local area network (LAN).

Local area networks (LANs), such as the one in Figure 6-16, are local networks that do not utilize a host computer as such. Instead, computers within the network itself manage the devices as they demand the shared facilities. These computers (not shown in Figure 6-16) are commonly called **servers.** For example, a *file server* might be used to manage disk-storage activities, enabling workstation users to access any of several available operating systems, applications programs, or data files. Similarly, a *print server* is used to handle printing-related activities, such as managing devices and user outputs. One also sees on LANs such devices as *mail servers* and *fax servers,* which are dedicated to managing electronic mail and facsimile transmissions, respectively. Because many servers need to manage large databases and need to interact with several other computers, powerful microcomputers like those based on the Intel 80486 chip are often chosen as servers.

LANs are used today for a variety of applications, the simplest of which involve just sharing expensive hard disks and laser printers. Although these were among the first types of LAN applications, LAN tech-

Figure 6-16 A local area network (LAN).
The surge in microcomputer usage has made local area networking a particularly attractive solution for sharing resources.

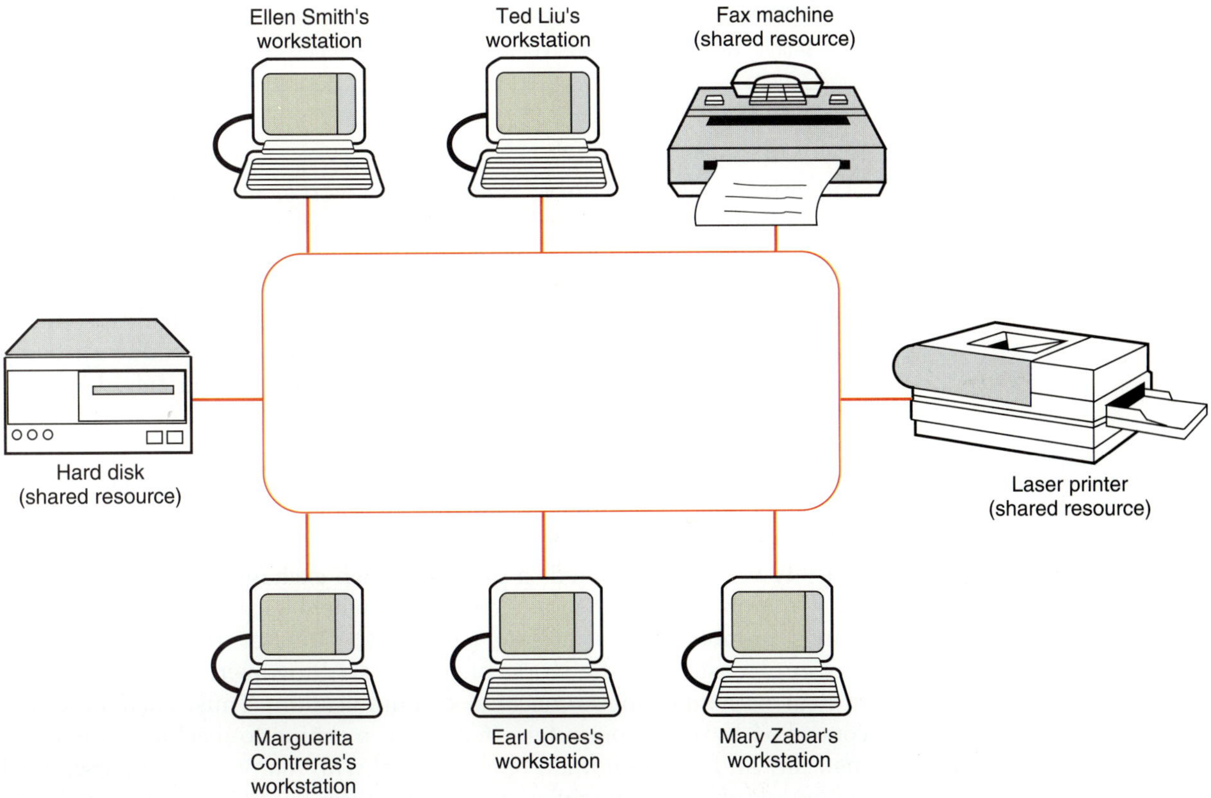

nology has evolved to include numerous other uses (see Figure 6-17). For instance, some firms that once would have centralized their transaction processing on mainframes are now doing the workload on microcomputer-based LANs. Also, many electronic mailbox systems (see Figure 6-18) and computer conferences are run on LANs. And, as *workgroup computing*—computing in which a common job, such as preparing a publication or solving a problem, is performed by people working simultaneously on a networked computer system (see User Solution 6-3)—takes hold, it, too, will use LANs. NBC even used local area networks to help in assembling footage for the 1988 Olympics in Seoul. Microcomputer-based LANs have a big advantage over systems based on larger computers: Organizations can inexpensively add small increments of extra computing power as their needs grow—say, by adding extra workstations or by adding more servers (see the Tomorrow box).

Some LANs—like those used to link soldiers in a battlefield—are wireless. Most, however, use coaxial cable or fiber-optic cable technology. Cable-based LANs usually employ either a baseband or broadband technology. *Baseband* products consist of a single, high-speed digital path over which text, graphics, voice, and video data can pass—but only one type

Figure 6-17
Uses for LANs.

- ☐ Sharing expensive devices among several users
- ☐ Handling certain types of transaction processing more efficiently than mainframes
- ☐ Performing electronic mail operations
- ☐ Sharing work among a group of users (called *workgroup computing*)

of data can pass at a time. *Broadband* networks, in contrast, consist of several paths, thereby allowing transmission of many dissimilar types of data simultaneously. Broadband, which involves analog transmission, can also cover much longer distances than baseband.

Xerox's Ethernet is one of the most widely used baseband products. Wang's Wangnet is a prominent broadband product. Broadband, being more complex and powerful than baseband, is, as you might expect, more expensive as well.

Private branch exchange (PBX).
A call-switching station that an organization acquires for its own use.

Private Branch Exchanges (PBXs). The phone system consists of numerous switching stations that essentially are public branch exchanges. When a company leases or purchases a switching station for its own use, such a facility becomes known as a **private branch exchange (PBX).** Most PBXs are commonly referred to as "company switchboards"—you call a company's number and a private (company) operator routes you to the proper extension. In the world of computers, however, many PBXs need to deal with machine-to-machine communication. Thus, such PBXs are controlled by host computers that route machine-to-machine calls automatically and let the human operator deal with many of the interpersonal communications. Sometimes these computer-based private branch exchanges are referred to as *CBXs* (*computerized branch exchanges*) or *PABXs* (*private automatic branch exchanges*).

Hierarchical local network.
A local network in which a relatively powerful "host" CPU is at the top of the hierarchy and communications terminals or less-powerful CPUs are at the bottom.

Hierarchical Local Networks. Hierarchical local networks are the oldest type of local network. At the top of the hierarchy is often a big host computer such as a mainframe or minicomputer. At the bottom are display terminals. Between the top and bottom are devices such as communications controllers, which manage exchanges between the host and the terminals.

In recent years, microcomputers have been used in hierarchical local networks. In some cases, microcomputer workstations serve as terminals that communicate with a host mainframe or mini through *terminal emulation software*. This type of software tricks the host into thinking that it is dealing with an ordinary display terminal when, in fact, it is communicating with a microcomputer. Thus, a computer like an IBM PS/2 may be made to behave similarly to an IBM 3270 display terminal when communicating with an IBM mainframe.

Downloading.
The process of transferring data or information from a large computer system to a smaller one.

Uploading.
The process of sending data from a small computer system to a larger computer system for storage or processing purposes.

Files in hierarchical local networks can be either downloaded from or uploaded to the host. **Downloading** means that copies of existing files can be sent from the host to the microcomputer workstations. **Uploading** means that new data can be created at the microcomputer workstations

Figure 6-18 LAN-based electronic mail.
This store-and-forward mail system connects two local area networks (LANs), each in a separate building. Mary, whose computer is connected to the mail server on network A, sends a copy of a memo to Joe and Linda. Server A stores the memo for Joe and Linda until it can make a delivery. Joe receives his copy as soon as he logs on to the network in his building. Linda's copy gets forwarded from the server in building A to the server in building B whenever the two networks are in contact. This could be immediately if the networks are always connected. The server on network B stores Linda's copy until she logs on to her network.

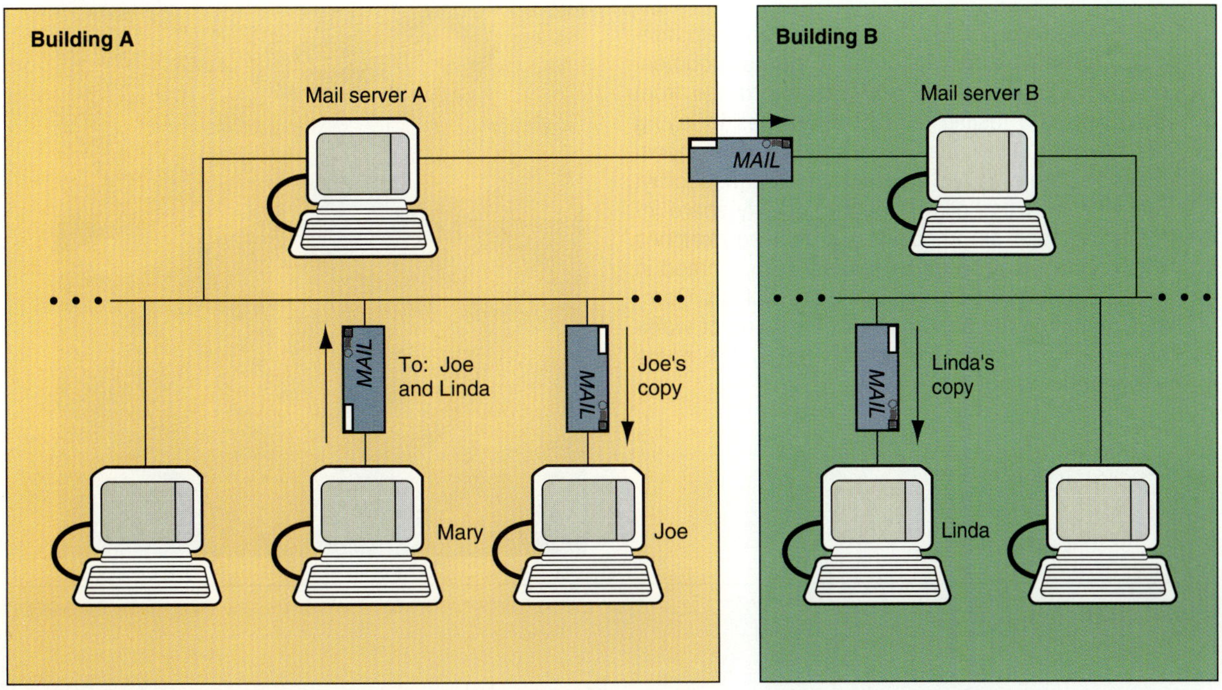

and sent to the host. Both downloading and uploading usually require stringent organizational control. Downloading presents the danger that data will be retrieved for unauthorized use, whereas uploading entails the risk of garbage data corrupting other applications.

Gateways and Bridges. Local networks often must communicate with outside resources, such as those on wide area networks and on other local networks.

Let's look at an example. An executive working at a microcomputer workstation on a LAN may wish to access a financial database such as Dow Jones News/Retrieval. In this particular case, a facility known as a gateway is necessary for linking the two networks—here, the LAN and the WAN. A **gateway** is a collection of hardware and software resources that enable devices on one network to communicate with devices on another, *dissimilar* network.

Gateway.
An interface that enables two dissimilar networks to communicate.

When the two networks being linked—say, a LAN in one campus building and an identical LAN in another nearby campus building—are based on similar technology, a device called a bridge is used to connect

User Solution 6-3

A LAN That Makes It Easy for Workers to Share Information

At Corning Incorporated, microcomputers help hundreds of engineers collaborate in the development of new products—doing activities that range from designing and testing product prototypes to laying out facilities in factories. The professionals shown here, at Corning's W.C. Decker engineering facility, are on a LAN that allows them to quickly share information such as proposals and revised sketches with engineers at a nearby research lab, located in another building. Because systems such as Corning's enhance the performance of a group of workers, they are commonly referred to by the name "workgroup computing."

Bridge.
An interface that enables two similar networks to communicate.

them. A **bridge** is a collection of hardware and software resources that enable devices on one network to communicate with devices on another, *similar* network.

Network Topologies

Telecommunications networks can be classified in terms of their *topology*, or shape. Three common topologies are the star, bus, and ring.

Star network.
A network consisting of a host device connected directly to several other devices.

Star Networks. A **star network** often consists of a host computer that's hierarchically connected to several display terminals in a point-to-point fashion. This configuration is illustrated in Figure 6-19a. In a common variant of this pattern, several microcomputer systems (the terminals) are connected to a larger host computer that switches data and programs between them. The private branch exchange (PBX), discussed earlier, is another example of a star network. Star networks are especially suited to an organization with several related plants or divisions, because each plant or division may need access to common centralized files but may also need to do its own local processing.

Tomorrow

Microcomputer-based Networks Challenge the Mainframes

Can the Mainframe Survive?

The LAN challenge. Downsizing to smaller computers has become a noticeable trend.

Just about three decades ago, all computer processing was done on mainframe computers. As supercomputers, minicomputers, and microcomputers were developed, they began to be used for such tasks as product design, film making, word processing and desktop publishing, spreadsheets, and control of physical processes—things that the mainframe was not particularly adept at doing. Even some of the mainframe's traditional jobs were sometimes transferred to these other computer systems. The mainframe, however, was never really threatened with extinction . . . until recently.

Today, the rise of powerful networks is making many people rethink the role of the mainframe. Within many organizations, the mainframe is still the computer system of choice for transaction processing and the control and storage of large, centralized databases. Transaction processing refers to work such as preparing customer bills and statements, paying employees and vendors, keeping track of inventories, and the like. Large, centralized databases are often used to store taxpayer records, data on stocks and bonds, information about goods available for sale, and many other voluminous banks of facts. Mainframes are designed with these types of applications in mind. Supercomputers are usually relegated to applications that need fast speeds and high degrees of accuracy (such as space exploration and weather forecasting). Minicomputers and microcomputers are just not powerful enough to deal with large databases.

But by linking several microcomputers together, especially powerful ones such as those based on new Intel and Motorola chips, you have a legitimate challenger to the mainframe. An especially attractive feature of microcomputer-based networks is that each end-user station is a microcomputer capable of doing much of its own processing. It's easy to expand the network simply by adding more microcomputer workstations and network servers. By contrast, mainframes are designed to communicate with "dumb" terminals and to do all of the processing themselves. Consequently, they are not easy to expand on as needs grow. Often, the only alternatives available are getting a more powerful mainframe or getting a second mainframe to handle the increased traffic. Either way, capacity expansion is expensive.

Although everyone seems to be predicting the mainframe's demise, chances are that this old standby will not be replaced overnight. Because mainframes have been around for nearly a half century, the systems protecting the security, accuracy, and privacy of data on them have been well tested by years of experience. Security, accuracy, and privacy are often as important as the data themselves, and networks—because they are exposed to so many access points—do not measure up to mainframes in these critical areas.

Another thing in favor of the mainframe is the fact that most corporations already own many millions of dollars of software that runs on mainframes. These organizations are not likely to discard these resources, especially when they still do useful work. Consequently, when looking at costs in the short term, many organizations would rather operate a bit inefficiently than spend a bundle tearing down a working system and starting over.

Most industry observers think that the end of the mainframe is just a matter of time. When that will occur, if it happens at all, is a matter of sheer speculation.

Figure 6-19 Three network topologies. (a) Star. (b) Bus. (c) Ring.

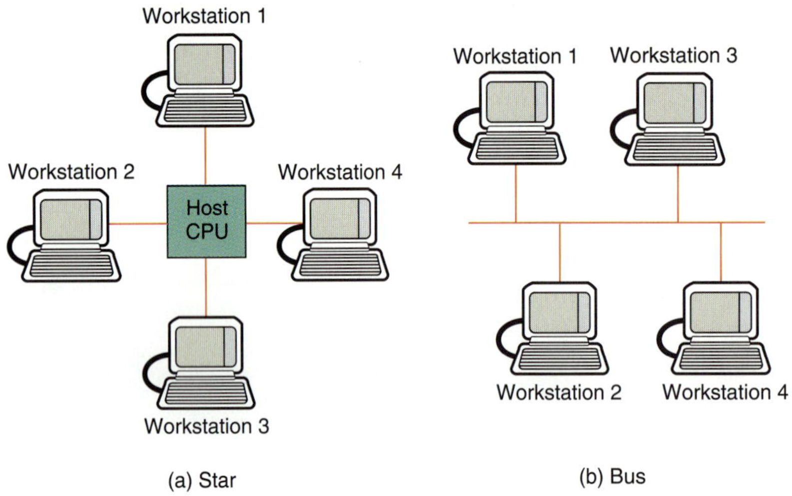

Bus network. A telecommunications network consisting of a line and several devices that are tapped into the line.

Bus Networks. A **bus network** works a lot like ordinary city buses in ground-based transportation systems. Moreover, the hardware devices are like "bus stops" and the data like "passengers." For example, the network in Figure 6-19b contains 10 terminal stations (bus stops) at which data (passengers) are "picked up" or "let off." Local area networks (LANs), discussed earlier, often use a bus topology. The bus line commonly consists of a high-capacity, high-speed coaxial cable, with inexpensive twisted-pair wires dropped off each terminal station. A bus network contains no host computer.

Ring network. A telecommunications network in which machines are connected serially in a closed loop.

Ring Networks. A less common and more expensive alternative to the star and the bus is the **ring network,** in which a host computer is absent and a number of computers or other devices are connected by a loop. A ring network is shown in Figure 6-19c. One popular form of ring network is the *token-ring* local area network (LAN) pattern, which we'll discuss in the next section.

Communications among Devices

In the last few sections, we covered various types of communications media and networks. In this section, we will discuss communications standards and special communications management techniques designed to optimize the flow of communications traffic.

Protocols

Because manufacturers have long produced devices that use a variety of transmission techniques, communications standards for the industry have been a major problem. Everyone recognizes the need for standardizing transmission methods, but the form such standards should take is still widely debated. What is needed is some common agreement on matters such as communications protocols.

The term *protocol* originates from the areas of diplomacy and etiquette. For instance, at a dinner party in the elegant home of a family on the social register, the protocol in effect may be formal attire, impeccable table manners, and remaining at the table until beckoned to the parlor by the host or hostess. At a backwoods country barbeque, a different protocol will probably exist. In the communications field, protocols have comparable rules.

A communications **protocol** is a collection of procedures used to establish, maintain, and terminate transmission between devices. Protocols specify how devices will physically connect into a network, how data will be packaged during transmission (e.g., asynchronously or synchronously), how receiver devices will acknowledge sender devices (a process called *handshaking*), how errors will be handled, and so on. Just as people need an agreed-upon set of rules to communicate effectively, so do machines need a common set of rules to help them get along with one another. Protocols are found in all types of networks. Two common protocols found in LANs, for instance, are token passing and CSMA/CD.

Protocol.
A set of conventions used by machines to establish communication with one another in a telecommunications environment.

Token passing often is used with a ring network topology. Here's how it works: A small packet called a *token* is sent around a loop or ring. The token has room for messages and addresses. As the token is passed around the ring, workstations either check to see if the token is addressed to them or try to seize it so that they can assign messages to it. A token traveling around the ring contains a control area, which specifies whether the token is free or carries a message. When a sender device captures a free token, it changes the status of the token from "free" to "busy," adds a message, and releases it. The message then travels around the ring to the receiver location. The receiver copies the message, puts an acknowledgement on the token, and sends the token back to the sender station. The sender notes the acknowledgement message and changes the status of the token to "free."

CSMA/CD is an acronym for *carrier sense multiple access with collision detection*. With CSMA/CD, which is most commonly used in bus networks, workstations try to seize the network's attention whenever they are ready. The collision detection feature ensures that the devices don't interfere with each other as they compete.

Hardware for Managing Communications Traffic

Now that we've covered some of the basic elements of telecommunications systems, let's see how these systems have been made more efficient. As an example, we'll look at several types of devices that enhance

Figure 6-20 Multiplexing.
Multiplexers enable several low-speed devices to share a high-speed line. Here multiplexer A combines the messages sent from four workstations. Multiplexer B "demultiplexes" the message for the CPU so that they look like standard local input.

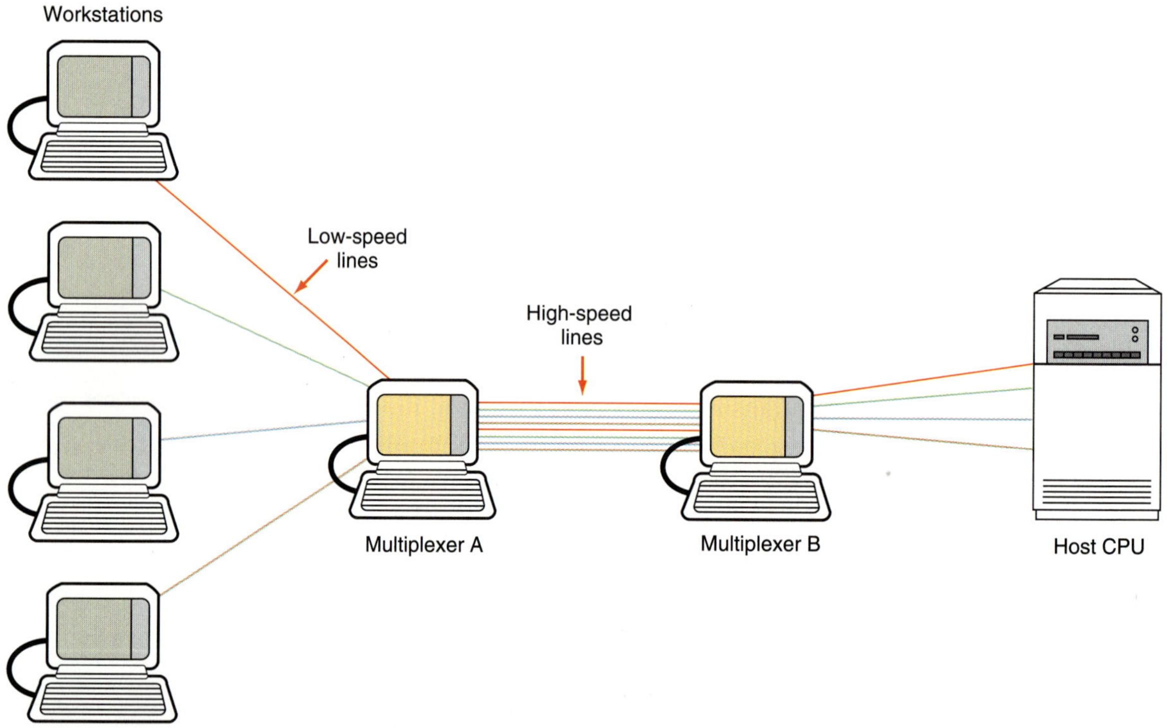

the efficiency of wide area telecommunications networks. The most notable of these *communications management devices* are multiplexers, concentrators, and front-end processors.

Multiplexer.
A communications device that interleaves the messages of several low-speed devices and sends them along a single high-speed path.

Multiplexers. Communications lines almost always have far greater capacity than a single terminal can use. Many workstations can work adequately at speeds of 300 bps, and voice-grade lines can transmit up to 9,600 bps. Since communications lines are expensive, it is desirable that several low-speed devices share the same line. A device called a **multiplexer** makes this possible.

Figure 6-20 illustrates the use of two multiplexers servicing several workstations and a host CPU. The first multiplexes, or combines, the data from low-speed lines into a high-speed line. The second demultiplexes the incoming character stream so that the CPU appears to get the messages from the workstations individually. Recently, with the appearance of high-speed digital lines, devices called *T1 multiplexers* have arrived on the telecommunications scene. These multiplexers have the capacity to carry as much voice and data traffic as 24 conventional (analog) phone lines.

Concentrators. A **concentrator** is a hardware device that combines control and multiplexing functions, among other things. Commonly it is a minicomputer with a memory that provides a store-and-forward capability. Thus, messages from slow devices such as asynchronous terminals can be stored at the concentrator until enough characters are collected to make forwarding to another device worthwhile.

Concentrator. A communications device that combines terminal control and multiplexing functions.

In airline passenger-reservations systems, concentrators placed at key sites, such as Boston, New York, Los Angeles, and other transportation centers, allow several agents to share communications lines economically. Messages initiated by agents are sent to the concentrator, stored, multiplexed with messages from other agents, and transmitted at very high speeds over long-distance lines to a central processing site. Using the long-distance line in this fashion minimizes communications costs.

Front-End Processors. The **front-end processor** is the most sophisticated type of communications management device. Generally it is a programmable minicomputer located at the site of the host CPU. It can perform all the communications functions of a concentrator as well as relieve the host of routine computational burdens. For example, a front-end processor can check for valid user account numbers and validate or change the format of incoming data.

Front-end processor. A computer that screens messages sent to the main computer and also relieves the main computer of certain computational chores.

Summary and Key Terms

Telecommunications refers to communications over a distance, such as over phone lines, via privately owned cable, or by satellite.

Telecommunications Applications. A wide variety of important business applications involve telecommunications. Among these are distributed transaction processing, interorganizational systems (IOSs), **electronic data interchange (EDI), electronic mailboxes, voice mail, electronic bulletin boards,** computer conferencing, **facsimile (fax) machine, cellular phones,** and information retrieval.

Communications Media. Messages transmitted in a telecommunications system are sent over some type of **communications medium.** Physical lines, such as **twisted-pair wires, coaxial cable,** and **fiber optic cable,** constitute one major class of media. Messages also are commonly sent through the air, in the form of **microwave** signals. **Terrestrial microwave stations** accommodate microwave transmission when either the sender or the receiver is on the ground. **Communications satellites** reduce the cost of long-distance transmission via terrestrial microwave stations and provide better overseas communications.

The *speed* of a data-communications medium is measured in **bits per second (bps).** The slowest speeds are referred to as **narrowband transmission.** Medium-speed lines, which are the type commonly found in the public phone network, are capable of **voice-grade transmission.** The highest speeds, referred to as **wideband transmission,** are possible only with coaxial cable, fiber optic cable, and microwaves.

Communications media can be in either the simplex, half-duplex, or full-duplex mode. In **simplex transmission,** messages can be sent only in a single, prespecified direction (such as with a doorbell). In **half-duplex transmission,** messages can be sent both ways but not simultaneously (for example, as with press-to-talk phones). **Full-duplex transmission** permits transmission in two directions simultaneously (as with traffic on a busy two-way street).

Signals sent along a phone line travel in an **analog** fashion—that is, as continuous waves. Computers and their support equipment, however, are **digital** devices that handle data coded into two discrete states—0s and 1s. For two or more digital devices to communicate with each other over analog phone lines, a device called a **modem** must be placed between each piece of equipment and the phone lines. Modems perform digital-to-analog and analog-to-digital conversion. Modems can be bypassed when *digital lines* are used to interconnect devices.

To exchange data along a communications medium, two machines must "agree" on a mode of transmission and on a method of packaging data. Transmission between machines is done either in **parallel,** in which each bit of a byte is sent along a different path, or in **serial,** in which bits of a byte follow one another serially along a single path. Serially transmitted data are packaged either **asynchronously** (one byte to a package) or **synchronously** (several bytes to a package).

Wide Area Networks and Local Networks. **Wide area networks (WANs)** are communications networks designed to encompass a relatively wide geographic area. Three types of WANs are public-access networks, value-added networks, and private wide area networks. **Public-access networks** generally are maintained by the phone companies, or **common carriers.** **Value-added network (VAN)** vendors are firms that use the facilities of a common carrier to offer the general subscribing public additional services using those facilities. These services include information retrieval, information processing, and electronic mail. Because many organizations today have such massive communications requirements, some of them have set up their own **private wide area networks.**

Many organizations take heavy advantage of these and also build their own **local networks**—networks that link devices in a single building or at a single site. Three common types of local networks are local area networks, private branch exchanges, and hierarchical networks.

Local area networks (LANs) typically utilize transparent processors within the network, called **servers,** to manage the network and its shared facilities. A **private branch exchange (PBX)** consists of a central, private switchboard that links to devices by switched lines. A **hierarchical local network** typically consists of a powerful host CPU at the top level of the hierarchy and microcomputer workstations and display terminals at lower levels. Data used by the workstations can be either **downloaded** from the host or **uploaded** to it. Devices on two *dissimilar* networks can communicate with each other if they are connected by a

gateway. Devices on two *similar* networks can communicate with each other if they are connected by a **bridge.**

Network Topologies. Telecommunications networks can be classified in terms of their topology, or shape. Three common topologies are the **star network,** the **bus network,** and the **ring network.**

Communication among Devices. A communications **protocol** is a collection of procedures used to establish, maintain, and terminate transmission between devices. Because there are so many ways to transmit data, many industry groups have pushed for certain protocols to become industry standards. These efforts notwithstanding, a number of incompatible guidelines remain in effect. Two major LAN protocols are *token passing* and *carrier sense multiple access with collision detection (CSMA/CD).*

Communications management devices enhance the efficiency of telecommunications traffic flow. Common devices are multiplexers, concentrators, and front-end processors. **Multiplexers** enable several low-speed devices to share a high-speed line. **Concentrators** perform multiplexing functions and can store and forward data as well. **Front-end processors** are the most sophisticated communications management devices. They can perform the concentrator's function as well as some of the tasks the computer normally does.

Review Exercises

Fill-in Questions

1. ______________ (EDI) refers to sending electronic purchase orders and invoices from company to company.
2. A(n) ______________ machine enables images of hard-copy documents to be sent over the phone lines.
3. ______________ , the communications medium employed by cable television, was developed primarily to deal with a phenomenon called crosstalk, which arises with lower-grade wire at high speeds.
4. In contrast to the continuous waves used to represent analog signals over phone lines, computers generate ______________ signals.
5. ______________ is a transmission medium that involves laser-generated light waves sent over transparent, hairlike strands.
6. Conversion from analog to digital and digital to analog is performed by a(n) ______________.
7. ______________ transmission involves sending data along a communications line in blocks of several characters at a time.
8. ______________ are companies licensed by the government to provide communications services to the public.
9. ______________ transmission is a type of serial transmission in which characters are sent along a line as they are generated.

10. A hierarchical local network is an example of a(n) ____________ network topology.

Matching Questions

Match each term with the description that fits best.

a. front-end processor
b. modem
c. gateway
d. multiplexer
e. concentrator
f. protocol

____ 1. A device that combines several low-speed lines into a high-speed line.

____ 2. A hardware device that collects messages and forwards them in a transmission-efficient fashion.

____ 3. A device that converts digital data for transmission over the phone lines.

____ 4. The most sophisticated type of communications management device.

____ 5. A standard used to make communications devices more compatible.

____ 6. A device that enables two dissimilar networks to communicate with each other.

Discussion Questions

1. What is the difference between an electronic mailbox and a computer bulletin board?
2. What are the differences between simplex, half-duplex, and full-duplex transmission?
3. What is the difference between a local area network (LAN) and a value-added network (VAN)?
4. Name some types of communications media and explain how they differ.
5. What is the difference between uploading and downloading?
6. What is the difference between baseband and broadband transmission?
7. How do parallel and serial communications differ?
8. What is a protocol?

Critical Thinking Questions

1. It has been said that advances in communications technology are collapsing the "information float"—the amount of time information spends in transit when being communicated from one point to another. Can you think of three business examples of collapsing information float? What is the benefit to a business in each example?
2. Identify two examples of computer applications that need the type of transmission that broadband cable provides.
3. You are asked by a teacher in your former high school to give a 45-minute presentation to her students on telecommunications. She has asked you specifically to prepare a list of the half dozen things that

every student today should know about telecommunications. What would be on your list?

4. EDI, its benefits notwithstanding, poses some new legal problems. One is that it's not clear who is at fault if transmission problems cause a miscommunicated transaction that results in a loss. Can you think of any ways in which an organization might protect itself from such legal headaches with EDI?
5. Should the government place special controls on operators of 900-prefix phone numbers? Defend your position by preparing a list of uses or practices you feel are not in the public interest and a list of uses or practices you feel are. If you believe there should be some controls, identify them.

How are operating systems keeping pace with the times? As discussed in this chapter and in Window 3, many operating systems and operating-system environments are sporting graphical interfaces, enabling users to select program options on the screen by pointing to them.

7 Systems Software

Outline

Learning Objectives

After completing this chapter, you will be able to:

1. Describe the types of systems software.
2. Explain the activities of an operating system and describe some of the differences between operating systems.
3. Describe several ways in which computer systems interleave operations to process data more efficiently.
4. Explain the role of a language translator and describe several types of language translators.
5. Explain the role of a utility program and describe several types of utility programs.

Overview

Systems software. Computer programs that enable computer systems to work rapidly and efficiently.

Systems software consists of programs that coordinate the various parts of the computer system to make it run rapidly and efficiently. They perform such tasks as formatting disks so that they are suitable for storing budgets or word-processed documents, copying program files or data files from one diskette to another, and enabling your brand of applications software to work on your printer or display device.

Most users aren't aware of what systems software is doing for them. On microcomputer systems, for example, issuing a save command to store a program onto disk requires that systems software look for adequate space on the disk, write the program onto "addresses" of this space, and update the disk's directory (indicating the addresses at which the program has been placed). And when users are having their systems communicate with remote mainframes, they may not realize that systems software goes to work checking the validity of their ID numbers and, later, translating their database commands or BASIC programs into machine language.

There are three basic types of systems software: operating systems, language translators, and utility programs.

In this chapter, we'll first look closely at the *operating system,* which is the main piece of systems software in any computer system. Here we'll discuss what operating systems do and examine the various differences among them. We'll also take a closer look at a few of today's most talked-about operating systems.

Next, we will look at *language translators.* A language translator is a program that translates a program in BASIC, COBOL, or some other programming language into machine language.

Finally, we will cover *utility programs,* or utilities. Utilities typically perform less-frequent or less-critical types of control functions, such as allowing you to recover inadvertently erased disk files. These packages are often sold by third-party vendors as add-ons to specific operating systems.

The Operating System

Before the 1960s, human operators generally ran computers manually. For each incoming job needing processing, the operator had to reset a number of circuits on the computer by hand. In fact, every function of the computer system—input, output, processing, and storage—required substantial operator supervision and intervention.

On these early computers, jobs could be processed only in a serial fashion—one program at a time. As a result, the computers sat idle for long periods while operators took care of manual procedures between jobs.

The development of operating systems greatly improved the efficiency of computers. An **operating system** is the main collection of programs that manage the computer system's activities. Operating systems have eliminated much of the manual work formerly required to process programs. Many of today's operating systems enable processing of several jobs concurrently and permit the computer to be left completely unattended by the operator while programs are running.

Operating system. The main collection of systems software that enables the computer system to manage the resources under its control.

The primary chores of the operating system are management and control. The operating system ensures that each valid incoming program is processed in an orderly fashion and that the computer system's resources are made available to run the programs optimally. For example, on a large computer system, the operating system checks to see that people trying to gain access to the computer system are authorized users. When a user's identification number is found to be valid, he or she is signed in, or "logged on." Next, the operating system determines which of the computer system's resources will be needed to do the user's job. Then it automatically assigns these resources to the work request if and when they are available.

Generally, the user will need to tap a number of the system's resources. For example, a typical job might need the number-crunching power of the CPU, a language translator that understands the BASIC programming language, primary memory for storing intermediate results, secondary storage for storing data and programs, and a printer for output. The operating system makes all these facilities available. Finally, when the user finishes with the computer system, he or she is logged off. In effect, the operating system is the go-between, meshing the user's applications program with the system's hardware resources.

Figure 7-1 depicts the hierarchical principle by which computer systems work. The operating system serves as the gateway to applications programs, their data, and other system resources. As soon as you turn on your computer system or terminal, you are confronted with the operating system. From there, you choose the program with which you wish to work—say, word processor or spreadsheet—and the operating system retrieves it from disk for you. When finished, you generally must exit back to the operating system before you can invoke another program.

Because of the central role of the operating system in managing the computer system's activities, many consider the operating system to be the most critical piece of software in the computer system. Without an operating system, none of the other programs can run.

Differences among Operating Systems

The marketplace offers a wide selection of operating systems (see Figure 7-2). Like the executives who manage and control large corporations, the various operating systems differ in many important respects. For example, some operating systems are designed for only one "brand" of computer, whereas others are compatible with several. Other important differences concern ease of use, speed, number of features available,

Figure 7-1 The gateway role of the operating system.
The operating system makes computer system resources available to the user. Everyone using a computer system must interact with the operating system in some say.

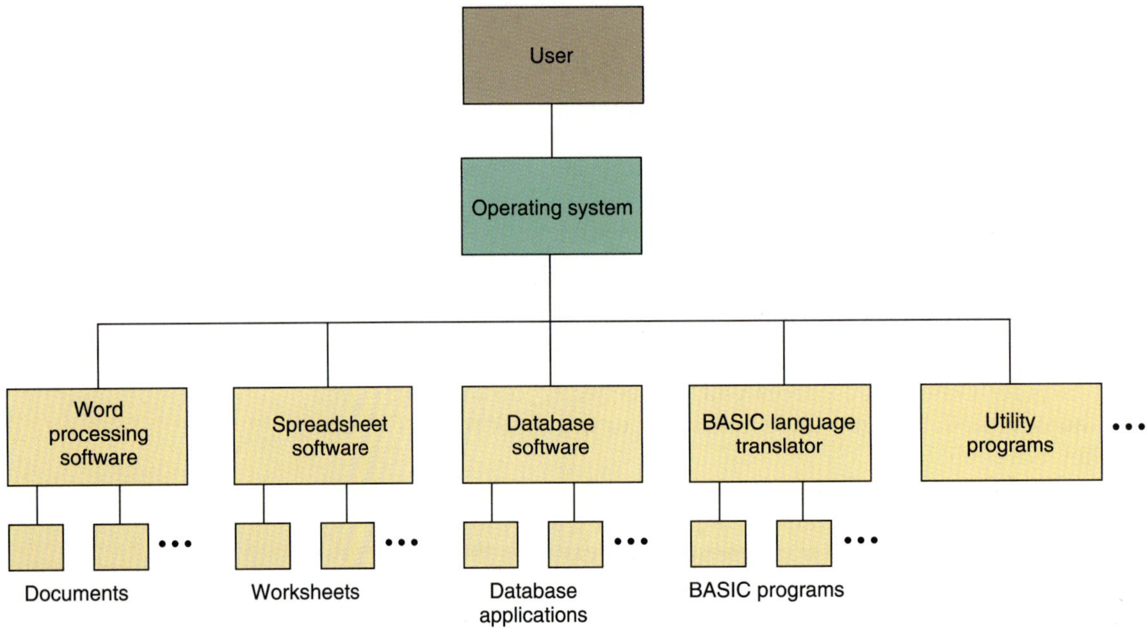

Figure 7-2 Some popular operating systems. Operating systems can differ substantially with respect to ease of use, speed, number of features available, portability, and cost. Each operating system is targeted to one or more specific types of computers.

AOS, DG Operating systems used on Data General minicomputers

CPF, SSP Operating systems available on IBM's small business systems

Macintosh System Software The icon-oriented operating system used on Apple Macintosh microcomputers

MCP/AS, OS/1100 Operating systems used on Unisys mainframes

MS-DOS The most widely used operating system on IBM-compatible microcomputers

MVS, VM Operating systems used on IBM mainframes

NetWare The most widely used operating system on local area networks (LANs)

NT A 32-bit version of MS-DOS

OS/2 The operating system designed for the high end of IBM's PS/2 line of microcomputers

PC-DOS The operating system most widely used by IBM microcomputers

UNICOS, COS Operating systems used by Cray supercomputers

UNIX A multiuser, multitasking operating system used by small computers

VAX/VMS An operating system used by DEC VAX minicomputers

Xenix, Venix, Ultrix, A/UX Four UNIX-like operating systems

portability, and cost. Often these criteria conflict. For example, an operating system that's designed to be either easy to use or flexible generally isn't fast. In other words, the more overhead the operating system must carry, the slower it will be. And, as you might expect, a system that's packaged with an assortment of sophisticated or powerful features isn't likely to be inexpensive.

On large computers such as mainframes, operating systems can be quite powerful. There may be hundreds of users seeking access to the mainframe at more or less the same time. Many of those users will be running several programs concurrently. For instance, someone may be working on a set of database retrievals while having a 50-page report printed out. On large computer systems there are sophisticated facilities for interleaving users' work, for keeping the computer safe from unauthorized access, for bookkeeping, and for a number of other complex tasks. Because these systems often have several megabytes or more of primary memory, their operating systems can afford to be large and sophisticated.

Microcomputers, in contrast, have almost always been hampered by a limited amount of primary memory. For instance, the original IBM PC of 1981 came with only 128 KB RAM. Thus, PC-DOS, the flagship operating system of the IBM PC, was originally limited to this amount. Although later models of the IBM PC came with greater amounts of RAM, allowing DOS to grow, DOS—which is based on the Intel 8088 chip—has a theoretical RAM limit of 640 KB. This situation forced DOS to become essentially just a partial operating system (by mainframe standards). In other words, some of the systems tasks that one would normally expect operating systems to do are not carried out by DOS; instead, these tasks are carried out by applications programs. For instance, applications programs manage RAM in their own way, once DOS has ceded control to them. Furthermore, some of the tasks that a mainframe operating system would perform transparently must be handled manually by DOS users.

Now that powerful 32-bit chips such as the Intel 80386, Intel 80486, Motorola 68030, and Motorola 68040 are available—and powerful operating systems such as UNIX and OS/2 are here to make use of them—we are beginning to see microcomputer operating-system environments that are approaching those of mainframes.

Functions of the Operating System

Now that you have a general idea of what operating systems do and what some of the differences among them are, we can discuss their functions in greater detail. As we examine these functions, keep in mind that not all of them—especially functions that deal with more than one user or one program—will apply to the operating system on your computer.

Assignment of System Resources. When most computers are first activated, a major component of the operating system—a program called the **supervisor**—is also activated. On some systems, this program may be referred to as the *monitor*, the *kernel*, or something else. The supervisor will always be in primary memory when the computer is on. On many computers, other programs in the operating system are brought into primary memory from secondary storage only as they are needed. The su-

Supervisor.
The central program in an operating system.

pervisor mobilizes these other programs to perform system tasks for applications programs.

Once the supervisor activates any other program in the operating system, it relinquishes control to that program until the program has performed its role. At that point, control returns to the supervisor, which may then call up other systems programs that the job requires. The supervisor operates somewhat like a master of ceremonies, repeatedly introducing the next speaker on the program after the previous one has finished his or her talk.

Command-language translator. Systems software that translates instructions written in a command language into machine-language instructions.

Command language. A programming language used to communicate with the operating system.

In addition to the supervisor, a number of other operating system programs have a hand in determining which parts of the computer system will be mobilized for any given job. One of these is the **command-language translator.** This program reads instructions to the operating system that the user or programmer initiates. These instructions, which often are coded in a **command language** (sometimes referred to as a *job-control language,* or *JCL*), permit the user and programmer to specify: orders for retrieving, saving, deleting, copying, or moving files; which I/O devices are to be used; which language the user or programmer is employing; any customized requests for output format; and any other special processing needs of the applications program. The command language, in effect, gives the user or programmer a channel for communicating directly with the operating system.

Operating systems can differ significantly in how command-language instructions are invoked. Take deleting a file, for example. With operating systems such as MS-DOS and PC-DOS, which are used on many IBM microcomputers and similar machines from other manufacturers, you generally type in a command such as

```
ERASE FRED
```

to delete a file named FRED. Both MS-DOS and PC-DOS employ a *language interface,* meaning that users generally must know the syntax of a particular command language to communicate with these operating systems.

On the Apple Macintosh line of computers, icons representing operating-system commands have traditionally been used in conjunction with a mouse to carry out similar operations. So, to delete FRED, you can use the mouse to point first to a file-folder-shaped icon labeled FRED and then to a wastebasket-shaped icon to activate the delete operation. Operating systems such as Macintosh System Software employ a *graphical interface,* meaning that users need only point to graphical icons to issue commands rather than remembering a specific syntax (see Figure 7-3).

Operating environment. A term that refers to a graphical interface or to the combination of an operating system and graphical interface.

Virtually any operating system that naturally uses a language interface can be complemented with a graphically oriented "shell" program, thereby overlaying it with a graphical interface. These shell programs are commonly called **operating environments.** Probably the most well-known operating environment is Microsoft Windows, which fits over the MS-DOS and PC-DOS operating systems (see Figure 7-4). Another prominent

Figure 7-3 Graphical interface.
Graphical interfaces available for operating systems enable users to do such things as (a) activate applications programs or data files and (b) save, copy, or delete their work. Typically, users point with a mouse to the operation they want and execute it by clicking a button on the mouse. Here, the user is activating a file named FRED and then deleting it.

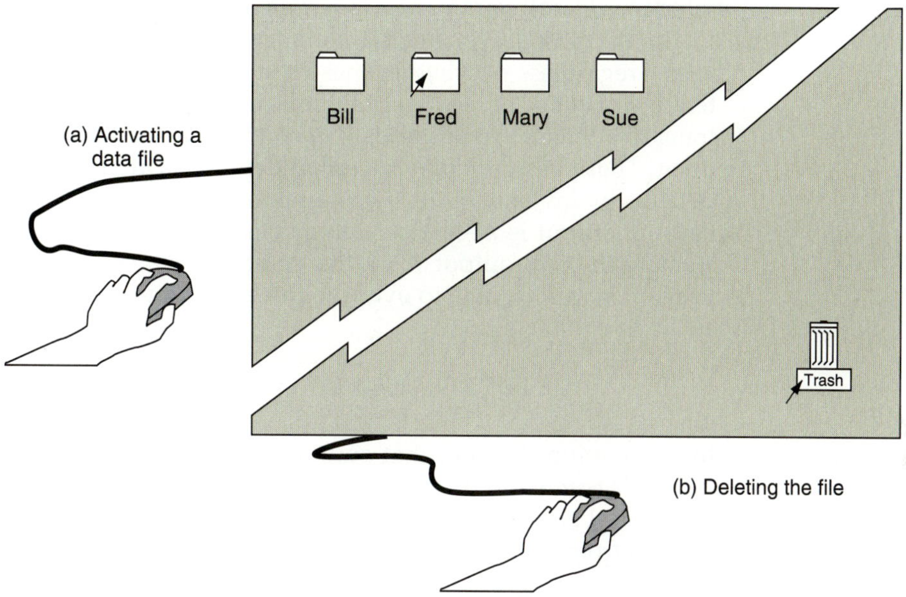

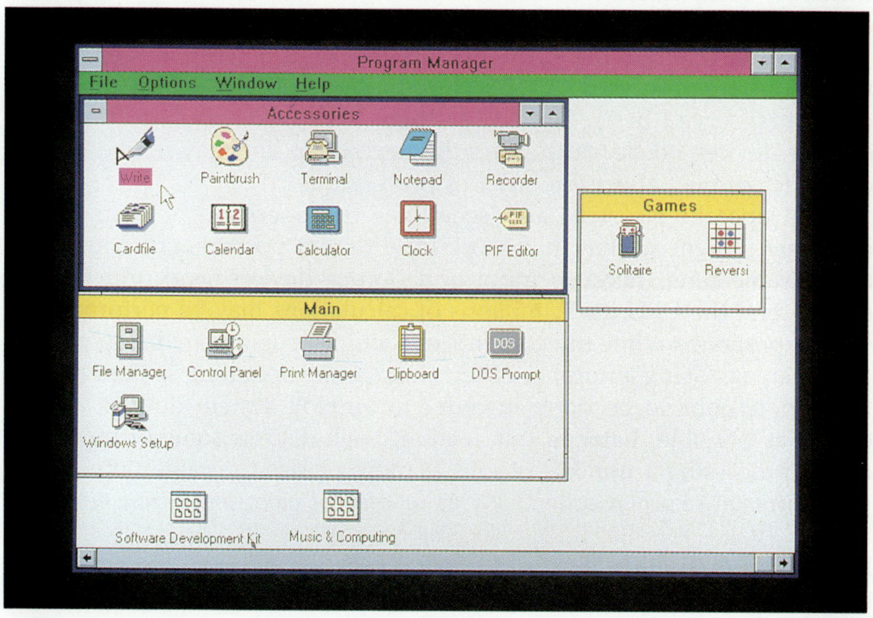

Figure 7-4
Microsoft Windows.
Microsoft Windows provides computers running the MS-DOS and PC-DOS operating systems with a graphical interface similar to the one accompanying Macintosh System Software.

example is Presentation Manager, a product derived from Microsoft Windows that provides a graphical environment for the OS/2 operating system. Still another example is Open Look, a graphical shell for UNIX created jointly by AT&T, Sun Microsystems, and Xerox. The use of graphical interfaces in software products is explored more fully in Window 3.

In the absence of special command-language instructions from the user—regardless of whether these instructions are invoked through written commands or via a graphical interface—the command-language translator makes some standard assumptions about how things are to be done. These assumptions are called **defaults.** Often you can override the defaults by invoking your own commands. For instance, suppose the default on output is 24-line screen images delivered to the display and you want hard-copy output from the printer—say, 5 copies at 50 lines per page. You may be able to override the default by issuing a command such as

Default.
The assumption a computer program makes when no specific choice is indicated by the user or programmer.

```
PRINTER, LINES = 50, COPIES = 5
```

In an operating system that supports written commands, you would invoke this command by typing it in as shown. In an operating system with a graphical interface, you might select the PRINTER, LINES, and COPIES options from menus and have to type in only the numbers 50 and 5.

Scheduling Resources and Jobs. Closely related to the process of assigning system resources to a job is that of scheduling resources and jobs. The operating system helps decide not only which resources to use (assignment) but when to use them (scheduling). Scheduling can become extremely complicated when the system must handle a number of jobs at once.

Scheduling programs in the operating system determine the order in which jobs are processed. A job's place in line is not necessarily on a first-come, first-served basis. Some users may have higher priority than others, the devices needed to process the next job in line may not be free, or other factors may affect the order of processing.

The operating system also schedules the operation of parts of the computer system so that they work on different portions of various jobs at the same time. Because input and output devices work much more slowly than the CPU itself, millions of calculations may be performed for several programs while the contents of a single program are being printed or displayed. Using a number of techniques, the operating system juggles the various jobs to be done in order to employ system devices as efficiently as possible. Later in this section, we'll discuss some of the methods of processing a number of jobs at more or less the same time. These procedures are known collectively as *interleaved processing techniques.*

Monitoring Activities. A third general function of operating systems is monitoring, or keeping track of, activities in the computer system while processing is under way. The operating system terminates programs that contain errors or exceed either their maximum running time or storage allocations. It also sends an appropriate message to the user or operator. Similarly, if any abnormalities arise in I/O devices or elsewhere in the system, the operating system sends a message to the user's or operator's terminal.

Bookkeeping and security are two other monitoring tasks of the operating system. Records may be kept of log-on and log-off times, programs' running times, programs that each user has run, and other information. In some environments, such records enable the organization to bill users. The operating system also can protect the system against unauthorized access by checking the validity of users' ID numbers and reporting attempts to breach system security. Moreover, it must protect memory so that an error in a program will not "crash" the computer system or, worse yet, corrupt vital data in other programs.

Interleaved Processing Techniques

In this section, we will examine some of the assignment and scheduling techniques that computers use to handle a large number of jobs at the same time. Sophisticated computers often take advantage of *interleaved processing techniques* such as multiprogramming, multitasking, time-sharing, virtual memory, and multiprocessing to operate more efficiently. These operating-system features enable computers to process many programs at almost the same time and, consequently, to increase the number of jobs the computer system can handle in any given period.

Multiprogramming. **Multiprogramming,** a term that refers to multiuser operating systems, is somewhat similar to the operation of a busy dentist's office. The dentist *concurrently* attends to several patients in different rooms within a given time period. The dentist may pull a tooth in room 1, move to room 2 to prepare a cavity for filling, move back to room 1 to treat the hole created by the pulled tooth, and so forth. As the dentist moves from patient to patient, assistants do minor tasks.

Multiprogramming. The execution of two or more programs *concurrently* on the same computer.

In a computer system with a multiprogrammed operating system, several applications programs may be stored in main memory at the same time. The CPU, like the dentist, works on only one program at a time. When it reaches a point in a program at which peripheral devices or other elements of the computer system must take over some of the work, the CPU interrupts processing to move on to another program, returning to the first program when that program is ready to be processed again. While the computer is waiting for data on one program to be accessed on disk, for example, it can perform calculations for another program. The systems software for the disk unit, like the dental assistants, does background work; in this case, it retrieves the data stored on disk.

Multiprogramming is feasible because computers can perform thousands of computations in the time it takes to ask for and receive a single piece of data from disk. Such disk I/O operations are much slower than computation, because the computer must interact with and receive communications from an external device to obtain the data it needs. It must also contend with the slower access speeds of secondary storage.

Multitasking.
The ability of a single-user operating system to enable two or more programs or program tasks to execute concurrently.

Multitasking. Multitasking refers to a multiprogramming capability on single-user operating systems. Thus, it refers to the ability of an operating system to enable two or more programs or program tasks from a single user to execute concurrently on one computer. This feature allows a user to do things such as edit one program while another program is executing or have two programs displayed on screen at the same time and modify them concurrently. Remember, one computer, like one dentist, can attend to only one task at a time. But the computer works so fast that the user often has the illusion that it is doing two things at once.

One situation in which multitasking is very helpful occurs when a program has an exceptionally long processing time and the computer is needed for other work. For example, suppose that you want to search through a large employee file for all people between the ages of 25 and 35 with six years of service and some experience with computers. On a relatively small computer, such a search may take several minutes, during which time you may want to use the computer for other work. With multitasking, you can use your computer to perform another task, on the same or a different program, while the search is taking place in the background.

Time-sharing.
Processing in a multiuser environment in which the computer handles users' jobs in a round-robin fashion.

Time-Sharing. Time-sharing is a very popular technique for computer systems that support numerous terminals. The operating system cycles through all the active programs in the system that need processing and gives each one a small time slice on each cycle.

For example, say there are 20 programs in the system and each program is to be allocated a time slice of 1 second (the time slice usually is much smaller than this, and all slices aren't necessarily equal). The computer will work on program 1 for one second, then on program 2 for one second, and so forth. When it finishes working on program 20 for one second, it will go back to program 1 for another second, program 2 for another second, and so on. Thus, if there is an average of 20 programs on the system, each program will get a total of 3 seconds of processing during each minute of actual clock time, or 1 second in every 20-second period. As you can see, in a time-sharing system it is difficult for a single program to dominate the CPU's attention, thereby holding up the processing of shorter programs.

Both time-sharing and multiprogramming are techniques for working on many programs concurrently by allotting short uninterrupted time periods to each. They differ in the way they allot time, however. In time-sharing, the computer spends a fixed amount of time on each program and then goes on to another. In multiprogramming, the computer works on a program until it encounters a logical stopping point, such as when more data must be read in, before going on to another program. Many computers today combine time-sharing and multiprogramming techniques to expedite processing.

Virtual Memory. In the early days of computing, users who had large programs faced numerous problems with loading them into main memory. Often they had to manually split such programs into pieces so that only small portions of them resided in the limited main memory space at any one time. In the early 1970s, a virtual-memory feature became available on some operating systems. It permitted users the luxury of writing extremely long programs that the operating system would automatically split up and manage.

Virtual memory refers to using disk to extend main memory. This is the way it usually works: The operating system delivers programs to be processed to the virtual-memory area on disk. Here the programs generally are divided into either fixed-length *pages* or variable-length *segments*. Whether the programs are subdivided into pages or segments depends on the operating system's capabilities.

Virtual memory.
An area on disk in which programs are "cut up" into manageable pieces so that they can be processed.

A virtual memory system using paging breaks a program into pages. If a program is 40 kilobytes long and the system divides programs into 4 kilobyte lengths, the program is divided into 10 pages. As the computer works on the program, it stores only a few pages at a time in main memory. As it requires other pages during program execution, it selects them from virtual memory and writes over the pages in main memory that it no longer needs. All the original pages, or modified ones, remain intact in virtual memory as the computer processes the program. So, if the computer again needs a page that has been written over in main memory, it can readily fetch it. This process, illustrated in Figure 7-5, continues until the program is finished.

Segmentation works somewhat like paging except that the segments are variable in length. Each segment normally consists of a contiguous block of logically interrelated material from the program. Some systems use a combination of segmentation and paging.

Not all operating systems on large computers use virtual memory. Although this technique permits a computer system to get by with a smaller main memory, it requires extra computer time to swap pages or segments in and out of main memory.

Multiprocessing. **Multiprocessing** refers to the use of two or more computers linked together to perform work at the same time. This, of course, requires systems software that will realize that multiple processors are in use and has the ability to assign work to them as efficiently as possible. Whereas multiprogramming involves processing several programs or tasks *concurrently* on a single computer, multiprocessing involves handling multiple programs or tasks *simultaneously* (at precisely the same instant) on several computers. There are many ways to implement multiprocessing; two common ones covered here are coprocessing and parallel processing.

Multiprocessing.
The *simultaneous* execution of two or more program sequences by multiple computers operating under common control.

With *coprocessing,* which we covered briefly in Chapter 3, a single CPU works in conjunction with specialized "slave" processors that perform dedicated chores. For instance, many microcomputer systems today have slave processors that handle tasks such as high-speed mathematical computation, display-screen graphics, and keyboard operations. At any point in time, two or more processors within the system unit may be performing work simultaneously. However, the time taken to perform an entire job will be largely constrained by the CPU.

Figure 7-5 Virtual memory based on a paging system.
In this system, programs awaiting processing are transferred from the input buffer area on disk to the virtual memory area. In the virtual memory area, programs are divided into pages of fixed length, perhaps 4,000 bytes each. When the computer is ready to process a program, the operating system transfers a certain number of pages (three in this example) into main memory. The computer then processes the program until it needs a new page, whereupon the required page is delivered to main memory, and the one that is no longer needed is written over. The computer system continues in this fashion, selecting desired pages of a program from virtual memory, until the program is completed. At that point, the program output is delivered to the output buffer area of the disk to await an output device, and a new program is read into its virtual memory area.

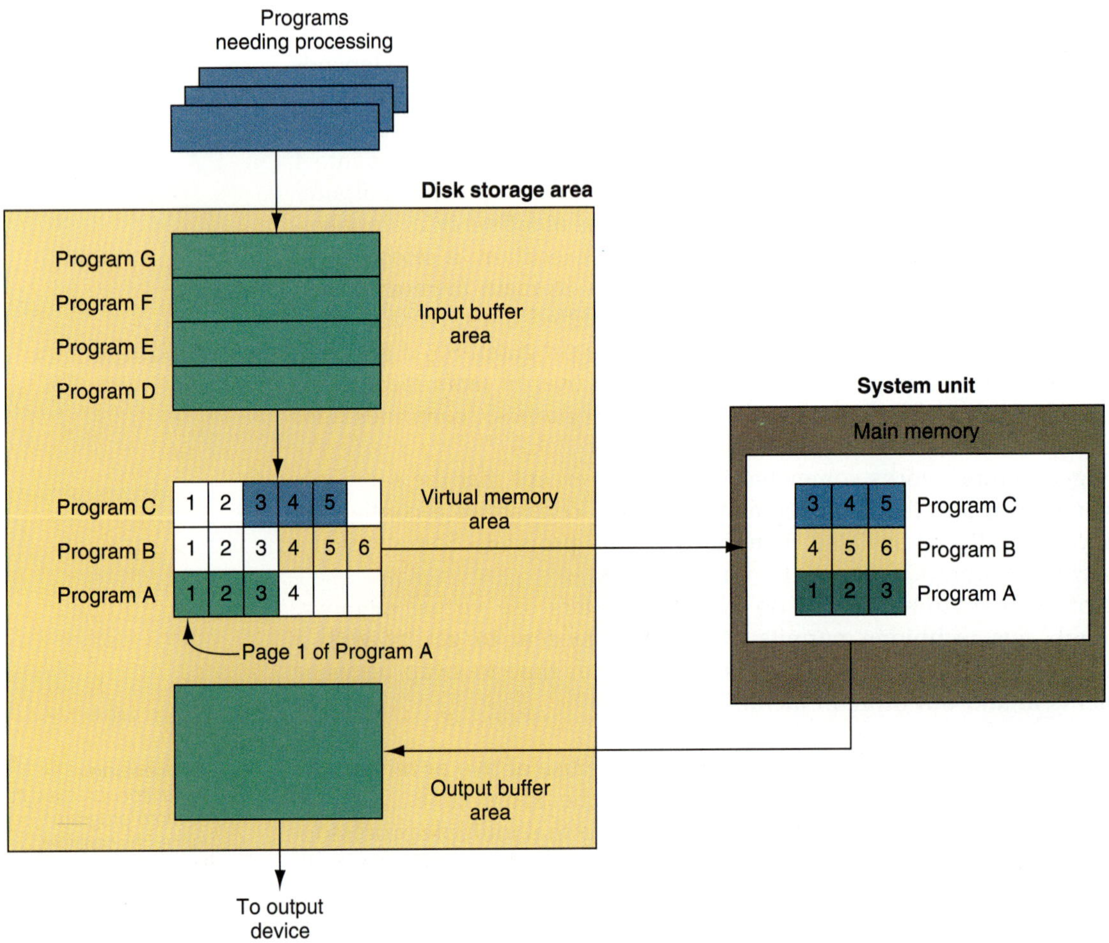

In *parallel processing,* which is the most sophisticated and fastest type of multiprocessing, the multiple processors involved are full-fledged, general-purpose CPUs. They are tightly integrated so that they can work together on a job by sharing memory. This may sound simple, but there are many practical complications, and special software is often required.

Multiprocessing is closely related to *fault-tolerant computing,* in which computer systems are built with important circuitry duplicated. If a critical component fails, an identical backup component takes over. Even though duplicate processors (or sets of processors) are involved, however, only one processor (or set of processors) will be in operation at any point in time.

A Closer Look at Several Operating Systems

Here, we briefly cover several of the most widely used operating systems to give you a feel for their principal characteristics and to help you understand how they differ from each other. The operating systems we discuss in this section include PC-DOS and MS-DOS, Macintosh System Software, UNIX, OS/2, and NetWare.

PC-DOS and MS-DOS

During the 1980s, DOS* (for Disk Operating System) was the predominant microcomputer-based operating system for most businesses. Over 15 million copies of it have been sold to date, making it the most widely used software package ever developed. Even though it has been made technologically obsolescent by newer products, well over 50 percent of today's microcomputer systems still use DOS.

There are two principal forms of DOS: PC-DOS and MS-DOS. Both were developed by Microsoft Corporation of Bellevue, Washington. Except for a few minor differences, these operating systems are virtually identical. **PC-DOS** was created originally for the IBM PC, whereas **MS-DOS** was devised to operate on computer systems that look and work a lot like the IBM PC. All of these computer systems use the 16-bit Intel 8088 chip or the closely related 16-bit Intel 8086 chip. These chips support less than a megabyte of RAM.

PC-DOS. The operating system most widely used on IBM microcomputers.

MS-DOS. The operating system most widely used by microcomputer systems similar to those made by IBM.

Both the PC-DOS and MS-DOS operating systems have been revised many times since they were first developed. Each major revision is referred to as a *version.* All versions starting with the number 1 (such as 1.0 and 1.1) were designed for the earliest microcomputer systems, such as the original IBM PC, which used only floppy disk and cassette tapes for secondary storage. Today, DOS is up to Version 5 and has been extended to work with hard disks and networks. Yet because it was originally designed around 16-bit chips—which supported limited amounts of RAM—DOS cannot take full advantage of the power of newer chips. When 80386-based machines arrived in 1987, with a whopping 4 gigabytes of RAM, an operating system that could support a full-fledged multitasking environment was needed.

*For simplicity, when used in this text, DOS refers strictly to MS-DOS and PC-DOS. DOS, however, is not a proprietary name, and there are other, lesser-known operating systems that use the name DOS—Radio Shack TRSDOS and Apple ProDOS, for instance.

Figure 7-6 Some widely used DOS commands, with examples.
Internal commands are always RAM-resident, whereas *external* commands need to be loaded from the DOS system disk every time they are used. All of the examples provided assume use of a two-diskette system and issuance of the command from the A drive.

Internal Commands

Command	Description	Example	Explanation
COPY	Copies individual files	COPY BOSS WORKER	Makes a copy of BOSS and stores it in WORKER
		COPY BOSS B:WORKER	Makes a copy of BOSS and stores it, on the B drive, in WORKER
DIR	Displays the names of files on a disk	DIR	Displays names of files on the A drive
		DIR B:	Displays names of files on the B drive
		DIR JILL	Tells whether a file named JILL is on the A drive
		DIR *.WKS	Displays names of files on the A drive with the extension WKS
		DIR/W	Displays names of files on the A drive in a table format
ERASE (DEL)	Erases individual files	ERASE DOLLAR	Erases DOLLAR from the A drive
		ERASE B:DOLLAR	Erases DOLLAR from the B drive
REN	Renames individual files	REN SAM BILL	Renames SAM to BILL
CLS	Clears the screen	CLS	Clears the display, leaving only the A> prompt at the top of the screen

External Commands

Command	Description	Example	Explanation
CHKDSK	Tells the amount of used and unused disk space	CHKDSK	Displays a status report for the disk on drive A
COMP	Compares the contents of two files to see whether they are identical	COMP FILEZ B:	Checks to see whether FILEZ on drive A is identical to FILEZ on drive B
DISKCOMP	Compares the contents of two disks to see whether they are identical	DISKCOMP A: B:	Checks to see whether the disk in drive A is identical to the disk in drive B
DISKCOPY	Copies the contents of one disk to another disk	DISKCOPY A: B:	Copies the contents of the disk in drive A to the disk in drive B
FORMAT	Prepares a disk for use, erasing what was there before	FORMAT	Formats the disk in the A drive
		FORMAT B:	Formats the disk in the B drive
		FORMAT B:/S	Formats the disk in the B drive and places the DOS system files onto disk

Today, it is not clear whether the successor to DOS will be OS/2, NT, UNIX, or another multitasking operating system. Despite the fact that DOS has become technologically obsolescent, it is likely that DOS and DOS-based applications will be prevalent for a good part of this decade. There are so many DOS-based computers around today that vendors of new software are still supplying—in force—DOS-based applications to the marketplace. Furthermore, products such as Microsoft Windows have extended the popularity of DOS. A sample of DOS commands is provided in Figure 7-6.

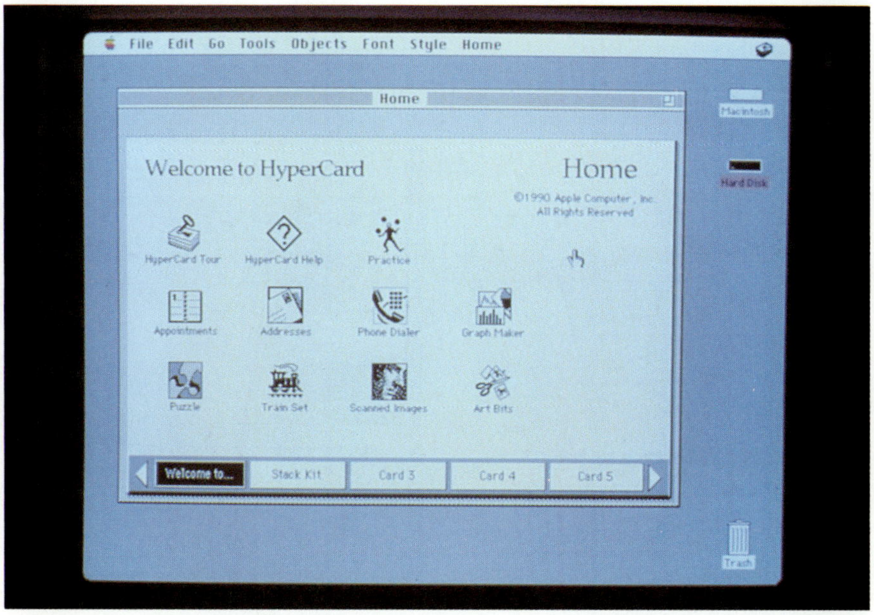

Figure 7-7
Macintosh System Software. Macintosh System Software sported the first commercially successful graphical interface for operating systems, and this interface is still one of the most popular. Here, an application called HyperCard (covered in Chapter 12) has just been summoned.

Macintosh System Software

Macintosh System Software is the proprietary, icon-oriented operating system that comes with the Apple Macintosh line of computers. The Apple Macintosh, introduced in 1984, has set the standard for graphical user interfaces. Today, many operating systems are trying to copy what the Mac originally started.

Macintosh System Software. The operating system that's primarily used on Apple's Macintosh line of computer systems.

Macintosh System Software has grown with the times, keeping pace with the increases in power made available with each new Motorola CPU chip and each new Macintosh computer system. The latest version of Macintosh System Software, Version 7, can be used on such computer systems as the Mac Plus, SE, SE/30, II, IIx, IIcx, IIci, and IIfx. On each of these machines, this version requires at least two megabytes of RAM. Some of the features it provides are typographic capabilities for display devices and printers, and multitasking.

Macintosh System Software is found, almost exclusively, on computers in the Apple Macintosh line. An example of the graphical user interface provided with the Macintosh is shown in Figure 7-7. Macintosh owners also frequently use UNIX, a flexible operating system that is not tied to any particular brand of computer.

UNIX

UNIX was originally developed almost two decades ago at Bell Laboratories as a highly portable operating system for minicomputers. Many properties make UNIX a compelling choice for the new breed of 32-bit microcomputers arriving in the marketplace.

UNIX. A multiuser, multitasking operating system.

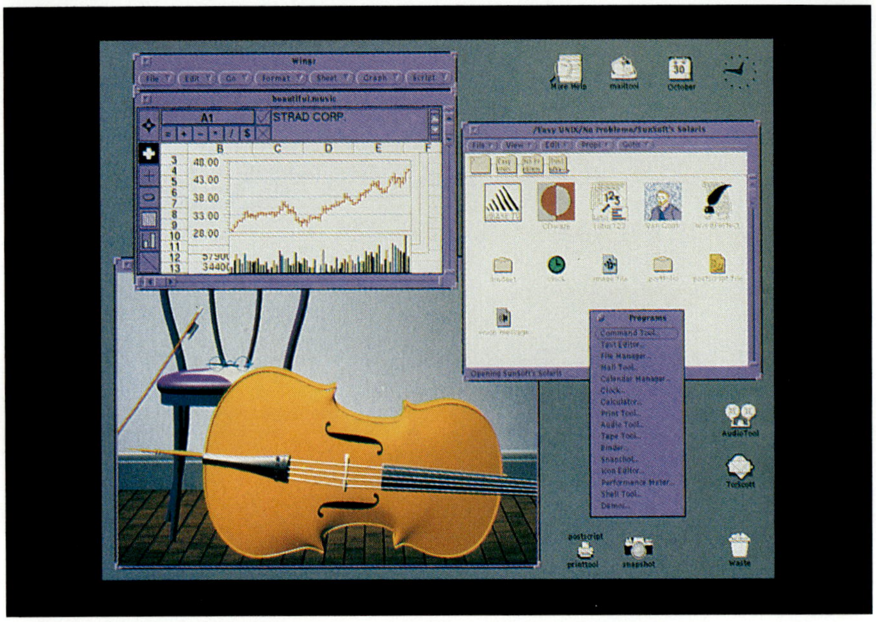

Figure 7-8
UNIX and Open Look.
Open Look is a graphically oriented operating environment used to provide a friendly user interface to UNIX. *(Shown here: SunSoft's Open Windows V3.) Copyright 1991 by Sun Microsystems, Inc.*

First, UNIX already has a relatively successful track record as a multiuser, multitasking operating system. During the 20 years it has been available, it has attracted a large, loyal following.

Second, UNIX is flexibly built, so it can be used on a wide variety of machines. Unlike other operating systems—such as DOS and OS/2, which are based on Intel chips, or Macintosh System Software, which is based on Motorola chips—UNIX is not built around a single family of processors. Computers from micros to mainframes can run UNIX, and a variety of devices from different manufacturers can easily run under UNIX while hooked into the same network. This flexibility gives UNIX a big advantage over competing operating systems for many types of applications.

But UNIX also has certain disadvantages. Many people complain that it isn't very easy to use. Also, its flexibility makes UNIX slower than operating systems tailored around a particular family of microprocessors when UNIX is used in an environment dominated by that particular family. Still another disadvantage of UNIX is that several "brands" of it are now available, many of them incompatible with each other.

Figure 7-8 shows a UNIX screen with an Open Look operating environment.

OS/2

OS/2.
The operating system designed for the high end of the IBM PS/2 line of microcomputers.

OS/2 is a single-user, multitasking operating system developed for the high end of the IBM PS/2 line of computers. It provides a graphical, display-screen interface called *Presentation Manager* (see Figure 7-9), which is

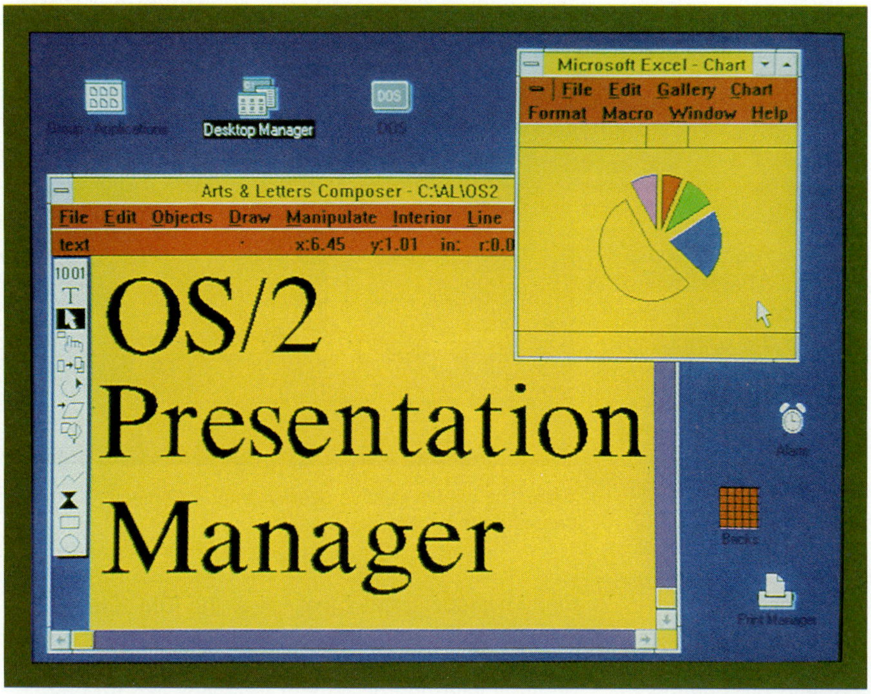

Figure 7-9
OS/2 and Presentation Manager.
Presentation Manager is a graphical interface used with the OS/2 operating system on high-end IBM microcomputers and compatibles.

similar to the Microsoft Windows interface. OS/2 is available in two versions. *OS/2 Extended Edition* contains built-in local area network (LAN) and database features, whereas *OS/2 Standard Edition* has no such capabilities.

Part of IBM's plan is to have all applications that run under OS/2 look similar to users—a concept IBM includes in its **Systems Applications Architecture (SAA).** This applications commonality will be shared by both the PS/2 line of computers and IBM mainframes. SAA is IBM's grand plan to interface many of its major product offerings (see the Tomorrow box).

Systems Applications Architecture (SAA).
An IBM strategy to interface major product offerings in a way that makes all applications running under OS/2 look similar to the user.

While both OS/2 and SAA are IBM concepts, they will also work with computers compatible with those in the IBM line, such as Compaq computers, as User Solution 7-1 shows.

The OS/2 operating system makes it possible to address 16 MB RAM. OS/2 can operate in either of two modes. In the *real (compatibility) mode,* OS/2 is capable of running programs that were created to run under DOS. Because DOS can address only 640 KB RAM, the real mode can address only this amount of space. In the *protected mode,* in contrast, OS/2 is designed to run applications that are created specifically for OS/2 and to take advantage of the fact that it can address 16 MB RAM and can do multitasking. When OS/2 runs in the protected mode, a *memory protection* feature ensures that multiple tasks won't collide with each other in RAM.

Tomorrow

Systems Applications Architecture (SAA)

IBM Looks to the Future

The computing industry has always had a problem with standards. Standards involve agreement on a common set of rules that will enable different types of hardware or software to work together. As the number of vendors and products in the computing industry has mushroomed, the standards problem has become more severe. Computer giant IBM has proposed a solution for the future . . . but will users accept it?

IBM's plan is called *Systems Applications Architecture* (*SAA*). Introduced in 1987, SAA proposes a consistent framework within which applications can fit together across IBM PS/2 computers, IBM small business systems (such as computers in the AS/400 line), and IBM mainframes. The framework is designed so that applications interfaces will have the same "look" to users and programmers, no matter what type of IBM computer the user or programmer is working on. The user or programmer does not even have to know where the programs or data used on the system are stored.

Basically, there are three levels to SAA. At the *user level,* a common user interface is employed for all IBM machines. This gives a consistent look to applications. At the *communications level,* communications support is given so that applications developed and used within an SAA environment can all "talk" to each other. At the *applications programming level,* consistent programming standards increase the transportability of programs across machines. The entry point to an SAA environment is IBM's OS/2 (Extended Edition) operating system.

IBM has held a commanding lead in mainframes for about the past 35 years. Mainframes and microcomputers are the leading types of computers for business applications, the principal market to which SAA is targeted. Although SAA is designed specifically around IBM equipment, there are so many microcomputers that follow the IBM standard that many of these, too, will be able to fit in an SAA environment. Apple Macintosh computers also can be fitted with boards so that they look like IBM microcomputers to the network server.

SAA. The goal is to have users master a single procedure to access any machine.

It will not be known for many years how successful SAA will be in drawing users. One determining factor will be what corporations decide to do as they download their transaction-processing systems from mainframes to microcomputer-based networks (see the Tomorrow box in Chapter 6). Even though SAA appears to be a logical choice for the migration of transaction-processing systems to networks, the actual choice may depend on how attractive both SAA and OS/2—IBM's "operating system of the future" for microcomputers—are when users decide to switch. OS/2 is still awaiting business acceptance, as many users have opted for Microsoft Windows to extend their use of DOS. Two other unknowns are UNIX and NT, OS/2's chief competitors. Even though UNIX is not designed around the equipment of a particular vendor, users have been reluctant to switch to it. NT is still extremely new and relatively untested by the marketplace.

NetWare

NetWare. The most widely used operating system on local area networks (LANs).

NetWare—developed by Novell, Inc. during the mid-1980s—is today the most widely used operating system on microcomputer-based local area networks (LANs). Most users of NetWare interact with it when they log

User Solution 7-1

A Newspaper's OS/2 Solution

The Chicago Tribune is one of the oldest newspapers in the United States and has a staff of more than 600 editors and programmers. The staff writes and edits stories using an Ethernet network. This network connects about 400 Compaq 386 microcomputers that use the OS/2 operating system with the Presentation Manager interface. The network allows access to other users, editing systems, remote databases and wire-service feeds, electronic mail, and a wide range of off-the-shelf applications software packages. OS/2 was selected because it was decided both to use computers that were IBM compatible and to have a state-of-the-art operating-system environment.

in to a network or when they deal with a print server or a file server on a network. NetWare provides a shell around the user's chosen operating system, thereby enabling files to be retrieved or saved on a shared hard disk and also printed on a shared printer (see Figure 7-10). The shell routine enables users to communicate with NetWare, which is located on the shared disk.

Here's a typical NetWare session on a network of IBM microcomputers or similar machines: When you turn on a workstation that is hooked into the network, the network will send a prompt to your display. Often, the prompt is

```
F>
```

At this point, you can decide to work on or off the network.

If you wish to work on the network, a log-in message must be typed in next. For instance, if the network recognizes you as KJOHNSON, you might have to type in

```
LOGIN KJOHNSON
```

When the log-in is accepted, you have *access rights* to the network, and you are free to do any network operation within the access rights that have been assigned to you. Access rights, managed by a person called the *network administrator*, will vary from user to user (see Figure 7-11).

Figure 7-10 NetWare shell.
At the workstation level, NetWare provides a shell around each user's local operating system (such as DOS). The shell routine enables users to communicate with NetWare, which is located on the file server. When the user asks for a job to be printed out, for instance, the user's applications program passes the job on to the local operating system, which sends it to the NetWare shell, which sends it on to NetWare. NetWare then lines the job up in the print queue on the appropriate server device.

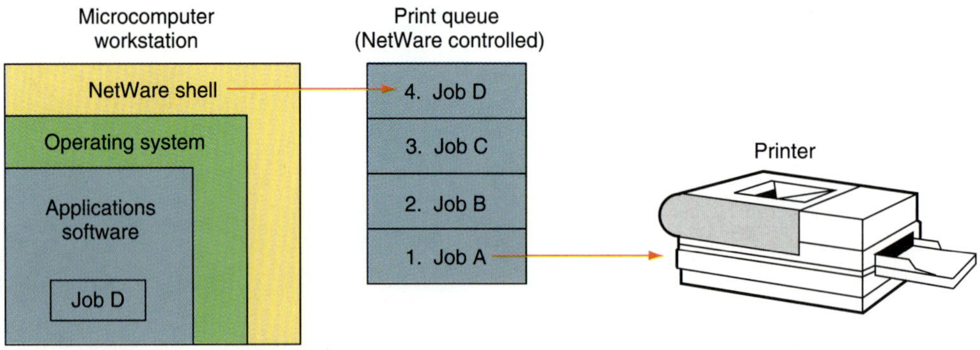

Figure 7-11
NetWare access rights.
The network administrator can grant a particular user any or all of the privileges listed here.

Right	Allows
READ	Reading from or executing files
WRITE	Writing to existing files
OPEN	Opening existing files
CREATE	Creating new files
DELETE (ERASE)	Deleting files
PARENTAL (ACCESS CONTROL)	Creating new subdirectories and controlling the rights to use those subdirectories
SEARCH (SCAN FILE)	Searching a directory's list of files
MODIFY	Changing filenames and file attributes
SUPERVISOR	Having all of the rights listed above

When you are working at the F> prompt, which typically corresponds to the shared hard disk on the network, you generally treat it as if it were just another disk drive.

If you choose not to work on the network, you simply respond A:, B:, or C: to the F> prompt, and you are then pointed to your local diskette drives or your local hard drive. You then work just as you would if you were on a non-networked computer system. Keep in mind, however, that if you need to gain access to a program stored on the shared hard disk, to save a program to the shared hard disk, or to output to a shared printer, you must first get network access.

Language Translators

As mentioned earlier, computers can execute programs only after the latter have been translated into machine language. There are two reasons why people don't generally write programs in this language. First, machine-language instructions consist of complex-looking strings of 0s and 1s—for example,

```
01011000011100000000000100000010
```

Few people enjoy or are successful at writing long programs consisting of statements like this. Second, machine-language instructions must be written at the most detailed level of exposition, which requires a technical knowledge beyond the grasp of most people.

A **language translator** is simply a systems program that converts into machine language an applications program written in a higher-level language. Three common types of language translators are compilers, interpreters, and assemblers.

Language translator. A systems program that converts an applications program into machine language.

Compilers. A **compiler** translates a high-level or very-high-level language program entirely into machine language before it is executed. Every compiler-oriented language requires its own special compiler. Thus, a COBOL program needs a COBOL compiler; it cannot run on a BASIC compiler.

Compiler. A systems program that translates a program entirely into machine language before the translated program is executed.

The program that you write in a high-level language and enter in the computer is called a **source module,** or *source program.* The machine-level program that the compiler then produces from it is called an **object module,** or *object program.*

Source module. The original form in which a program is entered into an input device by a user or programmer.

Object module. The machine-language program that is the output from a language translator.

Normally, before the object module is actually executed, it is bound together with other object modules that the CPU may need in order to process the program. For example, most computers can't compute square roots directly. To do so, they rely on small "subprograms," which are stored in secondary storage in object module form. Thus if your program calls for calculating a square root, the operating system will bind the object-module version of your program together with this square root routine to form an "executable package" for the computer. The binding process is referred to as *linkage editing,* or the *link-edit stage,* and the executable package that is formed is called a **load module.** A special systems program, called a **linkage editor,** is available on computer systems to do the binding automatically.

Load module. A complete machine-language program that is ready to be executed by the computer.

Linkage editor. A systems program that binds together related object-module program segments so that they may be run as a unit.

It is the load module that the computer actually executes, or runs. When your program is ready to run, it has reached the *Go (execution) stage.* Figure 7-12 shows the complete process from compiling to link editing to execution. Both object and load modules can be saved on disk for later use so that compilation and linkage editing need not be performed every time the program is executed.

Interpreters. An **interpreter,** unlike a compiler, does not create an object module. Interpreters read, translate, and execute source programs one line at a time. Thus, the translation into machine language is performed while the program is running.

Interpreter. A systems program that translates a program into machine language on a line-by-line basis, as each statement is executed.

Interpreters have advantages and disadvantages compared with compilers. Two major advantages are that interpreters are easier to use and they enable errors to be discovered in programs more quickly. The interpreter itself requires relatively little storage space, and it does not gener-

Figure 7-12
Compile, link-edit, go.
A compiler and a linkage editor convert a source module into a load module, which is processed by the CPU.

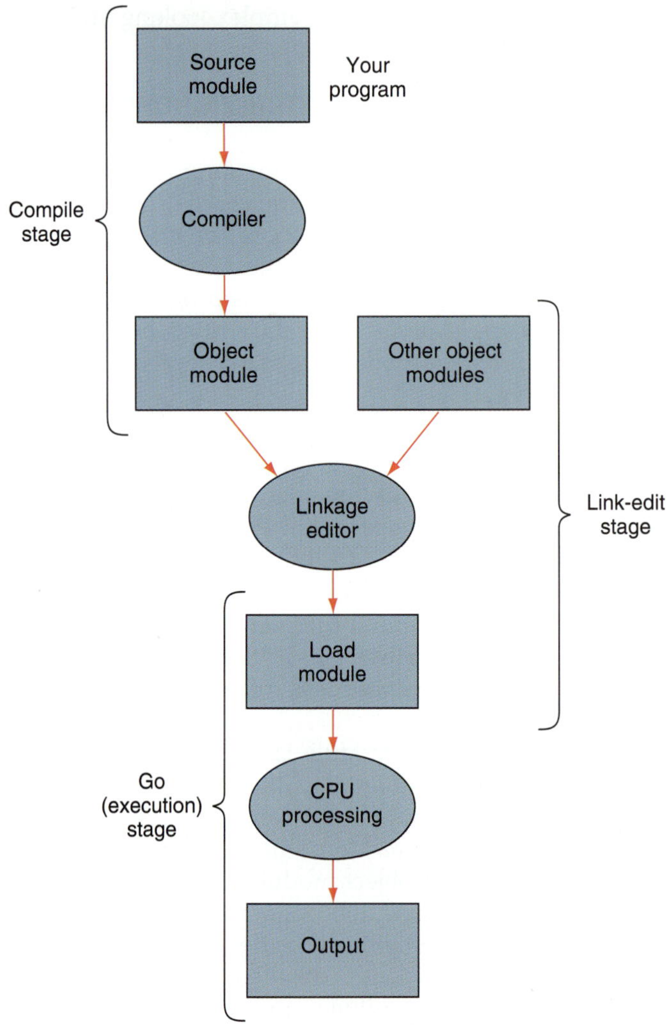

ate an object module that must be stored. For these reasons, interpreters are ideal for beginning programmers and for people with limited storage space on their systems.

The major disadvantage of interpreters is that they are less efficient than compilers, and, consequently, programs run more slowly on them. Because interpreters translate each program statement into machine language just before executing it, they can chew up a lot of time—especially when the same statements may be executed thousands of times during the course of program execution and must be reinterpreted every time they are encountered. With a compiler, in contrast, each program statement is translated only once—before the program is run. In addition, the object module of a compiled program can be saved on disk, so the source program doesn't have to be retranslated every time the program is executed.

Some programming-language packages are equipped with both an interpreter and compiler, giving the programmer the best of both worlds. This allows the programmer to work with the interpreter while rooting out program errors and, when the program is error-free, to use the compiler to save it in object-module form.

Assemblers. The third type of translator, the **assembler,** is used exclusively with assembly languages (discussed in Chapter 12). It works like a compiler, producing a stored object module. Each computer system typically has only one assembly language available to it; thus, only one assembler is required.

Assembler.
A computer program that takes assembly-language instructions and converts them to machine language.

Utility Programs

Some tasks are performed so often in the course of processing that it would be extremely inefficient if every user had to code them into programs over and over again. Sorting records, formatting disks and tapes, and copying programs from one medium to another are examples of such tasks. To eliminate the need for users and programmers to waste time writing such routines, computer systems normally have available a library of **utility programs** to perform these types of functions. Typically, utility programs reside in secondary storage and are summoned by the operating system's supervisor program or by the user when needed.

Utility program.
A program used to perform some frequently encountered operation in a computer system.

Utility programs are packaged in a variety of ways. Sometimes they are bundled into an operating system. For instance, utility programs for formatting disks, copying the contents of disks, and checking the allocation of disk space are built directly into the MS-DOS operating system. In other cases, utilities are independent programs that can be acquired from third-party vendors and made to run with a given operating system.

Four widely used types of utility programs that we will cover in depth here are disk utilities, spooling software, text editors, and device drivers. Feature 7-1 considers these and other types of utilities.

Disk Utilities. Many operating systems have built-in disk utility routines that format disks, copy disk files, copy the contents of one disk to another disk or to tape, compare disks, provide disk directories, and so on. A number of third-party, aftermarket companies have created packages of other, less-familiar **disk utility** programs that go well beyond those available with many operating systems. Four such types of utilities are disk toolkits, data compression utilities, disk optimizers, and backup utilities.

Disk utility.
A program that assists with such disk-related tasks as backup, data compression, space allocation, and recovering from accidental data destruction.

- *Disk toolkits,* the most famous of which is The Norton Utilities, are used to recover from accidental data destruction. They allow you to recover damaged or erased files, repair damaged format markings and directories, and recover from a disk crash (a crippling of the disk itself).

Feature 7-1

The World of Utilities

Small Programs That Can Make Big Differences

Utility programs have existed since the inception of many of the earliest operating systems. Utility programs are, essentially, add-on programs. They extend the duties of your computer's operating system, allowing it to do many tasks that the operating system's original designers probably never considered.

Operating-system utilities are of two principal types: those that load automatically into RAM when your computer is started up and those that you must explicitly call every time you need them.

In the IBM microcomputing world, the first types are called *TSR*s, for *terminate-and-stay-resident* utilities. These programs are so named because every time you use and finish with (i.e., terminate) them, they remain resident in RAM. In the Apple Macintosh world, TSRs are often referred to as *INIT*s, which stands for "initializing" utilities.

The second type of utility program, those that you call, comprises a variety of programs. For instance, DOS's external commands fall into this class, as do Microsoft Window's desk accessory (DA) programs. These programs must be reloaded into RAM every time you want to use them.

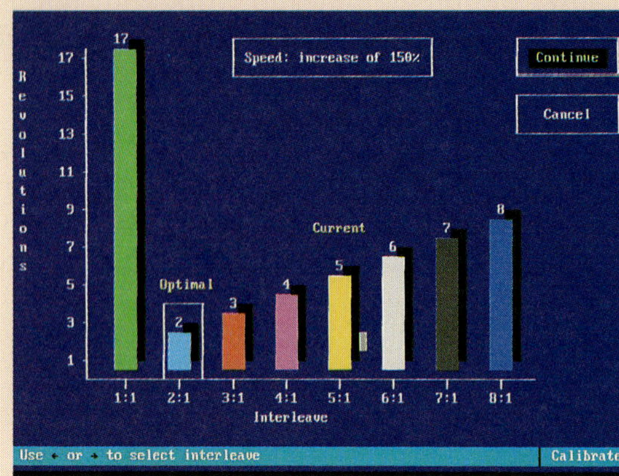

Performance monitors. Utility programs that help you test your system to see that it's working efficiently.

There are many utility programs in the marketplace. Chapter 7 covers only a few types in depth, but the accompanying list (page 245) is more comprehensive. Although many of these utilities may also exist as features in your operating system, keep in mind that such "tack ons" are usually limited in some way. Products from third-party vendors are generally more powerful.

- *Data compression programs* enable files to be compressed. This helps free up disk space and enables files to be sent over the phone lines faster. The person at the other end of the line must have the proper decompression program.
- *Disk optimizers* enable programs on disk to be accessed faster. They perform such tasks as allocating certain files to the outer cylinders (where they may be reached more quickly), rewriting fragmented files (that is, rewriting in contiguous sectors files that originally were written into many noncontiguous disk sectors), and sorting file directory names for faster access.
- *Backup utilities* are programs designed to back up the contents of a hard disk. One of the most widely used backup utilities is Fifth Generation Systems' Fastback Plus (see Figure 7-13). Backup is discussed in more detail in Chapter 13.

Spooling Software. Some input and output devices are extremely slow. Tape devices and printers, for example, work at a snail's pace compared to the CPU. If the CPU had to wait for these slower devices to finish their

Utility type	Description
Backup utilities	Quickly and easily back up the contents of a hard disk
Cosmetic utilities	Let you customize the user environment, for example, by changing the colors on your display or by changing the way in which menus are presented
Data compression utilities	Enable files to be compressed
Device drivers	Enable applications software to work on a specific configuration of hardware
Diagnostic software	Enable bugs to be more easily rooted out of your computer system
Disk optimizers	Better utilize space on disk
Disk toolkits	Recover and repair damaged or lost files
Extenders	Let you add new fonts, commands, or programs to your operating system
File transfer utilities	Make it possible for you to transfer files between two distinct programs or computer systems
Keyboard utilities	Let you construct keyboard macros (small programs that execute when you press a certain key) or let you reconfigure your keyboard
Performance monitors	Tell you how efficiently your computer system is performing its work (see photo)
Screen capture programs	Enable you to download any screen image onto a hard-copy output device
Screen savers	Turn the display off to prevent the phosphor coating from burning
Spooling programs	Control outputs going to the printer, thereby preventing your computer system from being tied up while the printer is outputting
Text editors	Allow text in a nondocument file to be manipulated
Text retrieval utilities	Enable you to find a lost file on your system by typing in part of its name or by typing in short strings of text known to be contained in the file
Vaccine programs	Protect your system from virus attacks (see Feature 7-2)
Workgroup utilities	Enable you to interconnect a small number of computers so that people working on them can pass messages back and forth

work, the computer system would face a horrendous bottleneck. For example, suppose the computer has just completed a 5-second job that generated 100 pages of hard copy for the printer. On a printer that prints 600 lines per minute, this job would take about 10 minutes to print. If the CPU had to deal directly with the printer, primary memory would be tied up for 10 minutes waiting for the printer to complete the job. As a result, other programs would have to wait for processing while this output was being transferred from main memory to paper.

To avoid such a delay, disks on almost all large systems contain *output spooling areas* to store output destined for the printer (see Figure 7-14). As the computer processes a program, a **spooling program** rapidly transfers, or "spools," the output from main memory to the disk spooling area. The computer is then free to process another program, leaving it to the spooling program to transfer the output of the first program from disk to printer.

Spooling program. A program that temporarily stages input or output in secondary storage to expedite processing.

At any given time, the spooling area of, say, a large computer system may contain more than 100 completed jobs waiting to be delivered to output devices. As long as space remains in the output spooling area, the

Figure 7-13
Backup utility.
Fifth Generation Systems' Fastback Plus is one of the most widely used backup programs for microcomputers. During any session, it lets you back up all of your hard-disk files or only selected ones.

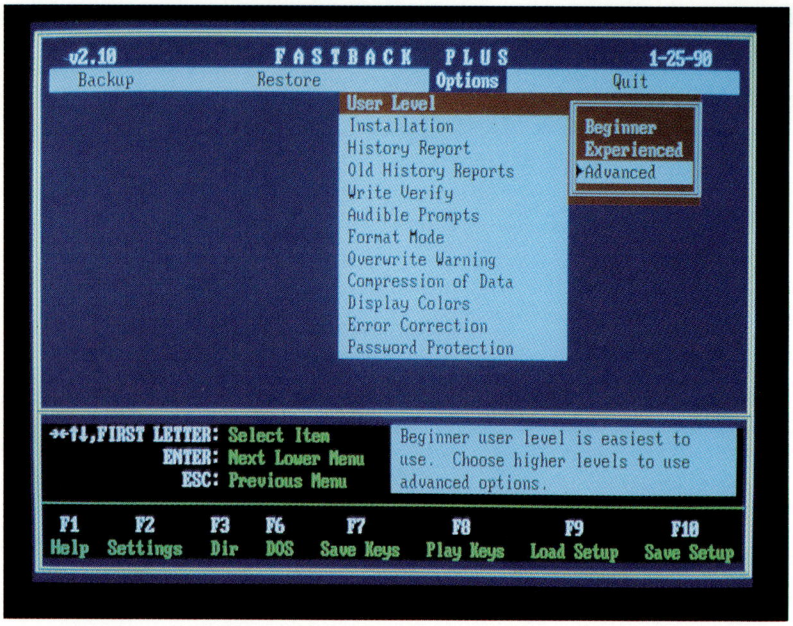

Figure 7-14 Spooling.
On large computer systems, input is spooled before it is processed and output is spooled before it is sent to the printer.

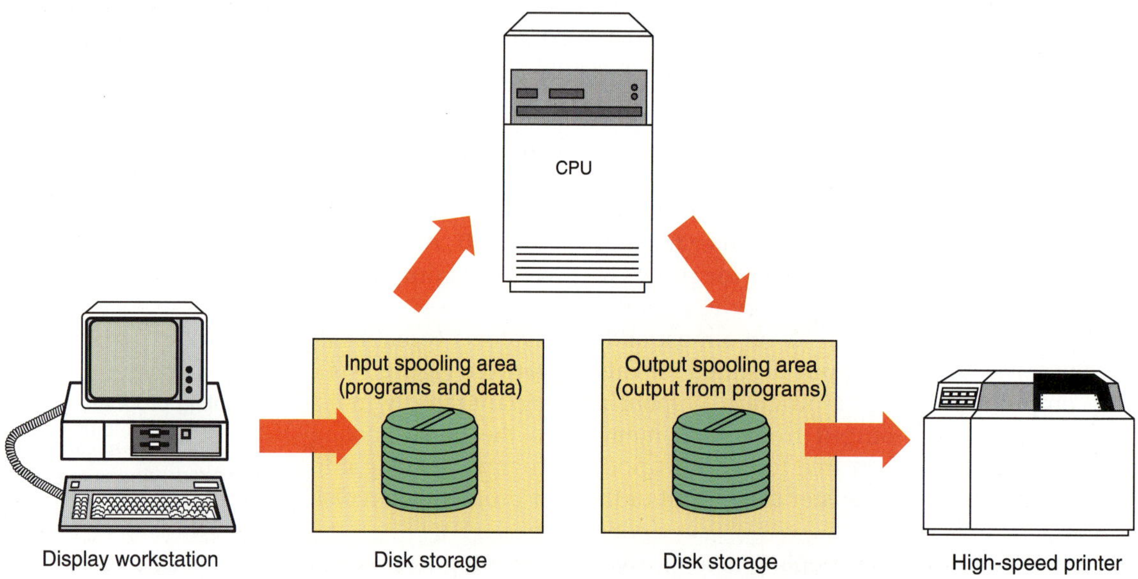

Feature 7-2

Virus Protection

What To Do When Your Computer System Catches a "Cold"

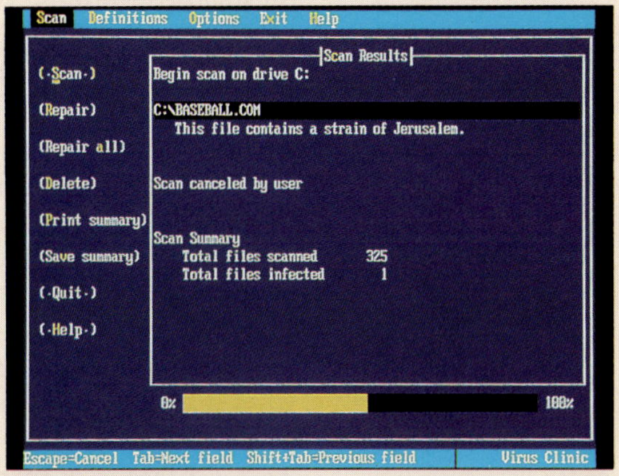

Vaccine program. Detecting a virus strain with Symantec's SAM program.

If your computer system comes down with nVir-a, nVir-f, INIT 29, ANTI, WDEF A or B, Michelangelo, Stoned, or Jerusalem, reach for your electronic medicine chest. It's got a computer virus.

A *computer virus* is a small block of code, often hidden inside a larger program, that is designed to create malicious damage or pull a harmless prank. Malicious damage includes such things as destroying programs and data or gumming up your computer system so that it's difficult or impossible to continue work. Pranks include such things as flashing messages on your display screen from time to time to let you know that your computer system has been invaded by someone who delights in this sort of practical joke.

Viruses often work by copying code onto programs or data on a disk or in memory. Many may even replicate themselves onto other disks, thereby spreading infection. The virus also contains a mechanism that at a specific time or moment (say, on a specific day or when an infected program performs a certain operation) destroys data or pulls pranks.

In November 1988, a virus implanted in a computer system disabled thousands of computers that were hooked into Arpanet, a nationwide network connecting dozens of colleges, universities, and research labs. When any computer system in the network read a program containing the viral code, the virus filled up the main memory of that computer system with garbage, effectively choking out legitimate applications and grinding the system to a halt.

The Michelangelo virus, named for the sixteenth-century Italian artist, has been devised to detonate any time the clock of an infected computer strikes March 6, the artist's birthday. On hard-disk systems, Michelangelo attaches itself to routines that *boot,* or start up, the computer, causing them to be moved to hard-to-find locations and causing vital directory data on the disk to be overwritten with random characters. Any diskettes inserted into a drive of an infected system are themselves infected, and data destroyed, during read/write operations.

Your system is vulnerable to viruses virtually any time you use it. At especially high risk are people who work on networks, people who use software that comes from unknown origins, and people who let others use their system. If you are concerned about viruses, you can protect yourself by (1) avoiding high-risk situations, (2) never using any new software unless all of the software and data that you can't afford to lose are backed up on offline diskettes, (3) locking up disks (a virus, for instance, can't write to a diskette when the latter has been made "read only" through the write-protect notch), (4) keeping high-risk software away from your hard disk, and (5) using some type of *vaccine program.*

To date, a number of vaccine programs have surfaced to combat computer viruses. Three of the most widely used are Symantec's SAM (see photo), Mainstay's AntiToxin, and HJC's Virex. Vaccine programs are priced at about $100 and are accompanied by a list of the specific strains of viruses that they can protect your system from picking up.

Vaccine programs scrutinize code for suspicious patterns. If something looks strange, they often can intercept an activity before it takes place and apprise you of what's going on. Many are also designed to repair damaged files in the event that a virus it is able to recognize has infected some programs or data, and some can prevent a program or data with a recognized virus from ever executing.

Many vaccine programs are designed to check for virus activity upon system log-in, during system use, and upon log-off. Some packages provide a log of all virus alerts, which lets you keep tabs on suspicious activity over a period of time.

Unfortunately, no vaccine program is foolproof. New viruses are being discovered all the time, so vaccine programs need to be updated constantly. Updates may cost anywhere from $10 to $25 annually.

CPU can continue to operate without delay. Output spooling is popular on microcomputers, too. For example, if your printer will be tied up for 15 minutes or so typing a long document, a spooling routine will let you use your computer to edit another document while the first one is printing.

As Figure 7-14 shows, spooling is also used to hold, or stage, input on its way to the computer. As programs enter the computer system, they are stored in an *input spooling area,* or *queue.* When the operating system is ready to deliver the next program to the CPU, it checks the queue to see which one to process next. On many computer systems, priorities can be assigned to programs. If this is possible, the computer will attend to high-priority jobs before it processes jobs that may have been waiting longer but have a lower priority.

Text editor.
A utility program that enables an operator to manipulate text in a file.

Text Editors. A **text editor** is a software package that enables you to manipulate text in a file. Whereas word processors are specifically targeted to manipulating text that exists in document form—say, memos, letters, and manuscripts—text editors are primarily aimed at text that exists in the form of records—say, lines of a computer program, columnar data, and so forth. With a text editor, you can often do things such as sort records in a file, delete or move fields in records, append fields to records, and so forth.

Let's look at an example. Say that you are creating records containing names and social security numbers. In each record, names are to begin in column 1 and the social security numbers in column 31. But you mistakenly type in the social security numbers first and then the names. Text editors will permit you to correct this mistake quickly, with a single command that reverses the positions of the social security number and name fields in all the records.

Some text editors are *full-screen editors,* meaning that they let you move the cursor anywhere on the screen to point as you manipulate text. *Line editors,* on the other hand, constrain the cursor to a single line position on the display screen. Normally, if you want to move back to an earlier line, you must depress a special sequence of keys to tell the line editor that you want to do something out of the normal sequence of operations.

Text editors are invaluable to programmers in creating and debugging programs. Many programming languages, such as BASIC, have their own built-in editors.

Device driver.
A utility program that enables an applications program to function with a specific hardware device.

Device Drivers. When communicating with output hardware such as display devices and printers, applications software packages commonly rely on utility programs known as device drivers. **Device drivers** act as interfaces between applications programs and specific hardware devices.

A device driver typically works as follows. A software package that you buy—say, a word processor—will often include both an installation program and a utilities disk that contains several device drivers. You install the word processor to work on a specific set of hardware devices by running the installation program. The installation program will ask you a number of questions—for instance, what type of printer and what type of monitor you are using. You answer these questions by selecting the appropriate devices from a list. As you make selections, the installation program retrieves the drivers corresponding to the selected devices and incorporates them into an "installed version" of the word processor, which it is building as the question-and-answer session is taking place. When this process is finished, the installed version of the program is ready for use on a specific hardware system.

As you later work with the installed version of the word processor, it will defer to the driver routines you have built into it to handle any hardware-specific commands. Generally, you will have to run the installation program only once—at the time you acquire the word processor. If, however, you replace one brand or model of hardware device with another, you will probably have to rerun the installation program to declare the new device.

Summary and Key Terms

Systems software consists of programs that coordinate the various parts of the computer system to make it run rapidly and efficiently. The basic role of systems software is to act as a mediator between applications programs and the computer system's hardware.

The Operating System. An **operating system** is a collection of programs that manage the computer's activities. The functions of the operating system—which include assignment of system resources, scheduling of resources and jobs, and monitoring activities—can be viewed as aspects of a single general mission: to control the computer system's operations.

Two of the most prominent programs of the operating system are the supervisor and the command-language translator. The **supervisor** controls all the other parts of the operating system. The **command-language translator** enables both users and programmers to communicate with the operating system by using a **command language.** When interfacing with the operating system, you can use the standard system **defaults,** chosen by the operating system, or can request customized service through command-language instructions.

On some computer systems, the operator uses a *language interface* to carry out command-language instructions. On others, which employ a *graphical interface,* the operator points on the screen to icons to carry out such instructions. An **operating environment** is a shell program that fits over an operating system, giving it a friendlier and more flexible user interface than its native one.

Sophisticated computers often take advantage of interleaved processing techniques, such as multiprogramming, multitasking, time-sharing, virtual memory, and multiprocessing, to operate more efficiently.

Multiprogramming is a term commonly used to describe some *multi-user* computer systems. In a computer system with multiprogramming, the computer works on several programs *concurrently*. For example, while the computer is waiting for data from one user's program to be accessed on disk, it can perform calculations for another user's program.

Multitasking refers to a multiprogramming-like capability on *single-user* operating systems. Thus, multitasking connotes the ability of two or more programs from any single user to execute *concurrently* on one computer or, more commonly, the ability of two or more tasks performed by a single program to execute concurrently.

Time-sharing is a technique in which the operating system cycles through all the active programs that need processing in the system and gives each one a small slice of time on each cycle.

Virtual memory refers to using disk to extend main memory. The operating system delivers programs to be processed to the virtual memory area, where they are subdivided into either fixed-length *pages* or variable-length *segments.*

Multiprocessing refers to the use of two or more computers, linked together, to perform work at the *same* time.

A Closer Look at Several Operating Systems. Some of today's most widely used operating systems include PC-DOS and MS-DOS, Macintosh System Software, UNIX, OS/2 (which is an integral part of IBM's **Systems Applications Architecture,** or **SAA**), and NetWare.

PC-DOS and **MS-DOS** are commonly found on IBM microcomputers and similar devices. DOS—as these operating systems are called for short—is the most widely used software package ever developed. **Macintosh System Software** is the operating system native to the Apple Macintosh line of computers. **OS/2** and **UNIX** are both multitasking operating systems that are targeted to today's most powerful microcomputer systems. **NetWare** is an operating system designed for the operation of local area networks (LANs).

Language Translators. A **language translator** is a systems program that converts into machine language an applications program written in a higher-level language. There are three common types of language translators: compilers, interpreters, and assemblers.

A **compiler** translates a high-level- or very-high-level-language program entirely into machine language before the program is executed. The program written by the user or programmer, called a **source module,** is first translated by the compiler into an **object module.** The object-module version of the program is then inputted to a **linkage editor,** which combines it with supplementary object modules needed to run the program to form a **load module.** It is the load module that the computer executes.

Interpreters read, translate, and execute source programs one line at a time. Thus, the translation into machine language occurs while the program is being run.

The third type of translator, the **assembler,** is used exclusively with assembly languages.

Utility Programs. A **utility program** is a type of systems program written to perform repetitive processing tasks. There are many types of utility programs. **Disk utility** routines extend the operating system's disk-handling capabilities, enabling users to do such things as recover erased files and reorganize disk data for faster access. **Spooling programs** free the CPU from time-consuming interaction with I/O devices such as printers. **Text editors** enable users to manipulate text in a file. **Device drivers** act as interfaces between applications programs and specific hardware devices.

Review Exercises

Fill-in Questions

1. ______________ software consists of programs that act as a mediator between applications software and the computer system's hardware.
2. A(n) ______________ is a collection of programs that manage the computer system's activities.
3. In a computer system with ______________ , the computer works on several users' programs concurrently, leaving one at some logical stopping point to begin work on another.
4. ______________ is a technique in which the operating system cycles through active programs in the system that need processing and gives each one a small slice of time on each cycle.
5. ______________ refers to the use of two or more computers, linked together, to perform work on programs at the same time.
6. The most widely used operating system on LANs is ______________ .
7. A(n) ______________ is a systems program that converts an applications program written in a high-level language or in an assembly language into machine language.
8. ______________ programs are systems programs written to perform repetitive processing tasks, such as formatting disks and text editing.

Matching Questions

Match each term with the description that fits best.

a. device driver
b. compiler
c. linkage editor
d. spooling software
e. interpreter
f. text editor
g. operating system

_____ 1. A language translator that reads, translates, and executes source programs a line at a time.

_____ 2. Enables a user to edit one document on a microcomputer system while printing out another.

_____ 3. A program that enables an applications software package to work on a specific hardware device.

_____ 4. Binds object modules together.

____ 5. A piece of systems software without which a computer will do nothing.

____ 6. A language translator that creates an object module.

____ 7. Can do things such as append fields to records and change the order of fields in records.

Discussion Questions

1. What is systems software?
2. What is an operating system and what are its major functions?
3. Describe multiprogramming, multitasking, time-sharing, virtual memory, and multiprocessing.
4. Describe the differences between UNIX and OS/2.
5. What are the differences between a compiler, an interpreter, and an assembler?
6. Identify several types of utility programs and explain what they do.

Critical Thinking Questions

1. UNIX has been available for about two decades, but it has only been during the last few years that it has received much attention. Why do you think this is so?
2. MS-DOS has sold millions of copies, making it the most widely used software package ever written. Now that powerful microcomputer systems are available and powerful operating systems are coming to take advantage of them, do you think a sizeable market will still exist for users who want these new computers but still want to use MS-DOS?
3. Many users of computer systems have argued that graphical interfaces, while potentially useful to some people, are totally undesirable for their needs. Where do you think these users are "coming from"?

Window 3

Graphical User Interfaces

Tools of the Electronic Desktop

In the decade or so that they've been available, graphical user interfaces (GUIs)—sometimes called electronic desktops, because they emulate the look of a real desktop—have become increasingly popular. In the 1980s, most users who wanted a GUI turned to the Apple Macintosh, which represented the biggest line of computers that fully supported graphics applications. In 1990, with the arrival of Microsoft Windows 3.0 as a shell for DOS, GUIs also became commonplace on IBM and IBM-compatible microcomputers. Today, virtually every new software product arriving in the marketplace sports a graphical interface of some type.

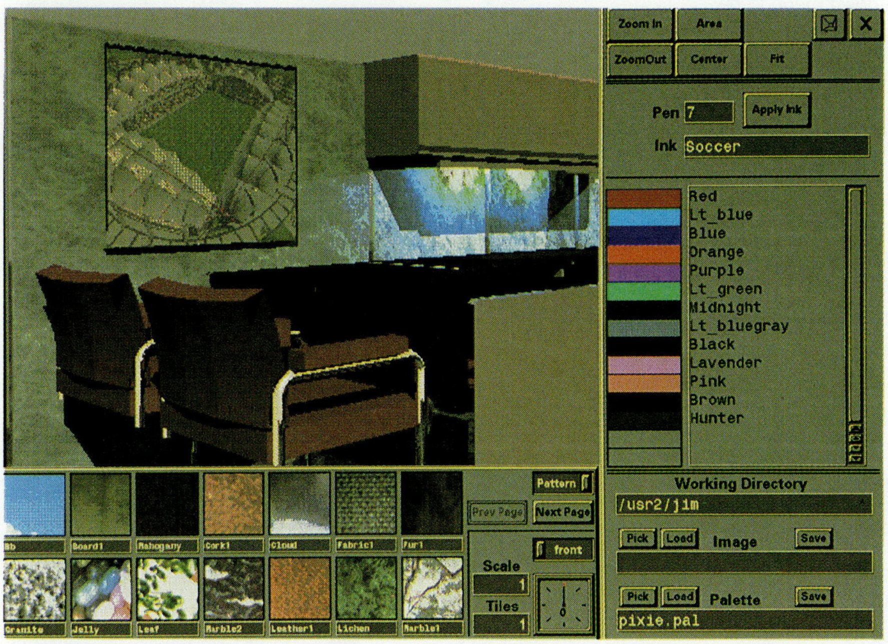

1. The state-of-the-art graphics interface in this architectural design package enables architects to choose colors and textures merely by pointing to them with a mouse and then pointing to the objects in the accompanying image that are to receive the coloring or texturing. The "buttons" at the right of the screen can be activated to perform other functions.

Menus

Most GUIs have some form of menu interface that users interact with to select commands or command options.

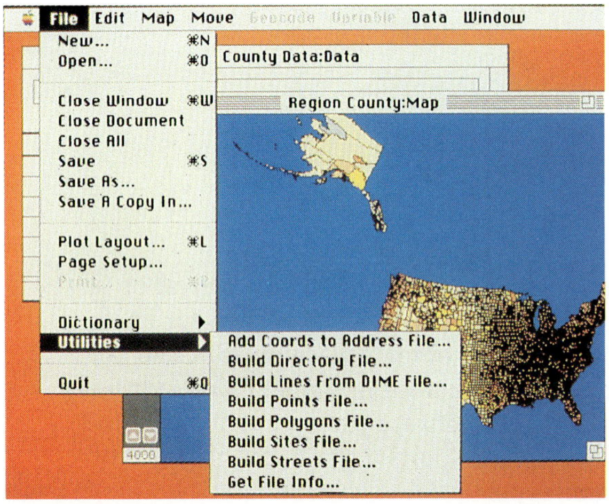

2. In many menu interfaces, there is a top-of-the-screen menu bar that shows the main commands and, for each command, a pull-down menu (or submenu) that shows other available options. Sometimes, as shown here, choosing an option on a pull-down menu causes another pull-down menu to be unfurled to the right of it.

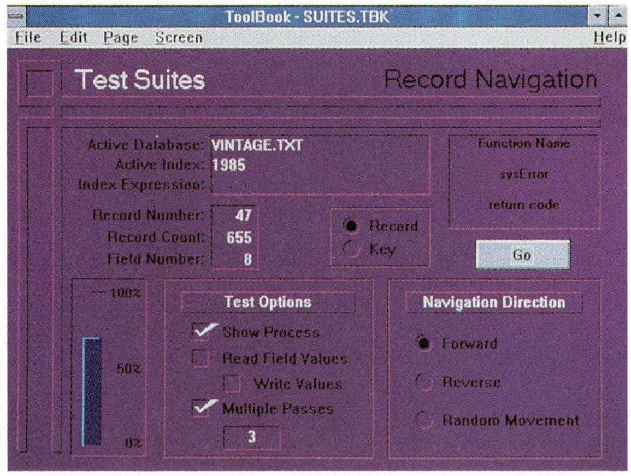

3. Dialogue, or pop-up, boxes often appear on the screen after a choice is made on a pull-down menu. Dialogue boxes require you to type something in or to choose (as shown by the white check marks and the black dots) among several items. When you are finished making selections, you press the go "button."

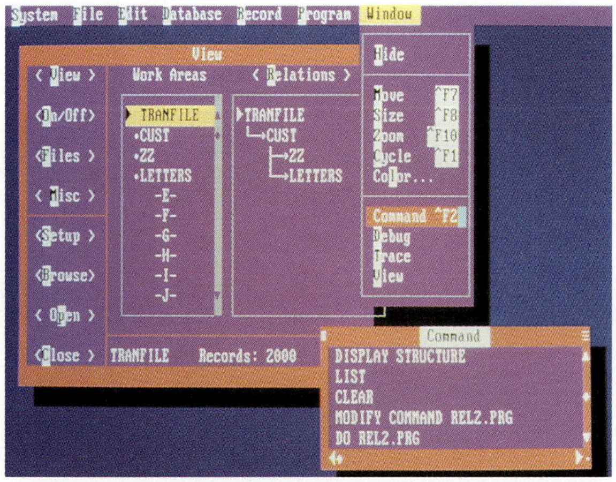

4. Many packages allow you to choose options on menus and submenus by typing in the letter that is highlighted in the name of the choice—for instance, "D" to select database.

Windows

Among favorite GUI tools are windows—small boxes of information that are created and stacked on the electronic desktop just as memos and file folders are created and stored on a regular desktop. Windows can be sized to your liking, resized, and moved around.

5

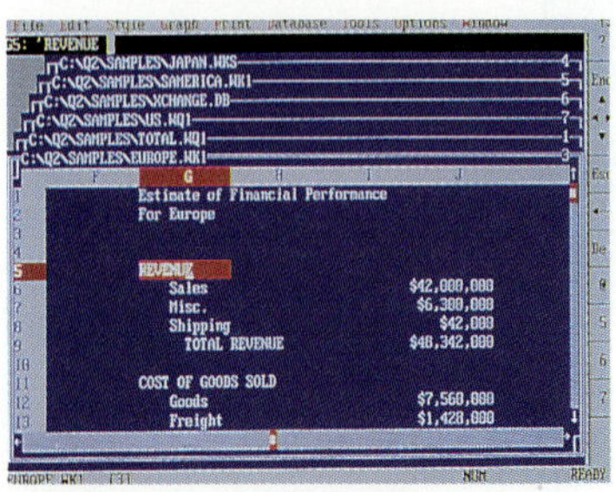

6

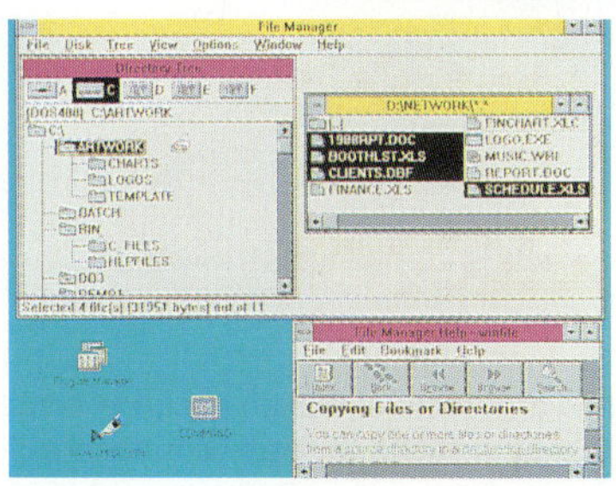

7

5–7. Multiple onscreen windows are generally (left to right) cascaded, tiled, or overlapped.

Major GUIs

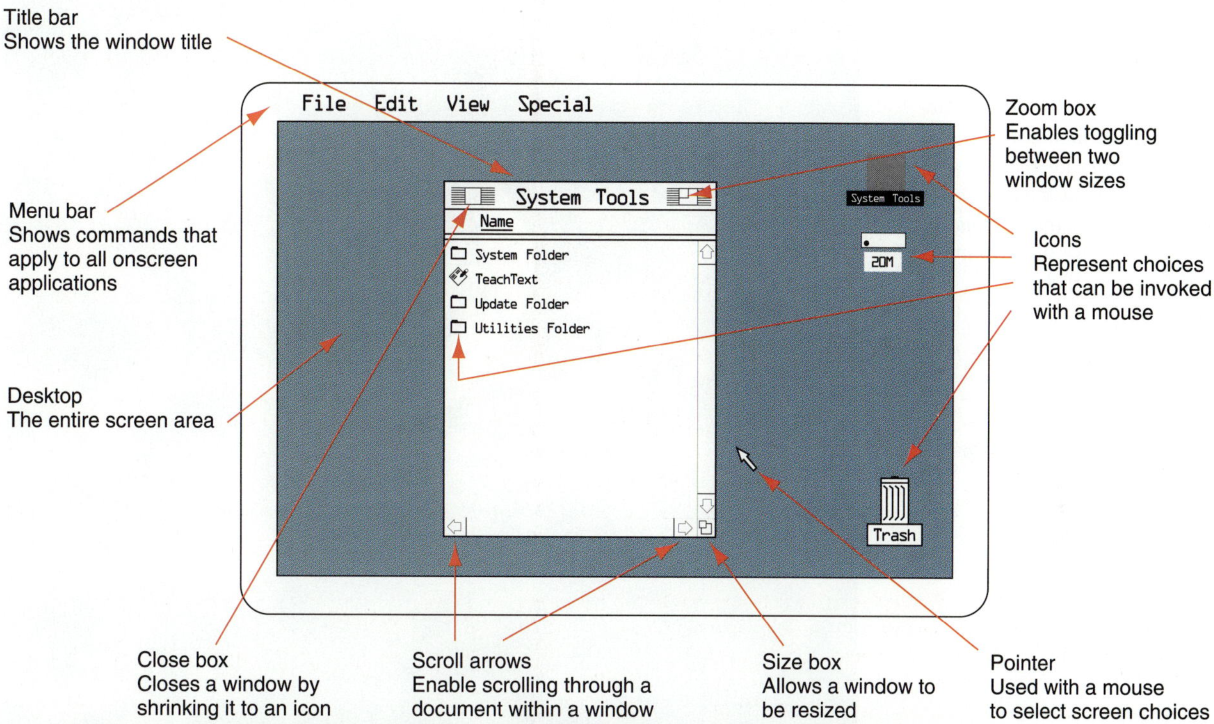

8. The Macintosh interface. As the first widely used GUI, the Macintosh interface automatically became the de facto standard for interfaces that followed it.

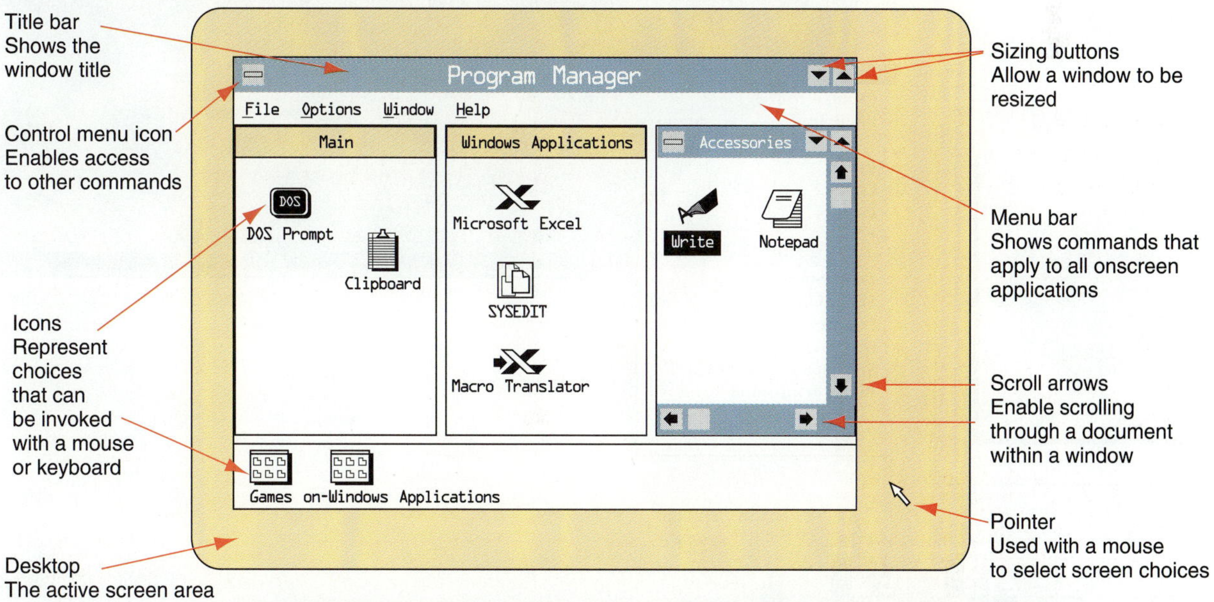

9. The Microsoft Windows interface. Although the names and appearance of many of the Windows features differ from those of the Macintosh, the types of tasks that you can perform with the Macintosh and Windows interfaces are almost identical.

Today software enables those who know how to use the computer to create an extremely wide variety of attractive-looking outputs. Tomorrow users will be able to order customized personalities for their computers, such as cartoonlike characters that help them use their computers if they get stuck.

Module D

Productivity Software

Over the last decade or so, computers have completely transformed the workplace. Look at the desktops of many managers, analysts, designers, engineers, secretaries, and even corporate presidents today and you will usually see a computer system. Managers and analysts regularly use computers to crunch numbers, send and receive electronic-mail messages, and prepare presentation materials for meetings. Designers and engineers typically employ computers to create products. Secretaries use computers on a daily basis to prepare correspondence and reports. And corporate presidents often rely on computers to access important facts about their organizations.

At the heart of this workplace transformation is productivity software. Productivity software refers to applications-software packages that enable end users to better perform their jobs. These packages help users save time, reduce costs, and perform types of work that couldn't possibly be done without the aid of a computer system.

Module D opens, in Chapter 8, with a look at word processors and desktop publishing systems, both of which assist in the development of documents. In Chapter 9 we cover spreadsheets and presentation graphics. Spreadsheets aid in the analysis of numbers, while presentation graphics packages help prepare graphs and charts showing numbers in a pictorial format. The module closes, in Chapter 10, with a discussion of file managers and database management systems. Both of these packages specialize in providing rapid access to electronically stored facts.

Have you ever wanted to create and publish your own magazine or book? As you will learn in this chapter, word processing and desktop publishing systems enable you to do just that—at a cost you can probably afford.

8 Word Processing and Desktop Publishing

Outline

Learning Objectives

After completing this chapter, you will be able to:

1. Describe what word processing is and name several ways in which it may be implemented on computer systems.
2. Identify the operations you must master to effectively use word processing software.
3. Explain the features common to many word processing packages.
4. Identify the software and hardware components found in many desktop publishing systems.

Overview

Word processing and desktop publishing are technologies that deal with the manipulation of words. *Word processing* enables a computer system to serve as a powerful typewriting tool. When using the computer in this way, one can quickly create, edit, and print documents and manage them as no ordinary typewriter can. *Desktop publishing,* available only since high-powered microcomputers entered the marketplace, carries word processing a step further. With desktop publishing hardware and software, one can create documents that look as though they were prepared by a professional print shop.

In this chapter, we'll first discuss word processors. Here we'll explore in detail some of the types of word processors currently available and many of the features that differentiate one word processor from another. We'll also look at some of the add-on packages that are available to make the word processing environment even more powerful. Then we'll turn to desktop publishing and the hardware and software found on desktop publishing systems.

A complaint often made about word processors and desktop publishing systems is that, like copying machines, they often contribute to the so-called "paper explosion" in organizations. One company's attempt in dealing with this problem is covered in User Solution 8-1.

Word Processing

Word processing. The use of computer technology to create, manipulate, and print text material such as letters, legal contracts, and manuscripts.

When you use your computer to do the kinds of work you normally do on a typewriter, you're doing word processing. **Word processing** is the use of computer technology to create, manipulate, and print text materials such as letters, legal contracts, manuscripts, and other documents. Word processing is such a timesaver, in fact, that most people who learn to do it let their typewriters gather dust. As you will discover in this chapter, the two primary features that differentiate word processing from ordinary typewriting are computer-assisted *text editing* and *print formatting* (see Figure 8-1). But before we examine how these tasks are carried out, let's look at some of the types of word processors currently available in the marketplace.

Types of Word Processors

There are several ways you can perform word processing. Four such alternatives are discussed in the following paragraphs.

Dedicated versus General-Purpose Computer Systems. One way to do word processing is to use a computer system specially dedicated to this purpose—that is, a *dedicated word processing system.* Generally these systems are microcomputers that are rigged with special keyboards and

User Solution 8-1

A Paperless Office Solution to Paperwork Reduction

Organizations usually create documents by word processing and printing them. At Westinghouse Security Systems, where traditional methods were resulting in an avalanche of internal paperwork, a paperless solution is being tried. Every worker in this 300-employee company has a desktop computer equipped with electronic "pens and paper." When a memo must be prepared, an employee picks up an electronic stylus and writes on a digitizing pad. The handwritten note appears on the display screen, and it can be routed to someone else's electronic mailbox or "stapled" to other electronic documents. Even the company mail is scanned into the system, so desks are as paper-free as possible.

monitors and packaged with special software to make word processing as painless as possible. For people who need a computer system exclusively for high-volume word processing, a dedicated system may be the best way to go. Unfortunately, the special-purpose nature of these systems makes them inefficient for and sometimes incapable of doing things other than word processing.

Since most people today need a single system for a wide variety of purposes—say, word processing, spreadsheets, and data management—they will acquire instead a *general-purpose computer system*. These systems are configured to do a variety of tasks. The familiar IBM PC, IBM PC AT, IBM PS/2, Apple Macintosh, and Apple II lines are examples of general-purpose computer systems. Word processing software packages are widely available for virtually all sizes of general-purpose computers. Among today's best-selling word processing packages are WordPerfect, Microsoft Word, and WordStar. WordPerfect is the undisputed leader in today's word processing marketplace, with close to a 30 percent market share (see Feature 8-1, "The WordPerfect Story").

WYSIWYG versus Embedded Formatting Codes. The vast majority of word processors in use today display on the screen an image that shows exactly, or almost exactly, how a document will appear before it's printed. Each screen line corresponds to a printed-page line, so you are rarely surprised at how the document looks when it's subsequently printed.

Ideally, the image on the screen and the image on the printed page correspond exactly. This feature is referred to as **WYSIWYG,** for What You See Is What You Get (see Figure 8-2a). WYSIWYG most often occurs in desktop publishing, where the design of a page can be critical. There,

WYSIWYG.
An acronym for "What You See Is What You Get," WYSIWYG refers to showing on the display screen an output image identical or very close to the final hard-copy image.

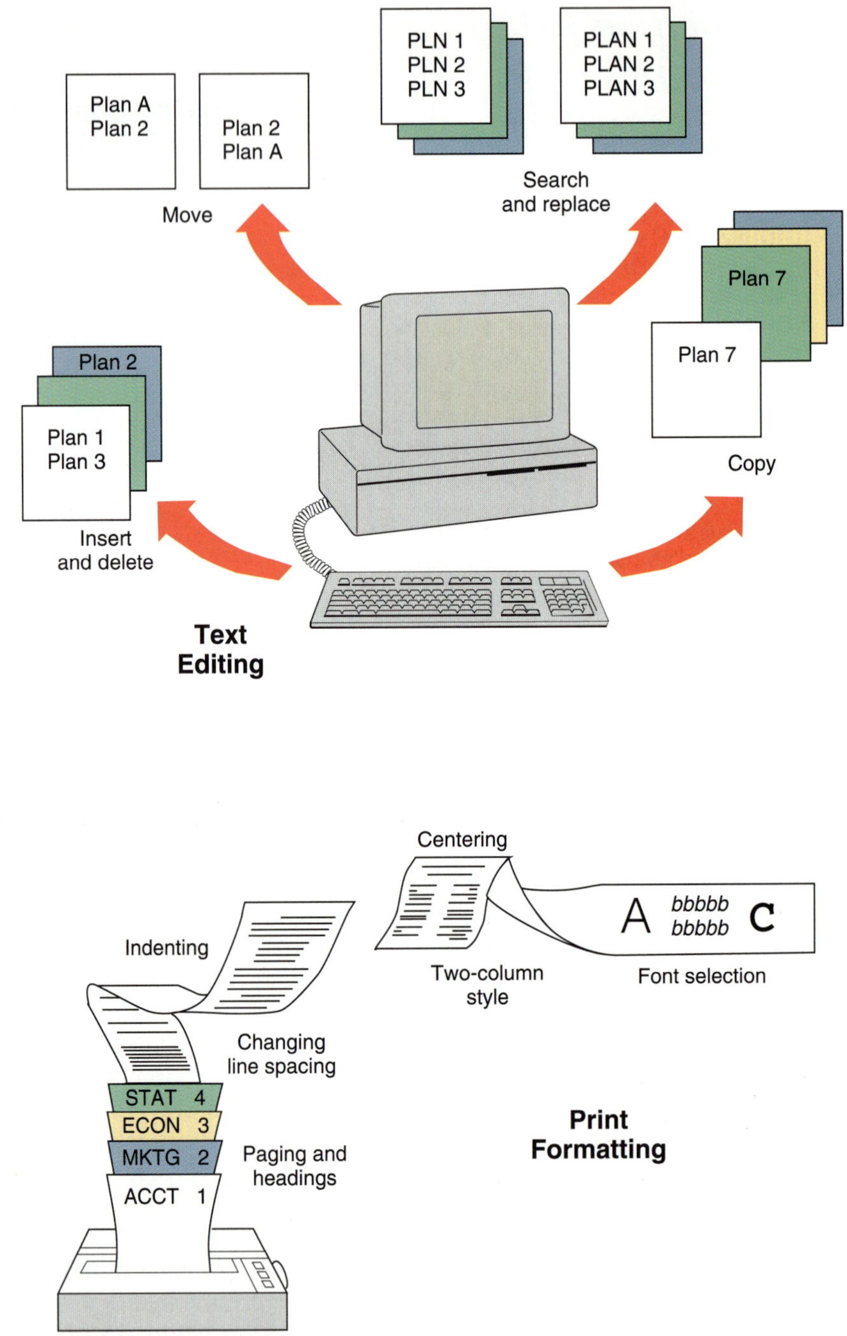

Figure 8-1
Text editing and print formatting.
Text-editing operations allow you to "cut and paste" text materials in electronic memory. Print-formatting operations let you output those materials in a visually appealing way.

users frequently employ high-resolution graphics monitors capable of simultaneously displaying a variety of type styles, sometimes scaled to different sizes. Users can experiment onscreen with several different page styles and inspect every document page in fine detail before committing anything to print.

Feature 9-1

The WordPerfect Story

Two Music Men Hit a High Note

Question: What happens when the leader of a college marching band takes a computer course from a trumpet-playing college professor? Answer: A partnership that gives birth to one of the world's largest software companies, a firm that has become the undisputed leader in the word processing marketplace.

WordPerfect began when a Brigham Young University student named Brian Bastian, who was also the $5,000-per-year leader of the school's marching band, took a course called "Computers and Music" taught by Professor Alan Ashton. Bastian wanted to produce a graphics program that showed how the band's marching formations would appear to spectators at field level, in the stands, or on TV (as from a camera in an overhead blimp). The student and the professor hit it off, and Ashton later persuaded Bastian to pursue a master's degree in computer science.

After Bastian graduated, he was hired to develop a word processing program for an Orem, Utah, research firm. Bastian and Ashton struck a deal with the firm; Bastian would work extra hours and Ashton would work free in his spare time if they could have the rights to the completed program. The program, originally called SSI*WP—for Satellite Software International (the name of their company) Word Processor—was first installed on a Data General minicomputer in Orem's city offices in 1979. As the 1980s began, Satellite Software International consisted of Bastian, Ashton, a programmer and bookkeeper, and someone to market the software.

Birthplace of WordPerfect. Brigham Young University Campus.

When the IBM PC made its debut in the early 1980s, Bastian and Ashton put all of their efforts into configuring their product to this machine. They changed the name of SSI*WP to WordPerfect (later renaming the company the same way). Success was rapid and phenomenal. Almost every year since the company was founded, revenues have been double or nearly double those of the previous year. WordPerfect quickly became the leading word processing program in the world. Annual sales are now over $100 million, and the company has more than 600 employees.

Today, most word processors and monitors in use fall far short of the WYSIWYG ideal. In fact, boldface, italic, and underlined characters often do not display conveniently onscreen even though they will be output as such on the printed document. To apprise users of such print-formatting effects, many word processors use *embedded formatting codes*. Typically, the user places these codes before and after a word or phrase that is to be output in a special way (see Figure 8-2b). The code placed before the word or phrase alerts the printer to turn on a formatting feature; the code following the word or phrase alerts it to turn off the feature. Some word processors display these codes onscreen at all times, whereas others reveal them only on demand.

General-Purpose versus Special-Purpose Word Processing Packages. Most word processing software products in use today are *general-purpose*

Figure 8-2 WYSIWYG versus embedded formatting codes.
With WYSIWYG, what you see on the screen is exactly what you get in print. Most users of word processors today must, however, rely on some type of embedded formatting codes to tell them if text is to be given special treatment.

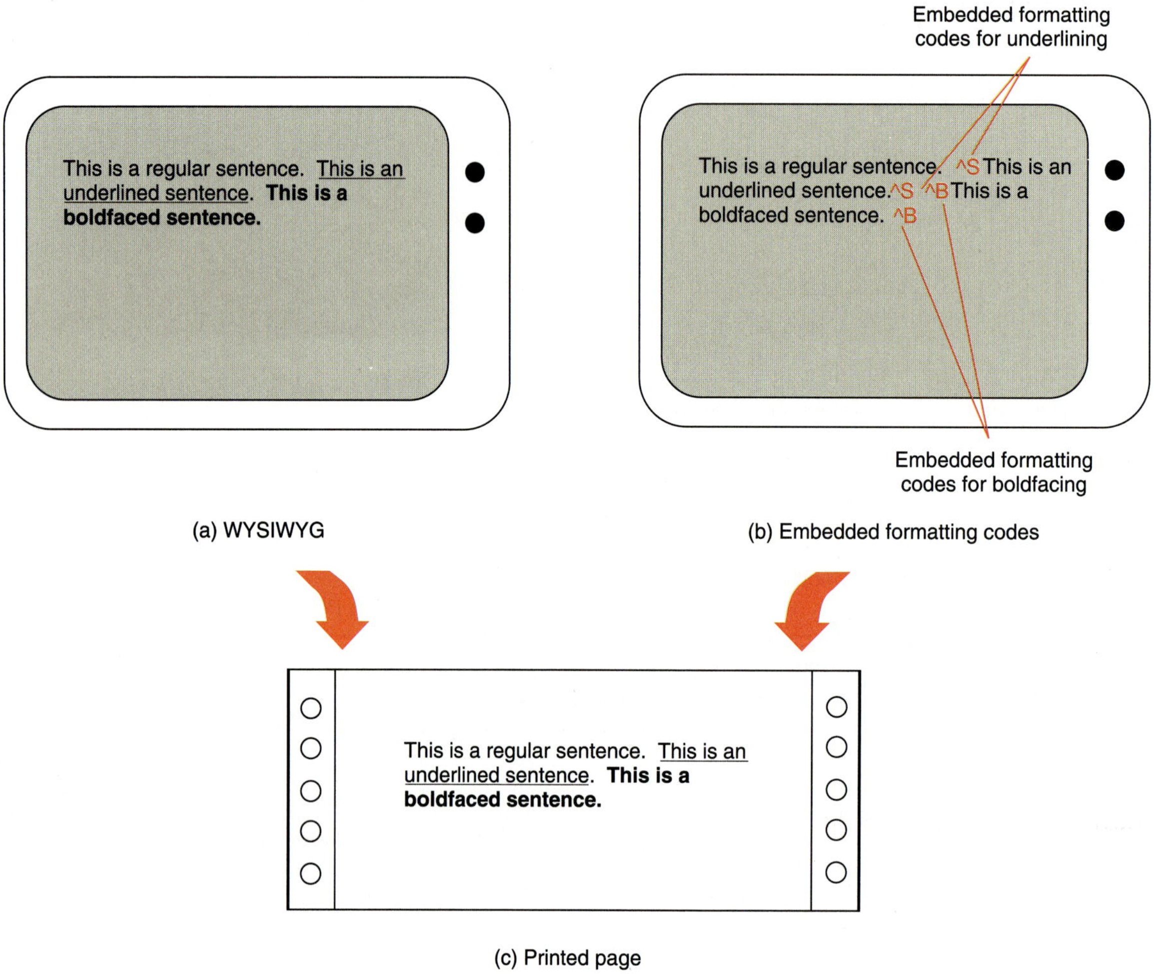

word processing packages; that is, they are designed to suit the needs of a variety of users, such as secretaries, authors, and average microcomputer users. However, a number of *specialized word processors* are commercially available to meet the unique demands of users in certain niche areas. For example, some word processors are designed to meet the unique needs of movie scriptwriters or musicians.

Dedicated Word Processing Packages versus Integrated Software Packages. Most people who do word processing use a *dedicated word processing package*—that is, a package targeted exclusively to meeting various word processing needs. The packages most familiar to the general public—WordPerfect, Word, and WordStar, for instance—fall into this category. However, some software products combine the ability to process words with the ability to perform other, dissimilar functions, such as spreadsheeting and database management. This latter category of products—which includes Symphony, Works, First Choice, and Framework—is most commonly referred to as *integrated software packages.* We'll discuss integrated software packages more fully in Chapter 9 (see Feature 9-1).

The remainder of this section will address dedicated, general-purpose word processing packages targeted to general-purpose computers. These are the types of word processors most commonly encountered in practice.

Learning to Use a Word Processor: The Basics

Even though many word processing packages have hundreds of features, usually only a handful of them account for 90 percent or more of what you will do during the course of word processing a typical document. This basic set of word processing operations may be classified as general operations, entering and editing operations, and print-formatting operations. The two primary features that differentiate word processing from ordinary typewriting are computer-assisted text editing and print formatting. In the future, many word processors will contain other text-entry features that distance them even further from the typewriting world (see the Tomorrow box, "Easy Input").

General Operations. To use virtually any type of productivity software package—word processor, spreadsheet, or whatever—you need to know how to carry out a number of general operations. These operations, listed in Figure 8-3, are functionally equivalent to activities like starting and stopping a car.

Entering and Editing Operations. Every word processor contains an assortment of entering and editing operations for keying in text and manipulating text on the screen. Among the most common of these operations are moving the cursor, scrolling, making a line return, inserting and deleting, moving and copying, and searching and replacing.

- ***Moving the Cursor.*** Many word processors offer well over a dozen ways to move the cursor around the screen. Usually you can move the cursor a character, a word, a line, or a screen at a time, as well as to the beginning or the end of a document. You can usually move the cursor either by typing in a short command or by depressing one of several function keys or cursor-movement keys. Many word processing users acquire a mouse to obtain additional cursor-movement capabilities.
- ***Scrolling.*** Scrolling lets you move contiguous lines of text up and down on the screen similarly to the way the roll on a player piano unwinds. When scrolling down, for example, as lines successively disappear from the top of the screen, new ones appear from the bottom. With many word processing packages, you can use the up-arrow and down-arrow keys to scroll a document line by line. By using

Tomorrow

Easy Input

The Potential for Voice and OCR Technologies in Word Processing

One of the most time-consuming word processing tasks is inputting documents. Generally, this task is carried out on a keyboard, and often it is done by a person who's not a skilled typist. While keyboards will probably be used extensively for document input for some time to come, both voice input and optical character recognition technology hold great promise for getting many of tomorrow's documents quickly into electronic form.

Voice input. Someday it will make many types of keyboard data entry superfluous.

Voice Input. Today, most voice-input systems recognize about 1,000 words. For voice input to be viable as an input medium for word processing, recognition of somewhere in the neighborhood of 12,000 words is necessary. Some people think that many of the upcoming breakthroughs in voice input will take place in Japan, because the Japanese will be among those who benefit most. Japan has a keyboarding problem; the Japanese use at least 2,000 characters in everyday reading and writing, and Japanese scholars may manipulate over 8,000 different characters in their work.

Voice-input systems merely copy sound; they do not try to understand what it is you are saying. Most systems record an electrical voice signal in analog form, filter it to remove background noises, and digitize the filtered output. Then software separates words and performs mathematical measurements on each one. These measurements form a "voiceprint." The voiceprint of each inputted word is compared with those stored in memory to form a match. Many PC-based voice-input systems must initially be trained by your voice to develop this working vocabulary of voiceprints.

OCR. OCR (optical character recognition) technology—machine recognition of characters by optical means—has been in use for some time but is still underutilized in the field of word processing. This is largely due to two things. First, a single scanned-in document often conforms to a variety of different fonts, some of which OCR readers may have trouble recognizing. Second, recognition-error rates on PC-based systems are still high enough that, in many cases, it is easier to type a document in from scratch. OCR systems for PCs are capable of recognizing up to about 2,500 characters per minute.

OCR systems for PCs can be classified into two basic types: nontrainable and trainable. *Nontrainable systems* have built-in font templates for the specific printers, typefaces, and point sizes that they support. If you want your system to read 12-point Helvetica type coming from a Toshiba P351, and the package you are using does not support that particular combination, you are out of luck. *Trainable systems,* by contrast, can be used to "teach" the OCR device a particular typeface. However, trainable systems are slower than nontrainable ones.

To recognize characters, OCR systems use one of two basic techniques. In *pattern matching,* each character to be recognized is compared to character templates in memory. When a match is found, the character is "recognized." In *feature extraction,* a table of several thousand individual shapes—lines, serifs, curves, and so on—is used to deduce the identity of the character being scanned in. For instance, the lowercase character *i* would be recognized by feature extraction techniques through its two distinctive features: a dot and a short vertical line. Some OCR systems use a combination of both pattern matching and feature extraction to recognize characters.

- ☐ **Accessing** your package from the operating system
- ☐ Informing the package that you either want to **create** a new file or **retrieve** an old one from disk
- ☐ Commanding the package to **save** a file onto disk
- ☐ Commanding the package to **print** a file
- ☐ Commanding the package to **delete** a file that's on disk
- ☐ Indicating to the package that you want to **quit** working on your current file and do something on another file
- ☐ **Terminating** your work on the package and getting back to the operating system

Figure 8-3
General operations needed for operating any productivity software package.
Depending on the package you use, the file that you work on may contain a word-processed document, a worksheet, a graph, a collection of database records, or something else.

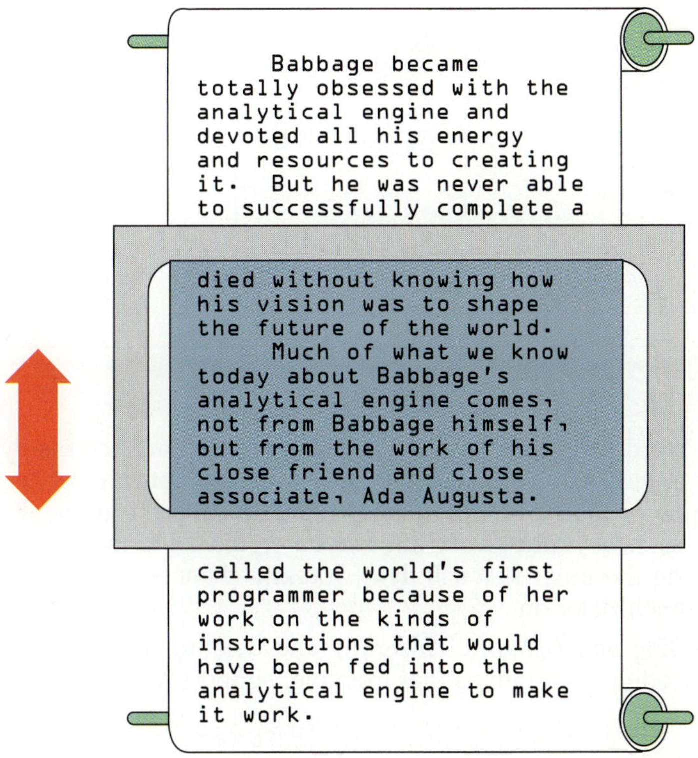

Figure 8-4
Scrolling.
With many word processors, depressing the PgUp or PgDn key enables you to scroll the document up or down to view contiguous, screen-size pages on the display. By starting at the beginning of the document and successively depressing the PgDn key, you can scroll through the entire document to proofread it. You can use the PgUp key to refer to preceding screen pages.

the PgUp and PgDn keys, you can scroll even faster—page by page instead of line by line (see Figure 8-4).

☐ ***Making a Line Return.*** On a conventional typewriter, you generally must hit the Return key every time you finish typing in a line. Not so on a word processor. Word processors provide an automatic line return when the cursor reaches a certain column position at the right-hand side of the screen. This return is called a **soft return,** and the built-in facility that provides soft returns is called a **wordwrap** feature (see Figure 8-5).

Soft return.
An automatic line return carried out by word-processing software.

Wordwrap.
The word processing feature that automatically produces soft carriage returns.

Figure 8-5 Wordwrap.
Wordwrapping produces a soft carriage return when the cursor reaches a certain position at the right-hand side of the screen.

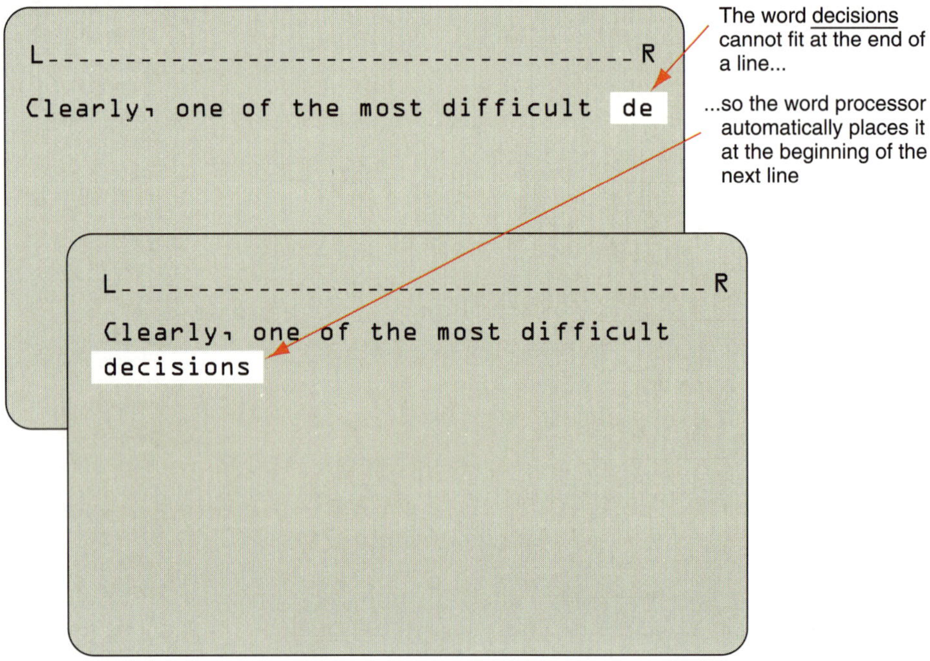

Hard return.
The use of the Enter key to provide line spacing in a document.

Word processors also allow you to key in **hard returns** by hitting the Enter key. Normally, you will use hard returns between paragraphs or blocks of text or after typing in titles. You should not hit the Enter key after every line as you would on a normal typewriter. Hitting the Enter key will deny you any chances of reformatting the document later on.

- ***Inserting and Deleting.*** Inserting and deleting are two of the most basic editing operations. For example, suppose you typed in

```
THE HAVE WON THE CHAMPIONSHIP
```

and forgot to type in the name of the winning team. If the Hoboken Zephyrs won the championship, you'd have to insert the phrase HOBOKEN ZEPHYRS between THE and HAVE. Virtually all word processors have an *insert mode* that lets you insert characters at the cursor position on the screen. Often, you enter the insert mode by depressing the Insert key on the keyboard. When you are not in the insert mode, you are automatically in the *typeover mode,* in which case every character you type into an already existing line replaces the character at the cursor position. On most systems, the Insert key is a *toggle key*—depressing it once activates the insert mode, and depressing it again deactivates the insert mode.

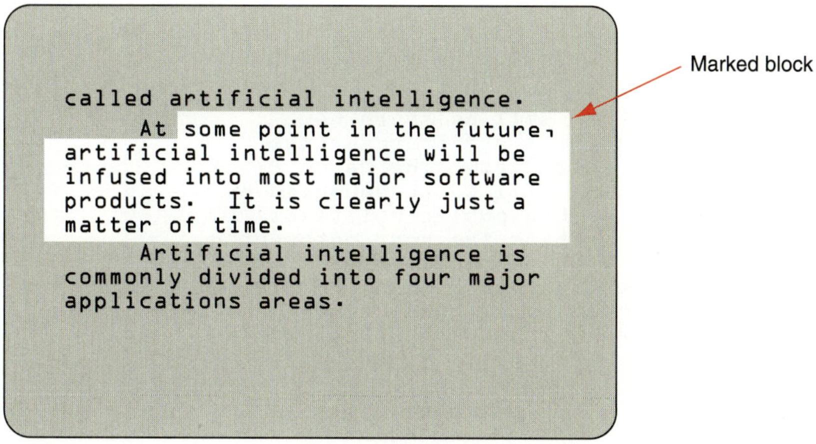

Figure 8-6
Marking a block of text.
A block is usually marked by highlighting it onscreen (as shown here) or by marking its beginning and end with special characters. Once a block has been marked, it can be moved, copied, formatted, or deleted.

Imagine that you later decided you wanted to delete the word HOBOKEN. Your word processor will generally allow you to delete a character, word, line, or block of characters at a time. Deleting a character at a time is normally done through either the Delete or Backspace key. Deleting a word or line at a time is generally done by positioning the cursor on the word or line to be deleted and depressing one or two keys. When you want to delete a block of characters, you normally must first identify the beginning and end of the block, an operation called *block marking,* and then invoke a delete command. Block marking, illustrated in Figure 8-6, is also necessary when you want to move, copy, boldface, or underline text.

- ***Moving and Copying.*** Moving and copying are operations that allow you to "cut and paste" text with a word processor. *Moving* means identifying a specific block of text and physically relocating it in a new place in the document. *Copying* is similar to moving except that a copy of the block remains in the original place as well.
- ***Searching and Replacing.*** Searching and replacing are extremely useful features. They enable you to search automatically for all occurrences of a particular word or phrase and change them to something else. For example, let's say you've typed out a long document that should repeatedly refer to a person named "Snider." If you've misspelled this name as "Schneider," you can instruct the word processor to look up all occurrences of "Schneider" and change them to "Snider."

  Some people take dangerous shortcuts in searching and replacing. For example, suppose you ask the word processor to change all occurrences of "chne" to "n." This will change all "Schneider" occurrences to "Snider," but it will also change a name such as "Schneymann" to "Snymann," which you probably did not intend to do.

  Figure 8-7 shows a document before and after a searching and replacing operation.

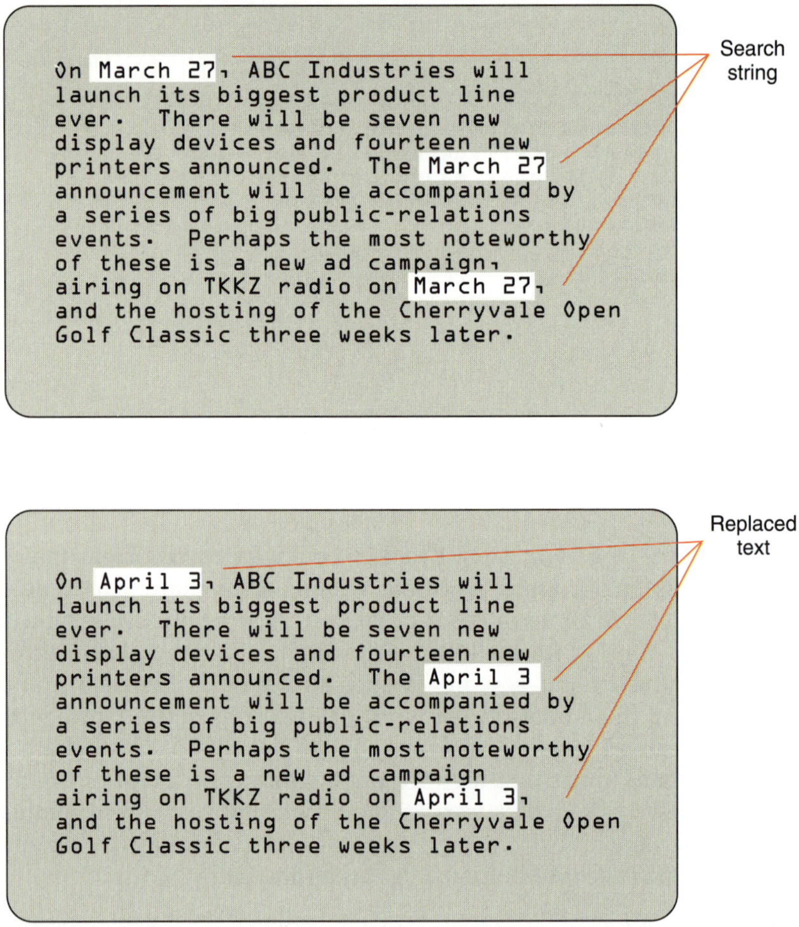

Figure 8-7
Searching and replacing. In the figure, the operator wishes to search for all occurrences of the date March 27 and replace them with the date April 3. Such an operation is called a global search-and-replace. Many word processors will also stop at each occurrence of the search string, if desired, and provide the operator the option of changing each one individually.

Print-Formatting Operations. Print-formatting operations tell the printer how to output the text onto paper. These operations include adjusting line spacing, indenting, justifying, establishing a page format, reformatting, centering, tabbing, paginating, setting up headers and footers, selecting typefaces, putting text into multiple columns, and footnoting.

- *Adjusting Line Spacing.* Adjusting line spacing is an important word processing operation. Suppose that you've single-spaced a paper, but your English 101 instructor wants all the essays you hand in to be double-spaced. Virtually all word processors will enable you to adjust the line spacing to a double space in a few seconds or minutes. Many packages will also permit triple-spacing, fractional blank lines between text lines, and several other line-spacing options.
- *Indenting.* Indenting, or adjusting margins, is useful when you are typing a paper with many quotations and want to set off these passages from the main text. Many word processors allow you to choose among several types of indenting styles. One of the most widely used

of these is the *hanging indent,* which is used to indent text in numbered and bulleted lists (such as the lists in the end-of-chapter Critical Thinking Questions in this book).

- ***Justifying.*** Virtually all word processing packages enable a printed document to be formatted with either a *ragged-right* or a *justified-right* margin. The text that you are reading at this instant has a straight, or justified-right, right margin. The text inside the screens of Figure 8-7, in contrast, has a ragged-right margin. Users who create business documents often would rather format with a ragged-right margin, as the extra blank spaces between words that often come with justified-right margins can make the document too difficult to read. Justified-right margins can look quite attractive, however, if the word processor and printer in use can handle proportional spacing (to be discussed shortly).
- ***Establishing a Page Format.*** Most word processors let you choose the way in which you would like your pages to be formatted. For instance, you can tell the word processor how many lines to print per page; the maximum number of characters to fit on each line; and the settings of the left, right, top, and bottom margins. A number of word processing packages will also automatically number lines for you—a useful feature if you are preparing legal documents or printer galleys. Having a number attached to each line makes it easy to identify text quickly and with less chance of error.
- ***Reformatting.*** Reformatting normally is necessary when you insert text, delete text, change line spacing, readjust margins in your document, change justification, or change the basic page format. Reformatting places the document in a form suitable for output, for instance, by ensuring that the document is properly fitted within the margins after an insertion or deletion is made. After making the format change, you may need to issue one or more commands to reformat the sections of the document affected. Some packages reformat automatically after each edit.
- ***Centering.*** Centering text is important for most users of word processors. Word processing packages usually require you to have the cursor on the line containing the text to be centered when invoking the centering command.
- ***Tabbing.*** Tabbing is a formatting feature that typists have relied on for years. Like typewriters, most word processors enable you to set your own tab stops. The tab-stop positions on the screen can normally be reached through the Tab key.
- ***Paginating.*** A pagination feature lets you choose whether to number pages in a document. For example, you may want page numbers placed on class reports but not on short letters. Many word processing packages will place page numbers wherever you specify.
- ***Setting Up Headers and Footers.*** *Headers* are titles automatically printed at the top of every page; *footers* are titles automatically printed at the bottom. Some word processors give you a great deal of flexibil-

Figure 8-8 Typefaces.
A typeface is a collection of visually consistent characters. Shown here are the (a) Courier, (b) Helvetica, and (c) Times typefaces.

(a) Courier (b) Helvetica (c) Times

ity with respect to headers and footers. For instance, you can print both headers and footers on the same page and even alternate the title placed in a header or a footer. This textbook, like many other books, alternates headers; module letter and title are on the left-facing pages and chapter number and title are on the right-facing pages. Many word processors also allow page numbers to appear in a header or footer and give you several choices about where to place them.

Typeface.
A collection of characters that share a common design.

Point size.
A measurement used in the scaling of typefaces.

Font.
A typeface in a particular point size—for instance, 12-point Helvetica.

☐ *Selecting Typefaces.* A **typeface** is a collection of characters that share a common design. Typeface selection features enable you to output characters in a variety of typefaces and typeface sizes (called **point sizes**). A typeface in a particular point size is referred to as a **font;** for instance, 12-point Courier is a font. Figures 8-8 and 8-9 illustrate typefaces, point sizes, and fonts.

Many word processors will also let you create boldface, italic, underlined, subscript, or superscript characters. Both the word processor and the printer on your system must support a particular styling feature for you to be able to use it.

Figure 8-9
Point size.
A typeface in a particular point size is commonly called a font.

This is 10-point Helvetica

This is 12-point Helvetica

This is 18-point Helvetica

This is 24-point Helvetica

- *Putting Text into Multiple Columns.* Multiple-column formatting lets you print text in a columnar format similar to that used in newspapers and magazines. If you are doing multiple-column formatting, it is especially useful to have a feature that eliminates orphans and widows (discussed later in the chapter).
- *Footnoting.* A footnoting feature allows you to create, edit, and delete footnotes in a document. Typically, the routine that manages the footnoting is designed to remember footnote references and automatically renumber footnotes if you insert or delete any.

Learning to Use a Word Processor: Advanced Operations

In addition to the basic operations we've just covered, the more sophisticated word processors enable you to do a number of other useful tasks. Some of these may be especially valuable if you are a professional typist or an author or if your business requires a lot of correspondence. Among such tasks are using proportional spacing, spelling checkers and thesauruses, mailing list and mail merge operations, and a math feature; setting up macros; redlining; preparing an index and table of contents; eliminating orphans and widows; sorting; embedding codes for typesetters; embedding presentation graphics into word processed text; and using style sheets.

Proportional Spacing. On many printers, text is **monospaced;** that is, each character takes up the same amount of horizontal space. This textbook, however, like most others, was typeset on a system that proportionally spaces characters. **Proportional spacing** is a feature that allocates more horizontal space on a line to some characters than to others. For example, a capital *M* takes up more space than a lowercase *i.* A microspacing feature may also be available. With **microspacing,** fractions of a full blank space are inserted within each line in places where they aren't likely to be noticed so that the left- and right-hand margins are flush. Proportional spacing and microspacing are shown in Figure 8-10.

Both your word processor and your printer must support proportional spacing and microspacing for your documents to achieve a typeset look.

Monospacing.
A printing feature that allocates the same amount of space on a line to each character.

Proportional spacing.
A printing feature that allocates more horizontal space on a line to some characters than to others.

Microspacing.
A technique used by some printers and software packages to insert fractional spaces between characters to give text a typeset look.

Spelling Checker. Most leading word processing packages today include a routine that reads through a document and searches for misspelled words. This routine and its accompanying dictionary are collectively known as a **spelling checker.**

The capabilities of spelling checkers can vary dramatically. Some spelling checkers have dictionaries that contain around 10,000 words, whereas others have 100,000 or more. A particularly important feature is the ability to place additional words into a dictionary. A writer of a computer text or medical article, for example, uses very specialized terms, most of which aren't in the dictionaries of standard spelling checkers.

Spelling checker.
A program or routine that is often used with a word processor to check for misspelled words.

Figure 8-10 Proportionally spaced characters with microspacing.
With proportional spacing, more horizontal space on a line is allotted to some characters than to others. Note, for instance, that a capital *H* takes up more space than the lowercase *t* and *i* combined. Microspacing inserts fractional spaces between characters to make a line appear more attractive to the eye.

How tight is tight?
How tight is tight?
How tight is tight?
How tight is tight?

Figure 8-11 Using a spelling checker.
Many spelling checkers stop to highlight words that they don't recognize when scanning a completed text document. Here the checker can't find "glossery" in its dictionary and, below the dotted line, offers the operator some replacement suggestions. Many spelling checkers automatically make a replacement when the operator depresses the assigned key—the *A* key, in this example.

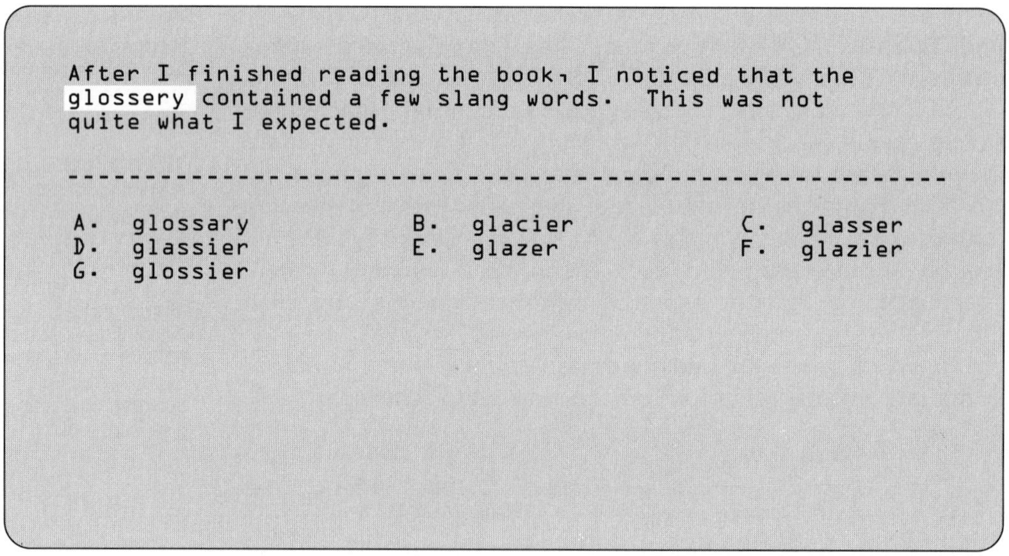

Many spelling checkers allow you to check for misspelled words either after you've finished typing or while you're typing a document. The latter feature, which is usually practical only if you have a hard disk, assists you as you type by beeping whenever you key in a word that it doesn't recognize. Spelling checkers usually also come with a feature that

Figure 8-12 Using a thesaurus.
In many word processors, the user points to a word to be "looked up" by positioning the cursor on it and then invokes the thesaurus feature. Here the operator has pointed to *want*, and the replacement suggestions in the middle of the screen have appeared. Many thesaurus routines automatically make a replacement when the key that corresponds to it is depressed.

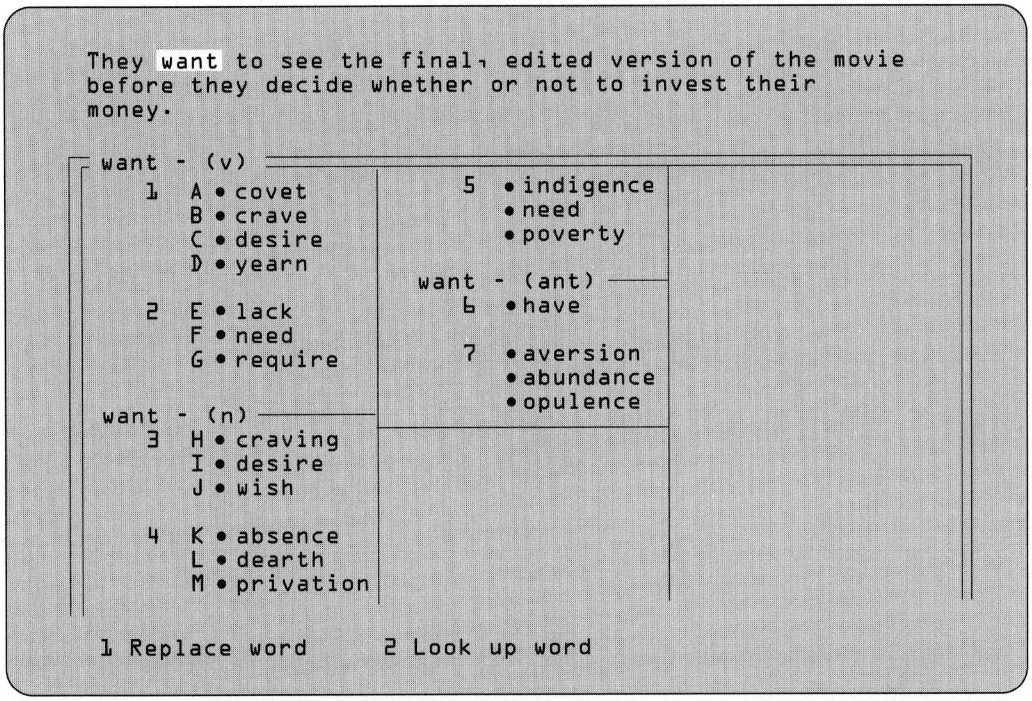

displays onscreen suggestions for how to properly spell a word they don't recognize (see Figure 8-11) and a feature that counts words.

Thesaurus Feature. A **thesaurus feature** allows you to check words for possible synonyms. To use a thesaurus, you first flag a word you wish to replace in your document. If the thesaurus feature recognizes the word, it will provide onscreen replacement suggestions in a form resembling that of a hard-copy thesaurus (see Figure 8-12). Often, when you see a word you like, you need only type in the key corresponding to it to perform the replacement. Many thesaurus routines automatically reformat text after replacing a word. In addition, several allow you to do word searches within other word searches, and many provide antonyms as well as synonyms. The thesauruses packaged with the leading word processors typically contain anywhere from 10,000 to 20,000 words. Some commercial-level electronic thesauruses used by newspapers and magazines have over a million words.

Thesaurus feature.
A word processing program or routine that enables electronic lookup of word synonyms.

Mailing List/Mail Merge Programs. A **mailing list program** is used to generate mailing labels. With such a feature, you can usually sort records

Mailing list program.
A program that is used to generate mailing labels.

by specific fields (such as zip code) or extract records having special characteristics (such as all alumni from the class of 1975 living in San Francisco) prior to processing the labels. Mailing list programs are specialized versions of file managers, which we will discuss in Chapter 10.

Mail merge program. A program that is specifically designed to produce form letters.

A **mail merge program** is specifically designed to produce form letters. This type of feature is so named because it usually prints such letters in volume by merging a file containing a list of names and addresses with a file containing the form letter.

Math Feature. A *math feature* allows you to perform modest amounts of computation during the course of word processing. Such a feature is useful for preparing expense reports, simple budgets, and other types of business documents that require little more than summing columns or rows of numbers. If you need to do more sophisticated forms of math, you might do well to acquire instead an integrated software package (with a spreadsheeting capability).

Macro. A predetermined series of keystrokes or commands that can be invoked by a single keystroke or command.

Macros. Many word processors allow users to create macros. A **macro** is a sequence of keystrokes that is saved in a special file so that you can use it whenever you wish. In the world of word processing, a macro can be either (1) a set of entering, editing, or print-formatting operations or (2) a prestored block of text. In other words, the macro can be either a program or data.

For instance, say you are going to be typing several letters containing your home address and a canned, "we-wish-you-were-here" paragraph. You would first invoke a "define macro" command in your word processor. Then you would type the address, saving it in a macro file. Next you would type the canned paragraph and save it in a different macro file. During the course of preparing your letters, you would invoke either of the macros at the point where you wanted the associated text placed in your document. This is normally done by pressing one or two keys followed by the name of the macro.

Redlining. A word processing facility that provides the electronic equivalent of the editor's red pen.

Redlining. When editing the hard-copy documents of others, many people use a red pen to cross out certain words or phrases and substitute others. This process is called **redlining.** After a document is redlined, the original author can see both what he or she originally wrote and the changes made by the editor. The redlining feature found in many word processors provides the electronic equivalent of the manual redlining process.

Index and Table of Contents Preparation. Many top-of-the-line word processors allow you to individually "tag" words or phrases so that you can later prepare an index or a table of contents. For instance, if you have tagged a few hundred words in a book for an index, you can later invoke an *indexing routine* that will arrange these words in alphabetical order and provide the page numbers on which the words appear. Most indexing routines also allow you to create index subheadings similar to the ones that appear in the index of this book.

Figure 8-13 Orphans and widows.
Orphans and widows are aesthetically undesirable line breaks that many word processors can eliminate.

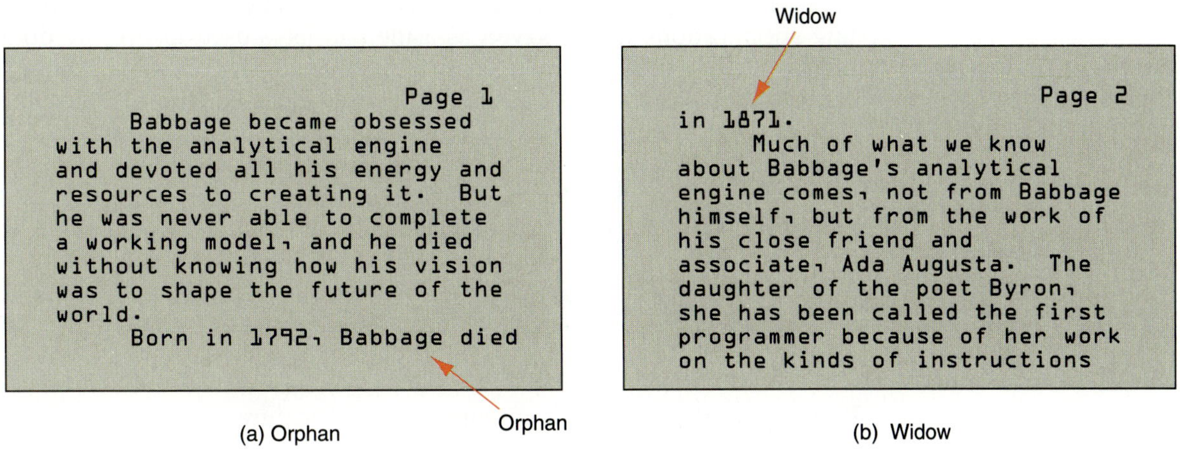

(a) Orphan (b) Widow

Orphan and Widow Elimination. Orphans and widows are aesthetically undesirable line breaks (see Figure 8-13). In document processing, the first line of a paragraph is called an **orphan** when it is separated from the rest of the paragraph by a page or column break. The last line of a paragraph is called a **widow** when it is separated from the rest of the paragraph by a page or column break. Many word processing packages allow you to eliminate widows and orphans by establishing a minimum number of lines that can be separated by a page or column break.

Orphan.
The first line of a paragraph when it is separated from the rest of the paragraph by a page or column break.

Widow.
The last line of a paragraph when it is separated from the rest of the paragraph by a page or column break.

Sorting. A useful word processing feature is *sorting*—for example, arranging a list of names in alphabetical order or arranging addresses by zip code for mailing purposes. As handy as this feature may be, however, it is either unavailable, somewhat limited, or relatively cumbersome to use in many word processors.

Embedded Typesetting Codes. Sometimes word-processed text is sent directly to a professional compositor for typesetting. When this is done, considerable savings can result if *typesetting codes,* such as codes for special fonts or complex printing effects, are embedded into the document before it is sent to the typesetter. Many of the more powerful word processing packages targeted for commercial environments offer this feature.

Presentation Graphics. Many business documents include presentation graphics such as bar charts, pie charts, and the like. Consequently, many word processors provide *interfacing* with presentation graphics packages to enable charts to be imported into a word-processed document. An alternative to using such an interface is obtaining an integrated software package that provides presentation graphics capabilities along with word processing.

Style sheet.
A collection of design specifications that can be saved as a file and later used to format documents in a particular way.

Style Sheets. A feature that several leading word processors have begun incorporating—and that is standard fare in desktop publishing packages—is the style sheet. A **style sheet** is a collection of font and formatting specifications that is saved as a file and later used to prepare documents in a particular way. For instance, if your letters to clients are to conform to a certain letterhead style, to use a specific typeface and point size, and to contain a personalized heading or footing on every page beyond the first one, you can declare all of these specifications in a style sheet that you invoke when preparing such letters. Reports, in contrast, would probably use a different style sheet.

Add-On Packages

When a word processor is missing a critical feature, chances are there's an aftermarket (third-party) vendor that offers such a feature as an add-on. Aftermarket vendors specialize in complementing a product made by another vendor with some type of "value-added" functionality. Five of the most widely used types of **add-on packages** are discussed in the following paragraphs.

Add-on package.
A software package that supplements the activities of a larger software package, either by providing new functions or improving on already existing functions.

Reference Shelves. *Reference shelves,* the most prominent of which is Microsoft Bookshelf (see Figure 8-14), provide a number of handy reference books online to the writer. For instance, Bookshelf packs electronic versions of the *American Heritage Dictionary,* a thesaurus, the *Chicago Manual of Style, Bartlett's Familiar Quotations,* an atlas, a zip-code directory, and a world almanac onto a single optical disk. Bookshelf enables any of its works to be summoned by a word processor with a couple of keystrokes. Once the computer system is pointing to a particular reference work on the "shelf," the work can be electronically searched for a particular block of text. When the block is found, it can be "cut and pasted" back into the document being word processed.

Bibliographic Databases. *Bibliographic databases* are specifically tailored to writers who prepare long reference lists or bibliographies. The programs use onscreen templates for entering information about references into specific fields and for entering lengthy notes. You can also select a style by which the entire bibliography will be automatically formatted.

Style/Grammar Checkers. *Style/grammar checkers* are designed to root out errors in grammar, punctuation, and word usage. They also analyze writing styles for specific weaknesses (such as overused words, overly long sentences, and words that are sexist or out-of-date). In addition, most packages will calculate some type of overall reading-level statistic for your written work. Unfortunately, good writing often depends on bending rules, so although style/grammar checkers may help people write in an understandable fashion, they are not geared to turning a wretched writer into an instant Hemingway.

Figure 8-14
Microsoft Bookshelf.
Users of this add-on package can summon any of the works shown in the photo with a couple of keystrokes.

Outline Processors. *Outline processors* enable you to mark headings in text and, upon issuing a specific command, have all other text but specific levels of headings disappear. If you want to look at text under a specific heading in more detail, the outline processor generally allows you to selectively open up lower levels of the document. Most outline processors let you choose among several different types of outline styles.

Font Libraries. Even though many word processors come packaged with a variety of fonts, you can add others by acquiring a font library. A font library is a collection of fonts that supplements those packaged into your word processor. Font libraries are particularly useful for users who want to give their documents a "desktop publishing" look.

Desktop Publishing

The late 1970s introduced desktop computing—an entire computer system capable of fitting on a desktop. Thanks to other major improvements on the software and hardware fronts, we now have desktop publishing—microcomputer-based publishing systems that fit on a desktop.

What Is Desktop Publishing?

Desktop publishing. A microcomputer-based publishing system that can fit on a desktop.

Desktop publishing systems are hardware/software systems that let you combine on a page such elements as text (in a variety of typefaces), art, and photos, thus creating attractive documents that look as if they came

Figure 8-15
Applications for desktop publishing.
Although low-end desktop publishing packages are adequate for simple outputs such as newsletters and price lists, high-end desktop publishing packages are usually required for sophisticated work such as books and brochures.

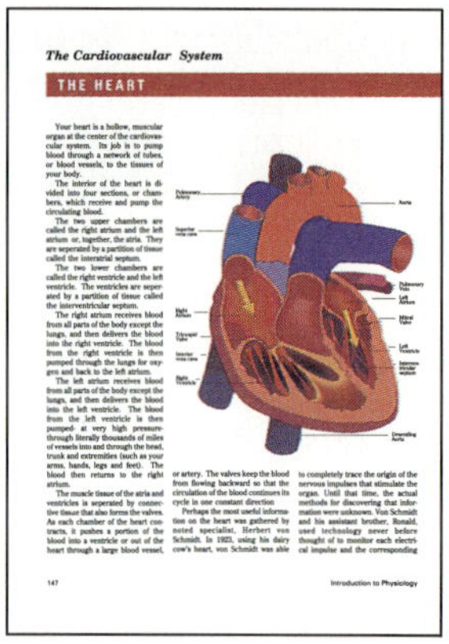

- ☐ Advertisements
- ☐ Annual reports
- ☐ Books
- ☐ Brochures
- ☐ Business reports
- ☐ Catalogs
- ☐ Business cards
- ☐ Resumes
- ☐ Restaurant menus

- ☐ Magazines
- ☐ Newsletters
- ☐ Newspapers
- ☐ Posters
- ☐ Price lists
- ☐ Software/system documentation
- ☐ Stationery and business forms
- ☐ Training manuals
- ☐ Signs

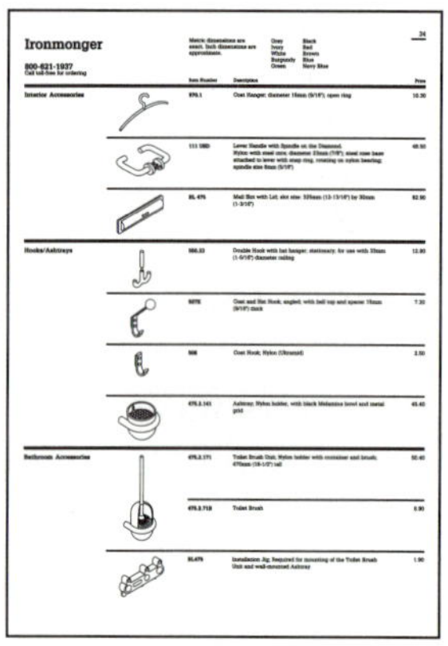

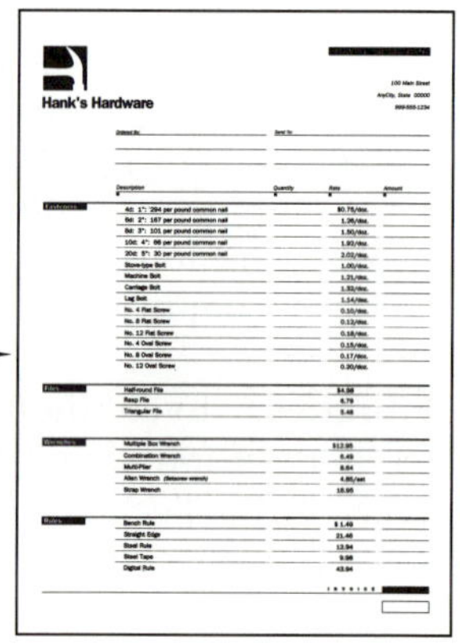

off a printer's press (see Figure 8-15). Desktop publishing systems are designed to replace many of the traditionally manual, labor-intensive tasks associated with cutting, arranging, and pasting elements onto a page. Because they make it possible for publishing to be done in-house, they also enable companies to save money, save time, and have more control over the look of finished documents. In the last decade or so, desktop publishing has rapidly evolved into a major applications area within the field of computers.

As you can see from studying the images in Figure 8-15, the basic difference between word processing and desktop publishing is one of document "look." Whereas word processing deals mainly with straight, nontypeset text—and maybe a few simple fonts for emphasis—desktop publishing involves full-fledged typesetting and imagesetting. *Typesetting* implies full control over type styles and sizes as well as spacing between words, letters, and lines. *Imagesetting* involves combining on a page both type and such artwork elements as drawings, photographs, and color. Although there is a theoretical distinction that separates desktop publishing from word processing, many of the leading word processors are increasingly being packaged with desktop publishing features.

Desktop publishing systems have come a long way in providing individuals with the capability to produce documents that look as if they were professionally prepared, but they are still a far cry from professional-level publishing systems. Systems falling into this latter category are the preferred choice for producing large volumes of high-quality printed materials such as corporate annual reports and four-color books like this one.

Components of a Desktop Publishing System

Naturally, not all desktop publishing systems are the same. You can spend a few thousand dollars for a system that produces simple newsletters, but you will have to pay several times that amount for one that creates stunning and creative color artwork. Desktop publishing systems targeted for commercial applications often consist of several hardware and software components. These components are described in this section, and the use of them is covered in Window 4.

Hardware. Hardware used to do high-end desktop publishing usually includes a high-end microcomputer system, a laser printer, a graphics-oriented monitor, an image scanner, and digitizing equipment. These devices were covered in depth in Chapter 5 of the text and are therefore addressed only briefly here.

- ***High-End Microcomputer System.*** High-quality desktop publishing requires a microprocessor that packs plenty of power, a respectable amount of RAM, and a hard disk with plenty of storage. Manipulation of graphical fonts, photos, and art can be computationally intensive. A mere two-page newsletter, for instance, can require 200 KB of storage, a 30-point character set uses about 150 KB, and a half-page scanned image needs another 500 KB. Such work requires a system unit like those based on the Intel 80386 or 80486 chips or the Motorola 68030 or 68040 processors. The systems should have at least 4 megabytes of RAM and at least 80 megabytes of hard-disk storage.
- ***Laser Printer.*** Most laser printers for microcomputer-based desktop publishing applications cost $1,000 to $10,000. These devices have their own built-in microprocessors, about 1 to 3 MB RAM, and several

ROM chips that carry popular fonts. Many such laser printers output at a resolution of either 300 dpi (dots per vertical and horizontal inch, or 90,000 dots to the inch) or 600 dpi. If you require higher resolution than this, you'll need software that will produce files that can be read by professional typesetting equipment (which works at 1,000 dpi or more).

Page description language (PDL). A language used to communicate instructions to a laser printer.

The laser printer in your computer system relies on a specific **page description language (PDL)** to carry out its work. The two most common PDLs are Adobe's *PostScript,* which is widely used in the fastest and most expensive laser printers, and Hewlett-Packard's *Printer Command Language (PCL),* which is more popular on slower and less expensive laser printers.

- *Graphics-Oriented Monitor.* Most monitors used with microcomputer systems contain a relatively small (13-inch) screen that can display about a third of a standard printed page at a time. On such screens, the resolution usually is adequate for text and some simple graphics. For desktop publishing applications, however, it generally is preferable to have a much higher screen resolution, both to fine-tune detailed graphics and to see either a full-page or a two-page layout on the screen at one time. Monitors designed for these purposes often have screens up to 50 percent larger than the typical microcomputer display screen, and they are generally capable of WYSIWYG (see Figure 8-16).
- *Image Scanner.* An image scanner (see Figure 5-21) allows you to scan photographs, drawings, or text and digitize them directly into computer memory. Later, you can edit the images with illustration software and hardware. Some image scanners also use optical character recognition (OCR) software, which enables them to recognize certain text characters instead of just digitizing them. Such a feature allows you to later edit any text that you enter with the scanner. Both color and grey-scale scanners are widely available.
- *Digitizers.* Hardware such as the penlike stylus, mouse, crosshair cursor, and digitizing tablet are commonly used with art and illustration packages in desktop publishing environments. All of these devices are examples of digitizers (see Figure 5-24). Desktop publishing users commonly trace over preexisting art using a stylus attached to a digitizing tablet, thereby providing an initial outline for a drawing or painting program.

Software. A variety of software and software-based products are used in desktop publishing environments. These include page-makeup software, word processing software, fonts, clip-art libraries, and art and illustration software.

- *Page-Makeup Software.* The programs that allow you to combine text, photos, and art elements into a finished page are collectively

Figure 8-16
Graphics-oriented monitor. Desktop publishing systems frequently use special monitors with oversized screens and the ability to output crisp images.

referred to as **page-makeup software.** Because page makeup is the central function in desktop publishing, page-makeup programs are often loosely referred to as "desktop publishing packages." Some of the leading page-makeup programs are Aldus Corporation's PageMaker, Xerox Corporation's Ventura Publisher, Quark Inc.'s Quark Xpress, and Letraset's Ready-Set-Go. Your page-makeup software must be compatible with the other desktop publishing products you use, such as fonts, clip-art libraries, and the software used to develop text or illustration files.

Page-makeup software. Programs used to compose page layouts in a desktop publishing system.

- ***Word Processing Software.*** Because most users already have their own word processing software, such as WordPerfect or Word, the vendors of the leading desktop publishing packages have designed their products to accept text prepared with several of the leading word processors. Thus, when acquiring a desktop publishing system, it is always wise to check out which word processors it recognizes. Although most page-makeup programs do contain built-in word processing features, enabling you to modify any text that you import to them, it is important to recognize that their primary function is page makeup. Consequently, they are not as easy to use for word processing as your average word processor.
- ***Fonts.*** A variety of *fonts*—that is, typefaces conforming to a specific style and size—are available for desktop publishing applications. Some fonts are available as ROM chips that are packaged into the laser printer you buy. You can acquire additional fonts in disk form

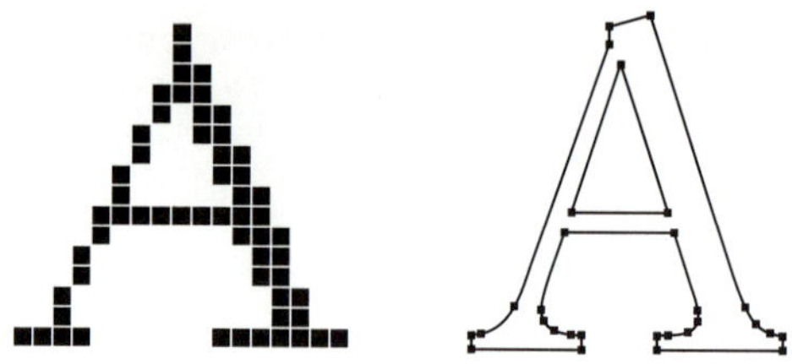

Figure 8-17
Bit-mapped versus outline fonts.
Bit-mapped fonts (left) are made up of a fixed pattern of dots, whereas outline fonts (right) are defined by a series of curves. Outline fonts can be resized to different point sizes; bit-mapped fonts can't.

and load them into the laser printer's RAM. When choosing type for desktop-published work, most people need to select both large and small fonts. Large fonts are widely used for banners and titles; small fonts are commonly used for body copy.

Fonts are of two types: bit-mapped and outline (see Figure 8-17). *Bit-mapped fonts* are described by a fixed configuration of dots. While they are the least expensive kind of font, you cannot scale them to different sizes. *Outline fonts* consist of mathematical curves that describe how characters are shaped. They are more expensive than bit-mapped fonts, but you can scale them to virtually any size you want. You can also create your own fonts.

Clip art.
Prepackaged artwork designed to be imported into text documents or charts, say, by desktop publishing or presentation graphics software.

□ *Clip-Art Libraries.* A **clip-art** library is a collection of prepared art images. You can use these images on their own or as building blocks to create other images. You can even modify them. A sample of clip-art pieces appears in Figure 8-18.

Clip-art libraries are bundled into many illustration packages and are also sold separately by third-party vendors. Vendors of illustration packages often use a proprietary format for their clip art, usually one that supports their other products, whereas third-party clip-art vendors typically make their clip art available in a variety of standard formats.

Figure 8-18
Clip art.
Clip-art libraries are bundled into many illustration software packages and are also sold separately.

Figure 8-19 Manipulating drawings with an illustration package.
Illustration packages enable images to be moved, copied, cut and pasted, rotated, colored and recolored, mirrored, distorted, and manipulated in virtually any other way you can imagine. Because images are manipulated at electronically fast speeds, it is possible to try out dozens of possibilities in the time it would take to produce only a single image by manual means.

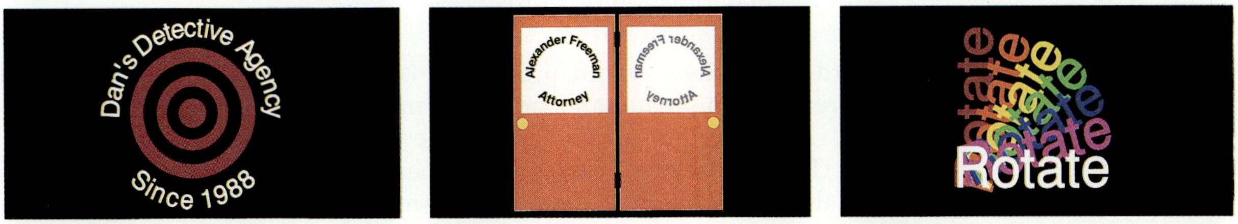

(a) Creating circular text and cutting holes in objects

(b) Creating mirror images

(c) Rotating text about a fixed point

□ ***Illustration Software.*** **Illustration software packages** enable artwork to be created from scratch. Also, they accept existing artwork as input and allow it to be modified using the software's image-manipulation facilities.

Illustration software package. A program package that enables users to paint or draw.

There are several ways to input an image to illustration software. If you have an image scanner, you can read a hard-copy image directly into RAM. If you have a digitizing tablet, you can trace over a hard-copy image with a stylus, thereby transferring the outline of the image to memory. Or, if the image is in a clip-art library, you can transfer the appropriate clip-art file directly to the illustration software if both use the same file formats.

High-quality illustration software enables you to size, rotate, flip, recolor, distort, and edit virtually any digitally stored drawing or photograph to your heart's content (see Figure 8-19 for several examples). Because images are manipulated at electronically fast speeds, it is possible to try out dozens of possibilities in the time it would normally take to produce only a single image by manual means. Once an image is satisfactory, it can be imported to a desktop publishing (page-makeup) program.

Sometimes illustration software packages are distinguished by whether they are primarily oriented toward painting or drawing. *Painting packages* enable you to create bit-mapped images and to color them pixel by pixel. Usually, the images you create cannot be resized without loss of resolution. For instance, blowing them up may result in jagged edges, whereas reducing them may result in a blurry mess. In contrast, *drawing packages* enable you to create outlines than can be resized. Once properly sized, these outlines can be filled in with colors.

Many illustration software packages are available today. Among the best-selling packages are Adobe's Illustrator, Aldus's Freehand, Corel's Corel Draw!, Z-Soft's PC Paintbrush, Claris's McDraw and McPaint, and Cricket's Stylist.

Summary and Key Terms

Both word processing and desktop publishing are technologies that deal with the manipulation of words.

Word Processing. **Word processing** is the use of computer technology to create, manipulate, and print text materials such as letters, legal contracts, manuscripts, and other documents.

There are several ways you can perform word processing. First, you can do it on either a *dedicated word processing system* or a *general-purpose computer*. Second, you can work with either a **WYSIWYG** (What You See Is What You Get) word processor or one that depends heavily on *embedded formatting codes* to show you what you will subsequently see in print. Third, you can use either a *general-purpose* or a *special-purpose word processing software package*. Fourth, you can choose between a *dedicated word processing package* or an *integrated software package*.

Using a word processor, or for that matter, any type of productivity software package, requires learning several general operations. These operations include accessing the package from the operating system, informing the package that you want to create a new file or retrieve an old one, commanding the package to save a file, commanding the package to print a file, commanding the package to delete a file, indicating to the package that you want to quit working on your current file and do something on another file, and terminating the package and getting back to the operating system.

Learning to use a word processor at a minimal level involves mastering a number of elementary editing operations as well as several print-formatting commands. Entering and editing operations include moving the cursor, scrolling, making line returns through either a **soft return** (the **wordwrap** feature) or a **hard return**, inserting and deleting, moving and copying, and searching and replacing. Among the print-formatting operations that one must learn are adjusting line spacing; indenting; justifying text; setting up page formats; reformatting body text; centering; tabbing; paginating; setting up headers and footers; selecting **typefaces**, **point sizes**, and **fonts**; multiple-column formatting; and footnoting.

More sophisticated use of word processing packages often requires software and hardware that provide **proportional spacing** and **microspacing** so that they can produce typeset-quality output. Without these features, text will be **monospaced.** In addition, advanced applications often make use of such features as **spelling checkers, thesauruses**, **mailing list programs**, **mail merge programs**, a math feature, **macros**, **redlining**, index and table of contents preparation, **orphan** and **widow** elimination, sorting, embedded typesetting codes, presentation graphics, and **style sheets.**

A wide variety of **add-on packages** can be acquired to enhance a word processing environment. Among such packages are reference shelves, bibliographic databases, style/grammar checkers, outline processors, and font libraries.

Desktop Publishing. **Desktop publishing** systems go a step further than word processors. They let you combine on a page such elements as text (in a variety of fonts), art, and photos, thus creating attractive documents that look as if they came off a printer's press.

Whereas word processing deals mainly with straight, nontypeset text—perhaps using a few simple fonts for emphasis—desktop publishing involves full-fledged *typesetting* and *imagesetting*. But as much as desktop publishing systems have improved, they are still not capable of the document quality possible with professional composition systems.

Desktop publishing systems are commonly configured with some of the following hardware and software components. Hardware includes a high-end microcomputer system, a laser printer (which is used in concert with a specific **page-description language**, or **PDL**), a graphics-oriented monitor capable of WYSIWYG display, an image scanner, and digitizing equipment. Software components include **page-makeup software**, word processing software, fonts, a **clip-art** library, and **illustration software packages** such as *painting* and *drawing packages.*

Review Exercises

Fill-in Questions

1. Most word processors have a(n) ____________ feature that automatically produces a soft carriage return.
2. ____________ is a word processing feature that allocates more horizontal space on a line to some characters than to others.
3. A(n) ____________ program is used to generate mailing labels.
4. A(n) ____________ word processing system is a computer system exclusively designed for word processing applications.
5. WYSIWYG is an acronym for ____________.
6. The first line of a paragraph is called a(n) ____________ when it is separated from the rest of the paragraph by a page or column break.
7. PDL is an acronym for ____________.
8. Prestored art images used in a desktop publishing environment are referred to as ____________.

Matching Questions

Match each term with the description that fits best.

a. copying	d. inserting
b. redlining	e. scrolling
c. proportional spacing	f. moving

____ 1. Moving contiguous lines of text up and down on screen similarly to the way the roll on a player piano is unwound.

____ 2. A feature particularly useful when one person must edit another's written work.

____ 3. An operation that involves replication.

____ 4. An operation that entails physically relocating text so that it no longer appears in its original location.

____ 5. A word processing feature that gives text a typeset-quality look.

____ 6. An operation you would use on a word processor to quickly change the string MISSIPPI to MISSISSIPPI.

Discussion Questions

1. Identify several ways in which word processing can be implemented on a computer system.
2. What is the difference between monospacing and proportional spacing?
3. What are orphans and widows?
4. What is a reference shelf?
5. Identify the components of a desktop publishing system.
6. Why is it getting increasingly more difficult to distinguish word processing from desktop publishing?

Critical Thinking Questions

1. Spelling checkers are said to be of greatest utility to people who can spell reasonably well. Why do you think this is so?
2. Comment on this statement: "Now that desktop publishing is available, the professional typesetting and print shop is doomed."
3. Word processing and desktop publishing present undeniable benefits to organizations that can effectively use them. Can you think of any problems that these technologies pose to the average organization?

Window 4

Desktop Publishing

A Step-by-Step Look at What's Involved

During the last decade, the desktop publishing industry has evolved from a dream to a highly sophisticated reality—one characterized by powerful art and illustration systems, electronic darkrooms, and a spate of fonts and clip art libraries to satisfy almost every need. In this window, we'll look at some of the steps involved in using a desktop publishing package—laying out pages, handling type, manipulating art and photos, and refining pages so that the finished product looks just right.

STONE

Italian Style

It assumes the same clumsy proportions and blocky silhouette outside Paris, Milan or Rio de Janeiro, and everywhere it reduces the idea of home to a polyester pant suit of the mind. But one innovative architect is fighting to keep natural fibers a part of homelife in the condos of Atlanta. Although constrained by economic limitations and modern building materials, architect Blue Argo and her Argonaut Construstruction Company have discovered clever ways of using wooden moldings and locally quarried marble to recreate ante-bellum architectural detail in low-rise condominium developments.The most impressive of these villages is located near Emory U Emory Ur Emory Use of proportion and well-being, the result of graceful white doric columns that gently lead the eye to the welcome of a wide porch framed by a wooden balustrade.

Many Italian families live in a home that is three to four centuries old.

59

1. A finished page produced using Adobe Photoshop and Adobe Illustrator software.

Page Layout

Desktop publishing generally begins after word processing ends. The first step in desktop publishing is designing the page layout.

2. Page layout is usually begun by creating or retrieving a page template. The template shows how the columns are to be formed on the page and where elements such as headings, art, and the main body of text are to go. Here, the areas shaded in blue will receive the text imported from a word processor.

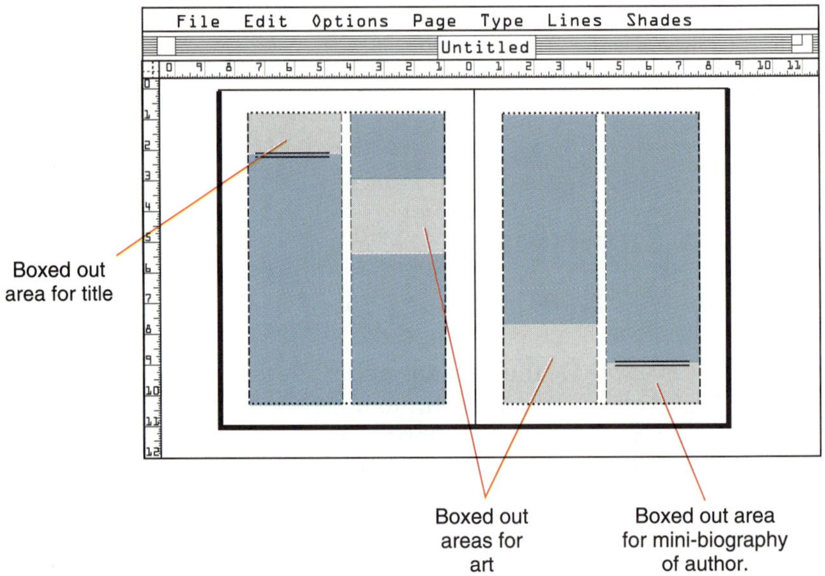

3, 4. The layout should be balanced so that it is pleasing to the eye. The piece at the left shows a good balance among the photo, heading, and body-copy text. The piece at the right, which has a "hole" in the middle, is unbalanced. Today, creating balance is largely a manual, judgmental process left to the talents of the user.

3

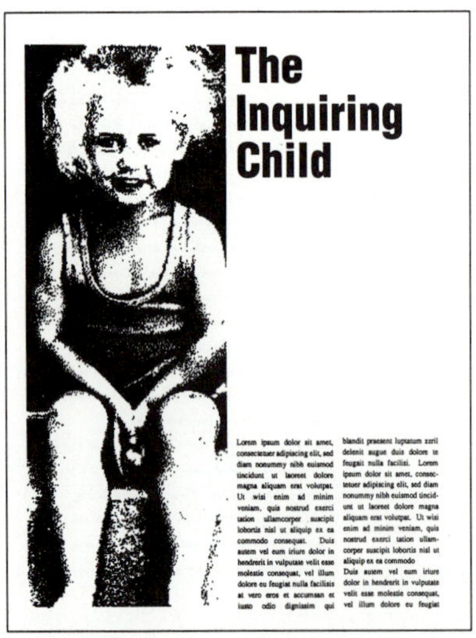

4

Type

A major element in any page layout is the typeface or typefaces used. In today's market, there are hundreds of typefaces available.

Goudy #20 **$185**

Goudy Old Style
abcdefghijklmnopqrstuvwxyz
ABCDEFGHIJKLMNOPQRSTUVW
XYZ&!?1234567890$¢

Goudy Old Style Italic
abcdefghijklmnopqrstuvwxyz
ABCDEFGHIJKLMNOPQRSTUVW
XYZ&!?1234567890$¢

Goudy Bold
abcdefghijklmnopqrstuvwxyz
ABCDEFGHIJKLMNOPQRSTUV
WXYZ&!?1234567890$¢

Goudy Bold Italic
abcdefghijklmnopqrstuvwxyz
ABCDEFGHIJKLMNOPQRSTUV
WXYZ&!?1234567890$¢

5. Many typefaces are available as a typeface family, as shown here for the Goudy typeface. Selecting typefaces from one family gives documents a consistent appearance.

6

6. Special effects with typefaces can be created with some art and illustration software packages.

7. Typeface selection affects the mood of the document.

7

Typeface Sample	Mood Imparted
THE ELEGANT GOURMET	Elegant and formal
The Elegant Gourmet	Elegant and informal
The Elegant Gourmet	Playful
THE ELEGANT GOURMET	Serious
THE ELEGANT GOURMET	Action-oriented

8

Tekton
abcdefghijklmnopqrstuvwxyz
ABCDEFGHIJKLMNOPQRSTUVWXYZ
&!?1234567890$¢
Tekton Oblique
abcdefghijklmnopqrstuvwxyz
ABCDEFGHIJKLMNOPQRSTUVWXYZ
&!?1234567890$¢

9
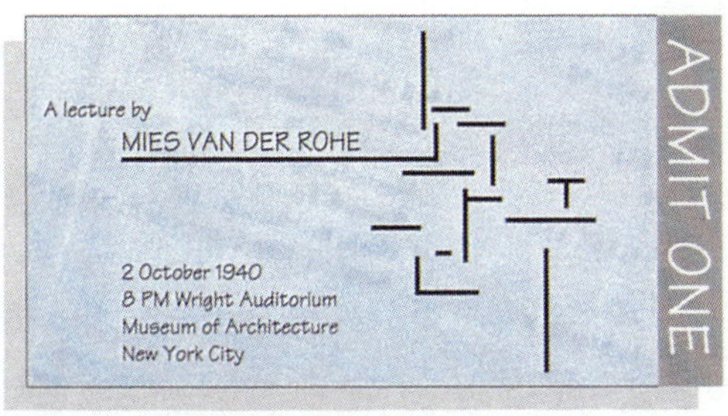

10

8–10. Examples of effective use of the Tekton typeface to create a mood.

Art

An important component of any page layout is the art used. Art elements may be illustrations, photos, or both.

11

12

11,12. Typically, illustrations are first prepared with an art or illustration software package. Then they are imported into the desktop publishing package, which sizes them and puts them into the place designated in the layout.

13

13. Most illustration packages come with a set of tools that enables the artist to use the computer as an electronic canvas. Here, an electronic blending tool was used to gradually change the face of the angel in the upper left to the face of the devil in the lower right.

14

15

14,15. Every photographic image that's published must be broken down into finely packed dots—a process called halftoning. As these two halftones suggest, the more dots that are used to represent the original image, the better the output quality.

Refinement

The last step in desktop publishing is refining pages so that they look exactly the way you want them to.

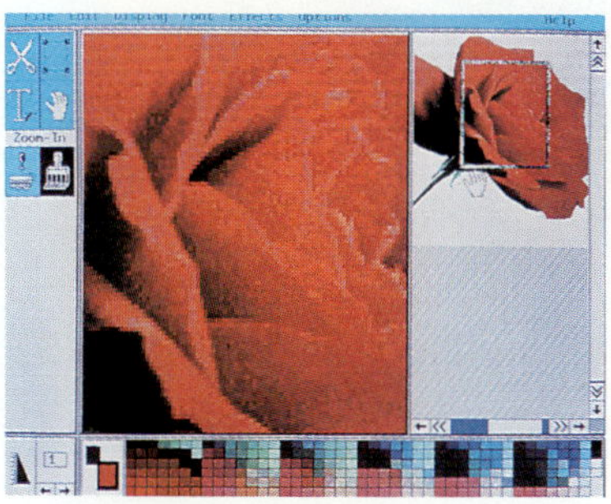

16. A zoom tool magnifies objects onscreen so that they may be inspected for detail.

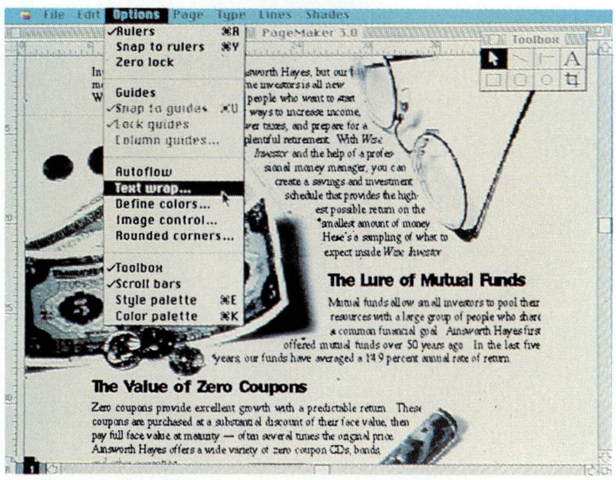

17. The text-wrap feature available in many desktop publishing packages fits text around the contours of art elements.

How do businesses condense large amounts of data into sophisticated but easy-to-follow graphs such as the one shown here? Often data are first analyzed and summarized with a spreadsheet package. Then, to be graphed, these data are read into and processed by a presentation graphics software package. Both spreadsheets and presentation graphics are covered in this chapter.

9

Spreadsheets and Presentation Graphics

Outline

Learning Objectives

After completing this chapter, you will be able to:

1. Describe what spreadsheet packages do and how they work.
2. Identify the basic operations you must master to effectively use spreadsheet software.
3. Explain the use of several advanced spreadsheet features.
4. Describe how presentation graphics packages work, some of the differences among them, and the images they let you create.

Overview

Today, one of the most important software packages that *any* businessperson—whether he or she is a manager, an office worker, or a sales representative—should learn is the *electronic spreadsheet.* Spreadsheet software is to the current generation of end users what the pocket calculator was to previous generations: a convenient means of performing calculations. But while most pocket calculators can compute and display only one result each time you enter new data, electronic spreadsheets can present you with hundreds or even thousands of results each time you enter a single new value or command. What spreadsheets can do and how they work are two of the primary subjects of this chapter.

From our discussion of spreadsheets we'll move on to *presentation graphics software,* which is designed to present the results of business computations in a visually oriented, easily understood way. This class of business software is easy to learn and use. Today many spreadsheet packages are equipped with built-in presentation graphics features and tools. Also, many dedicated presentation graphics packages, which enable you to produce higher-quality presentation images than those possible with spreadsheet packages, are commercially available.

The use of spreadsheets and presentation graphics software to assist in selling bank services to clients is illustrated in User Solution 9-1.

Spreadsheets

Electronic spreadsheet. A productivity software package that enables operators to develop tables and financial schedules quickly.

An **electronic spreadsheet** package produces computerized counterparts to the ruled, ledger-style worksheets with which accountants frequently work (see Figure 9-1). Electronic spreadsheets first came to public notice in the late 1970s when a Harvard Business School student named Dan Bricklin and a programmer friend produced a microcomputer package called VisiCalc ("The VISIble CALCulator"). Bricklin conceived of the idea while watching his accounting professor erase large chunks of blackboard computations every time a single number changed in an interdependent series of calculations. Awed by the amount of repetitive labor involved, Bricklin quickly saw the potential of computerized worksheets.

To call VisiCalc a huge success would be an understatement. It shattered sales records for applications software and made microcomputers valuable decision-making tools in business. It is also widely credited for moving Apple—the company that supported VisiCalc on its Apple II line of microcomputers—into the ranks of the computer-industry heavyweights. Both VisiCalc and the spreadsheet products that followed it have been easy to use and clearly made managers who mastered them more productive.

Today, although VisiCalc is gone from the scene, spreadsheet software for all sizes of computers abounds in the marketplace. Among the leading spreadsheet packages currently available for microcomputers are

User Solution 9-1

Computers as Selling Tools

At Texas Commerce Bank, a member of Chemical Banking Corporation, professional-looking presentation materials prepared by staff members on desktop computer systems help sell cash management and trust services to clients. Using spreadsheets and graphics software, staffers can customize charts that show prospective clients how well the bank's investment services are performing relative to the U.S. dollar, the S&P 500, and the price of West Texas crude oil. In the past, such presentation materials were prepared by outside firms, and the bank had less control over deadlines, quality, and cost.

(a) Manually prepared worksheet

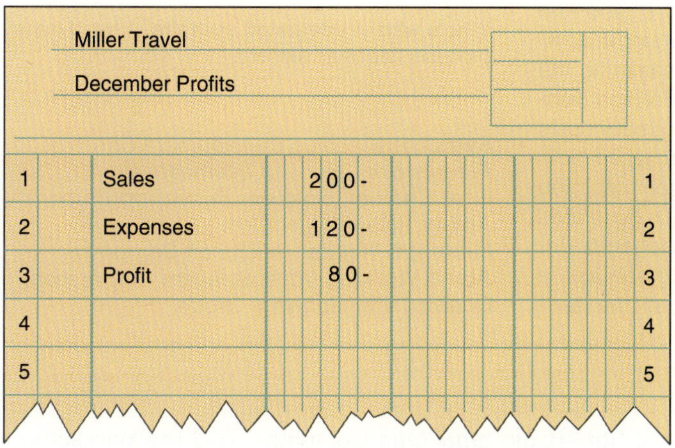

(b) Worksheet prepared by electronic spreadsheet package

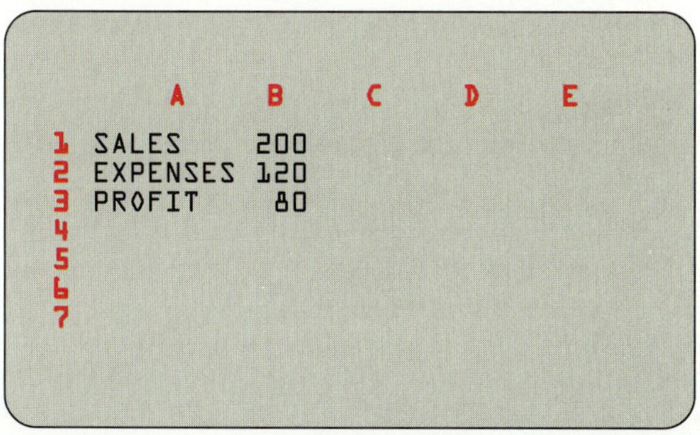

Figure 9-1
Manually prepared and electronic worksheets.
An electronic spreadsheet package produces computerized counterparts to the ruled, ledger-style worksheets with which accountants frequently work.

Feature 9-1

Integrated Software Packages

When You Need More than Just a Spreadsheet

For users who would like to tie together several applications under a single program "roof," an integrated software package may be the best choice.

An integrated software package bundles two or more relatively distinct productivity software functions into a single "megapackage." Symphony—which bundles together a spreadsheet, file manager, presentation graphics routine, word processor, and communications software—is an example of an integrated software product. So is Framework, which combines a spreadsheet, database management system, presentation graphics routine, word processor, and communications software (see accompanying list for names of leading packages).

Integrated software packages give you the convenience of having to learn only a single command or menu structure rather than mastering the different software approaches of three or four vendors. In addition, a bundled package normally costs less than a system of individually purchased software components. Perhaps more important, you automatically are able to integrate data generated from any of the various package components—for example, it is not difficult to insert a graph into a word-processed document—because all the software components are fully compatible with one another.

On the negative side, integrated packages typically have one or two strong components and several weak ones. Thus, an author, who probably requires a top-of-the-line word processor, would be better off getting a dedicated word processing package than an integrated package that also caters to spreadsheet or database users. Another disadvantage of these packages is that some of the features may be of little or no use to the user. For example, users who don't need to communicate with a remote location certainly wouldn't get their money's worth out of a communications software feature. Also, because integrated packages let you have several productivity functions at your fingertips, they require a lot of memory and result in some extra processing overhead.

Who's who in integrated software. A list of leading products and their vendors.

Symphony *Lotus Development Corporation*
Framework *Borland International*
First Choice *Software Publishing Corporation*
Ability Plus *Migent Inc.*
Microsoft Works *Microsoft Corporation*
Alpha Works *Alpha Software Corporation*
Enable *The Software Group*

1-2-3, Excel, SuperCalc, and Quattro, with 1-2-3 the pacesetter in sales. Technically speaking, most of these products are *integrated software packages;* they supplement spreadsheeting capabilities with one or more other functions (see Feature 9-1).

How Spreadsheets Work

Here we discuss some of the principles by which spreadsheets work.

Worksheet.
The computerized counterpart to the ruled, ledger-style paper used by accountants.

Cell.
The part of the worksheet that can hold a single label or value; a cell occurs where a row and column intersect.

The Anatomy of a Worksheet. In electronic spreadsheets, the display screen is viewed as a *window* looking in on a big grid, called a **worksheet** (see Figure 9-2). Most major spreadsheet packages allow worksheets that consist of thousands of *rows* and a couple hundred *columns.* In Microsoft Excel, for instance, a maximum of 16,384 rows and 256 columns is available to create worksheets. Each of the 4,194,304 (16,384 × 256) **cells** formed by the intersection of a row and column may contain text, a num-

Figure 9-2 A worksheet and a window to the worksheet.
Worksheets can be too large to view on the display screen at a single moment. The window allows users to see the worksheet in screen-sized chunks.

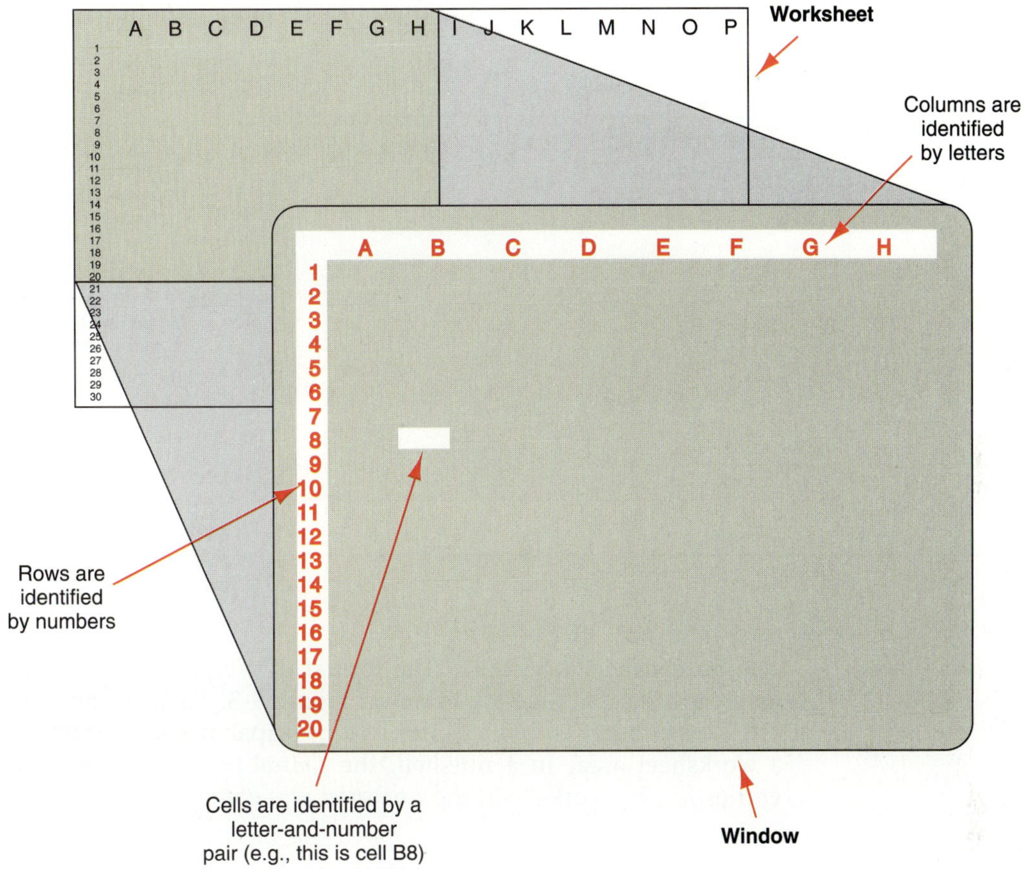

ber, or a formula. Each cell can be accessed through a **cell address,** such as B8 or E223.

Cell address.
The column/row combination that uniquely identifies a spreadsheet cell.

In most commercial spreadsheet packages, columns are identified by letters, rows by numbers, and each cell by a letter-and-number pair. For example, cell B8 is found at the intersection of column B and row 8. Of course, the display screen is too small to permit the viewing of more than a few rows and columns at any given time. However, users can press certain keys on the keyboard that will move the worksheet window around, letting them view other portions of the worksheet through it. After we've covered a couple of other important matters, we'll describe how to do this.

The discussion that immediately follows concerns two-dimensional spreadsheet applications. Later in the chapter, we'll look at the multidimensional capabilities rapidly being infused into most major spreadsheet packages.

Figure 9-3 Elements of spreadsheet-package screen.
Most screens are divided into two areas—a control panel, where cell contents are prepared, and a worksheet area, which holds the finished contents.

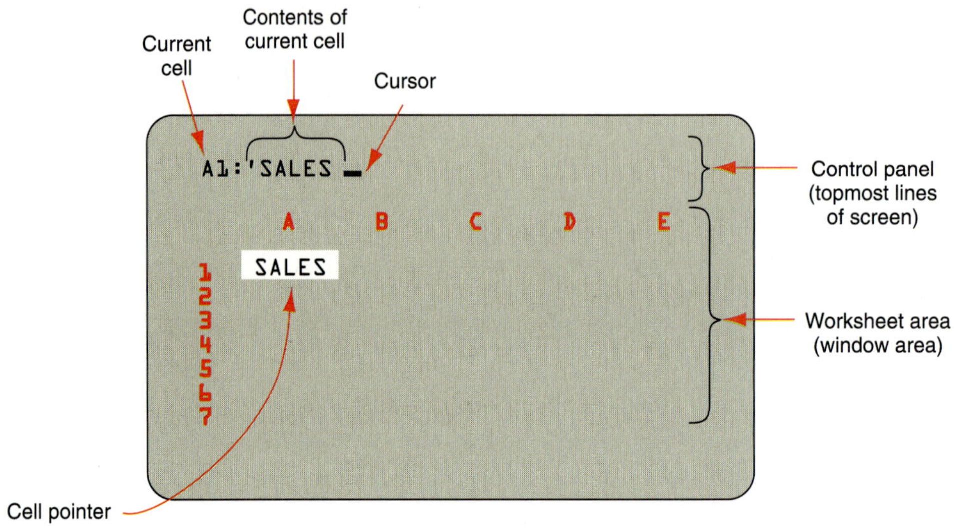

The Spreadsheet's Screen. The format of a typical-looking screen from a spreadsheet package is shown in Figure 9-3. Each screen, such as the one shown here, is divided into two principal areas: a control panel and a worksheet area. In a nutshell, the *control panel* is where you prepare entries for the worksheet; the *worksheet area* contains the worksheet itself.

Control panel.
The portion of the screen display that is used for issuing commands and observing what is being typed into the computer system.

Current cell.
In spreadsheet software, the worksheet cell at which the highlight is currently positioned.

Cursor.
A highlighting symbol in the control panel that appears where the next character to be typed in will be placed.

□ *The Control Panel.* The **control panel** in many spreadsheet packages consists of approximately three lines and is located in the top portion of the screen. The control panel serves several functions. Most important, it displays the address and contents of the current cell and the spreadsheet's command menu.

The **current cell** is the cell to which the spreadsheet package is currently pointing. Spreadsheet packages point to one cell at a time; you can always tell which cell is current by looking at the control panel. In Figure 9-3, the current cell is A1.

To the right of the address of the current cell are its contents. If the cell is empty, nothing will be showing in this portion of the screen. As you type in the contents of the current cell or edit the contents of this cell, each keystroke you hit will appear at the **cursor** position in this part of the control panel. In Figure 9-3, the content of cell A1 is SALES.

Every spreadsheet package has a set of commands for activities such as inserting or deleting rows or columns, moving and copying cell entries, and saving and printing worksheets. All of these tasks are accomplished by selecting commands off of a menu that is dis-

Figure 9-4 Scrolling to see other parts of the worksheet.
In this figure, the right-arrow key has been depressed once, producing the screen at the right from the screen at the left.

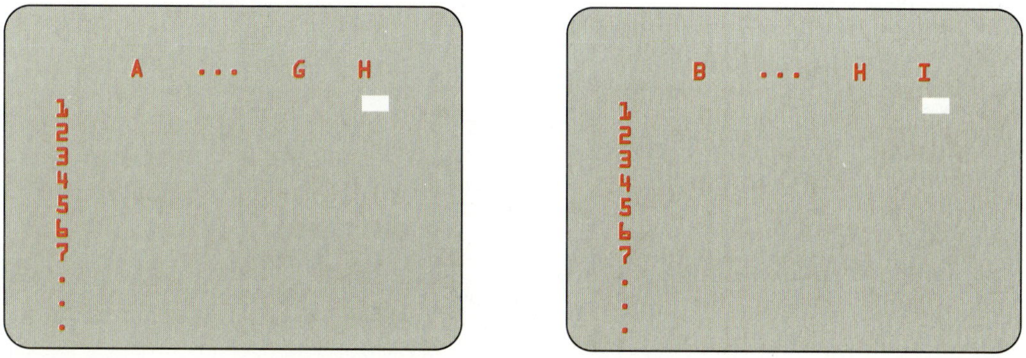

played in the control panel. For simplicity, we have not shown this menu in Figure 9-3. Later in the chapter, however, we'll cover a number of operations that can be performed from the command menu.

- *The Worksheet Area.* The worksheet itself is displayed in the part of the screen called the **worksheet area,** or **window area.** One important element in the worksheet area is the **cell pointer,** sometimes referred to as the **highlight** or simply the *pointer.* The cell pointer highlights the current cell. As you can see in Figure 9-3, the current cell (as indicated in the control panel) is cell A1, and this is the cell at which the cell pointer is positioned. As each cell is filled in the control panel, its contents are not entered into the worksheet area until the Enter key is depressed.

  Remember, the window area may not be large enough to show the whole worksheet at a single glance, but you can scroll the window about to see other parts of the worksheet if you desire. *Scrolling* is similar to moving a magnifying glass over a large map; the movable glass acts like the window, while the underlying map acts like the worksheet. We can scroll the worksheet a row or column at a time when the highlight is at the edge of the screen and we press one of the arrow keys (see Figure 9-4). Keys such as Tab, PgUp, and PgDn let us scroll the worksheet in window-sized blocks.

Worksheet area. The portion of the screen that contains the window onto the worksheet. Also called the **window area.**

Cell pointer. A cursorlike mechanism used in the worksheet area to point to cells, thereby making them active. Also called the **highlight.**

Creating a Worksheet. Now that you are familiar with a few of the basic mechanics of spreadsheet-package use, let's learn how to create a worksheet. Refer to Figure 9-5. In the worksheet shown in the figure, we are computing a business income statement in which expenses are 60 percent of sales and profit is the difference between sales and expenses. Here we will show how to enter the text and numbers in the figure into the computer. We'll also look at some of the details that the spreadsheet software will take care of for you.

Figure 9-5
An electronic spreadsheet package at work.
It's their *recalculation feature*—the ability to quickly rework thousands of tedious calculations—that makes spreadsheet packages so valuable to users.

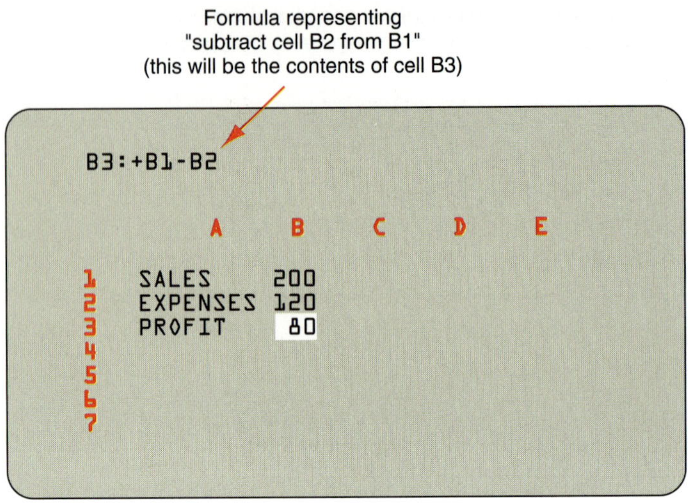

Label.
A cell entry that cannot be manipulated mathematically.

Value.
A cell entry that can be manipulated mathematically.

Into each worksheet cell the user can type either a label or a value. In the terminology of the spreadsheet world, a **label** is a cell entry that cannot be manipulated mathematically, whereas a **value** is an entry that can.

In the figure, we have entered—one at a time—the following six things into the control panel:

A1	SALES	(a label)
A2	EXPENSES	(a label)
A3	PROFIT	(a label)
B1	200	(a value)
B2	.6*B1	(a value)
B3	+B1-B2	(a value)

The spreadsheet package automatically assumes that each entry beginning with a letter (or a label-prefix character, which we'll cover shortly) is a label; otherwise, it's a value. (Incidentally, that's why we had to type the formula in cell B3 with a "+" in front of it.)

As we type each label or value into the control panel and enter it, that label or value is processed by the spreadsheet software, and the results are automatically transferred to the worksheet. For cells A1, A2, A3, and B1 in Figure 9-5, notice that a direct transfer occurs. For cells B2 and B3, the computer first makes the computation indicated by the *formulas* and then transfers the result to the corresponding worksheet cells.

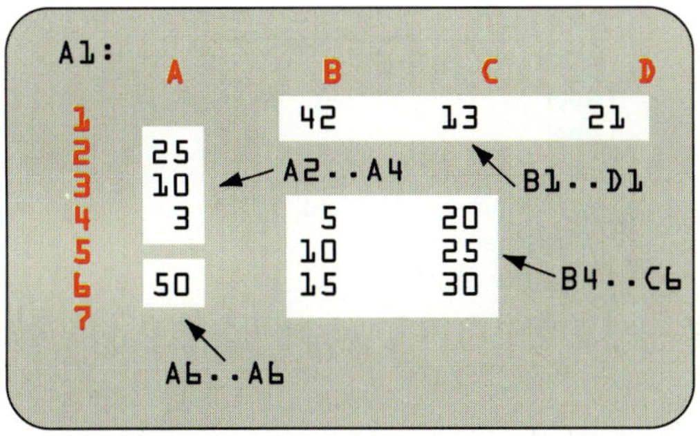

Figure 9-6
The range concept.
A range is any contiguous *rectangular* block of cells. It may be as small as a single cell or as large as a grid with several hundred cells on each side.

The Recalculation Feature. Electronic spreadsheet packages are particularly useful for "what-if" queries. For example, suppose we wish to know *what* profit will result in Figure 9-5 *if* sales are changed to $500. If we simply enter into cell B1 the value

```
500
```

the spreadsheet package automatically reworks all the figures according to the prestored formulas. Thus, the computer responds

SALES	500
EXPENSES	300
PROFIT	200

In seconds, electronic spreadsheets can perform recalculations that would require several hours to do manually or by writing a program in a regular programming language. In fact, it's this easy-to-use **recalculation feature** that makes spreadsheets so popular. You can learn to prepare budgets and financial schedules with them after only a few hours of training.

Recalculation feature. The ability of spreadsheet software to quickly and automatically recalculate the contents of several cells, based on new operator inputs.

Blocks of Cells: The Range Concept. Often, users need to be able to manipulate data in a set of contiguous cells—say, in a row or column of several cells or in a rectangular-shaped block of cells. To enable you to do this, spreadsheet packages have you declare **ranges** of cells. Figure 9-6 shows four examples of valid ranges. You will generally have to declare ranges of cells when you want to print, move, copy, insert, delete, sort, or graph parts of the worksheet.

Range. A set of contiguous cells arranged in a rectangle.

For instance, telling the spreadsheet package to print the range B4..C6 will result in the 3-by-2 block of cells in the southeast corner of Figure 9-6 being output. Generally, a range can be declared by explicitly typing it into the control panel—for instance, you would type in all six characters in the string "B4..C6" to declare it as a range—or by pointing to the range in the worksheet area.

Figure 9-7
Examples of labels and values.
Labels cannot be manipulated mathematically, whereas values can.

Example	Description
ABC Company	Label
Costs	Label
1.10	Value (numeric constant)
$300	Value (numeric constant)
.3*A1 − B2	Value (formula)
@AVG(B1..B4)	Value (function)
+A1 − B1	Value (formula)

Figure 9-8
Label prefixes.
In many spreadsheet packages, the apostrophe character, which left justifies labels, is the default label prefix and will not have to be typed in.

Character	Action Taken	Example
'	Left-justifies	FROG
^	Centers	FROG
"	Right-justifies	FROG
\	Repeats	FROG FROG FROG FROG

More on Labels and Values. As mentioned earlier, a cell can contain either a label or a value. A *label* is an entry that cannot be manipulated mathematically; a *value* is an entry that can. Several examples of labels and values are given in Figure 9-7.

Many spreadsheets automatically assume that an entry that starts with a letter or the ', ^, ", or \ character is a label; otherwise, it's a value. The ', ^, ", and \ characters are examples of *label-prefix characters* used in many packages. When typed as the first character in a label, these characters will, respectively, left justify, center, right justify, and repeat text placed into a cell (see Figure 9-8). When a label-prefix character is not explicitly typed in, the spreadsheet package typically assumes left justification as the default.

A value is generally one of three types: a numeric constant, a formula, or a function.

- ***Numeric Constants.*** *Numeric constants* are values that are in numeric form—for example, 200 or −10.
- ***Formulas.*** A *formula* consists of cell references and mathematical operators, such as those for addition (+), subtraction (−), and so on. An example of a formula is +B1 − B2, which tells the computer that the value in the current cell is computed as the value in cell B1 minus the value in cell B2.
- ***Functions.*** A *function* is a reference to a prestored formula or a preset value (such as today's date). An example is the SUM function; the string @SUM(B1..B3) tells the spreadsheet package that the value in the current cell is computed as the sum of the values in the range B1

Arithmetic and Statistical Functions	
@SUM (range)	Calculates the sum of all values in a range
@MAX (range)	Finds the highest value in a range
@MIN (range)	Finds the lowest value in a range
@COUNT (range)	Counts the number of nonempty cells in a range
@AVG (range)	Calculates the average of values in a range
@STD (range)	Calculates the standard deviation of values in a range
@ABS (cell or expression)	Calculates the absolute value of the argument
@LN (cell or expression)	Calculates the natural logarithm of the argument
@LOG (cell or expression)	Calculates the base-10 logarithm of the argument
@SQRT (cell or expression)	Calculates the square root of the expression
Financial Functions	
@PV (period payment, rate, number of payments)	Calculates the present value of an annuity at a specified interest rate
@FV (period payment, rate, number of payments)	Calculates the future value of an annuity at a specified interest rate
@PMT (present value, rate, number of payments)	Calculates an annuity (period payment) equivalent to a given present value at a specified interest rate
@NPV (rate, range)	Calculates the net present value of the cash flows in a range at a specified interest rate
Conditional Functions	
@IF (conditional expression, value if true, value if false)	Supplies to a cell a value that depends on whether the conditional expression is true or false
@CHOOSE (pointer value, list of possible values)	Chooses one value in a list of values, based on the pointer value
Date Functions	
@TODAY	Calculates today's date (in days since December 31, 1899)*
@DATE (month, day, year)	Calculates the number of days that have elapsed since the date specified in the argument and December 31, 1899*

*December 31, 1899, serves simply as a fixed reference point. In combination, the TODAY and DATE functions can be used to calculate the number of days past due on invoices or the number of days an account has existed.

Figure 9-9
Spreadsheet Functions. In many spreadsheet packages, functions always start with the @ key. A package may contain over a hundred built-in functions.

through B3. Figure 9-9 provides a listing of useful functions. Several examples of how to use functions are given in Figure 9-10.

When preparing value entries for a cell, you should note that numeric constants, formulas, and functions are often intermixed. By their basic nature, formulas consist of combinations of numeric constants and functions.

Commands and Menus. One of the most powerful features of any spreadsheet package is its command set. Commands enable you to save and print worksheets, copy the contents of one cell into other cells, sort

Figure 9-10
Using functions.
Most functions represent prestored formulas, such as those that compute an average, count up cells, or find maximum or minimum values. The functions shown here, and others, are described in Figure 9-9.

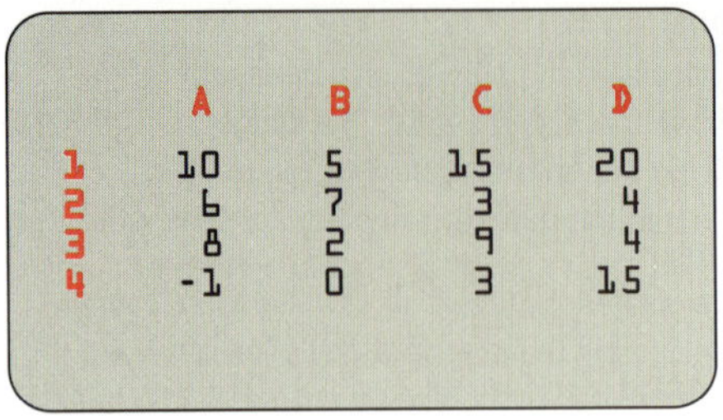

@ MIN (B2..C3) = 2

@ MAX (A1..D4) = 20

@ MAX (A1..D4, 100) = 100

@ AVG (A1..D1) = 12.5

@ AVG (B1..B4, 2) = 4

@ ABS (A4) = 1

@ SUM (A1..D1) = 50

@ SUM (C1..C4) = 30

@ SUM (A1..D4) = 110

@ MIN (A1..D4) = -1

@ SQRT (C3..C3) = 3

@ COUNT (A1..D4) = 16

@ SQRT (@ COUNT (A1..A4)) = 2

@ IF (A4 < 0, 10, 20) = 10

data, erase worksheets, and so forth. Figure 9-11 shows a typical sample of spreadsheet commands. In this subsection, we'll look at a number of general principles governing commands. Later, in the section entitled "Basic Entering and Editing Operations," we'll examine in greater detail some of the types of tasks that can be done through commands.

Spreadsheet packages use a hierarchical series of menus from which users can select commands. The *main menu (command menu)*—usually in the form of a top-of-screen menu bar that appears in the control panel when a special key is depressed—shows the principal command set. Subordinate to each command in the main menu are *submenus* that prompt users for finer and finer levels of detail. On either the main menu or submenus, selections are typically made by moving one of the arrow keys

Figure 9-11
Spreadsheet commands.
In many spreadsheet packages, there are about ten basic commands. Each of these commands, in turn, corresponds to a hierarchy of options.

Command	Explanation
Worksheet	Allows you to perform a variety of operations that affect either the entire worksheet or parts of it. For example, it allows you to change the width of one or more columns and to insert or delete columns or rows.
Range	Allows you to perform operations on a portion of the worksheet.
Copy	Allows you to reproduce any portion of the worksheet in another place on the worksheet.
Move	Lets you relocate any portion of the worksheet in another place on the worksheet.
File	Enables you to access your disk to save, retrieve, or combine worksheets.
Print	Allows you to print all or any portion of your worksheet.
Graph	Enables you to create graphs from your worksheet.
Data	Enables you to sort data, group data, or retrieve records with specific characteristics.
System	Lets you temporarily leave your spreadsheet package in order to issue operating system commands.
Quit	Ends your spreadsheeting session and enables you to return to the operating system.

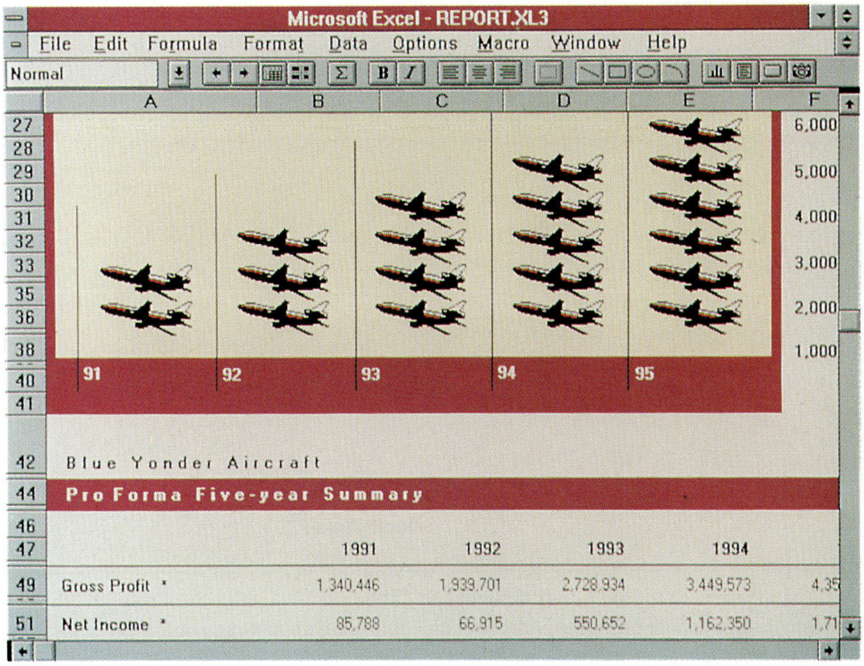

Figure 9-12
Graphical interface.
The current trend in spreadsheet software is toward graphical interfaces, which provide multiple windows and pull-down menus, allow presentation graphics to appear onscreen simultaneously with spreadsheet data, and provide options for scaling worksheets to different sizes.

to the choice and selecting it with the Enter key. As each selection is made by the user, successive submenus are presented onscreen until the spreadsheet package collects enough information to take a specific action.

Invoking spreadsheet commands can be thought of as a process of navigating through a *tree* of choices. Since you can point to the choices on the screen, there is no complicated command syntax to remember. Most packages are set up to enable ordinary users to apply their intuition, without constantly having to leaf through a reference manual. If you select the wrong option, you can, in most cases, easily void the choice and backtrack to where you were before.

Graphical Interfaces. An increasing number of spreadsheet packages are gravitating toward *graphical user interfaces* that sport pull-down menus and pop-up (dialog) boxes for submenus, multitasked windowing environments, mouse pointer control, and simultaneous viewing of spreadsheet and graphical data. Many of these features were pioneered by Microsoft's Excel (see Figure 9-12). *Windowing capabilities*—which enable users to create multiple windows of information within the main screen—vary tremendously among spreadsheet packages. Some packages allow you to create as many as two dozen windows that can be displayed onscreen at the same time and to size windows to your liking. With the success of Excel and with better graphics now available on all of the leading microcomputers, such interfaces are rapidly becoming an industry standard.

Figure 9-13 Entering and editing operations.

(a) Inserting a row. Both inserting and deleting involve moving the cell pointer to the apporopriate position in the worksheet and issuing the proper command.

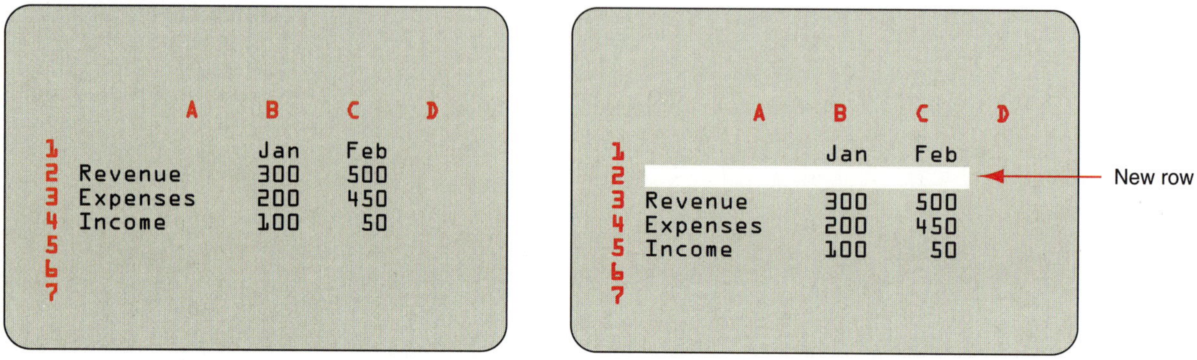

Before insertion After insertion

(b) Copying by relative replication. In most spreadsheet packages, relative replication is the default copy operation.

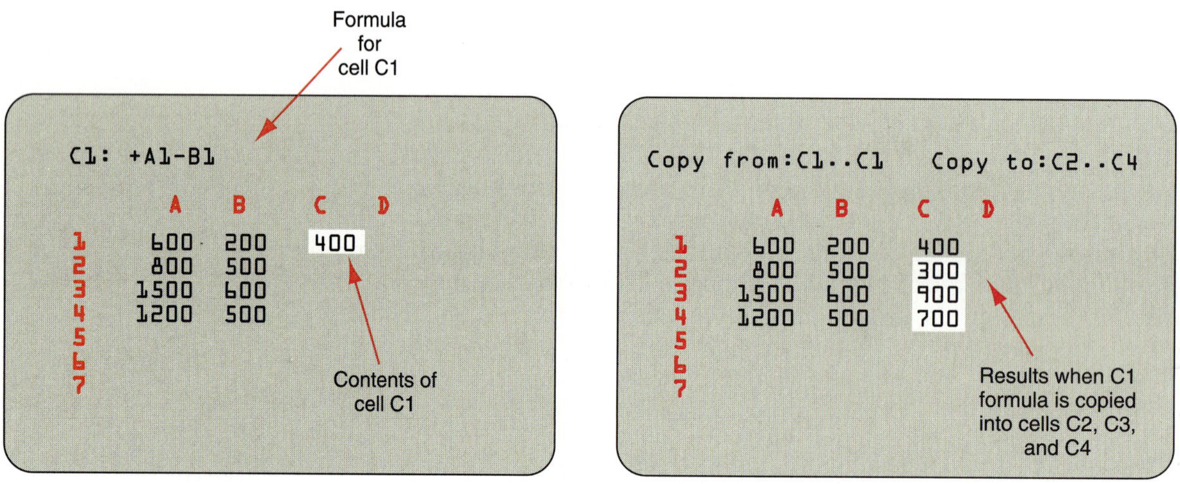

Before copy operation After copy operation

Basic Entering and Editing Operations

Spreadsheet packages have numerous command options that help you enter and edit data. A sampling of the most important of these features follows.

Inserting and Deleting. Virtually all spreadsheet packages allow you to insert a new column or row in a worksheet. Also, you can delete a column or row that you no longer need. Generally, inserting or deleting involves moving the cell pointer to the appropriate position on the worksheet and issuing the proper command. Figure 9-13a illustrates inserting a blank row to make a worksheet more attractive.

Figure 9-13 continued

(c) Copying by absolute replication. Copying by absolute replication involves marking each column and row reference in the cell address with a dollar ($) sign.

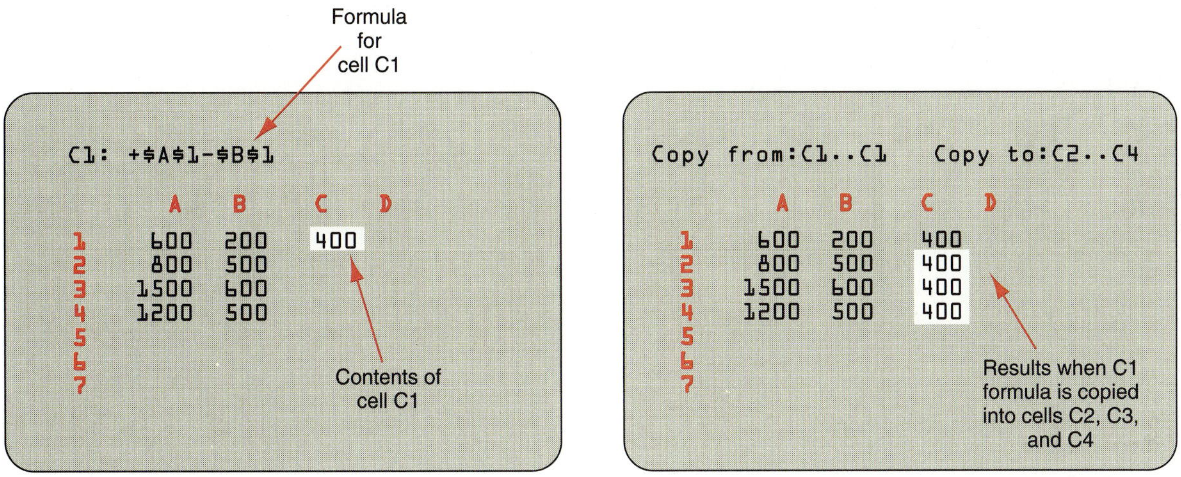

Before copy operation

After copy operation

(d) Copying by mixed replication. Mixed replication involves putting a dollar ($) sign in front of each column or row we wish to fix in place.

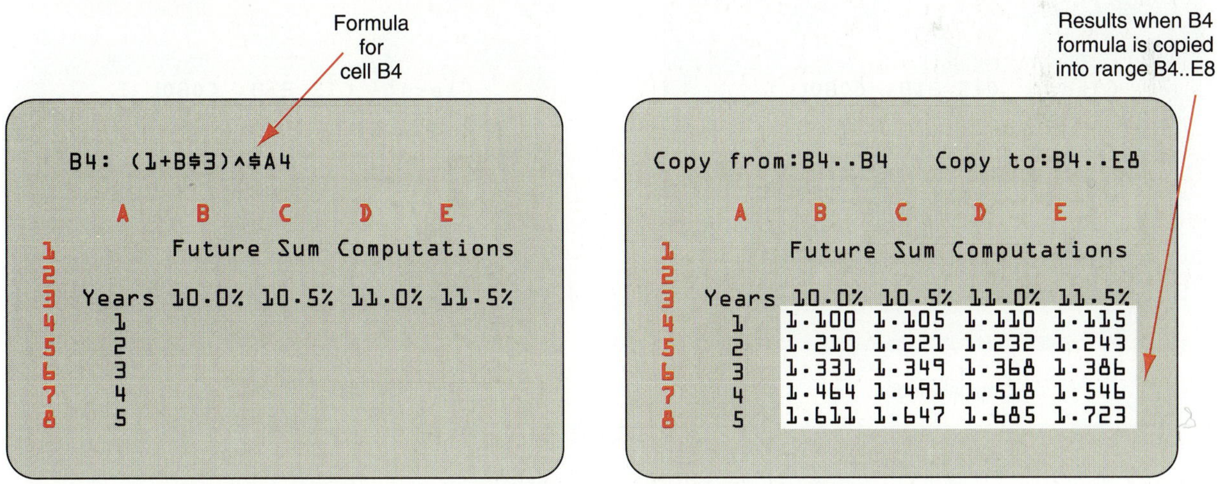

Before copy operation

After copy operation

continued

Copying. Most spreadsheets have a command that enables you to copy the contents of one cell (or several cells) into another cell (or several others). The command usually works by prompting you for a *source range* that contains the data to be copied and a *destination range* that will receive the copied data.

Figure 9-13 continued

(e) Moving a row. When the contents of a block (range) of cells are moved, they are "cut" out of one area of the worksheet and "pasted" into another of identical size.

Before move operation

After move operation

(f) Freezing titles. Freezing titles allows you to keep certain columns or rows of the worksheet in place while you are scrolling to other parts of it.

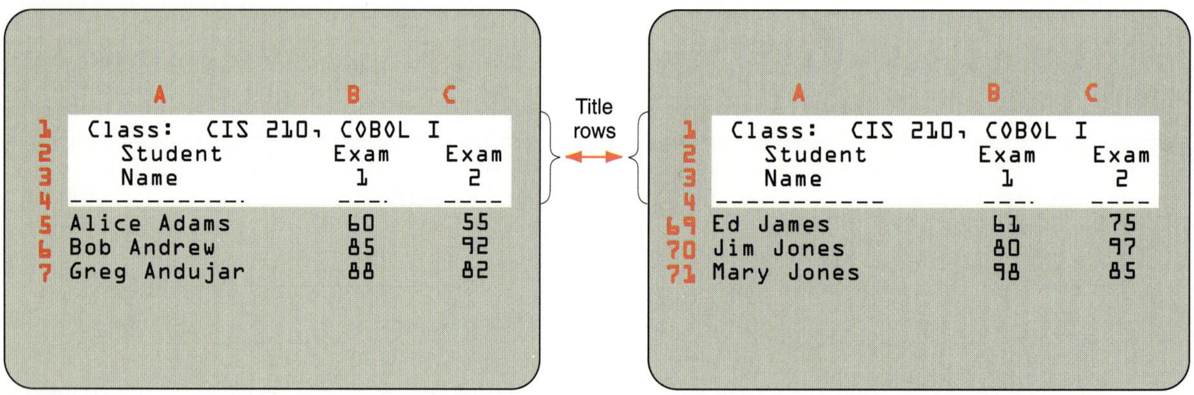

Original window

Scrolled worksheet with frozen titles

If you are copying from cells that contain formulas, you generally will be asked to state whether you want the cell references in the formulas to be "relative," "absolute," or "mixed." These three methods of copying are illustrated in Figures 9-13b, 9-13c, and 9-13d, respectively.

Relative replication. Copying formulas in a source range of cells into a target range of cells relative to the row and column coordinates of the cells in the target range.

□ ***Relative Replication.*** **Relative replication** allows you to copy the contents of a range of cells relative to the row and column coordinates of the destination range. For example, in Figure 9-13b, say that you

Figure 9-13 continued

(g) Using templates. The worksheet at the left contains both the blank template and the formulas to calculate the table amounts at the right (once the user supplies the interest rate, principal, and the number of years).

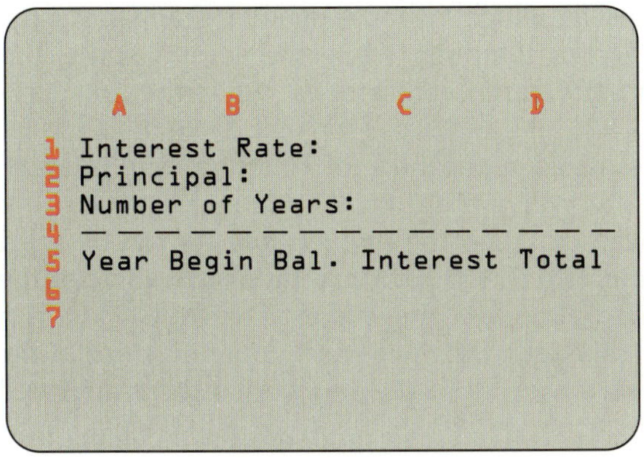

Blank template

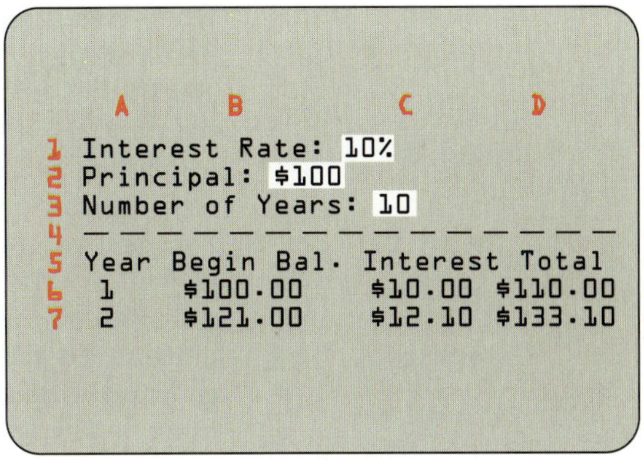

Filled-in template

want the value of each cell in column C to equal the corresponding column A entry minus the corresponding column B entry. In other words, you want

```
C1=A1-B1
C2=A2-B2
C3=A3-B3
C4=A4-B4
```

Generally you can do this by placing the cell pointer at C1 and typing +A1−B1. Then you can copy this formula into cells C2..C4 in the manner illustrated in the figure by specifying relative replication. In many packages, relative replication is the default when you copy, so the specification is implicit.

□ ***Absolute Replication.*** In the previous example, had you asked instead for **absolute replication,** the spreadsheet package would have copied the formula verbatim into all four cells so that each contained the expression +A1−B1 (see Figure 9-13c). Absolute replication is ideal when a certain computation yields a constant value and that constant is to repeat in a range of cells.

Absolute replication. Copying verbatim the contents in one range of cells into another range of cells.

The steps taken to perform absolute replication are exactly like those to perform relative replication in most spreadsheet packages, except for one difference: The formula in the source cell must be written in the form

```
+$A$1-$B$1
```

In other words, dollar signs must be placed before each row and column being referenced.

Mixed replication. Copying formulas in one range of cells into another range, while varying some cell references and leaving others constant.

☐ *Mixed Replication.* Many spreadsheet packages also allow **mixed replication**—a combination of absolute and relative replication—in which a row value can be kept constant while a column value is allowed to vary (or vice versa). Mixed replication is especially useful when handling formulas in which two parameters change. As the first parameter varies across columns (while the second stays constant), the second parameter varies across rows (while the first stays constant).

Figure 9-13d shows mixed replication for compounding interest. Note that interest rate and years are the two parameters in cell B4. For each column, we want to keep the interest rate (in row 3) fixed as we vary the year from 1 to 5. For each row, we want to keep the year (in column A) fixed as we vary the interest rate from 10 to 11.5 percent. To allow us to mix addresses, we put a $ sign in front of the coordinate that we want to fix; thus, the formula in the source cell must be written as

```
(1+B$3)^$A4
```

Moving. "Cutting and pasting" often is just as important in developing worksheets as it is in creating word-processed documents. Almost all spreadsheet packages enable you to move any row or column into another row or column position on the worksheet. As with the Copy command, you will need to specify a source range (the range you're moving from) and a destination range (the range you're moving to).

For example, suppose you decide to move row 5 into the row 2 position, as in Figure 9-13e. When moving, the software automatically makes all cell references point to the new worksheet locations. If your spreadsheet package also lets you cut and paste larger areas, as most do, you will be able to move, say, a contiguous 20-by-40 block of cells from one part of the worksheet to another.

Formatting Values. Because spreadsheets are particularly useful for preparing financial schedules, it follows that many of the worksheet cells will contain values that represent monetary amounts. Most packages enable you to quickly put dollar signs, commas, and decimal points into these values (for example, to change 90000 to $90,000.00). Generally, all you have to do is identify the range of cells that you want edited and select a Currency option that automatically inserts the proper symbols in the proper places. Adding percent signs (%) usually is an equally straightforward process.

Selecting Column Widths. Most packages allow you to change the width of columns on the worksheet. You can assign widths to each column individually, or you can select only a single, global width that applies to all columns. Many spreadsheet packages also have a spillover feature, which permits particularly long labels to spill over into adjacent columns, provided that those cells are empty.

Freezing Titles. Most spreadsheet packages have a Titles feature that allows you to keep a portion of the worksheet frozen in place on the screen when you are scrolling the rest of the worksheet. For example, if we used the Titles feature to freeze the first four rows of Figure 9-13f, we could use the down arrow key or PgDn key to scroll through data in the worksheet while the titles remained on the screen. When you freeze rows, you are working with a horizontally split screen. You can also freeze columns, resulting in a vertically split screen. You usually also have the option of freezing certain rows and certain columns at the same time.

Using Templates. A **template** is a worksheet in which rows and columns are prelabeled and many cells already contain formulas. Only the data are missing. Thus, the work involved in setting up the worksheet has already been done, leaving you more time to enter and analyze data. A template is shown in Figure 9-13g. In many spreadsheet packages, it is also possible to protect cells, such as those that contain the template's labels and formulas.

Template.
A prelabeled onscreen form that requires only that the operator fill in a limited number of input values.

Advanced Features

In addition to the basic operations we've just covered, many of the leading spreadsheet packages offer a rich variety of advanced features. In some cases, the spreadsheet package itself contains these features; in other cases, you have to buy the features from an aftermarket vendor that specializes in add-on routines.

Four features that advanced spreadsheet users find useful are data management, macro facilities, multidimensional spreadsheets, and presentation graphics. Here we discuss the first three features and defer discussing presentation graphics until the last section of the chapter.

Data Management. Most spreadsheets contain a facility for managing data. Two popular features in most spreadsheet programs' data management toolkits are sorting and searching (information retrieval).

- ***Sorting.*** The ability to sort is a handy feature in almost any type of business software package. With a word processor, sorting enables you to prepare alphabetical listings of names as well as indexes, directories, and glossaries. With a spreadsheet package, you might find a sort facility handy for preparing phone and office directories, ordered listings of overdue accounts, and reports identifying fast-moving or high-selling products. Most spreadsheet packages allow you to sort on more than one field.

  Many teachers use the spreadsheet's sort feature to keep grade books on students. Such a grade book can be maintained throughout the term in alphabetical order by student name, and at the end of the term, student records can be sorted according to final averages. Many spreadsheet packages also contain a *data distribution facility* so that a

Figure 9-14
Macro facility.
This 1-2-3 macro, named C, lets you set a column width to 20 characters by merely depressing the Alt key and hitting the C key.

teacher can, among other things, quickly find the number of students with averages between 90–100, 80–89, 70–79, and so on.

- *Searching.* Often each row in a worksheet represents some type of record. For example, if the worksheet stores company records, each row might contain a company name, a complete mailing address, a phone number, an employee record (see Figure 9-13e), and so on. If the worksheet is large (many can store thousands of records), it's handy to have a feature that will automatically extract records for you based on search criteria that you specify. For instance, you may wish to get a list of companies in Philadelphia, the address of Kane Publications, or a list of top employees. A search facility will enable you to gather this information rapidly and accurately.

Macro Facility. One of the things you'll appreciate about spreadsheet packages is that they let you do a great deal of information processing without having to know how to program. However, if you do have the talent to write programs and if the spreadsheet package you are using has a macro facility, you can really put your worksheets into high gear.

Macro.
A predetermined series of keystrokes or commands that can be invoked by a single keystroke or command.

A macro facility enables you to write programs within your worksheet. Each **macro** is, in fact, a program. It is identified by a name and consists of a series of keystrokes that the spreadsheet package executes every time you invoke the macro. In 1-2-3 and a number of other spreadsheet packages, for example, the macro shown in Figure 9-14 lets you automatically set column widths to 20 characters.

When you depress the Alt key followed by the name of the macro (C), seven keystrokes (/WCS20~) are automatically made for you. Roughly translated, these keystrokes mean invoke the command menu (/), pick the worksheet command (W) off of this menu, select the column-width option (C), choose the set option (S), set the column width to 20 characters (20), and hit the Return key (~).

Macros often are written in contiguous worksheet cells, as Figure 9-14 shows. Frequently the macro is written in a remote set of cells so it does not interfere with worksheet labels and values that will be output later. Also, you will want to place the macro far away from the main part of the worksheet so that it doesn't get erased when you are deleting rows or columns. It's a good idea to document the macro, as shown in cell AC101, so you can remember later what it is supposed to do.

If you are really skilled at writing macros, you can write long programs and even programs that loop. Macros can also be used to accept inputs by the operator of the spreadsheet package and to summon menu screens.

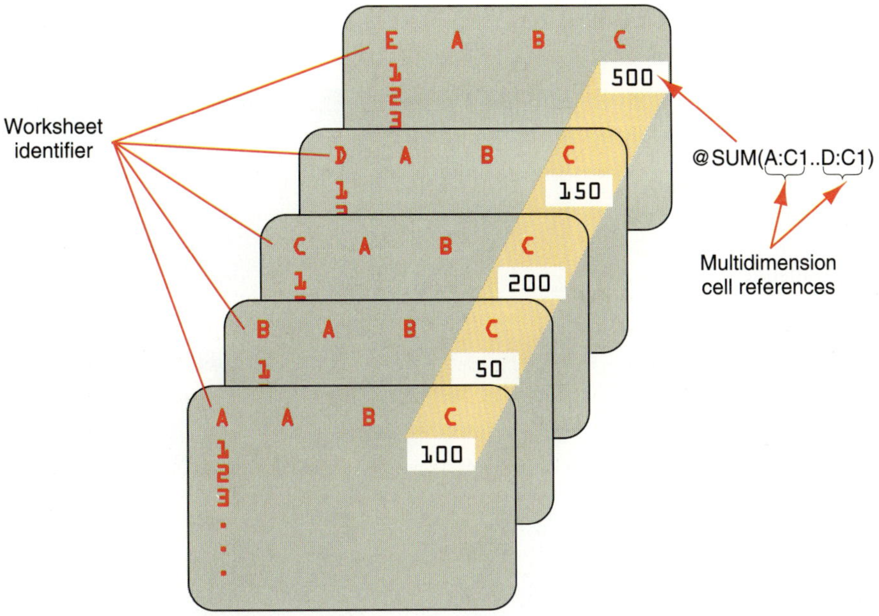

Figure 9-15 Multidimensional spreadsheet capability. Each worksheet in a multidimensional system is identified by the letter identifier in its upper left-hand corner. Cell references must include this identifier when several worksheets are being interrelated, as they are here to arrive at the sum in worksheet E.

Multidimensional Spreadsheets. In many cases, it is easier and more practical to create several interrelated worksheets than to cram all of your data into a single worksheet or to develop several independent worksheets. For instance, suppose you have four worksheets with sales data, each one pertaining to a different quarter of the year. Rather than have one busy worksheet or four independent worksheets, it is often easier to integrate the worksheets into a single system, as shown in Figure 9-15.

In the figure, the worksheet for first-quarter sales is referred to as worksheet A, the worksheet for second-quarter sales as worksheet B, and so on. In this three-dimensional (3-D) application, each cell in each worksheet has three coordinates. For instance, the cell in column A, row 1 of the fourth worksheet is referred to as cell D:A1 (because D is the fourth letter of the alphabet).

When worksheets are represented in a systematic way, as illustrated in Figure 9-15, users can easily specify both the relationships that apply among rows and columns of a single worksheet and the relationships that apply over the set of worksheets. So, for instance, you could create a fifth worksheet (representing a summary for the year) and specify that the cells in this worksheet are to be calculated by summing respective cells in worksheets A through D (representing the four quarters), as shown in the figure. You could even go so far as to create additional worksheets, such as one that computed a trend from the first four worksheets and reported the results.

Multidimensional spreadsheet. A program package that allows the construction of worksheets in which cells are referenced by more than two coordinates.

Spreadsheet packages that allow you to develop a system of worksheets in this way, with each worksheet having more than two coordinates to each cell, are often referred to as **multidimensional spreadsheets.**

Feature 9-2

Tax Software

Can It Make Doing Taxes Less Taxing?

Once the electronic spreadsheet was invented, it seemed inevitable that income-tax-preparation software would follow. Tax preparation is almost the perfect applications area for spreadsheets, because most of the work involved requires a high volume of simple, repetitive calculations; the transferring of numbers from line to line; and table lookups. Since spreadsheets are beginning their third decade of use, it is not surprising that a wide range of tax-preparation software has entered the marketplace.

Tax-preparation software is available as stand-alone programs or as add-ons that work with some of the more popular spreadsheet products (such as Lotus 1-2-3 or Microsoft Excel). Most stand-alone products are essentially just specialized, stripped-down spreadsheets.

One popular application served by tax software is tax planning. You are usually asked to enter several critical numbers off of last year's return, and the software projects your income taxes based on this year's tax tables. You can also do some what-if analysis, such as inputting this year's income in place of last year's, changing your IRA deduction, or checking the ramifications of some year-end stock selling. At best, you will get a ballpark estimate of your total tax bite for the past year, but using the tax software in this way also often uncovers some creative ways to lessen your tax burden.

Tax software. Packages let a user fill out tax returns onscreen, and they will automatically revise returns when changes are made.

Most of the leading spreadsheet packages now have a multidimensionality feature. Such a feature allows a set of worksheets to be read like an "electronic book," with each page (worksheet) capable of providing additional information, finer detail, or a consolidated summary of those worksheets that precede it.

Add-On Packages. During the last decade or so, a multimillion-dollar aftermarket industry has sprouted up to meet the continuing demands of spreadsheet users. The companies composing this industry make and sell **add-on packages**—utilities that enhance (or "add value" to) the major spreadsheet programs in the market, making them more powerful, easier to use, more flexible, and so forth. If you need your spreadsheet package to do something it isn't currently equipped to do, and if the package is widely used, chances are there's an aftermarket vendor that has just the feature you need available as an add-on package.

Add-on package. A software package that supplements the activities of a larger software package, either by providing new functions or improving on already existing functions.

Undeniably, the most important application for tax software is tax preparation. Several types of programs are available.

Some programs supply onscreen forms that are accurate facsimiles of those provided by the Internal Revenue Service (IRS). As you fill out the forms onscreen (see the figure), the spreadsheet feature in the package computes totals for you, looks up information in tax or rebate tables, and transfers numbers from ancillary schedules onto Form 1040. The spreadsheet feature also allows you to perform various types of what-if analysis to see how different numbers affect the bottom line of your return. Many packages allow you to jump freely from form to form as you are preparing your taxes, and a number of them do their own cross-checking to ensure that any numbers you provide are consistent with those already there. Some packages even have built-in instruction booklets, which are available as onscreen "help aids" as soon as you hit a special key or two.

Although professional tax preparers prefer onscreen forms that look like the official IRS ones, novices often prefer something simpler. To accommodate such users, there are tax packages that go through the tax-preparation process by asking the operator a graduated series of straightforward questions. At the end of the question-and-answer session, completed tax forms are output.

Printed output is available by any of several methods. If the package you use works with IRS form facsimiles and you have a laser printer, you can get the printer to create both the forms and the numbers on it. Some packages will output just the numbers on the form, but when you photocopy the outputted pages face to face with transparent overlays of the forms, you will produce filled-in forms that are suitable for submission. For professional tax accountants, some firms produce preprinted forms on fan-fold paper. When these forms are used in conjunction with a program that prints only numbers, filled-in forms result. Still another approach, of course, is transferring the numbers by hand from the screen onto the forms that you were sent by the IRS. Although this approach is prone to copying errors, it has the undeniable advantages of being straightforward and inexpensive.

Many tax software packages are available for under $100. Because tax laws change annually, a package is good only for a year. Many vendors of tax software enable people who have bought their products once to obtain updates at a reduced charge.

Although tax software can be extremely useful, especially to those in the business of tax accounting, spreadsheet users can themselves develop some simple worksheets to automate the tax-preparation process.

The number of add-on products available for the leading spreadsheet packages is enormous. Funk Software's Sideways (see Figure 9-16), a print utility that enables worksheets with lots of columns to be printed lengthwise on standard letter-sized paper, was one of the earliest add-on packages for spreadsheets. It is still one of the most popular. Personics Corporation's SeeMORE, another add-on package, can push more of a worksheet onto the screen by converting the characters on the display into one of four size modes—normal, medium, small, or tiny. The tiny mode can display up to 170 characters in 53 rows, depending on the graphics standard in use.

Figure 9-16
Spreadsheet utilities.
Spreadsheet aftermarket products make up a multimillion-dollar industry. Shown here is Funk Software's Sideways, which lets you print extra-long worksheets sideways.

Aftermarket vendors frequently sell templates that can be used with the leading spreadsheet programs. One of the most common examples is the federal income tax forms that all wage earners fill out each year (see Feature 9-2, "Tax Software"). Many tax-form templates also come equipped with built-in calculators, enabling them to be operated independently of any spreadsheet package. Today, income tax returns are com-

Figure 9-17 Types of presentation graphics.
Any type of graphical image that enhances the impact of information as it is shown to people is a presentation graphic. Although packages vary with respect to the number and type of presentation graphics they produce, most allow you to create simple bar, pie, and line charts.

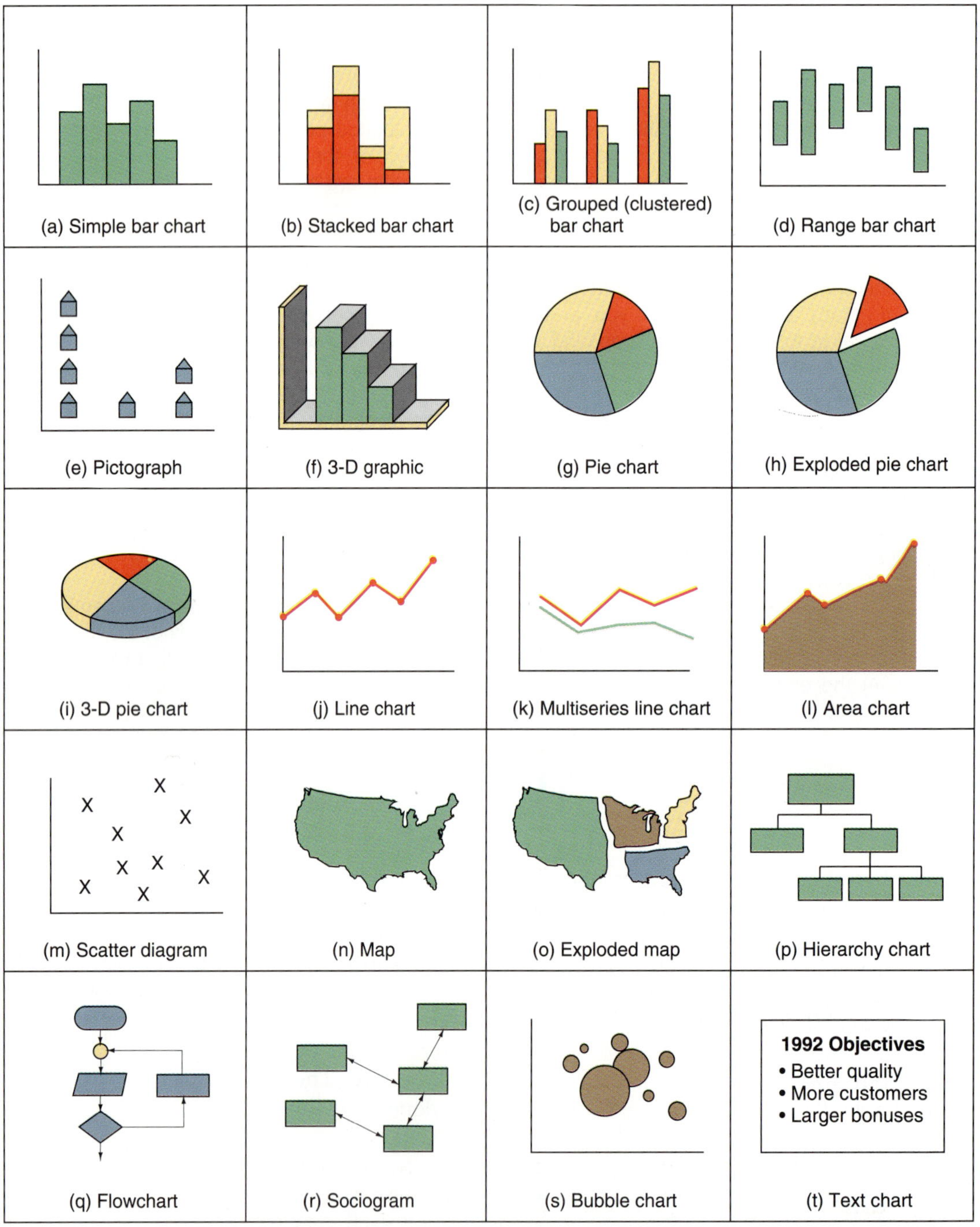

monly submitted on diskettes, and it is expected that electronic filing of returns will continue to become more popular in future years.

Presentation Graphics

Presentation graphics software enables you to draw bar charts, pie charts, and similar graphics to present data to others in an informative or convincing way (see Figure 9-17). Often a person can get the point suggested by the data much more quickly by looking at a presentation graphic than by reading text-based output with the same information content.

Presentation graphics software.
A program package used to prepare line charts, bar charts, pie charts, and other information-intensive images.

Types of Packages

A variety of presentation graphics packages exist in the marketplace. Most of them fall into one of two classes: dedicated presentation graphics packages and presentation graphics packages that are bundled (integrated) with spreadsheet software.

Dedicated Packages. Dedicated packages provide the most powerful types of graphics features—for instance, a wider selection of texturing patterns (such as solid, speckled, and cross-hatched patterns), legend fonts, graph types, and device drivers. Many also come with clip art libraries and slide sorters and enable you to interface with painting/drawing software routines to dress up the graphs you create (see Figure 9-18 and Window 5). In short, if your presentation graphics needs are extensive, a dedicated package is more likely to contain the types of features you require.

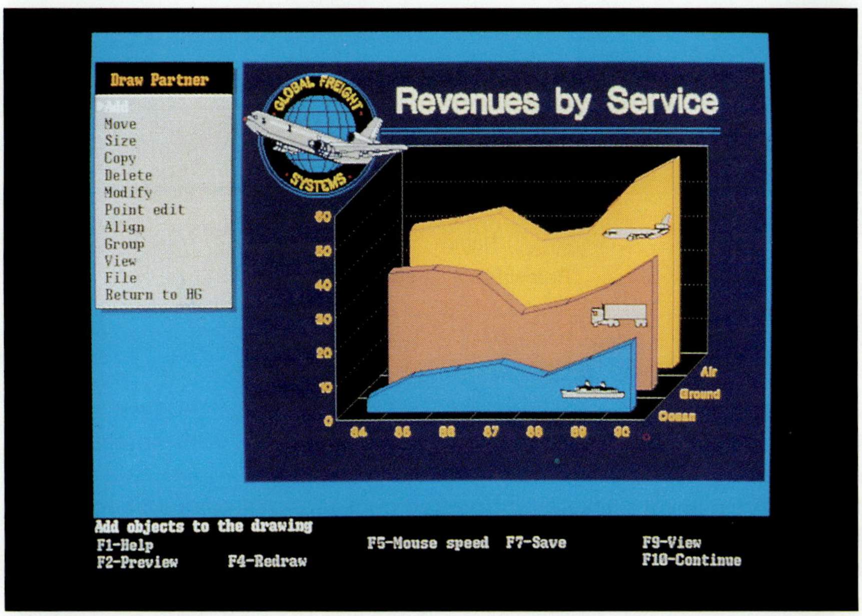

Figure 9-18
Creating area charts with a dedicated package.
Dedicated packages such as Harvard Graphics enable users to create a wide variety of color and three-dimensional charts with logos and clip art.

Figure 9-19 Creating a bar chart with an integrated package.
Integrated packages enable you to create graphs simply by describing the type of graph you want, pointing to the worksheet data that are to be graphed, and choosing colors and titles. The declarations in the upper right are the principal information you need to supply the spreadsheet package to produce the graph shown.

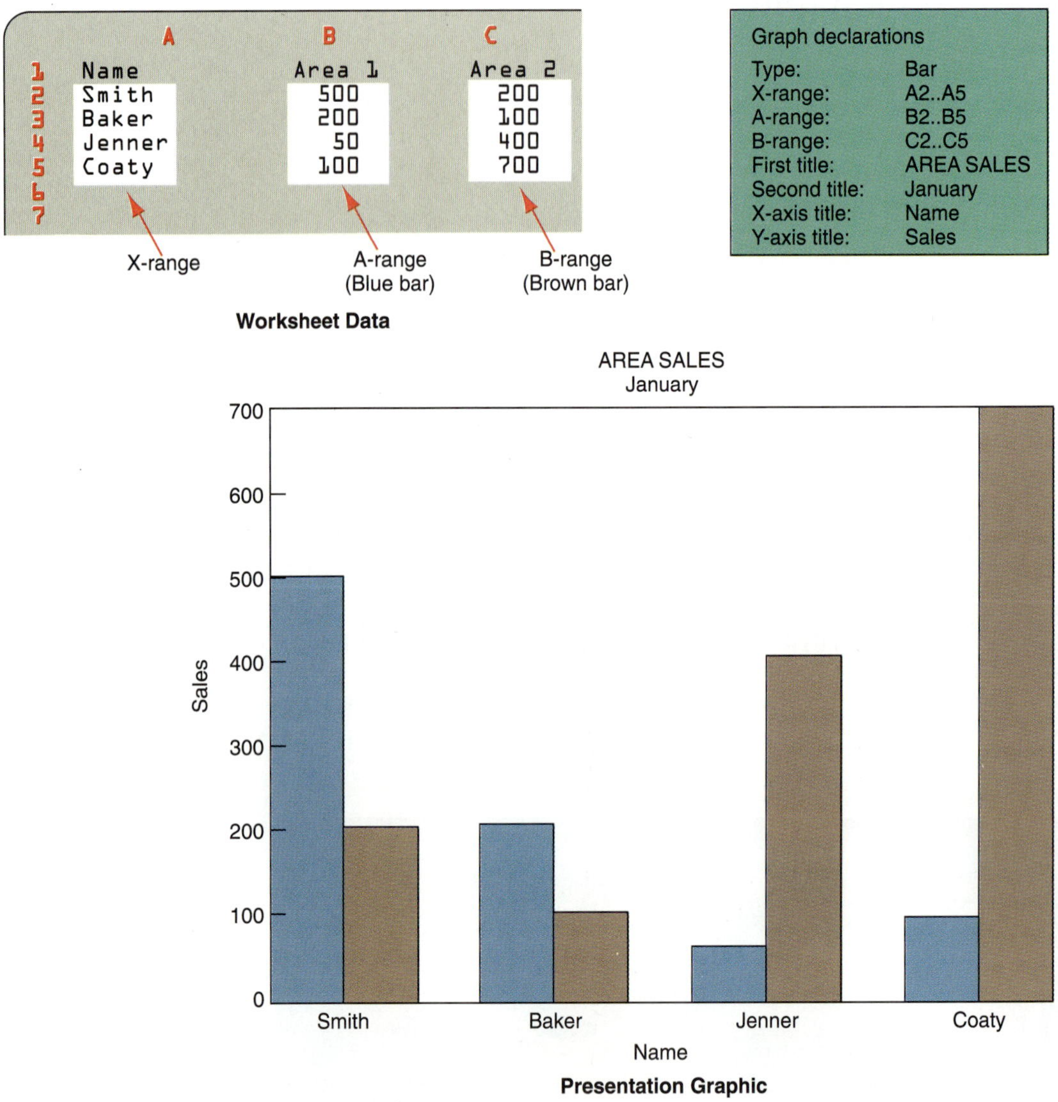

Integrated Packages. Unfortunately, dedicated packages lack some of the calculation and data-modeling features available with spreadsheets, so you either have to type data directly into them or import data to them from a spreadsheet package. Integrated packages overcome this limitation by integrating both functions into a single product (see Figure 9-19). Integrated packages are ideal for users who require the strong data manipulation or information processing capability that a spreadsheet package affords and whose presentation graphics needs are relatively modest.

Tomorrow

Intelligent Graphics

For Users Lacking Time or Expertise

To update for the computer era a phrase from H. L. Mencken, "No software vendor ever went broke by underestimating the capabilities of the average user." While presentation graphics packages of today offer a variety of sophisticated charting capabilities, many of them lack built-in intelligence features that make it easier for relatively unsophisticated users to create visuals. But this need will not go unrecognized, and, in the near future, we are likely to see the rise of intelligent presentation graphics packages.

Intelligent presentation graphics packages will strongly appeal to the user who is in a rush and to the user who has few graphic design skills. Intelligent packages will make decisions for and recommendations to these users, who can choose to accept or to override them. Features that these packages will offer include the following.

Automatic Chart Selection. Many users are not skilled at choosing the right chart type to present data. An intelligent package will ask the user questions about the target audience and the data to be graphed. With these details out of the way, it will then automatically create the type of presentation visual that best depicts the data under consideration. In fact, several visuals may be prepared, allowing the user to select the most appropriate one. The package will also have a modification feature that lets users point to any graph elements they want changed and correct them manually.

Automatic Styling. Styling involves such things as choosing colors, choosing fonts for titles and legends, balancing graphic elements visually, and scaling the axes and elements appropriately. A graphics artist may have the wherewithal to decide which colors out of a palette of 256,000 are most appropriate, but the average user does not. An intelligent graphics package will automatically choose effective, compatible colors for visuals. It will also be programmed not to make "rookie" design mistakes such as putting too many colors into a visual or making too many pie slices in a pie chart. In terms of color and font selection, this package of the future will make some assumptions based on the official corporate colors and the audience to which the presentation is targeted. For instance, if the corporate color is blue, the package may suggest a graduated blue background for each visual. Or, if a presentation is being made to top executives, the font chosen may be the type that one typically sees in an annual report.

Making design decisions. Intelligent graphics will help ordinary users make their point effectively.

Automatic Updates. Often, managers make the same types of presentations over and over again. For instance, a presentation made in February might show several pie charts based on January data; in March, the pie charts in the presentation would instead reflect what took place in February; and so on. In cases in which such repetitive presentations must be made, the intelligent package would allow the user to link into a spreadsheet containing the data and—after it is instructed what to do—would automatically make updates to visuals according to a predetermined schedule or on demand. As local area networks (LANs) become more commonplace, this feature will allow users on the network to view new graphs at their workstations as soon as a body of data has changed. In sports broadcasting, where visuals need to be updated as a game progresses, new charts could be calculated as soon as new data were entered into the system. These charts would then be immediately available to telecasters and analysts in the broadcast booth.

One of the features that probably will be incorporated into future presentation graphics packages—as the chapter Tomorrow box explains—is intelligence. Among other things, this feature will assist users who are not skilled in design matters to create professional-looking presentations.

Summary and Key Terms

Two useful types of program packages for summarizing data so that they make sense to others are spreadsheets and presentation graphics software.

Spreadsheets. An **electronic spreadsheet** package produces computerized counterparts to the ruled, ledger-style worksheets with which accountants frequently work. Spreadsheets first came to public notice in the late 1970s when a product named VisiCalc was developed. VisiCalc quickly convinced businesspeople of the usefulness of personal computers.

In electronic spreadsheets, the display screen is viewed as a *window* looking in on a big grid, called a **worksheet.** The worksheet consists of *rows* and *columns* that intersect to form **cells,** each of which can be accessed through a **cell address**. Columns are labeled by letters, and rows are labeled by numbers, so, for instance, cell (cell address) B3 is located at the intersection of the second column and third row.

Spreadsheet software often divides the screen into two principal areas. The worksheet itself is displayed in the **worksheet area,** or **window area.** The **control panel** is the area of the screen where users perform tasks such as preparing text (called *labels*) or numbers (called *values*) that are to be placed in the worksheet cells. A **label** is a cell entry that cannot be manipulated mathematically, whereas a **value** is an entry that can. The control panel also shows you the cell to which you are currently pointing, called the **current cell.** It is also the area used to display commands.

Most spreadsheet packages offer two pointing mechanisms: a cursor and a cell pointer (or highlight). The **cursor** is associated with the control panel, pointing to the place in that area where the next character typed in by the user will appear. The **cell pointer** (or **highlight**) is associated with the worksheet area, pointing to the current cell.

Spreadsheet packages are particularly valuable because they provide a **recalculation feature**—that is, they can perform recalculations in seconds that would require several hours to do manually or by writing a program in a regular programming language. It's this recalculation feature that makes spreadsheets so popular.

A contiguous, rectangular block of cells is called a **range.** A range can be typed in explicitly or pointed to on the screen.

Most spreadsheet packages use a hierarchical series of menus from which users can select commands. The *main menu* (or *command menu*) shows the principal command set, while *submenus* prompt users for finer and finer levels of detail.

Spreadsheet packages have numerous features to aid in entering and editing data. Some of the basic entering and editing operations include inserting and deleting rows or columns, moving or copying the contents of cells from one part of the worksheet to another (through **relative replication, absolute replication,** or **mixed replication**), formatting dollar amounts and other values, selecting column widths, and freezing titles.

Also, many packages have a **template** feature that permits the creation, saving, and protection of worksheets that have all of their rows and columns prelabeled, so that only the data need to be filled in.

A *data management* feature provides users with a variety of file-handling capabilities, including the ability to *search* for records with specific characteristics and to *sort* records on one or more fields.

A macro facility enables you to write programs within your worksheet. Each **macro** is, in fact, a program. It consists of a series of keystrokes that the spreadsheet package executes every time you invoke the macro.

Spreadsheet packages that allow you to develop worksheets with more than two cell dimensions are called **multidimensional spreadsheets.** A multidimensional feature allows a set of worksheets to be read like an "electronic book," with each page (worksheet) capable of adding detail to the one that precedes it.

During the last decade or so, a vigorous aftermarket industry has sprouted up to meet the continuing demands of spreadsheet users. The companies composing this industry make and sell **add-on packages**—utilities that enhance the major spreadsheet programs in the market. These packages allow you to print worksheets sideways, compress numbers on the screen so that you can see more of your worksheets, and so on.

Presentation Graphics. **Presentation graphics software** lets you draw bar charts, pie charts, and the like to present information to others in a visual, easily understandable way. Presentation graphics packages are either dedicated or integrated. *Dedicated* packages provide the most sophisticated types of graphing capabilities, whereas *integrated* packages consist of modest graphics routines that support a particular spreadsheet.

Review Exercises

Fill-in Questions

1. The principle behind electronic spreadsheets involves viewing the display screen as a(n) ______________ looking in on a big grid, called a(n) ______________.
2. Most spreadsheet packages provide two pointing mechanisms: a(n) ______________ and a(n) ______________.
3. Worksheet entries are created and edited in the ______________.
4. Three types of copying operations available in many spreadsheet packages are ______________, ______________, and ______________ replication.
5. A worksheet in which all rows and columns are prelabeled and formulas are supplied is called a(n) ______________.
6. The spreadsheet feature that allows users to embed small programs in a worksheet is called a(n) ______________ facility.

7. ______________ packages are spreadsheet utilities commonly sold by aftermarket vendors.
8. Most presentation graphics packages fall into one of two categories: ______________ packages and ______________ packages.

Matching Questions

Match each term with the description that fits best.

a. `+B1-B2*C2`
b. `@SUM`
c. `D4`
d. `JOHN SMITH`
e. `200`
f. `F18..F28`

_____ 1. A label.
_____ 2. A range.
_____ 3. A numeric constant.
_____ 4. A formula.
_____ 5. A cell address.
_____ 6. A function.

Discussion Questions

1. What purposes are served by electronic spreadsheets?
2. What is the difference between a label and a value?
3. What purpose does a range serve?
4. What are the differences between relative, absolute, and mixed replication?
5. Of what use is a template to users of spreadsheet software?
6. What does a spreadsheet's macro facility allow you to do?
7. What types of graphical images can you construct with presentation graphics software?
8. What is the difference between a dedicated and an integrated presentation graphics package?

Critical Thinking Questions

1. Is the average spreadsheet user actually "programming" when preparing a worksheet? Defend your response.
2. You need a plotter for your microcomputer system and want to spend no more than $500. You will use the plotter to prepare simple color graphs of bar charts, pie charts, and line charts. Some calls to local computer stores reveal that you can get about five or six product demonstrations. What questions should you get answered during these demonstrations?
3. Spreadsheets, oddly enough, evolved from word processors. What similarities are there between these two types of software packages?
4. Comment on this statement: "Nobody should graduate from a business school today without learning how to use a spreadsheet package."
5. Filing income-tax returns electronically (see Feature 9-2) has both advantages and disadvantages. Can you identify any of these?

Window 5

Creating Presentation Graphics

A Picture Is Worth a Thousand Words

Presentation graphics involves the use of computer graphics techniques to present information to others in a useful and interesting way. In this window we look at some techniques used by dedicated presentation graphics packages to create effective bar, pie, line, and text charts. Most of these packages go well beyond spreadsheets in their graphics-generating capabilities.

1. A full-color, three-dimensional grouped (clustered) bar chart. Many dedicated graphics packages enable you to put grid lines on graphs, embed library or custom work art, and create attractive titles.

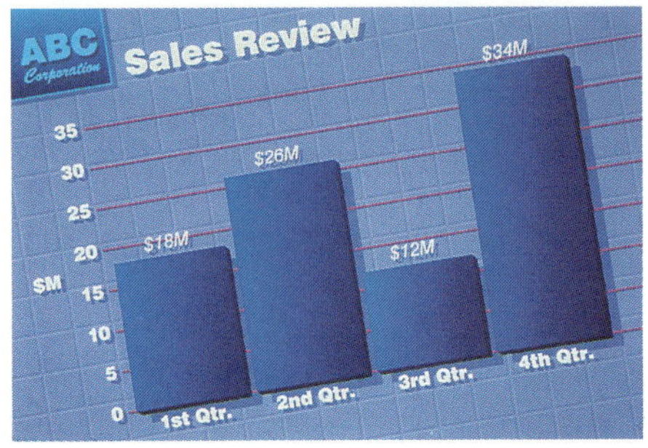

3

2

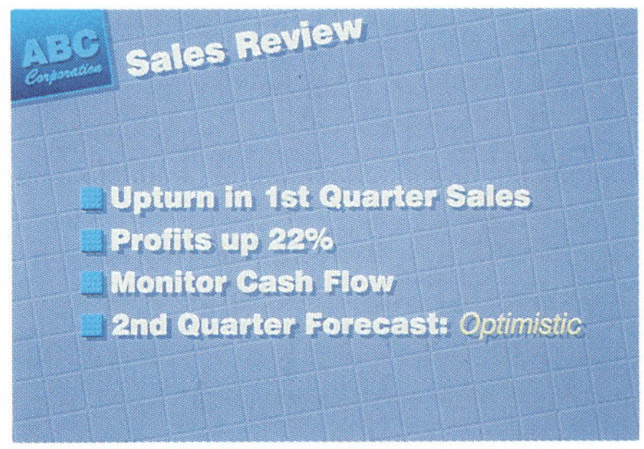

4

2–4. A presentation often consists of a series of slides that must have a consistent background or logo format. Dedicated packages enable you to create a "master slide" containing this format and to store it in a file. To prepare the series of three slides shown here, you simply summon the master slide three separate times, each time overlaying new information onto it.

5

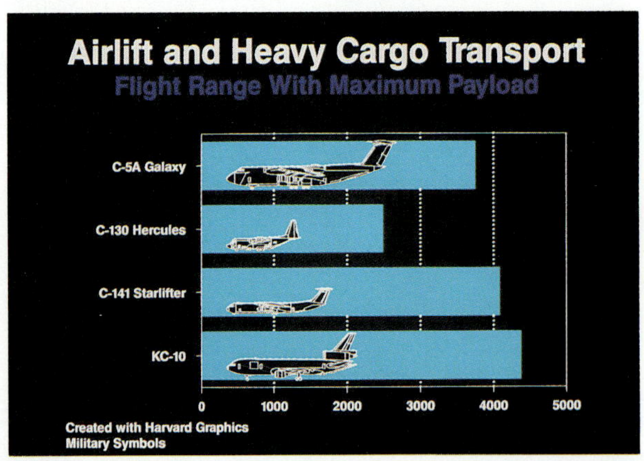

6

5, 6. Many dedicated packages have extensive clip-art libraries containing small pieces of ready-to-use art. Any art piece can be resized electronically and selectively placed on the chart being created.

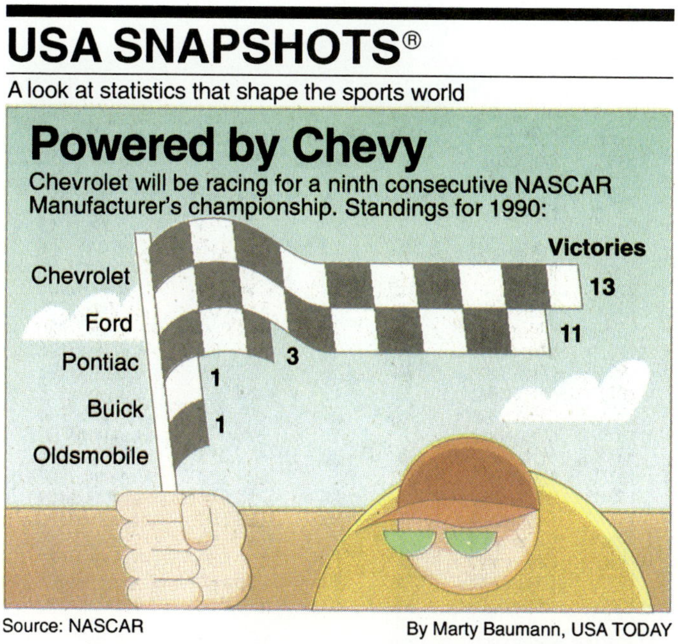

7

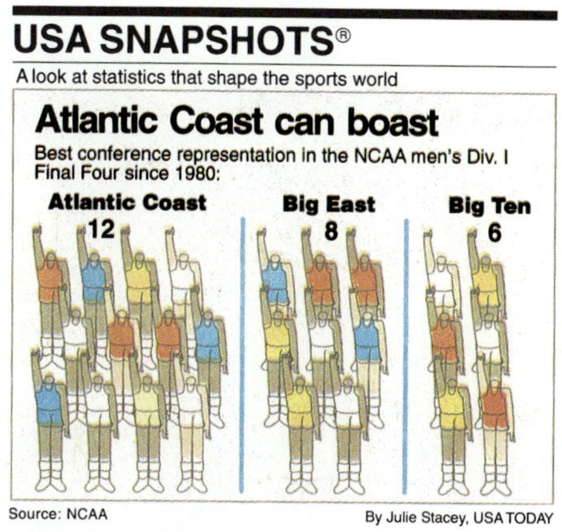

8

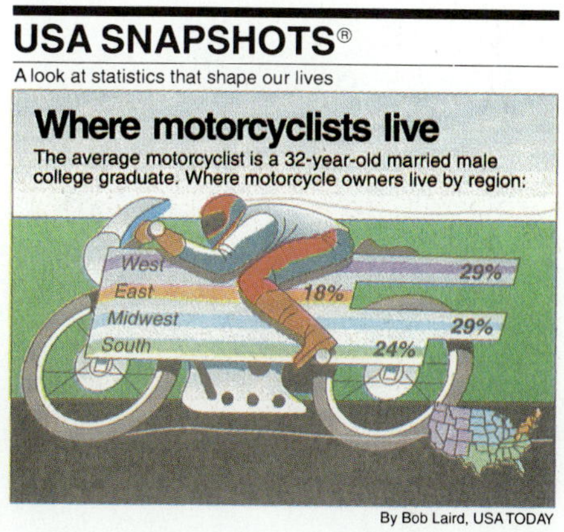

9

7–9. If you have an illustration software package available, you can completely customize your presentation graphics outputs. Some of the most creative and familiar uses of such presentation graphics are found in the daily newspaper *USA Today*. Shown here are several examples of bar charts, the most frequently observed type of visual. All of these bar charts were produced on a Macintosh computer.

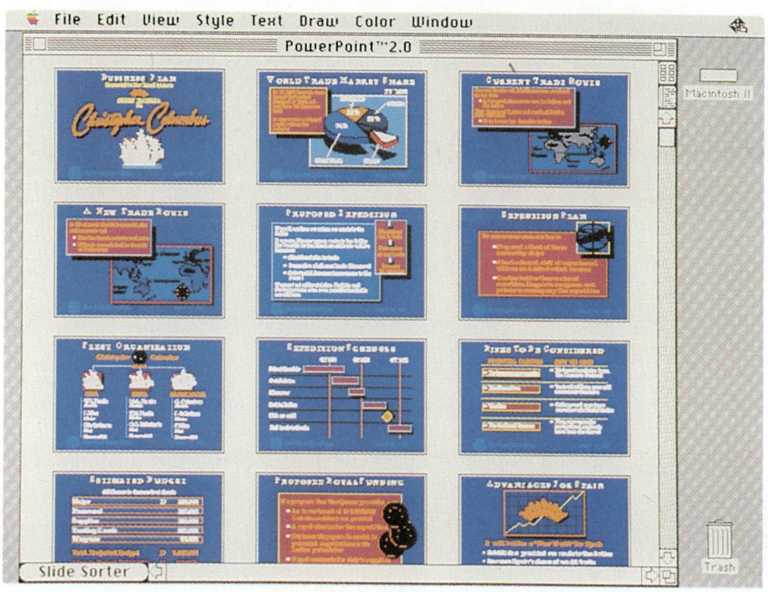

10

10. Slide shows are sometimes completely electronic, without hard copies ever being made of the slide images. When this is the case, it helps to have a slide sorter, such as the one shown here, which enables you to see miniature slide images onscreen and to arrange them (say, by selecting and dragging them with a mouse) in the correct order.

Have you wondered how computers keep track of the thousands of facts needed to assemble parts correctly, build skyscrapers so they meet specifications, and run complicated businesses? Often, it's through the use of data management software, which you'll be reading about in this chapter.

10

File Managers and Database Management Systems

Outline

Learning Objectives

After completing this chapter, you will be able to:

1. Describe what file managers can do and how they work.
2. Explain what database management systems are and how they differ from file managers.
3. Identify some of the strategies used for database management on both large and small computer systems.
4. Identify the advantages and disadvantages of database management.
5. Appreciate the emerging importance of multimedia data management.

Overview

People often need to summon large amounts of data rapidly. An airline agent on the phone to a client may need to search through mounds of data quickly to find the lowest-cost flight path from Tucson to Toronto two weeks hence. The registrar of a university may have to swiftly scan student records to find the grade point averages of all students who will graduate in June. An engineer may need to test several structural design alternatives against volumes of complicated safety and feasibility criteria before proceeding with a design strategy.

In this chapter and the next, we'll cover the type of software used specifically for such data management tasks. This class of software is rapidly replacing the thick, hard-copy manuals that people have had to wade through to find the information their jobs require.

Data management software often is categorized into two major types: *file managers* and *database management systems.* As with other popular types of software products, numerous data management software packages are available for both small and large computer systems. File managers are easier to use and understand, so we'll discuss them first. Then we'll turn to database management systems. Finally, we'll consider the topic of multimedia data management, in which voice, graphics, and video data are combined into applications with the most traditional type of data—text. The chapter Tomorrow box considers some of the hazards that modern database technology poses to personal privacy.

In Chapter 10 we will frequently be using terms such as *fields, records,* and *files.* These were covered in Chapter 2; you should review them before reading this chapter.

File Management Software

File manager.
A productivity software package used to organize data into records and to access data a single file at a time.

A **file manager,** or *record management system,* is a software package that enables you to organize data into files and to access the data a single file at a time. For example, you might first use the package to search for and print out the names of all recipes in a recipe file in which kumquats are an ingredient. Minutes later, you may summon the same package to scan an employee file and total the number of employees in your organization whose birthdays are in April.

You can use a file manager to create and store as many files as you want. You may even be able to keep several files resident in RAM at the same time and switch among them with a keystroke or two. But because you can work on only one file at a time, file managers can be cumbersome to use for interrelating data located in different files. For example, you'd be unable to easily find the birthday of the employee in your employee file who gave you the candied kumquats recipe in your recipe file. To get such information, you would first have to look up the name of the employee in the recipe file; then, using the name you found, you would

Tomorrow

Marketing Databases

How Far Will They Go?

Advocates have called them necessary and effective. Detractors have called them dangerous and diabolical. They're marketing databases, and what you've seen of them today is probably only the beginning.

Marketing databases contain information about the consuming public. These databases record where people live, what they are inclined to do, and what they buy. Using this information, marketers attempt to determine the best way to promote specific products to specific people. Virtually any time you leave traceable information about yourself anywhere, there's a good chance that it will eventually find its way into somebody's marketing database.

Micromarketing. Who you are is what you buy.

When you buy a house, for example, your name, address, and the sales price are recorded in a county courthouse. These records are available to the public, including micromarketers. *Micromarketers* are companies that specialize in creating marketing databases and selling them to companies that produce consumer goods and services. The micromarketer typically breaks down the neighborhoods in a region into several dozen categories. Consumers are placed into one of these categories according to their address. For instance, a "Blueblood Estates" category might be a neighborhood in which the very wealthy live. A "Shotguns and Pickups" category, by contrast, might refer to a rural area where trailers are the likely abode. There are also categories for urban professionals, the elderly, and so on.

Each category is correlated in the micromarketer's computer system with certain buying preferences, a technique known as *geodemographics.* "Blueblood Estates" types are likely to buy expensive cars and take trips to places such as Aspen, St. Thomas, and Patagonia. Those of the "Shotguns and Pickups" sort are more likely to be interested in fishing equipment, chainsaws, and Elvis collectables. This information helps the micromarketer customize a direct mail (unaffectionately called "junk mail") campaign to consumers' specific tastes.

In addition to geodemographic data, micromarketers also collect data showing consumers' past purchasing behavior. Every time you make a computerized purchase, valuable data can be gathered about your purchasing tastes and entered into a computer system. Records kept by stores, credit-card companies, banks, the companies whose magazines you subscribe to, and other organizations are sold to the micromarketer.

A shift in marketing trends has necessitated micromarketing. Not long ago, consumer-products companies produced a small line of products that had little variation. If you wanted a pair of jeans, for instance, you'd better have liked the blue denim variety; it was the only type there was. Today, you can get your jeans in different colors, in different styles, in different fabrics, prewashed, stone-washed, regular or boot cut, with or without rivets, ad nauseum. You've probably noticed that other products seem to come in endless variations. Mass marketing is out; niche marketing, or micromarketing, is in.

Micromarketing, in order to work optimally, requires, in the words of the late Arthur Miller, a "womb-to-tomb dossier" on every consumer. As more and more transactions and records become computerized, it will be easier for the micromarketer to know how much you earn, the names and ages of your children, and where you went and what you did last week. And consider this: In the future, as cars and televisions become more computerized, electronic data may be gathered about exactly where you go, what you are watching, and how much time you spend doing things. How much will you be willing to let the micromarketer know?

Figure 10-1
An onscreen form (template) representing an employee record.
Such forms can be filled out while displayed on the screen.

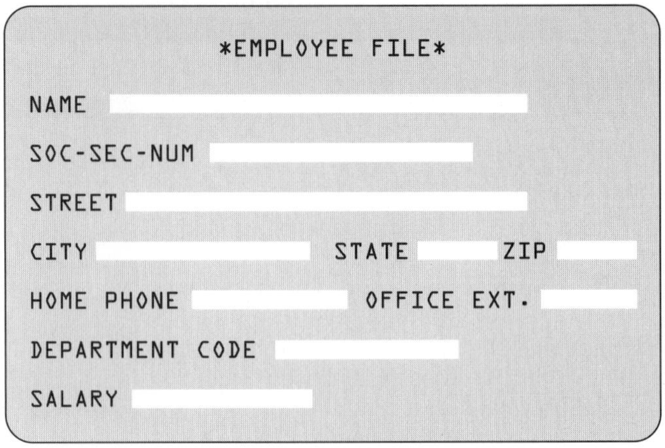

turn to the employee file to look up the birthday. With a database management system, which we'll be describing later in the chapter, you would be able to find the same information in a single step. In data management, files are sometimes referred to as **flat files,** meaning that they lack the multidimensionality imparted by the database structures.

Flat files.
A collection of related records that lack multidimensionality.

The one-file-at-a-time drawback aside, file managers are powerful and extremely useful. Besides enabling you to search for records with specific characteristics, most packages permit you to sort records and to produce both summary information and detailed reports from selected records. They also let you add, delete, and modify data.

How File Managers Work

Let's look at an example to get a feel for how file managers process data. Suppose an organization has 1,000 employees. The organization maintains a "form" on each employee like the one shown on the display screen in Figure 10-1. Such an *onscreen form,* or **template,** is commonly used for entering data into files or databases. Each file that needs to be created will have its own distinctive template.

Template.
A prelabeled onscreen form that requires only that the operator fill in a limited number of entries.

As you place data into the records of a file, you start with an unfilled template for each record to be keyed in. Then you repeatedly fill the template images at the keyboard and save the records onto disk. At any later point, you can modify or delete records from the file and add new ones.

Setting Up a File. Before we examine some of the ways in which we can process the employee file, let's look more closely at the template in Figure 10-1. Notice that it contains ten fields: NAME, SOC-SEC-NUM (social security number), STREET, and so on.

With most file management packages, you can design your own templates. In creating a template for a recipe file, for example, a chef will

```
        FILE MANAGEMENT PACKAGE
             OPENING MENU

1  DESIGN FILE       5  PRINT/SORT
2  ADD               6  REPORT GENERATION
3  COPY              7  REMOVE
4  SEARCH/UPDATE     8  EXIT PACKAGE

      SELECTION NUMBER:  1
      FILE NAME:  EMPLOYEE-FILE
```

KEY:

DESIGN FILE	Lets you create a template for a new file or modify a template for an existing file.
ADD	Lets you put new records into a file.
COPY	Lets you make a copy of a file or portions of a file.
SEARCH/UPDATE	Lets you retrieve information and update (modify) it.
PRINT/SORT	Lets you print records, print portions of records, or sort records.
REPORT GENERATION	Lets you prepare reports based on selected records.
REMOVE	Lets you delete forms (records) from a file.
EXIT PACKAGE	Lets you return to the operating system.

Figure 10-2
A typical opening menu for a file management package. In the highlighted areas, you key in the processing option you want and the file with which you wish to work.

probably set up a recipe-name field, an ingredients field, a directions field, and perhaps even a field for calories. Generally, the file management package will contain a DESIGN FILE option that gives you tools to design whatever types of templates you need for your applications. The records in a given file usually must have the same format and conform to the template you make.

To enable you to create templates or process file data, many file management packages provide you with an opening menu of choices, such as the one shown in Figure 10-2, as soon as you get into the package from the operating system. At this point, you must choose one of the given menu options and supply the name of the file you wish to process.

So, for example, if you were setting up a template for the 1,000-record employee file previously mentioned, you would select option 1, DESIGN FILE, and create a name for the file—say, EMPLOYEE-FILE. Then the package would summon a routine that would ask you a series of questions about how you wanted to design the template for this file. Here you would name the fields, define the maximum length of the data in each field, and make some choices about how the template should look on the screen. Many packages will let you set up templates that require more than one screen.

After designing the EMPLOYEE-FILE template, you would go back to the opening menu and select option 2, ADD, to fill out 1,000 copies of the form—one for each employee—and place them on disk.

File Maintenance. Once you have stored records on disk, you can add new records (opening menu option 2: ADD) or delete records representing departed employees (option 7: REMOVE). If a record contains outdated data, you can change them by requesting the update mode (option 4: SEARCH/UPDATE) on the menu.

Information Retrieval. Besides performing file maintenance operations, you can retrieve information for screen display and, if you desire, produce printed reports. For example, you might use the search/update feature on the opening menu to scan the file for the names of all employees in Department 544 or the names of all employees whose salaries exceed $40,000. You can direct any of this information to the screen and, if you wish, print it.

You may also want to produce mailing labels. You can extract the NAME, STREET, CITY, STATE, and ZIP fields from selected records by invoking opening menu option 5, PRINT/SORT. You can then sort these "reduced records" by zip code before sending them to the printer. (The postal service offers reduced rates for large mailings that are presorted by zip code.)

Most packages also allow you to produce sophisticated written reports. For example, you may wish to produce a salary report on all employees in departments 212 through 214, sorted by department and totaled. Again you go back to the opening menu, select option 6, REPORT GENERATION, and identify EMPLOYEE-FILE as the file you wish to process. Then the file management package is likely to present you with a report generation questionnaire, such as the one shown in Figure 10-3a, so that you can describe how to prepare the report. You merely fill out the questionnaire, hitting the Enter key after placing your responses into each field. The package will then produce the report (Figure 10-3b). In some cases, such as that in Figure 10-3, the file manager will automatically format the report, supply the current date, and number pages.

Increasingly, both file managers and database management systems are enabling storage and retrieval of information other than text, as shown in Figure 10-4 and Feature 10-1.

```
           FILE MANAGEMENT PACKAGE
      REPORT GENERATION QUESTIONNAIRE

FIELDS USED?   NAME, DEPARTMENT-CODE,
               SOC-SEC-NO, SALARY

RECORD SELECTION?  DEPT = 212-214

SORT FIELDS?  DEPT

TOTALS?  SALARY

HEADING?  SALARY REPORT

COLUMN TITLES?  NAME, DEPT, SS#, SALARY

OUTPUT?  PRINTER
```

(a) Describing the report on the display screen

```
    4/22/91   SALARY REPORT   PAGE 1

    NAME       DEPT      SS#          SALARY

 ABERNATHY     212   148-21-3224    $40,000
 BENSON        212   146-48-6211    $35,000
 GARRETSON     212   153-66-2150    $27,000
 RIGGINS       212   140-32-3562    $12,000
 COLES         213   139-64-3821    $52,000
 GRETSKY       213   153-11-4121    $32,000
 JACOBS        214   138-92-3005    $45,000

 TOTALS ...................        $243,000
```

(b) The report

Figure 10-3
Using a file manager to produce a report.
On the display screen, the user fills in blanks on a questionnaire that covers what the report is to look like. The file manager does the rest.

Database Management Systems

A **database management system (DBMS)** is a software system that integrates data in storage and provides easy access to them. The data themselves are placed on disk in a **database,** which can be thought of as an integrated collection of related files. The three files shown in Figure 10-5, which we will discuss shortly, collectively form a database. In a nondatabase environment, these data would normally exist as flat files.

A database management system performs many of the same types of tasks as a file manager. For instance, the work that file managers are asked to do—retrieving information, updating data, arranging data in a specific order, and the like—is essentially the same work done by database management systems. Database management systems and file managers also employ the same tools, such as templates. A template is designed for each of the files in a database, and the template is repeatedly filled with data representing records.

Database management system (DBMS).
A software package designed to integrate data and provide easy access to them.

Database.
An integrated collection of data.

Figure 10-4 Graphics data.
Data management packages are increasingly being used for storage and retrieval of graphics-oriented data. (a) Simple line drawings are used to create floor plans for a real-estate file management application. (b) and (c) Photographic data are included along with regular text data in applications that respectively feature maintaining insurance records and using an employee organization chart.

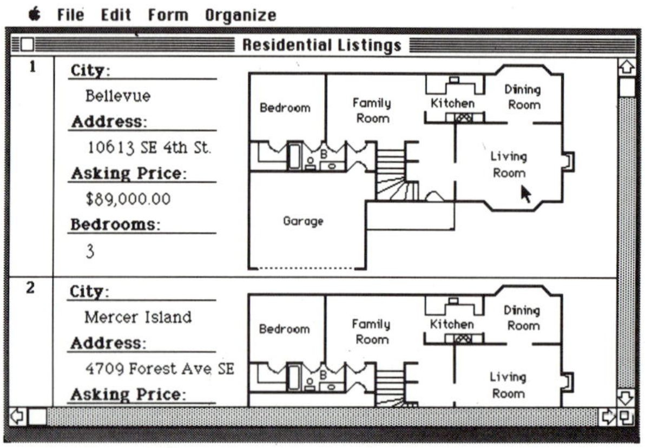

(a)

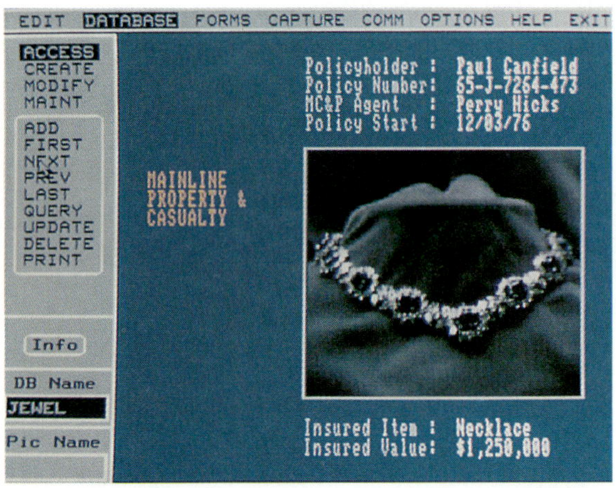

(b)

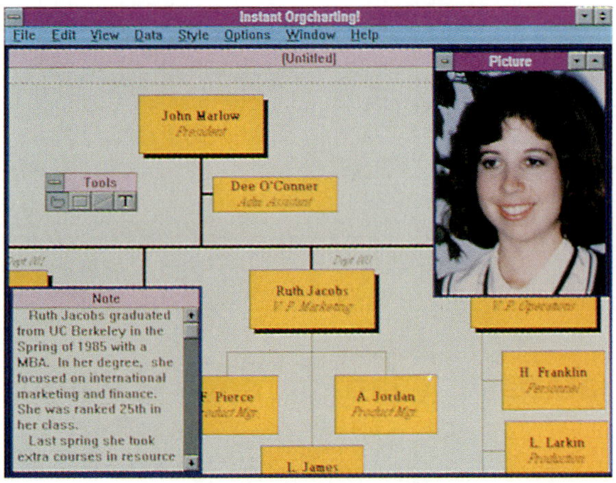

(c)

However, database management systems differ from file managers in that they enable immediate, "seamless" access to related data in *different* files. Put another way, if a file manager did not have the one-file-at-a-time drawback, many people would consider it a database management system.

As a rule, because database management systems are technically more complex than file managers, they are also more expensive and usually more difficult to master. Two applications of database management in organizations are covered in User Solutions 10-1 and 10-2.

Feature 10-1

Geographic Information Systems (GISs)

Data Management with Maps

For hundreds of years, when information had to be recorded on a map, it was drawn right on the map surface. Transparency overlays, introduced later, were a more sophisticated development, allowing different types of data to be layered on a single map. Sometimes the overlays were used jointly, but use of two or more overlays could make the maps confusing. Then, in the late 1980s, GISs were created.

Geographic information systems (GISs) are computerized display maps that are backed by powerful database systems. Advances in database technology, large-capacity storage (optical disk) devices, and improved computer graphics techniques have made GISs possible. Stored in the database are map images and useful geographic data such as demographic breakdowns, sales data, store and warehouse locations, trends, and market research data. Anything you can put on a map—including data on animal populations, land use, foliage growth, traffic patterns, mineral deposits, or pollution—is fair game for a GIS database.

GISs are a promising new area within the computing field. Following is a sampling of their wide range of applications.

- Oil companies such as Texaco, Shell, and Amoco use GISs to store exploration maps and data such as land-leasing arrangements, oil strikes, and terrain features. The systems have reduced the time needed to find promising places to drill and have made the process of locating drilling sites more accurate. GISs are also used by oil companies to locate profitable sites for gas stations.
- GISs have helped environmentalists in their attempt to control the 1989 *Exxon Valdez* oil spill at Prince William Sound in Alaska. A desktop mapping program called GeoREF has been used to collect environmental data, display it, and plan a cleanup strategy. Moreover, the maps have provided a useful electronic journal of the disaster so that its long-term impact can be more accurately assessed.

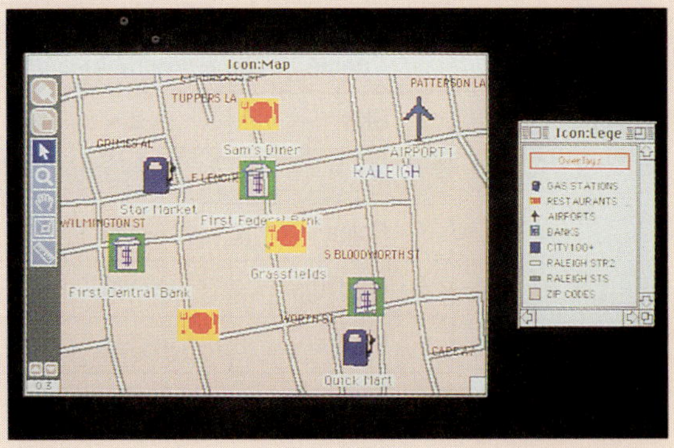

GISs. Computer maps backed by powerful DBMSs.

- Arby's uses GISs to assess the performance of its franchises and to select new sites. One of the key types of data it uses to select sites is traffic patterns. A spokesperson for the firm reports that the GISs have dramatically reduced the number of bad decisions.
- The U.S. Geographical Survey (USGS) is planning to computerize its large collection of maps showing every town, river, lake, and highway in the country. These maps will be used for governmental planning purposes and also made available to GIS users in the private sector.
- A feed company in Minnesota uses a GIS to estimate the amount of feed it can sell in a 12-state area. Data on animal populations and average consumption by each species by county are used to estimate demand.
- A growing roster of companies—including Coca-Cola, UPS, and Federal Express—uses GIS techniques to route trucks along the fastest routes. The city of Albuquerque, New Mexico, uses small display screens in ambulances that help drivers navigate to their destinations. Shaving minutes off driving time can be critical in emergency situations.
- The city of Tacoma, Washington, is a leader in using GISs. The police department uses a GIS to track crimes, the fire department uses a GIS to cut response time in getting to a fire, city planners use a GIS to keep track of properties for tax assessment, and the water company uses a GIS to locate meters and valves.

Figure 10-5 Using a relational database management system.
Data in various files can be pulled together quickly by their common fields (shaded here).

(a) Product description file

Product name	Product number	Supplier	Price
Skis	A-202	Ellis Ski Co.	90.00
Boots	A-211	Ajax Bros.	60.00
Poles	A-220	Bent Corp.	25.00
Bindings	A-240	Acme Co.	15.00
Wax	A-351	Candle Industries	3.00

(b) Inventory file

Product number	Uncommitted stock	On order?
A-202	15	Yes
A-211	90	Yes
A-220	30	Yes
A-240	25	Yes
A-351	80	No

(c) Order file

Shipment date	Product number	Amount
1/8	A-202	30
1/8	A-240	15
1/9	A-211	50
1/9	A-202	40
1/10	A-220	35
1/12	A-211	60

(d) Information screen

Product number	Product name	Date	Total stock
A-211	Boots	TODAY	90
		1/9	140
		1/12	200

User Solution 10-1
Using Databases to Fight Crime

Sometimes having little information to go on, crime analysts in the Los Angeles County Sheriff's Department scan large crime databases to develop new leads for detectives. Analysts can also generate maps—just like the ones discussed in Feature 10-1, on GISs—that enable them to discern crime patterns, track local gangs, and assign beats. If, say, a map shows a sharp increase in burglaries in an area, the database system can pull out the names of everyone living in the area who has committed a crime or who has been interrogated in connection with a crime during the last year—producing a quick list of "possibles."

Database Management on Microcomputers

The best way to understand what a microcomputer-based database management system does and how one works is to look at an example. Many different database management systems are commercially available. Not all of them work the same way nor are they all equally easy to comprehend. In the example that follows we'll look at **relational database management systems**—the type of database management system found on most microcomputers and probably the easiest type to understand.

Relational database management system. A database management system that links data in related files through common fields.

A Simple Example. Imagine that you're a sales manager at a ski-equipment warehouse, and an order comes in for 160 pairs of ski boots. You first need to find out if the order can be filled from stock in inventory. If it can't, you next need to know how long it will be before enough stock is available. You have an impatient client on the phone and require an immediate response.

Because rapid access to more than one file's worth of data is required, this type of task is especially suited to a database management system. Traditionally, an *inventory file* is used to store current stock levels, an *order file* is used to keep track of future shipments from vendors, and a *product description file* is used to store the product descriptions. The very notion of files is often transparent to the database end user, who sees only a screenful of information and usually has no idea from where the database system is extracting it.

The following scenario would be ideal for you. At the microcomputer workstation on your desk, you key in the product description, "Boots." The computer system responds with a screen that shows the status of this product, including the current level of uncommitted stock, future delivery dates, and future delivery amounts (see Figure 10-5d). Within sec-

User Solution 10-2

A Registrations Database That Organizes Paperwork

At Johnson Wax—the maker of Raid insect spray—a database solution was seen as the answer to dealing with the mounds of paperwork being handled by its registration department. Insect-control products are subject to strict state and federal restrictions. A seemingly minor discrepancy between the wording of the initial and final applications for product approval, for instance, can result in a product's being rejected during the registration process. A $50,000 object-oriented database installed by Johnson enabled it to centralize its product-registration information, thereby automating legal and clerical checking. It also makes it easy for users to retrieve customized information, such as determining the stage a product has reached in the registration process and finding out which states have approved or denied applications.

onds, you are able to pull together the information necessary to satisfy the client's request and place the order.

Data from several files are pulled together quickly by a relational database management system through the fields (columns) that the files have in common. Relational database management systems are so named because they *relate* data in different files by common fields in those files. In the example we just covered, data from the three files were pulled together through a common product-number field (highlighted in Figure 10-5).

You should observe that a file manager might be unsuitable for the type of information-retrieval task just described. With a file manager, you'd have to successively do the following: (1) access the product description file to get the product number; (2) check the inventory file to see if the order can be filled from current stock; and (3) if current stock is inadequate, look in the order file to determine when there will be enough stock to fill the order. Because this serial, "file-conscious" process would be slower than having the files integrated in a manner transparent to the user, both service to clients and efficiency would suffer.

Figure 10-6 Database environment.
The DBMS serves as an interface between users at one end and data and programs at the other.

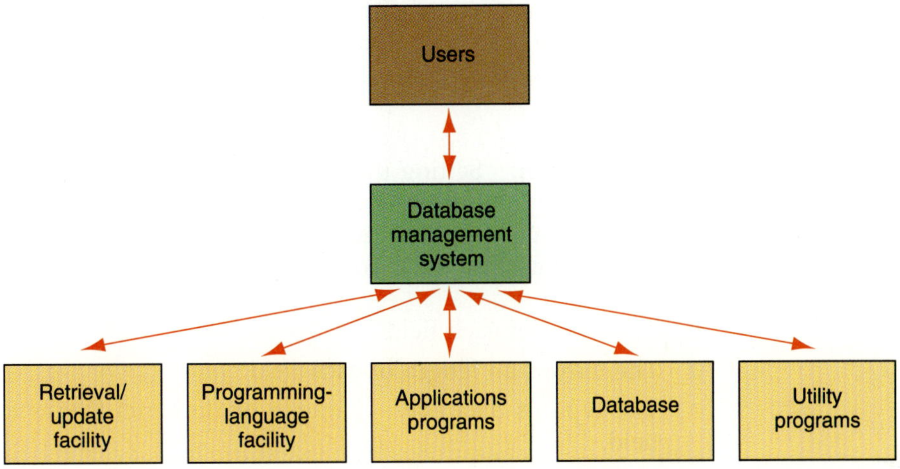

Interacting with the DBMS. Users interact with the database management system through either an easy-to-use retrieval/update facility that accompanies the database package or an applications program written in a programming language.

Usually the *retrieval/update facility* contains a graphical, menu-driven interface that lets users select choices onscreen and an easy-to-use language interface that allows commands to be typed in. Such a facility is designed primarily to satisfy the database needs of ordinary users. Among the most critical of these needs are creating the database, updating database data, and retrieving information from the database (making queries).

The *programming language facility* allows users to create complete computer programs. It often is targeted to more sophisticated users who want to design custom menus or screens or to create applications that go well beyond the standard ones offered with the database package. Most microcomputer-oriented DBMSs come equipped with their own proprietary programming language. A few also support applications developed in such public-domain programming languages as C, BASIC, or COBOL.

A database processing environment for a typical microcomputer system is illustrated in Figure 10-6. The DBMS serves as an interface between the user at one end and the data and programs at the other. As users develop programs and database data at their workstations, DBMS *utility programs* such as the data dictionary (to be discussed shortly) ensure that the data are properly prepared before storing them on disk. Other utility programs, such as a help facility, can be summoned quickly when the user needs assistance with executing a command or troubleshooting an error condition.

Users of microcomputer-based DBMSs must be able to do at least two principal tasks: (1) set up databases (an activity called *data definition*) and (2) create and use databases (an activity called *data manipulation*). Usually, database packages come with a single, proprietary language that can handle both these activities. Typically, this language can also be used to develop applications programs.

Data definition.
The process of describing the characteristics of data that are to be handled by a database management system.

Data Definition. Setting up the database, or **data definition,** mainly involves creating a template for each file in the database. Templates for the database shown in Figure 10-5 are given in Figure 10-7. Usually, each template will ask for the following types of information about the file:

- The name of each field.
- The maximum length of each field.
- The type of data (say, character or numeric) that is to go into each field.

File structure.
A collection of information about the records of a file, including the names, lengths, and types of the fields.

This information is commonly referred to as a **file structure.** Each file will have its own structure. For example, suppose you've informed your microcomputer's relational database package that you want to create a file called INVENTORY (see Figure 10-7b). The package will ask you to describe each data field of the records that will go into the file. You might respond as follows:

Field Name	Field Type	Width	Decimals
PRODUCT-NUMBER	Character	5	N/A
UNCOMMITTED-STOCK	Numeric	5	0
ON-ORDER?	Logical	1	N/A

Roughly translated, this structure declares that there will be three fields in the INVENTORY file—PRODUCT-NUMBER, UNCOMMITTED-STOCK, and ON-ORDER?. The PRODUCT-NUMBER field is composed of text, or *character,* data. The width of 5 means that product numbers will be five or fewer characters. The UNCOMMITTED-STOCK will consist of *numeric* data that will have a maximum width of five characters. Because stock is counted in units of product, there will be no decimal places. ON-ORDER? will be a *logical* field. A logical field contains either the value T (for true, or yes) or F (for false, or no). For instance, a product that was on order would typically be given the value T; a product not on order would receive the value F.

Field descriptor.
A code used to describe the type of data—say, numeric, character, logical—that occupy a given field in a data record.

In most DBMSs, arithmetic computations can be performed on data that have been declared as numeric but not on data declared as character or logical. The "character," "numeric," and "logical" designations are commonly called **field descriptors.** Many database packages have these three descriptors as well as ones for *date* and *memo* fields (see Figure 10-8).

Figure 10-7 Data definition.
Data definition requires developing a file structure, or template, for each database file. The template (shown to the right of each file) contains such data as field names, field widths, and field types.

(a) Product description file

Product name	Product number	Supplier	Price
Skis	A-202	Ellis Ski Co.	90.00
Boots	A-211	Ajax Bros.	60.00
Poles	A-220	Bent Corp.	25.00
Bindings	A-240	Acme Co.	15.00
Wax	A-351	Candle Industries	3.00

PRODUCT
PRODUCT-NAME
PRODUCT-NUMBER -
SUPPLIER
PRICE .

(b) Inventory file

Product number	Uncommitted stock	On order?
A-202	15	T
A-211	90	T
A-220	30	T
A-240	25	T
A-351	80	F

INVENTORY
PRODUCT-NUMBER -
UNCOMMITTED-STOCK
ON-ORDER?

Shipment date	Product number	Amount
1/8	A-202	30
1/8	A-240	15
1/9	A-211	50
1/9	A-202	40
1/10	A-220	35
1/12	A-211	60

ORDER
SHIPMENT-DATE / /
PRODUCT-NUMBER -
AMOUNT .

(c) Order file

File structures and other characteristics of the file are used by the DBMS to construct a **data dictionary** for the application. On most microcomputers, the data dictionary is kept *active* to the application. This means that when data are placed into the template and later used, the

Data dictionary.
A facility that manages characteristics of data or programs in a database environment.

Figure 10-8
Field descriptors.
Most business applications require use of five field descriptors—character, numeric, logical, date, and memo.

Field Type	Description
Character	*Character* fields store data that cannot be manipulated arithmetically. You can, however, sort, index, or compare on these fields.
Numeric	*Numeric* fields, which store integer numbers or numbers that contain decimal points, are those that can be arithmetically manipulated. Numbers on which you do not need to do arithmetic—such as employee identification numbers and product identification numbers—should be stored in character rather than numeric fields.
Logical	*Logical* fields store a single character of data—a "T" (for "true") or an "F" (for "false") or, alternatively, a "Y" (for "yes") and an "N" (for "no"). Tests on logical fields can be used to select records from a file, as can tests on character, numeric, and date fields.
Date	*Date* fields store dates, provided that they are in the format MM/DD/YY (such as 12/31/91). You can sort or index on date fields, and you can also subtract them to calculate the number of days elapsing between two dates.
Memo	*Memo* fields are used to store text information. They cannot be arithmetically manipulated or compared, but they can be edited and output, as can any other field.

data dictionary monitors the applications environment and ensures that no data are entered or used in any conflicting way. So, for instance, you couldn't enter a seven-character product number if the dictionary expected all product numbers to be five characters long. Nor would the dictionary allow you to add a character field and a numeric field.

In many database systems, the data dictionary is also used to protect certain data from unauthorized use or alteration. Sensitive data such as salaries can be hidden so that only certain users of the database, furnished with the proper password, are authorized to retrieve them. Also, only users with access to another password would be allowed to update these data.

Data manipulation.
The process of using language commands to add, delete, modify, or retrieve data in a file or database.

Data Manipulation. The process of using the database in some hands-on fashion is called **data manipulation.** There are generally two ways to manipulate data in a microcomputer-oriented DBMS—through the retrieval/update facility that is provided with the DBMS and through an applications program developed with the programming-language facility.

Data manipulation encompasses a variety of activities. Here we briefly cover some of the most important of them.

- ***Creation of Database Data.*** This task consists of developing records for the database. Each template in the database is successively brought to the screen and filled with the records that pertain to it. In Figure 10-7, for example, you might first summon the template for the product-description file. Then you would type in the first record in that file and enter it. After you did this, a fresh template would appear on the screen. You would type in the second record, and so forth. When you had finished entering all the records for the product-description file, you would do the same thing for the next file—say, the inventory file.

- *File Maintenance.* File maintenance consists primarily of updating records. This involves adding new records from time to time, deleting records that are no longer needed, and making modifications to records. Modifications are necessary because data such as prices and delivery schedules can change and also because errors are sometimes made in entering data.

- *Information Retrieval (Query).* The information on the screen in Figure 10-5d, where we needed to find out amounts and delivery dates of uncommitted stock, is an example of information retrieval, or query. Database queries can be simple or very complex. Figure 10-9 illustrates several queries from the database data described in Figures 10-5 and 10-7. Also provided are the DBMS's responses to those queries. One important fact you should keep in mind is that if you can *manually* pull together the data you need, you should be able to get your database management system to pull these same data together *automatically*—and a lot faster, too.

  Every database management system has its own way of letting users query the database for information. The style shown in Figure 10-9 is based largely on **SQL** (for **Structured Query Language**), which is recognized as today's de facto standard for information retrieval in relational databases.

Structured Query Language (SQL). A popular language standard for information retrieval in relational databases.

- *Reporting.* Reporting is the process of arranging the information you need in a formal report. Most database management systems require that you produce a *report form* for each type of report you need. The report form specifies what the report will look like when it is output—how the report title and column headings will look, which fields will be placed into which columns, the criteria used to select records for the report, how records are to be arranged in the report, and the like. Typically, a series of easy-to-use menus will guide users through report preparation (see Figure 10-10).

- *Sorting.* Sorting is the process of arranging records in some order. Most database management systems are equipped with the necessary tools to help you arrange records in virtually any sequence you desire. As with spreadsheets, you can choose several sort keys if you wish to do sorts within sorts.

- *Calculations.* Often it is necessary to compute sums for columns, take averages, count records, and so forth. Although spreadsheet software is especially suited to these particular applications, database management systems include such math features, too.

Database Management on Large Computers

On large computer systems, DBMSs perform exactly the same sorts of roles as they do on microcomputers, but they are necessarily more sophisticated, for several reasons. First, data are often organized in a more

Figure 10-9 Examples of database queries.
The queries given here can be directed to the database data described in Figures 10-5 and 10-7. Each of the queries conforms to SQL, the de facto standard for information retrieval from relational databases.

Query

```
SELECT   PRODUCT-NUMBER, PRODUCT-NAME
FROM     PRODUCT
WHERE    PRICE < 20.00
```

Selects all records in the product file that have a price of less than $20.00; outputs only the product number and product name on each selected record. That is,

Response

```
A-240   Bindings
A-351   Wax
```

Query

```
SELECT   PRODUCT-NUMBER, UNCOMMITTED-STOCK, ON-ORDER?
FROM     INVENTORY
WHERE    UNCOMMITTED-STOCK > 20    AND    ON-ORDER? = T
```

Selects all records in the inventory file that have an uncommitted stock level of over 20 and that are on order (i.e., the value of ON-ORDER is "T," for true); outputs all fields of each selected record. That is,

Response

```
A-211   90   T
A-220   30   T
A-240   25   T
```

Query

```
SELECT   SHIPMENT-DATE, PRODUCT-NUMBER
FROM     ORDER
WHERE    SHIPMENT-DATE >= 1/9 OR AMOUNT >= 30
```

Selects all records in the order file where the shipment date is 1/9 or beyond, amount is 30 or more units, or both. Outputs only dates and product numbers. That is,

Response

```
1/8    A-202
1/9    A-211
1/9    A-202
1/10   A-220
1/12   A-211
```

Query

```
SELECT   PRODUCT-NAME, ON-ORDER?
FROM     PRODUCT, INVENTORY
WHERE    PRODUCT.PRODUCT-NUMBER = INVENTORY.PRODUCT-NUMBER
```

Creates new records by linking the product and inventory files through their common field, PRODUCT-NUMBER. The new records show the name of each product and whether or not it is on order. That is,

Response

```
Skis       T
Boots      T
Poles      T
Bindings   T
Wax        F
```

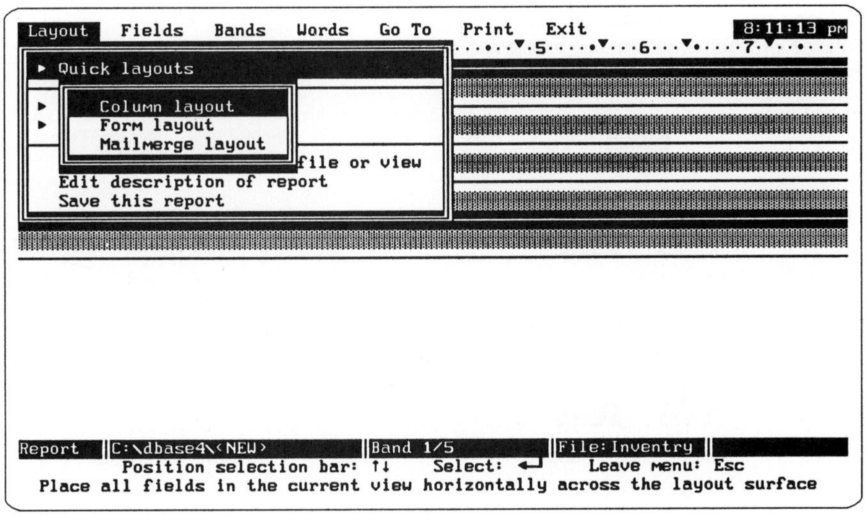

Figure 10-10
Using menus to develop a report form.
Users describe how a report is to look by selecting each report element on a menu and typing in its characteristics.

complex way to provide faster access. Second, DBMSs on large systems must deal with the problem of several users trying to access the database, perhaps simultaneously. Third, because database technology began evolving at a time when many organizations had thousands of dollars already invested in programs written in popular high-level languages, DBMS vendors had to design their products to interface with these languages.

Hierarchical and Network Data Models. The relational database model is particularly useful in managerial (decision-support) retrieval situations in which users are free to pose almost any sort of query to the database. In other situations, however, the types of queries that users need to make are highly predictable and limited. For instance, in banking, tellers usually have access only to the facts they need to perform their jobs, such as information on current customer account balances, deposits, and withdrawals. In these transaction processing environments, hierarchical and network database models are found more commonly than relational ones. *Relational* databases store data in tables, whereas *hierarchical* databases store data in trees and *network* databases store data in networks (see Figure 10-11).

Although an explanation of how hierarchical and relational models work goes beyond the scope of this book, suffice it to say that these models store data in a way that makes access faster for predefined and limited types of queries. Hierarchical and network databases have been around longer, too, so the security on these types of database systems is better than security on relational systems. Because hierarchical and relational databases are harder to set up and use, knowledgeable professionals known as *database administrators (DBAs)* are commonly hired to assist.

Figure 10-11 Relational, hierarchical, and network database models.
Most microcomputers use relational databases, which organize data into tables. Hierarchical and network databases are found mostly in transaction processing environments on large computer systems.

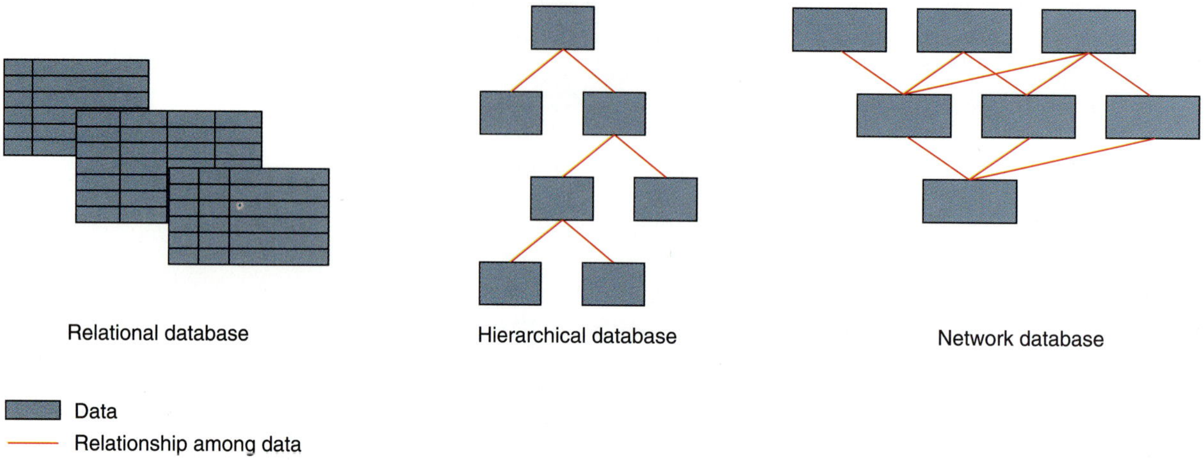

Data definition language (DDL).
A language used to create, store, and manage data in a database environment.

Setting Up the Database. Large DBMS packages usually have a special language dedicated to the data definition function. Such languages have generically come to be known as **data definition languages (DDLs).** Besides simply defining data, a major function of the DDL in these large packages is security—protecting the database from unauthorized use.

Because a large database management system in a firm is used by numerous people, the accompanying database is particularly vulnerable to security problems. For example, unscrupulous employees may attempt to alter payroll data, access privileged salary or financial account data, or even steal or erase data. To avoid these possibilities, the DBA may assign passwords when setting up the data dictionary, to determine which users access which data. This practice gives users only restricted views of the full database. For example, users working on a mailing list application that accesses an employee database will be locked out of access to data on employee salaries. Also, the DBA can allow some users to modify certain data and give other users of those data only retrieval privileges. For example, in an airline's passenger reservation database, a regular clerk or agent may not be allowed to rebook a special-rate passenger on an alternate flight, but a high-level supervisor, who knows the password, may be able to do so.

Processing Data. DBMSs targeted to larger computer systems often contain separate language packages to handle retrieval/update and programming tasks. Both sets of tasks pose their own array of problems that the typical microcomputer DBMS user doesn't encounter.

For example, on large computer systems (or microcomputer systems linked by a network), users often need to access the same data at more or less the same time. This can cause several problems. For example:

- Only one seat is available on a flight. Two agents seize it at the same moment and sell it to different customers.
- A program is tallying a series of customer balances in a database. When it is halfway finished, another program controlled by someone else transfers $5,000 from account 001 (which the first program already has tallied) to account 999 (which it hasn't). Thus, the first program will "double count" the $5,000 and obtain erroneous results.

To prevent such **concurrent access** problems, most database systems allow users to place a temporary "lock" on certain blocks of data to ensure that no other modifications to these data will be made during their processing.

Concurrent access.
A term that refers to two or more users attempting to interactively access the same data at more or less the same time.

Another problem unique to DBMSs on large computer systems relates to the need of these DBMSs to tie into programs coded in popular high-level programming languages. An interfacing feature known as a **data manipulation language (DML)** solves this problem, however. The DML is simply a set of commands that enable the language the programmer normally works with to function in a database environment. For example, if the programmer writes programs in COBOL, a COBOL DML must be used. The DML may consist of 30 or so commands, which the programmer uses to interact with data in the database (Figure 10-12 provides a sample of these commands).

Data manipulation language (DML).
A language used by programmers to supplement some high-level language supported in a database environment.

Thus, a COBOL program in a database environment consists of a mixture of standard COBOL statements and COBOL DML statements, such as the following small block of code, which deletes an employee's record from a database:

Standard COBOL Command → MOVE

COBOL DML Commands → FIND, DELETE

```
MOVE   '152364575' TO SOCIAL-SECURITY-NUMBER

FIND   EMPLOYEE RECORD
         .
         .
         .
DELETE EMPLOYEE ONLY
```

DML Command	Purpose
CREATE	Creates a record
STORE	Stores data in the database
FETCH	Retrieves data from the database
INSERT	Inserts a record
MODIFY	Changes data in a record
FIND	Locates a record
DELETE	Deletes a record

Figure 10-12
Some typical DML commands.
Where available, such commands extend the language with which the programmer normally works, tailoring it to a database environment.

Figure 10-13 Use of a COBOL precompiler.
The COBOL precompiler translates a COBOL program written with DML commands into a regular COBOL program, which can be run on a standard COBOL language translator.

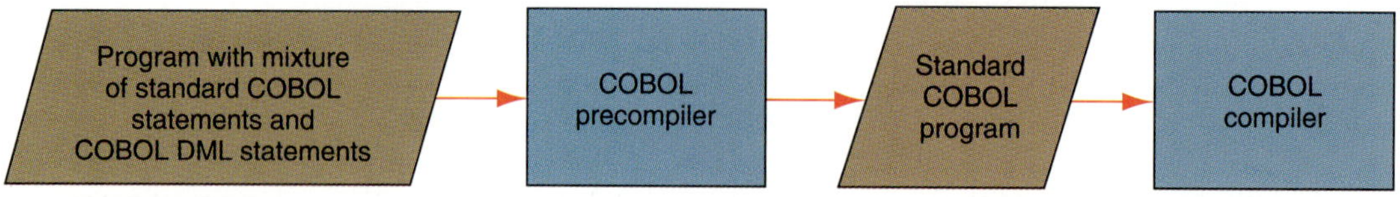

Precompiler.
A computer program that translates an extended set of programming language commands into standard commands of the language.

Host language.
A programming language used to code database applications.

The program containing this mixture of statements is then fed to the DBMS's COBOL precompiler, as shown in Figure 10-13. The **precompiler** translates this program into a standard COBOL program, which then can be executed with the regular COBOL compiler available on the system.

High-level languages that are supported by their own DMLs are called **host languages.** Several host languages may be available on any particular system. Languages that a DBMS commonly employs as hosts are COBOL, C, PL/1, and BASIC.

Advantages and Disadvantages of Database Management

A DBMS can offer several advantages over traditional flat-file systems. Several of these follow.

- *Better Information.* Because many more data are integrated in a database environment than in a flat-file environment, information that otherwise might be difficult or impossible to pull together can be collected easily.

- *Faster Response Time.* Data that would otherwise require several flat files are integrated into a single database, so complex requests can be handled much more quickly.

- *Lower Operating Costs.* Because response time is faster, more work can be done by users in less time.

- *Fewer Storage Requirements.* In a database system, integration often means that the same data need not appear over and over again in different files, thereby saving valuable disk space.

- *Better Data Integrity.* In a database system, integration often means that a data update need be made in only one place to be automatically reflected throughout the system, thereby avoiding the error that is often introduced when the same update has to be made manually in several independent files.

- *Better Data Management.* Since more data are centrally stored in a database than in flat files there is better control over such matters as the data dictionary, security, and standards.

However, there is a downside to database processing that an organization or individual should consider. The major problem is *cost*. Significant expenses are normally incurred in the following areas:

- ☐ ***Database Software.*** Relative to other types of software, a DBMS is expensive. Microcomputer packages typically cost somewhere from $300 to $800. File managers, in contrast, are often priced around $100.
- ☐ ***New Hardware.*** A DBMS requires a great deal of main memory and secondary storage, and accessing records can be time consuming. Thus, some users find it necessary to upgrade to a bigger, more powerful computer system after acquiring a DBMS.
- ☐ ***Training.*** Microcomputer-based database management systems are often considerably more difficult to master than file managers, spreadsheets, and word processors. Relating data in different files can be tricky at times. Also, if you want to custom design your own applications with the programming-language facility, prepare for a substantial investment in learning time.
- ☐ ***Conversion Effort.*** Moving from a traditional, flat-file system to a database management system can entail considerable conversion expense. Data must be reorganized and programs rewritten. Fortunately, this is a one-time expense.

Cost is not the only problem. Database processing can increase a system's vulnerability to failure. Because the data in the database are highly integrated, a problem with a key element might render the whole system inactive. Despite the disadvantages, however, DBMSs have become immensely popular with both organizations and individuals.

Multimedia Data Management

So far in this chapter we've concentrated on data management applications that involve text data. But, as you saw in Figure 10-4, graphic data such as drawings and photographs also need to be managed systematically. Carrying this thought further, there is no reason why voice and video data couldn't be included within a data management application. Applications in which several types of data are used to create files or databases are known as **multimedia** data management, or *multimedia computing*, applications. Currently, this is still a very new applications area for computers.

Multimedia.
A type of computing in which text, graphics, voice, and video are intermixed in applications.

The marriage by computer of text, graphics, sound, and video data in a single application is among the most exciting new technological frontiers we will explore in the 1990s. As many of the major hardware and software vendors position their products in what appears will soon be a multibillion-dollar market, one question remains unanswered: In which applications areas will multimedia data management take off?

Figure 10-14
Using a multimedia system to learn French.
Multimedia may soon revolutionize the teaching of languages.

A variety of applications are now being reported in the press. Four of these are discussed in the following paragraphs and several others in Window 6.

Education. Multimedia is increasingly being used as an educational tool. French students, for instance, can now pull up an onscreen video that shows someone speaking French and see the spoken words spelled out nearby (see Figure 10-14). Theoretically, if a word or phrase comes up that the student doesn't understand, the onscreen presentation could be halted by the press of a button, and the student could request an English translation. The student might also want to pause to view the local color at the boulangerie, see a graphic with a Paris street map, or listen to Edith Piaf or Jean-Luc Ponty belt out a few tunes in the background. Education is seen today as a prime area for multimedia product development. Some people have gone so far as to say that multimedia will completely change the way most people learn.

Entertainment. Entertainment is another area where multimedia is almost guaranteed to be a success. As computer technology enables more and more types of information to be presented, a different breed of show will evolve. Such a show will be both "infotaining" and entertaining, and it may ultimately transform the passive couch potato into an active participant.

Say, for instance, you wanted to learn about the Amazon. You could go to a videodisk rental store, where you would get an optical disk containing all sorts of text, voice, and picture information about the Amazon. You could take a tour of the river, learn about the wildlife there, or watch a show about the dangers of cutting down the forests. The disk also would allow you to temporarily halt any of these shows to pull up statistical data about the things you were viewing or even maps of the area. Basically, you create your own television program.

Live television is also likely to be packaged with a multimedia component in the future. Imagine watching a football game and being able to access football trivia or even another game in a window that you could blow up to any size. Multimedia may thus bring us to an age of "intelligent television."

Merchandising. Multimedia is beginning to catch on in merchandising. Some people in the know say that real estate will be one of the first areas to feel the boom in multimedia products. In the future you may shop for a home on a multimedia system. You begin by selecting an area where you want to purchase and by describing some of your personal preferences—say, a fireplace, at least five acres, three bedrooms, and a cost under $200,000. The system then fetches photographs of homes fitting the description you've given, as well as vital data on each. When you see a property you like, you press a button, thereby accessing a video that tours the home room by room, with spoken narration by the owner or a realtor. Such a presentation system would also allow you to access vital data about the area—weather statistics, facts about local schools, maps, nearby sights, and so on. It's possible that all of this will someday be available from a home TV set.

Training. Some companies have already started using multimedia applications to train their employees. One telecommunications firm uses a multimedia product to teach workers how to fix phone cables. Workers can access manuals from the system, manipulate pictures of tools (to see what happens visually), observe needles moving on simulated meters, and so on.

Summary and Key Terms

Database management software is often categorized into two major types: file managers and database management systems.

File Management Software. A **file manager** (or *record management system*) is a software package that enables users to organize data into files and to process the data a single file at a time. In data management, a "plain-vanilla" file is commonly referred to as a **flat file,** meaning that it lacks multidimensionality.

Many file managers employ an onscreen form, or **template,** to help users place data into the records of a file. At any later point, records can be modified or deleted from the file, and new records can be added.

Database Management Systems. A **database management system (DBMS)** is a software system that integrates data in storage and provides easy access to them. DBMSs differ from file managers in that they enable immediate access to data that could conceivably span several files.

The data in a DBMS are placed on disk in a **database,** which is an integrated collection of data.

There are several types of database management systems. **Relational database management systems** are the most common type found on microcomputer systems. These systems are so named because they relate data in various database files by common fields in those files.

Users gain access to the data they need through an easy-to-use *retrieval/update facility* that accompanies the DBMS or through an applications program written with a *programming language facility.* DBMSs also contain *utility programs* such as a data dictionary and a help facility.

One task performed by anyone setting up a database is **data definition**—the process of describing data to the DBMS prior to entering them. The descriptions of these data are used to create **file structures** and a **data dictionary** for the application. Both the file structure and data dictionary contain a **field descriptor** for each field of data in the database.

The process of using the database in some hands-on fashion is called **data manipulation.** Data manipulation encompasses a variety of activities, including the creation of database data, file maintenance, information retrieval (query), reporting, sorting, and calculating. **SQL** (for **Structured Query Language**) is today's de facto standard for information retrieval in relational databases. Database systems are generally one of three common types: relational, hierarchical, and network.

Many microcomputer-oriented DBMSs come with only a single proprietary language that has commands for data definition, retrieval/update, reporting, and programming functions. Large computer systems that use sophisticated DBMSs usually have a special language dedicated to each of these tasks. For example, a **data definition language (DDL)** handles data definition chores, placing key data for applications development and security purposes into a *data dictionary.* A **data manipulation language (DML)** extends the language the programmer normally works with into a database environment. Languages supported by their own DMLs are called **host languages.** A program called a **precompiler** translates DML commands into host-language commands, which in turn can be executed on the regular compilers available at the computer site.

On large computer systems, DBMS packages must also deal with the problem of several users trying to access the database at the same time. To prevent such **concurrent access** problems, most database systems allow users to place a temporary "lock" on certain blocks of data to ensure that no other modifications to these data will be made during their processing.

A DBMS can offer several advantages over traditional flat-file systems. Among these advantages are better information, faster response time, lower operating costs, fewer data storage requirements, better data integrity, and better data management. The biggest disadvantage is cost. Costs are normally incurred in the areas of new hardware and software, training, and conversion. Still another disadvantage is greater vulnerability to failure, because database data are integrated and a problem with a key element can render the whole system inactive.

Multimedia Data Management. **Multimedia** data management refers to data management in which a combination of text, graphics, voice, and video data are involved in a computing application. Four promising applications areas for multimedia data management are education, entertainment, merchandising, and training.

Review Exercises

Fill-in Questions

1. The two major types of data management packages are ________ and ________.
2. The onscreen form used to create records in a data management environment is often called a(n) ________.
3. An integrated collection of data is called a(n) ________.
4. ________ database management systems are the type of DBMSs typically found on microcomputers.
5. On hierarchical and network database management systems, a knowledgeable professional known as a(n) ________ often is called on to set up the database for users.
6. The problem of ________ access often arises when two or more people try to seize and modify data at the same time.
7. SQL is an acronym for ________.
8. Applications in which several types of data are intermingled are known as ________ data management.

Matching Questions

Match each term with the description that fits best.

a. precompiler
b. data definition language (DDL)
c. data manipulation
d. retrieval/update language
e. host language
f. data definition

____ 1. A language used to describe database data.

____ 2. A language supported by a DML (data manipulation language).

____ 3. A translator used to translate DML commands into commands that can be input to a regular language translator.

_____ 4. A database software product that permits programmers and nonprogrammers to easily retrieve, add, delete, or modify database data with simple, Englishlike commands.

_____ 5. Organizing data in the database so that programmers and users have good access to them, data are stored as efficiently as possible, and the database's security is maintained.

_____ 6. A task that can be performed through either a retrieval/update language or a programming language.

Discussion Questions

1. What is a file manager?
2. What is a database management system, and how does it differ from a file manager?
3. How do relational database management systems work?
4. What types of data are found in a file structure?
5. What is the difference between data description and data manipulation?
6. How do large database management systems solve the problem of concurrent access?
7. Identify the advantages and disadvantages of database management systems.
8. What is multimedia data management?

Critical Thinking Questions

1. An owner of a small personnel agency is about to purchase a well-known database package to manage a growing client list on a microcomputer system. One of her employees is a computer whiz and has suggested writing the database package himself, to make it better fit the agency's needs. What should the owner do in this situation—say yes, say no, or gather more information?
2. Many people believe that, to the average business, the choice of a particular database management system is much more important than the choice of a particular word processor or a spreadsheet package. What do you think?
3. As hinted in the Tomorrow box, there is considerable fear that marketing databases can be used to invade a person's privacy. What important issue areas do you feel should be addressed by the government to ensure the privacy of individuals isn't invaded by micromarketers? For instance, one critical issue area concerns *access;* that is, who will have access to the marketing data and under what circumstances will access be granted?

Window 6

Multimedia Computing

It May Revolutionize the Way We Deal with Information

Multimedia computing is a technology that might make an orchestra conductor envious of the ordinary user. Press a button, and screenfuls of information appear on a computer monitor. Press another, and related video images arise from an onscreen window. Press yet another, and related talk or music emerges out of an attached sound system. You control all of these media, each of which has a plethora of interesting information in the form of text, graphics, video, or sound ready at your beck and call. The possibilities of such a technology, which got started in earnest only in 1987, are almost endless and range from business to entertainment. In this window, we look at some of the environments in which multimedia is currently being applied.

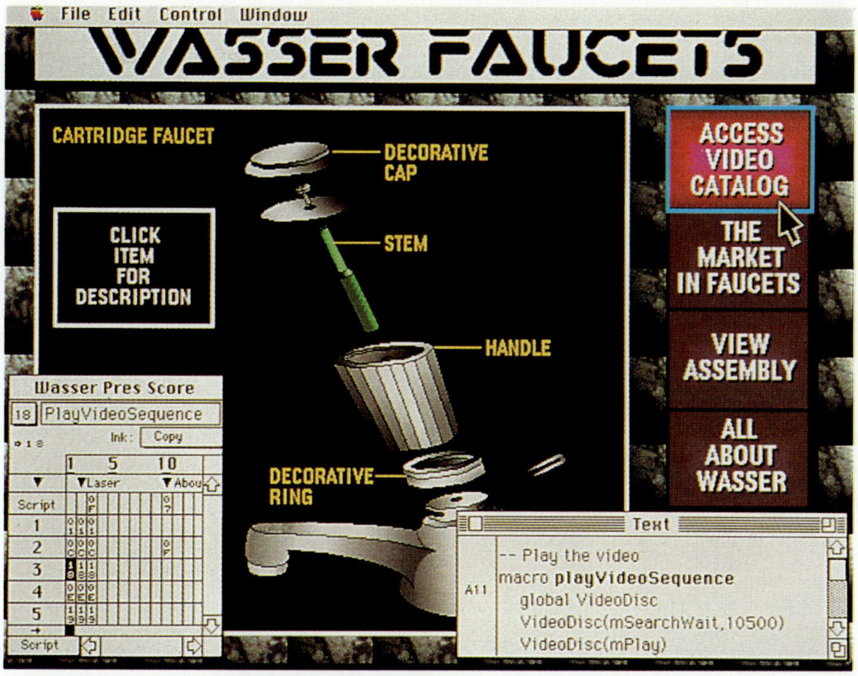

1. Multimedia computing is often used to prepare online parts catalogs as well as complete presentation systems that pitch products to clients.

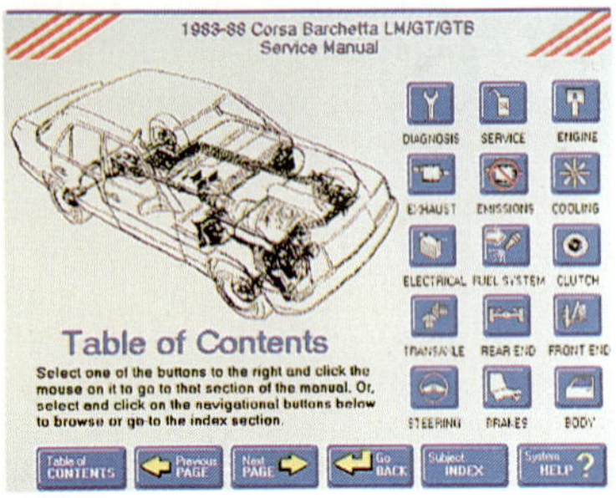

2

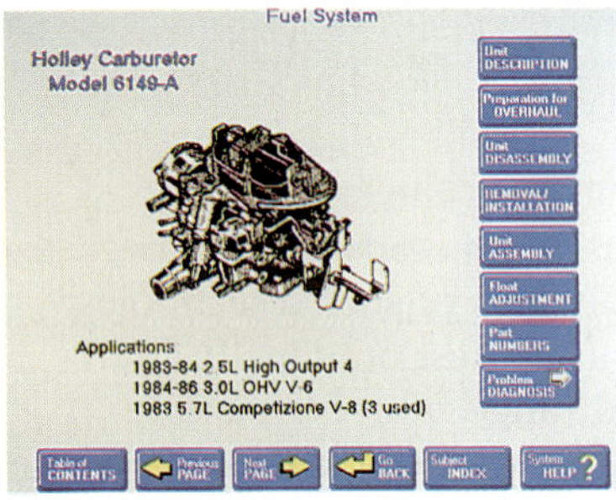

3

4

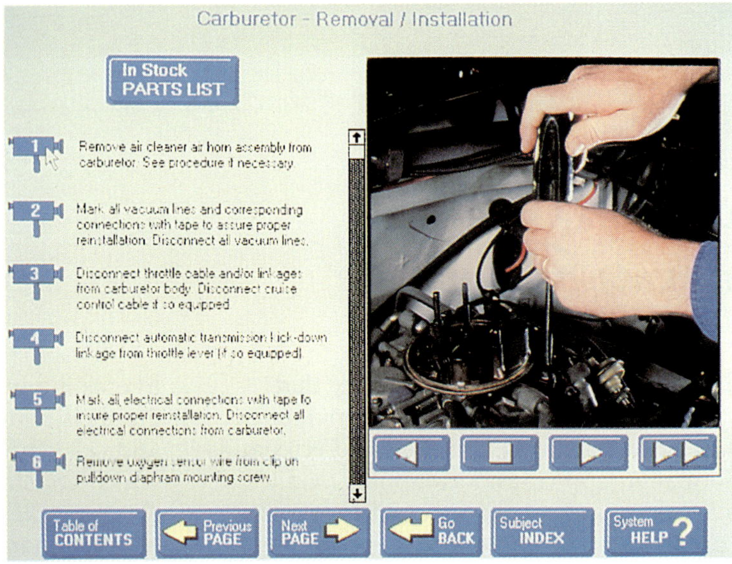

2–4. An online training application refers auto technicians to a set of manuals and lets them play video segments showing how certain types of repairs are done.

5

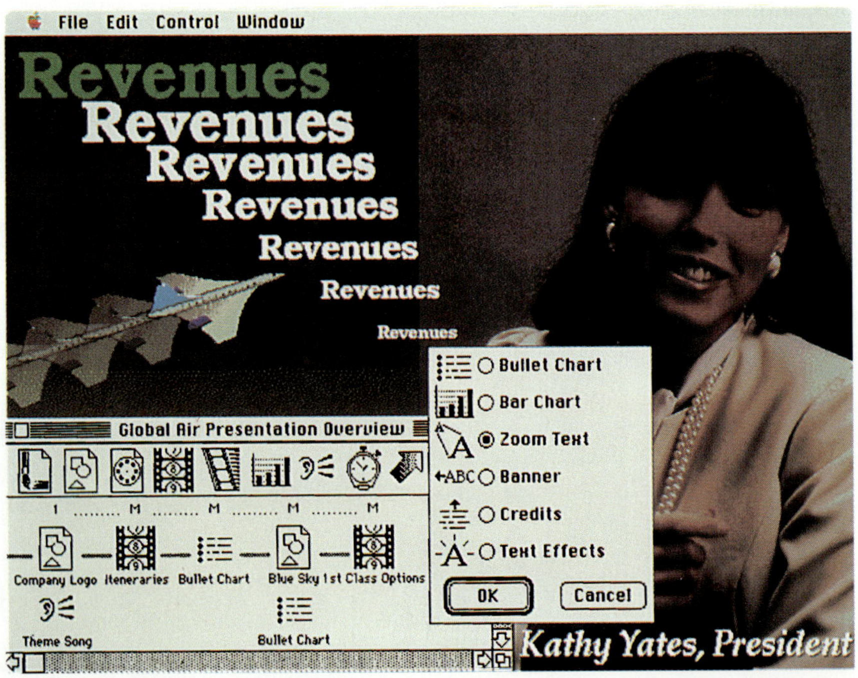

5. Multimedia kits are increasingly being packaged with "authoring software," which enables users to prepare their own multimedia presentations for colleagues or clients.

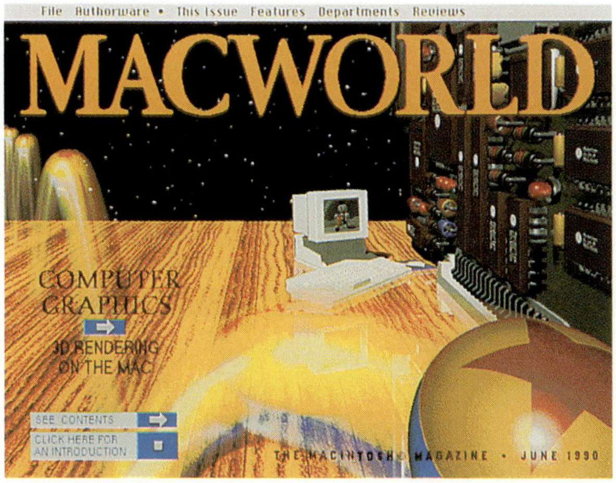

6

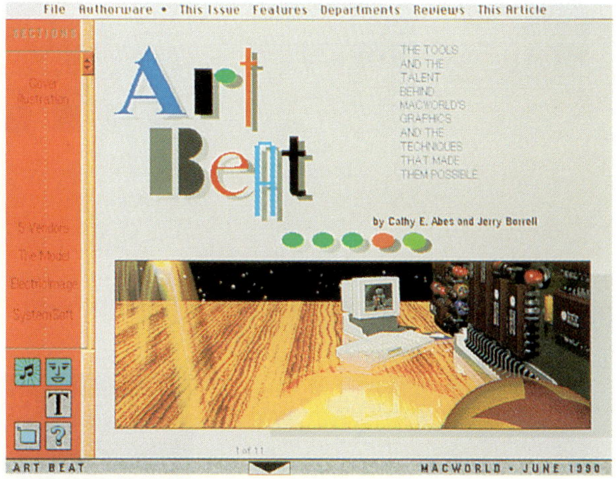

7

6, 7. In the future, many magazines will probably be available in multimedia versions. Instead of reading what your favorite columnist has written about a subject, you can press a button for a video clip that will have him or her speaking to you in a screen window.

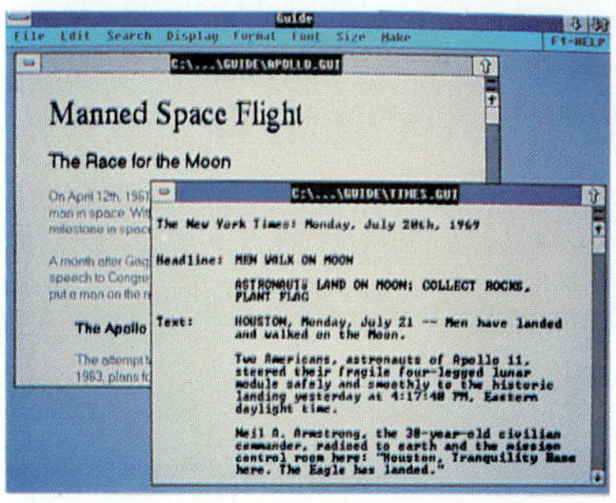

8

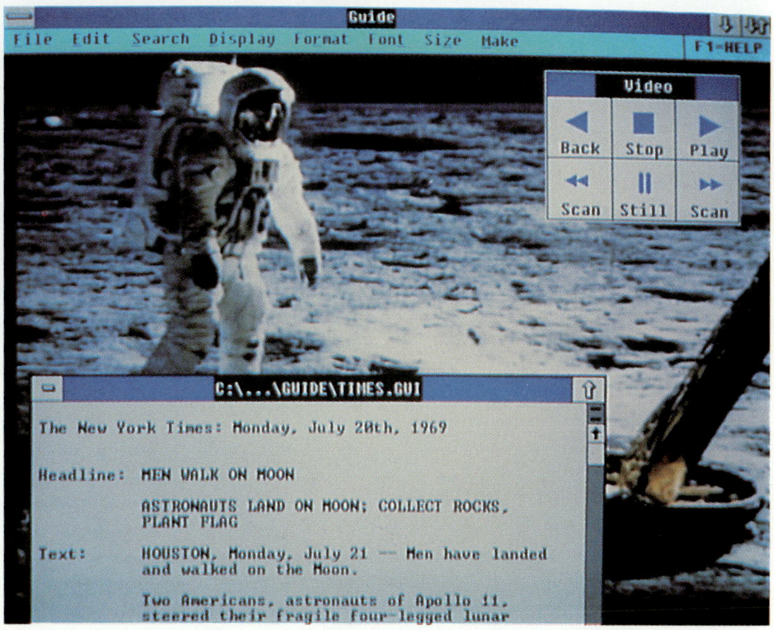

9

8, 9. In this application involving NASA's Apollo Space Program, ordinary users can choose from among related *New York Times* articles, documents, illustrations, and video clips. At any point while browsing through a particular piece, you can summon new materials that explore points of interest in increasing detail, and the system will keep track of your place in earlier pieces.

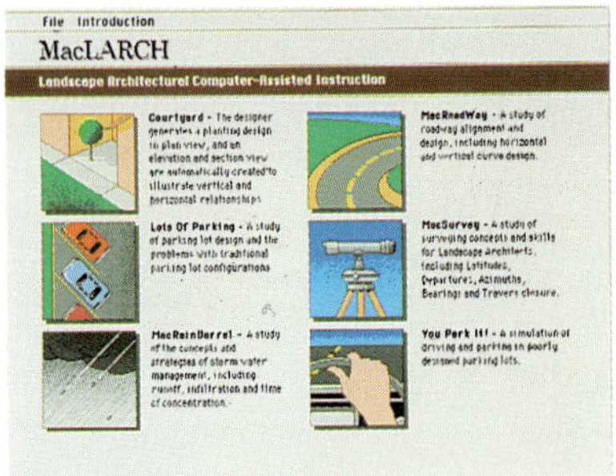

10

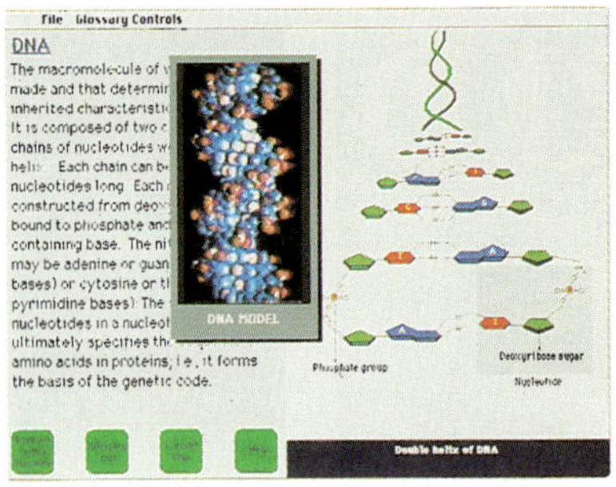

11

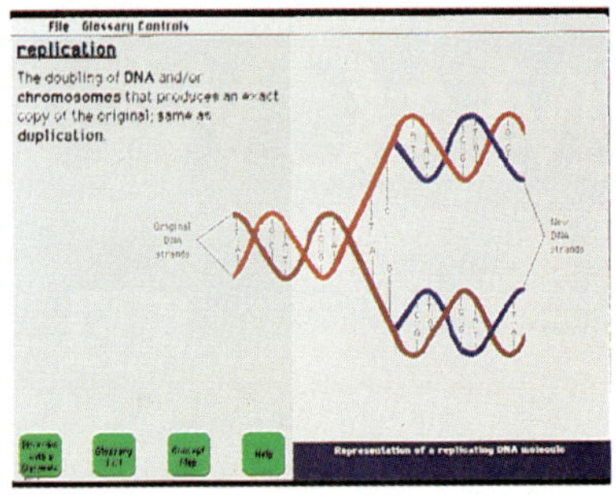

12

13

10–13. Books and other educational materials are a major applications area for multimedia computing. Students can read about subjects such as landscape architecture, chemistry, and the environment at their own pace, accompanied by sound and video clips.

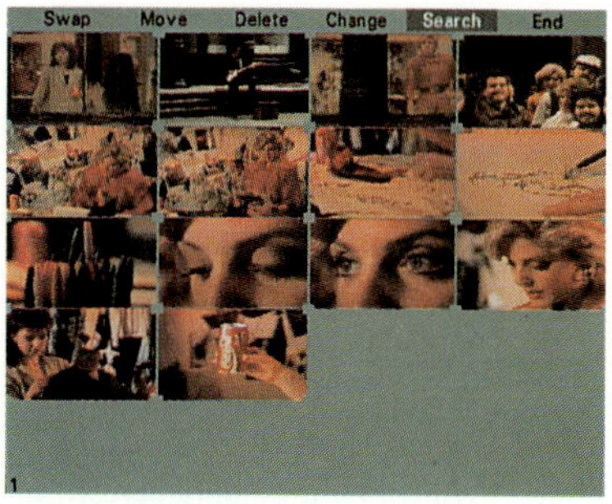

14

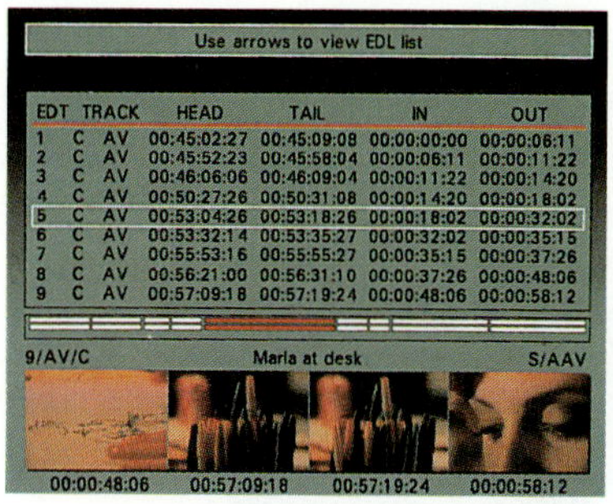

15

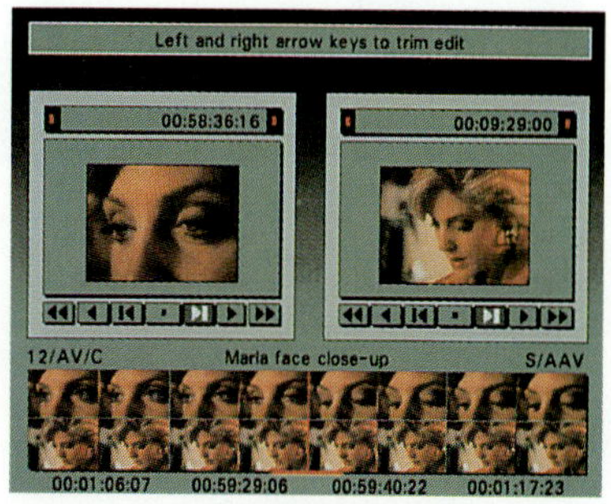

16

14–16. Multimedia computing is now widely used in film editing. Each screen window can capture a single frame or run a video segment (a series of frames). Frames can be rearranged or clipped electronically, as if one were word processing an electronic document.

17

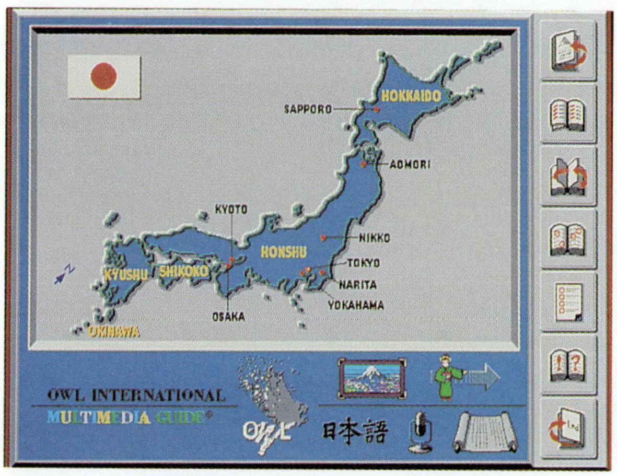

18

17–18. A multimedia application gives businesspeople in the United States and Canada a “crash course” in Japanese, in preparation for travel to the Orient.

Today's computer graphics packages make it easy for us to create distorted views of reality on a display screen, as seen in this fisheye view of a conventional airstrip. Tomorrow's packages, however, will enable us to create completely new realities—three-dimensional ones that exist in space and that are hard to distinguish from real life.

Module E

Information Systems

This module integrates several concepts from earlier chapters, tying together the parts of a computer system that involve hardware, software, data, people, and procedures.

Chapters 11 and 12 cover systems development and program development in organizations, respectively. In Chapter 11, we'll address types of systems, the various ways in which organizations build systems, and the sorts of activities performed and kinds of people involved in system building. In Chapter 12, we'll look in depth at applications software development and programming languages. Here, you'll learn about some of the tools used by computer professionals to design and code computer programs as well as the variety of languages commercially available.

Chapter 13, on end-user computing, covers many of the things you should know about computer systems if you decide to acquire one for your own use. Today, unprecedented numbers of people are purchasing their own microcomputer systems or being assigned to use one, making knowledge in this area essential for virtually everyone.

How is the move toward a global economy affecting the building of computer systems? The tearing down of world barriers and the rise of sophisticated computer and communications networks are why many companies are rebuilding a number of key systems today, making it possible for management to get a quick read on worldwide operations. The computer system in this Hewlett-Packard warehousing facility in Singapore illustrates the global reach of modern computer systems.

11 Developing Business Systems

Outline

Learning Objectives

After completing this chapter, you will be able to:

1. Explain what a system is.
2. Describe several types of computer systems commonly found in business.
3. Define the roles of various people and information-systems areas involved in the systems development process.
4. Identify and describe the components of the systems development life cycle (SDLC).
5. Describe several approaches used to develop systems.

Overview

In previous chapters we considered primarily hardware and software. Here we turn to the process of putting together these elements into complete computer systems.

All organizations have various sorts of systems—for example, systems that attend to accounting activities such as sending out bills and processing payrolls; systems that provide information to help managers make decisions; systems for word processing and electronic-mail tasks; systems that help run factories efficiently; and so on. Such systems require considerable effort to design, build, and maintain. The process that includes planning and implementing systems is called *systems development.*

Unfortunately, since no two situations are exactly alike, there is no surefire formula for successful systems development. A procedure that works well in one situation may fail in another. These facts notwithstanding, there is a set of general principles that, if understood, will enhance the likelihood of a system's success. Those principles are the subject of this chapter.

The chapter opens with a general discussion of systems and systems development. Then we cover the types of systems commonly found in business. From there we turn to the computer professionals who are hired to develop systems in organizations and consider some of their primary responsibilities. Then we look at the systems development life cycle—the set of activities that are at the heart of every serious systems-building effort. Chapter 11 concludes with a discussion of the major approaches to systems development.

On Systems

System.
A collection of elements and procedures that interact to accomplish a goal.

A **system** is a collection of elements and procedures that interact to accomplish a goal. A football game, for example, is played according to a system. It consists of a collection of elements (two teams, a playing field, referees) and procedures (the rules of the game) that interact to determine which team is the winner. A transit system is a collection of people, machines, work rules, fares, and schedules that get people from one place to another. Similarly, a computer system is a collection of people, hardware, software, data, and procedures that interact to perform information processing tasks.

Systems development.
The ongoing process of improving ways of doing work.

The function of many systems, whether manual or computerized, is to keep an organization well managed and running smoothly. Systems are created and altered in response to changing needs within an organization and shifting conditions in its surrounding environment. When problems arise in an existing system or a new system is needed, systems development comes into play. **Systems development** is a process that consists of analyzing an applications environment, designing a new system or making modifications to an old one, acquiring needed hardware and software, and getting the new or modified system to work.

Systems development may be required for any of a number of reasons. New laws may call for the collection of data never before assembled; for example, the government may require new data on personnel. The introduction of new technology, especially new computer technology, may prompt wholesale revision of a system. Or, as is the trend today, a company may decide to convert certain applications into a global, networked environment. These and other kinds of pressure often can bring about major changes in the systems by which work is done in an organization.

Business Systems

Undoubtedly, you've already encountered many types of business systems. When you go into the supermarket, you generally see in use electronic cash registers and various hand-held or laser scanning devices that are obviously a part of some supermarket system. Or, when you've registered for classes, perhaps you've observed someone at a display device checking to see whether a certain class you want to take is still open or whether you've paid all your bills—apparently as part of a registration system.

While there are hundreds of "types" of computer systems in existence today, many of those in business and most other organizations fall into one or more of four categories: transaction processing systems, information systems, office systems, and design and manufacturing systems. Here we'll look more closely at each of these. We will also explore the area of artificial intelligence, which can impart to a system certain characteristics that one would normally attribute to humans.

Transaction Processing Systems

Virtually every business must support a number of routine operations, most of which involve some form of tedious recordkeeping. These operations, such as payroll and accounts receivable, were some of the earliest commercial applications of computers in organizations and are still among the most important. Because these systems heavily involve processing of business transactions—such as paying employees, recording customer purchases and payments, and recording vendor receipts and payments—they are called **transaction processing systems** (see Figure 11-1).

Transaction processing system. A system that handles an organization's business transactions.

Some of the functions that one commonly finds as part of a transaction processing system are discussed below.

Payroll. *Payroll programs* compute deductions, subtract them from gross earnings, and write paychecks to employees for the remainder. These

Figure 11-1 Transaction processing systems.
Transaction processing systems are at the heart of most businesses, tracking goods being sold, monitoring inventory levels and orders of stock, and recording payments made by cash or credit. Transaction processing was the first business function to be computerized, and it is still one of the most critical computer applications.

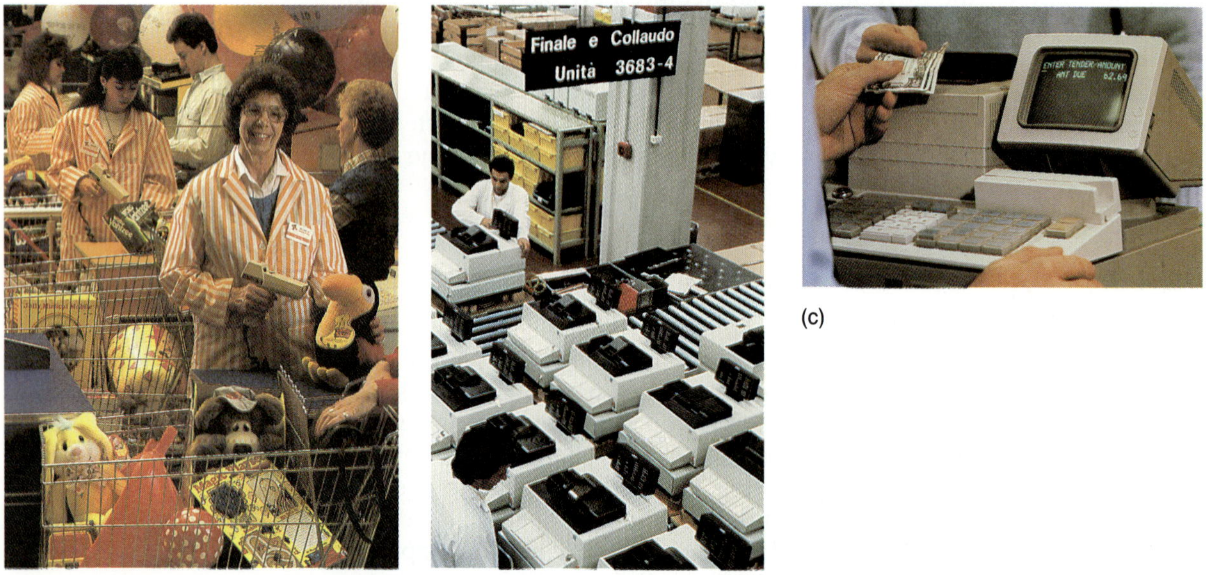

(a) (b) (c)

programs also contain routines that prepare reports for management and for taxing agencies of the federal, state, and local governments.

Accounts Receivable. The term *accounts receivable* refers to the amounts owed by customers who have made purchases on credit. Accounts receivable programs are charged with keeping track of customers' purchases, payments, and account balances. They also calculate and print customer statements and provide information to management. Other output includes sales analyses, which describe changing patterns of products and sales, as well as detailed or summary reports on current and past-due accounts.

Accounts Payable. The term *accounts payable* refers to the money a company owes to other companies for the goods and services it has received. Accounts payable programs keep track of bills and often generate checks to pay them. They record who gets paid and when, handle cash disbursements, and advise managers whether they should accept discounts offered by vendors in return for early payment.

Order Entry. Many businesses handle some type of order processing on a daily basis. Customers either call in orders by phone, send in written orders by ordinary mail or by computer, or place orders in person. The programs that record and help manage such transactions are called *order-entry software.*

Inventory Control. The units of products that a company has in stock to sell at a given moment are called its inventory. *Inventory control programs* closely monitor the number of units of each product in inventory and ensure that reasonable quantities of products are maintained.

General Ledger. *General ledger (G/L) programs* keep track of all financial summaries, including those originating from payroll, accounts receivable, accounts payable, and other sources (see Figure 11-2). They also ensure that the company's books balance properly. G/L programs also produce accounting reports such as income statements, balance sheets, and general ledger balances.

Information Systems

During the early days of commercial computing, businesses purchased computers almost exclusively to perform routine transaction processing tasks. Used in this way, the computer could cut clerical expenses considerably. However, as time passed, it became apparent that the computer could do much more than replace clerks. It could also provide information to assist management in its decision-making role.

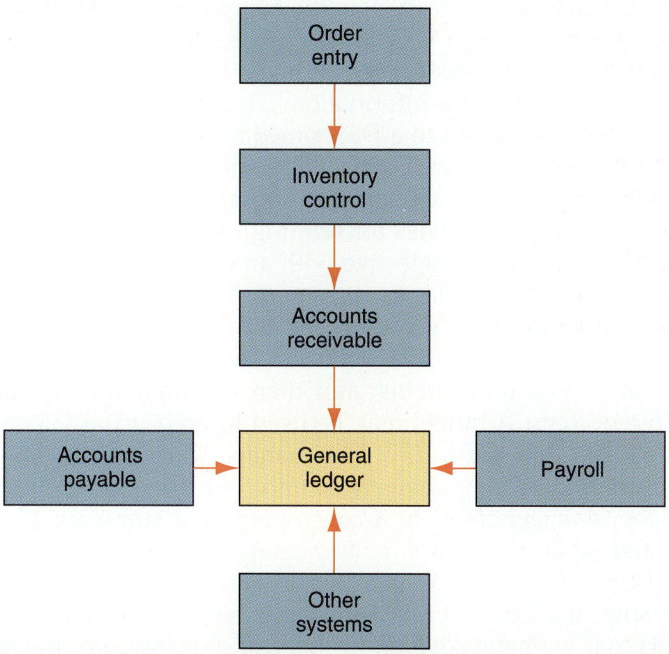

Figure 12-2
The relationship among transaction processing systems.

Information system. A system designed to provide information to managers to enable them to make decisions.

A system that generates information for use by decision makers is often called an **information system.** With an information system, management can incorporate much more information into decisions and spend less time gathering it. As a result, managers have more time to do the things that they do best—thinking creatively and interacting with people.

Two major types of information systems are information reporting systems and decision support systems.

Information reporting system. An information system whose principal outputs are preformatted reports.

Information Reporting Systems. **Information reporting systems** were the first type of information system. They provide management with preselected types of information, generally in the form of computer-generated reports. The types of information that some managers receive are preplanned, just like the information you see on your monthly checking account statements. The individual *values* on your statements, such as check numbers and amounts, may change from month to month, but the *types* of information you receive remain the same. Also, you and every other person mailed checking account statements by your bank receive exactly the same type of information.

Many information reporting systems provide managers with information that is a by-product of the data generated through transaction processing.

Decision Support Systems. During the 1970s, many companies began to call for systems that could field extemporaneous questions from managers. Such systems were expected to be particularly useful to top-level managers, whose requirements for information are somewhat unpredictable and unstructured. In response, the computer industry developed the decision support system.

Decision support system (DSS). A system that provides tools and capabilities to managers to help them satisfy their own information needs.

A **decision support system (DSS)** helps people organize and analyze their own decision-making information. Thus, a "sales support system" is the name typically given to a DSS aimed at the special decision-making needs of salespeople or marketing personnel. A "fire-suppression support system" might be a DSS targeted to helping the director of a forest area develop specific strategies for fighting forest fires.

Let's put DSSs into perspective with an example. To assist with making product pricing decisions, a sales manager uses a DSS that has been set up on a microcomputer system. At the keyboard, the manager first requests the price of an item. Then he or she decides to ask for the average price of several other items, and then for the inventory turnover of yet a different item. A model may be used to predict the sales volume of items five years into the future. The manager can pose questions as the need evolves and receive answers at once. At the end of the interactive session, the manager uses the DSS to prepare a summary of important findings and some bar charts for a meeting. The next time the manager uses the DSS, other types of information may be collected and analyzed.

Generally, the DSS is built from a number of other productivity software tools that we have covered in this text. For instance, the sales manager might acquire a spreadsheet package or a database management sys-

User Solution 11-1

Using a DSS to Rapidly Report Sales Data

Frito-Lay has one of the most powerful decision support systems (DSSs) in the world. On each store visit, salespeople equipped with handheld computers record the shelf space devoted to Frito-Lay products, record sales data, and record data about stale products removed. They also input facts about the movement of competitor products. This information is sent daily to Frito-Lay's headquarters, where mainframes assimilate it into a form that can be conveniently used by management. This is no small feat; Frito-Lay has 10,000 salespeople and 100 products in its line, and it sells to over 400,000 stores. Today, management has facts that would have taken months to discover in the pre-DSS days.

tem to build the sales support system just described. Figure 11-3 and User Solution 11-1 collectively illustrate three decision support systems at work.

Executive information system (EIS). A decision support system that is tailored to the needs of a specific, top-level individual in an organization.

Executive information systems (EISs) are DSSs customized to meet the special needs of individual executives—those people at the highest organizational level. As some executives see it, the business world today is so competitive and fast paced that they need instant access to fresh information. Among executives' favorite applications are using database management systems to access corporate and financial data, using electronic mail systems to streamline contact with subordinates, and using customized spreadsheet programs to display important ratios and trends in a graphical format. Because many executives can't type, many of them require easy-to-learn, easy-to-use graphical interfaces. With the right type of a system, it simply takes some pointing and, perhaps, a few keystrokes or mouse clicks to get what they want in exactly the form they require.

Office Systems

Office automation (OA). The use of computer-based, office-oriented technologies such as word processing, desktop publishing, electronic mail, video teleconferencing, and the like.

In recent years, computer technology has been applied to the task of increasing productivity in the office. The term **office automation (OA)** has been coined to describe this trend. Automating the office can be done through a wide variety of technologies and processing techniques, several of which are discussed below.

Document Processing. *Document processing* refers to the use of computer technology in the preparation of text-intensive documents such as letters,

Figure 11-3 Decision support systems at work.
(a) Electronic data collected through a transaction processing system can be provided immediately to managers, who can quickly spot problems and opportunities. (b) Geographic information systems (GISs) are frequently used to keep track of sales activity, and some, such as this Tactics International GIS, can provide pie charts showing relative salesperson activity.

(a)

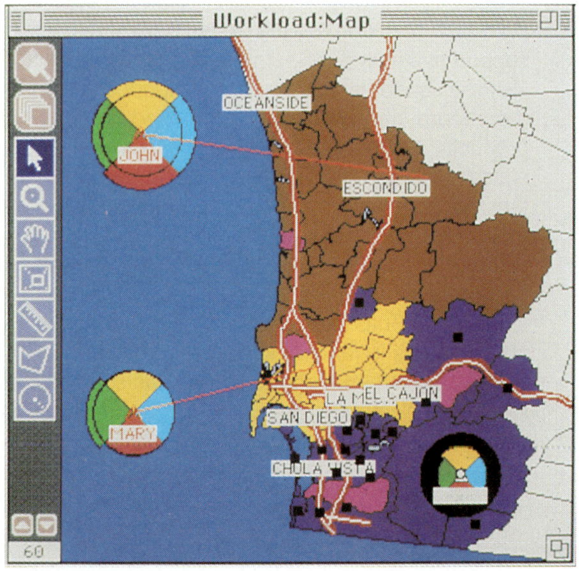

(b)

manuscripts, legal documents, articles, books, restaurant menus, reports, and the like. Two principal document-processing tools—word processing and desktop publishing—were covered extensively in Chapter 8.

Electronic mail.
A facility that enables users to send letters, memos, documents, and the like from one hardware device to another.

Electronic Mail. **Electronic mail** (or E-mail) makes it possible to send informative messages and documents from one terminal or computer system to another. Two familiar examples of electronic mail are the *fax (facsimile) machine* (such as the one pictured in Figure 6-4), which is used to transmit images of hard-copy documents over the phone wires, and *electronic mailboxes,* which are computer files that are set up to store any transmitted message that can be created in or converted to electronic form.

Desk Accessories. *Desk accessories,* or *desktop organizers,* are packages that provide the electronic equivalent of features commonly found on an office desktop. Desk accessory software varies from vendor to vendor, but many of them offer such features as a calendar (see Figure 11-4), clock, calculator, and Rolodex-type file. Often, the feature is implemented in a window, which appears when a specific sequence of keys is activated.

Decision Support Tools. Since many decisions are made by white-collar workers, in the office, it's understandable that many decision support systems are found in the office. Among the tools that are useful in such a setting are spreadsheets, presentation graphics, plotters and laser printers, color monitors, and relational database systems. All of these software and hardware tools have been discussed earlier in the book and have contributed to streamlining life at the office.

Teleconferencing. Teleconferencing makes it possible for a group of people to meet electronically, thereby avoiding the time and expense they would incur if they were to physically get together in one spot. *Audio teleconferencing*—also known as the conference phone call—allows a meeting to take place between several people on a phone system. *Video teleconferencing* systems, on the other hand, use specially equipped rooms that permit participants to see each other on video screens as well as to hear each other. *Computer teleconferencing,* which takes place at computer workstations, allows a conference to develop through messages sent to electronic mailboxes—even when the participants aren't all using their computer systems at the same time. Computer conferencing is an example of *workgroup computing* (see Feature 11-1).

Teleconferencing. Using computer and communications technology to carry out a meeting in which not all the participants need be present at the same place or time.

Figure 11-4
An electronic calendar.
Electronic calendars, such as the one shown here, often provide a graphical display of a full month's activity. At the far right of the screen are icons that can be activated to prepare or access a weekly planner, a daily planner, and a to-do list.

Feature 11-1

Working with Colleagues over Computer Networks

Workgroup Applications Take Off

We are now squarely in the age of computer networks. Company after company is finding it cost effective to downsize many mainframe operations onto networks and to build new applications on networks. This has led to the development of new software products that allow people to share their work, just as they would if they were sharing common file cabinets, bulletin boards, conference phone lines, and secretaries.

The linking of people on a common computer network to communicate with one another about a common job or problem is called *workgroup computing.* Although still in the pioneering stage, workgroup computing is beginning to take off in a big way. Five workgroup computing applications are in education, computer teleconferencing, publishing, claims processing, and CASE tools for program and system developers.

Education. Imagine taking a computer class in which everyone in the classroom, including the professor, is at a microcomputer workstation. As the professor lectures, everything she does at her keyboard appears on a large overhead monitor visible to the class. "Now it's your turn," she says, after showing students how to write a macro for a worksheet. With a keystroke or two, she downloads the worksheet over a local area network (LAN) that connects all of the workstations in the class and many other workstations on campus. When a problem occurs, a student simply types a short note, electronically cuts and pastes the error message or faulty macro into the note, and presses an "upload" key. The student's screen is then passed into a window on the professor's screen. The professor corrects the screen and sends it back to the student. Students can also receive the same type of help when the professor is holding office hours and they are on another part of campus. This is accomplished by getting on a LAN workstation (perhaps in a dorm room) and sending a message to the LAN workstation in the professor's office.

Computer Teleconferencing. Computer teleconferencing refers to the use of computers and an electronic bulletin board/electronic-mail system to conduct a conference. Workers can broadcast a bulletin-board message to everyone in a group or an electronic-mail message to certain individuals. Some groups that have used computer teleconferencing claim that it facilitates faster decision making, gets more people involved in the decision-making process, and avoids tying up time in routine staff meetings. In addition, higher-level managers can use their terminals to peek in on the conference bulletin board, eliminating the need for some formal reports. Although many such conferences are carried out locally, it's also possible to have "virtual workgroups" of people scattered geographically. In this type of arrangement, when a problem arises at one location, an organization can send a description to the electronic mailboxes of experts at other sites, who may be able to suggest solutions.

Publishing. In the publishing field, where deadlines can be tight and people need answers from colleagues quickly in order to proceed, workgroup computing is finding a home. When a writer or editor is part of a group, single-user workstations that are not part of a network can lead to chaos. For example, if a writer and two editors are working on an article at the same time, it can be difficult to make changes in a document to which everyone agrees. Publishing software, when implemented in a group environment, uses a locking feature so that concurrent access to the article is not possible while someone else is making changes to it. (This illustrates why software intended for workgroup computing is necessarily different than software intended for single-user environments.)

Insurance. In insurance, it's common for several types of photos and documents to be generated as a claim is being processed (see photos). For instance, an adjuster may take a picture of a damaged car and prepare an adjustment form. An estimate and a claim form will also be needed. Gradually, a file on each claim will be developed, and people within the insurance company's claims department will need to see the file, sign off on certain documents, and add other documents. In

(a)

(b)

(c)

(d)

Group processing of an insurance claim. (a) Accident photos, estimates, and reports are scanned into electronic files. (b) A customer representative can pull up any document on the screen when the customer has a question about a claim. (c) An appraiser electronically writes her comments on a form with a digitizing tablet and stylus and adds a digitized voice message. (d) The adjuster reviews all of the paperwork and approves the payment.

many firms, all of these documents are read into the computer system with an image scanner and put into a form that can be annotated and processed electronically.

CASE Tools. Software-development programmers often are assigned pieces of the same program to work on concurrently or sequentially. With the rise of automated program development tools—commonly referred to as *CASE (computer-aided software engineering)* products—programmers can share work more easily and synchronize work on-line.

Workgroup computing will evolve by trial and error. As pioneering vendors get workgroup computing products out to users and obtain feedback, they will come to understand more fully how people can use computers effectively when working in groups.

Telecommuting.
Working at home and being connected by means of electronic devices to other workers at remote locations.

Telecommuting. **Telecommuting** is the term used to describe people working at home and linking up to their employers through a microcomputer workstation, display terminal, fax machine, and/or other type of computer-age tool. Many typists and computer programmers, for example, telecommute to their jobs, perhaps because they prefer to do so or because they are more productive at home. Telecommuting can save workers both the time and expense involved in traveling to work. It can also save business the expense of maintaining office and parking space. On the negative side, telecommuting limits the interpersonal contact that often makes working in an office lively and productive.

Design and Manufacturing Systems: CAD/CAM

Computers are widely used in business to improve productivity both at the design stage—through computer-aided design (CAD)—and at the manufacturing stage—through computer-aided manufacturing (CAM).

Computer-aided design (CAD).
A general term applied to the use of computer technology to automate design functions.

Computer-Aided Design (CAD). Using **computer-aided design (CAD),** product designers can dramatically reduce the time they spend "at the drawing board." For example, using light pens and specialized graphics workstations (see Figure 11-5), engineers can sketch ideas directly into the computer system, which can then be instructed to analyze the proposed design in terms of how well it meets a number of design criteria. Taking into account the subsequent output of the computer, the designer can modify the drawings until a desirable design is achieved. Before the arrival of CAD, the designer had to produce by hand preliminary

Figure 11-5 Computer-aided design.
(a) High-resolution technical workstations enable design engineers to create a variety of products, ranging from cars and aircraft to rug patterns and running shoes. (b) A house being built with a CAD system.

(a)

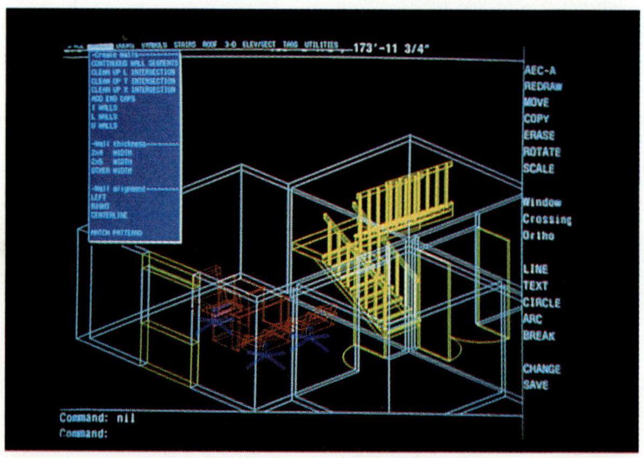

(b)

sketches and then advanced designs, representing refinements on the sketches. After models were built and tested, the designer had to prepare production drawings, which were used to build the equipment needed to manufacture the new product, whether it was a truck or a new toaster. Today, computer-aided assistance with all of these tasks is fairly common. CAD is especially helpful in the design of products such as automobiles, aircraft, ships, buildings, electrical circuits (including computer chips), and even running shoes. Window 7 provides several examples that provide insight into how CAD is implemented in design environments.

Computer-Aided Manufacturing (CAM). Computer applications are not limited to only the design phases of product development. In fact, computers were used on the factory floor well before engineers used them interactively for design. With each passing day, more and more of the actual process of production on the factory floor is becoming computerized.

Computer-aided manufacturing (CAM) includes the use of computers to help manage manufacturing operations and to control machinery used in manufacturing processes. One example is a system that observes production in an oil refinery, performs calculations, and opens and shuts appropriate valves when necessary. Another system, commonly used in the steel industry, works from preprogrammed specifications to automatically perform the shaping and assembly of steel parts. Increasingly, robots are used to carry out processes once solely in the human domain (see Figure 11-6). CAM is also widely employed to build cars and ships,

Computer-aided manufacturing (CAM). A general term applied to the use of computer technology to automate manufacturing functions.

Figure 11-6
An industrial robot.
Robots take on jobs that are too physically demanding, monotonous, dangerous, or expensive for humans to perform. The robot shown here is helping to assemble a keyboard at an IBM plant.

monitor power plants, manufacture food and chemicals, and perform a number of other functions.

Artificial Intelligence

Artificial intelligence (AI). The ability of a machine to perform actions that are characteristic of human intelligence, such as reasoning and learning.

Expert system. A program or computer system that provides the type of advice that would be expected of a human expert.

A computer is a device that, given some instructions, can perform work at extremely fast speeds, drawing upon a large memory. It can also be programmed with a set of rules or guidelines—enabling it to draw certain types of conclusions based on the input it receives. A good deal of human mental activity involves these very processes. For this reason, the ability of computer systems to perform in ways that would be considered intelligent if observed in humans is commonly referred to as **artificial intelligence (AI).**

Today, the four main areas of AI are expert systems, natural languages, vision systems, and robotics.

Expert Systems. **Expert systems** are programs that provide the type of advice that would normally be expected from a human expert. In medicine, for instance, an expert system might be used to incorporate the thinking patterns of some of the world's leading doctors. For example, the system might be given a configuration of symptoms exhibited by a patient. If these symptoms might lead to the diagnosis of a disease the program knows something about, the program might ask the attending physician for further information about specific details. Ultimately, through questioning and checking the patient's condition against a large database of successfully diagnosed cases, the program might draw conclusions that the attending physician may never have otherwise reached—and very quickly, no less.

Expert systems have enormous applications potential in business, where they can be used to capture the knowledge of expert business professionals into an active form and subsequently can be used to improve decision making within the firm or to train individuals. Today, the application of expert systems to the solution of business problems is just beginning to be felt. Figure 11-7 shows a number of present and proposed applications for expert systems in business. The Tomorrow box describes an expert-system technology called neural networks.

Natural Languages. One of the greatest challenges currently facing scientists in the field of AI is to equip computer systems with the ability to communicate in *natural languages*—English, Spanish, French, Japanese, and so forth. Unfortunately, this challenge is not easily met. People have personalized ways of communicating, and the meaning of words varies with the context in which they are used. Also, the rules people employ to reach an understanding of what others are saying are highly complex and still not well understood by language researchers. These hurdles notwithstanding, researchers have made some big strides in the direction of getting computers to listen to and respond in natural languages.

Business Area	Application
Tax accounting	Assisting tax accountants by providing advice on the best tax treatment for an individual or corporation
Repair	Assisting machine repairpeople by providing expert diagnosis of malfunctions
Insurance sales	Helping an insurance agent tailor an insurance package to a client, given the client's insurance, investment, financial planning, and tax needs
Portfolio planning	Determining the best securities portfolio for a client, given the client's growth and equity objectives
Manufacturing	Finding the best way to design, produce, stock, and ship a product
System design	Determining the optimal hardware and software configuration to meet a set of user requirements
Multinational planning	Providing expert advice on whether a given business strategy will work in different countries, each with its own laws and customs
Government tax auditing	Using a complex set of criteria and a knowledge base of past audit cases to decide which individuals and companies to audit to maximize overall return
Credit authorization	Deciding whether to grant credit to individuals and companies based on both their past histories and other similar credit cases
Training	Putting newly hired employees into computer-simulated situations in which their performance is aided by or compared with experts

Figure 11-7
Business examples of expert systems.
Within the coming decade, say industry analysts, expert system routines will become standard items in many software products.

Vision Systems. *Vision systems* enable computer-controlled devices to "see." A vision system might work as follows: Parts produced in a manufacturing process are sent along an assembly line for inspection. A vision system located at a station along the line takes a digital photograph of each part as it is going past the station. The photo is decomposed into vital data that are electronically compared to other data, showing how the part would compare if it were correctly produced. The vision system uses a set of rules to determine whether the part is correctly made or flawed. If the part is flawed, the vision system also identifies the nature of the flaw and the corrective action that should be taken.

Robotics. **Robotics** refers to the study of the design, building, and use of robots. Robots are machines that, with the help of a computer, can mimic a number of human motor activities in order to perform jobs that are too monotonous or dangerous for their flesh-and-blood counterparts. Although it may seem like many of these robots are "dumb," they are often aided by a number of artificial intelligence techniques so that they may identify objects and states in their environments and so that they may act accordingly. Some robots can even "see" by means of imbedded cameras and "feel" with sensors that permit them to assess the hardness, temperature, and other qualities of objects. Robots can represent a substantial savings to a corporation, since they don't go on strike, don't need vacations, and don't get sick.

Robotics.
The field devoted to the study of robot technology.

Tomorrow

Neural-Net Computing

Using Artificial Intelligence to Recognize Patterns

Most computing today is preprogrammed number crunching. Whether you are reformatting a document, doing spreadsheet computations, searching through a database, compiling a program, or coloring or rotating graphics images, you are simply executing a predetermined procedure at a high speed. Conventional computers are good at this type of thing. But if you ask them to recognize a handwritten letter, that's a different matter.

This is where neural nets come in. *Neural-net computing* refers to an artificial-intelligence technology in which the human brain's pattern-recognition process is emulated by a computer system. Neural-net systems aren't preprogrammed to provide predictable responses like conventional algorithms. Instead, they are designed to learn by observation and repetition.

Neural nets are usually software programs that work on conventional computers. Some research institutions have gone a step further, however, and have developed hardware-based neural nets—that is, computers with circuitry especially designed to solve pattern-recognition problems. This circuitry is often of analog design, in contrast to the digital (binary) circuitry that underlies conventional computers.

Neural-net computers translate pattern-recognition processes into small blocks of code that are processed in parallel. These computers simulate a network of hundreds or thousands of interconnected nodes, spanning several layers, that rapidly pass data to each other.

Although neural-net computing is largely a technology of tomorrow, several applications involving neural nets have already begun in earnest. These applications involve handwriting, speech, and image recognition; credit-risk assessment; crime analysis; and stock analysis.

Handwriting, Speech, and Image Recognition. Recognition of a person's signature, voice, or face happens so quickly that you scarcely notice how the underlying process works. Neural nets attempt to emulate this process. Consider character recognition, for instance. The lower levels of the neural net may recognize that a character is composed of curves and straight lines. This information is passed to the next layer, which may attempt to determine the number of curves and lines and how they fit together. Finally, conclusions are passed to a third level, which may recognize the character as a capital "B." If the character can't be recognized, the neural net attempts to learn from the mistake. One financial-services institution is already using such an algorithm to recognize handwritten numerals on checks.

Credit-Risk Assessment. Subtle patterns also exist in conventional text data, such as those found at financial institutions. If you were very sharp and studied the records of thousands of people who were granted and denied credit, you might eventually be able to discern which types of people were good credit risks and which types of people were poor ones. Of course, computers can work much faster than humans and can notice patterns that are hardly discernible. Neural nets are currently

Responsibility for Systems Development

In large organizations—with thousands of employees and thousands of operational details to keep track of—there are usually thousands of systems, ranging from personal systems to systems that operate at an enterprisewide level (see User Solution 11-2). Deciding which systems best support the direction of the enterprise, and how much attention to give being applied to solve credit-risk assessment problems at American Express and other companies. Perhaps in the future, use of neural nets will help to avert catastrophes such as the recent U.S. savings and loan crisis.

Crime Analysis. Neural nets are expected to offer some assistance in solving crimes. Many crimes, of course, display a pattern, and often this pattern is too subtle to be picked up without computer assistance. New York's Chase Manhattan Bank is currently using neural nets to examine hundreds of thousands of transactions daily and to look for fraudulent transactions.

Stock Analysis. One exciting neural-net application is a program that examines stock-market data for patterns and helps determine strategies for buying and selling stocks. Although such an application does not yet exist, some firms are currently attempting to use neural nets to forecast stock-market indexes.

Other applications for neural nets in the future abound. In medicine, neural nets may examine detailed records of patients having a specific disease and attempt to uncover an underlying pattern. In quality control, thousands of parts could be studied to uncover subtle structural problems. And, perhaps, the optimal mixture of glue, pulp, and water required to make top-quality paper can be determined with neural nets. Wherever there's a pattern to study, a neural-net application may be useful.

Technology taking a bite out of crime. Neural nets are expected to help.

each one, is essentially where systems responsibility begins. In the typical business organization, a number of computer professionals share responsibility for the development of all but the very smallest of systems.

The *chief information officer (CIO)* holds primary responsibility for systems development. Often this position is at the level of vice-president. One of the CIO's duties is to develop a corporate strategy that defines the role of information processing within the organization. Another is to oversee the formulation of a five-year plan that maps out which systems are to be studied and possibly revamped during that period.

User Solution 11-2

Systems Support at UPS

How much support does a big company need to build and maintain its computer systems? Consider UPS, the world's largest shipper of packages. Each day, UPS delivers about 12 million parcels domestically and to about 180 foreign countries or territories. It has a fleet of approximately 103,000 trucks, 350 jets (UPS is the tenth-largest airline), 230,000 employees, and 1,750 facilities worldwide. In terms of small computers alone, it has about 20,000 PCs and more than 300 LANs. Currently, UPS has a staff of around 1,700 computer professionals, many of whom work out of its computer and telecommunications support center in Mahwah, New Jersey.

Because information processing affects not only the accounting functions in most firms but also most other departments, including marketing, manufacturing, and personnel, a *steering committee* composed of top-level executives normally approves the plan. This committee also sets broad guidelines for performing computer-related activities. However, it does not become highly involved with technical details or the administration of particular projects, which are the responsibility of the information systems department.

The Information Systems Department

Information systems department. The area in an organization that consists of computer professionals.

The **information systems department** varies widely in structure from one company to another. In one form the department is divided into three parts, as shown in Figure 11-8. The *data processing area* has primary responsibility for the development of large transaction processing systems—that is, those systems costing over $100,000 or so and affecting the entire organization. The *information center* normally is involved with smaller projects, say, those that help individual end users or end-user departments select microcomputer resources for their own, local use. The *office automation (OA) area* is in charge of ensuring that the organization takes full advantage of technologies such as word processing, desktop publishing, electronic mail, and the like.

Data processing area. The group of computer professionals charged with building transaction processing systems.

Data Processing Area. The **data processing area** predates all other areas within the information systems department and is still considered by many to be the most important. After all, if their computers stopped processing high-volume business transactions, most large organizations would have to shut down.

Figure 11-8
A possible organizational structure for an information systems department.
Many information systems departments consist of three principal areas: data processing, an information center, and office automation.

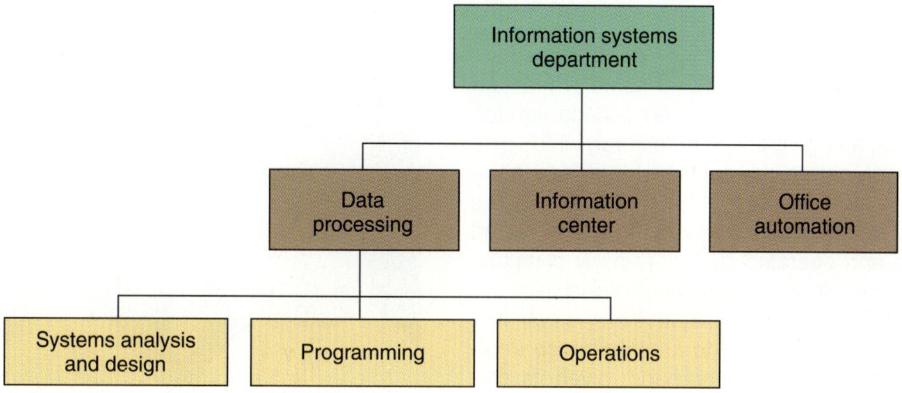

Within the data processing area, the *systems analysis and design group* analyzes, designs, and implements new software and hardware systems. The *programming group* codes computer programs from program design specifications. The *operations group* manages day-to-day processing once a system has become operational.

The person most involved with systems development is the **systems analyst.** Generally speaking, the systems analyst's job in the data processing area is to both plan and implement large systems that will use the computers the organization has or will acquire. When such a system is needed, the systems analyst interacts with current and potential end users to produce a solution. The analyst generally is involved in all stages of the development process, from beginning to end.

Systems analyst.
A person who studies systems in an organization in order to determine what actions need to be taken and how these actions may best be achieved with computer resources.

In most large projects, a team of people will be involved. A systems analyst will probably be appointed as a **project manager** to head up the team. Other people on the team might include users, programmers, an outside consultant, a cost accountant, and an auditor. In cases in which the organization doesn't have the staff on hand to build or operate the system it needs, an outsourcing option is often chosen (see Feature 11-2).

Project manager.
A systems analyst who is put in charge of a team that is building a large system.

Information Center. The **information center** (IC) was originally conceived to help the individual end users in the organization make intelligent choices about the microcomputer hardware and software they need to better perform their jobs, as well as to promote an orderly acquisition of microcomputing resources within the organization as a whole. Many ICs are staffed primarily with *information center consultants* (systems analysts having special skills in the microcomputing area) and with *trainers.*

Information center.
A facility in an organization charged with developing small systems.

ICs often are set up similarly to a typical microcomputer store. A user walks in and talks to a consultant about specific microcomputing needs. Perhaps the user is a sales manager who needs a small decision support system to keep track of a field sales force. The manager and consultant

Feature 11-2

Outsourcing

The Benefits and the Costs

At Andersen Consulting, a leading outsourcer, helping clients solve problems is a multimillion dollar business.

Outsourcing involves turning over some or most information systems functions to an outside vendor. For instance, a large paint manufacturer, which gets thousands of orders daily, might have only communications terminals at its main headquarters and plant. The remote mainframes doing the workload are owned and operated by a third-party company skilled at high-volume transaction processing.

Why do companies outsource? A small firm might find it too expensive to keep in-house information systems personnel on hand, given its current work volume. Or a large company might not have the capacity or capital to expand its operations in house, so it may outsource some of them temporarily. And many firms have found it easier to outsource operations in areas in which it's too hard to find or too expensive to hire new personnel. Many firms also turn to an outsourcer when they think that the outsourcer could do the job better or cheaper than they. Outsourcers often pay top dollar, and top dollar draws top talent.

Outsourcing may exist in a variety of different forms. In many cases, the outsourcer has its own computer center and supplies terminals and a network to the client. In other cases, the client firm has its own equipment and, needing someone to operate it, turns to the outsourcer to supply personnel. Personnel may be supplied on a short-term, project-specific basis, or they may work for the client long enough to seem like employees. Virtually any conceivable support arrangement is available through outsourcing.

Outsourcing is not a new concept. Throughout the last several decades, outsourcing firms have existed under a variety of names, calling themselves, for example, service bureaus, facilities managers, and systems integrators. Recently, outsourcing has become increasingly popular because there are almost too many technologies for a single firm to handle alone. In addition, several large, highly visible firms that have traditionally worked completely in house have gone on record in favor of outsourcing.

Along with the benefits to outsourcing come some serious drawbacks. Some firms simply hand over their work to an outsourcer and say "do me," hardly reading the contract and not requiring the outsourcer to be accountable for certain levels of performance. Consequently, they are "done to"—in a way they didn't expect. Leadership and control need to come from the client, not from the outsourcing firm. Also, when in-house personnel have to mix with personnel of the outsourcer, conflicts sometimes arise. The in-house personnel may feel that their jobs are threatened by the outsourcer's personnel, or, perhaps, there may be some disagreements about who is in charge. Finally, there is the matter of security. Although an outsourcer provides certain levels of security, the best security control is achieved when the client company attends to it at its own site. When work goes outside, anything can happen.

Despite the drawbacks, with both technology and business arrangements becoming more complex, outsourcing appears to be an unstoppable trend.

sit down at one or two machines and experiment with some appropriate, off-the-shelf software. Eventually, through trial and error, they put together a small system.

Office Automation (OA) Area. In many organizations, the **office automation (OA) area** is both the newest and the smallest group within the information systems department. The OA area is responsible for developing a cost-efficient, integrated approach to using office technologies such as electronic document processing and electronic mail. Typical duties, which resemble those of the IC, are arranging product demonstrations and helping end users and end-user departments select systems.

Office automation (OA) area. The group of computer professionals charged with managing office-related computer activities within the organization.

The Systems Development Life Cycle

Systems development often is subdivided into five steps, or phases:

- Phase 1: Preliminary investigation
- Phase 2: Systems analysis
- Phase 3: System design
- Phase 4: System acquisition
- Phase 5: System implementation

Collectively these phases often are referred to as the **systems development life cycle (SDLC),** because they describe a system from the time it is first studied until the time it is put into use. When a new business pressure necessitates a change in a system, the steps of the cycle begin anew. The five steps of the SDLC apply in principle both to the large, multimillion-dollar information systems that run large corporations and to the $3,000 microcomputer systems that sit on many desktops in homes.

Systems development life cycle (SDLC). The process consisting of the five phases of system development: preliminary investigation, systems analysis, system design, system acquisition, and system implementation.

The five steps of the systems development life cycle do not always follow in a predetermined sequence. Frequently, analysis and design are interleaved. For instance, to look at an example from everyday life, when people develop a seven-day vacation plan, they don't usually completely design the plan as the first step and execute it, without modification as the second step. They might design a plan for day 1, and when the day is over, analyze what has happened and use their experiences to design a plan for day 2. After day 2, further analysis is done to design day 3. And so on. Many systems are designed this way, "on the fly" as it were, as well.

The Preliminary Investigation

One of the first things to do when it is suggested that a new system is necessary is to conduct a **preliminary investigation,** or *feasibility study.* The purpose of this investigation is to quickly define and evaluate the

Preliminary investigation. A brief study of a problem area to assess whether or not a full-scale project should be undertaken. Also called a *feasibility study.*

problem at hand, to see if it is worthy of further study, and to suggest some possible courses of action. Accordingly, the investigation should examine such issues as the nature of the problem, the scope of the work involved with handling the problem, possible solution alternatives, and the approximate costs and benefits of the alternatives.

Systems Analysis

Systems analysis. The phase of the systems development life cycle in which a problem area is thoroughly examined to determine what should be done.

Systems analysis is the phase of systems development in which the problem area is studied in depth and the needs of system users are assessed. The main activities conducted during systems analysis are fact collection and fact analysis.

Fact Collection. The goal of fact collection is to gather information about the type of work being performed in the application under study and to ascertain what resources end users need. Later in this phase, the collection of facts should suggest some possible solutions. Deciding which facts to collect depends largely on the problem being studied. Four sources of information on the applications area and end-user needs are (1) written documents showing how the application under study is supposed to work, (2) questionnaires sent to users, (3) interviews of users, and (4) the personal observations of the systems analyst.

Fact Analysis. As information is gathered about the application, it must be analyzed to reach some conclusions. Two useful tools for performing analysis are data flow diagrams and checklists.

Data flow diagram. A graphically oriented systems development tool that enables a systems analyst to logically represent the flow of data through a system.

Data flow diagrams provide a visual representation of data movement in an organization. They show the relationship between activities that are part of a system as well as the data or information flowing into and out of each of the activities. Figure 11-9 shows a data flow diagram for the order-entry operation of a mail-order firm.

Checklists are often developed for such important matters as the goals of the system and the information needs of key people in the system. For example, an accounts receivable system should have such goals as getting bills out quickly, rapidly informing customers about late payments, and cutting losses due to bad debts. On the other hand, a decision support system that helps teachers advise students should increase the quality of information and decrease the time it takes to develop curricula for students.

Common sense eventually must dictate which type of checklist or diagram is most appropriate for the situation at hand. The principal purpose of these tools is to help the analyst organize thoughts so that conclusions can be drawn about what the system under study should be doing.

System Design

System design. The phase of the systems development life cycle in which the parts of a new system and the relationships among them are formally established.

System design focuses on specifying what the system will look like. The system design phase normally consists of developing a model of the new system and performing a detailed analysis of benefits and costs.

Figure 11-9 A data flow diagram for a mail-order firm.
An order triggers the processes of verification and assembly of the goods ordered, and payment is recorded by accounts receivable.

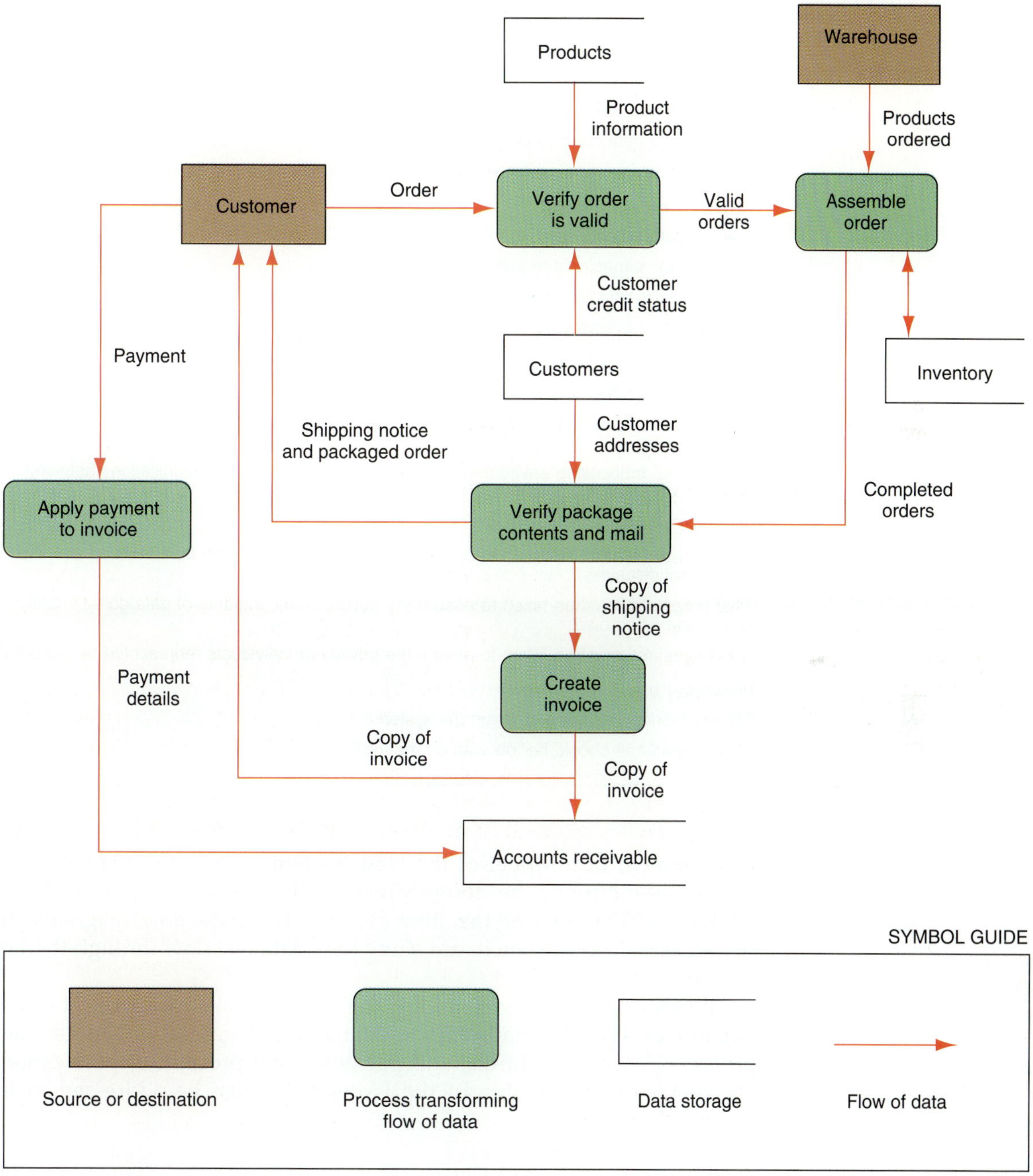

Figure 11-10
Issues to cover during the system design specification. System design ultimately addresses all major elements of a computer system—hardware, software, data, people, and procedures.

Output Considerations

What types of information do users need?

How often is this information needed? Annually? Monthly? Daily? On demand?

What output devices and media are necessary to provide the required information?

How should output be formatted or arranged so that it can easily be understood by users?

Input Considerations

What data need to be gathered?

How often do data need to be gathered?

What input devices and media are required for data collection and input?

Storage Considerations

How will data be accessed and therefore organized?

What storage capacity is required?

How fast must data be accessed?

What storage devices are appropriate?

Processing Considerations

What type of functionality is required in the software?

What type of processing power is required? A mainframe? A minicomputer? A microcomputer?

What special processing environments must be considered? A communications network? A database processing environment?

System Controls

What measures must be taken to ensure that data are secure from unauthorized use, theft, and natural disasters?

What measures must be taken to ensure the accuracy and integrity of data going in and information going out?

What measures must be taken to ensure the privacy of individuals represented by the data?

Personnel and Procedures

What personnel are needed to run the system?

What procedures should be followed on the job?

Development of a Model of the New System. Once the analyst understands the nature of the design problem, it is usually helpful to draw a number of diagrams of the new system. The data flow diagrams discussed earlier, for instance, can show how data will flow through the new system.

When designing a system, the analyst must take into account output requirements; input requirements; data access, organization, and storage; processing; system controls; and personnel and procedure specifications. Figure 11-10 covers some of the issues that must be addressed in the design specification.

Analysis of Benefits and Costs. Most organizations are acutely sensitive to costs, including computer system costs. Costs include both the initial investment in hardware and software and ongoing costs such as personnel and maintenance. Some benefits can be computed easily by calculating the amount of labor saved, the reduction in paperwork, and so on. These are called *tangible benefits,* because they are easy to quantify in dollars.

Other benefits, such as better service to customers or improved information for decision makers, are more difficult to convert into dollar amounts. These are called *intangible benefits.* Clearly the existence of intangible benefits makes it more difficult for management to reach firm decisions. On projects with a large number of such benefits, management must ask questions such as "Are the new services that we can offer to customers worth the $100,000 it will cost us?"

System Acquisition

Once a system has been designed and the required types of software and hardware have been specified, the analyst must decide from which vendors to buy the necessary components. This decision lies at the heart of the **system acquisition** phase.

System acquisition. The phase of the systems development life cycle in which equipment, software, or services are acquired from vendors.

RFPs and RFQs. Many organizations formulate their buying or leasing needs by preparing a document called a **request for proposal (RFP).** This document contains a list of technical specifications for equipment and software, determined during the system design phase. The RFP is sent to all vendors who might satisfy the organization's needs. In the proposal they send back to the initiating organization, vendors recommend a hardware and/or software solution to solve the problem at hand and quote a price.

Request for proposal (RFP). A document containing a general description of a system that an organization wishes to acquire.

In some cases, an organization knows exactly which hardware and software resources it needs from vendors and is interested only in a quote on a specific list of items. In this case, it sends vendors a document called a **request for quotation (RFQ),** which names those items and asks for a quote. Thus, whereas an RFP gives a vendor some leeway in making system suggestions, an RFQ does not.

Request for quotation (RFQ). A document containing a list of specific hardware, software, and services that an organization wishes to acquire.

Evaluating Bids. Once vendors have submitted their bids or quotes in response to the RFP or RFQ, the buyer organization must decide which bid to accept. Two useful tools for making this choice are a vendor rating system and a benchmark test.

In a **vendor rating system,** such as the one in Figure 11-11, important criteria for selecting computer system resources are identified and each is given a weight. For example, in the figure, the "60" for hardware and "30" for documentation may be loosely interpreted to mean that hardware is twice as important as documentation to this organization. Each vendor submitting an acceptable bid is rated on each criterion, with the associated weight representing the maximum possible score. The buyer then totals the scores and chooses—possibly—the vendor with the highest total. Such a rating tool does not guarantee that the best vendor will always have the highest point total, but it does have the advantage of being objective and simple to apply. If several people are involved in the selection decision, individual biases tend to be "averaged out."

Vendor rating system. A point-scoring procedure for evaluating competing vendors of computer products or services.

Figure 11-11
A point-scoring approach for evaluating vendors' bids.
Often, but not always, the vendor with the highest point total is the one selected.

Criterion	Weight (Maximum Score)	Vendor 1 Score	Vendor 2 Score
Hardware	60	60	40
Software	80	70	70
Cost	70	50	65
Ease of use	80	70	50
Modularity	50	30	30
Vendor support	50	50	50
Documentation	30	30	20
		360	325

Vendor 1 has highest total score

Benchmark test.
A test used to measure computer system performance under typical use conditions prior to purchase.

Some organizations, after tentatively selecting a vendor, make their choice conditional on the successful completion of a "test drive," or **benchmark test.** Such a test normally consists of running a pilot version of the new system on the hardware and software of the vendor under consideration. To do this, the acquiring organization generally visits the benchmark testing center of the vendor and attempts to determine how well the hardware/software configuration will work if installed. Benchmark tests are expensive and far from foolproof. It's very possible that the pilot system will perform admirably at the benchmark site but the real system, when eventually installed at the site of the acquiring organization, will not.

System Implementation

System implementation.
The phase of systems development that encompasses activities related to making the computer system operational and successful once it is delivered by the vendor.

Once arrangements for delivery of computer resources have been made with one or more vendors, the **system implementation** phase begins. This phase includes all the remaining tasks necessary to make the system operational and successful.

To ensure that the system will be working by a certain date, the analyst must prepare a timetable. One tool for helping with this task is *project management software,* illustrated in Figure 11-12. This software shows how implementation activities are related, shows when activities must start and finish, and pinpoints critical activities.

Implementation consists of converting programs and data files from the old system to the new one, debugging converted and new applications programs, training, and appraising the new system's performance. If the system has been designed well, it should be flexible enough to accommodate changes over a reasonable period of time with minimal disruption. However, if at some point a major change becomes necessary, another system will be needed to replace the current one. At this point, the systems development life cycle—from the preliminary investigation to implementation—will begin all over again.

Figure 11-12 Project management.
Large projects are often managed with the assistance of project management software. Many of the software products, like the one featured here, provide (a) a graphical project timetable and graphs of resource utilization and (b) a chart showing how pieces of the project fit together. The chart in (b) will also show the project's critical path—that is, the path along which any slippage means that the entire project is delayed.

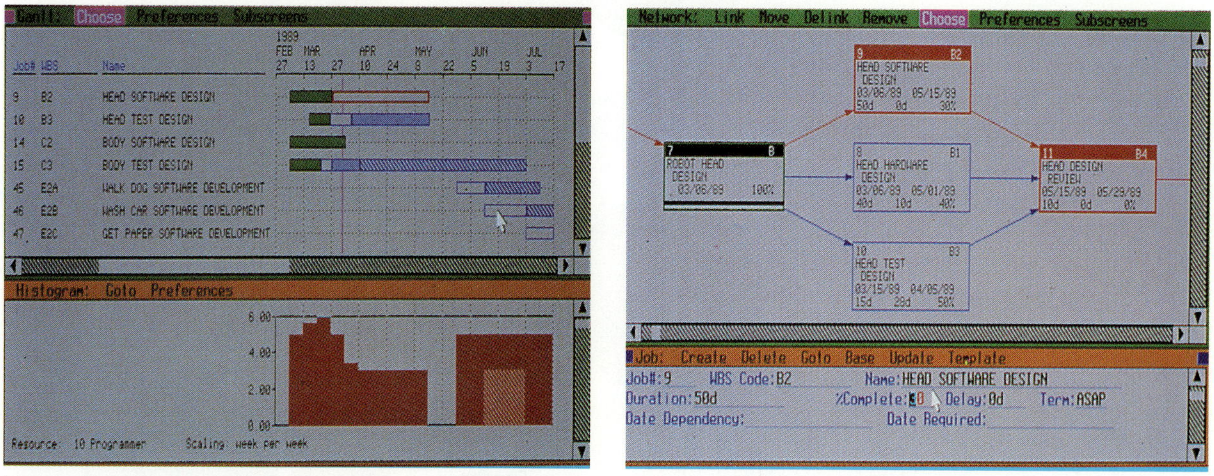

(a) (b)

Approaches to Systems Development

In this section, we'll closely examine three approaches to systems development: the traditional approach, prototyping, and end-user development.

The Traditional Approach

Traditional approach. An approach to systems development whereby the five phases of the systems development life cycle are carried out in a predetermined sequence.

In the **traditional approach,** the phases of systems development are carried out in a predetermined order: (1) preliminary investigation, (2) systems analysis, (3) system design, (4) system acquisition, and (5) implementation. Each phase is begun only when the one before it is completed. Often, the traditional approach is reserved for the development of large transaction processing systems. Because the traditional approach is usually expensive and extensive, it is normally carried out by knowledgeable professionals—that is, by systems analysts.

Traditional systems development requires system users to consider proposed system plans by looking at detailed diagrams, descriptive reports, and specifications of the proposed new system. The entire system is specified and built before anyone gets to use it. As each phase of development is completed, users "sign off" on the recommendations presented to them by the analyst, indicating their acceptance.

Figure 11-13
Prototyping.
Prototyping is an iterative process; after each prototype is built, the user and analyst try it out together and attempt to improve upon it. Eventually, the prototype evolves into a finished system.

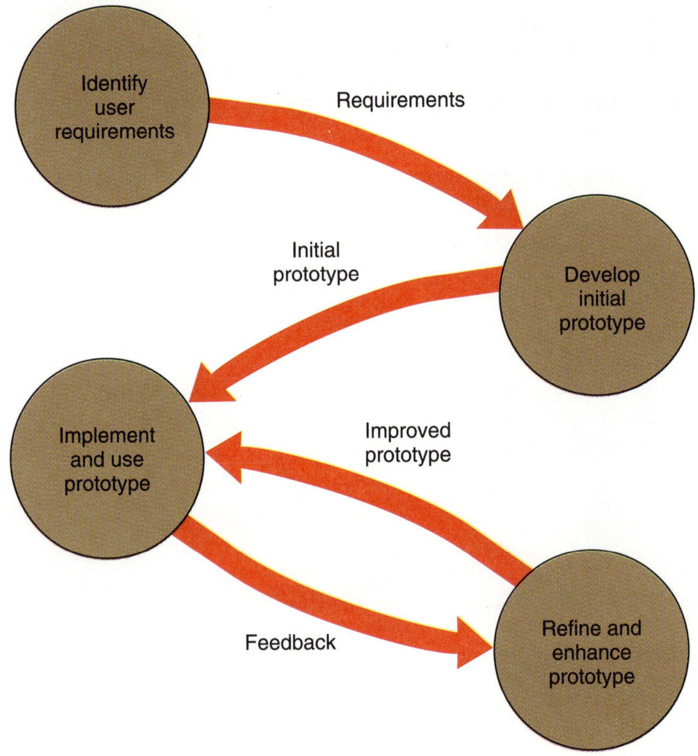

In many organizations, the traditional approach to systems development has recently fallen into disfavor for many systems projects. First, systems often take too long to analyze, design, and implement under the traditional approach. By the time a system is finally put into operation, important new needs that were not part of the original plan may surface. Second, the system being developed often is the wrong one. Managers almost always have difficulty expressing their information needs, and it is not until they begin to use a system that they discover what it is they really need.

Prototyping

Prototyping. A systems development alternative whereby a small model, or *prototype*, of the system is built before a full-scale systems development effort is undertaken.

To avoid the potentially expensive diaster that could result from completing every phase of systems development before users ever lay their hands on a system, many analysts have advocated prototyping as a means of systems development. In **prototyping,** the focus is on developing a small model, or *prototype,* of the overall system. Users work with the prototype and suggest modifications. The prototype is then modified, resulting in an improved prototype. As soon as the prototype is refined to the point where higher management feels confident that a larger version of the system will succeed, either the prototype can be gradually expanded or the organization can go "full steam ahead" with the remaining steps of systems development.

In prototyping, analysis and design generally proceed together, in small steps that finally result in a completed system. The idea behind the prototyping process is virtually identical to the one described on page 385 for developing vacation plans. Prototyping is illustrated in Figure 11-13.

End-User Development

End-user development is a relatively new form of systems development—one that has evolved from the microcomputing revolution. It is defined as a systems development effort in which the end user is primarily responsible for the development of the system. This is in contrast to other types of development, in which a qualified computer professional, such as a systems analyst, takes charge of the systems development process.

End-user development. Systems development carried out by the end user.

As you might guess, end-user development is feasible only in cases where the system being acquired is relatively inexpensive. A good example is the situation in which an end user purchases a microcomputer system and develops applications on his or her own. In developing the system, the end user might follow a prototyping approach or a method similar to traditional development.

Summary and Key Terms

Types of systems and how organizations build them are the principal subjects of this chapter.

On Systems. A **system** is a collection of elements and procedures that interact to accomplish a goal. The function of many systems, whether manual or computerized, is to keep an organization well managed and running smoothly.

Systems development is a process that consists of analyzing a system, designing a new system or making modifications to the old one, acquiring the needed hardware and software, and getting the new or modified system to work. Systems development may be required for any number of reasons; for example, changes in government regulations, new computer technology, and so forth.

Business Systems. There are many types of systems used in business.

Transaction processing systems generally perform tasks that involve the tedious recordkeeping that organizations handle regularly.

Information systems, which fall into two classes—**information reporting systems** and **decision support systems (DSSs)**—provide decision makers access to needed information and to tools that generate information.

Executive information systems (EISs) are DSSs customized to meet the special needs of individual executives. The term **office automation (OA)** refers to a wide range of systems, including those involving document processing, **electronic mail,** desk accessories, decision support tools, **teleconferencing,** and **telecommuting.**

Computers are also widely used to improve productivity both at the design stage—through **computer-aided design (CAD)**—and the manufacturing stage—through **computer-aided manufacturing (CAM).**

The ability of some computer systems to perform in ways that would be considered intelligent if observed in humans is called **artificial intelligence (AI).** The four main applications areas of AI are **expert systems,** natural languages, vision systems, and **robotics.**

Responsibility for Systems Development. The *chief information officer (CIO),* or someone with a similar title, holds primary responsibility for the overall direction of systems development. The technical details are the responsibility of the individual areas—the **data processing area,** the **information center,** and the **office automation (OA) area**—within the **information systems department. Systems analysts** are the people who are involved most closely with the development of systems from beginning to end. Often, a systems analyst is the **project manager** on the team assigned to the systems project.

The Systems Development Life Cycle. Systems development is often divided into five phases: preliminary investigation, systems analysis, system design, system acquisition, and system implementation. These phases are often collectively referred to as the **systems development life cycle (SDLC),** since they describe a system from the time it is first studied until the time it is put into use. When a new business pressure necessitates a change in a system, the steps of the cycle begin anew.

The first thing the systems analyst does when confronted with a new project assignment is to conduct a **preliminary investigation,** or *feasibility study.* This investigation addresses the nature of the problem under study, the potential scope of the systems development project, the possible solutions, and the costs and benefits of these solutions.

Next, the **systems analysis** phase begins. During this phase, the main objectives are to study the application in depth (to find out what work is being done), to assess the needs of users, and to prepare a list of specific requirements the new system must meet. These objectives are accomplished through fact collection and analysis. A number of tools can help with analysis, including **data flow diagrams** and *checklists.*

The **system design** phase of systems development consists of developing a model of the new system and performing a detailed analysis of benefits and costs.

Once a system has been designed and the required types of software and hardware have been specified, the analyst must decide from which vendors to buy the necessary components. This decision lies at the heart of the **system acquisition** phase. Many buying organizations notify vendors of an intention to acquire a system by submitting to the vendor a

request for proposal (RFP) or **request for quotation (RFQ).** Vendors submitting bids are then commonly evaluated through a **vendor rating system** and then, possibly, a **benchmark test.**

Once arrangements have been made with one or more vendors for delivery of computer resources, the **system implementation** phase begins. This phase includes all the remaining tasks that are necessary to make the system operational and successful, including converting files, debugging, training, and performance appraisal.

Approaches to Systems Development. In the **traditional approach** to systems development, the phases of the SDLC are carried out in a predetermined order—preliminary investigation, analysis, design, acquisition, and implementation. The focus in **prototyping** is on developing small models—or *prototypes*—of the target system in a series of graduated steps. **End-user development** is a systems development approach in which the user is primarily responsible for building the system. This is in contrast to other types of development, in which a qualified computer professional—such as a systems analyst—takes charge of the systems development process.

Review Exercises

Fill-in Questions

1. The term ____________ refers to money owed to a company by customers who have made purchases on credit.
2. CAD is an acronym for ____________.
3. The term ____________ refers to computer systems that perform humanlike tasks.
4. The study of the design, building, and use of robots comprises the field of ____________.
5. A(n) ____________ committee composed of executives in key departments and other members of top management normally approves a plan for systems development.
6. ____________ refers to systems development in which users are primarily responsible for the development effort.
7. Benefits that are easy to quantify in dollars are called ____ benefits.
8. A(n) ____________ consists of running a pilot version of a new system on the hardware and/or software of a vendor whose products are being considered for purchase or lease.

Matching Questions

Match each term with the description that best fits.

a. transaction processing system
b. CAM
c. expert system
d. DSS
e. CAD
f. prototyping

____ 1. A system possessing artificial intelligence.

____ 2. Pertains to the recordkeeping tasks that organizations handle on a day-to-day basis.

____ 3. A type of systems development.

____ 4. Refers to the use of computers in design.

____ 5. Pertains to the use of interactive computer systems for decision support.

____ 6. Refers to the use of computers in manufacturing.

Discussion Questions

1. What is systems development?
2. What are the main duties of the systems analyst?
3. Identify the five phases of the systems development life cycle.
4. What is the purpose of the preliminary investigation?
5. Name several functions performed by transaction processing systems.
6. What is the difference between an information reporting system and a decision support system?
7. What are the purposes of the RFP and RFQ?
8. What is meant by artificial intelligence?

Critical Thinking Questions

1. There is a great deal of confusion with regard to computer terminology. For instance, many people refer to almost every computer system as an "information system." Also, the term "artificial intelligence" is widely applied to systems that save people a great deal of work—even when such systems do not use techniques that mimic human intelligence. Why, do you think, is there such confusion?
2. Whereas robots can perform many jobs adequately, there are a number of other jobs for which robots may never be used. What are three such jobs?
3. What two devices in Chapter 5 does a fax machine most resemble? Identify any similarities.
4. What are several reasons why an organization using a vendor rating system may choose to buy from a vendor other than the most highly rated one?
5. Can the prototyping approach to development be useful in situations in which computer systems are not involved? If you think so, provide an example.
6. Many observers of the computing scene have pointed out that some of the biggest problems in getting a system to work properly are people-related. Provide several examples that show how people problems can make a system fail.

Window 7

The World of CAD

A Brief Pictorial Introduction to Computer-Aided Design

As you've seen in some of the other windows, computer systems are capable of producing spectacular images. How are these images created? It would take an entire book to adequately describe this process, but this window will give you some insights into several of the methods computer designers commonly use when confronted with a design challenge. In the first three pages, we'll study a few of designers' favorite techniques. Then we'll explore in depth several applications of computer graphics. You'll see how the so-called "optical illusion" is created, how marketers conceptualize a package design, and how architects can show clients the look and feel of a structure before it's ever built.

1. Computer graphics techniques make it possible to create realistic-looking images that resemble photographs. As you will see in this window, computer graphics can be used to create exciting, highly unrealistic images as well.

Basic Techniques

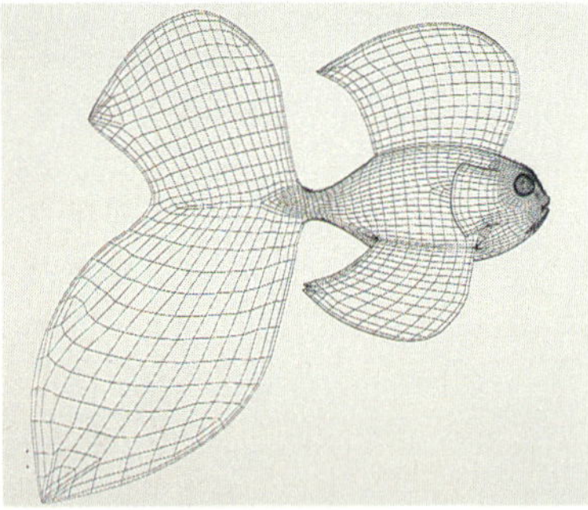

2

3

4

2–4. Three-dimensional computer graphics frequently start as wireframe images that are filled in, textured, and colored. Then the images are rotated, sized, and placed with other elements that form the final image.

5

5. Many realistic-looking computer graphics are formed by first scanning in an illustration or photograph and then enhancing it electronically.

7

7. A multicolored floor is mapped by computer onto the surface of a sphere, providing a reflection. A computer-generated, three-dimensional light source provides a realistic illuminating effect.

6

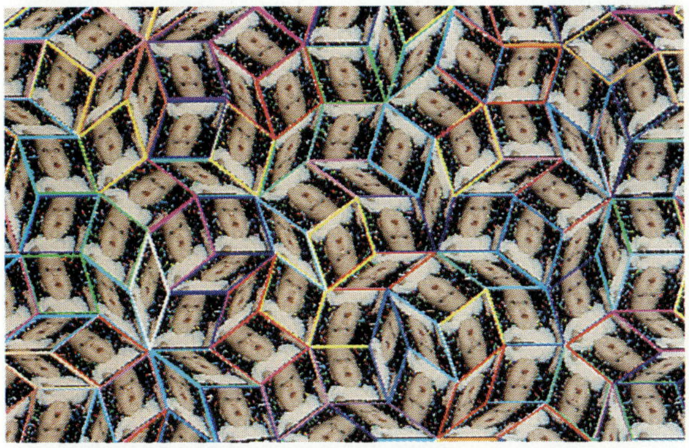

6. Two favorite techniques used by graphics artists are mapping and replication. Here, a baby's face is mapped onto a three-dimensional block, and the block is rotated and copied many times to produce the art effect.

9

8

8, 9. Graphics artists sometimes use "fractal" techniques so that images such as fluids and mountains look realistic. Fractals are tiny, randomly generated images that duplicate the natural appearance found in the earth's environment.

Applications

10

11

12

10–12. Computers are increasingly being recruited to generate the three-dimensional animated shorts that one sees on television to announce the news, the beginning of a basketball game, or a special event.

13

14

13, 14. Artists find the computer a useful tool because they can instantly recolor and reconfigure images, turning a day scene into a twilight scene in a minute or two, for example.

15

15, 16. Computers are often used to electronically combine images, creating an "impossible" scene. The Queens image, for instance, was produced from six different images—four separate facial images, a sky image, and a clouds image. Then the computer electronically blended the images into a composite piece.

16

17. A great deal of product packaging is computer generated. Because a package can be recolored or redesigned in seconds, advertising firms can present clients with many more options than in the days when all the artwork had to be done by hand.

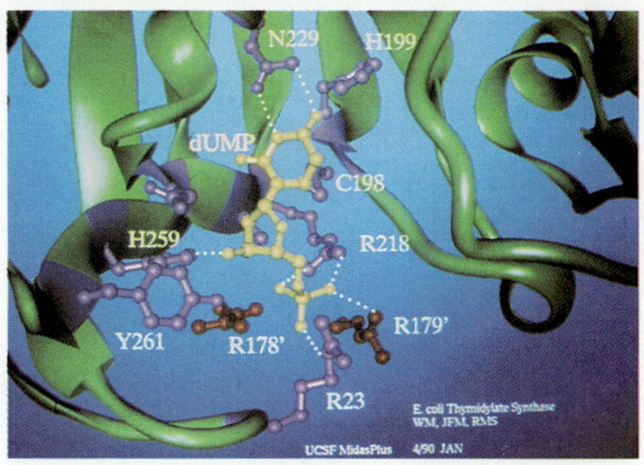

18. In medicine and chemistry, computer graphics are useful for representing strains of diseases and chemicals. The growth of disease organisms and the structure of chemical formations can be simulated on the computer and visualized by computer animation.

19

19. Computer graphic techniques are widely used in the design and testing of spacecraft.

20

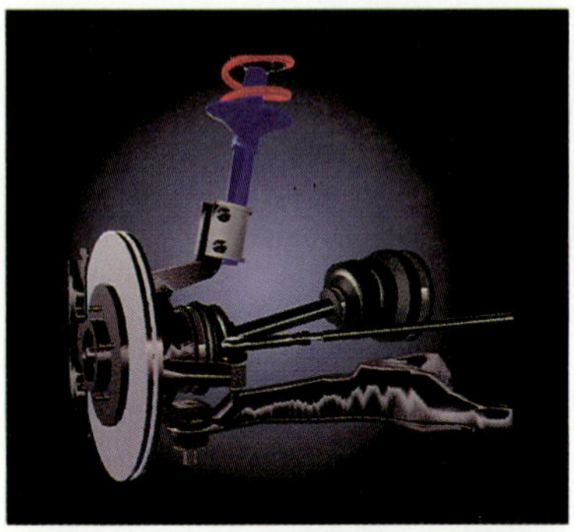

21

22

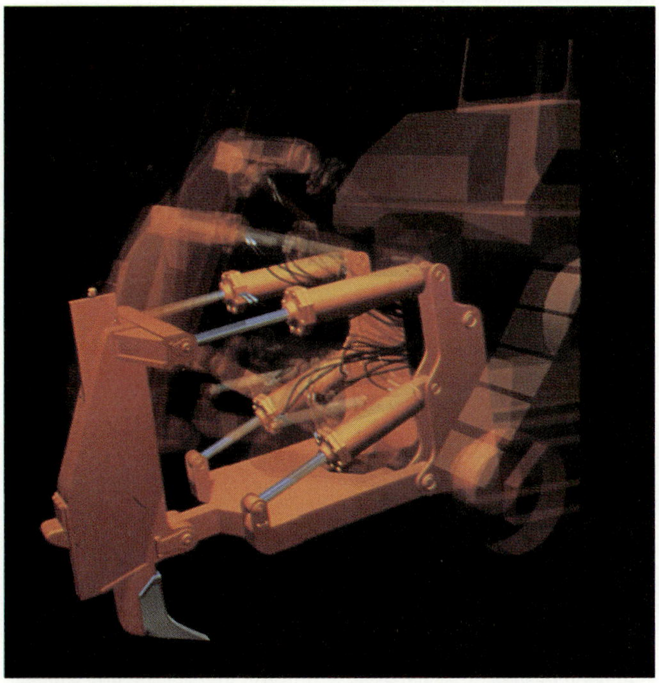

20–22. Many consumer and industrial products are designed and tested by computer. Here the wheel and braking assembly on a car and the motion of the shovel mechanism on a power shovel are illustrated.

23

24

25

26

23–26. (Top) In architecture, computer graphic techniques are frequently used to show clients how an undeveloped site will look with a structure on it. (Bottom) In many architectural packages, a building can be designed in three dimensions, enabling clients to see all sides of it and to tour the inside of the building as well—before the foundation is ever poured.

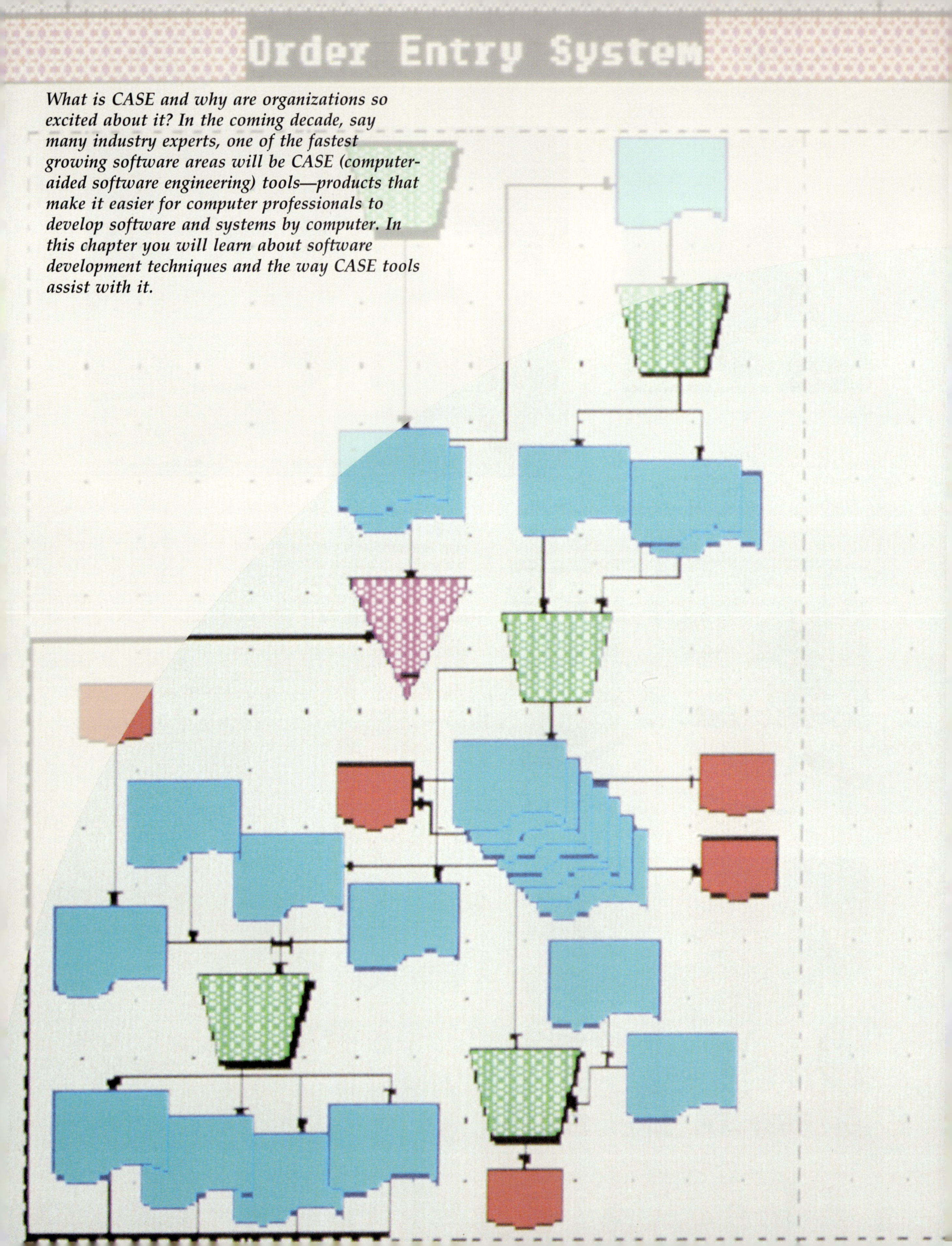

What is CASE and why are organizations so excited about it? In the coming decade, say many industry experts, one of the fastest growing software areas will be CASE (computer-aided software engineering) tools—products that make it easier for computer professionals to develop software and systems by computer. In this chapter you will learn about software development techniques and the way CASE tools assist with it.

12 Program Development and Programming Languages

Outline

Overview
Program Development Activities
The Make-or-Buy Decision
Program Design
- Program Design Tools
- Program Flowcharts
- Pseudocode
- Structure Charts

Programming Languages
- Low-level Languages
- High-level Languages
- Fourth-Generation Languages (4GLs)

Program Coding
Debugging Programs
Program Maintenance
Program Documentation
Computer-Aided Software Engineering (CASE)

Learning Objectives

After completing this chapter, you will be able to:

1. Identify and describe the activities involved with program development.
2. Recognize why it may be more advantageous to buy software in many instances than to develop it in-house.
3. Identify several of the language options available to code programs.
4. Describe a number of design and productivity tools used by computer professionals to develop software.
5. Explain some of the activities involved with debugging, maintaining, and documenting programs.
6. Explain the role played by CASE tools.

Overview

If you wanted to build a house, you'd probably begin with some research and planning. You might speak to various people about home design, draw up some floor plans, estimate the cost of materials, and so on. In other words, you wouldn't start digging a hole and pouring concrete on the very first day. Creating a successful applications program also requires considerable planning.

Computer professionals and advanced users often need to develop their own software from time to time. Applications software development involves using a programming language or similar tool to code new applications programs from scratch. In Chapter 12 we will spend a great deal of time studying useful practices for developing applications programs. As you read this chapter, keep in mind that it is never enough just to write a program that works. Good programs must also be easy to understand and to maintain. A well-planned program may take slightly longer to write initially, but the subsequent savings in maintenance costs usually will make the effort well worthwhile.

The chapter opens by covering the sorts of activities that need to be considered when new applications software is required. From there, we turn to the make-or-buy decision, which deals with choosing either to develop applications software from scratch or to buy it prepackaged. Next we address three of the chapter's most important topics: program design, programming languages, and program coding. Then we turn to a discussion of program debugging, testing, maintenance, and documentation. The chapter closes with a brief introduction to one of the hottest new software-development technologies—computer-aided software engineering (CASE).

Program Development Activities

There are two principal ways in which you can acquire applications programs: developing them from scratch and buying them in prepackaged form from an outside source. The method chosen generally depends on factors such as the quality of software available in the marketplace, the nature and importance of the application, the availability and capability of programmers, and cost. The developer of the software—whether it be you, a colleague, or an outside vendor—should follow certain steps to ensure that the software does its job.

Applications software development.
The process of designing, coding, debugging and testing, maintaining, and documenting applications software.

The steps associated with creating successful applications programs are called **applications software development.** Applications software development normally begins with the program specifications that are developed during the systems analysis and system design phases of the systems development life cycle (SDLC), which we discussed in detail in Chapter 11. Program specifications cover program outputs, the processing to take place, storage requirements, and program inputs. Applications software development consists of the four following activities or steps:

- *Program Design.* Planning the specific software solution to meet the program specifications.
- *Program Coding.* Writing the program.
- *Program Debugging and Testing.* Finding and eliminating errors in the program.
- *Program Maintenance.* Making changes to the program over time.

While each of these critical development activities is taking place, there should be ongoing documentation. *Documentation* is the process of "writing up" the details about what the program does and how it works.

In a typical organization, the responsibility for successful program development is the job of systems analysts and programmers. **Systems analysts,** or simply *analysts,* specify the requirements that the applications software must meet. They work with end users to assess applications needs and translate those needs into a plan. Then they determine the specific resources required to implement the plan. For every program, the analysts create a set of technical specifications outlining what the program must do, the timetable for completing the program, which programming language to use, how the program will be tested before being put into use, and what documentation is required. **Programmers** then use these specifications to design a software solution. Later they translate that design into code—a series of statements in a programming language. *Maintenance programmers* monitor the finished program on an ongoing basis, correcting errors and altering the program as technology or business conditions change.

Systems analyst.
A person who studies systems in an organization in order to determine what actions need to be taken and how these actions may best be achieved with computer resources.

Programmer.
A person whose job is to write, maintain, and test computer programs.

The Make-or-Buy Decision

Once an individual or organization has established a set of technical requirements for a software solution to a problem, it must be decided whether the programs should be created in house or acquired from a software vendor. This consideration is frequently called the *make-or-buy decision.*

During the last several years, prewritten applications programs for such tasks as payroll, general-ledger accounting, financial planning, manufacturing control, and project scheduling have become more widely available from specialized vendors. These programs, called **applications packages,** normally consist of an integrated set of programs, documentation (usually of fairly high quality), and possibly training. Because they often provide immediate results at a reasonable cost, applications packages are becoming increasingly popular.

Applications package.
A fourth-generation-language product that, when the user sets a few parameters, becomes a finished applications program ready to meet specific end-user needs.

But although applications packages offer many compelling advantages, they are not always appropriate. If a package was originally developed for a business that works differently from the one it's being sold to and the vendor has made only superficial attempts to adapt it for general use, it may prove to be more trouble than it's worth. Also, for some ap-

Feature 12-1

Developing Foreign Software

It's Where Today's Growth Is

While U.S. hardware manufacturers are in cutthroat competition with vendors in other countries for world dominance, U.S. software manufacturers are having a relatively easy time of it. Currently, it is estimated that 70 percent of the software used in the world is made by U.S. companies. Many large software companies in the United States report that one-third to one-half of their overall sales are made abroad. Most of the software growth in the next decade is expected to take place in foreign markets.

Foreign versions of software have to be carefully customized to meet the practices followed in each country. In France, for instance, users type on an AZERT keyboard, in contrast to the QWERTY keyboard so pervasive in the United States and Canada. Thus, the software developer has to be careful that a program's keystrokes don't tangle up the user's hands during typing. There are also special symbols used in French, as well as in many other languages, that need to be added to the standard character set. Users in Japan and China need thousands of characters. In England, dates are written in a different style, and decimal points and commas have different meanings in some cases. To complicate matters more, in some Arabic nations, sentences read from right to left.

Yet selling software to foreign markets normally involves much more than simply changing domestic software cosmetically to meet foreign practices. Foreign users have different needs than users in the United States, and the competition is stiff enough that these needs must be met if the software developer wishes to remain competitive. When Lotus Development Corporation went to Japan, for instance, it customized 1-2-3 so that the Japanese version included onscreen grid lines in graphs.

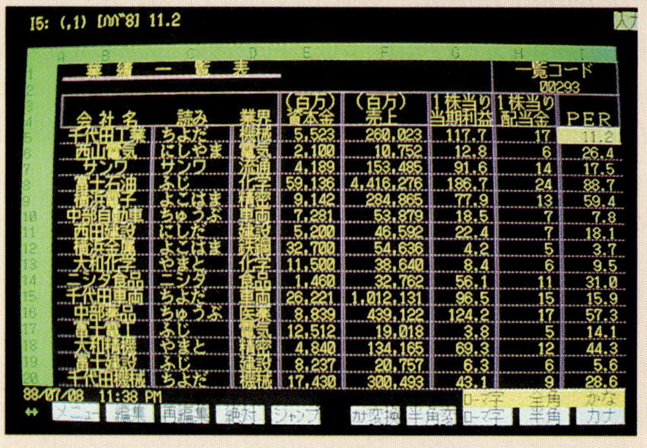

Foreign software. A Japanese version of 1-2-3 has been developed.

Although how the United States became the dominant player in foreign software is subject to debate, many observers point to the fact that the United States had a better head start on the rest of the world in developing packaged software. Also, venture capital is more available in the United States, and ownership of intellectual property is recognized and more carefully guarded in the United States. In Japan, most software is custom made, and only recently has packaged software started to become popular there. Some people think that the next big software boom will be in Japan.

Many people believe that the United States will be hard to unseat as a software power, basically because it has experienced so much success at home. This success includes knowing how to market products to end users. National pride was once a major barrier to selling a product abroad, but it is becoming less of a factor as people worldwide become more sophisticated and look to the vendor providing the greatest value. Also, in countries without tough copyright laws, few people would find it profitable to spend their time writing software; it would simply be stolen by someone else.

plications, little or no appropriate packaged software exists. In such cases, developing the software itself may be the organization's only alternative.

Many applications packages are also available in foreign-language versions, making it easier to develop applications across national borders (see Feature 12-1).

Program Design

In the design stage of applications software development, the program specifications developed by the systems analyst are used to spell out as precisely as possible the nature of the required programming solution. The design, or plan, derived from these specifications must address all the tasks that programs must do as well as how to organize or sequence these tasks when coding programs. Only when the design is complete does the next stage—the actual program coding—begin.

Program Design Tools

Program design tools are essentially planning tools. They consist of various kinds of diagrams, charts, and tables that outline either the organization of program tasks or the steps the program will follow. Once a program has been coded and implemented, program design tools serve as excellent documentation.

Program Flowcharts

Program flowcharts use *geometric symbols,* such as those in Figure 12-1, and familiar *relational symbols,* such as those in Figure 12-2, to graphically portray the sequence of steps involved in a program. The steps in a flowchart occur in the same logical sequence that their corresponding program statements follow in the program. To help you understand what these symbols mean and see how to use them, let's consider an example.

Program flowchart. A visual design tool showing step by step how a computer program will process data.

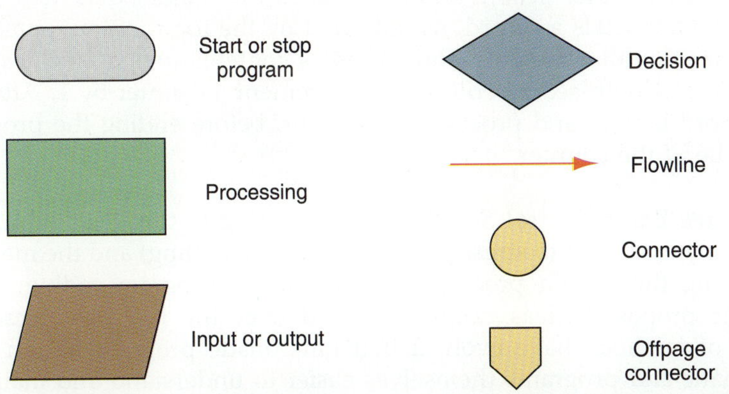

Figure 12-1
ANSI program flowchart symbols.

Figure 12-2
Relational symbols used in flowcharts.

Symbol	Meaning
<	Less than
≤	Less than or equal to
>	Greater than
≥	Greater than or equal to
=	Equal to
<>	Not equal to

Scanning a File for Employees with Certain Characteristics. A common activity in information processing is scanning an employee file for people with certain characteristics. Suppose, for example, a company's personnel department wants a printed list of all employees with computer experience and at least five years of company service. A flowchart that shows how to accomplish this task and also totals the number of employees who meet these criteria is shown in Figure 12-3.

This particular flowchart uses five symbols: start/stop, processing, decision, connector, and input/output. The lines with arrows that link the symbols are called *flowlines;* they indicate the flow of logic in the flowchart.

Every flowchart begins and ends with an oval-shaped *start/stop symbol.* The first of these symbols in the program contains the word *Start,* and the last contains the word *Stop.* The diamond-shaped *decision symbol* always indicates a question, which generally will have only two possible answers—yes or no (true or false). Decision symbols should always have one flowline entering and two flowlines (representing the two possible outcomes) exiting.

The rectangular *processing symbol* contains an action that needs to be taken—for example, "Set counter to 0" and "Add 1 to counter." The *connector symbol* provides a logical meeting point for several flowlines. The *input/output symbol* enables the logical process depicted in the flowchart to accept data or output them.

The flowchart in Figure 12-3 involves a looping operation. We "read" a record, inspect it, and take an action; then read another record, inspect it, and take another action; and so on until the file is exhausted. When the computer reads a record, as indicated by the input/output symbol, it brings it into main memory and stores its contents (or field values). If a record meets both search criteria, we increment a counter by 1. After the last record is read and processed, we print, before ending the program, the value of the counter.

The Three Basic Control Structures. Beginning in the 1960s, a number of researchers began to stress program design (planning) and the merits of separating the design process from the actual program coding. Many of their proposed ideas caught on, and over the last few decades a group of methods have evolved that have made program design more systematic and programs themselves easier to understand and maintain.

Figure 12-3 Scanning an employee file.
The situation that the flowchart represents is as follows: Print the names of all people in an employee file who have computer experience and at least five years of company service. Also, count the number of such people and print out this count.

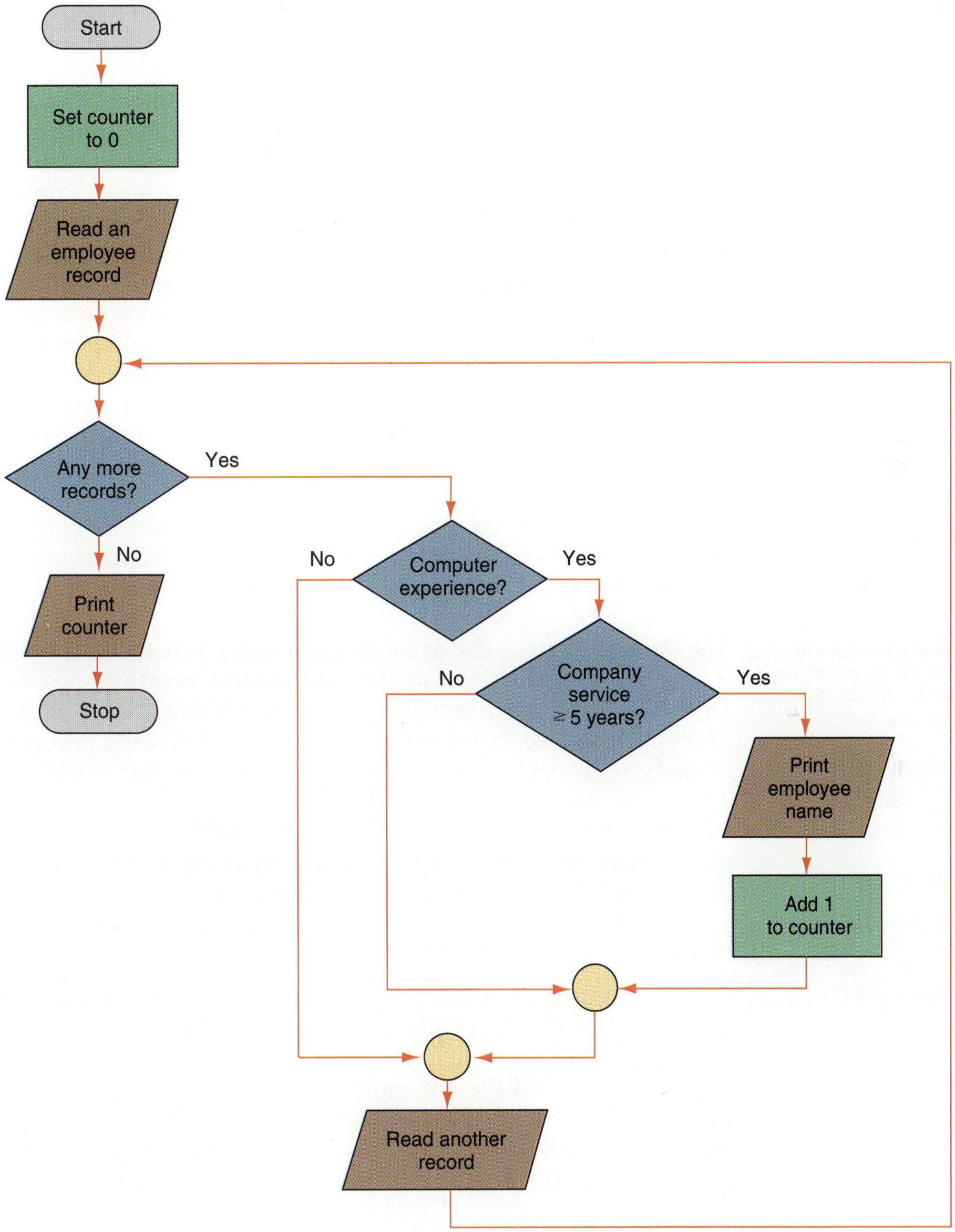

Structured programming.
An approach to program design that makes program code more systematic and maintainable.

Control structure.
A pattern for controlling the flow of logic in a computer program.

Sequence control structure.
The control structure used to represent operations that take place sequentially.

Selection (if-then-else) control structure.
The control structure used to represent a decision operation.

Looping (iteration) control structure.
The control structure used to represent a looping operation.

DOWHILE control structure.
A looping control structure in which the looping continues as long as a certain condition is true (i.e., "do while true").

DOUNTIL control structure.
A looping control structure in which the looping continues as long as a certain condition is false (i.e., "do until true").

Case control structure.
A control structure that can be formed by nesting two or more selection control structures.

One-entry-point/one-exit-point rule.
A rule stating that each program control structure will have only one entry point into it and one exit point out of it.

These methods usually are grouped together under the term **structured programming.**

Advocates of structured programming have shown that any program can be constructed out of three fundamental **control structures:** sequence, selection, and looping. Figure 12-4 illustrates these structures using flowchart symbols.

A **sequence control structure** is simply a series of procedures that follow one another. A **selection** (or **if-then-else**) **control structure** involves a choice: *If* a certain condition is true, *then* follow one procedure; *else,* if false, follow another. A *loop* is an operation that repeats until a certain condition is met. As Figure 12-4 shows, a **looping** (or **iteration**) **control structure** can take one of two forms: DOWHILE or DOUNTIL.

With **DOWHILE,** a loop is executed as long as a certain condition is true ("do *while* true"). With **DOUNTIL,** a loop continues as long as a certain condition is false ("do *until* true"). You should also note another major difference between these two forms of looping. With DOUNTIL, the loop procedure will always be executed at least once, because the procedure appears before any test is made about whether to exit the loop. With DOWHILE, the procedure may not be executed at all, because the loop-exit test appears before the procedure.

The three basic control structures are the major building blocks for structured program flowcharts and pseudocode. We discuss pseudocode later in the chapter.

The Case Structure. By nesting two or more if-then-else's, you can build a fourth structure known as the **case control structure.** For example, in Figure 12-3, the two individual choices—"Computer experience?" and "Company service ≥ 5 years?"—result in the following four possibilities, or cases:

Case I: No computer experience, company service < 5 years

Case II: No computer experience, company service ≥ 5 years

Case III: Computer experience, company service < 5 years

Case IV: Computer experience, company service ≥ 5 years

One Entry Point, One Exit Point. An extremely important characteristic of the control structures discussed so far is that each permits only one entry point into and one entry point out of any structure. This property is sometimes called the **one-entry-point/one-exit-point rule.** Observe the marked entry and exit points in Figure 12-4. The one-entry-point/one-exit-point convention encourages a modular, building-block programming approach that makes programs more readable and easier to maintain.

Pseudocode

Pseudocode.
A technique for structured program design that uses Englishlike statements to outline the logic of a program.

An alternative to the flowchart that has become extremely popular in recent years is **pseudocode.** This structured technique uses Englishlike statements in place of the flowchart's graphic symbols. An example of pseudocode is shown in Figure 12-5.

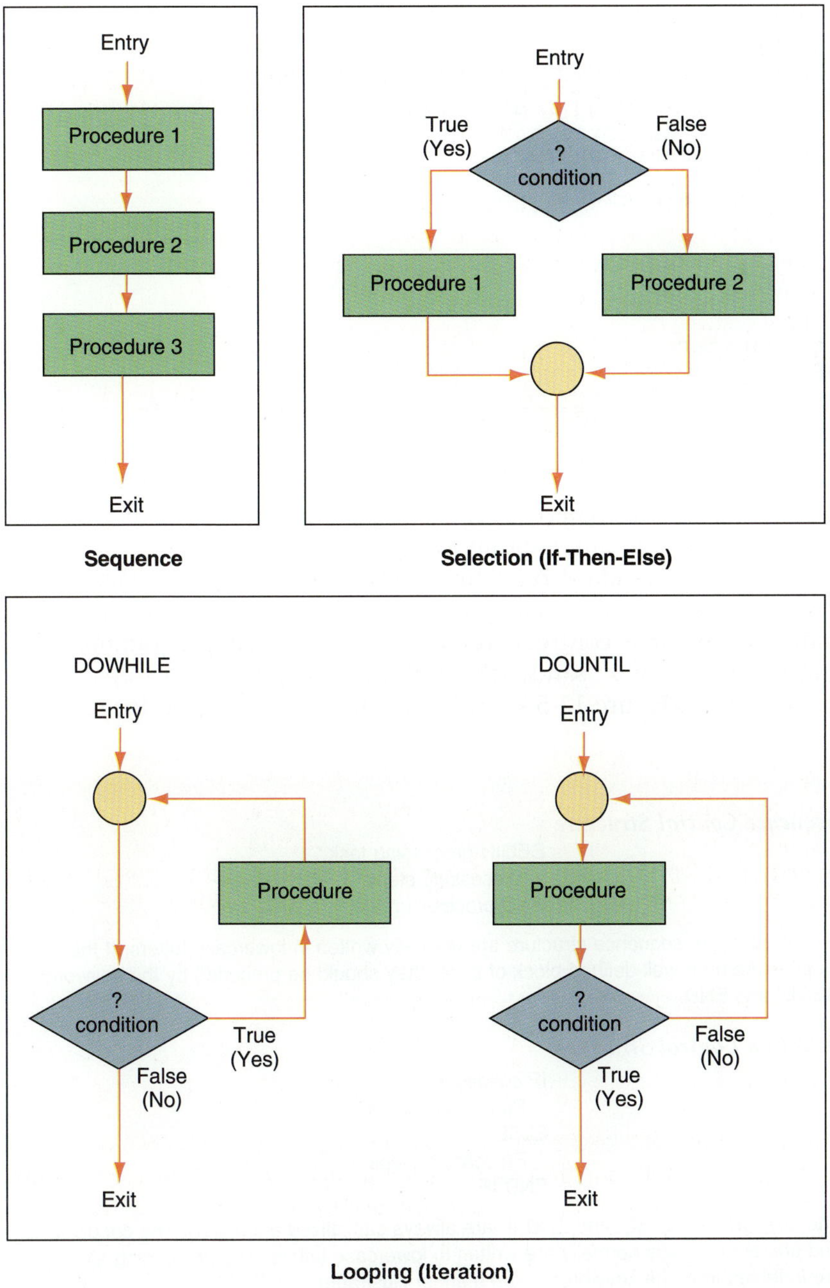

Figure 12-4
The three fundamental control structures of structured programming. Note that each structure has one entry point and one exit point.

Pseudocode looks more like a program than a flowchart. In fact, it's often easier to code a program from pseudocode than from a flowchart, because the former provides a codelike outline of the processing to take place. As a result, the program designer has more control over the end product—the program itself. Also unlike a flowchart, pseudocode is relatively easy to modify and can be embedded into the program as com-

Figure 12-5
Pseudocode for solving the employee file problem of Figure 12-3.
The problem requires printing the names of all people in an employee file with computer experience and at least five years of company service. A count of the number of such people is also required as output.

```
Start
Counter = 0
Read a record
DOWHILE there are more records to process
  IF computer experience
     IF company service ≥ 5 years
        Print employee name
        Increment counter
     ELSE
        Next statement
     END IF
  ELSE
     Next statement
  END IF
  Read another record
END DO
Print counter
Stop
```

ments. However, flowcharts, being visual, are sometimes better than pseudocode for designing logically complex problems.

There are no standard rules for writing pseudocode, but Figure 12-6 describes one set of rules that has a wide following. Note that all words relating to the three control structures of structured programming are capitalized and form a "sandwich" around other processing steps, which are indented. As Figure 12-5 shows, indentation is also used for readabil-

Figure 12-6
Some rules for pseudocode.
In addition to the rules shown here governing program control structures, pseudocode often begins with the keyword *Start* and ends with the keyword *Stop.*

Sequence Control Structure

```
BEGIN processing task
  Processing steps
END processing task
```

The steps in the sequence structure are normally written in lowercase letters. If the steps make up a well-defined block of code, they should be preceded by the keywords BEGIN and END.

Selection Control Structure

```
IF condition
  Processing steps
ELSE
  Processing steps
END IF
```

The keywords IF, ELSE, and END IF are always capitalized and tiered. The condition and processing steps normally are written in lowercase letters. The processing steps are indented from the keywords in the manner illustrated.

Loop (DOWHILE and DOUNTIL) Control Structures

```
DOWHILE condition        DOUNTIL condition
  Processing steps         Processing steps
END DO                   END DO
```

The keywords DOWHILE (or DOUNTIL) and END DO are always capitalized and tiered. The condition and processing steps follow the same lowercase convention and indentation rules as the selection control structure.

Figure 12-7 An action diagram.
Action diagrams, which are created and modified with a special editor, are used to design and code pseudocodelike programs that are capable of being executed.

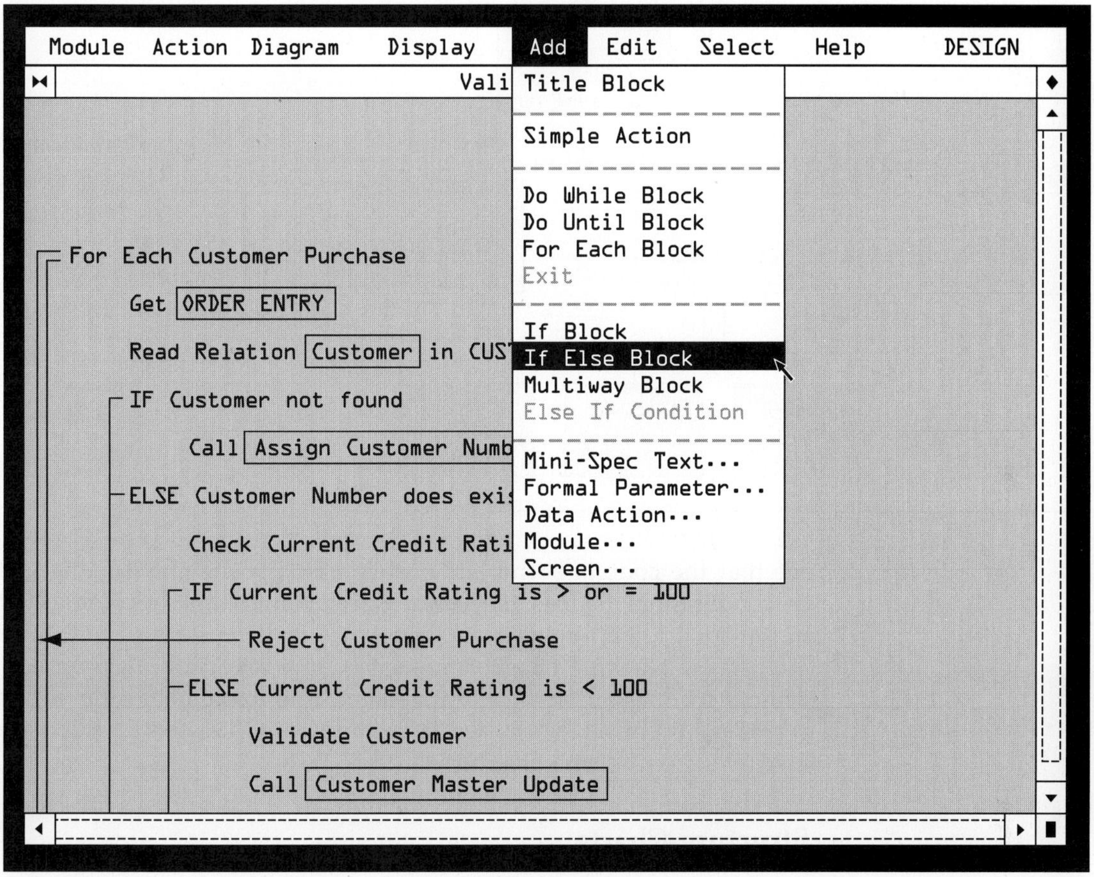

ity. The keywords *Start* and *Stop* are often used to begin and end pseudocode, respectively.

Action Diagrams. Pseudocode is now being widely employed in the creation of **action diagrams,** a tool used to develop applications programs rapidly while online to the CPU. Action diagrams are composed of brackets into which pseudocodelike statements are written (see Figure 12-7). These statements, from which the computer is automatically able to develop executable code, are usually created with an *action-diagram editor.* Each control structure used in the diagram—sequence, selection, looping, or case—has its own set of brackets.

Action diagram.
A programming tool that helps programmers code structured programs.

When the programmer signals that a particular control structure is to be used, the action-diagram editor creates both the appropriate pseudocode keywords and brackets. As programmers provide various conditions or field names at certain places within the brackets, the editor checks to

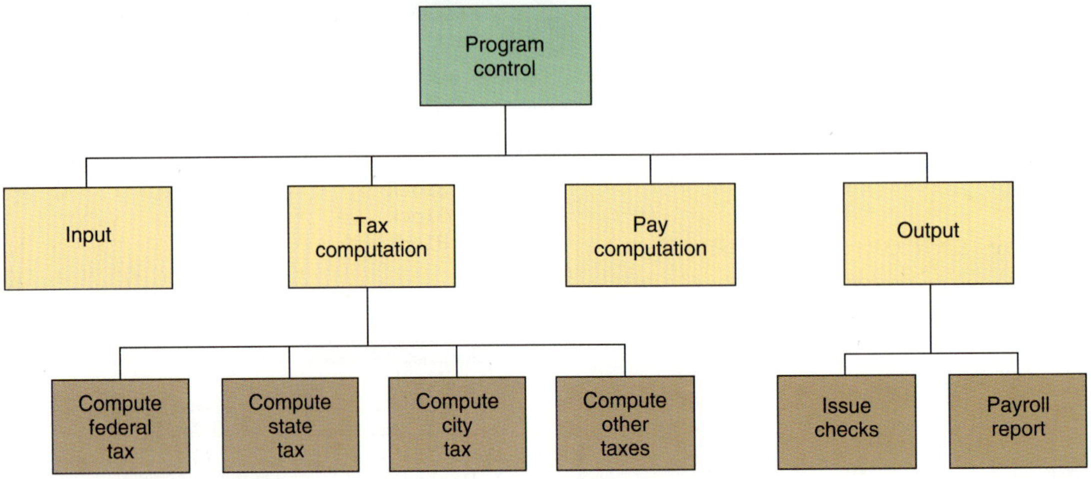

Figure 12-8 Structure charts.
This program-design technique subdivides a program into individual modules, each of which represents a well-defined processing task. The modules are then arranged hierarchically in a top-down fashion, as illustrated here for a payroll application.

see that the code is both valid and consistent with the existing code for the application. It does the latter by referring to the appropriate entries in the application's active data dictionary. If there is a problem, the editor will issue a warning or error message. Once an action diagram has been completed, it is automatically translated into executable code with a *code generator*. Action diagrams are an example of CASE tools, which are covered at the end of the chapter.

Structure Charts

Structure chart.
A program design tool that shows the hierarchical relationship between program modules.

Structure charts, unlike flowcharts and pseudocode, depict the overall organization of a program but not the specific, step-by-step processing logic. They show how the individual program segments, or modules, are defined and how they relate to one another. Each module may consist of one or more fundamental control structures.

A typical structure chart, with its several rows of boxes connected by lines, looks like a corporate organization chart. Each box represents a program *module*—that is, a set of logically related operations that perform a well-defined task. The modules in the upper rows serve control functions, directing the program to process modules under them as appropriate. The modules in the lower boxes serve specific processing functions. These modules do all the program "work." The lines connecting the boxes indicate the relationship between higher-level and lower-level modules. Figure 12-8 is a structure chart for a payroll application.

Top-down design.
A structured design philosophy whereby a program or system is subdivided into well-defined modules and organized into a hierarchy.

Structure charts commonly embody a top-down design. **Top-down design** indicates that modules are conceptualized first at the highest levels of the hierarchy and then at progressively lower levels.

Programming Languages

An important decision that must be made during the development of a program is the selection of a programming language. A **programming language** is a set of rules used to write instructions to the computer. Many users and organizations code the bulk of their applications in one or two prespecified languages, so this decision normally is very straightforward.

Programming language. A set of rules used to write computer programs.

Programming languages are commonly divided into three classes: low-level languages, high-level languages, and very-high-level (fourth-generation) languages.

Low-level Languages

The earliest programming languages—machine and assembly languages—are called **low-level languages** because programmers who code in them must write instructions at the finest level of detail: the base level of the machine. In both machine languages and assembly languages each line of code corresponds to a single action of the computer system.

Low-level language. A highly detailed, machine-dependent programming language.

Virtually no one writes machine-language programs anymore, which consist of strings of 0s and 1s. Nonetheless, all programs must automatically be translated into machine language (by, say, a compiler or interpreter) before they are executed.

Assembly languages were developed to replace the 0s and 1s of machine language with symbols that are easier to understand and remember. The big advantage of assembly-language programs is executional efficiency; they're fast and consume little storage compared with their higher-level counterparts. Unfortunately, assembly-language programs take longer to write and maintain than programs written in higher-level languages.

High-level Languages

High-level languages differ from their low-level predecessors in that they require less coding detail and make programs easier to write. Included in this class are what have come to be known as third-generation programming languages—BASIC, COBOL, FORTRAN, Pascal, PL/1, APL, and many others. A number of high-level languages that one commonly finds in computing environments are briefly discussed next.

High-level language. The class of programming languages that includes BASIC, COBOL, C, FORTRAN, and Pascal.

BASIC. *BASIC* (Beginner's All-purpose Symbolic Instruction Code) was designed to meet the need for an easy-to-learn beginner's language that would work in a "friendly," nonfrustrating programming environment. Over the years, it has evolved into one of the most popular and widely available programming languages. Because it is easy to learn and use, and because the storage requirements for its language translator are small, BASIC works well on almost all microcomputers. A BASIC program is illustrated in Figure 12-9.

Figure 12-9 A sample BASIC program and its output.
This program is designed to accept as input the name of a product, its unit selling price, and the number of units sold and to output this information along with the total dollar value of sales.

(a) BASIC program

```
10    REM PROGRAM TO COMPUTE SALES
20    REM AUTHOR - C.S. PARKER
30    PRINT "    DESCRIPTION              PRICE          UNITS          TOTAL VALUE"
40    A$="\                        \   $###.##         #,###          $###,###"
50    READ ITEM$, PRICE, UNITS
60    WHILE ITEM$ < > "LAST RECORD"
70       VALUE = PRICE * UNITS
80       PRINT USING A$; ITEM$, PRICE, UNITS, VALUE
90       READ ITEM$, PRICE, UNITS
100   WEND
110   DATA "SMALL WIDGETS",150,100
120   DATA "LARGE SKY HOOKS",200,50
130   DATA "BLIVETS",100,3000
140   DATA "LAST RECORD",0,0
150   END
```

(b) Output from the program

```
DESCRIPTION                PRICE       UNITS        TOTAL VALUE
SMALL WIDGETS             $150.00       100          $ 15,000
LARGE SKY HOOKS           $200.00        50          $ 10,000
BLIVETS                   $100.00     3,000          $300,000
```

Pascal. *Pascal,* named after the mathematician Blaise Pascal, was created primarily to fill the need for a teaching vehicle that would encourage structured programming. Pascal uses a modular, building-block approach to programming; that is, each program is created from smaller subprograms. Today, Pascal is widely used in academia as a model for how a programming language should be designed. A Pascal program is shown in Figure 12-10.

COBOL. *COBOL* (COmmon Business-Oriented Language) is the principal transaction processing language in use today. Currently, some 70 to 80 percent of transaction processing applications on mainframes in large organizations are coded in COBOL. Not too long ago, use of COBOL was restricted almost exclusively to large computer systems. Today, however, with many programmers developing mainframe-based applications on microcomputer workstations, microcomputer-based COBOL is a fast-growing trend. A COBOL program is shown in Figure 12-11.

C. *C* combines the best features of a structured, high-level language and an assembly language—that is, it's relatively easy to code and uses computer resources efficiently. Currently, it's one of the hottest languages for programmers to learn, largely because of its role in commercial software development. Many software vendors use C to code their products. A C program is shown in Figure 12-12.

Figure 12-10 A sample Pascal program and its output.
This program solves the same sales problem as the BASIC program in Figure 12-9.

(a) Pascal program

```
PROGRAM SALES (INPUT, OUTPUT);
(* PROGRAM TO COMPUTE SALES *)
(* AUTHOR -- C. S. PARKER *)

VAR  UNITS, INDEX          :INTEGER;
     PRICE, TOTAL          :REAL;
     PART                  :ARRAY [1..20] OF CHAR;

BEGIN
WRITELIN ('    DESCRIPTION             PRICE       UNITS       TOTAL VALUE ');
FOR INDEX := 1 TO 20 DO
  READ (PART[INDEX]);
  READLN (PRICE, UNITS);
WHILE NOT EOF DO
     BEGIN
     TOTAL := PRICE * UNITS;
     FOR INDEX := 1 TO 20 DO
       WRITE (PART[INDEX]);
       WRITELIN ('       $', PRICE:6:2, UNITS:11,'     $', TOTAL:9:2);
     FOR INDEX := 1 TO 20 DO
       READ (PART [INDEX]);
       READLN (PRICE, UNITS);
     END;
END.
```

(b) Output from the program

```
    DESCRIPTION            PRICE       UNITS        TOTAL VALUE
SMALL WIDGETS            $150.00         100         $ 15,000
LARGE SKY HOOKS          $200.00          50         $ 10,000
BLIVETS                  $100.00       3,000         $300,000
```

Figure 12-11 A sample COBOL program and its output.
This program solves the same sales problem as the BASIC program in Figure 12-9.

(a) COBOL program

```
IDENTIFICATION DIVISION.
  PROGRAM-ID. SALES.
  AUTHOR. PARKER.

ENVIRONMENT DIVISION.
CONFIGURATION SECTION.
  SOURCE-COMPUTER. VS9.
  OBJECT-COMPUTER. VS9.
INPUT-OUTPUT SECTION.
  FILE-CONTROL.
    SELECT DISKFILE ASSIGN TO DISK-A1F2-V.
    SELECT PRINTFILE ASSIGN TO SYSLST.
```

continued

Figure 12-11 continued

```
DATA DIVISION.
FILE SECTION.
FD  DISKFILE
    LABEL RECORDS ARE STANDARD.
01  DISKREC.
    05 PART-DESCRIPTION-IN      PIC X(20).
    05 PRICE-IN                 PIC 999.
    05 UNITS-SOLD-IN            PIC 9(5).
FD  PRINTFILE
    LABEL RECORDS ARE OMITTED.
01  PRINTLINE                   PIC X(120).
WORKING-STORAGE SECTION.
01  FLAGS.
    05 WS-END-OF-FILE.          PIC X(3) VALUE 'NO'.
01  HEADING-LINE.
    05 FILLER                   PIC X(9)  VALUE SPACES.
    05 FILLER                   PIC X(11) VALUE 'DESCRIPTION'.
    05 FILLER                   PIC X(10) VALUE SPACES.
    05 FILLER                   PIC X(5)  VALUE 'PRICE'.
    05 FILLER                   PIC X(7)  VALUE SPACES.
    05 FILLER                   PIC X(5)  VALUE 'UNITS'.
    05 FILLER                   PIC X(4)  VALUE SPACES.
    05 FILLER                   PIC X(11) VALUE 'TOTAL VALUE'.
01  DETAIL-LINE.
    05 FILLER                   PIC X(5)  VALUE SPACES.
    05 PART-DESCRIPTION-OUT     PIC X(20).
    05 FILLER                   PIC X(4)  VALUE SPACES.
    05 PRICE-OUT                PIC $ZZ9.99.
    05 FILLER                   PIC X(5)  VALUE SPACES.
    05 UNITS-SOLD-OUT           PIC ZZ,ZZ9.
    05 FILLER                   PIC X(5)  VALUE SPACES.
    05 SALES-VALUE              PIC $ZZZ,ZZ9.

PROCEDURE DIVISION.
010-HOUSEKEEPING.
    OPEN INPUT DISKFILE
         OUTPUT PRINTFILE.
    READ DISKFILE
         AT END MOVE 'YES' TO WS-END-OF-FILE.
    PERFORM 020-HEADINGS.
    PERFORM 030-PROCESSIT
         UNTIL WS-END-OF-FILE = 'YES'.
    CLOSE DISKFILE
          PRINTFILE.
    STOP RUN.
020-HEADINGS.
    WRITE PRINTLINE FROM HEADING-LINE
         AFTER ADVANCING 1 LINE.
030-PROCESSIT.
    MULTIPLY    UNITS-SOLD-IN
         BY     PRICE-IN
         GIVING SALES-VALUE.
    MOVE PART-DESCRIPTION-IN TO PART-DESCRIPTION-OUT.
    MOVE PRICE-IN            TO PRICE-OUT.
    MOVE UNITS-SOLD-IN       TO UNITS-SOLD-OUT.
    WRITE PRINTLINE FROM DETAIL-LINE
         AFTER ADVANCING 1 LINE.
    READ DISKFILE
         AT END MOVE 'YES' TO WS-END-OF-FILE.
```

(b) Output from the program

```
    DESCRIPTION              PRICE       UNITS          TOTAL VALUE
SMALL WIDGETS               $150.00        100           $ 15,000
LARGE SKY HOOKS             $200.00         50           $ 10,000
BLIVETS                     $100.00      3,000           $300,000
```

Figure 12-12 A sample C program and its output.
This program solves the same sales problem as the BASIC program in Figure 12-9.

(a) C program

```
/ *Program to compute sales* /
/ *Author -- C. S. Parker* /

#include <stdio.h>

main() {

   char *item[3] = {"SMALL WIDGETS   ", "LARGE SKY HOOKS", "BLIVETS          "};
   float price[3] = {150, 200, 100}, value[3];
   int units[3] = {100, 50, 3000};
   int i=0;

   while (i<3) {
      value[i] = price[i] * units[i];
      i++;
   };

   printf("    DESCRIPTION          PRICE          UNITS               TOTAL VALUE\n");
   for (i=0;i<3;i++){
     printf("%s\t\t$%5.2f\t\t%4d\t\t$%6.0f\n",
                                 item[i], price[i], units[i], value[i]);
   };

}
```

(b) Output from the program

```
    DESCRIPTION               PRICE          UNITS          TOTAL VALUE
SMALL WIDGETS              $150.00           100            $ 15000
LARGE SKY HOOKS            $200.00            50            $ 10000
BLIVETS                    $100.00          3000            $300000
```

FORTRAN. *FORTRAN* (FORmula TRANslator), which dates back to 1954, is the oldest surviving high-level language still in wide use. It was designed by scientists and is oriented toward scientific, mathematical, and engineering problem solving. The key strengths of FORTRAN are fast program execution and a large bank of preprogrammed subroutines. A FORTRAN program is shown in Figure 12-13.

PL/1. *PL/1* (Programming Language/1) was introduced in the mid-1960s by IBM as a general-purpose language; that is, it was designed for both scientific and transaction processing applications. It's an extremely powerful language and has strong capabilities for structured programming.

APL. *APL* (A Programming Language) was developed in the early 1960s to enable programmers to code rapidly. It is an extremely compact language, with conventions that are quite different than those of other programming languages. APL requires a special keyboard.

Ada. *Ada,* a superset of Pascal, is a relatively new structured language initiated by the U.S. Department of Defense. As a superset of Pascal, it

Figure 12-13 A sample FORTRAN program and its output.
This program solves the same sales problem as the BASIC program in Figure 12-9.

(a) FORTRAN program

```
C THIS PROGRAM COMPUTES SALES
C AUTHOR - C.S. PARKER

       CHARACTER PART*20
       INTEGER COUNT, RECORDS, UNITS

       READ (5, 100) RECORDS
       WRITE (6, 200)

       DO 999 COUNT = 1, RECORDS
       READ (5, 110) PART, PRICE, UNITS
       TOTAL = PRICE * UNITS
       WRITE (6, 210) PART, PRICE, UNITS, TOTAL
999    CONTINUE

100    FORMAT (I4)
110    FORMAT (A20,F6.2,I4)
200    FORMAT (5X,'DESCRIPTION',12X,'PRICE',7X,'UNITS',5X,'TOTAL VALUE')
210    FORMAT (1X, A,'      $',F6.2,I11,'      $',F9.2)

       STOP
       END
```

(b) Output from the program

```
     DESCRIPTION           PRICE       UNITS      TOTAL VALUE
 SMALL WIDGETS            $150.00        100      $ 15000.00
 LARGE SKY HOOKS          $200.00         50      $ 10000.00
 BLIVETS                  $100.00      3,000      $300000.00
```

shares many of Pascal's properties. It is still too early, however, to guess how successful it will be in the business and academic worlds.

Logo. *Logo* is a programming language that also represents a philosophy of learning. It was developed in the 1970s by Seymour Paepert of MIT, who incorporated into its specification some of the learning theories of Swiss psychologist Jean Piaget. Logo has been very popular with children, many of whom find it both easy to learn and exciting.

RPG. *RPG* (Report Program Generator) was developed by IBM in the early 1960s to produce reports quickly on small computers. Programmers provide facts on special coding forms about what a report should look like, and, after the forms are machine coded, the RPG package determines how the job will be done and creates (generates) a computer program to produce the report.

Smalltalk. *Smalltalk,* pioneered at the University of Utah in the late 1960s, represents a significant departure from conventional programming languages. Specifically, Smalltalk is an *object-oriented programming language;* that is, it works with *objects* and *messages* that encapsulate both instructions and data rather than with a set of instructions and a separate set of data, as in traditional languages. Some experts think that at some point in the future, object-oriented languages will dominate the programming language landscape.

LISP and Prolog. *LISP* (LISt Processor) and *Prolog* are used to develop applications in the field of artificial intelligence, a topic we covered in Chapter 11. LISP, a programming language that is nearly as old as FORTRAN, is often implemented on a special, dedicated computer system. Prolog, created about 1970, is designed to run on an ordinary computer.

Fourth-Generation Languages (4GLs)

Machine language and assembly language characterized the first and second generations of computing, respectively. During the third generation, languages such as FORTRAN, BASIC, and COBOL became dominant. Today, in the so-called fourth generation of the computer age, a new breed of languages has arrived. These *very-high-level languages* are appropriately called **fourth-generation languages (4GLs).** In contrast to lower-level languages, they are much easier to use and, consequently, they result in increased on-the-job productivity.

Fourth-generation language (4GL). An easy-to-learn, easy-to-use language that enables users or programmers to code applications much more quickly than they could with third-generation languages.

The 4GLs found in the market are diverse and serve a wide range of application areas. Some are targeted to users, some to programmers, and some to both. Six types of 4GLs commonly found in commercial software products are described in the following list and summarized in Figure 12-14. Many of these language functions overlap in a single product. For instance, Lotus Development Corporation's 1-2-3 is a decision support system tool with facilities for report generation, retrieval and update, and graphics generation.

Report Generators. A *report generator* is a tool that enables you to prepare reports quickly and easily. For instance, report generators packaged with database management systems allow you to create reports by declaring which data fields are to be represented as report columns and which report columns are to be used to sort data. The report is then generated automatically.

Report generators Used to generate reports quickly

Retrieval and update languages Used to retrieve information from files or databases and to add, delete, or modify data

Decision support system tools Used to create financial schedules, budgets, models of decision environments, and the like

Graphics generators Used to quickly prepare presentation graphics

Applications packages Prewritten programs for applications such as word processing, payroll, and various accounting tasks

Applications generators Used to quickly prepare applications programs, without having to resort to programming in a third-generation language

Figure 12-14
Types of fourth-generation languages (4GLs).
4GLs have evolved to make both end users and programmers more productive.

Retrieval and Update Languages. As more and more busy people learned to use computers to search through large files and databases, it became increasingly important to develop language products that would make this process as painless as possible. *Retrieval and update 4GLs* allow you to retrieve or update data in large files or databases without having to spend weeks learning a complicated programming syntax to do so.

Decision Support System Tools. *Decision support system tools* provide computing capabilities that help people make decisions. Perhaps the most familiar of such tools is the spreadsheet package, which we covered in Chapter 9. Other examples are modeling packages, which allow you to create complex mathematical models, and statistical packages, which facilitate statistical analysis.

Graphics Generators. *Graphics generators,* often called presentation graphics routines, are tools that help you to prepare business graphs. When you invoke the graphics generator, it will ask you a number of questions about your graph—what type it is, where the data are to create the graph, what colors and titles you want, and so on. After you satisfactorily respond to all of the questions, the graph is automatically created. We covered graphics generators in some detail in Chapter 9.

Applications Packages. An *applications package* is a "canned" program designed to perform some common business application, such as payroll, accounts receivable, invoicing, or word processing. Like a graphics generator, an applications package usually asks the user a number of questions. The responses are subsequently used to assign values to parameters within the package, to customize it to specific needs. A word processor, for instance, asks each user questions about line spacing, margins, justification, and so forth. The responses to these questions facilitate customizing word processing environments to each user.

Applications Generators. An *applications generator* is a package that enables you to quickly code applications software. These packages work in a variety of ways. For instance, some applications generators enable users to create new menu screens for their applications. Others contain *code generators,* routines that allow shorthand code or pseudocode to be automatically translated into a third-generation language such as COBOL. Products such as Apple's HyperCard (see Feature 12-2) are also frequently used as applications generators.

Program Coding

Coding.
The writing of programming-language instructions.

Once the program design is complete and the development language has been chosen, the next step is to code the program. **Coding** is the actual process of writing the program in a programming language.

Programs often are keyed into the computer system with the help of a text editor, which we covered in Chapter 7. The text editor enables the

Feature 12-2

HyperCard

Not Just a Programming Language

Here's one for all you "Jeopardy" watchers out there.

Introduced by Apple Computer in 1987, it's a programming language, a set of applications programs, an operating-system shell, a set of utility programs, a file manager, a screen-painting program, and (whew!) too many other things to describe in a single sentence.

If you answered "What is HyperCard?" you may not have to read any further.

HyperCard is a personal toolkit that allows users to create, customize, and use information involving text, graphics, video, voice, music, and animation. It is accompanied by an easy-to-use English-like programming language called *HyperTalk*—an object-oriented language that is similar to Smalltalk. HyperTalk is not new to the programming world; it was introduced in 1965. However, powerful computers such as the Macintosh, with their graphical user interfaces, weren't available then. It wasn't until August 1987, when Bill Atkinson of Apple Computer introduced HyperCard to the world, that HyperTalk was actually implemented in a marketable product.

The basic concept behind HyperCard (and similar products that have followed it into the marketplace, such as Silicon Beach Software's SuperCard) is the card. Data are created and placed on electronic *cards,* which are similar in concept to traditional 3-by-5-inch index cards. Each card may consist of one or more screenfuls of data. On each card may be one or more *buttons,* which, when selected by a mouse, can pull up another card to the screen, create a sound, play music, cause a series of animated images to appear on the screen, and so on.

A collection of cards and their buttons is called a *stack,* and any program that can access a stack is called a *script.* Thus, stacks and scripts, in the world of HyperCard, are respectively equivalent to data and programs in such languages as BASIC or COBOL. HyperCard has several built-in stacks and scripts, and you can buy many others from third-party vendors. If you purchase a HyperCard stack or script, you need HyperCard to run it or alter it, just as you would need a BASIC language translator if you were creating BASIC programs and data. HyperCard and HyperTalk are capable of handling several different media—such as music and animation—in addition to conventional text, so the term *multimedia* is often used to describe HyperCard applications. Chapter 10 covers types of multimedia applications more extensively.

An assortment of HyperCard uses have surfaced. An auto repair shop uses it to manage maintenance records, calculate and print bills, and post all parts used to an inventory record. Another company has collected images of artifacts and treasures from the National Gallery of Art and has placed them on optical disk along with a video-guided tour and a videotaped history of the museum. These sounds and images can be accessed by lecturers and historians by means of a HyperCard program. Medical and pre-med students at many colleges study subjects such as pathology through HyperCard scripts. The list of potential applications is virtually endless.

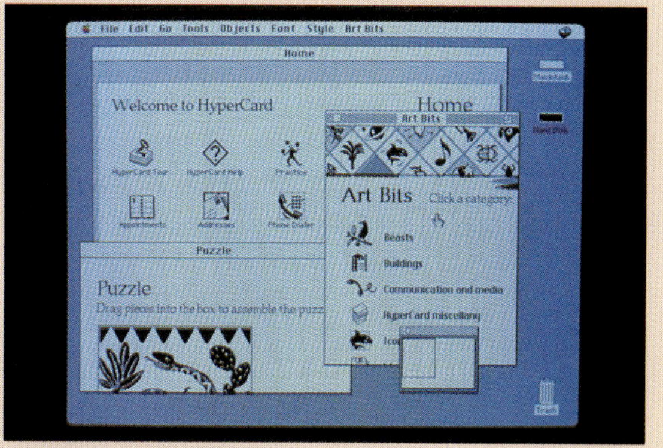

HyperCard. Apple Computer introduced this information-retrieval toolkit, containing its own programming language, in 1987.

programmer to copy blocks of code from one program to another; to replicate text strings so that they appear in several lines; to insert, delete, and move code; and to neatly format the program with indents and white space.

During the coding, computer professionals often take advantage of a number of special tools and methods that help make them more productive. The purpose of these techniques is to ensure that programmers produce code rapidly while creating programs that are both easy to maintain and as error-free as possible. Four techniques that are useful in many programming environments are coding standards, fourth-generation languages, reusable code, and data dictionaries.

Coding Standards. Many organizations and individuals follow a set of *coding standards,* which are essentially a list of rules designed to standardize programming style. These rules may cover items such as acceptable program structures, field-naming conventions, and comment conventions. Rules such as these help make programs readable and easy to maintain. If programs consistently use the same set of conventions, anyone making changes to the program knows what to expect.

Fourth-Generation Languages. In the last section we covered *fourth-generation languages*—languages that simplify using computers. Although many products using these languages—such as word processors and spreadsheets—are targeted primarily to the needs of end users, others have been created specifically to streamline the applications development process for professional programmers. For instance, applications generators enable programmers to quickly develop applications without having to deal directly with a traditional third-generation programming language such as COBOL or BASIC. Applications packages such as accounting programs provide an easy, off-the-shelf solution to many applications development problems.

Reusable Code. Related programs often use the same blocks of code. Take, for example, payroll programs. A company may have a dozen or more of them—programs that cut checks to employees; report every check issued by the treasurer's office; report payments to the city, state, or federal government; and so on. Rather than have programmers code each of these programs from scratch, most organizations keep libraries of reusable code available. **Reusable code,** as you might guess, refers to "generic" code segments that can be used over and over again by several programs. Thus, reusable code enables programs to be "cut and pasted" quickly from pretested, error-free code segments.

Reusable code.
Program segments that can be reused several times in constructing applications programs.

Data dictionary.
A facility that informs users and programmers about characteristics of data or programs in a database or a computer system.

Data Dictionaries. A **data dictionary** is similar to an ordinary dictionary in that it contains rules of usage for an alphabetical list of words. The words are those encountered in the company's information processing environment. Among them would be, for example, names of fields, records, files, and programs.

Data dictionaries can be active or passive. An *active* data dictionary is online to an application as a programmer is developing it. If, say, a programmer attempts to use a field name improperly or inconsistently, the active data dictionary will immediately warn the programmer, and it may prohibit the alleged infraction from being part of the finished software product. A data dictionary that is not online during application development is *passive.*

Debugging Programs

Debugging is the process of ensuring that a program is free of errors, or "bugs." Debugging is usually a lengthy process, sometimes amounting to over 50 percent of a program's total development time.

Debugging. The process of detecting and correcting errors in computer programs or in the computer system itself.

Preliminary Debugging. The debugging process often begins after the program is initially entered into the computer system. Rarely is any program error-free the first time the programmer attempts to execute it. A very long program may have well over a hundred errors of one sort or another—and maybe even thousands—at the outset. The computer's systems software usually provides the programmer with a list of informative "error messages" indicating the source of many of the bugs. At this point, the programmer again checks the code to see what's wrong, makes the necessary corrections, and reexecutes the program. This "execute, check, and correct" process will probably be repeated several more times before the program is free of bugs.

Testing. At some point in the debugging process, the program will appear to be correct. At this point, the original programmer—or, preferably, someone else—runs the program with extensive *test data.* Good test data will subject the program to all the conditions it might conceivably encounter when it is finally implemented. The test data should also check for likely sources of coding omissions. For example, will the program issue a check or a bill in the amount of $0.00? Does the program provide for leap years when dating reports? Although rigorous testing significantly decreases the chance of malfunctioning when a program is implemented, there is no foolproof guarantee that the completed program will be bug-free.

Proper debugging is vital, because an error that may cost a few dollars to fix at this stage in the development process may cost many thousands of dollars to correct after the program is implemented. As the Tomorrow box suggests, the cost of an error may be incalculable.

Program Maintenance

Virtually every program, if it is to last a long time, requires ongoing maintenance. Program **maintenance** is the process of updating software so that it continues to be useful. For instance, if new types of data are added to a database and existing programs must be modified to use these data,

Maintenance. The process of making upgrades and minor modifications to systems or software over time.

Tomorrow

Worrying about Bugs

To What Extent Can We Trust Software?

An oil field worker in Texas lay face down on a table waiting to receive another routine radiation treatment for a tumor in his shoulder. Although his previous eight treatments had been painless, this time the machine hurt him—so much so that he had to call out for help. He was told that the machine had flashed a malfunction message on its console screen but that he need not worry; it indicated that he was getting an underdose rather than an overdose. Within days his injury worsened severely. Six months later he was dead.

Subsequent testing of the machine, when another patient voiced a similar complaint and the same malfunction message was displayed, showed that strange things happened to the machine when the up-arrow key was used to edit certain parameters on the screen. The malfunction appeared to be traceable to a software error.

This incident and others like it have raised several moral and legal questions. To what extent can we trust software? When an error causes injury, how morally responsible are the programmers who code critical systems as well as those who determine when it's time to bring a product to market? Who is legally responsible when damages or deaths occur?

Many people believe that we are at the beginning of a software reliability crisis. Computer software is controlling more and more processes every year—communications, automobiles, air traffic control, election results, machines that monitor hospital patients, and so on. In the meantime—with their user-friendly interfaces, multiple options, graphics, color, and artificial-intelligence components—computer programs have become much more complex and much longer. Programs are now so complex and long, in fact, that certifying a substantial program as bug free could take a lifetime or longer. Given this fact and the competitive pressure to bring programs online as soon as possible, it's safe to assume that virtually no large program today is released without bugs. Typically, there are hundreds or thousands of them.

Compounding the software reliability crisis, some think, is the fact that, unlike doctors and air traffic controllers, programmers do not need to be certified to be hired in most places. Consequently, a programmer whose only experience has been designing computer games could be hired by a hospital to write programs that determine the dosage of drugs given to patients, a life-or-death decision. The programmer-certification problem may not have a simple solution, however. If programmers had to be certified, many of the good ones would probably find other jobs. This would create a critical labor shortage in an area that will largely determine the power of nations in the coming decade.

A recent Congressional report estimated that computer bugs cost the nation more than a billion dollars annually. (This cost does not take human fatalities into account.) One bug, for instance, caused a bank to borrow funds unnecessarily, causing it to rack up millions of dollars in interest payments. A patient in a large county hospital died when a computer system misreported a blood type. A bug in the nation's phone system in January 1990 caused long-distance lines to be tied up for hours. Yet another bug, which fortunately was discovered before anyone was seriously hurt, would have caused a fighter jet to flip upside down when passing over the equator.

Computer bugs have left many concerned people in the computer industry pondering the same questions that are in the minds of earthquake watchers: What will happen when the big one hits?

program maintenance is necessary. Program maintenance is also commonly triggered by new software releases, new equipment announcements, and changes in the way business is conducted.

Program maintenance is costly to organizations. It has been estimated that many organizations spend well over half of their programming time just maintaining existing applications programs. One of the major reasons why such tools as coding standards, fourth-generation languages, reusable code, and data dictionaries are so popular today is because these tools can result in lower program-creation costs or lower maintenance costs.

Program Documentation

Program **documentation** includes manuals that enable users, maintenance programmers, and operators to interact successfully with a program. If you've ever had the frustration of trying to get something to work from poorly written instructions, you can appreciate how valuable good documentation can be.

Documentation.
A detailed written description of a program, procedure, or system.

User documentation normally consists of a user's manual. This manual should provide instructions for running the program, a description of language commands, several examples of situations the end user is likely to encounter, and a troubleshooting guide to help with difficulties.

Programmer documentation usually consists of any tools that will simplify maintenance of the program. These might include a program narrative, design tools such as flowcharts and structure charts, a listing of the program, and a description of inputs and outputs. There should also be a set of procedures to help programmers test the program.

Operator documentation includes manuals that assist machine operators in setting up hardware devices, learning the ins and outs of successful hardware operation, and diagnosing machine malfunctions. Operator documentation is machine-dependent, and, unless you have a good grounding in computer fundamentals, it can be difficult to read through.

Computer-Aided Software Engineering (CASE)

Software development has never been an easy process. In fact, a partner at Arthur Andersen & Co. recently estimated that the average business applications program takes some 32,000 hours to develop from start to finish—an effort worthy of a team of three dozen programmers working for almost three years. And that represents only the programs that get finished! No wonder managers are looking for a better way to get programs developed.

In the last dozen years, a number of solutions have surfaced. Among the most promising are **CASE (computer-aided software engineering)** tools. The objective of CASE tools is automating one or more stages of applications software development. Although CASE is in its infancy now and has numerous bugs to be worked out, many people believe that most commercial software will be developed through a CASE-type approach at a not-too-distant future point.

Computer-aided software engineering (CASE).
Program products that automate systems and program development activities.

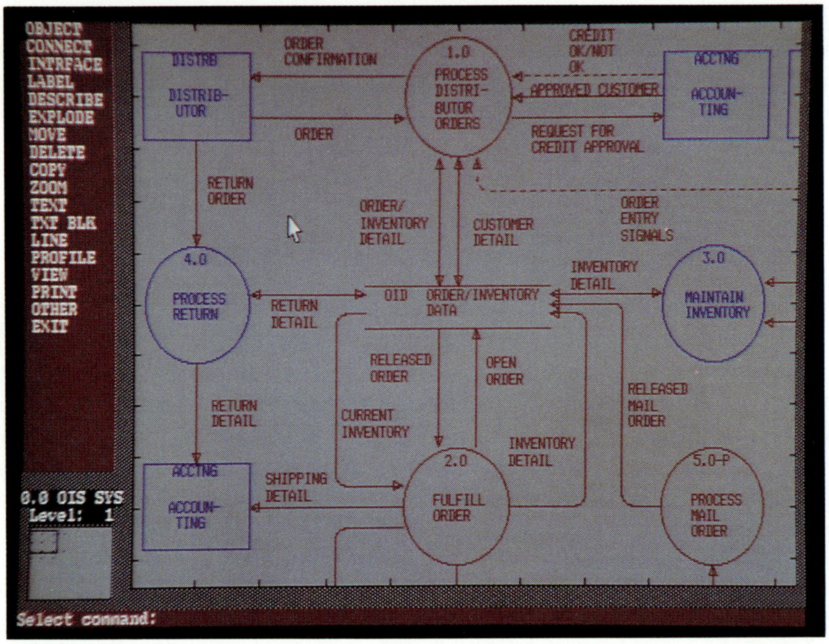

Figure 12-15
Excelerator.
Index Technology's Excelerator is today's leading CASE package and commands a hefty market share.

Many of the CASE products now offered in the marketplace are called *software engineering workbenches.* Like a carpenter's workbench, which comprises a number of the tools of the carpentry trade—hammers, saws, chisels, drill bits, and the like—software engineering workbenches contain a number of design, programming, and maintenance tools that get software products developed faster. For instance, such a workbench might consist of an action-diagram editor, a fourth-generation language, a code generator, a feature that facilitates the development of reusable code libraries, an active data dictionary, and tools that help turn unstructured programs into structured ones. The specific tools included in the workbench vary from one vendor to another.

No company has yet developed an everything-but-the-kitchen-sink CASE package, the panacea that will cure every company's applications software development headaches. Consequently, an organization may have to shop around for several CASE products that will meet its needs collectively. This is easier said than done; many CASE tools are incompatible with one another and may not interface well with other proprietary software products that the organization is using. Fortunately, CASE vendors realize this and currently are attempting to forge alliances with other vendors to establish standards that will increase CASE applicability. Currently the most successful product in the CASE marketplace is Index Technology Corporation's Excelerator (see Figure 12-15), a PC-based workbench product targeted primarily to systems analysis and design and to documentation. User Solution 12-1 describes one company's search for a CASE tool to meet its particular applications environment.

User Solution 12-1

Finding the Right CASE Tool

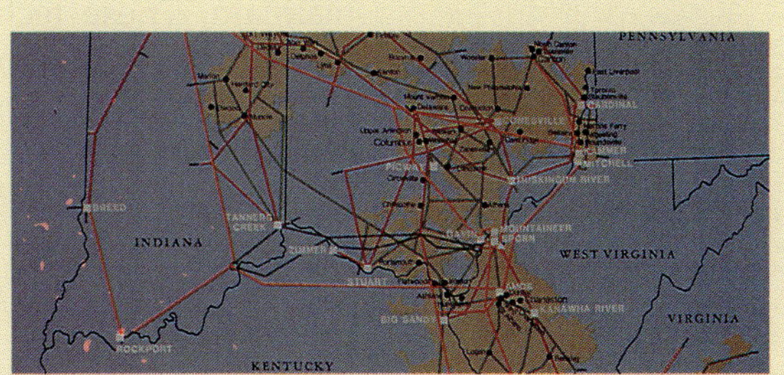

When Columbus, Ohio-based American Electric Power Service Corporation selected a CASE product, it had several specific objectives in mind. One was applications consistency. In the past, the company had found that programs written strictly with traditional languages were difficult to maintain, given the demand for new systems. To management, fourth-generation languages seemed to be only a quicker way to develop inconsistent, unmaintainable code. A second objective was the ability to integrate applications, which favored a single multi-tool vendor. Being a major IBM user, the firm's third objective was the ability to develop applications within an IBM environment. The company eventually chose Andersen Consulting's Foundation.

Summary and Key Terms

Like building a house, creating a successful applications program requires considerable planning.

Program Development Activities. The steps associated with creating successful applications programs are called **applications software development.**

In most large organizations, the development of applications software is the job of systems analysts and programmers. **Systems analysts** are the people who work with users to assess needs, translate those needs into a list of technical requirements, and design the necessary software specifications. The design specification is then handed to a **programmer,** who codes the program from it. Maintenance programmers monitor the software on an ongoing basis, correcting errors and altering the software as applications needs change.

The Make-or-Buy Decision. Many organizations choose to buy their software in the form of prewritten **applications packages** rather than creating it in house. The consideration to create software or acquire it from a vendor, which often takes place after the analysis and design stages of systems development, is frequently called the *make-or-buy decision.*

Program Design. Many tools are available to help the analyst design programs, including program flowcharts, pseudocode, and structure charts.

Program flowcharts use geometric symbols and familiar logical symbols to provide a graphic display of the sequence of steps involved in a program. The steps in a flowchart follow each other in the same logical sequence as their corresponding statements will follow in a program.

A group of techniques has evolved that has made program design more systematic and programs themselves easier to understand and maintain. These techniques are often grouped together under the term **structured programming.** Advocates of structured programming have shown that any program can be constructed out of three fundamental **control structures**—sequence, selection, and looping.

A **sequence control structure** is simply a series of procedures that follow one another. The **selection** (or **if-then-else**) **control structure** involves a choice: *If* a certain condition is true, *then* follow one procedure; *else,* if false, follow another. A **looping** (or **iteration**) **control structure** repeats until a certain condition is met. A *loop* can take two forms: **DO-WHILE** and **DOUNTIL.** By nesting two or more if-then-else's, you can build a fourth control structure, known as a **case control structure.** All of these control structures follow the **one-entry-point/one-exit-point rule**—that is, a structure can have only one way into it and one way out of it.

Pseudocode is a structured technique that uses Englishlike statements in place of the graphic symbols of the flowchart. Pseudocode is commonly employed in the creation of **action diagrams.**

Structure charts, unlike flowcharts and pseudocode, depict the overall, hierarchical organization of program modules and not the specific, step-by-step processing logic involved. **Top-down design** indicates that modules are defined first at the highest levels of the hierarchy and then at successively lower levels.

Programming Languages. An important decision that must be made during the design phase is the selection of a **programming language.** Programming languages are either **low-level languages,** such as machine and assembly languages; **high-level languages,** such as BASIC, Pascal, COBOL, C, FORTRAN, PL/1, APL, Ada, Logo, RPG, Smalltalk, LISP, and Prolog; or *very-high-level* languages, which are also called **fourth-generation languages (4GLs).** Six types of 4GLs commonly used are report generators, retrieval and update languages, decision support system tools, graphics generators, applications packages, and applications generators.

Program Coding. Once analysts have finished the program design for an application, the next stage is to code the program. **Coding,** which is the job of programmers, is the process of writing a program from scratch from a set of design specifications. Among the techniques that have been developed to increase programmer productivity are coding standards, fourth-generation languages, **reusable code,** and **data dictionaries.**

Debugging Programs. Debugging is the process of making sure that a program is free of errors, or "bugs." Debugging is usually a lengthy process, sometimes amounting to over 50 percent of the total development time for an in-house program. Once preliminary debugging is complete, programs will also have to be *tested.* Good test data will subject the program to all the conditions it might conceivably encounter when finally implemented.

Program Maintenance. Program **maintenance** is the process of updating software so that it continues to be useful. Program maintenance is costly; it has been estimated that some organizations spend well over half of their programming time just maintaining existing applications.

Program Documentation. Program **documentation** includes manuals that enable users, maintenance programmers, and operators to interact successfully with a program. Although noted as the final stage of the program development cycle, documentation is an ongoing process that must be addressed throughout the life of the project.

Computer-Aided Software Engineering (CASE). Computer-aided software engineering (CASE) refers to computer programs that assist in the development of other software. CASE packages differ widely, and no one vendor has produced a product that will cure every applications development headache.

Review Exercises

Fill-in Questions

1. ____________ define the requirements that applications software must meet to satisfy users' needs.
2. ____________ refers to the writing of computer programs.
3. The process of detecting and correcting errors in computer programs is called ____________.
4. A program ____________ uses geometric symbols and familiar relational symbols to provide a graphic display of the steps involved in a program.
5. ____________ is a program design tool that uses Englishlike statements.
6. ____________ is the principal transaction processing language in use today.
7. Report generators, retrieval and update languages, applications packages, and applications generators are all examples of ____________ languages.
8. Program pieces designed to be "cut and pasted" into several programs are called ____________.

Matching Questions

Match each term with the description that best fits.

a. Excelerator
b. sequence
c. debugging
d. documentation
e. flowchart
f. pseudocode
g. Pascal
h. program design tool

____ 1. A structure chart, for example.
____ 2. The process of ridding a program of errors.
____ 3. A graphical design tool with boxes and arrows showing step by step how a computer program will process data.
____ 4. A program control structure.
____ 5. A technique for designing programs that uses Englishlike statements resembling actual program statements to show the step-by-step processing a program will follow.
____ 6. A high-level programming language.
____ 7. A written description of a program, such as a manual.
____ 8. A CASE tool.

Discussion Questions

1. What is done during applications software development?
2. What is an applications package? Provide two examples.
3. Name some advantages and disadvantages of applications packages relative to in-house systems development.
4. Why have structured techniques evolved as a major strategy in program design?
5. Name three fundamental control structures of structured programming and provide an example of each.
6. What is the difference between the DOWHILE and DOUNTIL control structures?
7. What is the difference between a flowchart and a structure chart?
8. What need is met by each of the following programming languages: BASIC, COBOL, FORTRAN, C, Pascal?
9. Identify several types of fourth-generation languages and the principal purpose each one serves.
10. Identify some ways to increase programmer productivity.
11. What is the purpose of program maintenance?
12. Why is program documentation important?

Critical Thinking Questions

1. Most end users and programmers within organizations would prefer to work with a widely used applications package than a comparable software product developed in-house. Why is this so, and what benefits and/or problems does the widely used applications package present to the organization?
2. Computer programs have been created that distinguish people who are good credit risks from those who are not. How, would you suppose, do computer programs make this distinction?
3. If there are so many programming languages around today, why are new ones constantly being developed? Do any of these new programming languages really have a chance at wide acceptance, given the number of languages now in use?
4. Chapter 12 discusses the use of CASE tools in software development. If you had to justify the purchase of a $10,000 CASE package to your busy boss—who doesn't have even the vaguest notion of what CASE is—what would you say in that all-important first 60 seconds of your pitch?

How do you go about buying a microcomputer system, taking care of it and upgrading it over time, troubleshooting problems when something goes wrong, and deciding when to call for help? You'll find the answers to such questions in this chapter. Today, as greater numbers of people acquire microcomputers for their own use, it is becoming more important to be knowledgeable about developing and maintaining them.

13 End-User Development

Outline

Overview

The Microcomputer Marketplace

- Microcomputer Products
- Sales and Distribution

Selecting a Computer System

- Analyzing Needs
- Listing Alternatives
- Evaluating Alternatives
- Choosing a System

Operating a Computer System

- Backup
- Proper Maintenance of Resources
- Troubleshooting and Repairs

Upgrading

- Functional versus Technological Obsolescence

Learning More about Microcomputers

Learning Objectives

After completing this chapter, you will be able to:

1. Identify some of the leading companies in critical market segments of the microcomputer industry, as well as the key sales and distribution alternatives for microcomputing products.
2. Explain how to go about selecting a microcomputer system for home or office use.
3. Name some practices designed to protect software, hardware, and data resources from damage, and list some important guidelines that you should follow when troubleshooting problems and having equipment repaired.
4. Describe some of the ways in which a computer system can be upgraded, and explain under what conditions an upgrade should take place.
5. Name several sources for learning more about microcomputer systems.

Overview

It is becoming more common for a person to own a microcomputer or to use one at work. Consequently, more people than ever before are acquiring their own microcomputer resources, taking care of a system, deciding when to call for outside help, upgrading a system on their own, and so on.

End-user development. Systems development activities carried out by the end user.

The term *end-user development* is often used to describe activities such as the ones just mentioned. **End-user development** refers to systems development in which end users assume the responsibilities associated with building and maintaining their own computer systems. These responsibilities extend from initially acquiring a microcomputer system to solving the implementation problems that are bound to occur over time. Although end users may seek technical assistance in solving these problems, it is they who have to decide when it is better to solve problems themselves or call in a specialist. The purpose of this chapter is to make you aware of the many ins and outs connected with being an end user.

Chapter 13 opens with a discussion of the vendors in the microcomputer marketplace and the distribution channels they use to sell their products at the retail level. Then we look at some of the things you should know when acquiring a microcomputer system for home or work. From there we turn to several operation and maintenance issues. Next, upgrading a computer system is covered. Finally, we discuss some of the sources that are at your disposal for learning more about microcomputers.

The Microcomputer Marketplace

The microcomputer marketplace comprises a wide variety of firms that make hardware and software products. Because many hardware and software manufacturers do not sell directly to the public, several companies are in business solely for sales and distribution purposes.

Microcomputer Products

Only about a decade ago, many of the companies that make today's most familiar microcomputer products didn't even exist. Today, several of them earn more than a billion dollars a year in revenues. Almost overnight, the microcomputer industry has become both the fastest-growing and the largest segment of the computer industry.

Some of the big names in each of the major market segments of the microcomputer industry are covered in the following paragraphs.

System Units. IBM, Apple, and Compaq are the big three in the desktop microcomputer marketplace (see Figure 13-1 for a guide to major IBM, Apple, and Compaq microcomputer product lines). There are other companies—such as Tandy, Hewlett-Packard, and Dell—who, like Com-

Figure 13-1
A brief guide to IBM, Apple, and Compaq microcomputers.

IBM

PC

Introduced in 1981, the IBM PC was IBM's first major entry into the microcomputer marketplace. It was a highly successful product; over three million were sold before IBM stopped making them in 1985.

PC/XT

Introduced in 1983, the XT was, more or less, an IBM PC with a built-in hard-disk unit. It was another successful product, with over two million units sold.

PC AT

The AT, introduced in 1984, was the first IBM microcomputer based on the Intel 80286 chip. This chip provided increased performance over the 8088 chip used in the PC and PC/XT.

PS/2

Introduced in 1987, PS/2 refers to a line of several computers, ranging from the Model 25 at the low end to the Model 95 at the high end. The computers in the PS/2 line are based predominantly on advanced Intel chips, such as the 80286, 80386, and 80486.

PS/1

Introduced by IBM in 1990, the PS/1 is targeted primarily for the home, school, and personal computing markets.

Apple

Apple II

The original Apple II, circa 1977, was the first preassembled microcomputer system to achieve superstar status. Since then, Apple has launched improved versions of this machine, such as the Apple IIe and Apple IIc. The Apple II line today is more popular in the home and in schools than it is in business environments.

Apple Macintosh

Introduced in 1984, the Apple Macintosh was the first highly successful microcomputer system to employ onscreen computer graphics. Although the original Macintosh is no longer made, it lives on through the Macintosh Classic, SE, and LC series of computers, which feature a built-in hard disk and newer chip technology.

Apple Macintosh II Series and Quadra Series

Introduced in 1987, the Macintosh II is a powerful, graphically oriented series of desktop computer systems that is roughly comparable in performance to those in the IBM PS/2 line. Models in the series include the Macintosh II, IIx, IIcx, IIfx, IIcxi, IIci, IIsi, and Ic. The Quadra series marks the high end of the Macintosh line.

Macintosh Powerbook Series

Apple's laptop computer, this line of portables is targeted to home and business use.

Compaq

Compaq Portable Computer

Compaq's original computer, a portable, was introduced in 1982. Later versions of it, based on more powerful Intel chips, were known as the Compaq Plus, Compaq Portable 286, Compaq Portable II, Compaq Portable 386, and Compaq Portable III.

Compaq Deskpro

The Deskpro refers to Compaq's principal line of desktop computers. Devices in the line include the Compaq Deskpro, Compaq Deskpro 286, Compaq Deskpro 386, and Compaq Deskpro 486.

Compaq Systempro

Introduced in 1989, the Systempro is a line of advanced desktop computers targeted to high-end business and networking uses.

Compaq SLT and Compaq LTE

The SLT and LTE make up Compaq's line of laptop and notebook computers, respectively.

IBM-compatible computer. A computer that can run the same software as IBM computers run.

paq, have become highly successful largely by producing IBM-compatible computers. **IBM-compatible computers** are microcomputers that can run the same software as that targeted to IBM microcomputers. Most IBM-compatible machines made today will run virtually any major applications software product designed to work on IBM microcomputers.

Laptop computers are currently the fastest-growing segment within the microcomputer marketplace. In laptops, three of the biggest names are Toshiba, GRiD, and Tandy.

Software. Among the largest independent software producers (and their leading products) are Lotus Development Corporation (1-2-3 and Symphony), Microsoft Corporation (MS-DOS and Windows operating system software; BASIC language translators; Word; Excel; and Works), Computer Associates International (SuperCalc), Borland International (Sidekick, Quattro, Paradox, dBASE, and Turbo Pascal), and WordPerfect Corporation (WordPerfect). At one time, many of these companies could have been characterized as single-product firms. Today, the leaders in this segment are in a period of aggressive diversification, internally developing new products and acquiring smaller companies that have successful, related product lines.

Monitors and Printers. With the exception of a few U.S. companies such as IBM, Qume, Wyse, and Hewlett-Packard, these two segments are dominated by the Japanese. Some of the major players are Epson, Toshiba, Amdek, Brother, Fujitsu, Canon, NEC, and C. Itoh.

Computer and Memory Chips. The chip markets are ruled by Intel, Motorola, and Japanese companies. Intel makes CPU chips for most of the leading IBM and IBM-compatible system units, whereas Motorola makes chips for the Apple Macintosh line of computers.

Modems. Ten years ago, who would have thought that they'd someday watch a college football bowl game and see an award called the "Hayes Microcomputer Player of the Game"? Hayes is the dominant name in microcomputer modems today. Many other manufacturers are in the market of selling Hayes-compatible modems.

Add-In Boards. Hercules was one of the first big names in add-in boards. Like Hayes with its modems, Hercules's monochrome display board—which made possible monochrome graphics on a display screen—became somewhat of a de facto standard in the industry. Because there are many different products and specifications around today, a large variety of board products are available (refer back to Figure 3-11 in Chapter 3). Other major manufacturers of boards are Quadram, AST, and Tallgrass.

Disk Systems. Some of the more familiar firms in the marketplace for diskette drives and hard-disk drives are Conner, Control Data, IBM, Seagate, and Tandon. In the optical-disk-drive marketplace, Canon and

Company	Principal Product(s)
Adobe	Assorted desktop publishing software products
Aldus	PageMaker desktop publishing program
Apple	Microcomputer systems
AST	A wide variety of hardware products
Autodesk	AutoCAD design software
Borland	A wide variety of software products
Canon	Printers and related products
Commodore	Amiga microcomputer system
Compaq	Microcomputer systems
Computer Associates	A wide variety of software products
Dell	Microcomputer systems
Hayes	Modems
Hewlett-Packard	Microcomputer systems and laser printers
IBM	A wide variety of microcomputing products
Index Technology	Excelerator, a CASE product
Intel	Chips for IBM and IBM-compatible computers
Lotus Development	1-2-3 spreadsheet package
Microsoft	A wide variety of software products
Motorola	Chips for Apple computers
NEC	A wide variety of hardware products
Novell	NetWare operating system
Quadram	A wide variety of hardware products
Qume	Printers
Seagate	Hard disks
Software Publishing	Harvard Graphics presentation software
Symantec	A wide variety of software products
Tandy/Radio Shack	A wide variety of microcomputing products
Toshiba	A wide variety of hardware products
WordPerfect	WordPerfect word processing package

Figure 13-2
Who's who in the microcomputer marketplace. This list shows the products or product lines for which several leading companies are most famous.

Philips are big names. Such companies as Iomega and Plus Development have done well with their hard cards and hard-disk cartridges.

Diskettes. The competition in the diskette segment is among the fiercest imaginable, because there are not many important ways to differentiate diskettes. If the diskette "works" (that is, the quality level is sufficiently high—which is usually the case if you purchase a familiar brand), price is the only factor on which to compete. Most diskettes are sold by companies that don't make diskettes; instead, they buy them from someone else and put their own labels on them. If you want a familiar name on the label, you may pay $1 or more per (5¼-inch) diskette. However, generic diskettes (which may be made by the same manufacturer as the more expensive variety) may cost as little as a quarter each in quantities of 100.

A roster of some of the most familiar companies in the microcomputer marketplace appears in Figure 13-2, along with a description of the major product offerings that have made these companies famous.

Figure 13-3
A retail computer store.
Retail computer stores are often authorized dealers for name-brand equipment and usually provide local repair support.

Sales and Distribution

Hardware and software microcomputing products are most often acquired from retail computer stores, mail-order houses, and manufacturers.

Retail Computer Stores. Organizations that need strong local support often turn to retail computer stores (see Figure 13-3). Generally, the salespeople at these stores are relatively knowledgeable about computers and help buyers try out hardware and software before making a commitment. If a purchased item does not work as advertised, some stores take great pains to resolve any problems. Typically, retail computer stores also offer consulting, repair, and other support services to users.

Mail-Order Firms. Another source of computer products is mail-order firms. These companies regularly publish price lists in microcomputer journals and can ship products within 24 hours of a request (see Figure 13-4). Because these companies don't have to pay for a showroom and a large staff of knowledgeable salespeople, their prices usually are lower than those of computer stores. Also, some mail-order firms have access to an enormous stock of goods and can get almost any item to buyers quickly via UPS or Federal Express. A disadvantage of mail-order shop-

Figure 13-4
Mail-order houses.
Mail-order houses like MacConnection (featured here) and PC Connection, which respectively specialize in Apple Macintosh products and IBM-compatible microcomputing products, regularly advertise their prices in the leading microcomputer journals.

ping is that buyers need to know exactly what they want, because most mail-order firms don't maintain showrooms or an informative staff.

Manufacturers. A third alternative for buying hardware and software is going directly to the manufacturer, although this is not always possible. Many manufacturers have exclusive selling arrangements with certain wholesalers and with buying consortiums such as schools and large computer clubs. Also, when manufacturers do sell directly to the general public, they usually sell only in large quantities—perhaps only *very* large quantities. Buying directly from the manufacturer usually means lower prices but often does not include ongoing support. Such support, if needed, must be purchased from another firm.

When buying a computer system, don't overlook used equipment. Ads for used equipment can usually be found in the classified section of local newspapers. If you take this route, ask to try out the equipment before you buy it. If the equipment functions properly during the trial period, it will probably work fine. Be especially careful to check how the monitor works over a period of a couple of hours, and evaluate the output quality of the printer as well. You should pay considerably less for a used system than you would for a new one.

Selecting a Computer System

Chances are good that at some point in your life you will need to select a microcomputer system to better perform your job. Selecting a microcomputer system for home or for business use must begin with the all-important question: "What do I want the system to do?" Once you've determined the purposes to which the system will be put, you must choose among the software and hardware alternatives available. Finally, you need a method to evaluate the alternatives and to select a system.

Analyzing Needs

With regard to computer systems, a *need* refers to a requirement that the computer system must be capable of meeting. For instance, at a videotape rental store, a computer system must be able to enter bar codes automatically from tapes being checked in and out, identify customers with overdue tapes, manage tape inventories, and do routine accounting operations. All four of these uses are needs.

A person owning a computer system will find dozens of ways to use it, but he or she may often justify the acquisition of a microcomputer system on the basis of only one or two needs. For example, many managers do so much financial planning that a spreadsheeting capability alone is enough to justify the entire computer-system cost. Many writers find word processing so indispensable to their livelihoods that it matters little what else the computer system can do. And sales personnel working out of the office can often justify a laptop computer simply on the basis of its usefulness as an account-closing tool at client sites. Figure 13-5 provides a list of potential needs that are met by microcomputer systems.

If you're not really sure what you want a system to do, you should think twice about buying one. Because computer systems that are specially configured to serve certain applications (say, games) are often poor at others (such as word processing), you can easily make some expensive mistakes if you're uncertain.

As part of the needs analysis, you should look closely at budgetary constraints. Every user has many needs, but it is their affordability that separates the real needs from the pipe dreams.

Listing Alternatives

Once a set of needs has been established, the next step is to list some alternative systems that might satisfy those needs. You should almost always consider software first, then hardware.

Software is selected first because it most closely relates to needs. For instance, if you want a computer system to perform desktop publishing, it would be wise to first look at the various desktop publishing packages available. It makes no sense to choose the computer first and then find out that it doesn't support the type of desktop publishing package you prefer.

Word Processing
Most people purchase microcomputers to create memos, letters, manuscripts, and other documents.

Spreadsheets
Business users find microcomputers handy for preparing budgets and other financial schedules and for analyzing information to improve decision making.

Organizing, Scheduling, and Mailing
Microcomputers are commonly being used as electronic desktops to coordinate office activities and to provide an environment in which people can communicate more effectively.

Desktop Publishing
Microcomputer systems are useful for preparing books and articles whose quality is comparable to that of products done on a professional printer's press.

Preparing Slides and Presentation Materials
35mm slides, automated slide shows, overhead transparencies, and handout materials are frequently produced on a microcomputer.

Retrieving Information from Local or Remote Databases
Users of all types find the microcomputer a handy device for looking up information.

Transaction Processing
Many database services let people use their microcomputer systems to shop, bank, and buy and sell stocks from the home—and businesses use microcomputers, too, to process these and other transactions.

Learning
An abundance of microcomputer software—some of it in multimedia form—is available today to provide instruction on virtually any subject.

Software Development
By using microcomputer systems with CASE tools, programmers are developing software for all sizes of computers.

Design
Artists and designers find the microcomputer indispensable for creating products that would be impossible or too expensive to do manually.

Games and Entertainment
Electronic games have always been popular on microcomputer systems; today, devices such as televisions, VCRs, and music synthesizers are teaming up with microcomputers to take entertainment potential further.

Figure 13-5
Microcomputer needs.
Most users buy a microcomputer system on the basis of one or two of the needs listed here.

Often, in the world of microcomputers, decisions are highly interrelated, so that software and hardware must be selected jointly. A software product may work only with a specific set of hardware. For instance, a certain word processor might be available only for an Apple Macintosh computer system, and it might also require a laser printer to work most effectively. An illustration software package may work effectively only if a specific type of graphics interface hardware is used—say, a digitizing tablet and a cursor movement device. Also, most illustration packages require a hard disk, because graphics images require large amounts of storage. Because of the interrelated nature of many software and hardware products, it sometimes helps to make a list of system alternatives, in which each alternative listed is a complete configuration of hardware and software elements.

You can get a list of software and hardware products from the leading microcomputer journals. (We'll discuss some of these journals later in the chapter.) Many of these journals also periodically describe the best and worst features of products and give each product an overall rating (see Window 8). The ratings can be used as input for evaluating products, your next step in acquiring a microcomputer system.

Evaluating Alternatives

Alternative products are best examined by "test driving" them. You must keep in mind that when observing the performance of a software package, you are viewing its performance on a given configuration of hardware. A software package that runs smoothly on a Dell 80486-based computer system won't necessarily run as well on a Compaq 80386 system, which uses a slightly different architecture and a less powerful chip. Also, the look, feel, and performance of a software package on a computer in the Apple Macintosh line will be notably different than they are on an IBM or IBM-compatible machine. Sometimes it's quite difficult, when selecting a configuration of hardware and software, to see the entire system running together, but it's certainly advisable to do this whenever possible.

Selection Criteria. In evaluating software and hardware products, a number of criteria will help you make your final selection.

The most important selection criterion is usually *functionality*—the type of work the product does. For many people, ease of learning and ease of use follow closely behind. Also, most people prefer widely used products rather than unknown ones, because the large user base with the popular products ensures that vendor support will be around for a long time. In addition, if you are considering using a microcomputer system in an office environment dominated by, say, Apple Macintoshes, choosing that type of computer would probably be more convenient from the standpoint of having local expertise available for support. Good written documentation showing how to use the hardware or software is also important; when a helping hand isn't readily available, documentation is often the best alternative for answering a tough question.

A list of important criteria for selecting a microcomputer system is provided in Figure 13-6.

Software and Hardware Specifics. Before looking over software or hardware, you should make a checklist of properties that the software or hardware should possess—and be sure to watch for these during the test drive. A rehearsed presentation made by a salesperson is likely to point out only the strengths of a product, not its weaknesses.

For instance, in examining word processors, you should consider the type of text they output (e.g., do they allow proportionally spaced characters, half lines, subscripts and superscripts, and so on?), ask how easy it is to execute standard commands (such as moving the cursor, centering, moving and copying text, indenting, reformatting, or footnoting), check the quality of the spelling checker and thesaurus features, and find

- ☐ Product functionality
- ☐ Ease of learning and use
- ☐ Cost
- ☐ Vendor reputation
- ☐ Support
- ☐ Expandability
- ☐ Meets industry standards
- ☐ Speed
- ☐ Favorable reviews
- ☐ Delivery
- ☐ Documentation

Figure 13-6
Important selection criteria. Buyers generally select computer systems on the basis of some combination of these criteria.

out what advanced features the word processors possess (e.g., multiple-column formatting, redlining, sorting, and desktop publishing features). Again, consider the entire system. For example, if you are planning to buy an inexpensive dot-matrix printer that can't handle proportional spacing, certain types of graphics, or subscripts and superscripts, it makes little difference that a word processor supports these features. Some of the items that you should watch for particularly when buying specific types of software packages are enumerated in Feature 13-1.

Hardware items that usually will need to be considered when buying a microcomputer system are the system unit and RAM, diskette and hard-disk units, a monitor, a keyboard, and a printer. Some of the questions that need to be addressed when buying these types of hardware are shown in Feature 13-2.

Choosing a System

After you have considered the alternatives, it's time to choose a system and purchase it.

People choose between system alternatives in a number of ways. For instance, some people make a formal list of selection criteria (such as those shown in Figure 13-6) and quantitatively rate each alternative on each of these criteria. They then select the alternative that scores the highest. This method was discussed in Chapter 11 (see Figure 11-11).

Others prefer to make their choices less formally. After thinking about needs and the criteria that they will use to evaluate alternatives, they select a computer system as soon as it "feels right." In fact, several researchers have found that a large number of microcomputers are acquired in small quantities and that very little formal analysis, if any, is undertaken before the purchase. Although such an acquisition process could be criticized for lack of thoroughness, many managers claim that they are too busy to spend the time researching choices with greater care. There is, of course, a negative side to rushed selections. Just as a car owner can go through years of torture driving around in the wrong type

Feature 13-1

Buying Software

Some Important Questions to Ask

When buying software such as word processors, spreadsheets, and database management systems, be sure to get answers to the following questions:

Word Processing

Does the package contain all the features that you want? Make a list of features and check a reference manual, trade book, or product review to see what the package has or lacks.

Will the package work on your hardware configuration? Keep in mind that printing attractive fonts, proportionally spaced text, and graphics usually requires a laser printer. If the package lets you preview graphics outputs before printing them, you will need a graphics-oriented monitor. If you plan to use a spelling checker or thesaurus, you will almost certainly need a hard disk.

Will the package fit on your system? Look closely at the RAM and hard-disk requirements of the package to see if it fits.

Does the package implement word processing features in a way you find compatible with your work style? The best way to answer this question is to try out the system at a store, in school, or at a friend's house. Of course, don't forget to check that the package exists in a version that will work on your system.

Spreadsheets

Does the package contain all the features that you want, and does it implement them in a way that is comfortable with your work style? Most major spreadsheet packages are remarkably alike. They contain virtually the same types of commands and closely follow the user interface of Lotus Development Corporation's 1-2-3. Microsoft's Excel, with its graphics-oriented interface, is one of the few packages that differs somewhat from the pack in terms of look and feel.

Will the package fit on your system? Consider the RAM and hard-disk requirements of the package.

Will the package work on your hardware configuration? Check the graphics requirements of the package. If you are going to be using a great deal of presentation graphics, you will probably want a hard disk and laser printer. Of course, check that the package exists in a version that will work on your system.

of car, so too can a computer buyer wind up with years of headaches resulting from a poor computer-system choice. The expense of a computer-system mistake may be much greater, however.

Operating a Computer System

Once you've acquired a computer system, it is important that you develop a set of practices to protect your software, hardware, and data from damage and from costly mistakes. Three important areas in this regard are backup of programs and data, proper maintenance of hardware and I/O media, and troubleshooting and repairs. A fourth area, securing the data on your computer system, is covered in the chapter's Tomorrow box.

Database Management Systems and File Managers

Will you need to relate data appearing in different files? If the answer is yes, forget about a file manager. You will need a database management system.

Do you have a hard disk? Compared to other types of productivity software, database management systems and file managers are very data-intensive. If you need to relate files so that the contents of several files are available simultaneously, you will almost certainly need a hard disk.

Does the package contain all of the features that you want and implement them in a way that you find comfortable with your work style? Database management systems and file managers are like word processors, in that both a software package's features and its look and feel can vary tremendously from vendor to vendor. Before buying a package, make a checklist of the features that you need and see how they are implemented in the packages under consideration.

Will the package work on your hardware configuration? Check that the package exists in a version that will work on your system.

How easy is the package to learn and use? Data management is generally harder to master than word processing or spreadsheets. Some packages, in fact, are targeted more toward programmers than toward ordinary users. Make sure that the package you want to buy comes with documentation, demo disks, or learning manuals that you are able to read and understand. If the vendor learning and documentation tools are mediocre, look for some good trade books to help you get started.

How fast is the package? Because data management packages are data-intensive, the speed with which the package can retrieve information is extremely critical. It will probably be difficult for you to design a benchmark test to test speed yourself before you buy, so to judge the package under consideration, read closely the results of the comparative product tests published regularly in the computer journals.

What type of backup procedures do you plan to use? One of the worst of all computer nightmares is having a large database destroyed when a hard disk malfunctions and there is no backup. When considering buying a database management system, you should consider what backup options are available to you. A backup tape unit is most convenient for large databases but will add to the cost of having database management in your applications portfolio.

Backup

Virtually everyone who has logged months or years of his or her life on a computer system will swear to you that, sooner or later, you will lose some critical files. Maybe lightning will strike nearby, zapping your RAM. Or maybe a small brownout will cause the heads on your hard disk to drop out of orbit and crash onto the disk surface, carving a miniature canyon through the electronic version of a 45-page term paper that's due tomorrow. Computer veterans will also tell you that these file losses always seem to happen at the worst possible times.

Fortunately, there is a solution to most of these problems—backup. Creating **backup** means making a duplicate version of any file that you can't afford to lose so that, when the fickle finger of fate causes inadvertent erasure, you're confronted with only a minor irritant rather than an outright catastrophe. Theoretically, you can back up any file on your com-

Backup.
Making duplicate copies of programs or data.

Feature 13-2

Buying Hardware

Some Important Questions To Ask

When buying a system unit, storage, a monitor, a keyboard, or a printer, be sure to get answers to the following questions:

System Unit

What brand of system is best for your needs? Buy a system that runs the type of software with which you wish to work and that is widely supported. Buying a bargain-basement system could leave you completely on your own, and it could cost you more in the long run than you save on the purchase price.

Does the system unit have enough power to meet current and future applications needs? Most computers sold today are 32-bit machines and run at speeds of from 12 to 50 MHz. You should buy a system that will last for several years.

RAM

How much memory does your most memory-intensive application require? If you are planning to move up to OS/2 at some point in the future, for instance, applications will require at least 2 MB of RAM. Other sophisticated operating systems and operating environments can also be memory intensive.

Can memory be expanded later if you need more? Determine in what increments and to what maximum it can be extended. As an example, many machines allow memory expansion in 1-MB increments up to a maximum of 8 MB.

Secondary Storage

Will you need one or two diskette drives? What disk diameter and capacity will you need? Recall from Chapter 4 that drives accommodate either 3½-inch or 5¼-inch disks and that disk capacities usually run from 360 KB to 1.44 MB. Many people today buy systems that have one 1.44 MB 3½-inch drive and one 1.2 MB 5¼-inch drive, which enables them to read almost any disk.

Will you need a hard disk? Increasingly, business software requires a hard disk to run. If you do need a hard disk, what capacity and format will you choose? Recall from Chapter 4 that hard disks today range from 20 to a few hundred megabytes in capacity, and most use either an RLL, ESDI, or SCSI format. Computer professionals often advise that you figure out the minimum amount of storage you will need and at least double or triple that figure in order to meet future needs.

Monitor

How readable is the screen? Always inspect the output of the monitor you are considering before making a purchase.

Do you need a color or monochrome monitor? Color monitors differ in output quality and number of colors available; monochrome monitors may display in either green, amber, or white foregrounds.

What type of resolution do you require? If some of the work you do requires especially fine resolution, make sure that you evaluate how well the monitor produces such outputs.

Which graphics standards (for example, VGA) does the monitor support? Older and less expen-

puter system. The backups you create—through, say, a file-copy, disk-copy, or backup command—can be on diskette, hard disk, optical disk, streaming tape, or virtually any other secondary storage medium.

One common form of backup is making a duplicate of a long file that is being developed in RAM. For instance, suppose you are word processing a paper for a class. About every half hour or hour, you should make sure that you save the current version of the document file onto disk.

sive monitors may not be capable of running software that adheres to newer, more sophisticated graphics standards.

Does the monitor have adjustable features? Especially important are an adjustable base, which helps ward off glare, and brightness and contrast controls.

Keyboard

Does the keyboard feel comfortable as you type on it? If possible, type on the keyboard before buying; notice especially the key spacing and how the keys feel to your touch.

Does the keyboard have an assortment of special keys and features? Many people like light indicators showing if certain keys are active.

Are the keys placed in an arrangement that you prefer? Even though most people use the QWERTY key arrangement, there are several other keyboard layouts available. Also, make sure that the special keys are conveniently located.

Does the keyboard have adjustable features? It is especially important that the keyboard is detachable, enabling you to move it about to suit your comfort, and that it has an adjustable slope.

Printer

What type of printer (for example, impact dot matrix, laser, color thermal transfer) is best for your needs? For most people, the choice will be between an impact dot-matrix printer and a laser printer.

How fast is the printer? Impact dot-matrix printers typically are rated at several hundred characters per second (cps), whereas most microcomputer-oriented laser printers print anywhere from two to eight pages per minute.

What types of outputs can the printer produce (e.g., text or both text and graphics)? Be sure to examine closely both the range and the quality of outputs. Some laser printers, for instance, will print large-point-size text with jagged contours. You should never buy a printer unless you first see its outputs—and as wide a range of outputs as possible.

Can the printer be run in several modes? Impact dot-matrix printers should be capable of being run in a fast, draft-quality mode and a slow, letter-quality mode. Many laser printers have an adjustment for darkness that enables you to get lighter copies for drafts, which extends the life of the toner cartridge. Check the output quality in each of the available modes.

Other Hardware

If you are buying other hardware, make sure that there are enough ports and expansion slots to accommodate it.

If you are buying a modem, decide whether you want it to be internal or external, how fast it must be, and whether or not it meets the communications standards prescribed by the application for which you intend it.

If you are thinking about buying a mouse, consider also the possibility of getting a trackball. Many people dislike using a mouse because it must be moved around a desktop; trackballs, in contrast, are stationary.

That way, if the power goes out on your system, you will have lost only what you have typed in since the last save command. Many commercial packages provide certain types of automatic backup of files, but unless you know for sure what is being backed up and when, it's safer to do it yourself.

There are many different strategies for backing up files on a hard disk or a diskette. One is to perform a **full backup,** in which you back up all

Full backup.
A procedure that produces a duplicate copy of all files onto a secondary storage medium.

Tomorrow

Data Security for Your Microcomputer

Will Your Data Be There Tomorrow?

Yesterday seemed like a typical day. You worked on your desktop computer and put it to bed for the night by simply turning it off. But this morning, when you started it up, you noticed that some of your files had been tampered with, and others had been erased. Checking the hard disk's directory revealed that someone had been on your computer system early in the morning. Who was there and what they were doing seem minor when you speculate about the damage that might have been done.

Fortunately, there are a variety of solutions available today to ensure that the preceding scenario never happens.

The first line of defense for any microcomputer user is physical security. *Physical security* refers to the use of devices that inhibit physical access to property. For instance, people who have private offices can lock their doors while they are gone, making it unlikely that other people can get to their computer systems. For computer systems in open offices, various physical locking devices are available. Widely used are lockable security plates that can vacuum-attach computer hardware to a desk, without defacing the latter. Also, many system units today come with built-in locks. By turning a key, you can lock up your computer system so that nobody can use it while you are away. Removable disk cartridges are also excellent devices for security-conscious users. Disk cartridges enable you to remove large volumes of data from the computer system and to store them at another site.

A number of software products can also help you protect data. Access to computer systems is most often restricted by *passwords*. Passwords are commonly used on networks to keep unauthorized people from gaining access to the network. Passwords can also be used at the file and operator level. For instance, a certain password may be necessary to access a specific set of files, and another password may be necessary if the operator wants to update these files in any way.

Another popular software-based security product is the *disklock accessory*, which allows you to lock your hard disk, or selected portions of it, while you are away from your desk. You can make a request to lock a disk at any time, and, if you wish, you can also program the accessory to lock the disk if the computer system is unused for a certain number of minutes. Then, if you are unexpectedly away from your desk for a meeting, the screen will go blank on its own and a pop-up box will appear asking that a password be entered to unlock the system. Because many disklock accessories allow portions of a disk to be protected, security for a computer system is extended to networks and to environments in which several people share the same desktop computer system.

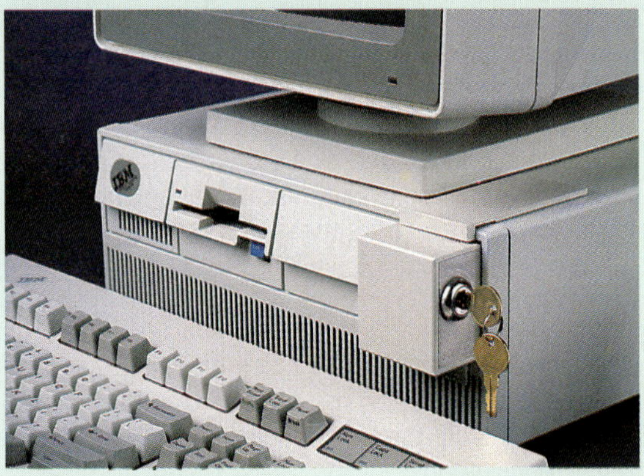

Physical security. A lockbox can prevent power-switch access.

Another popular software solution to security is encryption. *Encryption* allows you to encode files so that they appear as gibberish to anyone trying to read them. Naturally, there is also a decoding algorithm in the encryption package. The main disadvantages to encryption are that it takes a long time to encrypt a file and that files sometimes can get destroyed during the encryption process. If you encrypt a file, make sure that you also have an unencrypted version stored in a safe place.

Virtually everyone concerned about security will want to protect data from computer viruses, which are small blocks of renegade code that can destroy data or disable a computer system. Viruses are commonly countered through so-called *vaccine programs*. Viruses and vaccine software are covered in Feature 7-2.

It is important to note that no security strategy can give your computer system full protection. Nonetheless, taking a few simple precautions today can save you big headaches tomorrow.

Why Backup?

- ☐ A disk sector goes bad, destroying part of a file.
- ☐ A file that you thought you no longer had a need for and erased turns out to be important.
- ☐ You modify a file in an undesirable way, and the damage done is irreversible.
- ☐ You accidentally reformat a disk.
- ☐ The disk suffers a head crash.
- ☐ A power brownout or failure at the time of saving a file causes "garbage" to be saved.
- ☐ You save a file to the wrong subdirectory, overwriting a different file that has the same name.
- ☐ While rushing your work, you make a mistake that causes the wrong files to be erased.
- ☐ You unwittingly destroy a file while working on it—say, by deleting parts of it erroneously and then saving the file.
- ☐ Malfunctioning hardware or software causes files to be erased.
- ☐ A computer virus enters your system and destroys files.
- ☐ Your disk is physically destroyed—for instance, a diskette is left in the sun or the hard disk is given a jolt. Alternatively, a fire or flood may destroy the disk.
- ☐ Someone steals your diskette or hard disk.

Figure 13-7
Good reasons for backing up files.
Taking a few extra minutes to make duplicate copies of important files can avert a potential disaster.

of the files on disk several times throughout the day or at the end of a day or a session. The advantage to a full backup is that it is relatively straightforward, and, since it employs a "shotgun" approach to backup, it sometimes saves "treasures" that you neglected to copy previously. On the down side, a full backup takes longer than a backup in which selected files are targeted for copying. Also, you need more storage space to contain the copied files.

An alternative to the full backup is a **partial backup,** in which only files created or altered since the last backup are copied. Many people who have hard disks will perform a partial backup daily and a full backup weekly.

Partial backup.
A procedure that produces a duplicate copy of selected files onto a secondary storage medium.

Whenever you make backup copies on a disk, make sure that the backup files are not stored on the same disk as the originals. In theory, they shouldn't even be in the same room or building. Then, if a serious accident such as a fire or flood occurs at one location, the files at the other location will be safe. A variety of accidents that can destroy programs and data—accidents that are all good reasons to do disk backup—are listed in Figure 13-7.

Proper Maintenance of Resources

Microcomputer systems consist of sensitive electronic devices, so they must be treated with appropriate care. In this section we discuss protecting your computer system with a surge suppressor; caring for disks; protecting your computer system from dust, heat, and static; and protecting printers and monitors.

Surge Suppression. One of the best devices to have on your computer system to minimize the chance of unexpected damage is a surge suppres-

Figure 13-8
Surge suppressor.
The system unit and its support devices feed into the surge suppressor, which is plugged into a standard wall outlet. This permits you to turn on all of your equipment, as well as a nearby lamp or two, with the flick of a single switch.

Surge suppressor.
A device that protects a computer system from random electrical power spikes.

sor. A **surge suppressor,** which is installed between your system unit and the electrical outlet providing the power, is a hardware device that prevents random electrical power spikes from causing damage to your system (see Figure 13-8).

The power going into most homes is uneven. Power spikes, such as those caused from electrical storms, and power brownouts caused by drops in power can damage data or your system. Probably the most common problem caused by a spike or brownout is loss of data in RAM. Cases have also been reported, however, of loss of data in secondary storage and destruction of equipment.

A surge suppressor cannot guarantee complete protection. If lightning strikes your house, even a top-of-the-line surge suppressor will probably fail to protect your equipment. If you live in an area prone to severe lightning storms, the best thing that you can do if you are working on your computer system when a storm hits is save to disk what you've been working on, turn off your system, and unplug the surge suppressor. Lightning can cause damage to electrical equipment—whether it's turned on or off—if it is plugged in.

Disk Care. Precautions taken with diskettes and hard disks will safeguard any data stored on them.

Diskettes may look like inert slabs of plastic, but they are extremely sensitive items and must be cared for accordingly. Never touch the exposed diskette surface or bend the diskette in any way. Also, keep the diskette away from magnetic objects, motors, stereo speakers, and extreme temperatures. Figure 13-9 covers a number of precautions that should be taken when handling diskettes.

You should have the heads cleaned on your disk drives periodically, and at the same time, check to see that the heads haven't slipped out of alignment. Misregistered heads can usually be adjusted easily. Of course, never insert a warped disk into a drive. With a hard disk, the most important precaution to take is ensuring that the disk is in a place where it is not likely to be bumped.

Dust, Heat, and Static. Each of the tiny processor and memory chips in your hardware units are packed tightly with hundreds or thousands of circuits. Dust particles circulating in the air can settle on a chip, causing a short circuit. Many people buy dust covers that fit snugly over each of their hardware devices to prevent foreign particles in the air from causing hardware failure.

System units that support add-in boards require cooling fans. These boards generate heat, and too much heat inside the system unit can cause all sorts of problems. When inserting add-in boards, you should place them as far apart as possible to avoid heat buildup. Also, most boards draw power off the system's main power unit (as do many internal hard disks), so be particularly careful about overtaxing the power unit.

Static electricity is especially dangerous because it can damage chips, destroy programs and data in memory, or disable your keyboard. So that those nasty little electrical discharges from your fingertips don't wreak havoc, you might consider buying an antistatic mat for under your workstation chair or an antistatic spray for your keyboard. Static electricity is more likely in dry areas and in the wintertime, when there's less humidity in the air.

Other Concerns. CRT-type monitors have a phosphorescent surface that is "lit up" by an electronic gun. If you keep your monitor at a high brightness level and abandon it for an hour or two, the phosphorescent surface will be "torched" rather than merely lit up. This means that ghosty character images will be permanently etched on the screen, making it harder to read. Software packages called **screen savers** are available that either dim your monitor or create random patterns on the screen when the display remains unchanged for a given number of minutes.

Screen saver. A software product designed to protect the phosphor coating on the inside of a display screen from damage when the display is turned on but is not used for an extended period.

Printers are particularly prone to failure because they are electromechanical devices. If you have an impact dot-matrix printer, the most vulnerable mechanism in the unit is the print head. Like typewriter keys, these print heads will wear down over time. Still, you can take precautions to prevent rapid wear, such as making sure that the head is cleaned periodically, not using the printer excessively for graphics (which wear the head more rapidly), and making sure that the head is not adjusted

Figure 13-9 The DOs and DON'Ts of diskette care.
Diskettes are sensitive magnetic objects. A good rule when working with them is to avoid exposing them to heat, dust, pressure, and foreign substances.

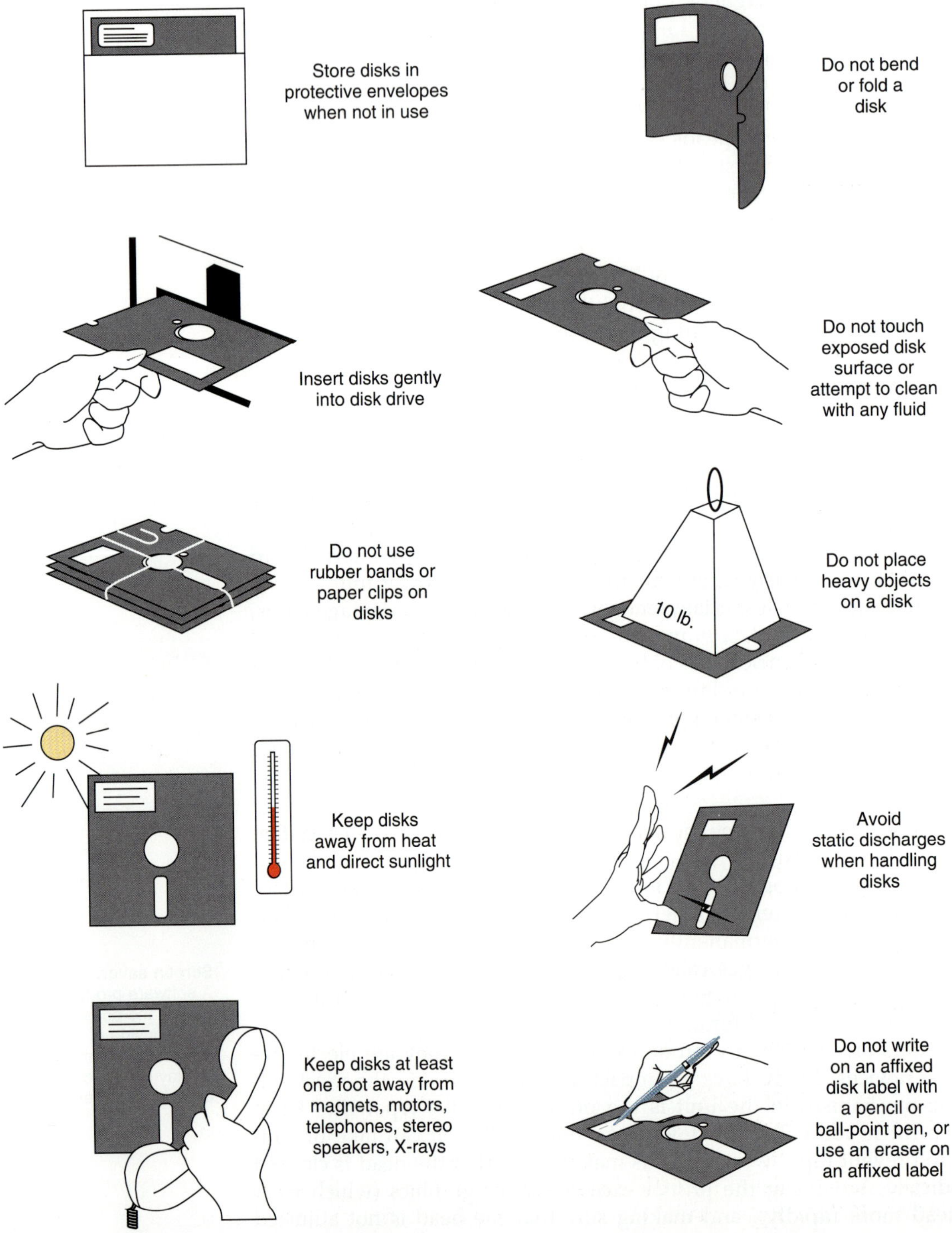

for carbon copies (which makes the head strike harder) if you want only single copies.

Naturally, as with other electronic devices, you shouldn't switch hardware units on and off excessively.

Troubleshooting and Repairs

If you work with computers for any length of time, at some point you will probably have an experience when your hardware or software does not work properly. You may turn on your computer system one day and get no response. Perhaps your monitor screen will begin flickering badly every few seconds. Or maybe you will issue a familiar command in a software package that you work with regularly and the keyboard will lock up or the command will remain unexecuted. When such an event takes place, you will need to troubleshoot to isolate the underlying problem. If the problem is serious enough, repairs may be necessary.

Troubleshooting. *Troubleshooting* refers to any actions taken to diagnose or solve a problem. Unfortunately, many problems are unique to specific types of hardware and software, so there's no simple troubleshooting remedy that works all of the time. Nonetheless, the following are some simple steps and guidelines that will help you out in a surprising number of instances.

- Recall exactly what happened between the time the system was operating properly and the time you began to encounter problems. There might have been an electrical storm outside, and your system was plugged in and damaged by lightning. Maybe someone disturbed the room where the computer is located; the hard disk may have been bumped, or the room may have been vacuumed and dust entered your keyboard or disk-drive bay. Perhaps you installed new systems software during your last session, and these changes are affecting the way your current application works.
- Try again. An unusual number of procedures work when you try a second or third time. You may have pressed the wrong keys the first time, or not pressed the keys hard enough. If the problem persists, attempt to save your work, restart (reboot) your computer system, and try again.
- Check to see that all of the equipment is plugged in and turned on and that none of the cables are detached or loose.
- If the problem seems traceable to software, try going through the same procedure again with a backup version of the software or with another set of data. The problem may simply be that the original program disk or data disk is defective.
- Be observant. If strange noises came out of the disk drives when you unsuccessfully tried to boot the system up, those noises might be important. If the output quality of your printer has deteriorated, check the printhead, observe the printer at work, and collect "before" and

"after" samples of outputs for further inspection. Also, if you were working successfully for several hours before the problem set in, that, too, could be significant. Even though solving the problem may be beyond your capabilities, you may be able to supply important facts to the people repairing your system. The faster the repair technicians can diagnose and fix your system, the less money you will spend in repair costs.

- If you can't solve the problem, temporarily abandon it, if possible, and work on something else. Sometimes solutions to seemingly insurmountable problems come to you when you are in the middle of doing another job, or when you approach the problem after a nap or exercise. If you are still stumped, call a repair shop and ask to speak with a repair technician. After you describe the "symptoms" to the technician, he or she might successfully diagnose the problem over the phone so that you can fix it yourself—for free.

Diagnostic disk.
A disk that's used to help pinpoint and correct computer-system malfunctions.

- Some hardware manufacturers produce **diagnostic disks** that enable you to run tests on your computer system. Other manufacturers allow you to link your computer by modem to their diagnostic centers so that they can run their own tests on your system over the phone lines. In some cases, you may be able to correct the problem without having to unplug your system and transport it to a repair center.

You should weigh the time that it takes to solve a problem yourself against the cost of outside repair. It's not a disgrace to have to give up if the problem is more than you can handle. It is simply an admission that your time is valuable and that you are wise enough to know when to call in a professional for assistance.

Repairs. In some cases, a problem is simple enough that no repair is necessary or you can do repairs yourself. However, when the repair is beyond the scope of your capabilities, you will need to seek professional help. Likely sources of professional help are the party that sold you the defective hardware or software, retail computer stores in your area, and computer repair technicians listed in the Yellow Pages of your local phone book (see Figure 13-10).

Things to consider when thinking about having someone else diagnose or repair your system are the following:

- Is it better to repair old equipment or to buy new equipment? For instance, if the equipment to be repaired costs less than $100, it may be cheaper to buy new equipment.

Warranty.
A conditional pledge made by a manufacturer to protect consumers from losses due to defective units of a product.

- Will the repair work be done under warranty? Most new equipment is sold with a **warranty** stating that the manufacturer will pay for certain repairs if the equipment fails within a given number of days or months after purchase. If the warranty hasn't expired, the repair may cost you nothing. Be aware that many manufacturers state in their warranty that the warranty becomes void if you attempt to repair the equipment yourself or if a repair is attempted by an unauthorized

Figure 13-10
Repair.
As technicians repair computer systems, many of them also field calls from users about problems.

person or shop. Most equipment manufacturers publish a list of authorized repair shops.

- Can you get an estimate before proceeding with the work? In many cases, repair technicians can provide a free estimate of what the repair will cost. If they can't, you might want them to diagnose the problem first and to call you when they are able to provide an estimate. You never, ever want to put yourself in a situation in which you are presented with an unexpected, outrageously expensive repair bill.
- Is priority service available? People who use their computers as part of their jobs often need repairs immediately. Many repair shops realize this and will provide same-day or next-day turnaround for an extra fee. Regular turnaround time can fluctuate tremendously in any given repair shop—from a matter of hours to a few weeks, depending on how many technicians are currently employed and how busy they are. Before requesting priority service, find out what the current turnaround time is on regular repair work.

When you buy a computer system, you often will have the option of buying a maintenance contract with it to cover certain types of repairs beyond those stated in the warranty. Figure 13-11 lists a number of the points covered by maintenance contracts.

Figure 13-11
Maintenance contracts.
A good maintenance contract should cover the clauses listed here.

Coverage
The contract should state clearly if both parts and labor are covered.

Contract Period
Many contracts cover a period of one or two years. Some vendors provide a "lifetime" guarantee on certain types of parts.

Repair Procedure
A procedure should spell out clearly what steps will be taken when a problem occurs. Often, the vendor will first try to diagnose the problem over the phone. If this fails, either you will have to bring or send the unit to an authorized repair center or a technician will be dispatched to your home or office within a certain number of hours or days. If you can't afford to be without your computer system for an appreciable period, this part of the contract may be the most critical. Some contracts will provide you with a "loaner" system while yours is being repaired.

Hotline
Many companies provide a hotline for you to call when you have a question or problem. Sometimes you can call toll free, and sometimes you won't be billed for the vendor's time. It's a good idea to check how easy it is to reach the hotline; some of them are so understaffed that it takes days for calls to be returned.

Other Clauses
Most maintenance contracts will be void if you attempt to repair the equipment yourself or let someone who's not an authorized repairperson do it.

User Solution 13-1 describes how one organization deals with the problem of equipment repair. Organizations spending a lot on microcomputer systems often attempt to motivate users to buy brand-name hardware and software products, to minimize the organization's having to support too many different types of products.

Upgrading

Upgrading.
The process of buying new hardware or software in order to extend the life of a computer system.

Hardware and software generally need to be upgraded over time. **Upgrading** a computer system means buying new hardware or software components that will extend the life of your current system. The question you must ask when considering a costly upgrade is the same one that you would ask when considering costly repairs to a car: Should I be spending this money on my current system, or start fresh and buy a completely new system?

When you acquire a microcomputer system initially, it is extremely important to have an upgrade strategy. Ideally, you should buy a microcomputer system that adheres to a well-supported standard and that is flexible enough and powerful enough to be upgraded to meet reasonable future needs over the course of its lifetime. Of course, it is not possible to anticipate all of those needs, but not putting any thinking into system growth can invite disaster.

Hardware. Some common types of hardware upgrades include adding more RAM to a system, installing a hard disk, adding boards to increase the speed of the CPU or to provide new types of functionality, and add-

User Solution 13-1

An In-House Repair Strategy

How do organizations handle equipment repair? Some of them let users or departments make their own decisions. Others contract with a repair outsourcer, an outside firm that does all of a client firm's repairs. But at the Tennessee Valley Authority (TVA), an arm of the federal government that sells electricity, an in-house solution is being used. The TVA supports some 14,000 pieces of equipment, including 4,000 PCs. It's experienced cost reductions of up to 50 percent in some areas by doing repair work itself. To cut down on purchasing and maintenance expenses, the TVA has adopted certain hardware and software products as standards, and it cross-trains its repair technicians on a broad line of products.

ing new input or output equipment such as an image scanner or a pen plotter.

Unless your system is big enough to handle growth, many upgrades will not be possible. For instance, if you have an Intel 8088-based processor, which limits RAM to a total of 640 KB, RAM-intensive hardware or software upgrades usually cannot be accommodated. Also, it's important to check both the number of expansion slots (used for add-in boards) and the power of the system unit. If new peripherals require add-in boards and all of the expansion slots that allow such boards to communicate with the CPU are used up, upgrading is not possible. Also, some upgrades, such as installing an internal hard disk or a streaming tape unit, require extra power; thus, upgrading the power supply may also be necessary.

Software. Software vendors typically enhance their products in some major way every year or so. Each of these upgrades—which are called **versions**—is assigned a number, such as 1.0, 2.0, 3.0, and so on. The higher the number, the more recent and more powerful the version. Minor versions, called **releases,** are typically numbered in increments of 0.1—say, 1.1, 1.2, 1.3, and so on.

Version.
A major upgrade of a software product.

Release.
A minor upgrade of a software product.

Each version of a software product is almost guaranteed to be more sophisticated and more complex and to require more RAM than its predecessors. For example, it's not unusual for a package that five years ago fit on one or two diskettes and worked with 256 KB to fit on eight or nine diskettes and require one or more megabytes of RAM today. The technical documentation accompanying the software is much more extensive than it was a few years ago and harder for the average person to understand. Fortunately, however, the quality of user training has increased dramatically and is geared to people at various levels of expertise.

Most software products tend to be *upward compatible*. This means that applications developed on earlier versions of the software will work on later versions of the software. Downward compatibility is generally rare.

Functional versus Technological Obsolescence

Functionally obsolete. Refers to a product that no longer meets the needs of an individual or business.

Technologically obsolete. Refers to a product that, although superseded by a newer version or release, still meets the needs of an individual or business.

Many microcomputer products serve needs for several years before they must be replaced. A product is said to be **functionally obsolete** when it no longer meets the needs of an individual or business. However, improvements to hardware and software products are continuous, and often a product is replaced on store shelves with a newer version or release before it is functionally obsolete. A product in this latter class is said to be **technologically obsolete.**

In upgrading, a common problem is that users believe the product they are using is functionally obsolete when it is merely technologically obsolete. Because of the rapid pace of technology, virtually anyone buying a computer system today will have at least one technologically obsolete component within a matter of months. Consequently, it's not feasible to keep current with versions or releases of products as soon as they become available. The most valid reasons for switching from a technologically obsolete product to a newer version are that the older product is also functionally obsolete, the older product results in considerably higher operating costs than the newer one, or support is no longer available for the older product. If you have an older product that many other people have, however, there will probably be vendors around for a long time ready to service applications needs.

Learning More about Microcomputers

A wealth of resources is available to those who want to learn more about microcomputer systems and their uses. Classes, computer clubs, computer shows, magazines, newspapers, newsletters, books, and electronic media are all sources of information about microcomputers.

Classes. A good way to learn any subject is to take an appropriate class. Many colleges, universities, and community colleges offer microcomputer-oriented courses for undergraduate and continuing-education students. Probably the fastest way to find out about such courses is to phone a local college and ask to speak to the registrar or to someone in a computer-related academic department.

Clubs. Computer clubs are another effective way to get an informal education in computers. They are also a good place to get an unbiased and knowledgeable viewpoint about a particular product or vendor. Generally clubs are organized by region, product line, or common interests. Apple computer enthusiasts join clubs such as Apple-Holics (Alaska), Apple Pie (Illinois), or Apple Core (California). Clubs such as The Boston Computer

Figure 13-12
Microcomputer books.
Today, you can find in many bookstores a comprehensive selection of microcomputer books on subjects such as popular brands of software, the use of laser printers and hard disks, and computer-system repair.

Society serve the needs of a more diverse group of microcomputer buffs. Many clubs also function as buying groups, obtaining software or hardware at reduced rates. Computer clubs range in size from two or three members to several thousand.

Shows. Computer shows give you a firsthand look at leading-edge hardware and software products. Such shows typically feature numerous vendor exhibits as well as seminars on various aspects of computing. The annual West Coast Computer Faire, held in the San Francisco area, is one event specifically oriented toward smaller computers.

Periodicals. Periodicals are another good source of information about microcomputers. Magazines such as *Byte, Popular Computing, PC,* and *Macworld* (see Window 8) focus on microcomputers. Computer magazines vary tremendously in reading level. You'll probably find and be able to browse through these publications and more at your local bookstore or computer store.

Books. One of the best ways to learn about any aspect of personal computing is to read a book on the subject. A host of softcover and hardcover books are available, covering topics ranging from the simple to the highly sophisticated (see Figure 13-12). Included are "how-to" books on subjects such as operating popular microcomputer systems or productivity software packages, programming in microcomputer-based languages, and the technical fundamentals of microcomputers. You can find such books in your local library, computer stores, and bookstores.

Electronic Media. One easy way to learn a subject in our electronic age is to pick up a training disk or view a videotape or television show devoted to the subject. Today many microcomputer-oriented software packages are sold with training disks that provide screen-oriented tutorials, showing you which keys to press and the results. Also, a large selection of videotapes are available for standard videocassette players, so you can see how something works simply by watching your television. Television shows such as PBS's "The Computer Chronicles," which may feature a program on optical disks one week and a program on bus architectures the next, are especially targeted to microcomputer users.

Summary and Key Terms

The term **end-user development** is often used to describe such activities as end users acquiring their own computer resources, using and taking care of their own systems, and upgrading systems on their own.

The Microcomputer Marketplace. The microcomputer marketplace comprises a wide variety of firms that make hardware and software products. One important market segment, composed of microcomputer system units, is dominated primarily by IBM, Apple, and **IBM-compatible computers.**

Hardware and software microcomputing products are most often acquired by users from retail computer stores, mail-order houses, and manufacturers.

Selecting a Computer System. When selecting a computer system, the steps include analyzing needs, listing system alternatives, evaluating alternatives, and choosing a system. Although software is normally selected before hardware, software and hardware choices for microcomputers are often interrelated so that you must consider them jointly.

Operating a Computer System. **Backup** refers to making a duplicate copy of valuable files. Two types of backup are **full backup** and **partial backup.** Microcomputer systems contain sensitive electronic devices, so they must be treated with care and protected from damage. A **surge suppressor** will prevent most random electrical spikes from entering your system and causing damage. Precautions taken with diskettes and hard disks will safeguard any data stored on them. Other practices can protect your system from dust, heat, and static. Software called **screen savers** can protect your monitor. Printer life can often be extended by taking precautions with the print head.

Although no two problems with a computer system are ever totally alike, some useful guidelines can be followed when troubleshooting problems and when having equipment repaired. For instance, **diagnostic disks** sometimes will help you to troubleshoot a problem. When considering a repair, you should check first to see what protection is granted under **warranty.**

Upgrading. **Upgrading** a computer system means buying new hardware or software components that will extend the life of your current system. When considering a hardware upgrade, you must consider such things as your current system's storage capacity, the number of expansion slots, and the power of the system unit. Software upgrades are often accomplished by acquiring a new **release** or **version** of the program that you are currently using. You need to ask yourself whether upgrading is better than starting fresh and buying a new computer system. You also must consider whether you are planning to replace a product that's only **technologically obsolete** instead of **functionally obsolete.**

Learning More about Microcomputers. A wealth of resources is available to those who want to learn more about microcomputer systems and their uses. Classes, computer clubs, computer shows, magazines, newspapers, newsletters, books, and electronic media are all sources of information about microcomputers.

Review Exercises

Fill-in Questions

1. ____________ development refers to users themselves taking responsibility in developing and maintaining computer systems.
2. A(n) ____________ computer runs the same software as that targeted to IBM microcomputers.
3. A minor upgrade of a software package is called a(n) ____________.
4. The most important selection criterion is ____________, which refers to the type of work a hardware or software product does.
5. ____________ refers to making, for security purposes, a duplicate copy of a file.
6. A(n) ____________ is a hardware device designed to stop power spikes from damaging a computer system.
7. A(n) ____________ usually states that a product manufacturer will pay for defective software or hardware for a given period of time under certain conditions.
8. A product that no longer meets the needs of a user is said to be ____________ obsolete.

Matching Questions

Match each term with the description that fits best.

a. Compaq
b. Toshiba
c. Hercules
d. Microsoft
e. Hayes
f. Motorola
g. Seagate
h. Lotus Development

____ 1. Makes CPU chips for the Apple Macintosh line of computers.
____ 2. The largest U.S.-based maker of IBM-compatible computers.
____ 3. Produces primarily disk products.
____ 4. Famous for Windows and MS-DOS, as well as a wide variety of other software products.
____ 5. Makes a widely used add-in board for graphic displays.
____ 6. Mostly known for its popular spreadsheet.

____ 7. Set the standard for microcomputer-based modems.

____ 8. A famous maker of laptop computers.

Discussion Questions

1. In the world of microcomputers, what is an IBM-compatible computer?
2. Who are the three leading manufacturers of desktop system units?
3. Name three ways in which microcomputer products are usually acquired by users.
4. Name several criteria that are important to consider when evaluating alternative computer systems for purchase.
5. Provide several examples that show why it is important to back up files.
6. Give several guidelines that are useful when troubleshooting a problem with your computer system.
7. What is the difference between a version and a release of a software package?
8. What is the difference between technological obsolescence and functional obsolescence?

Critical Thinking Questions

1. Almost every other year, a major new microprocessor chip is introduced, and it leads to the development of a new "family" of faster, more capable computer systems. What problems does this pose for a typical corporation?
2. Why, do you think, are so many companies in the business of producing IBM-compatible computer systems?
3. A number of newer microcomputer systems have multiuser capabilities, allowing several users to share the system at once. For instance, a single system unit, hard disk, and printer might be shared by four people, each with his or her own monitor and keyboard. But despite the multiuser capabilities of such systems, they are often bought for a single individual and are not shared. Why do you think this is so?

Window 8

Microcomputer Journals and Periodicals

Who They Are and What They Offer

Microcomputer journals and periodicals are an excellent resource for the average user to learn more about microcomputers. These publications regularly review new and existing products, feature interesting articles about technology areas and issues, present the viewpoints of experts about the present and future of computing, and provide tips on using products more effectively. In Window 8 we'll look at the wide variety of journals and periodicals in the computer marketplace. We'll also discuss some of the journals' features that readers find most useful.

1

2

3

4

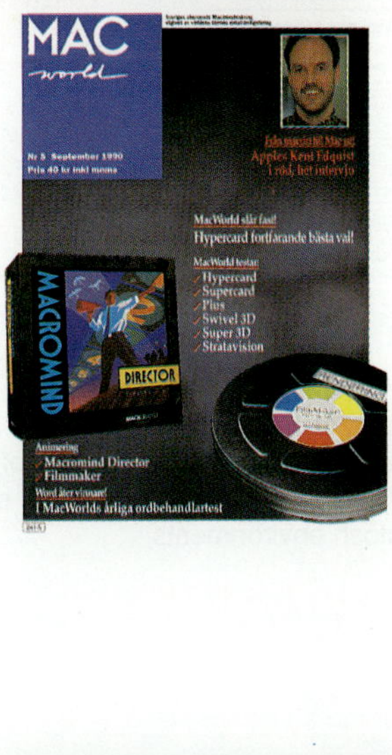

5

1–5. *MacWorld,* one of the most widely read journals on the Apple Macintosh, is among a growing number of U.S.-based magazines that are published in several foreign countries. Overall, the international market accounts for 40 percent of all Macintosh-related product sales.

A Brief Guide to the Journals

Virtually every microcomputing journal is aimed at a specific audience of readers—users of a specific type of computer, users of a certain software product, and so on.

6

THE NATIONAL NEWSPAPER OF CORPORATE COMPUTING, DECEMBER 17, 1990, VOL. 7 NO. 50, PRICE $3.95

PC WEEK

NCR Stands Firm Against AT&T Bid

Smaller-than-Ever Notebooks Just Around the Bend

Startup Looks Beyond Messaging Horizon

Add-Ins Could Revolutionize E-Mail

Apple Readies Smart Ethernet LAN Adapter

Slim, Trim OS/2 SE 1.3 Multitasks at Snail's Pace

Court Ruling Turns Table On A-T in dBASE Battle

Microsoft Eyes Remote Links For SQL Server

Thanks For the Memory Managers

7

ALL-HARDWARE SPECIAL ISSUE!

PC WORLD

HARDWARE FOR WINDOWS

270 Fresh Products That Do Windows NOW

NEW SYSTEMS
85 Price-Busting SXs
7 Windows-Ready SX Laptops
5 Compact 386 Dynamos

NEW DISPLAYS
126 Super Boards and Monitors

NEW PRINTERS
6 Smart PostScript Buys
31 LaserJet Workhorses

PLUS
10 Top Upgrades
How to Switch to Windows

8

PC MAGAZINE

GeoWorks Ensemble's Elegant Simplicity Challenges Windows On the Home Front

Math Coprocessor Facts and Fantasies: PC Labs Tells The Real Story

Why Wait for Microsoft? DR DOS 5.0 Is Here, Now

JOURNAL: The Effortless Way to Record and Report Your Expenses

FEBRUARY 12, 1991 THE INDEPENDENT GUIDE TO PERSONAL COMPUTING

486/33 Maximum Performance

PC Labs tests 30 ISA-based 33-MHz 486s

These speed kings are about to **explode all myths** about 486 price versus performance. These machines may be expensive, but if you need the **ultimate in ISA power** they're the ones to buy.

9

APPLE'S NEW LOW-COST LASER PRINTERS

MACWORLD

The Macintosh Magazine August 1990

NEW

Personal LaserWriters from Apple

17 ACCELERATORS
55 UTILITIES
21 FILE SERVER PRODUCTS
7 FAX MODEMS
21 COLOR SCANNERS
19 REVIEWS: PAGE 176

10

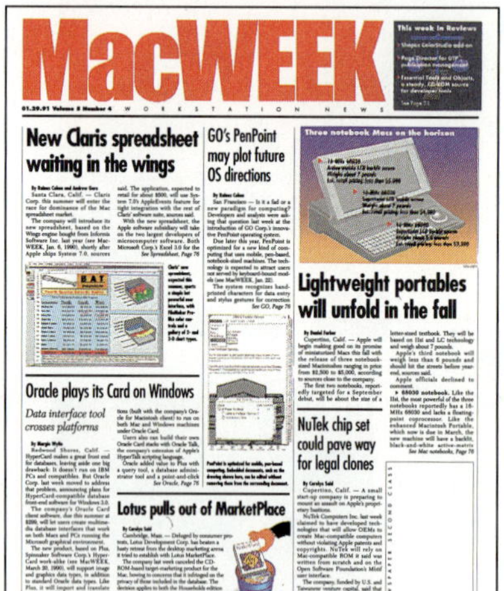

MacWEEK

New Claris spreadsheet waiting in the wings

GO's PenPoint may plot future OS directions

Three notebook Macs on the horizon

Lightweight portables will unfold in the fall

Oracle plays its Card on Windows

NuTek chip set could pave way for legal clones

Lotus pulls out of MarketPlace

11

INFO WORLD

The Critical Path

Independent's Toolkit Speeds IAC Development

A Quicker Route to IAC

Microsoft Preps Multimedia Spec

IBM, Tandy, Fujitsu, Zenith Expected to Endorse Windows Extensions

AST to Unfold Its Souped-Up SCSI Drive Technology

Microsoft Link Proposal Shrugged Off by Apple

Mac IIsi Power Design Limits System Expansion

6–11. One of the largest reader audiences consists of users who want information about specific types of systems environments. *PC Week, PC World,* and *PC Magazine,* for instance, are targeted largely to users of IBM and IBM-compatible microcomputers, whereas *MacWorld* and *MacWeek* are for users of the Apple Macintosh. *Infoworld* caters to both IBM and Macintosh environments.

12

13

12, 13. *Byte* and *Dr. Dobb's Journal* appeal to sophisticated, technically oriented microcomputer users.

14

15

16

14–16. Many journals, such as the ones featured here, are targeted to a specific type of hardware or software technology. *LAN Technology,* for instance, covers local area networks; *DBMS* and *UNIX Review* address database management systems and the UNIX operating systems, respectively.

17

18

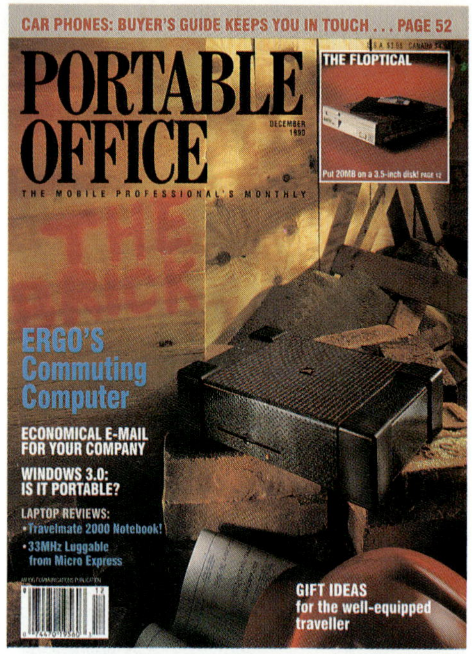

19

20

17–20. Office automation (OA) is an area that's particularly rich in publications. Among the topics most frequently found in OA journals are word processing, desktop publishing, slide and multimedia presentations, fax and copying machines, electronic mail, and printers.

21

22

21–24. Some microcomputing products are so widely used that they can support their own dedicated journals. In some cases these journals are published by subsidiaries of the software or hardware vendors themselves; in other cases, they're published by independent firms.

23

24

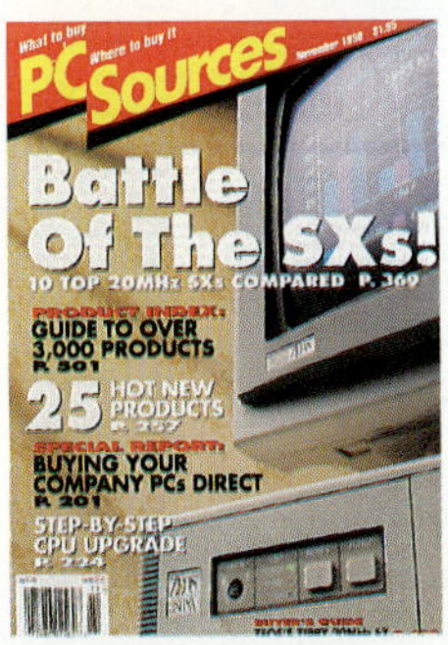

25

26

27

25–27. Some periodicals assist users in making buying decisions. *PC Sources* and *Computer Buyer's Guide and Handbook* are focused principally on new products. The semiannual *Computer Blue Book*—which lists about 30,000 different products—shows what you should pay for used equipment.

Product Evaluation

Product evaluation—making relative comparisons among a group of similar products and providing critical reviews of newly released products—is an important feature in many journals.

28

REPORT CARD — INFO WORLD

Workgroup Scheduler/Mail Packages

	(InfoWorld weighting)	(Your weighting)	The Coordinator II Version 2.1	Office Works Version 2.0	Right Hand Man Version 5.1	Word Perfect Office Version 3.0
List price			$1,800 (10-user)	$495 (six-user)	$1,169 (10-user)	$495 (five-user)
Performance						
Scheduling	(125)	( )	Good	Good	Excellent	Good
Messaging features	(150)	( )	Excellent	Good	Very Good	Very Good
Archiving	(50)	( )	Excellent	Good	Good	Good
Printing/ word processing	(50)	( )	Good	Poor	Good	Very Good
Gateways	(125)	( )	Very Good	Satisfactory	Very Good	Excellent
Documentation	(50)	( )	Very Good	Good	Good	Excellent
Ease of administration	(75)	( )	Very Good	Satisfactory	Very Good	Satisfactory
Ease of learning	(50)	( )	Good	Very Good	Very Good	Satisfactory
Ease of use	(100)	( )	Good	Good	Good	Good
Error handling	(50)	( )	Very Good	Very Good	Good	Very Good
Support						
Support policies	(25)	( )	Satisfactory	Good	Good	Excellent
Technical support	(25)	( )	Satisfactory	Very Good	Very Good	Very Good
Value	(125)	( )	Good	Good	Very Good	Very Good
Final scores			**7.3**	**5.9**	**7.4**	**7.3**
Use your own weightings to calculate your score						

GUIDE TO REPORT CARD SCORES

InfoWorld reviews only finished, production versions of products, never beta test versions.

Products receive ratings ranging from unacceptable to excellent in various categories. Scores are derived by multiplying the weighting (in parentheses) of each criterion by its rating, where:

Excellent = 1.0 — Outstanding in all areas.
Very Good = 0.75 — Meets all essential criteria and offers significant advantages.
Good = 0.625 — Meets essential criteria and includes some special features.
Satisfactory = 0.5 — Meets essential criteria.
Poor = 0.25 — Falls short in essential areas.
Unacceptable or N/A = 0.0 — Fails to meet minimum standards or lacks this feature.

Scores are summed, divided by 100, and rounded down to one decimal place to yield the final score out of a maximum possible score of 10 (plus bonus). Products rated within 0.2 points of one another differ little. Weightings represent average relative importance to *InfoWorld* readers involved in purchasing and using that product category. You can customize the report card to your company's needs by using your own weightings to calculate the final score.

28. Software evaluations are a regular feature in *Infoworld*. One week, six word processors might be compared; the next week, ten database management systems may be reviewed. Each multipage comparison is summed up in a "report card" (shown here for four workgroup scheduling packages) that provides an overall rating for each product evaluated.

29

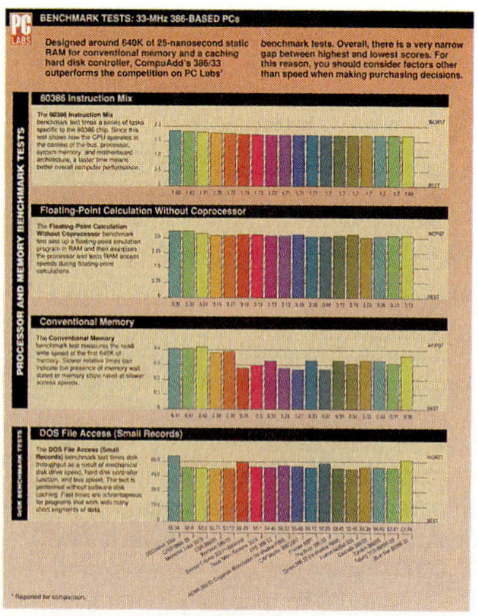

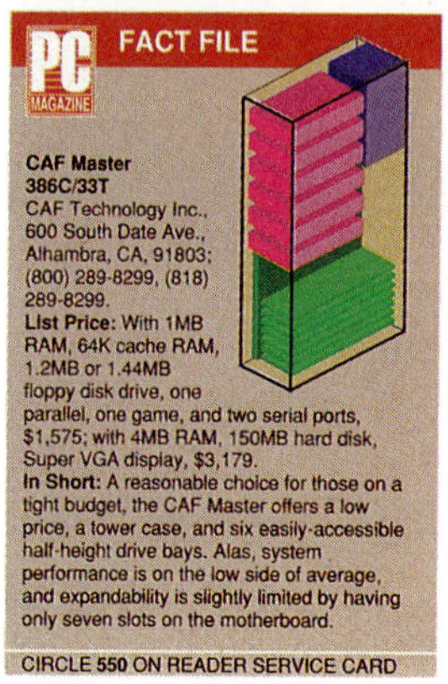

30

29, 30. *PC Magazine* is well known for its comparative evaluations of a very large number of products. Information is often summarized in both a tabular and a graphical format. Also included is a small "fact file" box, providing capsule summaries on each product evaluated.

31

31. In addition to comparative evaluations, many journals critically review products as soon as they are released.

Articles

Naturally, the main body of most journals is the article content. Regular features as well as stories on today's "hot" topics are included in most issues.

33

33. Many journals have regular columns that give users advice in specific computing areas—for instance, tips about using windows-based applications or developing spreadsheets.

32
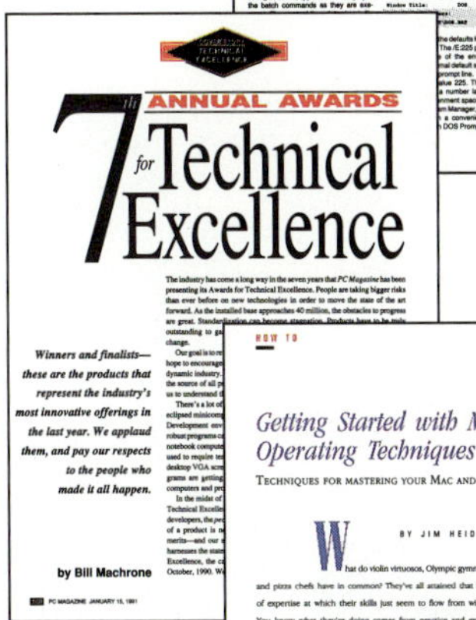

32. Journals such as *PC Magazine* and *Byte* produce a special issue in January featuring the best products in the previous year.

34

35

34, 35. Several of the leading microcomputer journals have regular columnists who appear in every issue. Jerry Pournelle—a science fiction writer seen in *Infoworld* and *Byte*—is legendary for relating his interesting opinions on products and technologies. *MacWorld's* Jim Heid has an easy-to-read "how to" column that helps readers get started on understanding some aspect of computers.

36

37

38

39
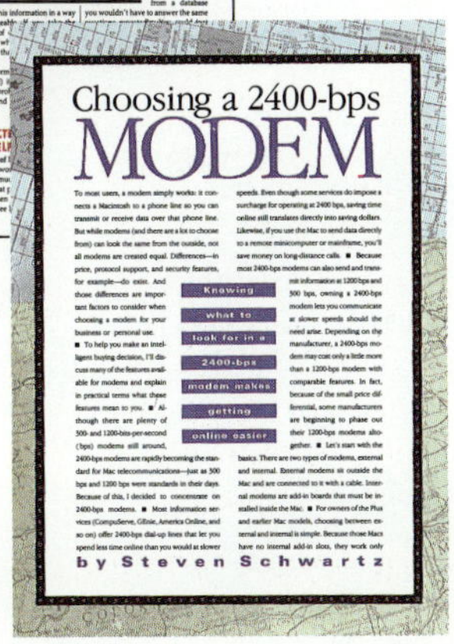

36–39. Collectively, microcomputer journals have articles on virtually everything you need to know about computers. Most libraries have a periodicals index that will enable you to find articles quickly on specific topics.

A

Numbering Systems

Outline

Numbering Systems
The Decimal Numbering System
The Binary Numbering System
The Hexadecimal Numbering System
Computer Arithmetic

Learning Objectives

After completing this appendix, you will be able to:

1. Describe how the decimal, binary, and hexadecimal numbering systems work.
2. Convert values in one numbering system to those of another.
3. Add and subtract with the binary and hexadecimal numbering systems.

In Chapter 3, you learned that fixed-length codes such as ASCII and EBCDIC are often used to represent numbers, letters of the alphabet, and special characters. Although these codes are handy for storing data and transporting them around a computer system, they are not designed to do arithmetic operations. For this type of use, numbers must be stored in a "true" binary form that can be manipulated quickly by the computer.

This appendix covers several fundamentals of numbering systems. The two primary systems discussed are the decimal numbering system (used by people) and the binary numbering system (used by computers). Also discussed is the hexadecimal numbering system, which is a shorthand way of representing long strings of binary numbers so that they are more understandable to people. The appendix also covers conversions between numbering systems and principles of computer arithmetic.

Numbering Systems

A *numbering system* is a way of representing numbers. The system we most commonly use is called the *decimal,* or base ten, system (the word *decimal* comes from the Latin word for *ten*). It is called *base 10* because it uses ten symbols—the digits 0, 1, 2, 3, 4, 5, 6, 7, 8, 9—to represent all possible numbers. Numbers greater than nine are represented by a combination of these symbols.

Because we are so familiar with the decimal system, it may never have occurred to most of us that we could represent numbers in any other way. In fact, however, nothing says that a numbering system has to have ten possible symbols. Many other numbers would do as a base.

We saw in Chapter 3 that the *binary,* or base 2, system is used extensively by computers to represent numbers and other characters. Computer systems can perform computations and transmit data thousands of times faster in binary form than they can using decimal representations. Thus, it's important for anyone studying computers to know how the binary system works. Anyone contemplating a professional career in computers should also understand the *hexadecimal* (base 16) system. Before we examine some of the numbering systems used in computing—and learn how to convert numbers from one system into another—let's look more closely at the decimal numbering system. Insight into how the decimal system works will help us understand more about the other numbering systems.

The Decimal Numbering System

Decimal.
A numbering system with ten symbols—0, 1, 2, 3, 4, 5, 6, 7, 8, and 9.

All numbering systems, including the decimal system with which we work in our everyday lives, represent numbers as a combination of ordered symbols. As stated earlier, the **decimal*** (or base 10) system has ten

*Boldfaced terms used in this appendix can be found in the Glossary at the end of the book.

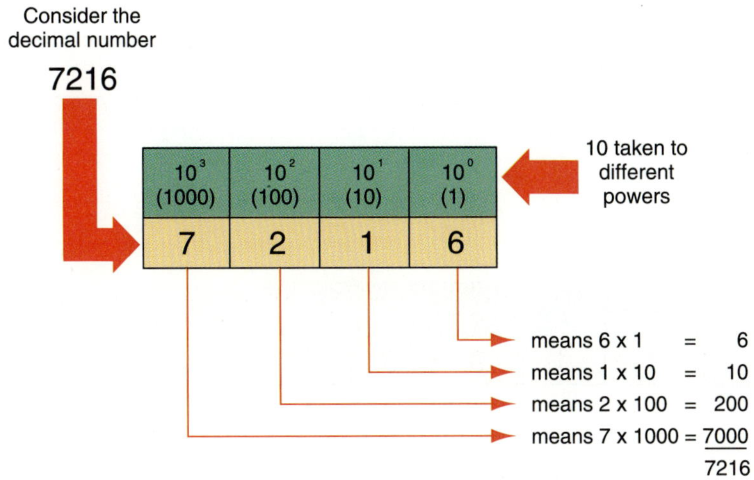

Figure A-1
How the decimal (base ten) system works.

acceptable symbols—the digits 0, 1, 2, . . . , 9. The positioning of the symbols in a decimal number is important. For example, 891 is a different number than 918 (with the same symbols occupying different positions).

The position of each symbol in any decimal number represents the number 10 (the base number) raised to a power, or exponent, that is based on that position. Going from right to left, the first position represents 10^0, or 1; the second position represents 10^1, or 10; the third position represents 10^2, or 100; and so forth. Thus, as Figure A-1 shows, a decimal number like 7,216 is understood as $7 \times 10^3 + 2 \times 10^2 + 1 \times 10^1 + 6 \times 10^0$.

The Binary Numbering System

Binary.
A numbering system with two possible states—0 and 1.

The **binary,** or base 2, system works in a manner similar to the decimal system. One major difference is that the binary system has only two symbols—0 and 1—instead of ten. A second major difference is that the position of each digit in a binary number represents the number 2 (the base number) raised to an exponent based on that position. Thus, the binary number 11100 represents

$$1 \times 2^4 + 1 \times 2^3 + 1 \times 2^2 + 0 \times 2^1 + 0 \times 2^0$$

which, translated into the decimal system, is 28. Another example of a binary-to-decimal conversion is provided in Figure A-2.

Converting in the reverse direction—from decimal to binary—is also rather easy. A popular approach for doing this is the *remainder method.* This procedure employs successive divisions by the base number of the system to which we are converting. Use of the remainder method to convert a decimal to a binary number is illustrated in Figure A-3.

Figure A-2 Binary-to-decimal conversion.
To convert any binary number to its decimal counterpart, take the rightmost digit and multiply it by 2^0 (or 1), the next-to-rightmost digit and multiply it by 2^1 (or 2), and so on, as illustrated here. Then add up all the products so formed.

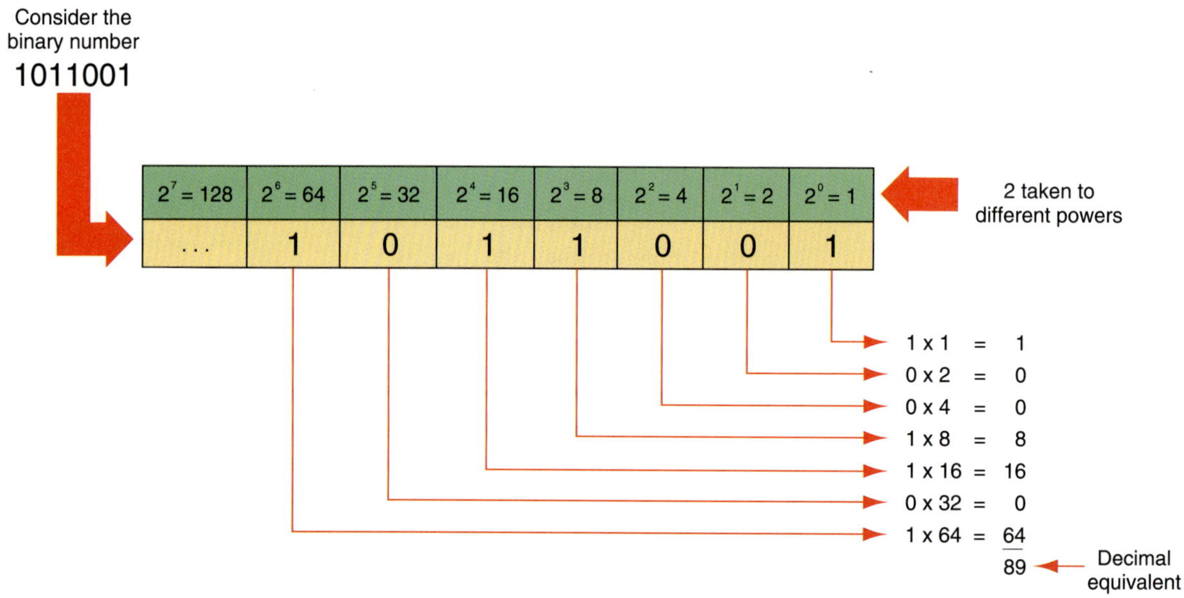

To avoid confusion when different number bases are being used, it is common to use the base as a subscript. So, referring to Figures A-2 and A-3, for example, we could write

$$89_{10} = 1011001_2$$

In addition, when we are using numbering systems other than the decimal system, it is customary to pronounce each symbol individually. For example, 101_2 is pronounced "one-zero-one" rather than "one hundred one." This convention is also used with other nondecimal systems.

The binary system described here is sometimes referred to as *true-binary representation*. True-binary representation does not use a fixed number of bits, as do ASCII and EBCDIC, nor is it used to represent letters or special characters.

The Hexadecimal Numbering System

Often diagnostic and memory-management messages are output to programmers and technically oriented users in hexadecimal (or *hex*) notation (see Figure A-4). Hex is a shorthand method for representing the binary

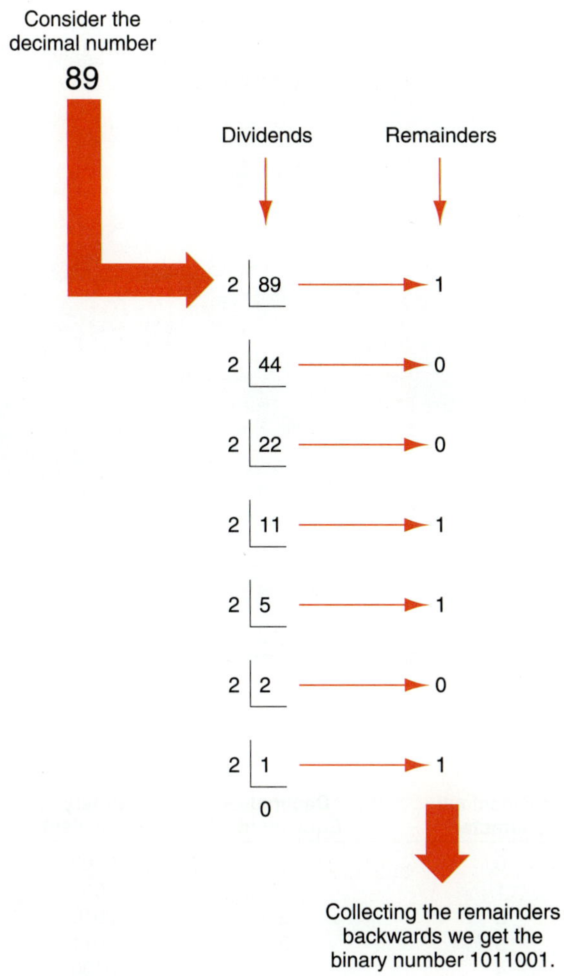

Figure A-3
Decimal-to-binary conversion using the remainder method. In this approach, we start by using the decimal number to be converted (89) as the initial dividend. Each successive dividend is the quotient of the previous division. We keep dividing until we've reached a zero quotient, whereupon the converted number is formed by the remainders taken in reverse order.

digits that are stored in the computer system. Because large binary numbers—for example, 1101010001001101_2—can easily be misread by programmers, binary digits are often grouped into units of four that, in turn, are represented by other symbols.

Hexadecimal. Pertaining to the numbering system with 16 symbols: 0, 1, 2, 3, 4, 5, 6, 7, 8, 9, A, B, C, D, E, and F.

Hexadecimal means base 16, implying that there are 16 different symbols in this numbering system. Since we have only ten possible digits to work with, letters are used instead of numbers for the extra six symbols. The 16 hexadecimal symbols and their decimal and binary counterparts are shown in Figure A-5.

Hexadecimal is not itself a code that the computer uses to perform computations or to communicate with other machines. It does, however, have a special relationship to the 8-bit bytes of ASCII-8 and EBCDIC that makes it ideal for displaying messages quickly. As you can see in Figure A-5, each hex character has a 4-binary-bit counterpart, so any combination of 8 bits can be represented by exactly two hexadecimal characters.

Figure A-4
Hexadecimal display. Programmers often rely on the hexadecimal numbering system to give them information about where programs and data are stored in memory. Here, Quarterdeck's Manifest—a diagnostics and resources-management software package—tells how the first megabyte of memory is allocated by the DOS operating system.

Figure A-5
Hexadecimal characters and their decimal and binary equivalents.

Hexadecimal Character	Decimal Equivalent	Binary Equivalent
0	0	0000
1	1	0001
2	2	0010
3	3	0011
4	4	0100
5	5	0101
6	6	0110
7	7	0111
8	8	1000
9	9	1001
A	10	1010
B	11	1011
C	12	1100
D	13	1101
E	14	1110
F	15	1111

Thus, the letter *A* (represented in EBCDIC by 11000001) has a hex representation of C1.

Let's look at an example to see how to convert from hex to decimal. Suppose you receive the following message on your display screen:

```
PROGRAM LOADED AT LOCATION 4F6A
```

Figure A-6 Hexadecimal-to-decimal conversion.
To convert any hexadecimal number to its decimal counterpart, take the rightmost digit and multiply it by 16^0 (or 1), the next-to-rightmost digit and multiply it by 16^1 (or 16), and so on, as illustrated here. Then add up all the products so formed.

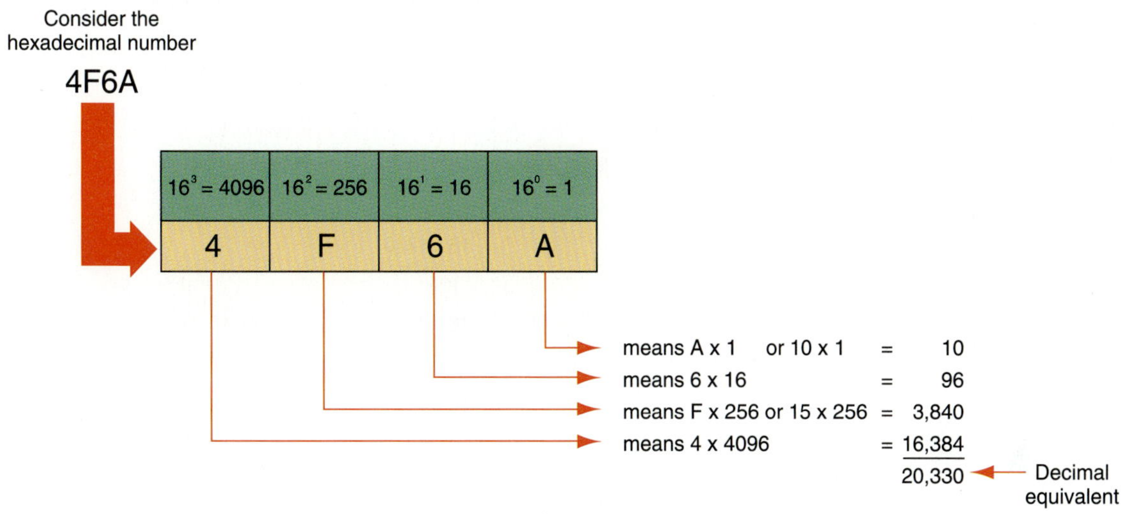

This message tells you the location in primary memory of the first byte in your program. To determine the decimal equivalent of a hexadecimal number such as 4F6A, you can use a procedure similar to the binary-to-decimal conversion shown in Figure A-2 (refer to Figure A-6).

To convert the other way—from decimal to hex—we again can use the remainder method, this time dividing by 16. A decimal-to-hex conversion using the remainder method is illustrated in Figure A-7.

To convert from base 16 to base 2, we convert each hex digit separately to four binary digits (using the table in Figure A-5). For example, to convert F6A9 to base 2, we get

F	6	A	9
1111	0110	1010	1001

or 1111011010101001_2. To convert from base 2 to base 16, we go through the reverse process. If the number of digits in the binary number is not divisible by 4, we add leading zeros to the binary number to force an even division. So, for example, to convert 1101101010011_2 to base 16, we get

0001	1011	0101	0011
1	B	5	3

or $1B53_{16}$. Note that three leading zeros were added to make this conversion.

One final word before we close. In Chapter 3 we mentioned that 32-bit computer chips, such as the Intel 80386 and 80486, are capable of ad-

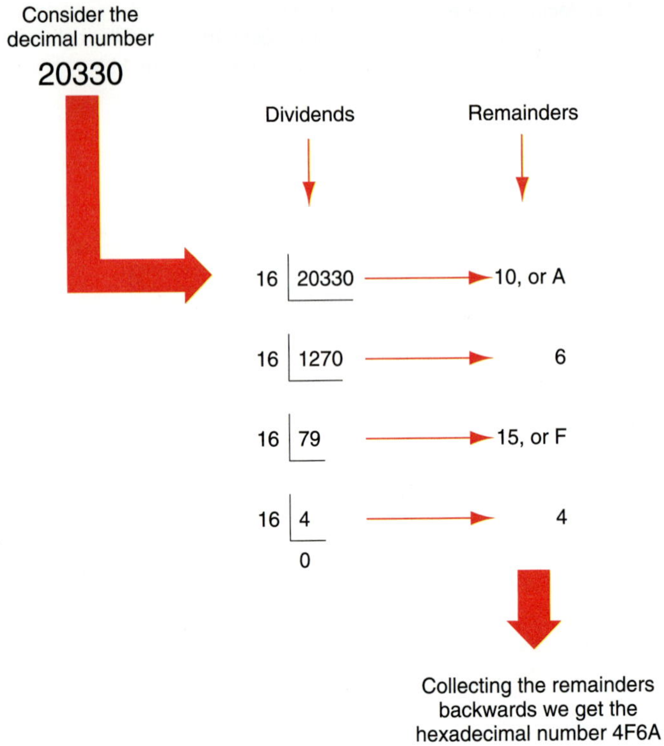

Figure A-7 Decimal-to-hexadecimal conversion using the remainder method. To convert 20330_{10} to a hexadecimal number, we start our successive divisions by 16 using 20330 as the initial dividend. Each successive dividend is the quotient of the previous division. As in Figure A-3, we divide until we've reached a zero quotient and form the converted number by taking the remainders in reverse order.

dressing about 4 billion bytes (4 gigabytes) of main memory. You may have wondered at that time, "Why 4 billion bytes?" Note that the maximum address in a 32-bit computer is a string of 32 1-bits, or

11111111111111111111111111111111

which, expressed in hex, is

FFFFFFFF

Note that the decimal equivalent is 4,294,967,296—or roughly 4 billion bytes.

A table summarizing all of the conversions covered in this appendix is provided in Figure A-8.

Computer Arithmetic

To most of us, decimal arithmetic is second nature. Addition and subtraction have been part of our education since kindergarten or first grade. Addition and subtraction using binary and hexadecimal numbers is not

From Base	To Base 2	10	16
2		Starting at rightmost digit, multiply binary digits by 2^0, 2^1, 2^2, etc., respectively. Then add products.	Starting at rightmost digit, convert each group of four binary digits to a hex digit.
10	Divide repeatedly by 2; then collect remainders in reverse order.		Divide repeatedly by 16; then collect remainders in reverse order.
16	Convert each hex digit to four binary digits.	Starting at rightmost digit, multiply hex digits by 16^0, 16^1, 16^2, etc., respectively. Then add products.	

Figure A-8
Summary of conversions.

	Decimal	Binary	Hexadecimal
Addition	142 +47 189	10001110 +101111 10111101	8E +2F BD
Subtraction	142 −47 95	10001110 −101111 1011111	8E −2F 5F

Figure A-9
Adding and subtracting with the decimal, binary, and hexadecimal numbering systems.

much harder than the same operations with decimal numbers. Practically the only difference is in the number of symbols used in each system.

Figure A-9 provides an example of addition and subtraction with decimal, binary, and hexadecimal numbers. Note that, as in decimal arithmetic, you carry to and borrow from adjacent positions as you move from right to left. Instead of carrying or borrowing 10, however—as you would in the decimal system—you carry or borrow 2 (binary) or 16 (hexadecimal).

Summary and Key Terms

This appendix covers several fundamentals of numbering systems.

Numbering Systems. A *numbering system* is a way of representing numbers.

The Decimal Numbering System. The number system we most commonly use is called the **decimal,** or base 10, system. It is called base 10 because it uses ten symbols—the digits 0, 1, 2, 3, 4, 5, 6, 7, 8, 9—to represent all possible numbers. The position of each symbol in any decimal number represents the number 10 (the base number) raised to a power, or exponent, which is based on that position.

The Binary Numbering System. The **binary,** or base 2, system works in a manner similar to the decimal system. One major difference is that the binary system has only two symbols—0 and 1—instead of ten. A second major difference is that the position of each digit in a binary number represents the number 2 (the base number) raised to an exponent based on that position.

The Hexadecimal Numbering System. Because large binary numbers can easily be misread by programmers, binary digits often are grouped and represented by other symbols. The **hexadecimal,** or base 16, system is used to represent a grouping of four binary digits. There are 16 different symbols in this system. Since we have only ten possible digits to work with, the letters A–F are used instead of numbers for the extra six symbols. The position of each digit in a hexadecimal number represents the number 16 raised to an exponent based on that position.

Computer Arithmetic. It is a relatively straightforward process to convert any value in one numbering system into a value in another system and to perform computer arithmetic on these values.

Exercises

Instructions: Provide an answer to each of the following questions.

1. Convert the following binary numbers to decimal numbers:
   a. 1011_2 ______________
   b. 101110_2 ______________
   c. 1010011_2 ______________
2. Convert the following decimal numbers to binary numbers:
   a. 51_{10} ______________
   b. 260_{10} ______________
   c. 500_{10} ______________
3. Convert the following binary numbers to hexadecimal numbers:
   a. 101_2 ______________
   b. 11010_2 ______________
   c. 111101000010_2 ______________
4. Convert the following hexadecimal numbers to binary numbers:
   a. $F2_{16}$ ______________
   b. $1A8_{16}$ ______________
   c. $39EB_{16}$ ______________
5. Convert the following hexadecimal numbers to decimal numbers:
   a. $B6_{16}$ ______________
   b. $5E9_{16}$ ______________
   c. $CAFF_{16}$ ______________

6. Drawing on techniques you've learned in this appendix, provide an expression to convert the base 6 (yes, six) number 451_6 to a decimal number: ______________ .
7. Adding the binary numbers 11011001 and 1011101 yields ____________.
8. Adding the hexadecimal numbers 8E and 5D yields ______________ .
9. Subtracting the binary number 1011 from 101110 yields ____________.
10. Subtracting the hexadecimal number B6 from F2 yields ____________.

Glossary

The terms shown in boldface are presented in the text as key terms. The number(s) in parentheses at the end of the definition of each term indicates the page (or pages) on which the term is boldfaced in the text. The terms shown in boldface italic are other commonly used and important words often encountered in information processing environments. The italic number in parentheses after the definition of each term indicates the page on which the term is first mentioned.

Absolute replication.
In spreadsheets, copying verbatim the contents in one range of cells into another range of cells. (311)

Access mechanism.
A mechanical device in the disk pack or disk unit that positions the read/write heads on the proper tracks. (104)

Accumulator.
A register that stores the result of an arithmetic or logical operation. (72)

Action diagram.
A programming tool that helps programmers code structured programs. (415)

Ada.
A structured programming language developed by the Department of Defense and named after Ada Augusta Byron, the world's first programmer. *(421)*

Add-in board.
A board that may be inserted into the computer's system unit to perform one or more functions. (86)

Add-on package.
A software package that supplements the activities of a larger software package, either by providing new functions or improving on already existing functions. (278, 316)

Address.
An identifiable location in storage where data are kept. Primary memory and direct-access secondary storage devices such as disk are addressable. *(71)*

Address register.
A register containing the memory location of data to be used. (72)

AI.
See Artificial intelligence. (378)

ALU.
See Arithmetic/logic unit. (68)

American National Standards Institute (ANSI).
An organization that acts as a national clearinghouse for standards in the United States. *(77)*

Analog transmission.
The transmission of data as continuous wave patterns. (198)

Analysis.
In program and systems development, the process of studying a problem area to determine what should be done. *(386)*

ANSI.
See American National Standards Institute. *(77)*

APL.
An acronym for A Programming Language. APL is a highly compact programming language popular for problem-solving applications. *(421)*

Applications generator.
A fourth-generation-language product that can be used to quickly create applications software. *(424)*

Applications package.
A fourth-generation-language product that, when the user sets a few parameters, becomes a finished applications program ready to meet specific end-user needs. *(407)*

Applications software.
Programs that do the useful work—such as payroll, inventory control, and accounting tasks—for end users of a computer system. Contrasts with systems software. (49)

Applications software development.
The process of designing, coding, debugging and testing, maintaining, and documenting applications software. *(406)*

Arithmetic/logic unit (ALU).
The part of the computer that contains the circuitry to perform addition, subtraction, multiplication, division, and comparison operations. (68)

Artificial intelligence (AI).
The ability of a machine to perform actions that are characteristic of human intelligence, such as reasoning and learning. (378)

ASCII.
An acronym for American Standard Code for Information Interchange. ASCII is a fixed-length, binary-based code widely used to represent data for processing and communications. (77)

Assembler.
A computer program that takes assembly-language instructions and converts them to machine language. (243)

Assembly language.
A low-level programming language that uses mnemonic codes in place of the 0s and 1s of machine language. *(417)*

Asynchronous transmission.
The transmission of data over a line one character at a time. Each character is preceded by a "start bit" and followed by a "stop bit." Contrasts with synchronous transmission. (201)

Auxiliary equipment.
Equipment that is designed to work in a "stand-alone" mode, independent of the main CPU. (46)

Backup.
Making duplicate copies of programs or data. (449)

Bar code.
A machine-readable code consisting of sets of bars of varying widths. The codes are prominently displayed on the packaging of many retail goods and are commonly read with special reading equipment. (157)

BASIC.
An acronym for Beginner's All-Purpose Symbolic Instruction Code. BASIC is an easy-to-learn, high-level programming language developed at Dartmouth College in the 1960s. *(417)*

Batch processing.
Processing transactions or other data in groups at periodic intervals. Contrasts with realtime processing. (54)

Benchmark test.
A test used to measure computer system performance under typical use conditions prior to purchase. The test is analogous to a rigorous "test drive" taken with a car before buying it. (390)

Binary.
A number system with two possible states. The binary system is fundamental to computers because electronic devices often function in two possible states—for example "on" or "off," "current present" or "current not present," "clockwise" or "counterclockwise," and so forth. (73, A-3)

Bit.
A binary digit, such as 0 or 1. The 0- or 1-states are used by computer systems to take advantage of the binary nature of electronics. Bits often are assembled into bytes and words when manipulated or stored. (73)

Bit mapping.
A term, used with certain display devices and dot-matrix printers, that means that each of the dots in the output image may be individually operator-controlled. (142)

Bits per second (bps).
A measure of the speed of a communications device. (197)

Board.
A hardware device into which processor chips and memory chips are fitted, along with related circuitry. *(81)*

Bps.
See Bits per second. (197)

Bridge.
An interface that enables two similar networks to communicate. Contrasts with gateway. (210)

Bug.
An error in a program or system. *(427)*

Bus.
A set of wires that acts as a data highway between the CPU and other devices. (88)

Bus network.
A telecommunications network consisting of a line and several devices that are tapped into the line. The network is so named because data are picked up and dropped off at devices similarly to the way in which passengers are picked up and dropped off at bus stops. (212)

Byte.
A configuration of seven or eight bits used to represent a single character of data. (78)

C.
A programming language that has the portability of a high-level language and the executional efficiency of an assembly language. *(418)*

Cache disk.
A disk management scheme whereby more data than necessary are read from disk during each time-consuming disk fetch and are stored in internal memory to minimize the number of fetches. (117)

CAD.
See Computer-aided design. (376)

CAD/CAM.
An acronym for *computer-aided design/computer-aided manufacturing.* CAD/CAM is a general term applied to the use of computer technology to automate design and manufacturing operations in industry. *(376)*

CAM.
See Computer-aided manufacturing. (377)

Cartridge disk.
Magnetic disk in which a single disk platter is contained in a sealed plastic case, which in turn is mounted onto a disk unit when data are to be read from or written to the disk inside. (115)

Cartridge tape.
Magnetic tape in which the supply and take-up reels are contained in a small plastic case, which in turn is mounted onto a tape unit when data are to be read from or written to the tape inside. (118)

CASE.
See Computer-aided software engineering. (429)

Case control structure.
A control structure that can be formed by nesting two or more selection control structures. (412)

Cathode-ray tube (CRT).
A display device that contains a long-necked display-tube mechanism similar to that used in television sets. (146)

Cell.
In spreadsheet software, an area of the worksheet that holds a single label or value. (298)

Cell address.
The column-row combination that uniquely identifies a spreadsheet cell. (299)

Cell pointer.
In spreadsheet software, a cursorlike mechanism used to point to cells on the display screen. (301)

Cellular phone.
A mobile phone that uses special stations called cells to communicate over the regular phone system. (193)

Central processing unit (CPU).
The piece of hardware, also known as the *computer,* that interprets and executes program instructions and communicates with input, output, and storage devices. (10)

Clip art.
Prepackaged artwork designed to be imported into text documents or charts, by desktop publishing or presentation graphics software. (284)

Coaxial cable.
A transmission line developed for transmitting data at high speeds. (195)

COBOL.
An acronym for Common Business-Oriented Language. COBOL is a high-level programming language developed for transaction processing applications. *(418)*

Coding.
The writing of instructions, in a programming language, that will cause the computer system to perform a specific set of operations. (424)

COM.
See Computer output microfilm. (165)

Command language.
A programming language used to communicate with the operating system. (226)

Command-language translator.
Systems software that translates instructions written in a command language into machine-language instructions. (226)

Common carrier.
A government-regulated private organization that provides communications services to the public. (202)

Communications medium.
The intervening substance, such as a telephone wire or cable, that connects two physically distant hardware devices. (194)

Communications satellite.
An earth-orbiting device that relays communications signals over long distances. (196)

Compiler.
A computer program that translates a source program written by a user or programmer in a high-level or very-high-level programming language into machine language. The translation takes place before the translated program is executed. Contrasts with interpreter. (241)

Computer.
See Central processing unit. (10, 40)

Computer-aided design (CAD).
A general term applied to the use of computer technology to automate design functions in industry. (376)

Computer-aided manufacturing (CAM).
A general term applied to the use of computer technology to automate manufacturing functions in industry. (377)

Computer-aided software engineering (CASE).
Program products that automate systems and program development activities. (429)

Computer output microfilm (COM).
A term referring to equipment and media that reduce computer output to microscopic form and put it on photosensitive film. (165)

Computer system.
When applied to buying a "computer system," the term generally refers to the equipment and programs being sold. When applied to a computer-based operation in an organization, it is commonly defined as all the equipment, programs, data, procedures, and personnel supporting that operation. (10)

Concentrator.
A communications device that combines control and multiplexing. Concentrators have a store-and-forward capability that enables them to store messages from several low-speed devices before forwarding them at high speeds to another device. (215)

Concurrent access.
A term that refers to two or more users attempting to interactively access the same data at more or less the same time. (349)

Control-break reporting.
A term that refers to "breaks" in the normal flow of information in a computer report that periodically occur for subtotals and totals. *(54)*

Control panel.
In spreadsheet software, the portion of the screen display that is used for issuing commands and observing what is being typed into the computer system. (300)

Control structure.
A pattern for controlling the flow of logic in a computer program. The three basic control structures are sequence, selection (if-then-else), and looping (iteration). (412)

Control unit.
The part of the CPU that coordinates the execution of program instructions. (71)

Coprocessor.
A dedicated processor chip that is summoned by the CPU to perform specialized types of processing. *(85)*

CPU.
See Central processing unit. (10)

Crosshair cursor.
A digitizing device that is often moved over hard-copy images of maps and drawings to enter those images into the computer system. (162)

CRT.
See Cathode-ray tube. (146)

Current cell.
In spreadsheet software, the worksheet cell at which the highlight is currently positioned. (300)

Cursor.
A highlighting symbol that appears on a display screen to indicate the position where the next character (or group of characters) typed in will appear. (140, 300)

Daisywheel printer.
A low-speed printer with a solid-font printing mechanism consisting of a spoked wheel of embossed characters. Daisywheel printers are capable of producing letter-quality output. *(147)*

Data.
A collection of raw, unorganized facts. (10)

Data access.
Fetching data from a device either sequentially or directly. (125)

Database.
An integrated collection of data stored on a direct-access storage device. (47, 335)

Database administrator (DBA).
The person or group of people in charge of designing, implementing, and managing the ongoing operation of a database. *(347)*

Database management system (DBMS).
A software package designed to integrate data and provide easy access to them. (5, 335)

Data definition.
The process of describing the characteristics of data that are to be handled by a database management system. (342)

Data definition language (DDL).
A language used by a database administrator to create, store, and manage data in a database environment. (348)

Data dictionary.
A facility that informs users and programmers about characteristics of data or programs in a database or a computer system. (343, 426)

Data flow diagram.
A graphically oriented systems development tool that enables a systems analyst to logically represent the flow of data through a system. (386)

Data manipulation.
The process of using language commands to add, delete, modify, or retrieve data in a file or database. (344)

Data manipulation language (DML).
A language used by programmers to supplement some high-level language supported in a database environment. (349)

Data organization.
The process of establishing a data file so that it may later be accessed in some desired way. Three common methods of organizing data are sequential organization, indexed-sequential organization, and direct organization. (125)

Data processing area.
The group of computer professionals within the information systems department who are charged with building transaction processing systems. (382)

Data processing system.
See Transaction processing system. *(367)*

DBA.
See Database administrator. *(347)*

DBMS.
See Database management system. (5, 335)

DDL.
See Data definition language. (348)

Debugging.
The process of detecting and correcting errors in computer programs or in the computer system itself. (427)

Decimal.
A number system with ten symbols—0, 1, 2, 3, 4, 5, 6, 7, 8, and 9. (A-2)

Decision support system (DSS).
A system that provides tools and capabilities to managers to enable them to satisfy their own information needs. (370)

Default.
The assumption that a computer program makes when no specific choice is indicated by the user or programmer. (228)

Design.
The process of planning a program or system. Design is normally undertaken after a problem has been thoroughly analyzed and a set of specifications for the solution established. *(386, 409)*

Desk accessory.
A software package that provides the electronic counterpart of tools commonly found on a desktop—a clock, calendar, notepad, and rolodex file, for instance. Also called a *desktop organizer.* (373)

Desktop computer.
A microcomputer system that can fit on a desktop. Some familiar examples are computers in the IBM PS/2 and Apple Macintosh II lines. *(16)*

Desktop publishing.
A microcomputer-based publishing system that can fit on a desktop. (279)

Detachable-reel tape.
Magnetic tape that is wound onto a single reel, which in turn is mounted onto a tape unit with an empty take-up reel when data are to be read from or written to the tape. (118)

Device driver.
A utility program that enables an applications program to function with a specific hardware device. (248)

Diagnostic disk.
A disk that's used to help pinpoint and correct computer-system malfunctions. (458)

Digital transmission.
The transmission of data as discrete impulses. (198)

Digitizer.
An input device that converts a measurement into a digital value. (159)

Digitizing tablet.
A digitizer that consists of a flat board and a device that traces over the board, storing the traced pattern in memory. (162)

Direct access.
Reading or writing data in storage so that the access time involved is relatively independent of the location of the data. (99)

Direct organization.
A method of organizing data on a device so that they can be accessed directly (randomly). (129)

Disk access time.
The time taken to locate and read (or position and write) data on a disk device. (107)

Disk cylinder.
All tracks on a disk pack that are accessible with a single movement of the access mechanism. (105)

Disk drive.
A mechanism within the disk storage unit on which disk packs, diskettes, or disk cartridges are placed to be accessed. *(21)*

Diskette.
A small, removable disk made of a tough, flexible plastic and coated with a magnetizable substance. (100)

Disk pack.
A group of tiered hard disks that are mounted on a shaft and treated as a unit. A disk pack must be placed on a disk unit in order to be accessed. (103)

Disk unit.
A direct-access secondary storage device that uses magnetic or optical disk as the principal I/O medium. (103)

Disk utility.
A program that assists with such disk-related tasks as backup, data compression, space allocation, and recovering from accidental data destruction. (243)

Display device.
A peripheral device that contains a viewing screen. (140)

Display terminal.
A communications workstation that consists of a display device and a keyboard. (140)

DML.
See Data manipulation language. (349)

Documentation.
A detailed written description of a program, procedure, or system. (429)

Dot-matrix character.
A character composed from a rectangular matrix of dots. *(148)*

DOUNTIL control structure.
A looping control structure in which the looping continues as long as a certain condition is false (i.e., "do until true"). (412)

DOWHILE control structure.
A looping control structure in which the looping continues as long as a certain condition is true (i.e., "do while true"). (412)

Downloading.
The process of transferring data or information from a large computer system to a smaller one. Contrasts with uploading. (208)

Drum plotter.
An output device that draws on paper that is rolled along a cylindrically shaped drum. *(167)*

DSS.
See Decision support system. (370)

EBCDIC.
An acronym for Extended Binary-Coded Decimal Interchange Code. EBCDIC is a fixed-length, binary-based code widely used to represent data on IBM mainframes. (77)

E-cycle.
The part of the machine cycle in which data are located, an instruction is executed, and the results are stored. (72)

EDI.
See Electronic data interchange. (187)

Electronic bulletin board.
A computer file that is shared by several people, enabling them to post or broadcast messages. (190)

Electronic data interchange (EDI).
A computer procedure that enables standard business documents, such as purchase orders and invoices, to be exchanged from one company's computer system to the computer system of another company. (187)

Electronic mail.
A facility that enables users to send letters, memos, documents, and the like from one hardware device to another. (372)

Electronic mailbox.
A storage area used to hold a recipient's electronic mail. (188)

Electronic spreadsheet.
A productivity software package that enables operators to create tables and financial schedules quickly by entering labels and values into cells on a display-screen grid. (296)

End user.
A person who needs computer-produced results in his or her job. (14)

End-user development.
Systems development activities carried out by the end user. (393, 438)

Executive information system (EIS).
A decision support system that is tailored to the needs of a specific, top-level individual in an organization. (371)

Expert system.
A program or computer system providing the type of advice that would be expected of a human expert. (378)

External disk.
A disk unit that is not housed within the computer's system unit. Contrasts with internal disk. *(112)*

External storage.
See Secondary storage. (13)

Facsimile (fax) machine.
A device that can transmit or receive hard-copy images of text, pictures, maps, diagrams, and the like over the phone lines. (190)

Fiber optic cable.
A cable composed of thousands of hair-thin, transparent fibers along which data are passed from lasers as light waves. (195)

Field.
A collection of related characters. (47)

Field descriptor.
A code used to describe the type of data—say, numeric, character, or logical—that occupy a given field in a data record. (342)

File.
A collection of related records. (47)

File directory.
A directory on an input/output medium that provides data such as file name, length, and starting address for each file on the medium. (111)

File manager.
A productivity software package used to manage records and files. (330)

File structure.
A collection of information about the fields of a file, including the names, lengths, and types of the fields. (342)

Film recorder.
A cameralike device that captures computer output on film. (167)

Firmware.
Software instructions that are written onto a hardware module. (85)

Flat file.
See File. (332)

Flatbed plotter.
An output device that draws on paper that is mounted on a flat drawing table. *(167)*

Flat-panel display.
A slim-profile display device. (146)

Floppy disk.
See Diskette. *(108)*

Flowchart.
See Program flowchart. *(409)*

Font.
A typeface in a particular point size—for instance, 12 point Helvetica. (272)

FORTRAN.
An acronym for FORmula TRANslator. FORTRAN is a high-level programming language used for mathematical, scientific, and engineering applications. *(421)*

Fourth-generation language (4GL).
An easy-to-learn, easy-to-use language that enables users or programmers to code applications much more quickly than they could with third-generation languages such as BASIC, FORTRAN, and COBOL. (423)

Front-end processor.
A computer that is positioned in a network to screen messages sent to the main computer and that also relieves the main computer of certain computational chores. (215)

Full backup.
A procedure that produces a duplicate copy of all files onto a secondary storage medium. (451)

Full-duplex transmission.
A type of transmission in which messages may be sent in two directions simultaneously along a communications path. (198)

Function key.
A special keyboard key that executes a preprogrammed routine when depressed. *(138)*

Functionally obsolete.
Refers to a product that no longer meets the needs of an individual or business. (462)

Gateway.
An interface that enables two dissimilar networks to communicate. Contrasts with bridge. (209)

GB.
See Gigabyte. (78)

General-purpose computer.
A computer capable of being programmed to solve a wide range of problems. *(11)*

Gigabyte (GB).
Approximately 1 billion bytes. (78)

Half-duplex transmission.
Any type of transmission in which messages may be sent in two directions—but only one way at a time—along a communications path. (198)

Handwriting recognition device.
A device that can read handwritten characters as input. (163)

Hard card.
A hard disk that has been configured onto an add-in board. (115)

Hard copy.
A permanent form of usable output; for example, output on paper or film. Contrasts with soft copy. (138)

Hard disk.
A rigid platter coated with a magnetizable substance. (100)

Hard return.
In word processing, the use of the Enter key to provide line spacing. Contrasts with soft return. (268)

Hardware.
Physical equipment in a computing environment, such as the computer and its support devices. (14)

Hashing.
A key-to-disk mathematical transformation in which the key field on each record determines where the record is stored. *(129)*

Hexadecimal.
Pertaining to the number system with 16 symbols: 0, 1, 2, 3, 4, 5, 6, 7, 8, 9, A, B, C, D, E, and F. (A-5)

Hierarchical local network.
A star-shaped local network in which a relatively powerful CPU is at the top of the hierarchy and communications terminals or less-powerful CPUs are at the bottom. (208)

High-level language.
See High-level programming language. (417)

High-level programming language.
The class of programming languages used by most professional programmers to solve a wide range of problems. Some examples are BASIC, COBOL, FORTRAN, and Pascal. (417).

Highlight.
See Cell pointer. (301)

Host computer.
In telecommunications, a computer that is used to control a communications network. *(206)*

Host language.
A programming language used to code applications within a specific software system, such as a database environment. (350)

HyperTalk.
A fourth-generation language that enables text, graphics, voice, and video data to be stored in a cardlike format and manipulated. *(425)*

IBM-compatible computer.
A computer that can run the same software as IBM computers run. (440)

Icon.
A graphical image on a display screen that invokes a particular program action when selected by the operator. (160)

I-cycle.
The part of the machine cycle in which the control unit fetches an instruction from main memory and prepares it for subsequent processing. (72)

If-then-else (selection) control structure.
See Selection control structure. (412)

Illustration software package.
A program package that enables users to paint or draw. (285)

Image scanner.
A device that can "read" into digital memory a hard-copy image such as a text page, photograph, map, or drawing. (157)

Impact dot-matrix mechanism.
A print head that forms dot-matrix characters through impact printing. (148)

Impact dot-matrix printer.
A printer whose print head is an impact dot-matrix mechanism. *(148)*

Impact printing.
The formation of characters by causing a metal hammer to strike a ribbon into paper or paper into a ribbon. Contrasts with nonimpact printing. (147)

Indexed-sequential organization.
A method of organizing data on a direct-access medium so that it can be accessed directly (through an index) or sequentially. (126)

Information.
Data that have been processed into a meaningful form. (11)

Information center.
A facility in an organization that develops small systems. (383)

Information processing.
Pertains to computer operations that transform data into meaningful information. (11)

Information reporting system.
An information system whose principal outputs are preformatted, hard-copy reports. (370)

Information retrieval.
Online inquiry, through a display terminal or microcomputer workstation, to computer files or databases. (54)

Information system.
A system designed to provide information to managers to enable them to make decisions. (370)

Information systems department.
The area in an organization that consists of computer professionals —managers, analysts, programmers, operations personnel, trainers, specialists, and the like. (382)

Input.
Anything supplied to a computer or computer-system process or involved with the beginning of such a process, such as the data to be keyed in. Contrasts with output. (8)

Input device.
A machine used to supply data to the computer. Contrasts with output device. (8, 42, 136)

Input/output (I/O) media.
Objects used to store data or information before or after processing. Examples include magnetic disk, magnetic tape, and paper. (8, 45)

Instruction register.
The register that holds the part of the instruction indicating what the computer is to do next. (72)

Integrated software package.
A software package that bundles two or more major software functions into a single package. *(265, 298)*

Internal disk.
A disk unit that is housed inside the computer's system unit. Contrasts with external disk. *(112)*

Internal memory.
See Primary memory. (13, 70)

Internal storage.
See Primary memory. *(13, 70)*

Interpreter.
A computer program that translates a source program written by a user or programmer in a high-level or very-high-level language into machine language. The translation takes place on a line-by-line basis as each statement is executed. Contrasts with compiler. (209)

I/O media.
See Input/output media. (8, 45)

Issuance.
The use of computers to produce transaction processing documents such as paychecks, bills, and customer reminder notices. (52)

Iteration control structure.
See Looping control structure. (412)

Joystick.
An input device, resembling a car's stick shift, that often is used for computer games and computer-aided design (CAD) work. (162)

KB.
See Kilobyte. (78)

Keyboard.
An input device composed of various typewriterlike keys, arranged in a configuration similar to that of a typewriter. Computer keyboards also have a number of special keys that initiate preprogrammed routines when activated. (138)

Key field.
A field used to identify a record. (120)

Kilobyte (KB).
Approximately 1,000 (1,024, to be exact) bytes. Primary memory on smaller computer systems often is measured in kilobytes. (78)

Label.
In spreadsheet software, a cell entry that cannot be manipulated mathematically. (302)

LAN.
See Local area network. (206)

Language translator.
A systems program that converts an applications program into machine language. (209)

Laptop computer.
A portable computer light enough to be operated while it rests on one's lap. *(5)*

Laser printer.
A nonimpact printer that works on a principle similar to that for a photocopier. *(152)*

Light pen.
An electrical device, resembling an ordinary pen, used to enter input by pointing to a display screen. (160)

Line printer.
A high-speed printer that produces output a line at a time. (154)

Linkage editor.
A systems program that binds together related object-module program segments so that they may be run as a unit. (209)

LISP.
A language widely used for artificial intelligence applications. *(423)*

Load module.
A complete machine-language program that is ready to be executed by the computer. Also called a *load program.* (209)

Local area network (LAN).
A local network, without a host computer, that usually consists entirely of microcomputer workstations and shared peripherals. (206)

Local network.
A privately run communications network of several machines located within a mile or so of one another. (205)

Looping (iteration) control structure.
The control structure used to represent a looping operation. Also see DOUNTIL control structure and DOWHILE control structure. (412)

Low-level language.
A highly detailed, machine-dependent programming language. Included in the class of low-level languages are machine and assembly languages. (417)

Machine cycle.
The series of operations involved in the execution of a single machine-language instruction. (72)

Machine language.
A binary-based programming language that the computer can execute directly. (79)

Machine-readable.
Any form in which data are represented so that they can be read by a machine. (10)

Macintosh System Software.
The operating system that's used primarily on Apple's Macintosh line of computer systems. (235)

Macro.
A predetermined series of keystrokes or commands that can be invoked by a single keystroke or command. (276, 314)

Magnetic bubble storage.
Storage that uses magnetic bubbles to indicate the 0- and 1-bit states. (124)

Magnetic disk.
A secondary storage medium consisting of platters made of rigid metal (hard disk) or flexible plastic (diskette). (100)

Magnetic ink character recognition (MICR).
A technology, confined almost exclusively to the banking industry, that involves the processing of checks inscribed with special characters set in a special magnetic ink. (158)

Magnetic tape.
A plastic tape with a magnetic surface for storing data as a series of magnetic spots. (118)

Mailing list program.
A program used to generate mailing labels. (275)

Mail merge program.
A program specifically designed to produce form letters. (276)

Mainframe.
A large, transaction-processing-oriented computer capable of supporting powerful peripheral devices. (17)

Main memory.
See Primary memory. (13, 70)

Maintenance.
A term that refers to making minor modifications and upgrades to systems or software over time to ensure that they continue to meet the needs of an organization. (427)

Maintenance programmer.
A programmer involved with keeping an organization's existing programs in proper working order. *(407)*

Mass storage unit.
A storage device capable of storing billions of bytes of data online. (121)

Master file.
A file containing relatively permanent data, such as customer names and addresses. (47)

MB.
See Megabyte. (78)

Megabyte (MB).
Approximately 1 million bytes. (78)

Memory.
See Primary memory. (13, 70)

Menu.
A set of options, provided at a display device, from which the operator makes a selection. *(23)*

MICR.
See Magnetic ink character recognition. (158)

Microcode.
Instructions that are built into the CPU to control the operation of its circuitry. (72)

Microcomputer.
See Microcomputer system. (16)

Microcomputer system.
The smallest and least expensive type of computer system. Also called a *personal computer system.* (16)

Microfiche.
A sheet of film, often 4 by 6 inches, on which computer output images are stored. *(165)*

Microprocessor.
A CPU on a silicon chip. *(15)*

Microsecond.
One millionth of a second. (73)

Microspacing.
A technique used by some printers and software packages to insert fractional spaces between characters to give text a typeset look. (273)

Microwave.
An electromagnetic wave in the high-frequency range. (195)

Millisecond.
One thousandth of a second. (73)

Minicomputer.
An intermediate-size and medium-priced type of computer. (17)

Mixed replication.
In spreadsheets, copying formulas in one range of cells into another range while varying some cell references and leaving others constant. (312)

Modem.
A contraction of the words MOdulation and DEModulation. A communications device that enables computers and their support devices to communicate over ordinary telephone lines. (198)

Monitor.
(1) A video display. (2) The supervisor program of an operating system. (140)

Monochrome.
A term used to refer to a display device that operates in a single foreground color. *(145)*

Monospacing.
A printing feature that allocates the same amount of space on a line to each character. Contrasts with proportional spacing. (273)

Mouse.
A device used to rapidly move a cursor around a display screen. (160)

MS-DOS.
An operating system widely used by microcomputer systems similar to those made by IBM. (233)

Multidimensional spreadsheet.
A program package that allows the construction of worksheets in which cells are referenced by more than two coordinates. (315)

Multimedia.
A type of computing in which text, graphics, voice, and video are intermixed in applications. (351)

Multiplexer.
A communications device that interleaves the messages of several low-speed devices and sends them along a single, high-speed transmission path. (214)

Multiprocessing.
The *simultaneous* execution of two or more program sequences by multiple computers operating under common control. (231)

Multiprogramming.
The execution of two or more programs, possibly being run by different users, *concurrently* on the same computer. (229)

Multitasking.
The ability of a single-user operating system to enable two or more programs or program tasks to execute concurrently. (230)

Nanosecond.
One-billionth of a second. (73)

Narrowband transmission.
Low-speed transmission, characterized by telegraph transmission. (197)

NetWare.
The most widely used operating system on local area networks (LANs). (238)

Network.
A system of machines that communicate with one another. *(210)*

Nonimpact printing.
The formation of characters on a surface by means of heat, lasers, photography, or ink jets. Contrasts with impact printing. (150)

Nonvolatile storage.
Storage that retains its contents when the power is shut off. Contrasts with volatile storage. (98)

OA.
See Office automation. (371)

Object module.
The machine-language program that is the output from a language translator. Also called an *object program.* (241)

Object-oriented programming.
Programming in which related blocks of programs and data are represented by screen icons. *(422)*

OCR.
See Optical character recognition. (156)

Office automation (OA).
The use of computer-based, office-oriented technologies such as word processing, desktop publishing, electronic mail, video teleconferencing, and the like. (371)

Office automation (OA) area.
The group of computer professionals within the information systems department that is charged with managing office-related computer activities within the organization. (385)

Offline.
Anything not in or prepared for communication with the CPU. Contrasts with online. (46)

One-entry-point/one-exit-point rule.
A rule stating that each program control structure will have only one entry point into it and one exit point out of it. (412)

Online.
Anything ready for or in communication with the CPU. Contrasts with offline. (46)

Operating environment.
A term that refers to a graphical interface or the combination of an operating system and graphical interface—for instance, MS-DOS running under Microsoft Windows. (226)

Operating system.
The main collection of systems software that enables the computer system to manage the resources under its control. (223)

Optical character recognition (OCR).
The use of light reflectivity to identify marks, characters, or codes and the subsequent conversion of such symbols into a form suitable for computer processing. (156)

Optical disk.
A disk read by laser beams rather than by magnetic means. (121)

Orphan.
The first line of a paragraph when it is separated from the rest of the paragraph by a page or column break. Contrasts with widow. (277)

OS/2.
An operating system designed for high-end microcomputers. (236)

Output.
Anything resulting from a computer or computer-system process or involved with the end result of such a process, such as information. Contrasts with input. (8)

Output device.
A machine used to output computer-processed data, or information. (8, 42, 136)

Page description language (PDL).
A language used to communicate instructions to a laser printer. (282)

Page-makeup software.
Programs used to compose page layouts in a desktop publishing system. (283)

Page printer.
A high-speed printer that delivers output one page at a time. (154)

Parallel processing.
A computer system that operates with two or more CPUs, which share work and process pieces of this work simultaneously. (92)

Parallel transmission.
Data transmission in which each bit in a byte has its own path and all of the bits in a byte are transmitted simultaneously. Contrasts with serial transmission. (200)

Parity bit.
An extra bit added to the byte representation of a character to ensure that there is always either an odd or an even number of 1-bits transmitted with every character. (79)

Partial backup.
A procedure that produces a duplicate copy of selected files onto a secondary storage medium. (453)

Pascal.
A structured high-level programming language that is often used to teach programming. *(418)*

PBX.
See Private branch exchange. (208)

PC-DOS.
The operating system most widely used on IBM microcomputers. (233)

PDL.
See Page description language. (282)

Peripheral equipment.
The input devices, output devices, and secondary storage devices in a computer system. (45)

Personal computer.
See Microcomputer system. (16)

Personal computer system.
See Microcomputer system. *(16)*

Picosecond.
A trillionth of a second. (73)

Pixel.
On a display screen, a single dot used to compose dot-matrix characters and other images. (141)

Plotter.
An output device used for drawing graphs and diagrams. (166)

PL/1.
An acronym for Programming Language/1. PL/1 is a structured, general-purpose, high-level programming language that can be used for scientific, engineering, and business applications. *(421)*

Point-of-sale (POS) system.
A computer system, commonly found in department stores and supermarkets, that uses electronic cash register terminals to process and record sales transactions. (156)

Point size.
A measurement used in the scaling of typefaces. (272)

Port.
An outlet on the computer's system unit through which a peripheral device may communicate. (88)

Portable computer.
A microcomputer system that is compact enough to be carried about easily. *(16)*

POS system.
See Point-of-sale system. (156)

Precompiler.
A computer program that translates an extended set of programming language commands into standard commands of the language. (350)

Preliminary investigation.
In systems development, a brief study of a problem area to assess whether or not a full-scale systems project should be undertaken. Also called a *feasibility study.* (385)

Presentation graphics software.
A program package used to prepare line charts, bar charts, pie charts, and other information-intensive images. (319)

Primary memory.
Also known as *main memory* and *internal storage,* a section of the computer system that temporarily holds data and program instructions awaiting processing, intermediate results, and output produced from processing. (13, 70)

Printer.
A device that places computer output onto paper. (147)

Private branch exchange (PBX).
A call-switching station that an organization acquires for its own use. (208)

Private wide area network.
A wide area network that is built by an organization for its own use. (203)

Processing.
See Information processing. (8)

Productivity software.
Fourth-generation-language-based software—such as word processors, spreadsheets, presentation-graphics packages, file managers, and database management systems—designed to make workers more productive at their jobs. *(49)*

Program.
A set of instructions that causes the computer system to perform specific actions. (10)

Program design tool.
A tool, such as a flowchart, pseudocode, or structure chart, that helps the systems analyst or programmer decide how a program is to work. *(409)*

Program flowchart.
A visual design tool showing step by step how a computer program will process data. (409)

Programmer.
A person whose job is to write, maintain, and test computer programs. (14, 407)

Programming language.
A set of rules used to write computer programs. (12, 417)

Project manager.
(a) A systems analyst who is put in charge of a team that is building a large system. (b) A software package that is used to manage projects. (383, 390)

Prolog.
A language widely used for artificial intelligence applications. *(423)*

Proportional spacing.
A printing feature that allocates more horizontal space on a line to some characters than to others. (273)

Protocol.
A set of conventions used by machines to establish communication with one another in a telecommunications environment. (213)

Prototyping.
A systems development alternative whereby a small model, or *prototype,* of the system is built before a full-scale systems development effort is undertaken. (392)

Pseudocode.
A technique for structured program design that uses Englishlike statements to outline the logic of a program. Pseudocode statements closely resemble actual programming code. (412)

Public access network.
A network, such as the phone system, that is designed to be used by the general public. (202)

Queue.
A group of items awaiting computer processing. *(221)*

RAM.
See Random access memory. (85)

RAM disk.
A disk management system in which a portion of RAM is set up to function as disk. (116)

Random access.
See Direct access. (99)

Random access memory (RAM).
Any memory capable of being accessed directly. In the world of microcomputers, the acronym RAM generally applies only to primary memory. (85)

Range.
In spreadsheets, a set of contiguous cells. (303)

Read-only memory (ROM).
A software-in-hardware module that can be read but not written on. (85)

Read/write head.
A magnetic station on a disk access mechanism or tape unit that reads or writes data. (98)

Realtime processing.
Updating data immediately in a master file as transactions take place. Contrasts with batch processing. (54)

Recalculation feature.
The ability of spreadsheet software to quickly and automatically recalculate the contents of several cells based on new operator inputs. (303)

Record.
A collection of related fields. (47)

Redlining.
A word processing facility that provides the electronic equivalent of the editor's red pen. (276)

Reduced instruction set computing (RISC).
A term referring to a computer system that gets by with a fewer number of instructions than conventional computer systems, thereby reducing system overhead and, in many cases, decreasing the time needed to process programs. (91)

Register.
A high-speed staging area within the computer that temporarily stores data during processing. (72)

Relational database management system.
A database management system that supports relational databases —that is, databases in which data records are placed into files and the files can be interrelated by common fields (columns). (339)

Relative replication.
In spreadsheets, copying formulas in a source range of cells into a target range of cells relative to the row and column coordinates of the cells in the target range. (310)

Release.
A minor upgrade of a software product. (461)

Report Program Generator (RPG).
A report-generation language popular with small businesses. *(422)*

Request for proposal (RFP).
A document containing a general description of a system that an organization wishes to acquire. The RFP is submitted to vendors, who subsequently recommend specific systems based on the resources they are able to supply. (389)

Request for quotation (RFQ).
A document containing a list of specific hardware, software, and services that an organization wishes to acquire. The RFQ is submitted to vendors, who subsequently prepare bids based on the resources they are able to supply. (389)

Resolution.
A term referring to the sharpness of the images on an output medium. *(141)*

Retrieval/update language.
A fourth-generation language specifically tailored to information retrieval and updating operations. *(341)*

Reusable code.
Program segments that can be reused several times in constructing applications programs. (426)

RFP.
See Request for proposal. (389)

RFQ.
See Request for quotation. (389)

Ring network.
A telecommunications network in which machines are connected serially in a closed loop. (212)

RISC.
See Reduced instruction set computing. (91)

Robotics.
The field devoted to the study of robot technology. (379)

ROM.
See Read-only memory. (85)

RPG.
See Report Program Generator. *(422)*

SAA.
See Systems Applications Architecture. (237)

Screen saver.
A software product designed to protect the phosphor coating on the inside of a display screen from damage when the display is turned on but is not used for an extended period. (455)

Secondary storage.
Storage, provided by technologies such as disk and tape, that supplements primary memory. Also called *external storage.* (13)

Secondary storage device.
A machine, such as a tape unit, disk unit, or mass storage device, capable of providing storage to supplement primary memory. (42)

Sector.
A pie-shaped area on a disk. Many disks are addressed through sectors. (109)

Selection.
The process of going through a set of data and picking out only those data elements that meet certain criteria. (51)

Selection (if-then-else) control structure.
The control structure used to represent a decision operation. (412)

Sequence control structure.
The control structure used to represent operations that take place sequentially. (412)

Sequential access.
Fetching records in storage ascendingly or descendingly by the key field on which they are physically ordered. (99)

Sequential organization.
Arranging data on a physical medium either ascendingly or descendingly by some key field. (125)

Serial transmission.
Data transmission in which every bit in a byte must travel down the same path in succession. Contrasts with parallel transmission. (200)

Server.
A computer that manages shared devices, such as laser printers or high-capacity hard disks, on a local area network (LAN). (206)

Simplex transmission.
Any type of transmission in which a message can be sent along a path in only a single prespecified direction. (198)

Smalltalk.
An object-oriented programming language. *(422)*

Smart card.
A credit-card-sized piece of plastic that contains a microprocessor and storage. (164)

Soft copy.
A nonpermanent form of usable output—for example, display output. Contrasts with hard copy. (138)

Soft return.
In word processing, an automatic line return carried out by the software when a typed word exceeds the rightmost margin. Contrasts with hard return. (267)

Software.
Computer programs. (14)

Solid-font mechanism.
The printing element on a printer, such as a daisywheel printer, that produces solid characters. Contrasts with dot-matrix mechanism. (147)

Sorting.
The process of arranging data in a specified order. (53)

Source-data automation.
Making data available in machine-readable form at the time they are collected. (155)

Source module.
The original form in which a program is entered into an input device by a user or programmer prior to its being translated into machine language. Also called a *source program.* (241)

Spelling checker.
A program often used adjunctively with a word processor to check for misspelled words. (273)

Spooling program.
A program that temporarily stores input or output in secondary storage to expedite processing. (245)

SQL.
See Structured Query Language. (345)

Star network.
A network consisting of a host device connected directly to several other devices. (210)

Storage.
Pertains to memory areas that hold programs and data in machine-readable form. (8)

Storage register.
A register that temporarily stores data that have been retrieved from primary memory prior to processing. (72)

Streaming tape.
A cartridge tape used exclusively for backup purposes. *(118)*

Structure chart.
A program design tool that shows the hierarchical relationship among program modules. A structure chart closely resembles the common organization chart. (416)

Structured programming.
An approach to program design that uses a restricted set of program control structures, the principles of top-down design, and numerous other design methodologies. (412)

Structured Query Language (SQL).
A popular language standard for information retrieval in relational databases. (345)

Style sheet.
A collection of font and formatting specifications that can be saved as a file and later used to format documents in a particular way. (278)

Summarizing.
The process of reducing a mass of data to a manageable form. (51)

Supercomputer.
The fastest type of computer. Typically, supercomputers are found in engineering or scientific research environments. (18)

Supervisor.
The central program in an operating system. The supervisor has the ability to invoke other operating system programs to perform various system tasks. (225)

Support equipment.
All the machines that make it possible to get data and programs into the CPU, get processed information out, and store data and programs for ready access to the CPU. (8, 40)

Surge suppressor.
A device that protects a computer system from random electrical power spikes. (454)

Synchronous transmission.
The transmission of data over a line a block of characters at a time. Contrasts with asynchronous transmission. (201)

System.
A collection of elements and procedures that interact to accomplish a goal. (366)

System acquisition.
The phase of the systems development life cycle in which equipment, software, or services are acquired from vendors. (389)

System board.
A board that contains the computer. Sometimes called a *motherboard.* (81)

System clock.
The timing mechanism within the computer that governs the transmission of instructions and data through the circuitry. (72)

System design.
The phase of the systems development life cycle in which the parts of a new system and the

relationships among them are formally established. (386)

System implementation.
The phase of systems development that encompasses activities related to making the computer system operational and successful once delivered by the vendor. (390)

System unit.
The hardware unit that houses the computer and its primary memory, as well as a number of other devices, such as add-in boards and related circuitry. (40, 81)

Systems analysis.
The phase of the systems development life cycle in which a problem area is thoroughly examined to determine what should be done. (386)

Systems analyst.
A person who studies systems in an organization to determine what actions need to be taken and how these actions may best be achieved with computer resources. (383, 407)

Systems Applications Architecture (SAA).
An IBM strategy to interface major product offerings in a way that makes all applications running under OS/2 look similar to the user. (237)

Systems development.
The process of studying a problem or opportunity area, designing a system solution for it, acquiring the resources necessary to support the solution, and implementing the solution. (366)

Systems development life cycle (SDLC).
The process consisting of the five phases of system development: preliminary investigation, systems analysis, system design, system acquisition, and system implementation. (385)

Systems software.
Computer programs, such as the operating system, language translators, and utility programs, that do background tasks for users and programmers. Contrasts with applications software. (50, 222)

Tape unit.
A secondary storage device on which magnetic tapes are mounted. (118)

Technologically obsolete.
Refers to a product that, although superseded by a newer version or release, still meets the needs of an individual or business. (462)

Telecommunications.
A term that refers to transmitting data over a distance—over the phone lines, via privately owned cable, or by satellite, for instance. (186)

Telecommuting.
The substitution of working at home, and being connected through electronic devices to other workers at remote locations, for the commute to work. (376)

Teleconferencing.
Using computer and communications technology to carry out a meeting in which the participants need not all be present at the same site. (373)

Template.
A prelabeled onscreen form that requires only that the operator fill in a limited number of input values. (313, 332)

Terabyte.
Approximately 1 trillion bytes. (78)

Terminal.
Technically speaking, any device that is not a host device. *(42)*

Terrestrial microwave station.
A ground station that receives microwave signals, amplifies them, and passes them on. (196)

Text editor.
A utility program that enables an operator to manipulate text in a file. (248)

Thesaurus feature.
A routine, often accompanying a word processor, that enables electronic lookup of word synonyms. (275)

Time-sharing.
Interactive processing in which the computer is shared by several users at more or less the same time. The computer system interleaves the processing of the programs so that it appears to each user that he or she has exclusive use of the computer. (230)

Top-down design.
A structured design philosophy whereby a program or system is subdivided into well-defined modules, organized in a hierarchy, which are developed from the top of the hierarchy down to the lowest level. (416)

Touch-screen device.
A display device that can be activated by touching a finger to the screen. (160)

Track.
A path on an input/output medium on which data are recorded. (103)

Trackball.
A cursor-movement device that consists of a sphere resting on rollers, with only the top of the sphere exposed outside its case. (162)

Traditional approach.
An approach to systems development whereby the five phases of the systems development life cycle are carried out in a predetermined sequence. (391)

Transaction file.
A file of occurrences, such as customer payments and purchases, that have taken place over a period of time. (48)

Transaction processing system.
A system that processes an organization's business transactions. Operations falling into the transaction processing category include payroll, order entry, accounts receivable, accounts payable, inventory, and general ledger. (367)

Twisted-pair wires.
A communications medium consisting of pairs of wires twisted

together and bound into a cable. The public-access telephone system consists mainly of twisted-wire cabling. (194)

Typeface.
A collection of printed characters that share a common design. (272)

UNIX.
A multiuser, multitasking operating system. (235)

Universal product code (UPC).
The bar code that is prominently displayed on the packaging of almost all supermarket goods, identifying the product and manufacturer. A variety of optical scanning devices may be used to read the codes. *(157)*

UPC.
See Universal product code. *(157)*

Updating.
The process of bringing something up to date by making corrections, adding new data, and so forth. (54)

Upgrading.
The process of buying new hardware or software to extend the life of a computer system. Contrasts with replacement. (460)

Uploading.
The process of sending data from a small computer system to a larger computer system for storage or processing purposes. Contrasts with downloading. (208)

Utility program.
A program used to perform some frequently encountered operation in a computer system. (243)

Value.
In spreadsheet programs, a cell entry that can be manipulated mathematically. Contrasts with label. (302)

Value-added network (VAN).
A term that most commonly refers to a service offered over the public-access phone network by a firm other than the phone company, thereby adding value to the network. (203)

VAN.
See Value-added network. (203)

Vendor rating system.
An objective point-scoring procedure for evaluating competing vendors of computer products or services. (389)

Version.
A major upgrade of a software product. (461)

Very-high-level language.
A problem-specific language that is generally much easier to learn and use than conventional high-level languages such as BASIC, FORTRAN, COBOL, and Pascal. *(423)*

Virtual memory.
An area on disk in which programs are "cut up" into manageable pieces and staged as they are processed. While the computer is processing a program, it fetches the pieces that are needed from virtual memory and places them into main memory. (231)

Voice-grade transmission.
Medium-speed transmission characterized by the rates of speed available over ordinary telephone lines. (197)

Voice-input device.
A device capable of recognizing the human voice. (162)

Voice mail.
An electronic mail system in which spoken phone messages are digitally recorded and stored in an electronic mailbox. (188)

Voice-output device.
A device that enables the computer system to produce spoken output. (167)

Volatile storage.
Storage that loses its contents when the power is shut off. Contrasts with nonvolatile storage. (99)

WAN.
See Wide area network. (202)

Warranty.
A conditional pledge made by a manufacturer to protect the consumer from losses due to defective units of product. (458)

Wide area network (WAN).
A network that covers a wide geographical area. (202)

Wideband transmission.
High-speed transmission characterized by the rates of speed available over coaxial cable, fiber optic cable, and microwave. (198)

Widow.
The last line of a paragraph when it is separated from the rest of the paragraph by a page or column break. (277)

Winchester disk.
A sealed data module that contains a disk, access arms, and read/write heads. *(112)*

Window.
Refers to either (1) using the display screen as a "peek hole" to inspect contiguous portions of a large worksheet or (2) dividing up the display screen into independent boxes of information. *(298)*

Window area.
In spreadsheet software, the portion of the screen that contains the window onto the worksheet. Also called the *worksheet area.* (301)

Word.
A group of bits or characters that are treated by the computer system as a unit. (81)

Word processing.
The use of computer technology to create, manipulate, and print text material such as letters, legal contracts, and manuscripts. (5, 260)

Wordwrap.
In word processing, the feature that automatically produces soft carriage returns. (265)

Workgroup computing.
A computer application in which a group of workers interdependently use the same set of software and data on a network. *(207)*

Worksheet.
In spreadsheet software, the grid that contains the actual labels and values. (298)

Worksheet area.
See Window area. (301)

WYSIWYG.
An acronym for "What You See Is What You Get," WYSIWYG shows on the display screen an output image identical or very close to the desired, final hard-copy image. (261)

Answers to Fill-in and Matching Review Exercises

Chapter 1

Fill-in Questions

1. processing
2. primary, internal, or main
3. information
4. software
5. secondary or external
6. hardware
7. program
8. computer system

Matching Questions

1. e 2. f 3. a 4. c
5. b 6. d

Chapter 2

Fill-in Questions

1. input/output medium
2. auxiliary
3. online
4. Applications
5. Systems
6. field
7. Batch
8. realtime

Matching Questions

1. b 2. f 3. c 4. e
5. a 6. d

Chapter 3

Fill-in Questions

1. accumulator
2. thousandth
3. terabyte
4. read-only memory
5. open
6. reduced instruction set computing
7. parallel

Matching Questions

1. b 2. d 3. g 4. e
5. h 6. a 7. f 8. c

Chapter 4

Fill-in Questions

1. volatile
2. disk pack
3. cylinder
4. hard card
5. small computer system interface
6. tracks
7. file-protection ring
8. mass storage unit

Matching Questions

1. d 2. a 3. c 4. f
5. e 6. b

Chapter 5

Fill-in Questions

1. hard copy
2. pixels
3. cursor
4. monochrome
5. near-letter-quality
6. thermal-transfer
7. ink-jet
8. flatbed, drum
9. bit-mapped
10. film recorder

Matching Questions

1. e 2. f 3. g 4. b
5. d 6. a 7. h 8. c

Chapter 6

Fill-in Questions

1. Electronic data interchange
2. facsimile (fax)
3. Coaxial cable
4. digital
5. Fiber optic cable
6. modem
7. Synchronous
8. Common carriers
9. Asynchronous
10. star

Matching Questions

1. d 2. e 3. b 4. a
5. f 6. c

Chapter 7

Fill-in Questions

1. Systems
2. operating system
3. multiprogramming
4. Time-sharing
5. Multiprocessing
6. NetWare
7. language translator
8. Utility

Matching Questions

1. e 2. d 3. a 4. c
5. g 6. b 7. f

Chapter 8

Fill-in Questions

1. wordwrap
2. Proportional spacing
3. mailing list
4. dedicated
5. what you see is what you get
6. orphan
7. page-description language
8. clip art

Matching Questions

1. e 2. b 3. a 4. f
5. c 6. d

Chapter 9

Fill-in Questions

1. window, worksheet
2. cursor, cell pointer (highlight)
3. control panel
4. absolute, relative, mixed

5. template
6. macro
7. Add-on
8. dedicated, integrated

Matching Questions

1. d 2. f 3. e 4. a
5. c 6. b

Chapter 10

Fill-in Questions

1. file managers, database management systems
2. template
3. database
4. Relational
5. database administrator
6. concurrent
7. Structured Query Language
8. multimedia

Matching Questions

1. b 2. e 3. a 4. d
5. f 6. c

Chapter 11

Fill-in Questions

1. Systems analysts
2. Coding
3. debugging
4. flowchart
5. Pseudocode
6. COBOL
7. fourth-generation
8. reusable code

Matching Questions

1. h 2. c 3. e 4. b
5. f 6. g 7. d 8. a

Chapter 12

Fill-in Questions

1. accounts receivable
2. computer-aided design
3. artificial intelligence
4. robotics
5. steering
6. End-user development
7. tangible
8. benchmark test

Matching Questions

1. c 2. a 3. f 4. e
5. d 6. b

Chapter 13

Fill-in Questions

1. End-user
2. IBM-compatible
3. release
4. functionality
5. Backup
6. surge suppressor
7. warranty
8. functionally

Matching Questions

1. f 2. a 3. g 4. d
5. c 6. h 7. e 8. b

Appendix A

1. a. 11
   b. 46
   c. 83
2. a. 110011
   b. 100000100
   c. 111110100
3. a. 5
   b. 1A
   c. F42
4. a. 11110010
   b. 000110101001
   c. 0011100111101011
5. a. 182
   b. 1513
   c. 51967
6. $(4 \times 6^2) + (5 \times 6^1) + (1 \times 6^0) = 175$
7. 100110110
8. EB
9. 100011
10. 3C

Credits

Text Photographs

Module A opening photos *Circular:* Courtesy of General Motors Corporation. *Rectangular:* Thomas Ives/The Stock Market.

Chapter 1 opening photo Courtesy of Compaq Computer Corporation.

Figure 1-1 (a) Courtesy of Compaq Computer Corporation. (b) Courtesy of American President Companies, Ltd.

Figure 1-3 (a) Courtesy of Compaq Computer Corporation. (b) Courtesy of International Business Machines Corporation. (c) Courtesy of Apple Computer, Inc. (d) Courtesy of Texas Instruments.

Figures 1-4, 1-5 Courtesy of International Business Machines Corporation.

Figure 1-6 Courtesy of Cray Research, Inc.

Feature 1-1 photo Courtesy of Hewlett-Packard Company.

Tomorrow box photo Courtesy of International Business Machines Corporation.

User Solution 1-1 photo Courtesy of Compaq Computer Corporation.

User Solution 1-2 photo Courtesy of Fleming Companies, Inc.

User Solution 1-3 photo Courtesy of British Airways/Annual Report 1989/90.

Chapter 2 opening photo Courtesy of Evans and Sutherland Computer Corporation.

Figures 2-1, 2-2, 2-3 Courtesy of International Business Machines Corporation.

Figure 2-4 Courtesy of Hewlett-Packard Company.

Figure 2-5 (a) Courtesy of Nashua Computer Products. (b) Courtesy of Memory Media Products, Tustin, CA.

Figure 2-6 (a) Courtesy of GRiD Systems Corporation. (b) Courtesy of International Business Machines Corporation.

Figure 2-12 Courtesy of International Business Machines Corporation.

Figure 2-13 Courtesy of Tactics International Limited.

Tomorrow box photo Courtesy of Eastern Indoor Golf; photographer, Bob Malik Studio, Brooklyn, N.Y.

User Solution 2-1 photo Courtesy of Pier 1 Imports.

User Solution 2-2 photo Courtesy of Compaq Computer Corporation.

Module B opening photos *Rectangular:* Courtesy of GRiD Systems Corp. *Circular:* © Robert Tinney/The Stock Market.

Chapter 3 opening photo Courtesy of International Business Machines Corporation.

Figure 3-8 Courtesy of Intel Corporation.

Figure 3-9 Courtesy of Apple Computer, Inc.

Feature 3-1 photo Courtesy of International Business Machines Corporation.

Feature 3-2 photo Courtesy of Hewlett-Packard Company.

User Solution 3-1 photo Courtesy of Federal Express Corporation. All rights reserved.

User Solution 3-2 photo Courtesy of Compaq Computer Corporation.

Chapter 4 opening photo Courtesy of American Airlines.

Figure 4-2 Courtesy of BASF Corporation.

Figure 4-7 Courtesy of BASF Corporation.

Figure 4-11 Courtesy of International Business Machines Corporation.

Figures 4-13, 4-14 Courtesy of Plus Development Corporation, a Quantum Company.

Figure 4-15 Courtesy of BASF Corporation.

Figure 4-16 Courtesy of Memory Media Products, Tustin, CA.

Figure 4-17 (a) Courtesy of Compuserve, Incorporated. (b) Courtesy of International Business Machines Corporation.

Figure 4-19 Charles S. Parker.

Figures 4-20, 4-21a Courtesy of International Business Machines Corporation.

Figure 4-21 (b) Courtesy of Pioneer Communications of America.

Figure 4-22 (a) Courtesy of Britannica Software, Inc. (b) Courtesy of University of Cincinnati Medical Center.

Feature 4-1 photo Courtesy of International Business Machines Corporation.

Feature 4-2 photo Courtesy of The SoftAd Group.

User Solution 4-1 photo Courtesy of North American Van Lines.

Chapter 5 opening photo Courtesy of Sony Corporation of America.

Figure 5-2 (a), (b), (c) Courtesy of International Business Machines Corporation. (d) Courtesy of RasterOps Corporation.

Figure 5-4 Courtesy of Brilliant Image (NYC).

Figure 5-5 Courtesy of International Business Machines Corporation.

Figure 5-6 Courtesy of Dataproducts Corporation.

Figure 5-7 Courtesy of Storage Technology Corporation.

Figure 5-10 Courtesy of Okidata, a division of OKI America, Inc.

Figure 5-11 Courtesy of General Parametrics Corporation.

Figure 5-12 Courtesy of GCC Technologies.

Figure 5-13 Courtesy of Hewlett-Packard Company.

Figure 5-15, 5-16 Courtesy of International Business Machines Corporation.

Figure 5-20 (a) Courtesy of Synchronics. (b) Courtesy of International Business Machines Corporation.

Figure 5-21 Courtesy of International Business Machines Corporation.

Figure 5-24 (a) Courtesy of International Business Machines Corporation. (b) Courtesy of Hewlett-Packard Company. (c) Courtesy of Apple Computer Company, Inc. (d) Courtesy of Curtis Manufacturing Co., Inc. (e) Courtesy of Calcomp. (f) Courtesy of MicroTouch Systems.

Figure 5-25 Courtesy of GRiD Systems Corp.

Figure 5-27 Courtesy of Houston Instruments.

Feature 5-1 photo Courtesy of International Business Machines Corporation.

Tomorrow box photo © Jeff Smith.

User Solution 5-1 photo Courtesy of Compaq Computer Corporation.

User Solution 5-2 photo Courtesy of VideOcart, Inc., Chicago, IL.

User Solution 5-3 photo Courtesy of Mercy Hospital, Springfield, MA.

Module C opening photos *Circular:* Courtesy of Hewlett-Packard Company. *Rectangular:* Created by Genigraphics. © 1990 Genigraphics Corporation.

Chapter 6 opening photo Courtesy of General Motors Corporation.

Figure 6-2 *Datamation,* March 15, 1988. © 1988 by Cahners/Ziff Publishing Associates, L.P.

Figure 6-3 Microsoft Screen shots 1990 Microsoft Corporation. Reprinted with permission from Microsoft Corporation.

Figure 6-5 (a), (b) Prodigy Services Company.

Figure 6-6 © Mark Joseph.

Figure 6-8 Courtesy of Corning Incorporated.

Figure 6-9 Courtesy of Harris Corporation.

Tomorrow box photo Courtesy of Hewlett-Packard Company.

User Solution 6-1 photo Courtesy of Wal-Mart Stores, Inc.

User Solution 6-2 photo Courtesy of American President Companies.

User Solution 6-3 photo Courtesy of Compaq Computer Corporation.

Chapter 7 opening photo Courtesy of MacroMind, Incorporated.

Figure 7-4 Reprinted with permission from Microsoft Corporation.

Figure 7-7 © 1987–1990 Apple Computer, Inc. All Rights Reserved. HyperCard is a registered trademark of Apple Computer, Inc., licensed to Claris Corporation.

Figure 7-8 Courtesy of Sun Microsystem, Inc. The OPEN LOOK® and Sun™ Graphical User Interfaces were developed by Sun Microsystems, Inc. for its users and licensees. Sun acknowledges the pioneering efforts of Xerox in researching and developing the concept of visual or graphical user interfaces for the computer industry. Sun holds a non-exclusive license from Xerox to the Xerox Graphical User Interface, which license also covers Sun's licensees who implement OPEN LOOK GUI's and otherwise comply with Sun's written license agreements.

Figure 7-9 Reprinted with permission from Microsoft Corporation.

Figure 7-13 Courtesy of Fifth Generation Systems, Inc.

Feature 7-1 photo Courtesy of Symantec Corporation.

Feature 7-2 photo Courtesy of Symantec Corporation.

Tomorrow box photo Courtesy of International Business Machines Corporation.

User Solution 7-1 photo Courtesy of Compaq Computer Corporation.

Module D opening photos *Rectangular:* Created by Genigraphics. © 1990 Genigraphics Corporation. *Circular:* Courtesy of Bright Star Technology, Inc.

Chapter 8 opening photo Courtesy of Quark.

Figure 8-8 (a), (b), (c) and **8-10** Courtesy of Adobe Systems Incorporated. All rights reserved.

Figure 8-14 Courtesy of Microsoft Corporation.

Figure 8-15 (a), (b) *What Can Adobe Illustrator 88 Do For You?* © 1988 Adobe Systems Incorporated. All rights reserved. (c) *Architrave Magazine,* © 1990 Adobe Systems Incorporated. (d) *What Can Adobe Illustrator 88 Do For You?* © 1988 Adobe Systems Incorporated. All rights reserved.

Figure 8-16 Courtesy of Cornerstone Technology.

Figure 8-18 Artright Software Corporation.

Figure 8-19 (a), (b), (c) Used with permission of Software Publishing Corporation. Harvard Graphics® is a registered trademark of Software Publishing Corporation.

Feature 8-1 photo Courtesy of Brigham Young University; photographer, Mark A. Philbrick.

Tomorrow box photo Courtesy of International Business Machines Corporation.

User Solution 8-1 photo Courtesy of Compaq Computer Corporation.

Chapter 9 opening photo Courtesy of Fox Software, Inc.

Figure 9-12 Courtesy of Microsoft Corporation.

Figure 9-16 Courtesy of Funk Software, Inc.

Figure 9-18 Used with permission of Software Publishing Corporation. Harvard Graphics® is a registered trademark of Software Corporation.

Feature 9-2 photo Courtesy of Kofax Image Products.

Tomorrow box photo Courtesy of International Business Machines Corporation.

User Solution 9-1 photo Courtesy of Compaq Computer Corporation.

Chapter 10 opening photo Courtesy of International Business Machines Corporation.

Figure 10-4 (a) Courtesy of Microsoft Corporation. (b) Courtesy of Pictureware, a Norick Company. (c) Courtesy of Roykore.

Figure 10-14 Ben Davis, Courtesy of MIT Athena Language Learning Project.

Feature 10-1 photo Courtesy of Tactics International Limited.

Tomorrow box photo Courtesy of International Business Machines Corporation.

User Solution 10-1 photo Courtesy of Compaq Computer Corporation.

User Solution 10-2 photo Charles S. Parker.

Module E opening photos *Circular:* Courtesy of Evans & Sutherland Computer Corporation. *Rectangular:* ESoft Corporation.

Chapter 11 opening photo Courtesy of Hewlett-Packard Company.

Figure 11-1 (a) Courtesy of Toys-R-Us®. (b), (c) Courtesy of International Business Machines Corporation.

Figure 11-3 (a) Courtesy of International Business Machines Corporation. (b) Courtesy of Tactics International Limited.

Figure 11-4 Courtesy of Asymetrix.

Figure 11-5 (a) Courtesy of Hewlett-Packard Company. (b) Courtesy of Autodesk, Inc.

Figure 11-6 Courtesy of International Business Machines Corporation.

Figure 11-12 (a), (b) Courtesy of Scitor Corporation.

Feature 11-1 photos (a), (b), (c), (d) Courtesy of Wang Laboratories Inc., Copyright © 1990.

Feature 11-2 photo Courtesy of Andersen Consulting, Arthur Andersen & Co. S.C.

Tomorrow box photo Courtesy of International Business Machines Corporation.

User Solution 11-1 photo Courtesy of Frito-Lay, Inc.

User Solution 11-2 photo Courtesy of United Parcel Service.

Chapter 12 opening photo Courtesy of Roykore, Inc.

Figure 12-15 Courtesy of Index Technology Corporation.

Feature 12-1 photo Courtesy of Lotus Development Corporation.

Feature 12-2 photo © 1987–1990 Apple Computer, Inc. All Rights Reserved. HyperCard is a registered trademark of Apple Computer, Inc., licensed to Claris Corporation.

User Solution 12-1 photo Courtesy of American Electric Power Service Corporation.

Chapter 13 opening photo Courtesy of International Business Machines Corporation.

Figure 13-3 Courtesy of Hewlett-Packard Company and ERA Computers (Ken Broussard, Bob Waller and Lillian Kellogg).

Figure 13-8 Courtesy of Curtis Manufacturing Co., Inc.

Figure 13-10 Courtesy of International Business Machines Corporation.

Figure 13-12 Courtesy of Macmillan Computer Publishing.

Tomorrow box photo Courtesy of Qualtec Data Products Inc.

User Solution 13-1 photo Reprinted from *Datamation,* October 15, 1990, Cahners/Ziff Publishing Associates, L.P.

Figure A-4 Courtesy of Quarterdeck Office Systems.

Windows

Window 1

1 Courtesy of Silicon Graphics Computer Systems.

2 Courtesy of International Business Machines Corporation.

3, 4 Screen shots 1990 Microsoft Corporation. Reprinted with permission from Microsoft Corporation.

5 Courtesy of Genigraphics Corporation.

6 Courtesy of Comshare.

7, 8 Courtesy of International Business Machines Corporation.

9 Courtesy of Compaq Computer Corporation.

10, 11 Courtesy of International Business Machines Corporation.

12 Courtesy of YRM Partnership, Ltd., London and Intergraph Corporation.

13 Courtesy of Adobe Systems Incorporated.

14 Courtesy of International Business Machines Corporation.

15 Courtesy of Genigraphics Corporation.

16 Courtesy of Truevision, Inc. (untitled/Paul Coffin—Ottawa, Ontario, Canada).

17, 18 Courtesy of Pacific Data Images.

19, 20 Courtesy of International Business Machines Corporation.

21 Courtesy of Hewlett-Packard Company.

22 Courtesy of MacroMind Incorporated.

23 Courtesy of Raytheon Company.

24 Courtesy of International Business Machines Corporation.

25 Courtesy of Hewlett-Packard Company.

26 Courtesy of Tactics International Limited.

Window 2

1 Courtesy of Genigraphics Corporation.

2 Courtesy of Truevision Inc., "Zach's Toys," Steven Barnier.

3 Courtesy of Genigraphics Corporation.

4 Courtesy of Truevision Inc., "Robotoquine," Leonard McVicker.

5 Courtesy of Time Arts, Inc.

6 Courtesy of MacroMind, Inc.

7 © 1991 SuperMac Technology.

8 Courtesy of Silicon Graphics Computer Systems.

9 Courtesy of Silicon Graphics Computer Systems.

10, 11 Courtesy of Genigraphics Corporation.

12 Courtesy of Truevision Inc., "One on One," Martin A. Ebube.

13 © 1991 SuperMac Technology.

14 Courtesy of Time Arts, Inc.

15 Courtesy of Truevision Inc., "Race" by John Perry.

16, 17, 18 Courtesy of Silicon Graphics Computer Systems.

19, 20 Courtesy of Symbolics, Inc.

21 © Adobe Systems Inc. All rights reserved.

22 Courtesy of Time Arts, Inc.

23 Courtesy of Quantel.

24 Courtesy of Jay Crawford, Intergraph Hardware/Software.

Window 3

1 Courtesy of Intergraph Corporation.

2 Courtesy of Tactics International Limited.

3 Courtesy of Asymetrix.

4 Courtesy of Fox Software, Inc.

5 Courtesy of Borland International.

6 Screen shots 1990 Microsoft Corporation. Reprinted with permission from Microsoft Corporation.

7 Courtesy of Digital Vision, Inc.

Window 4

1 © 1990 Adobe Systems Incorporated. All rights reserved.

3, 4 Courtesy of Aldus Corporation.

5, 6, 8, 9, 10 © Adobe Systems Inc. All rights reserved.

11, 12 Courtesy of Quark.

13 © 1989 Adobe Systems Incorporated. Art produced using Adobe Illustrator 88™. All rights reserved.

16 Courtesy of ZSoft Corporation. Image created in PC Paintbrush IV™. PC Paintbrush IV and ZSoft are trademarks of ZSoft Corporation.

17 Courtesy of Aldus Corporation.

Window 5

1 Courtesy of Wasatch Computer Technology/Brian Johnson.

2, 3, 4 Courtesy of Genigraphics Corporation.

5, 6 Used with permission of Software Publishing Corporation. Harvard Graphics® is a registered trademark of Software Publishing Corporation.

7, 8, 9 Copyright 1991, USA TODAY. Reprinted with permission.

10 Screen shots © Microsoft Corporation. Reprinted with permission from Microsoft Corporation.

Window 6

1 Courtesy of MacroMind Incorporated.

2, 3, 4 Courtesy of Owl International, Inc.

5 Courtesy of MacroMind Incorporated.

6, 7 Courtesy of Authorware, Inc.

8, 9 Courtesy of Owl International, Inc.

10, 11, 12, 13 Courtesy of Authorware, Inc.

14, 15, 16 Courtesy of Editing Machines Corporation.

17, 18 Courtesy of Owl International, Inc.

Window 7

1 Courtesy of Pixelerator System marketed by BTS Broadcast Television Systems.

2, 3, 4 Courtesy of Symbolics, Inc.

5 Courtesy of Silicon Graphics Computer Systems.

6 Created by Genigraphics. © 1990 Genigraphics Corporation.

7, 8, 9 Courtesy of Silicon Graphics Computer Systems.

10, 11, 12 Courtesy of Wasatch Computer Technology.

13, 14 Courtesy of Genigraphics Computer Systems.

15, 16 Courtesy of Quantel.

17 Courtesy of Wasatch Computer Technology.

18 Courtesy of Silicon Graphics Computer Systems.

19 Courtesy of Evans & Sutherland Computer Corporation.

20, 21, 22 Courtesy of Silicon Graphics Computer Systems.

23, 24 © 1989 New World Graphics Inc.

25, 26 Courtesy of Silicon Graphics Computer Systems.

Index

Productivity Software Guide

FOURTH EDITION

Productivity Software Guide

FOURTH EDITION

Charles S. Parker
The College of Santa Fe, Santa Fe, New Mexico

The Dryden Press
Harcourt Brace Jovanovich College Publishers
Fort Worth Philadelphia San Diego New York Orlando Austin San Antonio
Toronto Montreal London Sydney Tokyo

Editor in Chief	Robert A. Pawlik
Acquisitions Editor	Richard Bonacci
Developmental Editor	Michele Tomiak
Project Editor	Jennifer Johnson
Production Manager	Alison Howell, Eddie Dawson
Book Designer	Beverly Baker

Address for Editorial Correspondence
The Dryden Press, 301 Commerce Street, Suite 3700, Fort Worth, TX 76102

Address for Orders
The Dryden Press, 6277 Sea Harbor Drive, Orlando, FL 32887
1-800-782-4479, or 1-800-433-0001 (in Florida)

Printed in the United States of America

Library of Congress Catalog Number: 92-072677

ISBN: 0-03-096591-8

3 4 5 6 7 8 9 0 1 2   048   9 8 7 6 5 4 3 2 1

The Dryden Press
Harcourt Brace Jovanovich

Cover Source: Horticultural Photography, Corvallis, Oregon.

The Dryden Press Series in Information Systems

Arthur Andersen & Co./Flaatten, McCubbrey, O'Riordan, and Burgess
Foundations of Business Systems
Second Edition

Arthur Andersen & Co./Boynton and Shank
Foundations of Business Systems: Projects and Cases

Anderson
Structured Programming Using Turbo Pascal: A Brief Introduction
Second Edition

Bradley
Introduction to Data Base Management in Business
Second Edition

Brown and McKeown
Structured Programming with Microsoft BASIC

Carney
Advanced Structured BASIC for the IBM PC

Coburn
Advanced Structured COBOL

Coburn
Beginning Structured COBOL

Dean and Effinger
Common-Sense BASIC: Structured Programming with Microsoft QuickBASIC

Electronic Learning Facilitators, Inc.
The DOS Book

Electronic Learning Facilitators, Inc.
The Lotus 1-2-3 Book

Electronic Learning Facilitators, Inc.
Stepping Through Excel 4.0 for Windows

Electronic Learning Facilitators, Inc.
Stepping Through Harvard Graphics for Windows

Electronic Learning Facilitators, Inc.
Stepping Through Windows 3.1

Electronic Learning Facilitators, Inc.
Stepping Through Word for Windows

Electronic Learning Facilitators, Inc.
Working Smarter with DOS 5.0

Electronic Learning Facilitators, Inc.
Working with WordPerfect 5.0

Electronic Learning Facilitators, Inc.
Working with WordPerfect 5.1

Ellis and Lodi
Structured Programming Using True BASIC

Federico
WordPerfect 5.1 Primer

Goldstein Software, Inc.
Joe Spreadsheet, Macintosh Version

Goldstein Software, Inc.
Joe Spreadsheet, Statistical

Harrington
Making Database Management Work

Harrington
Microsoft Works: A Window to Computing

Harrington
Relational Database Management for Microcomputers: Design and Implementation

Laudon and Laudon
Business Information Systems: A Problem-Solving Approach
Second Edition

Laudon, Laudon, and Weill
The Integrated Solution

Lawlor
Computer Information Systems
Second Edition

Lawlor
Introducing BASIC: A Structured Approach

Liebowitz
The Dynamics of Decision Support Systems and Expert Systems

McKeown
Living with Computers
Fourth Edition

McKeown
Living with Computers with BASIC
Fourth Edition

McKeown
Working with Computers

McKeown
Working with Computers with Software Tutorials

McKeown and Leitch
Managing with Computers

Martin and Burstein
Computer Systems Fundamentals

Martin and Parker
Mastering Today's Software with DOS, WordPerfect 5.0/5.1, Lotus 1-2-3, dBASE III PLUS (or dBASE IV)

Martin and Parker
Mastering Today's Software with DOS, WordPerfect 5.0/5.1, Lotus 1-2-3, dBASE III PLUS (or dBASE IV) and BASIC

Mason
Using IBM Microcomputers in Business: Decision Making with Lotus 1-2-3 and dBASE III Plus (or dBASE IV)

O'Brien
The Nature of Computers

O'Brien
The Nature of Computers with Tutorials

Parker
A Beginner's Guide to BASIC

Parker
Computers and Their Applications
Third Edition

Parker
Computers and Their Applications with Productivity Software Tools
Third Edition

Parker
Microcomputers: Concepts and Applications

Parker
Productivity Software Guide
Fourth Edition

Parker
Understanding Computers and Information Processing: Today and Tomorrow
Fourth Edition

Parker
Understanding Computers and Information Processing: Today and Tomorrow with BASIC
Fourth Edition

Robertson and Robertson
Microcomputer Applications and Programming: A Complete Computer Course with DOS, WordPerfect 5.1, Lotus 1-2-3, dBASE III PLUS (or dBASE IV) and BASIC

Robertson and Robertson
Using Microcomputer Applications (A Series of Computer Lab Manuals)

Roche
Telecommunications and Business Strategy

Swafford and Haff
dBASE III PLUS

The HBJ College Outline Series

Kreitzberg
Introduction to BASIC

Kreitzberg
Introduction to Fortran

Pierson
Introduction to Business Information Systems

Veklerov and Pekelny
Computer Language C

TRADE NAMES

dBASE, dBASE III PLUS, and dBASE IV are trademarks of Borland International.

WordPerfect is a trademark of WordPerfect Corporation.

Lotus and 1-2-3 are trademarks of Lotus Development Corporation.

IBM PC, IBM PC XT, IBM PC AT, PS/2, and PC-DOS are trademarks of International Business Machines Corporation.

MS-DOS is a trademark of Microsoft Corporation.

PREFACE

The purpose of the *Productivity Software Guide,* Fourth Edition, is to teach some basic, hands-on skills in using microcomputers—skills designed to make someone more productive in virtually any field. No matter what career a person chooses—accounting, engineering, stockbroking, real-estate, law, architecture, medicine, or teaching—chances are that he or she will be able to work both faster and smarter by mastering such skills.

With microcomputers spreading into almost every business and occupation today, there has been an explosive growth in high-quality computer products. *Word processors* help people type and write letters, documents, and books; *spreadsheets* let a person analyze numbers up, down, and sideways; and *database management systems* provide access to virtually any kind of fact stored electronically. And the list doesn't end here. There are also products that keep track of stocks and other financial instruments, products that help in filing taxes, products that provide electronic access to thousands of newspapers and journals from home, and so on. We are currently in the midst of a computer applications revolution that is showing no signs of slowing down. Today it is almost mandatory for anyone working in an office—from a clerk to a president—to know how to use a microcomputer.

At the heart of the applications revolution lies the class of products that are the major focus of the *Guide:* productivity software. *Productivity software* refers to computer programs that turn microcomputers into useful work tools, thereby making people more productive at their jobs. Among the most important and widely used types of productivity software are word processors, spreadsheets, and database management systems, all of which are discussed in the *Guide.* We also cover the computer's *operating system*—the software package that serves as the gateway to every computer system.

Coverage

Productivity Software Guide is a set of easy-to-use, hands-on tutorial instructions designed primarily for users of computer systems running under either the MS-DOS or PC-DOS operating system. The *Guide* is written with a set of instructions that assist both users on hard-disk systems and users on dual-diskette computer systems (with either 5¼-inch or 3½-inch diskettes).

The *Guide* opens with coverage of basics that are important to know about when first getting started on a computer system, followed by tutorials on MS-DOS (PC-DOS). Next are the tutorials covering the productivity software packages: word processing with WordPerfect, spreadsheets with Lotus 1-2-3, and database management with dBASE. The particular versions of these software packages addressed by the *Guide* are

☐ *Word Processing:* WordPerfect Version 5.1

- *Spreadsheets:* Lotus 1-2-3 Version 2 series
- *Database Management:* dBASE III PLUS and dBASE IV

Because they differ significantly, dBASE III PLUS and dBASE IV are covered in separate sections.

Teaching and Learning Tools

Each section of *Productivity Software Guide* contains a number of features that help students master the materials:

- **Detailed Table of Contents** The detailed table of contents shows the major headings within each section. It is comprehensive enough also to serve as an index, enabling quick lookup of key features in each software package.
- **Learning Objectives** A list of learning objectives is provided to serve as a yardstick, measuring what should be learned as the section is being read.
- **Overview** Each section starts with an overview that puts the subject matter of the section into perspective and lets students know what they will be studying.
- **Boldfaced Terms and Glossary** Important terms appear in boldface type as they are introduced in each section. These terms are also defined in a glossary at the end of each section.
- **Step-by-Step Command Layout** Commands in each software package are laid out in an easy-to-execute, step-by-step fashion—one designed to be unintimidating to beginners.
- **Double-Column Command Format** A double-column format is used whenever keystroke sequences for accomplishing tasks differ. For example, in the DOS section, when commands pertain to either hard-disk or dual-diskette systems, a double-column format is used so that students have to read *only* the column that corresponds to their particular system. A double-column format is also used in the dBASE section to distinguish dot-prompt-command actions from actions taken from menus (from ASSIST or from the Control Center).
- **Color Highlighting** Special keyboard keys—such as Enter, Ctrl, Alt, and Shift—are color highlighted for easy use.
- **Illustrations** Illustrations are provided for further pedagogical support, showing such items as computer hardware, outputs that result when commands are executed, handy summaries of commands and keystroke sequences, and informative tables that help with data entry.
- **Command Reference** At the end of every section is a handy alphabetical command reference that briefly summarizes the key

commands of the software under study. This feature makes the *Guide* a useful tool even after the last tutorial is finished.

- ☐ **Review Questions** Also at the end of every section is a set of review questions, covering important commands and features of the software under study, and the answers to these questions.
- ☐ **Hands-on Exercises** The last (or next-to-last) item in most sections is a set of practice exercises. These facilitate further experimentation with the software, helping students build their skills.
- ☐ **Appendix Materials** At the end of the sections on DOS and WordPerfect are appendix materials showing how to respectively use DOS and WordPerfect in the menu mode.

Instructor's Manual and Test Bank

The *Instructor's Manual* provides materials that help teachers organize materials in the *Guide* for classroom use. For each section of the *Guide* the *Instructor's Manual* provides a(n)

- ☐ **Outline** of major section headings
- ☐ List of student **Learning Objectives**
- ☐ Brief **Summary** of the section materials
- ☐ **Teaching Outline** that summarizes the most important materials covered under each of the major section headings
- ☐ **Additional Commands,** which cover information about using advanced software features; you may wish to copy and distribute some of these materials to your students if you want to go beyond coverage in the *Guide*
- ☐ **Solution Hints** to many of the end-of-section Hands-on exercises. Some of the solutions are available in disk form
- ☐ **Additional Exercises,** and **Answers** for you to cover in class or to use for testing students
- ☐ **Discussion Questions** for in-class discussion and the **Answers** to these questions

The *Test Bank* portion of the *Instructor's Manual* contains nearly 1000 test items in various formats, including true/false, multiple-choice, matching, fill-in, and short-answer questions. Answers are provided for all but the short-answer questions. The *Test Bank* is available in both hard-copy and computerized forms. The electronic versions—available for use with IBM and IBM-compatible microcomputers—allow instructors to preview, edit, or delete questions as well as to add their own questions, print scrambled forms of tests, and print answer keys.

A useful feature of the *Test Bank* is a key indicating the section from which each question was taken. Keys are included with each question, except for the matching questions. Also included is a ten-question, ready-to-copy-and-distribute multiple-choice quiz for every section, which allows students to be tested on a representative sample of important topics.

Acknowledgments

A project of this magnitude could never be completed alone. I am very grateful for the efforts of several people, working in a variety of capacities, for the development of this textbook. First, I wish to thank the following reviewers, whose thoughtful comments on preliminary drafts of the *Guide* improved both the technical accuracy and selection of materials: Hilda Federico, *Jacksonville University, Florida;* Susan Hansen, *University of Nebraska, Nebraska;* LaVonne Manning, *University of the District of Columbia, Washington, D.C.;* Sandra Stalker, *North Shore Community College, Massachusetts;* Laura Rao, *Central Missouri State University, Missouri;* Kay Gray, *Jacksonville State University, Florida;* Shelly Langman, *Bellevue Community College, Washington;* Cathy Brotherton, *Riverside Community College, California;* Ed Martin, *Kingsborough Community College, New York;* Dick Callahan, *Mississippi State University, Mississippi;* Susan Silvera, *Los Angeles Trade–Technical College, California;* Marilyn Moore, *Indiana University Northwest, Indiana;* Milton Brawer, *Western Michigan University;* Lister Wayne Horn, *Pensacola Junior College,* Florida; and Sandra McMinnis, *Pennsylvania State University–Harrisburg.*

Next, at The Dryden Press, I would especially like to thank my editors, Michele Tomiak and Richard Bonacci, for their help in the design and shaping of the Fourth Edition of the *Guide.* Their suggestions improved the quality of this work substantially. I would also like to thank Jennifer Johnson, Eddie Dawson, Alison Howell, Beverly Baker, Kevin Cottingim, Lynne Bush, Lisa Rittby, Bob Pawlik, Bill Barnett, and the many others at HBJ/Dryden who worked hard on behalf of the book. Finally, I am especially indebted to Ed Martin of Kingsborough Community College for preparing the dBASE IV section of the *Guide.*

Charles S. Parker

CONTENTS

Productivity Software Guide

FOURTH EDITION

DISK OPERATING SYSTEM (DOS)

CONTENTS

LEARNING OBJECTIVES

After completing these tutorials, you will be able to:

1. Identify the basic components of a computer system.
2. Describe how various keys on the computer keyboard are used.
3. Start your computer system with directions specific to your system configuration.
4. Execute several common DOS commands.

OVERVIEW

Learning to operate a computer is a bit like learning to drive a car. When operating the car, you must first insert the key. You then follow a *procedure*—one that consists of a sequence of steps such as turning the key in a certain direction, waiting for the car engine to start, changing gears, pressing on the accelerator, and turning the steering wheel. The steps in this procedure may seem second nature to you now, but initially they may have caused you some apprehension. With time, though, you probably learned to enjoy driving. Driving makes it possible for you to accomplish more with your life. The car is a powerful tool that both expedites getting work done and provides pleasure, improving the quality of our lives. Learning to operate a computer also requires learning time and may cause some apprehension at first. But today's computer systems are so easy to use that it will not take long for you to become proficient. As you discover the many useful tasks made easier by the computer, it will become a valuable tool in your life.

When you drove a car for the first time, someone was probably in the car with you giving you step-by-step instructions. This guide provides the same type of assistance by teaching you how to operate your computer in a step-by-step fashion. This module on DOS provides an introduction to the equipment on which you'll work and a simple explanation of how the computer operates. You'll learn what you need to know to get started on your computer system, including a few simple procedures as integral to computing as steering and braking are to driving. So fasten your seat belt and let's get started.

COMPUTER SYSTEM COMPONENTS

A device that can store, retrieve, and process facts is called a *computer.* When a computer is put together with other elements so that it can perform useful work, the result is a *computer system.* Let's consider the

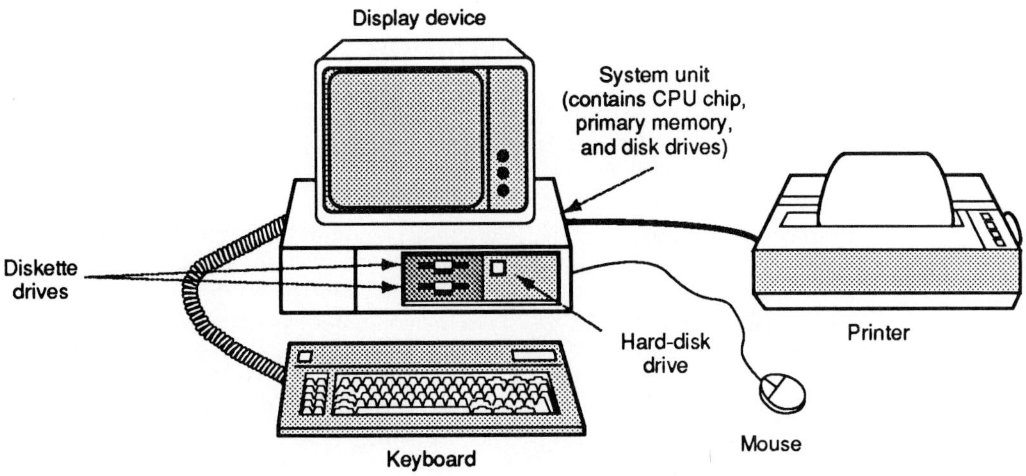

FIGURE DOS-1
A typical microcomputer system.

principal kinds of computer system components you'll be interacting with. These include software, data files, and hardware.

Software refers to computer programs. Software directs the computer system to perform specific tasks to produce the results that you, the computer user, want.

The facts that software uses or produces are often referred to as **data.** In order for the computer system to work efficiently, each batch of related data is organized into a data *file* that can be stored, retrieved, and processed as a whole or in part.

Hardware refers to the equipment on which you'll be working. Later in this section you'll learn about the role of such hardware components as the system unit, keyboard, monitor, and printer. Figure DOS-1 shows some of the devices in a typical microcomputer system.

Software

There are two types of software that direct the operation of a computer system: systems software and applications software.

Systems Software. The background computer programs that keep the various components of the computer system running efficiently are referred to as **systems software.** Many different programs are part of systems software. One of the most important is the **operating system,** which on IBM microcomputers or *IBM compatibles*—systems sold by a different vendor but using the same software—is called either PC-DOS or MS-DOS.

FIGURE DOS-2

Types of productivity software. Productivity software packages are designed to make end users more productive at their jobs.

Package Type	Description
Word processor	Turns the computer system into a powerful typewriting tool
Spreadsheet	Turns the computer system into a sophisticated electronic calculator and analysis tool
Presentation graphics	Turns the computer into a tool that can be used to prepare overheads, slides, and presentation materials for meetings
File manager and database manager	Turn the computer system into an electronic research assistant, capable of searching through mounds of data to prepare reports or answer queries for information
Communications software	Enables managers to call up remote computers for such things as financial information, marketing information, and news
Desktop publishing	Turns the computer system into a tool that can be used to produce documents that look like they were produced at a professional print shop
Desk accessory	Provides the electronic equivalent of tools commonly found on an office desktop—calendars, address files, and calculators, for instance
CASE (computer-assisted software engineering)	Automates and integrates many of the tasks performed by computer professionals, thus enabling them to develop systems and software faster and more effectively
Expert system	Enables workers to tap into expert knowledge to support them in their work

This guide will refer to the operating system simply as DOS. Later you'll learn how to activate some important DOS procedures necessary for the operation of your computer system.

Applications Software. While systems software coordinates the overall operation of the computer system, **applications software** instructs the computer to perform specific tasks that serve the end user. Among such tasks are producing letters, research papers, budgets, mathematical graphs, and sales invoices. Applications software designed to make workers more productive at their jobs is called **productivity software.** Figure DOS-2 lists a few of the many types of productivity software packages available to computer users.

Data Files

Data to be processed in a computer system must be organized in a systematic way. As mentioned earlier, related data are stored in a *file*. For every project you do on the computer, you will create one or more files to store your data.

When you use WordPerfect, for example, a file could hold a letter or short report. With Lotus 1-2-3, files often contain budgets, asset amortization tables, or profit-and-loss statements. And with dBASE III PLUS or dBASE IV, you might create files containing such items as employee, vendor, or client records. You assign each file a name to help you remember what it contains and to help you locate it among other files stored on your system.

Hardware

Software instructions and data files are manipulated electronically inside the hardware components of the computer system. As you begin to work on your computer system, you should know about the operation of hardware components like the system unit, disk drives, monitor, printer, keyboard, and mouse.

The System Unit. The "box" that contains the computer itself is called the **system unit.** If you looked inside your system unit, you would see a mass of wires and chips as well as the disk drives.

On the floor of the system unit is a circuit board called the *system board,* with a special chip plugged into it that performs the main computing for the entire system. This chip, called the "computer" or *central processing unit (CPU),* performs arithmetic operations such as adding and subtracting, compares items to see which is larger or smaller, and coordinates the flow of data being brought to and sent from its internal circuitry.

The system unit contains two principal types of storage: primary storage and secondary storage.

On microcomputer systems, primary storage is commonly referred to as **RAM,** which stands for **random access memory.** It consists of silicon-backed chips that are plugged into the system board. When the computer system is in operation, RAM temporarily holds all software instructions and data being used by the CPU for your current project. While you are using an applications program like WordPerfect, parts of it are temporarily stored in RAM along with the document file on which you are working.

When you turn off the computer system, everything in RAM is erased. If you want to store data for a longer period, you "save" or write the data to a *secondary storage medium* such as a diskette (or floppy disk) or a hard disk. The medium you use will depend upon the particular task you are doing and the configuration of your computer system.

The Disk Drives. In most microcomputer systems, you will find one or more **diskette** *(floppy disk)* drives and, also, a **hard-disk** drive fitted into the system unit. The term "drive" refers to the mechanism that spins a disk.

FIGURE DOS-3
Diskettes.
Diskettes are the principal medium used to transfer electronic data and programs to and from microcomputer systems.

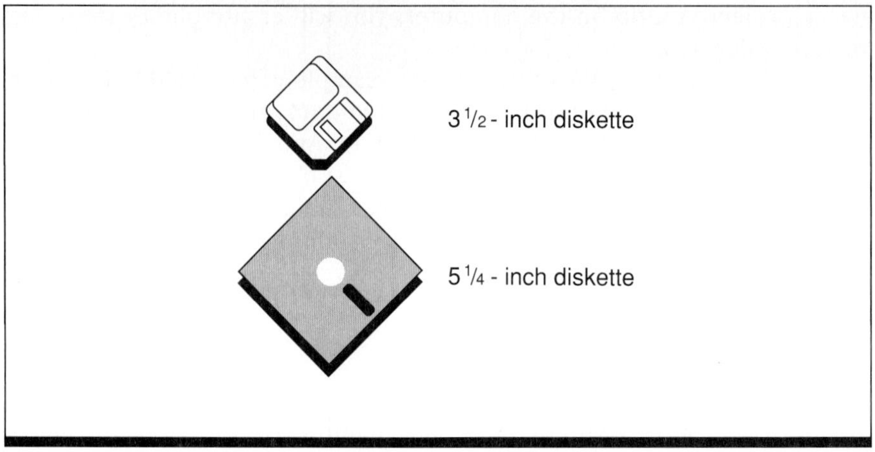

Each diskette drive is built to accept a removable diskette of a certain size (diameter). Diskettes are most widely available in two sizes—$3^1/_2$ inches and $5^1/_4$ inches—as shown in Figure DOS-3. Historically, the $5^1/_4$-inch diskettes came along first, then their $3^1/_2$-inch counterparts. The $5^1/_4$-inch diskettes are encased in flexible, plastic-coated cardboard jackets, whereas the $3^1/_2$-inch diskettes are contained in rugged plastic cases that can fit into a shirt pocket. Strange as it may seem, $3^1/_2$-inch diskettes can store more data than $5^1/_4$-inch ones.

Despite their small size, diskettes can store a respectable amount of data. Disk capacities are measured in *bytes,* or characters of data. Common capacities are 360 *kilobytes* (360 thousand characters) and 1.2 *megabytes* (1.2 million characters) for $5^1/_4$-inch diskettes, and 720 kilobytes and 1.44 megabytes for $3^1/_2$-inch diskettes. A 360-kilobyte diskette can store over 100 typewritten pages of information; thus, 1.44-megabyte diskettes can store up to 400 pages. The 1.2- and 1.44-megabyte diskettes are often called *high-density* diskettes; the 360- and 720-kilobyte diskettes are called *double-density* or *low density.* (Density refers to how tightly data are packed on the diskette.)

The diskettes that contain applications programs like WordPerfect are commonly called *program disks* while the diskettes that store your project files are called *data disks.* When you insert a diskette into a drive, the data or programs stored on the disk can be "read" or loaded into RAM and then processed by the CPU.

In contrast to diskettes, which are inserted when you start working on the computer and removed when you finish, a hard disk is permanently installed on a hard-disk drive inside the system unit. Later, you'll learn more about other differences among various disk-drive configurations.

The Display. As you work on the computer system, you can see the contents of your data files on the **display,** which resembles a TV screen. For example, when you're doing word processing, the display shows the words you are typing and instructions from the WordPerfect program about what to do next. If you direct the software to process any changes in your document, such as centering a title or indenting a line, you'll see those changes made on the display as well. Most display screens are either *monochrome* (one color for the characters and another color for the background) or *full-color* (eight or more colors for both characters and background). Sometimes people refer to displays as *monitors*.

The Printer. To complete many of the tasks you do on the computer, you need a **printer** to output on paper. In recent years the printers available for microcomputer systems have improved dramatically in terms of speed and print quality. There are so many variations among printers that it is impossible to catalog all of them here. The output of some printers resembles that of a simple typewriter, while other printers produce material that looks professionally published. The two most common types of printers are impact dot-matrix printers and laser printers.

Impact dot-matrix printers are the most inexpensive type of microcomputer printer. Characters are printed serially—that is, one after another—by pins in the printhead that strike the paper. Many dot-matrix printers sold today use a single row of nine pins. Several high-end printers that use two rows of 12 pins are also available. The more pins in the printhead, the higher the print quality.

Laser printers produce one page of output at a time, just as a copying machine does. In fact, many laser printers use the same "engine" (usually made by Canon or Ricoh) and the same principle (putting electrically charged toner onto paper) as copying machines do. Laser printers are superior to impact dot-matrix printers with respect to print quality, speed, and doing graphics applications such as desktop publishing and business charts. For commercial applications, laser printers are by far the printer of choice.

The Keyboard. Many **keyboards,** such as the ones for the IBM PC and PS/2 lines (see Figure DOS-4), have three sections. In the center is the *typewriter section.* The arrangement of the keys is similar to that on a conventional typewriter. There are, however, many special keys that you may not have encountered before, such as the Alt, Esc, and Prt Sc keys. We'll discuss these and other special keys shortly. One thing you should know right now, however, is that every productivity software package uses these special keys in its own way.

On the keyboard that accompanies the IBM PC (see Figure DOS-4a), to the left of the typewriter section are the *function keys* (see Figure DOS-4b for the PS/2 arrangement). These, too, are special keys and each of them has a different meaning in each software package. For example, if you are using WordPerfect on the IBM PC, the F2 key is used to search through text. In 1-2-3, F2 is used to switch into the edit mode.

Not all keyboards, incidentally, have 10 or 12 function keys. Also, these keys may be positioned differently from keyboard to keyboard and may even have different meanings for the same software package. In spite

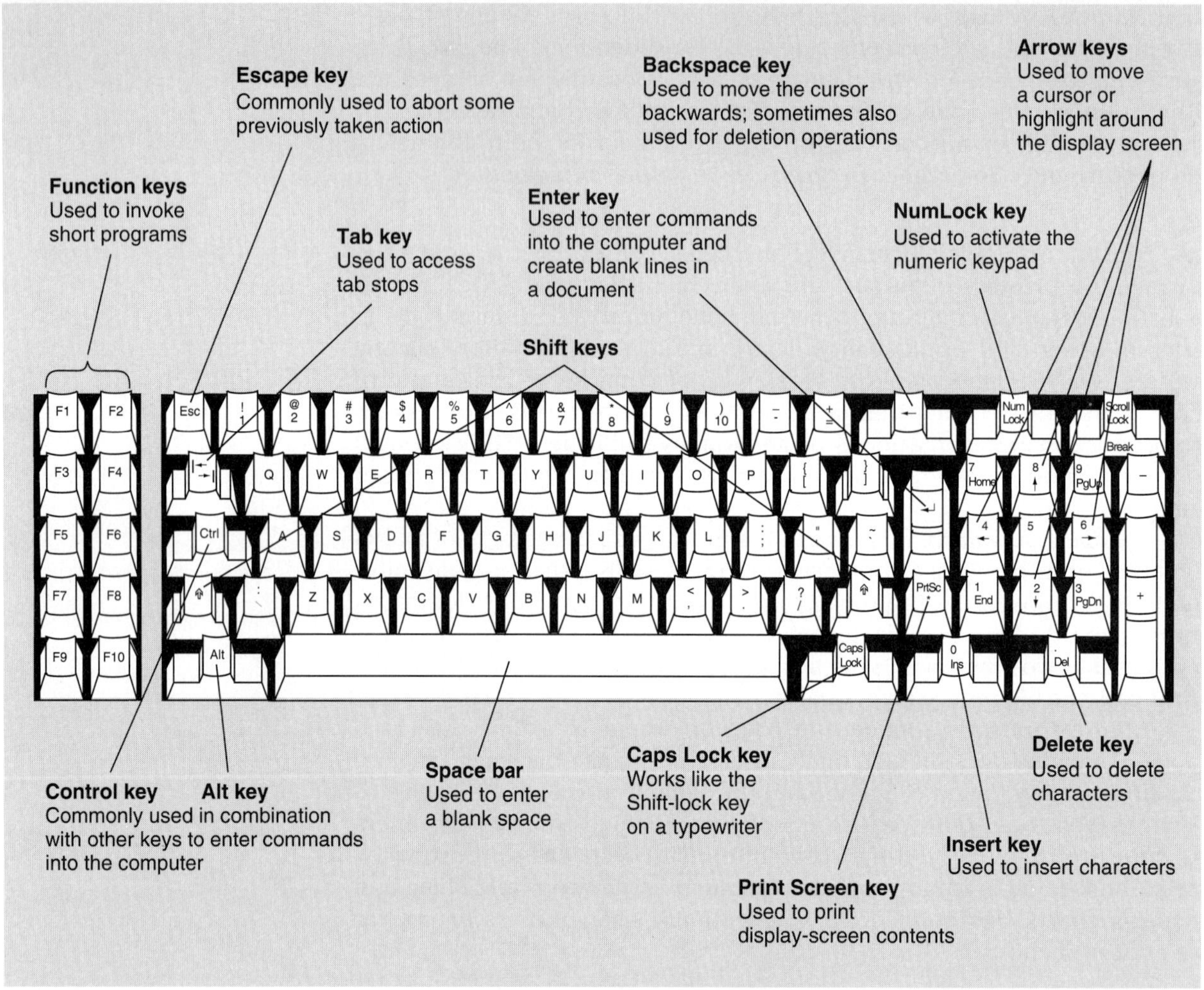

(a) IBM PC standard keyboard

FIGURE DOS-4
IBM PC and PS/2 keyboards.

of such differences, function keys are really easy to use and tremendously helpful. Each of them is designed to perform an operation through a single keystroke, saving you keying time.

The *numeric keypad section* is a cluster of number keys and special keys. On most keyboards it is located to the right of the typewriter section. The numeric keypad is handy to use if you are trained—as are many people—to enter numbers from a cluster of keys arranged in this configuration.

The computer keyboard is connected to the computer by a cable so that messages go directly to the computer's memory when the keys

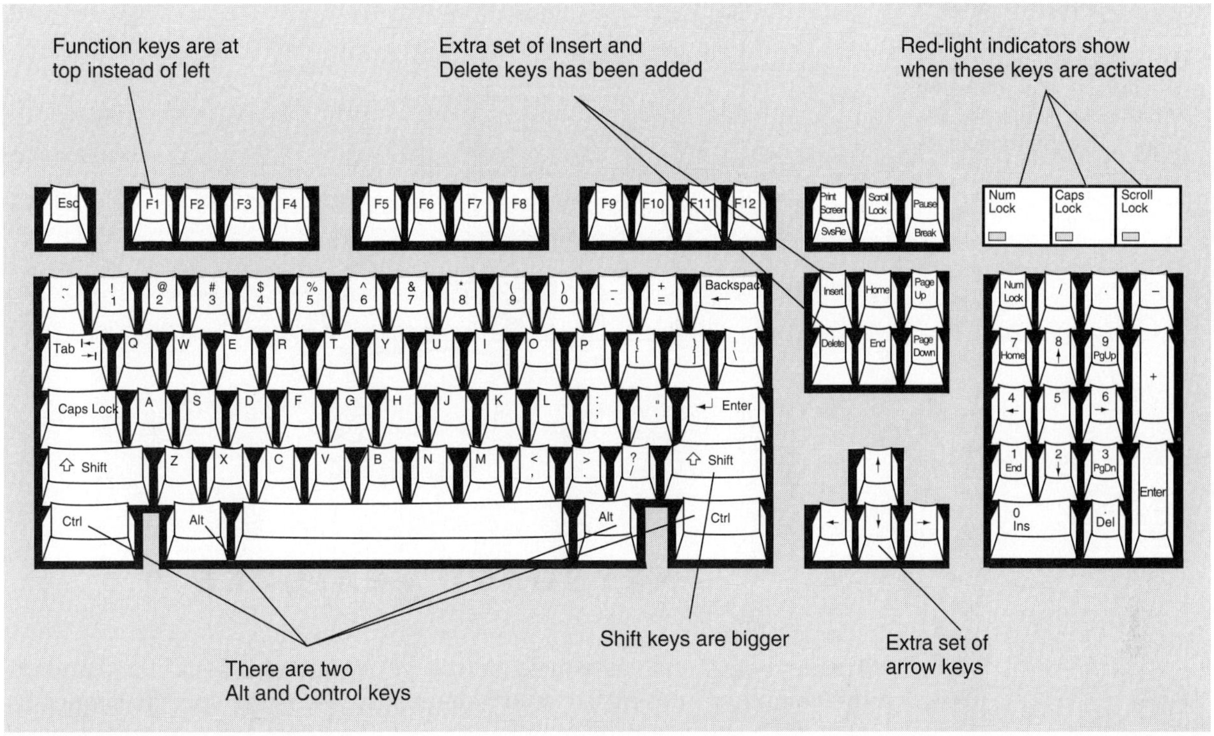

(b) IBM PS/2 enhanced keyboard

FIGURE DOS-4 *continued*

are pressed. On many keyboards the keys are *typematic;* that is, they repeat as long as you hold them down.

The Mouse. Many people supplement keyboard operations with a **mouse** (see Figure DOS-5). When a mouse is moved along a flat surface, the pointer on the display screen moves correspondingly. Mice are very useful for moving the pointer rapidly from one location to another on a display screen, and for dragging images from one part of the screen to another. Using a mouse often is much faster than pressing combinations of keys. Mice are especially handy when pointing to *icons* on the screen—small geometric symbols that represent commands or program options. When you use the mouse, say, to move to an icon on the display screen, you select or activate that icon by clicking a button on the mouse once or twice. Mice are popular for software products that have a graphical user interface, such as Microsoft Windows and DOS's shell program.

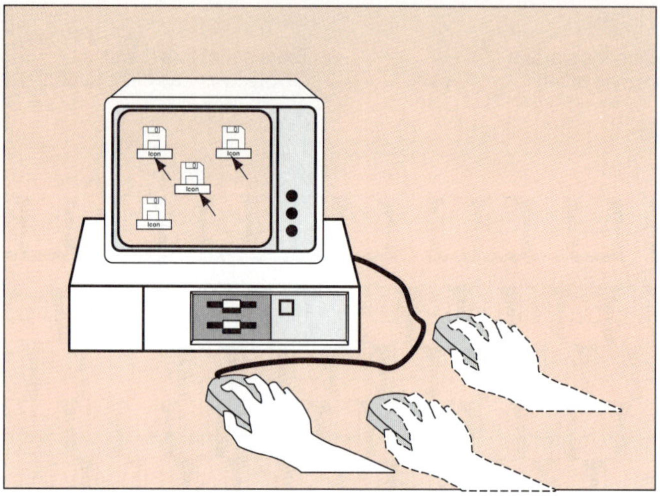

FIGURE DOS-5
Mouse input.
When a mouse is moved along a flat surface, the pointer on the display screen moves correspondingly.

KEYBOARD FEATURES

The keyboard enables you to both type in data and send commands to the computer system. To send commands, you press specific sequences of keys to activate programs in either the systems software or the applications software currently in use. The software then directs the operation of other system components.

Although the various applications software packages use keys in somewhat different ways, there are many similarities. For general use you'll want to become especially familiar with the location and features of the following keys on your keyboard.

↵ or Enter ↵

The Enter Key. This key is used to enter commands to the computer system in whatever software package you are using. In many cases, before this key is depressed, everything you type is held in a special memory area called an *input buffer,* awaiting corrections, before being sent on.

→ ← ↑ ↓

The Arrow Keys. These four keys are used to move some pointer—such as a *cursor* or *mouse pointer*—around the screen. In addition, these keys can be used to scroll offscreen portions of a file onto the screen. In 1-2-3, the arrow keys can also be used effectively at certain times to enter data.

Esc

The Escape Key. Escape is commonly used to abort some action that you've previously taken at the keyboard. In 1-2-3, you can also use this key to backtrack to some previous point in a command sequence.

Del

The Delete Key. In each of the packages we cover in this *Guide,* the Delete key enables you to remove characters at the cursor position.

Ins

The Insert Key. This key allows you to insert characters. In WordPerfect and dBASE, characters will be inserted wherever you position the cursor.

It works as a *toggle key,* that is, it activates a command (INSERT) when you depress it once and deactivates the command when you depress it again. In 1-2-3, the Insert key is inactive unless you are in EDIT mode.

The Backspace Key. Backspace moves the cursor back one space. In all of the packages covered in the *Guide,* this key will also erase characters as it backspaces to their positions.

← Backspace

The Shift, Ctrl, and Alt Keys. Many software packages use the Shift, Ctrl, and Alt keys—in combination with other keys—to issue commands. For example, in WordPerfect, the Shift key and the F6 function key are used to center text. It is important to note that you must hold down the Shift key while pressing the F6 key. Both the Ctrl and the Alt keys work similarly to the Shift key; that is, they must be held down while you strike the other key needed for the command.

↑ Shift

Ctrl

Alt

When used in combination with a key in the keyboard's typewriter section, the Shift key works like it does on a normal typewriter.

The Num Lock Key. Num Lock is used to activate the numeric keypad section of the keyboard. This key also can be an annoyance because it can easily be pressed by mistake and deactivate the arrow keys. So, if depressing the arrow keys produces numbers on your screen, hit the Num Lock key again (it's also a toggle key) to deactivate the numeric keypad.

Num Lock

The Tab Key. This key is used to reach preset tab stops in WordPerfect. In 1-2-3, Tab is used to move the cell pointer.

⇆ or Tab ⇆

The Function Keys. The function keys are used to perform preprogrammed routines. Check the *reference manual* available with the productivity software you are using to determine how the function keys are assigned.

F1 F2 . . .

The Caps Lock Key. You can use this key to produce uppercase letters on your keyboard, saving you from having to depress the Shift key. This key can be very handy when typing titles that consist only of uppercase letters. Caps Lock is also a toggle key, so you can deactivate it by pressing it again.

Caps Lock

The Ctrl-Alt-Delete Sequence. If you hold down the Ctrl and Alt keys (which work like Shift keys) and then press the Delete key, the sequence will cause a *warm boot* of your computer system. This is virtually equivalent to turning your computer off and then on again by activating the power switch (which is called a *cold boot*). Probably everyone working on a microcomputer system has faced some situation where proceeding with an applications software package was not possible, necessitating this drastic action. If you execute this key sequence, everything you currently have saved in RAM will be lost.

Ctrl Alt Del

↑ Shift PrtSc

The Shift-Prt Sc Sequence. Holding down the Shift key while you press the Prt Sc key enables you to send whatever is currently on your display screen to the printer. If what you want to send to the printer can fit onto a single screen, and you're not overly concerned about getting some extraneous characters that you see on the screen on your output, this is the best (and the fastest) way to get output. Using this sequence of keys provides an excellent way to copy a file or error message from the display screen, so that you can later discuss it with your instructor.

GETTING STARTED

Now that you have been introduced to the principal components of a computer system, there are a few more things you should know before sitting down to work. Just as it is important to memorize the rules of the road before starting to drive, you'll be better prepared to operate the computer if you first become familiar with the disk drives on your computer system and learn some tips on how to use diskettes.

Drive Configurations

Your computer system will probably include one or more diskette drives and, perhaps, a hard disk drive. Each drive on your system is referred to by a letter of the alphabet such as A, B, or C. The collection of drives is commonly called a "drive configuration."

You should know how your system is configured for several reasons. Many common procedures vary depending on what drive configuration you have. Also, to issue commands regarding specific data or programs, you'll often need to type the letter of the drive where the data and programs are stored, as part of the command.

Figure DOS-6 shows some drive configurations on IBM microcomputer systems and IBM compatibles. The two most common types of configurations are dual-diskette systems and hard-disk systems.

Dual-Diskette System. A system with two diskette drives (Drive A and Drive B) and no hard disk is commonly called a *dual-diskette system* (see Figure DOS-6b and DOS-6c). To use such a system, you insert a diskette into each drive's door or "slot." (On many machines, you also need to close the drive doors.) For dual-diskette systems, users often find it convenient to keep their data (i.e., letters and reports, budget worksheets, customer and sales records) and software programs (DOS, WordPerfect, 1-2-3, etc.) on separate diskettes. Generally, program diskettes go in the A drive and data diskettes go in the B drive.

Hard-Disk System. Although dual-diskette systems are still in wide use, *hard-disk systems* now dominate in the business world and are rapidly becoming the standard for personal and educational use. Compared to

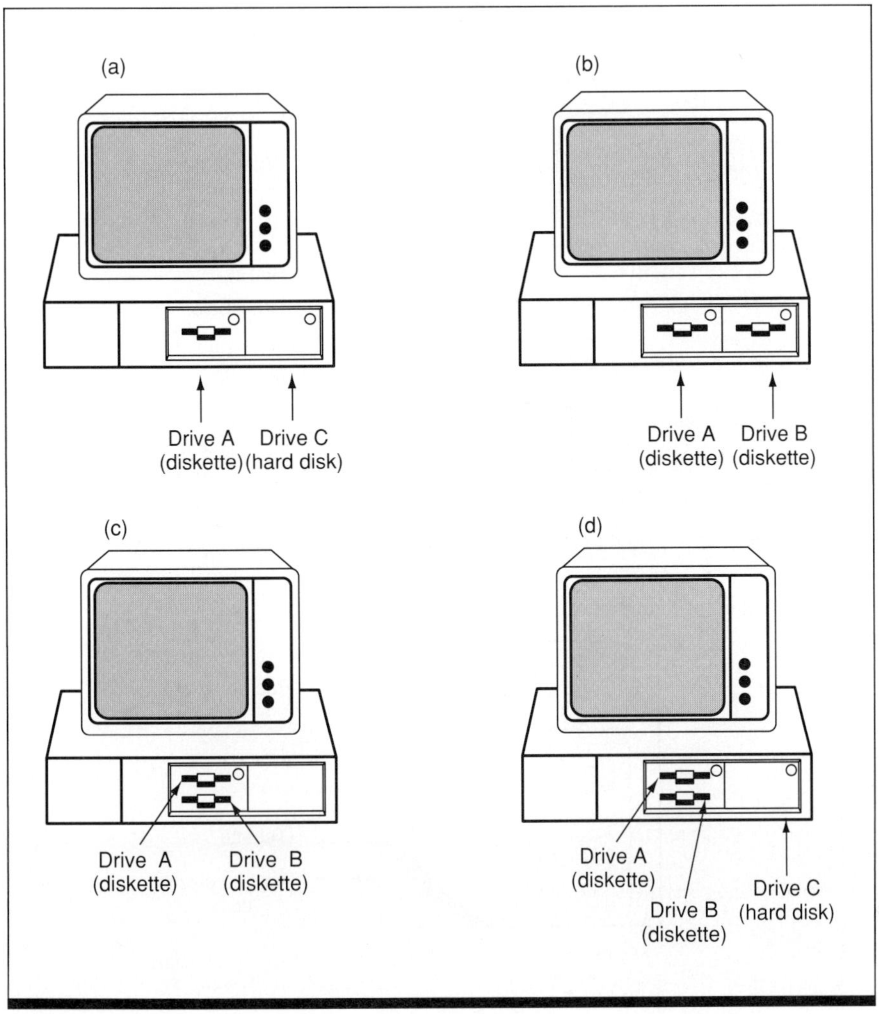

FIGURE DOS-6
Some disk-drive configurations.

dual-diskette systems, hard-disk systems offer the user more storage capacity and faster access to programs and data.

Two examples of a hard-disk configuration are shown in Figure DOS-6a and DOS-6d. In Figure DOS-6a, Drive C is the hard-disk drive and Drive A holds a diskette. The system unit in Figure DOS-6d has a hard-disk drive (Drive C) and two diskette drives (Drives A and B). In hard-disk systems with two diskette drives, it is common for the A diskette drive to accept $5^1/_4$-inch disks and the B drive to accept $3^1/_2$-inch disks.

It is also possible that you may be working on either a dual-diskette system or a hard-disk system that is configured to a network. In such an event, the network will usually have its own drive designator, such as the letter F ("drive F"). The hard disk on the network will assume many of the roles that would otherwise be undertaken by the local hard disk.

FIGURE DOS-7
5¼″ and 3½″ diskettes compared.
In addition to having a more rugged cover and a more compact size, 3½″ diskettes can store more data than can 5¼″ diskettes.

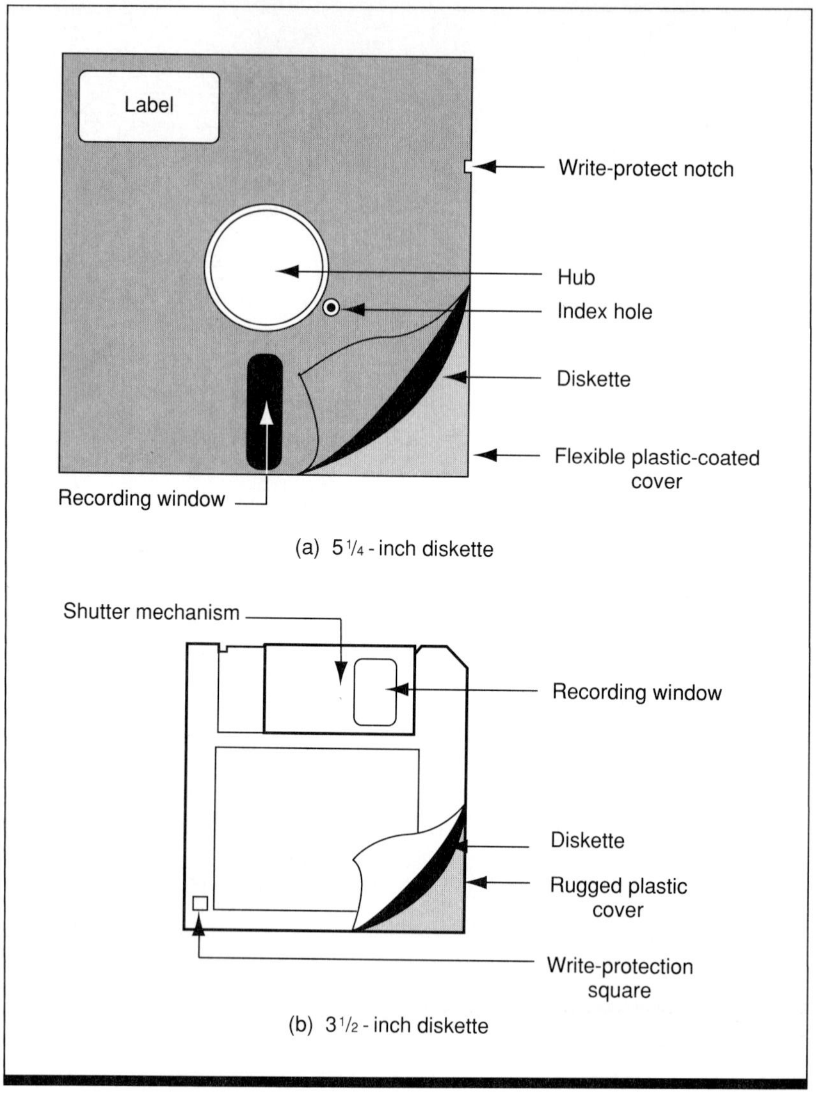

How to Use Diskettes

The diskettes you mount onto the drives of your system will probably store all of the software and data you will need to do your work. Your instructor will explain what type of diskettes you should use and what should be stored on them, based on your system's configuration.

Figure DOS-7 describes the features of 3½″ and 5¼″ diskettes. Each diskette consists of a round platter encased in a plastic jacket. The platters are made of a tough but flexible Mylar plastic and are coated with a magnetizable substance. The outer jacket is lined with a soft material that cleans the diskette as it spins. The disk spins when the computer is reading its contents or writing to it. A diskette is read or written to through its recording window.

To protect data, diskettes also contain a *write-protect notch* or *square* (see figure). This prevents the user from accidentally writing on the disk. Covering the notch on 5¼-inch diskettes makes it impossible to write on the surface. The convention on 3½-inch diskettes is the opposite: exposing the notch or square makes writing impossible.

You can protect programs and data by taking good care of your diskettes and by making regular backup copies.

Care of Diskettes. Diskettes may look like inert slabs of plastic, but they are extremely sensitive items and must be cared for accordingly. For instance, never touch an exposed diskette surface or bend the diskette in any way. Also, keep the diskette away from magnetic objects, motors, stereo speakers, and extreme temperatures. Furthermore, never subject the diskette to pressure; for example, never write on a label with a ballpoint pen after you attach it to the diskette.

If the diskette is damaged in any way, all or part of its contents may be destroyed. Imagine working at the computer for hours on a term paper and inadvertently causing half of your file to be erased from the diskette. Although some mishaps are caused by problems in the computer system or in your home's electrical system, most disasters happen because of carelessness. Careful handling of diskettes can vastly reduce the risk of an accident.

Backing Up Disks. Because some accidents on both diskette and hard disk are almost impossible to avoid, another important safety precaution is making *backup copies,* duplicates of any files you cannot afford to lose. Figure DOS-8 explains some of the reasons backup copies are needed. Though you may not understand all of these technical problems now, any of them could cause you difficulties once you start to work on the computer. The best insurance is to get in the habit of making backups. Later in this section you'll learn how to use DOS commands to make backup copies of individual files or entire diskettes.

When you purchase a software diskette, before using it you should make a backup copy. Then store the original diskette in a safe place and use your backup copy for working on the computer system. That way there is little chance of destroying the original, and you can use the original to make a new backup copy if necessary.

There are several strategies for backing up the data files you create on either a diskette or a hard disk. One strategy is to perform a *full backup* in which you back up all of the files on disk while working or at the end of a session. An alternative to the lengthy global backup is a *partial backup,* in which only files created since the last backup are copied. Whenever you back up a disk, make sure that backup files are not stored on the same disk as the originals.

Inserting Diskettes into a Drive. It is important to insert a diskette carefully and correctly into its drive. Slightly different procedures apply to 5¼″ and 3½″ diskettes.

With a 5¼″ diskette, you will usually start by removing the diskette from its envelope. You then insert the diskette with the label

FIGURE DOS-8

Good reasons for backing up a disk.
Taking a few extra minutes to make duplicate copies of important files can avert a potential disaster.

WHY BACKUP?

Part of the disk goes bad, destroying a file.

A file you thought you no longer had need for, and erased, turns out to be important.

You modify a file in an undesirable way, and the damage done is irreversible.

You accidentally reformat a disk.

The disk suffers a head crash.

A power brownout or failure, at the time of saving a file, causes "garbage" to be saved.

You save a file to the wrong subdirectory, overwriting a different file that has the same name.

While rushing your work, you make a mistake that causes the wrong files to be erased.

You unwittingly destroy a file while working on it—say, by deleting parts of it erroneously and then saving the file.

Malfunctioning hardware or software causes files to be erased.

A computer virus enters your system and destroys files.

Your disk is physically destroyed—for instance, a diskette is left in the sun or the hard disk is given a jolt. Alternatively, a fire or flood may destroy the disk.

Someone steals your diskette or hard disk.

side up and with the oval-cutout end going first into the slot. Be careful not to bend or force the diskette. Sometimes you may need to pull the diskette back out slowly and try again. When the diskette is securely inserted, your drive will probably have a door to close or a knob to pull down over the slot.

You insert a 3½″ diskette with the label side up and with the metal end going first into the slot. On the surface of the diskette is an arrow showing the correct direction. When you've done that properly, the diskette will lock into place.

You should never attempt to remove or install a disk in a drive when that drive's *indicator light* is on. The drive's indicator light shows when the drive is spinning. Inserting or removing a disk when the light is on can damage both the disk and the read/write heads.

How to Use Hard Disks

Hard disks differ functionally from diskettes in that they have huge storage capacities. A hard disk on a microcomputer system may be capable of storing 100 to 1,000 or more times the amount of information that can be stored on a single diskette. Consequently, special features are required to help users organize files.

Subdirectories. Files on hard disks commonly are organized hierarchically into a main directory and several subordinate subdirectories, as

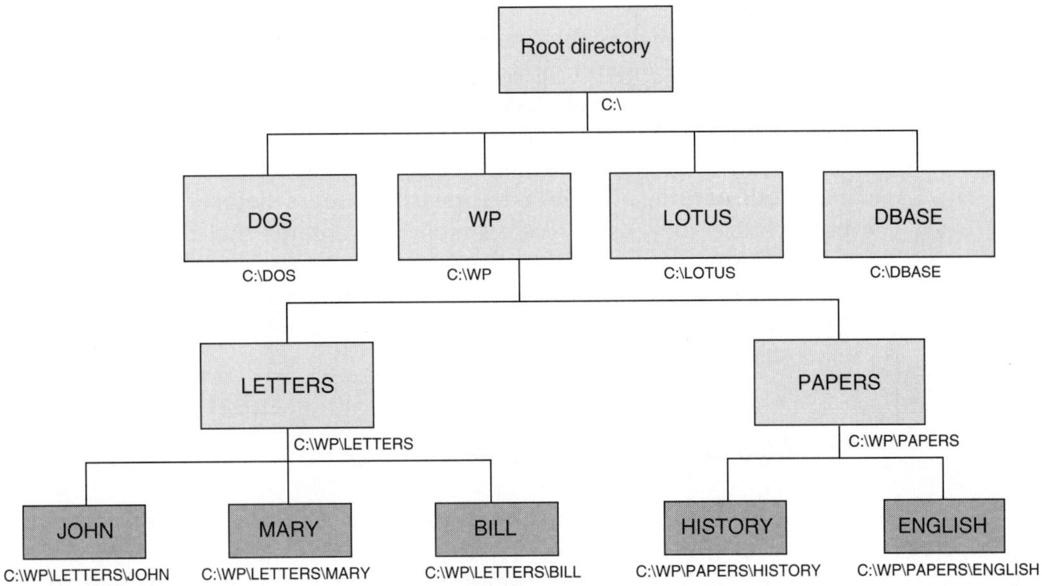

FIGURE DOS-9
A directory structure.
Shown here is a root directory and three levels of subdirectories. The subdirectory MARY, for instance, would contain all letters (files) written to Mary. Below each of the directories is its path name.

shown in Figure DOS-9. Such a hierarchy is commonly called a **directory structure.**

At the top of the structure is the main directory, known as the **root directory.** The root directory will often contain, at a minimum, some key operating system files. You can also put any other files into it. However, we will choose to store these other files in **subdirectories.**

The first level of subdirectories is often set aside, as indicated in the figure, for the operating system and for other software files. For example, the figure shows that this first level of subdirectories contains DOS, WordPerfect, Lotus 1-2-3, and dBASE. These subdirectories can be further subdivided into other, subordinate subdirectories containing program files, data files, and even other subdirectories. For instance, as shown in Figure DOS-9, you can organize the WordPerfect subdirectory by dividing letters and school papers, respectively, into lower subdirectories. If you so wish, you can add additional levels of subdirectories beyond those shown in the figure.

Later, when you want to access a file in any subdirectory, you must specify the **path** through the subdirectories to the file, for example:

C:\WP\LETTERS\MARY

Here, the hard disk is the C drive and C:\ is the designation for the root directory pertaining to this drive. WP (for WordPerfect) and LETTERS are the names of the two subdirectories on the path to a subdirectory named MARY. The MARY subdirectory contains all letters (files) written to Mary. The sequence of backward slashes (\) is used to separate the names of the subdirectories. When a backslash appears before the name of the first subdirectory, as in this example, it indicates that the path starts at the root directory.

It is also possible to set up subdirectories on diskettes. You may especially find this handy to do if you are using high-density diskettes, which have large storage capacities.

The DOS System Files and Booting

DOS consists primarily of three *system files* and several utility programs. In PC-DOS (MS-DOS), the system files may be known as IBMBIO.COM (BIO.SYS), IBMDOS.COM (MSDOS.SYS), and COMMAND.COM (COMMAND.SYS). The disk on which the system files and utilities are located is known as the **system disk,** or *DOS disk.*

The COMMAND.COM system file contains DOS's *command processor,* a set of programs that translates whatever you type in on the keyboard into a language the computer understands. COMMAND.COM also contains DOS's *internal commands* (discussed shortly). COMMAND.COM is displayed in the disk's directory, which provides a listing of the files on the disk. The other two system files, which serve control purposes, are "hidden" and not listed in the directory. A disk's directory can be seen using DOS's DIR command.

The DOS system files must always be present on a disk in order to boot from it. **Booting** is the process of getting the computer system ready to work with, or, put another way, the process of transferring the system files from the DOS disk into RAM. When you see DOS's "A> prompt" or "C> prompt" on the screen after turning your computer system on, this means that the system has been successfully booted up. This booting process will take place automatically if the system files are present on the A-drive diskette or hard disk when you flip on the power switch.

How to Boot Your Computer

Generally when you boot up your computer, DOS must be on one of the disk drives. If you have a dual-diskette system, your DOS disk must be inserted in Drive A. If you have a hard-disk system, DOS is probably stored permanently on the hard disk.

If DOS is mounted on the proper drive, the next step you take is to turn on your monitor and system unit. (It is not usually necessary to

```
Current date is Tue  1-01-1980
Enter new date (mm-dd-yy): 10-16-92


Current time is  0:03:09.65
Enter new time: 10:19
```

FIGURE DOS-10

Date and time screen messages.

turn on your printer until you have something to print.) After you turn on the computer system, it will take about 15 seconds for anything more to happen. You'll hear some whirring sounds inside the system unit. Then you will see a screen message called a **prompt,** which asks for a response from you. In many cases you'll see a prompt about the current date and time, similar to Figure DOS-10. (If you don't see a date or time prompt, but instead get an A> or C:\> prompt, skip to the next section.)

The first two lines of the prompt in Figure DOS-10 appear first; when you enter a date after the colon, the third and fourth lines appear.

It is not necessary to enter the date and time when you start the computer, but doing so allows the correct date and time to be recorded when files are saved. On some hard-disk systems, the first and third lines of the prompt will show the correct date and time because these have been preset and remain accurate; in this case, you need not type in any changes to the date and time.

You enter the date and time in exactly the format shown on the screen or in a similar format. Notice that the second line shows a format of mm-dd-yy. This means that you can type the data as one- or two-digit numbers separated by hyphens (for example, 10-16-92). In response to the date prompt, follow these two steps:

1. Type the current date (if desired)

2. Press ↵

The time prompt will next appear on the screen. To change the time shown on the third line of the prompt, type the hour and minute separated by a colon, such as 10:35. (Note, for example, if it is 10:35 a.m. you enter the time as 10:35. Or, if it is 6:23 p.m. you enter 18:23.) In response to the time prompt, follow these two steps:

1. Type the current time (if desired)

2. Press ↵

If you make an error, a new date or time prompt may appear so that you can type the entry again.

How to Change the Default Drive

When you press the Enter key after responding to the time prompt, you will see a message with DOS copyright information. Below that is the *DOS prompt* (or *system prompt*), a message that indicates what the **default drive** is—the drive the computer will read and write to unless you instruct otherwise. For instance, when you see the prompt A> or A:\> on the screen, DOS is telling you that it is ready for you to issue a command or enter data and that it is pointing to the A drive to interpret the command or write the data to.

When you want the computer to read or write to another drive, you'll need to change the default drive. Later, you'll see how to do this.

With a Hard-Disk System. If Drive C, the hard drive, is the default drive, the system prompt will look similar to C:\>. To change the default to Drive A, a diskette drive,

1. Type **A:**

2. Press ↵

The prompt on the screen will be A:\>. To change the default drive back to Drive C,

3. Type **C:**

4. Press ↵

The screen prompt will again be C:\>.

With a Dual-Diskette System. If Drive A is the default drive, A> is the DOS prompt you will see on the screen. To make Drive B the default drive,

1. Type **B:**

2. Press ↵

The prompt B> will now be on the screen. To change back to Drive A as the default,

3. Type **A:**

4. Press ↵

The screen prompt will again be A>.

Responding to an Error Message. If you try to change to a diskette drive that is not ready for reading or writing, the following *error message* will appear on the screen:

```
Abort, Retry, or Ignore?
```

When you receive that error message, be sure that the drive contains a diskette that is not damaged or write protected. The diskette should be properly inserted with the drive door closed.

After you correct the problem and still want to change the default drive, you can

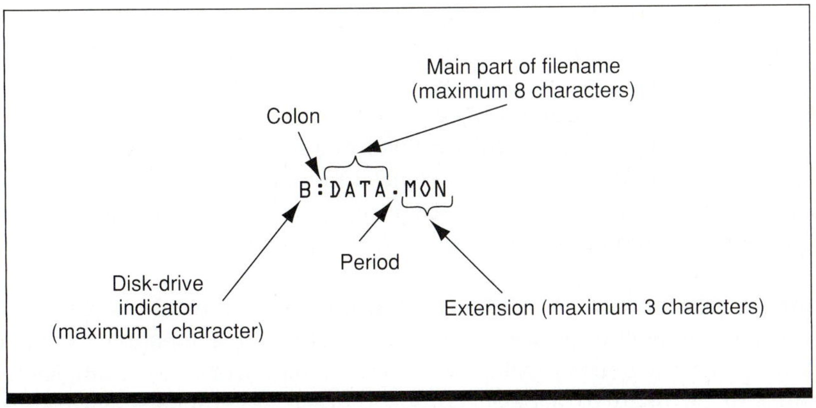

FIGURE DOS-11

DOS filename. Filenames in DOS consist of three parts. They include, from left to right, a disk-drive indicator (optional), the main part of the filename (mandatory), and an extension (optional).

1. Type **R** for Retry

2. Press ↵

How to Name Files in DOS

As you work on the computer, you'll need to assign unique names to the files you create. When you want to work on a previously created file at a later point, you must be able to recall or remember the filename you gave it.

Filenames in DOS have a maximum of three parts, which are shown in Figure DOS-11 for the filename B:DATA.MON.

The first (optional and temporary) component is the drive on which the file physically resides. It is only necessary to type in this component when the file is located on a drive other than the default drive. So, for instance, we would have to type the B: in front of the DATA.MON if A were the default drive; if B were the default drive, it wouldn't have been necessary to declare the B: explicitly. The drive specification is not saved as a permanent part of the filename because the file will likely be assigned to different drives during the course of its lifetime.

The second (mandatory) component is the main part of the filename, which consists of one to eight characters. In many software packages, this part of the filename must begin with a letter and cannot contain special characters. If you type a name that exceeds eight characters, DOS will truncate (eliminate) all characters after the first eight.

The third (optional) component is the **extension** to the main part of the filename. The extension consists of a period followed by one to three characters. Extensions are useful for qualifying related files, for example,

```
DATA.MON
DATA.TUE
DATA.WED
```

You should be careful to choose names for your files that will help you to remember what is on them and how to locate them. If you choose a filename that is obscure, you may have great difficulty locating it again if you have a large number of files.

You may find it helpful to develop a system for naming files. For example, you could start each file related to a particular academic course with an abbreviation (ENG, BIO, SOC) followed by some further identifier (TERM for term paper, REP for report; SPCH for speech).

Wildcard Characters. A **wildcard character** is a special character that can stand for one or more regular characters in a filename. Wildcard characters have been developed to save users work, so a single command can be used to access, copy, or erase several files with similar names. Wildcard characters are not used to name files but instead are used to refer to files when working with the DOS commands that we will be covering shortly.

In DOS, there are two principal wildcard characters:

```
? and *
```

The ? wildcard character is used to stand for a *single* character in a filename. For instance, let's say you've created four files on the default drive, naming them FRED1, FRED2, FRED3, and FRED4. If you wanted to erase all of them later you would tell DOS to erase

```
FRED?
```

If, instead, the files you wished to erase were named FRED11, FRED12, FRED13, and FRED14, you would have to tell DOS to erase

```
FRED??
```

With the ? wildcard character, every question mark that you declare is assigned to a specific character position in the filename. Each acts as a substitute for any character that occupies that particular position in the filename.

If you wanted to use the ? wildcard character to erase FRED1, FRED2, FRED3, FRED4, FRED11, FRED12, FRED13, and FRED14, you would have to do it in two passes, erasing the first four with FRED? and the last four with FRED?? You could, however, do the erasure in a single pass by using the * wildcard character. This character can be used to represent *several* character positions in a filename; for instance,

```
FRED*
```

Since the main part of the filename can consist of up to eight characters, we are telling DOS in this example to erase all files having FRED as the first four letters in the main part of the filename; any remaining characters of the filename are unimportant.

If, instead, we have named the files FRED1.X, FRED2.X, FRED3.X, and FRED4.Y, asking DOS to erase

```
FRED*.X
```

would erase the first three FRED files but not the fourth. To erase all four files, we would have to ask DOS to erase

```
FRED*.*
```

Wildcard characters can prove disastrous if we make mistakes when taking shortcuts. For instance, if we had told DOS to erase from disk

```
FR*.*
```

and there were files named FRIEND1 and FRIEND2 that we wanted to keep on the disk, they would be erased, too.

AUTOEXEC.BAT File. AUTOEXEC.BAT is a special file that DOS looks for when the system is being booted up. If it finds the AUTOEXEC.BAT filename in its directory, it will automatically issue all of the commands in the file; if it doesn't, it will immediately default to the system prompt. AUTOEXEC.BAT is used to do such tasks as set up a path to subdirectories, personalize the system prompt, and start an applications package when the system is booted. AUTOEXEC.BAT must be in the root directory of the system disk.

So, for instance, if DOS found the command

```
LOTUS
```

in the AUTOEXEC.BAT file—a command that says invoke Lotus 1-2-3—it would automatically execute this command and put you into Lotus 1-2-3. In other words, the results will be the same as if you had issued the LOTUS command to the system prompt. You can put as many commands as you like in the AUTOEXEC.BAT file.

Incidentally, BAT is a special DOS extension that stands for "batch." Whenever DOS sees a filename with this extension, it automatically assumes that the associated file contains a collection, or batch, of DOS commands. Keep in mind, however, that the AUTOEXEC.BAT file is the only batch file that DOS looks for as it is booting up the computer system.

Possibly, your instructor has already established an AUTOEXEC.BAT file on your computer system, so you will not need to create one.

CONFIG.SYS File. CONFIG.SYS is another special file that DOS reads during booting. This file establishes such things as the maximum number of files that can be used at one time, the number of file buffers and stacks to be put into use, communications with nonstandard system devices (such as a scanner or a mouse), and a number of other system directives. Whenever you are installing a new software package, the documentation included with it will specify acceptable settings of CONFIG.SYS directives.

Your instructor may have already established a CONFIG.SYS file on your computer system so you will not need to create one.

How to Turn Off the Computer

Your instructor will give you specific instructions about what to do when you are ready to end your work session on the computer.

Before you turn off a computer, your screen must show the system prompt, which is usually A> on a dual-diskette system and C:\> on a hard-disk system. These prompts will be your starting and ending screen messages. Generally, whatever equipment you turned on to start the computer system will need to be turned off when you finish your session.

USING DOS COMMANDS

Once the DOS prompt is on the screen, the computer is ready to receive instructions from you. Each time you type in a DOS command, you instruct a DOS program to do a specific task for you, such as preparing a diskette to store data, examining the files on a disk, or copying files from one disk to a backup disk.

DOS commands are either internal or external. **Internal commands** are transferred to RAM when the computer system is turned on, and can be used at any time. All internal commands are located in DOS's COMMAND.COM file. **External commands**—which are sometimes called *DOS utilities*—are not put in RAM when the computer system is turned on and are stored in separate files on the system disk. To use an external command, you need to specify the drive that contains its file if it isn't on the default drive (by typing the letter of the drive followed by a colon) as well as the name of the file. With a dual-diskette system, your DOS disk will need to be in a drive to carry out an external command. With a hard-disk system, you may first need to access the subdirectory where your external files are stored before you can invoke an external command. (Usually this will automatically be done for you through a PATH command in the AUTOEXEC.BAT file.)

To issue each DOS command, you will be directed to type some characters, after which you press Enter to start the execution of the command. In the subsections to follow, each direction is a numbered sentence in which the character(s) you type and the key(s) you press appear in bold print. Though the commands are printed in uppercase (capital) letters to make them easier to see, you can type with any combination of upper- and lowercase letters. However, if you see a space between the characters in a command, be sure to press the space bar at that point as you type.

The VER Command

The **VER** command displays the DOS version number currently in use. DOS comes in two principal forms: PC-DOS and MS-DOS. Both were developed by Microsoft Corporation of Bellevue, Washington. Except for a few minor differences, these operating systems are virtually identical. PC-DOS was created originally for the IBM PC, while MS-DOS was devised to operate on computer systems that look and work very much like the IBM PC. Both the PC-DOS and MS-DOS operating systems have been revised many times since they were first developed. Each major revision is referred to as a *version* (sometimes also called a *revision* or *release*).

If you want to know which version of DOS you are using, follow these instructions, starting at your DOS prompt.

1. Type **VER**

2. Press ↵

VER is an internal command.

The CLS Command

CLS, for Clear Screen, is perhaps the easiest DOS command to use. Entering this command clears the screen, leaving only the command prompt. To clear the screen,

1. Type **CLS**

2. Press ↵

CLS is an internal command.

The DIR Command

To see a list of the names of files on a disk or in a particular **directory** (root directory or subdirectory), you can use any of several variations of the **DIR** command. DIR is an internal command.

The DOS Directory. One important directory, which is informally called the "DOS directory," usually contains all DOS files.

On hard disks, the DOS directory is often located in a subdirectory named DOS. Before issuing an external DOS command, you must be at the prompt of the directory or in a subdirectory that contains or is linked to the file for that command.

On dual-diskette systems with the system disk in Drive A, the Drive A directory normally contains all DOS files.

With DOS Files in a Subdirectory. If your subdirectory is not called "DOS," substitute the name of your DOS subdirectory for "DOS" below. Start at the system prompt and

1. Type **CD\DOS** and press ↵

You will see a DOS directory prompt similar to C:\DOS>. To view the DOS directory

2. Type **DIR** and press ↵

With DOS Files in the Default Directory. To see a directory of DOS files, start at the DOS system prompt and

1. Type **DIR**

2. Press ↵

On the screen you'll see the directory files scrolling rapidly. *Scrolling* is the way the computer lets you see lines of text on the screen when there is too much text to fit on just one screen. Once the screen initially fills, as you see another line at the bottom, the line at the top disappears. With the DIR command, the scrolling is automatic to the end of the directory.

The directory screen will look similar to Figure DOS-12. You'll notice that each file occupies one line of the directory. Listed from left to right are the file's name, extension, size (expressed as the number of bytes of storage space it occupies on the disk), and date and time of creation. The most important information is the filename and extension, which you'll need to specify when retrieving a file.

At the end of the directory is a message showing the total number of files and the total number of bytes free on the disk (storage space not now occupied by files).

The DIR/P Command. When you use the DIR command to see a long directory, the filenames scroll too fast for you to read them. The DIR/P command allows you to view a directory one screen (also called a *screen page*) at a time. This command can be invoked at the prompt of any drive, directory, or subdirectory. To practice it now

1. Type **DIR/P**

2. Press ↵ to see the first page

3. To see subsequent pages, keep pressing ↵ until the end of the directory

The DIR/W Command. Sometimes you check a directory just to get one or more specific filenames from a long list. The DIR/W command allows you to see more filenames at one time, since just filenames and extensions are listed across the width of the screen. To practice this command

1. Type **DIR/W**

2. Press ↵

To View the Nondefault Directory. When you give the DIR command without specifying a disk drive, the computer assumes you want a directory of the default drive. You can use a variation of the DIR command to

```
A>DIR

 Volume in drive A has no label
 Directory of  A:\

COMMAND  COM    25307    3-17-92  12:00p
FORMAT   COM    11616    3-18-92  12:00p
DISKCOPY COM     6295    3-17-92  12:00p
EDLIN    COM     7526    3-17-92  12:00p
CHKDSK   COM     9850    3-18-92  12:00p
ASSIGN   COM     1561    3-17-92  12:00p
ATTRIB   EXE     9529    3-17-92  12:00p
COMP     COM     4214    3-17-92  12:00p
        8 File(s)    281600 bytes free

A>
```

FIGURE DOS-12
DOS directory screen.

see a directory of a drive other than the default. The instructions below are intended for your future use when working in an applications program; they cannot be executed now since you have not yet inserted a diskette in your other drive.

With a Hard-Disk System. To see a directory of Drive A (a diskette drive)

1. Type **DIR A:**

2. Press ↵

If your hard-disk system has two diskette drives, you will use DIR B: to see a directory of the other diskette drive.

With a Dual-Diskette System. To see a directory of Drive B, start at the A> prompt.

1. Type **DIR B:**

2. Press ↵

Other Forms of the DIR Command. The DIR command can be used in a variety of other ways, as the following examples suggest.

- □ DIR *.PCT lists the names of all files on the default drive with a PCT extension.
- □ DIR B:MARY.* lists the names of all files on the B drive with MARY as the main part of the filename.
- □ DIR/W B:CHAP* lists, widthwise on the screen, the names of all files on the B drive with CHAP as the first four letters in the main part of the filename.
- □ DIR \WP lists the names of all files in the WP subdirectory (see Figure DOS-9).

□ DIR \WP\LETTERS lists the names of all files in the LETTERS subdirectory (see Figure DOS-9).

The FORMAT Command

FORMAT, an external command, is one of the most frequently used and important of the DOS commands. The FORMAT command prepares a new diskette for use or erases the contents of an old diskette, making it reusable.

You will need to format every new blank diskette. The computer will refuse to read or write to an unformatted diskette.

You must be very cautious about issuing the FORMAT command with a diskette that may already have been formatted and used. Formatting erases all data on the specified disk. To see if a diskette contains any files, use the DIR command before formatting.

Never issue the FORMAT command without specifying the drive letter that will contain the diskette you want to format. The FORMAT command without a drive letter (or with the wrong drive letter) could erase the contents of your DOS diskette or hard drive. Because FORMAT is an external command, you will need to place your DOS disk in Drive A with a dual-diskette system. If you are using a hard-drive system without an automatic linkage to the DOS subdirectory, you must change to this subdirectory before issuing the FORMAT command.

Before following the directions below, make sure that the diskette you wish to format matches the specifications on the diskette drive you are using. The instructions that follow apply to formatting low-density disks in low-density drives and high-density disks in high-density drives. To format low-density diskettes in high-density drives, read the section that immediately follows the double-column instructions.

With a Hard-Disk System. The following instructions for formatting a new diskette assume that you need to change to a subdirectory named DOS.

1. Type **CD\DOS** and press ↵

You will now be at the DOS subdirectory prompt. If the diskette to be formatted is to be placed in Drive A

2. Type **FORMAT A:**

3. Press ↵

4. Insert the diskette in Drive A and press ↵

You'll see a screen message similar to Figure DOS-13, but specify-

With a Dual-Diskette System. To format the B-drive diskette, your DOS disk should be in Drive A. At the A> prompt

1. Type **FORMAT B:**

2. Press ↵

You'll see a screen message telling you to

3. Insert a blank diskette in Drive B

4. Press ↵ to begin formatting

After you do this, you'll hear some whirring sounds in the computer and then see the screen message shown in Figure DOS-13 when the format is complete. In response to the final question

```
A>FORMAT B:
Insert new diskette for drive B:
and strike ENTER when ready

Formatting...Format complete

     362496 bytes total disk space
     362496 bytes available on disk

Format another (Y/N)? N
A>
```

This message indicates a successful format

FIGURE DOS-13
FORMAT screen message.

ing A: instead of B: as the drive. After formatting, when asked if you want to format another diskette

5. Type **N** for No and then press ↵

If DOS files are in a subdirectory, you can return to the system prompt if you

6. Type **CD** and press ↵

about formatting another disk, you'll type Y or N, depending on whether you want another disk formatted. In this case

5. Type **N** for No

6. Press ↵

Your screen shows the system prompt again, as indicated in the figure.

Formatting Low-Density Diskettes in High-Density Drives. The FORMAT command must be supplemented with special switches when you want to format a low-density (double-density) diskette in a high-density drive. When faced with this type of formatting situation, follow the rules below.

□ ***5¼-inch diskettes:*** To format a 360-kilobyte diskette in a 1.2 megabyte drive, use the /F:360 switch. For example, if Drive A is 1.2 megabytes and you are formatting a 360-kilobyte diskette there,

1. Type **FORMAT A: /F:360**

2. Press ↵

□ ***3½-inch diskettes:*** To format a 720-kilobyte diskette in a 1.44-megabyte drive, use the /F:720 switch. For example, if Drive B is 1.44 megabytes and you are formatting a 720-kilobyte diskette there,

1. Type **FORMAT B: /F:720**

2. Press ↵

Note that while it is possible to format low-density disks in high-density drives, it is *not* possible to format high-density disks in low-density drives.

The UNFORMAT Command. Version 5 of DOS introduces an UNFORMAT command that, under certain circumstances, lets you unformat (reconstruct) an accidentally reformatted hard disk or diskette to recover any files lost during the reformat. This command works optimally if you discover the inadvertent erasure immediately, before you have written anything new to the disk. At the command prompt, to unformat a diskette,

1. Depending on the drive on which you will be mounting the disk to be unformatted, type **UNFORMAT A:** and press ↵ or type **UNFORMAT B:** and press ↵
2. When the prompt appears onscreen, insert the diskette to be unformatted and press ↵

The CHKDSK Command

This external DOS command checks a disk for errors and for damage that might endanger files stored on the disk. **CHKDSK** displays special messages if it finds anything wrong with your disk and gives you a status report of its condition. This command should be run occasionally on all your diskettes, especially those containing important data files.

Follow these steps when you wish to use the CHKDSK command.

With a Hard-Disk System. You should start at the DOS subdirectory prompt and have the disk to be checked in Drive A.

1. Type **CHKDSK A:**
2. Press ↵

With a Dual-Diskette System. Your DOS disk should be in Drive A and the diskette you want to check in Drive B.

1. Type **CHKDSK B:**
2. Press ↵

If there are no errors on the disk that was checked, you'll see a screen message similar to the one in Figure DOS-14.

The COPY Command

One of the most useful DOS commands is **COPY,** an internal command. You generally will use this command to copy one or more files from the *source disk,* where they are now stored, to a *target disk,* where you want the copies stored. When you have completed copying the files, they are on both the source disk and the target disk.

There are many reasons to copy files. Your instructor or a friend may ask for a copy of a project you have completed. Or, you may want to store a file on several diskettes, where it can be used for different purposes. The COPY command is also used to make backup copies of your files.

Since COPY is an internal command, you can issue it at the system prompt at any time. You can copy one file or a group of files using the COPY command.

```
A>CHKDSK B:

   362496   bytes total disk space
    78848   bytes in 1 user files
   283648   bytes available on disk

   655360   bytes total memory
   590448   bytes free
```

FIGURE DOS-14
CHKDSK screen message.

Copying One File. Usually you will use the COPY command to copy a data file. Since you have not yet created a data file, you will copy the DOS file named ASSIGN.COM to your formatted data diskette. This is for practice purposes only. In general, you should not copy software like DOS that is protected by copyright. If you cannot locate ASSIGN.COM, pick another DOS file to copy.

When you are copying a file from one disk to another, you must type both the filename and the extension (separated by a period), along with the letter of the drive containing the target disk. If you make an error in the spacing or typing, simply backspace and retype to make the corrections before pressing the Enter key.

To avoid accidentally erasing a file on the DOS disk, you should copy protect it. For example, on a 5¼″ diskette, covering the write-protect notch (see Figure DOS-7a) with a piece of tape prevents the diskette from being written to or erased; however, you can still read or copy files from the diskette.

With a Hard-Disk System. Your source disk is usually the hard disk, and your target disk goes in Drive A. Starting at C:\DOS>

1. Type **COPY ASSIGN.COM A:**
2. Press ↵

With a Dual-Diskette System. The source disk (in this case, the DOS disk) should be in Drive A. The target disk goes in Drive B. Starting at A>

1. Type **COPY ASSIGN.COM B:**
2. Press ↵

A message will appear when the copying process is complete, saying

```
1 File(s) copied.
```

Copying More than One File. As with DIR, the COPY command can also be used with wildcard characters to duplicate a group of files. The files you copy from the source disk automatically replace target disk files that have the same name. Sometimes you want this replacement. However, if you want to save both versions of the material in the file, be sure the source or target disk's version has a slightly different name.

Below are some examples showing relatively simple uses for the COPY command:

- COPY BOB FRED copies a file named BOB on the default drive to a file named FRED on the same drive.
- COPY *.LET B: instructs the computer to copy all files with the .LET extension from the default-drive disk to the B-drive disk.
- COPY *.* B: copies all files on the source disk to the B-drive disk.

Follow the steps below to copy all DOS files with the extension .COM to your formatted diskette. The ASSIGN.COM file copied earlier will automatically be replaced by the source disk's file with the same name.

With a Hard-Disk System. Your source disk is usually the hard disk, and your target disk goes in Drive A. Starting at C:\DOS>

1. Type **COPY *.COM A:**

2. Press ↵

You can copy all files on the diskette in Drive A back to the hard disk (Drive C) using these steps:

3. Type **COPY A:*.* C:\DOS**

4. Press ↵

The files you just copied from the diskette will replace files of the same name on the hard disk. A message will appear when the copying process is complete, indicating the number of files copied.

With a Dual-Diskette System. The source disk (in this case, the DOS disk) should be in Drive A. The target disk goes in Drive B. Starting at A>

1. Type **COPY *.COM B:**

2. Press ↵

To copy all files from the source disk in Drive A to the target disk in Drive B,

3. Type **COPY *.* B:**

4. Press ↵

Copying Files between Subdirectories. You can also use the COPY command to copy a file from one subdirectory to another. The main thing to remember is that along with any filename you must specify the source and target subdirectory paths. The following examples will clarify this process:

- COPY \CHAPTER.* \BOOK copies all files in the root directory with CHAPTER as the main part of the filename into a subdirectory named book.
- COPY CHAPTER.* A:\BOOK\SECTION1 copies all files in the current directory with CHAPTER as the main part of the filename into a subdirectory named SECTION1 on the A drive.

The COPY CON Command

The **COPY CON** command enables you to create DOS files such as AUTOEXEC.BAT, CONFIG.SYS, and others at the keyboard. CON is short for "console," which, in the computer field, refers to the keyboard. COPY CON takes the file that you create at the keyboard and copies it onto disk, thereby enabling it to be executed whenever you wish.

Here we will create a small file with COPY CON. The file we create will contain the words, "THIS IS A TEST".

With a Hard-Disk System. Make sure you are at the C:\> prompt, and then

1. Type **A:**
2. Press ↵
3. At the A:\> prompt type **COPY CON TEST**
4. Press ↵
5. Type **THIS IS A TEST**
6. Hold down the Ctrl key while pressing the **Z** key
7. Press ↵
8. To make sure TEST is in the directory, type **DIR**
9. Press ↵

With a Dual-Diskette System. Make sure you are at the A> prompt, and then

1. Type **B:**
2. Press ↵
3. At the A> prompt type **COPY CON TEST**
4. Press ↵
5. Type **THIS IS A TEST**
6. Hold down the Ctrl key while pressing the **Z** key
7. Press ↵
8. To make sure TEST is in the directory, type **DIR**
9. Press ↵

Note that by holding down the Ctrl key and pressing the Z key, you are indicating the end of the file. By next hitting the Enter key, you are in effect telling DOS to copy (save) the file onto disk, and you should get a screen message saying

```
1 File(s) copied
```

followed by the system prompt. You can use DOS's TYPE command, discussed next, to examine the contents of TEST if you wish.

Like COPY, COPY CON is an internal command.

The Type Command

While the DIR command enables you to see the names of the files located in a particular directory, the **TYPE** command enables you to get a listing of any text (ASCII) file you create through DOS or through any other software package. So, for instance, it is a particularly handy command to use for getting a listing of the AUTOEXEC.BAT file, the CONFIG.SYS file, or any file created through the COPY CON command.

To use TYPE, first point to the disk that contains the TEST file that you just created with the COPY CON command. Then

1. Type **TYPE TEST**

2. Press ↵

At this point the contents of the file should display onscreen.

TYPE is an internal command.

The DISKCOPY Command

Like the COPY *.* command, the **DISKCOPY** command copies all files from one diskette to another. There are some important differences between the two commands, however. For one, DISKCOPY is an external command while COPY is an internal command. Also, DISKCOPY erases the contents of the target disk and formats the target disk before copying the source disk's files. You will want to use DISKCOPY when you have a new unformatted diskette onto which you want to copy the entire contents of another diskette. But be careful not to use DISKCOPY if the target disk has any files you want to save. (Use the DIR/P command to check the filenames.) If you use the COPY *.* command, the files originally on the target disk will still be there, with the exception of files replaced by identically named copies. Also, you cannot use DISKCOPY to copy the contents of a hard disk onto a diskette.

The DISKCOPY command also copies any imperfections the source disk may have. If the source disk may be bad, use the COPY *.* command.

With a Hard-Disk System. The diskette onto which you copied all files with the .COM extension will be the source disk. You'll need another blank diskette for the target disk. If Drive A is your only diskette drive, start at your DOS subdirectory prompt (C:\DOS>) and

1. Type **DISKCOPY A: A:**

2. Press ↵

Responding to the screen message,

3. Insert the source diskette in Drive A

4. Press ↵

Responding to the next screen message,

With a Dual-Diskette System. Your DOS disk should be in Drive A. Starting at A>

1. Type **DISKCOPY A: B:**

2. Press ↵

The screen message shown in Figure DOS-15 will direct you to insert the source and target diskettes. If you were going to use DISKCOPY with a source diskette other than your DOS disk, you would remove the DOS disk and insert the source diskette in Drive A. In this case, since your source (DOS) diskette is already there, you need only

3. Insert the target diskette in Drive B

```
A>DISKCOPY A: B:

Insert SOURCE diskette in drive A:

Insert TARGET diskette in drive B:

Press any key when ready . . .

Copying 40 tracks
9 Sectors/Track, 2 Side(s)

Copy another diskette (Y/N)? N

A>
```

FIGURE DOS-15
DISKCOPY screen message for a dual-diskette system.
When using the DISKCOPY command, double-check to make sure that the target diskette does not contain any files you wish to keep.

DOS

5. Remove the source diskette and insert the target diskette in Drive A

6. Press ↵

When the entire diskette has been copied, a message will ask if you want to copy another.

7. Type **N** for No

Note: If your system has two diskette drives, you could type DISKCOPY A: B: and follow the screen prompts for inserting the source and target disks.

4. Press ↵

When the entire diskette has been copied, a message will ask if you want to copy another.

5. Type **N** for No

The RENAME (REN) Command

RENAME (REN) is an internal command that allows you to change the name of an existing file. When you are creating new data files, it is common to rename old files for the purpose of clarity. For example, you may type a letter to your sister and name the file LETTER. Later when you want to type more letters, you can use the REN command to rename the first file. In this exercise you will rename one of the DOS files you just copied onto your data diskette. The ASSIGN.COM file will be renamed as FILE.NEW so that you can easily spot it in a directory.

With a Hard-Disk System. Your data diskette should be in Drive A. Starting at C:\>

1. Type **REN A:ASSIGN.COM FILE.NEW**
2. Press ↵
3. Type **DIR/P A:** and keep pressing ↵ until you see FILE.NEW in the list
4. Keep pressing ↵ until the end

With a Dual-Diskette System. Your data diskette should be in Drive B. Starting at A>

1. Type **REN B:ASSIGN.COM FILE.NEW**
2. Press ↵
3. Type **DIR/P B:** and keep pressing ↵ until you see FILE.NEW in the list
4. Keep pressing ↵ until the end

The ERASE Command

The **ERASE** command will erase one, some, or all files from a disk. The ERASE command needs to be used with caution. Be certain that you want to erase files permanently before using this command.

This internal command is useful for erasing unwanted files from your disk. Sometimes files are accidentally saved under different but similar filenames when the contents of the files are exactly the same. Occasionally a data file is accidentally saved on the DOS disk. In these instances, you can erase unwanted files from the disk and thus "clean" the disk so that you have more room to save files you create in the future.

To specify a group of files to erase, you can use the asterisk (*) wildcard character in the same way you used it with other commands; for instance

☐ ERASE B:*.LET erases all files on Drive B with the .LET extension.

☐ ERASE B:LETTER.* erases all files on Drive B with the name LETTER.

☐ ERASE B:*.* erases all files on Drive B.

For this exercise you will start by erasing the file named FILE.NEW that you renamed in the preceding section. Then you will erase all of the DOS files you copied onto your data diskette.

With a Hard-Disk System. Your data diskette should be in Drive A. Starting at C:\>

1. Type **ERASE A:FILE.NEW**
2. When you are sure the drive and filename are typed correctly, press ↵

You will return to the system prompt C:\>. To erase all files from the data diskette in Drive A,

3. Type **ERASE A:*.***

With a Dual-Diskette System. Your data diskette should be in Drive B. Starting at A>

1. Type **ERASE B:FILE.NEW**
2. When you are sure the drive and filename are typed correctly, press ↵

   You will return to the system prompt A>. To erase all files from the data diskette in Drive B,

3. Type **ERASE B:*.***

Double-check to be sure you have typed the correct drive designation in a global ERASE command. If you typed ERASE C: by mistake, you would erase your hard disk.

4. Press ↵

The screen will ask, Are you sure (Y/N)?

5. Type **Y** for Yes

Double-check to be sure you have typed the correct drive designation in a global ERASE command. If you typed ERASE A:, you would mistakenly erase the wrong disk. When you are sure,

4. Press ↵

The screen will ask, Are you sure (Y/N)?

5. Type **Y** for Yes

DOS also has a DELETE (DEL) command that works exactly like ERASE and produces the same results. To use DELETE, just substitute DELETE (or DEL) for ERASE in the preceding examples.

The UNDELETE Command. Version 5 of DOS introduces an UNDELETE command that, under certain circumstances, lets you restore files previously marked for deletion with the ERASE or DELETE commands. For best results, you should use this command *immediately* after you've made an inadvertent deletion, before you've written any more files to disk. To invoke UNDELETE, make sure you are in the directory in which you wish to undelete and

1. Type **UNDELETE <filename.ext>** (Note: Do *not* type in the angle brackets. They are used here only to show a filename is to be supplied.

2. Press ↵

Note that

☐ **UNDELETE FRED** lets you restore a previously deleted file named FRED from the default drive.

☐ **UNDELETE *.BAT** restores all files with a .BAT extension. DOS will prompt for a yes or no response on each recoverable .BAT file, asking you whether you want it undeleted or not. If you want to undelete a file, answer Y to the prompt and type in the first letter of the file's name, to replace the question mark DOS is displaying in that position in the name.

UNDELETE is an external command.

The MKDIR (MD) Command

Since diskettes and especially hard disks can store such a large number of files, users find it helpful to organize their files into subdirectories. You use the **MKDIR** (**MD** for short) command to create these subdirectories.

In the exercise below, you will use the MKDIR (MD) command to create a new subdirectory named WP on your data diskette for the

FIGURE DOS-16
WP subdirectory created with MKDIR command.

```
A>MD\WP

A>DIR A:

Volume in drive A has no label
Directory of A:\

WP         <DIR>       9-22-92  11:14a
       1 File(s)   361472 bytes free

A>
```

WordPerfect data files you will create in the next section of this guide. With your data diskette in Drive A,

1. Type **A:** and press ↵ to make Drive A the default
2. Type **MD\WP** and press ↵ to create the WP subdirectory
3. Type **DIR** to verify that WP is listed as a subdirectory

Your directory will look similar to Figure DOS-16.

To create a letters subdirectory *below* your WP directory, similar to what you see in Figure DOS-9,

1. Type **MD\WP\LETTERS**
2. Press ↵

Note that a complete path through the tree is specified—one that extends from the root directory (which is implied by the slash after MD), through the WP directory, to the directory being created. We could have issued this particular form of the MD command from any subdirectory, since specifying the complete path leaves no question about where the new directory will be created.

DOS also allows us to leave out the path to the directory being created when we are already in the directory or subdirectory which will be immediately above it. For instance, if we had been located in the WP subdirectory, we could have issued the following shortened version of the MD command:

```
MD LETTERS
```

MD is an internal DOS command.

The CHDIR (CD) Command

The **CHDIR** (**CD** for short) command allows you to change your default directory. You will now use this command to move to the WP subdirectory you just created on your data diskette, which should still be in Drive A.

1. Type **CD\WP**

2. Press ↵

This places you in the WP subdirectory. Note that the system prompt has changed to

```
A:\WP>
```

To get back to the root directory,

1. Type **CD**

2. Press ↵

Note that you are back at the A:\> prompt. To get to the LETTERS subdirectory,

1. Type **CD\WP\LETTERS**

2. Press ↵

Note that the system prompt has changed to

```
A:\WP\LETTERS>
```

Because the command you just typed in had a backslash after the CD, placing you back in the root directory, you could have issued it from any subdirectory (such as HISTORY in Figure DOS-9) and produced the same result.

As with the MD command, you do not have to specify the complete path to the directory to which you wish to move if you are already in one of the subdirectories that is superior to it. For instance, if you are already in the WP subdirectory, you need only issue the command

```
CD LETTERS
```

to get to the LETTERS subdirectory. Note that this command implicitly tells DOS exactly which path to take to get from the current subdirectory to the one it must change to.

Before we leave the CD command, go back to the WP subdirectory to see what's there by following the steps below.

1. Type **CD\WP** and press ↵

2. Type **DIR** and press ↵

Note that you will get output similar to the that in Figure DOS-17. If you had issued the DIR command from the root directory, you would *not* have

FIGURE DOS-17
Using the CHDIR command to switch directories.

```
A:\WP\LETTERS>CD\WP

A:\WP>DIR

 Volume in drive A has no label
 Directory of A:\WP

.            <DIR>      02-22-92  11:59a
..           <DIR>      02-22-92  11:59a
LETTERS      <DIR>      02-22-92  12:00p
        3 File(s)     361472 bytes free

A:\WP>
```

found the LETTERS subdirectory, because DIR only supplies names of *immediately subordinate* directories. To get a more complete directory structure, you would use the TREE command, discussed next.

CD is an internal DOS command.

The Tree Command

One of the problems with hard disks is that you may over time create so many subdirectories and files that it is easy to forget the names of subdirectories, how they are related to one another, and which files are in each. Fortunately, the **TREE** command enables DOS to supply any or all of this forgotten information to you upon request.

There are two widely used forms of the tree command. For instance, following the steps below

1. Type **CD** and press ↵ to get back to the root directory

2. Type **TREE** and press ↵

will provide a listing of the complete directory structure. Figure DOS-18 shows the output from this command.

On the other hand, the command

```
TREE/F
```

would list not only the information in Figure DOS-18 but also all of the names of the files contained in each of the subdirectories. This particular form of the TREE command can result in a lot of output if your disk has

```
A:\>tree
Directory PATH listing
A:.
└──WP
    └──LETTERS

A:\>
```

FIGURE DOS-18
Using the TREE command to show all subdirectories under the root directory.

hundreds of files. At this point, however, we have not created any files in our subdirectories.

TREE is an external DOS command.

The RMDIR (RD) Command

If you find that you no longer need a subdirectory, you can use the **RMDIR** (**RD** for short) command to remove the subdirectory from the disk. Before a subdirectory can be removed, however, it must be empty of files. Therefore, you will need to erase all files first or move them to a different subdirectory. Also, you cannot remove a subdirectory when you are in it.

If you wish to remove the LETTERS subdirectory you created on your data diskette, you can do so because it does not contain any files. To remove the LETTERS subdirectory, move to the subdirectory right above it, WP.

1. Type **CD\ WP** and press ↵ to return to the WP subdirectory of Drive A
2. Type **RD LETTERS** and press ↵
3. Type **DIR** and press ↵ to verify that the LETTERS subdirectory is not listed

RMDIR is an internal command.

The PATH Command

The **PATH** command is a relatively advanced DOS command and we will address it here only in passing.

To execute a program, you must be pointed to the directory or subdirectory in which that program is located. Fortunately, DOS's PATH command enables you to get around this problem by setting up a pointer to another directory when you want to use a program from it. The PATH command can only point to files with COM, EXE, or BAT extensions. Commonly, a PATH command is set up in the AUTOEXEC.BAT file.

Let's say we are in the SMITH subdirectory on drive C and wish to issue a DOS external command while in that subdirectory. By having the PATH command

```
PATH C:\DOS
```

in your AUTOEXEC.BAT file, the operating system will look in the DOS subdirectory for any file it cannot find in SMITH.

A PATH command will remain in effect until we issue another PATH command or issue the command

```
PATH;
```

which will cancel the current PATH command. If at any time we are unsure of the current PATH command and wish to have it displayed, we can issue the PATH command without anything appearing to the right of it—that is,

```
PATH
```

PATH is an internal DOS command.

COMMAND REFERENCE

This is a quick reference guide and should primarily be used to look up commands after completing the preceding tutorials. Upon completion of the tutorials, refer to this summary for quick reference to key commands. Do not type in the angle brackets (< >) used in a command syntax. They appear only to show that a name needs to be supplied.

With a Hard-Disk System. Invoke internal commands at C:\> (the system prompt) and external commands at C:\DOS> (the DOS subdirectory prompt).

With a Dual-Diskette System. Invoke all commands at A.> For external commands, the DOS disk must be in Drive A.

CHDIR (CD) Command

Internal command that moves you from one directory or subdirectory to another in the default drive.

Type **CD \<directory name>** and press ↵ *or* **CD <directory name>** and press ↵

CHKDSK Command

External command that displays a status report on a disk.

With a Hard-Disk System. With your data diskette in Drive A,

Type **CHKDSK A:** and press ↵

With a Dual-Diskette System. With your data diskette in Drive B,

Type **CHKDSK B:** and press ↵

CLS Command

Internal command that clears the screen, leaving only the command prompt.

Type **CLS** and press ↵

COPY Command

Internal command that allows you to copy one or more files.

With a Dual-Diskette System. The source disk goes in Drive A and the target disk in Drive B.

To copy one file,

Type **COPY <filename.ext> B:** and press ↵

To copy all files with the same extension,

Type **COPY *.<ext> B:** and press ↵

To copy all files with the same filename but different extensions,

Type **COPY <filename>.* B:** and press ↵

To copy all files,

Type **COPY *.* B:** and press ↵

With a Hard-Disk System. The target disk should be in Drive A.

To copy one file,

Type **COPY <filename.ext> A:** and press ↵

To copy all files with the same extension,

Type **COPY *.<ext> A:** and press ↵

To copy all files with the same filename but different extensions,

Type **COPY <filename>.* A:** and press ↵

To copy all files,

Type **COPY *.* A:** and press ↵

COPY CON Command

Internal command used to create files in DOS, at the keyboard, that are copied onto disk.

Type **COPY CON <filename>** and press ↵

DIR Command

Internal command that displays names of files on a disk.

- □ To see the default drive directory,
  Type **DIR** and press ↵
- □ To see the default drive directory one page at a time,
  Type **DIR/P** and press ↵
- □ To see a directory of filenames across the width of the screen,
  Type **DIR/W** and press ↵
- □ To see a directory of Drive B,
  Type **DIR B:** and press ↵

DISKCOPY Command

External command that erases all files on the target disk and formats it before copying the contents of the source disk onto the target disk.

With a Hard-Disk System. Starting at C:\DOS>,

Type **DISKCOPY A: A:** and press ↵. Then follow the screen prompts.

With a Dual-Diskette System. With your DOS disk in Drive A,

Type **DISKCOPY A: B:** and press ↵. Then follow the screen prompts.

ERASE Command

Internal command that permanently erases one or more files from a disk. Be sure you are at the prompt corresponding to the directory containing the files to be erased.

- □ To erase one file,
  Type **ERASE** <**filename.ext**> and press ↵
- □ To erase all files with the same extension,
  Type **ERASE *.** <**ext**> and press ↵
- □ To erase all files with the same filename,
  Type **ERASE** <**filename**>**.*** and press ↵
- □ To erase all files listed on the directory,
  Type **ERASE *.*** and press ↵
- □ To erase the contents of Drive B while logged onto Drive A,
  Type **ERASE B:*.*** and press ↵

FORMAT Command

External command that prepares a new diskette for use or erases what was on a disk used before.

With a Hard-Disk System. With your unformatted diskette in Drive A or B, type (respectively) either

> **FORMAT A:** and press ↵ or
>
> **FORMAT B:** and press ↵.

Then follow the screen prompts.

With a Dual-Diskette System. With your unformatted data diskette in Drive B,

> Type **FORMAT B:** and press ↵. Then follow the screen prompts.

MKDIR (MD) Command

Internal command that creates a new subdirectory on the default drive. Be sure you are at the prompt corresponding to the drive or directory where the new subdirectory will be located. Then

> Type **MD \\<directory name>** and press ↵ *or* **MD <directory name>** and press ↵

PATH Command

Internal command that tells DOS to search a specified area on disk if a program that is not in the current directory needs to be executed. At the system prompt,

> Type **PATH <path>** and press ↵

RMDIR (RD) Command

Internal command that removes a directory or subdirectory once all files in it have been erased. At the system prompt,

> Type **RD \\<directory name>** and press ↵ *or* **RD <directory name>** and press ↵

RENAME (REN) Command

Internal command that changes the name of a file. Be sure you are at the prompt of the directory containing the file to be renamed.

> Type **REN <old filename.ext new filename.ext>** and press ↵

TREE Command

External command that shows the hierarchy of directories and/or files on a disk. At the system prompt,

Type **TREE** and press ↵ *or* **TREE/F** and press ↵

TYPE Command

Internal command that enables you to display the contents of a file. At the system prompt,

Type **TYPE <filename>** and press ↵

VER Command

Internal command that displays the DOS version in use.

Type **VER** and press ↵

GLOSSARY

Applications software. The programs that do the type of work for which people buy computer systems.

AUTOEXEC.BAT. A personalized DOS file that is executed when the computer system is booted.

Booting. Starting the computer system.

CHDIR (CD). A DOS command used to move from one directory to another.

CHKDSK. A DOS command used to check the status of a disk.

CLS. A DOS command used to clear the display screen.

CONFIG.SYS. A DOS file used to configure hardware to the computer system.

COPY. A DOS command used to make duplicate versions of files.

COPY CON. A DOS command used to create DOS files at the keyboard and copy them to disk.

Data. A collection of facts.

Default drive. The disk drive to which the computer system is currently pointing.

DIR. A DOS command used to get a listing of files and subdirectories in a particular directory.

Directory. A group of files that form a distinct unit. Also refers to the listing that shows the files belonging to the unit.

Directory structure. The hierarchy of directories.

DISKCOPY. A DOS command used to copy the contents of one diskette onto another.

Diskette. A small, removable disk made of a tough, flexible plastic and coated with a magnetizable substance.

Display. A televisionlike device used to show computer output.

ERASE. A DOS command used to remove files.

Extension. A collection of one to three characters used to qualify a filename.

External command. A DOS command that is not loaded into RAM when the system is booted up.

Filename. A collection of one to eight characters used to identify a file.

FORMAT. A DOS command that prepares a disk for use.

Hard disk. A rigid, nonremovable platter that has been coated with a magnetizable substance.

Hardware. The equipment in a computer system.

Internal command. A DOS command that is loaded into RAM when the system is booted up.

Keyboard. A typewriterlike device used to input data and instructions to the computer system.

Kilobytes. Approximately one thousand characters of data.

Megabytes. Approximately one million characters of data.

MKDIR (MD). A DOS command used to create directories.

Mouse. A device used to rapidly move a pointer around a display screen.

Operating system. The main collection of systems software on the computer system.

Path. A chain of directories in a directory structure that begins with one directory and ends at a lower, subordinate directory.

PATH. A DOS command used to create a path to a particular directory.

Printer. A device used to produce output on paper.

Productivity software. Applications software—such as word processors, spreadsheets, and database management systems—designed to make ordinary workers more productive at their jobs.

Prompt. A set of screen characters that directs the user to enter data.

RAM (random access memory). The storage area used by the computer system to work on current projects.

RENAME (REN). A DOS command used to change the names of files.

RMDIR (RD). A DOS command used to remove directories.

Root directory. The highest directory in a directory structure.

Software. Computer programs.

Subdirectory. Any directory subordinate to the root directory.

System disk. The disk containing DOS.

System unit. The "box" that houses the computer chip and RAM.

Systems software. The collection of programs that does background work in a computer system.

TREE. A DOS command used to show a directory structure and, optionally, files within directories.

TYPE. A DOS command used to show the contents of files.

VER. A DOS command used to identify the version of DOS currently in use.

Wildcard character. A character that acts as a stand-in for other characters in a filename.

REVIEW QUESTIONS

Using the diagrams of the standard IBM keyboards in Figure DOS-4 as a guide, match each of the items listed to the correct location on the keyboard you are using in your lab.

1. **a.** the function keys
   b. the Esc key
   c. the Enter key
   d. the Backspace key
   e. the Shift keys
   f. the Insert (Ins) key
   g. the Del key
   h. the numeric keypad
   i. the Num Lock key
   j. the Alt key
   k. the Ctrl key
   l. the arrow keys
   m. the Tab key
   n. the Caps Lock key

Match each of the following hardware components to its definition.

a. secondary storage
b. primary storage
c. keyboard
d. printer
e. computer
f. display

______ **2.** An output device that uses paper.
______ **3.** Where documents can be saved permanently without much concern about the power being turned off.
______ **4.** An input device used to send messages to the computer.
______ **5.** The RAM of a microcomputer.
______ **6.** The CPU or central processing unit.
______ **7.** The screen where output is sent.

Answer each of the following True/False questions with a T or an F.

______ **8.** The FORMAT command is primarily used to prepare a new disk for receiving data files.

______ **9.** The computer system's hard disk is automatically designated the "default drive."

______ **10.** The COPY command can copy only one file at a time from one disk to another.

______ **11.** The DISKCOPY command is used to copy the entire contents of one hard disk to another.

______ **12.** You cannot remove a subdirectory that contains files.

ANSWERS

2. d **3.** a **4.** c **5.** b **6.** e **7.** f **8.** T **9.** F **10.** F **11.** F **12.** T

HANDS-ON EXERCISES

1. Determine the configuration of your computer system:

a. Who is the manufacturer of the system unit?

b. What type of CPU is in use?

c. What diameter diskettes does your system take and what are the byte capacities of the diskettes that can fit into the drives? Are the drives high-density or double-density (low-density)?

d. Is there a hard disk on your system? If so, what byte capacity does it have?

e. What version(s) of DOS is (are) available to you?

2. Use the TREE command to determine the directory structure on your system disk.

3. Use the DIR command to determine the software and/or files available on your system disk. What external DOS commands did you find? Move from subdirectory to subdirectory, repeatedly issuing the DIR command so that you can see what's there.

4. Use the COPY command to practice copying files. Try especially the following:

a. Copy a diskette file onto the same diskette.

b. Copy a diskette file onto another diskette or, alternatively, a hard-disk file onto a diskette.

c. Copy a file from one subdirectory into another subdirectory.

5. Use the TYPE command to inspect the contents of the AUTOEXEC.BAT and CONFIG.SYS files on your system. What are each of these files is supposed to do?

6. Use the COPY CON command to create the two-line file below on your computer system:

```
HELLO THERE
HELLO THERE A SECOND TIME
```

Save the file under the name HELLO1, and use the TYPE command to see that the file's contents are correct.

7. Try as many of the following formatting situations as you are able to complete in your computer lab:

a. Format a low-density (360 kilobyte), 5¹/₄-inch diskette in a low-density, 5¹/₄-inch drive.

b. Format a low-density (360 kilobyte), 5¹/₄-inch diskette in a high-density, 5¹/₄-inch drive.

c. Format a high-density (1.2 megabyte), 5¹/₄-inch diskette in a high-density, 5¹/₄-inch drive.

d. Format a low-density (720 kilobyte), 3¹/₂-inch diskette in a low-density, 3¹/₂-inch drive.

e. Format a low-density (720 kilobyte), 3¹/₂-inch diskette in a high-density, 3¹/₂-inch drive.

f. Format a high-density (1.44 megabyte), 3¹/₂-inch diskette in a high-density, 3¹/₂-inch drive.

8. Experiment with referring to files with wildcard characters. For instance, take the file you created in exercise 6, HELLO1, and make 4 additional copies that have the following names:

```
HELLO.2
HELLO.3
HEL.3
HERRO.2
```

Now try issuing the following commands and, after each, write down the names of the files that appear on the screen:

a. `DIR HELLO`

b. `DIR H*.*`

c. `DIR HELLO.*`

d. `DIR *.2`

e. `DIR HE??O.*`

9. Issue the CHKDSK command to check the status of one of your diskettes. What is the meaning of each line of information in the computer's screen response?

10. Using the directory structure in Figure DOS-9, try creating the LETTERS, JOHN, MARY, and BILL subdirectories and also the PAPERS, HISTORY, and ENGLISH subdirectories. When you are finished,

a. Use the TREE command to output the directory structure.

b. Use the CHDIR command to move from one subdirectory to another. For instance, find a way to move from BILL to LETTERS, from HISTORY to ENGLISH, and from MARY to HISTORY.

c. Use the COPY CON command to create two files under MARY.

d. Use the RMDIR command to remove all of the subdirectories.

APPENDIX: USING THE DOS 5 SHELL PROGRAM

In Versions 4 and 5 of MS-DOS, a built-in graphical shell program was made available so that users could work with the operating system from menus without having to remember a command syntax. This appendix covers the Version 5 shell and assumes that Version 5 of DOS is installed on your hard disk. (Remember, you can tell what version of DOS is on your computer system by entering VER at the system prompt.) The appendix is also organized so that you can work the shell program with either a mouse or a keyboard.

Entering and Exiting the Shell

Depending how Version 5 is installed on your hard disk, the shell program may or may not automatically appear when you boot up your computer. If the command prompt appears instead of the shell, you can invoke the shell at the C:\> prompt if you

1. Type **DOSSHELL**
2. Press ↵

At this point, the opening screen of the shell program will appear on your screen (see Figure DOS-19).

Note, first of all, that the screen consists of four principal parts, or *windows:* a disk-drives window, a directory-tree window, a files-list window, and a program-list window. Each of these windows allows you to do a different type of task. Shortly, you will learn how to move among them and to make choices from them. The principal purpose of each of the windows is as follows:

1. **Disk-drives window.** Shows the disk drives available on your system and allows you to choose the default drive. Note in Figure DOS-19 that the C drive, which is highlighted, is currently active. Active (current) choices are always highlighted.
2. **Directory-tree window.** Enables you to inspect the list of directories and subdirectories on the current drive and to make a directory active.

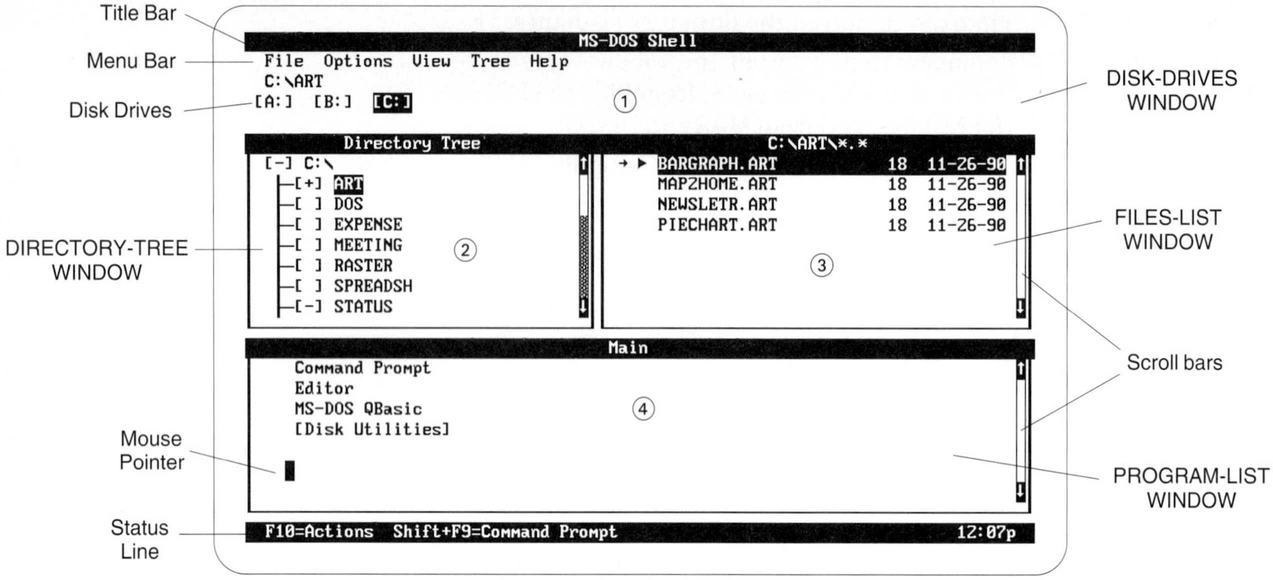

FIGURE DOS-19 The opening screen of the DOS shell program.
The screen consists of four parts (windows): (1) a disk-drives window, (2) a directory-tree window, (3) a files-list window, and (4) a program-list window.

The directory that is highlighted is the current directory, and the identity of the current directory is displayed in the disk-drives window and the files-list window.

3. **Files-list window.** Shows the names of files in the current directory. The highlight on BARGRAPH.ART indicates that this file is now active for processing.

4. **Program-list window.** Shows DOS programs that are currently available for you to run.

Scroll bars are placed on some of the windows to enable you to scroll currently hidden information into them. For instance, you may want to use the scroll bars when a window is too small to fit all of the directories or files on your system onscreen at one time. On many computer systems, because of the sizable number of directories and files present, the directory-tree window and the files-list window will often need to be scrolled.

Note also that a top-of-screen menu bar enables you to work with the DOS shell. The menu bar, among other things, makes it easy for you to issue standard DOS commands like COPY and DELETE.

The mouse pointer is relevant only if you have a mouse. If you have a mouse, try moving it along the desktop and observe that the mouse pointer moves in corresponding fashion on the screen. Mouse users make choices in the shell program either by clicking or double-clicking the leftmost mouse button. Clicking means the leftmost mouse button is pressed and released once; double-clicking means that the leftmost mouse button is pressed and released twice in rapid succession.

(Note: Some mice are configured for left-handed users so that the rightmost mouse button should instead be activated.)

You can exit DOS for the command prompt at any time by following the instructions below:

Using a Mouse.

1. Position the mouse pointer on the phrase "Command Prompt" in the program-list window
2. Double-click the left (or active) mouse button

Using a Keyboard.

1. Press **Alt** + **F9**

Note: In this appendix the "plus" symbol (+) between two keys indicates the first key is to be held down while the second is pressed.

Navigating through the Shell

Now that you know a little bit about what the opening screen of the shell looks like, and how to enter and exit the shell, you will learn to operate the menus and move among the windows. Before beginning, make sure that you are at the opening screen of the shell. (If you exited the shell in the previous exercise, again type DOSSHELL at the command prompt, followed by pressing the Enter key.)

Summoning Menus. You can see in turn each of the pull-down menus that unfurl from the menu bar by following the procedure below:

Using a Mouse.

1. Click on File on the menu bar to see the File pull-down menu
2. To see the other pull-down menus in turn, click on Options, then View, then Tree, and finally Help

Using a Keyboard.

1. Press **Alt** + **F9** to see the File pull-down menu
2. Press **Esc** to have the File pull-down menu disappear
3. To see another pull-down menu,
   a. Hold down the **Alt** key while pressing the highlighted or first letter in the menu's name (e.g., "O" for Options, "T" for Tree, etc.)
   b. Press **Esc** to get rid of the current pull-down menu before moving on to the next one
4. Repeat Step 3 if you wish to see any other pull-down menus

Figure DOS-20 shows an example of the File pull-down menu as it appears in many contexts. Note that each option on the menu represents a DOS command—running a program, copying a file, and deleting a file, for instance. Note that each option has a highlighted letter. With a key-

FIGURE DOS-20

The File pull-down menu. Each option capable of selection on the menu will have a colored or highlighted letter, enabling you to activate it.

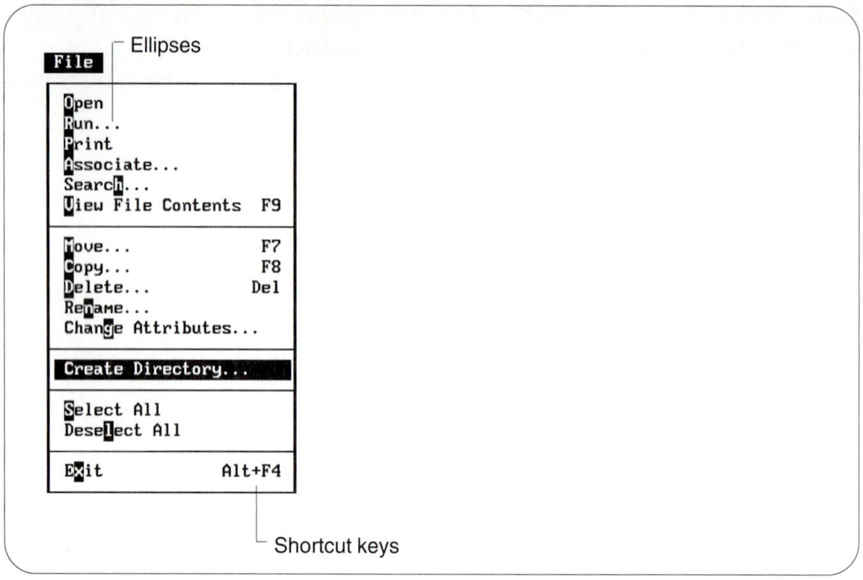

board, you can type in this letter to activate the command option from the menu. Or, you can use the arrow keys to highlight the option and then press the Enter key. With a mouse, on the other hand, you can merely click on the desired option to select it.

In some cases, not all of the entries in a pull-down menu will have a highlighted letter to facilitate their selection. Such entries will also likely be displayed in a dimmed color. Such entries represent choices that you cannot select in the current context. For instance, if a file isn't active, DOS won't let you use the Rename command. Also, if the Copy command is dimmed, it might be because a blank diskette is the default and there is nothing to copy.

Note also that some of the options contain ellipses (. . .). These are commands that require you to fill out a dialog box when you select them. You'll learn about using dialog boxes shortly.

Changing the Default Drive. You can change the default drive from the C drive to the A or B drive by following the procedure below. Before starting the procedure, make sure that there is a diskette in the drive you wish to make the default.

Using a Mouse.

1. Click on the appropriate icon, A or B, in the disk-drives window

Note: If you get an error message indicating there is no disk in the drive, click on "Do not try to read this disk again" and then click on "OK"

Using a Keyboard.

1. To activate the A drive, press **Ctrl** + **A**; to activate the B drive, press **Ctrl** + **B**

Note: If you get an error message indicating there is no disk in the drive, press ↓ to highlight "Do not try to read this disk again" and, then, press ↵ to select "OK"

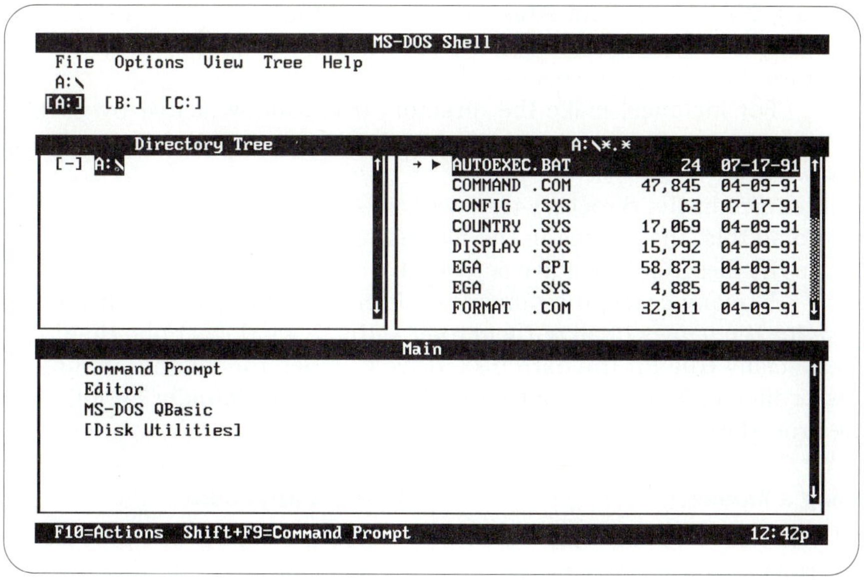

FIGURE DOS-21

Changing the default drive. When the default drive is changed from C to A, note that entries in the directory-tree and files-list windows change accordingly.

If, say, you had selected the A drive as a default, your screen might look similar to the one in Figure DOS-21. Note that when the default drive is changed, the entries in the directory-tree and files-list windows change accordingly.

Moving among the Windows. Only one of the four windows in the DOSSHELL screen can be active at any time. So far, the first (disk-drives) window has been active. You can make any of the other windows active by following the procedure below:

Using a Mouse.

1. Click the mouse in the window that you wish to activate.

Using a Keyboard.

1. Press the **Tab** key to move forward from window to window or press **Shift** + **Tab** to move backward

Note as you are moving from window to window that, except for the disk-drives window, a small arrow displays (→). This arrow, which is at the top of the files-list window of Figure DOS-21, tells you which window (and which choice within a window) is active. You can activate the menu bar from any window by using the procedure described earlier.

DOS Operations

Here, we will go through a few exercises that show you how to perform common DOS operations. To begin, make sure you are pointed to the C drive in the disk-drives window.

Viewing Directories and Files. You can see the directories and files on any of your system's disks through the directory-tree and files-list windows.

For instance, make the directory-tree window active by clicking on it (mouse) or by pressing the Tab key until you see the small arrow in this window. Next, use the mouse or up/down-arrow keys to highlight each choice in the directory-tree window successively. Note that as you are doing this, the entries in the files-list window change, displaying the files in the directory you have activated.

In many cases, the number of directories or files on a disk is too large for the names of all of them to fit within a window at one time. This is especially true for the hard disk, drive C. When the number of directories or files is large, you can *scroll* through the list rapidly by following the procedures below:

Using a Mouse.

1. Click on one of the scroll arrows of the active window

Using a Keyboard.

1. Use the **Pg Dn** or **Pg Up** keys to rapidly scroll through the list of names in the active window

You have probably also observed that some of the icons in front of the directory names in the directory-tree window have a plus (+) or minus (−) sign on them. Directories with a plus sign have subdirectories that are not currently displayed onscreen whereas directories with a minus sign do have their subdirectories displayed. You can "expand" a directory with a plus sign to display its hidden subdirectories or "collapse" a directory with a minus sign so it doesn't display subdirectories by following the procedure below:

Using a Mouse.

1. Click on the plus or minus sign

Using a Keyboard.

1. Use the ↓ or ↑ key to highlight the directory that you wish to expand or collapse
2. Press + to expand the directory or − to collapse it

Formatting a Disk. You can format a disk using the DOS shell just as you can format through the command prompt. To format a diskette in either the A or B drive, first activate the A or B drive in the disk-drives window and then follow the directions below:

Using a Mouse.

1. Place a blank diskette or a diskette whose contents are no longer important to you in the A or B drive

Using a Keyboard.

1. Place a blank diskette or a diskette whose contents are no longer important to you in the A or B drive

2. Activate the program-list window by clicking on it

3. Activate the [Disk Utilities] choice by double-clicking on it

Note that a new menu of choices opens up.

4. Double-click on the Format command

Note that a dialog box similar to the one in Figure DOS-22 appears in the foreground of your screen.

5. Do one of the following:

a. Drive A (5¼″): If you are formatting a 360 kilobyte disk in a 1.2 megabyte drive, type **A:/F:360** at the cursor and click on OK; if you are formatting a 1.2 megabyte disk in a 1.2 megabyte drive, just click on OK

b. Drive B (3½″): If you are formatting a 720 kilobyte disk in a 1.44 megabyte drive, type **B:/F:720** at the cursor and click on OK; if you are formatting a 1.44 megabyte disk in a 1.44 megabyte drive, just click on OK

Next, a message will appear asking you to insert a diskette and press Enter. Since your diskette is already inserted,

6. Press ↵

The disk will now be formatted.

7. If there is no volume label to enter, press **N**

8. Press ↵

9. If there are no more disks to format, press **N**

10. Press ↵

11. Press any key to renter the DOS shell

2. Activate the program-list window by pressing the **Tab** key the appropriate number of times

3. Activate the [Disk Utilities] choice by moving the highlight to it with the ↓ key and pressing ↵

Note that a new menu of choices opens up.

4. Activate the Format choice by moving the highlight to it with the ↓ key and pressing ↵

Note that a dialog box similar to the one in Figure DOS-22 appears in the foreground of your screen.

5. Do one of the following:

a. Drive A (5¼″): If you are formatting a 360 kilobyte disk in a 1.2 megabyte drive, type **A:/F:360** at the cursor and press ↵; if you are formatting a 1.2 megabyte disk in a 1.2 megabyte drive, just press ↵

b. Drive B (3½″): If you are formatting a 720 kilobyte disk in a 1.44 megabyte drive, type **B:/F:720** at the cursor and press ↵; if you are formatting a 1.44 megabyte disk in a 1.44 megabyte drive, just press ↵

Note that pressing Enter selects the OK button to invoke the formatting operation. If you should for some reason change your mind, you can use the left- or right-arrow keys to move to another button—such as Cancel, which aborts the formatting operation when activated.

Next, a message will appear asking you to insert a

FIGURE DOS-22

The Format dialog box. When the A drive is active, A: appears in the parameters list.

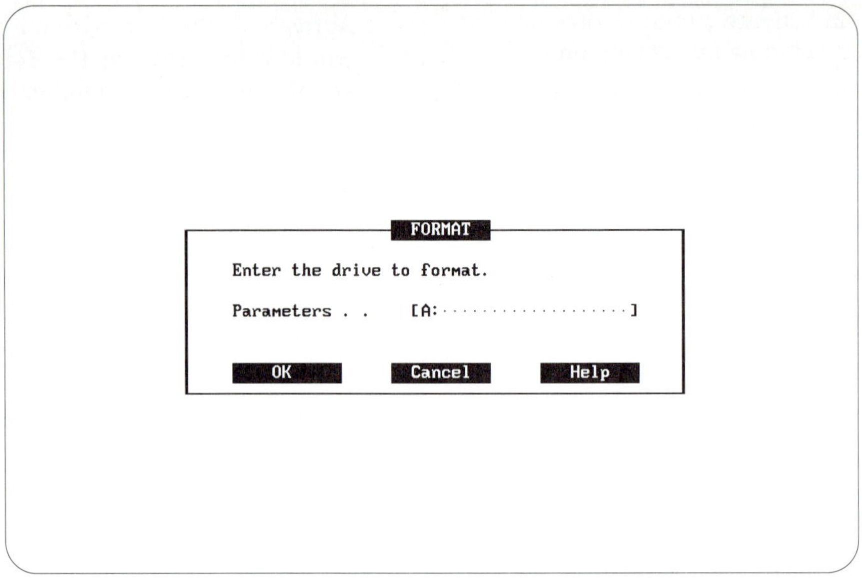

diskette and press Enter. Since your diskette is already inserted,

6. Press ↵

The disk will now be formatted.

7. If there is no volume label to enter, press **N**
8. Press ↵
9. If there are no more disks to format, press **N**
10. Press ↵
11. Press any key to return to the DOS shell

At this point, you can collapse the disk utilities list appearing in the program-list window by selecting [Main]. Note that the disk utilities window collapses back to the form suggested in the program-list window of Figure DOS-19.

You will note that a window with a listing of AUTOEXEC.BAT appears onscreen. You can get rid of this window by pressing the Esc key.

Copying a File. Copying a file is accomplished when the files-list window is active and you are pointing to the file you wish to copy. Since, in the previous exercise, you have activated AUTOEXEC.BAT, we'll assume here that this is the file you wish to copy. Actually, any file will do.

Also, since you have just created a fresh disk with the FORMAT command, we'll make a copy of AUTOEXEC.BAT on this disk. Assuming that the files-list window is active and that AUTOEXEC.BAT is highlighted,

Using a Mouse.

1. Click on File on the menu bar
2. Click on Copy on the File pull-down menu

Note that a dialog box similar to the one in Figure DOS-23 appears with AUTOEXEC.BAT already established as the file to copy. Let's assume that we would like to rename this file MISC8 when we copy it to our diskette.

3. At the cursor, type **A:MISC8** (if you are copying to the A drive) or **B:MISC8** (if you are copying to the B drive)
4. Click on Yes

Using a Keyboard.

1. Select File on the menu bar by pressing **Alt** + **F4**
2. Press **C** or **F8** to select Copy on the File pull-down menu

Note that a dialog box similar to the one in Figure DOS-23 appears, with AUTOEXEC.BAT already established as the file to copy. Let's assume that we would like to rename this file MISC8 when we copy it to our diskette.

3. At the cursor, type **A:MISC8** (if you are copying to the A drive) or **B:MISC8** (if you are copying to the B drive)
4. Press ↵ to select the Yes button

At this point the file will be copied. To make sure, activate the A- or B-drive icon in the disk-drives window and inspect the contents of the files-list window. MISC8 should be listed if the file has been successfully copied.

Copying Several Files. You can also copy several files at a time. Here, we will briefly discuss how to do this. You may wish to try to copy several files at a time on your own, however, after you finish the tutorials.

To copy several files at a time, you must first highlight the names of the files in the files-list window.

To highlight the names of the files with a mouse, press and hold down the Ctrl key while you click the name of each file you wish to select. If you make a mistake, release the Ctrl key and continue to click the mouse.

To highlight the names of the files with a keyboard, highlight the name of the first file you wish to select and press Ctrl+F8. The word "Add" will appear in the lower-right corner of the status bar. Then, use the up-arrow and/or down arrow keys to highlight the next file to be selected and press the spacebar to select it. Continue on with the arrow keys and spacebar in this fashion until all files are selected. Finally, press Ctrl+F8 again to turn off the Add feature. If you make a mistake, just use the arrow keys with the Add feature off.

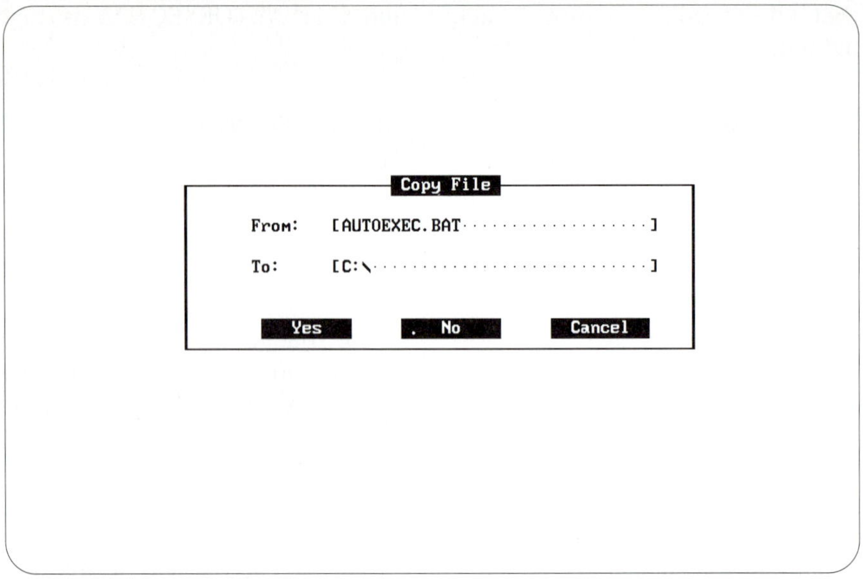

FIGURE DOS-23
The Copy dialog box. Note that the name of the active file—assumed by DOS as the file to copy—appears in the "From" box.

After you select the files and issue the COPY command, note that the names of all of the files you've chosen appear in the "From" part of the Copy dialog box. To copy all of the files to the A drive without renaming them, just type A:\ in the "To" part of the dialog box.

Moving Files. The MOVE command, which is also on the File pull-down menu, works almost exactly like the COPY command except the original files no longer appear in their original positions. You can test your understanding of the MOVE command by referring to the end-of-appendix exercises.

Renaming a File. Assuming you've just finished copying AUTOEXEC.BAT on the C drive into MISC8 on the A drive, you can rename MISC8 to something else by following the procedure below. With the files-list window active and the highlight on MISC8,

Using a Mouse.

1. Click on File on the menu bar
2. Click on Rename on the File pull-down menu

Note that a dialog box similar to the one in Figure DOS-24 appears with MISC8 already established as the file to be renamed. Let's assume that we would like to rename this file MISC8A.

3. At the cursor type, MISC8A

Using a Keyboard.

1. Press **Alt** + **F** to select File on the menu bar
2. Press **N** to select Rename on the File pull-down menu

Note that a dialog box similar to the one in Figure DOS-24 appears with MISC8 already established as the file to be renamed. Let's assume that we would like to rename this file MISC8A

4. Click on OK

3. At the cursor type **MISC8A**
4. Press ↵ to select the OK button

Note in the files-list window that the file has been renamed.

Deleting a File. Now, we will delete the file we just renamed MISC8A. Assuming that the files-list window is still active and that MISC8A is highlighted,

Using a Mouse.

1. Click on File on the menu bar
2. Click on Delete on the File pull-down menu

Note that a dialog box similar to the one in Figure DOS-25 appears with MISC8A already established as the file to be deleted.

3. Click on Yes

Using a Keyboard.

1. Press **Alt** + **F** to select File on the menu bar
2. Press **D** or **Del** to select Delete on the File pull-down menu

Note that a dialog box similar to the one in Figure DOS-25 appears with MISC8A already established as the file to be deleted.

3. Press ↵ to select the Yes button

Note in the files-list window that the file has been deleted.

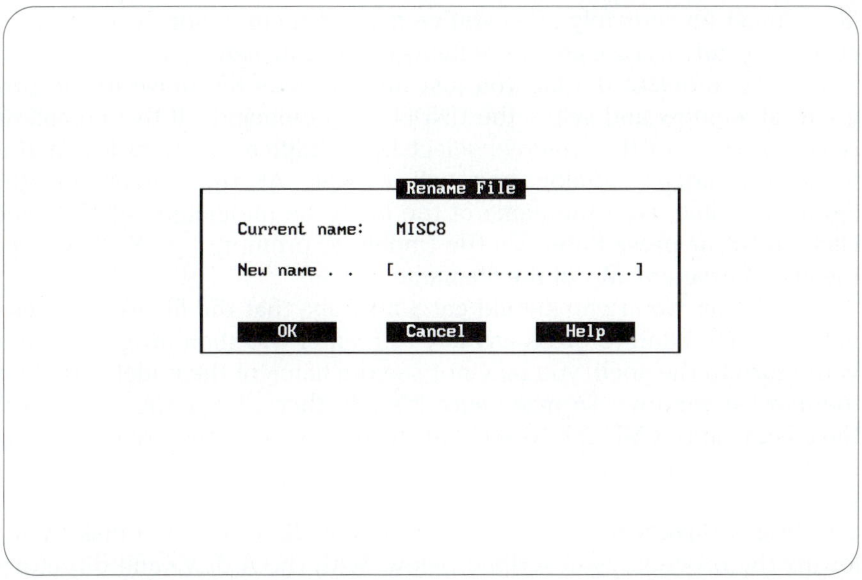

FIGURE DOS-24

The Rename dialog box. Note that the active file is assumed by DOS as the file to be renamed.

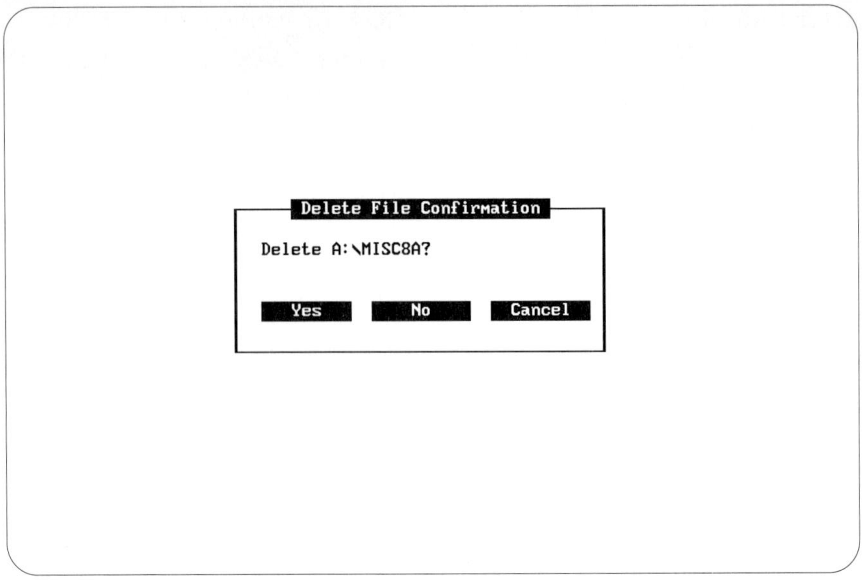

FIGURE DOS-25
The Delete File Confirmation dialog box.
Note that the active file is assumed by DOS as the file to be deleted.

You can also delete more than one file at a time. To do this you must mark the names of all of these files in the files-list window in the same manner discussed in the "Copying Several Files" subsection of this appendix. When the Delete File Confirmation dialog box appears, the names of all the files you selected will appear for you to confirm.

Undeleting a File. You can also undelete files in the DOS shell. Here, we will discuss how to do this only in passing, leaving it as an end-of-appendix exercise for you to try on your own. For best results, you should undelete files almost immediately after you've deleted them, before you've had a chance to add or erase any more items on your diskette.

To undelete the file you just deleted, MISC8A, move to the program-list window and select the UNDELETE command. (If this command is not showing in the window, select Disk Utilities to reveal it.) At this point an Undelete dialog box will appear. At the cursor, on the Parameters line, type the name of the file to be undeleted, MISC8A, and click on OK or press Enter. To the Undelete? prompt, type Y. Then type the first character—M—of the file name.

At this point you should get a message that the file was successfully undeleted and to press any key to reenter the shell program. When you return to the shell, you may not see the name of the undeleted file in the files-list window. To make sure it's still there, leave the shell, issue the command DIR MISC8A to see that the file has been restored, and reenter the shell again.

Creating a Directory. You can create a new directory on a disk by following the procedures described below. With the A drive and directory-tree window active,

Using a Mouse.

1. Click on File on the menu bar
2. Click on Create Directory on the File pull-down menu

Note that a dialog box similar to the one in Figure DOS-26 appears and asks you to supply a name for the directory.

3. Type **NEW** as the new directory name
4. Click on OK

Using a Keyboard.

1. Press **Alt** + **F** to select File on the menu bar
2. Press **E** to select Create Directory on the File pull-down menu

Note that a dialog box similar to the one in Figure DOS-26 appears and asks you to supply a name for the directory.

3. Type **NEW** as the new directory name
4. Press **↵**

Note in the directory-tree window that a new directory has been added as a subdirectory under the A-drive root directory.

Deleting a Directory. You can delete a directory by following the procedure described below. Note that a directory to be deleted must be empty. If the directory isn't empty, you will need to delete files from it by the method described earlier. Fortunately, NEW, the directory we just created, doesn't yet have any files in it. With the A drive and directory-tree window active, follow the directions on page 64. When you finish, note that the directory is deleted from the directory-tree window.

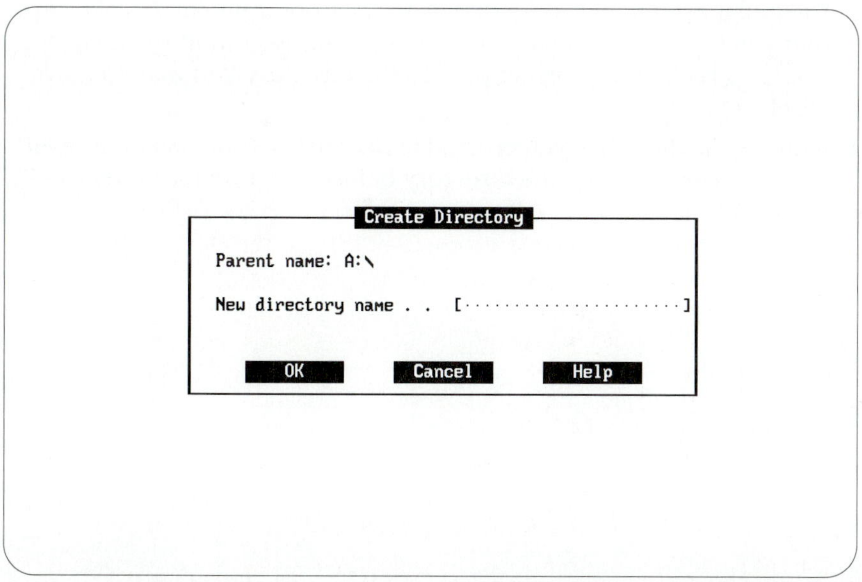

FIGURE DOS-26

The Create Directory dialog box.
Note that the first line of the box lists the name of the directory that will contain the subdirectory you enter on the second line. Here, the directory you identify on the second line will be placed under the A-drive root directory, A:\.

Using a Mouse.

1. Click on the NEW directory in the directory-tree window to make the NEW directory active
2. Click on File on the menu bar
3. Click on Delete on the File pull-down menu

Note that a dialog box similar to the ones you've seen earlier appears and asks you to confirm the directory deletion.

4. Click on Yes

Using a Keyboard.

1. Move the **↓** key to highlight the NEW directory in the directory-tree window to make the NEW directory active
2. Press **Alt** + **F** to activate File on the menu bar
3. Press **D** or **Del** for Delete on the File pull-down menu

Note that a dialog box similar to the ones you've seen earlier appears and asks you to confirm the directory deletion.

4. Press **↵** for Yes

SHELL EXERCISES

1. Use the COPY command to copy one of the files on your hard disk to a diskette. After you do this, try copying several files to the diskette at once.
2. Use the DELETE command to delete the files you copied in Exercise 1.
3. Use the UNDELETE command to undelete the files you deleted in Exercise 2. Verify that the files have been restored.
4. Create a new directory called NEWFILES on your diskette.
5. Move the files you copied and undeleted in the earlier exercises to the NEWFILES directory. (*Note:* The Move command, which appears on the File pull-down menu, works similar to the Copy command. Make sure that you begin the command on the directory you want to move files from and type in the correct path to the directory you wish to move files to.)
6. Remove the directory you created in Exercise 5. (*Note:* Make sure all files are removed from the directory before you attempt to remove it.)

WORD PROCESSING WITH WORDPERFECT

WP

CONTENTS

LEARNING OBJECTIVES

After completing these tutorials, you will be able to:

1. Type and edit documents.
2. Save and retrieve documents.
3. Make formatting changes that improve the appearance of documents.
4. Print documents.
5. Create tables.

OVERVIEW

Word processing is the use of computer technology to create, manipulate, and print text materials such as letters, memos, manuscripts, and other documents. Here you will learn to use WordPerfect, perhaps the most well-known and certainly the most widely used word processing package in the world. It is an extremely powerful program that is also reasonably easy to learn and operate. First you will learn how to start WordPerfect, use it to create and retrieve document files, and save files onto disk. Once you have practiced these basic skills, you will learn how to edit documents so that they say exactly what you want them to say and how to format documents to improve their appearance.

The instructions presented in the tutorials pertain to WordPerfect version 5.1. Step-by-step instructions on exactly what to do when using this word processing program at your computer are provided. Work through each of these steps in the order suggested. At the end of the main set of tutorial instructions is a set of review questions and hands-on exercises.

A "Command Reference" section immediately follows the main set of tutorials. This summary covers the most frequently used commands and keystroke sequences in WordPerfect. It is recommended that you use the feature primarily as a reference, after having completed the more detailed instructions in the tutorials.

Ending this discourse on word processing is an appendix on the pull-down-menu feature of WordPerfect 5.1. The pull-down-menu feature is an alternative to the approach covered throughout the main set of tutorials. Included in the appendix is a table showing you how to invoke most of the commands covered in the tutorials, both conventionally and with menus.

GETTING STARTED

Using WordPerfect will allow you to create, edit, format, save, revise, and print many different kinds of documents. The exercises that follow provide detailed instructions for creating several short documents. Keystroking has been kept to a minimum so that you can concentrate on learning the basic word processing functions. Before you begin, be certain you have all the necessary tools: you will need the WordPerfect program and a formatted data diskette on which you will store the documents created with the exercises.

Program Installation. You will need to install the WordPerfect program diskette(s) only if WordPerfect is not stored on your hard disk. Installing WordPerfect on a hard disk is a relatively simple matter; all you need to do is put the first program diskette into a drive, type INSTALL at the C:\> prompt, and follow the instructions on the screen. If WordPerfect is already on your hard disk, usually it will be assigned to the C drive in its own subdirectory. You should check with the instructor to find out the exact name of the directory.

While WordPerfect 5.1 is primarily designed for a hard disk, you can also run it without one. To do this, you will need the two program diskettes that come with the package. Also, to use 5.1 with a dual-diskette system, it is necessary to have two drives with a capacity of 720 kilobytes or larger.

How to Start WordPerfect

You will need to boot the operating system and be at the DOS system prompt (usually either A> or C:\>).

With a Hard-Disk System. For purposes of discussion, it is assumed that WordPerfect is in a subdirectory called WP51. Check with your instructor as to the exact directory name on your system. To access the hard disk, type **C:** and press Enter at the system prompt if the computer is not already pointing to the C drive.

1. Insert a data diskette into Drive A
2. Type **CD\WP51** to access the WordPerfect subdirectory (in which WordPerfect 5.1 is stored)

With a Dual-Diskette System. To start WordPerfect 5.1

1. Insert WordPerfect program disk 1 into Drive A
2. Insert your data disk into Drive B
3. Type **WP** ↵
4. Press
5. Remove WordPerfect program disk 1 when instructed to do so on the screen
6. Insert WordPerfect program disk 2 into Drive A

3. Press ↵

4. Type **WP** at the WordPerfect directory prompt.

5. Press ↵

7. Press ↵

As WordPerfect is booting up, you will see a WordPerfect title screen for a few seconds, followed by an Edit screen that is mostly blank (see Figure WP-1).

The Status Line

The Edit screen in Figure WP-1 is blank except for a *cursor* in the upper left corner and a line of information—called the **status line**—in the lower right corner. The cursor shows the position where the first or next keystroke you type in to your document will appear. The status line is used primarily to provide information about the cursor's current location. Below we describe this information more fully.

Doc 1. This message tells you which document file you are working on. WordPerfect can retain two document files in computer memory at the same time. If you think of the first file as a folder of paper on a desktop, this file is Doc 1 (for document 1). You might also have another document on your desktop that you can easily refer to. The second document would be called Doc 2 by WordPerfect.

It might happen that you accidentally switch from Doc 1 to Doc 2. If you suddenly see a blank screen, check the status line to see if you have changed to Doc 2. To switch back to Doc 1, hold down the Shift key and press F3 once. This key combination acts as a toggle between the two document screens. When you become more experienced you may want to work with two documents concurrently, but for now you will only work with one.

Pg 1. The *Pg* message shows you on which page in your document your cursor is located. If, for instance, you were typing a long document and were currently on page 3 of the document, the notation would read Pg 3.

Ln 1″. The *Ln* message tells you the position within the page of the line where the cursor is currently located. Ln is a measurement in inches from the top edge of your paper. The Ln message will change as you type.

Pos 1″. The *Pos* message shows the current position of your cursor on a line. Each line has space for 65 characters from left to right. If the cursor is at the left margin you will see 1″ on the status line. WordPerfect automatically leaves a one-inch left margin, so when you are at the far left edge of your document, you are at the one-inch position, or 10 blank character spaces from the edge of the page. Each time you press the spacebar or type a character, the Pos notation will change.

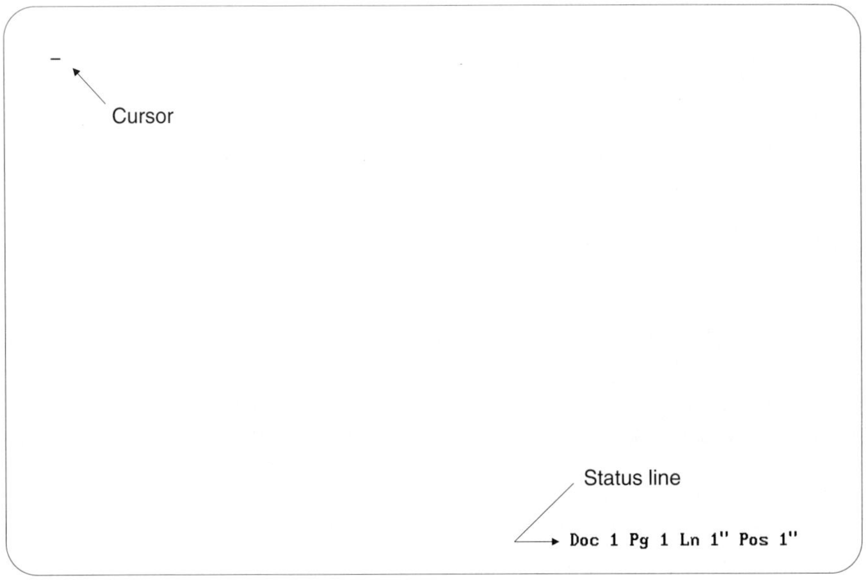

FIGURE WP-1
WordPerfect Edit screen.
The Edit screen represents the workspace used to create and edit documents.

You will now type a few lines so that you can see how the cursor moves and so that you can observe the changes on the status line.

Type your name and address in three lines as shown below:

name
address
city state zip

Start with the cursor in the upper left corner of the screen and press the Enter key after you type each line. Press Enter several times after the last line. (Do not worry about errors.)

As you are typing, watch the status line change. You should see changes in the Ln and Pos locations. Press the arrow keys to move around through text and watch the status line change as your cursor position changes.

The Function Keys

For just a moment, look away from your screen to your function keys. Most software programs have built-in commands that are invoked through the use of these function keys. The tasks that each function key performs vary from program to program. It is essential that you realize the important role that the function keys play in performing different tasks with WordPerfect.

In WordPerfect, you use the function keys either alone or in combination with the *Ctrl* key, the *Shift* key, or the *Alt* key. When you use one of these three keys with a function key, you hold down the key, then press the function key, and finally release both keys. Throughout the

Guide, to indicate that the Ctrl, Alt, or Shift key is to be held down while another key is depressed, we will insert the plus (+) symbol between the key that's to be held down and any other keys that are to be activated. The command to print out a document, for example, is

↑ Shift + **F7**

This means that you must hold down the Shift key first, then press the F7 key, and then release both keys. Occasionally in WordPerfect you will need to press keys in succession, releasing the previous key depressed; when this is the case, no + symbol will be shown between the keys.

Some keyboards have function keys arranged in two rows on the left side, and other keyboards have the function keys across the top. You should have a cardboard template that fits on your keyboard and matches the type of keyboard you are using.

You will notice on the template that there are four commands next to each function key. The color of the command determines which key is used in combination with the function key. For commands printed in red, you hold down the Ctrl key while pressing the appropriate function key. For commands printed in green, you use the Shift key. For commands printed in blue, you use the Alt key. For commands printed in black, you press the function key alone.

Figure WP-2 shows the actions produced by WordPerfect when you use the function keys, alone or in combination with the Shift, Ctrl, and Alt keys. These are the same actions shown on your template. As you progress through the WordPerfect tutorials, you will be working with a number of these commands.

FIGURE WP-2a
Commands invoked by depressing a function key.

Key	Action Taken
F1	Cancel last command/restore deleted text
F2	Forward search
F3	Request help
F4	Indent (from left margin only)
F5	List filenames
F6	Bold on/off
F7	Exit
F8	Underline on/off
F9	End field
F10	Save document and resume work
F11	Reveal codes
F12	Block

KEY	ACTION TAKEN
F1	Setup
F2	Backward search
F3	Switch to second document
F4	Indent (from both left and right margins)
F5	Date/outline
F6	Center text
F7	Print document
F8	Format document
F9	Merge codes
F10	Retrieve document

FIGURE WP-2b
Commands invoked by holding down the Shift key and depressing a function key.

KEY	ACTION TAKEN
F1	Shell/exit to DOS
F2	Spelling checker
F3	Screen/line drawing
F4	Move/copy text
F5	Text in/out
F6	Tab alignment
F7	Create/edit footnotes
F8	Font selection
F9	Merge/Sort
F10	Macro definition

FIGURE WP-2c
Commands invoked by holding down the Ctrl key and depressing a function key.

KEY	ACTION TAKEN
F1	Thesaurus
F2	Replace text
F3	Display reveal codes
F4	Mark a block of text
F5	Mark text for indexing, tables of contents, redlining/strikeout, etc.
F6	Flush right
F7	Table creation
F8	Style
F9	Graphics
F10	Start macro

FIGURE WP-2d
Commands invoked by holding down the Alt key and depressing a function key.

Cancelling Commands

During the course of word processing, you frequently will want to abort a command you started but didn't complete. When this is the case, you'll find WordPerfect's **cancel** key, F1, handy. You can also use the F1 key to *un*delete text—that is, to restore text that was previously deleted.

How to Exit WordPerfect

One of the most frequently used function keys is the F7 **(exit)** key. It is used to clear the screen, to leave command menus, and to exit WordPerfect for the operating system. For now, you are going to practice simply exiting the program.

On the template, find the commands associated with the F7 function key. Note that the word "Exit" appears in black at the bottom of the list of commands.

1. Press **F7** for EXIT

A message appears on the screen asking whether you want to save your document. The document with your name and address was just for practice, so

2. Type **N** for No.

You will learn how to save a document in a later exercise. To respond to the message Exit WP? No (Yes)

3. Type **Y** for Yes.

Note: If you had replied N to the prompt asking whether you wanted to exit, you would have returned to a blank WordPerfect document screen. This is the procedure used to clear the screen, erasing your document from memory, without exiting the program.

You are now back at the system prompt or perhaps a menu, and you may continue to the next exercise or quit.

CREATING A DOCUMENT

In this exercise you will create a short letter by entering text in much the same way that you would using a typewriter. You will also learn how to correct simple typing errors.

How to Enter Text

Start WordPerfect and type the letter shown in Figure WP-3. Press the Enter key only wherever you see the paragraph symbol ¶. Pressing the

```
(type today's date here)¶
¶
¶
¶
Patrick J. Pixby¶
32000 Randle Center, Suite 202¶
The Randle Scott Building¶
Seattle, WA 98101¶
¶
Dear Mr. Pixby:¶
¶
Thank you for your interest in the Wizzard's word
processing package. Wizzard is easy to use yet
sophisticated. It is not only a word processing
package, it is also a design tool, desktop publisher,
and organizer for your office.¶
¶
No matter what the size of your organization, the
Wizzard can handle your text typing needs.¶
¶
If you would like a demonstration of all of the
Wizzard's features, just give us a call. Our number is
on the attached brochure.¶
¶
Sincerely,¶
¶
¶
¶
(Type your name here)¶
Vice President, Sales¶
¶
```

FIGURE WP-3
PIXBY document.

Enter key produces what is known in the world of word processing as a **hard return.** A hard return puts a mark in the document that ends the current line and moves the cursor to the next line.

Do NOT press the Enter key at the end of each line as you would press the Return key on a typewriter. With WordPerfect and most other word processing programs, when the text you are entering reaches the right margin, it will wrap automatically to the next line as you continue typing. This action, called **wordwrap,** automatically inserts a **soft return** at the end of the line. This is important if you later add or delete text because WordPerfect will be able to reformat text that is wordwrapped; in other words, text between any two successive hard returns. The only times you will need to press the Enter key when you are word processing documents is when the text you enter must begin on a new line, such as in the case of an address line, a date line, the beginning of a new paragraph, or a blank line.

How to Make Corrections

There are many ways to make corrections when you make typing errors or when you want to change text. For instance, you can use the

Backspace key (←) or the Delete (Del) key to erase individual characters. You can also insert or delete whole words at a time, or simply type over text that you want to change.

As you type new text, it will be placed into the document at the cursor position. If the **insert mode** is on (the Ins key is automatically active when you enter WordPerfect), any text already on a line, to the right of the cursor, will automatically move to the right; otherwise, you'll type over existing text.

Below, we'll look at deleting and inserting in more detail.

Using the Del Key. The Del key will delete the character at the cursor position. Each time you press the Del key, another character will be deleted and any text to the right will move left to fill in the space. In the PIXBY document,

1. Press the **arrow keys** to move the cursor to the comma (,) on the second line of the address
2. Press **Del** until you have deleted the comma and the words "Suite 202"

Using the Backspace Key. The Backspace key will delete the character to the left of your cursor and move the cursor one space to the left. In the PIXBY document,

1. Press the **arrow keys** to move to the space before the word "easy" in the first paragraph
2. Press **←Backspace** several times until the words "is" and "Wizzard" are removed

Watch the screen as you are deleting the characters. Notice how the words to the right of your cursor move left as the cursor is moving left.

Using the Insert Mode. Next,

1. Type **Wizzard is extremely** at the beginning of the sentence

Watch as the characters to the right are automatically pushed to the right of the newly inserted text. *Note:* Some of the characters may be extending beyond the right margin. If this happens, simply go to the next step and keep your eyes on the right margin.

2. Press **↓** to move down in your paragraph

When you press the down arrow key, any text extending out from the right margin is automatically aligned and the line breaks in the paragraph change as necessary. This is called *automatic screen reformatting.* WordPerfect reformats all the text appearing from where you made the last insert to where it encounters a hard return. (This is why it's so important that you let wordwrap occur and don't press the Enter key after every line.)

Using Ctrl+Backspace. As you've already seen, deleting one character at a time is normally done with either the Del key or the Backspace key. You can delete an entire word more efficiently by using a combination of keystrokes.

1. Move your cursor to the **d** in the word "attached" in the last paragraph

Note: The cursor does not need to be on the last letter of the word you wish to delete. It can be positioned on any letter.

2. Press **Ctrl** + **←Backspace**

Remember to hold down the Ctrl key, press the Backspace key, and then release both.

3. Type the word **enclosed** in front of "brochure"

Watch as the text is moved right. Be sure to leave a space at the end of the added word.

4. Press **↓** to reformat text if needed

Using the Typeover Mode. Sometimes you do not want to insert text, thereby pushing over words to the right of the cursor. You would rather have the option of typing on top of existing text, thus deleting it as you type.

1. Move to the n in the word "needs" at the end of the first sentence in the second paragraph

2. Press **Ins** once

The word "Typeover" appears in the lower left corner of your screen. You are now in the **typeover mode** (originally you were in the insert mode).

3. Type **wants** over "needs"

This time the word "needs" is not pushed to the right. It is replaced with the word "wants."

The Insert key is a *toggle switch* that allows you to switch back and forth between the insert mode and typeover mode. Originally, when you enter WordPerfect, you are in the insert mode. When you press the Insert key for the first time, you are put in the typeover mode. Pressing it again puts you back in the insert mode, and so on.

4. Press the Ins key repeatedly. Watch as the word "Typeover" comes on and goes off the screen as you do this.

5. Make any other corrections (if necessary) in your document until all spacing and spelling are correct.

How to Save a Document

Now that you have a finished document on your screen, you should save it. There is one important step that may have to be completed prior to saving your document. You may need to set the default drive for saving and retrieving documents to B (dual-disk system) or A (hard-disk system). If you are on a hard-disk system without a preset default or a dual-diskette system, you must do this step each time you sign onto WordPerfect or are ready to save or retrieve your first file.

If you were to save your file right now, without changing the default drive, you would save the file on the same diskette or directory as your WordPerfect program files if the automatic default is on A or C. It is always wise to keep the data files (document files) separate from the program or system files, and so the default drive must be changed.

To Set the Default Drive. Follow the instructions for your system configuration.

With a Hard-Disk System. To set the default drive

1. Press **F5** for LIST FILES

A message appears in the lower right corner asking you to press the equal sign (=) to change the directory.

2. Press =

The C drive is shown (C:\WPDIR*.*).

3. Type **A:**

4. Press ↵

The new default directory prompt is now showing in the lower left corner of your screen (A:*.*).

5. Press **F7** to return to your document

With a Dual-Diskette System. To set the default drive

1. Press **F5** for LIST FILES

A message appears in the lower right corner asking you to press the equal sign (=) to change the directory.

2. Press=

The A drive is shown (A:*.*).

3. Type **B:**

4. Press ↵

The new default directory prompt is now showing in the lower left corner of your screen (B:*.*).

5. Press **F7** to return to your document.

Your default drive for saving and retrieving WordPerfect documents is now set. For as long as you are working with WordPerfect during your current session (until you exit the program), you will not need to reset the default. When you save (or retrieve) a document now, it will automatically be stored on (or fetched from) your data disk.

To Name the File and Save It. The SAVE command—which copies the most recent version of your document from RAM to disk—is good to use frequently as you are working on your document, particularly if it is a long, multipage document. By using the SAVE (F10) key frequently as you are working, you are assured that if power is lost for any reason, a relatively recent version of your document will be safely intact on the diskette.

1. Press **F10** for SAVE

2. Type **PIXBY** (the name of the document to be saved)

3. Press ↵

The drive light on the default drive will flash briefly, and you may hear the sound of the drive as the document is being saved. When the process is finished, you can resume working on your document if you wish.

To Clear the Screen. Now that your document is finished and saved, you will clear the screen (erasing the copy of your document in RAM) so that you can begin a new document. Clearing the screen is done with the Exit (F7) key. Pressing the F7 key will give you the options of (1) saving the document to disk and clearing the screen and (2) exiting or remaining in WordPerfect. Both of these options will be discussed here.

1. Press **F7** for EXIT

A message then appears asking whether you want to save your document. Whenever you press F7, this message will appear, whether you intend to clear the screen to work on a fresh document (option 1) or to exit WordPerfect (option 2). In this way, the program gives you the chance to save your document before you leave WordPerfect or clear the screen to work on another document. Otherwise, you might exit or clear the screen and lose your unsaved document.

You should note that the F7 key is an alternate way of saving your document (the other way was the F10 key). In general practice, use the F7 key for saving only if you forget to save before starting to exit the program or if you want to clear the screen. Ordinarily, use the F10 key as the standard way of saving your document as you are working on it.

To the message asking whether you want to save this document (it has already been saved, so you do not need to save it again),

2. Type **N** for No

To the message asking whether you want to exit the program,

3. Type **N** for No

Your screen is now clear. The PIXBY document has been erased from RAM and you can begin a new document.

Note: Generally you will clear the screen before retrieving a file from your default directory. If you do not, you will end up with both the document you just created and the retrieved document merged together in RAM. Of course, sometimes you will want to "cut and paste" two documents together, in which case you will not clear RAM before the retrieval.

How to List a Directory of Files

There are times when you will want to see a list of the files you have stored on your disk. You can check the directory now to see if your PIXBY file was saved

1. Press **F5** to invoke the LIST FILES command

The name of the default drive that you previously set appears in the lower left corner of your screen. This is the directory you want to look at, so

2. Press ↵

A directory similar to the one shown in Figure WP-4 appears.

At the top of the screen, you will see the current date and time. The name of the directory you are viewing is also shown on the first line. The second line shows the size of the document currently in RAM and the amount of free space remaining on your data disk. The names of any documents you've saved to disk (such as PIXBY) are displayed on the remainder of the screen.

How to Retrieve a Document

When you use the LIST FILES command (F5), there is a menu of choices at the bottom of the screen. Notice, in Figure WP-4, that a number appears in front of each choice: 1 for Retrieve, 2 for Delete, 3 for Rename, and so forth. To retrieve a file, for instance, you first use the arrow keys to highlight the filename in the directory. (If you are unsure of the contents of the file, you can simply press Enter—for "Look"—to temporarily view it. This is not a retrieval, however, because you have not really made the file available for editing.) To retrieve the file

1. Use the **arrow keys** to highlight the filename PIXBY in the directory

2. Choose **1** to Retrieve PIXBY

FIGURE WP-4
Directory of WordPerfect data files.

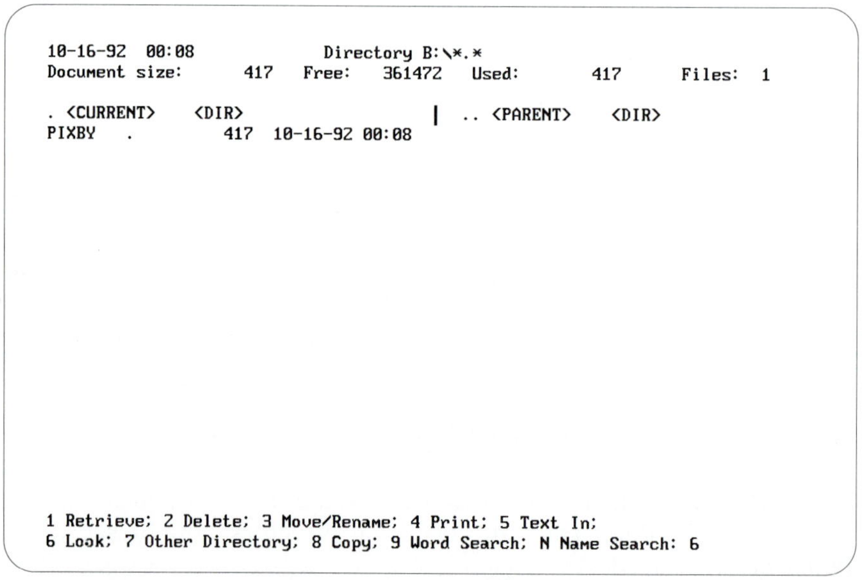

The PIXBY file is now retrieved and displayed on screen. At this point, the file can be edited. *Note:* An A:\ or B:\ and the filename appear in the lower left corner of the screen.

How to Check Spelling

A **spelling checker,** or *speller,* enables you to check each word in your document for correct spelling. It is a feature that can be quite useful, especially if you have problems spelling or typing. The speller that is available with the full-featured version of WordPerfect contains more than 100,000 words and allows you to add new words as you need them.

To Correct Misspelled Words. The spell-check feature allows you to correct words in several ways. The following exercise will give you a chance to practice some of these methods.

The PIXBY file should be displayed on your screen. If it is not, retrieve it. Enter some errors in the first paragraph of your document, as shown in the underlined portions of Figure WP-5. Ordinarily you would not make errors deliberately, but by doing so now, you will be able to get some practice with the spell-check feature.

If you are using a dual-diskette system, the speller is on a separate disk and must now be inserted into the drive where you normally keep your data disk. If you are using a hard-disk system, the speller was probably installed with the WordPerfect program, and it will not be necessary to switch disks. With the document you want spell-checked displayed on the screen, follow these instructions:

1. Press **Ctrl** + **F2** to invoke the speller

The following message appears at the bottom of the screen:

```
1 Word; 2 Page; 3 Document; 4 New Supplemental
        Dictionary; 5 Lookup; 6 count: 0
```

2. Choose **3** for Document

The first word in your document that is not in the WordPerfect dictionary will now be highlighted. The options you have at this time are listed at the bottom of the screen. You will need to make one of the following choices:

- □ Choose the letter on the spell-check screen that corresponds to the correct spelling of the highlighted word.

```
Thank yuo for your interest in tha Wizzard's wird
processing pakage. Wizzard is easy to use yet
zufistikated. It is is only a a word processing
package, it it is also a design tool, desktop
publisher, and organizer for your office.
```

FIGURE WP-5
PIXBY paragraph with errors underlined.

- Choose 1 to skip the highlighted word at this time without making the correction, and to have this misspelled word highlighted again if it appears later in the document.
- Choose 2 to skip the highlighted word now and for the remainder of the document. This is usually chosen for words like proper names that are spelled correctly but are not in the dictionary. Notice that the PIXBY file begins with a number of proper names that are not likely to be in the dictionary.
- For words that are spelled correctly and used often, choose 3 to add the word to the dictionary. You should not attempt to add words to the dictionary if you are not using your own computer system.
- Choose 4 to place the cursor in the document so you can correct the word that is misspelled. This is the choice that you must use when no correct alternative spellings are given. Press F7 to exit from the document when you are finished editing the word and wish to return to spell checking.

3. Choose **2** to skip each proper name the speller highlights at the start of the letter

The first word that is actually misspelled is "yuo." Figure WP-6 shows what you'll see on the screen when "yuo" is highlighted. A list of alternative spellings is on the lower half of the screen. If you see the word that you want, choose the corresponding letter to replace the misspelled word with the correct one. To change "yuo" to "you"

4. Choose the letter corresponding to the correct word. (In Figure WP-6, this letter is B.)

FIGURE WP-6
Spell check screen.
WordPerfect's speller contains a dictionary of over 100,000 words and allows you to add new words as you need them.

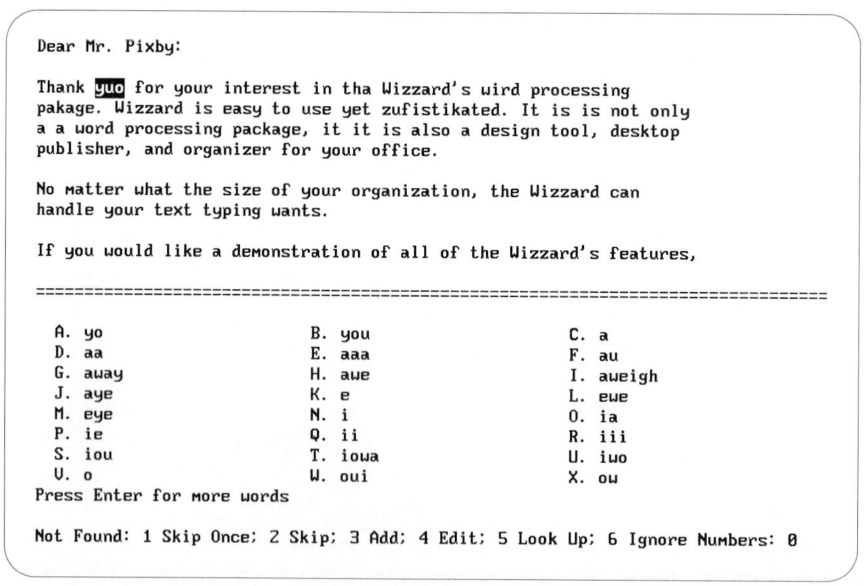

```
Dear Mr. Pixby:

Thank yuo for your interest in tha Wizzard's wird processing
pakage. Wizzard is easy to use yet zufistikated. It is is not only
a a word processing package, it it is also a design tool, desktop
publisher, and organizer for your office.

No matter what the size of your organization, the Wizzard can
handle your text typing wants.

If you would like a demonstration of all of the Wizzard's features,

================================================================================

  A. yo                     B. you                    C. a
  D. aa                     E. aaa                    F. au
  G. away                   H. awe                    I. aweigh
  J. aye                    K. e                      L. ewe
  M. eye                    N. i                      O. ia
  P. ie                     Q. ii                     R. iii
  S. iou                    T. iowa                   U. iwo
  V. o                      W. oui                    X. ow
Press Enter for more words

Not Found: 1 Skip Once; 2 Skip; 3 Add; 4 Edit; 5 Look Up; 6 Ignore Numbers: 0
```

5. Correct the next four misspelled words in the same way.

There are times when the speller finds a word it does not recognize, and no correct alternative spellings are given. In these instances, you will need to fully type the correct word. For instance, when the word "zufistikated" is highlighted

6. Choose **4** to edit the word

7. Use the **arrow keys** and **Del** or **←Backspace** to change the word to "sophisticated"

When the word is spelled correctly

8. Press **F7**

To Correct Double Words. When double words occur, such as "is is" in the first paragraph, you will see the following message:

```
Double Word: 1 2 Skip; 3 Delete 2nd; 4 Edit;
       5 Disable Double Word Checking
```

1. Choose **3** to delete the second word

Note: Choosing 5 would discontinue checking for double words.

2. Continue correcting your PIXBY document

The spell check will continue until no more allegedly misspelled words are found. Then it will give you a word count for your document. At this time

3. Press any key to leave spell check and return to your document

4. Save the corrected version to disk, replacing the original copy

To Find Synonyms and Antonyms

WordPerfect's **thesaurus feature** allows you to check words for possible synonyms. To use a thesaurus, you first flag a word you wish to replace in your document. If the thesaurus feature recognizes the word, it will provide onscreen replacement suggestions in a form resembling that of a hard-copy thesaurus. When you see a word you like, you can type it in directly or type in the key corresponding to it to perform the replacement. WordPerfect also automatically reformats text after automatically replacing a word. In addition, it allows you to do word searches within other word searches, and it provides antonyms as well as synonyms.

To see how WordPerfect's thesaurus feature works,

1. Use the arrow keys to move to the word "wants" in the second paragraph of the PIXBY document

2. Press **Alt** + **F1** to summon the thesaurus

You will now see the screen in Figure WP-7. Suppose you select choice

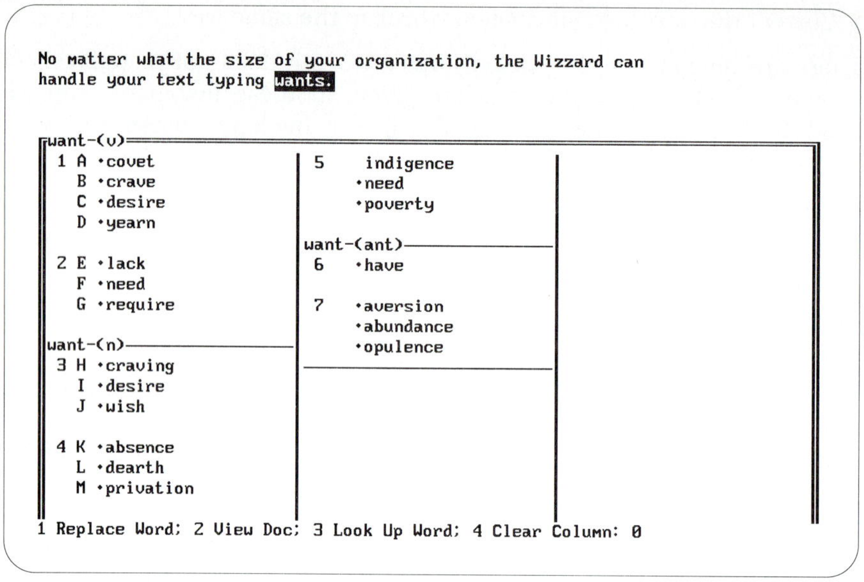

FIGURE WP-7

Thesaurus feature. In WordPerfect, you point to a word to be "looked up" by positioning the highlight on it and then invoking the thesaurus feature. Here the highlight is on *wants,* and the replacement suggestions in the middle of the screen have appeared. WordPerfect automatically makes a replacement when you depress the key that corresponds to it.

"I," corresponding to the word "desire." At this point you can follow either of the procedures below:

Procedure 1:

3. Press **F1** to return to the normal editing screen

4. Type **desires.** in place of "wants."

Procedure 2:

3. Press **1** for Replace Word

4. Type **I,** which corresponds to "desire"

5. When the normal editing screen appears, put an "s" at the end of desire to make it plural.

Note. WordPerfect does not automatically pluralize words that are substituted.

The screen in Figure WP-7 also gives hints as to how to do word lookups within word lookups. Any word preceded by a round bullet (•) has its own thesaurus listing—meaning you can look it up. To try this feature,

1. Move the highlight back to "desires" if it's not already there

2. Press **Alt** + **F1** to summon the thesaurus

3. When you get a screen similar to the one in Figure WP-7, type **3** for "Look Up Word"

4. Type in the letter **J** for "wish" (or alternatively, type in the word **wish**) and press ↵

Note that the last two columns give you a variety of synonyms and antonyms (see the "ant" column) for this word as well as letter choices that you can invoke by the "Procedure 2" method discussed earlier. Also, all of the bulleted words enable you to do further word lookups.

How to Print a Document

WordPerfect has several commands available for printing documents. There are a few, however, that are most used; they are the ones discussed in this exercise. The menu options appear on a separate screen from your document and are itemized vertically.

Before you print your document, be sure your computer is connected to a printer, the printer is turned on, and the paper is correctly aligned in the printer.

To Print a Full Document. One of the print commands that you will be using most often is the command to print your *full* document (that is, all pages of the document). Printing is done with the Shift+F7 key combination. To print the PIXBY document, retrieve it if it is not already on your screen. Then,

1. Press **Shift** + **F7** for PRINT

2. Choose **1** for Full Document

You will be returned to your document as it is printing.

To Print a Page. There will be times when you have made a correction on one page of a longer document and do not need to reprint the entire document. Fortunately, there is a print option that will allow you to print a single page.

Be sure that your cursor is somewhere on the page you want to print.

1. Press **Shift** + **F7** for PRINT

2. Choose **2** for Page

At this point, the page to which the screen cursor is pointing will print. Note that if your document is only one page long, choosing 1 for Full Document or 2 for Page will produce the same result. Later, on page WP-39, you will see how to print several selected pages at once.

EDITING A DOCUMENT

WordPerfect gives you the ability to apply a variety of editing tools as you are developing your document. In this section, you will learn how to edit your PIXBY document in simple ways and how to use the BLOCK command to perform more ambitious types of edits.

There are many ways to edit your document in WordPerfect. You can add or delete lines, insert text, and merge paragraphs, to name only a few examples.

How to Move through a Document

So far, you have been moving through documents by using the arrow keys. However, there are other, faster ways to move around within the document.

Figure WP-8 shows a number of ways to move the cursor through a document. Practice some of these movements with the PIXBY file.

How to Join Paragraphs

Follow the instructions below to merge two paragraphs into one. First retrieve your PIXBY document if it isn't already on the screen. Then,

1. Position the cursor immediately after the period at the end of the first paragraph

FIGURE WP-8
Using cursor movement keys. Keystrokes separated by the plus sign (+) mean you hold down the first key while pressing the second. Keys not separated by plus signs are pressed one after another.

THE CURSOR MOVES	WHEN YOU PRESS
one character to the right	→
one character to the left	←
one line up	↑
one line down	↓
one word to the right	**Ctrl** + →
one word to the left	**Ctrl** + ←
to the beginning of the current line	**Home** ←
to the end of the current line	**Home** →
to the top of the document	**Home** **Home** ↑
to the bottom of the document	**Home** **Home** ↓
to page *n*	**Ctrl** + **Home** **n**
one screen back (up)	− (from numeric keypad)
one screen forward (down)	+ (from numeric keypad)
one page back (up)	**Pg Up**
one page forward (down)	**Pg Dn**
one column to the right	**Ctrl** + **Home** →
one column to the left	**Ctrl** + **Home** ←

2. Press **Del** twice so that the second paragraph is joined to the first one

Note: Remember, the Del key deletes text or codes at the cursor position. What just happened is that you deleted the two hard returns you previously entered at the end of the paragraph. With these returns removed, the two paragraphs are no longer separated.

If your paragraphs are not joined after pressing the Del key twice, keep pressing Del until they are joined. Sometimes extra spaces have been added that are not visible on the screen. By continuing to press Del the paragraphs will eventually join.

Make sure "Typeover" doesn't appear at the lower left of the screen. If it does, press the Ins key to return to the insert mode.

3. Press the **Spacebar** once or twice so that two spaces appear between the two newly joined paragraphs

How to Split a Paragraph

You can also split a paragraph, thereby creating two paragraphs from one.

1. Position your cursor on the **W** of "Wizzard" at the start of the second sentence
2. Press ↵ twice

Because of WordPerfect's insert mode, the text at and to the right of the cursor position will automatically be moved right (in this case down).

How to Insert Blank Lines

You apply the same procedure used above to insert a blank line into your document. Suppose, for example, that you wanted to insert a blank line or two above the date line.

1. Move your cursor to the first character in the date line
2. Press ↵ three times

Your entire document is moved down on the page. If you had moved the cursor to any other location in your document, the same type of result—blank lines—would have occurred. Again, this is because of the automatic insert mode—anything from the cursor position to the right will be pushed to the right or down when additional material is entered.

How to Delete Blank Lines

You can also delete unwanted blank lines. To remove the three blank lines that you just inserted,

1. Press **Home** **Home** ↑ to move your cursor to the top of your document

2. Press **Del** two times

Your date should now be on the second line of your screen.

How to Save a Revised Document

Your document now has a few minor changes. You can quickly save the changes before continuing.

1. Press **F10** for SAVE

The name of your document will appear at the bottom left of your screen.

2. Press ↵

3. Type **Y** for Yes to replace the old file

This command will replace the original version with the revised copy showing on your screen. As mentioned earlier in this section, it is wise to save the document you are working on at regular intervals. It is your insurance against losing most of your work.

How to Block Text

So far you have learned how to use the Backspace, Del, and Ins keys to make corrections. There are other ways to make editing or formatting corrections to words, sentences, paragraphs, or entire documents at one time. By learning how to block text, for example, you can make changes to large areas of a document quickly. A **block** is a segment of continguous text. It can be as small as a few words or as large as a range of several document pages.

To block text, you use the Alt+F4 key combination. The BLOCK command highlights an area of text so that an action can be taken that will affect the entire block at once. Moving, copying, deleting, and formatting the block are four examples of such actions.

At this time you will add a paragraph to your PIXBY file and will then block the text. If your file is not already displayed on the screen, retrieve it.

1. Press **Pg Dn** once and move to the blank line following the title Vice President, Sales

2. Press ↵ twice to add two more blank lines

3. Type the paragraph shown in Figure WP-9.

Do not worry if the right margin aligns differently from the one shown.

4. Move your cursor to the **W** in "With" on the first line of the new paragraph

```
With the Wizzard, you can move or copy a block of text
to a new location in a document and repeat the command
one, two, three times, or more. You can also justify
text, center, add headings, and assign several fonts
to your document. The Wizzard is your own desktop
publisher and editor.
```

FIGURE WP-9
New paragraph for PIXBY document.

5. Press **Alt** + **F4** for BLOCK

The words "Block on" flash in the lower left corner of your screen.

6. Press **Home** **Home** ↓ (down arrow) to move quickly to the end of your document

The entire paragraph is now blocked and should be highlighted on your screen. Note that you block text by invoking the BLOCK command at the point where you want to begin the block and then use cursor-movement keys to move to the point where you want the block to end. When you are at the end of the block, it's time to tell WordPerfect which specific type of action—say, move or copy—you wish to take.

To Move a Block of Text. A *block move* is a process that allows you to identify a block of text and move it anywhere in a file. To move the blocked paragraph

1. Press **Ctrl** + **F4** for MOVE

This key combination is used for both MOVE and COPY commands.

2. Choose **1** or **B** for Block

3. Choose **1** or **M** for Move

You are now back in your normal document screen. Your next action is to position the cursor where you want to move the block of text.

4. Move the cursor to the space immediately after the period at the end of the second paragraph

5. Press the **spacebar** twice to add two spaces

6. Press ↵ to move the paragraph

Your block of text is now moved to its new location.

To Copy a Block of Text. Use the COPY command when you want to copy a block of text to another location, without deleting it from its original location. To copy a block of text, position the cursor at the start of the text to be blocked and

1. Press **Alt** + **F4** for BLOCK, and then press ↓ to block the third paragraph

2. Press **Ctrl** + **F4** for MOVE

3. Choose **1** or **B** for Block

WP

4. Choose **2** or **C** for Copy

5. Position the cursor at the place where you want to copy the text to (say, at the bottom of your document, two lines below your name)

6. Press ↵

Note: If you had a block of text that you wanted to copy several times to various locations in your document, you would follow the steps above the first time you copied it. For each additional location, you would position the cursor where you wanted the copy and press Ctrl + F4, then choose 4 for Retrieve and 1 for Block.

To Delete a Block of Text. Once text is blocked, you can also quickly delete it. As you will see, this is much faster than repeatedly holding down the Del key or the Backspace key to remove text.

1. Move the cursor to the first character of the paragraph you just moved to the bottom of your document

2. Press **Alt** + **F4** for BLOCK

3. Press **Home** **Home** ↓ to block to the end of the paragraph

4. Press **Del** or **←Backspace**

In response to the question at the bottom of the screen

5. Type **Y** for Yes to delete the block

The paragraph is gone.

To Restore a Deleted Block of Text. You have an option in WordPerfect to restore text that you wish you hadn't deleted. You must, however, remember to restore the text fairly soon after it has been deleted; WordPerfect retains the three most recent deletions.

You will now restore the paragraph that was just deleted.

1. Press **F1** for CANCEL

The most recent deletion is displayed and highlighted.

2. Choose **1** to restore the deletion

Note: You can first use the 2 key to cycle through the stored deletions until the one you wish to restore is highlighted.

To Save a Block of Text. Sometimes you will want to save a frequently used block of text so that you can recall it for later use. In the PIXBY document, assume that you want to save the second paragraph, describing the software being sold. You frequently write paragraphs using the same wording and are tired of retyping them each time.

1. Move the cursor to the first character in the second paragraph

2. Press **Alt** + **F4** and then keep pressing ↓ and ↑ to block the paragraph

3. Press **F10** for Save

Note: Normally this key is used to save your entire document. However, when a block command is active, pressing the F10 key will save only the block.

To respond to the message asking for a name for the block of text

4. Type **FeaPara** (for features paragraph)

5. Press ↵

The block of text is now saved as a separate file. To exit from the PIXBY file

6. Press **F7** for EXIT

7. Type **Y** to save the document

8. Press ↵

9. Type **Y** to replace the old version

10. Press ↵ or **N** to exit the document without exiting WordPerfect

To Retrieve a Saved Block of Text. You just saved a block of text under its own filename. It is permanently saved in your default directory. You will now retrieve it.

1. Press **Shift** + **F10** for RETRIEVE

Note: This is a quick way to retrieve when you know the name of the file. It may be used for retrieving either a block of text or any one of the other files in your directory.

2. Type **FeaPara** (the name of the stored block)

3. Press ↵

The paragraph is retrieved to the screen. You could also retrieve this paragraph at a time when another document is on the screen. When this is done, the block of text will be inserted into the other active document at the cursor position.

Note: The paragraph was stored by blocking it and then saving it using the F10 function key. The blocking was done only to select specific text to be saved rather than saving the entire document. Whether you save a block of text or an entire document, the result is the same—you are saving a file to disk.

4. Press **F7** and then type **N** (for No) two times to clear your screen without saving

WP

FORMATTING A DOCUMENT

Formatting commands allow you to control the final appearance of your document. Until now you have been using WordPerfect's *default settings* for such features as margins and line spacing. Defaults are standard settings that the word processor uses unless instructed otherwise by you. You can change margins, tab settings, line spacing, justification, and much more. You can also emphasize certain portions of text by underlining, bolding, and centering.

Now you will create a short document that will give you a chance to use many of these formatting features. If you are just beginning your work session, remember to change your default drive to the drive holding your data diskette.

How to Format Pages

WordPerfect offers a number of formatting features that can change the appearance of text on a page. These changes take effect at the cursor position and affect all following text until another formatting change is made.

To Change Margins. The default margins are set at one inch on both the left and right sides of the document. Margins are measured from the left and right edges of the page in inches. Often you may want to make margins larger or smaller. To change margins

1. Press **Shift** + **F8** for FORMAT

You will see the format menu shown in Figure WP-10

2. Choose **1** or **L** for Line

You will see the line format menu shown in Figure WP-11.

FIGURE WP-10
The Format menu.

```
Format

     1 - Line
              Hyphenation                       Line Spacing
              Justification                     Margins Left/Right
              Line Height                       Tab Set
              Line Numbering                    Widow/Orphan Protection

     2 - Page
              Center Page (top to bottom)       New Page Number
              Force Odd/Even Page               Page Numbering
              Headers and Footers               Paper Size/Type
              Margins Top/Bottom                Suppress

     3 - Document
              Display Pitch                     Redline Method
              Initial Codes/Font                Summary

     4 - Other
              Advance                           Overstrike
              Conditional End of Page           Printer Functions
              Decimal Characters                Underline Spaces/Tabs
              Language

Selection: 0
```

```
Format: Line

     1 - Hyphenation                      Off

     2 - Hyphenation Zone - Left          10%
                            Right         4%

     3 - Justification                    Yes

     4 - Line Height                      Auto

     5 - Line Numbering                   No

     6 - Line Spacing                     1

     7 - Margins - Left                   1"
                   Right                  1"

     8 - Tab Set                          0", every 0.5"

     9 - Widow/Orphan Protection          No


Selection: 0
```

FIGURE WP-11
The Line Format menu.

3. Choose **7** or **M** for Margins

Your cursor will move to the current left margin setting.

4. Type **1.5** to set the left margin

5. Press **↵**

6. Type **1.5** to set the right margin

7. Press **↵** and press **F7** to exit

Your margins have been reset and you are ready to begin typing the document shown in Figure WP-12. Press Enter after each of the first three lines. Do not worry about where the right margin wraps; as with other exercises in this guide, the right margin may align differently from the one shown. When finished, check for errors in the document and make any corrections. Save the document under the name REPORT.

To Change Line Spacing. The default setting for line spacing is single spacing. Now that you have finished the basic document, suppose you have decided that it needs to be double spaced. This is easy to do with WordPerfect's format options. To change line spacing to double space

1. Move to the first character at the top of the page (the D in "DEMAND")

2. Press **Shift** + **F8** for FORMAT

3. Choose **1** or **L** for Line

4. Choose **6** or **S** for Line Spacing

Your cursor will move to the current line spacing setting.

FIGURE WP-12
REPORT document.

```
DEMAND FOR QUALIFIED DATA PROCESSING PERSONNEL
Study Developed by the Human Resources Department
SeaTech Corporation


Background

As the area of data processing in the business
community grows, the demand for qualified personnel
also soars in our industry. SeaTech has increased in
size by 100 percent over the last five years, and the
need to fill an ever increasing number of data
processing vacancies is serious.

As employers, however, we need to differentiate
between potentially good employees and effective data
processing employees. Developing the basic criteria to
define a "qualified programmer," for instance, starts
with fundamental education background. In prior years,
the criterion was equipment operation skills. As the
field has expanded and the work become extremely
technical, business management has begun to reevaluate
the staffing needs of its data processing and MIS
departments.

The basic skills needed to write programs for SeaTech
cannot be learned on the job. Those skills must come
through an accredited institution offering courses in
computer science, software applications, and
programming skills.
```

5. Type **2** to set double spacing

6. Press ↵

7. Press **F7** to return to your document

To Justify Text. WordPerfect enables you to format a printed document with either a *ragged right* (*left* justification) or *justified right* (*full* justification) margin as shown in Figure WP-13. (You do not have to type in the document in Figure WP-13; it is shown merely for illustration.) Users who create business documents often would rather format with a ragged right margin, as the extra blank spaces between words in the fully justified format make the document harder to read. The default setting for **justification** in WordPerfect produces a justified right margin when a document is printed, though you will see only a ragged right margin on the screen.

To change justification in REPORT, your cursor should be at the top of the page. To produce a ragged-right edge

1. Press **Shift** + **F8** for FORMAT

2. Choose **1** or **L** for Line

3. Choose **3** or **J** for Justification

4. Choose **1** or **L** for Left Justification

FIGURE WP-13

Justification.

The two most popular text justification options are (a) ragged right edge (justified *left*) and (b) justified right edge (*full* justification). All documents are displayed onscreen with a ragged right edge but will justify correctly when printed.

```
     One of the most interesting
parts of the meeting was when
Elizabeth talked about corporate
strategy.  I think that everyone
realized that unless our information
systems are modernized, Platte
Company will no longer be in
business by year's end.
```

(a) Ragged right edge

```
     One  of  the  most  interesting
parts   of   the  meeting  was  when
Elizabeth  talked  about  corporate
strategy.   I  think  that  everyone
realized that unless our information
systems  are  modernized,   Platte
Company  will  no  longer  be   in
business by year's end.
```

(b) Justified right edge

To Preview Documents. You can check to see if your document has a ragged right margin through WordPerfect's **view document** feature. This feature shows you onscreen what the document will look like when it is printed. To preview your document at this point

1. Press **↑Shift** + **F7** for PRINT

2. Select **6** or **V** for View Document

3. Choose one of the following options:

- **1** for viewing the document at normal size (100%)
- **2** for viewing the document blown up (200%)
- **3** for viewing a full page
- **4** for viewing facing pages

If you have selected 1 or 2, use the cursor-movement keys to move the document around.

4. Press **F7** to return to your document

To Indent Paragraphs. The indent feature allows you to indent an entire paragraph without changing the margins elsewhere in the document. This feature is useful when you are typing a paper with lengthy quotes or lists that you want to set off from the main text.

You will now add some more text to the REPORT document. Before doing this you will change back to one-inch margins and single spacing for the new text.

1. Move your cursor to the bottom of your document
2. Press ↵ twice to move to a new blank line and to leave a blank line after the last paragraph
3. Change the left and right margins to 1″, in other words, left margin at 1″, right margin at 1″
4. Change the line spacing to 1 for single spacing

To add the itemized list shown in Figure WP-14 to the end of your document

5. Type the first sentence of the text shown in Figure WP-14.
6. Press ↵ twice after the word "are:"
7. Type **1.** at the left margin
8. Press **F4** to indent at the first tab stop

   Note: Tabs are discussed in detail in the next section.

9. Type the sentence after the "1."

Note that the second line of the sentence is automatically indented.

10. Press ↵ once after "terminology" to add a hard return (which will end the indent)
11. Continue to type the remaining items in the list, pressing **F4** to indent after typing each number
12. Press **F10** and resave your document under the name REPORT

To Change Tab Settings. Default tab settings are set every half inch. Each time you depress the Tab key, you will note that the cursor moves a half inch to the right. (Try this—then, move the cursor back to its original position with the Backspace key.)

FIGURE WP-14
List added to REPORT document.

```
The criteria on which we need to place an emphasis for
new industry recruits are:

1. The qualified applicant should possess skills in
   fundamental computer concepts and terminology.
2. The qualified applicant should possess at least a
   two-year degree in computer science, business, or a
   related field.
3. He/she should have a working knowledge of COBOL as
   well as three software application programs,
   including a word processing program, a spreadsheet
   program, and a database program.
4. He/she should have excellent written and oral
   communication skills.
```

There could be many reasons that you might want to change the tab settings. If you want to place a column of figures at the fifth tab stop of this document, for example, it would be awkward on each line to press the Tab key five times to move toward the center of your page. It would be very convenient to have only the necessary tab stop on your page so that pressing the Tab key once on a line would send you to the correct location.

There are four options for tab settings:

L for Left	Text is left-aligned at the tab stop
C for Center	Text is centered over the tab setting
R for Right	Text is right-aligned at the tab stop
D for Decimal	Text is aligned on a decimal point

Each of these tab settings can also be set to have a dot leader which fills the space in front of tabs with a line of dots.

Tab settings can be measured either from the left edge of the page or from the left margin. **Absolute tabs** are measured from the left edge of the page, regardless of the current margin setting. **Relative tabs** are measured from the left margin. When you use relative tabs, the distance between tab settings and the left margin always stays the same even if the margins are changed. Relative tabs are the default setting, and are the type you will probably use most often. To verify that you have relative tabs,

1. Press **Shift** + **F8** for FORMAT

2. Choose **1** or **L** for Line and make sure "Rel" is specified in option 8. If it's not, choose **8** or **T** for Tab set, choose **T** to change Type, and then choose **2** or **R** for Relative tab.

3. Press **F7** twice to exit the menu

To practice changing tab settings, you will begin by adding the table shown in Figure WP-15 to your REPORT document.

1. Move your cursor to the bottom of your document and press ↵ twice

2. Type the first three lines of Figure WP-15, and press ↵ twice after the word "positions":

```
At present, we have the following openings. The
criteria stated should be given priority in placement
for these positions:

          Data Entry                      6.50/hr
          Data Processing Asst. 1         7.00
          Data Processing Asst. 2         7.50
          Data Processing Senior Rep.     8.00
          Programmer 1                    8.00
          Programmer 2                   10.00
```

FIGURE WP-15
Table added to REPORT document.

WP

To summon the tab ruler

3. Press **Shift** + **F8** for FORMAT

4. Choose **1** or **L** for Line and **8** or **T** for Tab Set

A tab ruler line similar to the one in Figure WP-16 will be displayed at the bottom of your screen. Note, for instance, that 0″ signifies the left edge of the paper and +1″ is one inch from the left edge (which is also the left margin).

This ruler line shows all of the default tabs (L for left align at every half inch). It also shows the total number of character positions across the entire width of the paper.

Tabs can be set by moving the cursor with the arrow keys to the corresponding position on the tab ruler and then pressing L, C, R, or D for the type of tab. Left-aligned tabs can also be set by typing the inch position and pressing Enter. If you need a different type of tab at that position, you can then simply type the corresponding letter over the L that appears on the tab ruler. To set a dot leader type a period on top of the letter, which will show in reverse video.

To change the settings on the tab ruler to those needed for the table you will be adding to the REPORT document

5. Press **Ctrl** + **End** to delete all of the default tab settings

To set the tab for the first column in the table

6. Press **→** to move to +1.5″ (halfway between +1″ and +2″) on the ruler line

7. Type **L** to set a left-aligned tab setting at +1.5″

To set the tab for the second column in the table

8. Move to +**5**″ on the ruler line

9. Type **D** to set a decimal tab setting

10. Press **F7** twice to return to your document

Your tabs are now correctly set. To type the two columns in the table

11. Press **Tab** once to get to the first column and type **Data Entry**

12. Press **Tab** again, to get to the second column, and type **6.50/hr**

FIGURE WP-16
The Tab ruler.

```
L....L....L....L....L....L....L....L....L....L....L....L....L....L....L....L....L...
|    ^    |    ^    |    ^    |    ^    |    ^    |    ^    |    ^    |    ^
0"        +1"       +2"       +3"       +4"       +5"       +6"       +7"
Delete EOL (clear tabs); Enter Number (set tab); Del (clear tab);
Type; Left; Center; Right; Decimal; .= Dot Leader; Press Exit when done.
```

When you type the period, the decimal will automatically align at the tab stop.

13. Enter the remaining lines of the table in the same way

How to Use Reveal Codes

As you work on a document a number of formatting codes, such as the code for a hard return and the code for a soft return, are automatically inserted. These *codes* are not visible on the normal screen but can be seen by using the REVEAL CODES command to display a special **reveal codes** screen. To implement this command

1. Press **Alt** + **F3** or **F11** for REVEAL CODES

Note that your screen is split into two parts, similar to the screen shown in Figure WP-17. The top half shows your normal document screen and the bottom half shows the same part of your document with all the codes that were automatically entered as you typed. A few of the many codes you are likely to encounter now and during the course of using WordPerfect are shown in Figure WP-18. At first these codes look quite confusing but you will become accustomed to checking your work on the Reveal Codes screen. Many school labs have a WordPerfect reference manual available that describes all of the codes.

Use the arrow keys to scroll through your document. Note that there is a cursor in the upper half of the screen that is coordinated with a highlight in the lower part. When one is moved, the other moves to the same relative place at the same time.

```
      DEMAND FOR QUALIFIED DATA PROCESSING PERSONNEL

      Study Developed by the Human Resources Department

      SeaTech Corporation


      Background

                                                  Doc 1 Pg 1 Ln 1" Pos 1.5"
▲   {    ▲    ▲    ▲    ▲    ▲    ▲    ▲    ▲    ▲    ▲    }    ▲    ▲    ▲
[L/R Mar:1.5",1.5"][Ln Spacing:2]DEMAND FOR QUALIFIED DATA PROCESSING PERSONNEL[
HRt]
Study Developed by the Human Resources Department[HRt]
SeaTech Corporation[HRt]
[HRt]
Background[HRt]
[HRt]



Press Reveal Codes to restore screen
```

FIGURE WP-17
Reveal Codes screen.

FIGURE WP-18
Selected Reveal Codes.
A few of the codes used by WordPerfect to format text.

CODE*	DESCRIPTION
[-]	Hyphen
[Block]	Beginning of block
[Bold]	Bold
[Center]	Center
[Footer]	Footer
[Header]	Header
[HPg]	Hard page break
[HRt]	Hard return
[->Indent]	Indent
[Just]	Justification
[Ln Spacing]	Line spacing setting
[L/R Mar]	Left and right margins
[Pg Num]	New page number
[Pg Numbering]	Page numbering
[SPg]	Soft page break
[SRt]	Soft return
[T/B Margins]	Top and bottom margins
[Tab]	Tab
[Tab Set]	Tab setting
[Und]	Underline

*Uppercase letters indicate "on" status; lowercase letters indicate "off" as in[UND] [Und].

Now that your report is finished, suppose you realize that it is longer than expected and you want it to fit on one page. When you made your margins larger and double spaced the top of your report, your document expanded to cover more than a page. If you set your margins back to one inch and go back to single spaced lines, the report will fit on one page. It is easy to get it to fit by deleting the formatting codes corresponding to the margin and line-spacing settings from the reveal codes screen.

To Delete in the Reveal Codes Screen. If you want to change any formatting codes it is easiest to do this from the Reveal Codes screen because you can see exactly what you are doing. One of the most common reasons codes are deleted is that WordPerfect will be doing something that appears to be strange, such as not indenting properly. When an event like this happens, the only way to correct the problem is to retrieve the reveal codes screen. Sometimes, for instance, people delete text at the beginning of a paragraph but forget to remove the corresponding tab or indent, which is hidden. These extraneous codes can later cause difficulties.

You will now delete the codes for the margin setting and the double spacing that were entered at the beginning of your report.

1. Move to the top of your REPORT document by pressing **Home** **Home** ↑

2. Press **Alt** + **F3** or **F11** for REVEAL CODES

To delete in the Reveal Codes screen

3. Move your cursor directly onto the[L/R Mar: 1.5″, 1.5″] code

Notice how your cursor expands to cover the entire code.

4. Press **Del**

5. Delete the [Ln Spacing: 2] code in the same way

Your document reverts to the default settings of one-inch margins and single spacing and will now fit on one page. Compare your document with the one shown in Figure WP-19. Save your document as REPORT.

To get rid of the reveal codes screen, press the Cancel key, F1.

How to Format Text

It is easy to make formatting changes in WordPerfect—in other words, changes that emphasize certain portions of text. You may want to center headings, or to have text bolded or underlined, for instance. These formatting features can be specified before or after typing the text.

Several things could be done to make the REPORT document look even better than it already does. The following instructions will allow you to practice some text-formatting features. Since your document is already completed, you should follow the instructions below that pertain to formatting text *after* it has been typed.

To Center before Entering Text. Headings or titles are often centered. You can request centering before typing the text to be centered by following the instructions below:

1. Press **Shift** + **F6** for CENTER

2. Type the text you want centered

3. Press ↵

To Center after Text Has Been Typed. Often you will decide to center text after it has been typed. To practice centering, retrieve your REPORT file if necessary.

1. Move your cursor to the D in “DEMAND” in the main heading

2. Press **Shift** + **F6** to CENTER the line

FIGURE WP-19
Finished REPORT document.

DEMAND FOR QUALIFIED DATA PROCESSING PERSONNEL
Study Developed by the Human Resources Department
SeaTech Corporation

Background

As the area of data processing in the business community grows, the demand for qualified personnel also soars in our industry. SeaTech has increased in size by 100 percent over the last five years, and the need to fill an ever increasing number of data processing vacancies is serious.

As employers, however, we need to differentiate between potentially good employees and effective data processing employees. Developing the basic criteria to define a "qualified programmer," for instance, starts with fundamental education background. In prior years, the criterion was equipment operation skills. As the field has expanded and the work become extremely technical, business management has begun to reevaluate the staffing needs of its data processing and MIS departments.

The basic skills needed to write programs for SeaTech cannot be learned on the job. Those skills must come through an accredited institution offering courses in computer science, software applications, and programming skills.

The criteria on which we need to place an emphasis for new industry recruits are:

1. The qualified applicant should possess skills in fundamental computer concepts and terminology.
2. The qualified applicant should possess at least a two-year degree in computer science, business, or a related field.
3. He/she should have a working knowledge of COBOL as well as of three software applications programs, including a word processing program, a spreadsheet program, and a database program.
4. He/she should have excellent written and oral communication skills.

At present, we have the following openings. The criteria stated should be given priority in placement for these positions:

Data Entry	6.50/hr
Data Processing Asst. 1	7.00
Data Processing Asst. 2	7.50
Data Processing Senior Rep.	8.00
Programmer 1	8.00
Programmer 2	10.00

3. Center both the second and the third line headings

Note: To make the process go faster, block both lines at once and then issue the CENTER command. (Remember to answer **Y** for Yes at the screen prompt.)

To Bold before Entering Text. **Bold** is a feature in WordPerfect that allows the strokes of letters to look thicker and darker than normal text.

1. Press **F6** to turn on the BOLD feature
2. Type the text you want to make bold
3. Press **F6** to turn off the bold feature

To Bold after Text Has Been Typed. It is also possible to bold text that has already been typed in a document. In your REPORT document

1. Move to the D in "DEMAND" in the centered heading at the top of the page
2. Press **Alt** + **F4** and **End** to block the line
3. Press **F6**

Note: The way bolded text appears on your screen will depend on the kind of monitor you are using. On some monitors the text will appear bolded. On other monitors, bolded text may be different color or may show a different color background.

To Underline before Entering Text. *Underline* is another formatting feature used to emphasize text. To underline while entering text:

1. Press **F8** for UNDERLINE
2. Type the text you want underlined
3. Press **F8** to turn off underlining

To Underline after Text Has Been Typed. Follow the instructions below to underline text in the REPORT document.

1. Block the word "Background" prior to the first paragraph
2. Press **F8** for UNDERLINE

   Note: The way underlined text appears on your screen will depend on the kind of monitor you are using. On some monitors the text will appear underlined. On other monitors, underlined text may be a different color or may show a different color background.
3. Save your revised document and clear the screen or quit

How to Format Long Documents

Up until now, the documents that you have created have been very short. When you begin working with longer documents like reports or research papers there are a number of features that will be particularly useful. For instance, you will usually want to number pages. You may also want to use a header or a footer to provide information about your report on each page. And, you may choose to print only selected pages of a document.

WP

In the exercise that follows, you will retrieve your REPORT file and change the line spacing to double spacing to make it two pages long.

1. Retrieve REPORT

2. Move the cursor to the beginning of your document

3. Press **Shift** + **F8** and choose options as necessary to double space the document

To Number Pages. When you are typing a one-page letter or any other one-page document, it is not necessary to number your page. For documents that are at least two pages long, it is very helpful to include page numbers. These numbers usually start with page 2; the first page is usually left unnumbered.

The following instructions will number pages when your document is printed. You will not be able to see these page numbers on your screen (although you can rely on WordPerfect's status line to tell you which page you are on).

To number pages, start with your cursor positioned at the top of page 2.

1. Press **Shift** + **F8** for FORMAT

2. Choose **2** for Page

3. Choose **6** for Page Numbering

4. Choose **4** for Page Number Position

You will see a screen that shows several pages with numbers in different locations.

5. Select the number that corresponds to the position where you want your page numbers located

Example: Selection 6 would place page numbers at the bottom center of every page.

6. Press **F7** to return to your document

To Create a Header or Footer. Headers and footers are lines that appear on every page of a document. They contain descriptive information such as the title of the document or the name of a particular chapter in the document. **Headers** are used at the top of pages and **footers** are used at the bottom.

Usually headers and footers are one or two lines in length. You could make them longer, but this is generally not practical. WordPerfect will automatically calculate the number of lines needed for your header or footer and subtract them from the total number of lines available on your page. Headers and footers will not show on your regular document screen but you can check on the placement of the header or footer codes by looking at the Reveal Codes screen or the view-document feature.

Usually you will not want a header or footer on the first page of your document. Just as with page numbers, you will begin a header or footer on page 2. The following instructions will help you create a header for your REPORT document. A footer would be created in much the same way. To create a header

1. Move the cursor to the top of page 2 so the cursor is under the first character on that page

2. Press **Shift** + **F8** for FORMAT

3. Choose **2** or **P** for Page

4. Choose **3** or **H** for Headers

5. Choose **1** for Header A and then choose **2** for Every Page

You are in a blank screen now that looks similar to your document screen. This is the screen for typing and saving a header.

6. Type **Data Processing Report** as the header

7. Press **F7** to exit and save the header

8. Press **F7** again to return to your document

9. Save the revised document as REPORT2 so that you will not replace the single-spaced version

To Print Selected Pages. You have already used the Shift + F7 key combination to print a full document or a single page. Suppose you wanted to print only a range of pages of your document. To print selected pages:

1. Press **Shift** + **F7** for PRINT

2. Choose **3** for Document on Disk

In response to the message asking for the document name

3. Type **REPORT2**

4. Press ↵

When asked to specify pages

5. Type 1-2 as the range of pages that you want to print

Note: You could enter any combination of individual page numbers and page ranges, such as 5-11, 18, 21-24 or 6-11, 15, 21.

6. Press ↵

7. Press **F7** to return to your document

The pages of your document will begin printing.

To Create Hard Page Breaks. Occasionally during the course of formatting a long document, you will want certain text to start on a new page, such as when a document is divided into major "sections" (or chapters). You can force WordPerfect to type a page break as follows:

1. Place the cursor at the location in your document where you want a page break

2. Type **Ctrl** + ↵

Note that a double dotted line appears onscreen at the cursor position, indicating the page break. Such a break is referred to as a **hard page break.** This is in contrast to the **soft page break,** which shows onscreen as a single dotted line, that WordPerfect automatically produces. You can, of course, delete the hard break by deleting its reveal code.

SEARCHING AND REPLACING

There is a feature in virtually every word processor that allows you to **search** for particular text strings in your document—a string consisting of, say, a few characters, an entire word, or several contiguous words. You can also search for strings and **replace** them with other strings. If a date, for example, is entered many times throughout a long document, you can quickly change all occurrences of it by searching for the date and replacing it with a new one. This can be done with a single command so that in a long document all dates are replaced in one step. With WordPerfect, the search string can be as long as 59 characters.

Using the search option is also often the fastest way to move through a very long document to reach a specific section. You can do this by searching for a particular word or group of words in an area of a document, such as a chapter heading or other titles appearing on the page.

How to Start a Search

To practice searching for a specific string of text

1. Retrieve the REPORT document (if necessary)

2. Move your cursor to the beginning of your document

3. Press **F2** for FORWARD SEARCH

The cursor now appears to the right of the search prompt (Srch) in the lower left corner of the screen.

4. Type **data** as the string for which you are searching

5. Press **F2** again to start the search process

Note: DO NOT press the Enter key this time. If you do, you will see the [HRt] code that is also visible on the Reveal Codes screen. You begin and end a search process using the F2 (Search) key.

At this time, you can edit the word "data" or add text at this location in your document. Leave the word as is for now.

You can find other occurrences of the word "data" throughout the file. Since you entered the word at the beginning of the search process in lowercase letters, SEARCH will locate all occurrences of "data" in both upper- and lowercase. If you had entered the word in uppercase letters, however, SEARCH would locate only the word "DATA" in uppercase letters.

To continue searching for "data"

6. Keep pressing **F2** until all occurrences are found and the *Not found* message appears

You can press the F1 key at any time to cancel the search.

How to Replace Text

Use the REPLACE command when you wish to both search for and replace existing text. Do the following:

1. Move to the beginning of your document

2. Press **Alt** + **F2** for REPLACE

3. Press **Y** for Yes to confirm each replacement

Note: Pressing N for No would replace for every occurrence automatically without your confirmation. This action can lead to some very serious problems if you are not careful.

4. Type **data processing** in lowercase letters as the phrase to search for

5. Press **F2**

Note: Be sure not to press Enter. In response to the "replace with" message,

6. Type **MIS computer**

7. Press **F2**

Your cursor has moved to the first occurrence of the words "data processing."

8. Press **Y** for Yes to each occurrence of "data processing" to replace it with "MIS computer"

When the confirm message no longer appears, all occurrences have been located and replaced.

9. Clear the screen without saving the changed document

COMMAND REFERENCE

This is a quick reference guide and should primarily be used to look up commands and features only after completing all exercises. Upon completion of the tutorials, refer to this summary for quick reference to key commands and features.

Blocking Text

Use this command to assign special formats; to delete, move, or copy text; and to save blocks of text such as frequently used paragraphs.

1. Move the cursor to the beginning of the text to be blocked
2. Press **Alt** + **F4** for BLOCK
3. Use the arrow keys or another combination of keys to block the desired text
4. Perform editing or formatting procedures or save text
5. Press **Alt** + **F4** again to turn blocking off if necessary

Boldfacing Text

Boldfacing enables you to output text with thicker strokes than normal text.

Before Typing in the Text.

1. Press **F6** for BOLD, to turn on boldfacing
2. Type the text to be boldfaced
3. Press **F6** again, to turn off boldfacing

After Typing in the Text.

1. Block the text to be boldfaced
2. Press **F6** for BOLD

Cancelling a Command

Cancelling enables you to back out of a command and return to your document.

1. Press **F1** for CANCEL

Centering Text

The centering command enables text to be centered on a line, either before or after you type in the text.

Before Typing in the Text.

1. Press **Shift** + **F6** for CENTER
2. Type the text to be centered
3. Press ↵

After Typing in the Text.

1. Move cursor to beginning of the text to be centered
2. Press **Shift** + **F6** for CENTER

Changing the Default Drive

The default drive often must be changed when you enter WordPerfect so files are saved to and retrieved from a data diskette.

1. Press **F5** for LIST FILES

A message appears in the lower right corner asking you to press the equal sign (=) to change the directory.

2. Press =
3. Type **A:** (from a hard-disk system), or
   Type **B:** (from a dual-diskette system)
4. Press ↵

The new default directory prompt is now showing in the lower left corner of your screen

5. Press ↵ again to view the directory of the default drive
6. Press **F7** for EXIT, to return to your document

Clearing the Screen

Clearing the screen allows you to start on a fresh document.

1. Press **F7** for EXIT
2. Press **Y** or **N** depending on whether or not you want to save your document; if you type Y, you must provide a name for the document
3. Press **N** to clear the screen

Copying Text

Copying allows a duplicate version of a block of text to be placed in another section of a document.

1. Block the text to be copied

2. Press **Ctrl** + **F4** for MOVE

3. Choose **1** or **B** (for *Block*)

4. Choose **2** or **C** (for *Copy*)

5. Move the cursor to the location where you wish to copy the text

6. Press ↵

Deleting Text

Deleting removes text from a document.

Deleting a Character or a Word at a Time, or Deleting to the End of a Line or Page. Follow the instructions below:

To delete	Press
the current character	**Del**
the character to the left	**← Backspace**
the current word	**Ctrl** + **← Backspace**
the word to the left	**Home** **← Backspace**
the word to the right	**Home** **Del**
to the end of the line	**Ctrl** + **End**
to the end of the page	**Ctrl** + **Pg Dn**

Deleting a Block of Text.

1. Block the text to be deleted

2. Press **Del**

3. Press **Y**

Exiting WordPerfect

WordPerfect's Exit command, F7, lets you to leave WordPerfect for DOS and (optionally) save your document.

1. Press **F7** for EXIT

2. If you wish to save your document, type **Y** and follow the instructions for naming the document to be saved. If you do not wish to save your document, type **N**

3. Type **Y** to exit WordPerfect

Headers and Footers

Headers and footers contain brief information that identifies a page. You can create headers and/or footers for odd pages, even pages, or all pages.

1. Move the cursor to the very top of the page where you want the header or footer to begin
2. Press **Shift** + **F8** for FORMAT
3. Choose **2** or **P** (for *Page*)
4. Choose **3** or **H** for *Headers,* **4** or **F** for *Footers*
5. Choose **1** for *Header A or Footer A*
6. Choose the desired pages for the header or footer to appear
7. Type the header or footer
8. Press **F7** to exit and save the new changes

Indenting Paragraphs

Indenting is appropriate both for a numbered list of sentences or paragraphs and for sentences or paragraphs that are not numbered.

1. If preparing a numbered list, type the number and period at the left margin; otherwise go directly to step 2
2. Press **F4** (rather than the Tab key) to move to the tab position at which you want the indent to occur
3. Type the text, letting the right margin wrap
4. Press **↵** to end the indent.
5. Repeat this procedure for each item to be indented

Inserting Text

Inserting allows text to be added at the cursor position, pushing existing text over to the right. To insert text

1. Make sure the Insert mode is active

   Note: If the word "Typeover" appears at the bottom left of your screen you are not in the Insert mode and must strike the **Ins** key to get there.

2. Move the cursor to the place where you want to insert text.
3. Type the text to be inserted.

Justification

Most people choose to format a document with either a justified right edge or with a ragged right edge. WordPerfect automatically defaults to a justified right edge on printing. To change justification

1. Press **Shift** + **F8** for FORMAT
2. Choose **1** or **L** (for *Line*)
3. Choose **3** or **J** (for *Justification*)
4. When WordPerfect places your cursor in a position to change the justification, type **Left** (for a ragged right edge) or **Full** (for a justified right edge)

Margin Adjustment

WordPerfect allows you to adjust either or both left and right margins of your document.

1. Press **Shift** + **F8** for FORMAT
2. Type **1** or **L** (for *Line)*
3. Type **7** or **M** (for *Margins*)
4. Type in the left and/or right margins over the current margin setting(s)
5. Press **F7** for EXIT, to return to your document

Line Spacing

The line spacing option allows text to be single-spaced, double-spaced, and so on. Move to the beginning of the line in your text at which you want to begin the new spacing and

1. Press **Shift** + **F8** for FORMAT
2. Choose **1** or **L** (for *Line*)
3. Choose **6** or **S** (for *Line Spacing*)
4. Type **2** for double spacing or **3** for triple spacing (or whatever number you choose)
5. Press **↵**
6. Press **F7** to exit

Moving Text

Moving text is an action that physically removes a block of text from one place in a document and puts it in another.

1. Block the text to be moved
2. Press **Ctrl** + **F4** for MOVE
3. Choose **1** or **B** (for *Block*)
4. Choose **1** or **M** (for *Move*)
5. Move the cursor to new location in document
6. Press ↵

Numbering Pages

The WordPerfect default is no page numbers. When used, page numbers do not appear on the screen. To number pages of a WordPerfect document

1. Place the cursor at the beginning of the page where the page numbers will start
2. Press **Shift** + **F8** for FORMAT
3. Press **2** or **P** (for *Page Format*)
4. Press **6** for *Page Numbering*
5. Press **4** for *Page Number Position*

WordPerfect will now display eight page-numbering styles from which to choose. (For instance, style 1 allows you to print a number at the top left of every page.)

6. Type in a number from 1 to 8, corresponding to a page-numbering style
7. Press **F7** to return to your document

Note: You can also print page numbers within a header or a footer by placing the cursor where you want the number to print in the header or footer and pressing Ctrl+B

Page Breaks

The standard length of a WordPerfect page is 54 lines. The line of dashes (-) you see at the bottom of a standard 54-line page is called a *soft page break.* You can also force page breaks when you want a page to be shorter than standard length, thereby creating a *hard page break.* A hard page break will show as a line of equal signs (=). WordPerfect will automatically adjust pages following a hard break to be 54 lines in length. To produce a hard break

1. Place the cursor on the character that is to begin a new page
2. Press **Ctrl** + ↵

Printing Documents

WordPerfect allows several printing options, including printing an entire document, a single page, or a range of pages.

Printing the Entire Document.

1. Press **Shift** + **F7** for PRINT
2. Press **1** or **F** (for *Full Document*)

Printing a Single Page.

1. Position the cursor anywhere on the page you want to print
2. Press **Shift** + **F7**
3. Press **2** or **P** (for *Page*) to send the page to the printer

Printing a Range of Pages.

1. Press **Shift** + **F7**
2. Press **5** or **M** (for *Multiple Pages*)
3. Press ↵ to print all pages, or type the numbers corresponding to the range of pages to be printed

Examples:

- □ 11, 17 (means pages 11 and 17 only)
- □ 11-17 (means pages 11 through 17)
- □ 10, 12-14 (means pages 10, 12, 13, and 14)
- □ 11- (means from page 11 on)
- □ -11 (means up to page 11)

Printing from the Directory Listing.

1. Press **F5** for LIST FILES
2. Press ↵ to confirm directory
3. Highlight the filename
4. Press **4** or **P** (for *Print*)
5. Press ↵ to print the entire document or type in a range of pages and press ↵

Stopping or Cancelling a Print Job. To stop or cancel a job that is printing:

1. Press **Shift** + **F7** for PRINT
2. Press **4** or **C** (for *Control Printer*)

3. Press **5** or **S** to *Stop* printing

At this point you can resume or cancel the job. To resume the job,

4. Press **G,** for *Go*

To cancel the job,

5. Press **1** or **C** (for *Cancel*)

6. Press ↵ to cancel the current job (Cancelling may not work if the printer has a large buffer.)

Replacing Text

Replacement requires you to identify both the text string you want to search for in the document as well as the text string you want to replace it with. With the cursor placed where you wish to begin the search,

1. Press **Alt** + **F2** for REPLACE

2. Press **Y** for *Yes* to confirm replacement (if necessary)

3. Type the search string (up to 59 characters)

4. Press **F2**

5. Type the replacement text

6. Press **F2**

7. Confirm replacements and repeat

Retrieving a Document

Retrieving is the act of fetching a document from disk and loading it into RAM. To retrieve a document

From the Directory Listing.

1. Press **F5** for LIST FILES

2. Press ↵ to confirm directory

3. Highlight the filename

4. Choose **1** or **R** (for *Retrieve*)

5. If there is a document in memory, press **Y** to add new document or **N** to cancel the command

Using the F10 key.

1. Press **Shift** + **F10** for RETRIEVE

2. Type the name of the file

3. Press ↵

Revealing Codes

Use the REVEAL CODES command to see all formats, tabs, indents, and other formatting codes. You may edit and delete formats from the Reveal Codes screen as well as add text.

1. Press **Alt** + **F3** or **F11** for REVEAL CODES

2. Press **Alt** + **F3** or **F11** again to return to the regular document screen after editing

Saving a Document

Saving a document places onto disk a copy of the active document in RAM. To save

Using the F7 key.

1. Press **F7** for EXIT

2. Press **Y** to save

3. Type a document name or press ↵ to accept the name showing on the screen

4. Press **Y** to replace (if necessary)

5. Press **Y** to exit WordPerfect or **N** to clear the screen

Using the F10 key.

1. Press **F10** for SAVE

2. Type your document name or press ↵ to accept the name showing on the screen

3. Press **Y** to replace (if necessary)

Saving and Retrieving Blocks of Text

Use this feature to save frequently used blocks of text.

To Save.

1. Block the text to be saved

2. Press **F10** for SAVE

3. Give the block a name and press ↵

To Retrieve.

1. Press **F5** for RETRIEVE

2. Press ↵ to the directory name

3. Select the filename you gave to the block of text

4. Choose **1** or **R** to *Retrieve*

Searching for Text

Searching for text requires you to identify the string of characters you want to find. There is a separate command to *both* search and replace (see "Replacing Text"). With the cursor placed where you want to begin the search,

1. Press **F2** for FORWARD SEARCH

2. Type the search string (up to 59 characters)

3. Press **F2** to move to the first occurrence of this text

4. Keep pressing **F2** to move to the remaining occurrences or **F1** to end the search

Spelling

The spelling checker is used to flag and subsequently correct allegedly misspelled words and double words.

1. Press **Ctrl** + **F2** for SPELL

2. Choose **3** or **D** to check the *Document* (or make another selection)

Note: If using a dual-diskette system you should follow the screen messages for inserting the spelling program into Drive B (if necessary).

Tab Settings

WordPerfect, like most word processors, has default tab settings. However, you can change any of these by following a procedure such as the one described below (refer back to the text for several other options).

1. Press **Shift** + **F8** for FORMAT

2. Choose **1** or **L** (for *Line*)

3. Choose **8** or **T** (for *Tab Set*)

4. Press **Ctrl** + **End** to delete all of the current tab settings

5. Press → to move to the position on the ruler line where you want to set a tab

6. Type a letter corresponding to the type of tab you want— **L** (left justify), **R** (right justify), **C** (center text), **D** (decimal alignment), or **.** (preceding dot leader)

7. Repeat steps 5 and 6 to set tabs at other positions

8. Press **F7** to exit and save the settings

Thesaurus

The thesaurus is used to find synonyms and antonyms for words.

1. Place the cursor on the word you want to look up

2. Press **Alt** + **F1** for THESAURUS

Note: If you are using a dual-diskette system, insert the thesaurus disk in drive B before issuing this command.

3. If the word is found, you will see a list of synonyms and antonyms on the screen. To choose one of the words on the list, type **1** for *Replace Word*

4. Type the letter corresponding to the word you want to use to replace the word you highlighted in Step 1

Undeleting Text

WordPerfect allows you to see and restore the three most recent deletions.

1. Move the cursor to where you want the previously deleted text placed

2. Press **F1** for CANCEL

3. Choose **1** or **R** to *Restore* the last deletion, or

4. Choose **2** or **P** to cycle through the two previous deletions

Underlining Text

Underlining enables you to produce text that is underlined.

Before Typing in the Text.

1. Press **F8** for UNDERLINE, to turn on the underlining feature

2. Type the text to be underlined

3. Press **F8** again to turn off the underlining feature

After Typing in the Text.

1. Block the text to be underlined

2. Press **F8** for UNDERLINE

Viewing Documents

The View Document feature enables you to inspect, on the display, a fully formatted document before it is printed. Headers, footers, page numbers, footnotes, text of all sizes and appearances, special characters, and graphics are all displayed as close in appearance as possible to what you will see on the printed page.

1. Press **Shift** + **F7** for PRINT

2. Choose **6** or **V** (for *View Document*) on the Print menu

3. Select the number corresponding to the viewing option you want

The default is *100%,* selection 1. Selection 2, *200%,* will zoom into a piece of the document so you can inspect it in closer detail. You can also see a complete full page or facing pages. Whichever selection you make, you can use the cursor movement keys to move text about so you can see it.

4. Press **F7** to return to your document

GLOSSARY

Absolute tab. A tab that has been measured from the left edge of a page.

Block. Contiguous text.

Bold. Enhancing text so that it has thicker strokes.

Cancel. The WordPerfect feature that lets you back out of commands and retrieve previously deleted text.

Exit. The WordPerfect feature that allows you to leave documents and command menus.

Footer. A line or more of text that appears at the bottom of each page.

Hard page break. The use of the Enter key to start a new page.

Hard return. The use of the Enter key to start a new line or paragraph.

Header. A line or more of text that appears at the top of each page.

Insert mode. The WordPerfect setting that enables new text to be squeezed in between existing text.

Justification. A term that refers to whether the rightmost text margin is flush or ragged.

Relative tab. A tab that has been measured with respect to the left margin.

Replace. Exchanging all or some occurrences of a word or string with another word or string.

Reveal Codes. The WordPerfect feature that inserts hidden formatting codes into your document, any of which can be inspected by summoning a special screen.

Search. Inspecting text for specific words or text strings.

Soft page break. The word processing feature that automatically places you on a new page when you exceed the line limit imposed on the previous page.

Soft return. The word processing feature that automatically places the cursor on a new line when you keystroke beyond the right margin.

Spelling checker. An adjunct program that checks a document for misspelled words.

Status line. The bottom line of the normal WordPerfect editing screen, which shows such information as the name of the current file, the page on which you are working, and the cursor position.

Thesaurus feature. An adjunct feature that enables the electronic lookup of synonyms and antonyms.

Typeover mode. The WordPerfect setting that causes newly typed text to replace already existing text.

View document. The WordPerfect feature that lets you see a document before it is printed.

Wordwrap. The word processing feature that produces soft returns.

REVIEW QUESTIONS

1. What does each of the following status line remarks tell you?
   a. Doc 1
   b. Pg 1
   c. Ln 1″
   d. Pos 1″
2. Four commands are listed on your template opposite each of the function keys. Why are they color coded? Which key is used with each color?
3. What are the functions of the F7 key?
4. How do you save a revised copy of a document? (Assume that the revised copy is on the screen and is to be saved under the same name as the original.)
5. How do you move a block of text?
6. How do you copy a block of text?
7. What WordPerfect feature enables you to find words that have mistakenly been typed twice in succession.
8. What key is used to create a paragraph indent?
9. What key combination is used to center a line on a page?
10. How do you make text bold after it has been typed?
11. What key is used to underline text?
12. To continue the search process after finding the first match, which function key do you press?

ANSWERS

1. a. Doc 1: The document you are working on is the first of two possible documents.

b. Pg 1: Your cursor is located on the first page of your document.

c. Ln 1″: Ln 1″ says your cursor is located 1″ from the top edge of the page.

d. Pos 1″: Pos 1″ says your cursor is located 1″ from the left edge of the page.

2. The commands are color coded so that a second key may be used in conjunction with the function key. Black means to use the function key alone; red means to use Ctrl; green means to use Shift; and blue means to use Alt.

3. (1) To clear the screen, (2) to exit WordPerfect for the operating system, and (3) to save files

4. **F10** or **F7, Enter, Y** to save the revision

5. a. Press **Alt** + **F4** to block

b. Press **Ctrl** + **F4**

c. Choose **1**

d. Choose **1**

e. Position the cursor

f. Press **Enter**

6. a. Press **Alt** + **F4** to block

b. Press **Ctrl** + **F4**

c. Choose **1**

d. Choose **2**

e. Position cursor

f. Press **Enter**

7. The speller

8. **F4**

9. **Shift** + **F6**

10. Block it, then press the bolding key, **F6**

11. **F8**

12. **F2**

WP

HANDS-ON EXERCISES

Note to the Student

These exercises cover many of the WordPerfect features presented in this guide. They also introduce a few additional features that are useful when doing word processing. Six excercises are presented here.

Completing each of them as outlined in the instructions will reinforce your knowledge of most of the functions in this guide so that you will be able to use them in your future work without continual reference to the guide.

Hands-on Exercise 1: A Letter

In this exercise you will practice:

☐ using the CENTER command

☐ using the UNDERLINE command

☐ using the typeover mode

☐ making corrections

☐ printing

1. Begin typing the letter in Figure WP-20. Using four hard returns after the date
2. Single space the entire letter, except press ↵ twice to create blank lines between the city and salutation, the salutation and the first paragraph, and before "Yours very truly"
3. Press ↵ to enter four hard returns between the closing line ("Yours very truly") and the author's name, "J. T. College"

FIGURE WP-20
Hands-on Exercise 1: A letter.

```
(Type today's date)



Florence L. Smythe
SeaTech Corporation
East Coast Division
30 Industrial Avenue
Pittsburgh, PA 15230

Dear Ms. Smythe:

I certainly enjoyed my visit to SeaTech Corporation
and the lively talk we had over lunch. Of course, I am
still very interested in the opening in your
accounting department, and I will notify you of my
employment decision as soon as my last interview is
finished next month.

Enclosed is a copy of a recent curriculum vitae. I
apologize for not having a copy to give you during my
visit.

Yours very truly,



J. T. College
```

Note: Don't worry if the lines of text do not wrap exactly as shown in the letter. Let wordwrap take effect to control your line breaks within paragraphs.

4. Save the letter on disk as SMYTHE
5. Print a copy of the letter
6. Use the LIST FILES command to make sure your document has been saved on your data disk
7. Make the following changes to the second paragraph:
   a. insert the words **are two copies** after the word "Enclosed"
   b. delete the words "is a copy" in the same sentence
   c. insert **sincerely,** between "I" and "apologize" in the next sentence
   d. change the words "a copy" in the same sentence to the word **one**
8. Save the revised letter under the same filename, SMYTHE
9. Print a copy of the revised letter
10. Insert the following paragraph directly after the first paragraph in the letter:

```
Enclosed is a list of expenses I incurred on the trip.  I
would appreciate your reimbursing me at your earliest
possible convenience.
```

11. Move the paragraph just typed so that it is the third instead of the second paragraph
12. Save the letter again under the same filename, SMYTHE
13. Print another copy of the letter
14. Clear your screen so that you can get ready for the next exercise

WP

Hands-on Exercise 2: A Table

In this exercise you will practice:

☐ using the UNDERLINE command

☐ using the CENTER command

☐ clearing and setting tabs

☐ setting dot leaders

☐ creating indents

☐ formatting text

☐ using the BLOCK command

☐ using the UNDELETE feature

☐ changing line spacing

Type the document shown in Figure WP-21 using the following guidelines:

1. Type and center the three lines of the heading as shown, pressing **↵** twice after the third heading line

2. Clear all tabs

3. Set new tabs as follows:

☐ A left-aligned tab at +0.5 inches

☐ A dot leader tab at +4.5 inches

☐ A decimal tab at +5 inches

Note: Remember to exit with F7 to save the tab settings.

4. Type the itemized list using the following guidelines:

a. type the **1.**

b. press **Tab**

c. type **Airfare**

d. press **Tab** (the dots will automatically appear)

e. press **Tab** again to move to the decimal tab position

f. type **$300.00**

g. press **↵**

Repeat for the next two lines of the table and the total line, leaving a blank line before "Total"

5. Press **↵** twice after the total line

6. Type **<u>Notes</u>** and underline as shown

FIGURE WP-21
Hands-on Exercise 2: A table.

```
                 EXPENSES SUMMARY
                  J. T. COLLEGE
        Visit to SeaTech Corporation, date

1. Airfare.....................................$300.00
2. Hotel......................................   90.00
3. Meals......................................   65.00

   Total.......................................$455.00

Notes

1. The airfare consisted of a round-trip coach ticket
   from San Francisco. I have enclosed a copy of the
   receipt with this letter.
2. Receipt also enclosed.
3. I lost the meal receipts, but, since meals are
   being billed to my credit card, I can get receipts
   if you need them.
```

7. Type the itemized list under Notes. Be sure to press **F4** after the numbers, instead of the Tab key, to indent
8. Block and delete note number 3
9. Restore (undelete) note number 3 using **F1**
10. Use the Reveal Codes screen to inspect the formatting codes
11. Return to the normal document screen
12. Add the following to your document:
    a. make the first line of the heading bold
    b. underline "65.00" in the decimal tab column
    c. underline the total figure "$455.00"
13. Double space the notes section
14. Proof the document and save it as EXPENSES
15. Print a copy of the document
16. Clear the screen

WP

Hands-on Exercise 3: A Report

In this exercise you will practice

☐ using the UNDERLINE command

☐ using the CENTER command

☐ creating a header

☐ changing margins

☐ changing line spacing

☐ running a spelling check

☐ changing the right margin to a ragged right margin

☐ saving and printing a multipage document

Type the document in Figure WP-22, as shown. Do not worry about how the right margin wraps but do type the misspelled words as shown. If you make other errors do not stop to correct them.

1. Center the heading
2. Underline as shown
3. Save the document as HISTORY
4. With your cursor at the beginning of the document, run a spelling check on the document, correcting the misspelled words and double words

Note: Are there any further errors that the speller didn't catch? If so, correct them. (The spelling checker will not catch errors of grammar or punctuation.)

FIGURE WP-22
Hands-on Exercise 3: A report.

```
          WORD PROCESSING COMPUTER APPLICATIONS

Simply put, word processing is what it says: the
processing of words. Documents containing
predominantly sttraight-copy copy type use a word
processing system and/or aplication for processing.
Typically, documents such as letters, memos, reports,
manuscripts, and tabels come to mind.

Brief History:

In th early 1960s IBM developed and markted the
Magnetic Tape Selectric Typewriter (MTST). This
typeriter was the first turely automated word
processing system with tape memory for storage and
errorr-free playback. They were, of course, failry
expensive (around $10,000 initially), and thus IBM
also introducded the concept of centralized word
processing. It made much more sence to centrelize the
system in a business so that the machnine remained
continually in use. They were ismpmly too expensive
and too large to be a practical accessory in every
office

Centralisation became the commonly thought of method
of perfroming word processing duties at this time.
Often the bulky word processor was closeted away in
the basement with the unfortnate operater. They also
were not the quietest machines around, but the
technology was new and rather evolutionary. At that
time it was an exciting piece of euqipment which gave
typists and office assistants a tool by which to
elimijnate the need for retyping numberous drafts and
applying their artistic talents to paper with whiteout
and erasers. It also gave these oeperators a new kind
of status and a new title: word processors. They held
a new skills which was rapidly gorwing in demand.
Skilled wordprocessors became the elite of office
personnel and qcquired a better salery as a result.
```

5. Change the left margin to 1.5″ and the right margin to 2″ using the following guidelines:
   a. Press **Shift** + **F8**
   b. Choose **1** or **L** for Line
   c. Choose **7** or **M** for Margins
   d. Type the left margin setting
   e. Press ↵
   f. Type the right margin setting
   g. Press ↵
   h. Press **F7** to exit back to your document
6. Double space the entire document (**Hint: Shift** + **F8** again)
7. Make the main heading bold

8. Create a header for the document:

    `Word Processing History`

9. Provide page numbers for your document
10. Change the right margin to a ragged edge rather than right-justified.

    To change justification

    a. Move to the top of the document

    b. Press **Shift** + **F8**

    c. Choose **1** for Line

    d. Choose **3**

    e. Type **L** for Left

    f. Press **F7** to exit back to the document
11. Save the revised document under the same filename, HISTORY
12. Print a copy of the entire report
13. Print a copy of only the second page of the report

Clear your screen for the next exercise or exit WordPerfect.

WP

Hands-on Exercise 4: A Report with Table

In this exercise you will practice

□ creating various tab settings, including a center tab, a right-align tab, and a decimal tab

□ changing tabs throughout a document more than one time

□ setting up a multipage document

□ viewing a document prior to printing

Type the document in Figure WP-23 using the following guidelines:

1. Center the heading
2. Type the text in the first two paragraphs and center the "EXHIBIT C . . ." heading of the table
3. Delete all tabs. Set a center tab at +3″ and another center tab at +5″
4. Type the two column headings after you tab to them. Press ↵ twice after typing the second column heading
5. Clear all tabs and set the following new tabs:

    a. a right-align tab (R) at +3.5″

    b. a decimal tab (D) at +5.1″
6. Type all lines up to "Issaquah"
7. After typing "Issaquah," tab to the second column and press **F8** for underline. Press the **spacebar** twice and then type **19,001.** Tab to the third column, press the **spacebar** once and type **6.2%.** Press **F8** to turn off Underline.

FIGURE WP-23
Hands-on Exercise 4: A report with table.

GROSS POPULATION

Of the eight areas that make up the East King Council service area (as defined for this project), by far the most populous is the Bellevue area, with 1/3 of the total population in 1980. The areas north and northeast of Bellevue (Kirkland, Redmond, Bear Creek, Bothell/Woodinville, and the Snohomish County border tracts) together contain another 53-1/2 percent of the population, with Mercer Island and the growing East Sammamish/Issaquah area making up the remaining 13 percent.

Exhibit C displays the 1980 census figures for each of the eight areas and the proportion of the overall population residing in each.

EXHIBIT C: 1980 POPULATION

	1980 Population	Percentage of Total
Snohomish County border tracts	29,600	9.5%
Bothell/Woodinville	71,471	23.3
Kirkland	22,851	7.4
Redmond	31,464	10.3
Bear Creek	8,909	2.9
Bellevue	101,828	33.2
Mercer Island	21,527	7.0
East Sammamish/ Issaquah	19,001	6.2%
TOTAL	306,597	

Anticipated growth by the year 2000* shows remarkable population increases to the north and east of Bellevue, from 90 percent growth in Bothell/Woodinville to 125 percent growth in East Sammamish/Issaquah. Growth expected in East Sammamish is most striking--176 percent.

*Source: Puget Sound Council of Governments

8. Type the TOTAL line

9. Include the solid lines at the top and bottom of the table

10. Finish typing the document

11. Run a spelling check
12. Save the document as CENSUS
13. Print a copy of the document
14. Clear your screen

Hands-on Exercise 5: Miscellaneous Exercises

Here, we will practice

☐ searching and replacing

☐ using the thesaurus feature

☐ making hard page breaks

Type the document in Figure WP-24 and save it as BABBAGE1. Then do the following:

1. Use the search-and-replace feature to change all occurrences of the word "machine" to "device"

FIGURE WP-24

Hands-on Exercise 5: Editing and formatting.

BABBAGE AND HIS ENGINES

One of the most noteworthy figures in the history of computers was the nineteenth-century English mathematician Charles Babbage. About 150 years ago, he designed a machine with an amazing similarity to the first modern computers.

Babbage was able to get funds from the British government to build a machine that he called the difference engine. He succeeded in building a small prototype. His attempts to build a larger version of the machine failed, however, because the technology for creating the parts he needed did not yet exist.

While working on the difference engine, Babbage conceived another, much more powerful machine, which he called the analytical engine. Like the difference engine, it would consist of gears and shafts run by a steam engine. It is this machine that is so similar in concept to the modern computer.

Much of what we know about Charles Babbage's analytical engine comes not from Babbage himself but from the work of his close friend and associate Ada Augusta. She has been called "the first programmer" because of her work on the kinds of instructions that would have been fed into the analytical engine to make it work.

Babbage became obsessed with the analytical engine and devoted all of his energy and resources to creating it. But he was never able to complete a working model, and he died without knowing how his vision would shape the future.

2. Use the thesaurus feature to find synonym replacements for the following words:

amazing

consist

obsessed

devoted

If you can't locate these words by eye, use the search feature to find them.

3. Insert, flush left, the following headings in the document, adding a blank line before and after each heading.

Before paragraph #2: Babbage's Engines
Before paragraph #4: Babbage's Legacy

Then, insert hard page breaks before each of these headings so that your entire document spans three pages.

4. Save the document as BABBAGE2

5. Print a copy of the document

6. Clear your screen

Hands-on Exercise 6: Desktop Publishing with WordPerfect

This exercise is designed specifically for students with access to a laser printer. In it, you will learn how to enhance your documents with special fonts. Specifically we will cover

- changing the appearance of typefaces
- accessing special characters
- changing the size of typefaces

The document you will create should look something like the one shown in Figure WP-25. To create this document

1. Type the document in as you would any normal WordPerfect document. Don't worry at this point about such matters as boldfacing, italicizing, or sizing type. When you come to the square bullets, read the note below:

Note: The square bullets are an example of WordPerfect special characters. WordPerfect has about 1,500 such characters that are available to you, and you will find these in Appendix P (page 997) of the WordPerfect 5.1 Reference Manual that comes with the software package. The square bullet is a typographic character that you will find listed as character 38 in Character Set 4 of the appendix.

2. To get this character into your document, place the cursor where you want to enter the character and press **Ctrl** + **V**

CELLULAR PHONES

In a Nutshell, How They Work

Cellular phones operate by keeping in contact with transmitter stations called cell stations, or *cells*. These stations, which resemble tall metal telephone poles and are operated by private franchises that have successfully applied to the government for licenses to provide public communications services, are strategically placed throughout a calling area. Cells perform two essential functions:

- ☐ They provide an interface with the regular public phone network.
- ☐ They enable a moving vehicle with a phone to receive uninterrupted transmitting power by passing signals off to contiguous cells located in the zone into which the vehicle is moving.

Unlike many conventional mobile transmission solutions, cellular technology can maintain a quality transmission free from interference and eavesdropping.

FIGURE WP-25
Hands-on Exercise 6: Desktop publishing with WordPerfect 5.1.

3. At the "Key =" prompt, type in the number corresponding to the character set, followed by a comma, followed by the number corresponding to the symbol you want. So, type **4,38**

4. Press ↵

When you move the cursor, the character will appear. In some cases, the character displayed might not look exactly like the one you requested. Use the View Document option off the Print command to display the character onscreen.

At this point, it's time to create the heading effects and, also, to italicize "cells" in the first sentence.

5. Move the cursor to the "C" in "CELLULAR" of the first title

6. Block the title

7. Press **Ctrl** + **F8** for FONT

8. Select **1** for Size

9. Select **6** for Very Large

The text may have changed color on your screen or have been provided a background effect. You have now resized the text to very large, but you still have to boldface it. To do this,

WP

10. Reblock the title

11. Press **Ctrl** + **F8** again

12. Select **2** for Appearance

13. Select **1** for Boldface

Notice that the color or background effect has changed again. You now have very large boldface text. Again, you may want to call up the View Document feature to inspect the text onscreen.

You should have noticed as you went through the preceding steps that you had several choices for changing the size or appearance of your text when you pressed Ctrl+F8. Later, you will experiment with these choices to provide other effects in your document.

Now it's time to produce the large, italic, boldface title, "In a Nutshell, How They Work." To produce this effect on the title, you will have to block the text three separate times. The first time, you will make the block "large" (which is a size smaller than "very large" but bigger than the body copy); the second time, italic; and the third time, boldface. The steps to follow are summarized below:

14. For large: Block the heading; press **Ctrl** + **F8** and then **1** and **5**

15. For italic: Block the heading; press **Ctrl** + **F8** and then **2** and **4**

16. For boldface: Block the heading; press **Ctrl** + **F8** and then **2** and **1**

Next, you will need to italicize "cells" in the second line of body copy. To do this, move the cursor to the word and do the same thing you did in step 15. In other words,

17. For italic: Block the word; press **Ctrl** + **F8** and then **2** and **4**

At this point, the last thing to do is to change the typeface. The document in Figure WP-25 uses the Times font that is available within the WordPerfect software package. This typeface, as you have probably noticed, is much more attractive than the Courier font that you are probably used to using, which is the standard for typewritten material. Courier is a monospaced font, meaning that all characters are the same width. Times, on the other hand, is a proportionally spaced font, meaning that characters vary in width. You will notice, for instance, that a lowercase "i" takes up little width, while a lowercase "m" takes up a lot. To change the font to Times

18. Move the cursor to the first character of the document, the "C" in the title "CELLULAR PHONES"

19. Press **Ctrl** + **F8**

20. Select **4** or **F** for Base Font

21. Use the arrow keys to move the highlight to Times and press ↵

You will next be asked to choose a point size. This refers to the size of the type. The larger the number you supply, the larger the type in the body copy. Here, we will select the default of 12, so

22. Press ↵

At this point your document is finished. Before saving it and printing it out, use the View Document feature of the Print command to inspect it.

By selecting the “100%” or “200%” options, and moving the arrow keys, you can see the document in fine detail. If it is not yet satisfactory, edit it until the View Document feature provides a document that appears to be suitable. When the document is satisfactory,

23. Save the document as PHONES

24. Print a copy of the document

Additional Problems. After you have finished your first successful document, try the exercises below:

1. Change the base font to Univers or another option available to you, inspecting the document onscreen first and then printing it out
2. Try a couple of different point sizes for the body copy
3. Try resizing the titles. For instance, make the main title “extra large”
4. Change the appearance of the word “cells” from italic to double underline
5. Change the square bullets to round bullets (Round bullets are character 37 in Character Set 4.)

APPENDIX: OPERATING WORDPERFECT WITH PULL-DOWN MENUS

The WordPerfect 5.1 commands that users commonly invoke by pressing function keys—either alone or in combination with the Shift, Alt, or Ctrl keys—are also available on pull-down menus. Pull-down menus are so named because you pull them down from menu titles that are displayed on a top-of-screen menu bar. Choices can be made from pull-down menus using either a keyboard or a mouse.

Summoning the Pull-Down Menus

To get pull-down menus to display on a normal Edit screen, you must call the top-of-screen menu bar (see Figure WP-26). This menu bar can be displayed using any of the techniques described below:

Using a Mouse.

1. Press and release (i.e., click) the right mouse button

Using a Keyboard.

1. Press **Alt** + =

FIGURE WP-26
Menu Bar.
The menu bar is displayed at the top of the Edit screen when you press **Alt** + = or click the right mouse button. When you press the Escape key the menu-bar disappears.

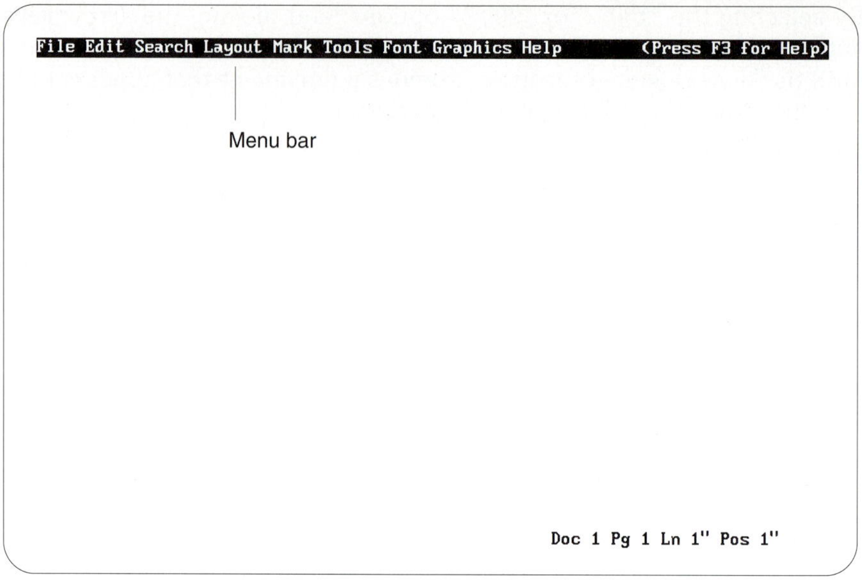

Each of the choices listed on the menu bar refers to the name of a pull-down menu. Pull-down menus may be seen and accessed in a variety of ways, including those listed below:

Using a Mouse.

1. Move the mouse pointer to the name of the choice on the menu bar whose pull-down menu you wish to see

Note: The mouse pointer is a colored, rectangular cursor that moves in relation to a mouse being slid along the desktop.

2. Click the left mouse button

Using a Keyboard.

1. Press the colored (highlighted) letter in the name of the choice on the menu bar whose pull-down menu you wish to see

or

Use the → or ← key to highlight the name of the choice on the menu bar whose pull-down menu you wish to see

2. Press ↵ or ↓

For instance, if you had clicked the mouse button on the File command on the menu bar or pressed the down-arrow key when File was highlighted, you would see the pull-down menu in Figure WP-27.

Choices are made from pull-down menus in the same way they are made from the menu bar. For instance, you can select Retrieve by pressing the R key, by pressing the Enter key (since Retrieve is already highlighted), or by clicking on Retrieve with the mouse. Alternatively, you will note on the list of shortcut keystrokes that you can also retrieve files by holding down the Shift key and pressing the F10 key—the method you learned in the main part of the tutorials.

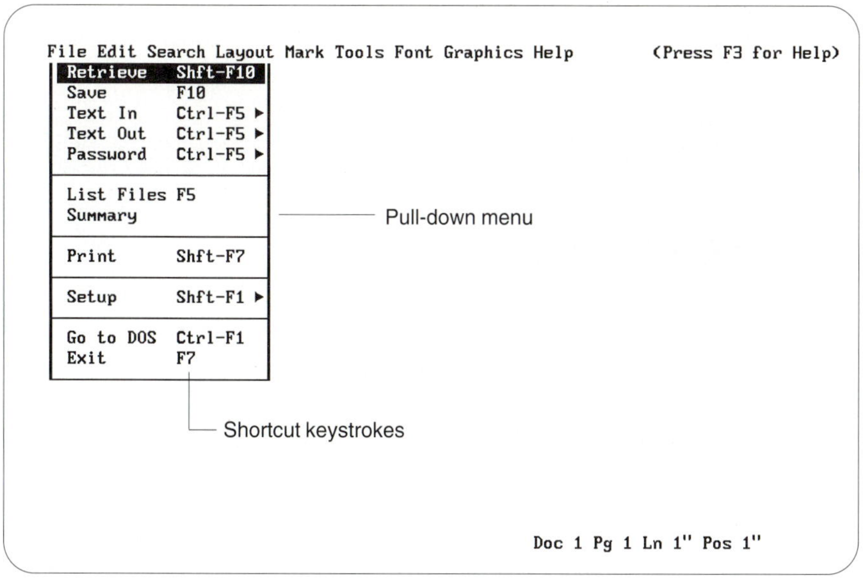

FIGURE WP-27

Pull-down menu.
When the menu bar is displayed onscreen, you can unfurl a pull-down menu by clicking a choice on the menu bar (mouse) or by typing in the colored or highlighted letter in the choice (keyboard).

At this point, select Retrieve from the menu by pressing Enter or by clicking it with a mouse. You will note that the menus have disappeared and that the message

`Document to be retrieved:`

is displayed at the bottom of the screen. At this point, you would follow the same steps to retrieve a file as you learned in the main part of the tutorials.

Since we aren't going to retrieve a file at this time and you are already familiar with the retrieval prompt, press the Esc key or F1 key to get rid of the prompt.

Submenus. You will notice also in Figure WP-27 that some of the pull-down menu commands have arrow symbols to the right of them. An arrow to the right of a command indicates that the command has a submenu. Submenus will display automatically when their pull-down menu commands are highlighted, and you can reach any of these submenus with a mouse click or with the right-arrow key. To get a submenu display like the one in Figure WP-28,

Using a Mouse.

1. Click on the Edit command on the menu bar
2. Click on the Select command on the Edit pull-down menu

Using a Keyboard.

1. Press the → or ← key the appropriate number of times to display the Edit pull-down menu
2. On the Edit submenu, press the ↓ or ↑ key the appropriate number of times to display the Select command

FIGURE WP-28

Submenus.

Certain commands on pull-down menus will contain submenus. These submenus will display automatically when the appropriate pull-down menu command is highlighted. Submenu choices can be selected in the same way as choices from the menu bar and pull down menus.

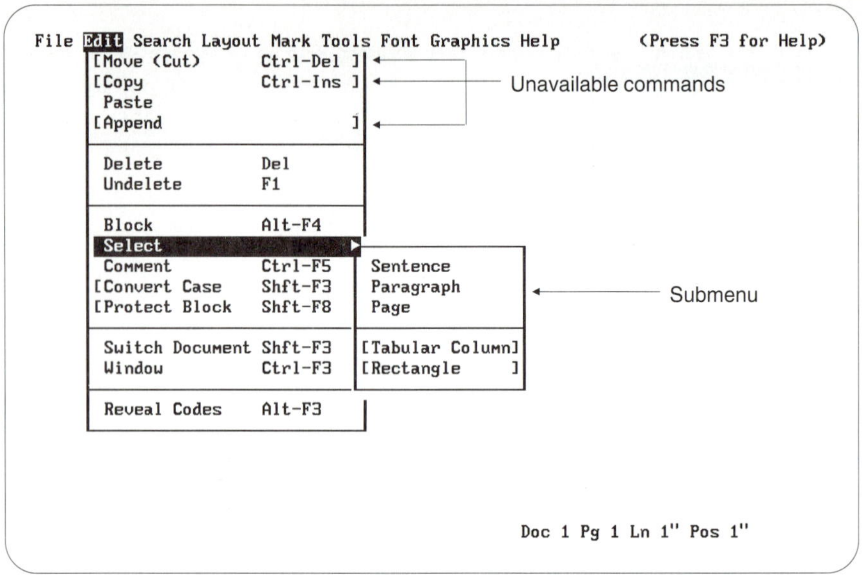

Choices are made from submenus in the same way as they are from the menu bar and pull-down menus—by clicking on them or by typing in the colored or highlighted letter (or by using the arrow keys to highlight the choice and then pressing Enter). At this point, select Sentence on the submenu.

Using a Mouse.

1. Click on Sentence

Using a Keyboard.

1. Press → to highlight Sentence

2. Press ↵

At this point, the menus will disappear and you will get a bottom-of-screen message asking you if you would like to move or copy the sentence upon which the cursor is currently positioned in your document. Since we are just exploring using the menus at this point, press the Esc key to return to the normal editing screen.

Note that once you've made a final selection from a pull-down menu or submenu, all of the menus disappear and the screens that you subsequently see are the same as if you had been operating WordPerfect without menus.

Bracketed Commands. You will also notice in Figure WP-28 that some of the pull-down menu commands are bracketed, meaning they are not available in the current context. For instance, you will not be allowed to select the Move or Copy commands if text is not blocked. Note that you cannot highlight bracketed commands with the arrow keys.

Backing Out of Pull-Down Menus

In some cases you may have summoned menus on your screen and then want to back out of them without making any choice. To back out one step at a time, press either the Esc key or Cancel (F1) key. To back out all the way—that is, to have all menus disappear from the screen—

Using a Mouse.

1. Click the right mouse button

Using a Keyboard.

1. Press the Exit key, **F7**, or press **Alt** + **=**

Guide to Commands

WP

In the event you wish to explore menus further, an additional aid is provided in this appendix to assist you. Figure WP-29 provides a list of common WordPerfect commands and a description of how to execute them with menus and with conventional keystroking through function keys. While many beginning WordPerfect users may prefer menus, conventional keystroking is almost always faster once you become familiar with WordPerfect and use it on a regular basis—especially if you are a touch-typist.

FIGURE WP-29
Executing common WordPerfect operations through menus and through conventional keystroking.

Operation	Menu Selections	Shortcut Keystrokes
Base font	Font/Base Font	Ctrl+F8 F
Block text	Edit/Block	Alt+F4 or F12
Center page	Layout/Page/C	Shift+F8 P C
Center text	Layout/Align/Center	Shift+F6
Copy block	Edit/Copy	Ctrl+F4 B C
Copy sentence, paragraph, page	Edit/Select	Ctrl+F4
Exit WordPerfect	File/Exit	F7
Font appearance and size	Font	Ctrl+F8
Footers	Layout/Page/F	Shift+F8 P F
Footnote	Layout/Footnote	Ctrl+F7 F
Full justification	Layout/Justify/Full	Shift+F8 L J F
Hard page break	Layout/Align/Hard Page	Ctrl+Enter
Headers	Layout/Page/H	Shift+F8 P H
Help	Help	F3
Hyphenation on/off	Layout/Line/Y	Shift+F8 L Y
→Indent	Layout/Align/Indent→	F4
→Indent←	Layout/Align/Indent→←	Shift+F4
Left justification	Layout/Justify/Left	Shift+F8 L J L
Line spacing	Layout/Line/S	Alt+F5 D L
List files	Files/List Files	F5

(continued)

FIGURE WP-29 (*continued*)

Margins (left,right)	Layout/Line/M	Shift+F8 L M
Margins (top, bottom)	Layout/Page/M	Shift+F8 P M
Move block	Edit/Move (Cut)	Ctrl+F4 L M
Move sentence, paragraph, page	Edit/Select	Ctrl+F4
Page numbering	Layout/Page/N	Shift+F8 P N
Print document	File/Print	Shift+F7
Replace text	Search/Replace	Alt+F2
Retrieve document	File/Retrieve	Shift+F10
Reveal codes	Edit/Reveal Codes	Alt+F3 or F11
Save document, block	File/Save	F10
Search backward	Search/Backward	Shift+F2
Search forward	Search/Forward	F2
Speller	Tools/Spell	Ctrl+F2
Switch documents	Edit/Switch Document	Shift+F3
Tab align	Layout/Align/Tab Align	Ctrl+F6
Tab settings	Layout/Line/T	Shift+F8 L T
Thesaurus	Tools/Thesaurus	Alt+F1
Undelete	Edit/Undelete	F1
View document	File/Print/V	Shift+F7 V

MENU EXERCISES

Redo the BABBAGE exercise with pull-down menus. Start with the BABBAGE1 document in Figure WP-24. Do you find the commands listed below easier or harder to issue with menus rather than conventional keystroking?

1. Using the search-and-replace feature

2. Using the thesaurus feature to find a synonym

3. Inserting a hard page break

4. Saving text

5. Printing text

Function Keys Templates for WordPerfect 5.1.

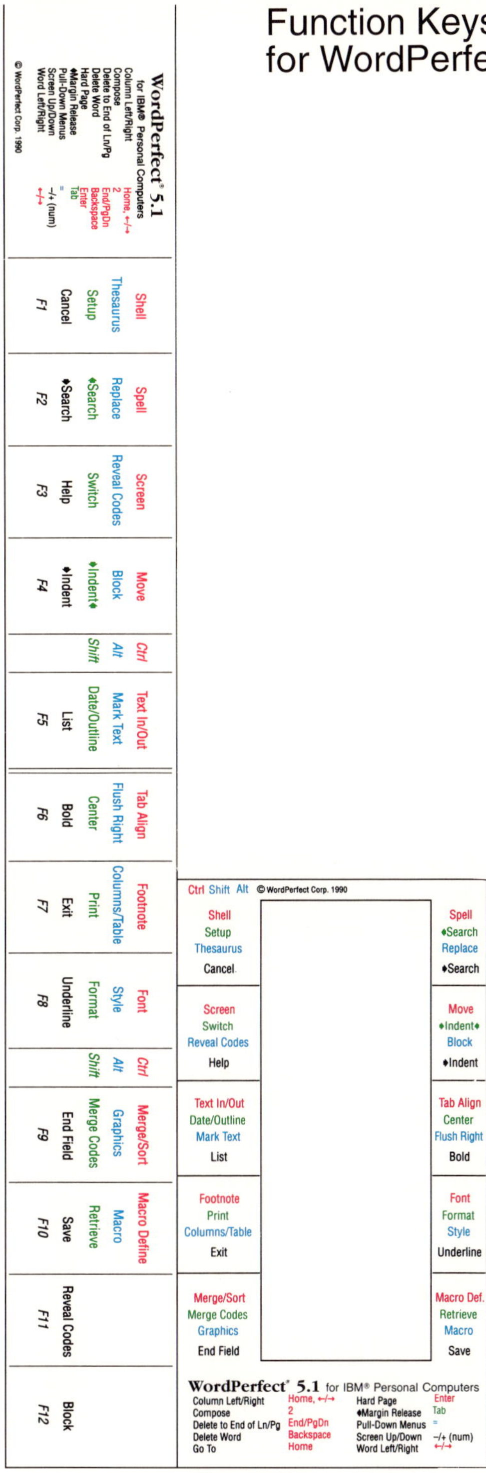

These keyboard templates for WordPerfect 5.1 appear here in reduced size for reference only. Full-size templates are available only through WordPerfect Corporation to purchasers of the software.

SPREADSHEETS WITH LOTUS 1-2-3

CONTENTS

LEARNING OBJECTIVES

After completing these tutorials, you will be able to:

1. Identify the basic components of a worksheet.
2. Enter labels and values to build a worksheet.
3. Execute commands to retrieve, edit, format, save, and print the worksheet.
4. Use a worksheet as an important information-organizing and analysis tool.
5. Create and print bar, pie, and line charts from worksheet data.

OVERVIEW

A **spreadsheet** is an electronic version of the large multicolumned paper accountants frequently use (see Figure SS-1). Spreadsheet programs like Lotus 1-2-3 can be used to create balance sheets, payroll reports, income statements, business forecasts, and a variety of other financial documents. Moreover, spreadsheets can be useful tools for analyzing data.

Today, Lotus 1-2-3 is widely acknowledged as the best-selling electronic spreadsheet product of all time. Many users favor 1-2-3 for its easy-to-use command structure, flexibility, power, and value as an industry standard. Lotus 1-2-3 combines several productivity functions—worksheets, presentation graphics, and data management—into a single package.

When you use a spreadsheet program, you create a *worksheet,* with your data organized into columns and rows. Your data can include words, numbers, and formulas. Each data item occupies a single cell at the intersection of a column and row. The display screen can show only a small section of the whole worksheet at a time. To bring different sections of a worksheet into view, you press cursor-movement keys—such as the arrow keys or the Pg Up and Pg Dn keys—on the keyboard. One of the most important features of a spreadsheet program is the recalculation feature that provides automatic recalculation of formulas on the worksheet when interdependent cell values are changed.

The *presentation graphics* feature allows users to quickly and easily graph spreadsheet data with bar charts, pie charts, and/or line charts. Normally, a chart is first prepared on the screen from an already existing worksheet. When an image is satisfactory, it may be saved on disk and sent to the printer.

The *data management* feature provides users with a variety of file-handling functions. The most notable of these are extracting records having specific characteristics and sorting records on one or more fields. In 1-2-3, each row of data is considered a record, and the worksheet columns divide the records into categories, or fields.

(a) Manually prepared worksheet

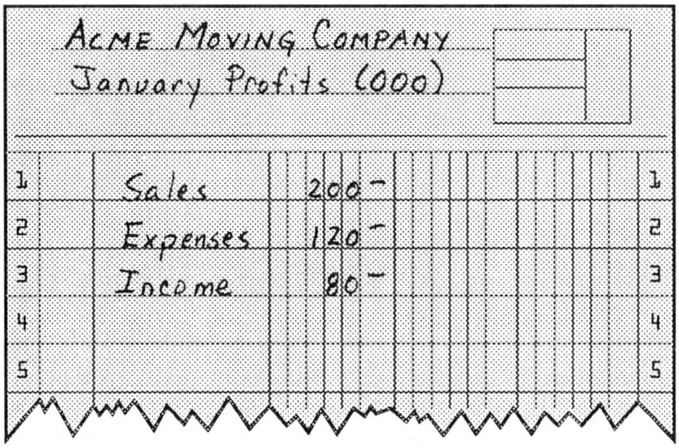

(b) Worksheet prepared by electronic spreadsheet package

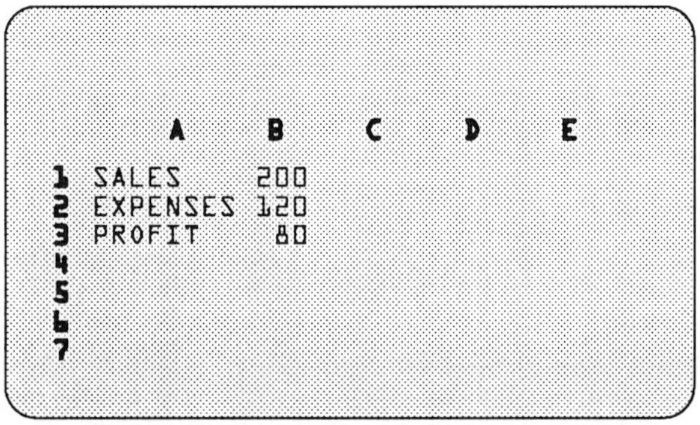

FIGURE SS-1
Manually prepared and electronic worksheets. An electronic spreadsheet package produces computerized counterparts to the ruled, ledger-style worksheets with which accountants frequently work.

GETTING STARTED

1-2-3 is a powerful program. Before you can use it in your work, you must first learn a few basic concepts and master a few basic skills. The steps used in the exercises that follow are numbered. The materials on the next several pages include practice exercises that introduce various concepts and functions of 1-2-3. Additional hands-on exercises are found at the end of the main set of tutorials. These exercises include some additional features, as well as providing practice using 1-2-3.

It is recommended that you proceed through the following materials in the order of presentation.

How to Invoke 1-2-3

To start your spreadsheet program, you must first turn on the computer and have the DOS prompt visible on the screen.

If you have a dual-diskette system, the spreadsheet software is on a program diskette that must be inserted in one of your diskette drives. It is assumed that on a hard-disk system, the spreadsheet program has already been installed on your hard drive, probably in a subdirectory. Get information from your instructor about the name of the subdirectory and the steps to invoke it.

When you are ready to begin working on the spreadsheet program, you'll need a formatted diskette on which to store your data files.

Following are directions for invoking 1-2-3. There are, incidentally, two ways to invoke 1-2-3. The easiest and most direct method is detailed in the steps that follow. It takes you to a blank worksheet screen, where you can immediately begin entering data. It is somewhat less convenient to invoke 1-2-3 through the *Access System,* which provides a menu for selecting a variety of 1-2-3 features not covered extensively in this guide. The Access System menu does, however, allow you to invoke the PrintGraph program, which enables you to print any graphs you create through 1-2-3. Later you will learn how to use PrintGraph.

With a Hard-Disk System. For these instructions, we will assume that 1-2-3 has already been installed on your hard drive in a subdirectory called SPREAD. (The actual name will usually be 123 in Version 2.2, 123R23 in Version 2.3, and 123R24 in Version 2.4.) Starting at the C:\> prompt,

1. Insert a blank formated diskette in your diskette drive
2. Type **CD\SPREAD** and press ↵ to get to the subdirectory
3. Type **123**
4. Press ↵

With a Dual-Diskette System. Starting at the A> prompt,

1. Remove your DOS diskette
2. Insert your 1-2-3 system diskette in Drive A
3. Insert a formatted data diskette in Drive B
4. Type **123**
5. Press ↵

You'll see an empty worksheet grid on your screen.

Using 1-2-3's Access System. With 1-2-3 on your hard drive or in Drive A of your dual-diskette system

1. Change to the directory containing the spreadsheet program
2. Type **LOTUS** and press ↵

This displays the Access System menu. To select the 1-2-3 spreadsheet program, which is already highlighted,

3. Press ↵

A fresh worksheet appears on your screen.

The Worksheet

The principle behind electronic spreadsheets is to view the display screen as a window looking in on a big grid, called a **worksheet** (see Figure SS-2). Worksheets can be very large. The screen you see represents only a small portion of the worksheet (a **window**). Repeatedly holding down one of the four arrow keys will scroll other portions of the worksheet into the window.

Figure SS-3 illustrates the basic format of a 1-2-3 worksheet. Worksheets are constructed of rows and columns, which intersect to form cells, or locations for data.

Columns, Rows, and Cells. Look at your screen and at Figure SS-3. The letters along the top border designate *columns* and the numbers along the left border identify *rows.* The intersection of each row and column forms a **cell.** Each cell is identified by its column and row coordinates. For example, Cell B5 is formed by Column B and Row 5. You can place text (called *labels*) or numbers (called *values*) into any cell. You can also expand or shrink the size of the cells in any column to accommodate larger or smaller cell entries whenever the need arises.

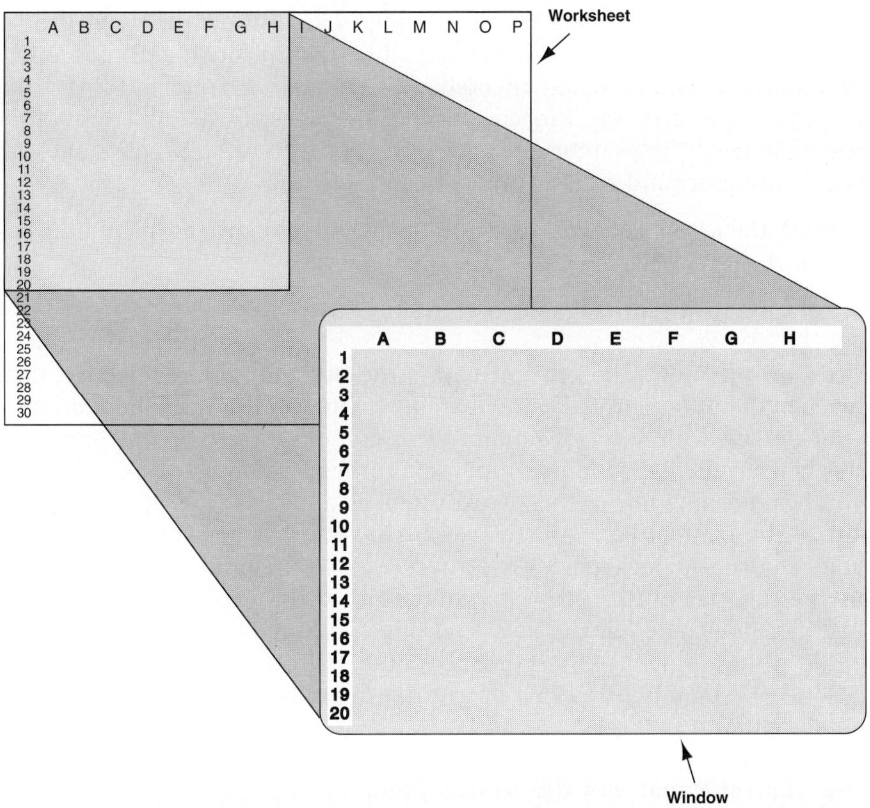

FIGURE SS-2
A worksheet and a window to the worksheet.
Worksheets can be too large to view on the display screen at a single moment. The window allows us to see the worksheet in screen-sized chunks.

SS

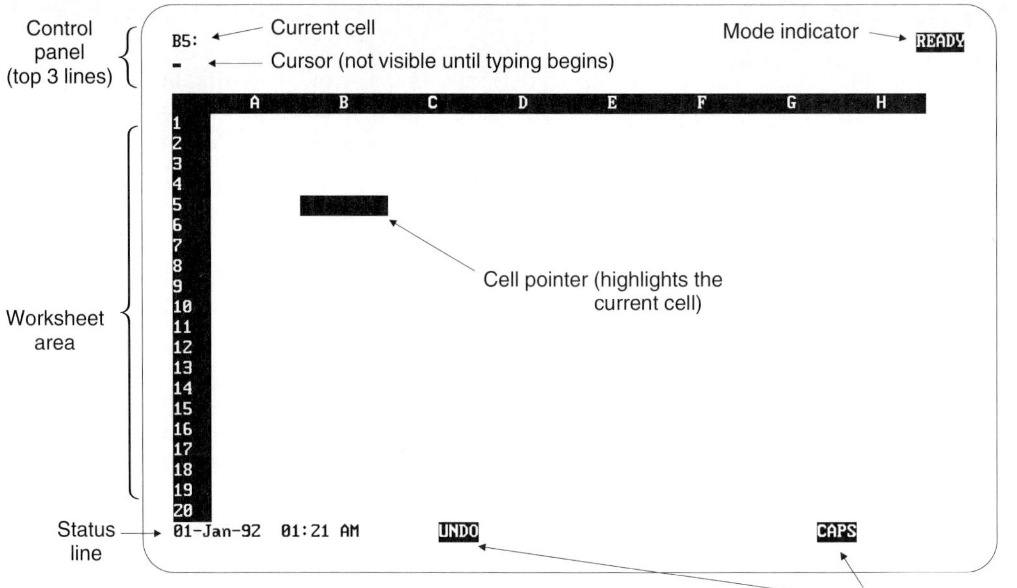

FIGURE SS-3 **1-2-3 worksheet.**

How to Move through the Worksheet. The **cell pointer**—often called the *pointer* or *highlight*—is the highlighted bar in the **worksheet area**—the window portion of your worksheet. It marks the location that is active for receiving data or being affected by a command. You can move from cell to cell by pressing the up, down, left, and right arrow keys. Other movements of the pointer are shown in Figure SS-4. To practice moving your pointer around on the spreadsheet

1. Press the arrow keys or other pointer-movement keys as many times as you wish
2. Relocate the pointer again in Cell A1

The Current Cell. The **current cell** is the one that will receive the next piece of data you enter. That cell is highlighted in the worksheet area on your screen with the cell pointer. The column and row coordinates of this cell are displayed in the upper left corner of the control panel. When you begin typing into a cell, the keystrokes appear in the upper left corner of the control panel, at the **cursor** position. If you make a mistake, you can use the Backspace key to backtrack to the point of the error and retype the rest of the entry. If you want to bail out of this cell entirely, you can press the Escape key. Pressing the Enter key or an arrow key enters your typing into the worksheet area. (If you use the arrow key, the pointer will be advanced one cell in the direction of the arrow after the data is entered.)

The Control Panel and the Status Line. The three-line area above the horizontal border, at the top of the worksheet, is called the **control**

FIGURE SS-4
Ways to move the cell pointer.

KEY(S)	ACTION
→	Moves one column to the right.
←	Moves one column to the left.
↓	Moves one row down.
↑	Moves one row up.
Pg Up	Moves a screen page up.
Pg Dn	Moves a screen page down.
Ctrl + → *or* **Tab**	Moves a screen page right.
Ctrl + ← *or* **Shift** + **Tab**	Moves a screen page left.
Home	Moves to home (A1) cell.
End + **Home**	Moves to the bottom right edge of a worksheet.
End + ←	Moves to the left edge of a list.
End + →	Moves to the right edge of a list.
End + ↑	Moves to the top of a list.
End + ↓	Moves to the bottom of a list.

SS

panel. This area displays information, command choices, and prompts. As shown in Figure SS-3, currently there are two messages in the control panel supplying you information. In the upper left corner, B5 indicates the current cell, or **cell address,** of the cell pointer.

The highlighted area in the upper right is the **mode indicator.** It tells you what the spreadsheet is currently doing. Since READY is now displayed, the program is ready for you to enter data or a command.

The bottom line of a 1-2-3 screen is called the *status line.* It displays a **status indicator** from time to time, a highlighted word that appears when you strike certain keys or when a particular type of condition exists in your worksheet. The status line also supplies date and time information. Figure SS-5 shows selected mode and status indicators that beginners to 1-2-3 may encounter.

The Command Set

One of the most powerful features of any spreadsheet package is its *command set.* Commands enable you to save and print worksheets, copy the contents of a cell into other cells, sort data, erase worksheets, and to initiate many other useful procedures.

You access the command set of 1-2-3 by making selections on a series of menus. Figure SS-6 describes the commands that are included in the topmost part of the *command menus* of 1-2-3.

FIGURE SS-5
Selected mode and status indicators.
Mode indicators, in the upper-right-hand corner of your screen, tell you the current state of the spreadsheet package. Status indicators appear from time to time at the bottom of your screen, when you use certain keys or when a particular type of condition exists.

MODE INDICATORS

Indicator	Description
EDIT	You are either in the EDIT mode or you attempted to enter an incorrect formula.
ERROR	An error message has been displayed on the screen. (Press F1, the HELP key, to display a screen explaining the error or Esc to erase the message.)
FILES	A menu of filenames is displayed in the control panel. (Press F3 to display a full-screen menu of names.)
FIND	1-2-3 is highlighting a data record you asked to locate, based on the criteria specified.
HELP	You are in the HELP mode; a Help screen is being displayed.
LABEL	You are entering a label.
MENU	You've summoned 1-2-3's system of menu commands and the main menu or some submenu is displaying.
NAMES	A menu of range names or graph names is being displayed.
POINT	You are being asked to declare a range or you are highlighting a range.
READY	You are able to enter data or invoke a command.
VALUE	You are entering a value.
WAIT	1-2-3 is working on a command or process.

STATUS INDICATORS

Indicator	Description
CALC	Worksheet formulas must be recalculated; press F9 (CALC).
CAPS	The Caps Lock key is activated.
CIRC	The worksheet contains a circular reference; that is, a formula that references itself.
END	The End key is activated.
MEM	The amount of unused RAM available for your worksheet has fallen below 4 kilobytes.
NUM	The Num Lock key is activated.
OVR	The Ins key is activated.
SCROLL	The Scroll Lock key is activated.
UNDO	Undo is activated.

You summon the command menus by using the slash **(/)** key.

1. Press /

You'll see the command menus shown in the control panel of Figure SS-7. To move the highlight across the commands on the topmost menu

2. Press →

FIGURE SS-6
1-2-3 command set.

COMMAND	EXPLANATION
Worksheet	This command allows you to do things that affect the entire worksheet. For example, it allows you to change the width of one or more columns, or to insert or delete columns or rows.
Range	This command allows you to perform operations on a portion of the worksheet.
Copy	This command allows you to copy any portion of the worksheet into another place on the worksheet.
Move	This command lets you relocate any portion of the worksheet into another place on the worksheet.
File	This command enables you to access your disk to save, retrieve, or combine worksheets.
Print	This command allows you to print any portion of your worksheet.
Graph	This command enables you to create graphs from your worksheet. The computer system must be equipped with a graphics display board for this command to be used effectively.
Data	This command enables you to use the data management routines, to sort data, group data, or retrieve records with specific characteristics.
System	This command lets you temporarily leave your spreadsheet package in order to issue DOS commands.
Add-In	This command allows you to attach other programs to 1-2-3 and to run these programs while using 1-2-3.
Quit	This command ends your 1-2-3 session and enables you to return to DOS.

As you do so, the third line of the panel changes, too. Often, this line will show you the subcommand options available under the main command option that is highlighted. In this way you can preview the choices available without leaving the main command menu.

How to Select Commands. Commands may be selected from the command menus in any one of three ways:

- □ Pressing the Enter key to select the highlighted command
- □ Using the arrow keys to move the highlight to the desired choice, and then pressing the Enter key
- □ Typing the first letter of the desired command on the menu or submenu (W for Worksheet, R for Range, C for Copy, etc.)

Instructions in the remainder of this chapter will specify typing the first letter to summon a command from any menu. Instructions will always include the name of the command being selected, so you can use the arrow keys if you prefer that method.

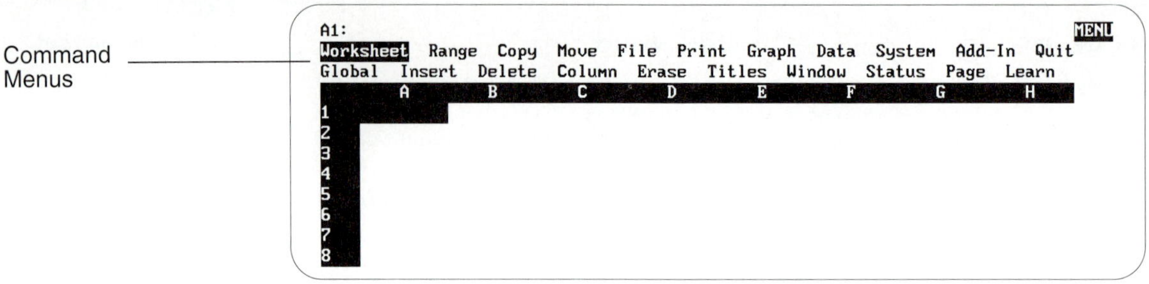

FIGURE SS-7
Invoking the command menu.

When you are instructed to type several letters in sequence, each letter selects an option on one menu and moves you to the next submenu. For example, when you type /FS to save a file, the / summons the main command menu, the F selects the File option and moves you to the next submenu, and the S selects the Save option from the submenu.

To begin the execution of a sequence of commands, you usually press the Enter key after performing the last step from the last submenu. In the preceding example, you would type /FS, then enter or highlight a filename, and then press Enter to save the file. If you change your mind before pressing Enter, and want to escape from the menu, you can do so by following the instructions below.

How to Escape from the Command Menu. Anytime you want to back out of a menu, simply press the Esc key. Pressing it once will take you back to the previous command menu; pressing it twice will take you back two menus, and so on. You can keep pressing the Esc key until you escape back to the READY mode in your worksheet. Practice this now.

1. Type **/FS** for File Save

2. Press **Esc** until you are back to READY mode

How to Quit 1-2-3

To leave the worksheet at the end of any session, you must access the command menus. These menus will be covered in more detail as you progress through the tutorials, but, for now, practice exiting the program as instructed below. You may then quit until the next session or continue by invoking the program again as directed at the beginning of this exercise.

1. Press **/** to access the command menus

2. Press **Q** to quit

A message appears asking if you are sure you want to leave.

3. Type **Y** for Yes

If you entered the program by using the access system, you will be returned to another menu and should select E for Exit. You will return to the system prompt.

ENTERING DATA ON A WORKSHEET

In this section you will create a simple worksheet and save it.

How to Set the Default Drive

One of the first things you should do each time you sign on to the spreadsheet program is tell the program the drive that holds your formatted data diskette (for saving and retrieving files). This is an essential step so that all of your worksheets are automatically saved on your data diskette and not with your program files in Drive A or C. If you have a hard-disk system, your data diskette will probably be in Drive A. If you have a dual-diskette system, your data diskette will probably be in Drive B.

To set the default, do the following:

1. Invoke 1-2-3
2. Type **/F** for File
3. Type **D** for Directory
4. Type **A:** (hard-disk system) or **B:** (dual-diskette system). In some cases you may need to follow the colon with a backslash, \
5. Press ↵

Labels and Values

The data you enter into a cell on a worksheet will be classified as either a label or a value. The difference is that values can be used in calculations; labels cannot. The first character of a cell entry tells the spreadsheet program if a label or value follows.

A **label** is used for descriptive spreadsheet entries and can consist of any combination of alphabetic, numeric, or special characters. Labels always start with either a letter of the alphabet or a **label prefix character.** Label prefix characters (see Figure SS-8) can be used to center, left-justify, right-justify, or repeat text. When used, the label-prefix character is typed as part of the label. The apostrophe character (left-justify) is the default label prefix character; that is, when you don't type in a label prefix character, your text is automatically left-justified within the cell.

There are three types of **values:** numeric constants, formulas, and functions. A *numeric constant* is simply a number. Sometimes you will fill a cell with a *formula* that directs the program to do a mathematical

FIGURE SS-8

Label prefix characters. In 1-2-3, the apostrophe character, which left-justifies labels, is the default and will not have to be typed in.

CHARACTER	ACTION TAKEN	EXAMPLE	RESULT
'	Left-justifies	'FROG	FROG
^	Centers	^FROG	FROG
"	Right-justifies	"FROG	FROG
\	Repeats	\FROG	FROG FROG FROG FROG

operation on numeric constants in other cells. A cell can also contain a **function,** which is a predefined formula built into the spreadsheet package. When you enter a formula or a function into the control panel, the numeric value resulting from the calculation will be placed into the cell that is current at the time. That value can in turn be used in other calculations. Also, the program will automatically recalculate the value of a formula or function if the values in related cells change.

Numeric constants generally start with a digit, a decimal point, a dollar sign, or a plus or minus symbol. Formulas usually begin with a plus or minus symbol, a decimal point, or a left parenthesis. Functions always begin with the @ sign. All values (numeric constants, formulas, functions) are automatically right-justified within the cell. If you change the justification of values, you may not be able to perform calculations with them. It is very important to get the first character of an entry correct so that the program is able to read the data and do the desired calculations.

Examples of labels and values are shown in Figure SS-9.

How to Enter Labels

You are now ready to type in data for the sales table worksheet shown in Figure SS-10. The procedure you will follow is to move to the appropriate cell using the arrow keys, type the value or label indicated, and then press Enter or one of the arrow keys.

FIGURE SS-9

Examples of labels and values.

EXAMPLE	DESCRIPTION	ENTERED ON THE KEYBOARD AS
Revenue	Label	Revenue
Expenses	Label	Expenses
.15	Numeric Constant	.15
$2,000,000	Numeric Constant	2000000
.6*A5/100−B2	Formula	.6*A5/100−B2
SUM(A1 . . A4)	Function	@SUM(A1 . . A4)
C3−D2	Formula	+C3−D2
3rd Quarter	Label	'3rd Quarter

	A	B	C	D
1	AGENT	Region A	Region B	Totals
2	Michaels	500	200	
3	Adams	200	100	
4	Williams	50	400	
5	Jones	100	700	
6	Totals			

FIGURE SS-10
DOC1 sales table data.

1. Move to Cell A1 using the arrow keys (you may already be there)
2. Type **AGENT** and press ↵

"AGENT" will automatically be recognized as a label because it begins with an alphabet character, and it will be left-justified within the cell.

If you make an error as you are keying values or labels into cells, use the Backspace key to backtrack to the point of the error and retype the remainder of the entry. You can watch this process in the control panel.

After you press Enter, you will notice that AGENT, a label, has been transferred to the very top line of the control panel and is shown as 'AGENT. The apostrophe is there to inform you that this entry is being stored as a left-justified label. You will also notice that "AGENT" has been sent to Cell A1 in the worksheet area.

3. Press → to move to Cell B1
4. Type **Region A**
5. Press ↵ (or you may press the right arrow key to both enter this label and move to the next cell on the right)
6. Repeat Steps 3 through 5 for Cells C1 and D1, entering the appropriate titles
7. Move to Cell A2 by pressing the arrow keys
8. Type **Michaels**
9. Move to Cell A3 by pressing ↓
10. Type **Adams**
11. Continue entering the labels through Cell A6

SS

How to Enter Numeric Constants

When you have finished entering all of the labels, you are ready to enter the numeric values. You will enter values in Cells B2 through C5 only. Do not enter values for B6 and C6 or in cells D2, D3, D4, D5, and D6. You will enter formulas in those cells later in this exercise so that all of the total amounts will be calculated automatically.

Note that B2 through C5 includes all cells between these two going both down and across. They are B2 through B5 and C2 through C5.

Locate this portion of the worksheet area on your screen. A block of cells such as this is called a range. A **range** is defined as one or more cells arranged in a rectangle. (Ranges are discussed in more detail later.)

1. Move to Cell B2

2. Type **500**

It will automatically be recognized as a value because it starts with a number and it will be right-justified, as all numeric constants are, within the cell.

3. Move to Cell C2

4. Type **200**

5. Move to Cell B3

6. Type **200**

Continue this procedure for Cells C3 through C5 and Cells B4 through B5.

How to Enter Formulas

You are now ready to enter formulas that will automatically compute the totals and enter the results in the worksheet cells.

1. Move to Cell D2

2. Type +**B2**+**C2**

This formula will compute the total for Cells B2 and C2, which contain all of Michaels's sales figures.

3. Press ↓ (down arrow) once to move to Cell D3

When you move, the correct sum, 700, is placed in Cell D2 on the worksheet.

4. Type the correct formula for computing Adams's total: +**B3**+**C3**

5. Enter the following formulas in the cells indicated

Cell D4	+**B4**+**C4**
Cell D5	+**B5**+**C5**
Cell B6	+**B2**+**B3**+**B4**+**B5**
Cell C6	+**C2**+**C3**+**C4**+**C5**
Cell D6	+**B6**+**C6**
	or
	+**D2**+**D3**+**D4**+**D5**

You are entering the formula for Cell D6 last since the value of this cell can be established only after formulas are set up for calculating the other totals. Your totals should appear as follows:

	A	B	C	D
1	AGENT	Region A	Region B	Totals
2	Michaels	500	200	700
3	Adams	200	100	300
4	Williams	50	400	450
5	Jones	100	700	800
6	Totals	850	1400	2250

Arithmetic Operators and the Hierarchy of Operations. An arithmetic *operator* is a character used in a formula that tells the program to perform a certain calculation. The plus sign (+) between the cell references in the formulas you just entered on your worksheet is one of the arithmetic operators recognized by 1-2-3.

Other operators you can use in addition to the plus sign:

^ exponentiation
* multiplication
/ division
– subtraction

The hierarchy of arithmetic operations, or order of precedence of the operators, is as follows:

a. Exponentiation is performed first.

b. Multiplication and division are performed next, in the order in which they occur reading from left to right.

c. Addition and subtraction are last, in the order in which they occur, reading from left to right.

To see how the hierarchy works, consider the formula below:

+B8/D23 + A2*F3^2

This formula results in the following sequence of computations:

a. First, the value in F3 is raised to the power of 2.

b. Next, the value in B8 is divided by the value in D23.

c. Then, the value in A2 is multiplied by the result of step a.

d. Finally, the result of step b is added to the result of step c.

When parentheses are used to surround parts of the formula, the operation inside the parentheses is given precedence over any other part of the formula. Consider, for instance,

SS

+D2 − (C23 + D23)

In this example, C23 and D23 are first added together. The result is then subtracted from the value in D2.

How to Save a Worksheet

You can save your worksheet onto your data diskette by again invoking the command menu.

1. Press / to get the command menu

2. Press **F** for File

3. Press **S** for Save

You now have a message on the screen asking for the name under which you want to save this worksheet (file).

4. Type the name **DOC1**

5. Press ↵

The worksheet is now saved under A:DOC1.WK1 on a hard-disk system (or B:DOC1.WK1 on a dual-diskette system).

With any of your documents, the file extensions will remain the same as those stated here. If you are using an older version of 1-2-3, files may have the .WKS extension. Extensions are provided automatically. You do not need to type them when you are referring to them in your spreadsheet package.

6. Press / to quit the program

7. Type **Q** for Quit

8. Type **Y** for Yes

EDITING AND PRINTING A WORKSHEET

In this section you will learn how to retrieve a worksheet, edit cell contents, use the recalculation feature to refigure the contents of cells, and widen or narrow columns.

How to Retrieve a Worksheet

Once the worksheet is saved, you can retrieve it from the data diskette. Each time you sign on at the beginning of a work session, you will want to either begin a new worksheet or retrieve a stored worksheet from the data diskette. You can also retrieve a stored file when a worksheet is in the window. The retrieved file will replace the one in the window. As long as the original worksheet in the window was saved, you do not need to worry about losing it.

From the operating system prompt,

1. Invoke 1-2-3

2. Set the default drive to where DOC1 is stored

3. Type **/F** to invoke the command menu and to choose File

4. Type **R** for Retrieve

The prompt asking for the name of the file to retrieve appears.

5. Move the arrow keys so that DOC1 is highlighted (the highlight may already be on DOC1)

6. Press ↵

As with saving, both the WK1 (or WKS) extension and the drive are assumed. You could also have typed the document name rather than highlighting it.

How to Edit Cells with the F2 Key

At some point, you may want to change the values and labels entered in cells. Perhaps a word was misspelled in a label, a value was entered incorrectly, or you wish to observe the effect of a change on the worksheet.

There are three basic ways in which you can change the contents of a cell:

☐ Simply move to the cell to be changed and retype the contents.

☐ Erase the contents through the command set.

☐ Use the EDIT mode (F2 key) to insert or delete characters or numbers.

Your DOC1 worksheet should now be displayed. To change the data entered previously, follow these steps.

1. Move to Cell B4

2. Press **F2**

At this time you can use the arrow keys and the Del key to make changes in the value now showing in the upper left corner of your screen.

3. Press ← to move the cursor to the 5 in 50

4. Type **1**

Watch the screen as you do so; the 50 moves to the right.

5. Press ↵ when the number reads 150

SS

Note: Not only did your value of 50 change to 150 but all totals affected by that number changed automatically as well. More is discussed on this later. Pressing the Enter key takes you out of the EDIT mode.

6. Press **F2** again with the cursor still in B4
7. Move your cursor to the 1 in 150
8. Press **Del** and ↵
9. Move to Cell A3
10. Press **F2**
11. To change the name "Adams" to "Adamson," move the cursor to the space right of s and type **on**
12. Press ↵
13. Press **F2**
14. Move your cursor to the o in Adamson
15. Press **Del** twice and press ↵ to change the name back to Adams

Note: Any value or label may be edited using the F2 key. This is particularly valuable when you have created long formulas and do not want to rekey them from the start.

How to Erase Cell Contents

You can also make changes through the command set by erasing the contents of a cell and then either leaving the cell blank or adding new data to it. To erase the contents of a cell

1. Move to Cell A1
2. Type **/RE** for Range Erase
3. Press ↵

The cell contents are gone.

4. Type **AGENTS** again in Cell A1
5. Press ↵

Note that you *cannot* erase a cell by entering blank spaces into it, since a series of blank spaces would be interpreted by 1-2-3 as a label.

How the Recalculation Feature Works

Now it's time to do some experimenting, to explore the power that spreadsheets give to you. The **automatic recalculation** feature in spreadsheets means that if a cell value being changed affects the amounts in other cells in the worksheet, the other cells will be adjusted automatically. Let's experiment with the recalculation feature.

1. Move to Cell B2

2. Change Michaels's Region A sales from 500 to 600

Note: Not only did the value in Cell B2 change, but values also changed in Cell B6 from 850 to 950, in Cell D2 from 700 to 800, and in Cell D6 from 2250 to 2350. Every cell whose value depended on the value in Cell B2 changed.

The recalculation feature makes electronic spreadsheets a valuable tool. Most businesses go through an extensive series of "what if" scenarios when making key decisions. For example, what if Region A totals are 10 percent lower next month? Or what if Williams increases Region A sales to 500? There is frequently a need to recalculate dozens of interdependent figures on schedules to find out the ultimate effect if something happens. Computations that spreadsheets can do in seconds could take hours to do by hand. Repeatedly having the spreadsheet package recalculate worksheets to reflect scenarios in a decision-making environment is called **what-if analysis.**

Continue using the recalculation feature on your worksheet by making the following changes, watching closely as the recalculations take place in related cells.

3. Change Adams's Region B sales from 100 to 500

4. Change Williams's Region A sales from 50 to 10

5. Try some other changes on your own

6. Change the cell contents back to the values that were shown in Figure SS-10

SS

How to Change Column Width

You will want to change the width of a column anytime the values or labels are wider than the default width of nine characters. In this exercise you will change the width of Column A to accommodate wide labels. With your highlight in any cell in Column A

1. Press / to invoke the command menu

2. Type **W** for Worksheet

A new list of options appears.

3. Type **C** for Column

This option allows you to change the width of your column. Your highlight is presently in Column A, so this is the one you will change.

Once again, a new list of commands appears. Remember, you are continuing to move down into submenus of your original choice, Worksheet.

You can see that you have a few choices open to you. To change the width of the column containing your highlight on the worksheet

4. Type **S** for Set-Width

You can now set the width. The message tells you that you can set widths in the range of 1 through 240. For this column, your longest name will not be more than 20 characters.

5. Type **20**

6. Press ↵

The menus now disappear, and you have returned to your worksheet in the Ready mode. You can see that the first column (Column A) is now much wider than the other columns. The steps that you have taken are illustrated in Figure SS-11.

7. Change each name in Column A by moving to the appropriate cell and then retyping as follows:

Ted Michaels
Elise Adams
Sam Williams
Terry Jones

8. Type **/FS** for File Save to save your worksheet again and press ↵

At the message asking whether you want to replace the existing file

9. Type **R** for Replace

This message will appear each time you are saving a file that has already been saved once.

Note that when attempts are made to place data into a cell whose width is too small, 1-2-3 will often display a series of asterisks in the cell in place of the data; for instance,

****

How to Print

As you work, you will want to print the worksheets that you created and, possibly, print some support information about the worksheets. Be sure the printer is turned on.

Printing the Worksheet. You can print your DOC1 worksheet by following these steps

1. Retrieve DOC1

2. Type **/PPR** for Print Printer Range

You must now enter the range of cells to print. The range includes the entire block on your worksheet that contains all of the cells you want to

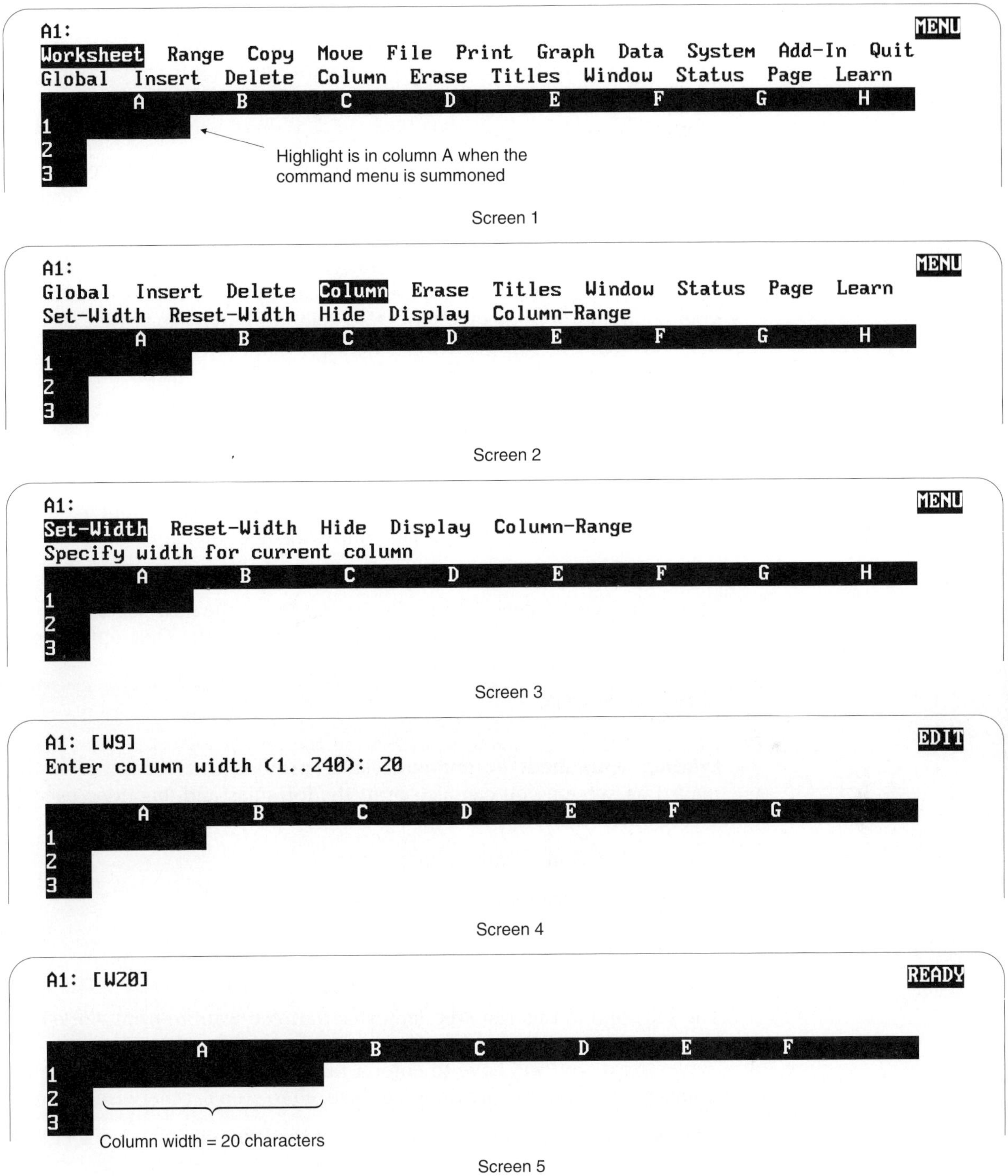

FIGURE SS-11

Using 1-2-3 to enlarge column A to 20 characters.

print. It is the area from the upper left corner to the lower right corner. This is usually Cell A1 through another cell on the lower right corner. The range of cells must always be entered before printing. To enter the range of cells in your DOC1 worksheet

3. Type **A1..D6**

Note: You only need to type one period between the cells designating the range. The program will add the second period automatically.

4. Press ↵

Next, you are ready to give the go-ahead instruction. The range is set, and you are ready to print the worksheet. Be sure your printer is on and that your computer is connected to it. Also make sure that the printer is set to begin printing at the top of a new page.

5. Press **A** for Align

Note: The Align command resets 1-2-3's line counter to the top of the page.

6. Type **G** for Go

Note: You could type G for Go several times without resetting the range to get multiple copies of your worksheet.

7. Type **P** for Page

This command advances your paper to the top of the next page.

To leave the command mode, you choose the Quit option from the same submenu.

8. Type **Q** for Quit

Printing Worksheet Formulas. Besides printing the worksheet as displayed on screen, you can also print the formulas and functions used to create the worksheet. To do this,

1. Type **/P** to again summon the print menu

2. Type **PO** for Printer Options

3. Type **O** for Other

4. Type **C** for Cell Formulas

The selection in this last step indicates that you want to print worksheet formulas and functions.

Next, you will have to enter a range of cells to print. If this range is unchanged from the previous exercise, go to step 6; otherwise,

5. Backtrack to the Range subcommand of the Print command, select it, and type in the range of cells to print, **A1..D6,** followed by ↵

6. Press **A** for Align

7. Press **G** for Go

8. Press **P** for Printer

9. Press **Q** for Quit

At this point, you will receive the output shown in Figure SS-12. Note that the square brackets with [W20] show that column A has been widened to 20 characters.

If you are through printing DOC1,

1. Quit the program by typing **/Q**

2. Type **Y** for Yes

USING RANGES FOR FORMATS AND FUNCTIONS

In this section you will learn important procedures that involve manipulating data in a group of cells. You will format your worksheet, adding special features such as dollar signs or percent signs to values entered as simple numbers. You will also learn how to use functions, which are special built-in formulas that simplify spreadsheet calculations.

When you format your worksheet or enter a function, a range of cells is affected. As discussed earlier, a *range* is defined as one or more cells arranged in a rectangle. A range is depicted by declaring the identity


```
A1: [W20] 'AGENT
B1: 'Region A
C1: 'Region B
D1: "Totals
A2: [W20] 'Ted Michaels
B2: 500
C2: 200
D2: +B2+C2
A3: [W20] 'Elise Adams
B3: 200
C3: 100
D3: +B3+C3
A4: [W20] 'Sam Williams
B4: 50
C4: 400
D4: +B4+C4
A5: [W20] 'Terry Jones
B5: 100
C5: 700
D5: +B5+C5
A6: [W20] 'Totals
B6: +B2+B3+B4+B5
C6: +C2+C3+C4+C5
D6: +B6+C6
```

FIGURE SS-12

Printing worksheet formulas. You can use 1-2-3 to print out the formulas in each cell, as shown here, or alternatively, as-displayed cell contents.

of the cell in the upper left corner of the rectangle, followed by one or two periods and the identity of the cell in the lower right corner. For example, in Figure SS-13, the range of values highlighted in the lower right corner of the screen would be defined as E8 . . G19.

Ranges are useful in spreadsheet packages for more than just printing, formatting, and creating functions. As you'll see later, they are also used for moving, copying, inserting, deleting, sorting, and graphing data. Several other examples of valid ranges are shown in Figure SS-13.

Now, we will go through an exercise involving ranges. If you are just beginning a work session, you'll need to invoke your spreadsheet program and set the default drive. If you are continuing from the previous section, you can erase your screen from the last exercise by typing /WEY and pressing Enter.

When you are at a blank worksheet, enter data for the worksheet shown in Figure SS-14 by following these steps:

1. Move to Cell B1 and type **SOFTWARE PRODUCT SALES,** and press ↵

Note: When there are no values or labels in the cells to the right of a long entry, it will overflow into the blank space. When there are values or labels in the cells to the right, however, the worksheet cell will show only the characters that can fit within the width of the cell, and the cell width must be adjusted.

2. Adjust the width of each column to accommodate the widest label or value in the column, as shown in Figure SS-14

FIGURE SS-13
Examples of ranges.

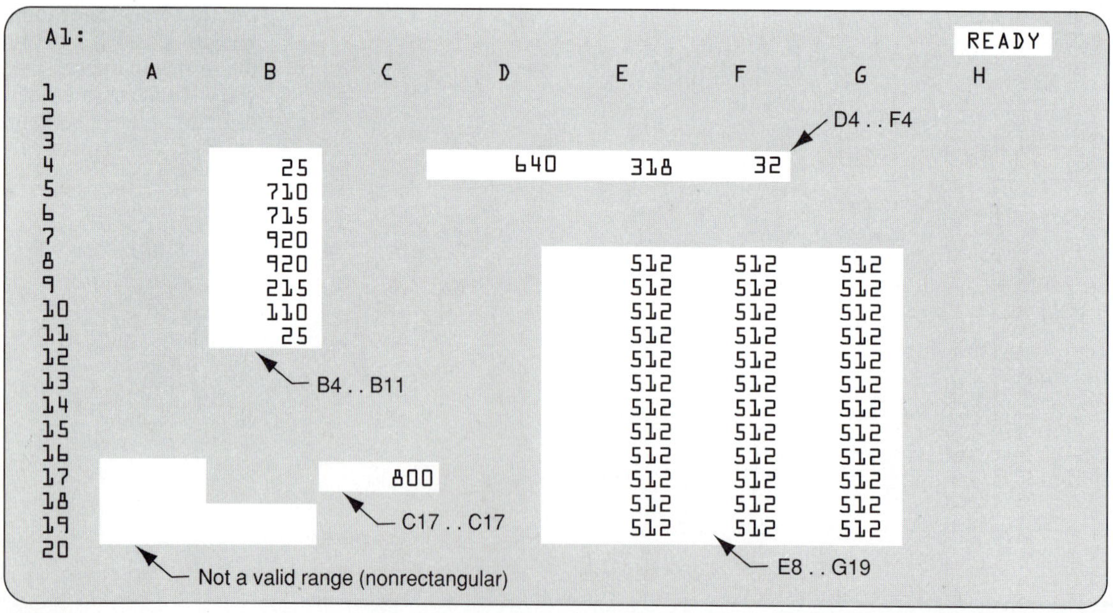

	A	B	C	D	E
1		SOFTWARE PRODUCT SALES			
2					%
3	Product	Last Month	This Month	Difference	Change
4					
5					
6	Word				
7	Processing				
8	Software:	5013.98	5589.18		
9					
10	Database				
11	Software:	4918.72	5890.2		
12					
13	Spreadsheet				
14	Software:	3981.9	3544.32		
15					
16	Graphics				
17	Software:	9873.2	9672.2		
18					
19	Other:	6988.1	5233.38		

FIGURE SS-14
DOC2 worksheet data.

Note: The trailing zeroes that belong in some of the values will not appear in the worksheet until after you have formatted. Formatting is discussed in the next section.

You may adjust the width of the columns to accommodate the widest label or value before or after entering the data. If you wait until after, however, the data will not completely show until you adjust the width. (*Hint:* use /WCS to widen the column width.) Next,

3. Enter the rest of the data in Figure SS-14

4. Type **/FS** for File Save

5. To save the worksheet as DOC2, type the name **DOC2** and press ↵

SS

How to Assign a Format

Formats for numbers in a worksheet may be assigned in either of two ways—through a global command or a range command. A **global command** affects the whole worksheet; a **range command** affects only a range of cells. Using either the Global or the Range command, you will have the format options shown in Figure SS-15.

Assigning a Range Format. To assign a range format for the values already in your DOC2 worksheet, you'll move through a series of command menus. On each menu, you'll type one letter to indicate your choice.

1. Type **/R** for Range

2. Type **F** for Format

FIGURE SS-15
Format choices for Global and Range commands.

Fixed	Fixes the number of decimal places as specified by the user, and numbers are rounded off accordingly. For instance, if two decimal places are specified, 2 becomes 2.00, 2.2 becomes 2.20, 2.015 becomes 2.02, and 2.014 becomes 2.01.
Scientific	Displays values in scientific format. The exponent is expressed as a power of 10 and is shown as an E, such as 1.45E + 02 (or 145).
Currency	Formats values with a dollar sign and commas (as appropriate). Normally business users will specify either zero or two decimal places. Parentheses surround negative numbers.
General	The number is displayed the way it is entered.
+/−	Values are converted into histograms.
Percent	Displays the values followed by a percent sign. The number of decimal places may also be set.
Date	You can specify the date format using this option. The date choices are DD-MMM-YY (Example: 05-Nov-92) DD-MMM (Example: 05-Nov) MMM-YY (Nov-92) (Long Intn'l) (05/05/92) (Short Intn'l) (05/05)
Text	Displays the formula used in a cell rather than the result of the formula.
Hidden	Will hide the contents of the cell so that it is not displayed on the screen or in print. This option is useful if you want to make comments that you want to read in the command line but do not want to see on the worksheet.
Reset	Will change a format from a range setting back to a global setting.
(comma)	Formats values with commas (as appropriate).
Time	Displays numbers as times, in the time format you select (e.g. 05:02:40 PM or 17:02)

You will see a format submenu with the options listed in the previous section.

3. Type **C** for Currency and press ↵ to accept the default of two places to the right of the decimal

In response to the prompt asking you to specify the range to format

4. Type **B8..C19** and press ↵

The values in B8 through C19 will now be displayed with dollar signs, and with commas and decimal points aligned, as shown in Figure SS-16.

Assigning a Global Format. You just gave a range format command to display some values on your worksheet in currency format. If you wanted all of the values to be formatted this way, you could assign a global format.

1. Type **/W** for Worksheet

	A	B	C	D	E
1		SOFTWARE PRODUCT SALES			
2					%
3	Product	Last Month	This Month	Difference	Change
4					
5					
6	Word				
7	Processing				
8	Software:	$5,013.98	$5,589.19		
9					
10	Database				
11	Software:	$4,918.72	$5,890.20		
12					
13	Spreadsheet				
14	Software:	$3,981.90	$3,544.32		
15					
16	Graphics				
17	Software:	$9,873.20	$9,672.20		
18					
19	Other:	$6,988.10	$5,233.38		

FIGURE SS-16
DOC2 worksheet with currency format.

2. Type **G** for Global

3. Type **F** for Format

From this format submenu you have the same selections that are offered for the range format. You can again choose the currency format, meaning that all values will appear with dollar signs, commas (where appropriate), and decimal digits.

4. Type **C** for Currency

5. Press ↵ to accept the default of two places to the right of the decimal

Because your DOC2 worksheet now has a global currency format, any values you enter after this point as simple numbers will be displayed with dollar signs and commas, and with decimal points aligned.

In this worksheet, your cells were changed earlier to be wide enough to accommodate the widest number after the dollar signs and decimal points were added. If you had not adjusted the cell width and the formatted numbers were too large to fit in the cells, a row of asterisks (*********) or a number in scientific format would appear in the cell where the number should be. The asterisks or scientific number disappear and the currency-format values replace them as soon as you increase the width of the column.

6. Remember to save your worksheet (again) as DOC2

How to Enter Functions

Lotus 1-2-3 has a number of useful, built-in functions, or prestored formulas. All functions in 1-2-3 are identified by some keyword (such as SUM, AVG, or IF) and preceded by the @ character. Two of the easiest functions to learn are @SUM and @AVG.

SS

When you use either the @SUM or the @AVG function, you need to identify the range of cells to be used to calculate your sum or average. We covered the concept of a range earlier. Remember, the correct form for identifying a range of cells is to separate the starting and ending cell names by one or two periods. For example, if your cursor is in Cell A1 and you type the function

```
@SUM(B4..B11)
```

you are adding the values in Cells B4 through B11. The answer will be placed in Cell A1.

You can, of course, position your highlight in any cell on the worksheet and use a formula or function that performs a calculation involving cells in any other location on the worksheet.

The @SUM Function. Use the @SUM function to add together Last Month's sales values in your DOC2 worksheet.

1. Move to Cell A21

2. Type the label **Total:**

3. Move to Cell B21

Watch the command line in the control panel as you

4. Type the function **@SUM (B8..B19)**

5. Press ↵

The sum ($30,775.90) appears in Cell B21. This method, as you can see, is much faster than typing +B8+B11+B14+B17, etc. This is particularly true as the range of cells becomes bigger.

The @AVG Function. The @AVG function works similarly to the @SUM. For example, @AVG(B8..B19) will calculate the average of the values in the range of cells B8 through B19. That is, the function @AVG will sum the values in B8 through B19 and then divide the number of values into the sum to get the average. To see how @AVG works,

1. Type the following label into Cells A23 and A24:

Monthly
Average:

2. Move to Cell B24

3. Type the function **@AVG(B8..B19)**

4. Press ↵

The average (6,155.18) appears in Cell B24.

5. Save the worksheet, replacing the original copy of DOC2

6. Quit

Other Spreadsheet Functions. More functions are shown in Figure SS-17 and some examples of their uses are shown in Figure SS-18. Further

FIGURE SS-17
Some common functions.

Arithmetic and Statistical Functions

@ INT (cell or formula) truncates a value to a whole number

@AVG (range) averages values in a range

@SUM (range) calculates the sum of all values in a range

@MAX (range) finds the highest value in a range

@MIN (range) finds the lowest value in a range

@COUNT (range) counts the number of nonempty cells in a range

@STD(range) calculates the standard deviation of values in a range

@SQRT (cell or formula) calculates the square root

@ABS (cell or formula) calculates the absolute value

Financial Functions

@PV (period payment, rate, number of periods) calculates the present value of an annuity, at a specified interest rate

@FV (period payment, rate, number of periods) calculates the future value of an annuity, at a specified interest rate

@PMT (present value, rate, number of periods) calculates an annuity (period payment) that is equivalent to a given present value at a specified interest rate

@NPV (rate, range) calculates the present value of the cash flows in a range, at a specified interest rate

@TERM (period payment, rate, future value) calculates the number of payment periods needed to reach a future value if each payment is invested at the end of each period at the specified periodic interest rate

@RATE (future value, present value, number of periods) calculates the periodic interest rate necessary for a present value to accrue to a future value, within a specified number of periods

@SLN (initial cost, salvage value, useful life) calculates the straight-line depreciation of an asset for each period, based upon the asset's initial cost, salvage value, and useful life

@SYD (initial cost, salvage value, useful life, period) calculates the sum-of-the-year's-digits depreciation of an asset for one period, based upon the asset's initial cost, salvage value, and useful life

Date Functions

@DATE (year, month, day) calculates the number of days that have elapsed since the date specified in parentheses and December 31, 1899*

@TODAY returns a number that corresponds to the current date according to your computer's clock. This number is expressed as a date number, such as 33866 or possibly 34292. The date number is calculated as the number of days that have elapsed since December 31, 1899

Other Functions

@HLOOKUP (*x*, range, offset) uses the value *x* to look across the first row in the range to find the value closest to but not larger than *x*; then, it goes down that column the number of *offset* rows specified and selects the contents of the cell there

@VLOOKUP (*x*, range, offset) uses the value *x* to look down the first column in the range to find the value closest to but not larger than *x*; then, it goes across that row the number of *offset* columns specified and selects the contents of the cell there

@IF (conditional expression, value if true, value if false) supplies a cell with a value that depends on whether the conditional expression is true or false

@CHOOSE (pointer value, list of possible values) chooses one value in a list of values, based on the pointer value

*December 31, 1899, serves as a fixed reference point. In combination, the TODAY and DATE functions can be used to calculate such things as the number of days past due on invoices or the number of days that an account has been in existence. In order for the value of a date function to look familiar (e.g., 12/15/95), you must appropriately format the cell in which the value appears.

SS

FIGURE SS-18
Using functions.

	A	B	C	D
1	10	5	15	20
2	6	7	3	4
3	8	2	9	4
4	-1	0	3	15

@ SUM (A1..D1) = 50

@ SUM (C1..C4) = 30

@ SUM (A1..D4) = 110

@ MIN (A1..D4) = -1

@ MIN (B2..C3) = 2

@ MAX (A1..D4) = 20

@ MAX (A1..D4, 100) = 100

@ AVG (A1..D1) = 12.5

@ AVG (B1..B4, 2) = 4

@ ABS (A4..A4) = 1

@ SQRT (C3..C3) = 3

@ COUNT (A1..D4) = 16

@ SQRT (@ COUNT (A1..A4)) = 2

@ IF (A4 < 0, 10, 20) = 10

explanation of these as well as a more extensive list of available functions is available in a 1-2-3 reference manual.

COMPLETING YOUR WORKSHEET

In this exercise, you will give your worksheet its finishing touches with the many other options available to you through the command set. When finished, your worksheet will take on a polished appearance.

How to Use Relative and Absolute Addressing

When you copy a formula in one cell to another, you will probably want some of the cell addresses within the formula to change and other cell addresses to remain the same. One of the most convenient and most used copy commands involves **relative addressing.** This concept means that when you copy a formula, the cell addresses within the formula change automatically to adjust to the addresses within the row and column to which you are copying. **Absolute addressing** allows you to designate certain cell addresses within a formula as those that will not change when copied.

How Relative Addressing Works When Copying a Formula. Watch what happens when you copy the formulas you have created on the DOC2 worksheet.

1. Invoke 1-2-3, set your default drive, and retrieve DOC2

2. Move to Cell B21

Note: The sum of the cells in the formula appears in this cell in the worksheet area, but the command line shows the formula used to arrive at this value.

3. Type **/C** for Copy

When the message appears asking for the range to copy from

4. Press ↵ (since your highlight is already in the cell from which you want to copy)

At the message asking for the range to copy to

5. Type **C21** (or **C21..C21**)

Note: You need to enter only the first cell of the location to which you are copying—the starting point. The remainder of the cells designated in the range will automatically follow.

6. Press ↵

The relative formula has been copied to C21, and the resulting value is inserted there in the worksheet area.

7. Move to Cell C21 and look at the formula in the command line.

Note in the command line that the cell ranges in the formula have automatically changed to C8..C19 from the original B8..B19. This is an example of relative addressing.

8. Copy the formula in B24 to C24 using the same procedure

To complete the "Difference" column in your worksheet

9. Move to Cell D8 and enter the formula **+C8−B8**

10. Copy the formula in D8 individually to cells D11, D14, D17, and D19

Note: You must use the copy command for each individual cell so that zeroes (0s) are not entered into the cells without values.

To complete the "% Change" column in your worksheet

11. Move to Cell E8 and enter the formula **+D8/B8**

Note: Ignore the currency format. You will change it later to percentage format.

12. Copy the formula in E8 individually to cells E11, E14, E17, and E19

How to Use an Absolute Address When Copying a Formula. Absolute addressing identifies certain cells in a formula as ones that will not change when the formula is copied. An absolute cell address includes a dollar sign before both the column letter and the row number, such as $B$5.

1. Move to Cell F2

2. Widen the column and then type the following labels in F2 and F3:

% of Total
This Month

The formulas you want to create for this column will divide this month's individual sales for each product by the total sales for this month. Of the two cell addresses used in the formula, you want the first one designating the product's total to change when the formula is copied and you want the address of the Total Amount for all Products this Month not to change since this amount is the same for all products.

3. Move to Cell F8

4. Type the formula +**C8/$C$21** to compute the % of Total

5. Press ↵

Note: Ignore the currency format. You will change it later.

When this formula is copied, the Cell C8 part will be relative (it will change when copied to a new cell address); both the column and row of Cell $C$21 are absolute (the address will not change when copied, so the divisor will always be the value in Cell C21).

You can also use **mixed addressing,** which employs a column-row address with only a single dollar sign. Examples are: $C19 (locks Column C but allows the row to change) and C$19 (locks the row but allows the column to change). You will use mixed addressing in a hands-on exercise toward the end of these spreadsheet tutorials.

6. Type **/C** for Copy to copy this formula individually from Cell F8 to each of the following cells: F11, F14, F17, F19

How to Use the MOVE Command

You can move the data in a cell or range of cells from one location to another. When you use the MOVE command, you remove the cell contents from their original location and place them in a new location.

You could, for example, move the worksheet title in DOC2 from Cell B1 to Cell C1. To do this

1. Move the cursor to Cell B1

2. Type **/M** for Move

For the range to move from

3. Press ↵ since your highlight is in the cell you want to move from

For the range to move to

4. Type **C1** (or **C1..C1**) and press ↵

The title will move one cell to the right so that it starts in Cell C1 and also fills part of the empty Cell D1.

Suppose, for another example, that you want to move the values of Column F of your worksheet to the next column so you can insert an additional heading and figures in Column F. For practice,

5. Move the cursor to Cell F8

6. Type **/M** for Move

For the range to move from

7. Type **F2..F19** and press ↵

For the range to move to

8. Type **G2** (or **G2..G2**) and press ↵

How to Set a Range by Pointing

You can also point to the cell(s) that you want to move (or copy). The following steps will direct you to restore the column you just moved to its original location.

1. Move to Cell G2

2. Type **/M** for Move

When the "from range" prompt appears, you'll use the period (.) key to lock the beginning of the range.

3. Type **.** (period)

4. Press ↓ to move to G19

Note: As you move, the cell location in the command line changes, and the entire cell range is highlighted on the worksheet.

5. Press ↵

The "target range" prompt appears.

6. Move to Cell F2 and press ↵

The range is back in its original location.

7. Save and replace the DOC2 worksheet again

How to Change a Format

Earlier you assigned a global currency format on your DOC2 worksheet. Follow these steps to change columns E and F to a percent format.

1. Move to Cell E8

2. Type **/RFP** and press ↵ (to accept 2 decimal places)

3. Type **E8..F19** as the range

4. Save and replace the worksheet again

How to Insert and Delete Rows and Columns

Inserting and deleting are both done through the Worksheet command.

To Insert a Row. Follow this procedure:

1. Move to Cell A2

The new row will be inserted above the current pointer position. This blank row will be inserted between the main heading and the sub–headings.

2. Press **/WIR** for Worksheet Insert Row

3. Press ↵

Note: You may also insert more than one row. After choosing Row, you can type a range of rows you would like to insert. You do not need to worry about entering a horizontal range since the Row insert automatically affects the entire width of the worksheet.

To insert three blank rows above the Total row

4. Move to the start of the Total row, now A22

5. Type **/WIR**

6. Type **A22..A24** to indicate the range of added rows

7. Press ↵

The Total row is pushed down on the worksheet.

To Insert a Column. Insert a column between Columns D and E by following the same steps as in the preceding activity, except this time you will choose Column rather than Row.

1. Move to Cell E1

2. Type **/WIC** for Worksheet Insert Column

3. Press ↵

As with rows, you could type a range of new columns if you wished to add more than one blank column to your worksheet. You can add columns or rows from anywhere in the worksheet; just type the range to be added and press Enter.

To Delete Columns and Rows. You can delete rows and columns the same way you inserted them. The only change in the command you give will be to substitute Delete for Insert. The position of your cursor will indicate the row or column to delete.

1. Move to Cell E1 (at the top of the column just added)

2. Type **/WDC** for Worksheet Delete Column

3. Press ↵

To delete the three added rows, A22..A24, this time type the range after choosing R for Rows:

4. Type **/WDR**

5. Type **A22..A24** to indicate the range to be deleted

6. Press ↵

How to Create Separator Lines

Business reports often use separator lines to neatly separate elements such as titles from the main body, or to separate a totals line from the figures above it. These lines usually consist of a string of dashes reaching from the leftmost column to the rightmost column of the worksheet (see Figure SS-19.

In the exercise to follow, you will add separator lines to your current worksheet, DOC2.

1. Move to Cell A21

Add a separator line just above the Totals line, using the spreadsheet's repeat label-prefix character (refer back to Figure SS-8). To do this, you'll use the backslash (\) and hyphen (-) characters.

2. Type \- and press ↵

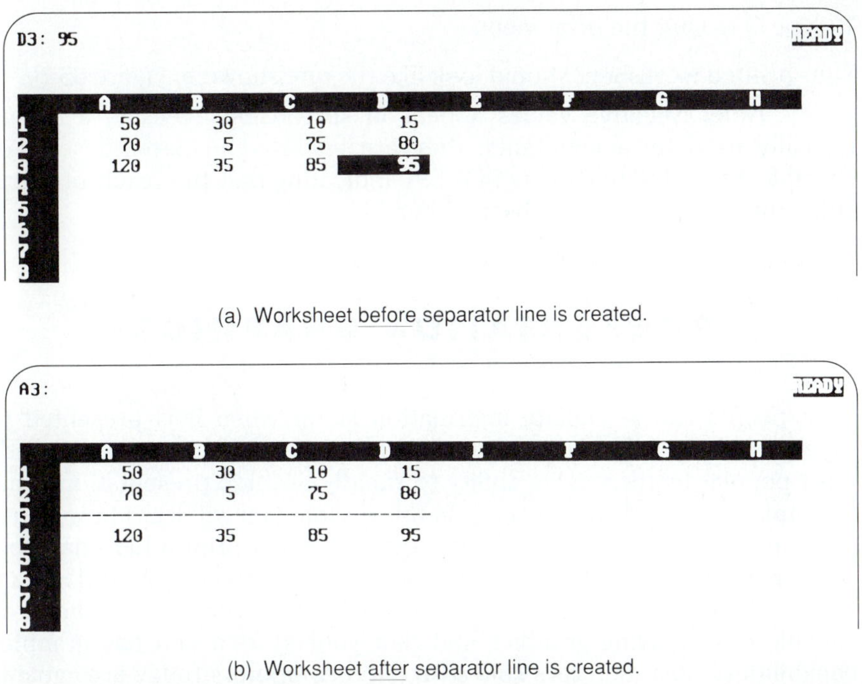

(a) Worksheet before separator line is created.

(b) Worksheet after separator line is created.

FIGURE SS-19
Using a separator line.

The backslash label-prefix character tells the program that you want the entire cell to be filled with the character after the backslash. In this case, that character is a hyphen (-).

Now all you need to do is copy this cell to the remaining cells in this row of your worksheet—in this case, Cells B21 through F21.

3. Type **/C** for Copy

4. Press ↵ at the "From:" prompt

5. Type **B21..F21** at the "To" prompt to specify the appropriate range

6. Press ↵

A row of dashes appears above the Total line.

7. Type **/FS** and press ↵ to save the file

8. Type **R** to Replace the earlier version

To Print the Revised Worksheet.

1. Type **/PPR** for Print Printer Range

2. To enter your range, type **A1..F25**

3. Press ↵

4. Press **A** for Align

5. Be sure the printer is ready and then type **G** for Go

6. Type **P** to reset printer to top of next page

7. Type **Q** to Quit the print menu

Your printed worksheet should look like the one shown in Figure SS-20.

Note: Negative values appear in spreadsheet cells in a format typically used by accountants: they are enclosed in parentheses. For example, the value of D14 is ($437.58), indicating that the result of calculating the formula is a negative number.

PRESENTATION GRAPHICS

Most people can assimilate information faster when it is presented to them in picture form. So it's not surprising that one of a spreadsheet's most popular features is its ability to rapidly develop presentation-quality **graphs** from worksheet values. In this lesson, you will learn how to use your spreadsheet program to construct, save, and print a bar chart, pie chart, and line chart. See the examples shown in Figures SS-21 and SS-22.

Before you begin, you should make sure that your monitor is capable of displaying graphics and that your system unit has graphics capabilities. Most monitors sold with microcomputers today are capable

SOFTWARE PRODUCT SALES					
Product	Last Month	This Month	Difference	% Change	% of Total This Month
Word Processing Software	$5,013.98	$5,589.18	$575.20	11.47%	18.67%
Database Software:	$4,918.72	$5,890.20	$971.48	19.75%	19.68%
Spreadsheet Software:	$3,981.90	$3,544.32	($437.58)	-10.99%	11.84%
Graphics Software:	$9,873.20	$9,672.20	($201.00)	-2.04%	32.32%
Other	$6.988.10	$5,233.38	($1,754.72)	-25.11%	17.49%
Total:	$30,775.90	$29.929.28			
Monthly Average:	$6,155.18	$5,985.86			

FIGURE SS-20
Printed DOC2 worksheet.

SS

of producing graphics. However, unless your system unit has graphics capability, and the spreadsheet software knows the graphics environment with which it is dealing, you will not be able to see any graphs on your display screen. You should also check to see that your printer supports graphics output before proceeding.

In the exercises to follow you're going to start off creating different types of graphs using the data in the DOC1 worksheet. Graphs are developed in 1-2-3 but they are printed by a separate program called PrintGraph, which is available off the Lotus Access System menu (see page SS-4 for details).

How to Create a Simple Bar Chart

A **bar chart** represents values in a range with columns of varying height. A **simple bar chart** is, as its name suggests, the most elementary type of bar chart. Each attribute assigned a column is accorded a single, dedicated column and these columns are equally spaced along the horizontal axis. Here, we will create the simple bar chart in Figure SS-23—comparing the totals of each agent's sales—with the DOC1 worksheet.

1. If necessary, invoke 1-2-3 and set the default drive

2. Type **/FR** to retrieve the worksheet called DOC1

3. Press the arrow keys to highlight DOC1

4. Press ↵

5. Type **/G** for Graph

FIGURE SS-21
Examples of presentation graphics.

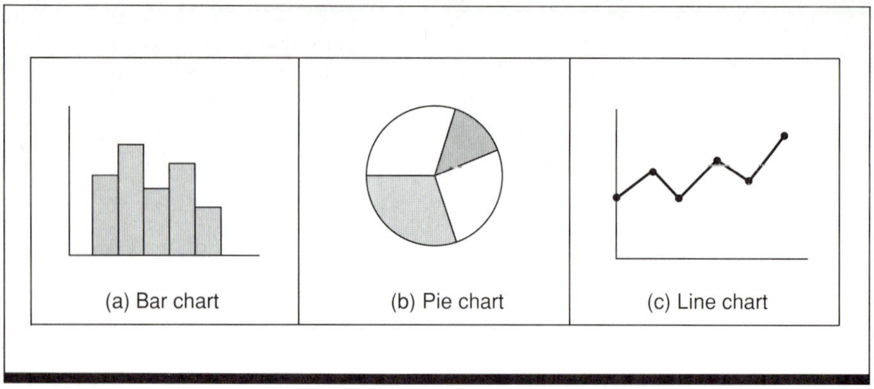

6. Type **T** for Type

The Type command on the submenu summons a list of subcommands. This submenu enables you to choose the type of graph you want.

7. Type **B** for Bar

To Label the X- and Y-Axes. You are now ready to select the worksheet values and labels that are to be graphed, and to tell the spreadsheet where these values or labels are to appear in the graph. To place the names of the sales agents along the graph's horizontal X-axis

1. Type **X** for X-axis from the graph submenu

When the computer prompts you for the X-axis range

2. Type **A2..A5** (or use the pointer method)

3. Press ↵

You are now back at the main graph commands.

4. Type **A** to identify the range of values that will be used to graph the bars for each sales agent (the Totals column)

FIGURE SS-22
Bar charts.
Bar charts are especially useful for comparing relative magnitudes of items and for showing the frequency with which events occur.

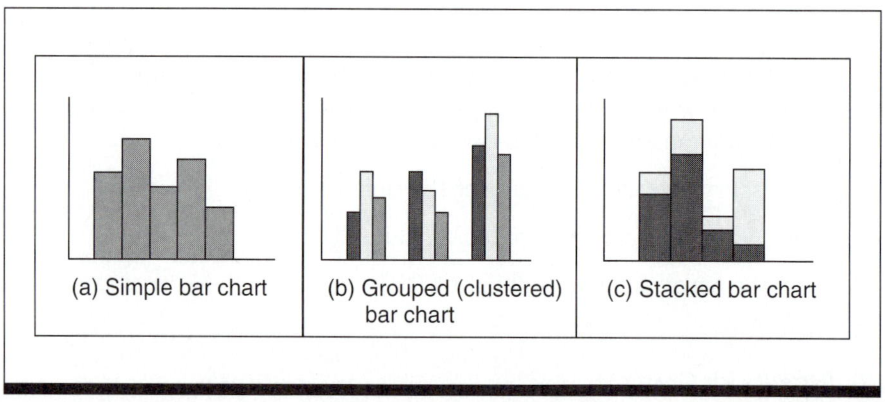

Worksheet

	A	B	C	D
1	AGENT	Region A	Region B	Totals
2	Ted Michaels	500	200	700
3	Elise Adams	200	100	300
4	Sam Williams	50	400	450
5	Terry Jones	100	700	800
6	Totals	850	1400	2250

X-range A-range

Graph declarations	
Type:	Bar
X-range:	A2..A5
A-range:	B2..B5
B-range:	C2..C5
First title:	SALES BY REGION
Second title:	January

Graph

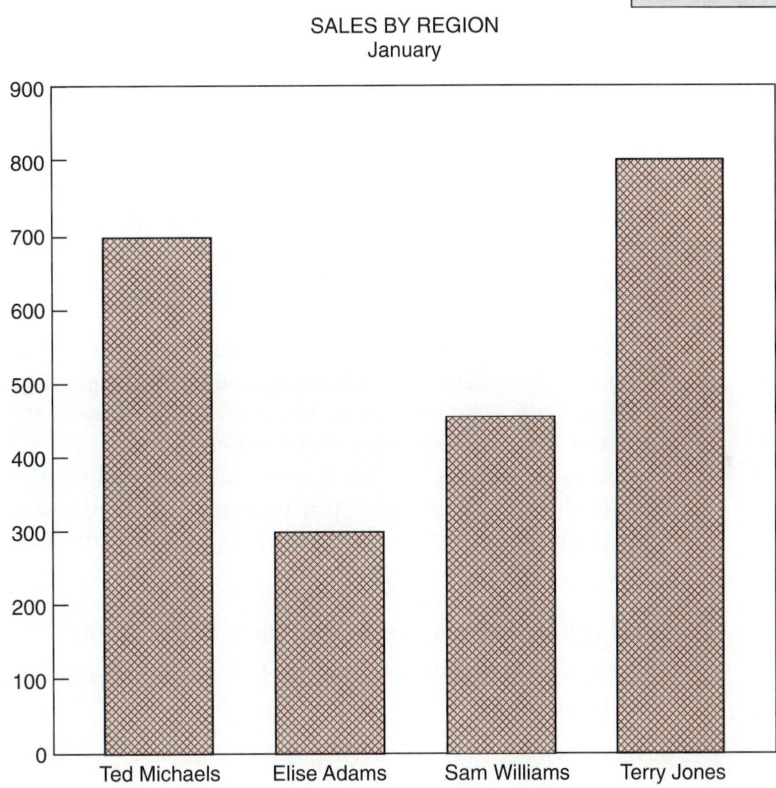

FIGURE SS-23
Simple bar chart.

These values appear in Column D of the worksheet. When the computer prompts you for the range,

5. Type **D2..D5** and press ↵

Now it's time to supply the title.

6. Type **O** for Options from the graph submenu

1-2-3 lets you supply titles of up to two lines.

7. Type **T** for Titles

8. Type **F** for First

9. Type **SALES BY REGION** and press ↵

To create the second title,

10. Type **TS** for Second

11. Type **January** and press ↵

To View the Graph. Now you are ready to view the graph. It is a good idea to view the graph prior to printing so that you can make any necessary adjustments to the graph. To do this,

1. Type **Q** for Quit

The Graph menu reappears.

2. Type **V** for View

At this point your graph should appear on the screen. If you wish to change the graph for any reason, reselect any of the graph-command options discussed so far and make the appropriate changes. As usual, you can either type your changes or use the pointer method to make them.

3. Press any key to return to the worksheet

To Name and Save the Graph. Although you can save your graph as a separate file, there are advantages to naming each graph you create and saving each as part of the worksheet. All graphs are then permanently connected to your worksheet and can be viewed on the screen. Changes made on the worksheet are then automatically reflected in the graphs. Each time changes are made, the worksheet and the associated graphs are retained by saving the worksheet again. To name the current bar graph

1. Type **N** to select Name

2. Type **C** to select Create and name a new graph

3. Type **DOC1BAR1** to indicate the name of this bar graph of worksheet DOC1

4. Press ↵

Note: When you name a graph, it is not saved permanently until you save the worksheet from which you are designing the graph.

5. Type **Q** to Quit graph menu

6. Type **/FS** to save your worksheet with the bar graph attached

How to Print a Graph

After the graph is created and named, it must be stored in a file for printing purposes. PrintGraph, a program supplied by 1-2-3, is used to print the graph file.

1. Retrieve DOC1 to your screen

2. Type **/GNU** for Graph Name Use

3. Move the menu pointer to **DOC1BAR1**

4. Press ↵

Your screen should now display the graph.

5. Press **Esc** to return to the Graph menu

Now you want to store this graph in a separate file so you can print it later with PrintGraph.

6. Type **S** for Save

The program prompts you for a file name.

7. Type **DOC1BAR1** and press ↵

The program adds the .PIC file extension to distinguish graph files from other kinds of files.

8. Type **Q** to Quit the Graph menu

To leave the 1-2-3 program and start PrintGraph,

9. Type **/QY** for Quit Yes

Hard-disk system users can skip step 10 if the PrintGraph portion of the program is already stored on hard disk.

10. Dual-diskette system users should replace the 1-2-3 system disk with the PrintGraph disk

11. Type **PGRAPH** and press ↵

12. Type **I** for Image-Select

You'll see a list of all .PIC files. (*Note:* You have only created one file, so only one will be listed.)

13. Highlight the file **DOC1BAR1**

14. Press the spacebar to mark the file

15. Press ↵ to return to the main menu

16. Type **A** for Align to set the printer's line counter

17. Type **G** for Go to print the graph

When the printer is ready

18. Type **P** for Page

19. Type **EY** for Exit Yes

How to Reset Settings for a New Graph

If you are creating several charts from a single worksheet, you need to reset the settings prior to creating each chart. Previous settings are stored as defaults for you to reuse. To reset the settings

1. Type **/GRG** for Graph Reset Graph

2. Type **Q** for Quit

This command will delete all headings, labels, ranges, etc., from the previous chart so that you may begin with new settings.

How to Create a Grouped (Clustered) Bar Chart

A **grouped (clustered) bar chart** is a bar chart in which similar columns are grouped side by side and separated by spacing from other such column groups. A grouped bar chart—showing each agent's sales for each region—appears in Figure SS-24. To create this chart

1. If necessary, invoke 1-2-3 and set the default drive

2. Type **/FR** to retrieve the worksheet called DOC1

3. Press the arrow keys to highlight DOC1

4. Press ↵

5. Type **/G** for Graph

6. Type **T** for Type

The TYPE command on the submenu summons a list of subcommands. This submenu enables you to choose the type of graph you want.

7. Type **B** for Bar

To Label the X- and Y-Axes. You are now ready to select the worksheet values and labels that are to be graphed, and to tell the spreadsheet where these values or labels are to appear in the graph. To place the names of the sales agents along the graph's horizontal X-axis

1. Type **X** for X-axis from the graph submenu

When the computer prompts you for the X-axis range

2. Type **A2..A5** (or use the pointer method)

3. Press ↵

You are now back at the main graph commands.

4. Type **A** to identify the range of values that will be used to graph the leftmost bar for each sales agent (the Region A totals)

These values appear in Column B of the worksheet. When the computer prompts you for the first range (or the A range),

5. Type **B2..B5** and press ↵

Worksheet

	A	B	C	D
1	AGENT	Region A	Region B	Totals
2	Ted Michaels	500	200	700
3	Elise Adams	200	100	300
4	Sam Williams	50	400	450
5	Terry Jones	100	700	800
6	Totals	850	1400	2250

X-range A-range B-range

Graph declarations	
Type:	Bar
X-range:	A2..A5
A-range:	B2..B5
B-range:	C2..C5
First title:	SALES BY REGION
Second title:	January

Graph

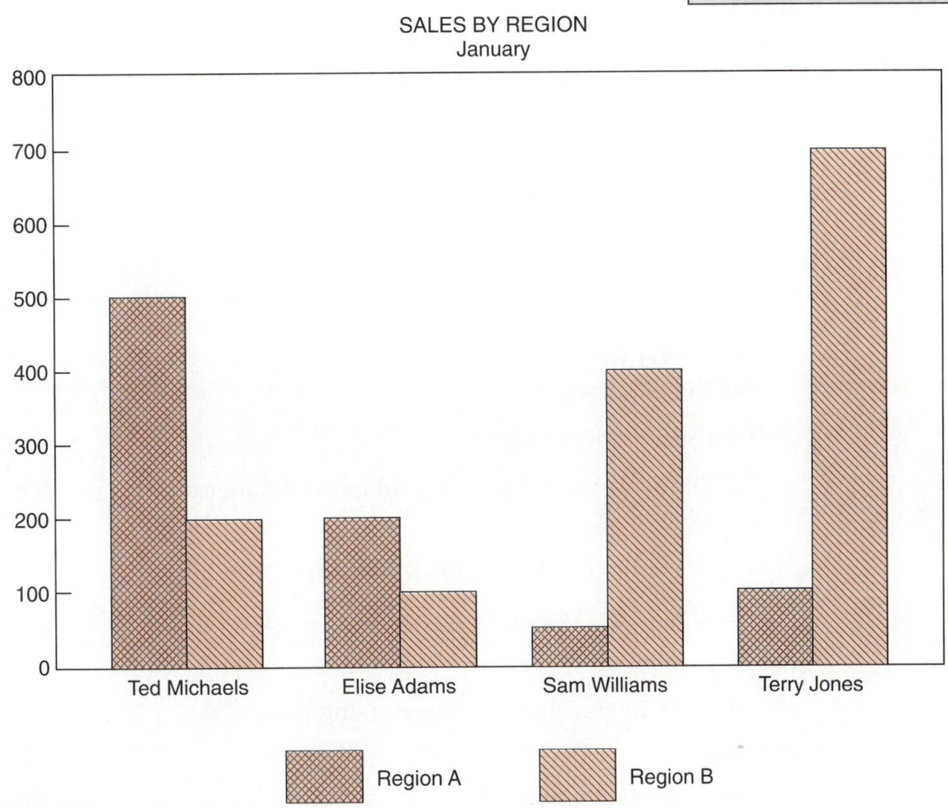

FIGURE SS-24
Grouped (clustered) bar chart.

At this time you will return to the main graph submenu.

6. Type **B** to identify the values for the rightmost bars for each agent in the chart

These bars will show the values contained in Column C of your worksheet. When prompted for the second data range,

7. Type **C2..C5** and press ↵

The graph is now finished except for the title.

8. Type **O** for Options from the graph submenu

1-2-3 lets you supply titles of up to two lines.

9. Type **T** for Titles

10. Type **F** for First

11. Type **SALES BY REGION** and press ↵

To create the second title,

12. Type **TS** for Second

13. Type **January** and press ↵

To Create Legends. The bar chart in Figure SS-24 contains legends. **Legends** are used to label the bars. To create legends for your graph

1. Press **Q** for Quit

The graph menu reappears

2. Press **O** for Options

3. Press **L** for Legend

Now you will have to tell 1-2-3 which legends you want to create for each of the data ranges.

4. Press **A** for A-range

5. To the prompt "Enter legend for first data range:" type **Region A** and press ↵

You will be returned to the options menu, so

6. Press **L** for Legend again

7. Press **B** for B-range

8. Type **Region B** to the prompt and press ↵

To View the Graph. Now you are ready to view the graph. To do this,

1. Type **Q** for Quit

The Graph menu reappears.

2. Type **V** for View

At this point your graph should appear on the screen. If you wish to change the graph for any reason, reselect any of the graph-command options discussed so far and make the appropriate changes.

3. Press any key to return to the worksheet

To Name and Save the Graph. To name the current bar graph

1. Type **N** to select Name
2. Type **C** to select Create and name a new graph
3. Type **DOC1BAR2** to indicate the name of this bar graph of worksheet DOC1
4. Press ↵
5. Type **Q** to Quit graph menu
6. Type **/FS** to save your worksheet with the bar graph attached

At this point your graph is named and saved. Before proceeding to the next exercise, print the graph and reset the graph settings through the procedures described earlier.

How to Create a Stacked Bar Chart

In a **stacked bar chart** columns are tiered one on top of another, such as those shown in Figure SS-25. To create a stacked bar chart

1. If necessary, invoke 1-2-3 and set the default drive
2. Type **/FR** to retrieve the worksheet called DOC1
3. Press the arrow keys to highlight DOC1
4. Press ↵
5. Type **/G** for Graph
6. Type **T** for Type

The TYPE command on the submenu summons a list of subcommands. This submenu enables you to choose the type of graph you want.

7. Type **S** for Stack-Bar

To Label the X- and Y-Axes. You are now ready to select the worksheet values and labels that are to be graphed, and to tell the spreadsheet where these values or labels are to appear in the graph. Your goal is to produce a bar chart like the one in Figure SS-25, showing each agent's sales for two different regions. To place the names of the sales agents along the graph's horizontal X-axis

1. Type **X** for X-axis from the graph submenu

When the computer prompts you for the X-axis range

2. Type **A2..A5** (or use the pointer method)
3. Press ↵

You are now back at the main graph commands.

Worksheet

	A	B	C	D
1	AGENT	Region A	Region B	Totals
2	Ted Michaels	500	200	700
3	Elise Adams	200	100	300
4	Sam Williams	50	400	450
5	Terry Jones	100	700	800
6	Totals	850	1400	2250

X-range A-range B-range

Graph declarations	
Type:	Bar
X-range:	A2..A5
A-range:	B2..B5
B-range:	C2..C5
First title:	SALES BY REGION
Second title:	January

Graph

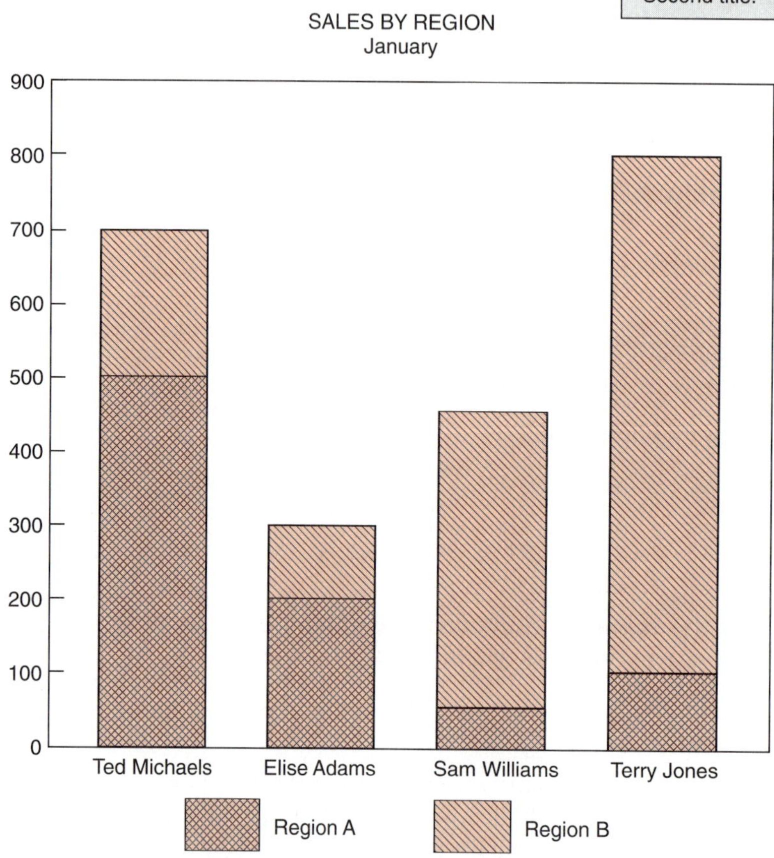

FIGURE SS-25
Stacked bar chart.

4. Type **A** to identify the range of values that will be used to graph the bottommost bar for each sales agent (the Region A totals)

These values appear in Column B of the worksheet. When the computer prompts you for the first range (or the A range),

5. Type **B2..B5** and press ↵

At this time you will return to the main graph submenu.

6. Type **B** to identify the values for the next tier of bars for each agent in the chart

These bars will show the values contained in Column C of your worksheet. When prompted for the second data range,

7. Type **C2..C5** and press ↵

The graph is now finished except for the title.

8. Type **O** for Options from the graph submenu

1-2-3 lets you supply titles of up to two lines.

9. Type **T** for Titles
10. Type **F** for First
11. Type **SALES BY REGION** and press ↵

To create the second title

12. Type **TS** for Second
13. Type **January** and press ↵

To Create Legends. Use the same procedure described earlier for grouped bar charts. In other words,

1. Press **Q** for Quit
2. Press **O** for Options
3. Press **L** for Legend
4. Press **A** for A-range
5. To the prompt "Enter legend for first data range:" type **Region A** and press ↵
6. Press **L** for Legend again
7. Press **B** for B-range
8. Type **Region B** to the prompt and press ↵

To View the Graph. Now you are ready to view the graph. To do this,

1. Type **Q** for Quit

The Graph menu reappears.

2. Type **V** for View

At this point your graph should appear on the screen. If you wish to change the graph for any reason, reselect any of the graph-command options discussed so far and make the appropriate changes.

3. Press any key to return to the worksheet

To Name and Save the Graph. To name the current bar graph

1. Type **N** to select Name
2. Type **C** to select Create and name a new graph
3. Type **DOC1BAR3** to indicate the name of this bar graph of worksheet DOC1
4. Press ↵
5. Type **Q** to Quit graph menu
6. Type **/FS** to save your worksheet with the bar graph attached

At this point your graph is named and saved. Before proceeding to the next exercise, print the graph and reset the graph settings through the procedures described earlier.

How to Create a Pie Chart

Pie charts show values in relation to a whole. They are constructed in a manner very similar to bar charts. The primary difference is that a pie chart typically uses only one range of data values.

With the DOC1 worksheet on the screen, follow these steps to create a pie chart like the one shown in Figure SS-26.

1. Type **/GTP** for Graph Type Pie

The procedures to identify the ranges and the one-line title for the graph are identical to the corresponding ones for bar charts.

2. Type **X** for X-axis
3. Type **A2..A5** and press ↵
4. Type **A** to identify the A range
5. Type **D2..D5** and press ↵
6. Type **OTF** to add the title
7. Type the title **TOTAL SALES** and press ↵

Follow the same steps as with bar charts to view, save, and print the pie chart.

8. Type **QV** to Quit the submenu and to View the chart
9. Type **NC** and **DOC1PIE1** to name the chart
10. Save your DOC1 worksheet
11. Follow the directions described earlier to print the graph
12. Press **Q** for Quit to return to the READY mode

Worksheet

	A	B	C	D
1	AGENT	Region A	Region B	Totals
2	Ted Michaels	500	200	700
3	Elise Adams	200	100	300
4	Sam Williams	50	400	450
5	Terry Jones	100	700	800
6	Totals	850	1400	2250

X-range (A2..A5)   A-range (D2..D5)

Graph declarations	
Type:	Pie
X-range:	A2..A5
A-range:	D2..D5
First title:	TOTAL SALES

Graph

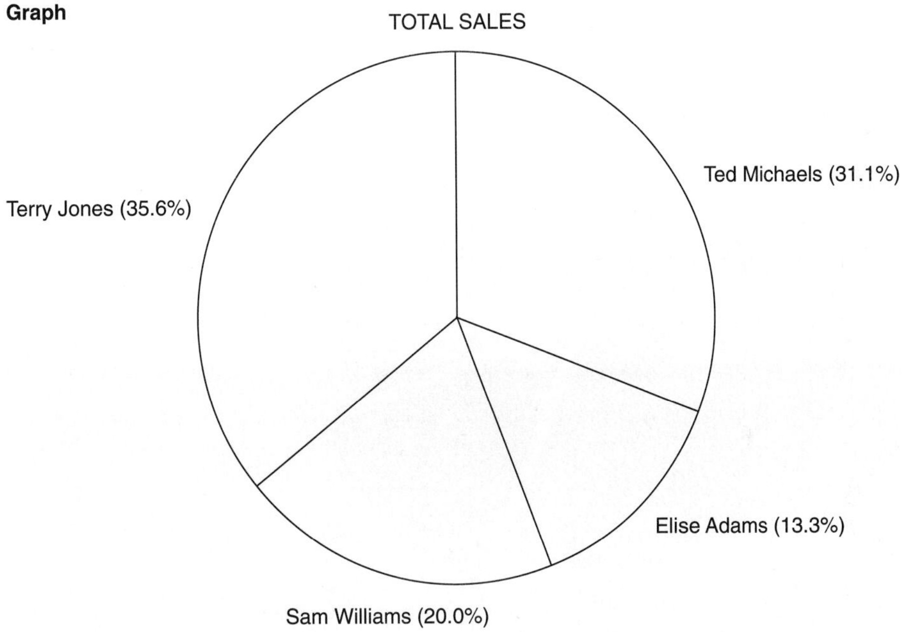

FIGURE SS-26
Pie chart.

How to Shade and Explode a Pie Chart. Sometimes it's advantageous to call to people's attention certain slices of a pie chart. To do this, you can **shade** and/or **explode** the pieces that you want people to notice. This is done in Figure SS-27.

To shade or explode a pie chart in 1-2-3, you create an extra column of data that tells the spreadsheet which pieces are to be shaded and/or exploded. Note that in Figure SS-27, a B-range has been created in

Worksheet

	A	B	C	D	E
1	AGENT	Region A	Region B	Totals	
2	Ted Michaels	500	200	700	1
3	Elise Adams	200	100	300	102
4	Sam Williams	50	400	450	3
5	Terry Jones	100	700	800	4
6	Totals	850	1400	2250	

X-range (A2..A5) A-range (D2..D5) B-range (E2..E5)

Graph

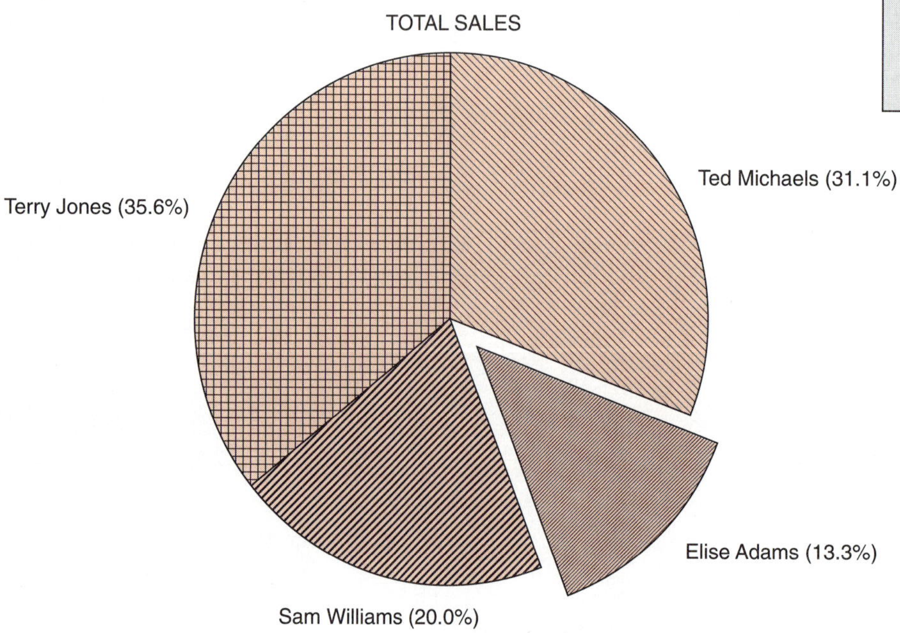

Graph declarations	
Type:	Pie
X-range:	A2..A5
A-range:	D2..D5
B-range:	E2..E5
First title:	TOTAL SALES

FIGURE SS-27
Exploded pie chart with shading.

column E. The B-range is numbered 1, 2, 3, 4, and so on if we want shading of the pie slices or 0, 1, 2, 3, and so on otherwise. In other words, we start the progression of digits with a 1 or 0 depending on whether or not we want shading.

You will also note that cell entry E3, for Elise Adams, is 102 instead of just 2. What 1-2-3 asks us to do is to add 100 to any number in the progression that we want to explode away from the main part of the chart. We can explode as many pieces as we want; here we will just explode Elise Adams' slice.

So, to shade and explode as in Figure SS-27, assuming your current settings are for the pie chart of Figure SS-26,

1. Return to DOC1 and create column E, as shown in Figure S-27

2. Type **/G** to summon the graph menu

3. Type **B** to select the B-range

4. In response to the prompt, type in the B-range **E2..E5** and press ↵

5. Type **V** to view the graph

At this point, if the graph is satisfactory, name it as DOC1PIE2 and follow the same steps as with bar charts to save and print the graph.

How to Create a Line Chart

Once you understand how to make bar and pie charts, the procedure for constructing **line charts** is simple. A line chart is similar to a bar chart except that it represents values as an unbroken line.

Suppose, for example, that the sales (in units) for a new product in a particular five-week period are as follows:

25 units the first week
45 units the second week
75 units the third week
70 units the fourth week
90 units the fifth week

From these figures you can create a line chart similar to the one shown in Figure SS-28. Your first step is to create a new worksheet containing the figures for each week. Starting with a blank worksheet screen

1. Type the labels as follows, including the apostrophe in front of each one to indicate that they are labels:

Cell A1 **'1**
Cell A2 **'2**
Cell A3 **'3**
Cell A4 **'4**
Cell A5 **'5**

Worksheet

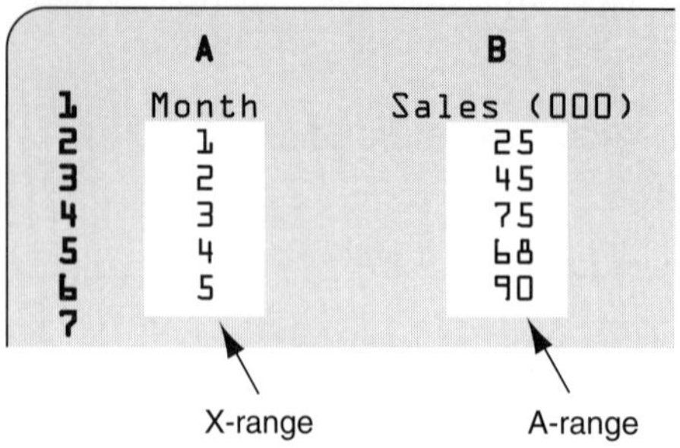

Graph declarations	
Type:	Line
X-range:	A2..A6
A-range:	B2..B6
First title:	SALES IN UNITS
Second title:	(First 5 Weeks)
X-axis title:	Week
Y-axis title:	Sales

Graph

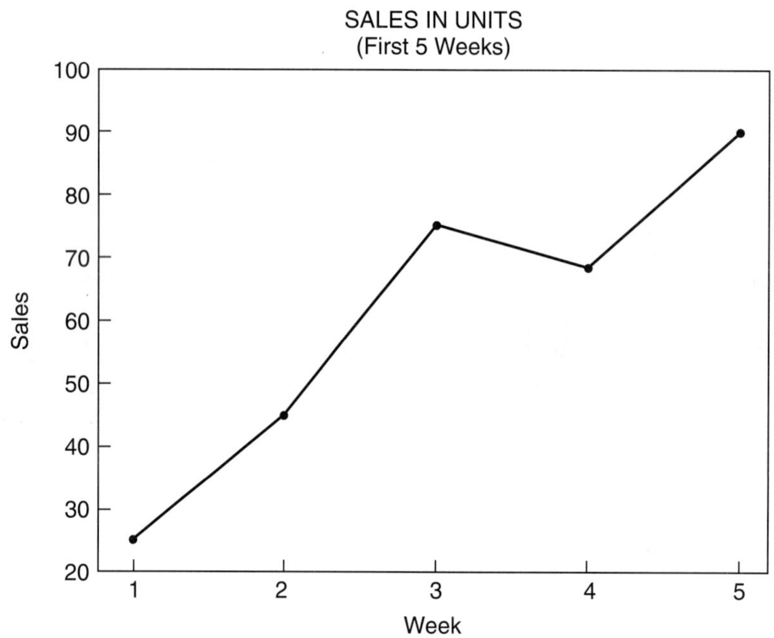

FIGURE SS-28
Line chart.

2. Type the following values (no apostrophe):

Cell B1	**25**
Cell B2	**45**
Cell B3	**75**
Cell B4	**70**
Cell B5	**90**

3. Save the worksheet as DOC3.

4. Type **/GTL** for Graph Type Line

When you return to the graph submenu,

5. Type **X** to identify the X range
6. Type **A1..A5** and press ↵
7. Type **A** to identify the A range
8. Type **B1..B5** and press ↵

To type in a two-line title,

9. Type **OTF** for Options Titles First
10. Type **SALES IN UNITS** and press ↵
11. Type **TS** for Titles Second
12. Type **(First 5 Weeks)** and press ↵

To label the X-axis from the graph submenu,

13. Type **OTX** for Options Titles X-axis

When the spreadsheet package prompts you for the X-axis title,

14. Type **Week** and press ↵

To label the Y-axis from the graph submenu,

15. Type **T** for Titles and then type **Y** for Y-axis

When the program prompts you for the Y-axis title,

16. Type **Sales** and press ↵

At this point, the graph is finished.

17. To view the graph, type **QV** for Quit and View
18. Name the graph as DOC3LINE
19. Type **Q** to return to the READY mode
20. Save your worksheet with the attached graph
21. Print a copy of the line chart following instructions in the section named "How to Print a Graph"

COMMAND REFERENCE

This section briefly summarizes many of the most-used instructions in 1-2-3. It is meant to be used only as a reference after completing the full 1-2-3 tutorials contained in the preceding exercises. New commands introduced in the Hands-on Exercises starting on page SS-67 are also listed here.

Aligning Labels

To align label data before data is placed into cells

1. Move to the cell to contain the data

2. Type a label prefix character, either " (for right justify), ^ (for center), or **** (for repeat)

Note: There is no need to type the apostrophe character ('), for left justify, since that is the default alignment.

3. Type the label

4. To enter the label, either type ↵ or press one of the arrow keys

To align label data after data have been placed into cells

1. Move to the cell containing the data or, if there are several cells, the first cell in the range

2. Type **/ RL** for *Range Label*

3. Type either **L** (for *Left* justify), **R** (for *Right* justify), or **C** (for *Center*)

4. Do one of the following:

a. If only a single cell is to be changed, press ↵

b. If the contents of a range of cells is to be changed, highlight the range and press ↵

Borders

To create borders, or frozen titles, on a printed worksheet

1. Move the cell pointer to the first cell to be included in the border

2. Press **/ PPOB** for *Printer Print Options Borders*

3. Press **C** for *Columns,* to print vertical headings on left side of each page, or **R,** for *Rows,* to print horizontal columns on the top

4. Highlight or type the range with the column or row borders and press ↵

5. Press **Q** for *Quit*

Note: Make sure that you remove the borders from the print range of your worksheet so that they won't print twice.

Cancelling Commands

To back up a menu level or command step at a time while you are in the process of completing a command

Press **Esc**

To undo the effects of the last-issued command

Press **Alt** + **F4**

Column Width Adjustments

To change the width of a specific column

1. With the cell pointer in the column, type **/ WCS** for *Worksheet Column Set-Width*

2. Type in the new width

3. Press ↵

Copying Data

To copy data from one part of the worksheet to another

1. Type **/ C** for *Copy*

2. Type or point to the range to copy from

3. Press ↵

4. Type or point to the range to copy to

5. Press ↵

Deleting Rows and Columns

To delete rows or columns

1. Type **/ WD** for *Worksheet Delete*

2. Type **R** for *Rows* or type **C** for *Columns*

3. Enter the range to be deleted

4. Press ↵

Directory Changes

To change the directory that 1-2-3 will default to in order to retrieve or save files

1. Press **/ FD** for *File Directory*

2. Type in the identity of the new directory; for instance, **B:** if you are working on a dual-diskette system or **A:** if you are working on a hard-disk system

3. Press ↵

Distributing Data

To set up a frequency distribution that tallies the number of data values in a range that fall into each of several contiguous intervals

1. Place the data values to be tallied into a range

   Note: In many cases, the data will already naturally be in a range, making this step unnecessary.

2. Set up a bin range (column), leaving the column to the right of the bin range empty
3. Press **/ DD** for *Data Distribution*
4. Type in the range of the data in step 1
5. Press ↵
6. Type in the bin range of step 2
7. Press ↵

Entering Data into a Cell

To enter data into a cell

1. Move the cell pointer to the cell in which the data are to be entered
2. Type in the data
3. Press ↵ or, if you wish to both enter data and move the cell pointer to the next cell at the same time, press one of the arrow keys

Erasing Cells

To erase the contents of one or more cells

1. Move to the first or only cell in the range
2. Press **/ RE** for *Range Erase*
3. If only one cell is to be erased, press ↵ ; otherwise, type the range and press ↵

Erasing Files

To erase the current worksheet from RAM

1. Press **/ WE** for *Worksheet Erase*
2. Type **Y** for *Yes,* to invoke the erasure

To erase a file on disk

1. Press **/ FE** for *File Erase*

   Note: If you have a dual-diskette system, the file to be erased must be mounted on one of the drives.

2. Either (a) type in the filename of the file to be erased, or (b) list the directory in which the file appears and highlight the filename

Note: If you type in the filename, make sure you include the disk drive and extension if 1-2-3 will not default to the proper ones.

3. Press ↵

4. Press **Y** for *Yes,* to invoke the erasure

Formatting Data

To format the entire worksheet a certain way

1. Press **/ WGF** for *Worksheet Global Format*

2. Select a format from the subsequent series of menus and prompts you receive

Note: Refer to page SS-26 in the text for a description of formatting options.

To format data in a specific range of cells

1. Press **/ RF** for *Range Format*

2. Select a format from the subsequent series of menus and prompts you receive

Note: Refer to page SS-26 in the text for a description of formatting options.

3. Type the range to which the format applies

4. Press ↵

Freezing Titles

To freeze worksheet titles horizontally

1. Place the cell pointer one row below the rows you wish to freeze

2. Press **/ WTH** for *Worksheet Titles Horizontal*

To freeze worksheet titles vertically

1. Place the cell pointer one column to the right of the columns you wish to freeze

2. Press **/ WTV** for *Worksheet Titles Vertical*

To freeze worksheet titles both horizontally and vertically

1. Place the cell pointer one row below and one column to the right of the rows and columns you wish to freeze

2. Press **/ WTB** for *Worksheet Titles Both*

To unfreeze, or clear, all frozen titles and rows

Press **/ WTC** for *Worksheet Titles Clear*

Graphs—Creating

To create a graph

1. Retrieve the worksheet on which the graph is to be based
2. Press **/ GT**, for *Graph Type*
3. Type the letter that corresponds to the graph type
4. To set the X-axis label range, press **X**
5. Identify the corresponding range in the worksheet
6. Press ↵
7. To set the Y-axis data range, press **A**

Note: In pie charts, *A* is the only data range (unless you wish to shade and explode, in which case there is a *B* range)

8. Identify the corresponding range in the worksheet
9. Press ↵
10. To set additional data ranges (*B* through *F*)
    a. Press **B**
    b. Identify the corresponding range in the worksheet
    c. Press ↵
    d. Repeat this procedure as is necessary, successively using in step 10a the letters C, D, E, and F

To create titles

1. Press **/ GOTF** for *Graph Options Title First*
2. Type the first title
3. Press ↵
4. To add a second title, press **TS** at the options submenu
5. Type the second title
6. Press ↵
7. Press **Q** for *Quit* to return to the Graph submenu

To create legends

1. Press **/ GO** for *Graph Options*
2. Press **L** for *Legends*
3. Press **A** for the first legend on the Y axis

Note: For subsequent legends, respectively use the letters B, C, D, E, and F.

4. Type the legend
5. Press ↵
6. For additional legends, repeat steps 2 through 5, observing the note in step 3

Graphs—Naming

To name a graph

1. Press **/ GNC** for *Graph Name Create*

2. Type in the name of the graph

3. Press ↵

Note: Remember to save your worksheet so that your graph will be saved.

Graphs—Printing

To print a graph in 1-2-3, you must first save your graph by typing S for *Save* from the Graph submenu.

1. Quit 1-2-3 and return to the system prompt (A: with a dual-diskette system or C: with a hard-disk system). Also, with a dual-diskette system, insert the PrintGraph diskette in Drive A

2. Type **Lotus** and press ↵

3. Select **PGraph** and press ↵

4. Press **I** for *Image-Select* and select the name of the graph you wish to print

5. Press ↵

6. Press **G** for *Go*

7. Press **P** for *Page* to advance to the top of the next page

8. Press **E** for *Exit* and **Y** for *Yes* to exit the PrintGraph program

Graphs—Resetting

It is necessary to reset if you are making several graphs from a single worksheet. Resetting erases all previous settings. To reset all graph settings

Press **/ GRG** for *Graph Reset Graph*

Note: You can also reset individual graph data ranges by typing the corresponding data-range letter.

Graphs—Saving

To save a graph onto disk

1. Press **/ GS** for *Graph Save*

2. Type the graph name

3. Press ↵

Graphs—Viewing

To inspect a graph onscreen

Press **/ GV** for *Graph View*

Help Feature

To enter the Help feature at any time

Press **F1**

To exit the Help feature at any time and return to your worksheet or graph

Press **Esc**

Inserting Rows and Columns

To insert rows or columns

1. Type **/ WI** for *Worksheet Insert*

2. Press **R** for *Rows* or **C** for *Columns*

3. Enter the range to be inserted

4. Press ↵

Listing Files

To display a list of files in a directory

Press **/ FL** for *File List*

Note: If you have a dual-diskette system, the files you wish to display must be mounted on one of the drives.

Moving Data

To move data within a worksheet

1. Type / **M** for *Move*

2. Type or point to the range to move from

3. Press ↵

4. Type or point to the range to move to

5. Press ↵

Page Breaks

To create a page break in your worksheet

1. Place the cell pointer in the leftmost column of the range you are printing, in the row where you want the new page to start
2. Press **/ WP** for *Worksheet Page*

Note: The page-break symbol (::) appears in the current cell. You can remove the page break by editing or deleting the contents of this cell.

Pointing to Ranges

Whenever you are setting a range, you can use the arrow keys to set the last cell location in the range.

1. Move the cursor to the cell
2. Select the operation (e.g., **/ M** for *Move* or **/ C** for *Copy*)
3. Type **.** (period) to anchor the first cell in the range
4. Press ↓ or → to move to the last cell in the range
5. Press ↵
6. Type in the cell of the target location or move the cursor to that cell
7. Press ↵

Printing Cell Formulas and Functions

To print the formulas or functions underlying the construction of a range of cells

1. Press **/ PPOOC** for *Print Printer Options Other Cell-Formulas*
2. Type in the range of cells to print
3. Type **A** for *Align*
4. Press **G** for *Go*
5. Press **P** for *Printer*
6. Press **Q** to *Quit* the Print menu

Printing Worksheets

To print a copy of your worksheet

1. Type **/ PPR** for *Print Printer Range*
2. Type in the range of cells to print
3. Type **A** for *Align*

4. Type **G** for *Go*
5. Type **P** for *Page*
6. Type **Q** for *Quit* the print menu

Quitting 1-2-3

To leave a 1-2-3 session

Press **/ QYY** for *Quit Yes Yes*

Depending on how you started 1-2-3, you will now be returned to either the operating system or the 1-2-3 Access System menu.

Retrieving Files

To display an existing file on your screen

1. Type **/ FR** for *File Retrieve*
2. Type the name of the file to retrieve or highlight the filename from the directory list
3. Press ↵

Saving Worksheets

To save your worksheet

1. Type **/ FS** for *File Save*
2. Type the name of the worksheet if this is the first time it has been saved or you are saving under a new name.
3. Press ↵
4. Type **R** to *Replace* the worksheet if this is not the first time it has been saved.

Separator Lines

Separator lines on the worksheet are formed from a series of hyphens (-). The backslash (\) is the repeat label-prefix character used to replicate the hyphen.

1. Position the cell pointer where you want the line to start
2. Type \-
3. Press ↵

4. Type **/ C** for *Copy*

5. Type the cell range where you want the line copied to

6. Press ↵

Sorting Data

To sort worksheet data

1. Press **/ DSD** for *Data Sort Data-Range*

2. Declare the range that corresponds to the data you wish to sort

Note: If the worksheet consists of a set of records, this range should cover the entire set of records (but not the field names that serve as columns).

3. Press ↵

4. Press **P** for *Primary-Key*

5. Type in the address of any cell of the column that will serve as the primary key

6. Enter the sort order for the primary key (**A** for *Ascending* or **D** for *Descending*)

If you wish to choose any secondary keys, follow steps 7 through 10 below; otherwise, go to step 11.

7. Press **S** for *Secondary-Key*

8. Type in the address of any cell of the column that will serve as the secondary key

9. Enter the sort order for the secondary key (**A** for *Ascending* or **D** for *Descending*)

10. If you wish to declare any other secondary keys, repeat steps 7 through 9.

Note: Each additional secondary key that you add will be subordinate to the secondary key declared before it.

11. Press **G** for *Go*

At this point, the sort will take place.

Starting 1-2-3

To start 1-2-3, at the operating-system prompt or Access System menu

1. Type **123**

2. Press ↵

SS

Table Lookups

To look up in a table an entry in a specified column (vertical lookup) or row (horizontal lookup) that corresponds to a value in a specific cell

1. Move the cell pointer to the cell that will contain the result of the lookup
2. Type either **@VLOOKUP** or **@HLOOKUP**, depending on whether you wish to do a vertical lookup or a horizontal lookup
3. Press **(** (open parenthesis)
4. Enter the cell address of the value upon which the search is to be based
5. Press **,** (comma)
6. Enter the range corresponding to the table to be searched
7. Press **,** (comma)
8. Type the offset, which is the number of columns (rows) that the lookup column (row) is from the first table column (row)
9. Press **)** (close parenthesis)
10. Press ↵

Undo

To cancel certain changes made to the worksheet since 1-2-3 was last in the READY mode,

Press **Alt** + **F4**

Note: 1-2-3 must be in the READY mode when Undo is invoked. Undo does not work when certain utilities are in use.

GLOSSARY

Absolute addressing. Writing a cell address so that the contents of a cell can be copied verbatim into other cells.

Automatic recalculation. The ability of spreadsheet software to quickly and automatically recalculate the contents of cells based on new operator inputs.

Bar chart. A graph in which spreadsheet values are represented as columns.

Cell. The part of the worksheet that can hold a single label or value; a cell occurs where a row and column intersect.

Cell address. The column/row combination that uniquely identifies a spreadsheet cell.

Cell pointer. A cursorlike mechanism used in the worksheet area to point to cells, thereby making them active. Sometimes referred to as the *pointer* or *highlight.*

Control panel. The topmost three lines of a normal 1-2-3 screen display; used for issuing commands and observing what is being typed into the computer system.

Current cell. The worksheet cell at which the cell pointer (highlight) is currently positioned.

Cursor. A flashing symbol in the control panel that appears where the next character to be typed in will be placed.

Explode. The act of setting off one or more pie slices from the main part of the pie chart.

Function. A prestored formula.

Global command. An instruction that impacts all cells in the worksheet.

Graph. A chart showing how values relate to each other.

Grouped (clustered) bar chart. A bar chart in which similar columns are grouped side by side and separated by spacing from other such column groups.

Label. A cell entry that cannot be manipulated mathematically.

Label-prefix character. A character preceding a label that specifies how the label is to be placed in a cell.

Legend. A descriptive label in a graph.

Line chart. A graph in which spreadsheet values are represented by a continuous line.

Mixed addressing. Writing a cell address so that if the column (row) is relative the row (column) is absolute.

Mode indicator. A highlighted system message at the top of the screen that tells what the spreadsheet package is doing.

Pie chart. A graph in which spreadsheet values are represented as percentages of a whole.

Range. A set of contiguous cells that are arranged in a rectangular pattern.

Range command. An instruction that impacts a range of cells in the worksheet.

Relative addressing. Writing a cell address so that the contents of a cell can be copied relative to new row and column positions.

Shade. A special texture applied to a chart element.

Simple bar chart. A bar chart in which each attribute assigned a column is accorded a single, dedicated column and these columns are equally spaced along the horizontal axis.

Spreadsheet. A productivity software package that enables operators to develop tables and financial schedules quickly and to graph the result.

Stacked bar chart. A bar chart in which columns are tiered one on top of the other.

Status indicator. A highlighted system message that sometimes appears at the bottom of the screen.

Value. A cell entry that can be manipulated mathematically.

What-if analysis. An approach to problem solving in which the decision maker repeatedly commands the computer system to recalculate a set of figures based on alternative inputs.

Window. Refers to the screen, through which can be seen any screen-sized portion of the worksheet.

Worksheet. The computerized counterpart to the ruled, ledger-style paper used by accountants.

Worksheet area. The portion of the screen that contains the window onto the worksheet area.

REVIEW QUESTIONS

1. The intersection of row and column in a worksheet is called a(n) ____________.
2. To load your spreadsheet program, what should you type at the system prompt?
3. The control panel consists of which lines in your screen?
4. The mode indicator is located where on your screen?
5. The command set (menus) are accessed by pressing which key?
6. Identify the main set of commands available in 1-2-3.
7. List the hierarchy of arithmetic operators used with 1-2-3.
8. If you are into your third set of subcommands and realize that you do not want to save the changes you have been making and would like to return to the READY mode, what can you do?
9. If the function @AVG(C12..C20) is typed into Cell C25, what will be the result?
10. State the difference between a relative and absolute address in a formula.
11. What is the label-prefix character used to repeat a character?
12. What is the difference between a pie chart and a bar chart?

ANSWERS **1.** cell **2.** 123 (or Lotus) **3.** the top three lines **4.** the upper right corner **5.** Slash key (/) **6.** See Figure SS-6 **7. a.** ^(exponentiation) **b.** / and * (division and multiplication, in the order in which they appear from left to right) **c.** + and – (addition and subtraction, in the order in which they appear from left to right) **8.** Press **Esc** several times

9. The values in C12 through C20 are summed and then the total is divided by the total number of nonempty cells in this range (9), and the result is put into Cell C25. **10.** In a relative address the cell locations change to match those in the range to which they are copied. An absolute cell address keeps the cell location the same regardless of where it is moved. **11.** \ (backslash) **12.** A pie chart shows values as part of a whole; a bar chart shows values as columns.

HANDS-ON EXERCISES

The following exercises will reinforce the knowledge you have acquired during the tutorials up to this point and will also introduce a few additional features that will be useful when doing worksheets on your own.

Hands-on Exercises 1 and 2 involve setting up a basic worksheet, editing it, copying cells, writing simple formulas, and saving and printing the worksheet. Exercises 3 through 6 cover graphs. Exercises 7 through 12 will not only reinforce many basic tasks but will also introduce a few new ones with each worksheet.

It is highly recommended that you proceed through each exercise in the order of presentation.

SS

Hands-on Exercise 1: Fundamentals #1

In this exercise, you will practice

☐ Copying values from cell to cell

☐ Saving a worksheet

☐ Retrieving a worksheet

☐ Printing a worksheet

☐ Adjusting column width

☐ Calculating an average

☐ Making changes to the worksheet

☐ Creating a formula for subtracting one value from another

1. Prepare the partial worksheet shown in Figure SS-29, right-justifying the dates in Cells B1 to F1
2. Compute profits by taking sales minus costs for each of the days presented. Create a formula for Cell B4 and copy it to other applicable cells in the Profits row

FIGURE SS-29
Hands-on Exercise 1.
Computing profits.

	A	B	C	D	E	F
1	Day	Jan 1	Jan 2	Jan 3	Jan 4	Jan 5
2	Sales	500	800	600	700	800
3	Costs	350	700	150	200	400
4	Profits					
5						
6						

3. Save the worksheet as HANDS1 (for Hands-on Exercise 1)

4. Quit the spreadsheet and go to the operating-system prompt

5. Sign back onto 1-2-3 and retrieve the worksheet

6. Print out the worksheet on your printer

Modifications to HANDS1. You are to make the following changes in HANDS1.

1. Adjust the column widths in HANDS1 as follows:

a. Column A: 20 characters

b. Columns B through F: 6 characters

2. Format sales and costs for the entire worksheet in Currency format (using 2 decimal places)

Note: The columns now show asterisks (******).

3. Adjust the width of the columns B through F (at least 8 spaces wide) so that all numeric values appear

4. Calculate the average sales, average costs, and average profits for the five days shown in Figure SS-29, placing these values into column G of the worksheet. Create an appropriate column heading, such as "Averages."

5. How would your worksheet change if the January 1 costs were actually $50 instead of $350? Print a copy of a revised worksheet showing the changes

Note: When you change the 350 to 50, you should not enter a dollar sign ($) or a decimal point (.). Enter the value as a whole number, 50, and press Enter. All formatting is done through the format commands.

6. How would the worksheet change if January 3 sales were $90 instead of $600? Print a copy of the revised worksheet showing these changes

7. Save the revised worksheet as HANDS1R. Print out a copy of HANDS1R

Hands-on Exercise 2: Fundamentals #2

In this exercise, you will practice

☐ Using the COPY command

☐ Using the MOVE command

☐ Creating separator lines

☐ Inserting rows

1. Prepare the worksheet shown in Figure SS-30. Remember to use a quote (") as the first character for the column headings in B, C, D, and E so they will be interpreted as labels. Remember also to format with dollar signs (currency) and not to type them in.

   Note: The example in Figure SS-30 was formatted with no decimal points.

2. Create a formula in Cell B4 to compute a row called "Income" (Revenue minus Expenses). Use a plus sign (+) at the beginning of the formula
3. Copy the formula in B4 to other applicable cells (Income in Columns C, D, and E)
4. Use the MOVE command to move the entire worksheet in this exercise to L7 (*Hint:* from A1..E4 to L7..P10)
5. Press **F5** to access the GOTO function and type **L7** and press ↵
6. Create separator lines on the worksheet:
   - **a.** Insert a new row above Revenue and one above Income
   - **b.** Create a separator line by using the repeat label-prefix character and the COPY command as follows:

     On the new Row 8: in Cells L8 through P8

     On the new Row 11: in Cells L11 through P11
7. Move the worksheet back to A1
8. Press **Home** to return the cursor to A1
9. Save the worksheet as HANDS2
10. Print a copy of the worksheet

SS

	A	B	C	D	E
1	Quarter	1st	2nd	3rd	4th
2	Revenue	$200	$100	$600	$500
3	Expenses	$130	$50	$100	$300
4	Income				

FIGURE SS-30
Hands-on Exercise 2. Computing income. Shown are 1992 quarterly figures.

Hands-on Exercise 3: Simple Bar Charts

In this exercise, you will practice

- □ Constructing a simple bar chart
- □ Saving a graph
- □ Printing a graph

1. Retrieve worksheet HANDS2 and construct a simple bar chart showing revenue (see Row 3 of the worksheet or Row 2 of Figure SS-30) for each quarter. Include the following:

a. A title as follows:

REVENUE REPORT
1992

b. Label the Y-axis:

Revenue

Use the **Graph Options Titles Y-axis** command to do this.

c. Labels on the X-axis for each quarter. Label the bars:

1st
2nd
3rd
4th

d. Label the entire x-axis itself:

Quarters

Use the **Graph Options Titles X-axis** command to do this.

2. Save the bar chart as HANDS3G

3. Save the worksheet as HANDS3

4. Print a copy of the bar chart

Hands-on Exercise 4: Grouped and Stacked Bar Charts

In this exercise, you will practice

- □ Constructing a grouped bar chart
- □ Constructing a stacked bar chart
- □ Creating legends

1. Retrieve worksheet HANDS2, which reports 1992 revenues and expenses

2. Assume that 1991 revenue and expense figures are as follows:

Quarter	1st	2nd	3rd	4th
Revenue	$350	$500	$400	$700
Expenses	$200	$100	$300	$500

3. Add the figures in step 2 to the HANDS2 worksheet, computing also the income (revenue minus expenses) for each quarter in 1991. Save the worksheet as HANDS4

   Hint: Put 1991 quarterly figures in columns B through E, moving 1992 figures over, to columns F through I.

4. Prepare a *grouped bar chart* that shows 1991quarterly incomes (in the final row of your worksheet) compared alongside those of 1992. In other words, the first group of two bars should compare income for the first quarter of each year; the second group of two bars, the second quarter; and so on. Include the following:

   a. A title as follows: **INCOME REPORT**
   1991 AND 1992 COMPARED

   b. Legends as follows:
   A-range legend: **1991**
   B-range legend: **1992**

   c. Label the Y-axis **Income**

   d. Labels on the X-axis for the bars in each quarter, as you did in Step 1c of Hands-on Exercise 3. Label the entire X-axis **Quarters**

5. Save the bar chart as HANDS4G1
6. Resave the worksheet as HANDS4
7. Print a copy of the bar chart
8. Repeat steps 4 through 7, preparing instead a *stacked bar chart.* In step 5, save the bar chart as HANDS4G2 and print it out; in step 6, resave the worksheet as HANDS4

Hands-on Exercise 5: Pie Charts

In this exercise, you will practice

☐ Constructing a pie chart

☐ Exploding and shading a pie chart

1. Retrieve HANDS2 again
2. Create a pie chart that compares income for each quarter in 1992. Title the chart **INCOME, 1992**
3. Shade the chart, viewing it to see that it has been properly shaded
4. Explode the most profitable quarter from the chart, again viewing the chart before proceeding
5. Save the chart as HANDS5G

6. Print a copy of the chart

7. Save the worksheet as HANDS5

Hands-on Exercise 6: Line Charts

In this exercise, you will practice

☐ Constructing a line chart

1. Retrieve worksheet HANDS4

2. Create a line chart that shows how income changed in the eight consecutive quarters extending from the first quarter of 1991 to the fourth quarter of 1992. Include the following

a. A title as follows:

INCOME REPORT
1991-1992

b. Label the Y-axis **Income**

c. Labels on the X-axis for each quarter, as you did in step 1c of Hands-on Exercise 3. Label the entire X-axis **Quarters, 1991-1992**

3. Save the chart as HANDS6G

4. Print a copy of the chart

5. Save the worksheet as HANDS6

Introduction to Hands-on Exercises 7 through 12

In preparing the remaining worksheets in this section, you will learn how to

☐ Prepare a multiperiod budget

☐ Prepare a check register for income taxes

☐ Freeze titles on the screen

☐ Sort data

☐ Do a frequency distribution

☐ Use some new functions

Hints accompany some of the exercises. It is important to read the hints thoroughly. They help to explain some new commands that are introduced and are necessary to completing the worksheet. Otherwise, suggestions are given as a part of the instructions. Some of the new functions covered are:

☐ Labeling tips (Exercise 7)

☐ Creating templates (Exercise 8)

- ☐ The range-formatting command (Exercise 8)
- ☐ The data-fill command (Exercise 8)
- ☐ The 1-2-3 hierarchy of arithmetic operations (Exercise 8)
- ☐ Using the SLN and SYD functions (Exercise 8)
- ☐ Preparing a frequency distribution (Exercise 9)
- ☐ Mixed cell addressing (Exercise 10)
- ☐ Sorting data (Exercise 11)
- ☐ Using the MIN function (Exercise 11)
- ☐ Freezing horizontal and vertical titles (Exercise 11)
- ☐ The @IF function (Exercise 12)

Hands-on Exercise 7: Preparing a Multiperiod Cash Budget

In this exercise, you will practice

- ☐ Filling in a worksheet from supplied data
- ☐ Creating formulas
- ☐ Saving the worksheet
- ☐ Printing the worksheet
- ☐ Changing the worksheet using different assumptions
- ☐ Positioning values and labels within a column
- ☐ Using the F2 key for editing

If asked to identify their most critical spreadsheet operation, many managers would name budgeting. Because budgets involve guesswork about the future, they often have to be recalculated over and over again under a variety of financial assumptions, commonly known as "what ifs." For example, what if sales projections are 10 percent too high (or too low), what if borrowing rates increase 1 or 2 percent, or what if a revenue or expense item is incurred earlier or later than expected?

Important note: Here you will prepare a cash budget for SeaTech Corporation. You are given a partial worksheet showing the various account titles involved, the expected beginning cash balance of $100,000, and the desired quarter-ending cash balances of $125,000, $165,000, $175,000, and $200,000.

Read the hints at the end of this document if you have problems completing the worksheet.

1. Create a worksheet with the data shown in Figure SS-31. (See the hints at the end of this exercise for typing in lines 1, 2, and 3. Also, enter the values in line 5 and 20 as whole numbers and format later.)

SS

	A	B	C	D	E	F
1		SeaTech Corporation -- Cash Budget				
2			-- Quarters --			
3		1	2	3	4	
4						
5	Beginning cash balance	$100,000				
6						
7	Total receipts					
8						
9	Disbursements:					
10	Payroll					
11	Supplies					
12	Utilities					
13	Services					
14	Taxes					
15	Equipment					
16	Rent					
17						
18	Total disbursements					
19						
20	Ending cash balance	$125,000	$165,000	$175,000	$200,000	

FIGURE SS-31
Hands-on Exercise 7. SeaTech Corporation budget.

2. Develop the worksheet further using the following assumptions:

a. Payroll: Payroll is expected to be $30,000 in Quarter 3, reflecting heavy summer employment. All other quarters are expected to be $20,000.

b. Supplies: Supplies generally run about $10,000 for the first three quarters and $15,000 for the 4th quarter.

c. Utilities: Utilities are usually 3 percent of payroll. (You will need to set up a formula to compute this.)

d. Services: Services are expected to be $10,000 for Quarter 1; $15,000 for Quarter 2; zero for Quarter 3; and $10,000 for Quarter 4.

e. Taxes: Taxes will be constant at $20,000 per quarter.

f. Equipment: Expected equipment purchases are $10,000 in Quarter 2; $25,000 in Quarter 3; and $40,000 in Quarter 4.

g. Rent: Rent will be constant at $12,000 per quarter.

3. Compute the Total receipts that will be needed in each quarter to cover expenses and to produce the required ending cash balances (as stated in the *Important note* at the beginning of this exercise). Assume that the beginning cash balance for any quarter is equivalent to the ending cash balance of the previous quarter. Use a formula for this computation. (HINT: Use the @SUM function or set up a formula to take the ending balance plus the total disbursements minus the beginning balance. Use cell addresses to copy the formula to the appropriate cells.)

4. Save the worksheet as HANDS7A

5. Print a copy of the completed worksheet

6. Rework the computations in Step 3 under the assumption that payroll and services will each be 10 percent higher than originally thought

7. Save the modified worksheet as HANDS7B

8. Print a copy of the revised version of the worksheet

9. Rework the computations from Step 3 again under the assumption that taxes will be 25 percent lower and that equipment purchases will occur a quarter earlier than expected

10. Save the modified worksheet as HANDS7C

11. Print a copy of the revised version of the worksheet

Hints: The title in Row 1 is created by moving to Cell B1 and pressing the spacebar several times, and then entering the title. When you enter this label onto the worksheet, you will notice that it spans several columns. If, when you complete the worksheet, the title isn't centered to your satisfaction, use the edit function key (F2) to insert or remove blank spaces.

The Quarters heading in Row 2 is created similarly, starting in Cell D2. Use an apostrophe label-prefix character in front of the dashes so the spreadsheet package doesn't think they are minus signs that go with a value.

Each of the quarters in Row 3 is centered in its respective column. This is done by placing a label prefix before the label (refer back to Figure SS-8). In Row 3, all Quarter labels should be entered as ^1, ^2, etc.

To check your figures for Total receipts in Row 7, set up a formula in Row 22, adding the Beginning balance and Total receipts and then subtracting the Total disbursements; the value should equal the Ending cash balance. Do not change the values in Row 20.

Hands-on Exercise 8: Computing a Depreciation Schedule

In this exercise, you will practice

- ☐ Creating formulas for depreciation
- ☐ Using the SLN and SYD functions
- ☐ Centering data within cells
- ☐ Using the automatic number generator
- ☐ Formatting ranges
- ☐ Formatting values
- ☐ Changing figures in the worksheet for "what if" speculations

SS

This exercise shows you how to compute a depreciation schedule. The straight-line depreciation method computes annual depreciation expenses by the formula below:

$$\text{Annual depreciation} = \frac{\text{Original cost} - \text{Salvage value}}{\text{Useful life}}$$

The straight-line depreciation schedule shown in Figure SS-32 represents an asset that originally cost $7,328 and is worth $600 at the end of its 10-year useful life. You will create these amounts through formulas.

To Set Up the Worksheet. Perform the following tasks to get started:

1. Type the main heading starting in Column B, and let it overflow into the other columns
2. Place the headings **Original Cost** and **Salvage Value** in Cells C3 and C4
3. Enter the following headings:

Column A	**YEAR**
Column C	**DEPRECIATION CHARGE**
Column E	**ACCUMULATED DEPRECIATION**
Column G	**UNDEPRECIATED BALANCE**

FIGURE SS-32

Hands-on Exercise 8. Depreciation schedule.

	A	B	C	D	E	F	G
1		TEN-YEAR ASSET DEPRECIATION SCHEDULE					
2							
3			Original cost		$7,328.00		
4			Salvage value		$600.00		
5							
6	---------	---------	---------	---------	---------	---------	---------
7	YEAR		DEPRECIATION		ACCUMULATED		UNDEPRECIATED
8			CHARGE		DEPRECIATION		BALANCE
9							
10	1		$672.80		$672.80		$6,655.20
11	2		$672.80		$1,345.60		$5,982.40
12	3		$672.80		$2,018.40		$5,309.60
13	4		$672.80		$2,691.20		$4,636.80
14	5		$672.80		$3,364.00		$3,964.00
15	6		$672.80		$4,036.80		$3,291.20
16	7		$672.80		$4,709.60		$2,618.40
17	8		$672.80		$5,382.40		$1,945.60
18	9		$672.80		$6,055.20		$1,272.80
19	10		$672.80		$6,728.00		$600.00
20							

Hint: Use the space bar or label-prefix characters to make headings look centered.

4. Enter the years using the following automatic number generator:

a. Type **/DF** for Data Fill

In response to the prompts that appear,

b. Type **A10..A19** as the fill range

c. Type **1** to Start

d. Type **1** to Step

e. Type **10** to Stop

This series of steps (b through e) tells the spreadsheet program that you want a pattern of numbers that starts with 1, ends with 10, and counts (steps) in units of 1.

5. Repeat the automatic numbering system for the Depreciation Charge amount of $672.80, which is consistent in Cells C10 through C19.

Hint: Start and Stop at the same number (672.80) and Step at zero (0). Note that, alternatively, you could type 672.80 into cell C10 and copy it into the range C11 . . C19.

Formatting. Format the dollar amounts (not the years) to include dollar signs.

1. Type **/RF** for Range Format

2. Choose the Currency option and set 2 decimal places

In response to the "Range to format" prompt

3. Type **C10..G19** and press ↵

Note: You may need to widen some of the columns to get the new formats to fit.

SS

Formulas. Follow these steps to enter the appropriate formulas.

1. Create the accumulated depreciation formula for Cell E10. Be sure the original cost value and the salvage value are inserted in Cells E3 and E4 respectively. This formula is computed using the following format:

In Cell E10
(Original cost − Salvage value)/10

In Cell E11
(Original cost − Salvage value)/10+ E10

Hint: Be sure to create a formula that includes the parentheses. Remember that the values within the parentheses will be computed first. This is critical to the correct working of the formula. Also remember that the cells in E3 and E4 must be absolute so that they do not change when copied. The cell addresses in the formula in E11, however, are relative—they should change.

2. Copy the accumulated depreciation formula to other applicable cells in the Accumulated Depreciation column
3. Create a formula to compute the undepreciated balance in column G: The original cost minus the accumulated depreciation
4. Copy the formula in Cell G10 to other applicable cells
5. Save the final worksheet as HANDS8A
6. Print a copy of the worksheet

Checking Your Work. Lotus 1-2-3 contains a function, @SLN (for straight-line depreciation) that enables you to calculate annual depreciation automatically (see Figure SS-17). Try this function in place of the formula you supplied for column C. Did you obtain the same results?

Modifications to the Worksheet. Enter the following changes and observe the results.

1. Redo the worksheet for an asset with an original cost of $11,000 and a salvage value of $1,000
2. Save the worksheet again as HANDS8B
3. Print a copy of the worksheet

Changing the Depreciation Method. Redo HANDS8A worksheet using the sum-of-the-year's digits depreciation method, which works as the following example shows: Assume that an asset originally costs $4000, has a salvage value of $1000, and has a useful life of 3 years. The asset will be depreciated by $3000 ($4000 minus $1000) over the 3-year period. The sum of the year's digits for 3 years is 1 + 2 + 3 = 6. The procedure to compute the depreciation charge for each of the 3 years is given below:

Year 1: (3/6) * $3000 = $1500
Year 2: (2/6) * $3000 = $1000
Year 3: (1/6) * $3000 = $ 500
$3000

Note, in the computations above, that the fraction's denominator is always the sum of the year's digits. This is computed by the formula $n(n + 1)/2$, where n is the asset's useful life. The fraction's numerator is, for year i, equal to $n - i + 1$. The fraction is always multiplied by a constant amount, which is equal to the cost minus the salvage value.

Call the resulting worksheet HANDS8C, and save and print it.

Hint: You can do this exercise by setting up your own formulas or by using the special 1-2-3 function, @SYD. @SYD calculates the sum-of-the-year's-digits depreciation of an asset for any year, based upon the asset's initial cost, salvage value, and useful life. The syntax of this function is

@SYD(initial cost,salvage value,useful life,year)

Hands-on Exercise 9: Preparing a Frequency Distribution

In this exercise, you will practice

- ☐ Setting up the format for a frequency distribution
- ☐ Using the GOTO command
- ☐ Using a scratchpad for entering values
- ☐ Using the DATA command

Suppose that in your statistics class you have been asked to prepare a frequency distribution of a class's test scores. Twenty-five people took an exam; the scores were distributed as follows:

91, 83, 69, 35, 99, 64, 78, 71, 52, 89, 72, 100, 56, 63, 72, 77, 82, 95, 85, 71, 66, 54, 63, 0, 5

Your professor would like you to prepare a simple table for output in the following format:

Range	**Number of scores**
90–100	?
80–89	?
and so forth	

One part of the worksheet in this exercise will need to be reserved for scratchpad computations; another part, for the desired output. Because 1-2-3 allows you to print only a portion (range) of the worksheet, you will be printing only the output portion. The scratchpad will be developed in a remote part of the worksheet and will not be used for output.

Both parts of the worksheet are shown in Figure SS-33. The output section is on the left; the scratchpad is on the right.

Column I shows only the first 17 scores. You'll need to enter the rest of the scores in that column.

Column K contains bins, which you set up. The 9 in Cell K4 catches all scores less than or equal to 9. The 19 in Cell K5 catches all scores greater than 9 but less than or equal to 19. And so on. You can see that these boundaries are also shown in the Range column in Column A. Starting from the bottom the same numbers appear: 9, 19, 29, etc. You will later declare column K as a "bin range," so the spreadsheet will interpret the values in the column as the bins we've just described.

With this column set up, the program will know that it is searching for the frequency of numbers falling within the specified ranges.

Column L shows the frequencies for all 25 scores. This column will receive the number of occurrences within each bin.

Follow these steps to create this worksheet:

1. Move to Cell A1 and type **FREQUENCY**

	A	B
1	FREQUENCY	
2		
3	Range	Number of
4		Scores
5		
6	90-100	4
7	80-89	4
8	70-79	6
9	60-69	5
10	50-59	3
11	40-49	0
12	30-39	1
13	20-29	0
14	10-19	0
15	0-9	2
16		
17		
18		
19		
20		
21		
22		

	I	J	K	L
1		Scratchpad Computations		
2				
3	Score		Bin	Frequency
4	91		9	2
5	83		19	0
6	69		29	0
7	35		39	1
8	99		49	0
9	64		59	3
10	78		69	5
11	71		79	6
12	52		89	4
13	89		100	4
14	72			0
15	100			
16	56			
17	63			
18	72			
19	77			
20	82			
21	•			
22	•			
	•			

FIGURE SS-33

Hands-on Exercise 9. The numbers in Columns B and L are not typed in but are calculated by the spreadsheet.

2. Type the following labels in the cells indicated:

Cell A3	**Range**
Cell B3	**Number of**
Cell B4	**Scores**

3. Type the ranges shown in Cells A6 through A15 as labels (use an apostrophe as the first character of each label that starts with a digit)

4. Move to Cell J1 (use the GOTO command) and type the label **Scratchpad Computations**

5. Type these labels in the cells indicated:

Cell I3	**Score**
Cell K3	**Bin**
Cell L3	**Frequency**

6. Enter the 25 scores listed at the start of this exercise in Cells I4 through I28

7. Enter the values for the bins in Cells K4 through K13

8. Move to Cell L4

9. To calculate bin frequencies,

a. Type **/DD** for Data Distribution

b. In response to the prompt "Enter values range," type **I4..I28** and press ↵

c. In response to the prompt "Enter bin range," type **K4..K13** and press ↵

The frequencies that will be calculated are shown in Column L. The zero at the bottom of the column is giving the information that there were no scores greater than 100.

You now need to transfer the frequencies in Column L to Column B. You'll notice from the example that Column B shows the scores in reverse, beginning with the highest range. You can have the program insert the scores by entering a formula.

10. Move to Cell B6 and type the formula +**L13**

11. Move to Cell B7 and type the formula +**L12**

12. Continue entering formulas in each cell as follows:

Cell B8	+**L11**
Cell B9	+**L10**
Cell B10	+**L9**
Cell B11	+**L8**
Cell B12	+**L7**
Cell B13	+**L6**
Cell B14	+**L5**
Cell B15	+**L4**

The scores are inserted in the cells in Column B.

13. Save the worksheet as HANDS9

14. Print a copy of the output of the worksheet (Columns A and B)

SS

Hands-on Exercise 10: Mixed-cell Addressing

In this exercise, you will practice creating a formula to compute future sums, using

☐ Addition

☐ Multiplication

☐ Exponentiation

☐ Mixed-cell addressing

This is a good exercise for practicing mixed-cell addressing. As you learned earlier, 1-2-3 can copy the contents of a cell in several ways. In *relative addressing*, the cell location[s] used in the formula adjusts to the cell[s] copied to. In *absolute addressing*, dollar signs are used to "fix" the cell positions in the formula so that they do not change when copied. There are many times, however, when you might want to mix these copying schemes; for example, when keeping a row value fixed while varying column values. You learned earlier that this is *mixed addressing.*

Many tables, such as the one you will set up here, require some form of mixed addressing. In the present case, this will allow you to write an interest-rate formula and copy it to other cells.

Partial output of the table you will produce is shown below, in Figure SS-34.

In this example, P dollars are invested in an account today at a compounded interest rate of R percent per period; the amount of the account at the end of N periods is given by the formula

$$S = P(1 + R/100)^N$$

The table shows the value of $1 at the end of 1, 2, 3, . . . , 10 years at interest rates of 10, 10.5, 11, 11.5, and 12 percent.

For this table, you will need to create only one formula. That formula will then be copied to all other cells.

1. Create the worksheet shown in Figure SS-34 by entering the following labels:

a. The centered heading Future Sum Computations

b. All column headings in Row 3 (this time enter the percentage column headings as values and format them as percents)

c. The years in Column A (as values!)

2. Type the formula **(1+ B$3)^$A4** in Cell B4:

Notice how this formula corresponds to the formula $P(1+R/100)^N$, where P = $1.

This formula tells 1-2-3 that you always want the rate value taken from Row 3 and the year value taken from Column A. Those values must

FIGURE SS-34

Hands-on Exercise 10. Future sum computations.

	A	B	C	D	E	F
1			Future Sum Computations			
2						
3	Years	10.0%	10.5%	11.0%	11.5%	12.0%
4	1	1.1	1.105	1.11	1.115	1.12
5	2	1.21	1.221025	1.2321	1.243225	1.2544
6	3	1.331	1.349232	1.367631	1.386195	1.404928
7	4	.				
8	5	.				
9	6	.				
10	7	.				
11	8	.				
12	9	.				
13	10	2.593742	2.714080	2.839420	2.969946	3.105848

remain constant, so dollar signs are placed in front of the 3 and the A in the formula. Everything else is relative to the row and column into which you are copying. When you copy this formula across to another column or down to another row, the program will always keep 3 and A intact.

3. Copy the formula from B4 to all other applicable cells in the worksheet (B4..F13)

Take time to look at the changes in the formula in other cells both down the rows and across the columns.

4. Save the worksheet as HANDS10

5. Print a copy of the worksheet

Hands-on Exercise 11: Sorting Data and Freezing Titles

In this exercise, you will practice

- ☐ Using Data Sort to sort labels and values
- ☐ Doing primary key sorts
- ☐ Freezing horizontal and vertical titles onscreen
- ☐ Unfreezing titles
- ☐ Using the MIN function

You have been asked by one of your professors to set up a grade book.

To Create the Worksheet. Create the partial gradebook as shown in Figure SS-35, adjusting column widths as necessary.

FIGURE SS-35
Hands-on Exercise 11. A grade book.

	A	B	C	D	E
1		Computer Information Systems 101			
2			Grade Book		
3			Fall Semester		
4		Professor Rufus J. Flywheel, Ph.D.			
5					
6					
7					
8	------------------------	------------------	------------------	------------------	------------------
9	Student Name	Exam 1	Exam 2	Exam 3	Exam 4
10	Zinn, Fred	85	81	76	74
11	Smith, Abel	55	76	88	46
12	Edwards, Frank	75	98	87	92
13	Rourke, Patricia	93	87	99	98
14					

1. Continue entering names of students and their scores as follows:

Gonzales, Jesus: 87, 94, 94, 75
Telzer, Marta: 66, 75, 78, 65
Robertson, Joe: 76, 81, 88, 92
Lyons, Katrina: 85, 83, 92, 88
Pritchard, C. J.: 65, 71, 68, 82
Littledog, Cyrus: 75, 85, 97, 86
Yamaguchi, Linda: 76, 88, 85, 72
Lewis, Bobbi: 65, 72, 75, 79
Wiggins, Percy: 84, 94, 85, 93
Williams, Van: 76, 58, 89, 84
Haji, Ali: 82, 89, 94, 86
Yazzie, Mary: 82, 97, 88, 75
Davidson, Norm: 76, 81, 75, 67
Lindstrom, Per: 88, 65, 82, 79
Lu, Tia: 66, 65, 74, 78
Barton, Mike: 76, 56, 67, 81

Sorting the Worksheet by Name. To sort your worksheet on the name column:

1. Type **/DSD** for Data Sort Data-range

2. Type the range **A10..E29.** This tells the spreadsheet that you want to involve all of the worksheet data—not just those in the names column—in the sort

3. Press ↵

4. Type **P** for Primary-key

5. Because you want to sort by the name column, type **A10..A29** in response to the primary-key prompt and press ↵

6. In response to the "Sort order" prompt, type **A** for Ascending (because you want to sort in alphabetical order) and press ↵

7. To start the sort, type **G** for Go

The spreadsheet program then rearranges the entire worksheet so that the student records are in alphabetical order. Save the worksheet as HANDS11A and print a copy of it.

Note: Lotus 1-2-3 also allows you to identify a "secondary key" (column), which will allow you to do sorts within a sort. For example, if your records for each student had a "majors" column (showing whether a student was majoring in accounting, financing, marketing, or some other field), you might want to sort the records first on the majors column (the primary key) and then on the name column (the secondary key). When you make changes to the worksheet, you can save the individual worksheets under different names and have a copy of each.

To Freeze the Horizontal Titles. Freezing titles enables you to keep titles and margin headings fixed on the screen as you scroll or page through the data in the worksheet. In the current 20-name example, it will allow you to keep the row titles and column headings in Rows 1-9 fixed.

To freeze horizontal titles (rows):

1. Place the highlight anywhere in Line 8 and type **/WTH** for Worksheet Titles Horizontal
2. Use **Pg Dn** and **Pg Up** to flip forward and backward through the data records. Note that the titles in rows 1–8 remain fixed. You can also use ↑ and ↓ to scroll a record at a time.

To Freeze the Vertical Titles. To freeze vertical titles (columns):

1. Place the highlight in Cell B9 (to freeze the titles to the left of that column)
2. Type **/WTV** for Worksheet Titles Vertical

This will freeze the titles in Column A.

3. Move to the right with **Tab** or the arrow keys and back again. Notice how the titles stay frozen.
4. Insert three additional blank columns to the right of Column E
5. Add these headings to the new columns:

Column F	**Exam 5**
Column G	**Exam 6**
Column H	**Exam 7**

6. Scroll to the right until you are immediately to the right of the names and aligned under Exam 5 (Cell F10)
7. Add the following scores for each of the students by pressing **Tab** or → to move from left to right (the scores are ready to be added in alphabetical order from the top, beginning with Barton):

80,54,78
85,75,84
90,73,81
95,80,85
75,90,82
82,90,78
67,80,80
78,91,74
90,82,86
78,65,75
92,83,76
59,80,78
89,95,90
82,75,89
75,83,78
78,87,87
72,72,100
89,82,85
95,92,90
94,82,74

When the vertical labels are frozen, notice how much easier it is to determine whom the scores belong to.

You can also set both of the titles at once by locating the cell pointer just to the right and below the columns and rows you wish to freeze and, then, typing /WTB for Worksheet Titles Both.

To Clear the Titles Lock. You can unfreeze titles through the WTC command sequence.

1. Type **/WTC** for Worksheet Titles Clear

2. Save the worksheet as HANDS11B

3. Print a copy of the worksheet

Additional Exercise #1. Add another column (column I) which averages the seven exam scores for each student. Then, resort the entire worksheet from the highest to lowest score. Don't forget, incidentally, to declare the entire set of names, scores, and averages as the data range, so you aren't just rearranging the averages column and nothing else. Call the finished worksheet HANDS11C, and save and print it.

Additional Exercise #2: Dropping the Lowest Test Score. Many teachers use a grading scheme in which the lowest score is dropped. If Professor Flywheel decided to drop the lowest of the seven test scores, this, too, could be incorporated into the worksheet. Looking for the moment at Fred Zinn in the seven-exam grade books, his lowest test score is 74, or

@MIN(B10..E10)

Thus, his average test score if the lowest score is dropped is

(@SUM(B10..E10) −@MIN(B10..E10))/7

The averages for the other students would be computed in a similar fashion.

Redo HANDS11C so that the student averages reflect the lowest score being dropped. Then, resort the worksheet by the column containing each student's average. Call the new worksheet HANDS11D and save and print it. Which students benefitted most by the drop-the-lowest score policy? Which students lost ground?

Hands-on Exercise 12: Preparing a Check Register

In this exercise, you will practice

- □ Writing @IF functions
- □ Creating @IF functions to test conditions in multiple columns

Most businesses, especially around tax time, need to pore over the checks they have written and determine which expenses fall into each of several expense categories, such as rent, supplies, utilities, services, and depreciable assets. Take KM Company, for instance. They were able to prepare the check register and expense summary in Figure SS-36, showing all of the checks paid out in the first quarter.

To calculate the "Summary of Expenses," you'll set up IF functions that evaluate each expense's code and add its amount to the correct category.

1. Begin by filling in all cells, except the contents of E1 . . F6, as shown in Figure SS-36. Adjust cell width as necessary. Enter the amounts in Column E without the dollar sign and then format them for currency.

2. Move to Cell G8 and type **Rent**

3. Type the following labels in the indicated cells:

Cell H8	**Supp.**	Cell J8	**Serv.**
Cell I8	**Util.**	Cell K8	**D.A.**

4. Type the function **@IF(F9=1,E9,0)** in Cell G9

This function reads as follows: If the value found in F9 equals 1 (or Code 1) then insert the amount found in E9 into this cell. Otherwise insert a zero.

Since you are presently in the column for Category 1, any Code 1 found will be inserted.

5. Type the following functions in the specified cells:

Cell H9	**@IF(F9=2,E9,0)**	Cell J9	**@IF(F9=4,E9,0)**
Cell I9	**@IF(F9=3,E9,0)**	Cell K9	**@IF(F9=5,E9,0)**

FIGURE SS-36 **Hands-on Exercise 12.** KM Co. check register.

	A	B	C	D	E	F
1					Summary of	Expenses
2		***************************			1-Rent	$2,100
3		KM COMPANY			2-Supp.	$60
4		FIRST QUARTER CHECK SUMMARY			3-Util.	$180
5		***************************			4-Serv.	$750
6					5-D.A.	$1,600
7	----------	----------	----------	----------	----------	----------
8	Check No.	Date		Paid To	Amount	Code
9	1503	1/93	XYZ Enterprises		$700	1
10	1509	2/93	XYZ Enterprises		$700	1
11	1499	1/93	Ace Suppliers		$45	2
12	1511	3/93	BZ Power and Elect.		$60	3
13	1510	2/93	Linda Smith Services		$400	4
14	1506	1/93	Larson's		$900	5
15	1504	1/93	Dave's Warehouse		$700	5
16	1505	1/93	BZ Power and Elect.		$55	3
17	1496	1/93	Ellis Services		$350	4
18	1502	1/93	Ace Suppliers		$15	2
19	1508	2/93	BZ Power and Elect.		$65	3
20	1512	3/93	XYZ Enterprises		$700	1
21						

6. Copy each of the functions in Row 9 down its respective column. Because the functions are all relative (containing no dollar signs), the cell location will change as you copy. Thus the function in G10, for example, will read @IF(F10=1,E10,0)

In this way the program will always be looking for conditions that exist in the current row.

Note: As each @IF function is evaluated by the spreadsheet package and a value is placed into the worksheet, you will see the table shown in Figure SS-37. Note that by summing each column, you will be able to calculate the total rent, supplies, utilities, and so on.

7. Move to Cell E1 and type **Summary of Expenses**

8. Type the following labels in the cells indicated, starting each with an apostrophe:

Cell E2	'**1=Rent**	Cell E5	'**4=Serv.**
Cell E3	'**2=Supp.**	Cell E6	'**5=D.A.**
Cell E4	'**3=Util.**		

9. To calculate the expense code totals for the Summary, type the following functions in the specified cells:

Cell F2	**@SUM(G9..G20)**	Cell F5	**@SUM(J9..J20)**
Cell F3	**@SUM(H9..H20)**	Cell F6	**@SUM(K9..K20)**
Cell F4	**@SUM(I9..I20)**		

10. Format the values in cell F2 through F6 for currency

11. Save the worksheet as HANDS12

12. Print a copy of the output range: A1 through F20

FIGURE SS-37
Output from Hands-on Exercise 12.

G23: READY

	G	H	I	J	K	L	M
8	Rent	Supp.	Util.	Serv.	D.A.		
9	700	0	0	0	0		
10	700	0	0	0	0		
11	0	45	0	0	0		
12	0	0	60	0	0		
13	0	0	0	400	0		
14	0	0	0	0	900		
15	0	0	0	0	700		
16	0	0	55	0	0		
17	0	0	0	350	0		
18	0	15	0	0	0		
19	0	0	65	0	0		
20	700	0	0	0	0		
21							
22							
23							
24							
25							
26							
27							

01-Jan-80 01:32 AM

APPENDIX: 1-2-3 COMMAND TREES

Following are the 1-2-3 menu trees for the commands that have subcommands. Note, on the main menu that immediately follows, that the Copy, Move, System, and Quit commands do not have subcommands. Command options that are highlighted in the trees are available only in Releases 2.3 and 2.4.

Main Menu Command Structure

Worksheet	Range	Copy	Move	File	Print	Graph	Data	System	Add-In	Quit
Global	Format			Retrieve	Printer	Type	Fill		Attach	
Insert	Label			Save	File	X	Table		Detach	
Delete	Erase			Combine	Encoded*	A	Sort		Invoke	
Column	Name			Xtract	Background*	B	Query		Clear	
Erase	Justify			Erase		C	Distribution		Quit	
Titles	Protect			List		D	Matrix			
Window	Unprotect			Import		E	Regression			
Status	Input			Directory		F	Parse			
Page	Value			Admin*		Reset				
Learn*	Transpose			View*		View				
	Search*					Save				
						Options				
						Name				
						Quit				

*Release 2.3 and 2.4

SS

Add-In Command Structure

Attach Detach Invoke Clear Quit

No-Key 7 8 9 10

Main options for Add-in command:

Attach	Brings an add-in program into RAM
Clear	Removes all attached add-in programs from RAM.
Detach	Removes an attached add-in program from RAM.
Invoke	Invokes an attached add-in program.
Quit	Returns to READY mode.

Worksheet Menu Command Structure

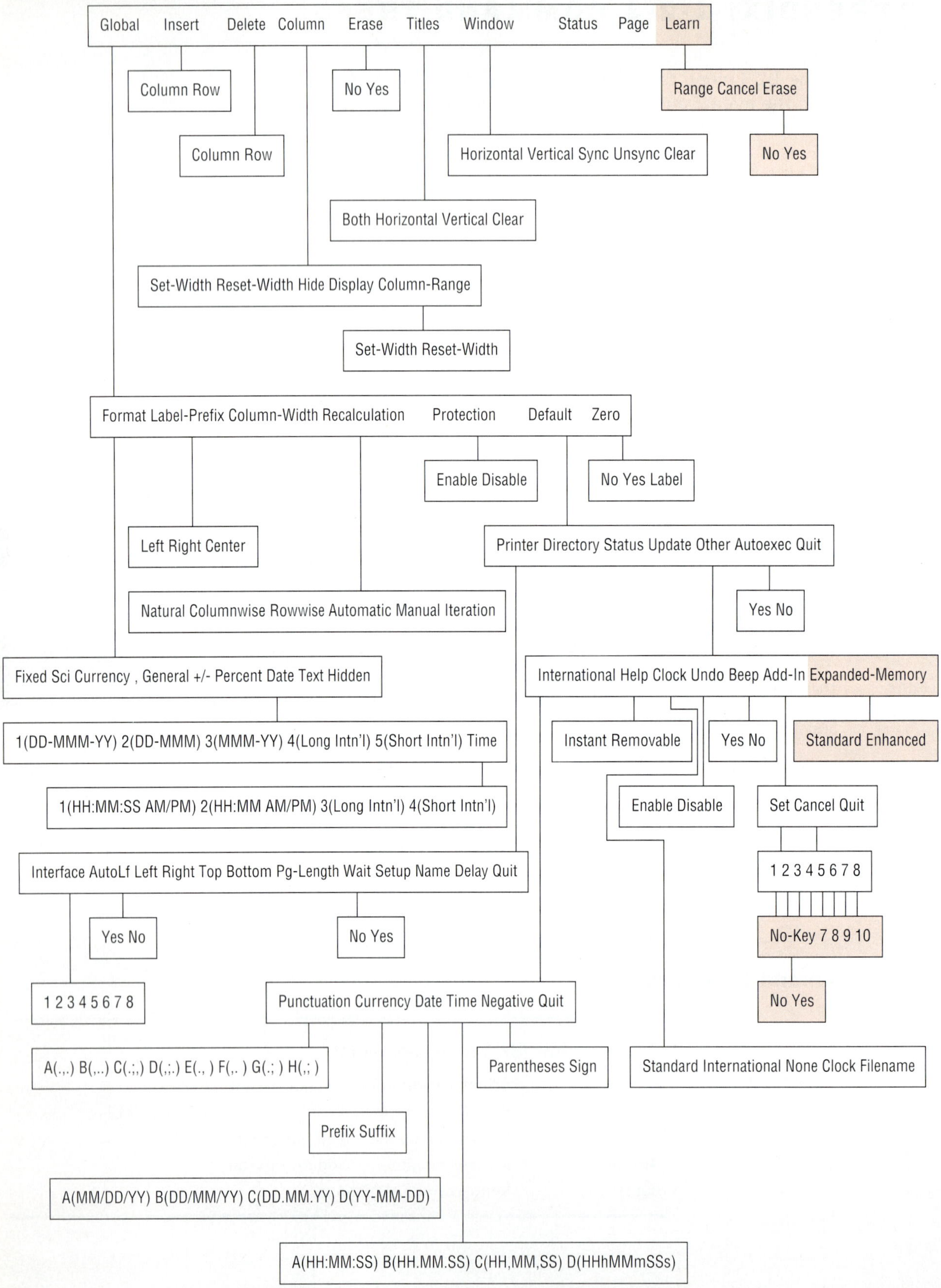

Main options for Worksheet command:

Column	Sets columns to a specified width, resets columns to the default width, and hides and redisplays columns.
Delete	Deletes columns and rows from a worksheet.
Erase	Deletes a worksheet from RAM.
Global	Establishes settings that hold for the entire worksheet.
Insert	Inserts blank columns and rows into a worksheet.
Learn	Specifies a range to record keystrokes when you invoke the Learn feature.
Page	Creates a page break in a worksheet.
Status	Displays current global settings.
Titles	Freezes rows on the left edge and columns on the top of the worksheet, so they remain onscreen while the rest of the worksheet is scrolled.
Window	Splits the screen into horizontal and vertical windows, unsplits the screen, and activates/deactivates synchronized scrolling.

Range Menu Command Structure

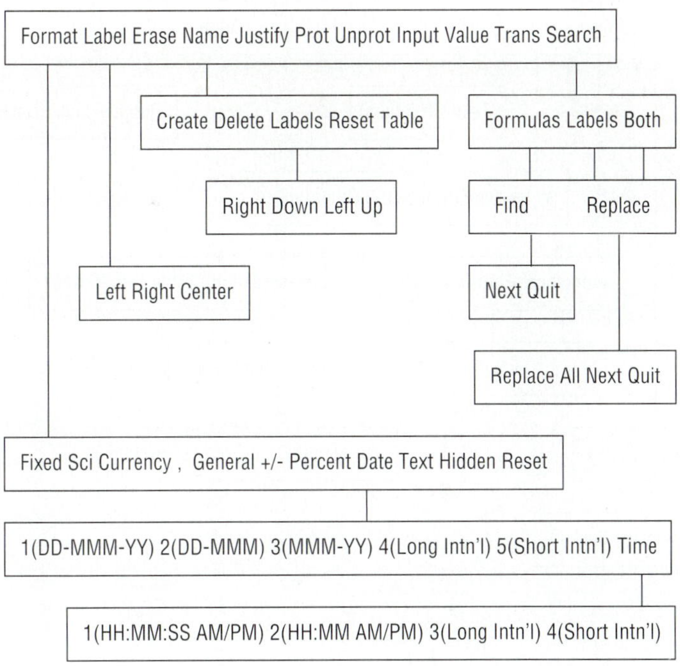

Main options for Range command:

Erase	Erases data in a specified range.
Format	Prepares cells to be output in a special format.
Input	Restricts cell-pointer movement to unprotected cells.
Justify	Rearranges text to fit within a specified width.
Label	Specifies whether you want labels centered, flush right, or flush left in a cell.
Name	Assigns a name to a range of cells.
Prot	Reprotects cells in a range when global worksheet protection is declared.
Search	Finds or replaces a specified string within a range of cells.
Trans	Copies a range of data while, at the same time, transposing its layout.
Unprot	Allows cells in a protected worksheet to be changed.
Value	Copies the contents of cells and, in the process, converts formulas in the destination range to their corresponding numeric constants.

File Menu Command Structure

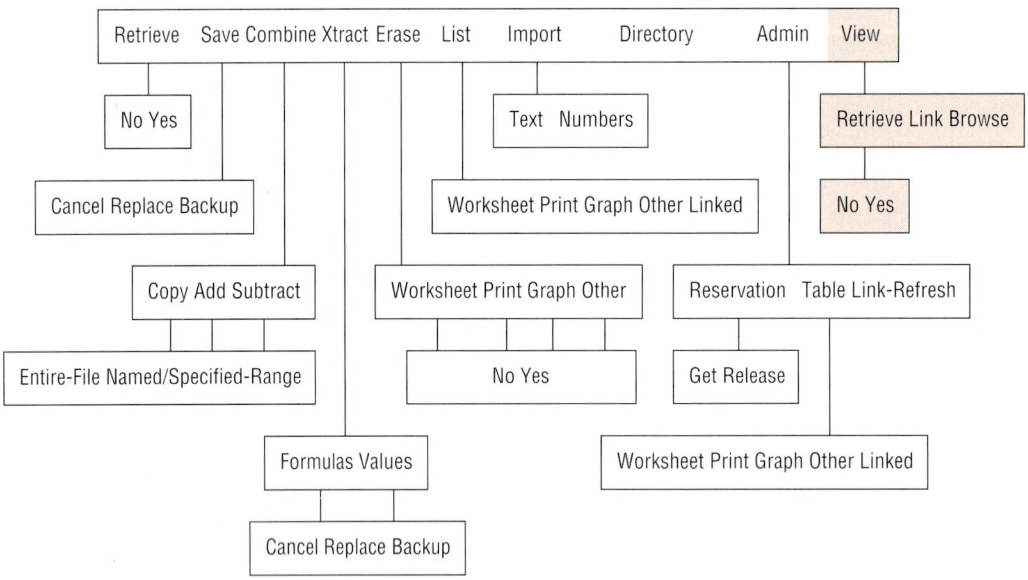

Main options for File command:

Admin	Creates a table of information about disk files, updates file links, and gets a file reservation so that you can save changes to a file on a network.
Combine	Combines data from a worksheet on disk into the active worksheet.
Directory	Changes the directory for the current work session.
Erase	Deletes files from disk.
Import	Reads data from an ASCII disk file into the current worksheet.
List	Displays all filenames of a specified type corresponding to files stored on the default directory.
Retrieve	Loads a file from disk into RAM.
Save	Saves the current worksheet and its settings.
View	Displays directory information and lets you scan through the text of both 1-2-3 files and other types of files.
Xtract	Saves a specified range of cells of the current worksheet to

Print Menu Command Structure

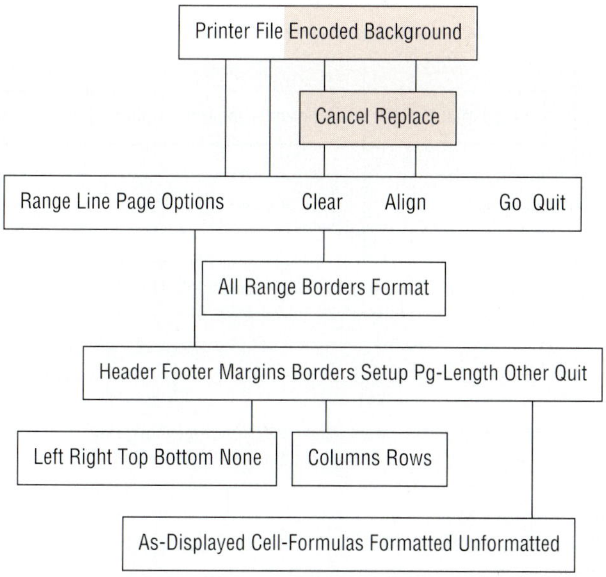

SS

Main options for Print command:

Align	Resets 1-2-3's internal line and page settings, and tells 1-2-3 that a page is ready to print.
Background	Enables printing to take place in the background, while you are doing other work.
Clear	Returns some or all print settings to their default states.
Encoded	Refers to a file that contains all data, borders, formatting and printing specifications, and graphics.
File	Directs output to a standard ASCII disk file.
Go	Allows printing to begin.
Line	Advances by one line the paper in the printer.
Options	Enables creation of headers and/or footers; controlling of margins, borders, and page length; and so on.
Page	Advances by one page the paper in the printer.
Printer	Directs output to the printer.
Quit	Returns to the READY mode.
Range	Specifies the range of the worksheet that is to be printed.

Data Menu Command Structure

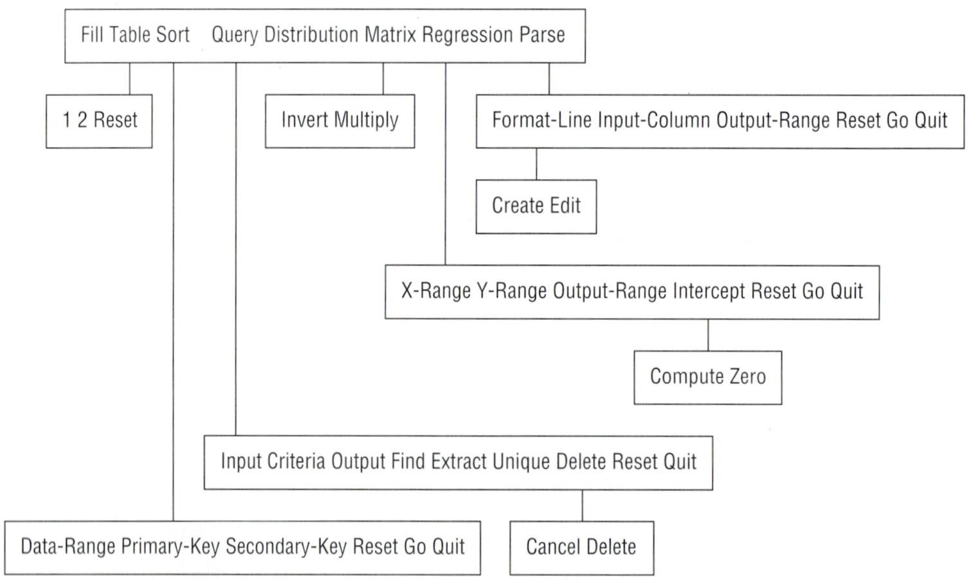

Main options for Data command:

Distribution	Tallies the number of values in a range of data falling into each of several contiguous numeric intervals.
Fill	Automatically fills a range with a sequence of values.

(continued)

Main options for Data command:	*(continued)*
Matrix	Inverts or multiplies matrix data.
Parse	Separates long labels into distinct text and numeric cell entries.
Query	Finds and edits database records.
Regression	Determines a curve that best fits a set of data.
Sort	Rearranges records in a database.
Table	Used for "what if" (sensitivity) analysis.

Graph Menu Command Structure

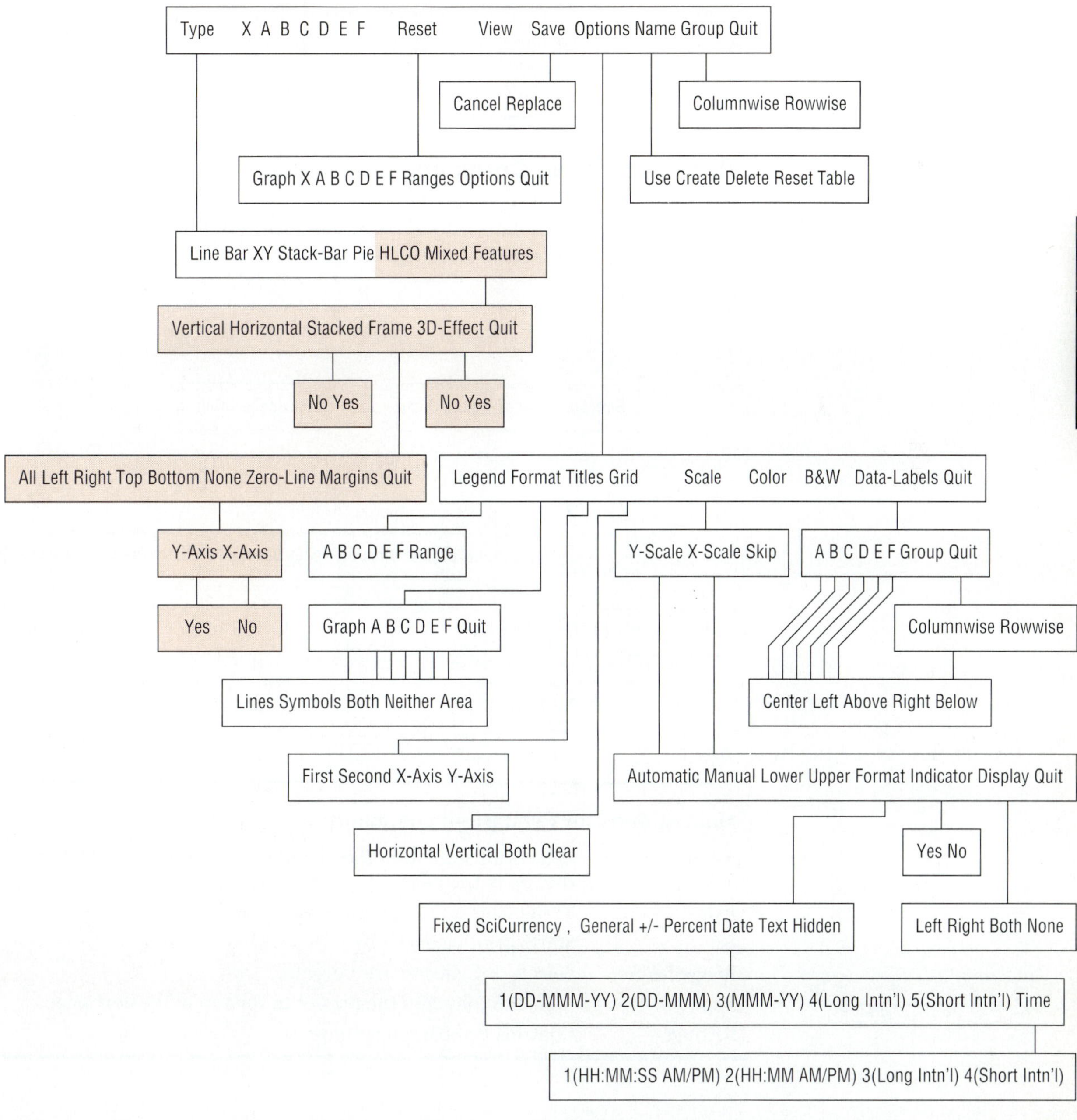

SS

Main options for Graph command:

A–F	Declares ranges that contain numeric data to be graphed.
Group	Used to select data ranges quickly for a graph when the ranges are in adjacent columns and rows.
Name	Creates, modifies, deletes, and creates tables of named graphs.
Options	Provides graphs with such enhancements as titles, legends, colors, and grid lines; also used to scale graphs.
Quit	Returns to the READY mode.
Reset	Used to reset graph settings.
Save	Saves the current graph in a .PIC file.
Type	Allows you to choose the kind of graph you would like.
View	Displays the current graph.
X	Declares the range that will contain the X-axis labels, the X-axis values (in an XY graph), and labels assigned to pie slices (in a pie chart).

PrintGraph Menu Command Structure

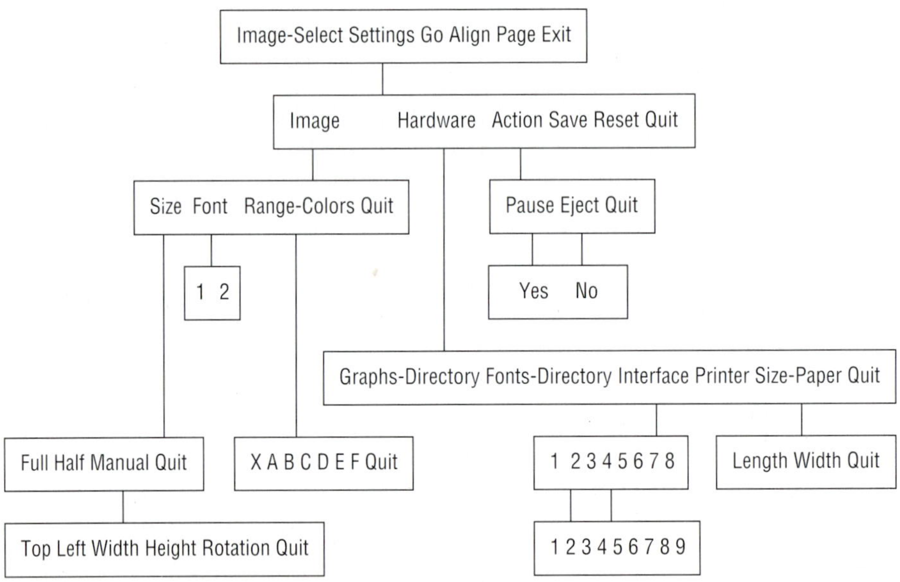

Main options for Printgraph command:

Align	Tells PrintGraph that the paper in the printer is aligned at the top of the page.
Exit	Terminates a PrintGraph session.
Go	Starts printing graph(s).
Image-Select	Selects .PIC files to print or view.
Page	Advances paper in the printer to the top of the next page.
Settings	Controls PrintGraph settings.

Help	Edit
Com-pose	**Step**
Name	Abs
Run	**Undo**
GoTo	Window
Learn	
Query	Table
APP1	**APP2**
Calc	Graph
APP3	**APP4**

ALT+

F1	Help	**Compose**
F2	Edit	**Step**
F3	Name	**Run**
F4	Abs	**Undo**
F5	GoTo	**Learn**
F6	Window	
F7	Query	**APP1**
F8	Table	**APP2**
F9	Calc	**APP3**
F10	Graph	**APP4**

ALT+

Function Keys Templates
for Lotus 1-2-3
(Releases 2.2 and 2.3)

DATABASE MANAGEMENT WITH dBASE III PLUS

CONTENTS

LEARNING OBJECTIVES

After completing these tutorials, you will be able to:

1. Understand basic database terminology, commands, and applications.
2. Create database files and enter data into them.
3. Access and manipulate data in database files.
4. Develop simple reports.

OVERVIEW

One of the major problems businesses face is that of storing, managing, and accessing large amounts of data. Information from such data is used for a variety of purposes—including reviewing facts about clients and products, preparing reports for upcoming decisions, studying levels of inventory and sales, and answering the many questions that arise in day-to-day business operations. These are but four of scores of examples.

Both large and small businesses have installed database management systems to effectively and efficiently organize, store, and access data coming from order forms, applications, payment slips, and other documents. Organizations such as hospitals, universities, and the government also rely on database management systems to handle huge quantities of data. Because database management systems are so predominant in our daily lives and most of us will wind up using them at one point or another to gather information, understanding how they work is important.

In these tutorials, you will be introduced to dBASE III PLUS, a powerful, microcomputer-based database management system. You will first create a simple database file. Then you will learn how to edit, manipulate, and access data from the file. Finally, you will learn some relatively advanced database operations such as preparing reports. After mastering the skills presented in these tutorials, you will be prepared to move on to the more advanced features of dBASE III and other database management systems.

GETTING STARTED

We will start by examining a sample database. Here you will see what a typical database looks like and how the data it contains can be processed.

Next, you will learn how to start dBASE on either a hard-disk or a dual-diskette system. Then, you will be introduced to dBASE's two operational modes: ASSIST and COMMAND. Finally, you will learn to set the default drive, to use the HELP feature, and to quit dBASE.

After studying and practicing these procedures, you will have acquired the basic skills necessary for moving on to the next step—creating your own database file.

What Is a Database and What Can You Do with It?

So you can fully grasp what a database is and what dBASE is capable of doing with one, let's look at a simple example. Refer to Figure DB-1. Figure DB-1a shows data on five customers of Avalanche Outfitters, a mail-order firm. Each type of data is known as a **field.** Thus there's a customer-number field (CUSTNUM), a name field (NAME), a street-address field (STREET), and so forth. The data collected on each person forms a **record.** As you can see, there are five records in Figure DB-1a, with each record consisting of seven fields. Collectively the five records comprise a **file** or **database file.** A collection of related database files is commonly called a **database.**

dBASE III PLUS requires you to provide a name for each field and a name for each database file. For example, we've called the entire customer database file CUSTOMER, and the customer-number field of this file, CUSTNUM. Notice that these names conform to DOS's naming conventions. In dBASE, we can create as many files as we wish to, although there are limitations on the number of files that can be **active** (i.e., in use) at once.

To see how dBASE can handle database files and relate data between them consider also the database files in Figures DB-1b, DB-1c, and DB-1d. We have a product file (PRODUCT), consisting of product descriptions and prices; an order file (ORDER), consisting of individual orders placed by customers (who are in the customer file); and a file showing some of the details of each order (ODETAILS). The ODETAILS file shows how many units of each product (of the product file) were shipped on each order (of the order file).

Even individually, each of these database files can provide a wealth of useful information. For example, we can tap the CUSTOMER file for a listing of all customers from Colorado. Or, we can use that same file to prepare mailing labels for catalogs that are to be sent out next month.

You may also have guessed that Avalanche Outfitters will want to *relate* data appearing in different database files. For example, if you've ever ordered anything through the mail, you've probably received an invoice such as the one in Figure DB-2. Note that this invoice contains data from several database files. When the order is placed, separate records are created in Avalanche's ORDER and ODETAILS files. To produce the invoice, name and shipping address are extracted from the CUSTOMER file, prices and descriptions are extracted from the PRODUCT file, the date is taken from the ORDER file, and the quantities ordered are taken from the ODETAILS file. The computational facilities of the database system then produce the totals in the last column. Thus, through the power of database technology, an invoice can be prepared quickly, with minimum error.

CUSTNUM	NAME	STREET	CITY	STATE	ZIP	CHARGE
810	John T. Smith	31 Cedarcrest	Boulder	CO	80302	.T.
775	Sally Jones	725 Aqua Fria	Santa Fe	NM	87501	.T.
690	William Holmes	3269 Fast Lane	Santa Fe	NM	87501	.F.
840	Artis Smith	2332 Alameda	Lakewood	CO	80215	.T.
574	Nellie Deutsch	23 E. Spruce	Olathe	KS	66061	.F.

(a) CUSTOMER file

PRODNUM	DESCRIP	PRICE
001	Nordic hat	10.00
002	Nylon windpants	40.00
003	Thermal ski socks	7.00
004	Indy Jones jacket, large	90.00
005	Rozelle headband	6.00

(b) PRODUCT file

ORDNUM	CUSTNUM	DATE
001	775	02/03/93
002	775	02/05/93
003	810	02/07/93
004	574	02/16/93
005	810	02/16/93
006	810	02/18/93

(c) ORDER file

ORDNUM	QTY	PRODNUM
001	2	003
001	1	002
002	1	001
003	1	001
003	3	003
004	1	001
004	1	003
005	2	003
006	1	004
006	1	005

(d) ODETAILS file

FIGURE DB-1
Database files for Avalanche Outfitters.

There are a number of other reasons we may want to relate data appearing in different database files. Avalanche's management may want the names of all customers who have ordered more than $1000 worth of merchandise during 1993. Or, an angry customer might call saying he ordered a Nordic hat rather than a large Indy Jones jacket, requiring Avalanche personnel to reconstruct the original order.

```
              Order number:  001
              Date placed: 02/03/93
              Ship to:   Sally Jones
                         725 Aqua Fria
                         Santa Fe, NM 87501

Quantity     Description           Unit Price       Total Price
--------     -----------           ----------       -----------
   2         Thermal ski socks       $ 7.00         $ 14.00
   1         Nylon windpants          40.00           40.00
                                                     ------
                                                    $ 54.00

              Remit check to:  AVALANCHE OUTFITTERS
                               P.O. Box 8000
                               Boulder, CO 80302
```

FIGURE DB-2

An invoice prepared from a relational database system (with data from the four database files in Figure DB-1).

For simplicity, the examples you'll see in this *Guide* involve working on only one database file at a time. In fact, many of the data management problems you'll probably face in your lifetime will be simple enough not to involve relating data between database files. Nonetheless, the ability to relate data between files is a relatively common application in database management.

How to Start dBASE

The procedure you use to start dBASE III PLUS will depend on the type of system you're working on. Instructions for starting dBASE III PLUS on both a hard-disk system and a dual-diskette system follow.

With a Hard-Disk System. The necessary dBASE program files should already be stored on the hard drive in their own subdirectory. If that subdirectory is named DBASE, as we will assume, follow these steps to start up the dBASE program. (However, you should check with your instructor to confirm instructions for accessing dBASE.) Starting at the C:\> prompt

1. Insert your formatted data diskette into Drive A
2. Type **CD DBASE**
3. Press ↵

At the C:\DBASE> prompt

With a Dual-Diskette System. Be sure your computer is booted with DOS and shows the system prompt, A>. To start dBASE you will need two disks, System Disk 1 and System Disk 2.

1. Insert System Disk 1 into Drive A
2. Insert your data diskette into Drive B
3. Type **DBASE** and press ↵

The copyright information screen appears.

4. Press ↵
5. At the next screen, take System Disk 1 out of Drive A and insert System Disk 2 into Drive A

4. Type **DBASE**

5. Press ↵

When the copyright information screen appears

6. Press ↵

6. Press ↵

You are now in dBASE's ASSIST mode.

ASSIST and COMMAND Modes

dBASE III PLUS commands can be issued in either of two modes, ASSIST or COMMAND.

The **ASSIST mode** is menu-driven and uses a routine called dBASE III PLUS Assistant, or *ASSIST.* When you start dBASE, your screen displays the main ASSIST menu, which is shown in Figure DB-3a. The ASSIST mode allows you to issue dBASE commands by selecting choices on a top-of-screen **menu bar** and on submenus—called **pull-down menus**—that appear when you highlight a command from the top-of-screen menu.

The interactive **COMMAND mode** is designed for the user who is familiar with dBASE commands and wants to issue commands as quickly as possible from the keyboard. The screen for the COMMAND mode is shown in Figure DB-3b. The COMMAND mode allows you to enter command words at the **dot prompt,** which is the dot that appears before a flashing cursor at the bottom of your screen. dBASE will display this prompt whenever it is ready for you, the user, to enter a command. The commands you type in COMMAND mode are the same as those you select from menus in ASSIST mode.

Using the ASSIST Mode. The ASSIST mode screen should now be displayed on your monitor. Notice the line at the bottom of the screen—the **status bar.** The first segment of the status bar shows the mode in which you are currently working, ASSIST. The second segment shows the current default drive, A: or B: (or C: with a hard-disk system). The third item in the status bar, Opt:1/6, states that you are now highlighting Option 1 of 6 options available in the pull-down menu.

The line below the status bar informs you that you can use the up or down arrow keys to move through the selections in the pull-down menu, press Enter to invoke the currently highlighted choice (which is "Set up a database file" in Figure DB-3a), press the left or right arrow keys to leave the highlighted choice on the top-of-screen menu bar and move to another choice, press F1 for help, or press the Esc key to exit the ASSIST mode.

You can also key in the first letter in the name of a menu-bar choice to point to that choice. It is only, however, when you press the Enter key that you execute, or *select,* the highlighted command.

Now, let's practice pointing to choices (without executing them).

1. Press ↓ twice to highlight Query on the pull-down menu belonging to the Set Up command on the menu bar

FIGURE DB-3
dBASE III PLUS modes.

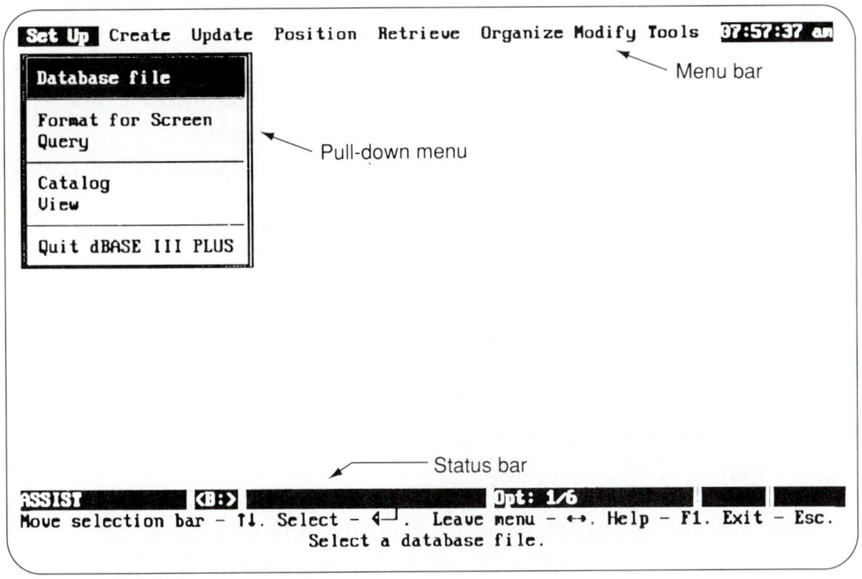

(a) Initial ASSIST-mode screen

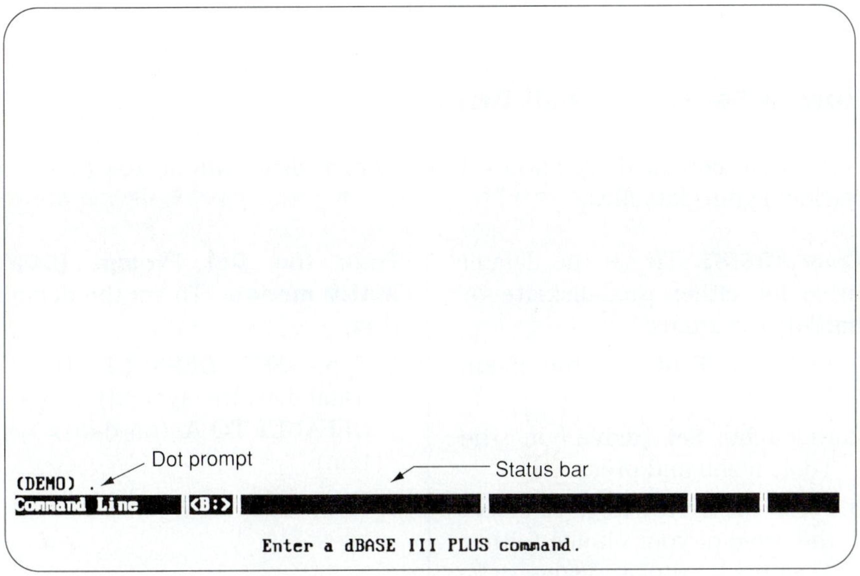

(b) Fresh COMMAND-mode screen

2. Press → twice to highlight the Update command on the menu bar

3. Type **C** to highlight the option Create on the menu bar

Notice the submenus that appear as you move across the menu bar.

4. Press **Esc** to move to the COMMAND mode

Using the COMMAND Mode. If, for example, you wanted to create a new file, you could start at the dot prompt and

DB III PLUS

1. Type **CREATE** and press ↵

Note: You may type commands in either uppercase or lowercase letters at the dot prompt. Instructions in this *Guide* show these commands in uppercase letters to make them easier to read.

When you issue the CREATE command, the prompt "Enter the name of the new file:" appears. For now, however,

2. Press **Esc** to return to the dot prompt

To temporarily remove the status bar from the screen

3. Type **SET STATUS OFF** and press ↵

To make the status bar reappear

4. Type **SET STATUS ON** and press ↵
5. Press **F2** to return to ASSIST

You can go from one mode to another easily. When in the ASSIST mode, press the Esc key to go to the COMMAND mode; when at the COMMAND mode's dot prompt, return to the ASSIST mode either by typing ASSIST or by pressing the F2 key.

How to Set the Default Drive

Setting the default drive shows dBASE which drive will access (save or retrieve) your data files.

From ASSIST. To set the default drive for either dual-diskette or hard-disk systems

1. Highlight **Tools** on the menu bar
2. Highlight **Set drive** on the Tools menu and press ↵
3. Press the **arrow keys** to select the drive of your choice (either A: with a hard-disk system or B: with a dual-diskette system)
4. Press ↵

From the Dot Prompt (COMMAND mode). To set the default drive

1. Type **SET DEFAULT TO B:** (dual-diskette system) or **SET DEFAULT TO A:** (hard-disk system)
2. Press ↵

Notice that the status bar now shows your default drive.

How to Use the HELP Feature

While working with dBASE, you may be confronted with an unfamiliar command. You can get help in either the ASSIST or the COMMAND mode.

From ASSIST. The HELP feature provides information about any command that has been highlighted on a menu but not yet executed by pressing the Enter key. To see how the HELP feature works

1. Press **→** to highlight any command on the menu bar
2. Press **F1** to access Help

A box with the description of the command as well as its syntax will appear on the screen (see Figure DB-4a). To make the box disappear and return to the screen from which you requested help

4. Press any key

From the Dot Prompt. When you access the HELP feature, you'll see a menu of commands about which information is available. To see how the HELP feature works

1. Press **F1** to access the Help menu
2. Use the **arrow keys** and press **↵** to select an option

A box with the description of the command as well as its syntax will appear on the screen (see Figure DB-4b). To make the box disappear and return to the dot prompt

3. Press any key

To request information about a specific command, you can type HELP and the name of the command. For example

4. Type **HELP SORT**
5. Press **↵**

This time you'll see a box with a description of the SORT command. To return to the dot prompt

6. Press **Esc**

DB III PLUS

How to Quit dBASE

Using the QUIT command when leaving dBASE closes (and thus saves) any files that might still be open.

It is important to use the QUIT command each time you leave dBASE so that records added to files are not lost when you shut off the system.

From ASSIST. To quit dBASE

1. Make sure the highlight is on SET UP on the top-of-screen menu bar.
2. Press **↓** (down arrow) the necessary number of times to highlight Quit dBASE III Plus
3. Press **↵**

From the Dot Prompt. To quit dBASE

1. Type **QUIT**
2. Press **↵**

FIGURE DB-4
dBASE III PLUS HELP screens.

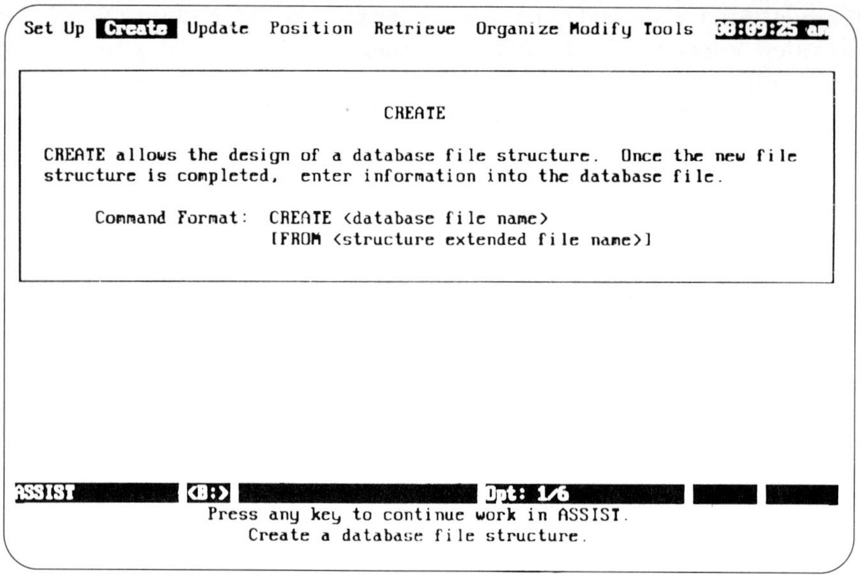

(a) ASSIST mode

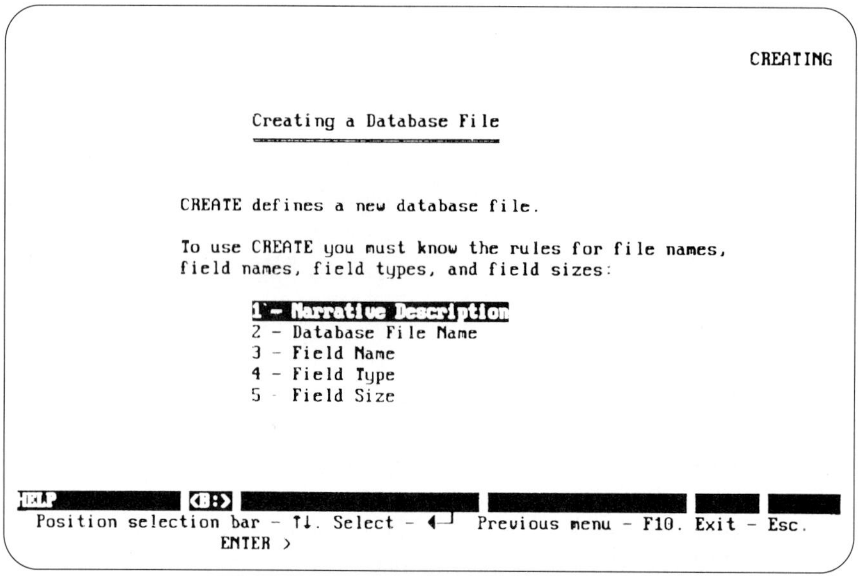

(b) COMMAND mode

CREATING A DATABASE FILE

Now that you've been introduced to dBASE and acquired some basic skills, you're ready to create a simple database file.

In this exercise, you will begin by naming the file and setting up its **structure.** This is done with the **CREATE** command. You must define a file's structure before you can put records into it or use it in any way.

Once the structure is defined, you will next learn how to append and list records, and finally, how to quit the file.

How to Name a File

First, you must provide dBASE with the name of the file you are going to create, and specify on which drive you want the new file stored.

Filenames generally conform to DOS's file-naming convention. In DOS, a filename can contain a maximum of eight characters. It must start with a letter and contain only letters, digits, and the underscore character (_); it must not contain embedded spaces. *Note:* You should not add an extension. dBASE will do this automatically, adding .DBF for Database File.

From ASSIST. To name your file and specify the drive that will store it

1. Start dBASE
2. Highlight **Create** on the menu bar
3. Highlight **Database file** on the Create menu and press ↵

A list of drives appears on the screen (see Figure DB-5). These are your options for the drive on which to store the new database file.

4. Highlight **B:** (dual-diskette system) or **A:** (hard-disk system) and press ↵

When dBASE prompts "Enter the name of the new file:"

5. Type **CUSTOMER** and press ↵

From the Dot Prompt. To name your file

1. At the dot prompt, type **CREATE**
2. Press ↵

When dBASE prompts "Enter the name of the new file:"

3. Type **CUSTOMER**
4. Press ↵

You are now in the fresh database screen shown in Figure DB-6a. Next, you will see how to fill out this screen. A completed screen is shown in Figure DB-6b.

How to Enter Field Descriptors

After naming a file, as you just did with CUSTOMER, and indicating the drive to store the file on, the next step is describing the characteristics of data going into the file. During this process, you specify the name, order of appearance, type, and width of each of the fields of the file. This step defines the structure the database file will have.

FIGURE DB-5
Using ASSIST to create a file.

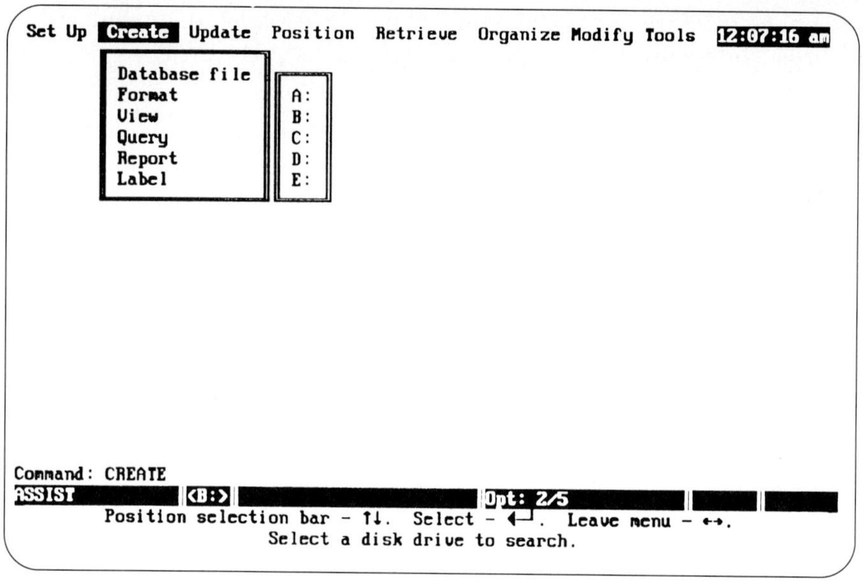

FIGURE DB-6a
Using the CREATE command to define the file structure for the CUSTOMER file.
A fresh screen

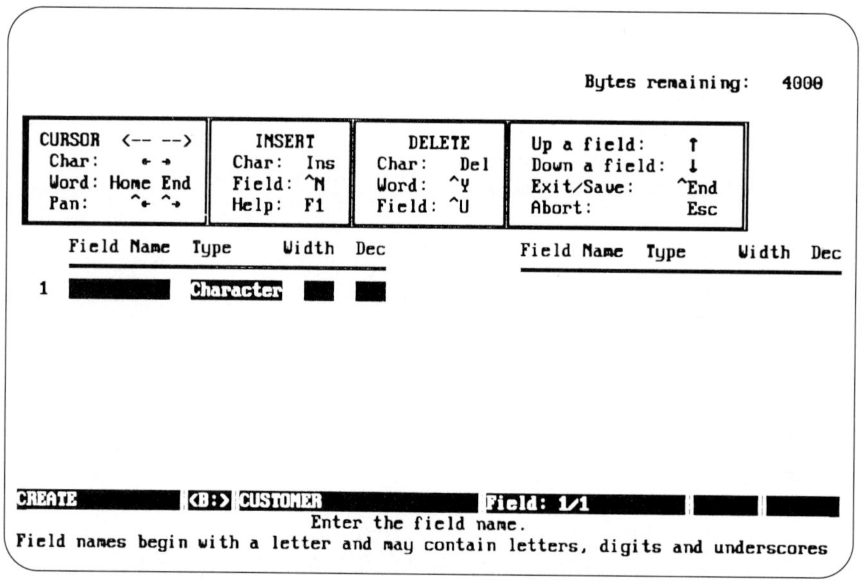

The field types are called **field descriptors.** Five of these descriptors are shown in Figure DB-7.

The most common field descriptors are *character* and *numeric.* Generally, fields that do not need to be involved in arithmetic computations, such as NAME, STREET, CITY, and STATE in the CUSTOMER file of Figure DB-1a are designated as character fields. Fields such as PRICE in the PRODUCT file, on the other hand, are used in computations (such as the invoice in Figure DB-2) and are designated numeric.

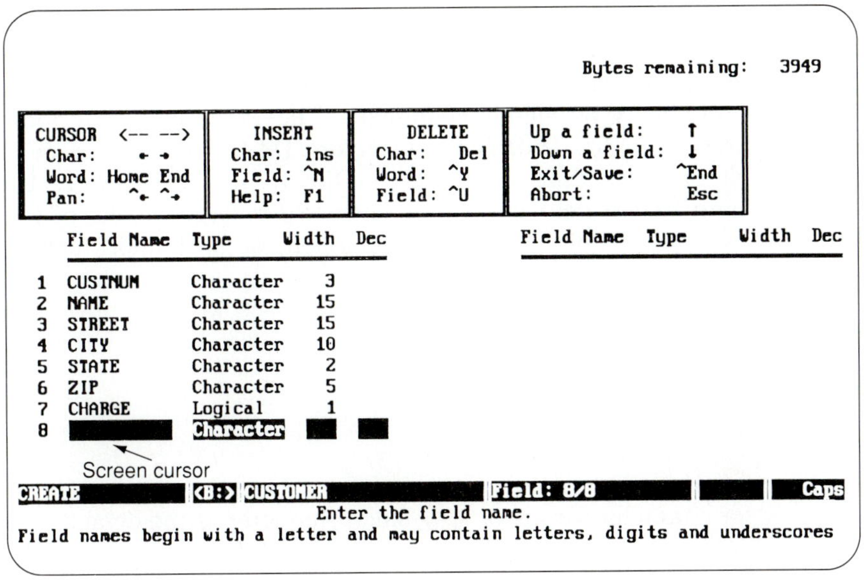

FIGURE DB-6b

Using the CREATE command to define the file structure for the CUSTOMER file.
A completed screen

FIGURE DB-7

Five dBASE III PLUS field descriptors.

FIELD TYPE	MAXIMUM DATA LENGTH	DESCRIPTION
Character	254 characters	Character fields store data that cannot be arithmetically manipulated. You can, however, sort, index, or compare on these fields.
Numeric	19 characters	Numeric fields, which store integer numbers or numbers that contain decimal points, can be arithmetically manipulated. Numbers upon which you do not need to do arithmetic—such as employee identification numbers—should be stored in character rather than numeric fields.
Logical	1 character	Logical fields store a single character of data—a T (meaning true, or yes) or an F (meaning false, or no). Tests on logical fields can be used to select records from a file, as can tests on character, numeric, and date fields.
Date	8 characters	Date fields store dates, provided they are in the format MM/DD/YY (such as 12/31/92). You can sort or index on date fields, and you can also subtract them in order to calculate the number of days elapsing between two dates.
Memo	5,000 characters	Memo fields are used to store text information. They cannot be arithmetically manipulated or compared, but they can be edited and output, as can any other field.

DB
III
PLUS

The *logical* field descriptor typically carries a value of either T or F (for True or False). In the CUSTOMER file in Figure DB-1a, the CHARGE field uses this descriptor to distinguish charge from cash customers (T indicates a charge customer). The *date* field descriptor, which is present in the ORDER file of Figure DB-1c, is used for fields that consist of dates that are stored in the format MM/DD/YY. The variable-length *memo* field descriptor is used for large blocks of text data that will not require sorting, comparison, or arithmetic manipulation.

Starting at the screen shown in Figure DB-6a, you will now enter information about each field in your CUSTOMER file. To enter the first field (as shown in Figure DB-6b),

1. Type **CUSTNUM** as the field name
2. Press ↵
3. Type **C** for character (or press ↵, since character is the default choice)
4. Type **3** as the field width
5. Press ↵
6. Follow these five steps again to enter each of the remaining field names, types, and widths for the CUSTOMER file (as shown in Figure DB-6b)

In some cases you will automatically be advanced to the next field; if not, press Enter. Use the arrow keys to move up or down a field if you wish to make corrections. Note that the width of the logical field, CHARGE, is automatically set to 1, after you type **L** as the field descriptor. This is because the data for any logical field is always just one character—either T or F (True or False).

7. Press **Ctrl** + **End** (hold down the Ctrl key while you press the End key) to save this file structure and exit

When dBASE prompts "ENTER to confirm?"

8. Press ↵

When dBASE asks "Input data records now? (Y/N)"

9. Type **N** for No

Note: If you had typed Y for Yes, you could begin to enter data immediately after defining the structure of your file.

After you press N for No, the ASSIST mode screen reappears. dBASE is awaiting your next command.

When you use the CREATE command to set up a database file, dBASE will allocate space on the disk for this file and record its name in your disk's directory (with a **.DBF** extension). Hence, the database file you have just defined has been saved as CUSTOMER.DBF on your disk, but you may refer to it as CUSTOMER when you are in dBASE.

How to Display a File Structure

After you create a structure for a database file, it's a good idea to check to see that the structure has been entered correctly. You can inspect a file's structure through the **DISPLAY STRUCTURE** command.

From ASSIST. To display a file's structure

1. Highlight **Tools** on the menu bar
2. Highlight **List Structure** from the Tools menu and press ↵

From the Dot Prompt. To display a file's structure

1. Type **DISPLAY STRUCTURE**
2. Press ↵

The screen you will see in response to issuing the DISPLAY STRUCTURE command is similar to the one in Figure DB-8. Note that the extension .DBF has automatically been added to the filename.

If you've made a mistake in creating the structure, don't worry—you can modify it at any time with the MODIFY STRUCTURE command, which you will learn shortly.

After you have correctly defined the structure of a file, you can enter records into it and, subsequently, get useful information from these records. For example, at some point, you will probably want to add, delete, or modify records. You may also want a listing on your printer of certain records in a particular file. Or, as you saw with Avalanche Outfitters, you may want to relate files to produce invoices or informative reports.

To develop or use file data in any way, dBASE requires that you first make the file active. This is done either by pointing to it or by

```
. DISPLAY STRUCTURE
Structure for database: A:CUSTOMER.dbf
Number of data records:       0
Date of last update   : 01/02/92
Field  Field Name  Type       Width    Dec
    1  CUSTNUM     Character      3
    2  NAME        Character     15
    3  STREET      Character     15
    4  CITY        Character     10
    5  STATE       Character      2
    6  ZIP         Character      5
    7  CHARGE      Logical        1
** Total **                      52

.
Command Line   |<A:>|CUSTOMER          |Rec: 1/8          |     |     Caps

                    Enter a dBASE III PLUS command.
```

FIGURE DB-8
Displaying a database structure.

identifying it in some other way. Later we'll show in detail how to make existing files active by opening them with the USE command. However, since the CUSTOMER file is still active at this point, we can proceed with work on the file.

In dBASE, you can only point to one file at a time. When you point to a file, you can add records to it, delete records from it, modify its records, extract records from it, sort it, and do a number of other useful tasks. With some commands dBASE also lets you identify "secondary" files that you might want to join, or relate, to the file you are currently using.

How to Modify a File Structure

Occasionally you will want to modify the structure of a database file. For instance, you may have made a mistake in initially setting up the structure. Or perhaps, after you've used a file successfully for a period, you will want to add a new field, delete a field, change a fieldname, or extend the width of a particular field. To modify a database structure in any of these ways or others, you use the **MODIFY STRUCTURE** command.

Here, we will talk about the command only in passing, leaving it as a hands-on exercise for you to try yourself when you have finished the tutorials.

Before You Modify, Have a Backup. It is a good idea to have a backup copy of any file whose structure you wish to modify in any way. This holds especially true if the file holds data and is large. By not having a backup copy of the file, you risk losing valuable data if you make a mistake in modifying the file.

You can make a backup copy of any file by using the COPY command available with DOS or by using dBASE's COPY command. The dBASE COPY command is not covered here, but it is relatively easy to execute and you can read about it in the Command Reference at the end of these tutorials.

The MODIFY STRUCTURE Command. To modify a structure, you first need to issue the MODIFY STRUCTURE command.

From ASSIST. To modify a structure

1. Highlight **Modify** on the menu bar
2. Highlight **Database file** from the Modify menu and press ↵

From the Dot Prompt. To modify a structure

1. Type **MODIFY STRUCTURE**
2. Press ↵

You will next be presented with a screen that looks like the one in Figure DB-9a. What you do next depends on which type of modification you wish to make. Three types of structure modifications are deleting fields, adding fields, and changing the definitions of fields.

To Delete a Field. To delete a field, highlight the field you want to delete on the screen (see Figure DB-9a, which highlights CUSTNUM) and hold down the Ctrl key while you press the U key—that is,

Ctrl + U

As soon as the new database structure has been saved, the field definition and any data that have been assigned to the field will be erased.

To Add a Field. To add a field, move the screen cursor to where you want to insert the field and press

Ctrl + N

For instance, to insert a field between NAME and STREET, move the screen cursor to the STREET field and press Ctrl+N. You will then see a screen similar to the one in Figure DB-9b, with the cursor positioned automatically where you need to enter the new field name.

To Change a Field Definition. To change a field name, a field width, a field type, or the number of decimal places, move the cursor to the item you wish to change in a field-definition screen such as the one in DB-9a, and just type the modification over the existing specification.

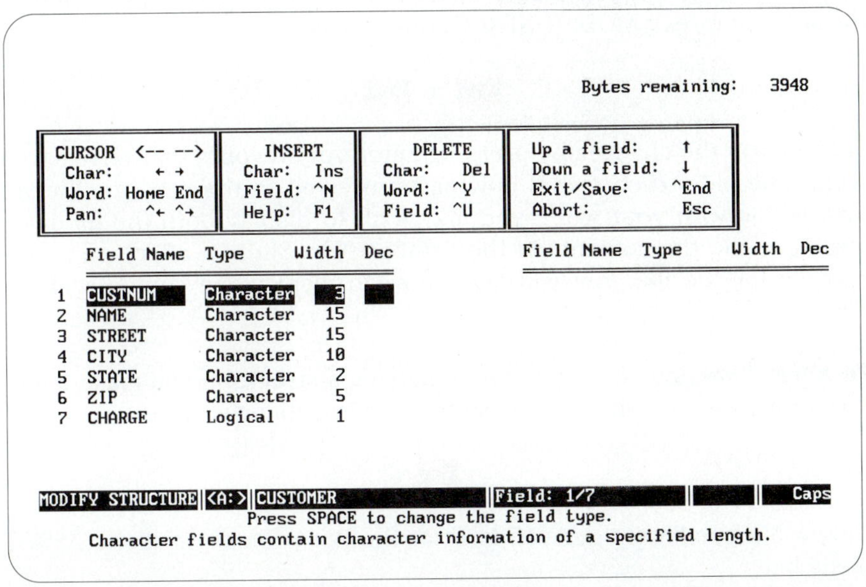

FIGURE DB-9a
Modifying a database structure—deletion.
To delete a field, move the cursor to the field and press Ctrl + U

FIGURE DB-9b

Modifying a database structure—insertion. To insert a field, move the cursor to the field above where you want the new field to be (i.e., STREET) and press Ctrl + N

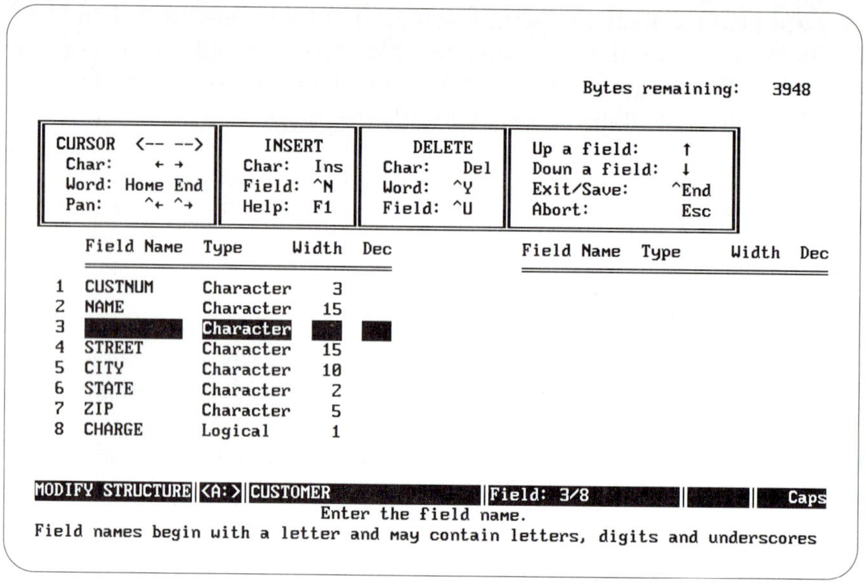

Caution: If you change the name of a field, you cannot make any other modifications to that field at this time; you will have to save the new structure and issue MODIFY STRUCTURE again to make any of these subsequent modifications.

As you are modifying a structure, you will either want to save the changes you make, or, if you get into trouble, abort the entire modification operation.

To Save a Modified Structure. To save the changes you've made and, at the same time, exit MODIFY STRUCTURE, press

Ctrl + **End**

and confirm the changes by pressing Enter. Any records that were saved within the old structure will now be transferred to the new one. Before proceeding with your work, you may wish to display both the modified structure and the contents of the database file. Shortly, after you create records for the file, you will learn how to display the contents of the file.

To Abort Changes. If, as you are modifying a structure, you make a mistake or get lost somehow and wish to abort the changes, press

Esc

This will immediately put you back at the dot prompt or at the ASSIST menu bar.

How to Add (Append) Records to a Database

The **APPEND** command is used to place records into a file. This command can be used to enter records whether the file is empty or already contains records.

If there are no records in the file, the APPEND command automatically points to the first record position. On the other hand, if, say, there are already 15 records in the file, APPEND will point to the 16th record position.

From ASSIST. To add records to a file

1. Highlight **Update** on the menu bar
2. Highlight **Append** on the Update menu and press ↵

From the Dot Prompt. To add records to a file

1. Type **APPEND**
2. Press ↵

Once you issue the APPEND command, you will see a template similar to the one in Figure DB-10a. The template has a highlighted data area sized to conform to the width structure you defined earlier. In dBASE as in many other packages, you will be given a fresh template on screen for each data record you type in.

As you enter records into the CUSTOMER file, follow the guidelines below:

a. When the data you are typing into a field fills up the entire shaded area for that field, you do not need to press Enter; the cursor will automatically move to the next line and a "beep" will sound

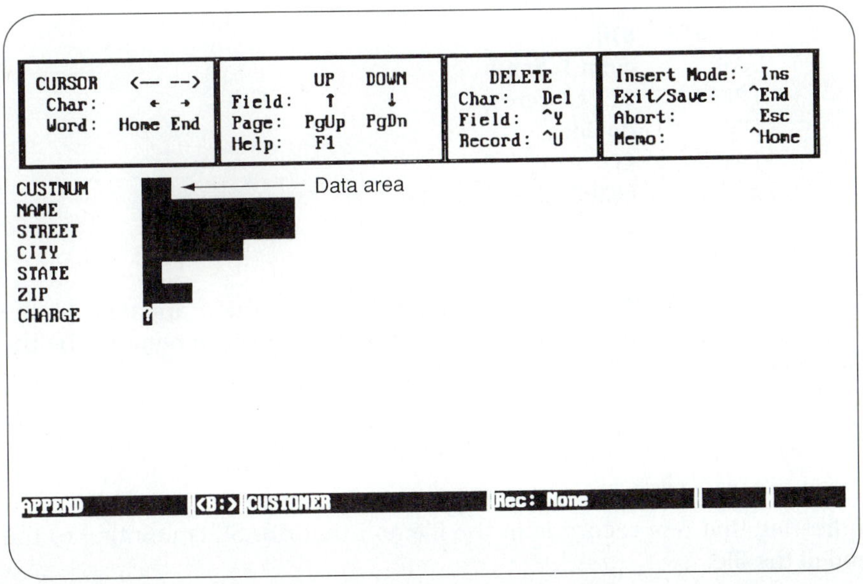

FIGURE DB-10a
APPENDing records to a file.
A blank dBASE template

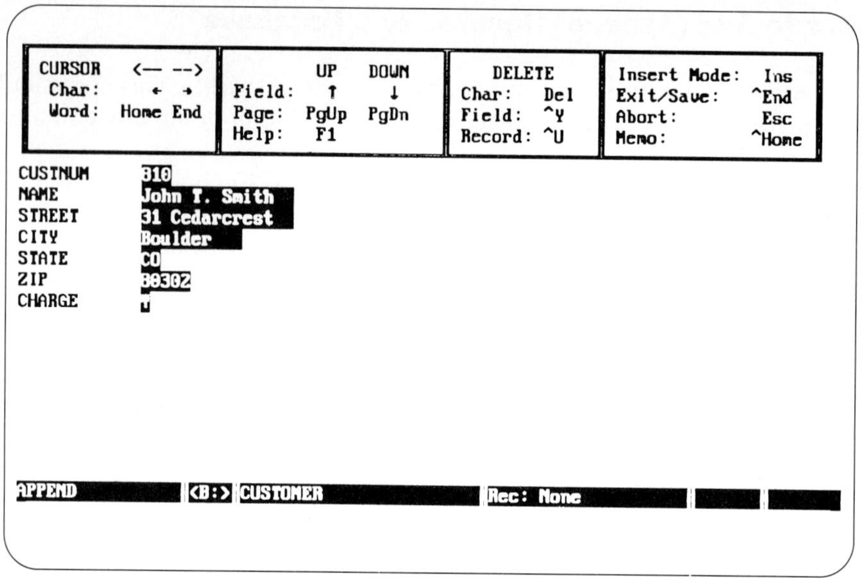

FIGURE DB-10b
APPENDing records to a file.
A filled-in dBASE template

b. When the data you are typing into a field does not fill up the shaded area for that field, press Enter to continue to the next field

c. Look at the menus at the top of the screen to note the keys to press to move from field to field and to invoke commands, such as SAVE

d. When you reach the last field, CHARGE, and enter T or F into it, a new blank record will be presented so you can continue filling in the data for the next record

3. Enter the following data for the first record (see Figure DB-10b)

CUSTNUM	**810**
NAME	**John T. Smith**
STREET	**31 Cedarcrest**
CITY	**Boulder**
STATE	**CO**
ZIP	**80302**
CHARGE	**T**

After you type in the CHARGE field, a fresh template appears. In the fourth segment of your status bar at the bottom of the screen will be the message

`REC:EOF/1`

indicating that one record is in the file and that dBASE is pointing to the end of the file.

4. Add the following records to the file, each record in a fresh template:

775
Sally Jones
725 Aqua Fria
Santa Fe
NM
87501
T

690
William Holmes
3269 Fast Lane
Santa Fe
NM
87501
F

840
Artis Smith
2332 Alameda
Lakewood
CO
80215
T

574
Nellie Deutsch
23 E. Spruce
Olathe
KS
66061
F

If you make an error while typing a record, use the arrow keys to move to the point of the error and type the correct data directly over the old. If the error is in an earlier record, use the Pg Up key to move backward to that record, make the correction, and then use the Pg Dn key to move forward again.

When you have entered all of the records, another fresh template will be showing. To save the file and exit

5. Press ↵

How to List Records

The LIST command allows you to look at the records a file contains. This command is especially useful if some time has passed since you created the file, and you need to review its contents.

From ASSIST. To list the records in the CUSTOMER file

1. Highlight **Retrieve** on the menu bar
2. Highlight **List** on the Retrieve menu and press ↵

A submenu appears with the Execute option highlighted.

3. Press ↵

At the prompt "Direct the output to the printer? [Y/N]"

4. Type **N**

From the Dot Prompt. To list the records in the CUSTOMER file

1. Type **LIST**
2. Press ↵

Whether you use the ASSIST or the COMMAND mode, you will get a listing like the one shown in Figure DB-11.

How to Halt a List. Sometimes the list of records in the file is too long to display on the screen all at one time and you would like to temporarily halt the listing so it doesn't scroll wildly and prevent you from looking at individual records. To temporarily halt the scrolling of all records so that you can view a portion of the file at a time

1. Press Ctrl + **S**

To restart the scrolling of the records, press any key

Note: Soon you will learn to use the DISPLAY command, which avoids the need for use of Ctrl+S by allowing you to view a selected number of records at a time.

How to Quit a File

The QUIT command closes and saves any files that might still be open at the time you are leaving the database.

Remember to use the QUIT command before shutting off the computer system so that you do not lose any records added to files.

FIGURE DB-11
Listed output from the CUSTOMER file.

Record#	CUSTNUM	NAME	STREET	CITY	STATE	ZIP	CHARGE
1	810	John T. Smith	31 Cedarcrest	Boulder	CO	80302	.T.
2	775	Sally Jones	725 Aqua Fria	Santa Fe	NM	87501	.T.
3	690	William Holmes	3269 Fast Lane	Santa Fe	NM	87501	.F.
4	840	Artis Smith	2332 Alameda	Lakewood	CO	80215	.T.
5	574	Nellie Deutsch	23 E. Spruce	Olathe	KS	66061	.F.

From ASSIST. To quit a file

1. Highlight **Quit dBASE III PLUS** on the Set Up menu
2. Press ↵

From the Dot Prompt. To quit a file

1. Type **QUIT**
2. Press ↵

EDITING A DATABASE FILE

Now that you know how to create database files, the next step is learning how to edit files. Because most databases need constant updating, understanding the procedures presented here is very important.

This section explains the methods for viewing a directory of database files, opening a file, deleting a record, modifying records, and adding new records.

How to View a Directory of Files

Before opening an existing database file, such as the CUSTOMER file, it often helps to see all of the database files on your data disk. It is easy to forget which files are stored on the disk or what exact name was given to a particular file.

In the ASSIST mode the Directory option on the Tools menu lists all files on your data disk, not just files with the .DBF extension. You just created a file named CUSTOMER with the .DBF extension. As was mentioned earlier, the .DBF extension is automatically inserted by dBASE for any file that is set up through the CREATE command. As you begin to create other kinds of files, such as index files and report files (discussed later), dBASE will insert other, different extensions for those. Some of the extensions one commonly sees in a directory are shown in Figure DB-12.

In the COMMAND mode, the DIR command will list only those files on your data disk with the .DBF file extension. One of the files (perhaps your only file at this time) is your CUSTOMER file. Other information given with the DIR command is the number of records in each database file, the date of the last revision of each file, and the size of each file. The DIR command may be used to check that your database file has been saved and that the number of records in the file is correct.

To view a directory of database files, do the following:

1. Start dBASE and set your default drive

From ASSIST. To view the directory

2. Highlight **Tools** on the menu bar
3. Highlight **Directory** on the Tools menu and press ↵

From the Dot Prompt. To view the directory

2. Type **DIR**
3. Press ↵

FIGURE DB-12
Some common dBASE III PLUS file extensions.

EXTENSION	DESCRIPTION
.DBF	Used for regular database files, such as those shown in Figure DB-1.
.DBT	Used for memo files and contains large blocks of information found in the memo fields of database files.
.NDX	Used for files created with the INDEX command. These files provide dBASE with the ability to rearrange information in a regular database file.
.FMT	Used for files that are custom screens.
.FRM	Used for files that have been created using the Creating a report form option.
.QRY	Used for information about conditions for displaying records from an existing database file.
.SCR	Used for information about the screen layout for custom data entry forms.

4. Highlight **B:** (dual-diskette system) or **A:** (hard-disk system) and press ↵

A list of file extensions appears.

5. Highlight **.DBF** and press ↵

A list of your database files appears. The CUSTOMER file is shown with the number of bytes used.

How to Retrieve a File

In order to use a database file—to make additions or deletions, for instance—you must first **open** the file. Opening files is done with the **USE** command. Now that, having viewed the directory, you know what files are contained on your disk, you will open one of them.

From ASSIST. To open a file

1. Highlight **Database File** on the Set Up menu and press ↵
2. Highlight **B:** (dual-diskette system) or **A:** (hard-disk system) and press ↵

A list of files with the .DBF extensions appears.

3. Highlight **CUSTOMER.DBF** and press ↵

From the Dot Prompt. To open a file

1. Type **USE CUSTOMER**
2. Press ↵

At the question "Is the file indexed? [Y/N]"

4. Type **N**

The CUSTOMER filename is now showing on the status bar, which means that it is the active, or open, file.

How to Delete Records

To keep a database current, deleting records is frequently necessary. Deleting a record permanently from a dBASE file requires two steps.

First, the **DELETE** command is issued to "flag" the record to be deleted. At this point, the record will be preceded by an asterisk (*), indicating it has been identified as one to be deleted. The record is still part of the file, however, and you can restore the record, if you wish, by issuing a RECALL command.

Second, the **PACK** command is issued to permanently delete the record. The PACK command causes dBASE to purge all records with delete flags (*) from the file. After the file has been packed, the deleted records no longer exist and cannot be recalled.

Marking records for deletion, permanently deleting them, and recalling them are all easier to accomplish in the COMMAND mode than in the ASSIST mode. However, the steps for both modes follow.

Using the DELETE Command. When you issue the DELETE command, a record is marked for deletion with an asterisk (*) but is not actually deleted. After marking the record, you have the option to recall it with the **RECALL** command, or permanently delete it with the PACK command.

From ASSIST. To issue the DELETE command

1. Highlight **Update** on the menu bar
2. Highlight **Delete** on the Update menu and press ↵
3. Highlight **Specify scope** in the submenu and press ↵
4. Highlight **Record** in the submenu and press ↵

At the prompt "Enter a numeric value:"

5. Type **5** (if record 5 is the one you wish to delete) and press ↵

From the Dot Prompt. To issue the DELETE command

1. Type **DELETE RECORD 5** (if record 5 is the one you wish to delete)
2. Press ↵

The message "1 record deleted" appears on your screen.

3. Type **LIST** and press ↵

DB III PLUS

6. Highlight **Execute the command** in the submenu and press ↵

The message "1 record deleted" appears.

7. Highlight **Retrieve** on the menu bar
8. Highlight **List** on the Retrieve menu and press ↵
9. Press ↵ to select Execute the command, which is already highlighted

At the question "Direct the output to the printer? [Y/N]"

10. Type **N**

Notice that Record 5 now has an asterisk next to it. It is marked for deletion, but is not yet permanently deleted, so you have the option of changing your mind.

Using the RECALL Command. You can recall a record that has been marked for deletion, removing the asterisk flag.

From ASSIST. To recall Record 5

1. Highlight **Update** on the menu bar
2. Highlight **Recall** on the Update menu and press ↵
3. Highlight **Specify scope** in the submenu and press ↵
4. Highlight **Record** in the submenu and press ↵

At the prompt "Enter a numeric value:"

5. Type **5** and press ↵
6. Highlight **Execute the command** and press ↵

The message "1 record recalled" appears. To confirm that the asterisk is gone

7. Highlight **Retrieve** on the menu bar
8. Highlight **List** on the Retrieve menu and press ↵

From the Dot Prompt. To recall Record 5

1. Type **RECALL RECORD 5**
2. Press ↵

The message "1 record recalled" appears. To confirm that the asterisk is gone

3. Type **LIST**
4. Press ↵

9. Press ↵ to select Execute the command, which is already highlighted
10. Type **N**

Figure DB-13 shows what your screen will look like when you delete and then recall a record.

Using the PACK Command. If, instead of recalling a record, you wanted to follow through with the deletion, you would invoke the PACK command to permanently delete the marked record.

From ASSIST. To flag Record 5 again and then eliminate it permanently

1. Highlight **Update** on the menu bar
2. Highlight **Delete** on the Update menu and press ↵
3. Highlight **Specify scope** in the submenu and press ↵
4. Highlight **Record** in the submenu and press ↵

At the prompt "Enter a numeric value:"

5. Type **5** and press ↵
6. Highlight **Execute the command** in the submenu and press ↵

The message "1 record deleted" appears.

7. List the file to be sure the record is marked
8. Highlight **Update** on the menu bar
9. Highlight **Pack** on the Update menu and press ↵

The message "4 records copied" appears. Record 5 has now been removed from the file. To add it back so we can continue to work with the complete file

10. Invoke the APPEND command and type Record 5's data into the template

From the Dot Prompt. To flag Record 5 again and then eliminate it permanently

1. Type **DELETE RECORD 5** and press ↵ to mark it for deletion
2. List the file to be sure the record is marked
3. Type **PACK**
4. Press ↵

The message "4 records copied" appears.

5. List the file again to confirm that the record is deleted

If the deleted record was in the middle of the file, the remaining records would be automatically renumbered sequentially. So that we can continue to work with the complete file,

6. Enter Record 5 back into the file by invoking the APPEND command and typing Record 5's data into the template

FIGURE DB-13
Using the DELETE and RECALL commands in the command mode.

```
(DEMO) . delete record 5
      1 record deleted
(DEMO) . list
Record#  CUSTNUM NAME             STREET          CITY       STATE ZIP   CHARGE
      1  810     John T. Smith    31 Cedarcrest   Boulder    CO    80302 .T.
      2  775     Sally Jones      725 Aqua Fria   Santa Fe   NM    87501 .T.
      3  690     William Holmes   3269 Fast Lane  Santa Fe   NM    87501 .F.
      4  840     Artis Smith      2332 Alameda    Lakewood   CO    80215 .T.
      5 *574     Nellie Deutsch   23 E. Spruce    Olathe     KS    66061 .F.

(DEMO) . recall record 5
      1 record recalled
(DEMO) . list
Record#  CUSTNUM NAME             STREET          CITY       STATE ZIP   CHARGE
      1  810     John T. Smith    31 Cedarcrest   Boulder    CO    80302 .T.
      2  775     Sally Jones      725 Aqua Fria   Santa Fe   NM    87501 .T.
      3  690     William Holmes   3269 Fast Lane  Santa Fe   NM    87501 .F.
      4  840     Artis Smith      2332 Alameda    Lakewood   CO    80215 .T.
      5  574     Nellie Deutsch   23 E. Spruce    Olathe     KS    66061 .F.

(DEMO) .
Command Line  <B:> CUSTOMER              Rec: EOF/5

                    Enter a dBASE III PLUS command.
```

How to Modify Records

Modifying data in records is another way to keep a database current. The changes may be necessary for various reasons. A customer may have moved, requiring a street address to be changed. The price of a product may have gone up. Data originally typed into a field may have been incorrect. Whatever the case, editing allows you to change the values contained in the fields of any records.

You can edit records by using either the EDIT or the BROWSE command.

Using the BROWSE Command. BROWSE is one of the fastest ways to edit your records. With BROWSE, you can display several records onscreen at the same time and edit them.

From ASSIST. To use BROWSE

1. Highlight **Update** on the menu bar
2. Highlight **Browse** on the Update menu and press ↵

From the Dot Prompt. To use BROWSE

1. Type **BROWSE**
2. Press ↵

Once you're in BROWSE, you can press Pg Up or Pg Dn to scroll through records in a longer file. You can use the arrow keys to move from record to record or from field to field. Whenever you see an item that needs to be updated, type in the update over the original data.

In your CUSTOMER file, make the following corrections:

3. Change Sally Jones's customer number to **778**

4. Change the Charge field for William Holmes to read **.T.**

Figure DB-14 shows what you'll see on your screen.

If you had a very large database file and were using the BROWSE command to edit it, you could press the F1 key to have the boxed menu at the top of the screen disappear, clearing additional screen space for your records.

Sometimes records are too long to fit on a BROWSE screen. When this happens, hold down the Ctrl key while pressing the right arrow key to pan to fields currently located offscreen. Use the Ctrl+left arrow key combination to pan in the other direction.

When you have finished making editing corrections

5. Press **Ctrl** + **End**

Note: Both Ctrl+End and Ctrl+W tell dBASE that you are finished with the edit and want to save the changes. These keystroke combinations also return you to the COMMAND (dot prompt) mode.

If you decided not to save the changes made in the Browse mode, you could press the Esc key to exit BROWSE. Be careful about using the Esc key for this purpose, however, because you will lose all the changes you made in BROWSE.

Using the EDIT Command for Single Records. Records can also be modified by using the **EDIT** command. However, with EDIT you can modify only one record at a time.

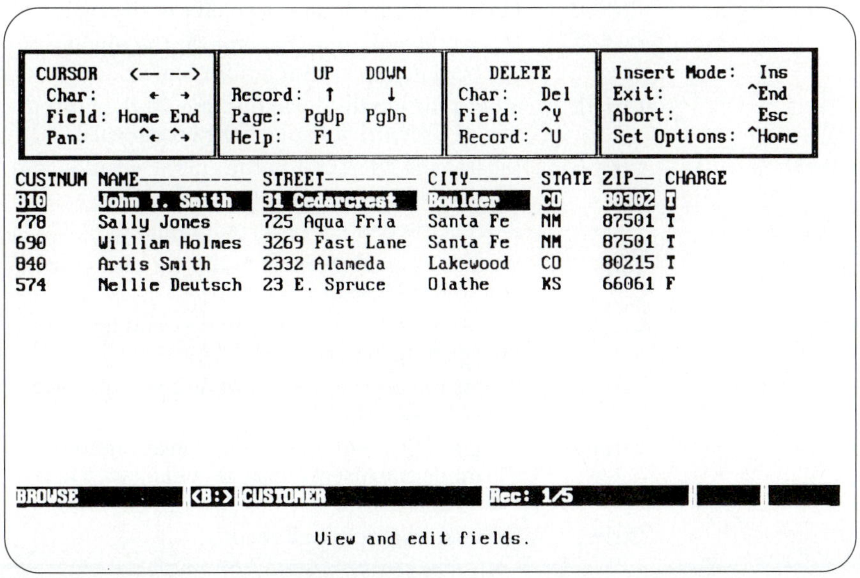

FIGURE DB-14
Using the BROWSE command.

DB III PLUS

From ASSIST. To use EDIT

1. Highlight **Update** on the menu bar
2. Highlight **Edit** on the Update menu and press ↵

From the Dot Prompt. To use EDIT

1. Type **EDIT**
2. Press ↵

Once you are in EDIT you can use a number of editing features available in dBASE III PLUS to make changes in a record. The options available to you are shown in Figure DB-15. For now, however, you will change Record 2 using the steps that follow.

3. Press **Pg Up** to go to Record 2 for Sally Jones
4. Type **813 Pine Bluff** over the old street address
5. Press **Ctrl** + **End** when finished

Using the EDIT Command for Selected Field Values. You can also use the EDIT command to edit specific types of records. For example, you might want to edit all Colorado records. This type of command is done more easily through the COMMAND mode. Starting at the dot prompt

FIGURE DB-15
Cursor movements to change records with the EDIT command.
The easiest way to take an action is by pressing a cursor control key. If there is no cursor control key to invoke the action you wish to take, press down on the control key while hitting the letter key named in the figure.

Cursor Control Key	*or*	dBASE Command	Action
		Ctrl+A	Moves the cursor one word to the left.
		Ctrl+F	Moves the cursor one word to the right.
←		Ctrl+S	Moves the cursor one character to the left.
→		Ctrl+D	Moves the cursor one character to the right.
↑		Ctrl+E	Moves the cursor up one line. At the top line of a record it displays the prior record.
↓		Ctrl+X	Moves the cursor down one line. At the bottom line of a record it displays the next record.
Del		Ctrl+G	Deletes the character at the cursor position and moves the text one position to the left.
		Ctrl+Y	Deletes the contents of an entire field.
		Ctrl+W	Writes the changes back to the file and returns you to the ASSIST menu.
Pg Up		Ctrl+R	Writes the current record to disk and displays the previous record.
Pg Dn		Ctrl+C	Writes the current record to disk and displays the next record.
Ins		Ctrl+V	Toggles between typeover and insert modes. In INS mode the insert message is displayed in the status bar.
		Ctrl+U	Deletes or undeletes a record.

1. Type **EDIT FOR STATE = "CO"**

2. Press ↵

All Colorado records (two of them) are retrieved for editing. You can move from record to record with the Pg Dn and Pg Up keys. The John T. Smith record is now showing.

3. Change the CUSTNUM data for the two Colorado records as follows:

Smith, John T. to **820**
Smith, Artis to **850**

4. Press **Ctrl** + **End** when finished

This EDIT command used the conditional expression STATE = "CO" to search for specific records. Conditional expressions will be discussed in detail later.

5. Use the LIST command to see that the records have been properly changed

How to Add More Records

Keeping a database current frequently requires that you add new records to it. You add records in the same way that you first entered information in the database, with the use of the APPEND command.

From ASSIST. To append records

1. Highlight **Update** on the menu bar

2. Highlight **Append** on the Update menu and press ↵

From the Dot Prompt. To append records

1. Type **APPEND**

2. Press ↵

You are now ready to add records to the current file. Notice that the status line tells you that you are at the end of your file (EOF). Remember that you will be adding records to the database file that is active, which currently is the CUSTOMER file. The name of the active file shows in the third segment of the status panel at the bottom of the screen. If you had opened other files while working with dBASE, the APPEND command would be in effect for the most recently opened file.

3. Enter the data shown in Figure DB-16 as new records in your CUSTOMER file

As you reach the end of each record, a new template will automatically appear.

4. Press ↵ when finished

5. List the file and check it for accuracy

Record#	CUSTNUM	NAME	STREET	CITY	STATE	ZIP	CHARGE
6	447	Vernon Pressy	5541 Canyon	Boulder	CO	80302	.T.
7	480	Benton Fink	440 Arapahoe	Boulder	CO	80302	.F.
8	401	Wayne Montoya	600 Tara Lane	Englewood	CO	80155	.F.
9	640	C. Foster Kane	P.O. Box 6000	Santa Fe	NM	87501	.T.
10	505	Alice Evans	5702 North St.	Boise	ID	83704	.T.
11	102	Maya Ellis	603 Oakwood	Aurora	CO	80011	.T.
12	754	Shane Williams	275 East Kiowa	Flagstaff	AZ	86001	.F.
13	801	Del Lopez	80 Williston	Austin	TX	78755	.F.
14	908	Duke Miller	CM Ranch	Stanley	NM	87056	.F.
15	665	Bette White	Box 20	Rowe	NM	87562	.T.
16	760	Kim Lundy	44 West St.	Missoula	MT	59802	.F.

FIGURE DB-16
Additional data for the CUSTOMER file.

Your file should match the one shown in Figure DB-17.

6. If necessary, use BROWSE or EDIT to make corrections to the records

7. Quit the file and dBASE

MANIPULATING DATA IN A FILE

Up to this point, you have learned how to use dBASE to create and edit files. Now it is time to find out how to manipulate the data in files to extract valuable information.

In this exercise you will be shown how to display records, perform calculations, and index or sort files to reorganize the contents.

FIGURE DB-17
An expanded version of the CUSTOMER file.

Record#	CUSTNUM	NAME	STREET	CITY	STATE	ZIP	CHARGE
1	820	John T. Smith	31 Cedarcrest	Boulder	CO	80302	.T.
2	778	Sally Jones	813 Pine Bluff	Santa Fe	NM	87501	.T.
3	690	William Holmes	3269 Fast Lane	Santa Fe	NM	87501	.T.
4	850	Artis Smith	2332 Alameda	Lakewood	CO	80215	.T.
5	574	Nellie Deutsch	23 E. Spruce	Olathe	KS	66061	.F.
6	447	Vernon Pressy	5541 Canyon	Boulder	CO	80302	.T.
7	480	Benton Fink	440 Arapahoe	Boulder	CO	80302	.F.
8	401	Wayne Montoya	600 Tara Lane	Englewood	CO	80155	.F.
9	640	C. Foster Kane	P.O. Box 6000	Santa Fe	NM	87501	.T.
10	505	Alice Evans	5702 North St.	Boise	ID	83704	.T.
11	102	Maya Ellis	603 Oakwood	Aurora	CO	80011	.T.
12	754	Shane Williams	275 East Kiowa	Flagstaff	AZ	86001	.F.
13	801	Del Lopez	80 Williston	Austin	TX	78755	.F.
14	908	Duke Miller	CM Ranch	Stanley	NM	87056	.F.
15	665	Bette White	Box 20	Rowe	NM	87562	.T.
16	760	Kim Lundy	44 West St.	Missoula	MT	59802	.F.

For these purposes, you will use your enlarged CUSTOMER file.

1. Start dBASE and open the CUSTOMER file
2. List the file to make sure all 16 records are present as shown in Figure DB-17

How to Display Records

This tutorial explains several ways to display records. The **DISPLAY** command, like the LIST command, lets you see the data in your files. However, there are some differences between the commands. LIST allows you to print records; DISPLAY doesn't. DISPLAY causes records to be displayed a screen at a time, whereas LIST causes them to scroll onto (and possibly off) the screen.

To display records in the COMMAND mode, you will type in variations of the DISPLAY ALL OFF command. The key word ALL causes all the records to be displayed on the screen. The key word OFF suppresses the record numbers.

To display records in ASSIST, a system of menus and submenus is used to construct the DISPLAY commands. When you choose the Display option from the Retrieve menu, a five-option submenu appears.

You may find it simpler to use the COMMAND mode to display records; however, examples of using the DISPLAY command in both modes follow.

Displaying All Records. The DISPLAY ALL command will cause all records to be displayed on the screen. Before starting the steps that follow, make sure you have activated the CUSTOMER file.

From ASSIST. To display all records

1. Highlight **Retrieve** from the menu bar
2. Highlight **Display** on the Retrieve menu and press ↵
3. Highlight **Specify scope** on the submenu and press ↵
4. Highlight **ALL** on the next submenu and press ↵
5. Highlight **Execute the command** on the Display submenu and press ↵

From the Dot Prompt. To display all records

1. Type **DISPLAY ALL OFF**
2. Press ↵

dBASE will automatically pause after 16 or 17 lines of the file are displayed on the screen. To display the next screen and subsequent files, press any key. You can continue this until you reach the end of the file you are viewing.

DB
III
PLUS

Displaying Specific Fields. This form of the DISPLAY command identifies specific fields to be displayed. In the exercise to follow, only the CUSTNUM, NAME, and CHARGE fields of your CUSTOMER file will be displayed.

From ASSIST. To display specific fields

1. Highlight **Retrieve** on the menu bar
2. Highlight **Display** on the Retrieve menu and press ↵
3. Highlight **Specify scope** on the submenu and press ↵
4. Highlight **ALL** on the next submenu and press ↵
5. Highlight **Construct a field list** on the Display submenu and press ↵

A list of all the fields in the database appears on the left of the screen.

6. Highlight **CUSTNUM** and press ↵; highlight **NAME** and press ↵; highlight **CHARGE** and press ↵
7. Press → (right arrow) to move to the Display submenu
8. Highlight **Execute the command** on the Display submenu and press ↵

From the Dot Prompt. To display specific fields

1. Type **DISPLAY ALL OFF CUSTNUM, NAME, CHARGE**
2. Press ↵

You'll see a list of the CUSTNUM, NAME, and CHARGE fields for all records in the CUSTOMER file.

Using Conditional Expressions. When a command includes a conditional expression, dBASE searches the file for records that fit the condition, and performs the command on those records only. Conditional expressions in dBASE are constructed much the same way as in some programming languages, such as BASIC, Pascal, COBOL, and FORTRAN. That is, they are typically formed by a field name, followed by one or more **relational operators** (see Figure DB-18) and a constant. For example,

```
STATE = "NM"
CITY = "Boulder"
ZIP = "80302"
CUSTNUM <= "505" (is less than or equal to)
```

SYMBOL	MEANING
<	Less than
≤	Less than or equal to
>	Greater than
≥	Greater than or equal to
=	Equal to
<>	Not equal to

FIGURE DB-18

Relational operators. Relational operators are used in conditional expressions to make comparisons between items. Conditional expressions reduce to the logical value "T" (for *true*) or "F" (for *false*).

Note: Constants (such as "NM" and "Boulder") that correspond to fields governed by the character field descriptor must appear in quotes. Also be aware that, regarding literal expressions within quotes, dBASE distinguishes upper from lowercase characters. Consequently, since NM has been entered in the fields in the file in uppercase, be sure to use uppercase in the conditional expression. Numeric fields cannot be in quotes.

From ASSIST. To produce a listing of all records with CO (Colorado) as the STATE field

1. Highlight **Retrieve** on the menu bar
2. Highlight **Display** on the Retrieve menu and press ↵
3. Highlight **Build a search condition** on the Display submenu and press ↵
4. Highlight **STATE** in the submenu and press ↵
5. Highlight = **Equal To** in the submenu and press ↵

At the prompt "Enter a character string:"

6. Type **CO**
7. Highlight **No more conditions** and press ↵
8. Highlight **Execute the command** and press ↵

From the Dot Prompt. To produce a listing of all records with CO (Colorado) as the STATE field

1. Type **DISPLAY ALL OFF FOR STATE = "CO"**

The FOR clause, used with the DISPLAY command, tells dBASE to select those records meeting the conditional expression that follows the key word FOR.

2. Press ↵

A listing of all records with CO (Colorado) as the STATE field appears.

Additional operators—called **logical connectives**—that can be used to combine conditional statements include

.NOT.	To select records that do not meet a condition
.AND.	To select records that meet both of two conditions
.OR.	To select records that meet either or both of two conditions

Using these operators in ASSIST is quite complex, requiring using the Build a search condition option in the Display submenu. Therefore, specific examples for using these operators will be given here for the COMMAND mode only.

To use the .NOT. operator starting at the dot prompt

1. Type **DISPLAY ALL OFF FOR .NOT. STATE = "CO"**

2. Press ↵

A list of all records representing states other than Colorado appears.

To use the .AND. operator

3. Type **DISPLAY ALL OFF FOR STATE = "NM" .AND. CHARGE**

You don't need to specify a value for CHARGE because the use of the logical field name CHARGE implies the logical relation CHARGE = ".T." This type of construction is used for logical field comparisons only.

4. Press ↵

A list of only those customers that *both* live in New Mexico and have charge accounts appears.

To use the .OR. operator

5. Type **DISPLAY ALL OFF FOR STATE = "NM" .OR. STATE = "CO"**

6. Press ↵

A listing of records representing customers from *either* New Mexico *or* Colorado appears. Another example of the .OR. follows:

7. Type **DISPLAY ALL OFF FOR STATE = "NM" .OR. CHARGE**

8. Press ↵

This statement finds customers who

- □ Are from New Mexico but don't have a charge account; or
- □ Are not from New Mexico but do have a charge account; or
- □ Are both from New Mexico and have a charge account.

There are many other forms of the DISPLAY command and forms of conditional expressions in addition to those shown here. A full discussion of these is beyond the scope of this guide. We will note here, however, that conditional expressions can be used with other dBASE commands, such as DELETE, LIST, and the computational commands that follow in the next subsection. For example, typing

```
DELETE FOR STATE = "CO"
```

would mark all Colorado records for deletion.

How to Perform Calculations

dBASE's ability to perform arithmetic operations on records or fields is a very useful feature. To perform calculations, dBASE uses three commands: COUNT, SUM, and AVERAGE.

When you understand how to use these commands, you will be able to extract valuable information from your files quickly.

Using the COUNT Command. COUNT is used for tallying records. Examples of how to count the records for an entire file or for specific fields follow. Your CUSTOMER file should be active.

From ASSIST. To count an entire file's records

1. Highlight **Retrieve** on the menu bar
2. Highlight **Count** on the Retrieve menu and press ↵

A submenu with the Execute the command option highlighted appears.

3. Press ↵

You'll see a message that there are 16 records in the file.

4. Highlight **Retrieve** on the menu bar
5. Highlight **Count** on the Retrieve menu and press ↵
6. Highlight **Build a search condition** and press ↵
7. Highlight **STATE** and press ↵
8. Highlight **= Equal To** and press ↵

At the prompt "Enter a character string:"

9. Type **CO**
10. Highlight **No more conditions** and press ↵
11. Highlight **Execute the command** and press ↵

The records in which the STATE is CO are tallied and the message "6 records" appears.

From the Dot Prompt. To count an entire file's records

1. Type **COUNT**
2. Press ↵

All the records are tallied and the message "16 records" appears.

To count records for a specific field

1. Type **COUNT FOR STATE = "CO"**
2. Press ↵

The records in which the STATE is CO are tallied and the message "6 records" appears.

DB III PLUS

Using the SUM Command. SUM is used to add the values in any numeric field of a file. Before using the SUM (and AVERAGE) commands, you will create a new database file so you can use these commands on its specified fields.

Please note that the following instructions for creating the new database file are designed for the COMMAND mode. At the dot prompt

1. Type **CREATE SALES** and press ↵
2. Define fields as shown in Figure DB-19.
3. Press **Ctrl** + **End** when you have finished creating the file's structure
4. Press ↵ to confirm and press **Y** for Yes to input data records
5. Fill in the data as shown in Figure DB-20

Note: When typing a number like 6.00, you need not press the spacebar to align it with the number above. The decimal place will automatically align as soon as you press the period when you type the number.

6. Press ↵ when finished
7. List the file to be sure you've entered the records properly

Now you are ready to perform a SUM calculation on numeric fields of your SALES file. You can do this from either ASSIST or the dot prompt.

From ASSIST. To sum the QUANTITY field

1. Highlight **Retrieve** from the menu bar
2. Highlight **Sum** on the Retrieve menu and press ↵
3. Highlight **Construct a field list** and press ↵

From the Dot Prompt. To sum the QUANTITY field

1. Type **SUM QUANTITY**
2. Press ↵

The sum 275 is produced.

As with the COUNT statement, you can also use a FOR clause to make a SUM statement conditional. For example

FIGURE DB-19
Fields for the SALES file.

Field name	Field type	Width	Decimal places
SUPPLIER	Character	4	
DESCRIP	Character	25	
QUANTITY	Numeric	3	0
PRICE	Numeric	6	2

FIGURE DB-20
Data for the SALES file.

SUPPLIER	DESCRIP	QUANTITY	PRICE
Funk	Indy Jones Jacket, large	30	90.00
Funk	Rozelle Headbands	10	6.00
Peak	Nordic Hats	85	10.00
Peak	Nylon Windpants	50	40.00
Peak	Thermal Ski Socks	100	7.00

4. Highlight **QUANTITY** and press ↵
5. Press → (right arrow) and select Execute the command
6. Press ↵

The sum 275 is produced.

3. Type **SUM QUANTITY FOR SUPPLIER = "Peak"** and press ↵

The sum of 235 is the total quantity ordered by Peak.

Using the AVERAGE Command. AVERAGE is used for averaging a field in the records of a file.

From ASSIST. To average the PRICE field

1. Highlight **Retrieve** on the menu bar
2. Highlight **Average** on the Retrieve menu and press ↵
3. Highlight **Construct a field list** and press ↵
4. Highlight **PRICE** and press ↵
5. Highlight Press → (right arrow) and select Execute the command
6. Press ↵

This produces the average of 30.60.

From the Dot Prompt. To average the PRICE field

1. Type **AVERAGE PRICE**
2. Press ↵

This produces the average of 30.60.

How to Index a File

You can sequentially reorganize records in a file in dBASE through either the **INDEX** or the **SORT** command.

An essential difference between the methods is that **indexing** creates an *index file* (a file with an **.NDX** extension) that is used to rearrange the records of a database file on the display screen or printer—without physically changing the original file—while sorting physically creates a new sorted database file.

Several indexing examples follow.

By Customer Number. You may, for instance, want to rearrange the order of records according to a certain field—called a **key field.** Assume that you want a listing of the records in the CUSTOMER file, in ascending order by customer number. In that case, CUSTNUM is your key field.

In the exercise that follows, you will create the index file NUMINDX.NDX, shown in Figure DB-21, with the records in the CUSTOMER file ordered by the CUSTNUM field. Remember that the CUSTOMER file will not change; the index file will merely show how its records are to be arranged on output. Note, for instance that the first

FIGURE DB-21
An index file (NUMINDX) for the CUSTOMER file. The key field, CUSTNUM, is used to arrange records in ascending order.

Indexing Order	Record #	CUSTNUM
1	11	102
2	8	401
3	6	447
4	7	480
5	10	505
6	5	574
7	9	640
8	15	665
9	3	690
10	12	754
11	16	760
12	2	778
13	13	801
14	1	820
15	4	850
16	14	908

record in the index file shows that the eleventh record in the database file, CUSTNUM 102, will be the first listed when that file is arranged numerically.

All index files created in dBASE have the extension .NDX. This extension, as mentioned earlier and as true with all dBASE extensions, is not typed and does not need to be entered by the user. All indexed files are saved by dBASE upon creation.

In the example that follows, you will be asked to use the CUSTOMER file. If this file isn't active, remember that you can activate it with the Set Up and Database file menu options in ASSIST or the USE command in the COMMAND mode.

From ASSIST. To create the index file in Figure DB-21 with the CUSTOMER file active

1. Highlight **Organize** on the menu bar
2. Highlight **Index** on the Organize menu and press ↵

At the prompt "Enter an index key expression:"

3. Type **CUSTNUM** and press ↵
4. Highlight **A:** (hard-disk system) or **B:** (dual-diskette system) as the disk drive to search

At the prompt "Enter the name of the file:"

From the Dot Prompt. To create the index file in Figure DB-21 with the CUSTOMER file active

1. Type **INDEX ON CUSTNUM TO NUMINDX**
2. Press ↵

The message "100% indexed" appears. To inspect the indexed records

3. Type **LIST**
4. Press ↵

5. Type **NUMINDX** and press ↵

The message "100% indexed" appears. To inspect the indexed records

6. Highlight **Retrieve** on the menu bar
7. Highlight **List** on the Retrieve menu and press ↵
8. Press ↵ to select the highlighted option, **Execute the command**

At the question, "Direct output to the printer? [Y/N]"

9. Type **N**

The customer numbers should now be displayed in ascending order as suggested by the last column of Figure DB-21.

Two similar indexing examples follow, using different key fields to sequence the records in the CUSTOMER file.

By Zip Codes. This sequence will produce a list of customers by zip in ascending order (see Figure DB-22).

```
(DEMO) . set index to zipindx
(DEMO) . list
Record# CUSTNUM NAME            STREET          CITY       STATE ZIP   CHARGE
     16 760     Kim Lundy       44 West St.     Missoula   MT    59802 .F.
      5 574     Nellie Deutsch  23 E. Spruce    Olathe     KS    66061 .F.
     13 801     Del Lopez       80 Williston    Austin     TX    78755 .F.
     11 102     Maya Ellis      603 Oakwood     Aurora     CO    80011 .T.
      8 401     Wayne Montoya   600 Tara Lane   Englewood  CO    80155 .F.
      4 850     Artis Smith     2332 Alameda    Lakewood   CO    80215 .T.
      1 820     John T. Smith   31 Cedarcrest   Boulder    CO    80302 .T.
      6 447     Vernon Pressy   5541 Canyon     Boulder    CO    80302 .T.
      7 480     Benton Fink     440 Arapahoe    Boulder    CO    80302 .F.
     10 505     Alice Evans     5702 North St.  Boise      ID    83704 .T.
     12 754     Shane Williams  275 East Kiowa  Flagstaff  AZ    86001 .F.
     14 908     Duke Miller     CM Ranch        Stanley    NM    87056 .F.
      2 778     Sally Jones     813 Pine Bluff  Santa Fe   NM    87501 .T.
      3 690     William Holmes  3269 Fast Lane  Santa Fe   NM    87501 .T.
      9 640     C. Foster Kane  P.O. Box 6000   Santa Fe   NM    87501 .T.
     15 665     Bette White     Box 20          Rowe       NM    87562 .T.

(DEMO) .
Command Line   <B:> CUSTOMER         Rec: EOF/16

                  Enter a dBASE III PLUS command.
```

FIGURE DB-22
Arranging the CUSTOMER file by ZIP code.

DB III PLUS

From ASSIST. With the CUSTOMER file active

1. Highlight **Organize** on the menu bar
2. Highlight **Index** on the Organize menu and press ↵

At the prompt "Enter an index key expression:"

3. Type **ZIP** and press ↵
4. Highlight **A:** (hard-disk system) or **B:** (dual-diskette system) as the disk drive to search

At the prompt "Enter the name of the file:"

5. Type **ZIPINDX** and press ↵

The message "100% indexed" appears.

6. List the indexed records

From the Dot Prompt. With the CUSTOMER file active

1. Type **INDEX ON ZIP TO ZIPINDX**
2. Press ↵
3. List the indexed records

By Customer Numbers within Each Zip Code. This sequence will produce a list that has customer numbers in ascending order within each zip code (see Figure DB-23).

FIGURE DB-23
Arranging the CUSTOMER file by ZIP code and, within ZIP codes, by customer number.

```
 100% indexed          16 Records indexed
(DEMO) . SET INDEX TO DBLINDX
(DEMO) . LIST
Record#  CUSTNUM NAME            STREET          CITY        STATE ZIP   CHARGE
     16  760     Kim Lundy       44 West St.     Missoula    MT    59802 .F.
      5  574     Nellie Deutsch  23 E. Spruce    Olathe      KS    66061 .F.
     13  801     Del Lopez       80 Williston    Austin      TX    78755 .F.
     11  102     Maya Ellis      603 Oakwood     Aurora      CO    80011 .T.
      8  401     Wayne Montoya   600 Tara Lane   Englewood   CO    80155 .F.
      4  850     Artis Smith     2332 Alameda    Lakewood    CO    80215 .T.
      6  447     Vernon Pressy   5541 Canyon     Boulder     CO    80302 .T.
      7  480     Benton Fink     440 Arapahoe    Boulder     CO    80302 .F.
      1  820     John T. Smith   31 Cedarcrest   Boulder     CO    80302 .T.
     10  505     Alice Evans     5702 North St.  Boise       ID    83704 .T.
     12  754     Shane Williams  275 East Kiowa  Flagstaff   AZ    86001 .F.
     14  908     Duke Miller     CM Ranch        Stanley     NM    87056 .F.
      9  640     C. Foster Kane  P.O. Box 6000   Santa Fe    NM    87501 .T.
      3  690     William Holmes  3269 Fast Lane  Santa Fe    NM    87501 .T.
      2  778     Sally Jones     813 Pine Bluff  Santa Fe    NM    87501 .T.
     15  665     Bette White     Box 20          Rowe        NM    87562 .T.

(DEMO) .
Command Line   <B:> CUSTOMER            Rec: EOF/16                  Caps

                    Enter a dBASE III PLUS command.
```

From ASSIST. With the CUSTOMER file active

1. Highlight **Organize** on the menu bar
2. Highlight **Index** on the Organize menu and press ↵

At the prompt "Enter an index key expression:"

3. Type **ZIP** + **CUSTNUM** and press ↵
4. Highlight **A:** (hard-disk) or **B:** (dual-diskette) as the disk drive to search

At the prompt "Enter the name of the file:"

5. Type **DBLINDX** and press ↵

The message "100% indexed" appears.

6. List the indexed records.

From the Dot Prompt. With the CUSTOMER file active

1. Type **INDEX ON ZIP + CUSTNUM TO DBLINDX**
2. Press ↵

The message "100% indexed" appears.

3. List the indexed records.

If you wish to temporarily turn off the active index

4. Type **SET INDEX TO**

How to Sort a File

Sorting is dBASE's second method for sequentially reorganizing records in a file. The SORT command, although conceptually more straightforward than indexing, is far less efficient. Using SORT creates a new DBF file, and thus uses more memory than INDEX.

Your CUSTOMER file should still be active, from the previous sorting exercise.

From ASSIST. To sort the CUSTOMER file by CUSTNUM

1. Highlight **Organize** on the menu bar
2. Highlight **Sort** on the Organize menu and press ↵
3. Highlight **CUSTNUM** and press ↵
4. Press → to select the drive to store the sorted field—either **A:** (hard-disk system) or **B:** (dual-diskette system)
5. Press ↵

At the prompt "Enter the name of the file:"

From the Dot Prompt. To sort the CUSTOMER file by CUSTNUM

1. Type **SORT ON CUSTNUM TO NEWFILE**
2. Press ↵

Two versions of CUSTOMER now exist—an unsorted version (CUSTOMER) and a sorted version (NEWFILE).

To view the file

3. Type **USE NEWFILE** and press ↵
4. Type **LIST** and press ↵

Note: To sort a file on more than one field and to sort a

6. Type **NEWFILE** and press ↵

The message "100% sorted" appears. Two versions of CUSTOMER now exist—the unsorted version (CUSTOMER) and a sorted version (NEWFILE).

7. Highlight **Set Up** on the menu bar
8. Highlight **Database file** on the Set Up menu
9. Highlight **B:** (dual-diskette system) or **A:** (hard-disk system) and press ↵
10. Highlight **NEWFILE.DBF** and press ↵
11. Type **N**

Your status bar should now show that you are using NEWFILE.

12. List the file to inspect the newly sorted records

Note: To Sort a file on more than one field in ASSIST, select the fields in the order you desire the sort (for example, first CITY and then CUSTNUM).

key in descending order—for example, to sort with CITY as the primary key field sorted in ascending order, and CUSTNUM as the secondary key field sorted in descending order—you would type

```
SORT ON CITY,
CUSTNUM/D TO NEWFILE2
```

The /D here tells dBASE to sort CUSTNUM in descending order.

Remember to have the main database file (CUSTOMER) open each time you execute the SORT command on it.

ACCESSING DATA IN A FILE

Several useful commands to help you access the data of a file are presented next. Specifically, you will learn additional options of the LIST command, and will be introduced to the SKIP, GOTO TOP and GOTO BOTTOM, REPLACE, LOCATE, and SEEK commands.

Knowing what these commands do and how to use them will allow you to efficiently access the data in your files.

Using the LIST Command

LIST offers options in addition to those previously discussed. LIST, like DISPLAY, may be used to show selected records of a file.

This tutorial will show you how to list selected fields of a file's records, to list records with fields in a specified order, and to list a single record. The CUSTOMER file should be active.

From ASSIST. To list just the NAME field of CUSTOMER records

1. Highlight **Retrieve** on the menu bar
2. Highlight **List** on the Retrieve menu and press ↵
3. Highlight **Construct a field list** on the submenu and press ↵
4. Highlight **NAME** in the submenu of field names and press ↵
5. Press → to leave the submenu
6. Highlight **Execute the command** in the submenu and press ↵

At the question "Direct the output to the printer? [Y/N]"

7. Type **N**

Only the names in the CUSTOMER file are displayed. You may use this command to list any field(s) of a file's records. If there is more than one field you want to list, repeat step 4 again with the other fields.

To list the records in CUSTOMER with the NAME and CUSTNUM fields in reverse order

8. Repeat Steps 1 through 3
9. Highlight **NAME** in the submenu and press ↵
10. Highlight **CUSTNUM** and press ↵
11. Repeat Steps 5 through 7

Notice that in this list of CUSTOMER records the CUSTNUM field follows the NAME field.

To list Record 8 only

12. Highlight **Retrieve** on the menu bar
13. Highlight **List** on the Retrieve menu and press ↵
14. Highlight **Specify scope** and press ↵

From the Dot Prompt. To list just the NAME field of CUSTOMER's records

1. Type **LIST NAME**
2. Press ↵

Only the names in the CUSTOMER file are displayed. You may use this command to list any field(s) of a file's records. If there is more than one field you want to list, separate the field names by commas.

To list the records in CUSTOMER with the NAME and CUSTNUM fields in reverse order

3. Type **LIST NAME, CUSTNUM**
4. Press ↵

Notice that in this list of CUSTOMER records, CUSTNUM field follows the NAME field.

To list Record 8 only

5. Type **LIST RECORD 8** and press ↵

DB III PLUS

15. Highlight **Record** and press ↵

At the prompt "Enter a numeric value:"

16. Type **8** and press ↵

17. Highlight **Execute the command** and press ↵

At the question "Direct the output to the printer? [Y/N]"

18. Type **N**

Using the SKIP Command

This command will advance the pointer forward one or more records. (Remember the record pointer indicates the current record.) You can enter either a positive number to move forward that number of records in the file or a negative number to move backwards that number of records.

By using the SKIP command, you can quickly move through the records in your file.

From ASSIST. To use the SKIP command with CUSTOMER active

1. Highlight **Retrieve** on the menu bar
2. Highlight **List** on the Retrieve menu and press ↵
3. Highlight **Specify scope** and press ↵
4. Highlight **Record** and press ↵

To display record 15, at the prompt "Enter a numeric value:"

5. Type **15** and press ↵
6. Highlight **Execute the command** and press ↵
7. Press **N**
8. Press ← to highlight **Skip** on the Position menu
9. Press ↵

To skip backwards 5 records, at the prompt "Enter a numeric value:"

From the Dot Prompt. To use the SKIP command with CUSTOMER active

1. Type **LIST RECORD 14** and press ↵ to display record 14
2. Type **SKIP** and press ↵

The message "Record No. 15" is showing.

3. Type **DISPLAY** and press ↵ to display Record 15
4. Type **SKIP −5** and press ↵ to move backwards 5 records
5. Type **DISPLAY** and press ↵ to inspect the current record, Record 10

10. Type **–5** and press ↵

To display Record 10

11. Highlight **Retrieve** on the menu bar

12. Highlight **Display** on the Retrieve menu and press ↵

13. Highlight **Execute the command** and press ↵

Using the GOTO TOP and GOTO BOTTOM Commands

Two additional commands, GOTO TOP and GOTO BOTTOM, can help you move quickly through your files. These commands do just what they suggest; they respectively go to the first or last record in the file.

From ASSIST. To go to the top of your CUSTOMER file

1. Highlight **Position** on the menu bar
2. Highlight **Go To Record** on the Position menu and press ↵
3. Highlight **Top** on the submenu and press ↵
4. Highlight **Retrieve** on the menu bar
5. Highlight **Display** on the Retrieve menu and press ↵
6. Highlight **Execute the command** and press ↵

The first record is shown. To go to the bottom of your file

7. Repeat Steps 1 and 2
8. Highlight **Bottom** in the submenu and press ↵
9. Repeat Steps 4 through 6

The last record (number 16) is shown.

From the Dot Prompt. To go to the top of your CUSTOMER file

1. Type **GOTO TOP** and press ↵
2. Type **DISPLAY** and press ↵

The first record is shown. To go to the bottom of your file

3. Type **GOTO BOTTOM** and press ↵
4. Type **DISPLAY** and press ↵

The last record (number 16) is shown.

DB III PLUS

Using the REPLACE Command

You can use the **REPLACE** command to quickly replace the contents of certain fields throughout a file. This command will replace one numeric string or character string in a field with another.

From ASSIST. To replace the F in the CHARGE field for customer Wayne Montoya with a T

1. Highlight **Retrieve** on the menu bar
2. Highlight **List** on the Retrieve menu and press ↵
3. Highlight **Specify scope** and press ↵
4. Highlight **Record** and press ↵

At the prompt "Enter a numeric value:"

5. Type **8** and press ↵
6. Highlight **Update** on the menu bar
7. Highlight **Replace** on the Update menu and press ↵
8. Highlight **CHARGE** and press ↵

At the prompt "Enter a character string:"

9. Type **.T.** and press ↵
10. Press → to highlight **Execute the command**
11. Press ↵

The message "1 record replaced" appears.

12. List all of the records (or just Record 8) to see the change in Montoya's CHARGE field

From the Dot Prompt. To replace the F in the CHARGE field for customer Wayne Montoya with a T

1. Type **REPLACE CHARGE WITH .T. FOR NAME = "Wayne Montoya"**
2. Press ↵

The message "1 record replaced" appears.

3. List all of the records (or just Record 8) to see the change in Montoya's CHARGE field

Using the LOCATE Command

The **LOCATE** command will search a field for specific occurrences of data and list the number of each record containing these occurrences. In this exercise, you will locate all records for the city of Boulder.

Make sure that you are at the top of the CUSTOMER file before beginning.

From ASSIST. To use the LOCATE command

1. Highlight **Position** on the menu bar

From the Dot Prompt. To use the LOCATE command

1. Type **LOCATE FOR CITY = "Boulder"**
2. Press ↵

2. Highlight **Locate** on the Position menu and press ↵

3. Highlight **Build a search condition** and press ↵

At the prompt "Enter a character string:"

4. Highlight **CITY** and press ↵

5. Highlight **= Equal To** and press ↵

At the prompt "Enter a character string:"

6. Type **Boulder** and press ↵

7. Highlight **No more conditions** and press ↵

8. Highlight **Execute the command** and press ↵

The statement "Record=1" appears. To inspect further occurrences

9. Highlight **Position** on the menu bar

10. Highlight **Continue** on the Position menu and continue to press ↵ until all occurrences are found

At this point, the message "End of LOCATE scope" appears.

The statement "Record = #######1" appears. To continue to the next occurrence (Record = #######6)

3. Type **CONTINUE**

4. Press ↵

When you locate an occurrence, you may, of course, display the record contents.

5. Keep typing **CONTINUE** and pressing ↵ until all occurrences are found

At this point the message "End of LOCATE scope" appears.

DB III PLUS

Using the SEEK Command

The **SEEK** command is used to find records having specific characteristics in any file that has an index. Both the database file and its index file must be referenced prior to issuing the SEEK command. The index is used to find records during a SEEK process.

From ASSIST. To start the SEEK process with the CUSTOMER file and its ZIPINDX file

1. Activate the CUSTOMER file as usual, but when dBASE asks "Is the file indexed?"

2. Type **Y**

3. Highlight **ZIPINDX** on the submenu and press ↵

From the Dot Prompt. To start the SEEK process with the CUSTOMER file and its ZIPINDX file

1. Type **USE CUSTOMER INDEX ZIPINDX**

2. Press ↵

Note: Any index file can be used.

4. Press the → to leave the submenu
5. Highlight **Position** on the menu bar
6. Highlight **Seek** on the Position menu and press ↵

At the prompt "Enter an expression:"

7. Type **"80302"** and press ↵

The first occurrence of zip code 80302 is located. To see the record

8. Highlight **Retrieve** on the menu bar
9. Highlight **Display** on the Retrieve menu and press ↵
10. Highlight **Execute the command** and press ↵

3. Type **SEEK "80302"** and press ↵

The first occurrence of zip code 80302 is located. To see the record

4. Type **DISPLAY** and press ↵

Repeatedly using the SKIP command and DISPLAY will respectively show and display subsequent occurrences of the 80302 zip.

PREPARING REPORTS

One of dBASE's most useful features is its report-generation capability. A report differs significantly from a list in that you can format a report extensively and gain additional flexibility in the type of information being output.

Preparing a dBASE report involves three steps: establishing a source-data file, defining the report format, and outputting the report.

By following the steps that will be given shortly, you will be able to create the report shown in Figure DB-24. It uses the source data from the SALES file you created earlier (refer back to Figure DB-20).

Figure DB-24, in addition to showing the format of the report you'll prepare, illustrates two interesting characteristics commonly found in business reports: the *calculated field* and the *control break.*

The Amount column in Figure DB-24 is a **calculated field** that was created from two fields of the SALES file—QUANTITY and PRICE. When the values in these two fields are multiplied together, the result is the values shown in the Amount column.

After each supplier, Funk Fashions (Funk) and Peak Mountaineering (Peak), dBASE breaks to print a subtotal of the Quantity Sold and Amount columns. Such breaks are called **control breaks.** Also, at the end of the report, a final break is taken to print totals. In dBASE and in other report generators you can specify which fields you want to use to

```
Page No. 1
02/10/93

                       January Sales

                                   Quantity
Vendor     Description                 Sold        Price        Amount

** Funk
Funk    Indy Jones jacket, large         30        90.00       2700.00
Funk    Rozelle headband                 10         6.00         60.00
** Subtotal **
                                         40                    2760.00
** Peak
Peak    Nordic hat                       85        10.00        850.00
Peak    Nylon windpants                  50        40.00       2000.00
Peak    Thermal ski socks               100         7.00        700.00

** Subtotal **                          235                    3550.00

*** Total ***                           275                    6310.00
```

FIGURE DB-24
Report using data in the SALES file.

control the breaks in the report and which columns you want totaled. In Figure DB-24, the SUPPLIER field in the file (which is retitled "Vendor" as a report column) is used to control the breaks, while the Quantity Sold and Amount columns are designated as columns that will be totaled during a break.

How to Establish a Source File

The file containing the source data for the report will generally be an ordinary .DBF file. You have already created the data file SALES that you'll use to prepare the report. You must, however, have the file sorted on the SUPPLIER column in order to use this column to initiate control breaks. Control breaks are automatically taken on this column each time its value changes. Fortunately, the SALES file of Figure DB-20 is already in correct sorted order.

If the SALES file is not already open, open it now, before you define the report format.

How to Define the Report Format

This step is perhaps the most important one in creating a report. It is the step in which you tell dBASE what the report will look like, how it will be titled, what fields will be calculated or used for control breaks, and so forth. dBASE uses a special file to store all of this information about how the report will be prepared. This file is called a **report form** and has the extension of **.FRM.**

From ASSIST. To begin creating the report form (with the SALES file active)

1. Highlight **Create** on the menu bar and **Report** on the Create menu and press ↵. Highlight the drive to store the report on—**A:** (hard disk) or **B:** (dual-diskette)—and press ↵

At the prompt "Enter the name of the file:"

2. Type **SALESR** and press ↵

From the Dot Prompt. To begin creating the report form (with the SALES file active)

1. Type **CREATE REPORT SALESR**
2. Press ↵

Note: SALESR (SALESR.FRM) will be the name of our report form.

The menu in FIGURE DB-25 appears.

The menu bar at the top of the screen contains report-generation commands that you will use to prepare various parts of the report. The pull-down menu under the OPTIONS command contains a list of the default settings for the output of the report. It shows the standard page width, the left margin and right margin, as well as the lines per page. Usually these default settings will be suitable; however, you may adjust them if you wish. For this exercise, we will leave the settings as they are.

3. Press ↵ to select the Page title option

Next to the Options menu appears a box that allows you to enter a title of up to four lines for the main heading of the report. (See Figure DB-26.)

4. Type **January Sales** and press ↵

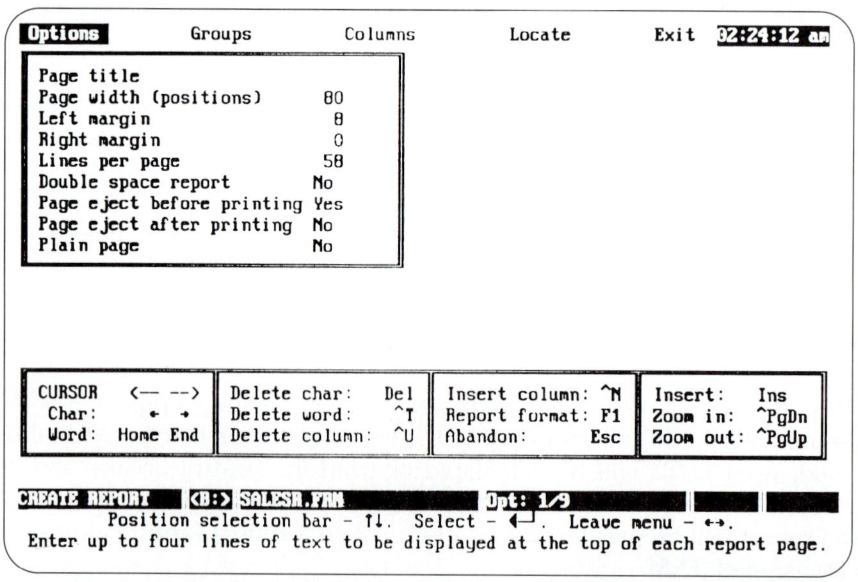

FIGURE DB-25
Initial screen for report preparation.

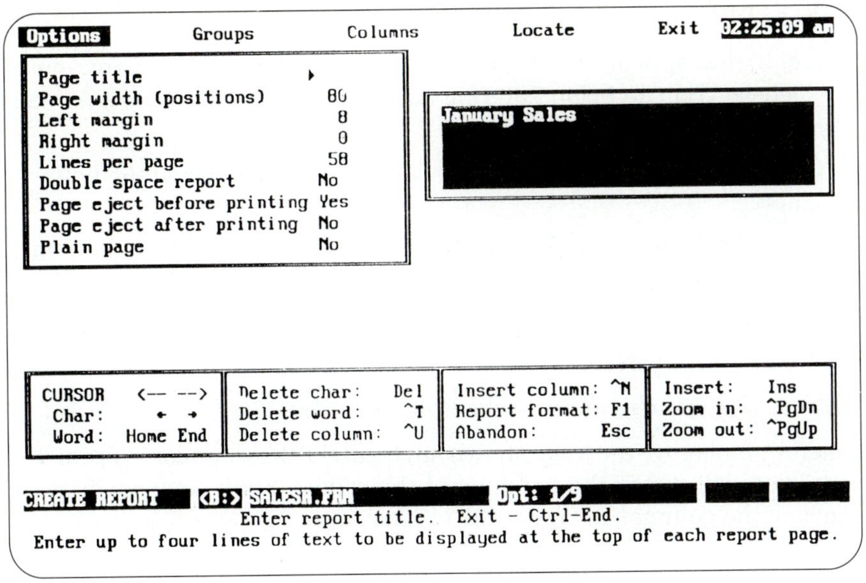

FIGURE DB-26
Establishing the report title.

5. Press **Ctrl** + **End** to save the title and exit from this screen

6. Press → once to move to the Groups menu

A screen similar to the one in Figure DB-27 appears. From this menu you can identify the field that will serve as the control-break field, which determines where subtotals will appear in the final report. When you identify SUPPLIER, each time SUPPLIER changes, a subtotal for the previous supplier will be output.

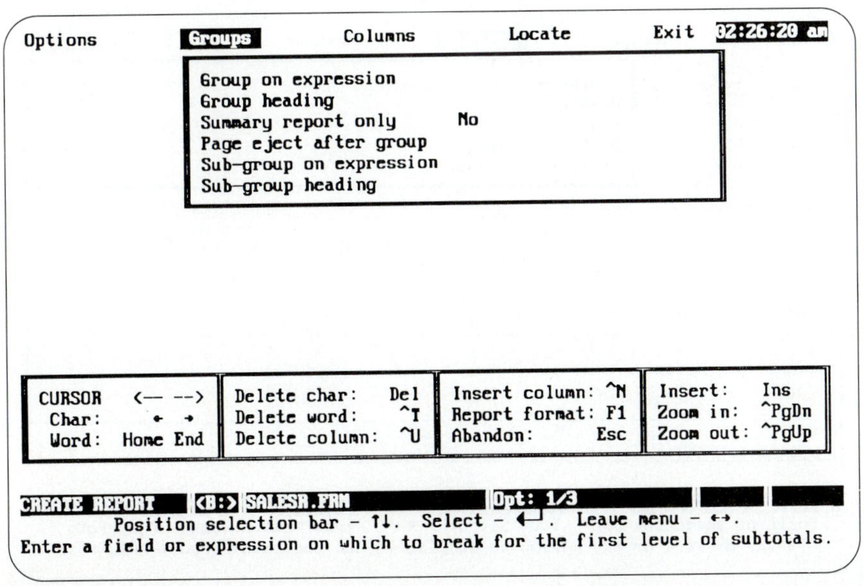

FIGURE DB-27
Identifying the control group.

DB III PLUS

7. Press ↵ to select the Group on expression option

A small arrow appears to the right of the expression. The arrow designates where you can begin entering data and signals that dBASE is ready for you to enter data.

8. Type **SUPPLIER** (in capital letters, exactly as you entered the field name)

Note: You could also press F10 to see a list of your field names. You would then highlight the correct field name and press Enter.

9. Press ↵

The arrow disappears.

10. Press → once to move to the Columns menu.

A menu similar to the one shown in Figure DB-28 appears. From this menu, you will define the columns of the report. Look once again at the names of the columns in Figure DB-24. They are

```
Vendor
Description
Quantity Sold
Price
Amount
```

A total of five columns needs to be defined for this report.

11. Press ↵ to select the first command in this menu, Contents

Note: Once again the arrow appears, indicating that you are ready to type the contents for the first column. The contents will be from one of the fields in the database file SALES.

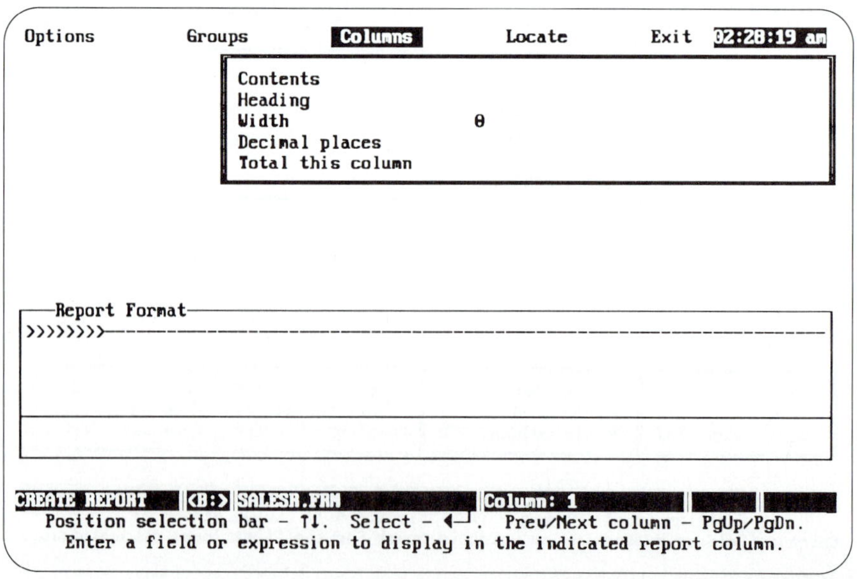

FIGURE DB-28
Menu for identifying fieldnames that will supply data for report columns.

12. Type **SUPPLIER** and press ↵ (or press **F10** to highlight SUPPLIER from a list and press ↵ twice)

Note: SUPPLIER is the field in SALES that corresponds to the Vendor column in your report, the first column in Figure DB-24).

13. Use ↓ to move to the next option, Heading

14. Press ↵

A small arrow appears to the right of Heading. A box then appears in which you can type up to four lines for the column heading.

15. Type **Vendor** for the heading and press ↵

16. Press **Ctrl** + **End** to indicate you're finished typing

That is all you need to define for this column of your report. Leave the width set at 6, which is the width of the column. The program allows you to widen columns when this is necessary.

You can leave "Decimal places" blank for this column. This specification applies only to numeric fields and is used to declare the number of places to the right of the decimal.

"Total this Column" also applies only to numeric data. When you want a field to be totaled during a control break (as in the case of the Quantity and Amount columns of this report), you would type Y (for yes) for this item; otherwise, type N (for no).

17. Press **Pg Dn** to begin identifying the next column

18. Set the remaining columns as shown in Figure DB-29

As you type column headings, you can improve their placement over the data by pressing the spacebar to add leading blanks (shown in Figure DB-29 as *b*'s).

For a two-line heading like "Quantity Sold," press the Enter key after typing "Quantity" to start the "Sold" line. On the pull-down menu, the line break for a heading will be indicated with a semicolon (Quantity; Sold).

As you are entering the remaining column headings, watch the bottom of the screen. A sample report format shows exactly what the layout of your report will look like when printed. The XXXXs represent the width of a character column. The #####s represent the width of a column

Contents field	Headings field	Width field	Total-this-column field
SUPPLIER	Vendor	6	–
DESCRIP	*bbb*Description	25	–
QUANTITY	*b*Quantity *bbb*Sold	9	Yes
PRICE	*bbb*Price	8	No
QUANTITY*PRICE	*bbbb*Amount	10	Yes

b = leading blank

FIGURE DB-29

Data specified under "Columns" option on Report menu bar.

Adding leading blanks before a column title will help center it over the column's contents on output.

DB III PLUS

that contains a totaled numeric field. The 999s represent the width of a nontotaled numeric column.

Pg Up and Pg Dn will move you back and forth through your columns to let you make a change in the layout.

When you have finished with the description of the report layout, the Report Format section of the screen should look like Figure DB-30. (Press Pg Up until "Vendor" can be seen at the left of this section.)

19. Press → twice to exit the menu

20. Press ↵ on the Save option

The report form is saved, and you return to the ASSIST mode.

How to Output the Report

In this step you point dBASE to the report form that you want to output and instruct dBASE to display the report or to send the report to the printer.

From ASSIST. To output the report

1. Highlight **Retrieve** on the menu bar
2. Highlight **Report** on the Retrieve menu and press ↵
3. Highlight the drive the report is stored on—B: (dual-diskette

From the Dot Prompt. To output the report

1. Type **REPORT FORM SALESR TO PRINT**
2. Press ↵

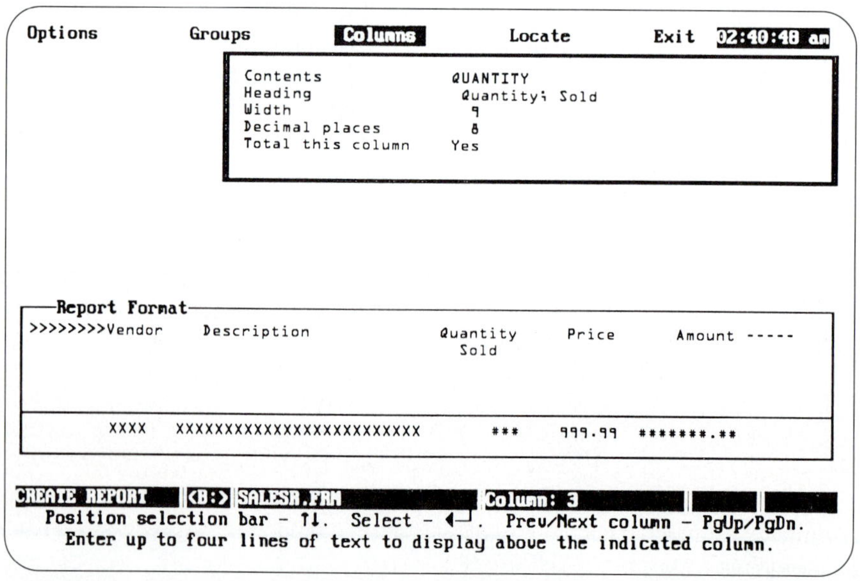

FIGURE DB-30
Final report mockup, when leaving the Columns command on the menu bar.

system) or A: (hard-disk system)—and press ↵

4. Highlight **SALESR.FRM** from the submenu and press ↵
5. Highlight **Execute the command** and press ↵

At the question "Direct output to the printer?"

6. Type **Y**

Advanced Reports

dBASE also enables you to perform a number of other operations in developing reports. Here, we will mention these only in passing, leaving it as an end-of-tutorials, hands-on exercise for you to do.

Preparing a Report from Selected Records. Doing this is relatively easy. Suppose, for instance, that we wish to prepare a report from only those records of the SALES file where the PRICE field exceeds $8.00. Such a condition would allow only the Indy Jones jacket, the nordic hat, and the nylon windpants to be used in the report; the other two records would be ignored. To produce such a report

From ASSIST.

1. Highlight **Report** from the Retrieve menu and press ↵
2. Choose the drive containing SALESR.FRM and select this report form
3. Build the search condition PRICE > 8
4. Execute the command and press any key when you're through looking at the report

From the Dot Prompt.

1. Type **REPORT FORM SALESR FOR PRICE > 8**
2. Press ↵

DB III PLUS

Preparing a Report That Contains Only Subtotals. To do this, you will need to use dBASE's MODIFY REPORT command, which enables you to change your report form. MODIFY REPORT lets you add or delete columns to reports, alter such report definitions as column widths and column titles, and change a variety of other characteristics about the report. Before you make any modifications to a report form, however, you should first back up the existing report form, using either the COPY command of DOS or the COPY command of dBASE (covered in the Command Reference). This ensures that you will easily be able to recover if you make a mistake modifying the form.

To prepare a report containing only subtotals,

From ASSIST.

1. Highlight **Report** from the Modify menu and press ↵
2. Highlight the name of the report form, SALESR.FRM, and press ↵

From the Dot Prompt.

1. Type **MODIFY REPORT SALESR**
2. Press ↵

When the report-form screen appears, highlight Groups and change the "Summary Report Only" line from "No" to "Yes" (refer back to Figure DB-27 to see a sample of this screen). To save the modified report form

1. Highlight **Exit** on the menu bar
2. Press ↵

When you subsequently run the report on the screen or the printer, you should get a report that looks like the one in Figure DB-31.

Inserting and Deleting Report Columns. Again, you would use the MODIFY REPORT command for such tasks.

To *delete* a column in a report form, you first highlight the Locate command on the report-form menu bar. This will display the column names in a pull-down menu. Simply select the name you wish to delete and press

Ctrl + **U**

The associated column, as you will notice, will be deleted from the report. To save the change, follow the exiting procedure described in the previous subsection.

FIGURE DB-31

Summary report using data in the SALES file.

```
Page No.  1
02/10/93

                         January Sales

Vendor    Description                   Quantity      Price        Amount
                                            Sold

** Funk
** Subtotal **
                                              40                  2760.00
** Peak
** Subtotal **
                                             235                  3550.00

*** Total ***                                275                  6310.00
```

To *insert* a column, you follow a similar procedure. From the pull-down menu on the Columns command, select the already present column name you want to come *after* the new column you are inserting and press

Ctrl + **N**

Then, insert the new column name. Remember also at this point that you will have to use the Columns command to define what the new column will look like—that is, its contents, heading, width, and so on (refer back to Figure DB-28). (dBASE places a question mark (?) in the bottom-of-screen report mockup, in the place where the new column is to be inserted, cautioning you that it won't know what the new column will look like until you reinvoke the Columns command.) To save changes after you've fully defined the new column, follow the exiting procedure described in the subtotals-only subsection.

COMMAND REFERENCE

This section briefly summarizes many of the most-used commands in dBASE III PLUS. It is meant to be used only as a reference after completing the full dBASE instructions contained in the preceding chapters.

Note: In this reference

1. The examples contain general terms, such as field name, filename, record number, and so on, within angle brackets (< >). When you issue the commands shown in the examples, you must enter the *actual* field name, filename, record number, etc. Do not type in the brackets.
2. To "select" an item from a menu means the same thing as highlighting it and pressing the Enter key ↵.

DB III PLUS

Adding Records to a File

To add records to a file:

From ASSIST.

Select **Append** from the Update menu

From the Dot Prompt.

Type **APPEND** ↵

Averaging Values in a Field

To average the values in a field:

From ASSIST.

1. Select **Average** from the Retrieve menu
2. Select **Construct a field list**
3. Select a numeric field name
4. Select **Execute the command**

From the Dot Prompt.

Type **AVERAGE <field name>** ↵

Canceling a Command

To cancel a command:

From ASSIST.

Press **Esc**

From the Dot Prompt.

Press **Esc**

Changing the Structure of a Database File

To modify the structure of a database file:

From ASSIST.

Select **Database file** from the Modify menu

From the Dot Prompt.

Type **MODIFY STRUCTURE** ↵

Closing a File

To close a database file:

From ASSIST. When a new database file is opened in the active file's work area, or you quit dBASE, the active database is automatically closed.

From the Dot Prompt. Close files as you would in ASSIST or

Type **CLOSE DATABASES** ↵

Copying Records

To copy all records to a new database file:

From ASSIST.

1. Select **Copy** from the Organize menu

2. Highlight the target drive and press ↵

3. Type the name of the new database file and press ↵

4. Select **Execute the command**

From the Dot Prompt.

Type **COPY TO <new filename>** ↵

Counting Records

To count all records in a file:

From ASSIST.

1. Select **Count** from the Retrieve menu

2. Select **Execute the command**

From the Dot Prompt.

Type **COUNT** ↵

To count only those records meeting specific conditions:

From ASSIST.
Example: Counting records from the state of Washington

1. Select **Count** from the Retrieve menu

2. Select **Build a search condition**

3. Select **STATE**

4. Select = **Equal to**

5. Type **WA**

6. Select **No more conditions**

7. Select **Execute the command**

From the Dot Prompt.
Example: Counting records from the state of Washington

Type **COUNT FOR STATE = "WA"** ↵

Creating a Database File

To create, name, and define the structure of a database file:

From ASSIST.

1. Select **Database file** from the Create menu
2. Select **A:** (hard-disk system) or **B:** (dual-diskette system) as the default drive
3. Type in the name of the file and press ↵
4. With the field-definition form onscreen, for each field in the database file:
   - **a.** Type a field name and press ↵
   - **b.** Type the first letter of the field descriptor
   - **c.** Type the field width and press ↵
   - **d.** If appropriate, type the number of decimals and press ↵
5. When finished, press ↵ to save and exit
6. Type **Y** or **N** to respond to the "Input data records now?" prompt

From the Dot Prompt.

1. Type **SET DEFAULT TO A:** (hard-disk system) or **SET DEFAULT TO B:** (dual-diskette system) and press ↵
2. Type **CREATE** <**filename**> ↵
3. With the field-definition form onscreen, for each field in the database file:
   - **a.** Type a field name and press ↵
   - **b.** Type the first letter of the field descriptor
   - **c.** Type the field width and press ↵
   - **d.** If appropriate, type the number of decimals and press ↵
4. When finished, press ↵ to save and exit
5. Type **Y** or **N** to respond to "Input data records now?" prompt

Defining the Structure of a Database File

See "Creating a Database File."

Deleting Records

The DELETE command marks a record for deletion with an asterisk (*) without actually physically removing it.

To mark a single record for deletion:

From ASSIST.

1. Select **Delete** from the Update menu
2. Select **Specify scope**
3. Select **Record**
4. Type in the number of the record to be deleted and press ↵
5. Select **Execute the command**

From the Dot Prompt.

Type **DELETE RECORD <record number>** ↵

To mark several records meeting a specific condition for deletion:

From ASSIST.
Example: Deleting records where STATE = 'CO'

1. Select **Delete** from the Update menu
2. Select **Build a search condition**
3. Select **STATE**
4. Select = **Equal To** and type **CO**
5. Select **No more conditions**
6. Select **Execute the command**

From the Dot Prompt.
Example: Deleting records where STATE = 'CO'

Type **DELETE FOR STATE = "CO"** ↵

To delete records permanently after they are marked with an asterisk (*) with the DELETE command:

From ASSIST.

Select **Pack** from the Update menu

From the Dot Prompt.

Type **PACK** ↵

Displaying a Database Structure

To display the structure of an active database file:

From ASSIST.

1. Select **List structure** from the Tools menu
2. Type **Y** to print or **N**

From the Dot Prompt.

Type **DISPLAY STRUCTURE** ↵

Displaying a File Directory

To display the names of all files with a .DBF extension:

From ASSIST.

1. Select **Directory** from the Tools menu
2. Select **A:** (hard-disk system) or **B:** (dual-diskette system)
3. Select **.DBF Database Files**

From the Dot Prompt.

Type **DIR** ↵

To display the names of all files with a specific extension:

From ASSIST.

1. Select **Directory** from the Tools menu
2. Select **A:** (hard-disk system) or **B:** (dual-diskette system)
3. Select desired file extension

From the Dot Prompt.

Type **DIR *.<file extension>** ↵

Displaying Records and Fields

To display all records in the file, one screen at a time:

From ASSIST.

1. Select **Display** from the Retrieve menu
2. Select **Specify scope**

3. Select **All**

4. Select **Execute the command**

From the Dot Prompt.

Type **DISPLAY ALL** ↵

To display all records in the file, but only specific fields in them:

From ASSIST.

1. Select **Display** from the Retrieve menu

2. Select **Specify scope**

3. Select **All**

4. Select **Construct a field list**

5. For each field, highlight the field name and press ↵

6. Press →

7. Select **Execute the command**

From the Dot Prompt.

Type **DISPLAY ALL OFF <field name>, <field name>, . . .** ↵

To display all records in the file that meet a specific condition:

From ASSIST.
Example: Displaying records from the state of Washington (STATE = "WA")

1. Select **Display** from the Retrieve menu

2. Select **Build a search condition**

3. Select **State**

4. Select = **Equal to**

5. Type **WA**

6. Select **No more conditions**

7. Select **Execute the command**

From the Dot Prompt.
Examples:
To display records from the state of Washington (STATE = "WA"),

Type **DISPLAY ALL OFF FOR STATE = "WA"** ↵

To display records from Washington and Colorado (STATE = "WA" and STATE = "CO"),

Type **DISPLAY ALL OFF FOR STATE = "WA" .AND. STATE = "CO"** ↵

To display records from Washington or Colorado (STATE = "WA" or STATE = "CO"),

Type **DISPLAY ALL OFF FOR STATE = "WA" .OR. STATE = "CO"** ↵

To show all records without the record numbers,

Type **DISPLAY ALL OFF** ↵

Editing Records

To edit records using the BROWSE command:

From ASSIST.

1. Select **Browse** from the Update menu

2. For each edit:

a. Use the arrow keys to go to the place in a record you would like to make an edit

b. Type in the change and press ↵

From the Dot Prompt.

1. Type **BROWSE** ↵

2. For each edit:

a. Use the arrow keys to go to the place in a record you would like to make an edit

b. Type in the change and press ↵

To edit records using the EDIT command:

From ASSIST.

1. Select **Edit** from the Update menu

2. For each edit:

a. Use the arrow keys to go to the place in a record you would like to make an edit

b. Type in the change and press ↵

From the Dot Prompt.

1. Type **EDIT RECORD <record number>** ↵

2. For each edit:

a. Use the arrow keys to go to the place in a record you would like to make an edit

b. Type in the change and press ↵

Help Feature

To get help while working in dBASE, from either mode:

Press **F1**

Indexing Records

Indexing records in a .DBF file allows them to be output in an order different from the one in which they are physically stored.

From ASSIST. To create a single-key-field index for the file you are currently pointed to:

1. Select **Index** from the Organize menu

2. Press the **F10** function key for a field list

3. Highlight the field name that will be used to arrange the file

4. Select **A:** (hard-disk system) or **B:** (dual-diskette system) as the drive

5. Type in the index name and press ↵

From the Dot Prompt. To create a single-key index for any field of the active database file:

Type **INDEX ON <field name> TO <index name>** ↵

To create a two-key index for the active database file,

Type **INDEX ON <field name> + <field name> . . . TO <index name>** ↵

To activate one or more indexes for use,

Type **SET INDEX TO <index name>, < index name> . . .** ↵

To update all active indexes,

Type **REINDEX** ↵

Listing Records

To list all records of the active file:

From ASSIST.

1. Select **List** from the Retrieve menu

2. Select **Execute the command**

3. Type **N**

From the Dot Prompt.

Type **LIST** ↵

To list selected fields:

From ASSIST.

1. Select **List** from the Retrieve menu

2. Select **Construct a field list**

3. Select the first field name

4. Select the second field name, third field name, etc.

5. Select **Execute the command**

6. Type **N**

From the Dot Prompt.

Type **LIST <field name>, <field name>, . . .** ↵

To List a single record:

From ASSIST.

1. Select **List** from the Retrieve menu

2. Select **Specify scope**

3. Select **Record**

4. Type <**record number**> and press ↵

5. Select **Execute the command**

6. Type **N**

From the Dot Prompt.

Type **LIST RECORD** <**record number**> ↵

Opening a File

To open a previously created database file:

From ASSIST.

1. Select **Database file** from the Set Up menu

2. Select **A:** (hard-disk system) or **B:** (dual-diskette system)

3. Select the filename

4. Type **Y** if the file is indexed or **N** if the file is not indexed.

5. If the file is indexed, highlight the filename and press ↵

From the Dot Prompt.

Type **USE <filename>** ↵

Positioning the Record Pointer

To go to the top of a file:

From ASSIST.

1. Select **Goto Record** from the Position menu

2. Select **Top**

From the Dot Prompt.

Type **GOTO TOP** ↵

To go to the bottom of a file:

From ASSIST.

1. Select **Goto Record** from the Position menu

2. Select **Bottom**

From the Dot Prompt.

Type **GOTO BOTTOM** ↵

To go to a specific record in a file:

From ASSIST.

1. Select **Goto Record** from the Position menu

2. Select **Record**

3. Type the record number and press ↵

From the Dot Prompt.

Type **GOTO <record number>** ↵

To go to the next record in a file:

From ASSIST.

1. Select **Skip** from the Position menu

2. Type **1** and press ↵

From the Dot Prompt.

Type **SKIP** ↵

To go to the previous record in a file:

From ASSIST.

1. Select **Skip** from the Position menu

2. Type **−1** and press ↵

From the Dot Prompt.

Type **SKIP −1** ↵

Printing Records

To print all records:

From ASSIST.

1. Select **List** from the Retrieve menu

2. Select **Execute the command**

3. Type **Y**

From the Dot Prompt.

Type **LIST TO PRINT** ↵

To print selected fields of all records:

From ASSIST.

1. Select **List** from the Retrieve menu

2. Select **Construct a field list**

3. For each field, highlight the field name and press ↵

4. Press →

5. Select **Execute the command**

6. Press **Y**

From the Dot Prompt.

Type **LIST TO PRINT <field name>, <field name>, . . .** ↵

To print selected records:

From ASSIST.

1. Select **List** from the Retrieve menu

2. Select **Build a search condition**

3. For each condition:

  a. Highlight the field name and press ↵

  b. Highlight the operator and press ↵

  c. Type a value and press ↵

4. Select **No more conditions**

5. Select **Execute the command**

6. Type **Y**

From the Dot Prompt.

Type **LIST TO PRINT FOR <fieldname,operator,value>, <field name,operator,value>, . . .** ↵

Quitting dBASE

To quit dBASE:

From ASSIST.

Select **Quit dBASE III PLUS** from the Set Up menu

From the Dot Prompt.

Type **QUIT** ↵

Recalling Records Marked for Deletion

To recall records marked with an asterisk (*) through the DELETE command:

From ASSIST.

1. Select **Recall** from the Update menu

2. Select **Specify scope**

3. Select **record**

4. Type in a record number and press ↵

5. Select **Execute the command**

From the Dot Prompt.

Type **RECALL RECORD <record number>** ↵

You can also recall all records or selected records. To recall all records, select *ALL* instead of *Record* in step 3 of the ASSIST mode or type **RECALL ALL** ↵ in COMMAND mode. To recall selected records, follow the same types of procedures that you would for building conditions when deleting selected records.

Replacing Data

From ASSIST. To replace data in records (starting from the top of the file):

1. Select **Replace** from the Update menu

2. Select a field name

3. Type in the new data and press ↵

4. Select **Execute the command**

From the Dot Prompt. To replace data in records (starting from the top of the file):

Type **REPLACE <field name> WITH <new data>** ↵

To replace data in records that meet specific conditions:

Type **REPLACE <field name> WITH <new data> FOR <field name,operator,value>** ↵

Example:

Type **REPLACE STATUS WITH .Y. FOR NAME = "Sam Jones"** ↵

Reports

To create a report:

From ASSIST.

1. Select **Report** from the Create menu

2. Select **A:** (hard-disk system) or **B:** (dual-diskette system) as the default drive

3. Type in the report name and press ↵

From the Dot Prompt.

Type **CREATE REPORT <report name>** ↵

To display a report on the screen:

From ASSIST.

1. Select **Report** from the Retrieve menu
2. Select **A:** (hard-disk system) or **B:** (dual-diskette system)
3. Select the report name
4. Select **Execute the command**
5. Type **N**

From the Dot Prompt.

Type **REPORT FORM <report name>** ↵

To modify a report:

From ASSIST.

1. Select **Report** from the Modify menu
2. Select **A:** (hard-disk system) or **B:** (dual-diskette system)
3. Select the report name

From the Dot Prompt.

Type **MODIFY REPORT <report name>** ↵

To print a report:

From ASSIST.

1. Select **Report** from the Retrieve menu
2. Select **A:** (hard-disk system) or **B:** (dual-diskette system)
3. Select the report name
4. Select **Execute the command**
5. Type **Y**

From the Dot Prompt.

Type **REPORT FORM <report name> TO PRINT** ↵

Saving Changes

To save changes to a database file:

From ASSIST and the Dot Prompt.

Close the database file

To save changes to a record:

From ASSIST and the Dot Prompt.

Move to another record in the file

To save changes to a database structure, or report form:

From ASSIST and the Dot Prompt.

Exit the structure or form, choosing the Save option when prompted

Searching for Records

Use the LOCATE command to make searches. To locate the first occurrence of a specific value in a field (starting from the top of the file):

From ASSIST.
Example: Locating the first Seattle record

1. Select **Locate** from the Position menu
2. Select **Build a search condition**
3. Select **CITY**
4. Select = **Equal to**
5. Type **SEATTLE**
6. Select **No more conditions**
7. Select **Execute the command**

From the Dot Prompt.
Example: Locating the first Seattle record

Type **LOCATE FOR CITY = "SEATTLE"** ↵

To locate the next occurrence, you would issue the CONTINUE command. Keep issuing the CONTINUE command until all occurrences of the condition you specified are found. The message "End of Locate Scope" will appear when all occurrences have been found.

From ASSIST.

Select **Continue** from the Position menu

From the Dot Prompt.

Type **CONTINUE** ↵

Use the SEEK command to search for records *only* when the file has been indexed. To search for records using the SEEK command (starting from the top of the file):

From ASSIST.

1. Select **Database file** from the Set Up menu

2. Select **A:** (hard-disk system) or **B:** (dual-diskette system)

3. Select the database file

4. Type **Y**

5. Select the index file

6. Select **Seek** from the Position menu

7. Type in the data and press ↵

8. Select **Display** from the Retrieve menu

9. Select **Execute the command**

From the Dot Prompt.

1. Type **USE < database file> INDEX < index file>** ↵

2. Type **SEEK < data>** ↵

3. Type **DISPLAY** ↵

Setting the Default Drive

To set the default drive:

From ASSIST.

1. Select **Set drive** from the Tools menu

2. Select **A:** (hard-disk system) or **B:** (dual-diskette system)

From the Dot Prompt.

Type **SET DEFAULT TO A:** (hard-disk system) or **SET DEFAULT TO B:** (dual-diskette system) ↵

Sorting Records

To reorganize the order of records in a file:

From ASSIST.

1. Select **Sort** from the Organize menu
2. Select the field name(s) that will be used to arrange the file (If more than one field name is selected, use → to exit the field list.)
3. Select **A:** (hard-disk system) or **B:** (dual-diskette system)
4. Type in the name of the new file and press ↵

From the Dot Prompt.

To sort on a single key field, type **SORT ON** < **field name**> **TO** <**new sorted filename**> ↵

To list a sorted file:

From ASSIST.

1. Select **Database file** from the Set Up menu
2. Select **A:** (hard-disk system) or **B:** (dual-diskette system)
3. Select the name of the new file
4. Type **N**
5. Select **List** from the Retrieve menu
6. Select **Execute the command**
7. Type **N**

From the Dot Prompt.

1. Type **USE** < **new sorted filename**> ↵
2. Type **LIST** ↵

Starting dBASE III PLUS

To start the program:

With a Hard-Disk System

1. Change to the dBASE subdirectory
2. At the dBASE prompt, type **dBASE** (in upper or lower case) and press ↵

With a Dual-Diskette System

1. Insert the System 1 disk in Drive A
2. Insert the data disk in Drive B
3. Type **dBASE** at the A> prompt
4. Press ↵
5. Follow the screen messages and insert the System 2 disk in Drive A when prompted to do so
6. Press ↵

Summing Values in a Field

To sum the values in a field

From ASSIST.

1. Select **Sum** from the Retrieve menu
2. Select **Construct a field list**
3. Select the field name
4. Select **Execute the command**

From the Dot Prompt.

Type **SUM** < **field name**> ↵

Example: To sum values in records that meet a specific condition:

Type **SUM PRICE FOR SUPPLIER = "SeaTech Corp."** ↵

Switching Modes

When in ASSIST Mode, to switch to the Dot Prompt

Press **Esc**

When in the Dot Prompt, to switch to ASSIST:

Press **F2** or type **ASSIST** ↵

GLOSSARY

Active. Refers to a dBASE file that is open and ready for use.

APPEND. The dBASE command used to place records into a file.

ASSIST mode. The system of menus by which dBASE lets users invoke commands by simply selecting them. Contrast with COMMAND mode.

BROWSE. A dBASE command that enables users to perform full-screen editing and appending.

Calculated field. A report field that is calculated from fields within the file structure.

COMMAND mode. Refers to operating dBASE by typing in commands at the dot prompt. Contrast with ASSIST mode.

Control break. A term that refers to "breaks" in the normal flow of record information in a report that periodically occur for subtotals and totals.

CREATE. The dBASE command used to develop a database file structure.

Database. A term that is commonly used to refer to a set of related files.

Database file. See File.

DBF. The extension dBASE uses for a database file.

DELETE. The dBASE command used to mark records for removal.

DISPLAY. The dBASE command used to output records onscreen.

DISPLAY STRUCTURE. The dBASE command used to output a file structure onscreen.

Dot prompt. The period character, used to tell dBASE operators that dBASE expects a command to be entered from the command mode.

EDIT. A dBASE command that enables you to modify records.

Field. A collection of related characters.

Field descriptors. A code or word used to describe the type of data—say, numeric, character, or logical—that occupies a given field in a data record.

File. A collection of related records.

FRM. The extension used by dBASE for a file that stores a report form.

INDEX. The dBASE command used to index files.

Indexing. A method used to specify how records are arranged in a file, without physically sorting the data records.

Key field. A field used to arrange records.

LOCATE. A dBASE command that repositions the record pointer.

Logical connective. The keywords AND, OR, and NOT, when used in a field having a logical value.

Menu bar. The top-of-screen line of choices in the initial ASSIST screen.

MODIFY STRUCTURE. The dBASE command used to change the structure of a database file.

NDX. The extension used by dBASE for index files.

Open. The act of making a file available for processing.

PACK. The dBASE command used to permanently remove data records from a database file.

Pull-down menus. In ASSIST, the vertical menus that can be accessed off the top-of-screen menu bar.

RECALL. The dBASE command that restores records made temporarily inaccessable by the DELETE command.

Record. A collection of related fields.

Relational operator. A character in a logical expression—such as < (less than), > (greater than), or = (equal to)—that compares the contents of two fields.

REPLACE. The dBASE command used to make mass alterations to records in a database file.

Report form. A specification telling what a report is supposed to look like.

SEEK. The dBASE command used to find, in an indexed file, records with specific characteristics.

SORT. The dBASE command used to physically rearrange a file.

Status bar. The bottom-of-screen display bar that shows specific characteristics about the current dBASE file or operation.

Structure. A collection of information about the fields of a file, including the names, lengths, and the types of the fields.

USE. The dBASE command used to open files, thereby making them available for processing.

REVIEW QUESTIONS

1. List the following database elements in order from largest to smallest: record, file, field, database.
2. How do you move from one choice to another on ASSIST's main menu bar?
3. What five field descriptors are used in dBASE III PLUS?
4. How are records
   - a. Marked for deletion?
   - b. Permanently deleted?
5. What command is used to add records to a database file?
6. Write the DISPLAY statement that you would type at the dot prompt to list each of the following:
   - a. The fields NAME, ADDRESS, and ZIP of the current database file
   - b. All records for those persons with a zip code of 98026 (assume the zip-code field is called ZIP)
   - c. All persons whose NAME is Smith and whose ZIP is 98112

7. What command in ASSIST and COMMAND tallies all records in a database field?
8. What command in ASSIST or COMMAND sums a numeric field in several records?
9. In COMMAND mode, what command would you type to create an index on the NAME field for a new index file called NAMEINDX?
10. What command is used in either ASSIST or COMMAND to move quickly to the
    a. First record in a file?
    b. Last record in a file?
11. **a.** To quickly replace the contents of certain fields throughout an entire database, what command would you use in either ASSIST or COMMAND?
    b. What command would you type at the dot prompt to replace the logical field MEMBER with .F. for all zip code areas of 98027 throughout an entire database?
12. How would you locate the first record in a file having a ZIP of 98027 in COMMAND mode?

ANSWERS

1. Database, file, record, and field. **2.** Press the left and right arrow keys or type the first character of the menu. **3.** Numeric, character, memo, logical, date. **4. a.** Issuing the DELETE command **b.** Issuing the PACK command **5.** APPEND. **6. a.** DISPLAY ALL NAME, ADDRESS, ZIP **b.** DISPLAY ALL FOR ZIP = "98026" **c.** DISPLAY ALL FOR NAME = "Smith" .AND. ZIP = "98112" **7.** COUNT. **8.** SUM. **9.** INDEX ON NAME TO NAMEINDX. **10. a.** GOTO TOP **b.** GOTO BOTTOM **11. a.** REPLACE **b.** REPLACE MEMBER WITH .F. FOR ZIP = "98027" **12.** LOCATE FOR ZIP = "98027"

HANDS-ON EXERCISES

Hands-on Exercise 1: Employee Donations Records

In this exercise you will practice

☐ Creating a database file

☐ Defining the fields in a file

☐ Adding records to a file

☐ Listing records

☐ Leaving and reentering the database file

☐ Viewing the directory

☐ Setting the default drive

☐ Using a stored file

☐ Printing a file

1. Create a database file called EMPLOYEE for the records described below. Count the maximum number of characters used in each column to decide on the width of each of the fields. Define SALARY and DONATION as numeric, EMPLOYED as date, and all other fields as character fields.

The fields are:

EMPLOYEE
TELEPHONE
GENDER
EMPLOYED
SALARY
DONATION

The employees are:

Pratt, John
225-1234
M
06/22/92
1949.00
200.00

Jones, David
292-3832
M
06/15/88
1500.00
225.00

Smoller, Ellen
225-3212
F
09/15/88
1650.00
300.00

Sill, Sally
224-4321
F
02/15/87
1800.00
150.00

Knat, Michael
221-1235
M
09/15/80
1700.00
350.00

Smith, Paul
223-8251
M
11/01/85
1800.00
200.50

2. After defining the fields, exit without entering data
3. Use the APPEND command to enter data
4. Exit from the program
5. Sign on to the program
6. Set the default drive
7. View the directory to be sure EMPLOYEE is listed
8. Open the database file, EMPLOYEE
9. List the file to be sure it is accurate
10. Add the following three records:

Martins, Mary
222-2123
F
11/01/93
1850.00
175.00

Beam, Sandy
225-6912
F
02/15/93
1450.00
275.00

Johnson, Frank
223-7928
M
03/20/93
1500.00
0.00

11. Print a copy of the file's records

Hands-on Exercise 2: Payroll Reporting

In this exercise you will practice

- ☐ Creating a database file
- ☐ Defining the fields in a file
- ☐ Using the APPEND command
- ☐ Deleting, recalling, and packing records
- ☐ Sorting data
- ☐ Listing specific records and fields
- ☐ Using the DISPLAY command
- ☐ Using the EDIT and BROWSE commands

1. Create a database file called PAYROLL. It will contain the following fields:

   ID_NUMBER
   EMP_NAME
   DEPARTMENT
   PAY_RATE

   Count the maximum number of characters used in each column to decide the width of each of the fields. PAY_RATE is a numeric field; all other fields are character.

2. Immediately after defining the fields, enter the data shown below:

   278
   Dougherty, Ronald H.
   MIS
   12.50

   178
   Jordan, James
   Payroll
   15.50

   292
   Smith, Bonnie
   Customer Services
   13.40

   346
   Clement, Cynthia
   MIS
   18.90

415
Zonguldake, Helen
Personnel
12.00

595
Foster, Donald
MIS
22.00

150
VanderZee, Charles
Personnel
20.00

420
Aiken, Helen
Payroll
17.50

3. Sort the file in alphabetical order on EMP_NAME

4. Print a copy of the file

5. Use the BROWSE command to change the following:
   a. Ronald Dougherty's pay rate to $13.00
   b. Bonnie Smith's department to Personnel
   c. Helen Zonguldake's department to Customer Services

6. Use the LIST command to show all persons working in the MIS department. Show the names and departments only.

7. Use the DISPLAY command to show the following:
   a. The names of all persons in the Payroll department
   b. The names of all persons earning more than $15.00 an hour
   c. the names of all persons who are either working in MIS or making less than $20.00 an hour

8. Mark Record 4, Cynthia Clement, for deletion. List the file to be sure it is marked. Recall the record. List or browse the file again to be sure the record is no longer marked.

9. Delete Helen Aiken's record permanently from the file, using the DELETE and PACK commands. List or browse the file again to be sure the record is gone.

10. Sort the file by DEPARTMENT in descending order and by NAME in ascending order. Print a copy of the sorted file.

11. Use the LIST command to show Record 3, Bonnie Smith

12. Use the EDIT command to edit Record 3, making the following changes:

a. Add a J. as the middle initial

b. Change the pay rate to 24.00

13. Print the file

Hands-on Exercise 3: Software Sales Sheet

In this exercise you will practice

☐ Creating a database file

☐ Modifying the file

☐ Creating an index

☐ Creating a report

1. Create a database file called SOFTWARE for the first five columns of the table shown in Figure DB-32. (Do not create the sixth column, TOTAL, yet. We will use the database system's report generation feature to create this column in part 4 of this exercise.) Make PRICE and QUANTITY numeric fields, DATE SOLD a date field, and CUSTNUM and ITEM character fields.

2. Create an index file called ITEMINDX using ITEM as the key field. The index should arrange records in alphabetical order.

3. List the records

CUSTNUM	ITEM	DATE SOLD	PRICE	QUANTITY	TOTAL
1232	Database Text	01/10/93	200.00	1	200.00
2388	Database Text	01/10/93	200.00	1	200.00
3445	Database Tutor	01/08/93	70.00	1	70.00
3442	Database Tutor	01/08/93	70.00	1	70.00
1232	Graphics	01/09/93	200.00	2	400.00
6224	Database Tutor	01/09/93	70.00	1	70.00
1232	Reports Pkg	01/09/93	150.00	1	150.00
1332	Spreadsheet	01/09/93	150.00	3	450.00
2445	Spreadsheet	01/11/93	150.00	1	150.00
2443	Time Mgt	01/09/93	300.00	2	600.00
6223	Time Mgt	01/10/93	300.00	3	900.00
3445	Database Text	01/11/93	200.00	3	600.00
5122	Database Text	01/11/93	200.00	5	1000.00
5223	Database Text	01/11/93	200.00	3	600.00
5432	Database Text	02/10/93	200.00	1	200.00
6223	Graphics	01/20/93	200.00	5	1000.00
2883	Reports Pkg	02/10/93	150.00	2	300.00
2443	Reports Pkg	02/05/93	150.00	3	450.00

FIGURE DB-32
Hands-on Exercise 3: Software sales file.

4. Create a report with the following specifications:

a. Specify the report title as

SOFTWARE MANUAL SALES
JANUARY 10 THROUGH FEBRUARY 10, 1992

b. Use the following column headings:

CUSTOMER NUMBER	ITEM SOLD	DATE SOLD	UNIT PRICE	QUANTITY SOLD	TOTAL SALE

Note that the data in the Total Sale column (see TOTAL column in Figure DB-32) is computed by multiplying PRICE by QUANTITY.

c. Arrange the report on the ITEM field. Use this field for control breaks in your report and subtotal the Quantity Sold and Total Sale columns at each break. Also provide a final total.

5. Print the report

Hands-on Exercise 4: Modifying a Database File Structure

In this exercise you will practice modifying a database file structure by

- ☐ Backing up the existing file
- ☐ Deleting a field
- ☐ Adding a field
- ☐ Changing the width of a field

Using the EMPLOYEE file you developed in Hands-on Exercise 1, do the following:

1. Back up the copy of the existing file, including its file structure and data contents. Use the COPY command in DOS or dBASE to do this.

2. Delete the GENDER field

After you do this, save the change and inspect the file structure and the data contents of EMPLOYEE. If the change has been made properly, continue; otherwise, start over.

3. Modify the TELEPHONE field to accommodate a three-digit area code

Again, save the change and inspect your work.

4. Add a field called DEPT, which will contain an employee's department. Assume this field will contain character data and have a length of three characters; for instance, ACC might stand for the accounting department, FIN for the finance department, and so on.

Again, save the change and inspect your work.

5. Add data to the file to fill the DEPT field. Assume that Pratt, Knat, and Beam work in the ACC department, Sill works in the MIS (Management Information Systems) department, and all other employees work in the FIN department.

6. Add area codes to the TELEPHONE field. Assume that all employees, except Smoller, are in area code 201. Smoller is in area code 212.

Save the changes and inspect your work.

7. Print a copy of the final database file contents and file structure

Hands-on Exercise 5: Advanced Reports

In this exercise you will extend your report-development skills by practicing how to

- ☐ Prepare reports from records that meet certain conditions
- ☐ Prepare reports that contain only subtotals and totals
- ☐ Delete and insert report columns

To do the exercise, you will be using the SALES file of Figures DB-19 and DB-20 and modifying the report of Figure DB-24 (which is based on the SALESR report form you created in the tutorials).

1. Produce a report that is restricted to only items that are priced above $15.00
2. Using the SALESR report form, produce a summary report similar to the one in Figure DB-31. Call this new report form SALESR2.
3. Using SALESR, delete the "Amount" column (the last column in Figure DB-24). Output the associated report and call the new report form SALESR3.
4. Using SALESR3, restore by insertion the amount column deleted in step 3. Output the associated report.

APPENDIX: ASSIST COMMANDS

The ASSIST menu bar consists of eight commands: Set Up, Create, Update, Position, Retrieve, Organize, Modify, and Tools. Each of these commands has its own pull-down menu of subcommands (see figure below). In the material that follows is a description of each of these subcommands along with a set of menu trees showing available options.

Set Up

- Database file
- Format for Screen
- Query
- Catalog
- View
- Quit dBASE III Plus

Create

- Database file
- Format
- View
- Query
- Report
- Label

Update

- Append
- Edit
- Display
- Browse
- Replace
- Delete
- Recall
- Pack

Position

- Seek
- Locate
- Continue
- Skip
- Goto Record

Retrieve

- List
- Display
- Report
- Label
- Sum
- Average
- Count

Organize

- Index
- Sort
- Copy

Modify

- Database file
- Format
- View
- Query
- Report
- Label

Tools

- Set drive
- Copy file
- Directory
- Rename
- Erase
- List structure
- Import
- Export

Set Up Command

SUBCOMMAND ON PULL-DOWN MENU	SUBCOMMAND DESCRIPTION
Database file	Opens a DBF File; optionally activates one or more index files
Format for screen	Selects a file that will contain a customized screen
Query	Selects a file that will contain a filter
Catalog	Sets up a data dictionary on each database file and its supporting files
View	Selects database files that are to be included in a view
Quit dBASE III PLUS	Ends a dBASE III PLUS session

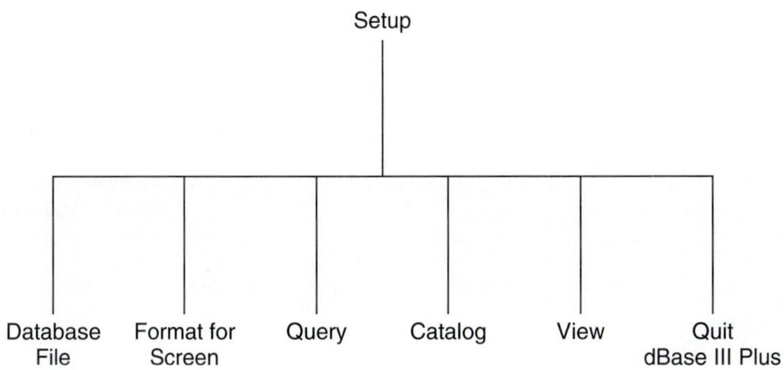

Create Command

Subcommand on Pull-Down Menu	Command Description
Database file	Creates a DBF file structure; optionally allows data entry
Format	Creates a customized screen
View	Creates a special operating environment
Query	Creates a saveable filter that is used to limit work to specified records and fields
Report	Defines a report form (FRM file)
Label	Defines a label form (LBL file), which can be used to generate mailing labels

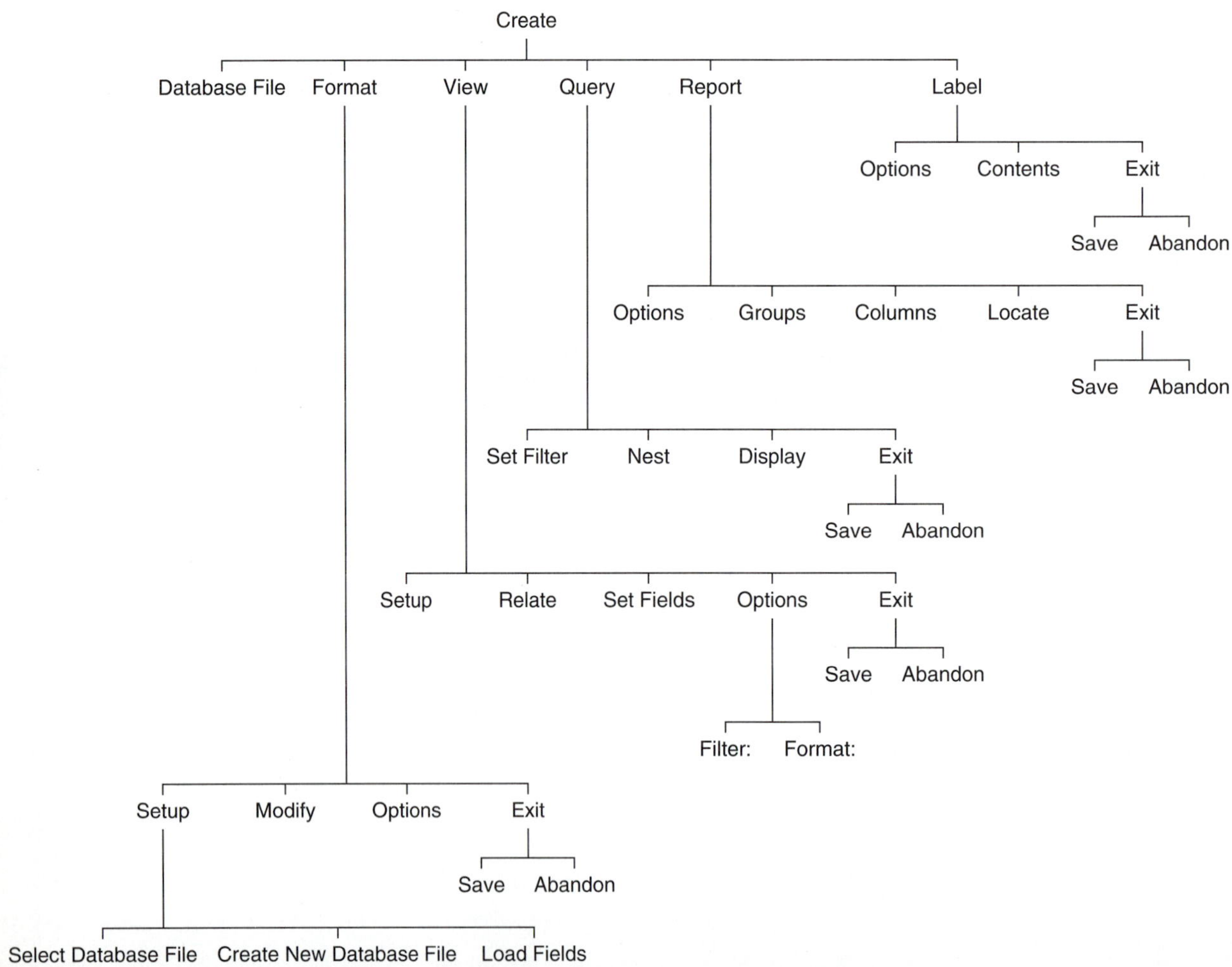

Update Command

Subcommand on Pull-Down Menu	Subcommand Description
Append	Adds records to a DBF file
Edit	Permits the modification of database records
Display	Lists specified database records and fields on the display or printer, a screenful at a time
Browse	Displays records in a database file, enabling them to be inspected or edited
Replace	Replaces the contents of a specified database field with new data
Delete	Flags specified database records for deletion
Recall	Undeletes specified database records
Pack	Permanently deletes database records flagged with the Delete command

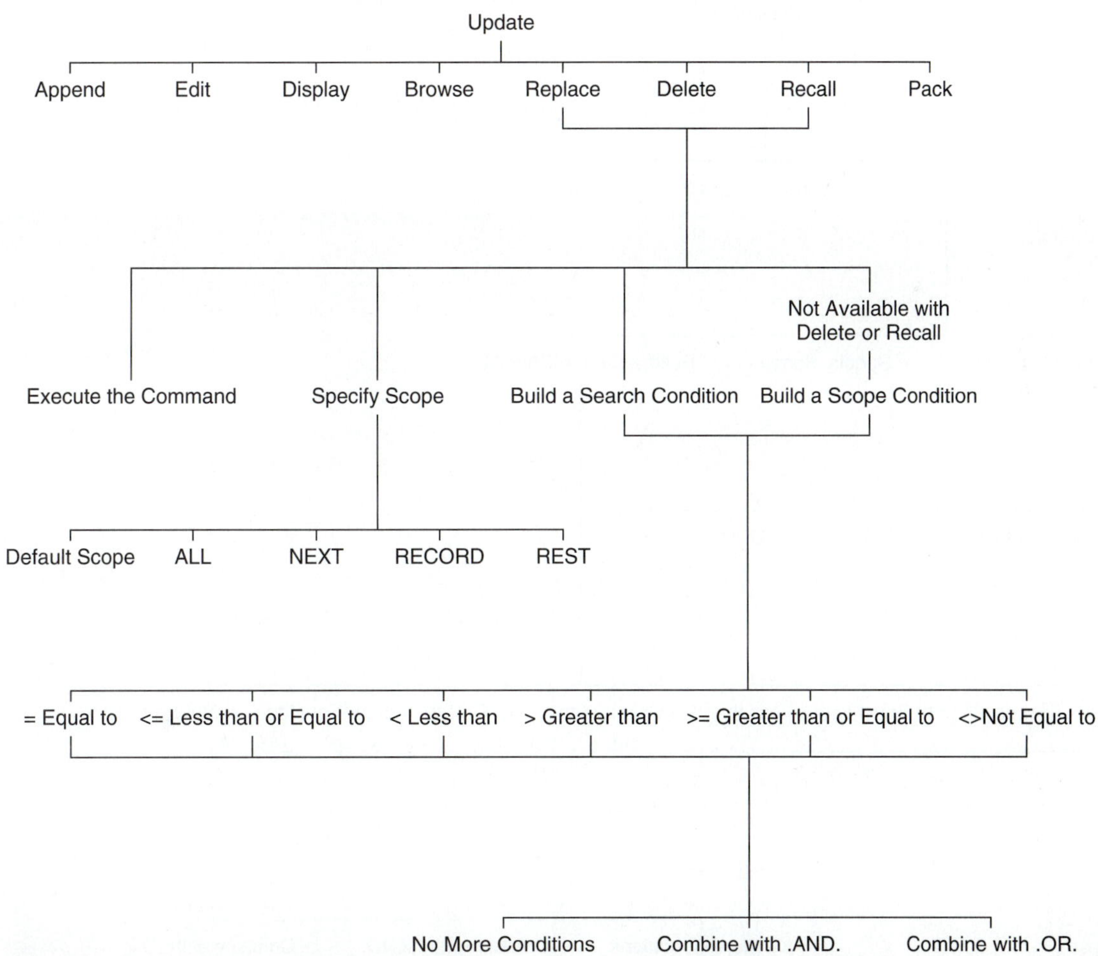

Position Command

Subcommand on Pull-Down Menu	Subcommand Description
Seek	Locates an expression in an indexed field of a database record
Locate	Locates the first database record meeting a specified condition
Continue	Used with the Locate command to locate other database records meeting a specified condition
Skip	Moves record pointer in a database up or down a specified number of times
Goto Record	Positions the record pointer at a specified database record

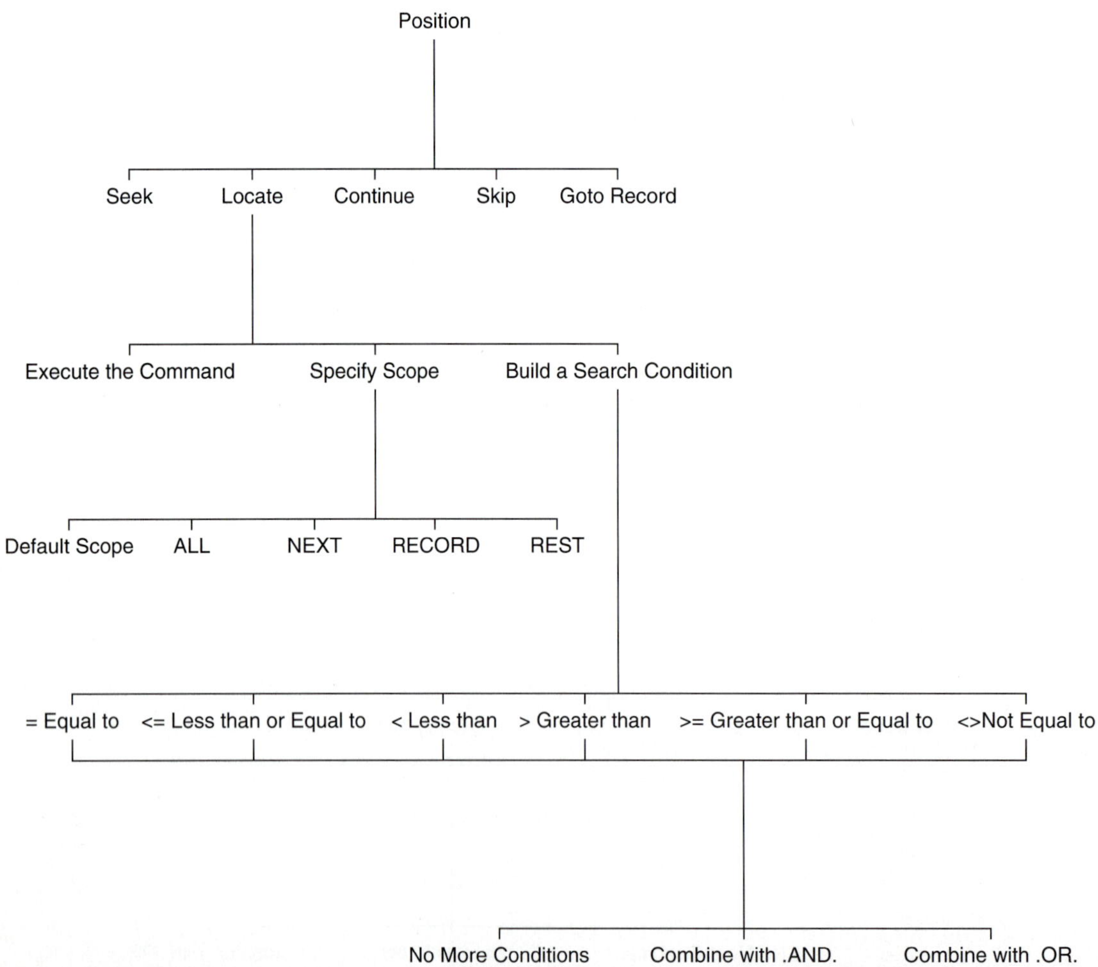

Retrieve Command

Subcommand on Pull-Down Menu	Subcommand Description
List	Lists specified database records and fields on the display or printer, without pause
Display	Lists specified database records and fields on the display or printer, a screenful at a time
Report	Retrieves a report form, so that a report may be output
Label	Retrieves a label form, so that mailing labels may be printed
Sum	Adds values in a numeric field for specified database records
Average	Averages values in a numeric field for specified database records
Count	Counts the number of database records that meet certain conditions

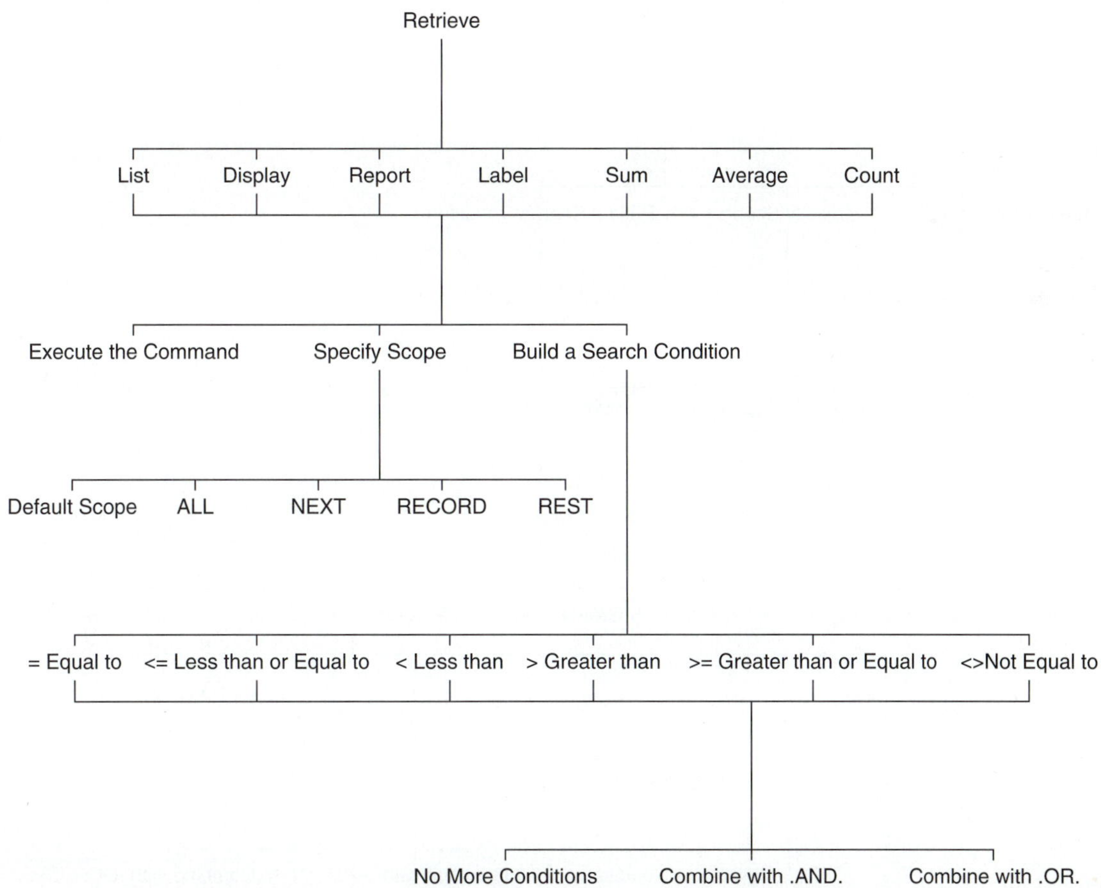

Organize Command

Subcommand on Pull-Down Menu	Subcommand Description
Index	Creates an index file (NDX file)
Sort	Creates a permanent, sorted version of a DBF file
Copy	Creates a database file out of selected records or fields of another database file

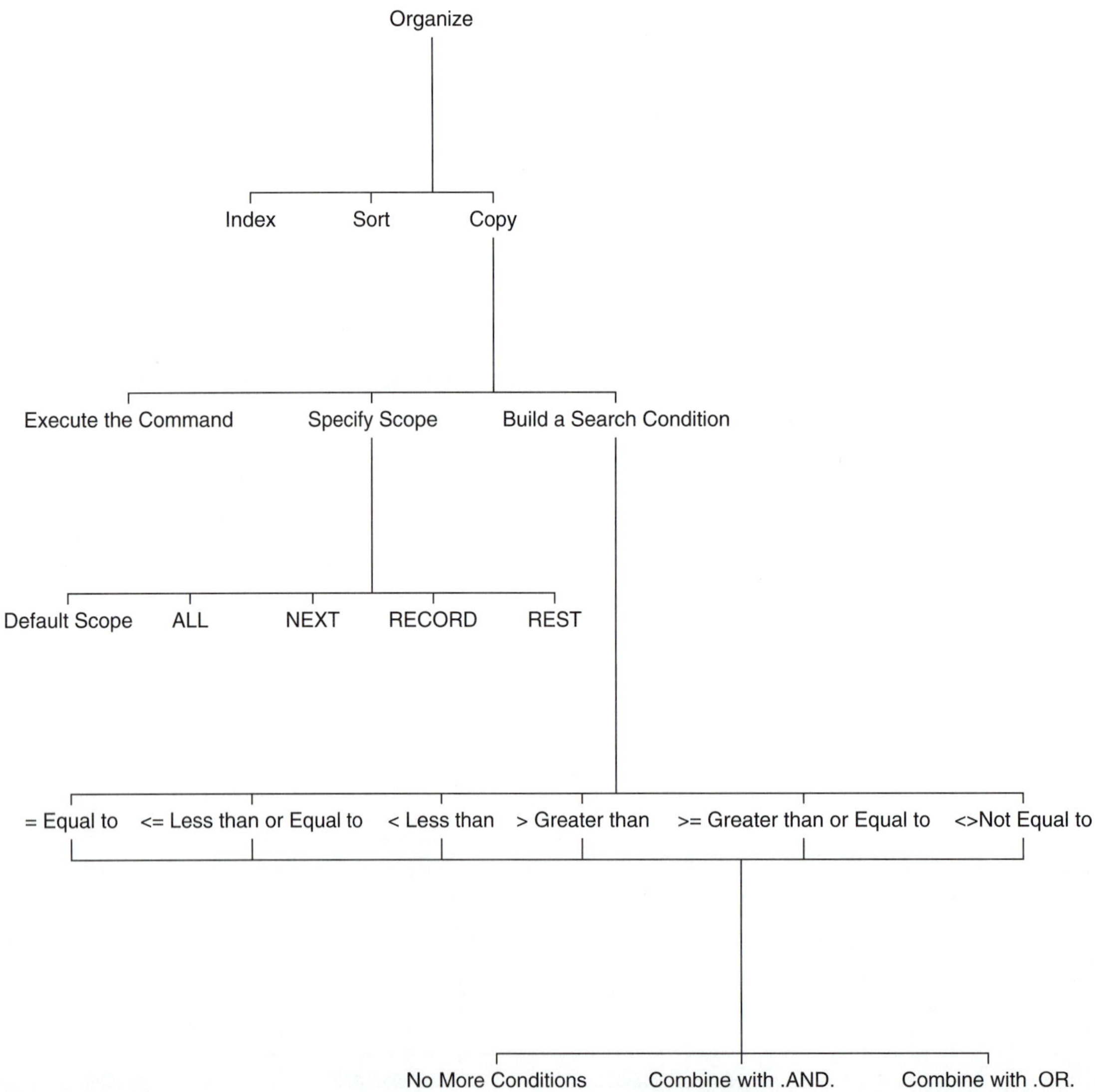

Modify Command

Subcommand on Pull-Down Menu	Subcommand Description
Database file	Modifies the structure of a DBF file
Format	Modifies a customized screen
View	Modifies an operating environment
Query	Modifies a saved filter
Report	Modifies a report form
Label	Modifies an existing label form (LBL file)

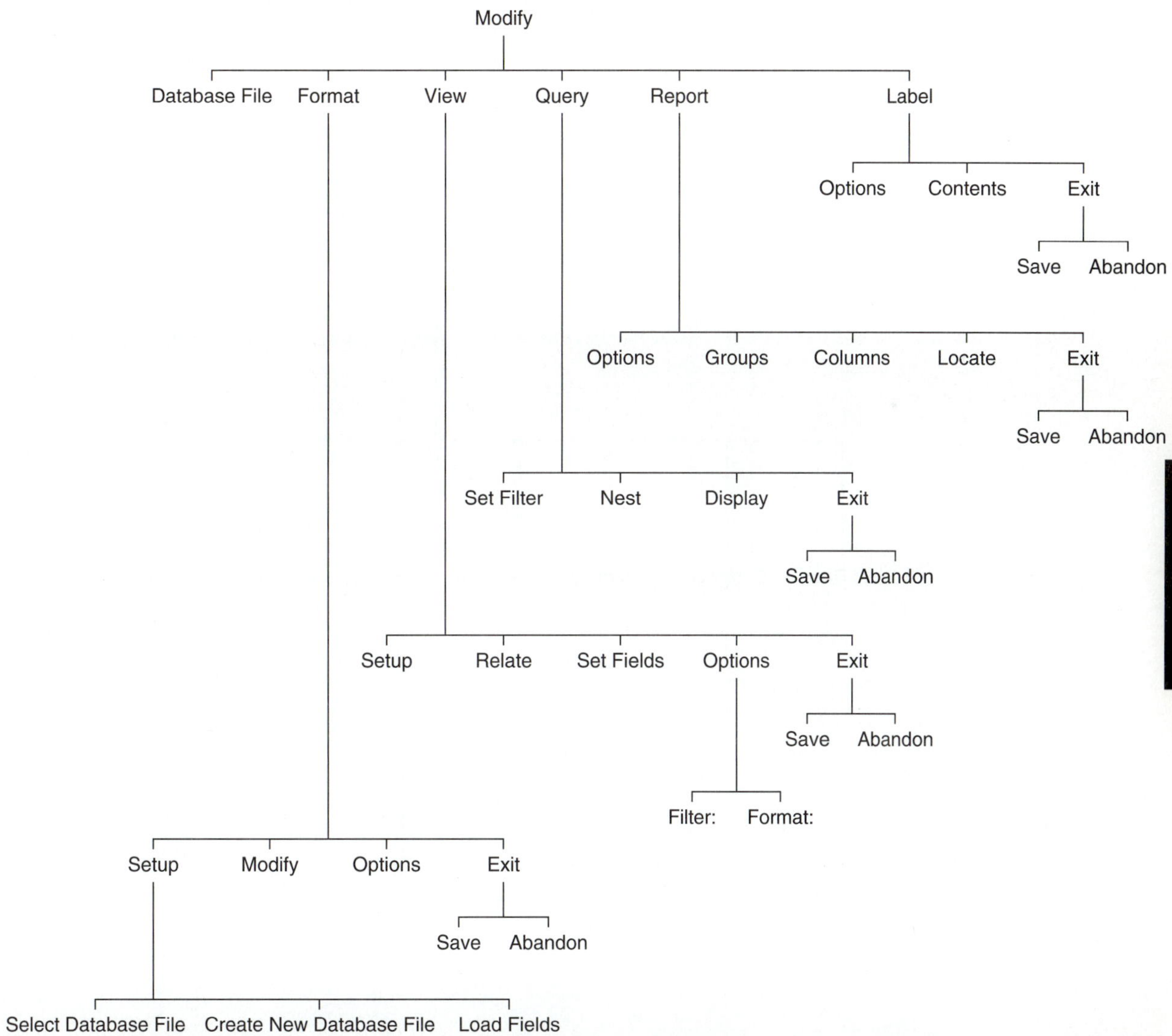

Tools Command

Subcommand on Pull-Down Menu	Subcommand Description
Set drive	Establishes the default drive for the data disk
Copy file	Makes duplicates of files
Directory	Displays the names of files on any of the disk drives
Rename	Renames files
Erase	Erases files
List structure	Outputs the structure of the active database file on the display or printer
Import	Used to make data created with another software package acceptable to dBASE
Export	Used to make dBASE data acceptable to another software package

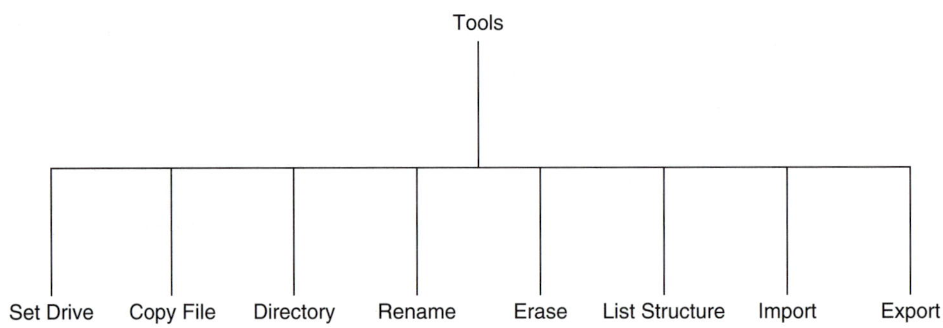

Help	Assist
List	Dir
Display Struc	Display Status
Display Memory	Display
Append	Edit

Function Keys Template
for dBase III PLUS

DATABASE MANAGEMENT WITH dBASE IV

CONTENTS

LEARNING OBJECTIVES

After completing these tutorials, you will be able to:

1. Understand basic database terminology, commands, and applications.
2. Create database files and enter data into them.
3. Access and manipulate data in database files.
4. Develop simple reports.

OVERVIEW

One of the major problems businesses face is that of storing, managing, and accessing large amounts of data. Information from such data is used for a variety of purposes—including reviewing facts about clients and products, preparing reports for upcoming decisions, studying levels of inventory and sales, and answering the many questions that arise in day-to-day business operations. These are but four of scores of examples.

Both large and small businesses have installed database management systems to effectively and efficiently organize, store, and access data coming from order forms, applications, payment slips, and other documents. Organizations such as hospitals, universities, and the government also rely on database management systems to handle huge quantities of data. Because database management systems are so predominant in our daily lives and most of us will wind up using them at one point or another to gather information, understanding how they work is important.

In these tutorials, you will be introduced to dBASE IV, a powerful, microcomputer-based database management system. You will first create a simple database file. Then you will learn how to edit, manipulate, and access data from the file. Finally, you will learn some relatively advanced database operations such as preparing reports. After mastering the skills presented in these tutorials, you will be prepared to move on to the more advanced features of dBASE IV and other database management systems.

GETTING STARTED

We will start by examining a sample database. Here you will see what a typical database looks like and how the data it contains can be processed.

Next, you will learn how to start dBASE on a hard-disk system. Then, you will be introduced to dBASE's two operational modes: Control Center and Command. Finally, you will learn to set the default drive, to use the HELP feature, and to quit dBASE.

After studying and practicing these procedures, you will have acquired the basic skills necessary for moving on to the next step—creating your own database file.

What Is a Database and What Can You Do with It?

So you can fully grasp what a database is and what dBASE is capable of doing with one, let's look at a simple example. Refer to Figure DB-1. Figure DB-1a shows data on five customers of Avalanche Outfitters, a mail-order firm. Each type of data is known as a **field.** Thus there's a customer-number field (CUSTNUM), a name field (NAME), a street-address field (STREET), and so forth. The data collected on each person forms a **record.** As you can see, there are five records in Figure DB-1a, with each record consisting of seven fields. Collectively the five records comprise a **file** or **database file.** A collection of related database files is commonly called a **database.**

dBASE IV requires you to provide a name for each field and a name for each database file. For example, we've called the entire customer database file CUSTOMER, and the customer-number field of this file, CUSTNUM. Notice that these names conform to DOS's naming conventions. In dBASE, we can create as many files as we wish to, although there are limitations on the number of files that can be **active** (i.e., in use) at once.

To see how dBASE can handle database files and relate data between them consider also the database files in Figures DB-1b, DB-1c, and DB-1d. We have a product file (PRODUCT), consisting of product descriptions and prices; an order file (ORDER), consisting of individual orders placed by customers (who are in the customer file); and a file showing some of the details of each order (ODETAILS). The ODETAILS file shows how many units of each product (of the product file) were shipped on each order (of the order file).

Even individually, each of these database files can provide a wealth of useful information. For example, we can tap the CUSTOMER file for a listing of all customers from Colorado. Or, we can use that same file to prepare mailing labels for catalogs that are to be sent out next month.

You may also have guessed that Avalanche Outfitters will want to *relate* data appearing in different database files. For example, if you've ever ordered anything through the mail, you've probably received an invoice such as the one in Figure DB-2. Note that this invoice contains data from several database files. When the order is placed, separate records are created in Avalanche's ORDER and ODETAILS files. To produce the invoice, name and shipping address are extracted from the CUSTOMER file, prices and descriptions are extracted from the PRODUCT file, the date is taken from the ORDER file, and the quantities ordered are taken from the ODETAILS file. The computational facilities of the database system then produce the totals in the last column. Thus, through the power of database technology, an invoice can be prepared quickly, with minimum error.

Fields →
Records →

CUSTNUM	NAME	STREET	CITY	STATE	ZIP	CHARGE
810	John T. Smith	31 Cedarcrest	Boulder	CO	80302	.T.
775	Sally Jones	725 Aqua Fria	Santa Fe	NM	87501	.T.
690	William Holmes	3269 Fast Lane	Santa Fe	NM	87501	.F.
840	Artis Smith	2332 Alameda	Lakewood	CO	80215	.T.
574	Nellie Deutsch	23 E. Spruce	Olathe	KS	66061	.F.

(a) CUSTOMER file

Fields →
Records →

PRODNUM	DESCRIP	PRICE
001	Nordic hat	10.00
002	Nylon windpants	40.00
003	Thermal ski socks	7.00
004	Indy Jones jacket, large	90.00
005	Rozelle headband	6.00

(b) PRODUCT file

Fields →
Records →

ORDNUM	CUSTNUM	DATE
001	775	02/03/93
002	775	02/05/93
003	810	02/07/93
004	574	02/16/93
005	810	02/16/93
006	810	02/18/93

(c) ORDER file

Fields →
Records →

ORDNUM	QTY	PRODNUM
001	2	003
001	1	002
002	1	001
003	1	001
003	3	003
004	1	001
004	1	003
005	2	003
006	1	004
006	1	005

(d) ODETAILS file

FIGURE DB-1
Database files.

There are a number of other reasons we may want to relate data appearing in different database files. Avalanche's management may want the names of all customers who have ordered more than $1000 worth of merchandise during 1993. Or, an angry customer might call saying she ordered a Nordic hat rather than a large Indy Jones jacket, requiring Avalanche personnel to reconstruct the original order.

```
          Order number : 001
          Date placed: 02/03/93
          Ship to:  Sally Jones
                    725 Aqua Fria
                    Santa Fe, NM 87501

Quantity  Description          Unit Price     Total Price
--------  -----------          ----------     -----------
   2      Thermal ski socks       $ 7.00       $ 14.00
   1      Nylon windpants          40.00         40.00
                                                 ------
                                                 $54.00

          Remit check to:  AVALANCHE OUTFITTERS
                           P.O. Box 8000
                           Boulder, CO 80302
```

FIGURE DB-2

An invoice prepared from a relational database system (with data from the four database files in Figure DB-1).

For simplicity, the examples you'll see in this *Guide* involve working on only one database file at a time. In fact, many of the data management problems you'll probably face in your lifetime will be simple enough not to involve relating data between database files. Nonetheless, the ability to relate data between files is a relatively common application in database management.

How to Start dBASE

The procedure you use to start dBASE IV will depend on the type of system you're working on. Instructions for starting dBASE IV on a hard-disk system follow.

The necessary dBASE program files should already be stored on the hard drive in their own subdirectory. If that subdirectory is named DBASE, as we will assume, follow these steps to start up the dBASE program. (However, you should check with your instructor to confirm instructions for accessing dBASE.) Starting at the C:\> prompt

1. Insert your formatted data diskette into Drive A

2. Type **CD DBASE**

3. Press ↵

At the C:\DBASE> prompt

4. Type **DBASE**

5. Press ↵

When the copyright information screen appears

6. Press ↵

You are now in dBASE's Control Center mode.

Control Center and Command Modes

dBASE IV commands can be issued in either of two modes, Control Center or Command.

The **Control Center mode** is menu-driven and uses a routine called dBASE Assistant, or *ASSIST.* When you start dBASE, your screen displays the main Control Center menu, which is shown in Figure DB-3a. The Control Center mode allows you to issue dBASE commands by selecting choices on a top-of-screen **menu bar** and on submenus—called **pull-down menus**—that appear when you highlight a command from the top-of-screen menu.

The interactive **Command mode** is designed for the user who is familiar with dBASE commands and wants to issue commands as quickly as possible from the keyboard. The screen for the Command mode is shown in Figure DB-3b. The Command mode allows you to enter command words at the **dot prompt,** which is the dot that appears before a flashing cursor at the bottom of your screen. dBASE will display this prompt whenever it is ready for you, the user, to enter a command. The commands you type in Command mode for the most part, produce the same result as those you select from menus in Control Center mode.

As shown in Figure DB-3b, a highlighted line—called the **status bar**—is usually displayed at the bottom of the Command mode screen. The status line identifies the current working conditions in dBASE. The first box lists the current command, the second box shows the file in use, the third displays the current record or option. The last box displays various

FIGURE DB-3a
dBASE IV modes.

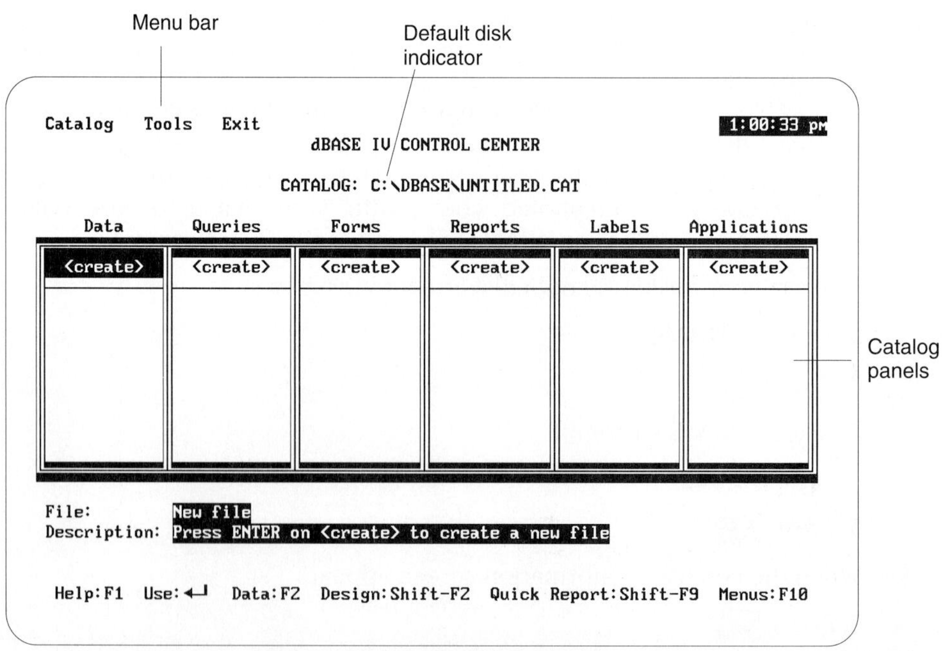

Initial Control Center

FIGURE DB-3b
dBASE IV modes.

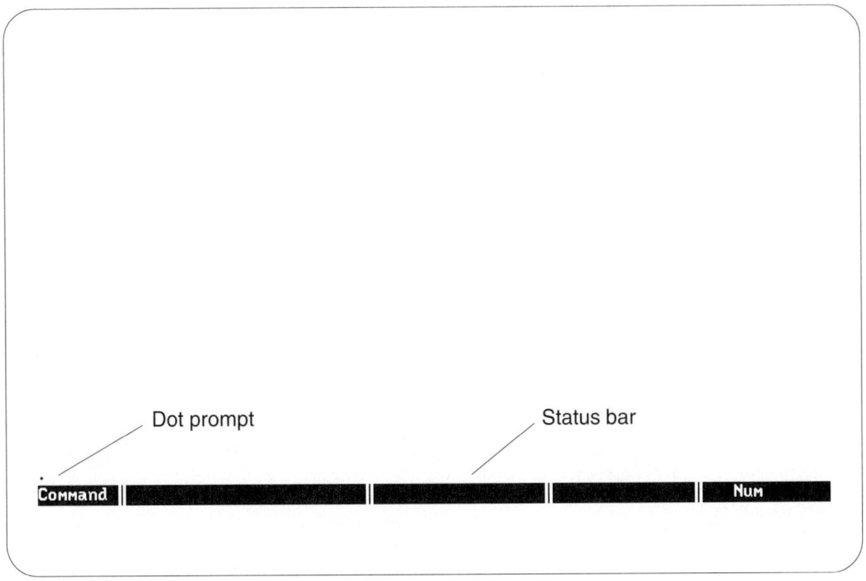

Fresh Command-mode screen

FIGURE DB-3c
dBASE IV modes.

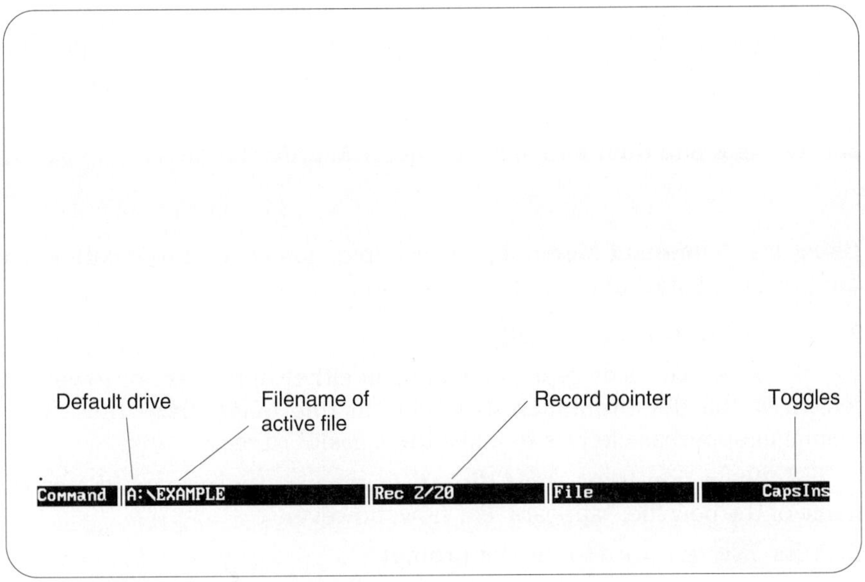

Sample Status Bar

toggles that have been set. For example, Figure DB-3c shows that you are in the Command mode, a file named EXAMPLE is in use on drive A, the active record is number 2 of 20 records, and the Ins and CapsLock toggles are on.

You may prefer some commands invoked through the Command mode; others might be easier through the Control Center. Both modes are presented side-by-side for your use.

Using the Control Center. The Control Center displays information about dBASE and allows easy access to its menu system. The top-of-screen menu bar can be accessed by pressing F10 and then moving the highlight, or by pressing the Alt key while typing the first letter of the desired command. Now, let's practice pointing to choices (without executing them).

1. Press **F10** to access the menu bar

2. Press → to highlight the Tools option

3. Press ↵ to select it

4. Press **Esc** to cancel the command and leave the menu

Centered two lines beneath the menu bar is the word "CATALOG:" followed by a disk designation. This message displays the default drive in use (and will change when you change the default drive shortly).

As seen in Figure DB-3a, the middle portion of the Control Center presents the **catalog**—a table of six columns (or "panels") that display all the dBASE files currently available on the default drive. These files are grouped by type, namely, data files, queries, forms, reports, labels, and applications. New files can be created by highlighting the word *<create>* in the appropriate panel. Active files are displayed *above* the single horizontal line in each panel. Inactive files are listed below the line (as we will see).

5. Press **Esc** and then **Y** to move to the COMMAND mode

Using the Command Mode. If, for example, you wanted to create a new file, you could start at the dot prompt and

1. Type **CREATE** and press ↵

Note: You may type commands in either uppercase or lowercase letters at the dot prompt. Instructions in this *Guide* show these commands in uppercase letters to make them easier to read.

When you issue the **CREATE** command, the prompt "Enter the name of the new file:" appears. For now, however,

2. Press **Esc** to return to the dot prompt

To temporarily remove the status bar from the screen

3. Type **SET STATUS OFF** and press ↵

To make the status bar reappear

4. Type **SET STATUS ON** and press ↵

5. Press **F2** to return to the Control Center

You can go from one mode to another easily. When in the Control Center press the Esc key and then the Y key to go to the Command mode; when at the Command mode's dot prompt, return to the Control Center mode by pressing the F2 key.

How to Set the Default Drive

Setting the default drive shows dBASE which drive will access (save or retrieve) your data files. Although you can set the default drive from the Control Center, it is much easier to invoke the command from the Command mode.

From the Control Center. To set the default drive for hard-disk systems

1. Press **Alt** + **T** for Tools
2. Type **D** for DOS Utilities
3. Press **Alt** + **D** to select DOS
4. Type **S** to set default drive
5. Type **A:**
6. Delete any other characters on the line
7. Press ↵
8. Press **Esc** and then **Y**

Notice that the catalog now lists the default drive as A:.

From the Dot Prompt (Command mode). To set the default drive

1. Type **SET DEFAULT TO A:**
2. Press ↵

Notice that the status bar now shows your default drive.

How to Use the HELP Feature

While working with dBASE, you may be confronted with an unfamiliar command. You can get help in either the Control Center or the Command mode.

From the Control Center. The HELP feature provides information about any command that has been highlighted on a menu but not yet executed by pressing the Enter key. To see how the HELP feature works

1. Press **F10**
2. Press → to highlight any command on the menu bar
3. Press **F1** to access Help

A box with the description of the

From the Dot Prompt. When you access the HELP feature, you'll see a menu of commands about which information is available. To see how the HELP feature works

1. Press **F1** to access the Help menu
2. Use the **arrow keys** and press ↵ to select an option

A box with the description of the command as well as its syntax will appear on the screen (see command as well as its syntax will appear on the screen (see Figure DB-4a). To see other topics, press space and then ↵. To make the box disappear and return to the screen from which you requested help

4. Press **Esc**

Figure DB-4b). To make the box disappear and return to the dot prompt

3. Press **Esc**

To request information about a specific command, you can type HELP and the name of the command. For example

4. Type **HELP SORT**

5. Press ↵

This time you'll see a box with a description of the SORT command. To return to the dot prompt

6. Press **Esc**

How to Quit dBASE

Using the QUIT command when leaving dBASE closes (and thus saves) any files that might still be open.

It is important to use the QUIT command each time you leave dBASE so that records added to files are not lost when you shut off the system.

FIGURE DB-4a
dBASE IV HELP screen.

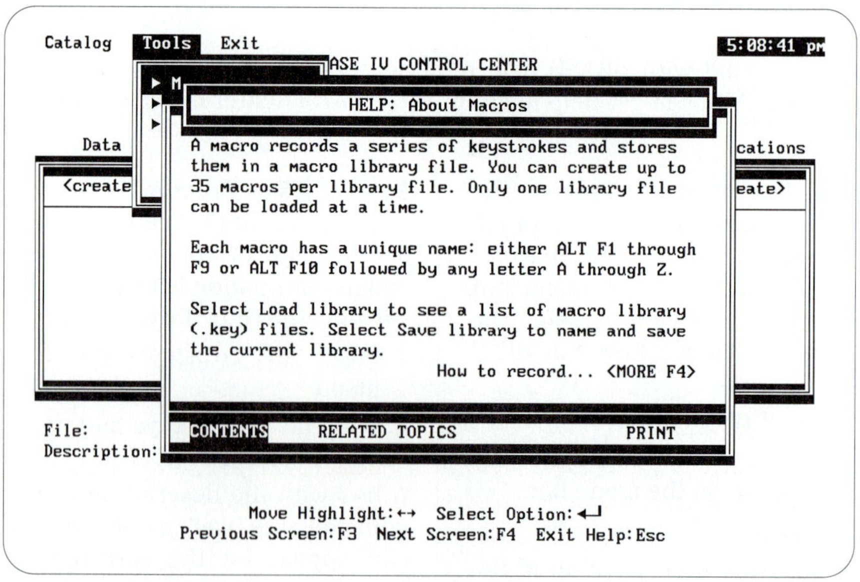

Control Center mode

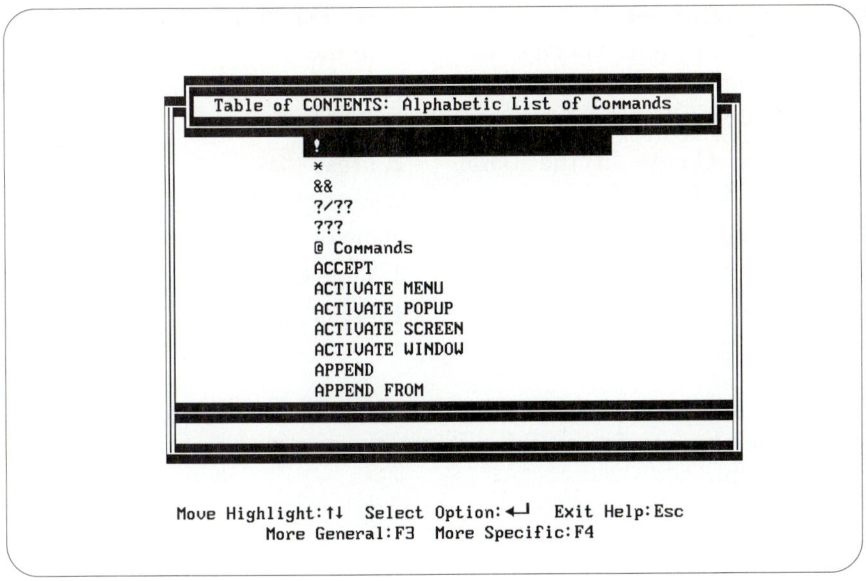

Command mode

FIGURE DB-4b
dBASE IV HELP screen.

From the Control Center. To quit dBASE

1. Press **Alt** + **E** to Exit

2. Type **Q** to Quit to DOS

From the Dot Prompt. To quit dBASE

1. Type **QUIT**

2. Press ↵

CREATING A DATABASE FILE

Now that you've been introduced to dBASE and acquired some basic skills, you're ready to create a simple database file.

In this exercise, you will begin by naming the file and setting up its **structure.** This is done with the CREATE command. You must define a file's structure before you can put records into it or use it in any way. Once the structure is defined, you will next learn how to append and list records, and finally, how to quit the file.

How to Name a File

First, you must provide dBASE with the name of the file you are going to create, and specify on which drive you want the new file stored.

Filenames generally conform to DOS's file-naming convention. In DOS, a filename can contain a maximum of eight characters. It must start with a letter and contain only letters, digits, and the underscore character (/); it must not contain embedded spaces. *Note:* You should not add an extension, dBASE will do this automatically.

DB IV

From the Control Center. To name your file and specify the drive that will store it

1. Start dBASE
2. Highlight **Create** in the Data panel (as in Figure DB-5)
3. Press ↵

From the Dot Prompt. To name your file

1. At the dot prompt, type **CREATE**
2. Press ↵

When dBASE prompts "Enter the name of the new file:"

3. Type **CUSTOMER**
4. Press ↵

You are now in the fresh database screen shown in Figure DB-6a. Next, you will see how to fill out this screen. A completed screen is shown in Figure DB-6b.

How to Enter Field Descriptors

After naming a file, as you just did with CUSTOMER, and indicating the drive to store the file on, the next step is describing the characteristics of data going into the file. During this process, you specify the name, order of appearance, type, and width of each of the fields of the file. This step defines the structure the database file will have.

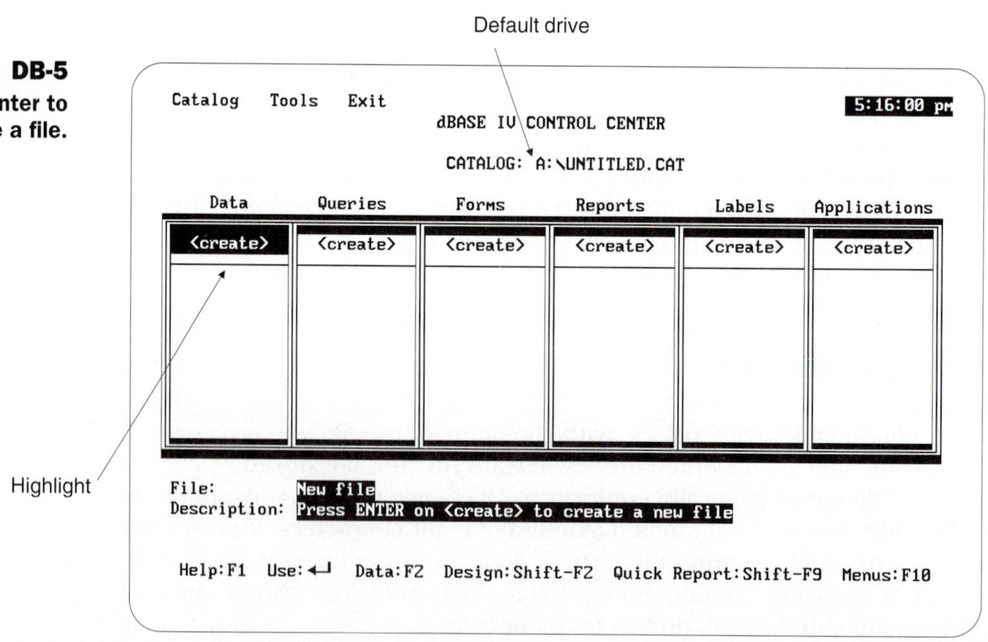

FIGURE DB-5
Using the Control Center to create a file.

FIGURE DB-6

Using the CREATE command to define the file structure for the CUSTOMER file.

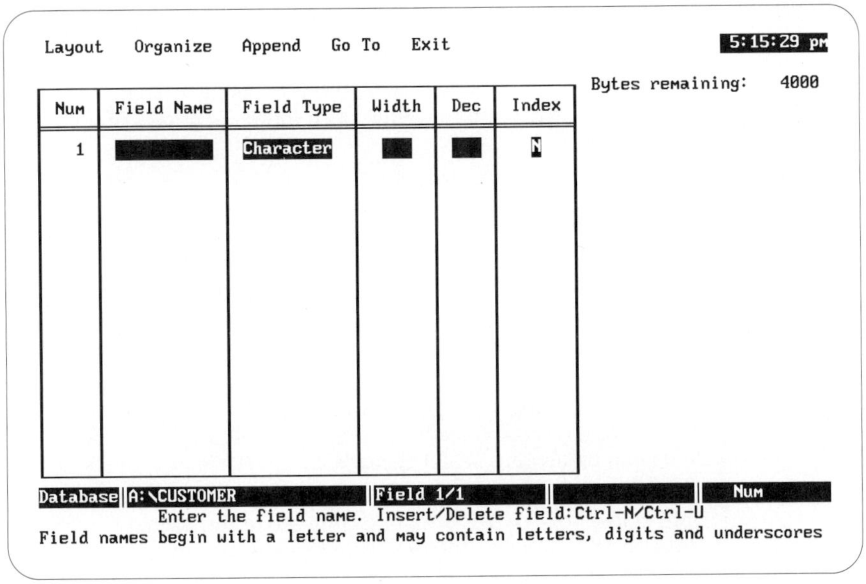

(a) Fresh screen

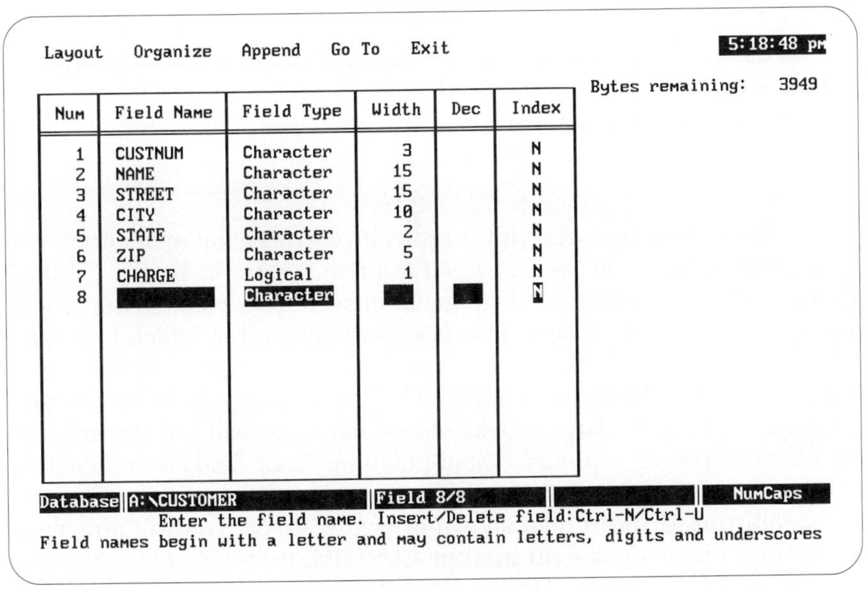

(b) Completed screen

The field types are called **field descriptors.** Six of these descriptors are shown in Figure DB-7.

The most common field descriptors are *character* and *numeric.* Generally, fields that do not need to be involved in arithmetic computations, such as NAME, STREET, CITY, and STATE in the CUSTOMER file of Figure DB-1a are designated as character fields. Fields such as PRICE in the PRODUCT file, on the other hand, are used in computations (such as the invoice in Figure DB-2) and are designated numeric.

Field Type	Maximum Data Length	Description
Character	254 characters	Character fields store data that cannot be arithmetically manipulated. You can, however, sort, index, or compare on these fields.
Numeric	1 to 20 characters	Numeric fields, which store integer numbers or numbers that contain fixed decimal points, can be arithmetically manipulated. Numbers upon which you do not need to do arithmetic—such as employee identification numbers—should be stored in character rather than numeric fields.
Float	1 to 20 characters	Float fields store floating point numbers frequently used in scientific applications involving either very large or very small numbers.
Logical	1 character	Logical fields store a single character of data—a T (meaning true, or yes) or an F (meaning false, or no). Tests on logical fields can be used to select records from a file, as can tests on character, numeric, and date fields.
Date	8 characters	Date fields store dates, provided they are in the format MM/DD/YY (such as 12/31/92). You can sort or index on date fields, and you can also subtract them in order to calculate the number of days elapsing between two dates.
Memo	5,000 characters	Memo fields are used to store text information. They cannot be arithmetically manipulated or compared, but they can be edited and output, as can any other field.

FIGURE DB-7
Six dBASE IV field descriptors.

The *logical* field descriptor typically carries a value of either T or F (for True or False). In the CUSTOMER file in Figure DB-1a, the CHARGE field uses this descriptor to distinguish charge from cash customers (T indicates a charge customer). The *date* field descriptor, which is present in the ORDER file of Figure DB-1c, is used for fields that consist of dates that are stored in the format MM/DD/YY. The variable-length *memo* field descriptor is used for large blocks of text data that will not require sorting, comparison, or arithmetic manipulation. *Float* fields store floating-point numbers used in scientific applications.

Starting at the screen shown in Figure DB-6a, you will now enter information about each field in your CUSTOMER file. To enter the first field (as shown in Figure DB-6b),

1. Type **CUSTNUM** as the field name
2. Press ↵
3. Type **C** for character (or press ↵ since character is the default choice)
4. Type **3** as the field width
5. Press ↵
6. Press ↵ or **N** for no index

7. Follow these six steps again to enter each of the remaining field names, types, and widths for the CUSTOMER file (as shown in Figure DB-6b)

In some cases you will automatically be advanced to the next field; if not, press Enter. Use the arrow keys to move up or down a field if you wish to make corrections. Note that the width of the logical field, CHARGE, is automatically set to 1, after you type **L** as the field descriptor. This is because the data for any logical field is always just one character—either T or F (True or False).

8. Press **Ctrl** + **End** (hold down the Ctrl key while you press the End key) to save this file structure and exit

In the Control Center, dBASE now asks for a filename and prompts "Save as:"

9. Type **CUSTOMER**
10. Press ↵

When dBASE asks "Input data records now? (Y/N)"

11. Type **N** for No

Note: If you had typed Y for Yes, you could begin to enter data immediately after defining the structure of your file.

After you press **N** for No, the appropriate mode screen reappears. dBASE is awaiting your next command.

When you use the CREATE command to set up a database file, dBASE will allocate space on the disk for this file and record its name in your disk's directory (with a **.DBF** extension). Hence, the database file you have just defined has been saved as CUSTOMER.DBF on your disk, but you may refer to it as CUSTOMER when you are in dBASE.

How to Display a File Structure

After you create a structure for a database file, it's a good idea to check to see that the structure has been entered correctly. You can inspect a file's structure through the **DISPLAY STRUCTURE** command.

From ASSIST. To display a file's structure

1. Press **Shift** + **F2** for Design
2. Press **Esc**

When you are finished looking at the structure (as in Figure DB-8b),

3. Press **Esc** and then **Y** to exit

From the Dot Prompt. To display a file's structure

1. Type **DISPLAY STRUCTURE**
2. Press ↵

The screen you will see in response to issuing the DISPLAY STRUCTURE command is similar to the one in Figure DB-8a or b. Note that the extension .DBF has automatically been added to the filename in the Command mode's display.

If you've made a mistake in creating the structure, don't worry—you can modify it at any time with the MODIFY STRUCTURE command, which you will learn shortly.

FIGURE DB-8
Displaying a file structure.

```
. DISPLAY STRUCTURE
Structure for database: A:\CUSTOMER.DBF
Number of data records:        5
Date of last update   : 03/23/92
Field  Field Name  Type       Width    Dec    Index
    1  CUSTNUM     Character      3                N
    2  NAME        Character     15                N
    3  STREET      Character     15                N
    4  CITY        Character     10                N
    5  STATE       Character      2                N
    6  ZIP         Character      5                N
    7  CHARGE      Logical        1                N
** Total **                      52

.
Command ||A:\CUSTOMER            ||Rec 1/5         ||File ||      ||  Num
```

(a) DISPLAY STRUCTURE in the Command mode

```
Layout   Organize   Append   Go To   Exit                        9:00:53 pm

                                                      Bytes remaining:   3949
 Num | Field Name | Field Type | Width | Dec | Index
   1 | CUSTNUM    | Character  |     3 |     |   N
   2 | NAME       | Character  |    15 |     |   N
   3 | STREET     | Character  |    15 |     |   N
   4 | CITY       | Character  |    10 |     |   N
   5 | STATE      | Character  |     2 |     |   N
   6 | ZIP        | Character  |     5 |     |   N
   7 | CHARGE     | Logical    |     1 |     |   N

Database||A:\CUSTOMER            ||Field 1/7        ||          ||  Num
          Enter the field name. Insert/Delete field:Ctrl-N/Ctrl-U
Field names begin with a letter and may contain letters, digits and underscores
```

(b) Design in the Control Center

After you have correctly defined the structure of a file, you can enter records into it and, subsequently, get useful information from these records. For example, at some point, you will probably want to add, delete, or modify records. You may also want a listing on your printer of certain records in a particular file. Or, as you saw with Avalanche Outfitters, you may want to relate files to produce invoices or informative reports.

To develop or use file data in any way, dBASE requires that you first make the file active. This is done either by pointing to it or by identifying it in some other way. Later we'll show in detail how to make existing files active by opening them with the USE command. However, since the CUSTOMER file is still active at this point, we can proceed with work on the file.

In dBASE, you can only point to one file at a time. When you point to a file, you can add records to it, delete records from it, modify its records, extract records from it, sort it, and do a number of other useful tasks. With some commands dBASE also lets you identify "secondary" files that you might want to join, or relate, to the file you are currently using.

How to Modify a File Structure

Occasionally you will want to modify the structure of a database file. For instance, you may have made a mistake in initially setting up the structure. Or perhaps, after you've used a file successfully for a period, you will want to add a new field, delete a field, change a fieldname, or extend the width of a particular field. To modify a database structure in any of these ways or others, you use the **MODIFY STRUCTURE** command.

Here, we will talk about the command only in passing, leaving it as a hands-on exercise for you to try yourself when you have finished the tutorials.

Before You Modify, Have a Backup. It is a good idea to have a backup copy of any file whose structure you wish to modify in any way. This holds especially true if the file holds data and is large. By not having a backup copy of the file, you risk losing valuable data if you make a mistake in modifying the file.

You can make a backup copy of any file by using the COPY command available with DOS or by using dBASE's COPY command. The dBASE COPY command is not covered here, but it is relatively easy to execute and you can read about it in the Command Reference at the end of these tutorials or in Hands-on Exercise 6.

The MODIFY STRUCTURE Command. To modify a structure, you first need to issue the MODIFY STRUCTURE command.

From the Control Center. To modify a structure

1. Highlight **CUSTOMER** in the Data panel
2. Press **↵**
3. Type **M** to modify
4. Press **Esc**

From the Dot Prompt. To modify a structure

1. Type **MODIFY STRUCTURE**
2. Press **↵**

You will next be presented with a screen that looks like the one in Figure DB-9a. What you do next depends on which type of modification you wish to make. Three types of structure modifications are deleting fields, adding fields, and changing the definitions of fields.

To Delete a Field. To delete a field, highlight the field you want to delete on the screen (see Figure DB-9a, which highlights CUSTNUM) and hold down the Ctrl key while you press the U key—that is,

Ctrl + **U**

As soon as the new database structure has been saved, the field definition and any data that have been assigned to the field will be erased.

To Add a Field. To add a field, move the screen cursor to where you want to insert the field and press

Ctrl + **N**

For instance, to insert a field between NAME and STREET, move the screen cursor to the STREET field and press Ctrl+N. You will then see a screen similar to the one in Figure DB-9b, with the cursor positioned automatically where you need to enter the new field name.

To Change a Field Definition. To change a field name, a field width, a field type, or the number of decimal places, move the cursor to the item you wish to change in a field-definition screen, such as the one in DB-9a, and just type the modification over the existing specification. **Caution:** If you change the name of a field, you cannot make any other modifications to that field at this time; you will have to save the new structure and issue MODIFY STRUCTURE again to make these modifications.

As you are modifying a structure, you will either want to save the changes you make, or, if you get into trouble, abort the entire modification operation.

To Save a Modified Structure. To save the changes you've made and, at the same time, exit MODIFY STRUCTURE, press

Ctrl + **End**

FIGURE DB-9
Modifying a file structure.

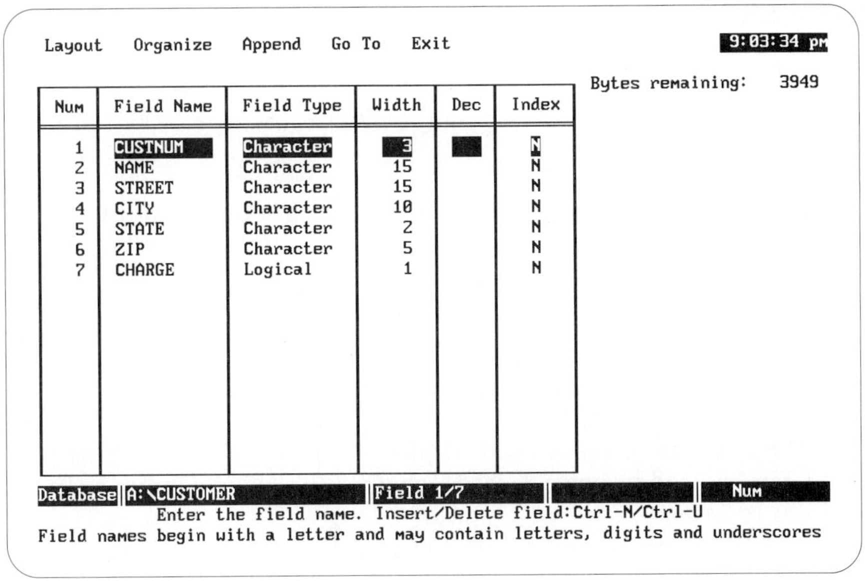

(a) The original file structure

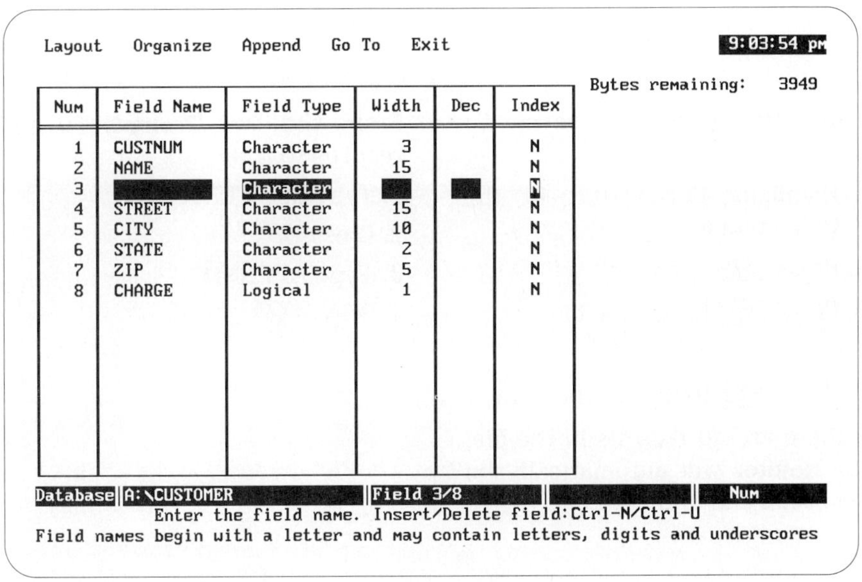

(b) Adding a field

and confirm the changes by pressing Enter. Any records that were saved within the old structure will now be transferred to the new one. Before proceeding with your work, you may wish to display both the modified structure and the contents of the database file. Shortly, after you create records for the file, you will learn how to display the contents of the file.

To Abort Changes. If, as you are modifying a structure, you make a mistake or get lost somehow, and wish to abort the changes, press

Esc

This will immediately put you back at the dot prompt or in the Control Center.

How to Add (Append) Records to a Database

The **APPEND** command is used to place records into a file. This command can be used to enter records whether the file is empty or already contains records.

If there are no records in the file, the APPEND command automatically points to the first record position. On the other hand, if, say, there are already 15 records in the file, APPEND will point to the 16th record position. In this example, you will first reopen the CUSTOMER file for use.

From the Control Center. To add records to a file

1. Highlight **CUSTOMER** in the Data column
2. Press ↵ to select
3. Press ↵ to use the file

To append records:

4. Press **F10** to access the data

If there are no records in the file, the pointer will automatically be set at the end of the file.

From the Dot Prompt. To add records to a file

1. Type **USE CUSTOMER**
2. Press ↵
3. Type **APPEND**
4. Press ↵

Once you issue the APPEND command, you will see a template similar to the one in Figure DB-10a. The template has a reverse-video, highlighted data area sized to conform to the width structure you defined earlier. In dBASE as in many other packages, you will be given a fresh template on screen for each data record you type in.

As you enter records into the CUSTOMER file, follow the guidelines below:

a. When the data you are typing into a field fills up the entire shaded area for that field, you do not need to press Enter; the cursor will automatically move to the next line and a "beep" will sound

FIGURE DB-10
APPENDing records to a file.

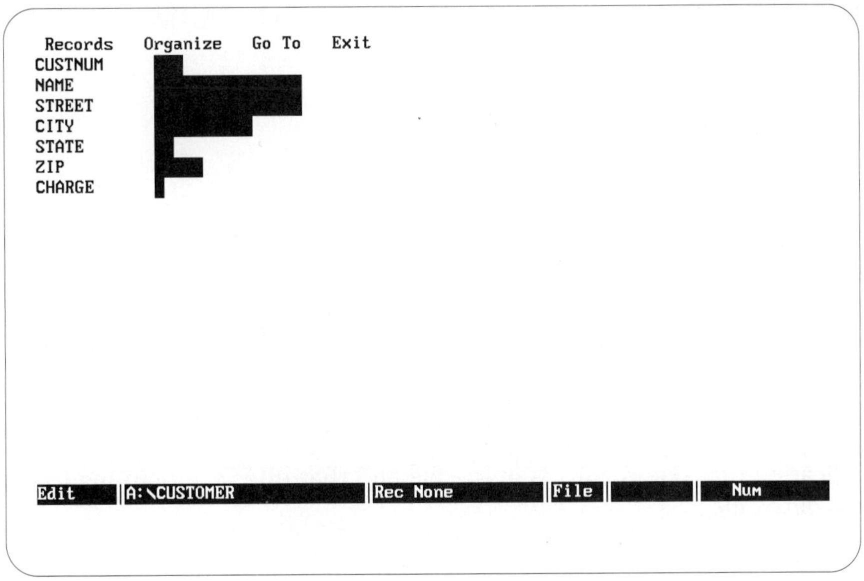

(a) A blank dBASE IV record template

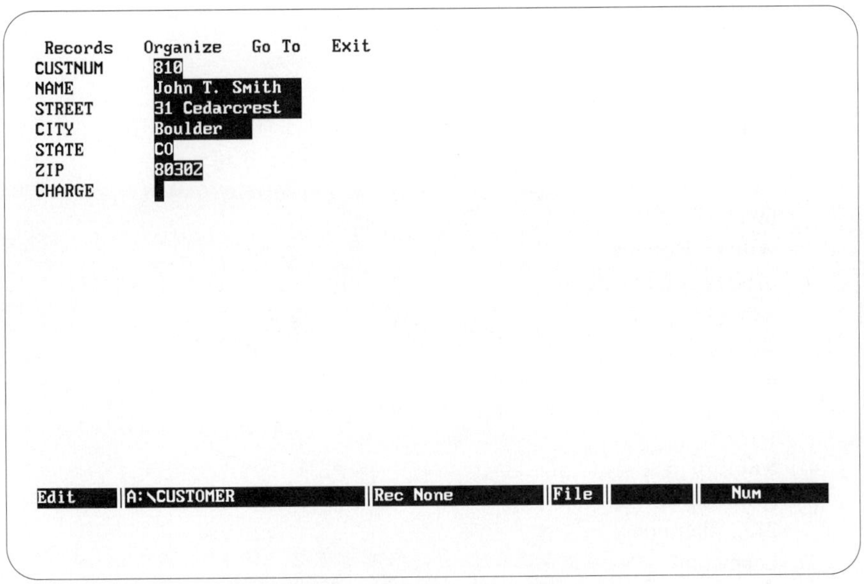

(b) A filled-in dBASE IV record template

b. When the data you are typing into a field does not fill up the shaded area for that field, press Enter to continue to the next field

c. Look at the menus at the top of the screen to note the keys to press to move from field to field and to invoke commands, such as SAVE

d. When you reach the last field, CHARGE, and enter T into it, a new blank record will be presented so you can continue filling in the data for the next record

3. Enter the following data for the first record (see Figure DB-10b)

CUSTNUM	**810**
NAME	**John T. Smith**
STREET	**31 Cedarcrest**
CITY	**Boulder**
STATE	**CO**
ZIP	**80302**
CHARGE	**T**

After you type in the CHARGE field, a fresh template appears. In the fourth segment of your status bar at the bottom of the screen will be the message

```
REC EOF/1
```

indicating that one record is in the file and that dBASE is pointing to the end of the file.

4. Add the following records to the file, each record in a fresh template:

775
Sally Jones
725 Aqua Fria
Santa Fe
NM
87501
T

690
William Holmes
3269 Fast Lane
Santa Fe
NM
87501
F

840
Artis Smith
2332 Alameda
Lakewood
CO
80215
T

574
Nellie Deutsch
23 E. Spruce
Olathe
KS
66061
F

If you make an error while typing a record, use the arrow keys to move to the point of the error and type the correct data directly over the old. If the error is in an earlier record, use the Pg Up key to move backward to that record, make the correction, and then use the Pg Dn key to move forward again.

When you have entered all of the records, another fresh template will be showing. To save the file and exit

5. Press ↵

How to List Records

The LIST command allows you to look at the records a file contains. This command is especially useful if some time has passed since you created the file, and you need to review its contents.

From the Control Center. To list the records in the CUSTOMER file create a quick report as follows:

1. Press **Shift** + **F9** for a quick report

2. Type **V** to view

When you are done viewing,

3. Press **Esc**

4. Press any key to continue

From the Dot Prompt. To list the records in the CUSTOMER file

1. Type **LIST**

2. Press ↵

If you use the COMMAND mode, you will get a listing like the one shown in Figure DB-11a. The Control Center's quick report will resemble Figure DB-11b.

How to Halt a List. Sometimes the list of records in the file is too long to display on the screen all at one time and you would like to temporarily halt the listing so it doesn't scroll wildly and prevent you from looking at individual records. To temporarily halt the scrolling of all records in the Command mode so that you can view a portion of the file at a time

1. Press **Ctrl** + **S**

To restart the scrolling of the records, press any key

Note: Soon you will learn to use the DISPLAY command, which avoids the need for use of Ctrl+S by allowing you to view a selected number of records at a time.

How to Quit a File

The QUIT command closes and saves any files that might still be open at the time you are leaving the database.

FIGURE DB-11
Listed output from the CUSTOMER file.

```
. LIST
Record#  CUSTNUM NAME             STREET          CITY        STATE ZIP    CHARGE
      1  810     John T. Smith    31 Cedarhurst   Boulder     CO    80302 .T.
      2  775     Sally Jones      725 Aqua Fria   Santa Fe    NM    87501 .T.
      3  690     William Holmes   3269 Fast Lane  Santa Fe    NM    87501 .F.
      4  840     Artis Smith      2332 Alameda    Lakewood    CO    80215 .T.
      5  574     Nellie Deutsch   23 E. Spruce    Olathe      KS    66061 .F.

.
Command ║A:\CUSTOMER              ║Rec EOF/5        ║File ║      ║  Num
```

(a) The Command mode's LIST

```
Page No.    1
03/27/92

CUSTNUM  NAME            STREET          CITY        STATE  ZIP    CHARGE

810      John T. Smith   31 Cedarhurst   Boulder     CO     80302  Y
775      Sally Jones     725 Aqua Fria   Santa Fe    NM     87501  Y
690      William Holmes  3269 Fast Lane  Santa Fe    NM     87501  N
840      Artis Smith     2332 Alameda    Lakewood    CO     80215  Y
574      Nellie Deutsch  23 E. Spruce    Olathe      KS     66061  N




              Cancel viewing: ESC,  Continue viewing: SPACEBAR
```

(b) The Control Center's Quick Report

Remember to use the QUIT command before shutting off the computer system so that you do not lose any records added to files.

From the Control Center. To quit a file

1. Press **Alt** + **E** to Exit
2. Press **Q** to Quit

From the Dot Prompt. To quit a file

1. Type **QUIT**
2. Press ↵

EDITING A DATABASE FILE

Now that you know how to create database files, the next step is learning how to edit files. Because most databases need constant updating, understanding the procedures presented here is very important.

This section explains the methods for viewing a directory of database files, opening a file, deleting a record, modifying records, and adding new records.

How to View a Directory of Files

Before opening an existing database file, such as the CUSTOMER file, it often helps to see all of the database files on your data disk. It is easy to forget which files are stored on the disk or what exact name was given to a particular file.

In the ASSIST mode the Directory option on the Tools menu lists all files on your data disk, not just files with the .DBF extension. You just created a file named CUSTOMER with the .DBF extension. As was mentioned earlier, the .DBF extension is automatically inserted by dBASE for any file that is set up through the CREATE command. As you begin to create other kinds of files, such as index files and report files (discussed later), dBASE will insert other, different extensions for those. Some of the extensions one commonly sees in a directory are shown in Figure DB-12.

In the Command mode, the DIR command will list only those files on your data disk with the .DBF file extension. One of the files (perhaps your only file at this time) is your CUSTOMER file. Other information given with the DIR command is the number of records in each database file, the date of the last revision of each file, and the size of each file. The

EXTENSION	DESCRIPTION
.DBF	Used for regular database files, such as those shown in Figure DB-1.
.DBT	Used for memo files and contains large blocks of information found in the memo fields of database files.
.MDX	The Master Index file created with the INDEX command. Files in this master file provide dBASE with the ability to rearrange information in a regular database file.
.FMT	Used for files that are custom screens.
.FRM	Used for files that have been created using the Creating a report form option.
.QRY	Used for information about conditions for displaying records from an existing database file.
.SCR	Used for information about the screen layout for custom data entry forms.

FIGURE DB-12
Some common dBASE IV file extensions.

DIR command may be used to check that your database file has been saved and that the number of records in the file is correct.

To view a directory of database files, do the following:

1. Start dBASE and set your default drive

From the Control Center. To view the directory

The Control Center already displays the directory of the default disk in the middle of the screen. A set of six vertical panels (or columns) displays all current files in their appropriate category.

From the Dot Prompt. To view the directory

2. Type **DIR**
3. Press ↵

A list of your database files appears. The CUSTOMER file is shown with the number of bytes used.

HOW TO RETRIEVE A FILE

In order to use a database file—to make additions or deletions, for instance—you must first **open** the file. Opening files is done with the **USE** command. Now that, having viewed the directory, you know what files are contained on your disk, you will open one of them.

From the Control Center. To open a file

1. Highlight **CUSTOMER** in the Data panel
2. Press ↵
3. Press ↵ to use the file

Note that the filename moves *above* the active line in the Data panel.

From the Dot Prompt. To open a file

1. Type **USE CUSTOMER**
2. Press ↵

In the Command mode, the CUSTOMER filename is now showing on the status bar, which means that it is the active, or open file.

How to Delete Records

To keep a database current, deleting records is frequently necessary. Deleting a record permanently from a dBASE file requires two steps.

First, the **DELETE** command is issued to "flag" the record to be deleted. At this point, the record will be preceded by an asterisk (*), indicating it has been identified as one to be deleted. The record is still part of the file, however, and you can restore the record, if you wish, by issuing a RECALL command.

Second, the **PACK** command is issued to permanently delete the record. The PACK command causes dBASE to purge all records with delete flags (*) from the file. After the file has been packed, the deleted records no longer exist and cannot be recalled.

Marking records for deletion, permanently deleting them, and recalling them are all easier to accomplish in the COMMAND mode than in the Control Center. However, the steps for both modes follow.

Using the DELETE Command. When you issue the DELETE command, a record is marked for deletion with an asterisk (*) but is not actually deleted. After marking the record, you have the option to recall it with the **RECALL** command, or permanently delete it with the PACK command.

From the Control Center. To issue the DELETE command

1. Press **F2** for data
2. If a single record appears, press **F2** again
3. Move the highlight to the record to be deleted (in this case, record 5/5)
4. Press **Ctrl** + **U** to mark the record

Note that "Del" appears in the rightmost box in the status line

5. Press **Alt** + **E** and then **E**

From the Dot Prompt. To issue the DELETE command

1. Type **DELETE RECORD 5** (if record 5 is the one you wish to delete)
2. Press ↵

The message "1 record deleted" appears on your screen.

3. Type **LIST** and press ↵

Notice that Record 5 now is marked for deletion, but is not yet permanently deleted, so you have the option of changing your mind.

Using the RECALL Command. You can recall a record that has been marked for deletion, removing the asterisk flag.

From the Control Center. To recall Record 5

Repeat the identical procedure used to mark Record 5 for deletion, namely

1. Press **F2**
2. Highlight **Record 5**
3. Press **Ctrl** + **U**

The "Del" message is removed from the status line.

4. Press **Alt** + **E** and then **E**

From the Dot Prompt. To recall Record 5

1. Type **RECALL RECORD 5**
2. Press ↵

The message "1 record recalled" appears. To confirm that the asterisk is gone

3. Type **LIST**
4. Press ↵

Figure DB-13 shows what your screen will look like when you delete and then recall a record in the Command mode.

Using the PACK Command. If, instead of recalling a record, you wanted to follow through with the deletion, you would invoke the PACK command to permanently delete the marked record.

From the Control Center. To flag Record 5 again and then eliminate it permanently

1. Press F2
2. Highlight **Record 5/5**
3. Press Ctrl + **U** to delete
4. Press Alt + **O** to organize
5. Type **E** to Erase
6. Type **Y**

The screen responds with "Pack" and "4 records copied." Record 5 has now been removed.

To add it back so we can continue to work with the complete file

7. Press the ↓ key to move to the end of the list.

From the Dot Prompt. To flag Record 5 again and then eliminate it permanently

1. Type **DELETE RECORD 5** and press ↵ to mark it for deletion
2. List the file to be sure the record is marked
3. Type **PACK**
4. Press ↵

The message "4 records copied" appears.

5. List the file again to confirm that the record is deleted

If the deleted record was in the middle of the file, the remaining records would be automatically renumbered sequentially. So that

FIGURE DB-13
Using the DELETE and RECALL commands in the Command mode.

```
. delete record 5
      1 record deleted
. list
Record# CUSTNUM NAME            STREET          CITY        STATE ZIP   CHARGE
      1  820     John T. Smith   31 Cedarhurst   Boulder     CO    80302 .T.
      2  778     Sally Jones     813 Pine Bluff  Santa Fe    NM    87501 .T.
      3  690     William Holmes  3269 Fast Lane  Santa Fe    NM    87501 .T.
      4  850     Artis Smith     2332 Alameda    Lakewood    CO    80215 .T.
      5 *574     Nellie Deutsch  23 E. Spruce    Olathe      KS    66061 .F.

. recall record 5
      1 record recalled
. list
Record# CUSTNUM NAME            STREET          CITY        STATE ZIP   CHARGE
      1  820     John T. Smith   31 Cedarhurst   Boulder     CO    80302 .T.
      2  778     Sally Jones     813 Pine Bluff  Santa Fe    NM    87501 .T.
      3  690     William Holmes  3269 Fast Lane  Santa Fe    NM    87501 .T.
      4  850     Artis Smith     2332 Alameda    Lakewood    CO    80215 .T.
      5  574     Nellie Deutsch  23 E. Spruce    Olathe      KS    66061 .F.

.
Command ||A:\CUSTOMER        ||Rec EOF/5   ||File ||      ||  Num
```

The screen asks "Add new records? (Y/N)"

8. Type **Y**
9. Type Record 5's data across the row as in Figure DB-14
10. Press **Ctrl** + **End** when we can continue to work with the complete file,

6. Enter Record 5 back into the file by invoking the APPEND command and typing Record 5's data into the template

How to Modify Records

Modifying data in records is another way to keep a database current. The changes may be necessary for various reasons. A customer may have moved, requiring a street address to be changed. The price of a product may have gone up. Data originally typed into a field may have been incorrect. Whatever the case, editing allows you to change the values contained in the fields of any records.

You can edit records by using either the EDIT or the BROWSE command.

Using the BROWSE Command. BROWSE is one of the fastest ways to edit your records. With BROWSE, you can display several records onscreen at the same time and edit them.

From the Control Center. To use BROWSE

1. Press **F2** for data
2. If a single record appears, press **F2** again

From the Dot Prompt. To use BROWSE

1. Type **BROWSE**
2. Press **↵**

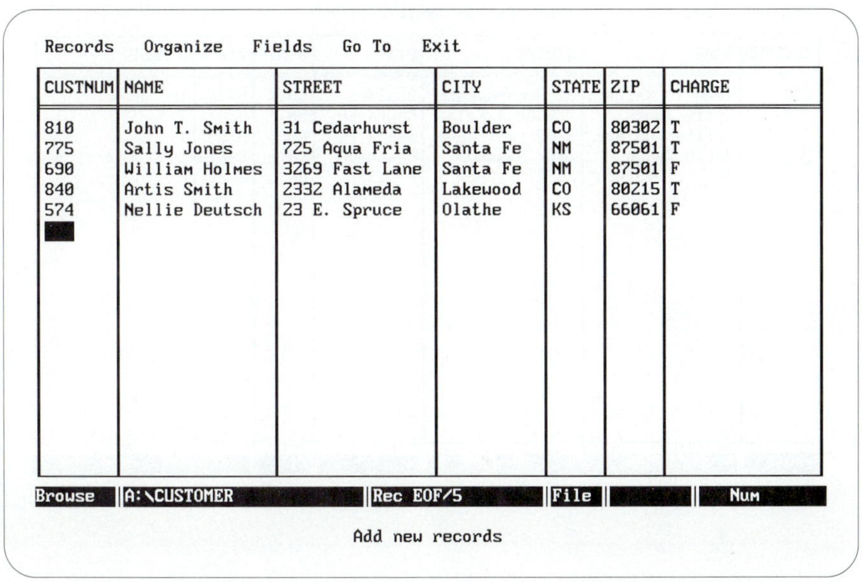

FIGURE DB-14
Using the BROWSE command.

DB IV

Once you're in BROWSE, you can press Pg Up or Pg Dn to scroll through records in a longer file. You can use the arrow keys to move from record to record or from field to field. Whenever you see an item that needs to be updated, type in the update over the original data.

In your CUSTOMER file, make the following corrections:

3. Change Sally Jones's customer number to **778**

4. Change the Charge field for William Holmes to read **.T.**

Figure DB-15 shows what you'll see on your screen.

Sometimes records are too long to fit on a BROWSE screen. When this happens, hold down the Ctrl key while pressing the right arrow key to pan to fields currently located offscreen. Use the Ctrl+left arrow key combination to pan in the other direction.

When you have finished making editing corrections

5. Press **Ctrl** + **End**

Note: Both Ctrl+End and Ctrl+W tell dBASE that you are finished with the edit and want to save the changes. These keystroke combinations also return you to the Command (dot prompt) mode.

If you decided not to save the changes made in the Browse mode, you could press the Esc key to exit BROWSE. Be careful about using the Esc key for this purpose, however, because you will lose all the changes you made in BROWSE.

Using the EDIT Command for Single Records. Records can also be modified by using the **EDIT** command. However, with EDIT you can modify only one record at a time.

FIGURE DB-15

The BROWSE screen after William Holmes's record has been changed.

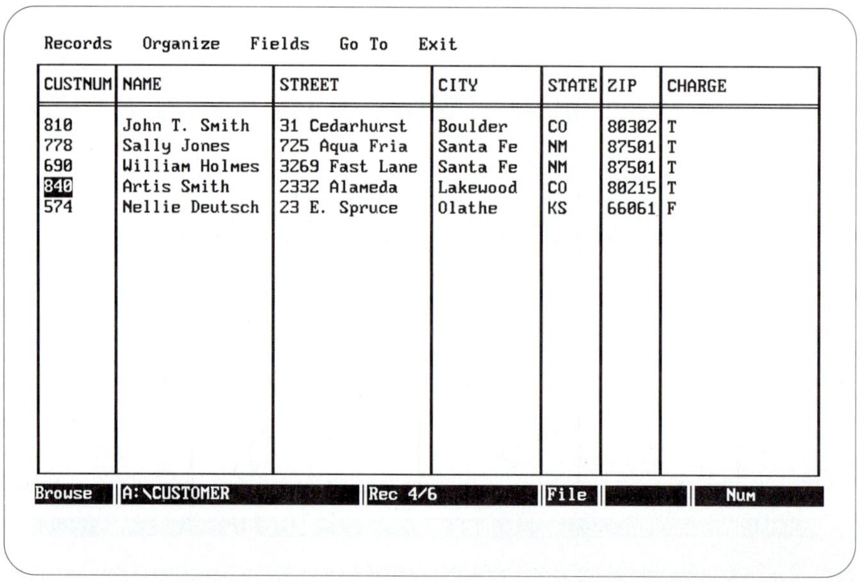

From the Control Center. To use EDIT

1. Press **F2** for data
2. If a BROWSE screen appears, press **F2** again to get the EDIT screen.

From the Dot Prompt. To use EDIT

1. Type **EDIT**
2. Press **↵**

Once you are in EDIT you can use a number of editing features available in dBASE IV to make changes in a record. The options available to you are shown in Figure DB-16. For now, however, you will change Record 2 using the steps that follow.

3. Press **Pg Up** to go to Record 2 for Sally Jones
4. Type **813 Pine Bluff** over the old street address
5. Press **Ctrl** + **End** when finished

Using the EDIT Command for Selected Field Values. You can also use the EDIT command to edit specific types of records. For example, you

CURSOR CONTROL KEY	*OR*	dBASE COMMAND	ACTION
		Ctrl/A	Moves the cursor one word to the left.
		Ctrl/F	Moves the cursor one word to the right.
←		Ctrl/S	Moves the cursor one character to the left.
→		Ctrl/D	Moves the cursor one character to the right.
↑		Ctrl/E	Moves the cursor up one line. At the top line of a record it displays the prior record.
↓		Ctrl/X	Moves the cursor down one line. At the bottom line of a record it displays the next record.
Del		Ctrl/G	Deletes the character at the cursor position and moves the text one position to the left.
		Ctrl/Y	Deletes the contents of an entire field.
		Ctrl/W	Writes the changes back to the file and returns you to the control center or dot prompt.
Pg Up		Ctrl/R	Writes the current record to disk and displays the previous record.
Pg Dn		Ctrl/C	Writes the current record to disk and displays the next record.
Ins		Ctrl/V	Toggles between typeover and insert modes. In INS mode the insert message is displayed in the status bar.
		Ctrl/U	Deletes or undeletes a record.

FIGURE DB-16
Cursor movements to change records with the EDIT command.
Use the cursor control key if listed; otherwise, press and hold the Ctrl key, hit the letter named in the figure, and then release both.

might want to edit all Colorado records. This type of command is done more easily through the Command mode. Starting at the dot prompt

1. Type **EDIT FOR STATE = "CO"**

2. Press ↵

All Colorado records (two of them) are available for editing. You can move from record to record with the Pg Dn and Pg Up keys. The John T. Smith record is now showing.

3. Change the CUSTNUM data for the two Colorado records as follows:

Smith, John T. to **820**
Smith, Artis to **850**

4. Press **Ctrl** + **End** when finished

This EDIT command used the conditional expression STATE = "CO" to search for specific records. Conditional expressions will be discussed in detail later.

5. Use the LIST command to see that the records have been properly changed

How to Add More Records

Keeping a database current frequently requires that you add new records to it. You add records in the same way that you first entered information in the database, with the use of the APPEND command.

From the Control Center. To append records

1. Press **F2**

2. If the BROWSE screen appears, press **F2** again to access the EDIT screen

3. Press **Alt** + **G** to Go to

4. Type **L** for last record

5. Press **Pg Dn**

The screen responds "Add new records? (Y/N)"

6. Type **Y**

From the Dot Prompt. To append records

1. Type **APPEND**

2. Press ↵

You are now ready to add records to the current file. Notice that the status line tells you that you are at the end of your file (EOF). Remember that you will be adding records to the database file that is active, which currently is the CUSTOMER file. The name of the active file shows in the status panel at the bottom of the screen. If you had opened other files while working with dBASE, the APPEND command would be in effect for the most recently opened file.

Entering new data.

1. Enter the data shown in Figure DB-17a as new records in your CUSTOMER file

As you reach the end of each record, a new template will automatically appear.

2. Press ↵ when finished

3. List the file and check it for accuracy

Your file should match the one shown in Figure DB-17b.

4. If necessary, use BROWSE or EDIT to make corrections to the records

5. Quit the file and dBASE

MANIPULATING DATA IN A FILE

Up to this point, you have learned how to use dBASE to create and edit files. Now it is time to find out how to manipulate the data in files to extract valuable information.

In this exercise you will be shown how to display records, perform calculations, and index or sort files to reorganize the contents.

For these purposes, you will use your enlarged CUSTOMER file.

1. Start dBASE and open the CUSTOMER file

2. List (or BROWSE) the file to make sure all 16 records are present as shown in Figure DB-17b.

FIGURE DB-17a
Additional data for the CUSTOMER file.

Record#	CUSTNUM	NAME	STREET	CITY	STATE	ZIP	CHARGE
6	447	Vernon Pressy	5541 Canyon	Boulder	CO	80302	.T.
7	480	Benton Fink	440 Arapahoe	Boulder	CO	80302	.F.
8	401	Wayne Montoya	600 Tara Lane	Englewood	CO	80155	.F.
9	640	C. Foster Kane	P.O. Box 6000	Santa Fe	NM	87501	.T.
10	505	Alice Evans	5702 North St.	Boise	ID	83704	.T.
11	102	Maya Ellis	603 Oakwood	Aurora	CO	80011	.T.
12	754	Shane Williams	275 East Kiowa	Flagstaff	AZ	86001	.F.
13	801	Del Lopez	80 Williston	Austin	TX	78755	.F.
14	908	Duke Miller	CM Ranch	Stanley	NM	87056	.F.
15	665	Bette White	Box 20	Rowe	NM	87562	.T.
16	760	Kim Lundy	44 West St.	Missoula	MT	59802	.F.

Record#	CUSTNUM	NAME	STREET	CITY	STATE	ZIP	CHARGE
1	820	John T. Smith	31 Cedarcrest	Boulder	CO	80302	.T.
2	778	Sally Jones	813 Pine Bluff	Santa Fe	NM	87501	.T.
3	690	William Holmes	3269 Fast Lane	Santa Fe	NM	87501	.T.
4	850	Artis Smith	2332 Alameda	Lakewood	CO	80215	.T.
5	574	Nellie Deutsch	23 E. Spruce	Olathe	KS	66061	.F.
6	447	Vernon Pressy	5541 Canyon	Boulder	CO	80302	.T.
7	480	Benton Fink	440 Arapahoe	Boulder	CO	80302	.F.
8	401	Wayne Montoya	600 Tara Lane	Englewood	CO	80155	.F.
9	640	C. Foster Kane	P.O. Box 6000	Santa Fe	NM	87501	.T.
10	505	Alice Evans	5702 North St.	Boise	ID	83704	.T.
11	102	Maya Ellis	603 Oakwood	Aurora	CO	80011	.T.
12	754	Shane Williams	275 East Kiowa	Flagstaff	AZ	86001	.F.
13	801	Del Lopez	80 Williston	Austin	TX	78755	.F.
14	908	Duke Miller	CM Ranch	Stanley	NM	87056	.F.
15	665	Bette White	Box 20	Rowe	NM	87562	.T.
16	760	Kim Lundy	44 West St.	Missoula	MT	59802	.F.

FIGURE DB-17b

An expanded version of the CUSTOMER file.

How to Display Records

This tutorial explains several ways to display records. The **DISPLAY** command, like the LIST command, lets you see the data in your files. However, there are some differences between the commands. LIST allows you to print files; DISPLAY doesn't. DISPLAY causes records to be displayed a screen at a time, whereas LIST causes them to scroll onto (and possibly off) the screen.

To display records in the Command mode, you will type in variations of the DISPLAY ALL OFF command. The key word ALL causes all the records to be displayed on the screen. The key word OFF suppresses the record numbers.

The Control Center uses the BROWSE screen and a *query* feature instead of display. We will see this shortly.

Use the Command mode to display records as follows:

Displaying All Records

The DISPLAY ALL command will cause all records to be displayed on the screen. Before starting the steps that follow, make sure you have activated the CUSTOMER file.

To display all records in the Command mode

1. Type **DISPLAY ALL OFF**

2. Press ↵

dBASE will automatically pause after 16 or 17 lines of the file are displayed on the screen. To display the next screen and subsequent files, press any key. You can continue this until you reach the end of the file you are viewing.

Displaying Specific Fields. This form of the DISPLAY command identifies specific fields to be displayed. In the exercise to follow, only the CUSTNUM, NAME, and CHARGE fields of your CUSTOMER file will be displayed.

To display specific fields

1. Type **DISPLAY ALL OFF CUSTNUM, NAME, CHARGE**
2. Press ↵

You'll see a list of the CUSTNUM, NAME, and CHARGE fields for all records in the CUSTOMER file.

Using Conditional Expressions. When a command includes a conditional expression, dBASE searches the file for records that fit the condition, and performs the command on those records only. Conditional expressions in dBASE are constructed much the same way as in some programming languages, such as BASIC, Pascal, COBOL, and FORTRAN. That is, they are typically formed by a field name, followed by one or more **relational operators** (see Figure DB-18) and a constant. For example,

```
STATE = "NM"
CITY = "Boulder"
ZIP = "80302"
CUSTNUM <= "505" (is less than or equal to)
```

Note: Constants (such as "NM" and "Boulder") that correspond to fields governed by the character field descriptor must appear in quotes. Also be aware that, regarding literal expressions within quotes, dBASE distinguishes upper- from lowercase characters. Consequently, since NM has

OPERATOR	EXAMPLE	EXPLANATION
<	A<500	Less than
>	A>B	Greater than
=	A=500	Equal
<> or #	A<>B	Not equal
<=	A<=500	Less than or equal
>=	A>=500	Greater than or equal
$	C$"York"	Substring comparison. X$Y is true if the string X is identical to the string Y *or contained within it.*
.AND.	A>B .AND. C=D	Logical "and" connector. *Both* conditions must be true.
.OR.	A>B .OR. C<D	Logical "or" connector. *Either* condition must be true.
.NOT.	A .NOT. B	Logical "not" expression. All values for A *Except* B

FIGURE DB-18
Relational and logical operators.

DB IV

been entered in the fields in the file in uppercase, be sure to use uppercase in the conditional expression. Numeric fields cannot be in quotes.

To produce a listing of all records with CO (Colorado) as the STATE field

1. Type **DISPLAY ALL OFF FOR STATE = "CO"**

The FOR clause, used with the DISPLAY command, tells dBASE to select those records meeting the conditional expression that follows the key word FOR.

2. Press ↵

A listing of all records with CO (Colorado) as the STATE field appears.

Additional operators—called **logical connectives**—that can be used to combine conditional statements include

.NOT.	To select records that do not meet a condition
.AND.	To select records that meet both of two conditions
.OR.	To select records that meet either or both of two conditions

To use the .NOT. operator starting at the dot prompt

1. Type **DISPLAY ALL OFF FOR .NOT. STATE = "CO"**

2. Press ↵

A list of all records representing states other than Colorado appears.

To use the .AND. operator

3. Type **DISPLAY ALL OFF FOR STATE = "NM" .AND. CHARGE**

You don't need to specify a value for CHARGE because the use of the logical field name CHARGE implies the logical relation CHARGE = ".T." This type of construction is used for logical field comparisons only.

4. Press ↵

A list of only those customers that *both* live in New Mexico and have charge accounts appears.

To use the .OR. operator

5. Type **DISPLAY ALL OFF FOR STATE = "NM" .OR. STATE = "CO"**

6. Press ↵

A listing of records representing customers from *either* New Mexico *or* Colorado appears. Another example of the .OR. follows:

7. Type **DISPLAY ALL OFF FOR STATE = "NM" .OR. CHARGE**

8. Press ↵

This statement finds customers who

□ Are from New Mexico but don't have a charge account; or

□ Are not from New Mexico but do have a charge account; or

□ Are from New Mexico and have a charge account.

There are many other forms of the DISPLAY command and forms of conditional expressions in addition to those shown here. A full discussion of these is beyond the scope of this guide. We will note here, however, that conditional expressions can be used with other dBASE commands, such as DELETE, LIST, and the computational commands that follow in the next subsection. For example, typing

```
DELETE FOR STATE = "CO"
```

would mark all Colorado records for deletion.

The QUERY Command

If you search for records using FOR conditions often, you may want to create a **query file** that saves conditions on disk for future use.

How to Create a Query File. Assume you want to create a query file called *CUST1* that includes only those records whose STATE is "NM." dBASE offers a menu-driven screen that creates this query for you as follows:

From the Control Center. To create a QUERY file

1. Highlight **<create>** in the Queries panel

2. Press ↵

From the Dot Prompt. To create a QUERY file

1. Type **CREATE QUERY**

2. Press ↵

When the screen prompts you for a query filename

3. Type **CUST1** and press ↵

The QUERY screen appears as shown in Figure DB-19a. (If you are using the Command mode, the filename CUST1 will appear on the status line.) The highlight appears beneath the main file name (Customer.DBF) in the left column. Each field name is presented in a separate column across the top row, preceded by a ↓. This symbol indicates that the field will be included in the query listing. The "view" at the bottom of the screen shows the order and width of the fields that will be displayed.

To specify query limits, you simply press the Tab key to move the highlight to an appropriate field column, and then type the desired condition.

3. Press **Tab** until the highlight moves under the *STATE* field column

Now indicate the desired condition

4. Type =**"NM"** and press ↵

FIGURE DB-19
Creating a QUERY.

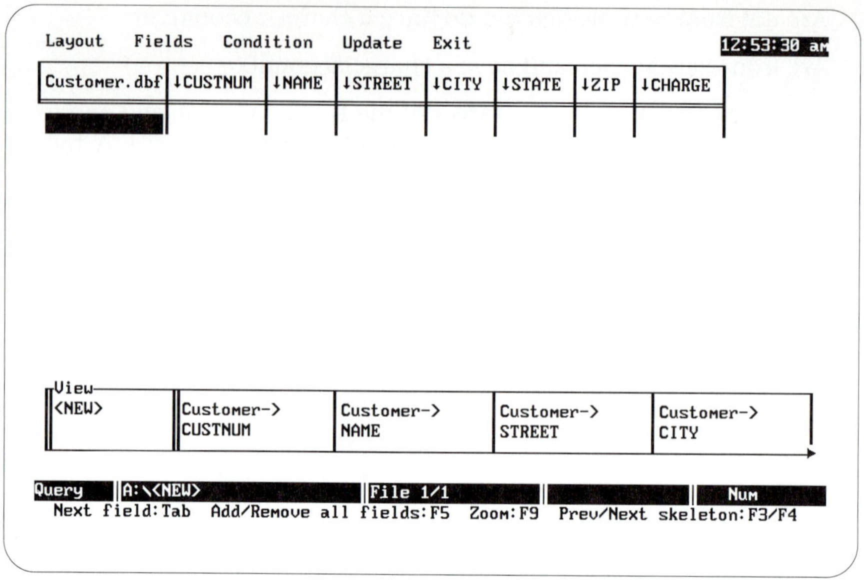

(a) A dBASE IV fresh Query screen

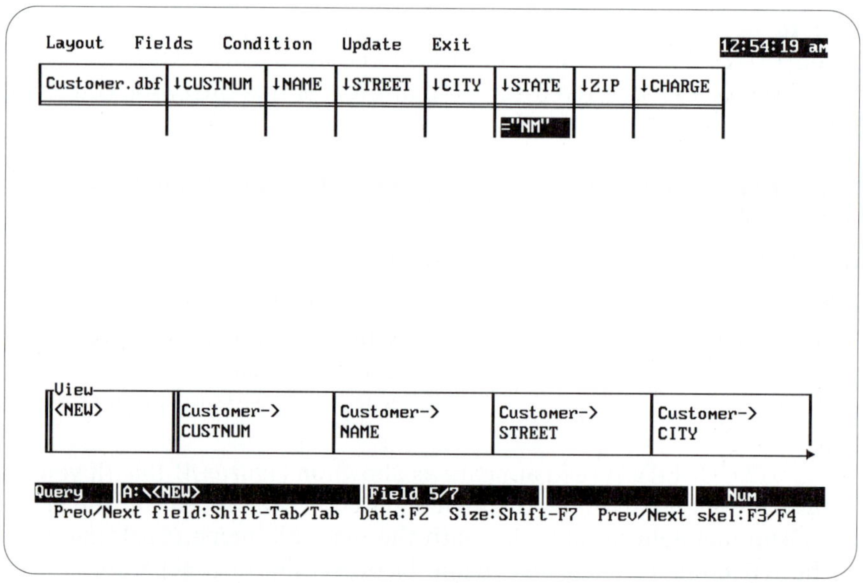

(b) Adding a query condition to select records whose state = "NM"

Your screen should resemble Figure DB-19b. If not, delete the condition and retype it correctly.

5. Press **Alt** + **E** to *Exit*

6. Type **S** to *Save*

If you entered the QUERY screen from the Control Center, you will now be asked for a query file name.

7. If "Save as:" appears, type **CUST1** and press ↵

The query is now saved to disk and available for use.

How to Use a Query. When you use a query, the conditions specified in the query control the records that are displayed.

From the Control Center.

Note: If CUST1 appears above the active line in the Queries panel, it is already in use and you should skip this section for now. Perform these steps only if CUST1 is not yet active.

1. Highlight **CUST1** in the Queries panel
2. Press ↵ twice to use the view

The query moves above the active line, showing that it is in use.

From the Dot Prompt.

1. Type **SET VIEW TO CUST1**
2. Press ↵

3. Browse the file

Only five records should appear—the ones whose state is "NM." This query "filter" will remain in effect until you cancel it. If you list, display, delete, recall, or edit, only those records that meet the query condition will be used.

How to Cancel a Query Command. When a query is no longer needed, you can cancel it easily.

From the Control Center.

1. Highlight **CUST1** in the Queries panel
2. Press ↵
3. Press ↵ twice to close the view

Notice how the query file moves below the active line.

From the Dot Prompt.

1. Type **SET FILTER TO**
2. Press ↵

A final note about queries: You can specify more than one condition in your query search. Conditions placed on the same line (as in Figure DB-20a) are treated as if they are joined by an "AND" connector. That is, the query in Figure DB1-20a will select records whose STATE is "NM" *AND* whose CHARGE is true. Conditions placed on separate lines as in Figure DB-20b (using the down arrow between entries) are joined by an "OR" connector. That is, the query in Figure DB-20b will select records whose STATE is "NM" *OR* whose CHARGE is true. The QUERY technique offers

FIGURE DB-20
Using multiple QUERY conditions.

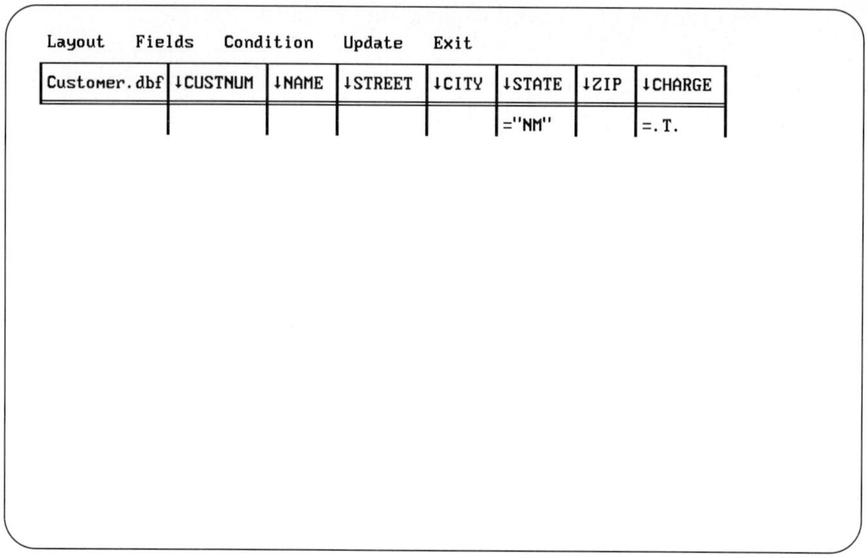

(a) The .AND. connector

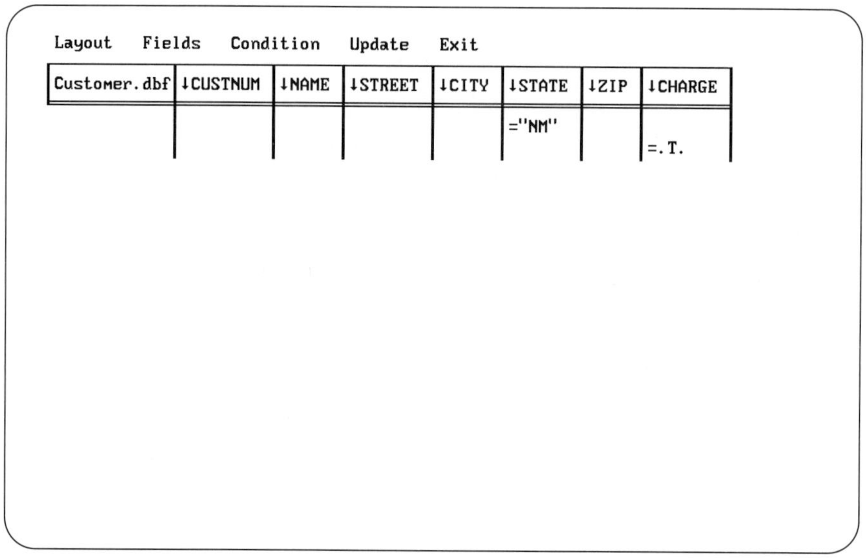

(b) The .OR. connector

many other useful searches and views. You may want to explore these using dBASE's *Help* feature.

How to Perform Calculations

dBASE's ability to perform arithmetic operations on records or fields is a very useful feature. To perform calculations, dBASE Command mode uses three commands: COUNT, SUM, and AVERAGE. The Control Center uses a query.

When you understand how to use these commands, you will be able to extract valuable information from your files quickly.

Using the COUNT Command. COUNT is used for tallying records. It is more easily invoked in the Command mode although both methods are shown. Examples of how to count the records for an entire file or for specific fields follow. Your CUSTOMER file should be active.

From the Control Center. To count an entire file's records

1. Highlight <**create**> in the Queries panel
2. Press ↵
3. Tab to any field and type **count**
4. Press ↵
5. Press **F2** to see the data

The total number of records (16) will be shown in the field you selected.

6. Press **Alt** + **E** and **T** to transfer to the query screen
7. Tab to the STATE column
8. Type **="CO"** and press ↵
9. Press **F2**

The number 6 now appears.

10. Press **Alt** + **E**
11. Type **E** to exit
12. Type **N**

From the Dot Prompt. To count an entire file's records

1. Type **COUNT**
2. Press ↵

All the records are tallied and the message "16 records" appears.

To count records for a specific field,

1. Type **COUNT FOR STATE = "CO"**
2. Press ↵

The records in which the STATE is CO are tallied and the message "6 records" appears.

DB IV

Using the SUM Command. SUM is used to add the values in any numeric field of a file. Before performing SUM (and AVERAGE) commands, you will create a new database file so you can use these commands on its specified fields.

Please note that the following instructions for creating the new database file are designed for the Command mode. At the dot prompt

1. Type **CREATE SALES** and press ↵
2. Define fields as shown in Figure DB-21
3. Press **Ctrl** + **End** when you have finished creating the file's structure
4. Press ↵ to confirm and press **Y** for Yes to input data records
5. Fill in the data as shown in Figure DB-22

Note: When typing a number like 6.00, you need not press the spacebar to align it with the number above. The decimal place will automatically align as soon as you press the period when you type the number.

6. Press ↵ when finished
7. List or Browse the file to be sure you've entered the records properly

Now you are ready to perform a SUM calculation on numeric fields of your SALES file. You can do this from either the Control Center or the dot prompt.

From the Control Center. To sum the QUANTITY field

1. Highlight <**create**> in the Queries panel
2. Press ↵
3. Tab to the QUANTITY column
4. Type **SUM** and press ↵
5. Press **F2**

The SUM 275 is produced.

6. Press **Alt** + **E**
7. Type **E** and then **N**

You could add a condition for SUPPLIER if desired.

From the Dot Prompt. To sum the QUANTITY field

1. Type **SUM QUANTITY**
2. Press ↵

The sum 275 is produced.

As with the COUNT statement, you can also use a FOR clause to make a SUM statement conditional. For example

3. Type **SUM QUANTITY FOR SUPPLIER = "Peak"** and press ↵

The sum of 235 is the total quantity ordered by Peak.

FIGURE DB-21
Fields for the SALES file.

Layout Organize Append Go To Exit 1:12:14 am

Bytes remaining: 3962

Num	Field Name	Field Type	Width	Dec	Index
1	SUPPLIER	Character	4		N
2	DESCRIP	Character	25		N
3	QUANTITY	Numeric	3	0	N
4	PRICE	Numeric	6	2	N

SUPPLIER	DESCRIP	QUANTITY	PRICE
Funk	Indy Jones Jacket, large	30	90.00
Funk	Rozelle Headbands	10	6.00
Peak	Nordic Hats	85	10.00
Peak	Nylon Windpants	50	40.00
Peak	Thermal Ski Socks	100	7.00

FIGURE DB-22
Data for the SALES file.

Using the AVERAGE Command. AVERAGE is used for averaging a field in the records of a file.

From the Control Center. To average the PRICE field

1. Highlight **<create>** in the Queries panel
2. Press ↵
3. Tab to the PRICE column
4. Type **AVERAGE** and press ↵
5. Press **F2**

This produces the average of 30.60

6. Exit the query as before

From the Dot Prompt. To average the PRICE field

1. Type **AVERAGE PRICE**
2. Press ↵

This produces the average of 30.60.

How to Index a File

You can sequentially reorganize records in a file in dBASE through either the **INDEX** or the **SORT** command.

An essential difference between the methods is that **indexing** creates an *index file* (a file with an **.MDX** extension) that is used to rearrange the records of a database file on the display screen or printer—without physically changing the original file—while sorting physically creates a new sorted database file.

Several indexing examples follow.

By Customer Number. You may, for instance, want to rearrange the order of records according to a certain field—called a **key field.** Assume that you want a listing of the records in the CUSTOMER file, in ascending order by customer number. In that case, CUSTNUM is your key field.

In the exercise that follows, you will create an index file with the records in the CUSTOMER file ordered by the CUSTNUM field. Remember that the CUSTOMER file will not change; the index file will merely show how its records are to be arranged on output. Note, for instance, that CUSTNUM 102 will be the first listed when that file is indexed numerically.

Index files created in dBASE have the extension .MDX. This extension, as mentioned earlier and as true with all dBASE extensions, is not typed and does not need to be entered by the user. All indexed files are saved by dBASE upon creation.

In the example that follows, you will be asked to use the CUSTOMER file. If this file isn't active, remember that you can activate it by highlighting it and pressing the Enter key in the Control Center, or the USE command in the Command mode.

From the Control Center. To create the CUSTNUM index file with the CUSTOMER file active

1. Press **F2** for data
2. Press **Alt** + **O** to organize
3. Type **C** to create new index
4. Press ↵
5. Type **CUSTNUM** and press ↵
6. Press ↵
7. Type **CUSTNUM** and press ↵

Your screen should resemble Figure DB-23

8. Press **Ctrl** + **End**

Note the new order.

9. Press **Esc**

From the Dot Prompt. To create the CUSTNUM index file with the CUSTOMER file active

1. Type **INDEX ON CUSTNUM TAG NUMINDX**
2. Press ↵

The message "100% indexed" appears. To inspect the indexed records

3. Type **LIST**
4. Press ↵

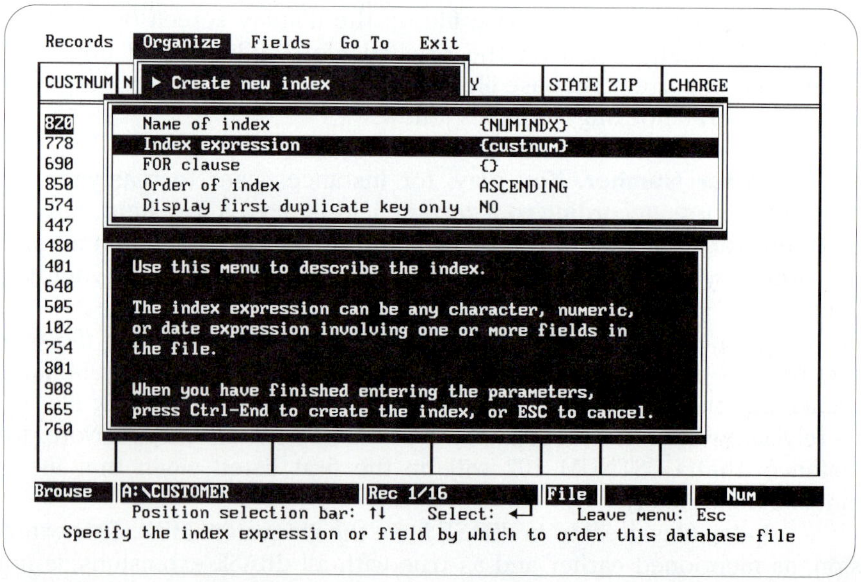

FIGURE DB-23

Creating an index file.
An index file named NUMINDX will present records arranged in ascending order based on the CUSTNUM key field.

```
. LIST
Record# CUSTNUM NAME             STREET           CITY       STATE ZIP   CHARGE
     11  102    Maya Ellis       603 Oakwood      Aurora     CO    80011 .T.
      8  401    Wayne Montoya    600 Tara Lane    Englewood  CO    80155 .F.
      6  447    Vernon Pressy    5541 Canyon      Boulder    CO    80302 .T.
      7  480    Benton Fink      440 Arapahoe     Boulder    CO    80302 .F.
     10  505    Alice Evans      5702 North St.   Boise      ID    83704 .T.
      5  574    Nellie Deutsch   23 E. Spruce     Olathe     KS    66061 .F.
      9  640    C. Foster Kane   P.O. Box 6000    Santa Fe   NM    87501 .T.
     15  665    Bette White      Box 20           Rowe       NM    87562 .T.
      3  690    William Holmes   3269 Fast Lane   Santa Fe   NM    87501 .T.
     12  754    Shane Williams   275 East Kiowa   Flagstaff  AZ    86001 .F.
     16  760    Kim Lundy        44 West St.      Missoula   MT    59802 .F.
      2  778    Sally Jones      813 Pine Bluff   Santa Fe   NM    87501 .T.
     13  801    Del Lopez        80 Williston     Austin     TX    78755 .F.
      1  820    John T. Smith    31 Cedarhurst    Boulder    CO    80302 .T.
      4  850    Artis Smith      2332 Alameda     Lakewood   CO    80215 .T.
     14  908    Duke Miller      CM Ranch         Stanley    NM    87056 .F.

.
Command ║A:\CUSTOMER          ║Rec EOF/16      ║File ║       ║    Num
```

FIGURE DB-24

Using an index file.

The NUMINDX presents the rearranged records in CUSTNUM order.

The customer numbers should now be displayed in ascending order as in Figure DB-24.

Two similar indexing examples follow, using different key fields to sequence the records in the CUSTOMER file.

By Zip Codes. This sequence will produce a list of customers by zip in ascending order.

From the Control Center. With the CUSTOMER file active

1. Press **F2**
2. Press **Alt** + O
3. Type **C**
4. Press ↵
5. Type **ZIPINDX** and press ↵
6. Type **ZIP** and press ↵
7. Press **Ctrl** + **End**

Note the records are rearranged by zip.

8. Press **Esc**

From the Dot Prompt. With the CUSTOMER file active

1. Type **INDEX ON ZIP TAG ZIPINDX**
2. Press ↵
3. List the indexed records

By Customer Numbers within Each Zip Code. This sequence will produce a list that has customer numbers in ascending order within each zip code.

DB IV

From the Control Center. With the CUSTOMER file active

1. Press **F2**
2. Press **Alt** + **O**
3. Type **C**
4. Press **↵**
5. Type **DBLINDX** and press **↵**
6. Type **ZIP** + **CUSTNUM** and press **↵**
7. Press **Ctrl** + **End**

The records are now re-ordered appropriately.

8. Press **Esc**

From the Dot Prompt. With the CUSTOMER file active

1. Type **INDEX ON ZIP + CUSTNUM TAG DBLINDX**
2. Press **↵**

The message "100% indexed" appears.

3. List the indexed records.

If you wish to temporarily turn off the active index

4. Type **SET INDEX TO**

How to Sort a File

Sorting is dBASE's second method for sequentially reorganizing records in a file. The SORT command, although conceptually more straightforward than indexing, is far less efficient. Using SORT creates a new DBF file, and thus uses more memory than INDEX.

Your CUSTOMER file should still be active, from the previous sorting exercise.

From the Control Center. To sort the CUSTOMER file by CUSTNUM

1. Press **F2**
2. Press **Alt** + **O**
3. Type **S** to sort database
4. Type **CUSTNUM** and press **↵**
5. Press **Ctrl** + **End**

The message "Enter name of sorted file:" appears.

6. Type **NEWFILE** and press **↵**
7. Press **↵** to skip the description

Two versions of CUSTOMER now exist—the unsorted version (CUSTOMER) and a sorted version (NEWFILE).

8. Press **Esc**
9. Highlight **NEWFILE** in the data panel

From the Dot Prompt. To sort the CUSTOMER file by CUSTNUM

1. Type **SORT ON CUSTNUM TAG NEWFILE**
2. Press **↵**

Two versions of CUSTOMER now exist—an unsorted version (CUSTOMER) and a sorted version (NEWFILE).

To view the file

3. Type **USE NEWFILE** and press **↵**
4. Type **LIST** and press **↵**

Note: To sort a file on more than one field and to sort a key in descending order—for example, to sort with CITY as the primary key field sorted in ascending order, and CUSTNUM as the secondary key field sorted in descending order—you would type

10. Press ↵
11. Press ↵ to use the file
12. Browse the file to see the new order, then press **Esc**

```
SORT ON CITY,
CUSTNUM/D TO NEWFILE2
```

The /D here tells dBASE to sort CUSTNUM in descending order.

Remember to have the main database file (CUSTOMER) open each time you execute the SORT command on it.

Quit or continue to the next section.

ACCESSING DATA IN A FILE

Several useful commands to help you access the data of a file are presented next. Specifically, you will learn additional options of the LIST command, and will be introduced to the SKIP, GOTO TOP and GOTO BOTTOM, REPLACE, LOCATE, and SEEK commands.

Knowing what these commands do and how to use them will allow you to efficiently access the data in your files.

Using the LIST Command

LIST offers options in addition to those previously discussed. LIST, like DISPLAY, may be used to show selected records of a file. The Control Center uses BROWSE and a query to achieve a similar result.

This tutorial will show you how to list selected fields of a file's records, to list records with fields in a specified order, and to list a single record. The CUSTOMER file should be active.

From the Control Center. To list just the NAME field of CUSTOMER records

1. Highlight <**create**> in the Queries panel
2. Press ↵
3. Press **F5** to remove all fields
4. Tab to the NAME column
5. Press **F5** to include it

Notice that a down arrow appears in front of NAME and the field is listed in the view as in Figure DB-25.

6. Press **F2** for data

A list of names appears. If you want to include other fields,

From the Dot Prompt. To list just the NAME field of CUSTOMER's records

1. Type **LIST NAME**
2. Press ↵

Only the names in the CUSTOMER file are displayed. You may use this command to list any field(s) of a file's records. If there is more than one field you want to list, separate the field names by commas.

To list the records in CUSTOMER with the NAME and CUSTNUM fields in reverse order

3. Type **LIST NAME, CUSTNUM**
4. Press ↵

DB IV

return to the query and repeat the F5 procedure.

7. Press **Alt** + **E**

8. Press **E** and then **N**

To list the records in CUSTOMER with the NAME and CUSTNUM fields in reverse order

9. Repeat Steps 1 through 5

10. Press **Shift** + **Tab** to move to the **CUSTNUM** column

11. Press **F5** to include it

Notice that the view shows both fields *in the order they were selected.*

12. Press **F2**

Notice that in this list of CUSTOMER records, the CUSTNUM field follows the name field.

13. Repeat Steps 7 and 8

Notice that in this list of CUSTOMER records, CUSTNUM field follows the NAME field.

To list Record 8 only

5. Type **LIST RECORD 8** and press ↵

Using the SKIP Command

This command will advance the pointer forward one or more records. (Remember the record pointer indicates the current record.) You can enter either a positive number to move forward that number of records

FIGURE DB-25
Using a QUERY to create a VIEW.

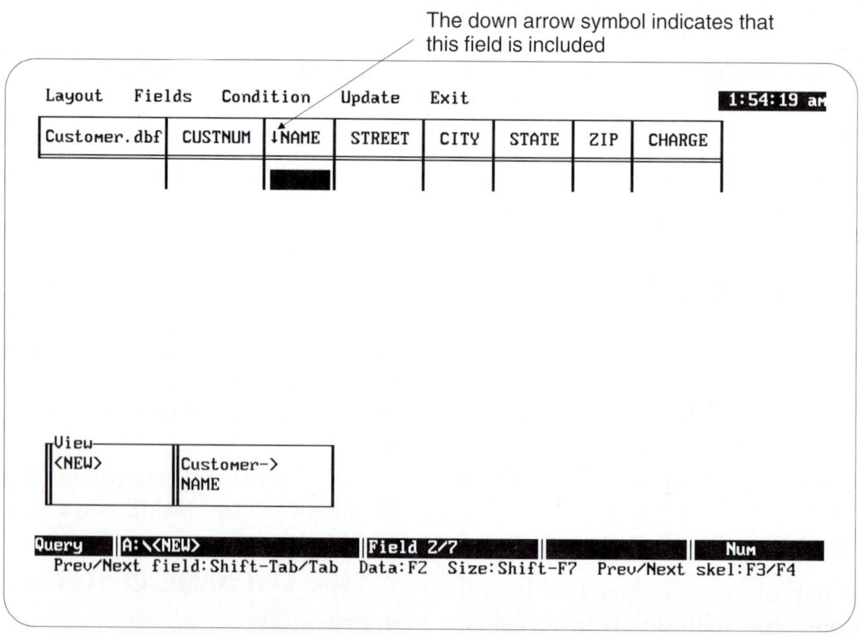

in the file or a negative number to move backwards that number of records.

By using the SKIP command, you can quickly move through the records in your file.

From the Control Center. To use the SKIP command with CUSTOMER active

1. Press **F2** for data
2. Press **Alt** + **G** for GOTO
3. Type **R** for record
4. Press **Backspace** to delete the current record number
5. Type **14** and press ↵

The screen points to Record 14.

6. Press **Alt** + **G**
7. Type **S** to skip
8. Press **Backspace** to delete the current number
9. Type **−5** and press ↵

The screen now repositions itself backwards 5 records

10. Press **Esc**

From the Dot Prompt. To use the SKIP command with CUSTOMER active

1. Type **LIST RECORD 14** and press ↵ to display record 14
2. Type **SKIP** and press ↵

The message "Record No. 15" is showing.

3. Type **DISPLAY** and press ↵ to display Record 15
4. Type **SKIP −5** and press ↵ to move backwards 5 records
5. Type **DISPLAY** and press ↵ to inspect the current record, Record 10

Using the GOTO TOP and GOTO BOTTOM Commands

Two additional commands, GOTO TOP and GOTO BOTTOM, can help you move quickly through your files. These commands do just what they suggest; they respectively go to the first or last record in the file.

From the Control Center. To go to the top of your CUSTOMER file

1. Press **F2**
2. Press **Alt** + **G**
3. Type **T** for top record

The screen is adjusted to show the top record. To go to the bottom of your file

4. Press **Alt** + **G**
5. Type **L** for last record

The last record (16/16) is shown.

6. Press **Esc**

From the Dot Prompt. To go to the top of your CUSTOMER file

1. Type **GOTO TOP** and press ↵
2. Type **DISPLAY** and press ↵

The first record is shown. To go to the bottom of your file

3. Type **GOTO BOTTOM** and press ↵
4. Type **DISPLAY** and press ↵

The last record (number 16) is shown.

Using the REPLACE Command

You can use the **REPLACE** command to quickly replace the contents of certain fields throughout a file. This command will replace one numeric string or character string in a field with another.

From the Control Center. To replace the F in the CHARGE field for customer Wayne Montoya with a T

1. Highlight **<create>** in the Queries panel
2. Press ↵
3. Type **REPLACE** in the leftmost column
4. Press ↵ and **P** to proceed
5. Tab to the NAME column
6. Type = **"Wayne Montoya"**
7. Tab to the CHARGE column
8. Type **WITH .T.** and press ↵

Your screen should resemble Figure DB-26. If not, tab to the appropriate column and change it.

9. Press **Alt** + **U** to update
10. Type **P** to perform the update

The message "1 record replaced" appears.

11. Press any key
12. Press **Alt** + **E** then **A** and **Y**
13. List or browse all of the records (or just Record 8) to see the change in Montoya's CHARGE field

From the Dot Prompt. To replace the F in the CHARGE field for customer Wayne Montoya with a T

1. Type **REPLACE CHARGE WITH .T. FOR NAME = "Wayne Montoya"**
2. Press ↵

The message "1 record replaced" appears.

3. List all of the records (or just Record 8) to see the change in Montoya's CHARGE field

FIGURE DB-26
Using a QUERY to REPLACE record data.
The entries in the target, NAME, and CHARGE columns will cause all records for which NAME = "Wayne Montoya" to have their CHARGE data replaced with a logical "TRUE."

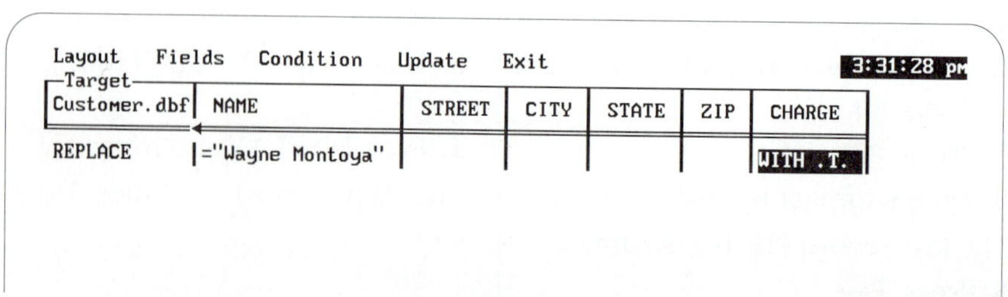

Using the LOCATE Command

The **LOCATE** command will search a field for specific occurrences of data and list the number of each record containing these occurrences. In this exercise, you will locate all records for the city of Boulder.

Make sure that you are at the top of the CUSTOMER file before beginning.

From the Control Center. To use the LOCATE command

1. Press **F2** for data

2. Move to the top record

Note that this search works in either the BROWSE or EDIT screen.

3. Tab to the CITY field

4. Press **Alt** + **G** to GoTo

5. Type **E** for Forward search

At the prompt "Enter search string:"

6. Type **Boulder** and press ↵

The pointer is relocated at the first record whose CITY is Boulder.

7. Press **Shift** + **F4** to continue the search

8. When done, press **Esc**

From the Dot Prompt. To use the LOCATE command

1. Type **LOCATE FOR CITY = "Boulder"**

2. Press ↵

The statement "Record = 1" appears. To continue to the next occurrence (Record = 6)

3. Type **CONTINUE**

4. Press ↵

When you locate an occurrence, you may, of course, display the record contents.

5. Keep typing **CONTINUE** and pressing ↵ until all occurrences are found

At this point the message "End of LOCATE scope" appears.

Using the SEEK Command

The **SEEK** command is used to find records having specific characteristics in any file that has an index. Both the database file and its index file must be referenced prior to issuing the SEEK command. The index is used to find records during a SEEK process.

From the Control Center. To start the SEEK process with the CUSTOMER file and its ZIPINDX file

1. Highlight **CUSTOMER** in the Data panel

2. Press ↵

3. Type **M** to Modify its order

4. Type **O** to order records by index

From the Dot Prompt. To start the SEEK process with the CUSTOMER file and its ZIPINDX file

1. Type **USE CUSTOMER INDEX CUSTOMER ORDER ZIPINDX**

2. Press ↵

Note: Any index file can be used.

3. Type **SEEK "80302"** and press ↵

5. Highlight **ZIPINDX** and press ↵

6. Press **Ctrl** + **End**

Now initiate the Index key search as follows:

7. Press **F2**

8. Press **Alt** + **G**

9. Type **I** for Index key search

At the prompt "Enter search string for zip:"

10. Type **80302** and press ↵

The first occurrence of zip code 80302 is located.

11. Press **Esc** to end

The first occurrence of zip code 80302 is located. To see the record

4. Type **DISPLAY** and press ↵

Repeatedly using the SKIP command and DISPLAY will respectively show and display subsequent occurrences of the 80302 zip.

PREPARING REPORTS

One of dBASE's most useful features is its report-generation capability. A report differs significantly from a list in that you can format a report extensively and gain additional flexibility in the type of information being output.

Preparing a dBASE report involves three steps: establishing a source-data file, defining the report format, and outputting the report.

By following the steps that will be given shortly, you will be able to create the report shown in Figure DB-27. It uses the source data from the SALES file you created earlier (refer back to Figure DB-27).

Figure DB-27, in addition to showing the format of the report you'll prepare, illustrates two interesting characteristics commonly found in business reports: the *calculated field* and the *control break*.

The Amount column in Figure DB-27 is a **calculated field** that was created from two fields of the SALES file—QUANTITY and PRICE. When the values in these two fields are multiplied together, the result is the values shown in the Amount column.

After each supplier, Funk Fashions (Funk) and Peak Mountaineering (Peak), dBASE breaks to print a subtotal of the Quantity Sold and Amount columns. Such breaks are called **control breaks.** Also, at the end of the report, a final break is taken to print totals. In dBASE and in other report generators you can specify which fields you want to use to control the breaks in the report and which columns you want totaled. In Figure DB-27, the SUPPLIER field is used to control the breaks, while the Quantity Sold and Amount columns are designated as columns that will be totaled during a break.

```
Page No.    1
03/28/92

                         JANUARY SALES

VENDOR     DESCRIPTION              QUANTITY     PRICE      AMOUNT
                                        SOLD

VENDOR: Funk
Funk       Indy Jones Jacket, large       30     90.00     2700.00
Funk       Rozelle Headbands              10      6.00       60.00
SUB-TOTAL:                                40               2760.00

VENDOR: Peak
Peak       Nordic Hats                    85     10.00      850.00
Peak       Nylon Windpants                50     40.00     2000.00
Peak       Thermal Ski Socks             100      7.00      700.00
SUB-TOTAL:                               235               3550.00

TOTAL:                                   275               6310.00


          Cancel viewing: ESC,  Continue viewing: SPACEBAR
```

FIGURE DB-27
Report using data in the SALES file.

How to Establish a Source File

The file containing the source data for the report will generally be an ordinary .DBF file. You have already created the data file SALES that you'll use to prepare the report. You must, however, have the file sorted on the SUPPLIER column in order to use this column to initiate control breaks. Control breaks are automatically taken on this column each time its value changes. Fortunately, the SALES file of Figure DB-22 is already in correct sorted order.

Open the SALES file for use as follows:

From the Control Center.

1. Highlight **SALES** in the Data panel
2. Press ↵
3. Type **U** to use

From the Dot Prompt.

1. Type **USE SALES**
2. Press ↵

How to Define the Report Format This step is perhaps the most important one in creating a report. It is the step in which you tell dBASE what the report will look like, how it will be titled, what fields will be calculated or used for control breaks, and so forth. dBASE uses a special file to store all of this information about how the report will be prepared. This file is called a **report form** and has the extension of **.FRM.**

From the Control Center. To begin creating the report form (with the SALES file active)

1. Highlight **<create>** in the Reports panel
2. Press ↵
3. Press **Esc**

From the Dot Prompt. To begin creating the report form (with the SALES file active)

1. Type **CREATE REPORT SALESR**
2. Press ↵

Note: SALESR (SALESR.FRM) will be the name of our report form.

The *Report* screen appears as in Figure DB-28. Seven categories are listed along the menu bar at the top. Each category can be selected in one of two ways: You can press F10 and then press the right arrow key to highlight a desired action, or you can press the Alt key and the first letter of the category (e.g., Alt+F for *Fields*).

As each category is highlighted, a pull-down menu appears offering options. Each of these options can be selected by moving the highlighted selection bar to it and pressing the Enter key.

Beneath the menu bar is a ruler line. This line shows the position of the left margin (with a "["symbol), tabs (shown by inverted triangles), and the right margin (shown by a "]" symbol, which is currently off the screen).

The remainder of the screen displays a representation of a report page, which is currently divided into five bands. These **bands** define the different components of the report. Each band contains a border and a shaded entry area beneath it. The five bands that begin each report include

FIGURE DB-28
A fresh dBASE IV report screen.

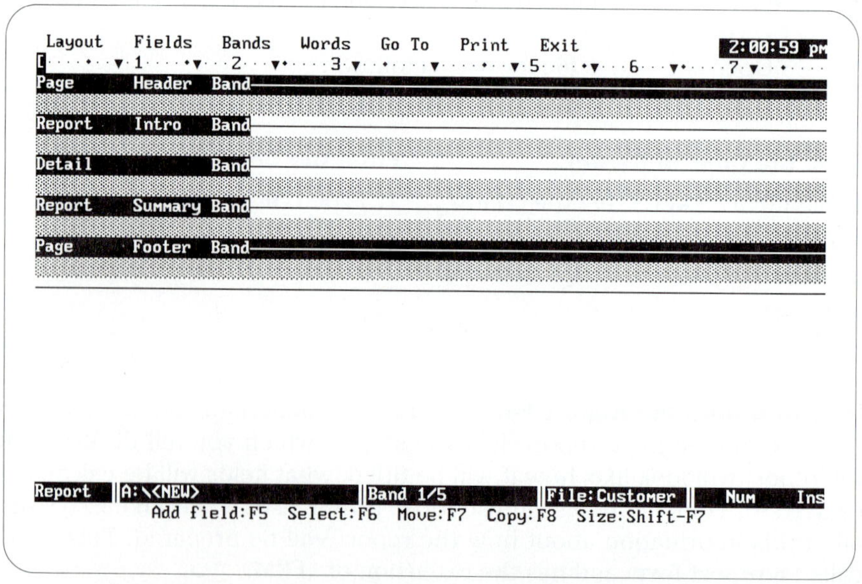

☐ A *Page Header* band, which contains text that will appear at the top of each page—usually report titles and column headings.

☐ A *Report Intro* band, which contains text that will appear once at the beginning of the report.

☐ A *Detail* band, which contains format symbols (or text) that show where data will appear in each row. "X" symbols show alphabetic text whereas "9" symbols show numbers.

☐ A *Report Summary* band, which displays summary data (such as totals, averages, and counts) for specific columns at the end of the report.

☐ A *Page Footer* band, which contains text that will appear at the bottom of each page.

Bands for control breaks (breaks between groups of data) may be added, and bands that are not desired may be hidden from the report (as you will see).

Invoking a Quick Layout. Although reports can be created line by line, it is much easier to let dBASE create the basic design for you using its *quick layouts* command. This is especially true if you are planning to use most of the database fields in the order they appear in your database file. You can then modify the form to better suit your specific needs. To create a quick layout,

1. Press **Alt** + **L** for layout

2. Type **Q** for quick layouts

3. Type **C** for column format

Your screen should resemble Figure DB-29. Note that a page number, date, and column headings (using actual field names) have been placed in the *Page Header* band. The *Detail* band and *Report Summary* band have been filled with templates for the appropriate data (X's or 9's). We can now modify this design to match the report shown in Figure DB-27. Note that the names we wish to use as headings differ slightly from those created by dBASE. They are

VENDOR

DESCRIPTION

QUANTITY SOLD

PRICE

AMOUNT

Modifying Titles and Headings. First, add a title to the report:

1. Move to *Line:3 Col:0* in the *Page Header* band

2. Press ↵ twice to add 2 new lines

DB IV

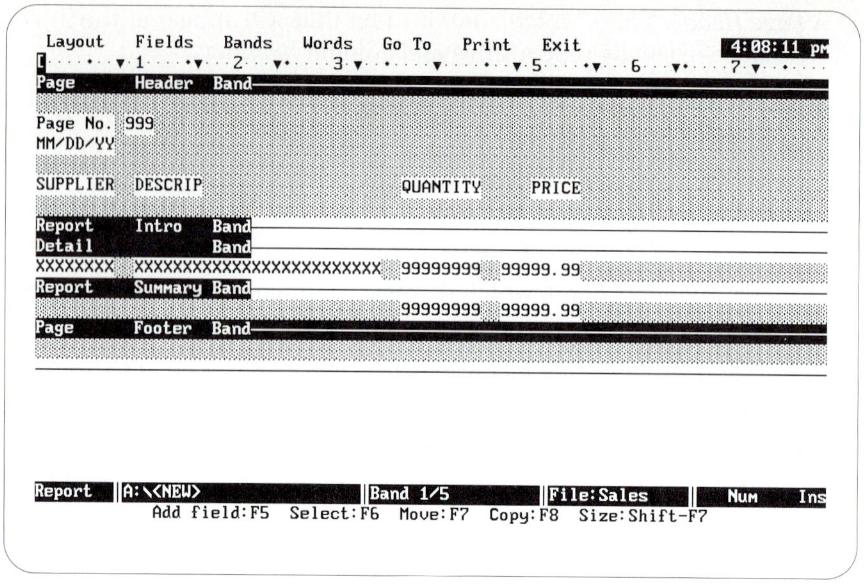

FIGURE DB-29
The Quick Layouts command creates appropriate entries in the Page Header, Detail, and Report Summary bands.

3. Move to *Line:4 Col:29*
4. Type **JANUARY SALES**

We can now change a few headings as follows:

5. At *Line:6 Col:0,* delete the word **SUPPLIER**
6. Type **VENDOR**

Note: "VENDOR" is the name we will give to the column that will display the SUPPLIER field.

7. At *Line:6 Col:17,* type **TION** so the heading reads "DESCRIPTION"
8. At *Line:6 Col:60,* type **AMOUNT**
9. At *Line:7 Col:0,* press **Ctrl** + **N** to add a line
10. At *Line:7 Col:41,* type **SOLD**

Adding Data Templates. We can add additional data fields to the *Detail* band to display other data in the report. Here, we will create the AMOUNT field, which will be calculated as QUANTITY times PRICE.

1. In the *Detail* band, move to *Line:0 Col:58*
2. Press **F5** to add a field

A menu box appears on the screen.

3. Highlight <**create**> in the Calculated column
4. Press ↵
5. Type **N** to open the Name entry line

6. Type **AMOUNT** and press **↵**

7. Type **E** to open the Expression entry line

8. Type **QUANTITY*PRICE** and press **↵**

We can now adjust the data template to adjust the number of digits that will be displayed in the answer.

9. Type **T** for Template

10. Press **Home** to move to the beginning

11. Press **Del** twice to remove two 9's

12. Press **Ctrl** + **End** to accept the data template

As seen in Figure DB-30a, the *Detail* band now shows that the new data will appear beneath the heading "AMOUNT."

Modifying Totals in the Summary Band. We can now modify the data templates in the *Summary* band to match our report needs. First, we'll delete an unwanted total.

1. In the *Summary* band, move to *Line:0 Col:47*

2. Press **Del** to remove the column's sum

Now, we can add a total for AMOUNT.

3. At *Line:0 Col:58,* press **F5**

4. Highlight **Sum** in the SUMMARY column

5. Type **N** to open the Name entry line

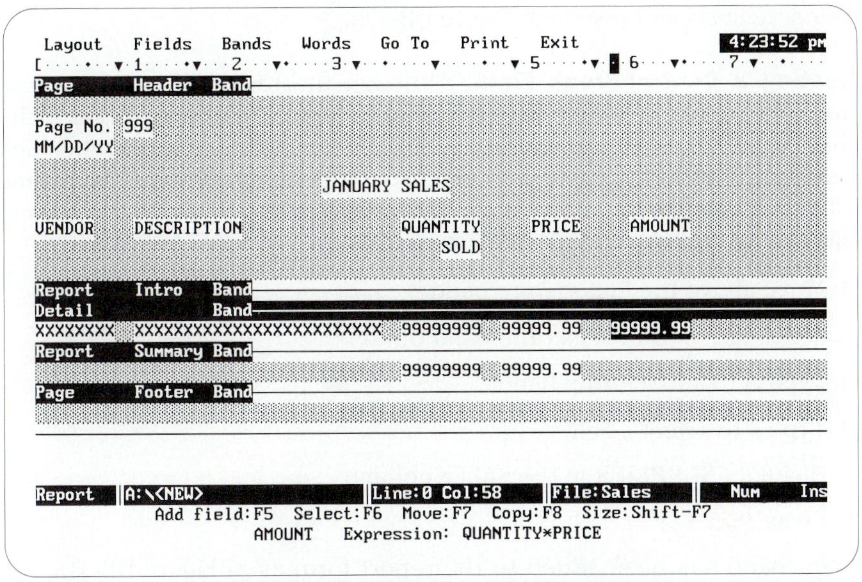

Changing column headings and data templates

FIGURE DB-30a
Modifying the Quick Layouts.

FIGURE DB-30b
Modifying the Quick Layouts.

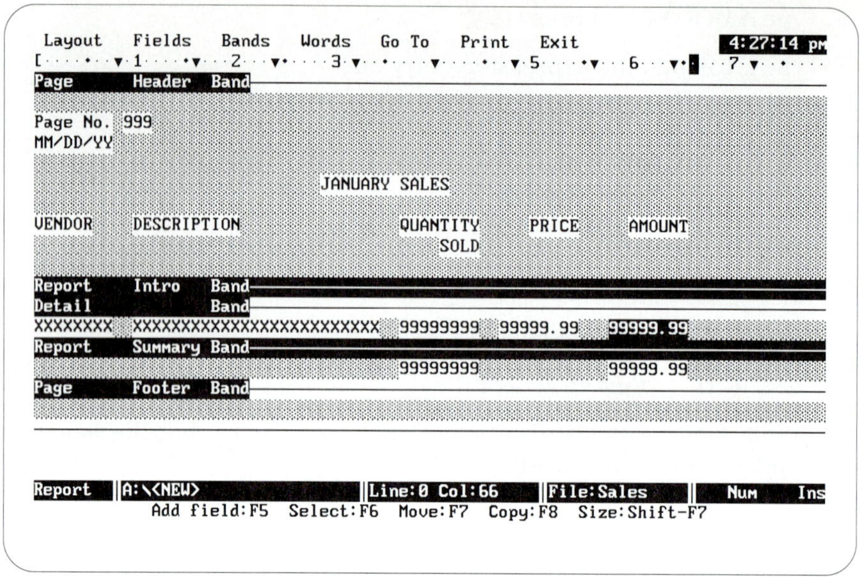

Completing the summary template for the AMOUNT column

6. Type **SUM_AMOUNT** and press ↵
7. Type **F** to select a field
8. Highlight **AMOUNT** in the CALCULATED Column
9. Type **T** for Template
10. Press **Home** to move to the beginning
11. Delete two 9's and press ↵
12. Press **Ctrl** + **End** to accept the template

Your screen should resemble Figure DB-30b.

Creating a Control-Break Field. Although the report can be saved in this form, remember that we also want to create a control-break field, which determines where subtotals will appear in the final report. When you identify SUPPLIER and its corresponding summary data, each time SUPPLIER changes, a subtotal for the previous supplier will be output. This can be done by adding a *Group* band to the report as follows.

1. Move above the *Report Intro* band
2. Press **Alt** + **B** to select the band option
3. Type **A** to add a group band
4. Type **F** to select a field
5. Highlight **SUPPLIER** in the SALES column
6. Press ↵

A new band has been added to the report form as in Figure DB-31a. We can now add some identifying text and data to this band.

FIGURE DB-31
Identifying the control group.

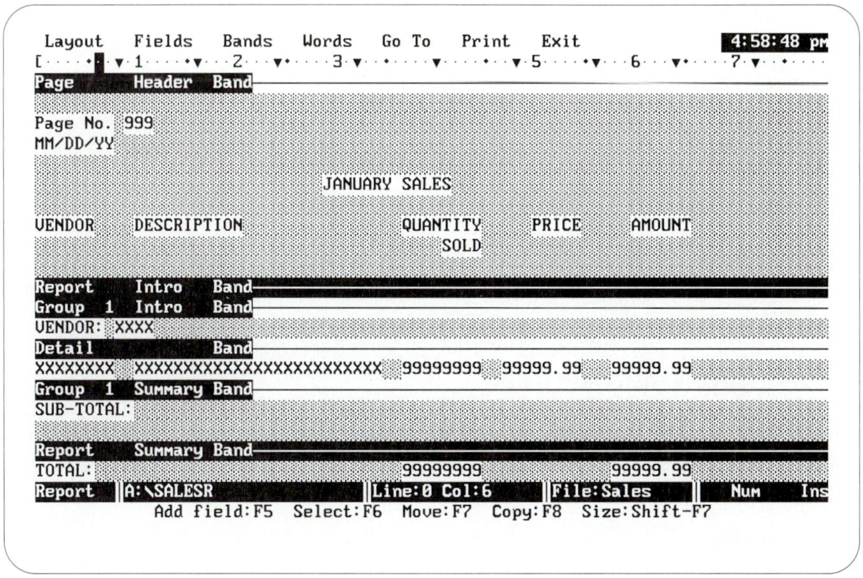

(a) A Group 1 Intro band is added to the report

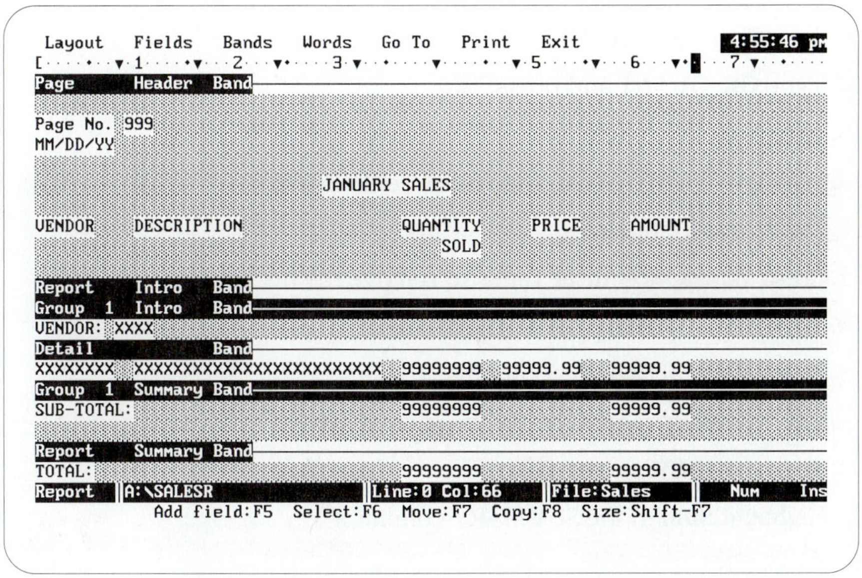

(b) Labels and sub-totals complete the report form

7. In the *Group1 Intro* band, move to *Line:0 Col:0*
8. Type **VENDOR:**
9. Move to *Line:0 Col:8* and press **F5**
10. Highlight **SUPPLIER** in the SALES column
11. Press **↵**
12. Press **Ctrl** + **End**

DB IV

We can now identify totals in the summary bands as well.

13. In the *Group1 Summary* band, move to *Line:0 Col:0*

14. Type **SUB-TOTAL:**

15. In the *Report Summary* band, move to *Line:0 Col:0*

16. Type **TOTAL:**

All that remains is to place data templates into the *Group1 Summary* band so that each vendor's data totals will be displayed in our report.

17. In the *Group1 Summary* band, move to *Line:0 Col:37*

18. Press **Ctrl** + **N** to add a line

Adding this second line to the summary band will make the report more readable by causing dBASE to leave a line before starting the next vendor's data.

19. Press **F5**

20. Highlight **Sum** in the SUMMARY column

21. Press ↵

22. Type **N** to open the Name entry line

23. Type **GR_QUANT** and press ↵

24. Type **F** to select a field

25. Highlight **QUANTITY** in the SALES Column

26. Type **T** for Template

27. Press **Backspace** three times to remove the decimals

28. Type **9** to add a final "9" to the template

29. Press **Ctrl** + **End** to accept it

Repeat a similar process to add the second sum as follows:

30. At *Line:0 Col:58,* press **F5**

31. Highlight **Sum** in the SUMMARY column

32. Press ↵

33. Type **N** then type **GR_AMOUNT** and press ↵

34. Type **F** then highlight **AMOUNT** in the CALCULATED Column

35. Type **T** for Template

36. Press **Home** then press **Del** twice

37. Press **Ctrl** + **End**

Your report form should now resemble Figure DB-31b. It is now ready to save.

How To Save a Report Form. You can save the report form on your disk as follows.

1. Press **Alt** + **E** to *Exit*

2. Type **S** to *Save changes and exit*

In the Command mode, your report is now saved. However, if you are using the Control Center, the screen will prompt you with "Save as:" and await an entry. If so,

3. Type **SALESR** and press ↵

How to Output the Report

Report forms can be sent to your screen or printer with a **REPORT FORM** command. When invoked, report forms present the data from the current database file in the record order specified by the active index (or in natural record order, if no index is used).

From the Control Center. To output a report form to the printer (with the SALES file active)

1. Make sure your printer is ready to receive output
2. Highlight **SALESR** in the Reports panel
3. Press ↵
4. Type **P** to print the report
5. Type **B** to begin printing the report

Note that you could press **V** to view the report on your screen without sending it to the printer. You would then have to follow the directions at the bottom of the screen to return to the Control Center.

From the Dot Prompt. To output a report form to the printer (with the SALES file active)

1. Type **REPORT FORM SALESR TO PRINT**
2. Press ↵

Note that you could view the report on your screen without sending it to the printer by omitting the words "TO PRINT" from the command.

The SALESR report is printed as shown in Figure DB-27. The records from the SALES file have been added to the report form. Note, too, that the date, page number, and totals are placed as dictated by the report form.

Advanced Reports

dBASE also enables you to perform a number of other operations in developing reports. Here, we will mention these only in passing, leaving it as an end-of-tutorials, hands-on exercise for you to do.

Preparing a Report from Selected Records. Doing this is relatively easy. Suppose, for instance, that we wish to prepare a report from only those records of the SALES file where the PRICE field exceeds $8.00. Such a condition would allow only the Indy Jones jacket, the nordic hat, and the nylon windpants to be used in the report; the other two records would be ignored. To produce such a report

From the Control Center. Selecting records in a report involves two steps: first, create (or activate) a query, and then generate the desired report.

1. Highlight <**create**> in the Queries panel
2. Press ↵
3. Tab to the PRICE column
4. Type >**8** and press ↵
5. Press **Alt** + **E** and then **S**

In response to *Save as:*

6. Type **CUSTP** and press ↵

The query is now active and you can generate the report to use selected records:

7. Highlight **SALESR** in the Reports panel
8. Press ↵
9. Type **P** to print the report
10. Type **C** to select the current view
11. Type **V** to view the report

When you are finished looking at the screen,

12. Press **Esc** and then any key

From the Dot Prompt.

1. Type **REPORT FORM SALESR FOR PRICE > 8**
2. Press ↵

Note: You can also first create a query, invoke it with a SET VIEW command, and then simply type REPORT FORM SALESR.

Preparing a Report That Contains Only Subtotals. To do this, you will need to use dBASE's MODIFY REPORT command, which enables you to change your report form. MODIFY REPORT lets you add or delete columns to reports, alter such report definitions as column widths and column titles, and change a variety of other characteristics about the report. Before you make any modifications to a report form, however, you should first back up the existing report form, using either the COPY command of DOS or the COPY command of dBASE. This ensures that you will easily be able to recover if you make a mistake modifying the form.

To prepare a report containing only subtotals,

From the Control Center.

1. Highlight **SALESR** in the Reports panel
2. Press ↵ and then **M** to modify

From the Dot Prompt.

1. Type **MODIFY REPORT SALESR**
2. Press ↵

The report form appears. A report form band that shows no entry lines under its border will not appear in the report. These bands are said to be "closed." Bands can be closed, or reopened, by moving to the band's border, and then pressing the Enter key. You can create a summary report by closing the *Detail* band in the report form, as follows:

3. Move to the *Detail* band border

The status line should display the message "Band 4/6."

4. Press ↵ to close it

As shown in Figure DB-32, the detail line disappears, indicating that the data templates will not appear in the report. (If the detail band is reopened, the text or data will reappear.)

5. Press **Alt** + **E** to Exit

6. Press **S** to Save

When you subsequently run the report on the screen or the printer, you should get a report that looks like the one in Figure DB-33.

Inserting and Deleting Report Columns. Again, you would use the MODIFY REPORT command for such tasks.

To *delete* a column in a report form, you must remove its column entry in each band. You do this by moving to the entry in each appropriate band, and pressing the Del key. Column entries should be removed from the *Page Header, Detail,* and all *Summary* bands.

After the column entries have been deleted, you may wish to move the position of other columns' text or data templates to close in any blank space.

To move text:

- ☐ Position the cursor at the start of the text
- ☐ Press **F6** to select
- ☐ Move the cursor so that the entire text block to be moved is highlighted
- ☐ Press **F7** to move the block
- ☐ Move the cursor to the start of the block's new location
- ☐ Press ↵ to accept this position
- ☐ Type **Y** to answer "Delete covered text and fields?"
- ☐ Press **Esc** to shut off the selection highlight

DB
IV

FIGURE DB-32
Creating a Summary Report.

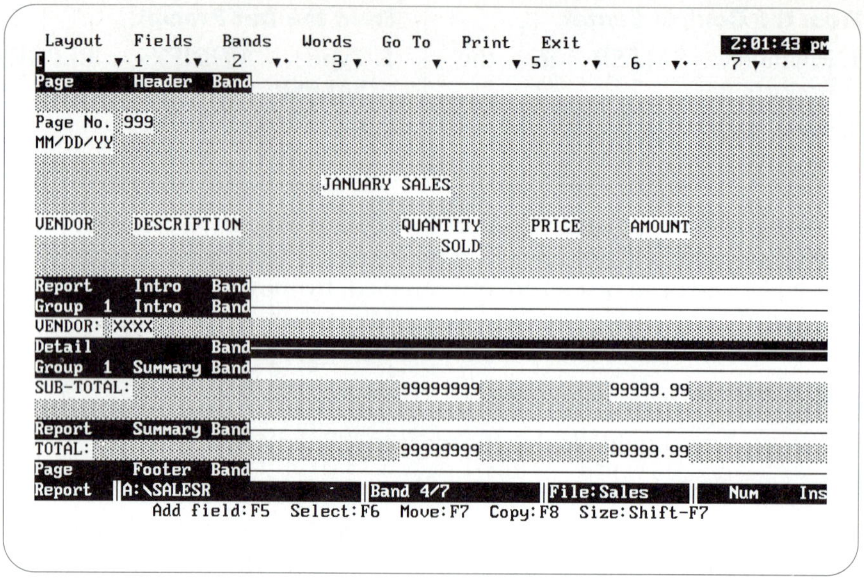

Closing the Detail band instructs dBASE IV to display only the summary statistics.

FIGURE DB-33
The printed Summary report.

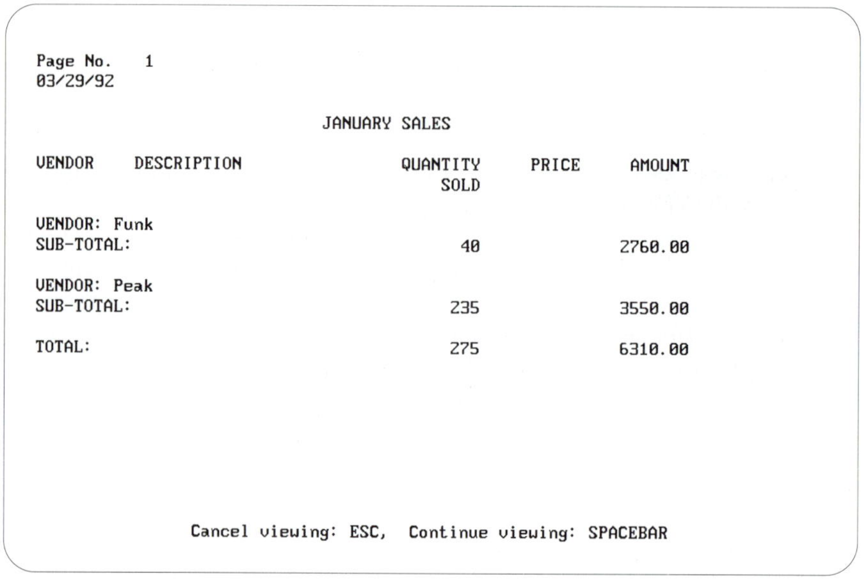

To move data or summary templates:

- ☐ Position the cursor at the start of the template
- ☐ Press **F6** to select
- ☐ Move the cursor so that all templates to be moved in the band are highlighted
- ☐ Press **F7** to move

☐ Move the cursor to the start of the new location

☐ Press ↵ then **Y** and **Esc**

To *insert* a new column, first use the techniques mentioned above to move existing columns aside to make room for the new one. Be sure to leave enough room for the width of the data and spacing between columns (usually 2 characters on each side). Of course, if you are adding a column at the extreme right of the report, no columns need be moved. Next, use the techniques described earlier in this chapter to type column headings and add data templates (using F5 as we did when creating the AMOUNT column).

To save changes after you've fully defined the new form, follow the exiting procedure described in the previous section (Alt+L, S, Enter).

COMMAND REFERENCE

This section briefly summarizes many of the most-used commands in dBASE IV. It is meant to be used only as a reference after completing the full dBASE instructions contained in the preceding chapters.

Note: In this reference

1. The examples contain general terms, such as field name, filename, record number, and so on, within angle brackets (< >). When you issue the commands shown in the examples, you must enter the *actual* field name, filename, record number, etc. Do not type in the brackets.
2. To "select" an item from a menu means the same thing as highlighting it and pressing the Enter key ↵.

Adding Records to a File

To add records with EDIT:

From the Dot Prompt

Type **APPEND** ↵

Control Center Mode

1. Highlight the name of the database file and press **F2** to access the BROWSE/EDIT screen

If no records are in the database, skip to step 5; otherwise, go to the next step.

2. If the BROWSE screen appears, press **F2** for the EDIT screen

3. Press **Alt** + **R** to reach the Records menu

4. Highlight **Add new records** and place the cursor on the first field of a blank record

5. For each field to be filled in the first appended record:

   a. Type data into the field or press ↵ to bypass entering data into the field

   b. If the data doesn't completely fill the field, press ↵ to advance to the next field

6. Enter data into the remaining records, in the manner described in step 5

7. When finished, press **Alt** + **E** to access the Exit pull-down menu

8. Highlight **Exit** from the Exit menu to save records and return to the Control Center

To add records using BROWSE:

From the Dot Prompt

1. Type **BROWSE** ↵

2. Move the cursor below the last record in the file

3. Type **Y** for Yes

Control Center Mode

1. Highlight the name of the database file and press **F2** to access the BROWSE/EDIT screen

2. If the EDIT screen appears, press **F2** for the BROWSE screen

3. Press **Alt** + **R** to reach the Records menu

4. Highlight **Add new records** ↵ and place the cursor on the first field of the first record to be appended

5. For this record and each subsequent one, enter data into the correct fields

6. When finished, press **Alt** + **E** to access the Exit pull-down menu

7. Highlight **Exit** from the Exit menu to save records and return to the Control Center ↵

Averaging Values in a Field

To average all the values in a field of an active database file:

From the Dot Prompt

Type **AVERAGE <field name>** ↵

Control Center Mode

1. Highlight <**create**> in the Queries panel ↵
2. Tab to the field to be averaged and type **AVERAGE**
3. Press **F2** to see the results

To average only those values in a field of an active database file meeting a given condition:

From the Dot Prompt

Type **AVERAGE <field name> FOR <condition>** ↵

Control Center Mode

1. Highlight <**create**> in the Queries panel ↵
2. Tab to the field to be averaged and type **AVERAGE**
3. Tab to the field to contain the condition and type in an operator followed by a value
4. Press **F2** to see the results

Cancelling a Command

To cancel a command:

In either mode, press **Esc**

Closing a File

To close a database file:

From the Dot Prompt

Close files just as you would in the Control Center mode or:

Type **CLOSE DATABASES** ↵

Control Center Mode

When a new database file is opened or you quit dBASE, the active database is automatically closed.

Counting Records

To count all records in a file:

From the Dot Prompt

Type **COUNT** ↵

Control Center Mode

1. Highlight <**create**> in the Queries panel ↵
2. Tab to any field and type **COUNT**
3. Press **F2** to see the results

To count all records that meet a given condition:

From the Dot Prompt

Type **COUNT FOR** <**condition**> ↵

Control Center Mode

1. Highlight <**create**> in the Queries panel ↵
2. Tab to any field and type **COUNT**
3. Tab to the field that is to contain the condition and type an operator followed by a value
4. Press **F2** to see the results

Creating a Database File

To create and define the structure of a database file:

From the Dot Prompt

1. Type **SET DEFAULT TO A:** ↵
2. Type **CREATE** <**filename**> ↵
3. With the database design screen displaying, for each field in the database file
   - **a.** Type a field name and press ↵
   - **b.** Type the first letter of the field descriptor
   - **c.** Type the field width and press ↵
   - **d.** If appropriate, type the number of decimals and press ↵
   - **e.** Press ↵ to ignore the Index column
4. When finished, press **Ctrl** + **W** to save the structure and exit to the dot prompt

Control Center Mode

1. Select the **Create** marker in the Data panel of the Control Center and press ↵
2. With the database design screen displaying, for each field in the database file
   - **a.** Type a field name and press ↵
   - **b.** Type the first letter of the field descriptor
   - **c.** Type the field width and press ↵
   - **d.** If appropriate, type the number of decimals and press ↵
   - **e.** Press ↵ to ignore the Index column
3. When satisfied that the database file is complete and correct, press **Alt** + **E** to access the Exit menu
4. Highlight **Save changes and exit** from the Exit menu ↵
5. If prompted for a filename, type **<filename>** ↵

Data Retrieval

All of the data retrieval commands listed below are typed in the COMMAND mode. LIST and DISPLAY produce identical actions.

To display the current record in an open database file:

Type **DISPLAY** ↵

To display multiple records in an open database file, for instance:

□ All the records in a file,

Type **DISPLAY ALL** ↵

or

Type **LIST** ↵

□ All records that match a condition,

Type **DISPLAY FOR <condition>** ↵

or

Type **LIST FOR <condition>** ↵

□ Selected fields,

Type **DISPLAY <field name> [, <field name>...]** ↵

or

Type **LIST <field name> [,<field name>...]** ↵

☐ The next several records,

Type **DISPLAY NEXT <number>** ↵

or

Type **LIST NEXT <number>** ↵

☐ Selected fields and records,

Type **DISPLAY <field name>[, <field name>...]**
[FOR <condition>] ↵

or

Type **LIST <field name> [, <field name>...]**
[FOR <condition>] ↵

Default Drive

To set the default drive:

From the Dot Prompt

Type **SET DEFAULT TO <drive identifier>** ↵

Control Center Mode

1. Press **Esc**

2. Type **Y** for Yes

3. Type **SET DEFAULT TO <drive identifier>** ↵

4. Press **F2**

Deleting Records

The DELETE command marks a record for deletion without physically removing it. To delete a single record:

From the Dot Prompt

Type **DELETE RECORD <record number>** ↵

Control Center Mode

1. Open the appropriate database file by highlighting the database name on the Control Center panel and pressing **F2**
2. Press **F2** again, if necessary, to get the BROWSE screen
3. Use ↑ and ↓ to position the cursor on a record you wish to mark
4. Press **Ctrl** + **U** to mark the record
5. Repeat steps 3 and 4 for every other record you wish to mark for deletion
6. Press **Alt** + **E** to access the Exit menu
7. To return to the Control Center, select **Exit** from the Exit menu

Note: Deleting only records that meet certain conditions can most easily be done at the dot prompt. To do this, type **DELETE FOR <condition>** ↵

Displaying a Database Structure

To display the structure of an active database file:

From the Dot Prompt

Type **DISPLAY STRUCTURE** ↵

Control Center Mode

1. Press **Shift** + **F2** for Design
2. Press **Esc**
3. When done, press **Esc** and then **Y**

Displaying a File Directory

To display the names of all files with a .DBF extension:

From the Dot Prompt

Type **DIR** ↵

Control Center Mode

All files are displayed in the six catalog panels under their appropriate type

To display the names of all file with a specific extension:

From the Dot Prompt

Type **DIR *.<file extension>** ↵

Displaying Records

(*See* Data Retrieval)

Dot Prompt (Command Prompt)

To access the dot (command) prompt from the Control Center:

Highlight **Exit to dot prompt** from the Exit menu ↵

or

1. Press **Esc**

2. Type **Y** for Yes

Editing Records

To edit records using the EDIT screen:

From the Dot Prompt

1. Type **EDIT RECORD <record number>** ↵

2. Make the necessary edits

Control Center Mode

1. Press **F2**

2. If the BROWSE screen appears, press **F2** again

3. Use the **Go To** menu to locate the record to be edited and make the necessary edits

To edit records using the BROWSE screen:

From the Dot Prompt

1. Type **BROWSE** ↵

2. Move the cursor to the record to be edited

3. Make the necessary edits

4. Press **Ctrl** + **End** when done with all edits

Control Center Mode

1. Press **F2**

2. If the EDIT screen appears, press **F2** again

3. Move the cursor to the record to be edited and make the necessary edits

4. Press **Ctrl** + **End** when done with all edits

HELP Feature

Use the following commands to access the HELP feature or to get various types of assistance:

☐ To access the HELP feature,

Press **F1**

☐ In the HELP feature, to remove the HELP box from the screen,

Press **Esc**

Indexing Records

Indexing records allows them to be output in an order different from the one in which they are physically stored.

From the Dot Prompt

☐ To create a single-key index for any field of the active database file,

Type **INDEX ON <field name> TO <index name>** ↵

☐ To create a multiple-key index for any field of the active database file,

Type **INDEX ON <field name> [+ field name. . .] TO <index name>** ↵

☐ To activate one or more indexes for use,

Type **SET INDEX TO <index name> [, index name. . .]** ↵

☐ To update all active indexes,

Type **REINDEX** ↵

Control Center Mode. To create an index for any field of the active database file:

1. Display the database design screen used to create database file structures
2. Move the highlight to the row of the field that is to be indexed
3. Move the highlight to the Index column
4. Type **Y** for Yes

Listing Records

(*See* Data Retrieval: Displaying Multiple Records)

Modifying a Database File Structure

To modify the structure of an active file:

From the Dot Prompt

Type **MODIFY STRUCTURE** ↵

Control Center Mode

1. Press **Shift** + **F2** to access the database design screen
2. Press **Esc** to get the Organize pull-down menu out of the way

Opening (Using) a File

To open a database file for use:

From the Dot Prompt

Type **USE <filename>** ↵

Control Center Mode

1. Move the cursor to the name of the database file
2. Press ↵
3. Type **U** for Use

Packing a File to Remove Records

To pack a file marked for deletion:

From the Dot Prompt

1. Open the database file

2. Type **PACK** ↵

Control Center Mode

1. Open and display the database file

2. Highlight **Erase marked records** from the Organize menu ↵

3. Press **Y** for Yes

Positioning the Record Pointer

All of the commands below are issued from the Dot Prompt.

To set the record pointer in an open database file to the:

□ First record,

  Type **GO TOP** ↵

□ Last record,

  Type **GO BOTTOM** ↵

□ Next record,

  Type **SKIP** ↵

□ *n*the record from the current one,

  Type **SKIP <n>** ↵

□ First record that matches a condition in a sequential search,

  Type **LOCATE FOR <condition>** ↵

□ Next record that matches a condition in a sequential search, assuming that no intervening command has moved the record pointer,

  Type **CONTINUE** ↵

□ First record that matches an index field value in an indexed search,

  Type **SEEK '<index field value>'** ↵

Quitting dBASE

To quit dBASE:

From the Dot Prompt

Type **QUIT** ↵

Control Center Mode

1. Press **Alt** + **E** to Exit
2. Type **Q** to Quit to DOS

Recalling Records Marked for Deletion

To recall records marked for deletion:

From the Dot Prompt

Type **RECALL RECORD <record number>** ↵

Control Center Mode

1. Open the appropriate database file by highlighting the database name in the Control Center and pressing **F2**
2. Press **F2** again, if necessary, to get to the BROWSE screen
3. Move the pointer to the record marked for deletion
4. Press **Ctrl** + **U** to remove "Del" mark
5. Repeat Steps 3 and 4 for every other record you wish to recall
6. Press **Alt** + **E** to access the Exit menu
7. To return to the Control Center, select **Exit** from the Exit menu

Note: Recalling all records or only records meeting a certain condition can most easily be done at the dot prompt. To recall all records, type *RECALL ALL* and press Enter; to recall only records meeting a certain condition, type *RECALL FOR <condition>* and press Enter.

Replacing Data

From the Dot Prompt. To replace data in records (starting from the top of the file):

Type **REPLACE <field name> WITH <new data>** ↵

To replace data in records that meet specific conditions:

Type **REPLACE <field name> WITH <new data> FOR <field name><operator><value>** ↵

Example:

Type **REPLACE STATUS WITH .Y. FOR NAME = "Sam Jones"** ↵

Control Center Mode. To replace data in records (starting from the top of the file):

1. Highlight **Replace** from the Update menu ↵
2. Highlight a field name ↵
3. Type in the new data and press ↵
4. Highlight **Execute the command** ↵

Reports

To create a report for the active database file:

From the Dot Prompt

Type **CREATE REPORT <report name>** ↵

Control Center Mode

1. Move the cursor to **Create** in the Reports panel
2. Press ↵

To output a report on the display screen:

From the Dot Prompt

Type **REPORT FORM <report name>** ↵

Control Center Mode

1. Move the cursor to the report name in the Reports panel
2. Press ↵
3. Type **P** to get the Print menu
4. Type **V** to View the report

To output a report on the printer:

From the Dot Prompt

Type **REPORT FORM <report name> TO PRINT** ↵

Control Center Mode

1. Move the cursor to the report name in the Reports panel

2. Press ↵

3. Type **P** to get the Print menu

4. Type **B** to Begin printing

To modify reports:

From the Dot Prompt

Type **MODIFY REPORT <report name>** ↵

Control Center Mode

1. Move the cursor to the report name in the Reports panel

2. Press ↵

3. Type **M** for Modify

Searching for Records

(*See* Data Retrieval)

Sorting Records

To sort files:

From the Dot Prompt

1. Open the database file that is to be sorted

2. Type **SORT TO <new filename> ON <field name> [,<field name>...]** ↵

Control Center Mode

1. Move the cursor to the database filename in the Data panel

2. Press ↵

3. Type **M** for Modify

4. Highlight **Sort database on field list** on the Organize menu ↵

Setting the Default Drive

To set the default drive:

From the Dot Prompt

Type **SET DEFAULT TO A:** ↵

Control Center Mode

1. Highlight **DOS Utilities** from the Tools menu ↵
2. Press **Alt** + **D** to select DOS
3. Type **S** to Set Default Drive
4. Type **A:**, delete other characters and press ↵
5. Press **Esc** and then **Y**

Starting dBASE IV

To start dBASE:

1. Type **CD<directory name>** ↵
2. Type **DBASE** ↵

Summing Values in a Field

To sum all the values in a field of an active database file:

From the Dot Prompt

Type **SUM <field name>** ↵

Control Center Mode

1. Highlight <**create**> in the Queries panel ↵
2. Tab to the field to be summed and type **SUM**
3. Press **F2** to see the results

To sum only the values in a field of an active database file meeting a specific condition:

From the Dot Prompt

Type **SUM <field name> FOR <condition>** ↵

Control Center Mode

1. Highlight <**create**> in the Queries panel ↵
2. Tab to the field to be summed and type **SUM**

3. Tab to the field to contain the condition and type in an operator followed by a value

4. Press **F2** to see the results

In Command Mode, to switch to the Control Center:

Press **F2** or type **ASSIST**

Switching Modes

In the Control Center, to switch to the Command mode:

Press **F2** and then **Y**

GLOSSARY

Active. Refers to a dBASE file that is open and ready for use.

APPEND. The dBASE command used to place records into a file.

Band. A screen division that defines an area of a report.

BROWSE. A dBASE command that enables users to perform fullscreen editing and appending.

Calculated field. A report field that is calculated from fields within the file structure.

Catalog. A table of six columns that display all available dBASE files.

Command mode. Refers to operating dBASE by typing in commands at the dot prompt. Contrast with ASSIST mode.

Control break. A term that refers to "breaks" in the normal flow of record information in a report that periodically occur for subtotals and totals.

Control Center. The system of menus by which dBASE lets users invoke commands by simply selecting them. Contrast with Command mode.

CREATE. The dBASE command used to develop a database file structure.

Database. A term that is commonly used to refer to a set of related files.

Database file. See File.

DBF. The extension dBASE uses for a database file.

DELETE. The dBASE command used to mark records for removal.

DISPLAY. The dBASE command used to output records onscreen.

DISPLAY STRUCTURE. The dBASE command used to output a file.

Dot prompt. The period character, used to tell dBASE operators that dBASE expects a command to be entered from the command mode.

EDIT. A dBASE command that enables you to modify records.

Field. A collection of related characters.

Field descriptors. A code or word used to describe the type of data—say, numeric, character, or logical—that occupy a given field in a data record.

File. A collection of related records.

FRM. The extension used by dBASE for a file that stores a report form.

INDEX. The dBASE command used to index files.

Indexing. A method used to specify how records are arranged in a file, without physically sorting the data records.

Key field. A field used to arrange records.

LOCATE. A dBASE command that repositions the record pointer.

Logical connective. The keywords AND, OR, and NOT, when used in a field having a logical value.

MDX. The extension used by dBASE for index files.

Menu bar. The top-of-screen line of choices in the initial Control Center screen.

MODIFY STRUCTURE. The dBASE command used to change the structure of a database file.

Open. The act of making a file available for processing.

PACK. The dBASE command used to permanently remove data records from a database file.

Pull-down menus. In the Control Center, the vertical menus that can be accessed off the top-of-screen menu bar.

RECALL. The dBASE command that restores records made temporarily inaccessable by the DELETE command.

Query. A dBASE file that saves search conditions on disk for future use.

Record. A collection of related fields.

Relational operator. A character in a logical expression—such as < (less than), > (greater than), or = (equal to)—that compares the contents of two fields.

REPLACE. The dBASE command used to make mass alterations to records in a database file.

Report form. A specification telling what a report is supposed to look like.

SEEK. The dBASE command used to find, in an indexed file, records with specific characteristics.

SORT. The dBASE command used to physically rearrange a file.

Status bar. In the Command mode, the bottom-of-screen display bar that shows specific characteristics about the current dBASE file or operation.

Structure. A collection of information about the fields of a file, including the names, lengths, and the types of the fields.

USE. The dBASE command used to open files, thereby making them available for processing.

REVIEW QUESTIONS

1. List the following database elements in order from largest to smallest: record, file, field, database.

2. How do you move from one choice to another in the Control Center's main menu bar?

3. What six field descriptors are used in dBASE IV?

4. How are records

a. Marked for deletion?

b. Permanently deleted?

5. What command is used to add records to a database file?

6. Write the DISPLAY statement that you would type at the dot prompt to list each of the following:

a. The fields NAME, ADDRESS, and ZIP of the current database file

b. All records for those persons with a zip code of 98026 (assume the zip-code field is called ZIP)

c. All persons whose NAME is Smith and whose ZIP is 98112

7. What command in the Control Center and Command mode tallies all records in a database field?

8. What command in the Control Center or Command mode sums a numeric field in several records?

9. In COMMAND mode, what command would you type to create an index on the NAME field for a new index file called NAMEINDX?

10. What command is used in either the Control Center or Command mode to move quickly to the

a. First record in a file?

b. Last record in a file?

11. a. To quickly replace the contents of certain fields throughout an entire database, what command would you use in either the Control Center or Command mode?

b. What command would you type at the dot prompt to replace the logical field MEMBER with .F. for all zip code areas of 98027 throughout an entire database?

12. How would you locate the first record in a file having a ZIP of 98027 in Command mode?

ANSWERS

1. Database, file, record, and field. **2.** Press the left and right arrow keys or type the first character of the menu. **3.** Numeric, character, float, memo, logical, date. **4. a.** Issuing the DELETE command **b.** Issuing the PACK command **5.** APPEND. **6. a.** DISPLAY ALL NAME, ADDRESS, ZIP **b.** DISPLAY ALL FOR ZIP = "98026" **c.** DISPLAY ALL FOR NAME = "Smith" .AND. ZIP = "98112" **7.** COUNT. **8.** SUM. **9.** INDEX ON NAME TAG NAMEINDX. **10. a.** GOTO TOP **b.** GOTO

BOTTOM (GOTO LAST in the Control Center) **11. a.** REPLACE **b.** REPLACE MEMBER WITH .F. FOR ZIP = "98027 **12.** LOCATE FOR ZIP = "98027"

HANDS-ON EXERCISES

Hands-on Exercise 1: Employee Donations Record

In this exercise you will practice:

- ☐ Creating a database file
- ☐ Defining the fields in a file
- ☐ Adding records to a file
- ☐ Listing records
- ☐ Leaving and reentering the database file
- ☐ Viewing the directory
- ☐ Setting the default drive
- ☐ Using a stored file
- ☐ Printing a file

1. Create a database file called EMPLOYEE for the records described below. Count the maximum number of characters used in each column to decide on the width of each of the fields. Define SALARY and DONATION as numeric, EMPLOYED as date, and all other fields as character fields.

The fields are:

EMPLOYEE
TELEPHONE
GENDER
EMPLOYED
SALARY
DONATION

The employees are:

Pratt, John
225-1234
M
06/22/92
1949.00
200.00

Jones, David
292-3832
M
06/15/88
1500.00
225.00

Smoller, Ellen
225-3212
F
09/15/88
1650.00
300.00

Sill, Sally
224-4321
F
02/15/87
1800.00
150.00

Knat, Michael
221-1235
M
09/15/80
1700.00
350.00

Smith, Paul
223-8251
M
11/01/85
1800.00
200.50

2. After defining the fields, exit without entering data

3. Use the APPEND command to enter data

4. Exit from the program

5. Sign on to the program

6. Set the default drive

7. View the directory (or Data Panel) to be sure EMPLOYEE is listed

8. Open the database file, EMPLOYEE

9. List (or Browse) the file to be sure it is accurate

10. Add the following three records:

Martins, Mary
222-2123
F
11/01/93
1850.00
175.00

Beam, Sandy
225-6912
F
02/15/93
1450.00
275.00

Johnson, Frank
223-7928
M
03/20/93
1500.00
0.00

11. Print a copy of the file's records

Hands-on Exercise 2: Payroll Reporting

In this exercise you will practice

☐ Creating a database file

☐ Defining the fields in a file

☐ Using the APPEND command

☐ Deleting, recalling, and packing records

☐ Sorting data

☐ Listing specific records and fields

☐ Using the DISPLAY command

☐ Using the EDIT and BROWSE commands

1. Create a database file called PAYROLL. It will contain the following fields:

ID_NUMBER
EMP_NAME
DEPARTMENT
PAY_RATE

2. Immediately after defining the fields, enter the data shown below:

278
Dougherty, Ronald H.
MIS
12.50

178
Jordan, James
Payroll
15.50

292
Smith, Bonnie
Customer Services
13.40

346
Clement, Cynthia
MIS
18.90

415
Zonguldake, Helen
Personnel
12.00

595
Foster, Donald
MIS
22.00

150
VanderZee, Charles
Personnel
20.00

420
Aiken, Helen
Payroll
17.50

3. Sort the file in alphabetical order on EMP_NAME

4. Print a copy of the file

5. Use the BROWSE command to change the following:

a. Ronald Dougherty's pay rate to $13.00

b. Bonnie Smith's department to Personnel

c. Helen Zonguldake's department to Customer Services

6. Use the LIST command to show all persons working in the MIS department. Show the names and departments only.

7. Use the DISPLAY command to show the following:

   a. The names of all persons in the Payroll department

   b. The names of all persons earning more than $15.00 an hour

   c. the names of all persons who are either working in MIS or making less than $20.00 an hour

8. Mark Record 4, Cynthia Clement, for deletion. List or browse the file to be sure it is marked. Recall the record. List or browse the file again to be sure the record is no longer marked.

9. Delete Helen Aiken's record permanently from the file, using the DELETE and PACK commands. List or browse the file again to be sure the record is gone.

10. Sort the file by DEPARTMENT in descending order and by NAME in ascending order. Print a copy of the sorted file.

11. Use the LIST command to show Record 3, Bonnie Smith

12. Use the EDIT command to edit Record 3, making the following changes:

    a. Add a J. as the middle initial

    b. Change the pay rate to 24.00

13. Print the file

Hands-on Exercise 3: Software Sales Sheet

In this exercise you will practice:

- ☐ Creating a database file
- ☐ Modifying the file
- ☐ Creating an index
- ☐ Creating a report

1. Create a database file called SOFTWARE for the first five columns of the table shown in Figure DB-34. (Do not create the sixth column, TOTAL, yet. We will use the database system's report generation feature to create this column in part 4 of this exercise.)

2. Create an index file called ITEMINDX using ITEM as the key field. The index should arrange records in alphabetical order.

3. List the records

4. Create a report with the following specifications:

   a. Specify the report title as

SOFTWARE MANUAL SALES
JANUARY 10 THROUGH FEBRUARY 10, 1992

b. Use the following column headings:

CUSTOMER NUMBER	ITEM SOLD	DATE SOLD	UNIT PRICE	QUANTITY SOLD	TOTAL SALE

Note that the data in the Total Sale column (see TOTAL column in Figure DB-34) is computed by multiplying PRICE by QUANTITY.

c. Arrange the records on the ITEM field. Use this field for control breaks in your report and subtotal the Quantity Sold and Total Sale columns at each break. Also provide a final total.

5. Print the report

Hands-on Exercise 4: Modifying a Database File Structure

In this exercise you will practice modifying a database file structure by

- □ Backing up the existing file
- □ Deleting a field
- □ Adding a field
- □ Changing the width of a field

FIGURE DB-34

Hands-on Exercise 3: Software sales file.

CUSTNUM	ITEM	DATE SOLD	PRICE	QUANTITY	TOTAL
1232	Database Text	01/10/93	200.00	1	200.00
2388	Database Text	01/10/93	200.00	1	200.00
3445	Database Tutor	01/08/93	70.00	1	70.00
3442	Database Tutor	01/08/93	70.00	1	70.00
1232	Graphics	01/09/93	200.00	2	400.00
6224	Database Tutor	01/09/93	70.00	1	70.00
1232	Reports Pkg	01/09/93	150.00	1	150.00
1332	Spreadsheet	01/09/93	150.00	3	450.00
2445	Spreadsheet	01/11/93	150.00	1	150.00
2443	Time Mgt	01/09/93	300.00	2	600.00
6223	Time Mgt	01/10/93	300.00	3	900.00
3445	Database Text	01/11/93	200.00	3	600.00
5122	Database Text	01/11/93	200.00	5	1000.00
5223	Database Text	01/11/93	200.00	3	600.00
5432	Database Text	02/10/93	200.00	1	200.00
6223	Graphics	01/20/93	200.00	5	1000.00
2883	Reports Pkg	02/10/93	150.00	2	300.00
2443	Reports Pkg	02/05/93	150.00	3	450.00

Using the EMPLOYEE file you developed in Hands-On Exercise 1, do the following:

1. Back up the copy of the existing file, including its file structure and data contents
2. Delete the GENDER field

After you do this, save the change and inspect the file structure and the data contents of EMPLOYEE. If the change has been made properly, continue; otherwise, start over.

3. Modify the TELEPHONE field to accommodate a three-digit area code

Again, save the change and inspect your work.

4. Add a field called DEPT, which will contain an employee's department. Assume this field will contain character data and have a length of three characters; for instance, ACC might stand for the accounting department, FIN for the finance department, and so on.

Again, save the change and inspect your work.

5. Add data to the file to fill the DEPT field. Assume that Pratt, Knat, and Beam work in the ACC department, Sill works in the MIS (Management Information Systems) department, and all other employees work in the FIN department.
6. Add area codes to the TELEPHONE field. Assume that all employees, except Smoller, are in area code 201. Smoller is in area code 212.

Save the changes and inspect your work.

7. Print a copy of the final database file contents and file structure

Hands-on Exercise 5: Advanced Reports

In this exercise you will extend your report-development skills by practicing how to

- □ Prepare reports from records that meet certain conditions
- □ Prepare reports that contains only subtotals and totals
- □ Delete and insert report columns

To do the exercise, you will be using the SALES file of Figure DB-21 and modifying the report of Figure DB-27 (which is based on the SALESR report form you created in the tutorials).

1. Produce a report that is based on only items that are priced above $15.00
2. Using the SALESR report form, produce a summary report similar to the one in Figure DB-33. Call this new report form SALESR2.

3. Using SALESR, delete the "Amount" column (the last column in Figure DB-27). Call the new report form SALESR3 and output the associated report

4. Using SALESR3, restore by insertion the amount column deleted in step 3. Output the associated report.

Hands-on Exercise 6: File Management Basics

In this exercise you will learn, and then practice, additional file management techniques to

- □ Copy one file to another
- □ Copy only selected records and fields
- □ Append records to the current file
- □ Rename a file
- □ Erase a file

To do this exercise, you will be using the CUSTOMER file, which you created earlier. The examples are presented in pairs—the first demonstrates the technique; the second provides you with additional practice. You may use either the Command mode (dot prompt) or Control Center mode as you prefer. If you use the Control Center mode, refer to query techniques as needed in the chapter or command reference.

COPYING SELECTED RECORDS

A. Using either procedure described below, copy the CUSTOMER database file into a new file called BUYER. (Examine Figure DB-35 for additional COPY techniques).

FIGURE DB-35
Hands-on Exercise 6: COPY Command Samples.

COPY Command	Description
COPY STRUCTURE TO XXX.DBF	Copies the current file structure alone (no records) to a new file named XXX.
COPY TO XXX.DBF	Copies the current file structure and all records to a new file named XXX.
COPY TO XXX.DBF FOR DEPT="A"	Copies the current file structure, and records that meet the condition (DEPT="A") to a new file named XXX.
COPY TO XXX.DBF FIELDS DEPT, ID	Copies only the named fields (DEPT and ID) from the current file structure and records to a new file named XXX.
COPY FILE XXX.DBF TO YYY.DBF	Copies the entire file named XXX to a new file named YYY.

From the Dot Prompt

1. Type COPY CUSTOMER.DBF TO BUYER.DBF (Both the file and extension must appear.)
2. Press ↵

Control Center Mode.

1. Press **Alt** + **T** (*Tools*)
2. Select *DOS Utilities*
3. Highlight *Customer.DBF*
4. Press **Alt** + **O** (*Operations*)
5. Select *Copy, Single File*
6. Press ↵
7. Type **BUYER.DBF** ↵
8. Press **Ctrl** + **End**, **Esc** **Y**

Now, add the BUYER file to the catalog,

9. Press **Alt** + **C** and then **A**
10. Highlight BUYER
11. Press ↵ twice

B. Using the procedure you learned in Example A, copy the BUYER database file into a new file called PATRON1. Output a list of the file's contents.

COPYING SELECTED RECORDS

A. Using either procedure described below, copy from the CUSTOMER file to the BUYER file only those customers who live in Colorado (CO.)

From the Dot Prompt

1. Type **COPY TO BUYER FOR STATE = "CO"**
2. Press ↵
3. Press **O** to overwrite (if asked)

Control Center Mode

1. Open the CUSTOMER file
2. Create a query for *State* = **"CO"**
3. Press **Alt** + **L** (*Layout*)
4. Select *Write view as database file*

5. Type **BUYER.DBF** ↵

6. Select *Overwrite* (if asked)

7. Press **Esc** **Y**

B. Using the procedure you learned in Example A, copy from the CUSTOMER file to the PATRON2 file only those customers who live in the city of Santa Fe. Output a list of the file's contents.

COPYING SELECTED FIELDS

A. Using either procedure described below, copy from the CUSTOMER file only the CUSTNUM and NAME fields into a new file called BUYER.

From the Dot Prompt

1. Type **COPY TO BUYER FIELDS CUSTNUM, NAME**

2. Press ↵

3. Press **O** to overwrite

Control Center Mode

1. Create a query

2. Remove all fields (**F5**)

3. Include the CUSTNUM and NAME fields(**F5**)

4. Press **Alt** +L (*Layout*)

5. Select *Write view as database file*

6. Type **BUYER.DBF** ↵

7. Select Overwrite

8. Press **Esc** **Y**

B. Using the procedure you learned in Example A, copy from the CUSTOMER file only the NAME, CITY, and STATE fields into a new file called PATRON3. Output a list of the file's contents.

APPENDING RECORDS

A. Using the procedure described below, append records from the CUSTOMER file into the BUYER file.

1. Open the BUYER file

2. Exit the Control Center (if needed)

3. Type **APPEND FROM CUSTOMER** ↵

B. Using the procedure you learned in Example A, append records from the CUSTOMER file into the PATRON3 file. Output a list of the file's contents.

RENAMING A FILE

A. Using either procedure described below, rename the BUYER.DBF file as BUYER2.DBF.

From the Dot Prompt

1. Type **RENAME BUYER.DBF TO BUYER2.DBF**

2. Press ↵

Control Center Mode

1. Press **Alt** +**T** (*Tools*)

2. Select *DOS Utilities*

3. Highlight *Buyer.DBF*

4. Press **Alt** +**O** (*Operations*)

5. Select *Rename, Single File*

6. Type **BUYER2.DBF** ↵

7. Press **Esc** **Y**

8. Add BUYER2 to the catalog

B. Using the procedure you learned in Example A, rename the PATRON3.DBF file as PATRON4.DBF. Output a list of the file's contents.

ERASING A FILE

A. Using either procedure described below, erase the BUYER2 file from your disk. (Note: You cannot erase a file that is in use. Either open another file first, or type CLOSE ALL in the Command mode.)

From the Dot Prompt

1. Type **ERASE BUYER2.DBF**

2. Press ↵

Control Center Mode

1. Press **Alt** +**T** (*Tools*)

2. Select *DOS Utilities*

3. Highlight *Buyer2.DBF* and press ↵

4. Press **Alt** +**O** (*Operations*)

5. Select *Delete, Single file*

6. Select *Proceed*

7. Press **Esc** **Y**

B. Using the procedure you learned in Example A, erase the PATRON 3 file from your disk. Output a list of the file's contents.

Hands-On Exercise 7: Final Exercise in dBASE File Basics

In this final exercise you will practice a few of the basic techniques you have learned in the chapter.

1. Create a database file called ITEMS with the following file structure:

FIELD NAME	FIELD TYPE	WIDTH	DEC
STOCK_NUM:	Character	4	
DESCRIP	Character	20	
COST	Numeric	6	2
QUANT	Numeric	4	0
PRICE	Numeric	6	2

2. Append these seven records to the ITEMS file:

STOCK_NUM: D301
DESCRIP: DISK, 3.5″ DD
COST: .17
QUANT: 2110
PRICE: .40

STOCK_NUM: D302
DESCRIP: DISK, 3.5″ HD
COST: .20
QUANT: 1500
PRICE: .55

STOCK_NUM: D501
DESCRIP: DISK, 5.25″ DD
COST: .15
QUANT: 2250
PRICE: .30

STOCK_NUM: T157
DESCRIP: TONER, LASER
COST: 25.00
QUANT: 200
PRICE: 49.95

STOCK_NUM: R155
DESCRIP: RIBBON, STANDARD
COST: 2.50
QUANT: 750
PRICE: 4.95

STOCK_NUM:	P670
DESCRIP:	PAPER, REAM, WHITE
COST:	5.25
QUANT:	3025
PRICE:	7.49

STOCK_NUM:	P718
DESCRIP:	PAPER, REAM, YELLOW
COST:	5.50
QUANT:	1540
PRICE:	7.99

3. Print a copy of the file's records.

4. Index the file in alphabetical order by STOCK_NUM and print a copy of the file's records.

5. Using the BROWSE command, change the following:
a. D301's QUANT to 2055
b. P718's COST to 5.65

6. Use the LIST command to show all items whose PRICE exceeds one dollar. Show STOCK_NUM and PRICE only.

7. Mark the record for item P670 for deletion. List or browse to make sure it is marked. Recall the record and list or browse to verify that it is no longer marked.

8. Delete the record for item P718 permanently from the file, using DELETE and PACK commands. Verify that it is gone.

9. Create a report entitled ITEMRPT that displays all fields with appropriate column headings. Include, at the rightmost position, a column entitled "VALUE" that is computed by multiplying the QUANT by COST. Show a total for the QUANT field only. Print the report.

10. Modify the structure of the ITEMS file as follows:
a. Add a character field for LOCATION with a width of 1
b. Change the width of the DESCRIP field to 25

11. Add data to the file to fill the LOCATION field. Assume that disks are in location "A," paper is in location "B," and all other items are in location "C." Print a list of all records.

12. Copy the entire ITEMS file into a new file called ITEMS-A.

13. Copy only the STOCK_NUM and PRICE fields to a new file called ITEMS-B for those records whose STOCK_NUM starts with a "D" and whose COST exceeds sixteen cents.

14. Append to the ITEMS-B file all records from the ITEMS-A file.

15. Rename the ITEMS-A file as ITEMS-D.